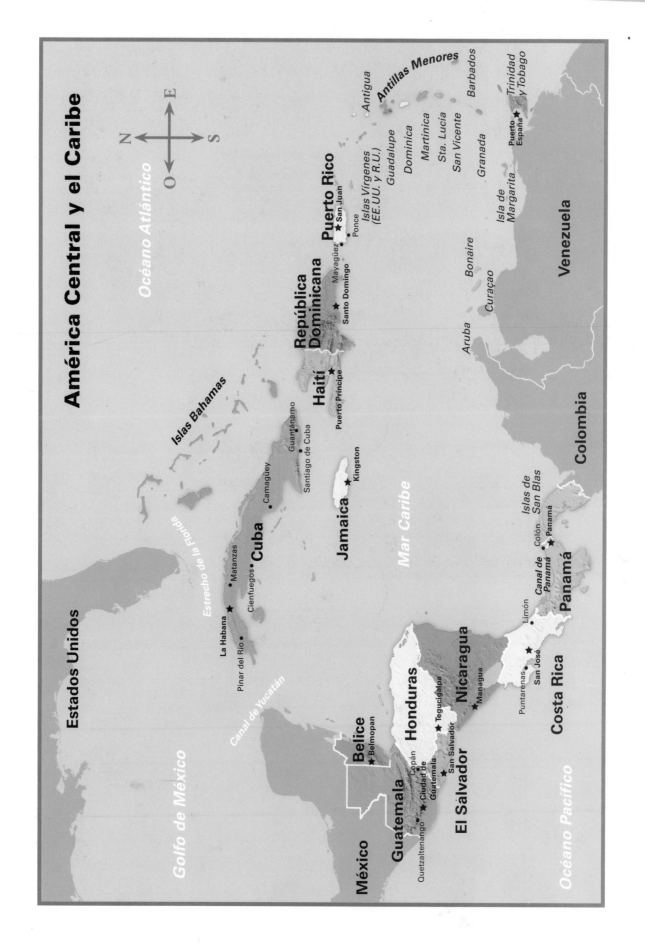

# América Central y el Caribe

**Instructor's Annotated Edition**

# PANORAMA

Introducción a la lengua española

**THIRD EDITION**

**José A. Blanco**

**Philip Redwine Donley, Late**
Austin Community College

**VISTA**
HIGHER LEARNING

Boston, Massachusetts

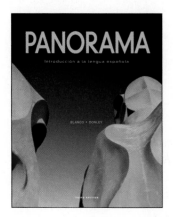

The **PANORAMA, Third Edition,** cover features a detail from Antoni Gaudí's **La Pedrera** in Barcelona, Spain. This remarkable architectural feat is one of the many landmarks from the Spanish-speaking world that you will learn about in **PANORAMA**.

**Publisher:** José A. Blanco
**Vice President and Editorial Director:** Beth Kramer
**Managing Editor:** Sarah Kenney
**Project Manager:** Isabelle Alouane
**Editor:** Gabriela Ferland
**Director of Art and Design:** Linda Jurras
**Director of Production and Manufacturing:** Lisa Perrier
**Design Manager:** Polo Barrera
**Photo Researcher and Art Buyer:** Rachel Distler
**Production Coordinator:** Nick Ventullo
**Production and Manufacturing Team:** Oscar Diez, Mauricio Henao, María Eugenia Castaño, Jeff Perron

**President:** Janet L. Dracksdorf
**Sr. Vice President of Operations:** Tom Delano
**Vice President of Sales and Marketing:** Scott Burns
**Executive Marketing Manager:** Benjamín Rivera

Student Text ISBN-13: 978-1-60007-594-0
           ISBN-10: 1-60007-594-0
Instructor's Annotated Edition ISBN-13: 978-1-60007-599-5
           ISBN-10: 1-60007-599-1

1 2 3 4 5 6 7 8 9 R 12 11 10 09 08 07

# Instructor's Annotated Edition

## Table of Contents

# Exciting new **PANORAMA** Supersite, powered by **MAESTRO**™!

Using the **MAESTRO**™ Language Learning System, you will be able to set up a course for your students to enroll in your class and automatically populate the rosters for different sections. Within your rosters you can communicate easily with your sections, or with individual students at a moment's notice. In addition, you will have access to a powerful gradebook and assignment manager that will allow you to assign, track, and assess student progress. Both the gradebook and assignment options are highly customizable.

## Instructor Resources, available on the Supersite (panorama.vhlcentral.com)

▶ **MAESTRO**™ course management system, featuring roster, gradebook, and customizable assignment functionalities

▶ the complete Instructor's Resource Manual *

▶ the complete Testing Program *
- Ready-to-print PDF files
- Editable word processing files
- Testing Program Audio MP3s

▶ Information Gap activities for select lessons *

▶ the Workbook / Video Manual / Lab Manual Answer Key *

▶ the Overhead Transparencies *

▶ the **Contextos** and **Estructura** PowerPoints

▶ lesson plans for semester and quarter courses

▶ complete access to the student track

  * Available as downloadable and printable PDFs

*Your students' Supersite passcodes are free with the purchase of a new student text.*

 For information on the student side of the Supersite, see p. xxviii.

**FREE WITH NEW BOOK PURCHASE**

New! **MAESTRO**™ WebSAM (premium content)

Because this electronic Workbook, Video Manual, and Lab Manual is built on the **MAESTRO**™ platform, it fully integrates with the Supersite course management system, allowing you to set assignments and track their progress right alongside their textbook work. This new option, an alternative to the traditional print ancillaries, delivers the same high-quality content with auto-grading capabilities.

# Getting to Know PANORAMA

**PANORAMA 3/e** retains the successful underpinnings of the first and second editions. It takes a fresh, student-friendly approach to introductory Spanish that tries to make students' learning and instructors' teaching easier, more enjoyable, and more successful. At the same time, **PANORAMA's** communicative approach to language learning develops students' speaking, listening, reading, and writing skills so that they can express their own ideas meaningfully. The program presents frequently used vocabulary and grammar as the necessary tools for effective communication. Finally, because cultural knowledge is integral to language learning and successful communication, **PANORAMA** introduces students to the everyday lives of Spanish speakers, as well as the countries of the Spanish-speaking world.

**PANORAMA's** distinctive features make it truly different.

- **PANORAMA**, and its parent program **VISTAS** were the first introductory college Spanish textbooks to incorporate graphic design—page layout, use of colors, typefaces, and other graphic elements—as an integral part of the learning process. To enhance learning and make navigation easy, lesson sections are color-coded and appear either completely on one page or on spreads of two facing pages. The textbook pages themselves are also visually dramatic.

- **PANORAMA** offers sidebars with on-the-spot linguistic, cultural, and language-learning information, as well as **Recursos** boxes with on-page correlations of student supplements.

- **PANORAMA** integrates video with the student textbook in a distinct, cohesive way in each lesson's **Fotonovela** section and throughout every lesson's **Estructura** section. **PANORAMA** also provides two cultural videos, *Flash cultura* and *Panorama cultural,* as well as authentic TV clips in **En pantalla**.

- **PANORAMA** offers a unique four-part practice sequence for virtually every grammar point. It moves from form-focused **¡Inténtalo!** exercises to directed **Práctica** exercises. Interactive **Comunicación** activities then progress into cumulative, open-ended **Síntesis** activities.

- **PANORAMA** incorporates groundbreaking, text-specific technology, powered by MAESTRO, that is specially designed to expand learning and teaching options.

- The **PANORAMA** Supersite, new to the Third Edition, now offers even more support for both students and instructors than ever before. Students can access all of the program's multimedia components as well as activities from the textbook with auto-grading and additional activities. Instructors can access a powerful course-management system, powered by MAESTRO, as well as all the instructor resources. For more information on the Supersite, turn to page xxviii.

Take a moment to familiarize yourself with the following pages of the Student Text front matter: page iii (To the Student), pages xii-xxv (**PANORAMA**-At-A Glance), pages xxvi-xxvii (Video Program), and pages xxix-xxx (Supersite, Icons and Ancillaries).

# Getting to Know Your Instructor's Annotated Edition

**PANORAMA** offers you a thorough Instructor's Annotated Edition that places a wealth of teaching resources at your fingertips. The annotations were written to complement and support varied teaching styles, to extend the already rich content of the student textbook, and to save you time in class preparation and course management. In response to instructor input, the **Third Edition** IAE features larger surrounding side and bottom panels for increased readability. Reduced student text pages provide overprinted answers to all activities with discrete responses.

Here is a quick orientation to the principal types of instructor annotations you will find in your textbook. These annotations are only suggestions, and any Spanish questions, sentences, models, or simulated instructor-student exchanges are not meant to be prescriptive or limiting. You are encouraged to view these suggested "scripts" as flexible points of departure that will help you achieve your instructional goals.

## On the Lesson Opener Pages

- **Lesson Goals** A list of the lexical, grammatical, and sociocultural goals of the lesson, including language-learning strategies and skill-building techniques

- **A primera vista** Personalized questions for jump-starting the lesson, based on the full-page photograph

- **Instructional Resources** A correlation, including page references, to all student and instructor supplements available to accompany the lesson

## In the Side Panels

- **Section Goals** A list of the lexical, grammatical, and/or sociocultural goals of the section

- **Instructional Resources** A correlation, including page references, to all ancillaries specific to a given strand

- **Teaching Tips** Teaching suggestions for presenting the section, working with on-page materials, and carrying out specific activities, as well as quick ways to start classes or activities by recycling language or ideas

- **Expansion** Expansions and variations on activities

- **Script** Transcripts of the audio recordings for the first two **Práctica** activities in each **Contextos** section and the **Estrategia** and **Ahora escucha** features in each **Escuchar** section

- **Possible Conversation** Sample answers based on known vocabulary, grammar, and language functions that students might produce

- **Video Recap** Questions to help students recall the events of the previous lesson's **Fotonovela** episode

- **Video Synopsis** Summaries in the **Fotonovela** sections that recap that lesson's video module

- **Expresiones útiles** Suggestions for introducing upcoming **Estructura** grammar points incorporated into the **Fotonovela** episode

- **Estrategia** Suggestions for working with the reading, writing, and listening strategies presented in the **Lectura, Escritura,** and **Escuchar** sections

- **Tema** Ideas for presenting and expanding the writing-assignment topic in **Escritura**

- **El país en cifras** Additional information expanding on the data presented for each Spanish-speaking country featured in the **Panorama** sections

- **¡Increíble pero cierto!** Curious facts about a lesser-known aspect of the country featured in the **Panorama** sections

- **Section-specific Annotations** Suggestions for presenting, expanding, varying, and reinforcing individual instructional elements

- **Student Text Sidebar Annotations** Suggestions for incorporating the information provided in sidebars (**¡Atención!, Ayuda, Nota cultural,** etc.)

- **Successful Language Learning** Tips and strategies to enhance students' language-learning experience

- **The Affective Dimension** Suggestions for reducing students' language-learning anxieties

## In the *Teaching Options* Boxes

- **Extra Practice, Pairs, Small Groups, and Large Groups** Additional activities beyond those included in the student textbook

- **Game** Games that practice the section's language or recycle previously learned language

- **TPR** Total Physical Response activities that physically engage students in learning Spanish

- **Variación léxica** Extra information related to the **Variación léxica** in **Contextos** or the Spanish-speaking countries in **Panorama**

- **Worth Noting** More detailed information about an interesting aspect of the Spanish-speaking countries in **Panorama**

- **Heritage Speakers** Suggestions and activities tailored to heritage speakers

- **Video** Techniques and activities for using the **PANORAMA** video program with **Fotonovela** and other lesson sections

- **Evaluation** Suggested rubrics for grading students' writing and oral presentations

Please check the Supersite (**panorama.vhlcentral.com**) for additional teaching support and program updates.

# General Teaching Considerations

## Orienting Students to the Student Textbook

Because **PANORAMA 3/e** treats design as an integral part of students' language-learning experience, you may want to take a few minutes to orient students to their textbooks. Have them flip through one lesson, and point out that all lessons are organized exactly the same way. Show how the major sections of each lesson are color-coded for easy navigation: red for **Contextos,** purple for **Fotonovela,** orange for **Cultura,** blue for **Estructura,** green for **Adelante,** and gold for **Vocabulario.** Let them know that, because of the design, they can be confident that they will always know "where they are" in their textbook.

Emphasize that sections are self-contained, occupying either a full page or a spread of two facing pages, thereby eliminating the need to flip back and forth to do activities or to work with explanatory material. Finally, call students' attention to the use of color to highlight key information in elements such as charts, diagrams, word lists, and activity **modelos,** titles, and sidebars.

## Flexible Lesson Organization

**PANORAMA 3/e** uses a flexible lesson organization designed to meet the needs of diverse teaching styles, institutions, and instructional goals. For example, you can begin with the lesson-opener page and progress sequentially through a lesson. If you do not want to devote class time to grammar, you can assign the **Estructura** explanations for outside study, freeing up class time for other purposes such as developing oral communication skills, learning more about the Spanish-speaking world, or working with the video program. You might work extensively with the **Cultura** and **Adelante** sections to focus on students' reading, writing, and listening skills and their knowledge of the Spanish-speaking world, or, you might prefer to use these sections periodically in response to your students' interests, as the opportunities arise. If you plan on using the **PANORAMA** Testing Program, however, be aware that its tests and exams test the language presented in **Contextos, Estructura,** and the **Expresiones útiles** boxes of **Fotonovela.**

## Identifying Active Vocabulary

All words and expressions taught in the illustrations and **Más vocabulario** lists in **Contextos** are considered active, testable vocabulary. However, any items in the **Variación léxica** or **Así se dice** boxes are intended for receptive learning and are presented for enrichment only. The words and expressions in the **Expresiones útiles** boxes in **Fotonovela,** as well as words in charts, word lists, ¡**Atención!** sidebars, and sample sentences in **Estructura,** are also part of the active vocabulary. Point out to students that at the end of each lesson, **Vocabulario** provides a convenient one-page summary of the items they should know and that may appear on tests and exams. You might also tell them that an easy way to study the **Vocabulario** list is to cover up the Spanish half of each section, leaving only the English equivalents exposed, or vice-versa, so they can quiz themselves.

## Taking into Account the Affective Dimension

While many factors contribute to the quality and success of the learning experience, two factors are particularly important: students' beliefs about how language is learned and language-learning anxiety.

Students often come to modern-language courses either with a lack of knowledge about how to approach language learning or with mistaken notions about how to do so. Many students believe that making mistakes when speaking the target language must be avoided. Others are convinced that learning another language is like learning any other academic subject; they believe that success is guaranteed, provided they attend class regularly, learn the assigned vocabulary words and grammar rules, and study for exams. In fact, in a study of college-level beginning language learners in the United States, more than one-third of the participants thought that they could become fluent if they studied the language for only one hour a day for two years or less. Mistaken and unrealistic beliefs such as these can cause frustration and ultimately loss of motivation.

Another factor that can negatively impact students is language-learning anxiety. As Professor Elaine K. Horwitz of The University of Texas at Austin and Senior Consulting Editor of **PANORAMA 1/e** wrote, "Surveys indicate that up to one-third of American foreign-language students feel moderately to highly anxious about studying another language. Physical symptoms of foreign-language anxiety can include heart-pounding or palpitations, sweating, trembling, fast breathing, and general feelings of unease." The late Dr. Philip Redwine Donley, **PANORAMA** co-author and author of articles on language-learning anxiety, spoke with many students who reported feeling nervous or apprehensive in their classes. They mentioned freezing when called on by their instructors or going inexplicably blank when taking tests. Some so dreaded their classes that they skipped them or dropped the course.

**PANORAMA** contains several features aimed at reducing students' language-learning anxiety and supporting a successful experience. Its highly structured, visually dramatic interior design was conceived as a learning tool to make students feel comfortable with the content and confident about navigating the lessons. The Instructor's Annotated Edition includes recurring *Affective Dimension* annotations with suggestions for reducing language-learning anxieties, as well as *Successful Language Learning* annotations that provide learning strategies for enhancing the learning experiences. In addition, the student text provides a wealth of helpful sidebars that assist students by making relevant connections with new information or reminding them of previously learned concepts.

### Student Sidebars

| | |
|---|---|
| **¡Atención!** | Provides active, testable information about the vocabulary or grammar point |
| **Ayuda** | Offers specific grammar and vocabulary reminders related to a particular activity or suggests pertinent language-learning strategies |
| **Consulta** | References related material introduced in previous or upcoming lessons |
| **¡Lengua viva!** | Presents immediately relevant information on everyday language use |
| **Nota cultural** | Provides a wide range of cultural information relevant to the topic of an activity |

# General Suggestions for Using the PANORAMA *Flash cultura* and *Panorama cultural* Videos

The *Flash cultura* Video is presented in the format of a news broadcast and accompanies the thematic presentations and readings in the **Cultura** section. The *Panorama cultural* Video contains documentary and travelogue footage of each country featured in the lessons' **Panorama** section. The visually appealing episodes were designed to cover a wide range of topics; they present interesting new information about each country that is included in the textbook. Like the conversations in the *Fotonovela* Video, these video segments deliver comprehensible input. Each was written to emphasize the vocabulary and grammar students learned in the corresponding and previous lessons, while providing a small amount of unknown language.

Activities for the *Panorama cultural* Video are located in the Video Manual section of the **PANORAMA 3/e** Workbook/Video Manual; activities for *Flash cultura* are on the Supersite. These varied activity formats follow a process approach that moves through pre-viewing, while-viewing, and post-viewing activities. This approach prepares students for watching the video segments, focuses them while they watch, and checks their comprehension after they have finished viewing the footage.

When showing the videos in your classes, you might implement a process approach. Start with an activity that prepares students for the video segment by taking advantage of what they learned in previous lessons or going over new vocabulary. This could be followed by an activity that students do while you play parts or all of the video segment. The final activity, done in the same class period or in the next one as warm-up, could recap what students saw and heard and then move beyond the video segment's topic. The following suggestions for working with the *Flash cultura* or *Panorama cultural* Video in class can be carried out as described or expanded upon in any number of ways.

## Before viewing

- After students have practiced the lesson's vocabulary and grammar and worked through the **Cultura** or **Panorama** section of the student textbook, mention the video segment's title and ask them to guess what the segment might be about.

- Based on their predictions, have pairs of students make a list of the lesson vocabulary they expect to hear in the video segment.

- Read the class a list of true-false or multiple-choice questions about the video. Students must use what they learned in the **Cultura** or **Panorama** section to guess the answers. Confirm their guesses after watching the segment.

## While viewing

- After having introduced the lesson's theme using the lesson-opening page, show the video segment *before* moving on to **Contextos** to jump-start the lesson. Have students tell you what vocabulary and grammar they recognize. Briefly present the new lesson's theme and grammar structures for recognition.

- Show the video segment with the audio turned off and ask students to use lesson vocabulary and structures to describe what is happening. Have them confirm their guesses by showing the segment again with the audio on.

- Have students refer to the list of words they brainstormed before viewing the video and put a check in front of any words they actually see in the segment.

- Turn the sound on and have students watch the video. Show it again and ask students to take notes. Finally, have them compare their notes in pairs or groups for confirmation.

- Photocopy the segment's videoscript from the Supersite and white out expressions related to the lesson theme. Distribute the scripts for pairs or groups to complete as cloze paragraphs.

## After viewing

- Have students say what aspects of the information presented in the **Cultura** or **Panorama** section they can see in the video segment.

- Ask groups to write a brief summary of the content of the video segment. Have them exchange papers with another group for peer editing.

- Ask students to discuss any new aspects of the featured country that they learned from watching the video. Encourage them to say how the new information was different from their expectations.

- Have students pick one characteristic about the country that they learned from watching the video segment. Have them research more about that topic and write a brief composition that expands on it.

For more information on the complete **PANORAMA** video program, see pages xxvi-xxvii of the Student Text.

# General Suggestions for Using
## the PANORAMA *Fotonovela* Video

The **Fotonovela** section in each of the student textbook's lessons and the **PANORAMA** *Fotonovela* Video were created as interlocking pieces. All photos in **Fotonovela** are video stills from the corresponding episode, while the printed conversations are abbreviated versions of the video module's dramatic content. Both the **Fotonovela** conversations and their expanded video versions represent comprehensible input at the discourse level; they were written to use language from the corresponding lesson's **Contextos** and **Estructura** sections. They recycle known language (starting with **Lección 2**), preview grammar points students will study later in the lesson, and, in keeping with the concept of "i + 1," contain a small amount of unknown language.

You may use this section in many different ways. No matter which approach you choose, students have ample materials to help them view the video independently and process it in a meaningful way. For each episode, there are activities in both the textbook lesson and in the Video Manual.

Here are some of the many ways you can use the **Fotonovela** Video and its corresponding textbook section.

- You can use **Fotonovela** as an advance organizer, presenting it before showing the video module.

- You can also show the video module first and then follow up with **Fotonovela**.

- You can use **Fotonovela** as a stand-alone, video-independent section.

- You might use the **PANORAMA** *Fotonovela* Video in class when working with the **Estructura** sections. You could play the parts of the dramatic episode that correspond to the video stills in the grammar explanations or show selected scenes and ask students to identify certain grammar points.

- You could focus on the video's **Resumen** sections. In these, one of the main video characters recaps the dramatic episode by reminiscing about its key events. These reminiscences, which emphasize the lesson's active vocabulary and grammar points, take the form of footage pulled out of the dramatic episode and repeated in black and white images. The main character who "hosts" each **Resumen** begins and ends the section with a few lines that do not appear in the live segment. These sentences provide additional opportunities for students to process the language they have been studying within the context of the video storyline.

- In class, you could play the parts of the **Resumen** section that exemplify individual grammar points as you progress through each **Estructura** section. You could also wait until you complete an **Estructura** section and then review it by showing the corresponding **Resumen** section in its entirety.

# PANORAMA and the *Standards for Foreign Language Learning*

Since 1982, when the *ACTFL Proficiency Guidelines* were first published, that document and its subsequent revisions have influenced the teaching of modern languages in the United States. **PANORAMA** and its parent book, **VISTAS**, were written with the concerns and philosophy of the *ACTFL Proficiency Guidelines* in mind, incorporating a proficiency-oriented approach from its planning stages.

The pedagogy of **PANORAMA** and **VISTAS** was also informed by the *Standards for Foreign Language Learning in the 21st Century*. First published in 1996 under the auspices of the National Standards in Foreign Language Education Project, the Standards are organized into five goal areas, often called the Five Cs: Communication, Cultures, Connections, Comparisons, and Communities.

Special Standards icons appear on the textbook pages of your IAE to call out sections that have a particularly strong relationship with the Standards. The following are a few examples of how **PANORAMA** was written with the Standards firmly in mind, but you will find many more as you work with the student textbook and its ancillaries.

- Because **PANORAMA** takes a communicative approach to the teaching and learning of Spanish, the Communication goal is obvious throughout the student text. For example, the diverse activity formats used in the **Comunicación** and **Síntesis** sections—pair work, small group work, class circulation, information gap, task-based, and so on—engage students in communicative exchanges such as providing and obtaining information and expressing feelings and emotions.

- The Cultures goal is most evident in the **Nota cultural** student sidebars, and the lessons' **Cultura, En pantalla, Oye cómo va,** and **Panorama** sections. **PANORAMA** weaves culture into virtually every page, exposing students to the multiple facets of the cultural practices, products, and perspectives of the Spanish-speaking world.

- In keeping with the Connections goal, students can connect with other disciplines such as geography, history, fine arts, and science in the **Panorama** section; they can acquire information and recognize distinctive cultural viewpoints in the non-literary and literary texts of the **Lectura** sections.

- The **Estructura** sections, with their clear explanations and special *Compare & Contrast* features, reflect the Comparisons goal.

- Students also work toward the Connections and Communities goal when they do the **Cultura** and **Panorama** sections' **Conexión Internet** activities, as well as the activities and information on the **PANORAMA** Supersite.

# COURSE PLANNING

The entire **PANORAMA** program was developed with an eye to flexibility and ease of use in a wide variety of courses. **PANORAMA** can be used in courses taught on a semester or quarter system, as well as in courses that complete the book in two or three semesters. Here are some sample course plans that illustrate how **PANORAMA** can be used in a variety of academic situations. Visit the **PANORAMA** Supersite (panorama.vhlcentral.com) for more course planning tips and detailed suggestions, as well as an essay on course planning by the late Dr. Philip Redwine Donley, **PANORAMA** co-author. You should, of course, feel free to organize your courses in the way that best suits your students' needs and your instructional objectives.

## Two-Semester System

This chart illustrates how **PANORAMA** can be completed in a two-semester course. This division of material allows the present and the present progressive, including reflexive verbs, and the preterite tenses to be presented in the first semester; the second semester focuses on the imperfect tense, the subjunctive, and the perfect tenses, as well as the future and the conditional.

| Semester 1 | Semester 2 |
|---|---|
| Lecciones 1–7 | Lecciones 8–15 |

## Three-Semester System

This chart shows how **PANORAMA** can be used in a three-semester course. The lessons are equally divided among the three semesters, allowing students to absorb the material at a steady pace.

| Semester 1 | Semester 2 | Semester 3 |
|---|---|---|
| Lecciones 1–5 | Lecciones 6–10 | Lecciones 11–15 |

## Quarter System

In this chart, the **PANORAMA** materials are organized in three balanced segments for use in the quarter system, allowing ample time for learning and review in each quarter.

| First Quarter | Second Quarter | Third Quarter |
|---|---|---|
| Lecciones 1–5 | Lecciones 6–10 | Lecciones 11–15 |

# LESSON PLANNING

**PANORAMA** has been carefully planned to meet your instructional needs, whether you teach on a semester or quarter system and whether you plan to use the textbook for two or three semesters or over three quarters.

The following lesson plan for **Lección 1** illustrates how **PANORAMA 3/e** can be used in a two-semester program with four contact hours per week. It deals with order of presentation rather than specific instructional techniques and suggestions. This is because pedagogical suggestions are provided in the annotations of the **PANORAMA 3/e** IAE. Lesson plans for alternate course configurations are available on the Supersite.

## Sample Lesson Plan for *Lección 1*

### Day 1

1. Introduce yourself and present the course syllabus.
2. Present the **Lección 1** objectives.
3. Preview the **Contextos** section; present the **Contextos** vocabulary.
4. Work through the **Práctica** activities with the class; have students read over the **Comunicación** activities for the next class.
5. Preview the **Fotonovela** and **Expresiones útiles**.
6. Have students read through the **Fotonovela** and prepare the first **¿Qué pasó?** activity for the next class.

### Day 2

1. Review **Contextos** vocabulary; have the class do the **Comunicación** activities.
2. Present the **Fotonovela** and **Expresiones útiles**.
3. Do the first **¿Qué pasó?** activity with the class.
4. Have students do the next three **¿Qué pasó?** activities.
5. Preview the **Pronunciación** section and **Estructura 1.1**.
6. Have students read **Estructura 1.1** and prepare the **¡Inténtalo!** and **Práctica** activities for the next class.
7. Have students read **En detalle** in **Cultura** and prepare the first activity for the next class.

### Day 3

1. Review the **Expresiones útiles**.
2. Do the first **Cultura** activity with the class.
3. Present the remaining **Cultura** features and have students do the activities.
4. Present **Estructura 1.1**.
5. Work through the **¡Inténtalo!** and **Práctica** activities with the class.
6. Have students do the **Comunicación** activity in class.
7. Preview **Estructura 1.2**.
8. Have students read **Estructura 1.2** and prepare the **¡Inténtalo!** and **Práctica** activities for the next class.

### Day 4

1. Review **Estructura 1.1**.
2. Present **Estructura 1.2** and work through the **¡Inténtalo!** and **Práctica** activities with the class.
3. Have students do the **Comunicación** activities during class.
4. Preview **Estructura 1.3**.
5. Have students read **Estructura 1.3** and prepare the **¡Inténtalo!** and **Práctica** activities for the next class.

### Day 5

1. Review **Estructura 1.2**.
2. Present **Estructura 1.3** and work through the **¡Inténtalo!** and **Práctica** activities with the class.
3. Have students do the **Comunicación** activities during class.
4. Preview **Estructura 1.4**.
5. Have students read **Estructura 1.4** and prepare the **¡Inténtalo!** and **Práctica** activities for the next class.

### Day 6

1. Quickly review **Estructura 1.3**.
2. Present **Estructura 1.4** and work through the **¡Inténtalo!** and **Práctica** activities with the class.
3. Have students do the **Comunicación** activities and the **Síntesis** activity.
4. Assign material from the **Adelante** section as desired for integrated practice and review.

### Day 7

1. Go over assigned material from the **Adelante** section.
2. Present the **Panorama** section.
3. Review **Lección 1** with the class.
4. Have students prepare the **Recapitulación** activities on the Supersite.
5. Have students prepare to take one of the four **Pruebas** for **Lección 1** during the next class session.

### Day 8

1. Administer **Prueba A** or **Prueba B** for **Lección 1**.
2. Preview the **Lección 2** objectives.
3. Have students read the **Contextos** section and prepare the **Práctica** activities for the next class.

---

The lesson plan presented here is not prescriptive. You should present lesson materials as you see fit, tailoring them to your own teaching preferences and to your students' learning styles. You may want to allow extra time for concepts students find challenging and less time to topics they comprehend without difficulty. Based on your students' needs, you may want to omit certain topics or activities altogether. If you have fewer than five contact hours per semester or are on a quarter system, you will find the **PANORAMA** program very flexible: simply pick and choose from its array of instructional resources and sequence them in the way that makes the most sense for your program.

# PANORAMA

Introducción a la lengua española

**THIRD EDITION**

**José A. Blanco**

**Philip Redwine Donley, Late**
Austin Community College

VISTA
HIGHER LEARNING

Boston, Massachusetts

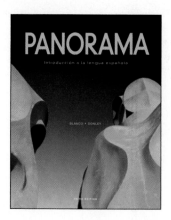

The **PANORAMA, Third Edition,** cover features a detail from Antoni Gaudí's **La Pedrera** in Barcelona, Spain. This remarkable architectural feat is one of the many landmarks from the Spanish-speaking world that you will learn about in **PANORAMA**.

**Publisher:** José A. Blanco
**Vice President and Editorial Director:** Beth Kramer
**Managing Editor:** Sarah Kenney
**Project Manager:** Isabelle Alouane
**Editor:** Gabriela Ferland
**Director of Art and Design:** Linda Jurras
**Director of Production and Manufacturing:** Lisa Perrier
**Design Manager:** Polo Barrera
**Photo Researcher and Art Buyer:** Rachel Distler
**Production Coordinator:** Nick Ventullo
**Production and Manufacturing Team:** Oscar Diez, Mauricio Henao, María Eugenia Castaño, Jeff Perron

**President:** Janet L. Dracksdorf
**Sr. Vice President of Operations:** Tom Delano
**Vice President of Sales and Marketing:** Scott Burns
**Executive Marketing Manager:** Benjamín Rivera

Student Text ISBN-13: 978-1-60007-594-0
       ISBN-10: 1-60007-594-0
Instructor's Annotated Edition ISBN-13: 978-1-60007-599-5
       ISBN-10: 1-60007-599-1

1 2 3 4 5 6 7 8 9 R 12 11 10 09 08 07

# TO THE STUDENT

To Vista Higher Learning's great pride, **PANORAMA** and **VISTAS**, the parent text from which **PANORAMA** is derived, became the best-selling new introductory college Spanish programs in more than a decade in their first editions. The success of the second editions followed suit, and it is now our pleasure to welcome you to **PANORAMA**, **Third Edition**, your gateway to the Spanish language and to the vibrant cultures of the Spanish-speaking world.

A direct result of extensive reviews and ongoing input from students and instructors, **PANORAMA 3/e** includes both the highly successful, ground-breaking features of the original program, plus many exciting new elements designed to keep **PANORAMA** the most student-friendly program available. Here are just some of the features you will encounter:

## Original, hallmark features

- A unique, easy-to-navigate design built around color-coded sections that appear either completely on one page or on spreads of two facing pages
- Integration of an appealing video, up-front in each lesson of the student text
- Practical, high-frequency vocabulary in meaningful contexts
- Clear, comprehensive grammar explanations with high-impact graphics and other special features that make structures easier to learn and use
- Ample guided, focused practice to make you comfortable with the vocabulary and grammar you are learning and to give you a solid foundation for communication
- An emphasis on communicative interactions with a classmate, small groups, the full class, and your instructor
- Careful development of reading, writing, and listening skills incorporating learning strategies and a process approach
- Integration of the culture of the everyday lives of Spanish speakers and coverage of the entire Spanish-speaking world
- Unprecedented learning support through on-the-spot student sidebars and on-page correlations of the print and technology ancillaries for each lesson section
- A complete set of print and technology ancillaries to help you learn Spanish

## New to the Third Edition

- Revised grammar scope for improved coverage within and across lessons
- Increased reading and coverage of culture in the new **Cultura** section
- The **Recapitulación** grammar review at the end of **Estructura**, available with auto-scoring and diagnostics at <u>panorama.vhlcentral.com</u>
- Exciting multimedia components, such as **En pantalla** and **Oye cómo va**
- New ancillaries, like the ***Flash cultura*** Video and the **PANORAMA, Third Edition**, Supersite at <u>panorama.vhlcentral.com</u>, all closely integrated with the student text

**PANORAMA 3/e** has fifteen lessons, each of which is organized exactly the same way. To familiarize yourself with the organization of the text, as well as its original and new features, turn to page xii and take the **at-a-glance** tour.

# table of contents

| | contextos | fotonovela |
|---|---|---|

# table of contents

| | contextos | fotonovela |
|---|---|---|

# table of contents

| | **contextos** | **fotonovela** |
|---|---|---|

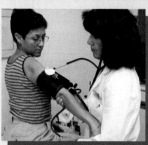

| cultura | estructura | adelante |
|---------|-----------|----------|

# table of contents

| | contextos | fotonovela |
|---|---|---|

## Consulta (*Reference*)

| cultura | estructura | adelante |
|---|---|---|

# PANORAMA-at-a-glance

## Lesson Openers
## outline the content and features of each lesson.

### Los pasatiempos 4

**Communicative Goals**

*You will learn how to:*

- Talk about pastimes, weekend activities, and sports
- Make plans and invitations

**contextos**

**pages 108–111**
- Pastimes
- Sports
- Places in the city

**fotonovela**

**pages 112–115**
Don Francisco informs the students that they have an hour of free time. Inés and Javier decide to take a walk through the city. Maite and Álex go to a park where they are involved in a minor accident. On their way back, Álex invites Maite to go running.

**cultura**

**pages 116–117**
- Soccer rivalries
- Anier García and Luciana Aymar

**estructura**

**pages 118–133**
- Present tense of **ir**
- Stem-changing verbs: **e→ie; o→ue**
- Stem-changing verbs: **e→i**
- Verbs with irregular **yo** forms
- Recapitulación

**adelante**

**pages 134–137**
**Lectura:** Popular sports in Latin America
**Panorama:** México

**A PRIMERA VISTA**
- ¿Qué son estas personas, atletas o artistas?
- ¿En qué tienen interés, en el fútbol o el tenis?
- ¿Son viejos? ¿Son delgados?
- ¿Tienen frío o calor?

**A primera vista** activities jump-start the lessons, allowing you to use the Spanish you know to talk about the photos.

**Communicative goals** highlight the real-life tasks you will be able to carry out in Spanish by the end of each lesson.

# Contextos
## presents vocabulary in meaningful contexts.

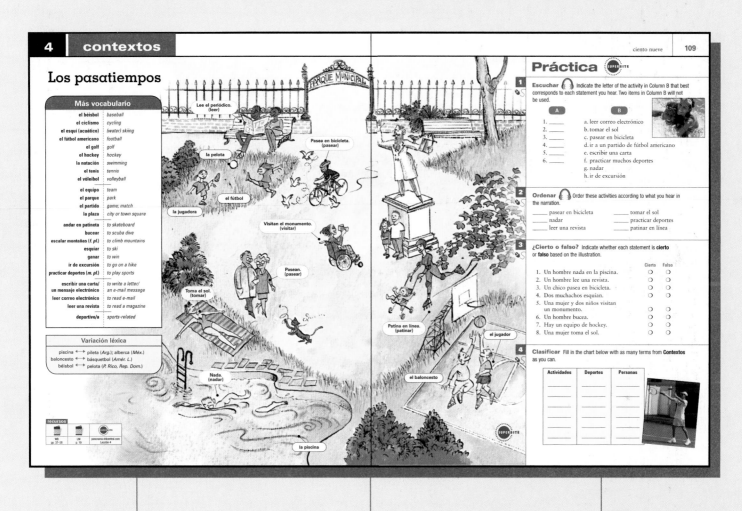

**Más vocabulario** boxes call out other important theme-related vocabulary in easy-to-reference Spanish-English lists.

**Illustrations** High-frequency vocabulary is introduced through expansive, full-color illustrations.

**Práctica** This section always begins with two listening exercises and continues with activities that practice the new vocabulary in meaningful contexts.

**Variación léxica** presents alternate words and expressions used throughout the Spanish-speaking world.

**Recursos** The icons in the **Recursos** boxes let you know exactly which print and technology ancillaries you can use to reinforce and expand on every section of every lesson.

**Comunicación** activities allow you to use the vocabulary creatively in interactions with a partner, a small group, or the entire class.

# PANORAMA-at-a-glance

## Fotonovela
# tells the story of four students traveling in Ecuador.

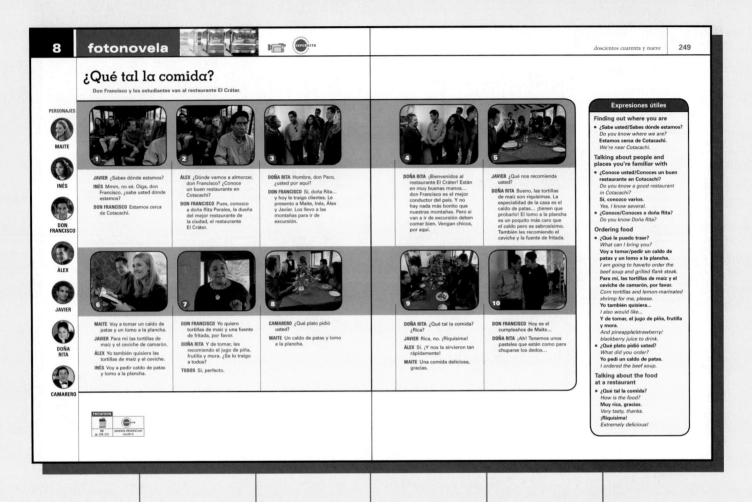

**Personajes** The photo-based conversations take place among a cast of recurring characters—four college students on vacation in Ecuador and the bus driver who accompanies them.

***Fotonovela* Video** The ***Fotonovela*** episode appears in the ***Fotonovela*** Video Program. To learn more about the video, turn to page xxvi.

**Conversations** Taken from the ***Fotonovela*** Video, the conversations reinforce vocabulary from **Contextos**. They also preview structures from the upcoming **Estructura** section in context *and* in a comprehensible way.

**Icons** provide on-the-spot visual cues for various types of activities: pair, small group, listening-based, video-related, handout-based, information gap, and Supersite. For a legend explaining all icons used in the student text, see page xxix.

**Expresiones útiles** These expressions organize new, active structures by language function so you can focus on using them for real-life, practical purposes.

# Pronunciación & Ortografía
## present the rules of Spanish pronunciation and spelling.

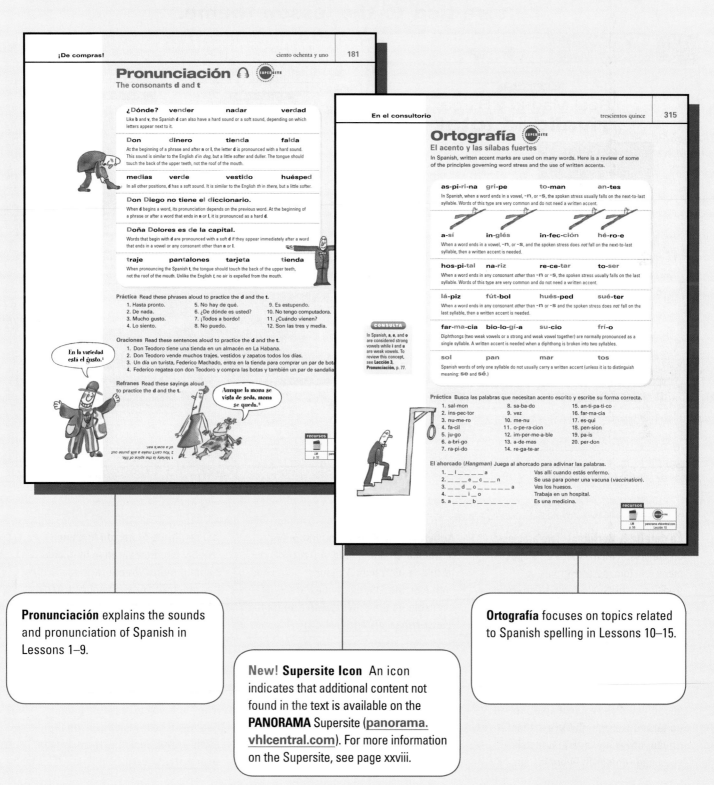

**Pronunciación** explains the sounds and pronunciation of Spanish in Lessons 1–9.

**New! Supersite Icon** An icon indicates that additional content not found in the text is available on the **PANORAMA** Supersite (panorama. vhlcentral.com). For more information on the Supersite, see page xxviii.

**Ortografía** focuses on topics related to Spanish spelling in Lessons 10–15.

# PANORAMA-at-a-glance

NEW SECTION!

## Cultura
# exposes you to different aspects of Hispanic culture tied to the lesson theme.

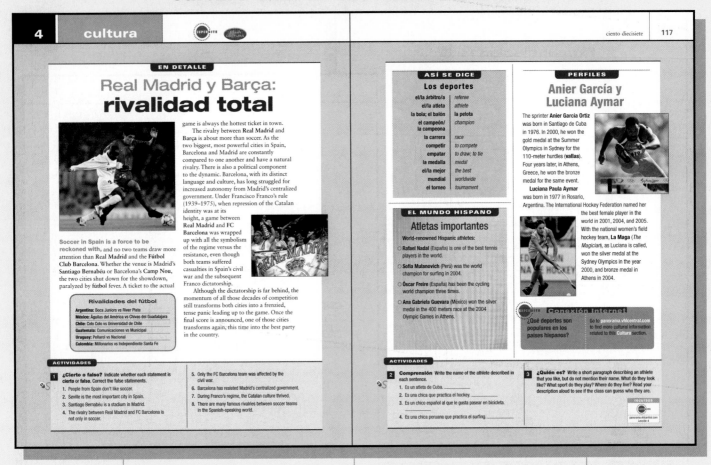

**En detalle & Perfil(es)** Two articles on the lesson theme focus on a specific place, custom, person, group, or tradition in the Spanish-speaking world. In Spanish starting in **Lección 7**, these features also provide reading practice.

**Activities** check your understanding of the material and lead you to further exploration. A mouse icon indicates that activities are available on the **PANORAMA** Supersite (**panorama.vhlcentral.com**).

**Así se dice & El mundo hispano** Lexical and comparative features expand cultural coverage to people, traditions, customs, trends, and vocabulary throughout the Spanish-speaking world.

**Coverage** While the **Panorama** section takes a regional approach to cultural coverage, **Cultura** is theme-driven, covering several Spanish-speaking regions in every lesson.

**Video** An icon lets you know that the brand-new **Flash cultura** Video offers specially-shot content tied to the feature article. To learn more about the video, turn to page xxvii.

**Conexión Internet** An Internet icon leads you to research a topic related to the lesson theme on the **PANORAMA** Supersite (**panorama. vhlcentral.com**).

# Estructura
## presents Spanish grammar in a graphic-intensive format.

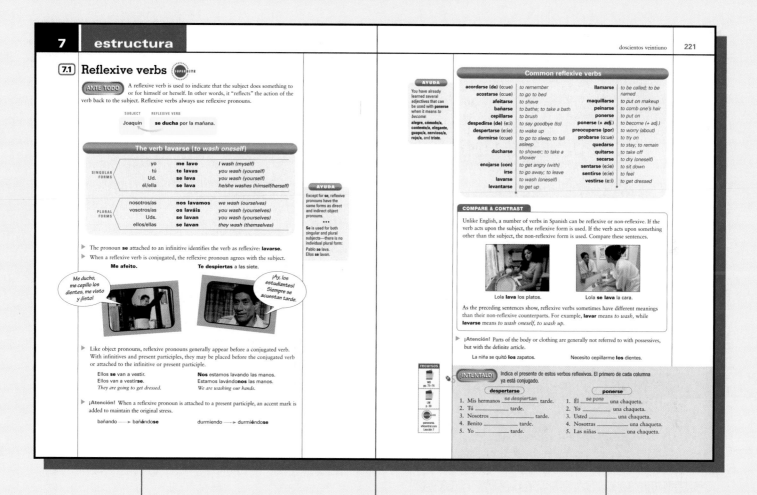

**Ante todo** This introduction eases you into the grammar with definitions of grammatical terms, reminders about what you already know of English grammar, and Spanish grammar you have learned in earlier lessons.

**Compare & Contrast** This feature focuses on aspects of grammar that native speakers of English may find difficult, clarifying similarities and differences between Spanish and English.

**Diagrams** To clarify concepts, clear and easy-to-grasp grammar explanations are reinforced by diagrams that colorfully present sample words, phrases, and sentences.

**Charts** To help you learn, colorful, easy-to-use charts call out key grammatical structures and forms, as well as important related vocabulary.

**Student sidebars** On-the-spot linguistic, cultural, or language-learning information directly relates to the materials in front of you.

**¡Inténtalo!** offers an easy first step into each grammar point. A mouse icon indicates these activities are available with auto-grading at **panorama.vhlcentral.com**.

## Estructura
## provides directed and communicative practice.

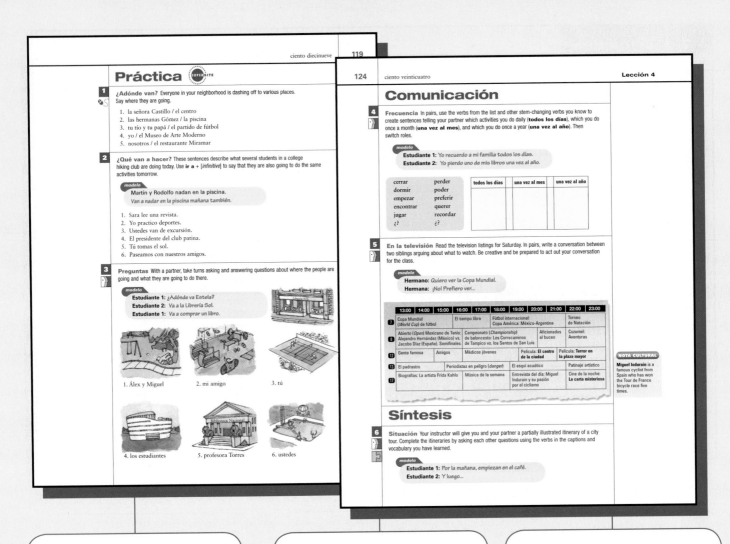

**Práctica** A wide range of guided, yet meaningful exercises weave current and previously learned vocabulary together with the current grammar point.

**Comunicación** Opportunities for creative expression use the lesson's grammar and vocabulary. These activities take place with a partner, in small groups, or with the whole class.

**Síntesis** activities integrate the current grammar point with previously learned points, providing built-in, consistent review and recycling as you progress through the text.

**New! Supersite Icon** An icon at the top of the page indicates that new content is available on the **PANORAMA** Supersite (**panorama.vhlcentral.com**); mouse icons next to individual activities signal that these are available with auto-grading on the Supersite.

**Information Gap activities** engage you and a partner in problem-solving and other situations based on handouts your instructor gives you. However, you and your partner each have only half of the information you need, so you must work together to accomplish the task at hand.

**Sidebars** The **Notas culturales** expand coverage of the cultures of Spanish-speaking peoples and countries, while **Ayuda** sidebars provide on-the-spot language support.

# Recapitulación
## provides review and a short quiz, available with auto-grading on the Supersite, for each lesson.

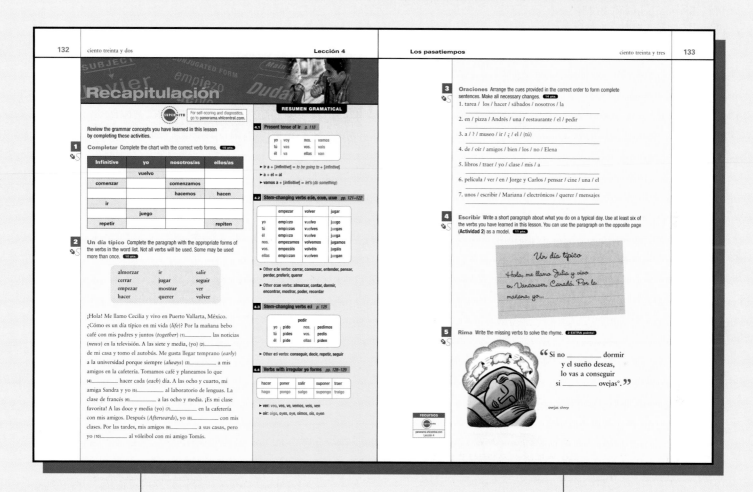

**Resumen gramatical** This review panel provides you with an easy-to-study summary of the basic concepts of the lesson's grammar, with page references to the full explanation.

**Activities** A series of activities, moving from directed to open-ended, systematically tests your mastery of the lesson's grammar. The section ends with a riddle or puzzle using the lesson's grammar.

**Points** Each activity is assigned a point value to help you track your progress. All **Recapitulación** sections add up to fifty points, with two extra-credit points for the last activity.

**Supersite Icon** An icon lets you know that the **Recapitulación** activities can be completed online with automatic scoring and diagnostics to help you identify where you are strong or where you might need review.

# PANORAMA-at-a-glance

## Adelante
## *Lectura* develops reading skills in the context of the lesson theme.

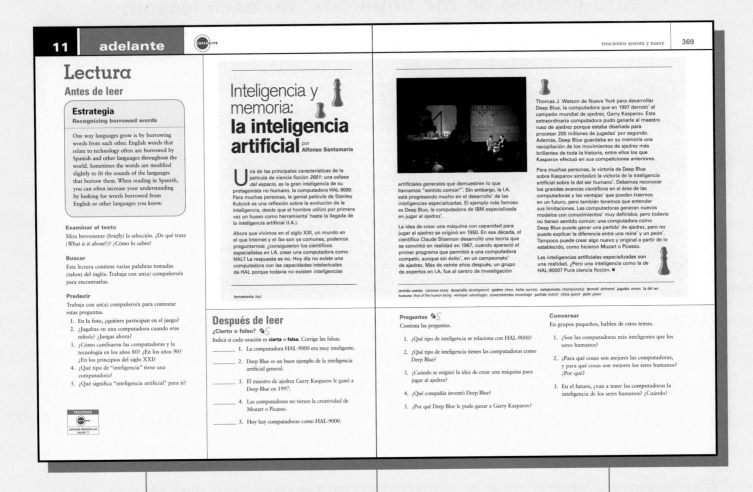

**Antes de leer** Valuable reading strategies and pre-reading activities strengthen your reading abilities in Spanish.

**Readings** Selections related to the lesson theme recycle vocabulary and grammar you have learned. The selections in Lessons 1–12 are cultural texts, while those in Lessons 13–15 are literary pieces.

**Después de leer** Activities include post-reading exercises that review and check your comprehension of the reading and expansion activities.

**New!** Three literary readings are new to this edition. Lessons 13–15 offer highly accessible poems, short stories, and excerpts from novels by important literary figures in the Spanish-speaking world.

# Adelante

## In lessons 3, 6, 9, 12, and 15, *Escritura* and *Escuchar* develop writing and listening skills.

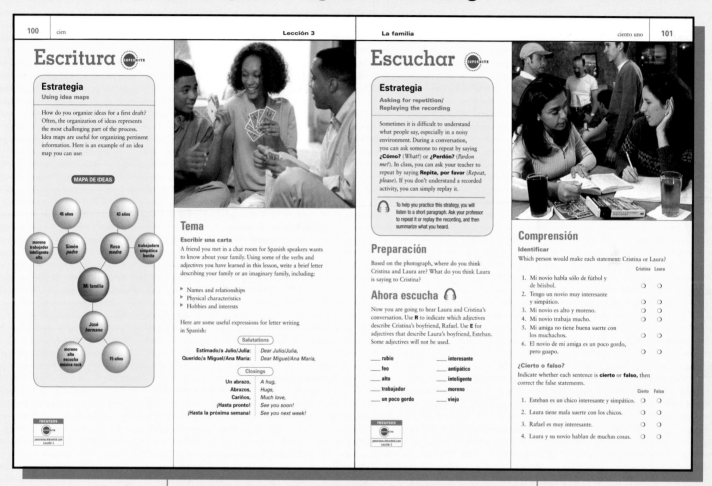

**Estrategia** Strategies help you prepare for the writing and listening tasks to come.

**Escuchar** A recorded conversation or narration develops your listening skills in Spanish. **Preparación** prepares you for listening to the recorded passage.

**Escritura** The **Tema** describes the writing topic and includes suggestions for approaching it.

**Ahora escucha** walks you through the passage, and **Comprensión** checks your listening comprehension.

# PANORAMA-at-a-glance

**Adelante**

## Every third lesson, *En pantalla* presents an authentic television clip tied to the lesson theme.

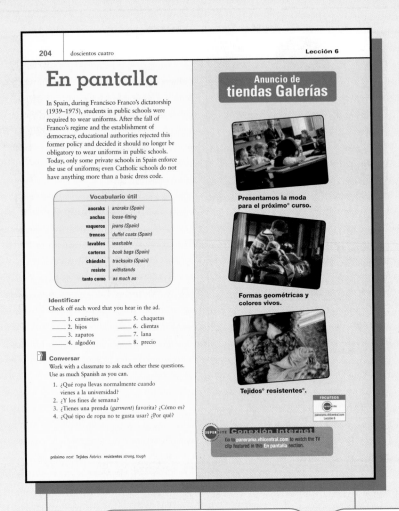

**En pantalla** TV clips from all over the Spanish-speaking world give you additional exposure to authentic language. The clips, in lessons 3, 6, 9, 12, and 15, include commercials, newscasts, and TV shows, and feature the language, vocabulary, and theme of the lesson.

**Presentation** Cultural notes, video stills with abbreviated excerpts, and vocabulary support all prepare you to view the clip. A series of activities checks your comprehension of the material and expands on the ideas presented.

**Supersite Icon** Icons and **Recursos** boxes lead you to the Supersite (**panorama.vhlcentral.com**), where you can view the TV clip and get further practice.

## Adelante

# Also every third lesson, *Oye cómo va* presents a song by an artist from the featured country or region.

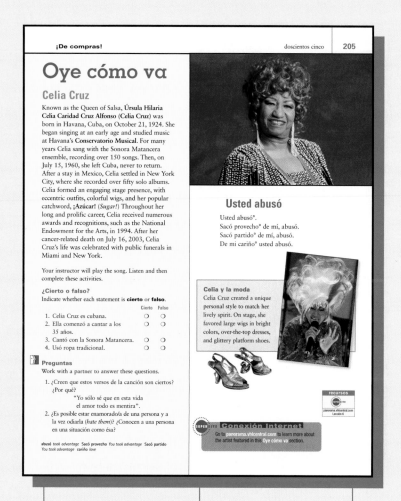

**Oye cómo va** A biography of an artist or group from the featured country introduces you to the music of the Spanish-speaking world. Excerpts from the song lyrics, photos, and explanations of the genre or other related information accompany the biography.

**Activities** A series of activities checks your comprehension of the material and expands on the ideas presented.

**Supersite Icon** Icons and **Recursos** boxes lead you to the Supersite (**panorama.vhlcentral.com**) for more information and further practice.

# PANORAMA-at-a-glance

## Panorama
## presents the nations of the Spanish-speaking world.

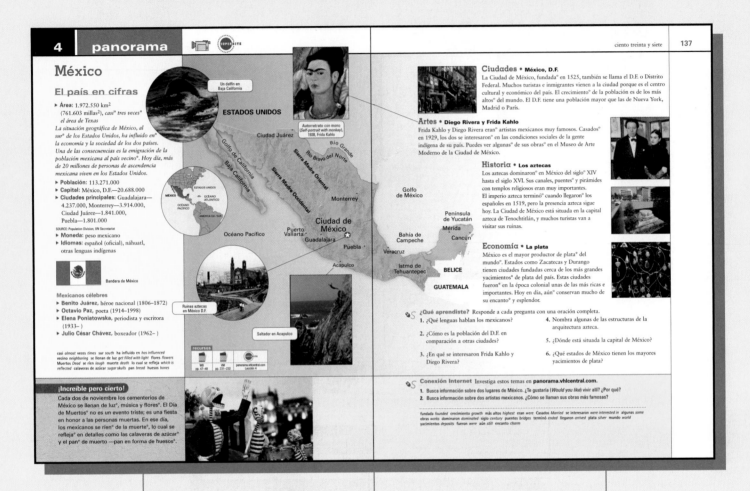

**El país en cifras** presents interesting key facts about the featured country.

**Maps** point out major cities, rivers, and geographical features and situate the country in the context of its immediate surroundings and the world.

**Readings** A series of brief paragraphs explores facets of the country's culture such as history, places, fine arts, literature, and aspects of everyday life.

**¡Increíble pero cierto!** highlights an intriguing fact about the country or its people.

**Conexión Internet** offers Internet activities on the **PANORAMA** Supersite (**panorama.vhlcentral. com**) for additional avenues of discovery.

***Panorama cultural* Video** The authentic footage of this video takes you to the featured Spanish-speaking country, letting you experience the sights and sounds of an aspect of its culture. To learn more about the video, turn to page xxvii.

# Vocabulario
## summarizes all the active vocabulary of the lesson.

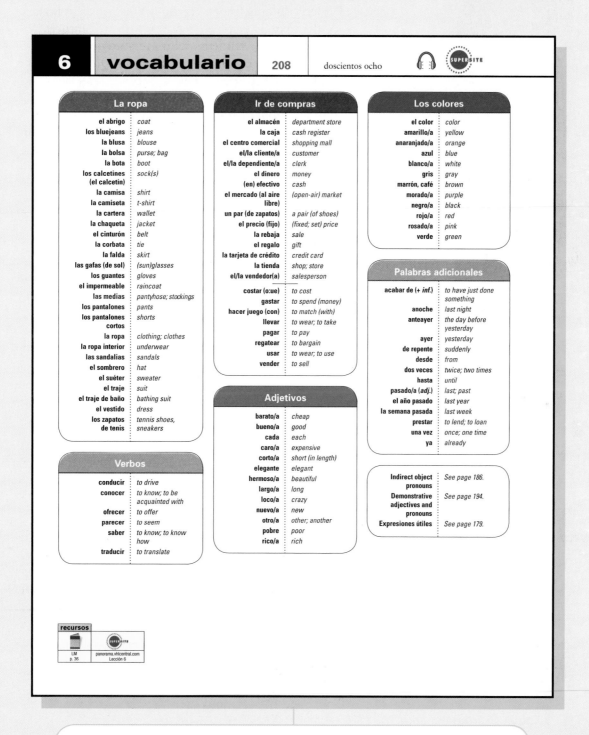

**6 vocabulario** 208 doscientos ocho

### La ropa

| | |
|---|---|
| el abrigo | coat |
| los bluejeans | jeans |
| la blusa | blouse |
| la bolsa | purse; bag |
| la bota | boot |
| los calcetines (el calcetín) | sock(s) |
| la camisa | shirt |
| la camiseta | t-shirt |
| la cartera | wallet |
| la chaqueta | jacket |
| el cinturón | belt |
| la corbata | tie |
| la falda | skirt |
| las gafas (de sol) | (sun)glasses |
| los guantes | gloves |
| el impermeable | raincoat |
| las medias | pantyhose; stockings |
| los pantalones | pants |
| los pantalones cortos | shorts |
| la ropa | clothing; clothes |
| la ropa interior | underwear |
| las sandalias | sandals |
| el sombrero | hat |
| el suéter | sweater |
| el traje | suit |
| el traje de baño | bathing suit |
| el vestido | dress |
| los zapatos de tenis | tennis shoes, sneakers |

### Verbos

| | |
|---|---|
| conducir | to drive |
| conocer | to know; to be acquainted with |
| ofrecer | to offer |
| parecer | to seem |
| saber | to know; to know how |
| traducir | to translate |

### Ir de compras

| | |
|---|---|
| el almacén | department store |
| la caja | cash register |
| el centro comercial | shopping mall |
| el/la cliente/a | customer |
| el/la dependiente/a | clerk |
| el dinero | money |
| (en) efectivo | cash |
| el mercado (al aire libre) | (open-air) market |
| un par (de zapatos) | a pair (of shoes) |
| el precio (fijo) | (fixed; set) price |
| la rebaja | sale |
| el regalo | gift |
| la tarjeta de crédito | credit card |
| la tienda | shop; store |
| el/la vendedor(a) | salesperson |
| costar (o:ue) | to cost |
| gastar | to spend (money) |
| hacer juego (con) | to match (with) |
| llevar | to wear; to take |
| pagar | to pay |
| regatear | to bargain |
| usar | to wear; to use |
| vender | to sell |

### Adjetivos

| | |
|---|---|
| barato/a | cheap |
| bueno/a | good |
| cada | each |
| caro/a | expensive |
| corto/a | short (in length) |
| elegante | elegant |
| hermoso/a | beautiful |
| largo/a | long |
| loco/a | crazy |
| nuevo/a | new |
| otro/a | other; another |
| pobre | poor |
| rico/a | rich |

### Los colores

| | |
|---|---|
| el color | color |
| amarillo/a | yellow |
| anaranjado/a | orange |
| azul | blue |
| blanco/a | white |
| gris | gray |
| marrón, café | brown |
| morado/a | purple |
| negro/a | black |
| rojo/a | red |
| rosado/a | pink |
| verde | green |

### Palabras adicionales

| | |
|---|---|
| acabar de (+ inf.) | to have just done something |
| anoche | last night |
| anteayer | the day before yesterday |
| ayer | yesterday |
| de repente | suddenly |
| desde | from |
| dos veces | twice; two times |
| hasta | until |
| pasado/a (adj.) | last; past |
| el año pasado | last year |
| la semana pasada | last week |
| prestar | to lend; to loan |
| una vez | once; one time |
| ya | already |

| | |
|---|---|
| Indirect object pronouns | See page 186. |
| Demonstrative adjectives and pronouns | See page 194. |
| Expresiones útiles | See page 179. |

**recursos**

LM p. 36

panorama.vhlcentral.com Lección 6

**Recorded vocabulary** The headset icon at the top of the page and the **Recursos** boxes at the bottom of the page highlight that the active lesson vocabulary is recorded for convenient study on the **PANORAMA** Supersite (panorama.vhlcentral.com).

## FOTONOVELA VIDEO PROGRAM

Fully integrated with your textbook, the *Fotonovela* Video contains fifteen episodes, one for each lesson of the text. The episodes present the adventures of four college students who are studying at the **Universidad de San Francisco** in Quito, Ecuador. They decide to spend their vacation break on a bus tour of the Ecuadorian countryside with the ultimate goal of hiking up a volcano. The video, shot in various locations in Ecuador, tells their story and the story of Don Francisco, the tour bus driver who accompanies them.

The **Fotonovela** section in each textbook lesson is an abbreviated version of the dramatic episode featured in the video. Therefore, each **Fotonovela** section can be done before you see the corresponding video episode, after it, or as a section that stands alone.

As you watch each video episode, you will first see a live segment in which the characters interact using vocabulary and grammar you are studying. As the video progresses, the live segments carefully combine new vocabulary and grammar with previously taught language. You will then see a **Resumen** section in which one of the main video characters recaps the live segment, emphasizing the grammar and vocabulary you are studying within the context of the episode's key events.

In addition, in most of the video episodes, there are brief pauses to allow the characters to reminisce about their home country. These flashbacks—montages of real-life images shot in Spain, Mexico, Puerto Rico, and various parts of Ecuador—connect the theme of the video to everyday life in various parts of the Spanish-speaking world.

### THE CAST

Here are the main characters you will meet when you watch the *Fotonovela* Video:

From Ecuador,
**Inés Ayala Loor**

From Spain,
**María Teresa (Maite) Fuentes de Alba**

From México,
**Alejandro (Álex) Morales Paredes**

From Puerto Rico,
**Javier Gómez Lozano**

And, also from Ecuador,
**don Francisco Castillo Moreno**

## NEW! *FLASH CULTURA* VIDEO PROGRAM

The dynamic, new **Flash cultura** Video provides an entertaining supplement to the **Cultura** section of each lesson. Young people from all over the Spanish-speaking world share aspects of life in their countries; the similarities and differences among Spanish-speaking countries that come up through their experiences will challenge you to think about your own cultural practices and values.

The segments provide valuable cultural insights as well as linguistic input; the episodes will expose you to a wide variety of accents and vocabulary as they gradually move into Spanish.

## PANORAMA CULTURAL VIDEO PROGRAM

The **Panorama cultural** Video is integrated with the **Panorama** section in each lesson of **PANORAMA, Third Edition**. Each segment is 2–3 minutes long and consists of documentary footage from each of the countries featured. The images were specially chosen for interest level and visual appeal, while the all-Spanish narrations were carefully written to reflect the vocabulary and grammar covered in the textbook.

As you watch the video segments, you will experience a diversity of images and topics: cities, monuments, traditions, festivals, archeological sites, geographical wonders, and more. You will be transported to each Spanish-speaking country, including the United States and Canada, thereby having the opportunity to expand your cultural perspectives with information directly related to the content of **PANORAMA, Third Edition**.

## MAESTRO™ Supersite

The **PANORAMA** Supersite, powered by **MAESTRO**™, provides a wealth of resources for both students and instructors.

**SUPERSITE** Access to the **Supersite** comes free with the purchase of a new student text.

### Learning tools available to students:

▶ interactive practice activities with auto-grading and real-time feedback
- ◐ directed practice from the textbook, including audio activities
- additional practice for each and every textbook section

▶ open-ended activities where students explore and search the Internet
- activities for the **NEW! Cultura** and **Panorama** cultural sections, including annotated interactive maps
- **NEW! Oye cómo va** music section spotlights Spanish-speaking musicians and leads students to explore further

▶ expanded audio practice
- **NEW!** record-and-compare audio activities

▶ the complete **PANORAMA** Video Program
- **Fotonovela:** These dramatic video episodes follow four students on their adventures through Ecuador.
- **NEW! Flash cultura:** Shot on location in Latin America and Spain, this video in the form of a news program expands on the theme of each lesson in the book.
- **Panorama cultural:** One episode for every country in the Spanish-speaking world highlights different aspects of each country's culture.
- **NEW! En pantalla:** Real TV clips, one every three lessons, offer you an authentic window into Spanish-language media

▶ MP3 files for the complete **PANORAMA** Audio Program
- textbook audio files
- lab program audio files

▶ and more...
- auto-scored practice quizzes with feedback in every lesson
- **NEW!** flashcards with audio
- **NEW!** flash-animated grammar tutorials (Premium content)

# ICONS AND *RECURSOS* BOXES

## Icons

Familiarize yourself with these icons that appear throughout **PANORAMA, Third Edition**.

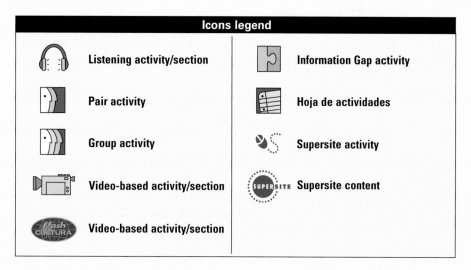

| Icons legend | |
|---|---|
| Listening activity/section | Information Gap activity |
| Pair activity | Hoja de actividades |
| Group activity | Supersite activity |
| Video-based activity/section | Supersite content |
| Video-based activity/section | |

- The Information Gap activities and those involving **Hojas de actividades** (*activity sheets*) require handouts that your instructor will give you.

- You will see the listening icon in each lesson's **Contextos**, **Pronunciación**, **Escuchar,** and **Vocabulario** sections.

- The video icons appear in the **Fotonovela, Cultura,** and **Panorama** sections of each lesson.

- **New!** Both Supersite icons appear in every strand of every lesson. Visit **panorama.vhlcentral.com**.

## Recursos

**Recursos** boxes let you know exactly what print and technology ancillaries you can use to reinforce and expand on every section of the lessons in your textbook. They even include page numbers when applicable. In **PANORAMA 3/e**, the colors of the icons match those of the actual ancillaries, making it even easier for you to use the complete program. See the next page for a description of the ancillaries.

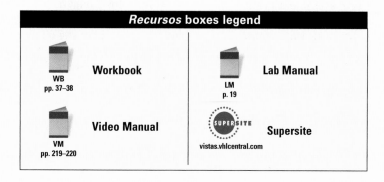

| *Recursos* boxes legend | |
|---|---|
| **WB** pp. 37–38 — Workbook | **LM** p. 19 — Lab Manual |
| **VM** pp. 219–220 — Video Manual | vistas.vhlcentral.com — Supersite |

# Supersite, icons, and ancillaries

## STUDENT ANCILLARIES

► **Workbook/Video Manual**
The Workbook/Video Manual contains the workbook activities for each textbook lesson, activities for the *Fotonovela* Video, and pre-, while-, and post-viewing activities for the *Panorama cultural* Video.

► **New! Cuaderno para hispanohablantes**
This new workbook parallels the traditional workbook and video manual with additional material directed to a heritage speaker audience.

► **Lab Manual**
The Lab Manual contains lab activities for each textbook lesson for use with the Lab Audio Program.

► **Lab Audio Program**
Available on the Supersite.

► **Textbook Audio Program**
The Textbook Audio Program MP3s, available on the Supersite, are the audio recordings for the listening-based activities and recordings of the active vocabulary in each lesson of the student text.

► **New! *Fotonovela* Video DVD**
The *Fotonovela* DVD provides the complete *Fotonovela* Video Program with subtitles.

► **VHL Intro Spanish Pocket Dictionary & Language Guide***
This portable reference for Spanish was created expressly to complement and extend the student text.

► **New! Web-SAM** (online Workbook/Video Manual/Lab Manual). New to the Third Edition, **PANORAMA** now offers two Web-SAM options: the traditional Quia version, and the new **Maestro™** version. Besides offering the entire Workbook, Video Manual, and Lab Manual online, the **Maestro** Web-SAM offers a robust learning management system that completely integrates with the **PANORAMA 3/e** Supersite.

► **New! Maestro™ Supersite***
Newly developed for **PANORAMA, Third Edition**, your passcode to the Supersite (**panorama.vhlcentral.com**) is free with the purchase of a new text. Here you will find activities found in your text, available with auto-grading capability, additional activities for practice, all of the audio and video material for the **PANORAMA, Third Edition**, and much more.

*Free with purchase of a new Student Text

## INSTRUCTOR ANCILLARIES

► **Instructor's Annotated Edition (IAE)**
The IAE contains a wealth of teaching information. The expanded trim size and enhanced design of **PANORAMA 3/e** make the annotations and facsimile student pages easy to read and reference in the classroom.

► **New! Instructor's Resource CD-ROM (IRCD)**
All of the traditional components of the **PANORAMA** Ancillary Program are now on one convenient CD-ROM.

  ► **Instructor's Resource Manual (IRM)**
  The IRM contains classroom handouts for the textbook, answers to directed activities in the textbook, audioscripts, and transcripts and translations of the video programs.

  ► **PowerPoint Presentations**
  This feature provides the Overhead Transparencies as PowerPoint slides, including maps of all Spanish-speaking countries, the **Contextos** vocabulary drawings, and other selected drawings from the student text. Also included on PowerPoint are presentations of each grammar point in **Estructura**.

  ► **Workbook/Lab Manual/Video Manual Answer Key**

  ► **Testing Program**
  The Testing Program contains four versions of tests for each textbook lesson, semester exams and quarter exams, listening scripts, test answer keys, and optional cultural, video, and reading test items. The Testing Program is provided in three formats: within a powerful Test Generator, in customizable RTF files, and as PDFs.

► **New! Instructor's Resource CD & DVD Set**
  ► Instructor's Resource CD-ROM (see above)

  ► Two video DVDs (*Fotonovela* and *Panorama cultural*) available with subtitles in English and Spanish. In addition, a third DVD of the brand-new *Flash cultura* video program hosts a tour of eight countries in the Spanish-speaking world.

► **New! Maestro™ Supersite**
In addition to access to the student site, the password-protected instructor site offers a robust course management system that allows instructors to assign and track student progress. The Supersite contains the full contents of the IRCD (with the exception of the Test Generator), and other resources, such as lesson plans and sample syllabi.

# acknowledgments

On behalf of its authors and editors, Vista Higher Learning would like to express our appreciation to the many instructors nationwide who provided feedback on this program. Their comments and suggestions have been invaluable to this revision.

▶ We especially thank Stewart James-Lejárcegui, Associate Professor of Spanish at Iowa Wesleyan College, for his many careful and thoughtful observations.

▶ We thank Mercedes Valle of the University of Massachusetts at Amherst for her review of the **Recapitulación** section.

▶ We extend our gratitude to José Cruz of Fayetteville Technical Community College for his insight and input on the WebSAM.

## Reviewers

Ellen Abrams
Northern Essex Community College, AZ

Yamandu P. Acosta
Andrew College, GA

Alma Alfaro
Walla Walla College, WA

Blanca Anderson
Loyola University New Orleans, LA

Eileen M. Angelini
Philadelphia University, PA

Karyn Armstrong
Mission College, CA

Bruno Arzola
Tacoma Community College, WA

Clara H. Becerra
Mount Union College, OH

Dennis Bricault
North Park University, IL

Maria Brucato
Merrimack College, MA

Carmela Bruni-Bossio
University of Alberta, AB, Canada

Ana Caldero
Valencia Community College/
West Campus, FL

Marla A. Calico
Georgia Perimeter College, GA

Beth Cardon
Georgia Perimeter College, GA

Lisa Celona
Tunxis Community College, CT

Robert O. Chase
Tunxis Community College, CT

Anita L. Coffey
Lander University, SC

Dominic Corraro
Albertus Magnus College, CT

Jose A. Cortes-Caballero
Georgia Perimeter College, GA

Javier A. Cortes de Jorge
Loyola University New Orleans, LA

Xuchitl N. Coso
Georgia Perimeter College, GA

Catherine Crater
Spring Arbor University, MI

Jan Coulson
Oklahoma State University-Okmulgee, OK

Gregg O. Courtad
Mount Union College, OH

Yonghu Dai
Southern Arkansas University, AR

Janan Fallon
Georgia Perimeter College, GA

Ronna Feit
Nassau Community College, NY

Bruce Gartner
Ohio Dominican University, OH

Jill Gauthier
Miami University Hamilton, OH

Beata Gesicka
University of Alberta, AB, Canada

E. Ginnett Rollins
Asbury College, KY

Don Goetz
North Country Community College, CT

Yolanda L Gonzalez
Valencia Community College, FL

Esperanza Granados
Erskine College, SC

Dr. Robert Harding
Lynchburg College, VA

Esther Holtermann
American University, VA

Robert Howell
Skagit Valley College, WA

Kib Hunt
Columbia College, SC

Harriet Hutchinson
Bunker Hill Community College, MA

Maria Italiano-McGreevy
Pikeville College, KY

William F Jimenez
Tunxis Community College, CT

Herman Johnson
Xavier University of Louisiana, LA

Michael Keathley
Ivy Tech Community College, IN

Todd Lakin
Richard J. Daley College, IL

Kimberly Z. Lowry
Asbury College, KY

Wendy W. Martin
Cleveland Community College, NC

Marco Mena
University of Wisconsin Oshkosh, WI

Joseph A Menig
Valencia Community College, FL

Carl Mentley
Erskine College, SC

Joshua Mora
Angelo State University, TX

Jennifer L. Omana
Texas Wesleyan University, TX

Ruth Owens
Arkansas State University, AR

Joy Parker
Southwestern Oregon Community
College, OR

Noelle Parris
Trident Technical College, SC

Maria C. Perez
Iowa Western Community College, IA

Mercedes Rahilly
Lansing Community College, MI

Angelica Ramirez-Roa
University of Alberta, AB, Canada

Gabriel Rico
Victor Valley College, CA

John Riley
Greenville Technical College, SC

Fernando Rubio
University of Utah, UT

Laura Ruiz-Scott
Scottsdale Community College, AZ

Jose E. Sanchez
Skagit Valley College, WA

Virginia Shen
Chicago State University, IL

Nancy Stites
Jackson Community College, MI

Angela Tavares-Sogocio
Miami Dade College, FL

Jessica Treat
Northwestern Connecticut Community
College, CT

Candice Tucker
Jackson Community College, MI

Marco Tulio Cedillo
Lynchburg College, VA

Jorge de Villasante
Middlesex Community College, MA

Antonia H. Wagner
Greenville Technical College, SC

Juping Wang
Southern Arkansas University, AR

Janice Wiberg
Montana State University-Northern, MT

Jean Zenor
Springfield Technical Community
College, MA

# Hola, ¿qué tal?

**1**

## A PRIMERA VISTA
- Guess what the people in the photo are saying:
  a. Adiós  b. Hola  c. Salsa
- Most likely they would also say:
  a. Gracias  b. Fiesta  c. Buenos días
- The women are:
  a. amigas  b. chicos  c. señores

## Lesson Goals

In **Lección 1**, students will be introduced to the following:
- terms for greetings and leave-takings
- identifying where one is from
- expressions of courtesy
- greetings in the Spanish-speaking world
- the **plaza principal**
- nouns and articles (definite and indefinite)
- numbers 0–30
- present tense of **ser**
- telling time
- recognizing cognates
- reading a telephone list rich in cognates
- demographic and cultural information about Hispanics in the United States and Canada

**A primera vista** Have students look at the photo. Ask: *What do you think the young women are doing?* Say: *It is common in Hispanic cultures for friends to greet each other with a kiss (or two) on the cheek.* Ask: *How do you greet your friends?*

**INSTRUCTIONAL RESOURCES**

**MAESTRO™ SUPERSITE (panorama.vhlcentral.com)**
Textbook, Vocabulary, & Lab MP3 Audio Files
Additional Practice
Learning Management System (Assignment Task Manager, Gradebook)
*Also on DVD*
  *Fotonovela*

*Flash cultura*
*Panorama cultural*
*Also on Instructor's Resource CD-ROM*
  *PowerPoints* (**Contextos** & **Estructura** Presentations, Overheads)
  *Instructor's Resource Manual* (Handouts, Textbook Answer Key, WBs/VM/LM Answer Key,

Audioscripts, Videoscripts & Translations)
  *Testing Program* (**Pruebas,** Test Generator, MP3s)
**WebSAM** (Workbook/Video Manual/Lab Manual)
**Workbook/Video Manual**
*Cuaderno para hispanohablantes*
**Lab Manual**

# Hola, ¿qué tal?

## Más vocabulario

| | |
|---|---|
| Buenos días. | *Good morning.* |
| Buenas noches. | *Good evening; Good night.* |
| Hasta la vista. | *See you later.* |
| Hasta pronto. | *See you soon.* |
| ¿Cómo se llama usted? | *What's your name? (form.)* |
| Le presento a… | *I would like to introduce (name) to you. (form.)* |
| Te presento a… | *I would like to introduce (name) to you. (fam.)* |
| el nombre | *name* |
| ¿Cómo estás? | *How are you? (fam.)* |
| No muy bien. | *Not very well.* |
| ¿Qué pasa? | *What's happening?; What's going on?* |
| por favor | *please* |
| De nada. | *You're welcome.* |
| No hay de qué. | *You're welcome.* |
| Lo siento. | *I'm sorry.* |
| Gracias. | *Thank you; Thanks.* |
| Muchas gracias. | *Thank you very much; Thanks a lot.* |

## Variación léxica

*Items are presented for recognition purposes only.*

| | | |
|---|---|---|
| Buenos días. | ⟷ | Buenas. |
| De nada. | ⟷ | A la orden. |
| Lo siento. | ⟷ | Perdón. |
| ¿Qué tal? | ⟷ | ¿Qué hubo? *(Col.)* |
| chau | ⟷ | ciao |

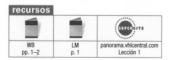

**recursos**

WB pp. 1–2 | LM p. 1 | SUPERSITE panorama.vhlcentral.com Lección 1

**1**

**ELENA** Patricia, éste es el señor Perales.
**PATRICIA** Encantada.
**SEÑOR PERALES** Igualmente. ¿De dónde es usted, señorita?
**PATRICIA** Soy de México. ¿Y usted?
**SEÑOR PERALES** De Puerto Rico.

**2**

**TOMÁS** ¿Qué tal, Alberto?
**ALBERTO** Regular. ¿Y tú?
**TOMÁS** Bien. ¿Qué hay de nuevo?
**ALBERTO** Nada.

**3**

**SEÑOR VARGAS** Buenas tardes, señora Wong. ¿Cómo está usted?
**SEÑORA WONG** Muy bien, gracias. ¿Y usted, señor Vargas?
**SEÑOR VARGAS** Bien, gracias.
**SEÑORA WONG** Hasta mañana, señor Vargas. Saludos a la señora Vargas.
**SEÑOR VARGAS** Adiós.

**AYUDA**

In Spanish, people can be addressed either formally or informally. Dialogues 1 and 3 are formal exchanges and use **usted** (*you*) forms. Dialogues 2, 4, and 5 are informal and use the familiar **tú** (*you*) form or other informal expressions. You will learn more about this in **Estructura 1.3.**

**BERTA** Hasta luego, Tere.
**TERESA** Chau, Berta. Nos vemos mañana.

**CARMEN** Buenas tardes. Me llamo Carmen. ¿Cómo te llamas tú?
**ANTONIO** Buenas tardes. Me llamo Antonio. Mucho gusto.
**CARMEN** El gusto es mío. ¿De dónde eres?
**ANTONIO** Soy de los Estados Unidos, de California.

# Práctica

**1**

**Escuchar** Listen to each question or statement, then choose the correct response.

1. a. Muy bien, gracias.     b. Me llamo Graciela. b
2. a. Lo siento.     b. Mucho gusto. b
3. a. Soy de Puerto Rico.     b. No muy bien. a
4. a. No hay de qué.     b. Regular. a
5. a. Mucho gusto.     b. Hasta pronto. b
6. a. Nada.     b. Igualmente. a
7. a. Me llamo Guillermo Montero.     b. Muy bien, gracias. b
8. a. Buenas tardes. ¿Cómo estás?     b. El gusto es mío. a
9. a. Saludos a la Sra. Ramírez.     b. Encantada. b
10. a. Adiós.     b. Regular. b

**2**

**Identificar** You will hear a series of expressions. Identify the expression (**a**, **b**, **c**, or **d**) that does not belong in each series.

1. _c_     3. _b_
2. _a_     4. _c_

**3**

**Escoger** For each expression, write another word or phrase that expresses a similar idea.

> **modelo**
> ¿Cómo estás? ¿Qué tal?

1. De nada. No hay de qué.
2. Encantado. Mucho gusto.
3. Adiós. Chau o Hasta luego/mañana/pronto.
4. Te presento a Antonio. Éste es Antonio.
5. Hasta la vista. Hasta luego.
6. Mucho gusto. El gusto es mío.

**4**

**Ordenar** Work with a classmate to put this scrambled conversation in order. Then act it out.

—Muy bien, gracias. Soy Rosabel.
—Soy del Ecuador. ¿Y tú?
—Mucho gusto, Rosabel.
—Hola. Me llamo Carlos. ¿Cómo estás?
—Soy de Argentina.
—Igualmente. ¿De dónde eres, Carlos?

**CARLOS** Hola. Me llamo Carlos. ¿Cómo estás?
**ROSABEL** Muy bien, gracias. Soy Rosabel.
**CARLOS** Mucho gusto, Rosabel.
**ROSABEL** Igualmente. ¿De dónde eres, Carlos?
**CARLOS** Soy del Ecuador. ¿Y tú?
**ROSABEL** Soy de Argentina.

SUPERSITE

**1 Teaching Tip** Before students listen, ask them to read through the items and jot down the questions or statements they think would elicit those responses.

**1 Script** 1. ¿Cómo te llamas? 2. Te presento a Juan Pablo. 3. ¿De dónde es usted? 4. Muchas gracias. 5. Nos vemos. 6. ¿Qué pasa? 7. ¿Cómo está usted? 8. Buenas tardes, señor Fernández. 9. Susana, éste es el señor Ramírez. 10. ¿Qué tal?
*Textbook MP3s*

**2 Teaching Tip** To simplify, provide two categories for each item. Ex: 1. a. asking how you are; b. asking where you are from. Then, as students listen to the audio, have them write the letter of the appropriate category.

**2 Script** 1. a. ¿Qué tal? b. ¿Cómo estás? c. ¿De dónde eres? d. ¿Qué hay de nuevo? 2. a. De nada. b. Adiós. c. Hasta luego. d. Nos vemos mañana. 3. a. Mucho gusto. b. Lo siento. c. Encantada. d. El gusto es mío. 4. a. Buenos días. b. Hola. c. Bien, gracias. d. Buenas tardes.
*Textbook MP3s*

**3 Expansion** To challenge students, have them provide the question or statement that would elicit each item. Ex: **1. —Gracias. —De nada.**

**4 Teaching Tip** Have pairs role-play their conversations for the class.

**4 Expansion** In small groups, ask students to write a new conversation and then to scramble the order of the dialogue. Have groups exchange papers and put the conversations in order.

**TEACHING OPTIONS**

**Game** Divide the class into two teams. Point to a team member and call out an original statement or question based on **Contextos**. If the student responds appropriately, his or her team earns one point. The team with the most points at the end wins.
**Pairs** Write several times on the board. Ex: **9:00 a.m., 4:00 p.m., 10:30 p.m.** Have students work in pairs to greet each other according to the time of day.

**Heritage Speakers** Ask heritage speakers to mention other greetings and expressions of courtesy that are used in their families' countries of origin. Have them indicate if the expressions are used in formal or informal situations, and write the phrases on the board in these categories. Then ask volunteers to state who in the **Contextos** illustration would use each expression.

**5** **Completar** Work with a partner to complete these exchanges.

**modelo**

**Estudiante 1:** ¿Cómo estás?
**Estudiante 2:** _Muy bien, gracias._

1. **Estudiante 1:** _Buenos días._
   **Estudiante 2:** Buenos días. ¿Qué tal?
2. **Estudiante 1:** _¿Cómo te llamas?_
   **Estudiante 2:** Me llamo Carmen Sánchez.
3. **Estudiante 1:** _¿De dónde eres?_
   **Estudiante 2:** De Canadá.
4. **Estudiante 1:** Te presento a Marisol.
   **Estudiante 2:** _Encantado/a._

5. **Estudiante 1:** Gracias.
   **Estudiante 2:** _De nada._
6. **Estudiante 1:** _¿Qué tal?_
   **Estudiante 2:** Regular.
7. **Estudiante 1:** _¿Qué pasa?_
   **Estudiante 2:** Nada.
8. **Estudiante 1:** ¡Hasta la vista!
   **Estudiante 2:** _Answers will vary._

**6** **Cambiar** Work with a partner and correct the second part of each conversation to make it logical. Answers will vary.

**modelo**

**Estudiante 1:** ¿Qué tal?
**Estudiante 2:** ~~No hay de qué.~~ Bien. ¿Y tú?

1. **Estudiante 1:** Hasta mañana, señora Ramírez. Saludos al señor Ramírez.
   **Estudiante 2:** *Muy bien, gracias.*
2. **Estudiante 1:** ¿Qué hay de nuevo, Alberto?
   **Estudiante 2:** *Sí, me llamo Alberto. ¿Cómo te llamas tú?*
3. **Estudiante 1:** Gracias, Tomás.
   **Estudiante 2:** *Regular. ¿Y tú?*
4. **Estudiante 1:** Miguel, ésta es la señorita Perales.
   **Estudiante 2:** *No hay de qué, señorita.*
5. **Estudiante 1:** ¿De dónde eres, Antonio?
   **Estudiante 2:** *Muy bien, gracias. ¿Y tú?*
6. **Estudiante 1:** ¿Cómo se llama usted?
   **Estudiante 2:** *El gusto es mío.*
7. **Estudiante 1:** ¿Qué pasa?
   **Estudiante 2:** *Hasta luego, Alicia.*
8. **Estudiante 1:** Buenas tardes, señor. ¿Cómo está usted?
   **Estudiante 2:** *Soy de Puerto Rico.*

◄ **¡LENGUA VIVA!**

The titles **señor, señora**, and **señorita** are abbreviated **Sr., Sra.,** and **Srta.** Note that these abbreviations are capitalized, while the titles themselves are not.

• • •

There is no Spanish equivalent for the English title *Ms.;* women are addressed as **señora** or **señorita**.

# Comunicación

**7** **Diálogos** With a partner, complete and act out these conversations. Answers will vary.

**Conversación 1**
—Hola. Me llamo Teresa. ¿Cómo te llamas tú?

—_____

—Soy de Puerto Rico. ¿Y tú?

—_____

**Conversación 2**
—_____

—Muy bien, gracias. ¿Y usted, señora López?

—_____

—Hasta luego, señora. Saludos al señor López.

—_____

**Conversación 3**
—_____

—Regular. ¿Y tú?

—_____

—Nada.

**8** **Conversaciones** This is the first day of class. Write four short conversations based on what the people in this scene would say. Answers will vary.

**9** **Situaciones** In groups of three, write and act out these situations. Answers will vary.

1. On your way out of class on the first day of school, you strike up a conversation with the two students who were sitting next to you. You find out each student's name and where he or she is from before you say goodbye and go to your next class.
2. At the next class you meet up with a friend and find out how he or she is doing. As you are talking, your friend Elena enters. Introduce her to your friend.
3. As you're leaving the bookstore, you meet your parents' friends Mrs. Sánchez and Mr. Rodríguez. You greet them and ask how each person is. As you say goodbye, you send greetings to Mrs. Rodríguez.
4. Make up and act out a real-life situation that you and your classmates can role-play.

**7** **Expansion**
- Have students work in small groups to write a few mini-conversations modeled on this activity. Then ask them to copy the dialogues, omitting a few words or phrases. Have groups exchange papers and fill in the blanks.
- Have students rewrite **Conversaciones 1** and **3** in the formal register and **Conversación 2** in the informal register.

**8** **Teaching Tip** To simplify, have students brainstorm who the people in the illustration are and what they are talking about. Ask students which groups would use the **usted** form and which would use **tú**.

**9** **Teaching Tip** To challenge students, have each group pick a situation to prepare and perform. Tell groups not to memorize every word of the conversation. Instead, they should rehearse the situation a few times and then recreate the conversation for the class.

**The Affective Dimension** Have students rehearse the situations a few times, so that they will feel more comfortable with the material and less anxious when presenting before the class.

**TEACHING OPTIONS**

**Extra Practice** Have students circulate around the classroom and conduct unrehearsed mini-conversations in Spanish with other students, using the words and expressions that they learned on pages 2–3. Monitor students' work and offer assistance if requested.

**Heritage Speakers** Ask heritage speakers to role-play some of the conversations and situations in these **Comunicación** activities, modeling correct pronunciation and intonation for the class. Remind students that, just as in English, there are regional differences in the way Spanish is pronounced. Help clarify unfamiliar vocabulary as necessary.

## Section Goals

In **Fotonovela**, students will:
- receive comprehensible input from free-flowing discourse
- learn functional phrases that preview lesson grammatical structures

**Instructional Resources**
**Supersite/DVD:** *Fotonovela*
**Supersite/IRCD:** *IRM*
(*Fotonovela* Videoscript & Translation, WBs/VM/LM Answer Key)
**WebSAM**
**Video Manual**, pp. 195–196

## Video Synopsis

**Don Francisco**, the bus driver, and **Sra. Ramos**, a representative of Ecuatur, meet the four travelers at the university. **Sra. Ramos** passes out travel documents. **Inés** and **Maite** introduce themselves, as do **Javier** and **Álex**. The travelers board the bus.

## Teaching Tips

- Have students cover the captions and guess the plot based on the video stills. Record their predictions. After students have watched the video, compare their predictions to what actually happened in the episode.
- Point out that **don** is a title of respect and neither equivalent nor related to the Anglo name *Don*. Ask if students think **Francisco** is the conductor's first or last name. (It is his first name.) Students will learn more about the titles **don** and **doña** on page 8.
- Tell students that all items in **Expresiones útiles** on page 7 are active vocabulary for which they are responsible. Model the pronunciation of each item and have the class repeat. Also, practice the **Expresiones útiles** by using them in short conversations with individual students.

# ¡Todos a bordo!

Los cuatro estudiantes, don Francisco y la Sra. Ramos se reúnen (*meet*) en la universidad.

**PERSONAJES**

**DON FRANCISCO**

**SRA. RAMOS**

**ÁLEX**

**JAVIER**

**INÉS**

**MAITE**

**1** **SRA. RAMOS** Buenos días, chicos. Yo soy Isabel Ramos de la agencia Ecuatur.
**DON FRANCISCO** Y yo soy don Francisco, el conductor.

**2** **SRA. RAMOS** Bueno, ¿quién es María Teresa Fuentes de Alba?
**MAITE** ¡Soy yo!
**SRA. RAMOS** Ah, bien. Aquí tienes los documentos de viaje.
**MAITE** Gracias.

**3** **SRA. RAMOS** ¿Javier Gómez Lozano?
**JAVIER** Aquí... soy yo.

**6** **JAVIER** ¿Qué tal? Me llamo Javier.
**ÁLEX** Mucho gusto, Javier. Yo soy Álex. ¿De dónde eres?
**JAVIER** De Puerto Rico. ¿Y tú?
**ÁLEX** Yo soy de México.

**7** **DON FRANCISCO** Bueno, chicos, ¡todos a bordo!

**8** **INÉS** Con permiso.

**recursos**

VM
pp. 195–196

panorama.vhlcentral.com
Lección 1

---

**TEACHING OPTIONS**

**Video Tips** General suggestions for using video clips in the classroom can be found on page IAE-12 of this Instructor's Annotated Edition.
**¡Todos a bordo!** Have students make a three-column chart with the headings *Greetings, Self-Identification,* and *Courtesy Expressions.* Have students suggest two or three possible phrases for each category. Then play the **¡Todos a bordo!** episode once and ask students to fill in the first column with the basic greetings that they hear. Repeat this process for the second column, where they should list the expressions the characters use to identify themselves. Play the video a third time for students to jot down courtesy expressions, such as ways to say "pleased to meet you" and "excuse me."

**SRA. RAMOS** Y tú eres Inés Ayala Loor, ¿verdad?

**INÉS** Sí, yo soy Inés.

**SRA. RAMOS** Y tú eres Alejandro Morales Paredes, ¿no?

**ÁLEX** Sí, señora.

**INÉS** Hola. Soy Inés.

**MAITE** Encantada. Yo me llamo Maite. ¿De dónde eres?

**INÉS** Soy del Ecuador, de Portoviejo. ¿Y tú?

**MAITE** De España. Soy de Madrid, la capital. Oye, ¿qué hora es?

**INÉS** Son las diez y tres minutos.

**ÁLEX** Perdón.

**DON FRANCISCO** ¿Y los otros?

**SRA. RAMOS** Son todos.

**DON FRANCISCO** Está bien.

## Expresiones útiles

### Identifying yourself and others

- **¿Cómo se llama usted?**
  *What's your name?*
  **Yo soy don Francisco, el conductor.**
  *I'm Don Francisco, the driver.*

- **¿Cómo te llamas?**
  *What's your name?*
  **Me llamo Javier.**
  *My name is Javier.*

- **¿Quién es...?**
  *Who is...?*
  **Aquí... soy yo.**
  *Here... that's me.*

- **Tú eres..., ¿verdad?/¿no?**
  *You are..., right?/no?*
  **Sí, señora.**
  *Yes, ma'am.*

### Saying what time it is

- **¿Qué hora es?**
  *What time is it?*
  **Es la una.**
  *It's one o'clock.*
  **Son las dos.**
  *It's two o'clock.*
  **Son las diez y tres minutos.**
  *It's 10:03.*

### Saying "excuse me"

- **Con permiso.**
  *Pardon me; Excuse me.*
  *(to request permission)*
- **Perdón.**
  *Pardon me; Excuse me.*
  *(to get someone's attention or to ask forgiveness)*

### When starting a trip

- **¡Todos a bordo!**
  *All aboard!*
- **¡Buen viaje!**
  *Have a good trip!*

### Getting someone's attention

- **Oye/Oiga(n)...**
  *Listen (fam./form.)...*

# ¿Qué pasó?

**1 Expansion** Give students these true-false statements as items 8–10: **8. Maite es de la capital de España. (Cierto.) 9. Son las tres y diez minutos. (Falso. Son las diez y tres minutos.) 10. Inés es de Quito, la capital del Ecuador. (Falso. Inés es de Portoviejo.)**

**2 Expansion** Ask students to call out additional statements that were made in the **Fotonovela**. The class should guess which character made each statement.

**¡Lengua viva!** Ask students how they might address **Sra. Ramos (doña Isabel).**

**3 Teaching Tip** Go over the activity by asking volunteers to take the roles of **Maite** and **Inés.**

**4 Teaching Tip** To simplify, ask students to read through the cues and jot down phrases for each step of the conversation.

**4 Possible Conversation**
E1: Buenas tardes. ¿Cómo te llamas?
E2: Hola. Me llamo Felipe. Y tú, ¿cómo te llamas?
E1: Me llamo Denisa. Mucho gusto.
E2: El gusto es mío.
E1: ¿Cómo estás?
E2: Bien, gracias.
E1: ¿De dónde eres?
E2: Soy de Venezuela.
E1: ¡Buen viaje!
E2: Gracias. ¡Adiós!

**The Affective Dimension**
Point out that many people feel a bit nervous about speaking in front of a group. Encourage students to think of anxious feelings as extra energy that will help them accomplish their goals.

**1 ¿Cierto o falso?** Indicate if each statement is **cierto** or **falso**. Then correct the false statements.

|  | Cierto | Falso |
|---|---|---|
| 1. Javier y Álex son pasajeros (*passengers*). | ☑ | ○ |
| 2. Javier Gómez Lozano es el conductor. | ○ | ☑ Don Francisco es el conductor. |
| 3. Inés Ayala Loor es de la agencia Ecuatur. | ○ | ☑ Isabel Ramos es de la agencia Ecuatur. |
| 4. Inés es del Ecuador. | ☑ | ○ |
| 5. Maite es de España. | ☑ | ○ |
| 6. Javier es de Puerto Rico. | ☑ | ○ |
| 7. Álex es del Ecuador. | ○ | ☑ Álex es de México. |

**NOTA CULTURAL**

**Maite** is a shortened version of the name **María Teresa.** Other popular "combination names" in Spanish are **Juanjo (Juan José)** and **Maruja (María Eugenia).**

**2 Identificar** Indicate which persons would make each statement. Two names will be used twice.

1. Yo soy de México. ¿De dónde eres tú? Álex
2. ¡Atención! ¡Todos a bordo! Don Francisco
3. ¿Yo? Soy de la capital de España. Maite
4. Y yo soy del Ecuador. Inés, don Francisco
5. ¿Qué hora es, Inés? Maite
6. Yo soy de Puerto Rico. ¿Y tú? Javier

ÁLEX    INÉS    MAITE

DON FRANCISCO    JAVIER

**¡LENGUA VIVA!**

In Spanish-speaking countries, **don** and **doña** are used with men's and women's first names to show respect: **don Francisco, doña Rita.** Note that these words are not capitalized.

**3 Completar** Complete this slightly altered version of the conversation that Inés and Maite had.

**INÉS**   Hola. ¿Cómo te (1) llamas ?
**MAITE**  Me llamo Maite. ¿Y (2) tú ?
**INÉS**   Inés. Mucho (3) gusto .
**MAITE**  (4) El gusto es mío.
**INÉS**   ¿De (5) dónde eres?
**MAITE**  (6) De España. ¿Y (7) tú ?
**INÉS**   Del (8) Ecuador .

**4 Conversar** Imagine that you are chatting with a traveler you just met at the airport. With a partner, prepare a conversation using these cues. Some answers will vary.

| Estudiante 1 | Estudiante 2 |
|---|---|
| Say "good afternoon" to your partner and ask for his or her name. → | Say hello and what your name is. Then ask what your partner's name is. |
| Say what your name is and that you are glad to meet your partner. → | Say that the pleasure is yours. |
| Ask how your partner is. → | Say that you're doing well, thank you. |
| Ask where your partner is from. → | Say where you're from. |
| Wish your partner a good trip. → | Say thank you and goodbye. |

**TEACHING OPTIONS**

**Pairs** Ask students to work in pairs to ad-lib the exchanges between **don Francisco** and **Sra. Ramos, Inés** and **Maite,** and **Álex** and **Javier.** Tell them to convey the general meaning using vocabulary and expressions they know, and assure them that they do not have to stick to the original dialogues word for word. Then, ask volunteers to present their exchanges to the class.

**Extra Practice** Choose four or five lines of the **Fotonovela** to use as a dictation. Read the lines twice slowly to give students sufficient time to write. Then read them again at normal speed to allow students to correct any errors or fill in any gaps. You may have students correct their own work by checking it against the **Fotonovela** text.

# Pronunciación

## The Spanish alphabet

The Spanish alphabet consists of 29 letters. The Spanish letter **ñ (eñe)** doesn't appear in the English alphabet. The letters **k (ka)** and **w (doble ve)** are used only in words of foreign origin.

| Letra | Nombre(s) | Ejemplos | Letra | Nombre(s) | Ejemplos |
|-------|-----------|----------|-------|-----------|----------|
| a | a | adiós | m | eme | mapa |
| b | be | bien, problema | n | ene | nacionalidad |
| c | ce | cosa, cero | ñ | eñe | mañana |
| ch | che | chico | o | o | once |
| d | de | diario, nada | p | pe | profesor |
| e | e | estudiante | q | cu | qué |
| f | efe | foto | r | ere | regular, señora |
| g | ge | gracias, Gerardo, regular | s | ese | señor |
| | | | t | te | tú |
| h | hache | hola | u | u | usted |
| i | i | igualmente | v | ve | vista, nuevo |
| j | jota | Javier | w | doble ve | *walkman* |
| k | ka, ca | kilómetro | x | equis | existir, México |
| l | ele | lápiz | y | i griega, ye | yo |
| ll | elle | llave | z | zeta, ceta | zona |

**El alfabeto** Repeat the Spanish alphabet and example words after your instructor.

**Práctica** Spell these words aloud in Spanish.

1. nada
2. maleta
3. quince
4. muy
5. hombre
6. por favor
7. San Fernando
8. Estados Unidos
9. Puerto Rico
10. España
11. Javier
12. Ecuador
13. Maite
14. gracias
15. Nueva York

**Refranes** Read these sayings aloud.

Ver es creer.[1]

En boca cerrada no entran moscas.[2]

1 Seeing is believing.    2 Silence is golden.

recursos

LM p. 2     panorama.vhlcentral.com Lección 1

---

**AYUDA**

The letter combination **rr** produces a strong trilled sound which does not have an English equivalent. English speakers commonly make this sound when imitating the sound of a motor. This combination only occurs between vowels: **puertorriqueño, terrible**. See **Lección 7**, p. 217 for more information.

**¡LENGUA VIVA!**

In 1994, the **Real Academia** subsumed **ch** and **ll** under **c** and **l** in alphabetized lists. For example, in dictionaries, entries starting with **ch** come between **ce** and **ci**, not under a separate letter between **c** and **d**.

---

**Section Goals**

In **Pronunciación**, students will be introduced to:
• the Spanish alphabet and how it contrasts with the English alphabet
• the names of the letters

**Instructional Resources**
**Supersite:** Textbook & Lab MP3 Audio Files **Lección 1**
**Supersite/IRCD:** *IRM* (Textbook Audio Script, Lab Audio Script, WBs/VM/LM Answer Key)
**WebSAM**
**Lab Manual**, p. 2
*Cuaderno para hispanohablantes*

**Teaching Tips**
• Model pronunciation of the alphabet and example words. Have students repeat.
• You may want to point out that to distinguish between **b** and **v**, **be alta, be grande** and **ve baja, ve chica** may be used. For a detailed explanation of the Spanish **b** and **v**, see **Lección 5, Pronunciación**, page 149.
• Drill the alphabet by having students repeat letters in overlapping sets of three. Ex: **a, be, ce; be, ce, che**…
• Draw attention to words on posters, signs, or maps in the classroom. Point out letters and have the class identify them.
• Write Spanish acronyms of famous organizations (Ex: **ONU**), and have students spell them out. Explain what each represents. Ex: **ONU** = **Organización de Naciones Unidas** (*United Nations, UN*).

**Ayuda** Draw attention to the sidebar and model trilling. Provide additional examples, such as **carro** and **perro**.

**El alfabeto/Práctica/Refranes** These exercises are recorded in the *Textbook MP3s*. You may want to play the audio so students practice the pronunciation point by listening to Spanish spoken by speakers other than yourself.

---

**TEACHING OPTIONS**

**Extra Practice** Do a dictation activity in which you spell aloud Spanish words (e.g., world capitals and countries). Spell each word twice to allow students sufficient time to write. After you have finished, write your list on the board or project it on a transparency and have students check their work. You can also have students spell their names in Spanish.

**Extra Practice** Here are four additional **refranes** to practice the alphabet: **De tal palo, tal astilla** (*A chip off the old block*); **Los ojos son el espejo del alma** (*Eyes are the window to the soul*); **El rayo nunca cae dos veces en el mismo lugar** (*Lightning never strikes twice in the same place*); **No dejes para mañana lo que puedas hacer hoy** (*Don't put off until tomorrow what you can do today*).

### EN DETALLE

# Saludos y besos en los países hispanos

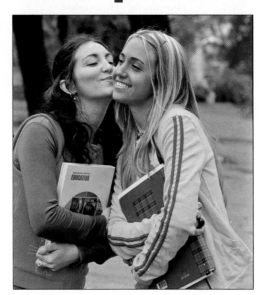

**In Spanish-speaking countries,** kissing on the cheek is a customary way to greet friends and family members. It is common to kiss someone upon introduction, particularly in a non-business setting. Whereas North Americans maintain considerable personal space when greeting, Spaniards and Latin Americans tend to decrease interpersonal space and give one or two kisses (**besos**) on the cheek, sometimes accompanied by a handshake or a hug. In formal business settings, where associates do not know one another on a personal level,

greetings entail a simple handshake.

Greeting someone with a **beso** varies according to region, gender, and context. With the exception of Argentina—where male friends and relatives lightly kiss on the cheek—men generally greet each other with a hug or warm handshake. Greetings between men and women, and between women, can differ depending on the country and context, but generally include kissing. In Spain, it is customary to give **dos besos,** starting with the right cheek first. In Latin American countries, including Mexico, Costa Rica, Colombia, and Chile, a greeting consists of a single "air kiss" on the right cheek. Peruvians also "air kiss," but strangers will simply shake hands. In Colombia, female acquaintances tend to simply pat each other on the right forearm or shoulder.

### Tendencias

| País | Beso | País | Beso |
|---|---|---|---|
| Argentina | 💋 | España | 💋💋 |
| Bolivia | ⊘ | México | 💋 |
| Chile | 💋 | Paraguay | 💋💋 |
| Colombia | 💋 | Puerto Rico | 💋 |
| El Salvador | 💋 | Venezuela | 💋/💋💋 |

### ACTIVIDADES

**1** **¿Cierto o falso?** Indicate whether these statements are true (**cierto**) or false (**falso**). Correct the false statements.

1. Hispanic cultures leave less interpersonal space when greeting than in the U.S. **Cierto.**

2. Men never greet with a kiss in Spanish-speaking countries. **Falso.** Argentine men can greet with a light kiss.

3. Shaking hands is not appropriate for a business setting in Latin America. **Falso.** In most business settings, people greet one another by shaking hands.

4. Spaniards greet with one kiss on the right cheek. **Falso.** They greet with one kiss on each cheek.

5. In Mexico, people greet with an "air kiss". **Cierto.**

6. Gender can play a role in the type of greeting given. **Cierto.**

7. If two women acquaintances meet up in Colombia, they should exchange two kisses on the cheek. **Falso.** They pat one another on the right forearm or shoulder.

8. In Peru, a man and a woman meeting for the first time would probably greet each other with an "air kiss." **Falso.** They would probably shake hands.

### TEACHING OPTIONS

**Game** Divide the class into two teams. Give situations in which people greet one another and have one member from each team identify the appropriate way to greet. Ex: Two male friends in Argentina should greet each other with a light kiss on the cheek. Give one point for each correct answer. The team with the most points at the end wins.

**Un beso** Kisses are not only a form of greeting in Hispanic cultures. It is also common to end phone conversations and close letters or e-mails with the words **un beso** or **besos**. Additionally, friends may use **un abrazo** to end a written message. In a more formal e-mail, one can write **un saludo** or **saludos**.

## ASÍ SE DICE

### Saludos y despedidas

| | |
|---|---|
| Buenas. | Hello./Hi. |
| Chao./Ciao. | Chau. |
| ¿Cómo te/le va? | How are things going (for you)? |
| Hasta ahora. | See you soon. |
| ¿Qué hay? | What's new? |
| ¿Qué onda? (Méx.); ¿Qué hubo? (Col.) | What's going on? |

## EL MUNDO HISPANO

### Parejas y amigos famosos

Here are some famous couples and friends from the Spanish-speaking world.

○ **Jennifer López** y **Marc Anthony** (Estados Unidos/Puerto Rico) Not long after ending her relationship with Ben Affleck, Jennifer López married salsa singer Marc Anthony.

○ **Gael García Bernal** (México) y **Diego Luna** (México) These lifelong friends both starred in the 2001 Mexican film *Y tu mamá también.*

○ **Salma Hayek** (México) y **Penélope Cruz** (España) Close friends Salma Hayek and Penélope Cruz developed their acting skills in their countries of origin before meeting in Hollywood.

## PERFIL

# La plaza principal

In the Spanish-speaking world, public space is treasured. Small city and town life revolves around the **plaza principal**. Often surrounded by cathedrals or municipal buildings like the **ayuntamiento** (*city hall*), the pedestrian **plaza** is designated as a central meeting place for family and friends. During warmer months, when outdoor cafés usually line the **plaza**, it is a popular spot to have a leisurely cup of coffee, chat,

**La Plaza Mayor de Salamanca**

and people watch. Many town festivals, or **ferias**, also take place in this space. One of the most famous town

squares is the **Plaza Mayor** in the university town of Salamanca, Spain. Students gather underneath its famous clock tower to meet up with friends or simply take a coffee break.

**La Plaza de Armas, Lima, Perú**

**SUPERSITE** **Conexión Internet**

**What are the plazas principales in large cities such as Mexico City and Buenos Aires?**

Go to **panorama.vhlcentral.com** to find more cultural information related to this **Cultura** section.

## ACTIVIDADES

**2** **Comprensión** Answer these questions. *Some answers may vary. Suggested answers:*
1. What are two types of buildings found on the **plaza principal**? *municipal buildings and cathedrals*
2. What are two types of events or activities common at a **plaza principal**? *meeting with friends and festivals*
3. How would Diego Luna greet his friends? *¿Qué onda?*
4. Would Salma Hayek and Jennifer López greet with one kiss or two? *one*

**3** **Saludos** Role-play these greetings with a partner. Include a verbal greeting as well as a kiss or handshake, as appropriate. *Role-plays will vary according to student gender.*
1. friends in Mexico
2. business associates at a conference in Chile
3. friends meeting in Madrid's Plaza Mayor
4. Peruvians meeting for the first time
5. relatives in Argentina

**recursos**

**SUPERSITE**
panorama.vhlcentral.com
Lección 1

## [1.1] Nouns and articles

### Spanish nouns

**ANTE TODO** A noun is a word used to identify people, animals, places, things, or ideas. Unlike English, all Spanish nouns, even those that refer to non-living things, have gender; that is, they are considered either masculine or feminine. As in English, nouns in Spanish also have number, meaning that they are either singular or plural.

| Nouns that refer to living things | | | |
|---|---|---|---|
| **Masculine nouns** | | **Feminine nouns** | |
| el hombre | *the man* | la mujer | *the woman* |
| *ending in –o* | | *ending in –a* | |
| el chico | *the boy* | la chica | *the girl* |
| el pasajero | *the (male) passenger* | la pasajera | *the (female) passenger* |
| *ending in –or* | | *ending in –ora* | |
| el conductor | *the (male) driver* | la conductora | *the (female) driver* |
| el profesor | *the (male) teacher* | la profesora | *the (female) teacher* |
| *ending in –ista* | | *ending in –ista* | |
| el turista | *the (male) tourist* | la turista | *the (female) tourist* |

▶ As shown above, nouns that refer to males, like **el hombre**, are generally masculine, while nouns that refer to females, like **la mujer,** are generally feminine.

▶ Many nouns that refer to male beings end in **–o** or **–or**. Their corresponding feminine forms end in **–a** and **–ora**, respectively.

el conductor

la profesora

▶ The masculine and feminine forms of nouns that end in **–ista,** like **turista,** are the same, so gender is indicated by the article **el** (masculine) or **la** (feminine). Some other nouns have identical masculine and feminine forms.

| | |
|---|---|
| **el** joven | **la** joven |
| *the youth; the young man* | *the youth; the young woman* |
| **el** estudiante | **la** estudiante |
| *the (male) student* | *the (female) student* |

## Nouns that refer to non-living things

| Masculine nouns | | Feminine nouns | |
|---|---|---|---|
| **ending in –o** | | **ending in –a** | |
| el cuaderno | the notebook | la cosa | the thing |
| el diario | the diary | la escuela | the school |
| el diccionario | the dictionary | la grabadora | the tape recorder |
| el número | the number | la maleta | the suitcase |
| el video | the video | la palabra | the word |
| **ending in –ma** | | **ending in –ción** | |
| el problema | the problem | la lección | the lesson |
| el programa | the program | la conversación | the conversation |
| **ending in –s** | | **ending in –dad** | |
| el autobús | the bus | la nacionalidad | the nationality |
| el país | the country | la comunidad | the community |

**¡LENGUA VIVA!**

The Spanish word for *video* can be pronounced with the stress on the **i** or the **e**. For that reason, you might see the word written with or without an accent: **video** or **vídeo**.

▶ As shown above, certain noun endings are strongly associated with a specific gender, so you can use them to determine if a noun is masculine or feminine.

▶ Because the gender of nouns that refer to non-living things cannot be determined by foolproof rules, you should memorize the gender of each noun you learn. It is helpful to memorize each noun with its corresponding article, **el** for masculine and **la** for feminine.

▶ Another reason to memorize the gender of every noun is that there are common exceptions to the rules of gender. For example, **el mapa** (*map*) and **el día** (*day*) end in **–a,** but are masculine. **La mano** (*hand*) ends in **–o,** but is feminine.

## Plural of nouns

▶ In Spanish, nouns that end in a vowel form the plural by adding **–s.** Nouns that end in a consonant add **–es.** Nouns that end in **–z** change the **–z** to **–c,** then add **–es.**

el chico → los chic**os**    la nacionalidad → las nacionalida**des**

el diario → los diari**os**    el país → los paí**ses**

el problema → los problem**as**    el lápi**z** (*pencil*) → los lápi**ces**

**CONSULTA**

You will learn more about accent marks in **Lección 4, Pronunciación,** p. 115.

▶ In general, when a singular noun has an accent mark on the last syllable, the accent is dropped from the plural form.

la lecci**ó**n → las lecci**ones**    el autob**ú**s → los autob**uses**

▶ Use the masculine plural form to refer to a group that includes both males and females.

1 pasajer**o** + 2 pasajer**as** = 3 pasajer**os**    2 chic**os** + 2 chic**as** = 4 chic**os**

### Teaching Tips
- Work through the list of nouns, modeling their pronunciation. Point out patterns of gender, including word endings **–ma, –ción,** and **–dad.** Give cognate nouns with these endings and ask students to indicate the gender. Ex: **diagrama, acción, personalidad.** Point out common exceptions to gender agreement rules for **el mapa, el día,** and **la mano.**
- Stress the addition of **–s** to nouns that end in vowels and **–es** to nouns that end in consonants. Write ten nouns on the board and ask volunteers to give the plural forms, along with the appropriate articles.
- Point to three male students and ask if the group is **los** or **las estudiantes (los).** Next, point to three female students and ask the same question **(las).** Then indicate a group of males and females and ask for the correct term to refer to them **(los estudiantes).** Stress that even if a group contains 100 women and one man, the masculine plural form and article are used.
- Point out that words like **lección** and **autobús** lose the written accent in the plural form in order to maintain the original stress.

### The Affective Dimension
Tell students that many people feel anxious when learning grammar. Tell them that grammar will seem less intimidating if they think of it as a description of how the language works instead of a list of strict rules.

**TEACHING OPTIONS**

**TPR** Give four students each a card with a different definite article. Give the other students each a card with a noun (include a mix of masculine, feminine, singular, and plural). Have students form a circle; each student's card should be visible to others. Call out one of the nouns; that student must step forward. The student with the corresponding article has five seconds to join the noun student.

**Game** Divide the class into two teams. As team members come up one by one, call out a singular or plural noun. For singular nouns, the team member must write the plural form and definite article on the board, and vice-versa. Each correct response earns a point.

# Spanish articles

**ANTE TODO**  As you know, English often uses definite articles (*the*) and indefinite articles (*a, an*) before nouns. Spanish also has definite and indefinite articles. Unlike English, Spanish articles vary in form because they agree in gender and number with the nouns they modify.

## Definite articles

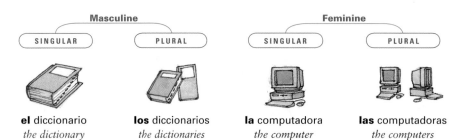

| Masculine | | Feminine | |
|---|---|---|---|
| SINGULAR | PLURAL | SINGULAR | PLURAL |
| **el** diccionario | **los** diccionarios | **la** computadora | **las** computadoras |
| *the dictionary* | *the dictionaries* | *the computer* | *the computers* |

▶ Spanish has four forms that are equivalent to the English definite article *the*. You use definite articles to refer to specific nouns.

**¡LENGUA VIVA!**
Feminine singular nouns that begin with **a-** or **ha-** require the masculine articles **el** and **un**. This is done in order to avoid repetition of the **a** sound:
**el agua** water
**las aguas** *waters*
**un hacha** *ax*
**unas hachas** *axes*

## Indefinite articles

| Masculine | | Feminine | |
|---|---|---|---|
| SINGULAR | PLURAL | SINGULAR | PLURAL |
| **un** pasajero | **unos** pasajeros | **una** fotografía | **unas** fotografías |
| *a (one) passenger* | *some passengers* | *a (one) photograph* | *some photographs* |

▶ Spanish has four forms that are equivalent to the English indefinite article, which according to context may mean *a*, *an*, or *some*. You use indefinite articles to refer to unspecified persons or things.

**¡LENGUA VIVA!**
Since **la fotografía** is feminine, so is its shortened form, **la foto**, even though it ends in **–o**.

**¡INTÉNTALO!**  Provide a definite article for each noun in the first column and an indefinite article for each noun in the second column. The first item has been done for you.

| **¿el, la, los o las?** | **¿un, una, unos o unas?** |
|---|---|
| 1. _la_ chica | 1. _un_ autobús |
| 2. _el_ chico | 2. _unas_ escuelas |
| 3. _la_ maleta | 3. _una_ computadora |
| 4. _los_ cuadernos | 4. _unos_ hombres |
| 5. _el_ lápiz | 5. _una_ señora |
| 6. _las_ mujeres | 6. _unos_ lápices |

**recursos**

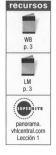

WB p. 3

LM p. 3

panorama. vhlcentral.com Lección 1

# Práctica SUPERSITE

**1** **¿Singular o plural?** If the word is singular, make it plural. If it is plural, make it singular.

1. el número  los números
2. un diario  unos diarios
3. la estudiante  las estudiantes
4. el conductor  los conductores
5. el país  los países
6. las cosas  la cosa
7. unos turistas  un turista
8. las nacionalidades  la nacionalidad
9. unas computadoras  una computadora
10. los problemas  el problema
11. una fotografía  unas fotografías
12. los profesores  el profesor
13. unas señoritas  una señorita
14. el hombre  los hombres
15. la grabadora  las grabadoras
16. la señora  las señoras

**2** **Identificar** For each drawing, provide the noun with its corresponding definite and indefinite articles.

> **modelo**
> las maletas, unas maletas

1. _la computadora, una computadora_
2. _los cuadernos, unos cuadernos_

3. _las mujeres, unas mujeres_
4. _el chico, un chico_
5. _la escuela, una escuela_

6. _las fotos, unas fotos_
7. _los autobuses, unos autobuses_
8. _el diario, un diario_

# Comunicación

**3** **Charadas** In groups, play a game of charades. Individually, think of two nouns for each charade, for example, a boy using a computer (**un chico; una computadora**). The first person to guess correctly acts out the next charade. Answers will vary.

---

**1** **Expansion** To reverse the activity, have students close their books. Read the on-page answers in random order and have students convert the singular to plural and vice-versa.

**2** **Expansion** As an additional visual exercise, bring in photos or magazine pictures that illustrate items whose names students know. Ask students to indicate the definite article and the noun. Include a mix of singular and plural nouns. Repeat the exercise with indefinite articles.

**3** **Teaching Tip** Explain the basic rules of charades relevant to what students know at this point: (1) the student acting out the charade may not speak and (2) he or she may show the number of syllables by using fingers.

**3** **Expansion** As a variant, split the class into two teams. A volunteer from Team A has one minute to act out the charade for his or her teammates. If Team A cannot come up with the correct answer, Team B has one chance to steal the point. Alternate teams until all students have taken a turn. The team with the most points wins.

---

### TEACHING OPTIONS

**Video** Show the **Fotonovela** episode again to offer more input on singular and plural nouns and articles. With their books closed, have students write down every noun and article that they hear. After viewing the video, ask volunteers to list the nouns and articles they heard. Explain that the **las** used when telling time refers to **las horas** (Ex: **Son las cinco = Son las cinco horas**).

**Extra Practice** To challenge students, slowly read a short passage from a novel, story, or poem written in Spanish, preferably one with a great number of nouns and articles. As a listening exercise, have students write down every noun and article they hear, even unfamiliar ones (the articles may cue when nouns appear).

## Section Goals

In **Estructura 1.2**, students will be introduced to:
• numbers 0–30
• the verb form **hay**

**Instructional Resources**
**Supersite:** Lab MP3 Audio Files **Lección 1**
**Supersite/IRCD:** *PowerPoints* (**Lección 1 Estructura** Presentation); *IRM* (Information Gap Activities, Lab Audio Script, WBs/VM/LM Answer Key)
**WebSAM**
**Workbook,** p. 4
**Lab Manual,** p. 4
*Cuaderno para hispanohablantes*

## Teaching Tips

• Introduce numbers by asking students if they can count to ten in Spanish. Model the pronunciation of each number. Write individual numbers on the board and call on students at random to say the number.
• Say numbers aloud at random and have students hold up the appropriate number of fingers. Then hold up varying numbers of fingers at random and ask students to shout out the corresponding number in Spanish.
• Emphasize the variable forms of **uno** and **veintiuno**, giving examples of each. Ex: **veintiún profesores, veintiuna profesoras.**
• Ask questions like these: **¿Cuántos estudiantes hay en la clase? (Hay _____ estudiantes en la clase.)**

---

## 1.2 Numbers 0–30 SUPERSITE

### Los números 0 a 30

| 0 | cero | | | | |
|---|---|---|---|---|---|
| 1 | uno | 11 | once | 21 | veintiuno |
| 2 | dos | 12 | doce | 22 | veintidós |
| 3 | tres | 13 | trece | 23 | veintitrés |
| 4 | cuatro | 14 | catorce | 24 | veinticuatro |
| 5 | cinco | 15 | quince | 25 | veinticinco |
| 6 | seis | 16 | dieciséis | 26 | veintiséis |
| 7 | siete | 17 | diecisiete | 27 | veintisiete |
| 8 | ocho | 18 | dieciocho | 28 | veintiocho |
| 9 | nueve | 19 | diecinueve | 29 | veintinueve |
| 10 | diez | 20 | veinte | 30 | treinta |

▶ The number **uno** (*one*) and numbers ending in **–uno**, such as **veintiuno**, have more than one form. Before masculine nouns, **uno** shortens to **un**. Before feminine nouns, **uno** changes to **una**.

**un** hombre → veinti**ún** hombres          **una** mujer → veinti**una** mujeres

▶ **¡Atención!** The forms **uno** and **veintiuno** are used when counting (**uno, dos, tres... veinte, veintiuno, veintidós...**). They are also used when the number *follows* a noun, even if the noun is feminine: **la lección uno**.

▶ To ask *how many people* or *things* there are, use **cuántos** before masculine nouns and **cuántas** before feminine nouns.

▶ The Spanish equivalent of both *there is* and *there are* is **hay**. Use **¿Hay...?** to ask *Is there...?* or *Are there...?* Use **no hay** to express *there is not* or *there are not*.

**AYUDA**

The numbers sixteen through nineteen can also be written as three words: **diez y seis, diez y siete...**

—**¿Cuántos** estudiantes **hay**?
*How many students are there?*

—**Hay** tres estudiantes en la foto.
*There are three students in the photo.*

—**¿Hay** chicas en la fotografía?
*Are there girls in the picture?*

—**Hay** cuatro chicos, y **no hay** chicas.
*There are four guys, and there are no girls.*

**recursos**

WB
p. 4

LM
p. 4

SUPERSITE
panorama.
vhlcentral.com
Lección 1

**¡INTÉNTALO!** Provide the Spanish words for these numbers.

| | | | | | | | |
|---|---|---|---|---|---|---|---|
| 1. **7** siete | 5. **0** cero | 9. **23** veintitrés | 13. **12** doce |
| 2. **16** dieciséis | 6. **15** quince | 10. **11** once | 14. **28** veintiocho |
| 3. **29** veintinueve | 7. **21** veintiuno | 11. **30** treinta | 15. **14** catorce |
| 4. **1** uno | 8. **9** nueve | 12. **4** cuatro | 16. **10** diez |

---

### TEACHING OPTIONS

**TPR** Assign ten students a number from 0–30 and line them up in front of the class. Call out one of the numbers at random, and have the student assigned that number step forward. When two students have stepped forward, ask them to repeat their numbers. Then ask individuals to add (Say: **Suma**) or subtract (Say: **Resta**) the two numbers, giving the result in Spanish.

**Game** Ask students to write B-I-N-G-O across the top of a blank piece of paper. Have them draw five squares vertically under each letter and randomly fill in the squares with numbers from 0–30, without repeating any numbers. Draw numbers from a hat and call them out in Spanish. The first student to mark five in a row (horizontally, vertically, or diagonally) yells **¡Bingo!** and wins. Have the winner confirm the numbers for you in Spanish.

# Práctica (SUPERSITE)

**1** **Contar** Following the pattern, provide the missing numbers in Spanish.

1. 1, 3, 5, ..., 29    7, 9, 11, 13, 15, 17, 19, 21, 23, 25, 27
2. 2, 4, 6, ..., 30    8, 10, 12, 14, 16, 18, 20, 22, 24, 26, 28
3. 3, 6, 9, ..., 30    12, 15, 18, 21, 24, 27
4. 30, 28, 26, ..., 0    24, 22, 20, 18, 16, 14, 12, 10, 8, 6, 4, 2
5. 30, 25, 20, ..., 0    15, 10, 5
6. 28, 24, 20, ..., 0    16, 12, 8, 4

**2** **Resolver** Solve these math problems with a partner.

**AYUDA**

+ → **más**
− → **menos**
= → **son**

**modelo**
5 + 3 =
**Estudiante 1:** *cinco más tres son...*
**Estudiante 2:** *ocho*

1. **2 + 15 =** Dos más quince son diecisiete.
2. **20 − 1 =** Veinte menos uno son diecinueve.
3. **5 + 7 =** Cinco más siete son doce.
4. **18 + 12 =** Dieciocho más doce son treinta.
5. **3 + 22 =** Tres más veintidós son veinticinco.
6. **6 − 3 =** Seis menos tres son tres.
7. **11 + 12 =** Once más doce son veintitrés.
8. **7 − 2 =** Siete menos dos son cinco.
9. **8 + 5 =** Ocho más cinco son trece.
10. **23 − 14 =** Veintitrés menos catorce son nueve.

**3** **¿Cuántos hay?** How many persons or things are there in these drawings?

**modelo**
Hay tres maletas.

1. Hay veinte lápices.    2. Hay un hombre.

3. Hay veinticinco chicos.    4. Hay una conductora.    5. Hay cuatro fotos.

6. Hay treinta cuadernos.    7. Hay seis turistas.    8. Hay diecisiete chicas.

**1** **Teaching Tips**
• Before beginning the activity, make sure students know each pattern: odds (**los números impares**), evens (**los números pares**), count by threes (**contar de tres en tres**).
• To simplify, write complete patterns out on the board.

**1** **Expansion** Explain that a prime number is any number that can only be divided by itself and 1. To challenge students, ask the class to list the prime numbers (**los números primos**) up to 30. Prime numbers to 30 are: 1, 2, 3, 5, 7, 11, 13, 17, 19, 23, 29.

**2** **Expansion** Do simple multiplication problems. Introduce the phrases **multiplicado por** and **dividido por**. Ex: **Cinco multiplicado por cinco son... (veinticinco). Veinte dividido por cuatro son... (cinco).**

**3** **Teaching Tip** Have students read the directions and the model. Cue student responses by asking questions related to the drawings. Ex: **¿Cuántos lápices hay? (Hay veinte lápices.)**

**3** **Expansion** Add an additional visual aspect to this activity. Hold up or point to classroom objects and ask how many there are. Since students will not know the names of many items, a simple number or **hay** + the number will suffice to signal comprehension. Ex: —**¿Cuántos bolígrafos hay aquí? —(Hay) Dos.**

**TEACHING OPTIONS**

**TPR** Give each student a card with a number from 0–30. Then call out simple math problems (addition or subtraction). When the first two numbers are called, each student steps forward, displaying his or her card. The student whose assigned number completes the math problem then has five seconds to join them.

**Extra Practice** Ask questions about your university and the town or city in which it is located. Ex: **¿Cuántos profesores hay en el departamento de español? ¿Cuántas universidades hay en _____? ¿Cuántas pizzerías hay en _____?** Encourage students to guess the number. If a number exceeds 30, write that number on the board and model its pronunciation.

# Comunicación

**4**

**4 Teaching Tip** For items 3, 4, 7, and 9, ask students: **¿Cuántos/as hay?** If there are no examples of the item listed, students should say: **No hay _____.**

**4 Expansion** After completing the activity, call on individuals to give rapid responses for the same items. To challenge students, mix up the order of items.

**5 Teaching Tip** Remind students that they will be forming sentences with **hay** and a number. Give them four minutes to do the activity. You might also have students write out their answers.

**5 Expansion** After pairs have finished analyzing the drawing, call on individuals to respond. Convert the statements into questions in Spanish. Ask: **¿Cuántos chicos hay? ¿Cuántas mujeres hay?**

**Teaching Tip** See the Information Gap Activities (Supersite/IRCD) for an additional activity to practice the material presented in this section.

**En la clase** With a classmate, take turns asking and answering these questions about your classroom. Answers will vary.

1. ¿Cuántos estudiantes hay?
2. ¿Cuántos profesores hay?
3. ¿Hay una computadora?
4. ¿Hay una maleta?
5. ¿Cuántos mapas hay?

6. ¿Cuántos lápices hay?
7. ¿Hay cuadernos?
8. ¿Cuántas grabadoras hay?
9. ¿Hay hombres?
10. ¿Cuántas mujeres hay?

**5**

**Preguntas** With a classmate, take turns asking and answering questions about the drawing. Talk about: Answers will vary.

1. how many children there are
2. how many women there are
3. if there are some photographs
4. if there is a boy
5. how many notebooks there are

6. if there is a bus
7. if there are tourists
8. how many pencils there are
9. if there is a man
10. how many computers there are

---

**TEACHING OPTIONS**

**Pairs** Have each student draw a scene similar to the one on this page. Of course, stick figures are perfectly acceptable! Give them three minutes to draw the scene. Encourage students to include multiple numbers of particular items (**cuadernos**, **maletas**, **lápices**). Then have pairs take turns describing what is in their partner's picture.

**Pairs** Divide the class into pairs. Give half of the pairs magazine pictures that contain images of familiar words or cognates. Give the other half written descriptions of the pictures, using **hay**. Ex: **En la foto hay dos mujeres, un chico y una chica.** Have pairs circulate around the room to match the descriptions with the corresponding pictures.

## [1.3] **Present tense of ser**

### Subject pronouns

**ANTE TODO**   In order to use verbs, you will need to learn about subject pronouns. A subject pronoun replaces the name or title of a person or thing and acts as the subject of a verb. In both Spanish and English, subject pronouns are divided into three groups: first person, second person, and third person.

| Subject pronouns | | | | |
|---|---|---|---|---|
| | **SINGULAR** | | **PLURAL** | |
| FIRST PERSON | yo | *I* | nosotros | *we* (masculine) |
| | | | nosotras | *we* (feminine) |
| SECOND PERSON | tú | *you* (familiar) | vosotros | *you* (masc., fam.) |
| | usted (Ud.) | *you* (formal) | vosotras | *you* (fem., fam.) |
| | | | ustedes (Uds.) | *you* (form.) |
| THIRD PERSON | él | *he* | ellos | *they* (masc.) |
| | ella | *she* | ellas | *they* (fem.) |

**¡LENGUA VIVA!**

In Latin America, **ustedes** is used as the plural for both **tú** and **usted**. In Spain, however, **vosotros** and **vosotras** are used as the plural of **tú**, and **ustedes** is used only as the plural of **usted**.

• • •

**Usted** and **ustedes** are abbreviated as **Ud.** and **Uds.**, or occasionally as **Vd.** and **Vds.**

▶ Spanish has two subject pronouns that mean *you* (singular). Address all friends, family members, and children as **tú**. Use **usted** to address a person with whom you have a formal or more distant relationship, such as a superior at work, a professor, or an older person.

**Tú** eres de Canadá, ¿verdad David?          ¿**Usted** es la profesora de español?
*You are from Canada, right David?*          *Are you the Spanish professor?*

▶ The masculine plural forms **nosotros**, **vosotros**, and **ellos** refer to a group of males or to a group of males and females. The feminine plural forms **nosotras**, **vosotras**, and **ellas** can refer only to groups made up exclusively of females.

nosotros, vosotros, ellos

nosotros, vosotros, ellos

nosotras, vosotras, ellas

▶ There is no Spanish equivalent of the English subject pronoun *it*, which is not expressed in Spanish.

Es un problema.                    Es una computadora.
*It's a problem.*                    *It's a computer.*

**Section Goals**

In **Estructura 1.3**, students will be introduced to:
• subject pronouns
• present tense of the verb **ser**
• using **ser** to identify, to indicate possession, to describe origin, and to talk about professions or occupations

**Instructional Resources**
**Supersite:** Lab MP3 Audio Files **Lección 1**
**Supersite/IRCD:** *PowerPoints* (**Lección 1 Estructura** Presentation); *IRM* (**Vocabulario adicional,** Lab Audio Script, WBs/VM/LM Answer Key)
**WebSAM**
**Workbook,** pp. 5–6
**Lab Manual,** p. 5
*Cuaderno para hispanohablantes*

**Teaching Tips**
• Point to yourself and say: **Yo soy profesor(a).** Then point to a student and ask: **¿Tú eres profesor(a) o estudiante?** (estudiante) Say: **Sí, tú eres estudiante.** Indicate the whole class and tell them: **Ustedes son estudiantes.** Once the pattern has been established, include other subject pronouns and forms of **ser** while indicating other students. Ex: **Él es..., Ella es..., Ellos son...**
• Remind students of familiar and formal forms of address they learned in **Contextos.**
• You may want to point out that while **usted** and **ustedes** are part of the second person *you*, they use third person forms.
• While the **vosotros/as** forms are listed in verb paradigms in **PANORAMA,** they will not be actively practiced.

**TEACHING OPTIONS**

**Extra Practice** Explain that students are to give subject pronouns based on their point of view. Ex: Point to yourself (**usted**), a female student (**ella**), everyone in the class (**nosotros**).
**Extra Practice** Ask students to indicate whether certain people would be addressed as **tú** or **usted**. Ex: A roommate, a friend's grandfather, a doctor, a neighbor's child.

**Heritage Speakers** Ask heritage speakers how they address elder members of their family, such as parents, grandparents, aunts, and uncles—whether they use **tú** or **usted**. Also ask them if they use **vosotros/as** (they typically will not unless they or their family are from Spain).

**Teaching Tips**

• Work through the explanation and the forms of **ser** in the chart. Emphasize that **es** is used for **usted**, **él**, and **ella**, and that **son** is used for **ustedes**, **ellos**, and **ellas**. Context, subject pronouns, or names will determine who is being addressed or talked about.

• Explain that **ser** is used to identify people and things. At this point there is no need to explain that **estar** also means *to be*; it will be introduced in **Lección 2**.

• Explain the meaning of **¿quién?** and ask questions about students. Ex: _____, **¿quién es ella? Sí, es** _____. **¿Quién soy yo? Sí, soy el/la profesor(a)** _____. Introduce **¿qué?** and ask questions about items in the class. Ex: (*Pointing to a map*) **¿Qué es? Sí, es un mapa**.

• Point out the construction of **ser** + **de** to indicate possession. Stress that there is no *'s* in Spanish. Pick up objects belonging to students and ask questions. Ex: **¿De quién es el cuaderno? (Es de** _____.) **¿De quién son los libros? (Son de** _____.) Then hold up items from two different students and ask: **¿De quiénes son las plumas? Son de** _____ **y** _____.

• Introduce the contraction **de + el = del**. Emphasize that **de** and other definite articles do not make contractions, and support with examples. Ex: **Soy del estado de** _____. **El diccionario no es de la profesora de** _____. Also use examples of possession to illustrate the contraction. Ex: **¿Es el mapa del presidente de la universidad?**

# The present tense of ser

**ANTE TODO** In **Contextos** and **Fotonovela**, you have already used several forms of the present tense of **ser** (*to be*) to identify yourself and others and to talk about where you and others are from. **Ser** is an irregular verb, which means its forms don't follow the regular patterns that most verbs follow. You need to memorize the forms, which appear in this chart.

| | | The verb ser (*to be*) | |
|---|---|---|---|
| **SINGULAR FORMS** | yo | **soy** | *I am* |
| | tú | **eres** | *you are* (fam.) |
| | Ud./él/ella | **es** | *you are* (form.); *he/she is* |
| **PLURAL FORMS** | nosotros/as | **somos** | *we are* |
| | vosotros/as | **sois** | *you are* (fam.) |
| | Uds./ellos/ellas | **son** | *you are* (form.); *they are* |

## Uses of *ser*

▶ Use **ser** to identify people and things.

—¿Quién **es** él?
*Who is he?*

—**Es** Javier Gómez Lozano.
*He's Javier Gómez Lozano.*

—¿Qué **es**?
*What is it?*

—**Es** un mapa de España.
*It's a map of Spain.*

Es Maite.

Es un autobús.

▶ **Ser** also expresses possession, with the preposition **de**. There is no Spanish equivalent of the English construction [*noun*] + 's (*Maite's*). In its place, Spanish uses [*noun*] + **de** + [*owner*].

—¿**De** quién **es**?
*Whose is it?*

—**Es** el diario **de** Maite.
*It's Maite's diary.*

—¿**De** quiénes **son**?
*Whose are they?*

—**Son** los lápices **de** la chica.
*They are the girl's pencils.*

▶ When **de** is followed by the article **el**, the two combine to form the contraction **del**. **De** does *not* contract with **la, las,** or **los**.

—**Es** la computadora **del** conductor.
*It's the driver's computer.*

—**Son** las maletas **del** chico.
*They are the boy's suitcases.*

**TEACHING OPTIONS**

**Extra Practice** As a rapid response drill, call out subject pronouns and have students answer with the correct form of **ser**. Ex: **tú (eres), ustedes (son)**. Reverse the drill by starting with forms of **ser**. Students must give the subject pronouns. Accept multiple answers for **es** and **son**.

**TPR** Have students form a circle. Toss a foam or paper ball to individual students. When a student catches it, call on another to state whose ball it is. Ex: **Es de** _____. Take two balls and toss them to different students to elicit **Son de** _____ **y** _____.

▶ **Ser** also uses the preposition **de** to express origin.

> ¿De dónde eres?

> Yo soy de México.

> ¿De dónde eres?

> Yo soy de España.

—¿**De** dónde **es** Javier?
*Where is Javier from?*

—Es **de** Puerto Rico.
*He's from Puerto Rico.*

—¿**De** dónde **es** Inés?
*Where is Inés from?*

—Es **del** Ecuador.
*She's from Ecuador.*

▶ Use **ser** to express profession or occupation.

Don Francisco **es conductor**.
*Don Francisco is a driver.*

Yo **soy estudiante**.
*I am a student.*

▶ Unlike English, Spanish does not use the indefinite article (**un**, **una**) after **ser** when referring to professions, unless accompanied by an adjective or other description.

Marta **es** profesora.
*Marta is a teacher.*

Marta **es una** profesora excelente.
*Marta is an excellent teacher.*

**Somos Perú**

**LanPerú**

**¡INTÉNTALO!** Provide the correct subject pronouns and the present forms of **ser**. The first item has been done for you.

| | | | | | | |
|---|---|---|---|---|---|---|
| 1. Gabriel | él | es | 5. las turistas | ellas | son | |
| 2. Juan y yo | nosotros | somos | 6. el chico | él | es | |
| 3. Óscar y Flora | ellos | son | 7. los conductores | ellos | son | |
| 4. Adriana | ella | es | 8. los señores Ruiz | ellos | son | |

■ **Teaching Tip** Review **tú** and **usted**, asking students which pronoun they would use in a formal situation and which they would use in an informal situation.

■ **Expansion** Once students have identified the correct subject pronouns, ask them to give the form of **ser** they would use when *addressing* each person and when *talking about* each person.

■ **Expansion** Give additional names of well-known Spanish speakers and ask students to tell where they are from. Have students give the country names in English if they do not know the Spanish equivalent. Ex: **¿De dónde es Andy García? (Es de Cuba.)**

■ **Teaching Tips**
• To simplify, before beginning the activity, guide students in identifying the objects.
• You might tell students to answer the second part of the question (**¿De quién es?**) with any answer they wish. Have students take turns asking and answering questions.

# Práctica

**1** **Pronombres** What subject pronouns would you use to (a) talk to these people directly and (b) talk about them?

> **modelo**
>
> un joven  tú, él

1. una chica  tú, ella
2. el presidente de México  Ud., él
3. tres chicas y un chico  Uds., ellos
4. un estudiante  tú, él
5. la señora Ochoa  Ud., ella
6. dos profesoras  Uds., ellas

**2** **Identidad y origen** With a partner, take turns asking and answering these questions about the people indicated: **¿Quién es?/¿Quiénes son?** and **¿De dónde es?/¿De dónde son?**

> **modelo**
>
> Ricky Martin (Puerto Rico)
> **Estudiante 1:** ¿Quién es?  **Estudiante 1:** ¿De dónde es?
> **Estudiante 2:** Es Ricky Martin.  **Estudiante 2:** Es de Puerto Rico.

1. Enrique Iglesias (España)
   E1: ¿Quién es? E2: Es Enrique Iglesias. E1: ¿De dónde es? E2: Es de España.
2. Sammy Sosa (República Dominicana)
   E2: ¿Quién es? E1: Es Sammy Sosa. E2: ¿De dónde es? E1: Es de la República Dominicana.
3. Rebecca Lobo y Martin Sheen (Estados Unidos)  E1: ¿Quiénes son? E2: Son Rebecca Lobo y Martin Sheen. E1: ¿De dónde son? E2: Son de los Estados Unidos.
4. Carlos Santana y Salma Hayek (México)  E2: ¿Quiénes son? E1: Son Carlos Santana y Salma Hayek. E2: ¿De dónde son? E1: Son de México.
5. Shakira (Colombia)
   E1: ¿Quién es? E2: Es Shakira. E1: ¿De dónde es? E2: Es de Colombia.
6. Antonio Banderas y Penélope Cruz (España)  E2: ¿Quiénes son? E1: Son Antonio Banderas y Penélope Cruz. E2: ¿De dónde son? E1: Son de España.
7. Edward James Olmos y Jimmy Smits (Estados Unidos)  E1: ¿Quiénes son? E2: Son Edward James Olmos y Jimmy Smits. E1: ¿De dónde son? E2: Son de los Estados Unidos.
8. Gloria Estefan (Cuba)  E2: ¿Quién es? E1: Es Gloria Estefan. E2: ¿De dónde es? E1: Es de Cuba.

**3** **¿Qué es?** Ask your partner what each object is and to whom it belongs.

> **modelo**
>
> **Estudiante 1:** ¿Qué es?  **Estudiante 1:** ¿De quién es?
> **Estudiante 2:** Es una grabadora.  **Estudiante 2:** Es del profesor.

1.  2.  3.  4.

1. E1: ¿Qué es?
   E2: Es una maleta.
   E1: ¿De quién es?
   E2: Es de la Sra. Valdés.

2. E1: ¿Qué es?
   E2: Es un cuaderno.
   E1: ¿De quién es?
   E2: Es de Gregorio.

3. E1: ¿Qué es?
   E2: Es una computadora.
   E1: ¿De quién es?
   E2: Es de Rafael.

4. E1: ¿Qué es?
   E2: Es un diario.
   E1: ¿De quién es?
   E2: Es de Marisa.

**TEACHING OPTIONS**

**Video** Replay the *Fotonovela*, having students focus on subject pronouns and the verb **ser**. Ask them to copy down as many examples of sentences that use forms of **ser** as they can. Stop the video where appropriate to ask comprehension questions on what the characters said.

**Heritage Speakers** Encourage heritage speakers to describe themselves and their family briefly. Make sure they use the cognates **familia**, **mamá**, and **papá**. Call on students to report the information given. Ex: **Francisco es de la Florida. La mamá de Francisco es de España. Ella es profesora. El papá de Francisco es de Cuba. Él es dentista.**

# Comunicación

**4 Preguntas** Using the items in the word bank, ask your partner questions about the ad. Be imaginative in your responses. Answers will vary.

| ¿Quién? | ¿De dónde? | ¿Cuántos? |
|---|---|---|
| ¿Qué? | ¿De quién? | ¿Cuántas? |

## SOMOS ECUATURISTA, S.A.
### El autobús nacional del Ecuador

- 25 autobuses en total
- 30 conductores del Ecuador
- pasajeros internacionales
- mapas de las regiones del país

### ¡Todos a bordo!

**5 ¿Quién es?** In small groups, take turns pretending to be a person from Spain, Mexico, Puerto Rico, Cuba, the United States, or another Spanish-speaking country who is famous in these professions. Your partners will try to guess who you are. Answers will vary.

| actor *actor* | deportista *athlete* | escritor(a) *writer* |
|---|---|---|
| actriz *actress* | cantante *singer* | músico/a *musician* |

**modelo**

**Estudiante 3:** ¿Eres de Puerto Rico?
**Estudiante 1:** No. Soy de Colombia.
**Estudiante 2:** ¿Eres hombre?
**Estudiante 1:** Sí. Soy hombre.
**Estudiante 3:** ¿Eres escritor?
**Estudiante 1:** No. Soy actor.
**Estudiante 2:** ¿Eres John Leguizamo?
**Estudiante 1:** ¡Sí! ¡Sí!

**4 Teaching Tip** If students ask, explain that the abbreviation **S.A.** in the ad stands for **Sociedad Anónima** and is equivalent to the English abbreviation *Inc.* (*Incorporated*).

**4 Expansion** Ask pairs to write four true-false statements about the ad. Call on volunteers to read their sentences. The class will indicate whether the statements are true (**cierto**) or false (**falso**) and correct the false statements.

**5 Teaching Tips**
- To simplify, have students brainstorm a list of names in the categories suggested.
- Have three students read the **modelo** aloud.

---

**TEACHING OPTIONS**

**Small Groups** Bring in personal photos or magazine pictures that show people. In small groups, have students invent stories about the people: who they are, where they are from, and what they do. Circulate around the room and assist with unfamiliar vocabulary as necessary, but encourage students to use terms they already know.

**Game** Hand out individual strips of paper with names of famous people on them. There should be several duplicates of each name. Then give descriptions of one of the famous people (**Es de _____. Es** [*profession*]**.**), including cognate adjectives if you wish (**inteligente, pesimista**). The first person to stand and indicate that the name they have is the one you are describing (**¡Yo lo tengo!**) wins that round.

# 1.4 Telling time

**ANTE TODO**  In both English and Spanish, the verb *to be* (**ser**) and numbers are used to tell time.

---

## Section Goals

In **Estructura 1.4**, students will be introduced to:
• asking and telling time
• times of day

---

**Instructional Resources**
**Supersite:** Lab MP3 Audio Files **Lección 1**
**Supersite/IRCD:** *PowerPoints* (**Lección 1 Estructura** Presentation, Overhead #11); *IRM* (Information Gap Activities, Lab Audio Script, WBs/VM/LM Answer Key)
**WebSAM**
**Workbook,** pp. 7–8
**Lab Manual,** p. 6
*Cuaderno para hispanohablantes*

---

## Teaching Tips

• To prepare students for telling time, review **es** and **son** and numbers 0–30.
• Introduce **es la una** and **son las dos (tres, cuatro...)**. Remind students that **las** in time constructions refers to **las horas**. Introduce **y cinco (diez, veinte...), y quince/ cuarto,** and **y treinta/media**.
• Show *Overhead PowerPoint #11*, use a paper plate clock, or any other clock where you can quickly move the hands to different positions. Display a number of different times for students to identify. Ask: **¿Qué hora es?** Concentrate on this until students are relatively comfortable with expressing the time in Spanish.
• Introduce **menos diez (cuarto, veinte...)** and explain this method of telling time in Spanish. It typically takes students longer to master this aspect of telling time. Spend about five minutes with your moveable-hands clock and ask students to state the times shown.

▶ To ask what time it is, use **¿Qué hora es?** When telling time, use **es + la** with **una** and **son + las** with all other hours.

**Es la** una.  **Son las** dos.  **Son las** seis.

▶ As in English, you express time from the hour to the half-hour in Spanish by adding minutes.

Son las cuatro **y cinco.**  Son las once **y veinte.**

▶ You may use either **y cuarto** or **y quince** to express fifteen minutes or quarter past the hour. For thirty minutes or half past the hour, you may use either **y media** or **y treinta**.

Es la una **y cuarto.**

Son las doce **y media.**

Son las nueve **y quince.**

Son las siete **y treinta.**

▶ You express time from the half-hour to the hour in Spanish by subtracting minutes or a portion of an hour from the next hour.

Es la una **menos cuarto.**  Son las tres **menos quince.**  Son las ocho **menos veinte.**  Son las tres **menos diez.**

---

**TEACHING OPTIONS**

**Extra Practice**  Draw a large clock face on the board with its numbers but without hands. Say a time and ask a volunteer to come up to the board and draw the hands to indicate that time. The rest of the class verifies that their classmate has written the correct time. Continue until several volunteers have participated.

**Pairs**  Tell the class **tengo** means *I have*. Have pairs take turns telling each other what time their classes are this semester/ quarter. (Ex: **Tengo una clase a las...**) For each time given, the other student draws a clock face with the corresponding time. The first student verifies the time. To challenge students, give a list of course names (**las matemáticas, la biología,** etc.)

▶ To ask at what time a particular event takes place, use the phrase **¿A qué hora (...)?**
To state at what time something takes place, use the construction **a la(s)** + *time*.

| | |
|---|---|
| **¿A qué hora** es la clase de biología? | La clase es **a las dos**. |
| *(At) what time is biology class?* | *The class is at two o'clock.* |
| **¿A qué hora** es la fiesta? | **A las ocho**. |
| *(At) what time is the party?* | *At eight.* |

▶ Here are some useful words and phrases associated with telling time.

| | |
|---|---|
| Son las ocho **en punto**. | Son las nueve **de la mañana**. |
| *It's 8 o'clock on the dot/sharp.* | *It's 9 a.m./in the morning.* |
| Es **el mediodía**. | Son las cuatro y cuarto **de la tarde**. |
| *It's noon.* | *It's 4:15 p.m./in the afternoon.* |
| Es **la medianoche**. | Son las diez y media **de la noche**. |
| *It's midnight.* | *It's 10:30 p.m./at night.* |

**¡LENGUA VIVA!**

Other useful expressions for telling time:

**Son las doce (del día).**
It is twelve o'clock (p.m.).

**Son las doce (de la noche).**
It is twelve o'clock (a.m.).

*Oye, ¿qué hora es?*

*Son las diez y tres minutos.*

*Oiga, ¿qué hora es?*

*Son las diez.*

**recursos**

WB
pp. 7–8

LM
p. 6

panorama.
vhlcentral.com
Lección 1

**¡INTÉNTALO!** Practice telling time by completing these sentences.
The first item has been done for you.

1. (1:00 a.m.) Es la _____una_____ de la mañana.
2. (2:50 a.m.) Son las tres _____menos_____ diez de la mañana.
3. (4:15 p.m.) Son las cuatro y ____cuarto/quince____ de la tarde.
4. (8:30 p.m.) Son las ocho y ____media/treinta____ de la noche.
5. (9:15 a.m.) Son las nueve y quince de la _____mañana_____.
6. (12:00 p.m.) Es el _____mediodía_____.
7. (6:00 a.m.) Son las seis de la _____mañana_____.
8. (4:05 p.m.) Son las cuatro y cinco de la _____tarde_____.
9. (12:00 a.m.) Es la _____medianoche_____.
10. (3:45 a.m.) Son las cuatro menos _____cuarto/quince_____ de la mañana.
11. (2:15 a.m.) Son las _____dos_____ y cuarto de la mañana.
12. (1:25 p.m.) Es la una y _____veinticinco_____ de la tarde.
13. (6:50 a.m.) Son las _____siete_____ menos diez de la mañana.
14. (10:40 p.m.) Son las once menos veinte de la _____noche_____.

**Teaching Tips**

• Ask students **¿Qué hora es?** and **¿A qué hora es la clase de español?** Emphasize the difference by looking at your watch when you ask the first question and shrugging your shoulders with a quizzical look when you ask the second question.

• Go over **en punto**, **mediodía**, and **medianoche**. Explain that **medio/a** means *half*.

• Go over **de la mañana/tarde/ noche**. Ask students what time it is now.

• You may wish to explain that Spanish speakers tend to view times of day differently than English speakers do. In many countries, only after someone has eaten lunch does one say **Buenas tardes**. Similarly, with the evening, Spanish speakers tend to view 6:00 and even 7:00 as **de la tarde**, not **de la noche**.

**¡Lengua viva!** Introduce the Spanish equivalents for noon (**las doce del día**) and midnight (**las doce de la noche**).

**TEACHING OPTIONS**

**Extra Practice** Give half of the class slips of paper with clock faces depicting certain times. Give the corresponding times written out in Spanish to the other half of the class. Have students circulate around the room to match their times. To increase difficulty, include duplicates of each time with **de la mañana** or **de la tarde/noche** on the written-out times and a sun or a moon on the clock faces.

**Heritage Speakers** Ask heritage speakers if they generally tell time as presented in the text or if they use different constructions. Some ways Hispanics use time constructions include (1) forgoing **menos** and using a number from 31–59 and (2) asking the question **¿Qué horas son?** Stress, however, that the constructions presented in the text are the ones students should focus on.

## Práctica  SUPERSITE

**1 Teaching Tip** To add a visual aspect to this activity, have students draw clock faces showing the times presented in the activity. Have them compare drawings with a partner to verify accuracy.

**1 Ordenar** Put these times in order, from the earliest to the latest.

a. Son las dos de la tarde. 4          d. Son las seis menos cuarto de la tarde. 5
b. Son las once de la mañana. 2        e. Son las dos menos diez de la tarde. 3
c. Son las siete y media de la noche. 6 f. Son las ocho y veintidós de la mañana. 1

**2 Teaching Tip** Read aloud the two ways of saying *4:15* in the model sentence. Point out that the clocks and watches indicate the part of day (morning, afternoon, or evening) as well as the hour. Have students include this information in their responses.

**2 ¿Qué hora es?** Give the times shown on each clock or watch.

**modelo**
Son las cuatro y cuarto/quince de la tarde.

NOTA CULTURAL

Many Spanish-speaking countries use both the 12-hour clock and the 24-hour clock (that is, military time). The 24-hour clock is commonly used in written form on signs and schedules. For example, 1 p.m. is **13h**, 2 p.m. is **14h** and so on.

p.m.
1. Son las doce y media/treinta de la tarde.
2. Es la una de la mañana.
3. Son las cinco y cuarto/quince de la tarde.
4. Son las ocho y diez de la noche.
5. Son las cinco y media/treinta de la mañana.

6. Son las once menos cuarto/quince de la mañana.
7. Son las dos y doce de la tarde.
8. Son las siete y cinco de la mañana.
9. Son las cuatro menos cinco de la tarde.
10. Son las doce menos veinticinco de la noche.

**2 Expansion** At random, say aloud times shown in the activity. Students must give the number of the clock or watch you describe. Ex: **Es la una de la mañana. (Es el número 2.)**

**3 Teaching Tip** To simplify, go over new vocabulary introduced in this activity and model pronunciation. Have students repeat the items after you to build confidence.

**3 ¿A qué hora?** Ask your partner at what time these events take place. Your partner will answer according to the cues provided.

**modelo**
la clase de matemáticas (2:30 p.m.)
**Estudiante 1:** ¿A qué hora es la clase de matemáticas?
**Estudiante 2:** Es a las dos y media de la tarde.

1. el programa *Las cuatro amigas* (11:30 a.m.)
2. el drama *La casa de Bernarda Alba* (7:00 p.m.)
3. el programa *Las computadoras* (8:30 a.m.)
4. la clase de español (10:30 a.m.)
5. la clase de biología (9:40 a.m.)
6. la clase de historia (10:50 a.m.)
7. el partido (*game*) de béisbol (5:15 p.m.)
8. el partido de tenis (12:45 p.m.)
9. el partido de baloncesto (*basketball*) (7:45 p.m.)

1. E1: ¿A qué hora es el programa *Las cuatro amigas*? E2: Es a las once y media/treinta de la mañana.
2. E1: ¿A qué hora es el drama *La casa de Bernarda Alba*? E2: Es a las siete de la noche.
3. E1: ¿A qué hora es el programa *Las computadoras*? E2: Es a las ocho y media/treinta de la mañana.
4. E1: ¿A qué hora es la clase de español? E2: Es a las diez y media/treinta de la mañana.
5. E1: ¿A qué hora es la clase de biología? E2: Es a las diez menos veinte de la mañana.
6. E1: ¿A qué hora es la clase de historia? E2: Es a las once menos diez de la mañana.
7. E1: ¿A qué hora es el partido de béisbol? E2: Es a las cinco y cuarto/quince de la tarde.
8. E1: ¿A qué hora es el partido de tenis? E2: Es a la una menos cuarto/quince de la tarde.
9. E1: ¿A qué hora es el partido de baloncesto? E2: Es a las ocho menos cuarto/quince de la noche.

**3 Expansion**
• Have partners switch roles and ask and answer the questions again.
• Have students come up with three additional items to ask their partner. The partner should respond with actual times. Ex: —¿A qué hora es el programa *ER*? —Es a las diez de la noche.

NOTA CULTURAL

**La casa de Bernarda Alba** is a famous play by Spanish poet and playwright **Federico García Lorca** (1898–1936). Lorca was one of the most famous writers of the 20th century and a close friend of Spain's most talented artists, including the painter Salvador Dalí and the filmmaker Luis Buñuel.

**TEACHING OPTIONS**

**Pairs** Have students work with a partner to create an original conversation in which they: (1) greet each other appropriately, (2) ask for the time, (3) ask what time a particular class is, and (4) say goodbye. Have pairs role-play their conversations for the class.
**Game** Divide the class into two teams and have each team form a line. Write two city names on the board. (Ex: **Los Ángeles**

and **Miami**) Check that students know the time difference and then list a time underneath the first city. (Ex: **10:30 a.m.**) Point to the first member of each team and ask: **En Los Ángeles son las diez y media de la mañana. ¿Qué hora es en Miami?** The first student to write the correct time in Spanish under the second column earns a point for their team. Vary the game with different times and cities. The team with the most points wins.

# Comunicación

**4** **En la televisión** With a partner, take turns asking and answering questions about these television listings. Answers will vary.

**modelo**

**Estudiante 1:** *¿A qué hora es el documental Las computadoras?*
**Estudiante 2:** *Es a las nueve en punto de la noche.*

**Telenovelas** are the Latin American version of soap operas, but they differ from North American soaps in many ways. Many **telenovelas** are prime-time shows enjoyed by a large segment of the population. They seldom run for more than one season and they are sometimes based on famous novels.

## TV Hoy – Programación

| | | | | |
|---|---|---|---|---|
| **11:00 am** | Telenovela: *Cuatro viajeros y un autobús* | | **5:00 pm** | Telenovela: *Tres mujeres* |
| **12:00 pm** | Película: *El cóndor* (drama) | | **6:00 pm** | Noticias |
| **2:00 pm** | Telenovela: *Dos mujeres y dos hombres* | | **7:00 pm** | Especial musical: *Música folklórica de México* |
| **3:00 pm** | Programa juvenil: *Fiesta* | | **7:30 pm** | La naturaleza: *Jardín secreto* |
| **3:30 pm** | Telenovela: *¡Sí, sí, sí!* | | **8:00 pm** | Noticiero: *Veinticuatro horas* |
| **4:00 pm** | Telenovela: *El diario de la Sra. González* | | **9:00 pm** | Documental: *Las computadoras* |

**5** **Preguntas** With a partner, answer these questions based on your own knowledge. Some answers will vary.

1. Son las tres de la tarde en Nueva York. ¿Qué hora es en Los Ángeles?
   Es el mediodía./ Son las doce.
2. Son las ocho y media en Chicago. ¿Qué hora es en Miami?
   Son las nueve y media.
3. Son las dos menos cinco en San Francisco. ¿Qué hora es en San Antonio?
   Son las cuatro menos cinco.
4. ¿A qué hora es el programa *60 Minutes*?; ¿A qué hora es el programa *Today Show*?
   Es a las siete de la noche.; Es a las siete de la mañana.

**6** **Más preguntas** Using the questions in the previous activity as a model, make up four questions of your own. Then, get together with a classmate and take turns asking and answering each other's questions. Answers will vary.

# Síntesis

**7** **Situación** With a partner, play the roles of a journalism student interviewing a visiting literature professor (**profesor(a) de literatura**) from Venezuela. Be prepared to act out the conversation for your classmates. Answers will vary.

| **Estudiante** | **Profesor(a) de literatura** |
|---|---|
| Ask the professor his/her name. | → Ask the student his/her name. |
| Ask the professor what time his/her literature class is. | → Ask the student where he/she is from. |
| Ask how many students are in his/her class. | → Ask to whom his/her tape recorder belongs. |
| Say thank you and goodbye. | → Say thank you and you are pleased to meet him/her. |

---

**TEACHING OPTIONS**

**Small Groups** Have small groups prepare skits. Students can choose any situation they wish, provided that they use material presented in the **Contextos** and **Estructura** sections. Possible situations include: meeting to go on an excursion (as in the *Fotonovela*), meeting between classes, and introducing friends to professors.

**Heritage Speakers** Ask heritage speakers what **telenovelas** are currently featured on Spanish-language television and the channel (**canal**) and time when they are shown.

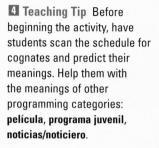

**4** **Teaching Tip** Before beginning the activity, have students scan the schedule for cognates and predict their meanings. Help them with the meanings of other programming categories: **película, programa juvenil, noticias/noticiero**.

**4** **Expansion** Ask students questions about what time popular TV programs are shown. Ex: —¿A qué hora es el programa **The Daily Show with Jon Stewart**? —**Es a las once.**

**5** **Teaching Tip** Remind students that there are four time zones in the continental United States, and that when it is noon in the Eastern Time zone, it is three hours earlier in the Pacific Time zone.

**6** **Expansion** Have pairs choose the two most challenging questions to share with the class.

**7** **Teaching Tip** Point out that this activity synthesizes everything students have learned in this lesson: greetings and leave-takings, nouns and articles, numbers 0–30 and **hay**, the verb **ser**, and telling time. Spend a few moments reviewing these topics.

**Teaching Tip** See the Information Gap Activities (Supersite/IRCD) for an additional activity to practice the material presented in this section.

## Section Goal

In **Recapitulación**, students will review the grammar concepts from this lesson.

**Instructional Resource**
**Supersite**

**1 Teaching Tips**

- Before beginning the activity, remind students that nouns ending in **-ma** tend to be masculine, despite ending in an **-a**.
- To add an auditory aspect to this activity, read aloud a masculine or feminine noun, then call on individuals to supply the other form. Do the same for plural and singular nouns. Keep a brisk pace.

**1 Expansion** Have students identify the corresponding definite and indefinite articles in both singular and plural forms for all of the nouns.

**2 Teaching Tips**

- Have students explain why they chose their answers. Ex: 1. **Cuántas** is feminine and modifies **chicas**.
- Ask students to explain the difference between **¿Tienes un diccionario?** and **¿Tienes el diccionario?** (general versus specific).

**2 Expansion**

- Ask students to rewrite the dialogue with information from one of their classes.
- Have volunteers ask class-mates questions using pos-sessives with **ser**. Ex: —¿**De quién es esta mochila?** —**Es de ella.**

# Recapitulación

SUPERSITE   For self-scoring and diagnostics, go to **panorama.vhlcentral.com**.

Review the grammar concepts you have learned in this lesson by completing these activities.

**1 Completar** Complete the charts according to the models. **14 pts.**

| MASCULINO | FEMENINO |
|---|---|
| el chico | la chica |
| el profesor | la profesora |
| el amigo | la amiga |
| el señor | la señora |
| el pasajero | la pasajera |
| el estudiante | la estudiante |
| el turista | la turista |
| el joven | la joven |

| SINGULAR | PLURAL |
|---|---|
| una cosa | unas cosas |
| un libro | unos libros |
| una clase | unas clases |
| una lección | unas lecciones |
| un conductor | unos conductores |
| un país | unos países |
| un lápiz | unos lápices |
| un problema | unos problemas |

**2 En la clase** Complete each conversation with the correct word. **11 pts.**

 César      Beatriz

**CÉSAR** ¿(1) __Cuántas__ (Cuántos/Cuántas) chicas hay en la (2) __clase__ (maleta/clase)?

**BEATRIZ** Hay (3) __catorce__ (catorce/cuatro) [14] chicas.

**CÉSAR** Y, ¿(4) __cuántos__ (cuántos/cuántas) chicos hay?

**BEATRIZ** Hay (5) __trece__ (tres/trece) [13] chicos.

**CÉSAR** Entonces (*Then*), en total hay (6) __veintisiete__ (veintiséis/veintisiete) (7) __estudiantes__ (estudiantes/chicas) en la clase.

 Ariana      Daniel

**ARIANA** ¿Tienes (*Do you have*) (8) __un__ (un/una) diccionario?

**DANIEL** No, pero (*but*) aquí (9) __hay__ (es/hay) uno.

**ARIANA** ¿De quién (10) __es__ (eres/es)?

**DANIEL** (11) __Es__ (Son/Es) de Carlos.

**RESUMEN GRAMATICAL**

**1.1 Nouns and articles** *pp. 12–14*

**Gender of nouns**

**Nouns that refer to living things**

| | Masculine | | Feminine |
|---|---|---|---|
| -o | el chico | -a | la chica |
| -or | el profesor | -ora | la profesora |
| -ista | el turista | -ista | la turista |

**Nouns that refer to non-living things**

| | Masculine | | Feminine |
|---|---|---|---|
| -o | el libro | -a | la cosa |
| -ma | el programa | -ción | la lección |
| -s | el autobús | -dad | la nacionalidad |

**Plural of nouns**

▶ ending in vowels + *-s*    la chica ➔ las chicas

▶ ending in consonant + *-es*
el señor ➔ los señores

(-z ➔ -ces   un lápiz ➔ unos lápices)

Definite articles: el, la, los, las

Indefinite articles: un, una, unos, unas

**1.2 Numbers 0–30** *p. 16*

| | | | | | |
|---|---|---|---|---|---|
| 0 | cero | 8 | ocho | 16 | dieciséis |
| 1 | uno | 9 | nueve | 17 | diecisiete |
| 2 | dos | 10 | diez | 18 | dieciocho |
| 3 | tres | 11 | once | 19 | diecinueve |
| 4 | cuatro | 12 | doce | 20 | veinte |
| 5 | cinco | 13 | trece | 21 | veintiuno |
| 6 | seis | 14 | catorce | 22 | veintidós |
| 7 | siete | 15 | quince | 30 | treinta |

**1.3 Present tense of *ser*** *pp. 19–21*

| yo | soy | nosotros/as | somos |
|---|---|---|---|
| tú | eres | vosotros/as | sois |
| Ud./él/ella | es | Uds./ellos/ellas | son |

---

**TEACHING OPTIONS**

**Extra Practice** To add a visual aspect to this grammar review, bring in pictures from newspapers, magazines, or the Internet of nouns that students have learned. Ask them to identify the people or objects using **ser**. As a variation, ask students questions about the photos, using **hay**. Ex: **¿Cuántos/as ____ hay en la foto?**

**TPR** Give certain times of day and night and ask students to identify who would be awake: **vigilante** (*night watchman*), **estudiante**, or **los dos**. Have students raise their left hand for the **vigilante**, right hand for the **estudiante**, and both hands for **los dos**. Ex: **Son las cinco menos veinte de la mañana.** (left hand) **Es la medianoche.** (both hands)

**3** **Presentaciones** Complete this conversation with the correct form of the verb **ser**. **6 pts.**

**JUAN** ¡Hola! Me llamo Juan. (1) _____Soy_____ estudiante en la clase de español.

**DANIELA** ¡Hola! Mucho gusto. Yo (2) _____soy_____ Daniela y ella (3) _____es_____ Mónica. ¿De dónde (4) _____eres_____ (tú), Juan?

**JUAN** De California. Y ustedes, ¿de dónde (5) _____son_____?

**MÓNICA** Nosotras (6) _____somos_____ de Florida.

---

**1.4** **Telling time** *pp. 24–25*

| | |
|---|---|
| Es la **una**. | *It's 1:00.* |
| Son las **dos**. | *It's 2:00.* |
| Son las **tres** y **diez**. | *It's 3:10.* |
| Es la **una** y **cuarto/quince**. | *It's 1:15.* |
| Son las **siete** y **media/treinta**. | *It's 7:30.* |
| Es la **una** menos **cuarto/quince**. | *It's 12:45.* |
| Son las **once** menos **veinte**. | *It's 10:40.* |
| Es el **mediodía/la medianoche**. | *It's noon/midnight.* |

---

**4** **¿Qué hora es?** Write out in words the following times, indicating whether it's morning, noon, afternoon, or night. **10 pts.**

1. It's 12:00 p.m.
Es el mediodía./Son las doce del día.

2. It's 7:05 a.m.
Son las siete y cinco de la mañana.

3. It's 9:35 p.m.
Son las diez menos veinticinco de la noche.

4. It's 5:15 p.m.
Son las cinco y cuarto/quince de la tarde.

5. It's 1:30 p.m.
Es la una y media/treinta de la tarde.

---

**5** **¡Hola!** Write five sentences introducing yourself and talking about your classes. You may want to include: your name, where you are from, who your Spanish teacher is, the time of your Spanish class, how many students are in the class, etc. **9 pts.** Answers will vary.

_____

_____

_____

_____

---

**6** **Canción** Write the missing words to complete this children's song. **2 EXTRA points!**

" ¿ _____Cuántas_____ patas° tiene un gato°? Una, dos, tres y _____cuatro_____ . "

patas *legs* tiene un gato *does a cat have*

---

---

**3** **Teaching Tip** Before beginning the activity, orally review the conjugation of **ser**.

**3** **Expansion** Ask questions about the characters in the dialogue. Ex: **¿Quién es Juan?** (Juan es un estudiante en la clase de español.) **¿De dónde es?** (Es de California.)

**4** **Teaching Tip** Remind students to make sure they use the correct form of **ser**.

**4** **Expansion** To challenge students, give them these times as items 6–10: **(6) It's 3:13 p.m., (7) It's 4:29 a.m., (8) It's 1:04 a.m., (9) It's 10:09 a.m., (10) It's 12:16 a.m.**

**5** **Expansion** For further practice with **ser** and **hay**, ask students to share the time and size of their other classes. Be certain to list necessary vocabulary on the board, such as **matemáticas, ciencias, literatura**, and **historia**.

**6** **Teaching Tip** Point out the word **Una** in line 3 of the song. To challenge students, have them work in pairs to come up with an explanation for why **Una** is used. (It refers to **pata** [una pata, dos patas… ]).

---

**TEACHING OPTIONS**

**Game** Have students make a five-column, five-row chart with B-I-N-G-O written across the top of the columns. Tell them to fill in the squares at random with different times of day. (Remind them to use only full, quarter, or half hours.) Draw times from a hat and call them out in Spanish. The first student to mark five in a row (horizontally, vertically, or diagonally) yells **¡Bingo!** and wins.

**Extra Practice** Have students imagine they have a new penpal in a Spanish-speaking country. Ask them to write a short e-mail in which they introduce themselves, state where they are from, and give information about their class schedule. (You may want to give students the verb form **tengo** and class subjects vocabulary.) Encourage them to finish the message with questions about their penpal.

# Lectura

## Antes de leer

### Estrategia
**Recognizing cognates**

As you learned earlier in this lesson, cognates are words that share similar meanings and spellings in two or more languages. When reading in Spanish, it's helpful to look for cognates and use them to guess the meaning of what you're reading. But watch out for false cognates. For example, **librería** means *bookstore*, not *library*, and **embarazada** means *pregnant*, not *embarrassed*. Look at this list of Spanish words, paying special attention to prefixes and suffixes. Can you guess the meaning of each word?

| | |
|---|---|
| importante | oportunidad |
| **farmacia** | **cultura** |
| inteligente | **activo** |
| dentista | sociología |
| decisión | **espectacular** |
| televisión | restaurante |
| **médico** | policía |

### Examinar el texto
Glance quickly at the reading selection and guess what type of document it is. Explain your answer.

### Cognados
Read the document and make a list of the cognates you find. Guess their English equivalents, then compare your answers with those of a classmate.

panorama.vhlcentral.com
Lección 1

### Teléfonos importantes

*Policía*

*Médico*

*Dentista*

*Pediatra*

*Farmacia*

*Banco Central*

*Aerolíneas Nacionales*

*Cine Metro*

*Hora/Temperatura*

*Profesora Salgado (universidad)*

*Felipe (oficina)*

*Gimnasio Gente Activa*

*Restaurante Roma*

*Supermercado Famoso*

*Librería El Inteligente*

54.11.11

54.36.92

54.87.11

53.14.57

54.03.06

54.90.83

54.87.40

53.45.96

53.24.81

54.15.33

54.84.99

54.36.04

53.75.44

54.77.23

54.66.04

## Después de leer

### ¿Cierto o falso?

Indicate whether each statement is **cierto** or **falso**. Then correct the false statements.

1. There is a child in this household.
   Cierto.

2. To renew a prescription you would dial 54.90.83.
   **Falso.** To renew a prescription you would dial 54.03.06.

3. If you wanted the exact time and information about the weather you'd dial 53.24.81.
   Cierto.

4. Felipe probably works outdoors.
   **Falso.** Felipe works in an office.

5. This household probably orders a lot of Chinese food.
   **Falso.** They probably order a lot of Italian food.

6. If you had a toothache, you would dial 54.87.11.
   Cierto.

7. You would dial 54.87.40 to make a flight reservation.
   Cierto.

8. To find out if a best-selling book were in stock, you would dial 54.66.04.
   Cierto.

9. If you needed information about aerobics classes, you would dial 54.15.33.
   **Falso.** If you needed information about aerobics classes, you would call Gimnasio Gente Activa at 54.36.04.

10. You would call **Cine Metro** to find out what time a movie starts.
    Cierto.

### Números de teléfono

Make your own list of phone numbers like the one shown in this reading. Include emergency phone numbers as well as frequently called numbers. Use as many cognates from the reading as you can. Answers will vary.

**¿Cierto o falso?**
- Go over the activity orally as a class. If students have trouble inferring the answer to any question, help them identify the cognate or provide additional corresponding context clues.
- Ask students to work with a partner to use cognates and context clues to determine whether each statement is **cierto** or **falso**. Go over the answers as a class.

**Números de teléfono**
- As a class, brainstorm possible categories of phone numbers students may wish to include in their lists. Begin an idea map on the board or overhead transparency, jotting down the students' responses in Spanish. Explain unfamiliar vocabulary as necessary.
- You may wish to have students include e-mail addresses (**direcciones electrónicas**) in their lists. If so, teach them how to read it aloud, including **arroba** for @ and **punto com** for ".com".
- To add an auditory aspect to this exercise, have groups of three read aloud entries from their lists. The listeners should copy down the items that they hear. Have group members switch roles so each has a chance to read. Have groups compare and contrast their lists.

**TEACHING OPTIONS**

**Variación léxica** How a Spanish speaker answers the telephone may reveal their origin. A telephone call in Mexico is likely answered **¿Bueno?** In other parts of the Spanish-speaking world you may hear the greetings **Diga**, **Dígame**, **Óigame**, **¿Sí?** and **Aló**.

**Heritage Speakers** Ask heritage speakers to share phone etiquette they may know, such as answering the phone or the equivalents of "Is _____ there?" (**¿Está _____?**), "Speaking" (**Soy yo.** or **Al habla.**), and identifying oneself, "This is _____." (**[Te/Le] Habla _____.** or **Soy _____.**).

# Estados Unidos

## El país en cifras°

▶ Población° de EE.UU.: 302 millones

▶ Población de origen hispano: 43 millones

▶ País de origen de hispanos en EE.UU.:

- 19,8% otros
- 3,5% Cuba
- 9,6% Puerto Rico
- 8,6% Centroamérica y Suramérica
- 58,5% México

SOURCE: U.S. Census Bureau

▶ Estados con la mayor° población hispana:

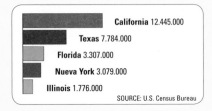

- California 12.445.000
- Texas 7.784.000
- Florida 3.307.000
- Nueva York 3.079.000
- Illinois 1.776.000

SOURCE: U.S. Census Bureau

# Canadá

## El país en cifras

▶ Población del Canadá: 33 millones

▶ Población de origen hispano: 300.000

▶ País de origen de hispanos en Canadá:

- 12,4% México
- 11,6% Chile
- 9% El Salvador
- 67% otros

SOURCE: Statistics Canada

▶ Ciudades° con la mayor población hispana:
Montreal, Toronto, Vancouver

en cifras *in figures* Población *Population* mayor *largest* Ciudades *Cities* creció *grew* cada *each* niños *children* Se estima *It is estimated* va a ser *it is going to be*

### ¡Increíble pero cierto!

La población hispana en los EE.UU. creció° un 3.3% entre los años 2004 (dos mil cuatro) y 2005 (dos mil cinco) (1.3 millones de personas más). Hoy, uno de cada° cinco niños° en los EE.UU. es de origen hispano. Se estima° que en el año 2050 va a ser° uno de cada cuatro.

SOURCE: U.S. Census Bureau and The Associated Press

Mission District, en San Francisco

AK    HI

CANADÁ

Vancouver · Calgary

San Francisco
Las Vegas
Los Ángeles
San Diego

EE.UU.

Chicago · Toronto · Nueva York

Ottawa · Mont

Washington, D.C.

San Antonio

Océano Atlántic

Miami

Golfo de México

MÉXICO

El Álamo, en San Antonio, Texas

Mar Caribe

**recursos**

| WB pp. 9–10 | VM pp. 225–226 | panorama.vhlcentral.com Lección 1 |

---

## Comida • La comida mexicana

La comida° mexicana es muy popular en los Estados Unidos. Los tacos, las enchiladas, las quesadillas y los frijoles son platos° mexicanos que frecuentemente forman parte de las comidas de muchos norteamericanos. También° son populares las variaciones de la comida mexicana en los Estados Unidos... el tex-mex y el cali-mex.

## Lugares • La Pequeña Habana

La Pequeña Habana° es un barrio° de Miami, Florida, donde viven° muchos cubanoamericanos. Es un lugar° donde se encuentran° las costumbres° de la cultura cubana, los aromas y sabores° de su comida y la música salsa. La Pequeña Habana es una parte de Cuba en los Estados Unidos.

## Costumbres • Desfile puertorriqueño

Cada junio desde° 1951 (mil novecientos cincuenta y uno), los puertorriqueños celebran su cultura con un desfile° en Nueva York. Es un gran espectáculo con carrozas° y música salsa, merengue y hip-hop. Muchos espectadores llevan° la bandera° de Puerto Rico en su ropa° o pintada en la cara°.

## Sociedad • La influencia hispánica en Canadá

La presencia hispana en Canadá es importante en la cultura del país. En 1998 (mil novecientos noventa y ocho) se establecieron° los *Latin American Achievement Awards Canada*, para reconocer° los logros° de la comunidad en varios campos°. Dos figuras importantes de origen argentino son Alberto Manguel (novelista) y Sergio Marchi (político°). Osvaldo Núñez es un político de origen chileno. Hay grupos musicales que son parte de la cultura hispana en Canadá: Dominicanada, Bomba, Norteño y Rasca.

 **¿Qué aprendiste?** Completa las frases con la información adecuada (*appropriate*).

1. Hay __43 millones__ de personas de origen hispano en los Estados Unidos.
2. Los cuatro estados con las poblaciones hispanas más grandes son (en orden) __California__, Texas, Florida y __Nueva York__.
3. Toronto, Montreal y __Vancouver__ son las tres ciudades con mayor población hispana del Canadá.
4. Las quesadillas y las enchiladas son platos __mexicanos__.
5. La Pequeña __Habana__ es un barrio de Miami.
6. En Miami hay muchas personas de origen __cubano__.
7. Cada junio se celebra en Nueva York un gran desfile para personas de origen __puertorriqueño__.
8. Dominicanada es un __grupo musical__ del Canadá.

 **Conexión Internet** Investiga estos temas en **panorama.vhlcentral.com**.

1. Haz (*Make*) una lista de seis hispanos célebres de los EE.UU. o Canadá. Explica (*Explain*) por qué (*why*) son célebres.
2. Escoge (*Choose*) seis lugares en los Estados Unidos con nombres hispanos e investiga sobre el origen y el significado (*meaning*) de cada nombre.

comida *food* platos *dishes* También *Also* La Pequeña Habana *Little Havana* barrio *neighborhood* viven *live* lugar *place* se encuentran *are found* costumbres *customs* sabores *flavors* Cada junio desde *Each June since* desfile *parade* con carrozas *with floats* llevan *wear* bandera *flag* ropa *clothing* cara *face* se establecieron *were established* reconocer *to recognize* logros *achievements* campos *fields* político *politician*

**Teaching Tip** Ask volunteers to read sentences from **¡Increíble pero cierto!**, **Comida**, **Lugares**, **Costumbres**, and **Sociedad**. As necessary, model pronunciation, pause to point out cognates, and clarify unfamiliar words.

**La comida mexicana** Ask students if they have tried these dishes. Have students look at illustrated cookbooks or recipes to identify the ingredients and variations of the dishes mentioned in the paragraph.

**La Pequeña Habana** Many large cities in the United States have neighborhoods where people of Hispanic origin predominate. Encourage students to speak of neighborhoods they know.

**Desfile puertorriqueño** The Puerto Rican Day Parade takes place on the weekend nearest the feast day of St. John the Baptist (**San Juan Bautista**), the patron saint of San Juan, capital of Puerto Rico.

**La influencia hispánica en Canadá** Ask students to research the names and achievements of recipients of the *Latin American Achievement Awards Canada*. Have them share the information with the class.

**Conexión Internet** Students will find supporting Internet activities and links at **panorama.vhlcentral.com**.

**Teaching Tip** You may want to wrap up this section by playing the *Panorama cultural* video footage for this lesson.

### TEACHING OPTIONS

**Variación léxica** Hispanic groups in the United States refer to themselves with various names. The most common of these terms, **hispano** and **latino**, refer to all people who come from Hispanic backgrounds, regardless of the country of origin of their ancestors. **Puertorriqueño, cubanoamericano**, and **mexicoamericano** refer to Hispanics whose ancestors came from Puerto Rico, Cuba, and Mexico, respectively. Many Mexican Americans also refer to themselves as **chicanos**. This word has stronger socio-political connotations than **mexicoamericano**. Use of the word **chicano** implies identification with Mexican Americans' struggle for civil rights and equal opportunity in the United States. It also suggests an appreciation of the indigenous aspects of Mexican and Mexican-American culture.

**Instructional Resources**
**Supersite:** Textbook &
Vocabulary MP3 Audio Files
**Lección 1**
**Supersite/IRCD:** *IRM* (WBs/
VM/LM Answer Key); *Testing
Program* (**Lección 1 Pruebas,**
Test Generator, Testing
Program MP3 Audio Files)
**WebSAM**
**Lab Manual,** p. 6

**Teaching Tip** Tell students
that this is active vocabulary
for which they are responsible
and that it will appear on tests
and exams.

## Saludos

| | |
|---|---|
| Hola. | Hello; Hi. |
| Buenos días. | Good morning. |
| Buenas tardes. | Good afternoon. |
| Buenas noches. | Good evening; Good night. |

## Despedidas

| | |
|---|---|
| Adiós. | Goodbye. |
| Nos vemos. | See you. |
| Hasta luego. | See you later. |
| Hasta la vista. | See you later. |
| Hasta pronto. | See you soon. |
| Hasta mañana. | See you tomorrow. |
| Saludos a... | Greetings to… |
| Chau. | Bye. |

## ¿Cómo está?

| | |
|---|---|
| ¿Cómo está usted? | How are you? (form.) |
| ¿Cómo estás? | How are you? (fam.) |
| ¿Qué hay de nuevo? | What's new? |
| ¿Qué pasa? | What's happening?; What's going on? |
| ¿Qué tal? | How are you?; How is it going? |
| (Muy) bien, gracias. | (Very) well, thanks. |
| Nada. | Nothing. |
| No muy bien. | Not very well. |
| Regular. | So-so; OK. |

## Expresiones de cortesía

| | |
|---|---|
| Con permiso. | Pardon me; Excuse me. |
| De nada. | You're welcome. |
| Lo siento. | I'm sorry. |
| (Muchas) gracias. | Thank you (very much); Thanks (a lot). |
| No hay de qué. | You're welcome. |
| Perdón. | Pardon me; Excuse me. |
| por favor | please |

## Títulos

| | |
|---|---|
| señor (Sr.); don | Mr.; sir |
| señora (Sra.); doña | Mrs.; ma'am |
| señorita (Srta.) | Miss |

## Presentaciones

| | |
|---|---|
| ¿Cómo se llama usted? | What's your name? (form.) |
| ¿Cómo te llamas (tú)? | What's your name? (fam.) |
| Me llamo... | My name is… |
| ¿Y tú? | And you? (fam.) |
| ¿Y usted? | And you? (form.) |
| Mucho gusto. | Pleased to meet you. |
| El gusto es mío. | The pleasure is mine. |
| Encantado/a. | Delighted; Pleased to meet you. |
| Igualmente. | Likewise. |
| Éste/Ésta es... | This is… |
| Le presento a... | I would like to introduce (name) to you… (form.) |
| Te presento a... | I would like to introduce (name) to you… (fam.) |
| el nombre | name |

## ¿De dónde es?

| | |
|---|---|
| ¿De dónde es usted? | Where are you from? (form.) |
| ¿De dónde eres? | Where are you from? (fam.) |
| Soy de... | I'm from… |

## Palabras adicionales

| | |
|---|---|
| ¿cuánto(s)/a(s)? | how much/many? |
| ¿de quién...? | whose…? (sing.) |
| ¿de quiénes...? | whose…? (plural) |
| (no) hay | there is (not); there are (not) |

## Países

| | |
|---|---|
| Ecuador | Ecuador |
| España | Spain |
| Estados Unidos (EE.UU.) | United States |
| México | Mexico |
| Puerto Rico | Puerto Rico |

## Verbo

| | |
|---|---|
| ser | to be |

## Sustantivos

| | |
|---|---|
| el autobús | bus |
| la capital | capital city |
| el chico | boy |
| la chica | girl |
| la computadora | computer |
| la comunidad | community |
| el/la conductor(a) | driver |
| la conversación | conversation |
| la cosa | thing |
| el cuaderno | notebook |
| el día | day |
| el diario | diary |
| el diccionario | dictionary |
| la escuela | school |
| el/la estudiante | student |
| la foto(grafía) | photograph |
| la grabadora | tape recorder |
| el hombre | man |
| el/la joven | youth; young person |
| el lápiz | pencil |
| la lección | lesson |
| la maleta | suitcase |
| la mano | hand |
| el mapa | map |
| la mujer | woman |
| la nacionalidad | nationality |
| el número | number |
| el país | country |
| la palabra | word |
| el/la pasajero/a | passenger |
| el problema | problem |
| el/la profesor(a) | teacher |
| el programa | program |
| el/la turista | tourist |
| el video | video |

| | |
|---|---|
| Numbers 0–30 | See page 16. |
| Telling time | See pages 24–25. |
| Expresiones útiles | See page 7. |

**recursos**

LM
p. 6 | panorama.vhlcentral.com
Lección 1

# En la universidad

## Communicative Goals

**You will learn how to:**

- Talk about your classes and school life
- Discuss everyday activities
- Ask questions in Spanish
- Describe the location of people and things

## Lesson Goals

In **Lección 2**, students will be introduced to the following:

- classroom- and university-related words
- names of academic courses and fields of study
- class schedules
- days of the week
- universities and majors in the Spanish-speaking world
- the **Universidad Nacional Autónoma de México (UNAM)**
- present tense of regular –ar verbs
- forming negative sentences
- the verb **gustar**
- forming questions
- the present tense of **estar**
- prepositions of location
- numbers 31 and higher
- using text formats to predict content
- cultural, geographic, and economic information about Spain

**A primera vista** Have students look at the photo. Say: **Es una foto de dos jóvenes en la universidad.** Then ask: **¿Qué son los jóvenes? (Son estudiantes.) ¿Qué hay en la mano del chico? (Hay un diccionario/libro.)**

### A PRIMERA VISTA
- ¿Hay dos chicas en la foto?
- ¿Hay un libro o dos?
- ¿Son turistas o estudiantes?
- ¿Qué hora es, la una de la mañana o de la tarde?

**INSTRUCTIONAL RESOURCES**

**MAESTRO™ SUPERSITE** (panorama.vhlcentral.com)
Textbook, Vocabulary, & Lab MP3 Audio Files
Additional Practice
Learning Management System (Assignment Task Manager, Gradebook)
*Also on DVD*
**Fotonovela**

*Flash cultura*
*Panorama cultural*
*Also on Instructor's Resource CD-ROM*
*PowerPoints* (**Contextos** & **Estructura** Presentations, Overheads)
*Instructor's Resource Manual* (Handouts, Textbook Answer Key, WBs/VM/LM Answer Key,

Audioscripts, Videoscripts & Translations)
*Testing Program* (**Pruebas,** Test Generator, MP3s)
**WebSAM** (Workbook/Video Manual/Lab Manual)
**Workbook/Video Manual**
*Cuaderno para hispanohablantes*
**Lab Manual**

## Section Goals

In **Contextos**, students will learn and practice:
• names for people, places, and things at the university
• names of academic courses

**Instructional Resources**
**Supersite:** Textbook, Vocabulary, & Lab MP3 Audio Files **Lección 2**
**Supersite/IRCD:** *PowerPoints* (**Lección 2 Contextos** Presentation, Overhead #13); *IRM* (**Vocabulario adicional,** Textbook Audio Script, Lab Audio Script, WBs/VM/LM Answer Key)
**WebSAM**
**Workbook,** pp. 11–12
**Lab Manual,** p. 7
*Cuaderno para hispanohablantes*

## Teaching Tips
• Introduce vocabulary for classroom objects such as **mesa, libro, pluma, lápiz, papel.** Hold up or point to an object and say: **Es un lápiz.** Ask questions that include **¿Hay/No hay…?** and **¿Cuántos/as…?**
• Using either objects in the classroom or *Overhead PowerPoint #13,* point to items and ask questions such as: **¿Qué es? ¿Es una mesa? ¿Es un reloj?** Vary by asking: **¿Qué hay en el escritorio? ¿Qué hay en la mesa? ¿Cuántas tizas hay en la pizarra? ¿Hay una pluma en el escritorio de ____?**

**Successful Language Learning** Encourage students to make flash cards to help them memorize new vocabulary words.

**Note:** At this point you may want to present *Vocabulario adicional: Más vocabulario para las clases,* from the Supersite/IRCD.

# En la universidad

## Más vocabulario

| | |
|---|---|
| la biblioteca | library |
| la cafetería | cafeteria |
| la casa | house; home |
| el estadio | stadium |
| el laboratorio | laboratory |
| la librería | bookstore |
| la residencia estudiantil | dormitory |
| la universidad | university; college |
| el/la compañero/a de clase | classmate |
| el/la compañero/a de cuarto | roommate |
| la clase | class |
| el curso | course |
| la especialización | major |
| el examen | test; exam |
| el horario | schedule |
| la prueba | test; quiz |
| el semestre | semester |
| la tarea | homework |
| el trimestre | trimester; quarter |
| la administración de empresas | business administration |
| el arte | art |
| la biología | biology |
| las ciencias | sciences |
| la computación | computer science |
| la contabilidad | accounting |
| la economía | economics |
| el español | Spanish |
| la física | physics |
| la geografía | geography |
| la música | music |

## Variación léxica

pluma ←→ bolígrafo
pizarra ←→ tablero (*Col.*)

**recursos**

WB pp. 11–12 | LM p. 7 | panorama.vhlcentral.com Lección 2

el reloj
la ventana
la puerta
la profesora
el estudiante
la mesa
el libro
la mochila
la pluma

**TEACHING OPTIONS**

**Variación léxica** Ask heritage speakers to tell the class any other terms they or their families use to talk about people, places, or things at school. Ask them to tell where these terms are used. Possible responses: **el boli, la ciudad universitaria, el profe, el catedrático, la facultad, el profesorado, la asignatura, el gimnasio, el pizarrón, el salón de clases, el aula, el pupitre, el gis, el alumno.**

**Game** Divide the class into two teams. Then, in English, name an academic course and ask one of the teams to provide the Spanish equivalent. If the team provides the correct term, it gets a point. If not, the second team gets a chance at the same item. Alternate between teams until you have read all the course names. The team with the most points at the end wins.

el mapa

la pizarra

**LAS MATERIAS** | *COURSES*
---|---
la historia | *history*
las humanidades | *humanities*
el inglés | *English*
las lenguas extranjeras | *foreign languages*
la literatura | *literature*
las matemáticas | *mathematics*
el periodismo | *journalism*
la psicología | *psychology*
la química | *chemistry*
la sociología | *sociology*

el papel

el borrador

la tiza

la papelera

el escritorio

la estudiante

la silla

# Práctica

**1**

**Escuchar** Listen to Professor Morales talk about her Spanish classroom, then check the items she mentions.

| | | | | | |
|---|---|---|---|---|---|
| puerta | ☑ | tiza | ☑ | plumas | ☑ |
| ventanas | ☑ | escritorios | ☑ | mochilas | ○ |
| pizarra | ☑ | sillas | ○ | papel | ☑ |
| borrador | ○ | libros | ☑ | reloj | ☑ |

**2**

**Identificar** You will hear a series of words. Write each one in the appropriate category.

| **Personas** | **Lugares** | **Materias** |
|---|---|---|
| el estudiante | el estadio | la química |
| la profesora | la biblioteca | las lenguas extranjeras |
| el compañero de clase | la residencia estudiantil | el inglés |

**3**

**Emparejar** Match each question with its most logical response. ¡Ojo! (*Careful!*) One response will not be used.

1. ¿Qué clase es? d
2. ¿Quiénes son? g
3. ¿Quién es? e
4. ¿De dónde es? c
5. ¿A qué hora es la clase de inglés? f
6. ¿Cuántos estudiantes hay? a

a. Hay veinticinco.
b. Es un reloj.
c. Es del Perú.
d. Es la clase de química.
e. Es el señor Bastos.
f. Es a las nueve en punto.
g. Son los profesores.

**4**

**Identificar** Identify the word that does not fit in each group.

1. examen • grabadora • tarea • prueba   grabadora
2. economía • matemáticas • biblioteca • contabilidad   biblioteca
3. pizarra • tiza • borrador • librería   librería
4. lápiz • cafetería • papel • cuaderno   cafetería
5. veinte • diez • pluma • treinta   pluma
6. conductor • laboratorio • autobús • pasajero   laboratorio

**5**

**¿Qué clase es?** Name the class associated with the subject matter.

> **modelo**
> los elementos, los átomos   *Es la clase de química.*

1. Abraham Lincoln, Winston Churchill   Es la clase de historia.
2. Picasso, Leonardo da Vinci   Es la clase de arte.
3. Freud, Jung   Es la clase de psicología.
4. África, el océano Pacífico   Es la clase de geografía.
5. la cultura de España, verbos   Es la clase de español.
6. Hemingway, Shakespeare   Es la clase de literatura.
7. geometría, trigonometría   Es la clase de matemáticas.

**1 Teaching Tip** Have students check their answers by going over **Actividad 1** as a class.

**1 Script** ¿Qué hay en mi clase de español? ¡Muchas cosas! Hay una puerta y cinco ventanas. Hay una pizarra con tiza. Hay muchos escritorios para los estudiantes. En los escritorios de los estudiantes hay libros y plumas. En la mesa de la profesora hay papel. Hay un mapa y un reloj en la clase también.
*Textbook MP3s*

**2 Teaching Tip** To simplify, have students prepare for listening by predicting a few words for each category.

**2 Script** el estudiante, la química, el estadio, las lenguas extranjeras, la profesora, la biblioteca, el inglés, el compañero de clase, la residencia estudiantil
*Textbook MP3s*

**3 Expansion** Have student pairs ask each other the questions and answer based on your class. Ex: **1. ¿Qué clase es? (Es la clase de español.)** For items 2–4, the questioner should indicate specific people in the classroom.

**4 Expansion** Give students these word groups as items 7–9: **7. humanidades, mesa, ciencias, lenguas extranjeras (mesa) 8. papelera, casa, residencia estudiantil, biblioteca (papelera) 9. pluma, lápiz, silla, tiza (silla)**

**5 Expansion** Have the class associate famous people with these fields: **periodismo, computación, humanidades**. Then have them guess the field associated with these people: Albert Einstein (**física**), Charles Darwin (**biología**).

**Teaching Tips**
- Write these questions and answers on the board, explaining their meaning as you do so:
  —¿Qué día es hoy?
  —Hoy es ____.
  —¿Qué día es mañana? (Students learned **mañana** in **Lección 1**.)
  —**Mañana es** ____.
  —**¿Cuándo es la prueba?**
  —**Es el** ____.
  Then ask students the questions on the board.
- Explain that Monday is considered the first day of the week in the Spanish-speaking world and usually appears as such on calendars.

**6 Expansion** To challenge students, ask them questions such as: **Mañana es viernes… ¿qué día fue ayer? (miércoles); Ayer fue domingo… ¿qué día es mañana? (martes)**

**7 Teaching Tip** To simplify, before doing this activity, have students review the list of **sustantivos** on page 34 and numbers 0–30 on page 16.

## Los días de la semana

**¡LENGUA VIVA!**

The days of the week are never capitalized in Spanish.

•••

Monday is considered the first day of the week in Spanish-speaking countries.

**CONSULTA**

Note that September in Spanish is **septiembre**. For all of the months of the year, go to **Contextos, Lección 5,** p. 142.

### septiembre

| lunes | martes | miércoles | jueves | viernes | sábado | domingo |
|-------|--------|-----------|--------|---------|--------|---------|
|       | 1      | 2         | 3      | 4       | 5      | 6       |
| 7     | 8      | 9         | 10     |         |        |         |

---

**6**

**¿Qué día es hoy?** Complete each statement with the correct day of the week.

1. Hoy es martes. Mañana es ___miércoles___. Ayer fue (*Yesterday was*) ___lunes___.
2. Ayer fue sábado. Mañana es ___lunes___. Hoy es ___domingo___.
3. Mañana es viernes. Hoy es ___jueves___. Ayer fue ___miércoles___.
4. Ayer fue domingo. Hoy es ___lunes___. Mañana es ___martes___.
5. Hoy es jueves. Ayer fue ___miércoles___. Mañana es ___viernes___.
6. Mañana es lunes. Hoy es ___domingo___. Ayer fue ___sábado___.

---

**7**

**Analogías** Use these words to complete the analogies. Some words will not be used.

| | | | |
|---|---|---|---|
| arte | día | martes | pizarra |
| biblioteca | domingo | matemáticas | profesor |
| catorce | estudiante | mujer | reloj |

1. maleta ⟷ pasajero ⊜ mochila ⟷ ___estudiante___
2. chico ⟷ chica ⊜ hombre ⟷ ___mujer___
3. pluma ⟷ papel ⊜ tiza ⟷ ___pizarra___
4. inglés ⟷ lengua ⊜ miércoles ⟷ ___día___
5. papel ⟷ cuaderno ⊜ libro ⟷ ___biblioteca___
6. quince ⟷ dieciséis ⊜ lunes ⟷ ___martes___
7. Cervantes ⟷ literatura ⊜ Dalí ⟷ ___arte___
8. autobús ⟷ conductor ⊜ clase ⟷ ___profesor___
9. los EE.UU. ⟷ mapa ⊜ hora ⟷ ___reloj___
10. veinte ⟷ veintitrés ⊜ jueves ⟷ ___domingo___

---

**TEACHING OPTIONS**

**Extra Practice** Have students prepare a day-planner for the upcoming week. Tell them to list each day of the week and the things they expect to do each day, including classes, homework, tests, appointments, and social events. Provide unfamiliar vocabulary as needed. Tell them to include the time each activity takes place. Have them exchange their day-planners with a partner and check each other's work for accuracy.

**Game** Have groups of five or six play a "word-chain" game in which the first group member says a word in Spanish (e.g., **estudiante**). The next student has to say a word that begins with the last letter of the first person's word (e.g., **español**). If a student cannot think of a word, he or she is eliminated and it is the next student's turn. The last student left in the game is the winner.

# Comunicación

**8** **Horario** Choose three classes to create your own class schedule, then discuss it with a classmate. Answers will vary.

| materia | hora | días | profesor(a) |
|---------|------|------|-------------|
| historia | 9–10 | lunes, miércoles | Ordóñez |
| biología | 12–1 | lunes, jueves | Dávila |
| periodismo | 2–3 | martes, jueves | Quiñones |
| matemáticas | 2–3 | miércoles, jueves | Jiménez |
| arte | 12–1:30 | lunes, miércoles | Molina |

**modelo**

**Estudiante 1:** Tomo (*I take*) biología los lunes y jueves con (*with*) la profesora Dávila.

**Estudiante 2:** ¿Sí? Yo no tomo biología. Yo tomo arte los lunes y miércoles con el profesor Molina.

**9** **La clase** First, look around your classroom to get a mental image, then close your eyes. Your partner will then use these words or other vocabulary to ask you questions about the classroom. After you have answered six questions, switch roles. Answers will vary.

**modelo**

**Estudiante 1:** ¿Cuántas ventanas hay?

**Estudiante 2:** Hay cuatro ventanas.

| | | |
|---|---|---|
| escritorio | mochila | puerta |
| estudiante | pizarra | reloj |
| libro | profesor(a) | silla |

**10** **Nuevos amigos** During the first week of class, you meet a new student in the cafeteria. With a partner, prepare a conversation using these cues. Answers will vary.

| Estudiante 1 | Estudiante 2 |
|--------------|--------------|
| Greet your new acquaintance. | → Introduce yourself. |
| Find out about him or her. | → Tell him or her about yourself. |
| Ask about your partner's class schedule. | → Compare your schedule to your partner's. |
| Say nice to meet you and goodbye. | → Say nice to meet you and goodbye. |

---

**8** **Expansion** Tell students to write their name at the top of their schedules and have pairs exchange papers with another pair. Then have them repeat the activity with the new schedules, asking and answering questions in the third person. Ex: —**¿Qué clases toma ____? —Los lunes y jueves ____ toma biología con la profesora Dávila.**

**9** **Expansion** Repeat the activity with campus-related vocabulary.

**Successful Language Learning** Remind the class that errors are a natural part of language learning. Point out that it is impossible to speak "perfectly" in any language. Emphasize that their spoken and written Spanish will improve if they make the effort to practice.

**10** **Teaching Tip** To simplify, quickly review the basic greetings, courtesy expressions, and introductions taught in **Lección 1, Contextos,** pages 2–3.

**10** **Expansion** Ask volunteers to introduce their new acquaintances to the class.

---

**TEACHING OPTIONS**

**Groups** Have students do **Actividad 10** in groups, imagining that they meet several new students in the cafeteria. Have the groups present this activity as a skit for the class. Give the groups time to prepare and rehearse, and tell them that they will be presenting it without a script or any other kind of notes.

**Game** Point out the **modelo** in **Actividad 8.** Have students write a few simple sentences that describe their course schedules. Ex: **Los lunes, miércoles y viernes tomo español con la profesora Morales. Los martes y jueves tomo arte con el profesor Casas.** Then collect the descriptions, shuffle them, and read them aloud. The class should guess who wrote each description.

SUPERSITE

# ¿Qué clases tomas?

communication
cultures
NATIONAL
STANDARDS

Maite, Inés, Javier y Álex hablan de las clases.

**PERSONAJES**

**MAITE**

**INÉS**

**ÁLEX**

**JAVIER**

**1**
**ÁLEX** Hola, Ricardo... Aquí estamos en la Mitad del Mundo. ¿Qué tal las clases en la UNAM?

**2**
**MAITE** Es exactamente como las fotos en los libros de geografía.
**INÉS** ¡Sí! ¿También tomas tú geografía?
**MAITE** Yo no. Yo tomo inglés y literatura. También tomo una clase de periodismo.

**3**
**MAITE** Muy buenos días. María Teresa Fuentes, de Radio Andina FM 93. Hoy estoy con estudiantes de la Universidad San Francisco de Quito. ¡A ver! La señorita que está cerca de la ventana... ¿Cómo te llamas y de dónde eres?

**6**
**MAITE** ¿En qué clase hay más chicos?
**INÉS** Bueno, eh... en la clase de historia.
**MAITE** ¿Y más chicas?
**INÉS** En la de sociología hay más chicas, casi un ochenta y cinco por ciento.

**7**
**MAITE** Y tú, joven, ¿cómo te llamas y de dónde eres?
**JAVIER** Me llamo Javier Gómez y soy de San Juan, Puerto Rico.
**MAITE** ¿Tomas muchas clases este semestre?
**JAVIER** Sí, tomo tres: historia y arte los lunes, miércoles y viernes y computación los martes y jueves.

**8**
**MAITE** ¿Te gustan las computadoras, Javier?
**JAVIER** No me gustan nada. Me gusta mucho más el arte... y sobre todo me gusta dibujar.
**ÁLEX** ¿Cómo que no? ¿No te gustan las computadoras?

**recursos**

VM
pp. 197–198

panorama.vhlcentral.com
Lección 2

---

**TEACHING OPTIONS**

**Video Tips** General suggestions for using video clips in the classroom can be found on page IAE-12 of this Instructor's Annotated Edition.
**¿Qué clases tomas?** Play the **¿Qué clases tomas?** segment of the *Fotonovela* and have students give you a "play-by-play" description of the action. Write their descriptions on the board. After playing the segment, give the class a moment to read the descriptions you have written on the board. Then play the segment a second time so that students can add more details to the descriptions or consolidate information. Finally, discuss the material on the board with the class and call attention to any incorrect information. Help students prepare a brief plot summary.

**INÉS** Hola. Me llamo Inés Ayala Loor y soy del Ecuador… de Portoviejo.

**MAITE** Encantada. ¿Qué clases tomas en la universidad?

**INÉS** Tomo geografía, inglés, historia, sociología y arte.

**MAITE** Tomas muchas clases, ¿no?

**INÉS** Pues sí, me gusta estudiar mucho.

**ÁLEX** Pero si son muy interesantes, hombre.

**JAVIER** Sí, ¡muy interesantes!

## Expresiones útiles

### Talking about classes

- **¿Qué tal las clases en la UNAM?**
  *How are classes going at UNAM?*
- **¿También tomas tú geografía?**
  *Are you also taking geography?*
  **No, tomo inglés y literatura.**
  *No, I'm taking English and literature.*

- **Tomas muchas clases, ¿no?**
  *You're taking lots of classes, aren't you?*
  **Pues sí.** *Well, yes.*

- **¿En qué clase hay más chicos?**
  *In which class are there more guys?*
  **En la clase de historia.**
  *In history class.*

### Talking about likes/dislikes

- **¿Te gusta estudiar?**
  *Do you like to study?*
  **Sí, me gusta mucho. Pero también me gusta mirar la televisión.**
  *Yes, I like it a lot. But I also like to watch television.*
- **¿Te gusta la clase de sociología?**
  *Do you like sociology class?*
  **Sí, me gusta muchísimo.**
  *Yes, I like it very much.*
- **¿Te gustan las computadoras?**
  *Do you like computers?*
  **No, no me gustan nada.**
  *No, I don't like them at all.*

### Talking about location

- **Aquí estamos en…**
  *Here we are at/in…*
- **¿Dónde está la señorita?**
  *Where is the young woman?*
  **Está cerca de la ventana.**
  *She's near the window.*

### Expressing hesitation

- **A ver…**
  *Let's see…*
- **Bueno…**
  *Well…*

**Teaching Tip** Have the class read through the entire **Fotonovela**, with volunteers playing the parts of **Álex**, **Maite**, **Inés**, and **Javier**.

**Expresiones útiles** Identify forms of **tomar** and **estar**. Point out question-forming devices and the accent marks over question words. Tell students that they will learn more about these concepts in **Estructura**. Point out that **gusta** is used when what is liked is singular, and **gustan** when what is liked is plural. A detailed discussion of the **gustar** construction (see **Estructura 2.1**, page 48) is unnecessary here.

# ¿Qué pasó? SUPERSITE

**1**

**Escoger** Choose the answer that best completes each sentence.

1. Maite toma (*is taking*) __c__ en la universidad.
   a. geografía, inglés y periodismo   b. economía, periodismo y literatura
   c. periodismo, inglés y literatura

2. Inés toma sociología, geografía, __a__.
   a. inglés, historia y arte   b. periodismo, computación y arte
   c. historia, literatura y biología

3. Javier toma __b__ clases este semestre.
   a. cuatro   b. tres   c. dos

4. Javier toma historia y __c__ los __c__.
   a. computación; martes y jueves   b. arte; lunes, martes y miércoles
   c. arte; lunes, miércoles y viernes

**2**

**Identificar** Indicate which person would make each statement.
The names may be used more than once.

1. Sí, me gusta estudiar. Inés
2. ¡Hola! ¿Te gustan las clases en la UNAM? Álex
3. ¿La clase de periodismo? Sí, me gusta mucho. Maite
4. Hay más chicas en la clase de sociología. Inés
5. Buenos días. Yo soy de Radio Andina FM 93. Maite
6. ¡Uf! ¡No me gustan las computadoras! Javier
7. Las computadoras son muy interesantes. Álex
8. Me gusta dibujar en la clase de arte. Javier

INÉS
JAVIER   MAITE
ÁLEX

**3**

**Completar** These sentences are similar to things said in the **Fotonovela**.
Complete each sentence with the correct word(s).

| la sociología | el arte | la Universidad San Francisco de Quito |
| la clase de historia | geografía | la Mitad del Mundo |

1. Maite, Javier, Inés y yo estamos en... la Mitad del Mundo
2. Hay fotos impresionantes de la Mitad del Mundo en los libros de... geografía
3. Me llamo Maite. Estoy aquí con estudiantes de... la Universidad San Francisco de Quito
4. Hay muchos chicos en... la clase de historia
5. No me gustan las computadoras. Me gusta más... el arte

**4**

**Preguntas personales** Interview a classmate about his/her university life.   Answers will vary.

1. ¿Qué clases tomas en la universidad?
2. ¿Qué clases tomas los martes?
3. ¿Qué clases tomas los viernes?
4. ¿En qué clase hay más chicos?
5. ¿En qué clase hay más chicas?
6. ¿Te gusta la clase de español?

**NOTA CULTURAL**

In the **Fotonovela**, Álex, Maite, Javier, and Inés visit **la Mitad del Mundo** (*Center of the World*), a monument north of Quito, Ecuador. It marks the line at which the equator divides the Earth's northern and southern hemispheres.

NATIONAL communication STANDARDS

## Sidebar (left margin)

**1 Teaching Tip** Before doing this activity, review the names of courses, pages 36–37, and the days of the week, page 38.

**2 Expansion** Give these statements to the class as items 9–12: **9. Hay muchos chicos en mi clase de historia. (Inés) 10. Tomo tres clases… computación, historia y arte. (Javier) 11. Yo tomo tres clases… inglés, literatura y periodismo. (Maite) 12. ¿Yo? Soy de la capital de Puerto Rico. (Javier)**

**3 Expansion** Point out that one of the answers in the word bank will not be used. After students complete this activity, have them write a sentence that includes the unused item (**la sociología**).

**4 Expansion** Ask volunteers to role-play their conversation for the class.

**The Affective Dimension** Reassure students who seem anxious about speaking that perfect pronunciation is not necessary for communication and that their pronunciation will improve with practice.

## TEACHING OPTIONS

**Small Groups** Have students work in small groups to create a skit in which a radio reporter asks local university students where they are from, which classes they are taking, and which classes they like. Encourage students to use the phrases in **Expresiones útiles** as much as possible. Have one or two groups role-play their skit for the class.

**Extra Practice** Have students close their books and complete these statements with information from the **Fotonovela**. You may present the sentences orally or write them on the board. **1. Hoy estoy con dos _____ de la Universidad San Francisco de Quito. (estudiantes) 2. ¿En qué _____ hay más chicos? (clase) 3. ¿_____ te llamas y de _____ eres? (Cómo; dónde)**

# Pronunciación

## Spanish vowels

**a     e     i     o     u**

Spanish vowels are never silent; they are always pronounced in a short, crisp way without the glide sounds used in English.

| | | | |
|---|---|---|---|
| **Álex** | **clase** | **nada** | **encantada** |

The letter **a** is pronounced like the *a* in *father*, but shorter.

| | | | |
|---|---|---|---|
| **el** | **ene** | **mesa** | **elefante** |

The letter **e** is pronounced like the *e* in *they*, but shorter.

| | | | |
|---|---|---|---|
| **Inés** | **chica** | **tiza** | **señorita** |

The letter **i** sounds like the *ee* in *beet*, but shorter.

| | | | |
|---|---|---|---|
| **hola** | **con** | **libro** | **don Francisco** |

The letter **o** is pronounced like the *o* in *tone*, but shorter.

| | | | |
|---|---|---|---|
| **uno** | **regular** | **saludos** | **gusto** |

The letter **u** sounds like the *oo* in *room*, but shorter.

**Práctica** Practice the vowels by saying the names of these places in Spain.

1. Madrid
2. Alicante
3. Tenerife
4. Toledo
5. Barcelona
6. Granada
7. Burgos
8. La Coruña

**Oraciones** Read the sentences aloud, focusing on the vowels.

1. Hola. Me llamo Ramiro Morgado.
2. Estudio arte en la Universidad de Salamanca.
3. Tomo también literatura y contabilidad.
4. Ay, tengo clase en cinco minutos. ¡Nos vemos!

**Refranes** Practice the vowels by reading these sayings aloud.

Del dicho al hecho hay un gran trecho.[1]

Cada loco con su tema.[2]

1 Easier said than done.
2 To each his own.

**recursos**

LM
p. 8

panorama.vhlcentral.com
Lección 2

---

**EN DETALLE**

# La elección de una carrera universitaria

**Since higher education is heavily state-subsidized** in the Spanish-speaking world, tuition is almost free and thus public universities see large enrollments. Spanish and Latin American students generally choose their **carrera universitaria** (major) around 18 years of age—either the year before or upon entering the university. In order to enroll, all students must complete a high school degree, known as the **bachillerato**. In countries like Bolivia, Mexico, and Peru, the last year of high school (**colegio\***) tends to be specialized toward an area of study, such as the arts or natural sciences.

Students then choose their major according to their area of specialization. Similarly, university-bound students in Argentina follow the **polimodal** track during the last three years of high school. **Polimodal** refers to exposure to various disciplines, such as business, social sciences, or design; based on this coursework, Argentine students choose their **carrera**. Finally, in Spain, students choose their major according to the score they receive on the **prueba de aptitud** (skills test or entrance exam).

University graduates receive a **licenciatura**, or bachelor's degree. In Argentina or Chile, a

**Universidad Central de Venezuela en Caracas**

**licenciatura** takes four to six years to complete, and may be considered equivalent to a master's degree. In Peru and Venezuela, a bachelor's degree is a five-year process. Spanish and Colombian **licenciaturas** take four to five years, although some fields, such as medicine, require six or more.

---

### Estudiantes hispanos en los EE.UU.

In the 2004–05 academic year, over 13,000 Mexican students (2.3% of all international students) studied at U.S. universities. Colombians were the second largest Spanish-speaking group, with over 7,000 students.

---

**\*¡Ojo! El colegio** is a false cognate. In most countries, it means *high school*, but in some regions it refers to an elementary school. All undergraduate study takes place at **la universidad**.

---

**ACTIVIDADES**

**1**  **¿Cierto o falso?** Indicate whether these statements are **cierto** or **falso**. Correct the false statements.

1. Students in Spanish-speaking countries must pay large amounts of money toward their college tuition. **Falso**. At public universities tuition is almost free.
2. After studying at a **colegio**, students receive their **bachillerato**. **Cierto.**
3. Undergraduates study at a **colegio** or an **universidad**. **Falso**. An undergraduate student takes classes at a **universidad**.

4. In Latin America and Spain, students usually choose their majors in their second year at the university. **Falso**. Students choose their majors either the year before or upon entering the university.
5. The **polimodal** system exposes students to many disciplines and helps them choose their university major. **Cierto.**
6. In Mexico, the **bachillerato** involves specialized study.
7. In Spain, majors depend on entrance exam scores. **Cierto.**
8. Venezuelans complete a **licenciatura** in five years. **Cierto.**

---

## ASÍ SE DICE

### Clases y exámenes

| | |
|---|---|
| aprobar | to pass |
| la asignatura (Esp.) | la clase, la materia |
| la clase anual | year-long course |
| el examen parcial | midterm exam |
| la facultad | department, school |
| la investigación | research |
| reprobar; suspender (Esp.) | to fail |
| sacar buenas/ malas notas | to get good/ bad grades |
| tomar apuntes | to take notes |

## EL MUNDO HISPANO

### Las universidades hispanas

Enrollment in Spanish and Latin American universities is often much higher than in the U.S.

○ **Universidad de Buenos Aires** (Argentina) 308.600 estudiantes

○ **Universidad Autónoma de Santo Domingo** (República Dominicana) 100.000 estudiantes

○ **Universidad Complutense de Madrid** (España) 92.000 estudiantes

○ **Universidad Central de Venezuela** (Venezuela) 60.000 estudiantes

## PERFIL

# La UNAM

The **Universidad Nacional Autónoma de México (UNAM)**, founded in 1551, is the second oldest university in North America. Its enrollment of about 270,000 students makes this one of the largest universities in the world. The main campus (or **ciudad universitaria**), located in Mexico City, has a famous library covered with the world's largest mosaic mural, which depicts scenes from Mexico's precolonial past, present, and future. The university has also established several locations in other parts of Mexico and abroad (including the United States and Canada). Today the **UNAM** is widely considered one of the best institutions of higher education in Latin America.

### SUPERSITE Conexión Internet

To which **facultad** does your major belong in Spain or Latin America?

Go to **panorama.vhlcentral.com** to find more cultural information related to this **Cultura** section.

## ACTIVIDADES

**2** **Comprensión** Complete these sentences.

1. The **UNAM** was founded in the year _____1551_____.
2. A __clase anual__ is a year-long course.
3. The world's largest __mosaic mural__ is part of the **UNAM**'s library.
4. Over 300,000 students attend the __Universidad de Buenos Aires__.
5. An __examen parcial__ occurs about halfway through a course.

**3** **La universidad en cifras** With a partner, research a Spanish or Latin American university online and find five statistics about that institution (for instance, the total enrollment, majors offered, year it was founded, etc.). Using the information you found, create a dialogue between a prospective student and a university representative. Present your dialogue to the class. Answers will vary.

**recursos**

SUPERSITE

panorama.vhlcentral.com
Lección 2

## TEACHING OPTIONS

**Extra Practice** Tell students to imagine they have the opportunity to study abroad at one of the universities listed in **El mundo hispano** or **Perfil**. Have them choose a location and explain why they would like to attend that particular school. You may want to assign this as homework, and ask students to research the universities on the Internet in order to reach their decision.

**Game** Play a Pictionary-style game. Divide the class into two teams, A and B. Have one member from each team go to the board, and hand each one an index card with a university-related vocabulary word. The member from team A has one minute to draw a representation of that word, while the rest of team A guesses what the word is. Alternate between teams and award one point for each correct answer. The team with the most points wins.

---

**Así se dice**
- Model the pronunciation of each term and have students repeat it.
- To challenge students, add these words to this list: **la beca** (scholarship); **el préstamo educativo** (student loan); **el/la profe** (professor, colloquial).
- Ask simple questions using the terms. Ex: **¿Hay un examen parcial en esta clase?**

**Perfil** Many **UNAM** alumni have become prominent figures in politics, science, and humanities. Some famous graduates include **Alfonso Caso** (archaeologist), **Carlos Fuentes** (writer), **Dr. Mario J. Molina** (Nobel Prize in Chemistry, 1995), **Abel Pacheco de la Espriella** (President of Costa Rica, 2002–2006), and **Octavio Paz** (writer/poet, Nobel Prize in Literature, 1990).

**El mundo hispano** Have students read the enrollment numbers. Ask a volunteer to state your university's enrollment. Then have students discuss the advantages and disadvantages of studying at a large university.

**2** **Expansion** Give students these sentences as items 6–8: 6. About _____ students take classes at the **UNAM**. (270,000) 7. A _____ is a university department or school. (**facultad**) 8. The _____ is located in the Dominican Republic. (**Universidad Autónoma de Santo Domingo**)

**3** **Expansion** To add a visual aspect to this exercise, have the same pairs design a university brochure to attract prospective students. Encourage students to highlight the university's strengths and unique traits.

## Section Goals

In **Estructura 2.1**, students will learn:
- the present tense of regular **–ar** verbs
- the formation of negative sentences
- the verb **gustar**

---

**Instructional Resources**
**Supersite:** Lab MP3 Audio Files **Lección 2**
**Supersite/IRCD:** *PowerPoints* (**Lección 2 Estructura** Presentation); *IRM* (Lab Audio Script, WBs/VM/LM Answer Key)
**WebSAM**
**Workbook,** pp. 13–14
**Lab Manual,** p. 9
***Cuaderno para hispanohablantes***

---

## Teaching Tips

- Point out that students have been using verbs and verb constructions from the start: **¿Cómo te llamas?, hay, ser,** and so forth. Ask a student: **¿Qué clases tomas?** Model student answer as **Yo tomo…** Then ask another student: **¿Qué clases toma ____? Sí, toma ____.**
- Explain that, because the verb endings mark the person speaking or spoken about, subject pronouns are usually optional in Spanish.
- Remind students that **vosotros/as** forms will not be practiced actively in **PANORAMA**.

**[2.1]** # Present tense of -ar verbs

**ANTE TODO** In order to talk about activities, you need to use verbs. Verbs express actions or states of being. In English and Spanish, the infinitive is the base form of the verb. In English, the infinitive is preceded by the word *to*: *to study, to be.* The infinitive in Spanish is a one-word form and can be recognized by its endings: **-ar, -er,** or **-ir.**

| *-ar* verb | | *-er* verb | | *-ir* verb | |
|---|---|---|---|---|---|
| **estudiar** | *to study* | **comer** | *to eat* | **escribir** | *to write* |

▶ In this lesson, you will learn the forms of regular **-ar** verbs.

### The verb estudiar (*to study*)

| | | | |
|---|---|---|---|
| SINGULAR FORMS | yo | estudi**o** | *I study* |
| | tú | estudi**as** | *you* (fam.) *study* |
| | Ud./él/ella | estudi**a** | *you* (form.) *study; he/she studies* |
| PLURAL FORMS | nosotros/as | estudi**amos** | *we study* |
| | vosotros/as | estudi**áis** | *you* (fam.) *study* |
| | Uds./ellos/ellas | estudi**an** | *you* (form.) *study; they study* |

*¿Tomas muchas clases este semestre?*

*Sí, tomo tres.*

▶ To create the forms of most regular verbs in Spanish, drop the infinitive endings (**-ar, -er, -ir**). You then add to the stem the endings that correspond to the different subject pronouns. This diagram will help you visualize the process by which verb forms are created.

### Conjugation of *-ar* verbs

| INFINITIVE | VERB STEM | CONJUGATED FORM |
|---|---|---|
| estudi**ar** | estudi- | yo estudi**o** |
| bail**ar** | bail- | tú bail**as** |
| trabaj**ar** | trabaj- | nosotros trabaj**amos** |

---

**TEACHING OPTIONS**

**Extra Practice** Do a pattern practice drill. Write an infinitive from the list of common –ar verbs on page 51 on the board and ask individual students to provide conjugations for the subject pronouns and names you suggest. Reverse the activity by saying a conjugated form and asking students to give the corresponding subject pronoun. Allow multiple answers for the third-person singular and plural.

**Extra Practice** Ask questions using **estudiar, bailar,** and **trabajar.** Students should answer in complete sentences. Ask additional questions to get more information. Ex: —____, ¿**trabajas?** —**Sí, trabajo.** —¿**Dónde trabajas?** —**Trabajo en ____.** • —¿**Quién baila los sábados?** —**Yo bailo los sábados.** —¿**Bailas merengue?** • —¿**Estudian ustedes mucho?** —¿**Quién estudia más?** —¿**Cuántas horas estudias los lunes? ¿Y los sábados?**

## Common -ar verbs

| | | | | |
|---|---|---|---|---|
| **bailar** | to dance | **estudiar** | to study |
| **buscar** | to look for | **explicar** | to explain |
| **caminar** | to walk | **hablar** | to talk; to speak |
| **cantar** | to sing | **llegar** | to arrive |
| **cenar** | to have dinner | **llevar** | to carry |
| **comprar** | to buy | **mirar** | to look (at); to watch |
| **contestar** | to answer | **necesitar (+ inf.)** | to need |
| **conversar** | to converse, to chat | **practicar** | to practice |
| **desayunar** | to have breakfast | **preguntar** | to ask (a question) |
| **descansar** | to rest | **preparar** | to prepare |
| **desear (+ inf.)** | to desire; to wish | **regresar** | to return |
| **dibujar** | to draw | **terminar** | to end; to finish |
| **enseñar** | to teach | **tomar** | to take; to drink |
| **escuchar** | to listen (to) | **trabajar** | to work |
| **esperar (+ inf.)** | to wait (for); to hope | **viajar** | to travel |

▶ **¡Atención!** The Spanish verbs **buscar, escuchar, esperar,** and **mirar** do not need to be followed by prepositions as they do in English.

**Busco** la tarea.
*I'm looking for the homework.*

**Escucho** la música.
*I'm listening to the music.*

**Espero** el autobús.
*I'm waiting for the bus.*

**Miro** la pizarra.
*I'm looking at the blackboard.*

### COMPARE & CONTRAST

English uses three sets of forms to talk about the present: (1) the simple present (*Paco works*), (2) the present progressive (*Paco is working*), and (3) the emphatic present (*Paco does work*). In Spanish, the simple present can be used in all three cases.

Paco **trabaja** en la cafetería.
1. *Paco works in the cafeteria.*
2. *Paco is working in the cafeteria.*
3. *Paco does work in the cafeteria.*

In Spanish and English, the present tense is also sometimes used to express future action.

Marina **viaja** a Madrid mañana.
1. *Marina travels to Madrid tomorrow.*
2. *Marina will travel to Madrid tomorrow.*
3. *Marina is traveling to Madrid tomorrow.*

▶ When two verbs are used together with no change of subject, the second verb is generally in the infinitive. To make a sentence negative in Spanish, the word **no** is placed before the conjugated verb. In this case, **no** means *not*.

**Deseo hablar** con don Francisco.
*I want to speak with Don Francisco.*

Alicia **no** desea bailar ahora.
*Alicia doesn't want to dance now.*

---

**Teaching Tips**
- Model the pronunciation of each infinitive and have students repeat it after you.
- Model the **yo** form of several verbs, creating simple sentences about yourself (Ex: **Bailo con mis amigos.**) and asking students if they do the same activities (Ex: **¿Bailas mucho con los amigos?**). Restate students' answers using the **él/ella** forms of the –ar verbs and then ask them to verify their classmates' answers. Ex: ¿_____ baila mucho? **No, _____ no baila.**
- Explain that the simple present tense in Spanish is the equivalent of the three present tense forms of English. Model sentences and give a few additional examples.
- Write additional examples of a conjugated verb followed by an infinitive on the board.
- Explain that, when answering questions negatively, **no** must be used twice. Ask questions of students that will most likely result in negative answers. Ex: —_____, ¿bailas tango? —**No, no bailo tango.**

---

### TEACHING OPTIONS

**Heritage Speakers** Ask heritage speakers to create sentences about their current semester/quarter: what they study, if/where they work, television programs they watch, etc. Ask the rest of the class comprehension questions.

**Extra Practice** Ask students to create a two-column chart with the heads **Necesito…** and **Espero…**, and have them complete it with six things they need to do this week and six things they

hope to do after the semester is over. Ex: **Necesito estudiar. Espero viajar.** Then have them interview a classmate and report back to the class.

**Pairs** Ask student pairs to write ten sentences, using verbs presented in this section. Point out that students can use vocabulary words from **Contextos** with these verbs. Have pairs share their sentences with the class.

▶ Spanish speakers often omit subject pronouns because the verb endings indicate who the subject is. In Spanish, subject pronouns are used for emphasis, clarification, or contrast.

**Clarification/Contrast**

—¿Qué enseñan?
*What do they teach?*

—**Ella** enseña arte y **él** enseña física.
*She teaches art, and he teaches physics.*

**Emphasis**

—¿Quién desea trabajar hoy?
*Who wants to work today?*

—**Yo** no deseo trabajar hoy.
*I don't want to work today.*

## The verb gustar

▶ To express your own likes and dislikes, use the expression **me gusta** + [*singular noun*] or **me gustan** + [*plural noun*]. Never use a subject pronoun (such as **yo**) with this structure.

**Me gusta la música** clásica.
*I like classical music.*

**Me gustan las clases** de español y biología.
*I like Spanish and biology classes.*

▶ To express what you like to do, use the expression **me gusta** + [*infinitive(s)*].

**Me gusta viajar.**
*I like to travel.*

**Me gusta cantar** y **bailar**.
*I like to sing and dance.*

▶ To use the verb **gustar** with reference to another person, use the expressions **te gusta(n)** (**tú**) or **a** + [*name/pronoun*] **le gusta(n)** (**usted, él, ella**). To say that someone does not like something, insert the word **no** before the expression.

**Te gusta la geografía.**
*You like geography.*

**A Javier no le gustan las computadoras.**
*Javier doesn't like computers.*

▶ To use the verb **gustar** with reference to more than one person, use **nos gusta(n)** (**nosotros**) or **a** + [*name/pronoun*] **les gusta(n)** (**ustedes, ellos, ellas**).

**Nos gusta dibujar.**
*We like to draw.*

**A ellos** no **les gustan los exámenes.**
*They don't like tests.*

**¡INTÉNTALO!**  Provide the present tense forms of these verbs. The first items have been done for you.

**hablar**

1. Yo ___hablo___ español.
2. Ellos ___hablan___ español.
3. Inés ___habla___ español.
4. Nosotras ___hablamos___ español.
5. Tú ___hablas___ español.

**gustar**

1. ___Me gusta___ el café. (yo)
2. ¿___Te gustan___ las clases? (tú)
3. No ___le gusta___ el café. (usted)
4. No ___le gustan___ las clases. (ella)
5. No ___nos gusta___ el café. (nosotros)

# Práctica ⬤SUPERSITE

**1**

**Completar** Complete the conversation with the appropriate forms of the verbs.

**JUAN** ¡Hola, Linda! ¿Qué tal las clases?

**LINDA** Bien. (1)___Tomo___ (tomar) tres clases… química, biología y computación. Y tú, ¿cuántas clases (2)___tomas___ (tomar)?

**JUAN** (3)___Tomo___ (tomar) tres también… biología, arte y literatura. Yo (4)___tomo___ (tomar) biología a las cuatro con el doctor Cárdenas. ¿Y tú?

**LINDA** Lily, Alberto y yo (5)___tomamos___ (tomar) biología a las diez, con la profesora Garza.

**JUAN** ¿(6)___Estudian___ (estudiar) ustedes mucho?

**LINDA** Sí, porque hay muchos exámenes. Alberto y yo (7)___estudiamos___ (estudiar) dos horas todos los días (*every day*).

**2**

**Oraciones** Form sentences using the words provided. Remember to conjugate the verbs and add any other necessary words.

1. ustedes / practicar / vocabulario   Ustedes practican el vocabulario.
2. ¿preparar (tú) / tarea?   ¿Preparas la tarea?
3. clase de español / terminar / once   La clase de español termina a las once.
4. ¿qué / buscar / ustedes?   ¿Qué buscan ustedes?
5. (nosotros) buscar / pluma   Buscamos una pluma.
6. (yo) comprar / computadora   Compro una computadora.

**3**

**Gustos** Read what these people do. Then use the information in parentheses to tell what they like or like to do.

> **modelo**
> Álvaro enseña en la universidad. (las clases)   *Le gustan las clases.*

1. Los jóvenes desean mirar cuadros (*paintings*) de Picasso. (el arte)   Les gusta el arte.
2. Soy estudiante de economía. (estudiar)   Me gusta estudiar.
3. Tú estudias italiano y español. (las lenguas extranjeras)   Te gustan las lenguas extranjeras.
4. Ustedes no descansan los sábados. (cantar y bailar)   Les gusta cantar y bailar.
5. Nosotros buscamos una computadora. (la computación)   Nos gusta la computación.

**4**

**Actividades** Get together with a classmate and take turns asking each other if you do these activities. Which activities does your partner like? Which do you both like?   Answers will vary.

| | | |
|---|---|---|
| bailar merengue | escuchar música rock | practicar el español |
| cantar bien | estudiar física | trabajar en la universidad |
| dibujar en clase | mirar la televisión | viajar a Europa |

> **modelo**
> tomar el autobús
> **Estudiante 1:** ¿Tomas el autobús?
> **Estudiante 2:** Sí, tomo el autobús, pero (*but*) no me gusta./ No, no tomo el autobús.

---

**TEACHING OPTIONS**

**Pairs** Have individual students write five dehydrated sentences and exchange them with a partner, who will complete them. After pairs have completed their sentences, ask volunteers to share some of their dehydrated sentences. Write them on the board and have the class "rehydrate" them.

**Game** Divide the class into two teams. Prepare brief descriptions of easily recognizable people, using **-ar** verbs. Write each name on a card, and give each team a set of names. Then read the descriptions aloud. The first team to hold up the correct name earns a point. Ex: **Ella canta, baila y viaja a muchos países. (Jennifer López)**

---

**1 Teaching Tip** To simplify, guide the class to first identify the subject and verb ending for each item.

**1 Expansion** Go over the answers quickly as a class. Then ask volunteers to role-play the dialogue.

**2 Teaching Tip** Point out that students will need to conjugate the verbs and add missing articles and other words to complete these dehydrated sentences. Tell them that subject pronouns in parentheses are not included in the completed sentences. Model completion of the first sentence for the class.

**2 Expansion** Give these dehydrated sentences to the class as items 7–10: **7. (yo) desear / practicar / verbos / hoy (Deseo practicar los verbos hoy.) 8. mi compañero de cuarto / regresar / lunes (Mi compañero de cuarto regresa el lunes.) 9. ella / cantar / y / bailar / muy bien (Ella canta y baila muy bien.) 10. jóvenes / necesitar / descansar / ahora (Los jóvenes necesitan descansar ahora.)**

**3 Teaching Tip** To simplify, start by reading the model aloud. Then ask students why **le** is used (**Álvaro** is third-person singular) and why **gustan** is needed (**las clases** is plural). Have students identify the indirect object pronoun and choose **gusta** or **gustan** for each item, then complete the activity.

**3 Expansion** Repeat the activity, providing different subjects for each item. Ex: **1. Deseamos mirar cuadros de Picasso. (Nos gusta el arte.)**

**4 Teaching Tip** Before beginning the activity, give a two- to three-minute oral rapid-response drill. Provide infinitives and subjects, and call on students to give the conjugated form.

# Comunicación

**5 Describir** With a partner, describe what you see in the pictures using the given verbs. Also ask your partner whether or not he/she likes one of the activities. *Answers will vary.*

**modelo**
enseñar
La profesora enseña química. ¿Te gusta la química?

1. caminar, hablar, llevar      2. buscar, descansar, estudiar

3. dibujar, cantar, escuchar      4. llevar, tomar, viajar

**6 Charadas** In groups of three students, play a game of charades using the verbs in the word bank. For example, if someone is studying, you say "**Estudias.**" The first person to guess correctly acts out the next charade. *Answers will vary.*

| bailar | cantar | descansar | enseñar | mirar |
| caminar | conversar | dibujar | escuchar | preguntar |

# Síntesis

**7 Conversación** Get together with a classmate and pretend that you are friends who have not seen each other on campus for a few days. Have a conversation in which you catch up on things. Mention how you're feeling, what classes you're taking, what days and times you have classes, and which classes you like and don't like. *Answers will vary.*

**TEACHING OPTIONS**

**Extra Practice** Have students write a description of themselves made up of activities they like or do not like to do, using sentences containing **(no) me gusta…** Collect the descriptions and read them aloud. Have the class guess who wrote each description.
**Game** To add a visual aspect to this grammar practice, play **Concentración**. Choose eight infinitives taught in this section, and write each one on a separate card. On another eight cards, draw or paste a picture that illustrates the action of each infinitive. Randomly place the cards facedown in four rows of four. Play with even-numbered groups of students. In pairs, students select two cards. If the two cards match, the pair keeps them. If the cards do not match, students return them to their original position. The pair that finishes with the most cards wins.

**2.2** Forming questions in Spanish

**ANTE TODO** There are three basic ways to ask questions in Spanish. Can you guess what they are by looking at the photos and photo captions on this page?

¿Dibujas mucho?

Las computadoras son muy interesantes, ¿no?

¿También tomas tú geografía?

▸ One way to form a question is to raise the pitch of your voice at the end of a declarative sentence. When writing any question in Spanish, be sure to use an upside down question mark (¿) at the beginning and a regular question mark (?) at the end of the sentence.

| Statement | Question |
|---|---|
| Ustedes trabajan los sábados. | ¿Ustedes trabajan los sábados? |
| *You work on Saturdays.* | *Do you work on Saturdays?* |
| Miguel busca un mapa. | ¿Miguel busca un mapa? |
| *Miguel is looking for a map.* | *Is Miguel looking for a map?* |

▸ You can also form a question by inverting the order of the subject and the verb of a declarative statement. The subject may even be placed at the end of the sentence.

| Statement | Question |
|---|---|
| SUBJECT VERB | VERB SUBJECT |
| **Ustedes trabajan** los sábados. | **¿Trabajan ustedes** los sábados? |
| *You work on Saturdays.* | *Do you work on Saturdays?* |
| SUBJECT VERB | VERB SUBJECT |
| **Carlota regresa** a las seis. | **¿Regresa** a las seis **Carlota**? |
| *Carlota returns at six.* | *Does Carlota return at six?* |

▸ Questions can also be formed by adding the tags **¿no?** or **¿verdad?** at the end of a statement.

| Statement | Question |
|---|---|
| Ustedes trabajan los sábados. | Ustedes trabajan los sábados, **¿no?** |
| *You work on Saturdays.* | *You work on Saturdays, don't you?* |
| Carlota regresa a las seis. | Carlota regresa a las seis, **¿verdad?** |
| *Carlota returns at six.* | *Carlota returns at six, right?* |

**Teaching Tips**
• Model pronunciation by asking questions. Ex: **¿Cómo estás? ¿Cuál es tu clase favorita?**
• Point out written accent marks on interrogative words.
• Briefly note that **¿qué?** and **¿cuál?** are not interchangeable. Before nouns, **¿qué?** is generally used; **¿cuál?** is typically used with verbs. Ex: **¿Qué clase te gusta?; ¿Cuál es tu clase favorita?** Write similar questions on the board but leave out the interrogative word. Ask students whether **¿qué?** or **¿cuál?** would be used.
• Point out **¿cuáles?** and **¿quiénes?** and give examples for each.
• Clarify singular/plural and masculine/feminine variants for **¿cuánto/a?** and **¿cuántos/as?** Ex: **¿Cuánta tarea hay? ¿Cuántos libros hay?**
• Model the pronunciation of example sentences, asking similar questions of students. Ex: ___, **¿dónde trabajas?** Ask other students to verify their classmates' answers. Ex: ____ **trabaja en ____.**
• Explain that the answer to the question **¿por qué?** is **porque**.
• Point out that a question such as **¿Caminan a la universidad?** has three possible answers: **Sí, caminamos a la universidad. No, no caminamos a la universidad. No, tomamos el autobús.**

# Question words

## Interrogative words

| | | | | |
|---|---|---|---|---|
| **¿Adónde?** | *Where (to)?* | | **¿De dónde?** | *From where?* |
| **¿Cómo?** | *How?* | | **¿Dónde?** | *Where?* |
| **¿Cuál?, ¿Cuáles?** | *Which?; Which one(s)?* | | **¿Por qué?** | *Why?* |
| **¿Cuándo?** | *When?* | | **¿Qué?** | *What?; Which?* |
| **¿Cuánto/a?** | *How much?* | | **¿Quién?** | *Who?* |
| **¿Cuántos/as?** | *How many?* | | **¿Quiénes?** | *Who (plural)?* |

**¡ATENCIÓN!**

To ask for clarification or repetition in Spanish, use **¿Cómo?** instead of **¿Qué?** to soften the request.
**¿Cómo?** No la escucho bien.
*Pardon? I can't hear you well.*

▶ To ask a question that requires more than a *yes* or *no* answer, use an interrogative word.

**¿Cuál** de ellos estudia en la biblioteca?
*Which of them studies in the library?*

**¿Adónde** caminamos?
*Where are we walking?*

**¿Cuántos** estudiantes hablan español?
*How many students speak Spanish?*

**¿Por qué** necesitas hablar con ella?
*Why do you need to talk to her?*

**¿Dónde** trabaja Ricardo?
*Where does Ricardo work?*

**¿Quién** enseña la clase de arte?
*Who teaches the art class?*

**¿Qué** clases tomas?
*What classes are you taking?*

**¿Cuánta** tarea hay?
*How much homework is there?*

**CONSULTA**

You will learn more about the difference between **qué** and **cuál** in **Estructura 9.3**, p. 292.

▶ When pronouncing this type of question, the pitch of your voice falls at the end of the sentence.

**¿Cómo** llegas a clase?
*How do you get to class?*

**¿Por qué** necesitas estudiar?
*Why do you need to study?*

▶ Notice the difference between **¿por qué?**, which is written as two words and has an accent, and **porque**, which is written as one word without an accent.

**¿Por qué** estudias español?
*Why do you study Spanish?*

**¡Porque** es divertido!
*Because it's fun!*

▶ In Spanish **no** can mean both *no* and *not*. Therefore, when answering a yes/no question in the negative, you need to use **no** twice.

**¿Caminan a la universidad?**
*Do you walk to the university?*

**No, no** caminamos a la universidad.
*No, we do not walk to the university.*

---

**¡INTÉNTALO!** Make questions out of these statements. Use intonation in column 1 and the tag **¿no?** in column 2. The first item has been done for you.

| Statement | Intonation | Tag questions |
|---|---|---|
| 1. Hablas inglés. | ¿Hablas inglés? | Hablas inglés, ¿no? |
| 2. Trabajamos mañana. | ¿Trabajamos mañana? | Trabajamos mañana, ¿no? |
| 3. Ustedes desean bailar. | ¿Ustedes desean bailar? | Ustedes desean bailar, ¿no? |
| 4. Raúl estudia mucho. | ¿Raúl estudia mucho? | Raúl estudia mucho, ¿no? |
| 5. Enseño a las nueve. | ¿Enseño a las nueve? | Enseño a las nueve, ¿no? |
| 6. Luz mira la televisión. | ¿Luz mira la televisión? | Luz mira la televisión, ¿no? |

**recursos**

WB
pp. 15–16

LM
p. 10

panorama.
vhlcentral.com
Lección 2

---

**TEACHING OPTIONS**

**Video** Show the *Fotonovela* again to give students more input on forming questions. Stop the video where appropriate to discuss how certain questions, including tag questions, are formed. Have students focus on characters' rising and falling intonation in questions and statements.

**Heritage Speakers** Ask heritage speakers to give original statements and questions at random. Have the rest of the class determine whether each sentence is a statement or a question.
**Pairs** Give pairs of students five minutes to write original questions using as many interrogative words as they can. Can any group come up with questions using all interrogative words?

# Práctica

**1** **Preguntas** Change these sentences into questions by inverting the word order.

> **modelo**
>
> Ernesto habla con su compañero de clase.
>
> ¿Habla Ernesto con su compañero de clase? /
> ¿Habla con su compañero de clase Ernesto?

1. La profesora Cruz prepara la prueba.
   ¿Prepara la profesora Cruz la prueba? / ¿Prepara la prueba la profesora Cruz?
2. Sandra y yo necesitamos estudiar.
   ¿Necesitamos Sandra y yo estudiar? / ¿Necesitamos estudiar Sandra y yo?
3. Los chicos practican el vocabulario.
   ¿Practican los chicos el vocabulario? / ¿Practican el vocabulario los chicos?
4. Jaime termina la tarea.
   ¿Termina Jaime la tarea? / ¿Termina la tarea Jaime?
5. Tú trabajas en la biblioteca.     ¿Trabajas tú en la biblioteca? / ¿Trabajas en la biblioteca tú?

**2** **Completar** Irene and Manolo are chatting in the library. Complete their conversation with the appropriate questions.   Answers will vary.

| | |
|---|---|
| **IRENE** | Hola, Manolo. (1)¿Cómo estás?/¿Qué tal? |
| **MANOLO** | Bien, gracias. (2)¿Y tú? |
| **IRENE** | Muy bien. (3)¿Qué hora es? |
| **MANOLO** | Son las nueve. |
| **IRENE** | (4)¿Qué estudias? |
| **MANOLO** | Estudio historia. |
| **IRENE** | (5)¿Por qué? |
| **MANOLO** | Porque hay un examen mañana. |
| **IRENE** | (6)¿Te gusta la clase? |
| **MANOLO** | Sí, me gusta mucho la clase. |
| **IRENE** | (7)¿Quién enseña la clase? |
| **MANOLO** | El profesor Padilla enseña la clase. |
| **IRENE** | (8)¿Tomas psicología este semestre? |
| **MANOLO** | No, no tomo psicología este semestre. |
| **IRENE** | (9)¿A qué hora regresas a la residencia? |
| **MANOLO** | Regreso a la residencia a las once. |
| **IRENE** | (10)¿Deseas tomar una soda? |
| **MANOLO** | No, no deseo tomar soda. ¡Deseo estudiar! |

**3** **Dos profesores** In pairs, create a dialogue, similar to the one in **Actividad 2**, between Professor Padilla and his colleague Professor Martínez. Use question words.   Answers will vary.

> **modelo**
>
> **Prof. Padilla:** ¿Qué enseñas este semestre?
> **Prof. Martínez:** Enseño dos cursos de sociología.

**1** **Teaching Tip** Ask students to give both ways of forming questions for each item. Explain that the last element in a question is emphatic; thus **¿Habla Ernesto con el Sr. Gómez?** and **¿Habla con el Sr. Gómez Ernesto?** have different emphases. In pairs, have students take turns making the statements and converting them into questions.

**1** **Expansion** Make the even statements negative. Then have students add tag questions to the statements.

**2** **Expansion** Have pairs of students create a similar conversation, replacing the answers with items that are true for them. Then ask volunteers to role-play their conversations for the class.

**3** **Teaching Tip** To prepare students for the activity, have them brainstorm possible topics of conversation.

---

**TEACHING OPTIONS**

**Heritage Speakers** Ask students to interview heritage speakers, whether in the class or outside. Students should prepare questions about who the person is, if they work and when/where, what they study and why, and so forth. Have students use the information they gather in the interviews to write a brief profile of the person.

**Large Groups** Divide the class into two groups, A and B. To each member of group A give a strip of paper with a question on it. Ex: **¿Cuántos estudiantes hay en la clase?** Give an answer to each member of group B. Ex: **Hay treinta estudiantes en la clase.** Have students find their partners. Be sure that each question has only one possible answer.

# Comunicación

**4** **Encuesta** Your instructor will give you a worksheet. Change the categories in the first column into questions, then use them to survey your classmates. Find at least one person for each category. Be prepared to report the results of your survey to the class. Answers will vary.

| Categorías | Nombres |
|---|---|
| 1. estudiar computación | |
| 2. tomar una clase de psicología | |
| 3. dibujar bien | |
| 4. cantar bien | |
| 5. escuchar música clásica | |

**5** **Un juego** In groups of four or five, play a game (**un juego**) of Jeopardy.® Each person has to write two clues. Then take turns reading the clues and guessing the questions. The person who guesses correctly reads the next clue. Answers will vary.

| **Es algo que...** | **Es un lugar donde...** | **Es una persona que...** |
|---|---|---|
| *It's something that...* | *It's a place where...* | *It's a person that...* |

**modelo**

**Estudiante 1:** Es un lugar donde estudiamos.
**Estudiante 2:** ¿Qué es la biblioteca?

**Estudiante 1:** Es algo que escuchamos.
**Estudiante 2:** ¿Qué es la música?

**Estudiante 1:** Es un director de España.
**Estudiante 2:** ¿Quién es Pedro Almodóvar?

# Síntesis

**6** **Entrevista** Imagine that you are a reporter for the school newspaper. Write five questions about student life at your school and use them to interview two classmates. Be prepared to report your findings to the class. Answers will vary.

---

## Teaching notes (left margin)

**4 Teaching Tips**
- Because this is the first activity in which the *Hojas de actividades* are used, explain to students that they will use the worksheets to complete the activity. For survey-type activities, encourage students to ask one question per person and move on. When they find someone who answers affirmatively, that student signs his or her name.
- Distribute the *Hojas de actividades* (Supersite/IRCD) and explain that students must actively approach their classmates with their *Hoja* in hand. When they find someone who answers affirmatively, that student signs his or her name.
- For survey-type activities, encourage students to ask one question per person and move on. This will promote circulation throughout the room and prevent students from remaining in clusters.

**4 Expansion** Ask students to say the name of someone who signed their *Hoja*. Then ask that student for more information. Ex: **¿Quién estudia computación? Ah, ¿sí? \_\_\_\_ estudia computación. ¿Dónde estudias computación, \_\_\_\_? ¿Quién es el/la profesor(a)?**

**5 Expansion** Play this game with the entire class. Select a few students to play the contestants and to "buzz in" their answers.

**6 Teaching Tip** Brainstorm ideas for interview questions and write them on the board, or have students prepare their questions as homework for an in-class interview session.

---

**TEACHING OPTIONS**

**Extra Practice** Have students go back to the **Fotonovela** on pages 40–41 and write as many questions as they can about what they see in the photos. Ask volunteers to share their questions as you write them on the board. Then call on individual students to answer them.

**Extra Practice** Prepare eight questions and answers. Write only the answers on the board in random order. Then read the questions aloud and have students identify the appropriate answer. Ex: **¿Cuándo es la clase de español? (Es los lunes, miércoles y viernes.)**

# [2.3] Present tense of estar

**ANTE TODO**   In **Lección 1**, you learned how to conjugate and use the verb **ser** *(to be)*. You will now learn a second verb which means *to be*, the verb **estar**. Although **estar** ends in **-ar**, it does not follow the pattern of regular **-ar** verbs. The **yo** form (**estoy**) is irregular. Also, all forms have an accented **á** except the **yo** and **nosotros/as** forms.

| The verb estar *(to be)* | | |
|---|---|---|
| **SINGULAR FORMS** | yo     est**oy** | *I am* |
| | tú     est**ás** | *you* (fam.) *are* |
| | Ud./él/ella     est**á** | *you* (form.) *are; he/she is* |
| **PLURAL FORMS** | nosotros/as     est**amos** | *we are* |
| | vosotros/as     est**áis** | *you* (fam.) *are* |
| | Uds./ellos/ellas     est**án** | *you* (form.) *are; they are* |

*Hola, Ricardo... Aquí estamos en la Mitad del Mundo.*

*María está en la biblioteca.*

## COMPARE & CONTRAST

Compare the uses of the verb **estar** to those of the verb **ser**.

### Uses of *estar*

**Location**
**Estoy** en casa.
*I am at home.*

Inés **está** al lado de Javier.
*Inés is next to Javier.*

**Health**
Álex **está** enfermo hoy.
*Álex is sick today.*

**Well-being**
—¿Cómo **estás**, Maite?
*How are you, Maite?*

—**Estoy** muy bien, gracias.
*I'm very well, thank you.*

### Uses of *ser*

**Identity**
Hola, **soy** Maite.
*Hello, I'm Maite.*

**Occupation**
**Soy** estudiante.
*I'm a student.*

**Origin**
—¿**Eres** de España?
*Are you from Spain?*

—Sí, **soy** de España.
*Yes, I'm from Spain.*

**Telling time**
**Son** las cuatro.
*It's four o'clock.*

▶ **Estar** is often used with certain prepositions to describe the location of a person or an object.

### Prepositions often used with estar

| | | | |
|---|---|---|---|
| **al lado de** | next to; beside | **delante de** | in front of |
| **a la derecha de** | to the right of | **detrás de** | behind |
| **a la izquierda de** | to the left of | **encima de** | on top of |
| **en** | in; on | **entre** | between; among |
| **cerca de** | near | **lejos de** | far from |
| **con** | with | **sin** | without |
| **debajo de** | below | **sobre** | on; over |

La clase **está al lado de** la biblioteca.
*The class is next to the library.*

Los libros **están encima del** escritorio.
*The books are on top of the desk.*

El laboratorio **está cerca de** la clase.
*The lab is near the classroom.*

Maribel **está delante de** José.
*Maribel is in front of José.*

El estadio no **está lejos de** la librería.
*The stadium isn't far from the bookstore..*

El mapa **está entre** la pizarra y la puerta.
*The map is between the blackboard and the door.*

Los estudiantes **están en** la clase.
*The students are in class.*

El libro **está sobre** la mesa.
*The book is on the table.*

¡A ver! La señorita que está cerca de la ventana…

Aquí estoy con cuatro estudiantes de la universidad…

**¡INTÉNTALO!**  Provide the present tense forms of **estar**. The first item has been done for you.

1. Ustedes ___están___ en la clase.
2. José ___está___ en la biblioteca.
3. Yo ___estoy___ bien, gracias.
4. Nosotras ___estamos___ en la cafetería.
5. Tú ___estás___ en el laboratorio.
6. Elena ___está___ en la librería.
7. Ellas ___están___ en la clase.

8. Ana y yo ___estamos___ en la clase.
9. ¿Cómo ___está___ usted?
10. Javier y Maribel ___están___ en el estadio.
11. Nosotros ___estamos___ en la cafetería.
12. Yo ___estoy___ en el laboratorio.
13. Carmen y María ___están___ enfermas.
14. Tú ___estás___ en la clase.

**recursos**

WB
pp. 17–18

LM
p. 11

SUPERSITE
panorama.
vhlcentral.com
Lección 2

# Práctica

**1**

**Completar** Daniela has just returned home from her classes at the local university. Complete this conversation with the appropriate forms of **ser** or **estar**.

**MAMÁ**    Hola, Daniela. ¿Cómo (1)____estás____?

▶ **DANIELA**    Hola, mamá. (2)____Estoy____ bien. ¿Dónde (3)____está____ papá?

           ¡Ya (*Already*) (4)____son____ las ocho de la noche!

**MAMÁ**    No (5)____está____ aquí. (6)____Está____ en la oficina.

**DANIELA**    Y Andrés y Margarita, ¿dónde (7)____están____ ellos?

**MAMÁ**    (8)____Están____ en el restaurante La Palma con Martín.

**DANIELA**    ¿Quién (9)____es____ Martín?

**MAMÁ**    (10)____Es____ un compañero de clase. (11)____Es____ de México.

**DANIELA**    Ah. Y el restaurante La Palma, ¿dónde (12)____está____?

**MAMÁ**    (13)____Está____ cerca de la Plaza Mayor, en San Modesto.

**DANIELA**    Gracias, mamá. Voy (*I'm going*) al restaurante. ¡Hasta pronto!

**2**

**Escoger** Choose the preposition that best completes each sentence.

1. La pluma está (**encima de**/ detrás de) la mesa.
2. La ventana está (**a la izquierda de**/ debajo de) la puerta.
3. La pizarra está (debajo de /**delante de**) los estudiantes.
4. Las sillas están (encima de / **detrás de**) los escritorios.
5. Los estudiantes llevan los libros (**en** / sobre) la mochila.
6. La biblioteca está (sobre / **al lado de**) la residencia estudiantil.
7. España está (cerca de /**lejos de**) Puerto Rico.
8. Cuba está (**cerca de** / lejos de) los Estados Unidos.
9. Felipe trabaja (**con**/ en) Ricardo en la cafetería.

**3**

**La librería** Imagine that you are in the school bookstore and can't find various items. Ask the clerk (your partner) where the items in the drawing are located. Then switch roles. Answers will vary.

▶ **modelo**

   **Estudiante 1:** ¿Dónde están los diccionarios?
   **Estudiante 2:** Los diccionarios están debajo de los libros de literatura.

**1 Teaching Tips**
- To simplify, guide students in choosing **ser** or **estar** for each item.
- Ask students to explain why they chose **ser** or **estar** in each case.

**1 Expansion** Ask two volunteers to role-play the conversation for the class.

**2 Expansion**
- To challenge students, rework items 1 through 6, asking questions about items in the classroom or places at the university. Ex: **¿Qué objeto está encima de la mesa? ¿Dónde está la ventana?**
- To add a visual aspect to this exercise, ask students to create simple illustrations for items 1–8.

**3 Teaching Tip** Using *Overhead PowerPoint #14* or the drawing in the textbook, quickly have volunteers name the objects they see in the illustration.

**3 Expansion** Assign one student the role of **vendedor(a)** and another the role of **cliente/a**. Then name one of the items in the drawing and ask the participants to create a conversation as in the activity.

# Comunicación

**4** Teaching Tips
- Ask two volunteers to read the model aloud.
- Have students scan the days and times and ask you for any additional vocabulary.

**4** Expansion After students have completed the activity, ask the same questions of selected individuals. Then expand on their answers by asking additional questions. Ex: —¿Dónde estás los sábados a las seis de la mañana? —Estoy en la residencia estudiantil. —¿Dónde está la residencia?

**5** Expansion
- To make more challenging for students, have them create statements about the buildings' locations from the point of view of the man in the drawing.
- Make copies of your campus map and distribute them to the class. Ask questions about where particular buildings are. Give yourself a starting point so that you can ask questions with as many prepositions as possible. Ex: **Estoy en la biblioteca. ¿Está lejos la librería?**

**6** Teaching Tip Remind students to jot down each interviewee's answers.

**6** Expansion Call on students to share the information they obtained with the class.

**4** **¿Dónde estás...?** Get together with a partner and take turns asking each other where you are at these times. Answers will vary.

> **modelo**
> lunes / 10:00 a.m.
> **Estudiante 1:** ¿Dónde estás los lunes a las diez de la mañana?
> **Estudiante 2:** Estoy en la clase de español.

1. sábados / 6:00 a.m.
2. miércoles / 9:15 a.m.
3. lunes / 11:10 a.m.
4. jueves / 12:30 a.m.
5. viernes / 2:25 p.m.
6. martes / 3:50 p.m.
7. jueves / 5:45 p.m.
8. miércoles / 8:20 p.m.

**5** **La ciudad universitaria** You are an exchange student at a Spanish university. Tell a classmate which buildings you are looking for and ask for their location relative to where you are. Answers will vary.

> **modelo**
> **Estudiante 1:** ¿La Facultad de Medicina está lejos?
> **Estudiante 2:** No, está cerca. Está a la izquierda de la Facultad de Administración de Empresas.

Facultad de Medicina
Facultad de Administración de Empresas
Biblioteca
Facultad de Química
Facultad de Bellas Artes
Colegio Mayor Cervantes

# Síntesis

**6** **Entrevista** Use these questions to interview two classmates. Then switch roles. Answers will vary.

1. ¿Cómo estás?
2. ¿Dónde estamos ahora?
3. ¿Dónde está tu (*your*) compañero/a de cuarto ahora?
4. ¿Cuántos estudiantes hay en la clase de español?
5. ¿Quién(es) no está(n) en la clase hoy?
6. ¿A qué hora termina la clase hoy?
7. ¿Estudias mucho?
8. ¿Cuántas horas estudias para (*for*) una prueba?

---

**TEACHING OPTIONS**

**Video** Show the *Fotonovela* again to give students more input. Stop the video where appropriate to discuss how **estar** and prepositions were used and to ask comprehension questions.
**Pairs** Write a list of well-known monuments, places, and people on the board. Ex: **las Torres Petrona, el Space Needle, Bill Gates, las Cataratas del Niágara, Madonna** Have student pairs take turns asking each other the location of each item. Ex: —**¿Dónde están**

**las Torres Petrona? —Están en Kuala Lumpur/Malasia.**
**Game** Divide the class into two teams. Select a student from team A to think of an item in the classroom. Team B can ask five questions about where this item is. The first student can respond only with **sí, no, caliente** (*hot*), or **frío** (*cold*). If a team guesses the item within five tries, award them a point. If not, give the other team a point. The team with the most points wins.

## 2.4 Numbers 31 and higher

**ANTE TODO** You have already learned numbers 0–30. Now you will learn the rest of the numbers.

### Numbers 31–100

▶ Numbers 31–99 follow the same basic pattern as 21–29.

#### Numbers 31–100

| | | | | | |
|---|---|---|---|---|---|
| 31 | treinta y uno | 40 | cuarenta | 50 | cincuenta |
| 32 | treinta y dos | 41 | cuarenta y uno | 51 | cincuenta y uno |
| 33 | treinta y tres | 42 | cuarenta y dos | 52 | cincuenta y dos |
| 34 | treinta y cuatro | 43 | cuarenta y tres | 60 | sesenta |
| 35 | treinta y cinco | 44 | cuarenta y cuatro | 63 | sesenta y tres |
| 36 | treinta y seis | 45 | cuarenta y cinco | 64 | sesenta y cuatro |
| 37 | treinta y siete | 46 | cuarenta y seis | 70 | setenta |
| 38 | treinta y ocho | 47 | cuarenta y siete | 80 | ochenta |
| 39 | treinta y nueve | 48 | cuarenta y ocho | 90 | noventa |
| | | 49 | cuarenta y nueve | 100 | cien, ciento |

▶ **Y** is used in most numbers from **31** through **99**. Unlike numbers 21–29, these numbers must be written as three separate words.

Hay **noventa y dos** exámenes.
*There are ninety-two exams.*

Hay **cuarenta y dos** estudiantes.
*There are forty-two students.*

¿En qué clase hay más chicas?

En la de sociología… casi un ochenta y cinco por ciento.

▶ With numbers that end in **uno** (31, 41, etc.), **uno** becomes **un** before a masculine noun and **una** before a feminine noun.

Hay **treinta y un** chicos.
*There are thirty-one guys.*

Hay **treinta y una** chicas.
*There are thirty-one girls.*

▶ **Cien** is used before nouns and in counting. The words **un**, **una**, and **uno** are never used before **cien** in Spanish. **Ciento** is used for numbers over one hundred.

¿Cuántos libros hay? **Cientos.**
*How many books are there?*
*Hundreds.*

Hay **cien** libros y **cien** sillas.
*There are one hundred books*
*and one hundred chairs.*

### Section Goal

In **Estructura 2.4**, students will be introduced to numbers 31 and higher.

**Instructional Resources**
**Supersite:** Lab MP3 Audio Files
**Lección 2**
**Supersite/IRCD:** *PowerPoints*
(**Lección 2 Estructura**
Presentation); *IRM* (Information Gap Activities, Lab Audio Script, WBs/VM/LM Answer Key)
**WebSAM**
**Workbook,** pp. 19–20
**Lab Manual,** p. 12
***Cuaderno para hispanohablantes***

**Teaching Tips**
• Review 0–30 by having the class count with you. When you reach 30, ask individual students to count through 39. Count 40 yourself and have students continue counting through 100.
• Write on the board numbers not included in the chart: 56, 68, 72, and so forth. Ask students to say the number in Spanish.
• Drill numbers 31–100 counting in sequences of twos and threes. Point to individuals at random and have them supply the next number in the series. Keep a brisk pace.
• Emphasize that from 31 to 99, numbers are written as three words (**treinta y nueve**).
• Remind students that **uno** changes into **un** and **una**, as in **veintiún** and **veintiuna**.
• Bring in a newspaper or magazine ad that shows phone numbers and prices. Call on volunteers to read the numbers aloud.

### TEACHING OPTIONS

**Extra Practice** Do simple math problems (addition and subtraction) with numbers 31 and higher. Include numbers 0–30 as well, for a balanced review. Remind students that **más** = *plus*, **menos** = *minus*, and **es/son** = *equals*.
**Extra Practice** Write the beginning of a series of numbers on the board and have students continue the sequence. Ex: **45, 50, 55,…** or **77, 80, 83, 86,…**

**Heritage Speakers** Add an auditory aspect to this grammar presentation. Ask heritage speakers to give the house or apartment number where they live (they do not have to give the street name). Ask them to give the addresses in tens (**1471 = catorce setenta y uno**). Have volunteers write the numbers they say on the board.

## Teaching Tips

- Write these phrases on the board: **cuatrocientos estudiantes, novecientas personas, dos mil libros, once millones de viajeros.** Help students deduce the meanings of the numbers.
- Write numbers on the board and call on volunteers to read them aloud.
- To practice agreement, write numbers from 101 to 999 followed by various nouns and have students read them aloud.
- To make sure that students do not say **un mil** for *one thousand*, list **1.000, 2.000, 3.000,** and **4.000** on the board. Have the class call out the numbers as you point to them randomly in rapid succession. Repeat this process for **cien mil.** Then emphasize that **un** is used with **millón.**
- Point out that **de** is used between **millón/millones** and a noun.
- Slowly dictate pairs of large numbers for students to write down on separate pieces of paper. Have them hold up the larger number. Ex: You say **seiscientos cincuenta y ocho mil, ciento catorce;** then **quinientos setenta y siete mil, novecientos treinta y seis.** Students hold up **658.114.**
- Point out how dates are expressed in Spanish and have volunteers read aloud the examples on this page. Then provide word groups that describe famous historical events. Ex: **Cristóbal Colón, las Américas; Neil Armstrong, la luna.** Have students state the year that they associate with each one. Ex: **Mil cuatrocientos noventa y dos.**

# Numbers 101 and higher

▶ As shown in the chart, Spanish uses a period to indicate thousands and millions, rather than a comma as used in English.

### Numbers 101 and higher

| | | | |
|---|---|---|---|
| 101 | ciento uno | 1.000 | mil |
| 200 | doscientos/as | 1.100 | mil cien |
| 300 | trescientos/as | 2.000 | dos mil |
| 400 | cuatrocientos/as | 5.000 | cinco mil |
| 500 | quinientos/as | 100.000 | cien mil |
| 600 | seiscientos/as | 200.000 | doscientos/as mil |
| 700 | setecientos/as | 550.000 | quinientos/as cincuenta mil |
| 800 | ochocientos/as | 1.000.000 | un millón (de) |
| 900 | novecientos/as | 8.000.000 | ocho millones (de) |

▶ The numbers 200 through 999 agree in gender with the nouns they modify.

324 plum**as**
trescient**as** veinticuatro plum**as**

605 libr**os**
seiscient**os** cinco libr**os**

Hay tres mil quinient**os** libr**os** en la biblioteca.

▶ The word **mil**, which can mean *a thousand* and *one thousand*, is not usually used in the plural form when referring to numbers. **Un millón** (*a million* or *one million*), has the plural form **millones,** in which the accent is dropped.

1.000 relojes          25.000 pizarras          2.000.000 de estudiantes
**mil** relojes          veinticinco **mil** pizarras          dos **millones** de estudiantes

▶ To express a complex number (including years), string together its component parts.

55.422   cincuenta y cinco mil cuatrocientos veintidós

 **¡INTÉNTALO!**  Give the Spanish equivalent of each number. The first item has been done for you.

1. **102** _ciento dos_
2. **5.000.000** cinco millones
3. **201** doscientos uno
4. **76** setenta y seis
5. **92** noventa y dos
6. **550.300** quinientos cincuenta mil trescientos
7. **235** doscientos treinta y cinco
8. **79** setenta y nueve
9. **113** ciento trece
10. **88** ochenta y ocho
11. **17.123** diecisiete mil ciento veintitrés
12. **497** cuatrocientos noventa y siete

**¡LENGUA VIVA!**
In Spanish, years are not expressed as pairs of 2-digit numbers as they are in English (1979, *nineteen seventy-nine*): 1776, **mil setecientos setenta y seis;** 1945, **mil novecientos cuarenta y cinco;** 2007, **dos mil siete.**

**¡ATENCIÓN!**
When **millón** or **millones** is used before a noun, the word **de** is placed between the two:
**1.000.000 de hombres = un millón de hombres**
**12.000.000 de aviones = doce millones de aviones.**

**recursos**
WB pp. 19–20
LM p. 12
panorama. vhlcentral.com Lección 2

### TEACHING OPTIONS

**TPR** Write number patterns on cards (one number per card) and distribute them among the class. Begin a number chain by calling out the first two numbers in the pattern. Ex: **veinticinco, cincuenta.** The students holding these cards have five seconds to get up and stand in front of the class. The rest of the class continues by calling out the numbers in the pattern for the students to join the chain. Continue until the chain is broken or complete; then begin a new pattern.

**Pairs** Ask students to list three numerals in the hundreds, three in the thousands, and three in the millions; each should be followed by a masculine or feminine noun. Have students exchange lists with a classmate, who will read the items aloud. Partners should listen for the correct number and gender agreement. Ex: **204 personas (doscientas cuatro personas)**

# Práctica y Comunicación

**1** **Baloncesto** Provide these basketball scores in Spanish.

1. Ohio State 76, Michigan 65
2. Florida 92, Florida State 104
3. Stanford 78, UCLA 89
4. Purdue 81, Indiana 78
5. Princeton 67, Harvard 55
6. Duke 115, Virginia 121

1. setenta y seis, sesenta y cinco   3. setenta y ocho, ochenta y nueve   5. sesenta y siete, cincuenta y cinco
2. noventa y dos, ciento cuatro   4. ochenta y uno, setenta y ocho   6. ciento quince, ciento veintiuno

**2** **Completar** Complete these sequences of numbers.

1. 50, 150, 250 ... 1.050 trescientos cincuenta, cuatrocientos cincuenta, quinientos cincuenta, seiscientos cincuenta, setecientos cincuenta, ochocientos cincuenta, novecientos cincuenta
2. 5.000, 20.000, 35.000 ... 95.000
cincuenta mil, sesenta y cinco mil, ochenta mil
3. 100.000, 200.000, 300.000 ... 1.000.000
cuatrocientos mil, quinientos mil, seiscientos mil, setecientos mil, ochocientos mil, novecientos mil
4. 100.000.000, 90.000.000, 80.000.000 ... 0 setenta millones, sesenta millones, cincuenta millones, cuarenta millones, treinta millones, veinte millones, diez millones

**3** **Resolver** Read the math problems aloud and solve them.

**AYUDA**

+ → más
− → menos
= → son

> *modelo*
>
> 200 + 300 = Doscientos más trescientos son quinientos.

1. 1.000 + 753 = Mil más setecientos cincuenta y tres son mil setecientos cincuenta y tres.
2. 1.000.000 − 30.000 = Un millón menos treinta mil son novecientos setenta mil.
3. 10.000 + 555 = Diez mil más quinientos cincuenta y cinco son diez mil quinientos cincuenta y cinco.
4. 15 + 150 = Quince más ciento cincuenta son ciento sesenta y cinco.
5. 100.000 + 205.000 = Cien mil más doscientos cinco mil son trescientos cinco mil.
6. 29.000 − 10.000 = Veintinueve mil menos diez mil son diecinueve mil.

**4** **Entrevista** Find out the telephone numbers and e-mail addresses of four classmates.

Answers will vary.

**AYUDA**

arroba *at* (@)
punto *dot* (.)

> *modelo*
>
> **Estudiante 1:** ¿Cuál es tu (*your*) número de teléfono?
> **Estudiante 2:** Es el 635-19-51.
> **Estudiante 1:** ¿Y tu dirección de correo electrónico?
> **Estudiante 2:** Es a-Smith-arroba-pe-ele-punto-e-de-u. (*asmith@pl.edu*)

# Síntesis

**5** **¿A qué distancia...?** Your instructor will give you and a partner incomplete charts that indicate the distances between Madrid and various locations. Fill in the missing information on your chart by asking your partner questions. Answers will vary.

> *modelo*
>
> **Estudiante 1:** ¿A qué distancia está Arganda del Rey?
> **Estudiante 2:** Está a veintisiete kilómetros de Madrid.

**1** **Expansion** In pairs, have each student write three additional basketball scores and dictate them to his or her partner, who writes them down.

**2** **Teaching Tip** To simplify, have students identify the pattern of each sequence. Ex: 1. Add one hundred.

**3** **Expansion** To challenge students, have them create four additional math problems for a partner to solve.

**4** **Teaching Tips**
• Write your own e-mail address on the board as you pronounce it.
• Point out that **el correo electrónico** means *e-mail*.
• Reassure students that, if they are uncomfortable revealing their personal information, they can invent a number and address.
• Ask volunteers to share their phone numbers and e-mail addresses. Other students write them on the board.

**5** **Teaching Tips**
• Distribute the corresponding handouts (Supersite/IRCD) and explain that this type of exercise is called an information gap activity. Each partner has information that the other needs. To obtain the missing information, partners must ask each other questions. Give students ten minutes to complete the activity.

**Teaching Tip** See the Information Gap Activities (Supersite/IRCD) for an additional activity to practice the material presented in this section.

---

**TEACHING OPTIONS**

**Small Groups** In groups of three or four, ask students to think of a city or town within a 100-mile radius of the university. Have them find out the distance in miles (**Está a _____ millas de la universidad.**) and what other cities or towns are nearby (**Está cerca de...**). Then have groups read their descriptions for the class to guess.

**Game** Ask for two volunteers and station them at opposite ends of the board so neither one can see what the other is writing. Say a number for them to write on the board. If both students are correct, continue to give numbers until one writes an incorrect number. The winner continues on to play against another student.

# Recapitulación

 For self-scoring and diagnostics, go to **panorama.vhlcentral.com**.

Review the grammar concepts you have learned in this lesson by completing these activities.

**1 Completar** Complete the chart with the correct verb forms. **12 pts.**

| yo | tú | nosotros | ellas |
|----|----|----------|-------|
| **compro** | compras | compramos | compran |
| deseo | **deseas** | deseamos | desean |
| miro | miras | **miramos** | miran |
| pregunto | preguntas | preguntamos | **preguntan** |

**2 Números** Write these numbers in Spanish. **8 pts.**

> **modelo**
> 645: *seiscientos cuarenta y cinco*

1. **49:** cuarenta y nueve
2. **97:** noventa y siete
3. **113:** ciento trece
4. **632:** seiscientos treinta y dos
5. **1.781:** mil setecientos ochenta y uno
6. **3.558:** tres mil quinientos cincuenta y ocho
7. **1.006.015:** un millón seis mil quince
8. **67.224.370:** sesenta y siete millones doscientos veinticuatro mil trescientos setenta

**3 Preguntas** Write questions for these answers. **12 pts.**

1. —¿ De dónde es _____ Patricia?
   —Patricia es de Colombia.
2. —¿ Quién es _____ él?
   —Él es mi amigo (*friend*).
3. —¿ Cuántos idiomas hablas _____ (tú)?
   —Hablo dos idiomas.
4. —¿ Qué desean (tomar) _____ (ustedes)?
   —Deseamos tomar dos cafés.
5. —¿ Por qué tomas biología _____ ?
   —Tomo biología porque me gusta.
6. —¿ Cuándo descansa Camilo _____ ?
   —Camilo descansa por las mañanas.

## RESUMEN GRAMATICAL

**2.1 Present tense of -ar verbs** *pp. 46–48*

| estudiar | |
|----------|----|
| estudio | estudiamos |
| estudias | estudiáis |
| estudia | estudian |

**The verb gustar**

SINGULAR  me, te, le   **gust**a ⟩ el chocolate / viajar / cantar y bailar

PLURAL  nos, os, les   **gust**an ⟩ los libros

**2.2 Forming questions in Spanish** *pp. 51–52*

▶ ¿Ustedes trabajan los sábados?
▶ ¿Trabajan ustedes los sábados?
▶ Ustedes trabajan los sábados, ¿verdad?/¿no?

**Interrogative words**

| ¿Adónde? | ¿Cuánto/a? | ¿Por qué? |
|----------|------------|-----------|
| ¿Cómo? | ¿Cuántos/as? | ¿Qué? |
| ¿Cuál(es)? | ¿(De) dónde? | ¿Quién(es)? |
| ¿Cuándo? | | |

**2.3 Present tense of estar** *pp. 55–56*

▶ estar: **est**oy, **est**ás, **est**á, **est**amos, **est**áis, **est**án

**2.4 Numbers 31 and higher** *pp. 59–60*

| 31 | treinta y uno | 101 | ciento uno |
|----|---------------|-----|------------|
| 32 | treinta y dos | 200 | doscientos/as |
| | (and so on) | 500 | quinientos/as |
| 40 | cuarenta | 700 | setecientos/as |
| 50 | cincuenta | 900 | novecientos/as |
| 60 | sesenta | 1.000 | mil |
| 70 | setenta | 2.000 | dos mil |
| 80 | ochenta | 5.100 | cinco mil cien |
| 90 | noventa | 100.000 | cien mil |
| 100 | cien, ciento | 1.000.000 | un millón (de) |

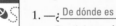

**4** **Al teléfono** Complete this telephone conversation with the correct forms of the verb **estar**. 〔8 pts.〕

**MARÍA TERESA** Hola, señora López. (1) ¿___Está___ Elisa en casa?

**SRA. LÓPEZ** ¿Quién es?

**MARÍA TERESA** Soy María Teresa. Elisa y yo (2) ___estamos___ en la misma (*same*) clase de literatura.

**SRA. LÓPEZ** ¡Ah, María Teresa! ¿Cómo (3) ___estás___?

**MARÍA TERESA** (4) ___Estoy___ muy bien, gracias. Y usted, ¿cómo (5) ___está___?

**SRA. LÓPEZ** Bien, gracias. Pues, no, Elisa no (6) ___está___ en casa. Ella y su hermano (*her brother*) (7) ___están___ en la Biblioteca Cervantes.

**MARÍA TERESA** ¿Cervantes?

**SRA. LÓPEZ** Es la biblioteca que (8) ___está___ al lado del Café Bambú.

**MARÍA TERESA** ¡Ah, sí! Gracias, señora López.

**SRA. LÓPEZ** Hasta luego, María Teresa.

**5** **¿Qué te gusta?** Write a paragraph of at least five sentences stating what you like and don't like about your university. If possible, explain your likes and dislikes. 〔10 pts.〕 Answers will vary.

> *Me gusta la clase de música porque no hay muchos exámenes. No me gusta cenar en la cafetería...*

**6** **Canción** Write the missing words to complete the beginning of a popular song by Manu Chao. 〔2 EXTRA points!〕

**❝** Me ___gustan___ los aviones°,
me gustas tú,
me ___gusta___ viajar,
me gustas tú,
me gusta la mañana,
me gustas tú. **❞**

aviones *airplanes*

**4** **Expansion** Ask student pairs to write a brief phone conversation based on the one in **Actividad 4**. Have volunteers role-play their dialogues for the class.

**5** **Teaching Tips**
• Before writing their paragraphs, have students brainstorm a list of words or phrases related to universities.
• Remind students of when to use **gusta** versus **gustan**. Write a few example sentences on the board.
• Have students exchange papers with a partner to peer-edit each other's paragraphs.

**6** **Teaching Tip** Point out the form **gustas** in lines 2, 4, and 6, and ask students to guess the translation of the phrase **me gustas** (*I like you*, literally, *you are pleasing to me*). Tell students that **me gustas** and **le gustas** are not used as often as their English counterparts. Most often they are used in romantic situations.

**6** **Canción** **Manu Chao**, originally Oscar Tramor, was born in Paris to Spanish parents. In 1987, he founded the group **Mano Negra** and recorded five albums. After the break-up of the band, he recorded *Clandestino*, his first solo album. He calls himself a musical journalist, as most of his songs are about worldwide social and economic problems.

**TEACHING OPTIONS**

**Pairs** Write **más, menos, multiplicado por,** and **dividido por** on the board. Model a few simple problems using numbers 31 and higher. Ex: **Cien mil trescientos menos diez mil son noventa mil trescientos. Mil dividido por veinte son cincuenta.** Then ask students to write two math problems of each type for a class-mate to solve. Have partners verify each other's work.

**Extra Practice** Collect the paragraphs that students wrote and redistribute them. Ask students to write a profile of the person whose paper they received. For instance, if Kim wrote **No me gusta la clase de música**, the profile should read **Kim estudia música, pero no le gusta la clase**.

## Section Goals

In **Lectura**, students will:
• learn to use text formats to predict content
• read documents in Spanish

**Instructional Resources**
**Supersite**
*Cuaderno para hispanohablantes*

**Estrategia** Introduce the strategy. Point out that many documents have easily identifiable formats that can help readers predict content. Have students look at the document in the **Estrategia** box and ask them to name the recognizable elements:
• days of the week
• time
• classes
Ask what kind of document it is (a student's weekly schedule).

**Cognados** Have pairs of students scan **¡Español en Madrid!** and identify cognates and guess their meanings.

**Examinar el texto** Ask students what type of information is contained in **¡Español en Madrid!** (It is a brochure for a summer intensive Spanish language program.) Discuss elements of the recognizable format that helped them predict the content, such as headings, list of courses, and course schedule with dates.

# Lectura

NATIONAL STANDARDS communication cultures

## Antes de leer

### Estrategia

**Predicting Content Through Formats**

Recognizing the format of a document can help you to predict its content. For instance, invitations, greeting cards, and classified ads follow an easily identifiable format, which usually gives you a general idea of the information they contain. Look at the text and identify it based on its format.

|       | lunes    | martes   | miércoles | jueves   | viernes  |
|-------|----------|----------|-----------|----------|----------|
| 8:30  | biología |          | biología  |          | biología |
| 9:00  |          | historia |           | historia |          |
| 9:30  | inglés   |          | inglés    |          | inglés   |
| 10:00 |          |          |           |          |          |
| 10:30 |          |          |           |          |          |
| 11:00 |          |          |           |          |          |
| 12:00 |          |          |           |          |          |
| 12:30 |          |          |           |          |          |
| 1:00  |          |          |           |          |          |
| 2:00  | arte     |          | arte      |          | arte     |

If you guessed that this is a page from a student's schedule, you are correct. You can now infer that the document contains information about a student's weekly schedule, including days, times, and activities.

### Cognados

With a classmate, make a list of the cognates in the text and guess their English meanings. What do the cognates reveal about the content of the document?

### Examinar el texto

Look at the format of the document entitled **¡Español en Madrid!** What type of text is it? What information do you expect to find in a document of this kind?

# ¡ESPAÑOL EN MADRID!

UAM

**Programa de Cursos Intensivos de Español**

**Universidad Autónoma de Madrid**

*Madrid, la capital cultural de Europa, y la UAM te ofrecen cursos intensivos de verano° para aprender° español como nunca antes°.*

## Después de leer

**Correspondencias**

Provide the letter of each item in Column B that matches the words in Column A. Two items will not be used.

**A**
1. profesores  f
2. vivienda  h
3. Madrid  d
4. número de teléfono  a
5. Español 2B  c
6. número de fax  g

**B**
a. (34) 91 523 4500
b. (34) 91 524 0210
c. 23 junio–30 julio
d. capital cultural de Europa
e. 16 junio–22 julio
f. especializados en enseñar español como lengua extranjera
g. (34) 91 523 4623
h. familias españolas

**TEACHING OPTIONS**

**Extra Practice** For homework, ask students to write a weekly schedule (**horario semanal**) of a friend or family member. Ask them to label the days of the week in Spanish and add notes for that person's appointments and activities as well. In class, ask students questions about the schedules they wrote. Ex: ¿**Qué clase toma** _____ **hoy?** ¿**Trabaja** _____ **mañana?** ¿**Cuántos días trabaja** _____ **esta semana?**

**Heritage Speakers** Ask heritage speakers who have attended or know about a school in the Spanish-speaking world to describe their schedule there, comparing and contrasting it with their schedule now. Invite them to make other comparisons between American or Canadian institutions and those in the Spanish-speaking world.

## ¿Dónde?
En la Facultad de Filosofía y Letras de la UAM.

## ¿Quiénes son los profesores?
Son todos hablantes nativos del español y catedráticos° de la UAM especializados en enseñar el español como lengua extranjera.

## ¿Qué niveles se ofrecen?
Se ofrecen tres niveles° básicos:
1. Español Elemental, A, B y C
2. Español Intermedio, A y B
3. Español Avanzado, A y B

## Viviendas
Para estudiantes extranjeros se ofrece vivienda° con familias españolas.

## ¿Cuándo?
Este verano desde° el 16 de junio hasta el 10 de agosto. Los cursos tienen una duración de 6 semanas.

| Cursos | Empieza° | Termina |
|--------|----------|---------|
| Español 1A | 16 junio | 22 julio |
| Español 1B | 23 junio | 30 julio |
| Español 1C | 30 junio | 10 agosto |
| Español 2A | 16 junio | 22 julio |
| Español 2B | 23 junio | 30 julio |
| Español 3A | 16 junio | 22 julio |
| Español 3B | 23 junio | 30 julio |

### Información
Para mayor información, sirvan comunicarse con la siguiente° oficina:

**Universidad Autónoma de Madrid**
**Programa de Español como Lengua Extranjera**
Ctra. Colmenar Viejo, Km. 15
28049 Madrid, ESPAÑA
Tel. (34) 91 523 4500
Fax (34) 91 523 4623
www.uam.es

verano *summer* aprender *to learn* nunca antes *never before* catedráticos *professors* niveles *levels* vivienda *housing*
desde *from* Empieza *Begins* siguiente *following*

---

## ¿Cierto o falso?

Indicate whether each statement is **cierto** or **falso**. Then correct the false statements.

|  | Cierto | Falso |
|---|:---:|:---:|
| 1. La Universidad Autónoma de Madrid ofrece (*offers*) cursos intensivos de italiano. <br> Ofrece cursos intensivos de español. | ○ | ⊘ |
| 2. La lengua nativa de los profesores del programa es el inglés. <br> La lengua nativa de los profesores es el español. | ○ | ⊘ |
| 3. Los cursos de español son en la Facultad de Ciencias. <br> Son en el edificio de la Facultad de Filosofía y Letras. | ○ | ⊘ |
| 4. Los estudiantes pueden vivir (*can live*) con familias españolas. | ⊘ | ○ |

|  | Cierto | Falso |
|---|:---:|:---:|
| 5. La universidad que ofrece los cursos intensivos está en Salamanca. <br> Está en Madrid. | ○ | ⊘ |
| 6. Español 3B termina en agosto. <br> Termina en julio. | ○ | ⊘ |
| 7. Si deseas información sobre (*about*) los cursos intensivos de español, es posible llamar al (34) 91 523 4500. | ⊘ | ○ |
| 8. Español 1A empieza en julio. <br> Empieza en junio. | ○ | ⊘ |

**Correspondencias** Go over the answers as a class or assign pairs of students to work together to check each other's answers.

**¿Cierto o falso?** Give students these true-false statements as items 9–16: **9. El campus de la UAM está en la Ciudad de México. (Falso; está en Madrid.) 10. Los cursos terminan en junio. (Falso; terminan en julio y agosto.) 11. Hay un curso de español intermedio. (Falso; hay dos cursos.) 12. Los cursos se ofrecen en el verano. (Cierto) 13. Hay una residencia estudiantil para los estudiantes extranjeros en el campus. (Falso; hay vivienda con familias españolas para estudiantes extranjeros.) 14. Hay un número de teléfono en la universidad para más información. (Cierto) 15. Todos los profesores son hablantes nativos. (Cierto) 16. Los cursos tienen una duración de doce semanas. (Falso; tienen una duración de seis semanas.)**

---

### TEACHING OPTIONS

**Language Notes** Explain that in Spanish dates are usually written in the order of day/month/year rather than month/day/year, as they are in the United States and Canada. Someone from Mexico with a birthdate of July 5, 1986, would write his or her birthdate as 5/7/86. To avoid confusion, the month is often written with a roman numeral, 5/VII/86.

**Pairs** Provide pairs of students with Spanish-language magazines and newspapers. Ask them to look for documents with easily recognizable formats, such as classified ads or advertisements. Ask them to use cognates and other context clues to predict the content. Then have partners present their examples and findings to the class.

## Section Goal

In **Panorama**, students will read about the geography, culture, and economy of Spain.

**Instructional Resources**
**Supersite/DVD:** *Panorama cultural*
**Supersite/IRCD:** *PowerPoints* (Overheads #7, #8, #15); *IRM* (*Panorama cultural* Videoscript & Translation, WBs/VM/LM Answer Key)
**WebSAM**
**Workbook**, pp. 21–22
**Video Manual**, pp. 227–228

**Teaching Tip** Show *Overhead PowerPoint #15* or have students use the map in their books to find the places mentioned. Explain that the Canary Islands are located in the Atlantic Ocean, off the northwestern coast of Africa. Point out the photos that accompany the map on this page.

**El país en cifras** After students have read **Idiomas**, associate the regional languages with the larger map by asking questions such as: **¿Hablan catalán en Barcelona? ¿Qué idioma hablan en Madrid?** Point out that the names of languages may be capitalized as map labels, but are not capitalized when they appear in running text.

**¡Increíble pero cierto!** In addition to festivals related to economic and agricultural resources, Spain has many festivals rooted in Catholic tradition. Among the most famous is **Semana Santa** (*Holy Week*) which is celebrated annually in Seville, and many other towns and cities, with great reverence and pageantry.

# España

## El país en cifras

► **Área:** 504.750 km² (kilómetros cuadrados) ó 194.884 millas cuadradas°, incluyendo las islas Baleares y las islas Canarias
► **Población:** 43.993.000
► **Capital:** Madrid—5.977.000
► **Ciudades° principales:** Barcelona—4.998.000, Valencia—806.000, Sevilla, Zaragoza
SOURCE: Population Division, UN Secretariat
► **Moneda°:** euro
► **Idiomas°:** español o castellano, catalán, gallego, valenciano, euskara

Gallego · Euskara · Catalán · Español · Valenciano

**Regiones lingüísticas**

Bandera de España

## Españoles célebres

► **Miguel de Cervantes,** escritor° (1547–1616)
► **Pedro Almodóvar,** director de cine° (1949– )
► **Rosa Montero,** escritora y periodista° (1951– )
► **Fernando Alonso,** corredor de autos° (1981– )
► **Paz Vega,** actriz° (1976– )

millas cuadradas *square miles* Ciudades *Cities* Moneda *Currency* Idiomas *Languages* escritor *writer* cine *film* periodista *reporter* corredor de autos *racing driver* actriz *actress* pueblo *town* Cada año *Every year* Durante todo un día *All day long* se tiran *throw at each other* varias toneladas *many tons*

La Sagrada Familia en Barcelona

Plaza Mayor en Madrid

**FRANCIA**

Mar Cantábrico
La Coruña
San Sebastián
**ANDORRA**
Salamanca
Zaragoza **Pirineos** Río Ebro
**PORTUGAL**
Barcelona
**ESPAÑA**
Menorca
★ **Madrid** Valencia
Mallorca
Ibiza
**Islas Baleares**
Sierra Nevada
Sevilla
Mar Mediterráneo
Estrecho de Gibraltar
Ceuta
Melilla
**MARRUECOS**

El baile flamenco

**Islas Canarias**
La Palma
Tenerife Gran Canaria
Lanzarote
Gomera
Fuerteventura
Hierro

**recursos**
WB pp. 21–22 | VM pp. 227–228 | panorama.vhlcentral.com Lección 2

## ¡Increíble pero cierto!

En Buñol, un pueblo° de Valencia, la producción de tomates es un recurso económico muy importante. Cada año° se celebra el festival de *La Tomatina*. Durante todo un día°, miles de personas se tiran° tomates. Llegan turistas de todo el país, y se usan varias toneladas° de tomates.

**TEACHING OPTIONS**

**Heritage Speakers Paella,** the national dish of Spain, is the ancestor of the popular Latin American dish **arroz con pollo**. Ask heritage speakers if they know of any dishes traditional in their families that have their roots in Spanish cuisine. Invite them to describe the dish to the class.

**Variación léxica** Tell students that they may also see the word **euskara** spelled **euskera** and **eusquera**. The letter **k** is used in Spanish only in words of foreign origin. **Euskera** is the Basque name of the Basque language, which linguists believe is unrelated to any other known language. The spelling students see on this page (**eusquera**) follows the principles of Spanish orthography. The Spanish name for *Basque* is **vascuence** or **vasco**.

## Lugares • La Universidad de Salamanca

La Universidad de Salamanca, fundada en 1218, es la más antigua° de España. Más de 35.000 estudiantes toman clases en la universidad. La universidad está en la ciudad de Salamanca, famosa por sus edificios° históricos, tales como° los puentes° romanos y las catedrales góticas.

## Economía • La Unión Europea

Desde° 1992 España es miembro de la Unión Europea, un grupo de países europeos que trabaja para desarrollar° una política° económica y social común en Europa. La moneda de la mayoría de los países de la Unión Europea es el euro.

*Las meninas,*
Diego Velázquez, 1656

## Artes • Velázquez y el Prado

El Prado, en Madrid, es uno de los museos más famosos del mundo°. En el Prado hay pinturas° importantes de Botticelli, de El Greco, y de los españoles Goya y Velázquez. *Las meninas* es la obra° más conocida° de Diego Velázquez, pintor° oficial de la corte real° durante el siglo° XVII.

## Comida • La paella

La paella es uno de los platos más típicos de España. Siempre se prepara° con arroz° y azafrán°, pero hay diferentes recetas°. La paella valenciana, por ejemplo, es de pollo° y conejo°, y la paella marinera es de mariscos°.

Una playa de Ibiza

**¿Qué aprendiste?** Completa las oraciones con la información adecuada.

1. La <u>Unión Europea</u> trabaja para desarrollar una política económica común en Europa.
2. El arroz y el azafrán son ingredientes básicos de la <u>paella</u>.
3. El Prado está en <u>Madrid</u>.
4. La universidad más antigua de España es la <u>Universidad de Salamanca</u>.
5. La ciudad de <u>Salamanca</u> es famosa por sus edificios históricos, tales como los puentes romanos.
6. El gallego es una de las lenguas oficiales de <u>España</u>.

**Conexión Internet** Investiga estos temas en **vistas.vhlcentral.com.**

1. Busca (*Look for*) información sobre la Universidad de Salamanca u otra universidad española. ¿Qué cursos ofrece (*does it offer*)? ¿Ofrece tu universidad cursos similares?
2. Busca información sobre un español o una española célebre (por ejemplo, un(a) político/a, un actor, una actriz, un(a) artista). ¿De qué parte de España es, y por qué es célebre?

más antigua *oldest* edificios *buildings* tales como *such as* puentes *bridges* Desde *Since* desarrollar *develop* política *policy* mundo *world* pinturas *paintings* obra *work* más conocida *best-known* pintor *painter* corte real *royal court* siglo *century* Siempre se prepara *It is always prepared* arroz *rice* azafrán *saffron* recetas *recipes* pollo *chicken* conejo *rabbit* mariscos *seafood*

**La Universidad de Salamanca** The University of Salamanca hosts many programs for foreign students, and your campus foreign-study office may have brochures. One of the oldest universities in Europe, Salamanca is famous for its medieval buildings and student musical societies, called **tunas**.

**La Unión Europea** Have students use the Internet, a newspaper, or a bank to learn the current exchange rate for euros on the international market.

**Velázquez y el Prado** Point out **la infanta Margarita**, the royal princess, with her attendants. The name **Las meninas** comes from the Portuguese word for "girls" used to refer to royal attendants. Reflected in the mirror are **Margarita's** parents, **los reyes Felipe IV y Mariana de Asturias**. Have students find **Velázquez** himself, standing paintbrush in hand, before an enormous canvas. You may wish to ask students to research the identity of the man in the doorway.

**La paella** Pairs can role-play a restaurant scene: the customer asks the waiter/waitress about the ingredients in the paella, then chooses **paella valenciana** or **paella marinera**.

**Conexión Internet** Students will find supporting Internet activities and links at **panorama.vhlcentral.com**.

**Teaching Tip** You may want to wrap up this section by playing the *Panorama cultural* video footage for this lesson.

**TEACHING OPTIONS**

**Variación léxica** Regional cultures and languages have remained strong in Spain, despite efforts made in the past to suppress them in the name of national unity. The language that has come to be called *Spanish*, **español**, is the language of the region of north central Spain called **Castilla**. Because Spain was unified under the Kingdom of Castile at the end of the Middle Ages, the language of Castile, **castellano**, became the principal language of government, business, and literature. Even today one is likely to hear Spanish speakers refer to Spanish as **castellano** or **español**. Efforts to suppress the regional languages, though often harsh, were ineffective, and after the death of the dictator **Francisco Franco** and the return of power to regional governing bodies, the regional languages of Spain were given co-official status.

**Instructional Resources**
**Supersite:** Textbook &
Vocabulary MP3 Audio Files
**Lección 2**
**Supersite/IRCD:** *IRM* (WBs/
VM/LM Answer Key); *Testing
Program* (**Lección 2 Pruebas**,
Test Generator, Testing
Program MP3 Audio Files)
**WebSAM**
Lab Manual, p. 12

## La clase y la universidad

| | |
|---|---|
| el/la compañero/a de clase | classmate |
| el/la compañero/a de cuarto | roommate |
| el/la estudiante | student |
| el/la profesor(a) | teacher |
| el borrador | eraser |
| el escritorio | desk |
| el libro | book |
| el mapa | map |
| la mesa | table |
| la mochila | backpack |
| el papel | paper |
| la papelera | wastebasket |
| la pizarra | blackboard |
| la pluma | pen |
| la puerta | door |
| el reloj | clock; watch |
| la silla | seat |
| la tiza | chalk |
| la ventana | window |
| la biblioteca | library |
| la cafetería | cafeteria |
| la casa | house; home |
| el estadio | stadium |
| el laboratorio | laboratory |
| la librería | bookstore |
| la residencia estudiantil | dormitory |
| la universidad | university; college |
| la clase | class |
| el curso, la materia | course |
| la especialización | major |
| el examen | test; exam |
| el horario | schedule |
| la prueba | test; quiz |
| el semestre | semester |
| la tarea | homework |
| el trimestre | trimester; quarter |

## Las materias

| | |
|---|---|
| la administración de empresas | business administration |
| el arte | art |
| la biología | biology |
| las ciencias | sciences |
| la computación | computer science |
| la contabilidad | accounting |
| la economía | economics |
| el español | Spanish |
| la física | physics |
| la geografía | geography |
| la historia | history |
| las humanidades | humanities |
| el inglés | English |
| las lenguas extranjeras | foreign languages |
| la literatura | literature |
| las matemáticas | mathematics |
| la música | music |
| el periodismo | journalism |
| la psicología | psychology |
| la química | chemistry |
| la sociología | sociology |

## Preposiciones

| | |
|---|---|
| al lado de | next to; beside |
| a la derecha de | to the right of |
| a la izquierda de | to the left of |
| en | in; on |
| cerca de | near |
| con | with |
| debajo de | below; under |
| delante de | in front of |
| detrás de | behind |
| encima de | on top of |
| entre | between; among |
| lejos de | far from |
| sin | without |
| sobre | on; over |

## Palabras adicionales

| | |
|---|---|
| ¿Adónde? | Where (to)? |
| ahora | now |
| ¿Cuál?, ¿Cuáles? | Which?; Which one(s)? |
| ¿Por qué? | Why? |
| porque | because |

## Verbos

| | |
|---|---|
| bailar | to dance |
| buscar | to look for |
| caminar | to walk |
| cantar | to sing |
| cenar | to have dinner |
| comprar | to buy |
| contestar | to answer |
| conversar | to converse, to chat |
| desayunar | to have breakfast |
| descansar | to rest |
| desear | to wish; to desire |
| dibujar | to draw |
| enseñar | to teach |
| escuchar la radio/ música | to listen (to) the radio/music |
| esperar (+ *inf.*) | to wait (for); to hope |
| estar | to be |
| estudiar | to study |
| explicar | to explain |
| gustar | to like |
| hablar | to talk; to speak |
| llegar | to arrive |
| llevar | to carry |
| mirar | to look (at); to watch |
| necesitar (+ *inf.*) | to need |
| practicar | to practice |
| preguntar | to ask (a question) |
| preparar | to prepare |
| regresar | to return |
| terminar | to end; to finish |
| tomar | to take; to drink |
| trabajar | to work |
| viajar | to travel |

## Los días de la semana

| | |
|---|---|
| ¿Cuándo? | When? |
| ¿Qué día es hoy? | What day is it? |
| Hoy es… | Today is… |
| la semana | week |
| lunes | Monday |
| martes | Tuesday |
| miércoles | Wednesday |
| jueves | Thursday |
| viernes | Friday |
| sábado | Saturday |
| domingo | Sunday |

| | |
|---|---|
| **Numbers 31 and higher** | See pages 59–60. |
| **Expresiones útiles** | See page 41. |

| | |
|---|---|
| **recursos** | |
| LM p. 12 | panorama.vhlcentral.com Lección 2 |

# La familia

## 3

### Communicative Goals

**You will learn how to:**
- Talk about your family and friends
- Describe people and things
- Express ownership

### Lesson Goals

In **Lección 3**, students will be introduced to the following:
- terms for family relationships
- names of various professions
- surnames and families in the Spanish-speaking world
- Spain's Royal Family
- descriptive adjectives
- possessive adjectives
- the present tense of common regular –er and –ir verbs
- the present tense of **tener** and **venir**
- context clues to unlock meaning of unfamiliar words
- using idea maps when writing
- how to write a friendly letter
- strategies for asking clarification in oral communication
- a television commercial for **Pentel**
- Ecuadorian singer **Olimpo Cárdenas**
- geographical and cultural information about Ecuador

**A primera vista** Here are some additional questions you can ask based on the photo: **¿Cuántas personas hay en tu familia? ¿De qué conversas con ellos? ¿Estudias lejos o cerca de la casa de tu familia? ¿Viajas mucho con ellos?**

---

### A PRIMERA VISTA
- ¿Hay cuatro personas en la foto?
- ¿Hay una mujer a la izquierda? ¿Y a la derecha?
- ¿Está el hombre al lado de la mujer?
- ¿Conversan ellos? ¿Trabajan? ¿Viajan? ¿Caminan?

---

**INSTRUCTIONAL RESOURCES**

**MAESTRO™ SUPERSITE (panorama.vhlcentral.com)**
Textbook, Vocabulary, & Lab MP3 Audio Files
Additional Practice
Learning Management System (Assignment Task Manager, Gradebook)
*Also on DVD*
  *Fotonovela*

*Flash cultura*
**Panorama cultural**
*Also on Instructor's Resource CD-ROM*
  *PowerPoints* (**Contextos** & **Estructura** Presentations, Overheads)
  *Instructor's Resource Manual* (Handouts, Textbook Answer Key, WBs/VM/LM Answer Key, Audioscripts,

Videoscripts & Translations)
  *Testing Program* (**Pruebas**, Test Generator, MP3s)
**Vista Higher Learning** *Cancionero*
**WebSAM** (Workbook/Video Manual/Lab Manual)
**Workbook/Video Manual**
*Cuaderno para hispanohablantes*
**Lab Manual**

## Section Goals

In **Contextos**, students will learn and practice:
- terms for family relationships
- names of professions

**Instructional Resources**
**Supersite:** Textbook, Vocabulary, & Lab MP3 Audio Files
**Lección 3**
**Supersite/IRCD:** *PowerPoints* (Lección 3 Contextos Presentation, Overheads #16, #17); *IRM* (**Vocabulario adicional,** Textbook Audio Script, Lab Audio Script, WBs/VM/LM Answer Key)
**WebSAM**
**Workbook,** pp. 23–24
**Lab Manual,** p. 13
*Cuaderno para hispanohablantes*

## Teaching Tips

- Point out the meanings of plural family terms and explain that the masculine plural forms can refer to mixed groups of males and females:
  **los hermanos** *brothers; siblings; brothers and sisters*
  **los primos** *male cousins; male and female cousins*
  **los sobrinos** *nephews; nieces and nephews*
  **los tíos** *uncles; aunts and uncles*
- Introduce active lesson vocabulary. Ask: **¿Cómo se llama tu hermano?** Ask another student: **¿Cómo se llama el hermano de ____?** Work your way through various family relationships.
- Show *Overhead PowerPoint #16.* Point out that the family tree is drawn from the point of view of **José Miguel Pérez Santoro.** Have students refer to the family tree to answer your questions about it. Ex: **¿Cómo se llama la madre de Víctor?**
- If students request vocabulary on pets, use *Vocabulario adicional: Más vocabulario para hablar de la familia,* from the Supersite/IRCD.

# La familia

## La familia de José Miguel Pérez Santoro

### Más vocabulario

| | |
|---|---|
| los abuelos | *grandparents* |
| el/la bisabuelo/a | *great-grandfather/great-grandmother* |
| el/la gemelo/a | *twin* |
| el/la hermanastro/a | *stepbrother/stepsister* |
| el/la hijastro/a | *stepson/stepdaughter* |
| la madrastra | *stepmother* |
| el medio hermano/ la media hermana | *half-brother/ half-sister* |
| el padrastro | *stepfather* |
| los padres | *parents* |
| los parientes | *relatives* |
| el/la cuñado/a | *brother-in-law/ sister-in-law* |
| la nuera | *daughter-in-law* |
| el/la suegro/a | *father-in-law/ mother-in-law* |
| el yerno | *son-in-law* |
| el/la amigo/a | *friend* |
| el apellido | *last name* |
| la gente | *people* |
| el/la muchacho/a | *boy/girl* |
| el/la niño/a | *child* |
| el/la novio/a | *boyfriend/girlfriend* |
| la persona | *person* |
| el/la artista | *artist* |
| el/la ingeniero/a | *engineer* |
| el/la doctor(a), el/la médico/a | *doctor; physician* |
| el/la periodista | *journalist* |
| el/la programador(a) | *computer programmer* |

### Variación léxica

madre ⟷ mamá, mami *(colloquial)*
padre ⟷ papá, papi *(colloquial)*
muchacho/a ⟷ chico/a

**recursos**

| | | |
|---|---|---|
| WB pp. 23–24 | LM p. 13 | panorama.vhlcentral.com Lección 3 |

**Juan Santoro Sánchez**

**mi abuelo** (*my grandfather*)

**Ernesto Santoro González**

**mi tío** (*uncle*)
hijo (*son*) **de Juan y Socorro**

**Marína Gutiérrez de Santoro**

**mi tía** (*aunt*)
esposa (*wife*) **de Ernesto**

**Silvia Socorro Santoro Gutiérrez**

**mi prima** (*cousin*)
hija (*daughter*) **de Ernesto y Marina**

**Héctor Manuel Santoro Gutiérrez**

**mi primo** (*cousin*)
nieto (*grandson*) **de Juan y Socorro**

**Carmen Santoro Gutiérrez**

**mi prima**
hija de Ernesto y Marina

### ¡LENGUA VIVA!

In Spanish-speaking countries, it is common for people to go by both first name and middle name, such as **José Miguel.** You will learn more about names and naming conventions on p. 78.

**TEACHING OPTIONS**

**Extra Practice** Draw your own family tree on a transparency or the board and label it with names. Ask students questions about it. Ex: **¿Es ____ mi tío o mi abuelo? ¿Cómo se llama mi madre? ____ es el primo de ____, ¿verdad? ¿____ es el sobrino o el hermano de ____? ¿Quién es el cuñado de ____?** Help students identify the relationships between members. Encourage them to ask you questions.

**Heritage speakers** Ask heritage speakers to tell the class any other terms they use to refer to members of their families. These may include terms of endearment. Ask them to tell where these terms are used. Possible responses: **nene/a, guagua, m'hijo/a, chamaco/a, chaval(a), cuñis, tata, viejo/a, cielo, cariño, corazón.**

Socorro González de Santoro

**mi abuela** (*my grandmother*)

Mirta Santoro de Pérez

Rubén Ernesto Pérez Gómez

**mi madre** (*mother*)
hija de Juan y Socorro

**mi padre** (*father*)
esposo de mi madre

José Miguel Pérez Santoro

Beatriz Alicia Pérez de Morales

Felipe Morales Zapata

hijo de Rubén y de Mirta

**mi hermana** (*sister*)

**esposo** (*husband*) de Beatriz Alicia

Víctor Miguel Morales Pérez

Anita Morales Pérez

**mi sobrino** (*nephew*)
hermano (*brother*) de Anita

**mi sobrina** (*niece*)
nieta (*granddaughter*) de mis padres

**los hijos** (*children*) de Beatriz Alicia y de Felipe

# Práctica  SUPERSITE

## 1 Escuchar
Listen to each statement made by José Miguel Pérez Santoro, then indicate whether it is **cierto** or **falso**, based on his family tree.

| | Cierto | Falso | | Cierto | Falso |
|---|---|---|---|---|---|
| 1. | ⊘ | ○ | 6. | ⊘ | ○ |
| 2. | ⊘ | ○ | 7. | ⊘ | ○ |
| 3. | ○ | ⊘ | 8. | ○ | ⊘ |
| 4. | ⊘ | ○ | 9. | ○ | ⊘ |
| 5. | ○ | ⊘ | 10. | ⊘ | ○ |

## 2 Personas
Indicate each word that you hear mentioned in the narration.

1. _____ cuñado
2. ✔ tía
3. ✔ periodista
4. ✔ niño
5. ✔ esposo
6. ✔ abuelos
7. _____ ingeniera
8. ✔ primo

## 3 Emparejar
Provide the letter of the phrase that matches each description. Two items will not be used.

1. Mi hermano programa las computadoras. c
2. Son los padres de mi esposo. e
3. Son los hijos de mis (*my*) tíos. h
4. Mi tía trabaja en un hospital. a
5. Es el hijo de mi madrastra y el hijastro de mi padre. b
6. Es el esposo de mi hija. l
7. Es el hijo de mi hermana. k
8. Mi primo dibuja y pinta mucho. i
9. Mi hermanastra enseña en la universidad. j
10. Mi padre trabaja con planos (*blueprints*). d

a. Es médica.
b. Es mi hermanastro.
c. Es programador.
d. Es ingeniero.
e. Son mis suegros.
f. Es mi novio.
g. Es mi padrastro.
h. Son mis primos.
i. Es artista.
j. Es profesora.
k. Es mi sobrino.
l. Es mi yerno.

## 4 Definiciones
Define these family terms in Spanish.

*modelo*
hijastro  Es el hijo de mi esposo/a, pero no es mi hijo.

1. abuela
2. bisabuelo
3. tío
4. parientes
5. suegra
6. cuñado
7. nietos
8. medio hermano

1. la madre de mi madre/padre
2. el abuelo de mi madre/padre
3. el hermano de mi madre/padre
4. la familia extendida
5. la madre de mi esposo/a
6. el esposo de mi hermana
7. los hijos de mis hijos
8. el hijo de mi padre pero no de mi madre

**1 Teaching Tip** To challenge students, have them correct the false statements by referring to the family tree.

**1 Script** 1. Beatriz Alicia es mi hermana. 2. Rubén es el abuelo de Víctor Miguel. 3. Silvia es mi sobrina. 4. Mirta y Rubén son los tíos de Héctor Manuel. 5. Anita es mi prima. 6. Ernesto es el hermano de mi madre. 7. Soy el tío de Anita. 8. Víctor Miguel es mi nieto. 9. Carmen, Beatriz Alicia y Marina son los nietos de Juan y Socorro. 10. El hijo de Juan y Socorro es el tío de Beatriz Alicia.
*Textbook MP3s*

**2 Teaching Tips**
• To simplify, read through the list as a class before playing the audio. Remind students to focus only on these words as they listen.
• Tell students that the words, if they appear in the narration, will not follow the sequence in the list.

**2 Script** Julia y Daniel son mis abuelos. Ellos viven en Montreal con mi tía Leti, que es periodista, y con mi primo César. César es un niño muy bueno y dibuja muy bien. Hoy voy a hablar por teléfono con todos ellos y con el esposo de Leti. Él es de Canadá.
*Textbook MP3s*

**3 Expansion** After students finish, ask volunteers to provide complete sentences combining elements from the numbered and lettered lists. Ex: **Los padres de mi esposo son mis suegros. Mis primos son los hijos de mis tíos.**

**4 Expansion** Have student pairs write five additional definitions following the pattern of those in the activity.

**5 Teaching Tip** To challenge students, ask them to provide other possible responses for items 2, 3, 4, 5, and 6.
Ex: **2. esposos 3. doctor 4. tío/ sobrino, hijastro/padrastro 5. niños, muchachos, amigos, primos, chicos, hermanastros, medios hermanos 6. bisabuelo, tío, padre, cuñado, padrastro**

**5 Expansion**
• Ask the class questions about the photos and captions in the textbook.
Ex: **¿Quién es artista? (Elena Vargas Soto es artista.) ¿Trabaja Irene? (Sí, es programadora.)**
• Bring to class family-related photos. Prepare a fill-in-the-blank sentence for each. Talk about the photos, and ask volunteers to complete the sentences.

**5**

**Escoger** Complete the description of each photo using words you have learned in **Contextos**. Some answers will vary.

1. La ___familia___ de Sara es muy grande.

2. Héctor y Lupita son ___novios___.

3. Alberto Díaz es ___médico___.

4. Rubén camina con su ___hijo/padre___.

5. Los dos ___hermanos___ están en el parque.

6. Don Manuel es el ___abuelo___ de Martín.

7. Elena Vargas Soto es ___artista___.

8. Irene es ___programadora___.

---

**TEACHING OPTIONS**

**Extra Practice** Add an additional visual aspect to this vocabulary practice. Ask students to bring in a family-related photo of their own or a photo from the Internet or a magazine. Have them write a fill-in-the-blank sentence to go with it. Working in pairs, have them guess what is happening in each other's photo and complete the sentence.

**Pairs** Have pairs of students create an additional sentence for each of the photos on this page. Ask one student to write sentences for the first four photos and the other student to write sentences for the remainder. Then have them exchange papers and check each other's work.

# Comunicación

**6** **Una familia** With a classmate, identify the members in the family tree by asking questions about how each family member is related to Graciela Vargas García.

> **modelo**
> **Estudiante 1:** ¿Quién es Beatriz Pardo de Vargas?
> **Estudiante 2:** Es la abuela de Graciela.

**CONSULTA**
To see the cities where these family members live, look at the map in **Panorama** on p. 104.

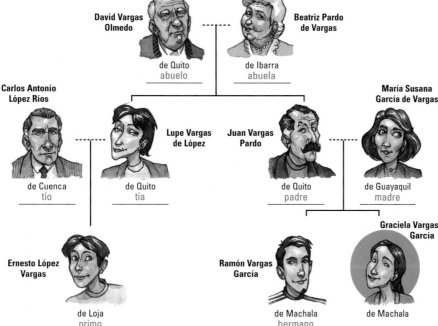

David Vargas Olmedo
de Quito
abuelo

Beatriz Pardo de Vargas
de Ibarra
abuela

Carlos Antonio López Ríos
de Cuenca
tío

Lupe Vargas de López
de Quito
tía

Juan Vargas Pardo
de Quito
padre

María Susana García de Vargas
de Guayaquil
madre

Ernesto López Vargas
de Loja
primo

Ramón Vargas García
de Machala
hermano

Graciela Vargas García
de Machala

Now take turns asking each other these questions. Then invent three original questions.

1. ¿Cómo se llama el primo de Graciela? Se llama Ernesto López Vargas.
2. ¿Cómo se llama la hija de David y de Beatriz? Se llama Lupe Vargas de López.
3. ¿De dónde es María Susana? Es de Guayaquil.
4. ¿De dónde son Ramón y Graciela? Son de Machala.
5. ¿Cómo se llama el yerno de David y de Beatriz? Se llama Carlos Antonio López Ríos.
6. ¿De dónde es Carlos Antonio? Es de Cuenca.
7. ¿De dónde es Ernesto? Es de Loja.
8. ¿Cuáles son los apellidos del sobrino de Lupe? Son Vargas García.

**7** **Preguntas personales** With a classmate, take turns asking each other these questions.
Answers will vary.
1. ¿Cuántas personas hay en tu familia?
2. ¿Cómo se llaman tus padres? ¿De dónde son? ¿Dónde trabajan?
3. ¿Cuántos hermanos tienes? ¿Cómo se llaman? ¿Dónde estudian o trabajan?
4. ¿Cuántos primos tienes? ¿Cuáles son los apellidos de ellos? ¿Cuántos son niños y cuántos son adultos? ¿Hay más chicos o más chicas en tu familia?
5. ¿Eres tío/a? ¿Cómo se llaman tus sobrinos/as? ¿Dónde estudian o trabajan?
6. ¿Quién es tu pariente favorito?
7. ¿Tienes novio/a? ¿Tienes esposo/a? ¿Cómo se llama?

**AYUDA**
**tu** *your* (sing.)
**tus** *your* (plural)
**mi** *my* (sing.)
**mis** *my* (plural)
**tienes** *you have*
**tengo** *I have*

---

**6** **Teaching Tip** Show *Overhead PowerPoint #17* to do this activity.

**6** **Expansion** Model the pronunciation of the Ecuadorian cities mentioned. Ask students to locate each on the map of Ecuador, page 104. Ask students to talk about each city based on the map. Ex: **Guayaquil y Machala son ciudades de la costa del Pacífico. Quito, Loja y Cuenca son ciudades de la cordillera de los Andes. Quito es la capital del Ecuador.**

**7** **Expansion**
- Emphasize that, for this activity and throughout the lesson, if students do not feel comfortable talking about their own families, they may refer to fictional family members or a family that they know.
- After modeling the activity with the whole class, have students circulate around the classroom asking their classmates these questions.
- Have pairs of students ask each other these questions, writing down the answers. After they have finished, ask students questions about their partner's answers. Ex: **¿Cuántas personas hay en la familia de _____? ¿Cómo se llaman los padres de _____? ¿De dónde son ellos? ¿Cuántos hermanos tiene _____?**

---

**TEACHING OPTIONS**

**Extra Practice** For homework, ask students to draw their own family tree or that of a fictional family. Have them label each position on the tree with the appropriate family term and the name of their family member. In class, ask students questions about their families. Ex: **¿Cómo se llama tu prima? ¿Cómo es ella? ¿Ella es estudiante? ¿Cómo se llama tu madre? ¿Quién es tu cuñado?**

**TPR** Start a family tree by calling on one student to stand in front of the class. Then indicate another student, telling them: **_____, eres el esposo/a de** (*first student*); the two should link arms. Complete the family tree by calling on students and stating their relationships. Students have five seconds to come to the front of the class and stand or kneel in the appropriate spot in the family tree.

# ¿Es grande tu familia?

Los chicos hablan de sus familias en el autobús.

**PERSONAJES**

**MAITE**

**INÉS**

**DON FRANCISCO**

**ÁLEX**

**JAVIER**

**1**

**MAITE** Inés, ¿tienes una familia grande?
**INÉS** Pues, sí... mis papás, mis abuelos, cuatro hermanas y muchos tíos y primos.

**2**

**INÉS** Sólo tengo un hermano mayor, Pablo. Su esposa, Francesca, es médica. No es ecuatoriana, es italiana. Sus papás viven en Roma, creo. Vienen de visita cada año. Ah... y Pablo es periodista.
**MAITE** ¡Qué interesante!

**3**

**INÉS** ¿Y tú, Javier? ¿Tienes hermanos?
**JAVIER** No, pero aquí tengo unas fotos de mi familia.
**INÉS** ¡Ah! ¡Qué bien! ¡A ver!

**6**

**INÉS** ¿Y cómo es él?
**JAVIER** Es muy simpático. Él es viejo pero es un hombre muy trabajador.

**7**

**MAITE** Oye, Javier, ¿qué dibujas?
**JAVIER** ¿Eh? ¿Quién? ¿Yo? ¡Nada!
**MAITE** ¡Venga! ¡No seas tonto!

**8**

**MAITE** Jaaavieeer... Oye, pero ¡qué bien dibujas!
**JAVIER** Este... pues... ¡Sí! ¡Gracias!

**recursos**

| VM pp. 199–200 | panorama.vhlcentral.com Lección 3 |

---

**TEACHING OPTIONS**

**Video Tips** General suggestions for using video clips in the classroom can be found on page IAE-12 of this Instructor's Annotated Edition.
**¿Es grande tu familia?** Before viewing the **¿Es grande tu familia?** segment of the *Fotonovela*, ask students to brainstorm a list of things that they think might happen in an episode in which the characters find out about each other's families. Then play the segment once without sound and have the class create a plot summary based on visual clues. Afterward, show the segment with sound and have the class correct any mistaken guesses and fill in any gaps in the plot summary they created.

Teaching Tip Ask students to read the **Fotonovela** captions in groups of five. Then ask one or two groups to role-play the conversation for the class.

Expresiones útiles Draw attention to the masculine, feminine, singular, and plural forms of descriptive adjectives and the present tense of **tener** in the video-still captions, **Expresiones útiles**, and as they occur in your conversation with the students. Point out that this material will be formally presented in **Estructura**. Correct students when they ask for correction, but do not expect them to be able to produce the forms correctly at this time.

**JAVIER** ¡Aquí están!

**INÉS** ¡Qué alto es tu papá! Y tu mamá, ¡qué bonita!

**JAVIER** Mira, aquí estoy yo. Y éste es mi abuelo. Es el padre de mi mamá.

**INÉS** ¿Cuántos años tiene tu abuelo?

**JAVIER** Noventa y dos.

**MAITE** Álex, mira, ¿te gusta?

**ÁLEX** Sí, mucho. ¡Es muy bonito!

**DON FRANCISCO** Epa, ¿qué pasa con Inés y Javier?

## Expresiones útiles

### Talking about your family

- **¿Tienes una familia grande?**
  *Do you have a large family?*
  **Sí... mis papás, mis abuelos, cuatro hermanas y muchos tíos.**
  *Yes... my parents, my grandparents, four sisters, and many (aunts and) uncles.*
  **Sólo tengo un hermano mayor/ menor.**
  *I only have one older/younger brother.*

- **¿Tienes hermanos?**
  *Do you have siblings (brothers or sisters)?*
  **No, soy hijo único.**
  *No, I'm an only (male) child.*

- **Su esposa, Francesca, es médica.**
  *His wife, Francesca, is a doctor.*
  **No es ecuatoriana, es italiana.**
  *She's not Ecuadorian; she's Italian.*
  **Pablo es periodista.**
  *Pablo is a journalist.*
  **Es el padre de mi mamá.**
  *He is my mother's father.*

### Describing people

- **¡Qué alto es tu papá!**
  *How tall your father is!*
- **Y tu mamá, ¡qué bonita!**
  *And your mother, how pretty!*

- **¿Cómo es tu abuelo?**
  *What is your grandfather like?*
  **Es simpático.**
  *He's nice.*
  **Es viejo.**
  *He's old.*
  **Es un hombre muy trabajador.**
  *He's a very hard-working man.*

### Saying how old people are

- **¿Cuántos años tienes?**
  *How old are you?*
- **¿Cuántos años tiene tu abuelo?**
  *How old is your grandfather?*
  **Noventa y dos.**
  *Ninety-two.*

# ¿Qué pasó?

**1 Expansion** Give these true-false statements to the class as items 7–10: **7. El padre de Javier es alto. (Cierto.) 8. Javier tiene tres hermanos. (Falso. Javier no tiene hermanos.) 9. Javier tiene unas fotos de su familia. (Cierto.) 10. Inés es italiana. (Falso. Inés es del Ecuador.)**

**2 Expansion** **Álex** is the only student not associated with a statement. Ask the class to look at the **Fotonovela** captions and **Expresiones útiles** on pages 74–75 and invent a statement for him. Remind students not to use his exact words. Ex: **¡Qué bonito! ¡Me gusta mucho!**

**3 Expansion** Have pairs who wrote about the same family exchange papers and compare their descriptions. Ask them to share the differences with the class.

**4 Teaching Tip** Model the activity for students by providing answers based on your own family.

**4 Expansion** Ask volunteers to share their partner's answers with the class.

**1** **¿Cierto o falso?** Indicate whether each sentence is **cierto** or **falso**. Correct the false statements.

| | Cierto | Falso |
|---|---|---|
| 1. Inés tiene una familia grande. | ☑ | ○ |
| 2. El hermano de Inés es médico. | ○ | ☑ Es periodista. |
| 3. Francesca es de Italia. | ☑ | ○ |
| 4. Javier tiene cuatro hermanos. | ○ | ☑ Javier no tiene hermanos. |
| 5. El abuelo de Javier tiene ochenta años. | ○ | ☑ Tiene noventa y dos años. |
| 6. Javier habla del padre de su (*his*) padre. | ○ | ☑ Javier habla del padre de su madre. |

**2** **Identificar** Indicate which person would make each statement. The names may be used more than once. **¡Ojo!** One name will not be used.

**ÁLEX** **JAVIER**
**INÉS** **MAITE**
**DON FRANCISCO**

1. Tengo una familia grande. Tengo un hermano, cuatro hermanas y muchos primos. Inés
2. Mi abuelo tiene mucha energía. Trabaja mucho. Javier
3. ¿Es tu mamá? ¡Es muy bonita! Inés
4. Oye, chico… ¿qué dibujas? Maite
5. ¿Fotos de mi familia? ¡Tengo muchas! Javier
6. Mmm… Inés y Javier… ¿qué pasa con ellos? don Francisco
7. ¡Dibujas muy bien! Eres un artista excelente. Maite
8. Mmm… ¿Yo? ¡No dibujo nada! Javier

**3** **Escribir** In pairs, choose Don Francisco, Álex, or Maite and write a brief description of his or her family. Be creative! Answers will vary.

**MAITE** **ÁLEX** **DON FRANCISCO**

Maite es de España. ¿Cómo es su familia?

Álex es de México. ¿Cómo es su familia?

Don Francisco es del Ecuador. ¿Cómo es su familia?

**4** **Conversar** With a partner, use these questions to talk about your families. Answers will vary.

1. ¿Cuántos años tienes?
2. ¿Tienes una familia grande?
3. ¿Tienes hermanos o hermanas?
4. ¿Cuántos años tiene tu abuelo (tu hermana, tu primo, etc.)?
5. ¿De dónde son tus padres?

**AYUDA**
Here are some expressions to help you talk about age.
**Yo tengo… años.** *I am… years old.*
**Mi abuelo tiene… años.** *My grandfather is… years old.*

**TEACHING OPTIONS**

**Extra Practice** Ask volunteers to ad-lib the **Fotonovela** episode for the class. Assure them that it is not necessary to memorize the **Fotonovela** or stick strictly to its content. They should try to get the general meaning across with the vocabulary and expressions they know, and they also should feel free to be creative. Give students time to prepare.

**Small Groups** Have groups of three interview each other about their families. Assign one person to be the interviewer, one the interviewee, and the third person to be the note taker. At three-minute intervals, have students switch roles. When everyone has been interviewed, have students report back to the class.

# Pronunciación
**Diphthongs and linking**

| **hermano** | **niña** | **cuñado** |
|---|---|---|

In Spanish, **a**, **e**, and **o** are considered strong vowels. The weak vowels are **i** and **u**.

| **ruido** | **parientes** | **periodista** |
|---|---|---|

A diphthong is a combination of two weak vowels or of a strong vowel and a weak vowel. Diphthongs are pronounced as a single syllable.

**mi hijo**    **una clase excelente**

Two identical vowel sounds that appear together are pronounced like one long vowel.

**la abuela**

| **con Natalia** | **sus sobrinos** | **las sillas** |
|---|---|---|

Two identical consonants together sound like a single consonant.

| **es ingeniera** | **mis abuelos** | **sus hijos** |
|---|---|---|

A consonant at the end of a word is linked with the vowel at the beginning of the next word.

| **mi hermano** | **su esposa** | **nuestro amigo** |
|---|---|---|

A vowel at the end of a word is linked with the vowel at the beginning of the next word.

**Práctica**  Say these words aloud, focusing on the diphthongs.

1. historia
2. nieto
3. parientes
4. novia
5. residencia
6. prueba
7. puerta
8. ciencias
9. lenguas
10. estudiar
11. izquierda
12. ecuatoriano

**Oraciones**  Read these sentences aloud to practice diphthongs and linking words.

1. Hola. Me llamo Anita Amaral. Soy del Ecuador.
2. Somos seis en mi familia.
3. Tengo dos hermanos y una hermana.
4. Mi papá es del Ecuador y mi mamá es de España.

**Refranes**  Read these sayings aloud to practice diphthongs and linking sounds.

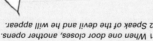

Cuando una puerta se cierra, otra se abre.[1]

Hablando del rey de Roma, por la puerta se asoma.[2]

2 Speak of the devil and he will appear.
1 When one door closes, another opens.

**recursos**

LM
p. 14

panorama.vhlcentral.com
Lección 3

**Section Goals**

In **Pronunciación**, students will be introduced to:
• the strong and weak vowels
• common diphthongs
• linking in pronunciation

**Instructional Resources**
**Supersite:** Textbook & Lab MP3 Audio Files **Lección 3**
**Supersite/IRCD:** *IRM* (Textbook Audio Script, Lab Audio Script, WBs/VM/LM Answer Key)
**WebSAM**
**Lab Manual**, p. 14
*Cuaderno para hispanohablantes*

**Teaching Tips**
• Write **hermano, niña**, and **cuñado** on the board. Ask students to identify the strong and weak vowels.
• Pronounce **ruido, parientes**, and **periodista**, and have students identify the diphthong in each word. Point out that the strong vowels (**a, e, o**) do not combine with each other to form diphthongs. When two strong vowels come together, they are in different syllables.
• Pronounce **mi hermano** and **su esposa** and ask volunteers to write them on the board. Point out that the linked vowels form a diphthong and are pronounced as one syllable.
• Follow the same procedure with **es ingeniera** and **mis abuelos**. You may want to introduce linking involving the other final consonants (**l, n, r, z**). Ex: **Son hermanos. El hermano mayor está aquí. ¿Cuál es tu hermana?**
• Ask students to provide words they learned in **Lecciones 1** and **2** and **Contextos** and **Fotonovela** of this lesson that exemplify each point.

**Práctica/Oraciones/Refranes**
These exercises are recorded in the *Textbook MP3s*. You may want to play the audio so that students practice the pronunciation point by listening to Spanish spoken by speakers other than yourself.

### EN DETALLE

# ¿Cómo te llamas?

**In the Spanish-speaking world,** it is common to have two last names. The first last name is inherited from the father and the second from the mother. In some cases, the conjunctions **de** or **y** are used to connect the two last names. For example, in the name **Juan Martínez de Velasco,** *Martínez* is the paternal surname (**el apellido paterno**), and *Velasco* is the maternal surname (**el apellido materno**); **de** simply links the two names. This convention of using two last names (**doble apellido**) is a European tradition that Spaniards brought to the Americas and continues to be practiced in many countries, including Chile, Colombia, Mexico, Peru, and Venezuela. There are exceptions, however; in Argentina, the prevailing custom is to use only the father's last name.

When a woman marries in a country where two last names are used, legally she retains her two maiden surnames. However, socially she may take her husband's paternal surname in

Gabriel García Márquez      Mercedes Barcha Pardo

Rodrigo García Barcha

place of her inherited maternal surname. Therefore, now that **Mercedes Barcha Pardo** is married to Colombian writer **Gabriel García Márquez,** she could use **Mercedes Barcha García** or **Mercedes Barcha de García** in social situations, although officially her name remains **Mercedes Barcha Pardo.** (Adopting a husband's last name for social purposes, though widespread, is only legally recognized in Ecuador and Peru.)

Regardless of the surnames the mother uses, most parents do not break tradition upon naming their children; they maintain the father's first surname followed by the mother's first surname, as in the name **Rodrigo García Barcha.** However, one should note that both surnames come from the grandfathers, and therefore all **apellidos** are effectively paternal.

### Hijos en la casa

In Spanish-speaking countries, family and society place very little pressure on young adults to live on one's own (**independizarse**), and children often live with their parents well into their thirties. Although reluctance to live on one's own is partly cultural, the main reason is economic—lack of job security or low wages coupled with a high cost of living make it impractical for young adults to live independently before they marry. For example, about 60% of Spaniards under 34 years of age live at home with their parents.

### ACTIVIDADES

**1**  **¿Cierto o falso?** Indicate whether these statements are **cierto** or **falso.** Correct the false statements.

1. Most Spanish-speaking people have three last names. **Falso.** Most people have two last names.
2. Hispanic last names generally consist of the paternal last name followed by the maternal last name. **Cierto.**
3. It is common to see **de** or **y** used in a Hispanic last name. **Cierto.**
4. Someone from Argentina would most likely have two last names. **Falso.** They would use only the father's last name.

5. Generally, married women legally retain two maiden surnames. **Cierto.**
6. In social situations, a married woman often uses her husband's last name in place of her inherited paternal surname. **Falso.** She often uses it in place of her inherited maternal surname.
7. Adopting a husband's surname is only legally recognized in Peru and Ecuador. **Cierto.**
8. Hispanic last names are effectively a combination of the maternal surnames from the previous generation. **Falso.** They are a combination of the paternal surnames from the previous generation.

## ASÍ SE DICE

### Familia y amigos

| | |
|---|---|
| el/la bisnieto/a | *great-grandson/daughter* |
| el/la chamaco/a (Méx.); el/la chamo/a (Ven.); el/la chaval(a) (Esp.) | el/la muchacho/a |
| el/la colega (Esp.) | el/la amigo/a |
| mi cuate (Méx.); mi llave (Col.); mi pana (Ven., P. Rico, Rep. Dom.) | *my pal; my buddy* |
| la madrina | *godmother* |
| el padrino | *godfather* |
| el/la tatarabuelo/a | *great-great-grandfather/ great-great-grandmother* |

## EL MUNDO HISPANO

### Las familias

Although worldwide population trends show a decrease in average family size, households in many Spanish-speaking countries are still larger than their U.S. counterparts.

- ○ **Colombia** 5,2 personas
- ○ **México** 5,0 personas
- ○ **Argentina** 3,7 personas
- ○ **Uruguay** 3,2 personas
- ○ **España** 2,9 personas
- ○ **Estados Unidos** 2,6 personas

## PERFIL

# La familia real española

Undoubtedly, Spain's most famous family is **la familia real** (*Royal*). In 1962, then-prince **Juan Carlos de Borbón**, living in exile in Italy, married Princess **Sofía** of Greece. Then, in the late 1970s, **el Rey** (*King*) **Juan Carlos** and **la Reina** (*Queen*) Sofía returned to Spain and helped to transition the country to democracy after a forty-year dictatorship. The royal couple, who enjoys immense public support, has three children: **las infantas** (*Princesses*) **Elena** and **Cristina**, and a son, **el príncipe** (*Prince*) **Felipe**, whose official title is **el príncipe de Asturias**. In 2004, Felipe married **Letizia Ortiz Rocasolano** (now **la princesa de Asturias**), a journalist and TV presenter. A year later, the future king and queen had their first child, **la infanta** Leonor.

 **Conexión internet**

**What role do padrinos and madrinas have in today's Hispanic family?**

Go to **panorama.vhlcentral.com** to find more cultural information related to this **Cultura** section.

## ACTIVIDADES

**2** **Comprensión** Complete these sentences.

1. Spain's royals were responsible for guiding in _democracy_.
2. In Spanish, your godmother is called _la madrina_.
3. Princess Leonor is the _granddaughter_ of Queen Sofía.
4. Uruguay's average household has _3.2_ people.
5. If a Venezuelan calls you **mi pana**, you are that person's _friend_.

**3** **Una familia famosa** Create a genealogical tree of a famous family, using photos or drawings labeled with names and ages. Present the family tree to a classmate and explain who the people are and their relationships to each other.
Answers will vary.

**recursos**

panorama.vhlcentral.com
Lección 3

## TEACHING OPTIONS

**Cultural Comparison** Have student pairs research a famous English-speaking family (such as the Kennedys) and write a brief comparison with the Spanish Royal Family. Ask students to include information about their prominence in the media, involvement in politics, and general popularity.

**La familia hispana** Explain to students that the concept **la familia** in Spanish-speaking countries is somewhat more inclusive than it is in English. When people say **la familia**, the majority of them are referring to their extended family. Extended families, if they do not live in the same dwelling, tend to live in closer geographical proximity in Latin America than they do in the U.S. and Canada.

## 3.1 Descriptive adjectives

**ANTE TODO**    Adjectives are words that describe people, places, and things. In Spanish, descriptive adjectives are used with the verb **ser** to point out characteristics such as nationality, size, color, shape, personality, and appearance.

## Forms and agreement of adjectives

**COMPARE & CONTRAST**

In English, the forms of descriptive adjectives do not change to reflect the gender (masculine/feminine) and number (singular/plural) of the noun or pronoun they describe.

    *Juan is **nice.***         *Elena is **nice.***         *They are **nice.***

In Spanish, the forms of descriptive adjectives agree in gender and/or number with the nouns or pronouns they describe.

    Juan es simpátic**o.**       Elena es simpátic**a.**       Ellos son simpátic**os.**

▶ Adjectives that end in **-o** have four different forms. The feminine singular is formed by changing the **-o** to **-a.** The plural is formed by adding **-s** to the singular forms.

| Masculine | | Feminine | |
|---|---|---|---|
| SINGULAR | PLURAL | SINGULAR | PLURAL |
| el muchach**o** alt**o** | los muchach**os** alt**os** | la muchach**a** alt**a** | las muchach**as** alt**as** |

 Mi abuelo es muy simpático.

 ¡Qué alto es tu papá! Y tu mamá, ¡qué bonita!

▶ Adjectives that end in **-e** or a consonant have the same masculine and feminine forms.

| Masculine | | Feminine | |
|---|---|---|---|
| SINGULAR | PLURAL | SINGULAR | PLURAL |
| el chico inteligent**e** | los chicos inteligent**es** | la chica inteligent**e** | las chicas inteligent**es** |
| el examen difíci**l** | los exámenes difíci**les** | la clase difíci**l** | las clases difíci**les** |

▶ Adjectives that end in **-or** are variable in both gender and number.

| Masculine | | Feminine | |
|---|---|---|---|
| SINGULAR | PLURAL | SINGULAR | PLURAL |
| el hombre trabajad**or** | los hombres trabajad**ores** | la mujer trabajad**ora** | las mujeres trabajad**oras** |

▶ Adjectives that refer to nouns of different genders use the masculine plural form.

Manuel es alt**o**.      Lola es alt**a**.      Manuel y Lola son alt**os**.

## Common adjectives

| | | | | | |
|---|---|---|---|---|---|
| **alto/a** | tall | **gordo/a** | fat | **moreno/a** | brunet(te) |
| **antipático/a** | unpleasant | **grande** | big; large | **mucho/a** | much; many; a lot of |
| **bajo/a** | short (in height) | **guapo/a** | handsome; good-looking | **pelirrojo/a** | red-haired |
| **bonito/a** | pretty | **importante** | important | **pequeño/a** | small |
| **bueno/a** | good | **inteligente** | intelligent | **rubio/a** | blond(e) |
| **delgado/a** | thin; slender | **interesante** | interesting | **simpático/a** | nice; likeable |
| **difícil** | hard; difficult | **joven** | young | **tonto/a** | silly; foolish |
| **fácil** | easy | **malo/a** | bad | **trabajador(a)** | hard-working |
| **feo/a** | ugly | **mismo/a** | same | **viejo/a** | old |

## Adjectives of nationality

▶ Unlike in English, Spanish adjectives of nationality are **not** capitalized. Proper names of countries, however, are capitalized.

## Some adjectives of nationality

| | | | |
|---|---|---|---|
| **alemán, alemana** | German | **inglés, inglesa** | English |
| **canadiense** | Canadian | **italiano/a** | Italian |
| **chino/a** | Chinese | **japonés, japonesa** | Japanese |
| **ecuatoriano/a** | Ecuadorian | **mexicano/a** | Mexican |
| **español(a)** | Spanish | **norteamericano/a** | (North) American |
| **estadounidense** | from the U.S. | **puertorriqueño/a** | Puerto Rican |
| **francés, francesa** | French | **ruso/a** | Russian |

▶ Adjectives of nationality are formed like other descriptive adjectives. Those that end in **-o** form the feminine by changing the **-o** to **-a**.

chin**o** ⟶ chin**a**          mexican**o** ⟶ mexican**a**

The plural is formed by adding an **-s** to the masculine or feminine form.

chin**o** ⟶ chin**os**          mexican**a** ⟶ mexican**as**

▶ Adjectives of nationality that end in **-e** have only two forms, singular and plural.

canadiens**e** ⟶ canadiens**es**          estadounidens**e** ⟶ estadounidens**es**

▶ Adjectives of nationality that end in a consonant form the feminine by adding **–a**.

alem**án** ⟶ alema**na**          españo**l** ⟶ españo**la**
japoné**s** ⟶ japone**sa**          inglé**s** ⟶ ingl**esa**

▶ Adjectives of nationality which carry an accent mark on the last syllable drop it in the feminine and plural forms.

ingl**és** ⟶ ingl**esa**          alem**án** ⟶ alem**anes**

**Teaching Tips**
- Point out that when referring to people, **bonito/a** can only be used for females, but **guapo/a** can be used for both males and females. Some heritage speakers may use **moreno/a** to refer to someone with dark skin, and **rubio/a** for someone with light brown hair.
- Use pictures or names of celebrities to teach descriptive adjectives in semantic pairs. Ex: ¿**Shaquille O'Neal es alto o bajo?** (Es alto.) ¿**Salma Hayek es fea?** (No, es bonita.) ¿**Los candidatos son inteligentes o tontos?** (Son inteligentes.)
- Use names of celebrities to practice adjectives of nationality. Ex: **Tony Blair, ¿es canadiense?** (No, es inglés.) **Condoleezza Rice, ¿es francesa?** (No, es norteamericana.)
- Point out that adjectives with an accent mark on the last syllable drop the accent mark in the feminine and plural forms. Ex: **irlandés, irlandesa, irlandeses, irlandesas.**
- Point out that adjectives of nationality also can be used as nouns. Ex: **La chica rusa es guapa. La rusa es guapa.** Like adjectives, nouns of nationality are not capitalized.
- At this point you may want to present *Vocabulario adicional: Más adjetivos de nacionalidad* and *Más vocabulario para hablar de la familia,* from the Supersite/IRCD.
- You may want to add to the list of nationalities. Ex: ¿**Los chicos del grupo ABBA son suecos?** (Sí, son suecos.) ¿**Cuáles son las formas singulares de suecos?** (*sueco/sueca*)

**Pairs** If the majority of your students are **norteamericanos**, have pairs ask each other their family's origin. Write ¿**Cuál es el origen de tu familia?** and **Mi familia es de origen…** on the board. Brainstorm other adjectives of nationality as necessary (Ex: **galés, indígena, nigeriano, polaco**). Point out that since **el origen** is masculine and singular, any adjectives they use will be as well.
**TPR** Create two sets of note cards with a city and a correspond-ing adjective of nationality. Shuffle the cards and distribute them. Have students circulate around the room to find the person who shares their nationality. Ex: ¿**De dónde eres? Soy de Managua. Soy nicaragüense.** Once pairs are complete, they should form a living map by asking other pairs' nationality (¿**De dónde son ustedes? Somos panameños.**) You may want to repeat this activity, focusing on a different region each time.

**Teaching Tips**
• After describing each grammar point, practice it by asking questions like these.

**Descriptive adjectives**
¿Tienes amigos inteligentes?
¿Tienes amigas guapas?
¿Tomas clases difíciles?
¿Tienes compañeros trabajadores? ¿Tienes profesores simpáticos o antipáticos?

**Adjectives of quantity**
¿Cuántos hermanos tienes?
¿Cuántas personas hay en la clase de español? ¿Cuántas materias estudias?

*Bueno/a* and *malo/a*
¿Tus amigos son buenos estudiantes? ¿Tienes un buen diccionario? ¿Hoy es un mal día? ¿Tu novio es una persona mala?

*Grande*
¿Vives en una residencia grande o pequeña? ¿Estudias en una universidad grande o pequeña?

• Ask simple questions about the **Fotonovela** characters using adjectives from this lesson. Ex: ¿**Son estadounidenses los cuatro estudiantes? ¿Es simpático o antipático el conductor? ¿Las dos muchachas son altas?**

## Position of adjectives

▶ Descriptive adjectives and adjectives of nationality generally follow the nouns they modify.

El niño **rubio** es de España.
*The blond boy is from Spain.*

La mujer **española** habla inglés.
*The Spanish woman speaks English.*

▶ Unlike descriptive adjectives, adjectives of quantity are placed before the modified noun.

Hay **muchos** libros en la biblioteca.
*There are many books in the library.*

Hablo con **dos** turistas puertorriqueños.
*I am talking with two Puerto Rican tourists.*

▶ **Bueno/a** and **malo/a** can be placed before or after a noun. When placed before a masculine singular noun, the forms are shortened: **bueno → buen; malo → mal.**

Joaquín es un **buen** amigo.
Joaquín es un amigo **bueno.**     → *Joaquín is a good friend.*

Hoy es un **mal** día.
Hoy es un día **malo.**     → *Today is a bad day.*

▶ When **grande** appears before a singular noun, it is shortened to **gran,** and the meaning of the word changes: **gran** = *great* and **grande** = *big, large.*

Don Francisco es un **gran** hombre.
*Don Francisco is a great man.*

La familia de Inés es **grande.**
*Inés' family is large.*

**¡LENGUA VIVA!**

Like **bueno** and **grande, santo** (*saint*) is also shortened before masculine nouns (unless they begin with **To-** or **Do-**): **San Francisco, San José, Santo Tomás. Santa** is used with names of female saints: **Santa Bárbara, Santa Clara.**

**¡INTÉNTALO!** Provide the appropriate forms of the adjectives. The first item in each group has been done for you.

**simpático**
1. Mi hermano es _simpático_.
2. La profesora Martínez es _simpática_.
3. Rosa y Teresa son _simpáticas_.
4. Nosotros somos _simpáticos_.

**alemán**
1. Hans es _alemán_.
2. Mis primas son _alemanas_.
3. Marcus y yo somos _alemanes_.
4. Mi tía es _alemana_.

**difícil**
1. La química es _difícil_.
2. El curso es _difícil_.
3. Las pruebas son _difíciles_.
4. Los libros son _difíciles_.

**guapo**
1. Su esposo es _guapo_.
2. Mis sobrinas son _guapas_.
3. Los padres de ella son _guapos_.
4. Marta es _guapa_.

**recursos**

WB
pp. 25–26

LM
p. 15

panorama.
vhlcentral.com
Lección 3

**TEACHING OPTIONS**

**Video** Show the **Fotonovela** episode again, stopping where appropriate to discuss how certain adjectives were used.
**TPR** Divide the class into two teams and have them line up. Point to a member from each team and give a certain form of an adjective (Ex: **rubios**). Then name another form that you want students to provide (Ex: feminine singular) and have them race to the board. The first student who writes the correct form earns one point for his or her team. Deduct one point for each wrong answer. The team with the most points at the end wins.
**Extra Practice** Create sentences similar to those in **¡Inténtalo!** Say the sentence, have students repeat it, then say a different subject. Have students say the sentence with the new subject, changing adjectives and verbs as necessary.

# Práctica  SUPERSITE

**1** **Emparejar** Find the words in column B that are the opposite of the words in column A. One word in B will not be used.

Jorge    Marcos

| A | | B |
|---|---|---|
| 1. guapo | d | a. delgado |
| 2. moreno | f | b. pequeño |
| 3. alto | h | c. malo |
| 4. gordo | a | d. feo |
| 5. joven | e | e. viejo |
| 6. grande | b | f. rubio |
| 7. simpático | g | g. antipático |
| | | h. bajo |

**2** **Completar** Indicate the nationalities of these people by selecting the correct adjectives and changing their forms when necessary.

1. Una persona del Ecuador es ___ecuatoriana___.
2. ▶ Carlos Fuentes es un gran escritor (*writer*) de México; es ___mexicano___.
3. Los habitantes de Vancouver son ___canadienses___.
4. Giorgio Armani es un diseñador de modas (*fashion designer*) ___italiano___.
5. Gérard Depardieu es un actor ___francés___.
6. Tony Blair y Margaret Thatcher son ___ingleses___.
7. Claudia Schiffer y Boris Becker son ___alemanes___.
8. Los habitantes de Puerto Rico son ___puertorriqueños___.

**3** **Describir** Look at the drawing and describe each family member using as many adjectives as possible. Some answers will vary.

Carlos Romero Sandoval    Josefina Barcos de Romero    Susana Romero Barcos

Tomás Romero Barcos    Alberto Romero Pereda

1. Susana Romero Barcos es ___delgada, rubia___.
2. Tomás Romero Barcos es ___pelirrojo, inteligente___.
3. Los dos hermanos son ___jóvenes___.
4. Josefina Barcos de Romero es ___alta, bonita, rubia___.
5. Carlos Romero Sandoval es ___bajo, gordo___.
6. Alberto Romero Pereda es ___viejo, bajo___.
7. Tomás y su (*his*) padre son ___pelirrojos___.
8. Susana y su (*her*) madre son ___altas, delgadas___.

## Comunicación

**4**

**¿Cómo es?** With a partner, take turns describing each item on the list. Tell your partner whether you agree (**Estoy de acuerdo**) or disagree (**No estoy de acuerdo**) with the descriptions. Answers will vary.

> **modelo**
>
> San Francisco
> **Estudiante 1:** *San Francisco es una ciudad (city) muy bonita.*
> **Estudiante 2:** *No estoy de acuerdo. Es muy fea.*

1. Nueva York
2. Jim Carrey
3. las canciones (*songs*) de Celine Dion
4. el presidente de los Estados Unidos
5. Steven Spielberg
6. la primera dama (*first lady*) de los Estados Unidos
7. el/la profesor(a) de español
8. las personas de Los Ángeles
9. las residencias de mi universidad
10. mi clase de español

**AYUDA**

Here are some tips to help you complete the descriptions:

- **Jim Carrey es actor de cine.**
- **Celine Dion es cantante.**
- **Steven Spielberg es director de cine.**

**5**

**Anuncio personal** Write a personal ad that describes yourself and your ideal boyfriend, girlfriend, or mate. Then compare your ad with a classmate's. How are you similar and how are you different? Are you looking for the same things in a boyfriend, girlfriend, or mate? Answers will vary.

**SOY ALTA,** morena y bonita. Soy ecuatoriana, de Quito. Estudio arte en la universidad. Busco un chico similar. Mi novio ideal es alto, moreno, inteligente y muy simpático.

**AYUDA**

| | |
|---|---|
| **casado/a** | *married* |
| **divorciado/a** | *divorced* |
| **soltero/a** | *single; unmarried* |

These words and others like them are presented in **Contextos, Lección 9**, p. 278.

## Síntesis

**6**

**Diferencias** Your instructor will give you and a partner each a drawing of a family. Find at least five more differences between your picture and your partner's. Answers will vary.

> **modelo**
>
> **Estudiante 1:** *Susana, la madre, es rubia.*
> **Estudiante 2:** *No, la madre es morena.*

---

**Sidebar (left column):**

**4 Expansion** Have small groups brainstorm a list of additional famous people, places, and things. Ask them to include some plural items. Then ask the groups to exchange papers and describe the people, places, and things on the lists they receive.

**5 Teaching Tip** Have students divide a sheet of paper into two columns, labeling one **Yo** and the other **Mi novio/a ideal** or **Mi esposo/a ideal**. Have them brainstorm Spanish adjectives for each column. Ask them to rank each adjective in the second column in terms of its importance to them.

**5 Expansion** Ask small groups to write a personal ad describing a fictional person and his or her ideal mate. Have groups exchange and respond to each other's ads.

**6 Teaching Tips**
- Divide the class into pairs and distribute the handouts from the Information Gap Activities (Supersite/IRCD) that correspond to this activity. Give students ten minutes to complete this activity.
- To simplify, have students brainstorm a list of adjectives for each person in their drawing, then have them proceed with the activity.

**6 Expansion**
- Ask questions based on the artwork. Ex: **¿Es alto el abuelo? ¿Es delgado el hijo menor?**
- Have volunteers take turns stating the differences. Then have them invent stories based on these families.

---

**TEACHING OPTIONS**

**Heritage Speakers** Ask heritage speakers to write descriptions of their extended families. Encourage them to illustrate the descriptions with a few family photos, if possible.

**Extra Practice** Research zodiac signs on the Internet and prepare a simple personality description for each sign, using cognates and adjectives from this lesson. Divide the class into pairs and distribute the descriptions. Have students guess their partners' sign. Ex: —**Eres Aries, ¿verdad?** —**No, no soy Aries. No soy impulsiva y no soy adventurera.**

**Extra Practice** For homework, have students collect several pictures of people from the Internet, magazines, or newspapers. Have them prepare a description of one of the pictures. Invite each student to display the pictures on the board and give their description orally. The class should guess which picture is being described.

## 3.2 Possessive adjectives

**ANTE TODO**   Possessive adjectives, like descriptive adjectives, are words that are used to qualify people, places, or things. Possessive adjectives express the quality of ownership or possession.

### Forms of possessive adjectives

| SINGULAR FORMS | PLURAL FORMS | |
|---|---|---|
| mi | mis | *my* |
| tu | tus | *your* (fam.) |
| su | sus | *his, her, its, your* (form.) |
| nuestro/a | nuestros/as | *our* |
| vuestro/a | vuestros/as | *your* (fam.) |
| su | sus | *their, your* (form.) |

#### COMPARE & CONTRAST

In English, possessive adjectives are invariable; that is, they do not agree in gender and number with the nouns they modify. Spanish possessive adjectives, however, do agree in number with the nouns they modify.

| *my cousin* | *my cousins* | *my aunt* | *my aunts* |
|---|---|---|---|
| **mi** primo | **mis** primos | **mi** tía | **mis** tías |

The forms **nuestro** and **vuestro** agree in both gender and number with the nouns they modify.

| nuestr**o** prim**o** | nuestr**os** prim**os** | nuestr**a** tí**a** | nuestr**as** tí**as** |
|---|---|---|---|

▶ Possessive adjectives are always placed before the nouns they modify.

—¿Está **tu novio** aquí?        —No, **mi novio** está en la biblioteca.
*Is your boyfriend here?*       *No, my boyfriend is in the library.*

▶ Because **su** and **sus** have multiple meanings (*your, his, her, their, its*), you can avoid confusion by using this construction instead: [*article*] + [*noun*] + **de** + [*subject pronoun*].

**AYUDA**
Look at the context, focusing on nouns and pronouns, to help you determine the meaning of **su(s)**.

| **sus** parientes ◀ | los parientes **de él/ella** | *his/her relatives* |
|---|---|---|
| | los parientes **de Ud./Uds.** | *your relatives* |
| | los parientes **de ellos/ellas** | *their relatives* |

**recursos**

WB
pp. 27–28

LM
p. 16

**SUPERSITE**
panorama.
vhlcentral.com
Lección 3

**¡INTÉNTALO!**   Provide the appropriate form of each possessive adjective. The first item in each column has been done for you.

1. Es ___mi___ (*my*) libro.
2. ___Mi___ (*My*) familia es ecuatoriana.
3. ___Tu___ (*Your,* fam.) esposo es italiano.
4. ___Nuestro___ (*Our*) profesor es español.
5. Es ___su___ (*her*) reloj.
6. Es ___tu___ (*your,* fam.) mochila.
7. Es ___su___ (*your,* form.) maleta.
8. ___Su___ (*Their*) sobrina es alemana.

1. ___Sus___ (*Her*) primos son franceses.
2. ___Nuestros___ (*Our*) primos son canadienses.
3. Son ___sus___ (*their*) lápices.
4. ___Sus___ (*Their*) nietos son japoneses.
5. Son ___nuestras___ (*our*) plumas.
6. Son ___mis___ (*my*) papeles.
7. ___Mis___ (*My*) amigas son inglesas.
8. Son ___sus___ (*his*) cuadernos.

#### TEACHING OPTIONS

**Video** Replay the *Fotonovela*, having students focus on possessive adjectives. Ask them to write down each one they hear, with the noun it modifies. Afterward, ask the class to describe **Inés** and **Javier**'s families. Remind them to use definite articles and **de** if necessary to avoid confusion with the possessive **su**.

**Small Groups** Give small groups three minutes to brainstorm as many words as they can associated with the phrases **nuestro país, nuestro estado, nuestra universidad,** and **nuestra clase de español**. Have them model their responses on **En nuestra clase hay ____** and **Nuestro país es ____**. Have the groups share their associations with the rest of the class.

**Section Goals**
In **Estructura 3.2**, students will be introduced to:
• possessive adjectives
• ways of clarifying **su(s)** when the referent is ambiguous

**Instructional Resources**
**Supersite:** Lab MP3 Audio Files **Lección 3**
**Supersite/IRCD:** *PowerPoints* (**Lección 3 Estructura** Presentation); *IRM* (Lab Audio Script, WBs/VM/LM Answer Key)
**WebSAM**
**Workbook,** pp. 27–28
**Lab Manual,** p. 16
***Cuaderno para hispanohablantes***

**Teaching Tips**
• Introduce the concept of possessive adjectives. Hold up your book, jacket, or other personal possession and ask individuals: **¿Es tu libro? (No.)** Then, as you point to one student, ask the class: **¿Es el libro de ____? ¿Es su libro?** Link arms with another student and ask the class: **¿Es nuestro libro?** Indicate the whole class and ask: **¿Es el libro de ustedes? ¿Es su libro?** Finally, hug the object dramatically and say: **No. Es mi libro.** Ask volunteers personalized questions. Ex: **¿Es simpática tu madre?**
• Use each possessive adjective with a noun to illustrate agreement. Point out that all agree in number with the noun they modify but that only **nuestro/a** and **vuestro/a** show gender. Point out that **tú** (subject) has an accent mark; **tu** (possessive) does not.
• Ask students to give the plural or singular of possessive adjectives with nouns. Say: **Da el plural: nuestra clase. (nuestras clases)** Say: **Da el singular: mis manos. (mi mano)**
• Write **su familia** and **sus amigos** on the board and ask volunteers to supply the equivalent phrases using **de**.

**1 Expansion**
• Have students change the number and gender of the nouns in items 1–7. Then have them say each new sentence, changing the possessives as necessary.
• Have students respond to the question in item 8.

**2 Expansion**
• Change the subject pronouns in parentheses and have the class provide new answers. Then have groups of students provide new nouns and the corresponding answers.
• Give the class sentences such as **Es su libro** and have volunteers rephrase them with a clarifying prepositional phrase.

**3 Teaching Tips**
• Before doing the activity, quickly review **estar** by writing the present-tense forms on the board.
• Remind students that **estar** is used to indicate location.

**3 Expansion** Ask questions about objects that are in the classroom. Ex: **¿Dónde está mi escritorio? ¿Dónde está el libro de ____? ¿Dónde están las plumas de ____? ¿Dónde están tus lápices?**

# Práctica

**1** **La familia de Manolo** Complete each sentence with the correct possessive adjective. Use the subject of each sentence as a guide.

1. Me llamo Manolo, y ____mi____ (nuestro, mi, sus) hermano es Federico.
2. ___Nuestra___ (Nuestra, Sus, Mis) madre Silvia es profesora y enseña química.
3. Ella admira a ____sus____ (tu, nuestro, sus) estudiantes porque trabajan mucho.
4. Yo estudio en la misma universidad, pero no tomo clases con ____mi____ (mi, nuestras, tus) madre.
5. Federico trabaja en una oficina con ____nuestro____ (mis, tu, nuestro) padre.
6. ____Su____ (Mi, Su, Tu) oficina está en el centro de Quito.
7. Javier y Óscar son ____mis____ (mis, mi, sus) tíos de Guayaquil.
8. ¿Y tú? ¿Cómo es ____tu____ (mi, su, tu) familia?

**2** **Clarificar** Clarify each sentence with a prepositional phrase. Follow the model.

> **modelo**
> Su hermana es muy bonita. (ella)
> *La hermana de ella es muy bonita.*

1. Su casa es muy grande. (ellos) _____La casa de ellos es muy grande._____
2. ¿Cómo se llama su hermano? (ellas) _____¿Cómo se llama el hermano de ellas?_____
3. Sus padres trabajan en el centro. (ella) _____Los padres de ella trabajan en el centro._____
4. Sus abuelos son muy simpáticos. (él) _____Los abuelos de él son muy simpáticos._____
5. Maribel es su prima. (ella) _____Maribel es la prima de ella._____
6. Su primo lee los libros. (ellos) _____El primo de ellos lee los libros._____

**3** **¿Dónde está?** With a partner, imagine that you can't remember where you put some of the belongings you see in the pictures. Your partner will help you by reminding you where your things are. Take turns playing each role. *Answers will vary.*

**CONSULTA**
For a list of useful prepositions, refer to the table *Prepositions often used with estar*, in **Estructura 2.3**, p. 56.

> **modelo**
> **Estudiante 1:** *¿Dónde está mi mochila?*
> **Estudiante 2:** *Tu mochila está encima del escritorio.*

1.    2.    3.

4.    5.    6.

**TEACHING OPTIONS**

**Extra Practice** Ask students a few questions about the members of their immediate and extended families. Ex: **¿Cómo son tus padres? ¿Cómo se llama tu tío favorito? ¿Es el hermano de tu madre o de tu padre? ¿Tienes muchos primos? ¿Cómo se llaman tus primos? ¿De dónde son tus abuelos? ¿Hablas mucho con tus abuelos?**

**Heritage Speakers** Ask heritage speakers to write a short paragraph about a favorite relative. Ask them to include the characteristics that make that relative their favorite. Have them explain what they have learned from that person.

# Comunicación

**4** **Describir** Get together with a partner and take turns describing the people and places on the list. Answers will vary.

> **modelo**
>
> la biblioteca de su universidad
> *La biblioteca de nuestra universidad es muy grande. Hay muchos libros en la biblioteca. Mis amigos y yo estudiamos en la biblioteca.*

1. tu profesor favorito
2. tu profesora favorita
3. su clase de español
4. la librería de su universidad
5. tus padres
6. tus abuelos
7. tu mejor (*best*) amigo
8. tu mejor amiga
9. su universidad
10. tu país de origen

**5** **Una familia** In small groups, each student pretends to be a different member of the family pictured and shares that person's private thoughts about the others in the family. Make two positive comments and two negative ones. Answers will vary.

> **modelo**
>
> **Estudiante 1:** *Mi hijo Roberto es muy trabajador. Estudia mucho y siempre termina su tarea.*
> **Estudiante 2:** *Nuestra familia es difícil. Mis padres no escuchan mis opiniones.*

# Síntesis

**6** **Describe a tu familia** Get together with two classmates and describe your family to them in several sentences (**Mi padre es alto y moreno. Mi madre es delgada y muy bonita. Mis hermanos son...**). They will work together to try to repeat your description (**Su padre es alto y moreno. Su madre...**). If they forget any details, they will ask you questions (**¿Es alto tu hermano?**). Alternate roles until all of you have described your families. Answers will vary.

---

**4** Teaching Tip Ask students to suggest a few more details to add to the **modelo**.

**5** Teaching Tips
- Quickly review the descriptive adjectives on page 81. You can do this by saying an adjective and having volunteers give its opposite (**palabra opuesta**).
- Explain the activity to the class. Have students give names to the people in the photo following Hispanic naming conventions.

**5** Expansion Ask a couple of groups to perform the activity for the class.

**6** Teaching Tips
- Review the family vocabulary on pages 70–71.
- Explain that the class will divide into groups of three. One student will describe his or her own family (using **mi**), and then the other two will describe the first student's family to one another (using **su**) and ask for clarification as necessary (using **tu**).
- You may want to model this for the class. Before beginning, ask students to list the family members they plan to describe.

---

**TEACHING OPTIONS**

**Extra Practice** Have students work in small groups to prepare a description of a famous person, such as a politician, a movie star, or a sports figure, and his or her extended family. Tell them to feel free to invent family members as necessary. Have groups present their descriptions to the class.

**Heritage Speakers** Ask heritage speakers to describe their families' home countries (**países de origen**) for the class. As they are giving their descriptions, ask them questions that elicit more information. Clarify for the class any unfamiliar words and expressions they may use.

## [3.3] Present tense of -er and -ir verbs

**ANTE TODO** In **Lección 2,** you learned how to form the present tense of regular -**ar** verbs. You also learned about the importance of verb forms, which change to show who is performing the action. The chart below shows the forms of verbs from two other important verb groups, -**er** verbs and -**ir** verbs.

**CONSULTA**

To review the conjugation of -**ar** verbs, see **Estructura 2.1,** p. 46.

| Present tense of -er and -ir verbs | | |
|---|---|---|
| | **comer** *(to eat)* | **escribir** *(to write)* |
| **SINGULAR FORMS** yo | com**o** | escrib**o** |
| tú | com**es** | escrib**es** |
| Ud./él/ella | com**e** | escrib**e** |
| **PLURAL FORMS** nosotros/as | com**emos** | escrib**imos** |
| vosotros/as | com**éis** | escrib**ís** |
| Uds./ellos/ellas | com**en** | escrib**en** |

▶ -**Er** and -**ir** verbs have very similar endings. Study the preceding chart to detect the patterns that make it easier for you to use them to communicate in Spanish.

Inés y Javier comen.

Maite escribe.

**AYUDA**

Here are some tips on learning Spanish verbs:
1) Learn to identify the stem of each verb, to which all endings attach.
2) Memorize the endings that go with each verb and verb tense.
3) As often as possible, practice using different forms of each verb in speech and writing.
4) Devote extra time to learning irregular verbs, such as **ser** and **estar.**

▶ Like -**ar** verbs, the **yo** forms of -**er** and -**ir** verbs end in -**o.**

Yo com**o.**      Yo escrib**o.**

▶ Except for the **yo** form, all of the verb endings for -**er** verbs begin with -**e.**

| -es | -emos | -en |
|---|---|---|
| -e | -éis | |

▶ -**Er** and -**ir** verbs have the exact same endings, except in the **nosotros/as** and **vosotros/as** forms.

nosotros ◀ com**emos** / escrib**imos**      vosotros ◀ com**éis** / escrib**ís**

## Common -er and -ir verbs

### -er verbs

| | |
|---|---|
| **aprender (a +** *inf.***)** | *to learn* |
| **beber** | *to drink* |
| **comer** | *to eat* |
| **comprender** | *to understand* |
| **correr** | *to run* |
| **creer (en)** | *to believe (in)* |
| **deber (+** *inf.***)** | *should; must; ought to* |
| **leer** | *to read* |

### -ir verbs

| | |
|---|---|
| **abrir** | *to open* |
| **asistir (a)** | *to attend* |
| **compartir** | *to share* |
| **decidir (+** *inf.***)** | *to decide* |
| **describir** | *to describe* |
| **escribir** | *to write* |
| **recibir** | *to receive* |
| **vivir** | *to live* |

Ellos **beben** café y **leen** el periódico.

Él **escribe** una carta.

**¡INTÉNTALO!** Provide the appropriate present tense forms of these verbs. The first item in each column has been done for you.

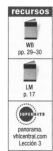

### correr

1. Graciela _corre_.
2. Tú _corres_.
3. Yo _corro_.
4. Sara y Ana _corren_.
5. Usted _corre_.
6. Ustedes _corren_.
7. La gente _corre_.
8. Marcos y yo _corremos_.

### abrir

1. Ellos _abren_ la puerta.
2. Carolina _abre_ la maleta.
3. Yo _abro_ las ventanas.
4. Nosotras _abrimos_ los libros.
5. Usted _abre_ el cuaderno.
6. Tú _abres_ la ventana.
7. Ustedes _abren_ las maletas.
8. Los muchachos _abren_ los cuadernos.

### aprender

1. Él _aprende_ español.
2. Maribel y yo _aprendemos_ inglés.
3. Tú _aprendes_ japonés.
4. Tú y tu hermanastra _aprenden_ francés.
5. Mi hijo _aprende_ chino.
6. Yo _aprendo_ alemán.
7. Usted _aprende_ inglés.
8. Nosotros _aprendemos_ italiano.

**recursos**

WB
pp. 29–30

LM
p. 17

SUPERSITE
panorama.
vhlcentral.com
Lección 3

**Teaching Tips**
- Point out the characteristic vowel (–e–) of –er verbs. Help students see that all the present-tense endings of regular –er/–ir verbs are the same except for the **nosotros/as** and **vosotros/as** forms.
- Reinforce –er/–ir endings and introduce the verbs by asking the class questions. First, ask a series of questions with a single verb until you have elicited all of its present-tense forms. Have students answer with complete sentences. Ex: **¿Aprenden ustedes historia en nuestra clase? ¿Aprendes álgebra en tu clase de matemáticas? ¿Qué aprenden ____ y ____ en la clase de computación? Aprendo mucho cuando leo, ¿verdad?** Then, ask questions using all the verbs at random.
- Ask questions based on the photos. Ex: **¿Quiénes corren en el parque en la foto? ¿Quiénes de ustedes corren? ¿Dónde corren? ¿A quién creen que escribe el muchacho? ¿Escribe a su novia? ¿Escribe a su mamá? ¿Ustedes escriben a sus mamás? ¿Escriben a sus novios/as?**
- Ask students to come up with a list of things they routinely do in Spanish class or in any of their other classes. Encourage them to use as many of the –er/–ir verbs that they can.

**TEACHING OPTIONS**

**Video** Replay the *Fotonovela*. Have students listen for –er/–ir verbs and write down those they hear. Afterward, write the verbs on the board and ask their meanings. Have students write original sentences using each verb.

**Extra Practice** Have students answer questions about their Spanish class. Have them answer in complete sentences. Ex: **Ustedes estudian mucho para la clase de español, ¿verdad?**

**Deben estudiar más, ¿no? Leen las lecciones, ¿no? Escriben mucho en clase, ¿verdad? Abren los libros, ¿no? Asisten al laboratorio de lenguas, ¿verdad? Comen sándwiches en la clase, ¿verdad? Beben café, ¿no? Comprenden el libro, ¿no?** Pairs may ask each other these questions by changing the verbs to the **tú** form.

# Práctica

**1 Completar** Complete Susana's sentences about her family with the correct forms of the verbs in parentheses. One of the verbs will remain in the infinitive.

1. Mi familia y yo ___vivimos___ (vivir) en Guayaquil.
2. Tengo muchos libros. Me gusta ___leer___ (leer).
3. Mi hermano Alfredo es muy inteligente. Alfredo ___asiste___ (asistir) a clases los lunes, miércoles y viernes.
4. Los martes y jueves Alfredo y yo ___corremos___ (correr).
5. Mis padres ___comen___ (comer) mucho.
6. Yo ___creo___ (creer) que (*that*) mis padres deben comer menos (*less*).

**2 Oraciones** Juan is talking about what he and his friends do after school. Form complete sentences.

> **modelo**
> yo / correr / amigos / lunes y miércoles
> *Yo corro con mis amigos los lunes y miércoles.*

1. Manuela / asistir / clase / yoga   Manuela asiste a la clase de yoga.
2. Eugenio / abrir / correo electrónico (*e-mail*)   Eugenio abre su correo electrónico.
3. Isabel y yo / leer / biblioteca   Isabel y yo leemos en la biblioteca.
4. Sofía y Roberto / aprender / hablar / inglés   Sofía y Roberto aprenden a hablar inglés.
5. tú / comer / cafetería / universidad   Tú comes en la cafetería de la universidad.
6. mi novia y yo / compartir / libro de historia   Mi novia y yo compartimos el libro de historia.

**3 Consejos** Mario teaches Japanese at a university in Quito and is spending a year in Tokyo with his family. In pairs, use the words below to say what he and/or his family members are doing or should do to adjust to life in Japan. Then, create one more sentence using a verb not in the list.
Answers will vary.

> **modelo**
> recibir libros / deber practicar japonés
> **Estudiante 1:** *Mario y su esposa reciben muchos libros en japonés.*
> **Estudiante 2:** *Los hijos deben practicar japonés.*

| | |
|---|---|
| aprender japonés | decidir explorar el país |
| asistir a clases | escribir listas de palabras en japonés |
| beber sake | leer novelas japonesas |
| deber comer cosas nuevas | vivir con una familia japonesa |
| ¿? | ¿? |

---

**TEACHING OPTIONS**

**Pairs** Have pairs of students role-play an interview with a movie star. Students can review previous lesson vocabulary lists in preparation. Give pairs sufficient time to plan and practice. When all pairs have completed the activity, ask a few of them to introduce their characters and perform the interview for the class.

**TPR** Add to the list of phrases in **Actividad 3**. In groups of three,

have students pantomime the activities for their classmates to guess.

**Heritage Speakers** Have heritage speakers brainstorm a list of things that a study-abroad student in a Spanish-speaking country might want to do. Have them base their list on **Actividad 3** using as many **–er/–ir** verbs as they can. Then have the rest of the class write complete sentences based on the list.

# Comunicación

**4** **Entrevista** Get together with a classmate and use these questions to interview each other. Be prepared to report the results of your interviews to the class. *Answers will vary.*

1. ¿Dónde comes al mediodía? ¿Comes mucho?
2. ¿Debes comer más (*more*) o menos (*less*)?
3. ¿Cuándo asistes a tus clases?
4. ¿Cuál es tu clase favorita? ¿Por qué?
5. ¿Dónde vives?
6. ¿Con quién vives?
7. ¿Qué cursos debes tomar el próximo (*next*) semestre?
8. ¿Lees el periódico (*newspaper*)? ¿Qué periódico lees y cuándo?
9. ¿Recibes muchas cartas (*letters*)? ¿De quién(es)?
10. ¿Escribes poemas?

**5**  **Encuesta** Your instructor will give you a worksheet. Walk around the class and ask a different classmate each question about his/her familiy members. Be prepared to report the results of your survey to the class. *Answers will vary.*

| Actividades | Miembros de la familia |
|---|---|
| 1. vivir en una casa | los padres de Juan |
| 2. beber café | |
| 3. correr todos los días (*every day*) | |
| 4. comer mucho en restaurantes | |
| 5. recibir mucho correo electrónico (*e-mail*) | |
| 6. comprender tres lenguas | |
| 7. deber estudiar más (*more*) | |
| 8. leer muchos libros | |

# Síntesis

**6**  **Horario** Your instructor will give you and a partner incomplete versions of Alicia's schedule. Fill in the missing information on the schedule by talking to your partner. Be prepared to reconstruct Alicia's complete schedule with the class. *Answers will vary.*

> **modelo**
> **Estudiante 1:** A las ocho, Alicia corre.
> **Estudiante 2:** ¡Ah, sí! (*Writes down information.*) A las nueve, ella...

**Small Groups** Have small groups talk about their favorite classes and teachers. They should describe the classes and the teachers and indicate why they like them. They should also mention what days and times they attend each class. Ask a few volunteers to present a summary of their conversation.

**Extra Practice** Add an auditory aspect to this grammar practice. Use these sentences as a dictation. Read each twice, pausing after the second time for students to write. **1. Mi hermana Juana y yo asistimos a la Universidad de Quito. 2. Ella vive en la casa de mis padres y yo vivo en una residencia. 3. Juana es estudiante de literatura y lee mucho. 4. Yo estudio computación y aprendo a programar computadoras.**

---

**4** **Teaching Tips**
- Tell students that one of them should complete their interview before switching roles.
- This activity is also suited to a group of three students, one of whom acts as note taker. They should switch roles at the end of each interview until each student has played all three roles.

**5** **Teaching Tips**
- Model one or two of the questions. Then distribute the *Hojas de actividades* (Supersite/IRCD).
- The activity can also be done in pairs. Have students change the heading of the second column to **¿Sí o no?**

**5** **Expansion** Go through the survey to find out how the items apply to the class. Record the results on the board. For example, ask: **¿Quiénes viven en una casa?**

**6** **Teaching Tip** Divide the class into pairs and distribute the handouts from the Information Gap Activities (Supersite/ IRCD) that correspond to this activity. Give students ten minutes to complete this activity.

**6** **Expansion**
- Ask questions based on **Alicia's** schedule. Ex: **¿Qué hace Alicia a las nueve? (Ella desayuna.)**
- Have volunteers take turns reading aloud **Alicia's** schedule. Then have them write their own schedules using as many **–er/–ir** verbs as they can.

## 3.4 Present tense of **tener** and **venir**

**ANTE TODO**  The verbs **tener** (*to have*) and **venir** (*to come*) are among the most frequently used in Spanish. Because most of their forms are irregular, you will have to learn each one individually.

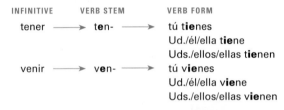

| | | **ten**er | **ven**ir |
|---|---|---|---|
| **SINGULAR FORMS** | yo | ten**go** | ven**go** |
| | tú | tien**es** | vien**es** |
| | Ud./él/ella | tien**e** | vien**e** |
| **PLURAL FORMS** | nosotros/as | ten**emos** | ven**imos** |
| | vosotros/as | ten**éis** | ven**ís** |
| | Uds./ellos/ellas | tien**en** | vien**en** |

▶ The endings are the same as those of regular **-er** and **-ir** verbs, except for the **yo** forms, which are irregular: **tengo, vengo.**

▶ In the **tú, Ud.,** and **Uds.** forms, the **e** of the stem changes to **ie** as shown below.

| INFINITIVE | VERB STEM | VERB FORM |
|---|---|---|
| tener ⟶ | ten- ⟶ | tú **tie**nes |
| | | Ud./él/ella **tie**ne |
| | | Uds./ellos/ellas **tie**nen |
| venir ⟶ | ven- ⟶ | tú **vie**nes |
| | | Ud./él/ella **vie**ne |
| | | Uds./ellos/ellas **vie**nen |

¿Tienes hermanos?

Sí, tengo cuatro hermanas y un hermano mayor.

▶ The **nosotros** and **vosotros** forms are the only ones which are regular. Compare them to the forms of **comer** and **escribir** that you learned on page 88.

| | tener | comer | venir | escribir |
|---|---|---|---|---|
| nosotros/as | ten**emos** | com**emos** | ven**imos** | escrib**imos** |
| vosotros/as | ten**éis** | com**éis** | ven**ís** | escrib**ís** |

## Expressions with tener

| tener... años | to be... years old | tener (mucha) prisa | to be in a (big) hurry |
|---|---|---|---|
| tener (mucho) calor | to be (very) hot | tener razón | to be right |
| tener (mucho) cuidado | to be (very) careful | no tener razón | to be wrong |
| tener (mucho) frío | to be (very) cold | tener (mucha) sed | to be (very) thirsty |
| tener (mucha) hambre | to be (very) hungry | tener (mucho) sueño | to be (very) sleepy |
| tener (mucho) miedo (de) | to be (very) afraid/ scared (of) | tener (mucha) suerte | to be (very) lucky |

▶ In certain idiomatic or set expressions in Spanish, you use the construction **tener** + [*noun*] to express *to be* + [*adjective*]. The chart above contains a list of the most common expressions with **tener**.

—¿**Tienen** hambre ustedes?       —Sí, y **tenemos** sed también.
*Are you hungry?*                   *Yes, and we're thirsty, too.*

▶ To express an obligation, use **tener que** (*to have to*) + [*infinitive*].

—¿Qué **tienes que** estudiar hoy?    —**Tengo que** estudiar biología.
*What do you have to study today?*    *I have to study biology.*

▶ To ask people if they feel like doing something, use **tener ganas de** (*to feel like*) + [*infinitive*].

—¿**Tienes ganas de** comer?       —No, **tengo ganas de** dormir.
*Do you feel like eating?*           *No, I feel like sleeping.*

MIciudad.COM

Usted tiene que visitarnos.

---

 **¡INTÉNTALO!**    Provide the appropriate forms of **tener** and **venir**. The first item in each column has been done for you.

**tener**

1. Ellos ___tienen___ dos hermanos.
2. Yo ___tengo___ una hermana.
3. El artista ___tiene___ tres primos.
4. Nosotros ___tenemos___ diez tíos.
5. Eva y Diana ___tienen___ un sobrino.
6. Usted ___tiene___ cinco nietos.
7. Tú ___tienes___ dos hermanastras.
8. Ustedes ___tienen___ cuatro hijos.
9. Ella ___tiene___ una hija.

**venir**

1. Mis padres ___vienen___ de México.
2. Tú ___vienes___ de España.
3. Nosotras ___venimos___ de Cuba.
4. Pepe ___viene___ de Italia.
5. Yo ___vengo___ de Francia.
6. Ustedes ___vienen___ de Canadá.
7. Alfonso y yo ___venimos___ de Portugal.
8. Ellos ___vienen___ de Alemania.
9. Usted ___viene___ de Venezuela.

**recursos**

WB
pp. 31–32

LM
p. 18

SUPERSITE
panorama.
vhlcentral.com
Lección 3

---

**Teaching Tips**
• Remind the class that Spanish uses **tener** + [*noun*] in many cases where English uses *to be* + [*adjective*].
• Model the use of the expressions by talking about yourself and asking students questions about themselves. Ex: **Tengo ____ años. Y tú, ¿cuántos años tienes? Esta mañana tengo frío. ¿Tienen frío ustedes? Y tú, ____, ¿tienes frío también o tienes calor? Yo no tengo sueño esta mañana. Me gusta enseñar por la mañana.**
• Present **tener que** + [*infinitive*] and **tener ganas de** + [*infinitive*] together. Go around the class asking questions that use the expressions, having students answer in complete sentences. Ex: **____, ¿tienes que estudiar más para la clase de español? ¿Tienes ganas de ir a la biblioteca ahora?**

---

**TEACHING OPTIONS**

**TPR** Assign gestures to each expression with **tener**. Ex: **tener calor:** *wipe brow;* **tener cuidado:** *look around suspiciously;* **tener frío:** *wrap arms around oneself and shiver;* **tener miedo:** *hold hand over mouth in fear.* Have students stand. Say an expression at random (Ex: **Tienes sueño**) and point at a student, who should perform the appropriate gesture. Vary by pointing to more than one student (Ex: **Ustedes tienen hambre**).

**Variación léxica** Point out that **tener que** + [*infinitive*] not only expresses obligation, but also need. **Tengo que estudiar más** can mean either *I have to (am obligated to) study more* or *I need to study more.* Another way of expressing need is with the regular –ar verb **necesitar** + [*infinitive*]. Ex: **Necesito estudiar más.** This can also be said with **deber** + [*infinitive*]. Ex: **Debo estudiar más.**

# Práctica

**1**

**Emparejar** Find the phrase in column B that matches best with the phrase in column A. One phrase in column B will not be used.

| A | | B |
|---|---|---|
| 1. el Polo Norte | c | a. tener calor |
| 2. una sauna | a | b. tener sed |
| 3. la comida salada (*salty food*) | b | c. tener frío |
| 4. una persona muy inteligente | d | d. tener razón |
| 5. un abuelo | g | e. tener ganas de |
| 6. una dieta | f | f. tener hambre |
| | | g. tener 75 años |

**2**

**Completar** Complete the sentences with the forms of **tener** or **venir**.

1. Hoy nosotros __tenemos__ una reunión familiar (*family reunion*).
2. Yo __vengo__ en autobús de la Universidad de Quito.
3. Todos mis parientes __vienen__, excepto mi tío Manolo y su esposa.
4. Ellos no __tienen__ ganas de venir porque viven en Portoviejo.
5. Mi prima Susana y su novio no __vienen__ hasta las ocho porque ella __tiene__ que trabajar.
6. En las fiestas, mi hermana siempre (*always*) __viene__ muy tarde (*late*).
7. Nosotros __tenemos__ mucha suerte porque las reuniones son divertidas (*fun*).
8. Mi madre cree que mis sobrinos son muy simpáticos. Creo que ella __tiene__ razón.

**3**

**Describir** Look at the drawings and describe what people are doing using an expression with **tener**.

1. ___Tiene (mucha) prisa.___

2. ___Tiene (mucho) calor.___

3. ___Tiene veintiún años.___

4. ___Tienen (mucha) hambre.___

5. ___Tienen (mucho) frío.___

6. ___Tiene (mucha) sed.___

# Comunicación

**4** **¿Sí o no?** Using complete sentences, indicate whether these statements apply to you.
Answers will vary.

1. Mi padre tiene 50 años.
2. Mis amigos vienen a mi casa todos los días (*every day*).
3. Vengo a la universidad los martes.
4. Tengo hambre.
5. Tengo dos computadoras.
6. Tengo sed.
7. Tengo que estudiar los domingos.
8. Tengo una familia grande.

Now interview a classmate by transforming each statement into a question. Be prepared to report the results of your interview to the class. Answers will vary.

> **modelo**
>
> **Estudiante 1:** ¿Tiene tu padre 50 años?
> **Estudiante 2:** No, no tiene 50 años. Tiene 65.

**5** **Preguntas** Get together with a classmate and ask each other these questions. Answers will vary.

1. ¿Tienes que estudiar hoy?
2. ¿Cuántos años tienes? ¿Y tus hermanos/as?
3. ¿Cuándo vienes a la clase de español?
4. ¿Cuándo vienen tus amigos a tu casa, apartamento o residencia estudiantil?
5. ¿De qué tienes miedo? ¿Por qué?
6. ¿Qué tienes ganas de hacer esta noche (*tonight*)?

**6** **Conversación** Use an expression with **tener** to hint at what's on your mind. Your partner will ask questions to find out why you feel that way. If your partner cannot guess what's on your mind after three attempts, tell him/her. Then switch roles. Answers will vary.

> **modelo**
>
> **Estudiante 1:** Tengo miedo.
> **Estudiante 2:** ¿Tienes que hablar en público?
> **Estudiante 1:** No.
> **Estudiante 2:** ¿Tienes un examen hoy?
> **Estudiante 1:** Sí, y no tengo tiempo para estudiar.

# Síntesis

**7** **Minidrama** Act out this situation with a partner: you are introducing your boyfriend/girlfriend to your extended family. To avoid any surprises before you go, talk about who is coming and what each family member is like. Switch roles. Answers will vary.

**4** **Teaching Tip** Give students three minutes to read the statements. Have them rephrase any statement that does not apply to them so that it does. Ex: **Mi padre tiene 80 años.** Then read the **modelo** and clarify the transformations involved.

**5** **Teaching Tip** Remind students that each partner should both ask and answer all the questions. Ask volunteers to summarize the responses. Record these responses on the board as a survey about the class's characteristics.

**6** **Teaching Tip** Model the activity by giving an expression with **tener**. Ex: **Tengo mucha prisa.** Encourage students to guess the reason, using **tener** and **venir**. If they guess incorrectly, give them more specific clues. Ex: **Tengo mucho que hacer hoy. Es un día especial. (Viene un amigo.)**

**6** **Expansion** In pairs, have students use **tener** and **venir** to invent a conversation between the characters in the drawing.

**7** **Teaching Tip** Before doing **Síntesis**, have students quickly review this material: family vocabulary on pages 70–71; descriptive adjectives on pages 80–82; possessive adjectives on page 85; and the forms of **tener** and **venir** on page 92.

---

**TEACHING OPTIONS**

**Small Groups** Have small groups prepare skits in which one person takes a few friends to a family reunion. The introducer should facilitate introductions and small talk. All group members should participate in the conversation.

**Pairs** Give pairs of students five minutes to write a conversation in which they use as many **tener** expressions as they can in a logical manner. Have the top three pairs perform their conversations for the class.

## Section Goal

In **Recapitulación**, students will review the grammar concepts from this lesson.

**Instructional Resource**
**Supersite**

### ◼1 Teaching Tips
• To add an auditory aspect to the activity, have students read their answers aloud, emphasizing the adjective ending sounds –a(s) and –o(s).
• Remind students that some adjectives have the same masculine and feminine forms.

### ◼1 Expansion
Ask students to rewrite the sentences to convey an opposite or different meaning. Ex: **1. Mi tía es francesa. Vive en París. 2. Mi primo no es moreno, es rubio.**

### ◼2 Teaching Tip
Remind students that possessive adjectives agree in number (and in gender for **nuestro/a** and **vuestro/a**) with the nouns they modify, not with the subject. Therefore, in item 1, even though **Esteban y Julio** is a plural subject, **su** is singular to agree with **tía**.

### ◼2 Expansion
Have students rewrite the sentences using different subjects. Ex: **Yo tengo una tía. Es mi tía.**

### ◼3 Teaching Tip
To simplify, have students circle the subject and underline the verb before forming the sentences.

### ◼3 Expansion
Have pairs create two additional dehydrated sentences for another pair to write out.

---

# Recapitulación

**SUPERSITE** For self-scoring and diagnostics, go to **panorama.vhlcentral.com**.

Review the grammar concepts you have learned in this lesson by completing these activities.

**1   Adjetivos** Complete each phrase with the appropriate adjective from the list. Make all necessary changes. **6 pts.**

| antipático | interesante | mexicano |
|---|---|---|
| difícil | joven | moreno |

1. Mi tía es __mexicana__. Vive en Guadalajara.
2. Mi primo no es rubio, es __moreno__.
3. Mi novio cree que la clase no es fácil; es __difícil__.
4. Los libros son __interesantes__; me gustan mucho.
5. Mis hermanos son __antipáticos__; no tienen muchos amigos.
6. Las gemelas tienen quince años. Son __jóvenes__.

**2   Completar** For each set of sentences, provide the appropriate form of the verb **tener** and the possessive adjective. Follow the model. **12 pts.**

> **modelo**
> Él tiene un libro. Es su libro.

1. Esteban y Julio __tienen__ una tía. Es __su__ tía.
2. Yo __tengo__ muchos amigos. Son __mis__ amigos.
3. Tú __tienes__ tres primas. Son __tus__ primas.
4. María y tú __tienen__ un hermano. Es __su__ hermano.
5. Nosotras __tenemos__ unas mochilas. Son __nuestras__ mochilas.
6. Usted __tiene__ dos sobrinos. Son __sus__ sobrinos.

**3   Oraciones** Arrange the words in the correct order to form complete logical sentences. **¡Ojo!** Don't forget to conjugate the verbs. **10 pts.**

1. libros / unos / tener / interesantes / tú / muy
   Tú tienes unos libros muy interesantes.
2. dos / tener / grandes / universidad / mi / bibliotecas
   Mi universidad tiene dos bibliotecas grandes.
3. mi / francés / ser / amigo / buen / Hugo
   Hugo es mi buen amigo francés./Mi buen amigo francés es Hugo.
4. ser / simpáticas / dos / personas / nosotras
   Nosotras somos dos personas simpáticas.
5. menores / rubios / sus / ser / hermanos
   Sus hermanos menores son rubios.

---

**RESUMEN GRAMATICAL**

**3.1 Descriptive adjectives** *pp. 80–82*

**Forms and agreement of adjectives**

| Masculine | | Feminine | |
|---|---|---|---|
| **Singular** | **Plural** | **Singular** | **Plural** |
| alto | altos | alta | altas |
| inteligente | inteligentes | inteligente | inteligentes |
| trabajador | trabajadores | trabajadora | trabajadoras |

▶ Descriptive adjectives follow the noun: **el chico rubio**
▶ Adjectives of nationality also follow the noun: **la mujer española**
▶ Adjectives of quantity precede the noun: **muchos libros, dos turistas**

**Note:** When placed before a masculine noun, these adjectives are shortened.

**bueno → buen   malo → mal   grande → gran**

**3.2 Possessive adjectives** *p. 85*

| Singular | | Plural | |
|---|---|---|---|
| mi | nuestro/a | mis | nuestros/as |
| tu | vuestro/a | tus | vuestros/as |
| su | su | sus | sus |

**3.3 Present tense of -er and -ir verbs** *pp. 88–89*

| com**er** | | escrib**ir** | |
|---|---|---|---|
| como | comemos | escribo | escribimos |
| comes | coméis | escribes | escribís |
| come | comen | escribe | escriben |

**3.4 Present tense of tener and venir** *pp. 92–93*

| tener | | venir | |
|---|---|---|---|
| tengo | tenemos | vengo | venimos |
| tienes | tenéis | vienes | venís |
| tiene | tienen | viene | vienen |

---

**TEACHING OPTIONS**

**TPR** Make sets of cards containing –er and –ir infinitives that are easy to act out. Divide the class into groups of five. Have students take turns drawing a card and acting out the verb for the group. Once someone has correctly guessed the verb, the group members must take turns providing the conjugated forms.

**Extra Practice** To add a visual aspect to this grammar review, bring in magazine or newspaper photos of people and places. Have students describe the people and places using descriptive adjectives.

**4**  **Carta** Complete this letter with the appropriate forms of the verbs in the word list. Not all verbs will be used. **10 pts.**

| abrir | correr | recibir |
|-------|--------|---------|
| asistir | creer | tener |
| compartir | escribir | venir |
| comprender | leer | vivir |

Hola, Ángel,

¿Qué tal? (Yo) (1) _Escribo_ esta carta (this letter) en la biblioteca. Todos los días (2) _vengo_ aquí y (3) _leo_ un buen libro. Yo (4) _creo_ que es importante leer por diversión. Mi compañero de apartamento no (5) _comprende_ por qué me gusta leer. Él sólo (6) _abre/lee_ los libros de texto. Pero nosotros (7) _compartimos_ unos intereses. Por ejemplo, los dos somos atléticos; por las mañanas nosotros (8) _corremos_ . También nos gustan las ciencias; por las tardes (9) _asistimos_ a nuestra clase de biología. Y tú, ¿cómo estás? ¿(Tú) (10) _Tienes_ mucho trabajo?

**5**  **Su familia** Write a brief description of a friend's family. Describe the family members using vocabulary and structures from this lesson. Write at least five sentences. **12 pts.**
Answers will vary.

**modelo**

La familia de mi amiga Gabriela es grande. Ella tiene tres hermanos y una hermana. Su hermana mayor es periodista...

**6**  **Proverbio** Write the missing words to complete this proverb. **2 EXTRA points!**

❝Dos andares° _tiene_ el dinero°,
_viene_ despacio°
y se va° ligero°.❞

andares *gaits* dinero *money* despacio *slowly*
se va *it leaves* ligero *fast*

**recursos**

panorama.vhlcentral.com
Lección 3

## Section Goals

In **Lectura**, students will:
- learn to use context clues in reading
- read context-rich selections about Hispanic families

**Instructional Resources**
**Supersite**
*Cuaderno para hispanohablantes*

**Estrategia** Tell students that they can often infer the meaning of an unfamiliar Spanish word by looking at the word's context and by using their common sense. Five types of context clues are:
- synonyms
- antonyms
- clarifications
- definitions
- additional details

Have students read the sentence **Ayer fui a ver a mi tía abuela, la hermana de mi abuela** from the letter. Point out that the meaning of **tía abuela** can be inferred from its similarity to the known word **abuela** and from the clarification that follows in the letter.

**Examinar el texto** Have students read Paragraph 1 silently, without looking up the glossed words. Point out the phrase **salgo a pasear** and ask a volunteer to explain how the context might give clues to the meaning. Afterward, point out that **salgo** is the first-person singular form of **salir** (*to go out*). Tell students they will learn all the forms of **salir** in **Lección 4**.

**Examinar el formato** Guide students to see that the photos and captions reveal that the paragraphs are about several different families.

# Lectura

## Antes de leer

### Estrategia
**Guessing meaning from context**

As you read in Spanish, you'll often come across words you haven't learned. You can guess what they mean by looking at the surrounding words and sentences. Look at the following text and guess what **tía abuela** means, based on the context.

> ¡Hola, Claudia!
> ¿Qué hay de nuevo?
> ¿Sabes qué? Ayer fui a ver a mi tía abuela, la hermana de mi abuela. Tiene 85 años pero es muy independiente. Vive en un apartamento en Quito con su prima Lorena, quien también tiene 85 años.

If you guessed *great-aunt*, you are correct, and you can conclude from this word and the format clues that this is a letter about someone's visit with his or her great-aunt.

### Examinar el texto

Quickly read through the paragraphs and find two or three words you don't know. Using the context as your guide, guess what these words mean. Then glance at the paragraphs where these words appear and try to predict what the paragraphs are about.

### Examinar el formato

Look at the format of the reading. What clues do the captions, photos, and layout give you about its content?

**recursos**

panorama.vhlcentral.com
Lección 3

# Gente ··· Las familias

**1.** Me llamo Armando y tengo setenta años pero no me considero viejo. Tengo seis nietas y un nieto. Vivo con mi hija y tengo la oportunidad de pasar mucho tiempo con ella y con mi nieto. Por las tardes salgo a pasear° por el parque con mi nieto y por la noche le leo cuentos°.

Armando. Tiene seis nietas y un nieto.

**2.** Mi prima Victoria y yo nos llevamos muy bien. Estudiamos juntas° en la universidad y compartimos un apartamento. Ella es muy inteligente y me ayuda° con los estudios. Además°, es muy simpática y generosa. Si no tengo dinero°, ¡ella me lo presta!

Diana. Vive con su prima.

**3.** Me llamo Ramona y soy paraguaya, aunque° ahora vivo en los Estados Unidos. Tengo tres hijos, uno de nueve años, uno de doce y el mayor de quince. Es difícil a veces, pero mi esposo y yo tratamos° de ayudarlos y comprenderlos siempre°.

Ramona. Sus hijos son muy importantes para ella.

---

**4.** Tengo mucha suerte.
Aunque mis padres están
divorciados, tengo una
familia muy unida. Tengo dos
hermanos y dos hermanas. Me
gusta hablar y salir a fiestas con
ellos. Ahora tengo novio en la
universidad y él no conoce a
mis hermanos. ¡Espero que se
lleven bien!

Ana María. Su familia
es muy unida.

**5.** Antes quería° tener hermanos pero ya no°
es tan importante. Ser hija única tiene muchas
ventajas°: no tengo que
compartir mis cosas
con hermanos, no hay
discusiones° y, como
soy nieta única también,
¡mis abuelos piensan°
que soy perfecta!

Fernanda.
Es hija única.

**6.** Como soy joven todavía°, no tengo ni esposa
ni hijos. Pero tengo un sobrino, el hijo de mi
hermano, que es muy especial para mí. Se llama
Benjamín y tiene diez años. Es un muchacho muy
simpático. Siempre tiene hambre y por lo tanto
vamos° frecuentemente a comer hamburguesas.
Nos gusta también ir al cine° a ver películas
de acción.
Hablamos de
todo. ¡Creo que
ser tío es mejor
que ser padre!

Santiago. Ser
tío es divertido.

salgo a pasear *I go take a walk* cuentos *stories* juntas *together*
me ayuda *she helps me* Además *Besides* dinero *money* aunque *although*
tratamos *we try* siempre *always* quería *I wanted* ya no *no longer*
ventajas *advantages* discusiones *arguments* piensan *think* todavía *still*
vamos *we go* ir al cine *to go to the movies*

# Después de leer

## Emparejar

Glance at the paragraphs and see how the words and
phrases in column A are used in context. Then find their
definitions in column B.

| **A** | | **B** |
|---|---|---|
| 1. me lo presta | d | a. the oldest |
| 2. nos llevamos bien | h | b. movies |
| 3. no conoce | g | c. the youngest |
| 4. películas | b | d. loans it to me |
| 5. mejor que | j | e. borrows it from me |
| 6. el mayor | a | f. we see each other |
| | | g. doesn't know |
| | | h. we get along |
| | | i. portraits |
| | | j. better than |

## Seleccionar

Choose the sentence that best summarizes each
paragraph.

1. Párrafo 1 a
   a. Me gusta mucho ser abuelo.
   b. No hablo mucho con mi nieto.
   c. No tengo nietos.
2. Párrafo 2 c
   a. Mi prima es antipática.
   b. Mi prima no es muy trabajadora.
   c. Mi prima y yo somos muy buenas amigas.
3. Párrafo 3 a
   a. Tener hijos es un gran sacrificio pero es muy
      bonito también.
   b. No comprendo a mis hijos.
   c. Mi esposo y yo no tenemos hijos.
4. Párrafo 4 c
   a. No hablo mucho con mis hermanos.
   b. Comparto mis cosas con mis hermanos.
   c. Mis hermanos y yo somos como (*like*) amigos.
5. Párrafo 5 a
   a. Me gusta ser hija única.
   b. Tengo hermanos y hermanas.
   c. Vivo con mis abuelos.
6. Párrafo 6 b
   a. Mi sobrino tiene diez años.
   b. Me gusta mucho ser tío.
   c. Mi esposa y yo no tenemos hijos.

## Section Goals

In **Escritura**, students will:
- learn to write a friendly letter in Spanish
- integrate vocabulary and structures taught in **Lección 3** and before

**Instructional Resources**
**Supersite**
*Cuaderno para hispanohablantes*

**Estrategia** Have students create their idea maps in Spanish. Some students may find it helpful to create their idea maps with note cards. They can write each detail that would be contained in a circle on a separate card to facilitate rearrangement.

**Tema**
- Introduce students to the common salutations (**saludos**) and closings (**despedidas**) used in friendly letters in Spanish. Point out that the salutation **Estimado/a** is more formal than **Querido/a**, which is rather familiar. Also point out that **Un abrazo** is less familiar in Spanish than its translation *A hug* would be in English.
- Point out that **Estimado/a** and **Querido/a** are adjectives and therefore agree in gender and number with the nouns they modify. Write these salutations on the board and have students supply the correct form:

  ____ **Señora Martínez:**
  (Estimada)
  ____ **Allison:** (Querida)
  ____ **padres:** (Queridos)
- Point out the use of the colon (**dos puntos**). Tell students that a colon is used instead of a comma in letter salutations.

# Escritura SUPERSITE

## Estrategia
### Using idea maps

How do you organize ideas for a first draft? Often, the organization of ideas represents the most challenging part of the process. Idea maps are useful for organizing pertinent information. Here is an example of an idea map you can use:

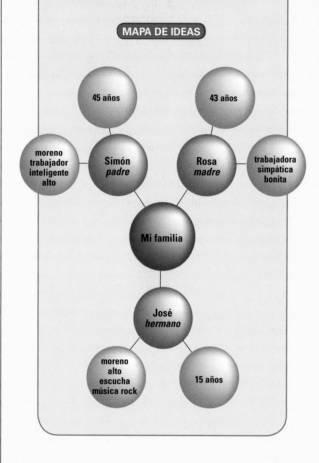

MAPA DE IDEAS

45 años

43 años

moreno trabajador inteligente alto

Simón *padre*

Rosa *madre*

trabajadora simpática bonita

Mi familia

José *hermano*

moreno alto escucha música rock

15 años

**recursos**
SUPERSITE
panorama.vhlcentral.com
Lección 3

## Tema

NATIONAL communication STANDARDS

### Escribir una carta

A friend you met in a chat room for Spanish speakers wants to know about your family. Using some of the verbs and adjectives you have learned in this lesson, write a brief letter describing your family or an imaginary family, including:

▸ Names and relationships
▸ Physical characteristics
▸ Hobbies and interests

Here are some useful expressions for letter writing in Spanish:

( Salutations )

| | |
|---|---|
| **Estimado/a Julio/Julia:** | *Dear Julio/Julia,* |
| **Querido/a Miguel/Ana María:** | *Dear Miguel/Ana María,* |

( Closings )

| | |
|---|---|
| **Un abrazo,** | *A hug,* |
| **Abrazos,** | *Hugs,* |
| **Cariños,** | *Much love,* |
| **¡Hasta pronto!** | *See you soon!* |
| **¡Hasta la próxima semana!** | *See you next week!* |

**EVALUATION: Carta**

| Criteria | Scale |
|---|---|
| Appropriate salutations/closings | 1 2 3 4 5 |
| Appropriate details | 1 2 3 4 5 |
| Organization | 1 2 3 4 5 |
| Accuracy | 1 2 3 4 5 |

| Scoring | |
|---|---|
| Excellent | 18–20 points |
| Good | 14–17 points |
| Satisfactory | 10–13 points |
| Unsatisfactory | < 10 points |

# Escuchar

## Estrategia

**Asking for repetition/
Replaying the recording**

Sometimes it is difficult to understand what people say, especially in a noisy environment. During a conversation, you can ask someone to repeat by saying **¿Cómo?** (*What?*) or **¿Perdón?** (*Pardon me?*). In class, you can ask your teacher to repeat by saying **Repita, por favor** (*Repeat, please*). If you don't understand a recorded activity, you can simply replay it.

 To help you practice this strategy, you will listen to a short paragraph. Ask your professor to repeat it or replay the recording, and then summarize what you heard.

## Preparación

Based on the photograph, where do you think Cristina and Laura are? What do you think Laura is saying to Cristina?

## Ahora escucha

Now you are going to hear Laura and Cristina's conversation. Use **R** to indicate which adjectives describe Cristina's boyfriend, Rafael. Use **E** for adjectives that describe Laura's boyfriend, Esteban. Some adjectives will not be used.

| | | | |
|---|---|---|---|
| ___ | rubio | _E_ | interesante |
| ___ | feo | ___ | antipático |
| _R_ | alto | _R_ | inteligente |
| _E_ | trabajador | _R_ | moreno |
| _E_ | un poco gordo | ___ | viejo |

**recursos**
panorama.vhlcentral.com
Lección 3

## Comprensión

### Identificar

Which person would make each statement: Cristina or Laura?

*(NATIONAL communication STANDARDS)*

| | Cristina | Laura |
|---|:---:|:---:|
| 1. Mi novio habla sólo de fútbol y de béisbol. | ☑ | ○ |
| 2. Tengo un novio muy interesante y simpático. | ○ | ☑ |
| 3. Mi novio es alto y moreno. | ☑ | ○ |
| 4. Mi novio trabaja mucho. | ○ | ☑ |
| 5. Mi amiga no tiene buena suerte con los muchachos. | ○ | ☑ |
| 6. El novio de mi amiga es un poco gordo, pero guapo. | ☑ | ○ |

### ¿Cierto o falso?

Indicate whether each sentence is **cierto** or **falso,** then correct the false statements.

| | Cierto | Falso |
|---|:---:|:---:|
| 1. Esteban es un chico interesante y simpático. | ☑ | ○ |
| 2. Laura tiene mala suerte con los chicos.<br>Cristina tiene mala suerte con los chicos. | ○ | ☑ |
| 3. Rafael es muy interesante.<br>Esteban es muy interesante. | ○ | ☑ |
| 4. Laura y su novio hablan de muchas cosas. | ☑ | ○ |

L: Esteban es muy simpático. Es un poco gordo pero creo que es muy guapo. También es muy trabajador.
C: ¿Es interesante?

L: Sí. Hablamos dos o tres horas cada día. Hablamos de muchas cosas… las clases, los amigos… de todo.
C: ¡Qué bien! Siempre tengo mala suerte con los novios.

## Section Goals

In **Escuchar**, students will:
- listen to and summarize a short paragraph
- learn strategies for asking for clarification in oral communication
- answer questions based on the content of a recorded conversation

**Instructional Resources**
**Supersite:** Textbook MP3 Audio Files
**Supersite/IRCD:** *IRM* (Textbook Audio Script)

**Estrategia**
**Script** La familia de María Dolores es muy grande. Tiene dos hermanos y tres hermanas. Su familia vive en España. Pero la familia de Alberto es muy pequeña. No tiene hermanos ni hermanas. Alberto y sus padres viven en el Ecuador.

**Teaching Tip** Have students look at the photo and describe what they see. Guide them to guess where they think **Cristina** and **Laura** are and what they are talking about.

**Ahora escucha**
**Script** LAURA: ¿Qué hay de nuevo, Cristina?
CRISTINA: No mucho… sólo problemas con mi novio.
L: ¿Perdón?
C: No hay mucho de nuevo… sólo problemas con mi novio, Rafael.
L: ¿Qué les pasa?
C: Bueno, Rafael es alto y moreno… es muy guapo. Y es buena gente. Es inteligente también… pero es que no lo encuentro muy interesante.
L: ¿Cómo?
C: No es muy interesante. Sólo habla del fútbol y del béisbol. No me gusta hablar del fútbol las veinticuatro horas al día. No comprendo a los muchachos. ¿Cómo es tu novio, Laura?

*(Script continues at far left in the bottom panels.)*

# En pantalla

The American concept of dating does not exist in the same way in countries like Mexico, Spain, and Argentina. In the Spanish-speaking world, at the beginning of a relationship couples can go out without the social or psychological pressures and expectations of "being on a date." Relationships develop just like in the rest of the world, but perhaps in a more spontaneous manner and without insisting on labels.

### Vocabulario útil

| | |
|---|---|
| has sido | you have been |
| maravillosa | wonderful |
| conmigo | with me |
| te sorprenda | it catches you by surprise |
| quiero que me dejes | I want you to let me |
| explicarte | explain to you |
| por muy bajo que te parezca | however low it seems to you |
| lo que hago | what I do |
| Gracias por haberme querido escuchar. | Thank you for having wanted to listen to me. |
| que me dejes | that you leave me |
| haberme querido | having loved me |
| vida | life |

### Preguntas

Answer these questions.

1. Who wrote the letter to the young woman? Her boyfriend wrote her the letter.
2. What do you think she was expecting from the letter? Answers will vary.
3. How does she feel at the end of the ad? Why? Answers will vary. Sample answer: She feels satisfied, because she turned the letter into something positive for her.

### Conversar

Answer these questions with a classmate. Answers will vary.

1. What is your opinion about the young woman's reaction to the letter?
2. What do you think about ending a relationship by mail?
3. What other ways do people use to break up?

algo falla *something is wrong*  por eso *that's why* hay que acabar *we must break up*  Sería *It would be*  lo que ha sido *what has been*

## Anuncio de Pentel

**Eres una buena chica.**

**Pero algo falla°, por eso° hay que acabar°.**

**Sería° tonto convertir en feo lo que ha sido° bonito.**

**recursos**

panorama.vhlcentral.com
Lección 3

**SUPERSITE** **Conexión Internet**

Go to **panorama.vhlcentral.com** to watch the TV clip featured in this **En pantalla** section.

# Oye cómo va

## Olimpo Cárdenas

Ecuadorian vocalist **Olimpo Cárdenas Moreira** was born in the town of Vinces in 1919. A singer from the age of eight, at ten years old he began participating in children's music competitions in Guayaquil and Quito. In 1946 Cárdenas recorded, as a duet with Carlos Rubira Infante, the song *En las lejanías*. Of the more than fifty albums he completed during his career, six were joint endeavors with another famous Ecuadorian singer, Julio Jaramillo. Some of the songs Cárdenas made famous are *Temeridad*, *Hay que saber perder*, *Nuestro juramento*, and *Lágrimas de amor*. He often performed internationally, in countries such as Colombia, Venezuela, Mexico, and the United States. In 1991, Olimpo Cárdenas died in Tuluá, Colombia, the country where he had resided for many years.

Your instructor will play the song. Listen and then complete these activities.

## Completar

Complete each sentence.

1. Olimpo Cárdenas started singing when he was ____eight____ years old.
2. He recorded _En las lejanías_ with Carlos Rubira Infante.
3. He visited Colombia, __Venezuela__, Mexico, and the U.S. with his music.
4. Cárdenas died in 1991 in ____Tuluá____, Colombia.

## Interpretación

Answer these questions in Spanish. Then, share your answers with a classmate.   Answers will vary.

1. Describe the girl to whom this song is dedicated.
2. What do you think her relationship is with the singer?
3. If the girl had to reply to this song, what do you think she would say?

## Chacha linda

National Standards — communication, cultures

Chacha°,
mi chacha linda°,
cómo te adoro, mi linda muchacha;
no sé° si pueda° dejar de° quererte°,
no sé si pueda dejarte de amar°.

### El pasillo

Olimpo Cárdenas and Julio Jaramillo were famous for their interpretations of **pasillo**, which is considered the national music of Ecuador. **El pasillo**, a sentimental and romantic musical style, descended from the waltz and is closely related to the **bolero**.

**Julio Jaramillo**

**recursos**

SUPERSITE

panorama.vhlcentral.com
Lección 3

**SUPERSITE Conexión Internet**

Go to **panorama.vhlcentral.com** to learn more about the artist featured in this **Oye cómo va** section.

chacha *short for* Muchacha   linda *pretty*   no sé *I don't know*   si pueda *if I could*   dejar de *stop*   quererte *loving you*   dejarte de amar *stop loving you*

## Section Goal

In **Panorama**, students will receive comprehensible input by reading about the geography and culture of Ecuador.

**Instructional Resources**
**Supersite/DVD:** *Panorama cultural*
**Supersite/IRCD:** *PowerPoints* (Overheads #5, #6, #18); *IRM* (*Panorama cultural* Videoscript & Translation, WBs/VM/LM Answer Key)
**WebSAM**
**Workbook,** pp. 33–34
**Video Manual,** pp. 229–230

**Teaching Tip** Have students look at the map of Ecuador or show *Overhead PowerPoint #18*. Then have them look at the call-out photos and read the captions. Encourage students to mention anything they may know about Ecuador.

**El país en cifras**
• Ask students to glance at the headings. Establish the kind of information contained in each and clarify unfamiliar words. Point out that every word in the headings has an English cognate.
• Point out that in September 2000, the U.S. dollar became the official currency of Ecuador.

**¡Increíble pero cierto!**
Mt. St. Helens in Washington and **Cotopaxi** in Ecuador are just two of a chain of volcanoes that stretches along the entire Pacific coast of North and South America, from Mt. McKinley in Alaska to **Monte Sarmiento** in the **Tierra del Fuego** of southern Chile.

# Ecuador

*connections cultures NATIONAL STANDARDS*

## El país en cifras

▶ **Área:** 283.560 km² (109.483 millas²), *incluyendo las islas Galápagos, aproximadamente el área de Colorado*

▶ **Población:** 14.192.000

▶ **Capital:** Quito — 1.680.000

▶ **Ciudades° principales:**
Guayaquil — 2.709.000, Cuenca, Machala, Portoviejo

SOURCE: Population Division, UN Secretariat

▶ **Moneda:** dólar estadounidense

▶ **Idiomas:** español (oficial), quichua

*La lengua oficial del Ecuador es el español, pero también se hablan° otras° lenguas en el país. Aproximadamente unos 4.000.000 de ecuatorianos hablan lenguas indígenas; la mayoría° de ellos habla quichua. El quichua es el dialecto ecuatoriano del quechua, la lengua de los incas.*

Bandera del Ecuador

### Ecuatorianos célebres

▶ **Francisco Eugenio De Santa Cruz y Espejo,** médico, periodista y patriota (1747–1795)

▶ **Juan León Mera,** novelista (1832–1894)

▶ **Eduardo Kingman,** pintor° (1913–1998)

▶ **Rosalía Arteaga,** abogada°, política y ex-vicepresidenta (1956– )

Ciudades *cities* se hablan *are spoken* otras *other* mayoría *majority* pintor *painter* abogada *lawyer* sur *south* mundo *world* pies *feet* dos veces más alto que *twice as tall as*

Las islas Galápagos

COLOMBIA

Indígenas de Amazonas

Río Esmeraldas

• Ibarra

Quito ☆

Volcán Cotopaxi

Río Napo

Portoviejo

Río Daule

Volcán Tungurahua

Río Pastaza

Cordillera de los Andes

Guayaquil

Volcán Chimborazo

Océano Pacífico

Cuenca

Los indígenas del Ecuador hablan quichua.

Machala

• Loja

La ciudad de Quito y la Cordillera de los Andes

PERÚ

Catedral de Guayaquil

**recursos**

WB pp. 33–34

VM pp. 229–230

SUPERSITE panorama.vhlcentral.com Lección 3

### ¡Increíble pero cierto!

El volcán Cotopaxi, situado a unos 60 kilómetros al sur° de Quito, es considerado el volcán activo más alto del mundo°. Tiene una altura de 5.897 metros (19.340 pies°). Es dos veces más alto que° el monte St. Helens (2.550 metros o 9.215 pies) en el estado de Washington.

---

**TEACHING OPTIONS**

**Heritage Speakers** If a heritage speaker is of Ecuadorian origin or has visited Ecuador, ask him or her to prepare a short presentation about his or her experiences there. If possible, the presentation should be illustrated with photos and articles of the country.

**Language Notes** Remind students that **km²** is the abbreviation for **kilómetros cuadrados** and that **millas²** is the abbreviation for **millas cuadradas**. Ask a volunteer to explain why **kilómetros** takes **cuadrados** and **millas** takes **cuadradas**.

### Lugares • Las islas Galápagos

Muchas personas vienen de lejos a visitar las islas Galápagos porque son un verdadero tesoro° ecológico. Aquí Charles Darwin estudió° las especies que inspiraron° sus ideas sobre la evolución. Como las islas están lejos del continente, sus plantas y animales son únicos. Las islas son famosas por sus tortugas° gigantes.

### Artes • Oswaldo Guayasamín

Oswaldo Guayasamín fue° uno de los artistas latinoamericanos más famosos del mundo. Fue escultor° y muralista. Su expresivo estilo viene del cubismo y sus temas preferidos son la injusticia y la pobreza° sufridas° por los indígenas de su país.

*Madre y niño en azul*, 1986, Oswaldo Guayasamín

### Deportes • El *trekking*

El sistema montañoso de los Andes cruza° y divide el Ecuador en varias regiones. La Sierra, que tiene volcanes, grandes valles y una variedad increíble de plantas y animales, es perfecta para el *trekking*. Muchos turistas visitan el Ecuador cada° año para hacer° *trekking* y escalar montañas°.

### Lugares • Latitud 0

Hay un monumento en el Ecuador, a unos 22 kilómetros (14 millas) de Quito, donde los visitantes están en el hemisferio norte y el hemisferio sur a la vez°. Este monumento se llama la Mitad del Mundo°, y es un destino turístico muy popular.

*Explosión del volcán Tungurahua en 1999*

**¿Qué aprendiste?** Completa las oraciones con la información correcta.

1. La ciudad más grande (*biggest*) del Ecuador es ___Guayaquil___.
2. La capital del Ecuador es ___Quito___.
3. Unos 4.000.000 de ecuatorianos hablan ___lenguas indígenas___
4. Darwin estudió el proceso de la evolución en ___las islas Galápagos___.
5. Dos temas del arte de ___Guayasamín___ son la pobreza y la ___injusticia___.
6. Un monumento muy popular es ___la Mitad del Mundo___.
7. La Sierra es un lugar perfecto para el ___trekking___.
8. El volcán ___Cotopaxi___ es el volcán activo más alto del mundo.

**Conexión Internet** Investiga estos temas en **panorama.vhlcentral.com**.

1. Busca información sobre una ciudad del Ecuador. ¿Te gustaría (*Would you like*) visitar la ciudad? ¿Por qué?
2. Haz una lista de tres animales o plantas que viven sólo en las islas Galápagos. ¿Dónde hay animales o plantas similares?

............................................................................................

**verdadero tesoro** *true treasure* **estudió** *studied* **inspiraron** *inspired* **tortugas** *tortoises* **fue** *was* **escultor** *sculptor* **pobreza** *poverty* **sufridas** *suffered* **cruza** *crosses* **cada** *every* **hacer** *to do* **escalar montañas** *to climb mountains* **a la vez** *at the same time* **Mitad del Mundo** *Equatorial Line Monument (lit. Midpoint of the World)*

**Instructional Resources**
**Supersite:** Textbook &
Vocabulary MP3 Audio Files
**Lección 3**
**Supersite/IRCD:** *IRM* (WBs/
VM/LM Answer Key); *Testing
Program* (**Lección 3 Pruebas,**
Test Generator, Testing
Program MP3 Audio Files)
**WebSAM**
**Lab Manual,** p. 18

## La familia

| | |
|---|---|
| el/la abuelo/a | grandfather/grandmother |
| los abuelos | grandparents |
| el apellido | last name |
| el/la bisabuelo/a | great-grandfather/great-grandmother |
| el/la cuñado/a | brother-in-law/sister-in-law |
| el/la esposo/a | husband; wife; spouse |
| la familia | family |
| el/la gemelo/a | twin |
| el/la hermanastro/a | stepbrother/stepsister |
| el/la hermano/a | brother/sister |
| el/la hijastro/a | stepson/stepdaughter |
| el/la hijo/a | son/daughter |
| los hijos | children |
| la madrastra | stepmother |
| la madre | mother |
| el/la medio/a hermano/a | half-brother/half-sister |
| el/la nieto/a | grandson/granddaughter |
| la nuera | daughter-in-law |
| el padrastro | stepfather |
| el padre | father |
| los padres | parents |
| los parientes | relatives |
| el/la primo/a | cousin |
| el/la sobrino/a | nephew/niece |
| el/la suegro/a | father-in-law/mother-in-law |
| el/la tío/a | uncle/aunt |
| el yerno | son-in-law |

## Otras personas

| | |
|---|---|
| el/la amigo/a | friend |
| la gente | people |
| el/la muchacho/a | boy/girl |
| el/la niño/a | child |
| el/la novio/a | boyfriend/girlfriend |
| la persona | person |

## Profesiones

| | |
|---|---|
| el/la artista | artist |
| el/la doctor(a), el/la médico/a | doctor; physician |
| el/la ingeniero/a | engineer |
| el/la periodista | journalist |
| el/la programador(a) | computer programmer |

## Adjetivos

| | |
|---|---|
| alto/a | tall |
| antipático/a | unpleasant |
| bajo/a | short (in height) |
| bonito/a | pretty |
| buen, bueno/a | good |
| delgado/a | thin; slender |
| difícil | difficult; hard |
| fácil | easy |
| feo/a | ugly |
| gordo/a | fat |
| gran, grande | big; large |
| guapo/a | handsome; good-looking |
| importante | important |
| inteligente | intelligent |
| interesante | interesting |
| joven | young |
| mal, malo/a | bad |
| mismo/a | same |
| moreno/a | brunet(te) |
| mucho/a | much; many; a lot of |
| pelirrojo/a | red-haired |
| pequeño/a | small |
| rubio/a | blond(e) |
| simpático/a | nice; likeable |
| tonto/a | silly; foolish |
| trabajador(a) | hard-working |
| viejo/a | old |

## Nacionalidades

| | |
|---|---|
| alemán, alemana | German |
| canadiense | Canadian |
| chino/a | Chinese |
| ecuatoriano/a | Ecuadorian |
| español(a) | Spanish |
| estadounidense | from the U.S. |
| francés, francesa | French |
| inglés, inglesa | English |
| italiano/a | Italian |
| japonés, japonesa | Japanese |
| mexicano/a | Mexican |
| norteamericano/a | (North) American |
| puertorriqueño/a | Puerto Rican |
| ruso/a | Russian |

## Verbos

| | |
|---|---|
| abrir | to open |
| aprender (a + *inf.*) | to learn |
| asistir (a) | to attend |
| beber | to drink |
| comer | to eat |
| compartir | to share |
| comprender | to understand |
| correr | to run |
| creer (en) | to believe (in) |
| deber (+ *inf.*) | should; must; ought to |
| decidir (+ *inf.*) | to decide |
| describir | to describe |
| escribir | to write |
| leer | to read |
| recibir | to receive |
| tener | to have |
| venir | to come |
| vivir | to live |

| | |
|---|---|
| Possessive adjectives | See page 85. |
| Expressions with *tener* | See page 93. |
| Expresiones útiles | See page 75. |

**recursos**

LM
p. 18

panorama.vhlcentral.com
Lección 3

# Los pasatiempos

## 4

### Communicative Goals

**You will learn how to:**

- **Talk about pastimes, weekend activities, and sports**
- **Make plans and invitations**

### A PRIMERA VISTA
- ¿Qué son estas personas, atletas o artistas?
- ¿En qué tienen interés, en el fútbol o el tenis?
- ¿Son viejos? ¿Son delgados?
- ¿Tienen frío o calor?

### Lesson Goals

In **Lección 4**, students will be introduced to the following:
- names of sports and other pastimes
- names of places in a city
- soccer rivalries
- Cuban sprinter **Anier García** and Argentine field hockey player **Luciana Aymar**
- present tense of **ir**
- the contraction **al**
- **ir a** + [*infinitive*]
- present tense of common stem-changing verbs
- verbs with irregular **yo** forms
- predicting content by surveying graphic elements
- cultural, historical, economic, and geographic information about Mexico

**A primera vista** Here are some additional questions you can ask based on the photo: **¿Te gusta el fútbol? ¿Crees que son importantes los pasatiempos? ¿Trabajas mucho los sábados y domingos? ¿Bailas? ¿Lees? ¿Escuchas música?**

**INSTRUCTIONAL RESOURCES**

**MAESTRO™ SUPERSITE (panorama.vhlcentral.com)**
Textbook, Vocabulary, & Lab MP3 Audio Files
Additional Practice
Learning Management System (Assignment Task Manager, Gradebook)
*Also on DVD*
 **Fotonovela**

**Flash cultura**
**Panorama cultural**
*Also on Instructor's Resource CD-ROM*
 *PowerPoints* (**Contextos** & **Estructura** Presentations, Overheads)
 *Instructor's Resource Manual* (Handouts, Textbook Answer Key, WBs/VM/LM Answer Key,

Audioscripts, Videoscripts & Translations)
 *Testing Program* (**Pruebas,** Test Generator, MP3s)
**WebSAM** (Workbook/Video Manual/Lab Manual)
**Workbook/Video Manual**
*Cuaderno para hispanohablantes*
**Lab Manual**

# Los pasatiempos

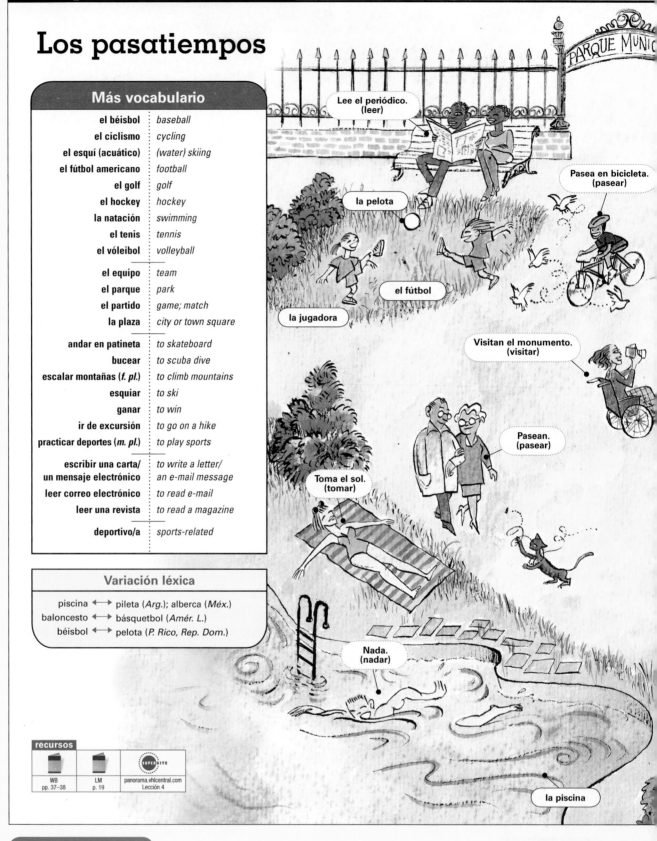

## Más vocabulario

| | |
|---|---|
| el béisbol | baseball |
| el ciclismo | cycling |
| el esquí (acuático) | (water) skiing |
| el fútbol americano | football |
| el golf | golf |
| el hockey | hockey |
| la natación | swimming |
| el tenis | tennis |
| el vóleibol | volleyball |
| el equipo | team |
| el parque | park |
| el partido | game; match |
| la plaza | city or town square |
| andar en patineta | to skateboard |
| bucear | to scuba dive |
| escalar montañas (f. pl.) | to climb mountains |
| esquiar | to ski |
| ganar | to win |
| ir de excursión | to go on a hike |
| practicar deportes (m. pl.) | to play sports |
| escribir una carta/ un mensaje electrónico | to write a letter/ an e-mail message |
| leer correo electrónico | to read e-mail |
| leer una revista | to read a magazine |
| deportivo/a | sports-related |

Lee el periódico. (leer)

Pasea en bicicleta. (pasear)

la pelota

el fútbol

la jugadora

Visitan el monumento. (visitar)

Pasean. (pasear)

Toma el sol. (tomar)

Nada. (nadar)

la piscina

## Variación léxica

| | |
|---|---|
| piscina ⟷ | pileta (*Arg.*); alberca (*Méx.*) |
| baloncesto ⟷ | básquetbol (*Amér. L.*) |
| béisbol ⟷ | pelota (*P. Rico, Rep. Dom.*) |

**recursos**

WB pp. 37–38

LM p. 19

**SUPERSITE** panorama.vhlcentral.com Lección 4

# Práctica

na en línea.
patinar)

el jugador

el baloncesto

**1** **Escuchar** 🎧 Indicate the letter of the activity in Column B that best corresponds to each statement you hear. Two items in Column B will not be used.

| A | B |
|---|---|
| 1. __b__ | a. leer correo electrónico |
| 2. __d__ | b. tomar el sol |
| 3. __f__ | c. pasear en bicicleta |
| 4. __c__ | d. ir a un partido de fútbol americano |
| 5. __g__ | e. escribir una carta |
| 6. __h__ | f. practicar muchos deportes |
| | g. nadar |
| | h. ir de excursión |

**2** **Ordenar** 🎧 Order these activities according to what you hear in the narration.

__5__ pasear en bicicleta        __3__ tomar el sol

__1__ nadar                              __6__ practicar deportes

__4__ leer una revista            __2__ patinar en línea

**3** **¿Cierto o falso?** Indicate whether each statement is **cierto** or **falso** based on the illustration.

| | Cierto | Falso |
|---|---|---|
| 1. Un hombre nada en la piscina. | ☑ | ○ |
| 2. Un hombre lee una revista. | ○ | ☑ |
| 3. Un chico pasea en bicicleta. | ☑ | ○ |
| 4. Dos muchachos esquían. | ○ | ☑ |
| 5. Una mujer y dos niños visitan un monumento. | ☑ | ○ |
| 6. Un hombre bucea. | ○ | ☑ |
| 7. Hay un equipo de hockey. | ○ | ☑ |
| 8. Una mujer toma el sol. | ☑ | ○ |

**4** **Clasificar** Fill in the chart below with as many terms from **Contextos** as you can. Answers will vary.

| Actividades | Deportes | Personas |
|---|---|---|
| | | |
| | | |
| | | |
| | | |
| | | |
| | | |

SUPERSITE

---

**TEACHING OPTIONS**

**Extra Practice** Add an auditory exercise to this vocabulary practice. Prepare short descriptions in which you mention sports and leisure activities. Read each description aloud and have students name an appropriate location. Ex: **Necesito estudiar en un lugar tranquilo. También deseo leer una revista y unos periódicos. (la biblioteca)**

**Game** Play a modified version of **20 Preguntas**. Ask a volunteer to think of an activity, person, or place from the scene or **Más vocabulario** that other students will take turns guessing by asking yes-no questions. Limit the attempts to ten questions, after which the volunteer will reveal the secret item. You may need to provide some phrases on the board.

---

**1** **Teaching Tip** Have students check their answers by going over **Actividad 1** with the class.

**1** **Script** 1. No me gusta nadar pero paso mucho tiempo al lado de la piscina. 2. Alicia y yo vamos al estadio a las cuatro. Creemos que nuestro equipo va a ganar. 3. Me gusta patinar en línea, esquiar y practicar el tenis. 4. El ciclismo es mi deporte favorito. 5. Me gusta mucho la natación. Paso mucho tiempo en la piscina. 6. Mi hermana es una gran excursionista.
*Textbook MP3s*

**2** **Teaching Tips**
• To simplify, prepare the class for listening by having students read the list aloud.
• Ask students if the verbs in the list are conjugated or if they are infinitives. Tell them that the verbs they hear in the audio recording may be in the infinitive or conjugated form.

**2** **Script** Hoy es sábado y mis amigos y yo estamos en el parque. Todos tenemos pasatiempos diferentes. Clara y Daniel nadan en la piscina. Luis patina en línea. Sergio y Paco toman el sol. Dalia lee una revista. Rosa y yo paseamos en bicicleta. Y tú, ¿practicas deportes?
*Textbook MP3s*

**3** **Expansion** Ask students to write three additional true-false sentences based on the scene. Have volunteers read sentences aloud for the rest of the class to answer.

**4** **Expansion** Ask students to provide complete sentences for each category. You can cue students to elicit more responses. Ex: **¿Qué es la natación? (La natación es un deporte.)**

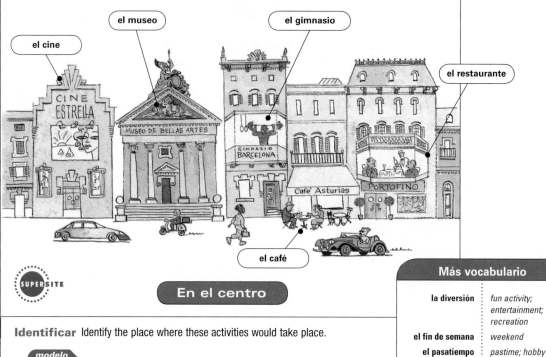

el cine

el museo

el gimnasio

el restaurante

CINE ESTRELLA

MUSEO DE BELLAS ARTES

GIMNASIO BARCELONA

Café Asturias

PORTOFINO

el café

**SUPERSITE**

**En el centro**

## Más vocabulario

| | |
|---|---|
| la diversión | fun activity; entertainment; recreation |
| el fin de semana | weekend |
| el pasatiempo | pastime; hobby |
| los ratos libres | spare (free) time |
| el videojuego | video game |
| la iglesia | church |
| el lugar | place |
| ver películas (*f. pl.*) | to see movies |
| favorito/a | favorite |

**Teaching Tip** Show *Overhead PowerPoint #20* and ask brief yes-no questions to review vocabulary in **En el centro** and **Más vocabulario.** Ex: **¿Hay muchas diversiones en el centro? No tienen ratos libres los fines de semana, ¿verdad? ¿Pasan ustedes los ratos libres en el museo?**

**5 Expansion**
• Read each item aloud and ask individuals to respond. After each answer is given, ask a different student to verify whether the answer is correct, using a complete sentence. Do the first verification yourself to model possible student responses. Ex: **—Tomamos una limonada. —Es un café/restaurante. —Sí. En un café/restaurante tomamos una limonada.**
• To challenge students, ask them to convert items into yes-no questions. Ex: **¿Tomamos una limonada en el café? (Sí.) ¿Vemos una película en el restaurante? (No.)** Have student pairs take turns answering questions.

**6 Teaching Tip** Before beginning the activity, review the verb **gustar** that students learned in **Lección 2.**

**6 Expansion** Have the same pairs ask each other additional questions. Then ask volunteers to share their mini-conversations with the class.

**5** **Identificar** Identify the place where these activities would take place.

**modelo**
Esquiamos.
Es una montaña.

1. Tomamos una limonada. Es un café./Es un restaurante.
2. Vemos una película. Es un cine.
3. Nadamos y tomamos el sol. Es una piscina./Es un parque.
4. Hay muchos monumentos. Es un parque./Es una ciudad.
5. Comemos tacos y fajitas. Es un restaurante.
6. Miramos pinturas (*paintings*) de Diego Rivera y Frida Kahlo. Es un museo.
7. Hay mucho tráfico. Es una ciudad./Es el centro.
8. Practicamos deportes. Es un gimnasio./Es un parque.

**6** **Entrevista** In pairs, take turns asking and answering the questions. Answers will vary.

1. ¿Hay un café cerca de la universidad? ¿Dónde está?
2. ¿Cuál es tu restaurante favorito?
3. ¿Te gusta viajar y visitar monumentos? ¿Por qué?
4. ¿Te gusta ir al cine los fines de semana?
5. ¿Cuáles son tus películas favoritas?
6. ¿Te gusta practicar deportes?
7. ¿Cuáles son tus deportes favoritos? ¿Por qué?
8. ¿Cuáles son tus pasatiempos favoritos?

**CONSULTA**

To review expressions with **gustar**, see **Estructura 2.1**, p. 48.

UN DÍA CON ÁNGELA

Un día inolvidable.

---

**TEACHING OPTIONS**

**Extra Practice** Give students five minutes to write a description of a typical weekend: what they do and where, and with whom they spend time. Circulate through the class and help with unfamiliar vocabulary. Have volunteers share their paragraphs with the class, who will decide if the weekend descriptions are "typical."

**Game** Have students tell a chain story. For example, one student begins with: **Es el sábado por la mañana y voy [al café].** The next student continues with: **Estoy en el café y tomo una Coca-Cola.** You may need to provide some phrases on the board: **voy a/al... , luego, después.** The story may change location; set a time limit for each response. The game ends after ten minutes or when all students have participated.

# Comunicación

**7** **Preguntar** Ask a classmate what he or she does in the places mentioned below. Your classmate will respond using verbs from the word bank. Answers will vary.

| | | |
|---|---|---|
| beber | escribir | patinar |
| caminar | leer | practicar |
| correr | mirar | tomar |
| escalar | nadar | visitar |

> **modelo**
> una plaza
> **Estudiante 1:** ¿Qué haces (*What do you do*) cuando estás en una plaza?
> **Estudiante 2:** Camino por la plaza y miro a las personas.

1. una biblioteca
2. un estadio
3. una plaza
4. una piscina
5. las montañas
6. un parque
7. un café
8. un museo

**8** **Conversación** Using the words and expressions provided, work with a partner to prepare a short conversation about your pastimes. Answers will vary.

| | | |
|---|---|---|
| ¿a qué hora? | ¿con quién(es)? | ¿dónde? |
| ¿cómo? | ¿cuándo? | ¿qué? |

> **modelo**
> **Estudiante 1:** ¿Cuándo patinas en línea?
> **Estudiante 2:** Patino en línea los domingos. Y tú, ¿patinas en línea?
> **Estudiante 1:** No, no me gusta patinar en línea. Me gusta practicar el béisbol.

**9** **Pasatiempos** In pairs, tell each other what pastimes three of your friends and family members enjoy. Be prepared to share with the class any pastimes you noticed they have in common. Answers will vary.

> **modelo**
> **Estudiante 1:** Mi hermana pasea mucho en bicicleta. Pero mis padres practican la natación. Mi hermano no nada, pero visita muchos museos.
> **Estudiante 2:** Mi primo lee muchas revistas, pero no practica muchos deportes. Mis tíos esquían y practican el golf...

---

**7** **Teaching Tip** Quickly review the verbs in the list. Make sure that students understand the meaning of **¿Qué haces... ?** Tell them that they will use this phrase throughout the activity.

**7** **Expansion**
- Ask additional questions and have volunteers answer. Ex: **¿Qué haces en la residencia estudiantil (el apartamento, la casa)?** Suggested places: **la casa de un amigo/una amiga, el centro, el gimnasio**
- Have students share their responses with the class. Then have them create a table based on the responses. Ex: **En la biblioteca: yo (leo, trabajo en la computadora)**

**8** **Expansion** After students have asked and answered questions, ask volunteers to report their partners' activities back to the class. The partners should verify the information.

**9** **Expansion**
- Ask volunteers to share any pastimes they and their partners, friends, and families have in common. Ask for a show of hands to find out which activities are most popular and where they do them. What are the general tendencies of the class?
- In pairs, have students write sentences about the pastimes of a famous person. Then have them work with another pair, who will guess who is the famous person being described.

---

**TEACHING OPTIONS**

**Large Group** Have students write down six activities they enjoy and then circulate the room to collect signatures from others who enjoy the same activities (**¿Te gusta... ? Firma aquí, por favor.**). Ask volunteers to report back to the class. What activities are most popular?

**Game** Have students use complete sentences with **gustar** to write down five activities they enjoy. Collect and shuffle the slips of paper. Divide the class into two teams. Pull out and read aloud each slip of paper, and have the teams take turns guessing the student's identity.

# ¡Vamos al parque!

*Los estudiantes pasean por la ciudad y hablan de sus pasatiempos.*

NATIONAL communication cultures STANDARDS

## Section Goals

In **Fotonovela**, students will:
- receive comprehensible input from free-flowing discourse
- learn functional phrases for making invitations and plans, talking about pastimes, and apologizing

**Instructional Resources**
**Supersite/DVD:** *Fotonovela*
**Supersite/IRCD:** *IRM* (*Fotonovela* Videoscript & Translation, WBs/VM/LM Answer Key)
**WebSAM**
**Video Manual,** pp. 201–202

**Video Recap: Lección 3**
Before doing this **Fotonovela** section, review the previous episode with this activity.
1. _____ tiene una familia grande. (Inés) 2. El _____ de Javier es viejo y trabajador. (abuelo) 3. _____ no tiene hermanos. (Javier) 4. Inés tiene _____ hermanas. (cuatro)

**Video Synopsis** The travelers have an hour to explore the city before heading to the cabins. **Javier** and **Inés** decide to stroll around the city. **Álex** and **Maite** go to the park. While **Maite** writes postcards, **Álex** and a young man play soccer. A stray ball hits **Maite**. **Álex** and **Maite** return to the bus, and **Álex** invites her to go running with him that evening.

**Teaching Tips**
- Have students quickly glance over the **Fotonovela** captions and make a list of the cognates they find. Then, ask them to predict what this episode is about.
- Have students tell you a few expressions used to talk about pastimes. Then ask a few questions. Ex: **¿Eres aficionado/a a un deporte? ¿Te gusta el fútbol?**

**PERSONAJES**

**DON FRANCISCO**

**JAVIER**

**INÉS**

**ÁLEX**

**MAITE**

**JOVEN**

**1** **DON FRANCISCO** Tienen una hora libre. Pueden explorar la ciudad, si quieren.

**2** **JAVIER** Inés, ¿quieres ir a pasear por la ciudad?
**INÉS** Sí, vamos.

**3** **ÁLEX** ¿Por qué no vamos al parque, Maite? Podemos hablar y tomar el sol.
**MAITE** ¡Buena idea! También quiero escribir unas postales.

**6** **ÁLEX** ¡Maite!
**MAITE** ¡Dios mío!

**7** **JOVEN** Mil perdones. Lo siento muchísimo.
**MAITE** ¡No es nada! Estoy bien.

**8** **ÁLEX** Ya son las dos y treinta. Debemos regresar al autobús, ¿no?
**MAITE** Tienes razón.
**ÁLEX** Oye, Maite, ¿qué vas a hacer esta noche?
**MAITE** No tengo planes. ¿Por qué?

**recursos**

VM
pp. 201–202

panorama.vhlcentral.com
Lección 4

**Video Tips** General suggestions for using video clips in the classroom can be found on page IAE-12 of this Instructor's Annotated Edition.
**¡Vamos al parque!** Play the last half of the **¡Vamos al parque!** episode and have the class give you a description of what they saw. Write their observations on the board, pointing out any incorrect information. Repeat this process to allow the class to pick up more details of the plot. Then ask students to use the information they have accumulated to guess what happened at the beginning of the **¡Vamos al parque!** episode. Write their guesses on the board. Then play the entire episode and, through discussion, help the class summarize the plot.

**Teaching Tip** Have the class read through the entire **Fotonovela**, with volunteers playing the parts of **Don Francisco, Javier, Inés, Álex, Maite,** and the **Joven**. Have students take turns playing the roles so that more students participate.

**Expresiones útiles**
- Point out the written accents in the words **¿qué?, ¿por qué?,** and **también.** Explain that accents indicate a stressed syllable in a word (**también**) and remind students that all question words have accent marks. Tell students that they will learn more about word stress and accent marks in **Pronunciación.**
- Mention that **voy, vas, va,** and **vamos** are present-tense forms of the verb **ir.** Point out that **ir a** is used with an infinitive to tell what is going to happen. Ask: **¿Qué vas a hacer esta noche? ¿Por qué no vamos al parque?** Explain that **quiero, quieres,** and **siento** are forms of **querer** and **sentir,** which undergo a stem change from **e** to **ie** in certain forms. Tell students that they will learn more about these concepts in **Estructura.**

**MAITE** ¿Eres aficionado a los deportes, Álex?

**ÁLEX** Sí, me gusta mucho el fútbol. Me gusta también nadar, correr e ir de excursión a las montañas.

**MAITE** Yo también corro mucho.

**ÁLEX** Oye, Maite, ¿por qué no jugamos al fútbol con él?

**MAITE** Mmm... no quiero. Voy a terminar de escribir unas postales.

**ÁLEX** Eh, este... a veces salgo a correr por la noche. ¿Quieres venir a correr conmigo?

**MAITE** Sí, vamos. ¿A qué hora?

**ÁLEX** ¿A las seis?

**MAITE** Perfecto.

**DON FRANCISCO** Esta noche van a correr. ¡Y yo no tengo energía para pasear!

## Expresiones útiles

### Making invitations
- **¿Por qué no vamos al parque?**
  *Why don't we go to the park?*
  **¡Buena idea!**
  *Good idea!*
- **¿Por qué no jugamos al fútbol?**
  *Why don't we play soccer?*
  **Mmm... no quiero.**
  *Hmm... I don't want to.*
  **Lo siento, pero no puedo.**
  *I'm sorry, but I can't.*
- **¿Quieres ir a pasear por la ciudad/ el pueblo conmigo?**
  *Do you want to walk around the city/the town with me?*
  **Sí, vamos.**
  *Yes, let's go.*
  **Sí, si tenemos tiempo.**
  *Yes, if we have time.*

### Making plans
- **¿Qué vas a hacer esta noche?**
  *What are you going to do tonight?*
  **No tengo planes.**
  *I don't have any plans.*
  **Voy a terminar de escribir unas postales.**
  *I'm going to finish writing some postcards.*

### Talking about pastimes
- **¿Eres aficionado/a a los deportes?**
  *Are you a sports fan?*
  **Sí, me gustan todos los deportes.**
  *Yes, I like all sports.*
  **Sí, me gusta mucho el fútbol.**
  *Yes, I like soccer a lot.*
- **Me gusta también nadar, correr e ir de excursión a las montañas.**
  *I also like to swim, run, and go hiking in the mountains.*
  **Yo también corro mucho.**
  *I also run a lot.*

### Apologizing
- **Mil perdones./Lo siento muchísimo.**
  *I'm so sorry.*

**TEACHING OPTIONS**

**Pairs** After viewing the **Fotonovela**, ask students what **Inés** and **Javier** are doing in the meantime (**pasean por la ciudad**). Have student pairs write a dialogue between **Inés** and **Javier** as they stroll through the city. Encourage them to be creative and mention at least three places that they visit on their walk. Then have pairs role-play the dialogue for the class.

**TPR** Go through the **Expresiones útiles** as a class. Then have students stand and form a circle. Call out a question or statement from **Expresiones útiles** (Ex: **¿Qué vas a hacer esta noche?**) and toss a foam or paper ball to a student. He or she must respond appropriately and toss the ball back to you. Ex: **Voy a mirar la televisión.** Encourage students to respond according to what is true for them.

# ¿Qué pasó?

**1** **Escoger** Choose the answer that best completes each sentence.

1. Inés y Javier ___b___.
   a. toman el sol  b. pasean por la ciudad  c. corren por el parque

2. Álex desea ___a___ en el parque.
   a. hablar y tomar el sol  b. hablar y leer el periódico  c. nadar y tomar el sol

3. A Álex le gusta nadar, ___c___.
   a. jugar al fútbol y escribir postales  b. escalar montañas y esquiar
   c. ir de excursión y correr

4. A Maite le gusta ___b___.
   a. nadar y correr  b. correr y escribir postales  c. correr y jugar al fútbol

5. Maite desea ___c___.
   a. ir de excursión  b. jugar al fútbol  c. ir al parque

**2** **Identificar** Identify the person who would make each statement.

1. No me gusta practicar el fútbol pero me gusta correr. ___Maite___

2. ¿Por qué no vamos a pasear por la ciudad? ___Javier___

3. ¿Por qué no exploran ustedes la ciudad? Tienen tiempo. ___don Francisco___

4. ¿Por qué no corres conmigo esta noche? ___Álex___

5. No voy al parque. Prefiero estar con mi amigo. ___Inés___

 **JAVIER**

 **INÉS**

 **MAITE**

 **ÁLEX**

**DON FRANCISCO**

**3** **Preguntas** Answer the questions using the information from the **Fotonovela**.

1. ¿Qué desean hacer Inés y Javier? Desean pasear por la ciudad.

2. ¿Qué desea hacer Álex en el parque? Desea jugar al fútbol.

3. ¿Qué desea hacer Maite en el parque? Maite desea escribir postales./Maite desea terminar de escribir unas postales.

4. ¿Qué deciden hacer Maite y Álex esta noche? Deciden ir a correr.

**4** **Conversación** With a partner, prepare a conversation in which you talk about pastimes and invite each other to do some activity together. Use these expressions and also look at **Expresiones útiles** on the previous page. Answers will vary.

| ¿A qué hora? (At) What time? | ¿Dónde? Where? | Nos vemos a las siete. See you at seven. |
|---|---|---|
| contigo with you | No puedo porque... I can't because... | |

▶ ¿Eres aficionado/a a...?  ▶ ¿Por qué no...?  ▶ ¿Qué vas a hacer esta noche?

▶ ¿Te gusta...?  ▶ ¿Quieres... conmigo?

 NATIONAL communication STANDARDS

# Pronunciación  SUPERSITE

## Word stress and accent marks

**pe-lí-cu-la**　　**e-di-fi-cio**　　**ver**　　**yo**

Every Spanish syllable contains at least one vowel. When two vowels (two weak vowels or one strong and one weak) are joined in the same syllable they form a **diphthong**. A **monosyllable** is a word formed by a single syllable.

**bi-blio-te-ca**　　**vi-si-tar**　　**par-que**　　**fút-bol**

The syllable of a Spanish word that is pronounced most emphatically is the "stressed" syllable.

**pe-lo-ta**　　**pis-ci-na**　　**ra-tos**　　**ha-blan**

Words that end in **n**, **s**, or a **vowel** are usually stressed on the next to last syllable.

**na-ta-ción**　　**pa-pá**　　**in-glés**　　**Jo-sé**

If words that end in **n**, **s**, or a **vowel** are stressed on the last syllable, they must carry an accent mark on the stressed syllable.

**bai-lar**　　**es-pa-ñol**　　**u-ni-ver-si-dad**　　**tra-ba-ja-dor**

Words that do *not* end in **n**, **s**, or a **vowel** are usually stressed on the last syllable.

**béis-bol**　　**lá-piz**　　**ár-bol**　　**Gó-mez**

If words that do *not* end in **n**, **s**, or a **vowel** are stressed on the next to last syllable, they must carry an accent mark on the stressed syllable.

**Práctica** Pronounce each word, stressing the correct syllable. Then give the word stress rule for each word.

1. profesor
2. Puebla
3. ¿Cuántos?
4. Mazatlán
5. examen
6. ¿Cómo?
7. niños
8. Guadalajara
9. programador
10. México
11. están
12. geografía

**Oraciones** Read the conversation aloud to practice word stress.

**MARINA** Hola, Carlos. ¿Qué tal?
**CARLOS** Bien. Oye, ¿a qué hora es el partido de fútbol?
**MARINA** Creo que es a las siete.
**CARLOS** ¿Quieres ir?
**MARINA** Lo siento, pero no puedo. Tengo que estudiar biología.

**Refranes** Read these sayings aloud to practice word stress.

*En la unión está la fuerza.²*

*Quien ríe de último, ríe mejor.¹*

¹ He who laughs last, laughs loudest.　² United we stand.

**recursos**

LM
p. 20

SUPERSITE
panorama.vhlcentral.com
Lección 4

**En detalle**

**Antes de leer** Ask students to predict the content of this reading based on the title and photos. Have them share what they know about these teams or about other sports rivalries.

**Lectura**
- Use the map on page 66 to point out the locations of Barcelona and Madrid. Briefly explain that Spain's regional cultures (Basque, Catalan, Galician, etc.) were at odds with the authoritarian, centralized approach of **Franco's** regime, which banned the public use of regional languages. Point out that the nickname **Barça** is Catalan, which is why it has an accent to mark a soft *c.*
- Describe the stadiums: **Camp Nou** (Catalan for *new field*) holds about 100,000 spectators and is the largest soccer stadium in Europe. Madrid's **Estadio Santiago Bernabéu**, named after an ex-player and club president, can seat about 80,000.
- Remind students that **el fútbol** is *soccer* and **el fútbol americano** is *football*.

**Después de leer** Ask students what facts in this reading are new or surprising to them.

**1** **Expansion** To challenge students, ask them to write two additional items. Then have them exchange papers with a classmate and complete the activity.

---

**EN DETALLE**

# Real Madrid y Barça: rivalidad total

**Soccer in Spain is a force to be reckoned with,** and no two teams draw more attention than **Real Madrid** and the **Fútbol Club Barcelona.** Whether the venue is Madrid's **Santiago Bernabéu** or Barcelona's **Camp Nou,** the two cities shut down for the showdown, paralyzed by **fútbol** fever. A ticket to the actual game is always the hottest ticket in town.

The rivalry between **Real Madrid** and **Barça** is about more than soccer. As the two biggest, most powerful cities in Spain, Barcelona and Madrid are constantly compared to one another and have a natural rivalry. There is also a political component to the dynamic. Barcelona, with its distinct language and culture, has long struggled for increased autonomy from Madrid's centralized government. Under Francisco Franco's rule (1939–1975), when repression of the Catalan identity was at its height, a game between **Real Madrid** and **FC Barcelona** was wrapped up with all the symbolism of the regime versus the resistance, even though both teams suffered casualties in Spain's civil war and the subsequent Franco dictatorship.

Although the dictatorship is far behind, the momentum of all those decades of competition still transforms both cities into a frenzied, tense panic leading up to the game. Once the final score is announced, one of those cities transforms again, this time into the best party in the country.

### Rivalidades del fútbol

**Argentina:** Boca Juniors vs River Plate
**México:** Águilas del América vs Chivas del Guadalajara
**Chile:** Colo Colo vs Universidad de Chile
**Guatemala:** Comunicaciones vs Municipal
**Uruguay:** Peñarol vs Nacional
**Colombia:** Millonarios vs Independiente Santa Fe

---

**ACTIVIDADES**

**1**  **¿Cierto o falso?** Indicate whether each statement is **cierto** or **falso**. Correct the false statements.

1. People from Spain don't like soccer. **Falso.** People from Spain like soccer very much.
2. Seville is the most important city in Spain. **Falso.** Barcelona and Madrid are the most important cities in Spain.
3. Santiago Bernabéu is a stadium in Madrid. **Cierto.**
4. The rivalry between Real Madrid and FC Barcelona is not only in soccer. **Cierto.**
5. Only the FC Barcelona team was affected by the civil war. **Falso.** Both teams were affected by the civil war.
6. Barcelona has resisted Madrid's centralized government. **Cierto.**
7. During Franco's regime, the Catalan culture thrived. **Falso.** Catalan culture was repressed during Franco's regime.
8. There are many famous rivalries between soccer teams in the Spanish-speaking world. **Cierto.**

---

**TEACHING OPTIONS**

**Project** Have groups of four choose famous soccer rivalries, then split into two to research and create a web page for each of the rival teams. The pages should feature each team's colors, players, home stadium, official song, and other significant or interesting information. Have the groups present their rivals' web pages to the class.

**¡Goooooooool!** Explain that sportscasters in the Spanish-speaking world are famous for their theatrical commentaries. One example is **Andrés Cantor**, who provides commentary for soccer matches on Spanish-language stations in the U.S. Each time a goal is scored, fans know they can hear a drawn-out bellow of **¡Goooooooool!** Cantor's call, which can last for nearly thirty seconds, was made into a ringtone for cell phones in the U.S.

## ASÍ SE DICE

### Los deportes

| | |
|---|---|
| el/la árbitro/a | referee |
| el/la atleta | athlete |
| la bola; el balón | la pelota |
| el campeón/ la campeona | champion |
| la carrera | race |
| competir | to compete |
| empatar | to draw; to tie |
| la medalla | medal |
| el/la mejor | the best |
| mundial | worldwide |
| el torneo | tournament |

## EL MUNDO HISPANO

### Atletas importantes

World-renowned Hispanic athletes:

○ **Rafael Nadal** (España) is one of the best tennis players in the world.

○ **Sofía Mulanovich** (Perú) was the world champion for surfing in 2004.

○ **Óscar Freire** (España) has been the cycling world champion three times.

○ **Ana Gabriela Guevara** (México) won the silver medal in the 400 meters race at the 2004 Olympic Games in Athens.

## PERFILES

### Anier García y Luciana Aymar

The sprinter **Anier García Ortiz** was born in Santiago de Cuba in 1976. In 2000, he won the gold medal at the Summer Olympics in Sydney for the 110-meter hurdles (**vallas**). Four years later, in Athens, Greece, he won the bronze medal for the same event.

**Luciana Paula Aymar** was born in 1977 in Rosario, Argentina. The International Hockey Federation named her the best female player in the world in 2001, 2004, and 2005. With the national women's field hockey team, **La Maga** (*The Magician*), as Luciana is called, won the silver medal at the Sydney Olympics in the year 2000, and bronze medal in Athens in 2004.

### Conexión Internet

¿Qué deportes son populares en los países hispanos?

Go to **panorama.vhlcentral.com** to find more cultural information related to this **Cultura** section.

## ACTIVIDADES

**2 Comprensión** Write the name of the athlete described in each sentence.

1. Es un atleta de Cuba. Anier García
2. Es una chica que practica el hockey. Luciana Aymar
3. Es un chico español al que le gusta pasear en bicicleta. Óscar Freire
4. Es una chica peruana que practica el surfing. Sofía Mulanovich

**3 ¿Quién es?** Write a short paragraph describing an athlete that you like, but do not mention their name. What do they look like? What sport do they play? Where do they live? Read your description aloud to see if the class can guess who they are. Answers will vary.

**recursos**

panorama.vhlcentral.com
Lección 4

**Así se dice**
- Model the pronunciation of each term and have students repeat it.
- To challenge students, add these words to the list: **el atletismo** (*track and field*); **marcar un gol** (*to score a goal*); **el/la portero/a** (*goalie*).

**Perfiles**
- In addition to his Olympic medals, **Anier García** has won gold medals at six international track events, most recently at the 2002 IAAF World Cup in Madrid, Spain.
- **Luciana Aymar**—known to her friends as **Lucha**—plays midfield. On being named the top female player in the world, she said it was like "touching the sky with your hands."

**El mundo hispano** Have students write three true-false sentences about this section. Then have them get together with a classmate and take turns reading and correcting their statements.

**2 Expansion** Give students these sentences as items 5–6: 5. ____ tiene una medalla de plata (*silver*). (Ana Gabriela Guevara/Luciana Aymar) 6. El ____ es el deporte favorito de Rafael Nadal. (tenis)

**3 Teaching Tip** Have students get together with a classmate and peer edit each other's paragraphs, paying close attention to gender agreement.

## TEACHING OPTIONS

**Los campeones** For homework, ask students to research one of the champions from **El mundo hispano**. They should write five Spanish sentences about the athlete's life and career, and bring in a photo from the Internet. Have students who researched the same person work as a group to present that athlete to the class.

**Heritage Speakers** Ask heritage speakers to describe sports preferences in their families' countries of origin, especially ones that are not widely known in the United States, such as **jai-alai**. What well-known athletes in the U.S. are from their families' countries of origin?

## Section Goals

In **Estructura 4.1**, students will learn:

- the present tense of **ir**
- the contraction **al**
- **ir a** + [*infinitive*] to express future events
- **vamos a** to express *let's . . .*

---

**Instructional Resources**
**Supersite:** Lab MP3 Audio Files **Lección 4**
**Supersite/IRCD:** *PowerPoints*
(**Lección 4 Estructura** Presentation); *IRM* (**Hojas de actividades,** Information Gap Activities, Lab Audio Script, WBs/VM/LM Answer Key)
**WebSAM**
**Workbook,** pp. 39–40
**Lab Manual,** p. 21
*Cuaderno para hispanohablantes*

---

## Teaching Tips

- Write your next day's schedule on the board. Ex: **8:00— la biblioteca; 12:00—comer**. Explain where you are going or what you are going to do, using the verb **ir**. Ask volunteers about their schedules, using forms of **ir**.
- Add a visual aspect to this grammar presentation. Call on several students to come to the front of the room and create a "living map" of Latin America, calling out their country names as you position them. Point to your destination "country," and as you pantomime flying there, ask students: **¿Adónde voy? (Vas a Chile.)** Once there, pantomime an activity, asking: **¿Qué voy a hacer? (Vas a esquiar.)**
- Practice **vamos a** to express the idea of *let's* by asking volunteers to suggest things to do. Ex: **Tengo hambre. (Vamos a la cafetería.)**

**Ayuda** Point out the difference in usage between **dónde** and **adónde**. Ask: **¿Adónde va el presidente para descansar? (Va a Camp David.) ¿Dónde está Camp David? (Está en Maryland.)**

---

## 4.1 Present tense of **ir** SUPERSITE

**ANTE TODO** The verb **ir** (*to go*) is irregular in the present tense. Note that, except for the **yo** form (**voy**) and the lack of a written accent on the **vosotros** form (**vais**), the endings are the same as those for **–ar** verbs.

### The verb **ir** (*to go*)

| Singular forms | | Plural forms | |
|---|---|---|---|
| yo | **voy** | nosotros/as | **vamos** |
| tú | **vas** | vosotros/as | **vais** |
| Ud./él/ella | **va** | Uds./ellos/ellas | **van** |

▶ **Ir** is often used with the preposition **a** (*to*). If **a** is followed by the definite article **el**, they combine to form the contraction **al**. If **a** is followed by the other definite articles (**la, las, los**), there is no contraction.

$$a + el = al$$

Voy **al** parque con Juan.
*I'm going to the park with Juan.*

Mis amigos van **a las** montañas.
*My friends are going to the mountains.*

▶ The construction **ir a** + [*infinitive*] is used to talk about actions that are going to happen in the future. It is equivalent to the English *to be going to* + [*infinitive*].

**Va a leer** el periódico.
*He is going to read the newspaper.*

**Van a pasear** por el pueblo.
*They are going to walk around town.*

Voy a escribir unas postales.

Álex y Maite van a volver al autobús.

▶ **Vamos a** + [*infinitive*] can also express the idea of *let's (do something)*.

**Vamos a** pasear.
*Let's take a stroll.*

**¡Vamos a** ver!
*Let's see!*

**CONSULTA**

To review the contraction **de** + **el**, see **Estructura 1.3,** pp. 20–21.

**AYUDA**

When asking a question that contains a form of the verb **ir**, remember to use **adónde**:
**¿Adónde vas?**
*(To) Where are you going?*

---

🔊 **¡INTÉNTALO!** Provide the present tense forms of **ir**. The first item has been done for you.

1. Ellos _____van_____.
2. Yo _____voy_____.
3. Tu novio _____va_____.
4. Adela _____va_____.
5. Mi prima y yo _____vamos_____.
6. Tú _____vas_____.
7. Ustedes _____van_____.
8. Nosotros _____vamos_____.
9. Usted _____va_____.
10. Nosotras _____vamos_____.
11. Miguel _____va_____.
12. Ellas _____van_____.

**recursos**

WB pp. 39–40

LM p. 21

SUPERSITE panorama. vhlcentral.com Lección 4

---

# Práctica (SUPERSITE)

**1** **¿Adónde van?** Everyone in your neighborhood is dashing off to various places. Say where they are going.

1. la señora Castillo / el centro   La señora Castillo va al centro.
2. las hermanas Gómez / la piscina   Las hermanas Gómez van a la piscina.
3. tu tío y tu papá / el partido de fútbol   Tu tío y tu papá van al partido de fútbol.
4. yo / el Museo de Arte Moderno   (Yo) Voy al Museo de Arte Moderno.
5. nosotros / el restaurante Miramar   (Nosotros) Vamos al restaurante Miramar.

**2** **¿Qué van a hacer?** These sentences describe what several students in a college hiking club are doing today. Use **ir a** + [*infinitive*] to say that they are also going to do the same activities tomorrow.

> **modelo**
>
> Martín y Rodolfo nadan en la piscina.
> Van a nadar en la piscina mañana también.

1. Sara lee una revista.   Va a leer una revista mañana también.
2. Yo practico deportes.   Voy a practicar deportes mañana también.
3. Ustedes van de excursión.   Van a ir de excursión mañana también.
4. El presidente del club patina.   Va a patinar mañana también.
5. Tú tomas el sol.   Vas a tomar el sol mañana también.
6. Paseamos con nuestros amigos.   Vamos a pasear con nuestros amigos mañana también.

**3** **Preguntas** With a partner, take turns asking and answering questions about where the people are going and what they are going to do there.   Some answers will vary.

> **modelo**
>
> **Estudiante 1:** ¿Adónde va Estela?
> **Estudiante 2:** Va a la Librería Sol.
> **Estudiante 1:** Va a comprar un libro.

1. Álex y Miguel
¿Adónde van Álex y Miguel?
Van al parque. Van a…

2. mi amigo ¿Adónde va
mi amigo? Va al gimnasio.
Va a…

3. tú ¿Adónde vas? Voy
al partido de tenis. Voy a…

4. los estudiantes
¿Adónde van los estudiantes?
Van al estadio. Van a…

5. profesora Torres
¿Adónde va la profesora
Torres? Va a la Biblioteca
Nacional. Va a…

6. ustedes ¿Adónde
van ustedes? Vamos a la
piscina. Vamos a…

---

**1 Teaching Tip** To add a visual aspect to this exercise, bring in photos of people dressed for a particular activity. As you hold up each photo, have the class say where they are going, using the verb **ir**. Ex: Show a photo of a basketball player. **(Va al gimnasio./Va a un partido.)**

**1 Expansion** After completing the activity, extend each answer with **pero** and a different name or pronoun, and have students complete the sentence. Ex: **La señora Castillo va al centro, pero el señor Castillo... (va al trabajo).**

**2 Expansion**
• Show the same photos you used for **Actividad 1** and ask students to describe what the people are going to do. Ex: **Va a jugar al baloncesto.**
• Ask students about tomorrow's activities. Ex: **¿Qué van a hacer tus amigos mañana? ¿Qué va a hacer tu compañero/a mañana?**

**3 Expansion** Ask student pairs to write a logic problem using **ir a** + [*infinitive*]. Ex: **Ángela, Laura, Tomás y Manuel van a hacer cosas diferentes. Tomás va a nadar y Laura va a comer, pero no en casa. Un chico y una chica van a ver una película. ¿Adónde van todos?** Then have pairs exchange papers to solve the problems.

---

**TEACHING OPTIONS**

**Heritage Speakers** Ask heritage speakers to write six sentences with the verb **ir** indicating places they go on weekends either by themselves or with friends and family. Ex: **Mi familia y yo vamos a visitar a mi abuela los domingos.**
**Game** Divide the class into teams of four. Ask each team to write a brief description of a well-known fictional character's activities for tomorrow, using the verb **ir**. Ex: **Mañana va**

a dormir de día. Va a caminar de noche. Va a buscar una muchacha bonita. La muchacha va a tener mucho miedo.** Have each team read their description aloud without naming the character. If another team correctly identifies the person **(Es Drácula.)**, they receive one point. The team with the most points at the end wins.

# Comunicación

**4** **Situaciones** Work with a partner and say where you and your friends go in these situations. Answers will vary.

1. Cuando deseo descansar…
2. Cuando mi novio/a tiene que estudiar…
3. Si mis compañeros de clase necesitan practicar el español…
4. Si deseo hablar con unos amigos…
5. Cuando tengo dinero (*money*)…
6. Cuando mis amigos y yo tenemos hambre…
7. En mis ratos libres…
8. Cuando mis amigos desean esquiar…
9. Si estoy de vacaciones…
10. Si tengo ganas de leer…

**5** **Encuesta** Your instructor will give you a worksheet. Walk around the class and ask your classmates if they are going to do these activities today. Find one person to answer **Sí** and one to answer **No** for each item and note their names on the worksheet in the appropriate column. Be prepared to report your findings to the class.

Answers will vary.

**modelo**
**Tú:** ¿Vas a leer el periódico hoy?
**Ana:** Sí, voy a leer el periódico hoy.
**Luis:** No, no voy a leer el periódico hoy.

| Actividades | Sí | No |
| --- | --- | --- |
| 1. comer en un restaurante chino | | |
| 2. leer el periódico | | |
| 3. escribir un mensaje electrónico | Ana | Luis |
| 4. correr 20 kilómetros | | |
| 5. ver una película de horror | | |
| 6. pasear en bicicleta | | |

**6** **Entrevista** Interview two classmates to find out where they are going and what they are going to do on their next vacation. Answers will vary.

**modelo**
**Estudiante 1:** ¿Adónde vas de vacaciones (*for vacation*)?
**Estudiante 2:** Voy a Guadalajara con mis amigos.
**Estudiante 1:** ¿Y qué van a hacer (*to do*) ustedes en Guadalajara?
**Estudiante 2:** Vamos a visitar unos monumentos y museos.

# Síntesis

**7** **El fin de semana** Create a schedule with your activities for this weekend. Answers will vary.

▶ For each day, list at least three things you have to do.
▶ For each day, list at least two things you will do for fun.
▶ Tell a classmate what your weekend schedule is like. He or she will write down what you say.
▶ Switch roles to see if you have any plans in common.
▶ Take turns asking each other to participate in some of the activities you listed.

## 4.2 Stem-changing verbs: e→ie, o→ue

**ANTE TODO** Stem-changing verbs deviate from the normal pattern of regular verbs. In stem-changing verbs, the stressed vowel of the stem changes when the verb is conjugated.

| INFINITIVE | VERB STEM | STEM CHANGE | CONJUGATED FORM |
|---|---|---|---|
| empezar<br>volver | empez-<br>volv- | emp**ie**z-<br>v**ue**lv- | emp**ie**zo<br>v**ue**lvo |

▶ In many verbs, such as **empezar** (*to begin*), the stem vowel changes from **e** to **ie**. Note that the **nosotros/as** and **vosotros/as** forms don't have a stem change.

### The verb empezar (e:ie) (*to begin*)

| Singular forms | | Plural forms | |
|---|---|---|---|
| yo | emp**ie**zo | nosotros/as | empezamos |
| tú | emp**ie**zas | vosotros/as | empezáis |
| Ud./él/ella | emp**ie**za | Uds./ellos/ellas | emp**ie**zan |

*Álex y Maite vuelven al autobús.*

*Álex empieza a enviar mensajes.*

▶ In many other verbs, such as **volver** (*to return*), the stem vowel changes from **o** to **ue**. The **nosotros/as** and **vosotros/as** forms have no stem change.

### The verb volver (o:ue) (*to return*)

| Singular forms | | Plural forms | |
|---|---|---|---|
| yo | v**ue**lvo | nosotros/as | volvemos |
| tú | v**ue**lves | vosotros/as | volvéis |
| Ud./él/ella | v**ue**lve | Uds./ellos/ellas | v**ue**lven |

▶ To help you identify stem-changing verbs, they will appear as follows throughout the text:

**empezar (e:ie), volver (o:ue)**

---

**CONSULTA**

To review the present tense of regular –ar verbs, see **Estructura 2.1**, p. 46.

• • •

To review the present tense of regular –er and –ir verbs, see **Estructura 3.3**, p. 88.

---

### Section Goals

In **Estructura 4.2**, students will be introduced to:
- present tense of stem-changing verbs: **e → ie**; **o → ue**
- common stem-changing verbs

**Instructional Resources**
**Supersite:** Lab MP3 Audio Files **Lección 4**
**Supersite/IRCD:** *PowerPoints* (**Lección 4 Estructura** Presentation); *IRM* (Information Gap Activities, Lab Audio Script, WBs/VM/LM Answer Key)
**WebSAM**
**Workbook,** pp. 41–42
**Lab Manual,** p. 22
*Cuaderno para hispanohablantes*

### Teaching Tips
- Take a survey of students' habits. Ask: **¿Quiénes empiezan las clases a las ocho?** Make a chart with students' names on the board. Ask: **¿Quiénes vuelven a casa a las seis?** Then create sentences based on the chart. Ex: **Tú vuelves a casa a las siete, pero Amanda vuelve a las seis. Daniel y yo volvemos a las cinco.**
- Copy the forms of **empezar** and **volver** on the board. Reiterate that the personal endings for the present tense of all the verbs listed in **Estructura 4.2** are the same as those for the present tense of regular –ar, –er, and –ir verbs.
- Explain that an easy way to remember which forms of these verbs have stem changes is to think of them as boot verbs. Draw a line around the stem-changing forms in each paradigm to show the boot-like shape.

---

**TEACHING OPTIONS**

**Extra Practice** Write a pattern sentence on the board. Ex: **Ella empieza una carta.** Have students write down the model, and then dictate a list of subjects (Ex: **Maite, nosotras, don Francisco**), pausing after each one to allow students to write a complete sentence. Ask volunteers to read their sentences aloud.

**Heritage Speakers** Ask heritage speakers to work in pairs to write a mock interview with a Spanish-speaking celebrity in which they use the verbs **empezar**, **volver**, **querer**, and **recordar**. Ask them to role-play their interview for the class, who will write down the stem-changing verb forms that they hear.

**Teaching Tips**
- Write **e:ie** and **o:ue** on the board and explain that some very common verbs have these types of stem changes. Point out that all the verbs listed are conjugated like **empezar** or **volver**. Model the pronunciation of the verbs and ask students a few questions using verbs of each type. Have them answer in complete sentences. Ex: **¿A qué hora cierra la biblioteca? ¿Duermen los estudiantes tarde, por lo general? ¿Qué piensan hacer este fin de semana? ¿Quién quiere comer en un restaurante esta noche?**
- Point out the structure **jugar al** used with sports. Practice it by asking students about the sports they play. Have them answer in complete sentences. Ex: ____, ¿te gusta jugar al fútbol? Y tú, ____, ¿juegas al fútbol? ¿Prefieres jugar al fútbol o ver un partido en el estadio? ¿Cuántos juegan al tenis? ¿Qué prefieres, ____, jugar al tenis o jugar al fútbol?
- Prepare a few dehydrated sentences. Ex: **Maite / empezar / la lección; ustedes / mostrar / los trabajos; nosotros / jugar / al fútbol.** Write them on the board one at a time, and ask students to form complete sentences based on the cues.

## Common stem-changing verbs

| e:ie | | o:ue | |
|---|---|---|---|
| cerrar | to close | almorzar | to have lunch |
| comenzar (a + *inf.*) | to begin | contar | to count; to tell |
| empezar (a + *inf.*) | to begin | dormir | to sleep |
| entender | to understand | encontrar | to find |
| pensar | to think | mostrar | to show |
| perder | to lose; to miss | poder (+ *inf.*) | to be able to; can |
| preferir (+ *inf.*) | to prefer | recordar | to remember |
| querer (+ *inf.*) | to want; to love | volver | to return |

**¡LENGUA VIVA!**
The verb **perder** can mean *to lose* or *to miss*, in the sense of "to miss a train": **Siempre pierdo mis llaves.** *I always lose my keys.* **Es importante no perder el autobús.** *It's important not to miss the bus.*

▶ **Jugar** (*to play* a sport or game) is the only Spanish verb that has a **u:ue** stem change. **Jugar** is followed by **a** + [*definite article*] when the name of a sport or game is mentioned.

Oye, Maite, ¿por qué no jugamos al fútbol?

Álex y el joven juegan al fútbol.

▶ **Comenzar** and **empezar** require the preposition **a** when they are followed by an infinitive.

**Comienzan a** jugar a las siete. / *They begin playing at seven.*
Ana **empieza a** escribir una postal. / *Ana starts to write a postcard.*

▶ **Pensar** + [*infinitive*] means *to plan* or *to intend to do something.* **Pensar en** means *to think about someone* or *something.*

**¿Piensan** ir al gimnasio? / *Are you planning to go to the gym?*
**¿En** qué **piensas**? / *What are you thinking about?*

**¡INTÉNTALO!** Provide the present tense forms of these verbs. The first item in each column has been done for you.

**cerrar (e:ie)**
1. Ustedes _cierran_.
2. Tú _cierras_.
3. Nosotras _cerramos_.
4. Mi hermano _cierra_.
5. Yo _cierro_.
6. Usted _cierra_.
7. Los chicos _cierran_.
8. Ella _cierra_.

**dormir (o:ue)**
1. Mi abuela no _duerme_.
2. Yo no _duermo_.
3. Tú no _duermes_.
4. Mis hijos no _duermen_.
5. Usted no _duerme_.
6. Nosotros no _dormimos_.
7. Él no _duerme_.
8. Ustedes no _duermen_.

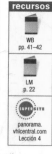
**recursos**
WB pp. 41–42
LM p. 22
panorama. vhlcentral.com Lección 4

**TEACHING OPTIONS**
**TPR** Add an auditory aspect to this grammar presentation. At random, call out infinitives of regular and **e:ie** stem-changing verbs. Have students raise their hands if the verb has a stem change. Repeat for **o:ue** stem-changing verbs.
**Extra Practice** For additional drills of stem-changing verbs, do the ¡Inténtalo! activity orally using infinitives other than **cerrar** and **dormir**. Keep a brisk pace.

**TPR** Have the class stand in a circle. As you toss a foam or paper ball to a student, call out the infinitive of a stem-changing verb, followed by a pronoun. (Ex: **querer, tú**) The student should say the appropriate verb form (**quieres**), then name a different pronoun (Ex: **usted**) and throw the ball to another student. When all subject pronouns have been covered, start over with another infinitive.

# Práctica

**1** **Completar** Complete this conversation with the appropriate forms of the verbs. Then act it out with a partner.

**PABLO** Óscar, voy al centro ahora.

**ÓSCAR** ¿A qué hora (1)_____piensas_____ (pensar) volver? El partido de fútbol (2)_____empieza_____ (empezar) a las dos.

**PABLO** (3)_____Vuelvo_____ (Volver) a la una. (4)_____Quiero_____ (Querer) ver el partido.

**ÓSCAR** (5)¿_____Recuerdas_____ (Recordar) que (*that*) nuestro equipo es muy bueno? (6)¡ _____Puede_____ (Poder) ganar!

**PABLO** No, (7)_____pienso_____ (pensar) que va a (8)_____perder_____ (perder). Los jugadores de Guadalajara son salvajes (*wild*) cuando (9)_____juegan_____ (jugar).

**2** **Preferencias** With a partner, take turns asking and answering questions about what these people want to do, using the cues provided.

> **modelo**
> Guillermo: estudiar / pasear en bicicleta
> **Estudiante 1:** ¿Quiere estudiar Guillermo?
> **Estudiante 2:** No, prefiere pasear en bicicleta.

1. tú: trabajar / dormir
   ¿Quieres trabajar? No, prefiero dormir.
2. ustedes: mirar la televisión / jugar al dominó
   ¿Quieren ustedes mirar la televisión? No, preferimos jugar al dominó.
3. tus amigos: ir de excursión / descansar
   ¿Quieren ir de excursión tus amigos? No, mis amigos prefieren descansar.
4. tú: comer en la cafetería / ir a un restaurante
   ¿Quieres comer en la cafetería? No, prefiero ir a un restaurante.
5. Elisa: ver una película / leer una revista
   ¿Quiere ver una película Elisa? No, prefiere leer una revista.
6. María y su hermana: tomar el sol / practicar el esquí acuático
   ¿Quieren tomar el sol María y su hermana? No, prefieren practicar el esquí acuático.

**3** **Describir** Use a verb from the list to describe what these people are doing.

almorzar · cerrar · contar · dormir · encontrar · mostrar

1. las niñas   Las niñas duermen.
2. yo   (Yo) Cierro la ventana.
3. nosotros   (Nosotros) Almorzamos.

4. tú   (Tú) Encuentras una maleta.
5. Pedro   Pedro muestra una foto.
6. Teresa   Teresa cuenta.

---

---

# Comunicación

**4** **Frecuencia** In pairs, use the verbs from the list and other stem-changing verbs you know to create sentences telling your partner which activities you do daily (**todos los días**), which you do once a month (**una vez al mes**), and which you do once a year (**una vez al año**). Then switch roles.  Answers will vary.

> **modelo**
> **Estudiante 1:** Yo recuerdo a mi familia todos los días.
> **Estudiante 2:** Yo pierdo uno de mis libros una vez al año.

| cerrar | perder |
| dormir | poder |
| empezar | preferir |
| encontrar | querer |
| jugar | recordar |
| ¿? | ¿? |

| todos los días | una vez al mes | una vez al año |
| --- | --- | --- |
|  |  |  |
|  |  |  |

**5** **En la televisión** Read the television listings for Saturday. In pairs, write a conversation between two siblings arguing about what to watch. Be creative and be prepared to act out your conversation for the class.  Answers will vary.

> **modelo**
> **Hermano:** Quiero ver la Copa Mundial.
> **Hermana:** ¡No! Prefiero ver...

| | 13:00 | 14:00 | 15:00 | 16:00 | 17:00 | 18:00 | 19:00 | 20:00 | 21:00 | 22:00 | 23:00 |
| --- | --- | --- | --- | --- | --- | --- | --- | --- | --- | --- | --- |
| **7** | Copa Mundial (*World Cup*) de fútbol | | | El tiempo libre | | Fútbol internacional: Copa América: México-Argentina | | | | Torneo de Natación | |
| **8** | Abierto (*Open*) Mexicano de Tenis: Alejandro Hernández (México) vs. Jacobo Díaz (España). Semifinales | | | Campeonato (*Championship*) de baloncesto: Los Correcaminos de Tampico vs. los Santos de San Luis | | | | Aficionados al buceo | | Cozumel: Aventuras | |
| **12** | Gente famosa | | Amigos | | Médicos jóvenes | | | Película: **El centro de la ciudad** | | Película: **Terror en la plaza mayor** | |
| **13** | El padrastro | | | Periodistas en peligro (*danger*) | | | El esquí acuático | | | Patinaje artístico | |
| **17** | Biografías: La artista Frida Kahlo | | | Música de la semana | | | Entrevista del día: Miguel Induráin y su pasión por el ciclismo | | | Cine de la noche: **La carta misteriosa** | |

# Síntesis

**6** **Situación** Your instructor will give you and your partner a partially illustrated itinerary of a city tour. Complete the itineraries by asking each other questions using the verbs in the captions and vocabulary you have learned.  Answers will vary.

> **modelo**
> **Estudiante 1:** Por la mañana, empiezan en el café.
> **Estudiante 2:** Y luego...

---

## Sidebar (left column)

**4 Teaching Tip** Model the activity by asking questions about famous people. Ex: **¿Con qué frecuencia juega al golf Tiger Woods?** Write the answers on the board.

**4 Expansion** After tallying results on the board, ask students to graph them. Have them refer to **Lectura**, pages 134–135, for models.

**5 Teaching Tips**
- Model the activity by stating two programs from the listing that you want to watch and asking the class to react.
- Remind students that the 24-hour clock is often used for schedules. Model a few of the program times. Then ask: **Quiero ver** *Amigos* **y mi amigo prefiere ver** *La carta misteriosa.* **¿Hay un conflicto? (No.) ¿Por qué? (Porque** *Amigos* **es a las 15:00 y** *La carta misteriosa* **es a las 22:00.)** Give students the option of answering with the 12-hour clock.

**5 Expansion** Have students personalize the activity by choosing their own favorite programs. You may wish to bring in a current television schedule. As a class, tally students' favorite shows.

**6 Teaching Tip** Divide the class into pairs and distribute the handouts from the Information Gap Activities (Supersite/IRCD) that correspond to this activity. Give students ten minutes to complete the activity.

**6 Expansion**
- Ask questions based on the artwork. Ex: **¿Dónde empiezan el día? (en el café) ¿Qué pueden hacer en la plaza mayor? (Pueden pasear.)**
- Have volunteers take turns completing the information in the puzzle. Then have students invent their own stories, using stem-changing verbs, about what happens to the same group of tourists.

---

**Small Groups** Have students choose their favorite pastime and work in groups of three with other students who have chosen that same activity. Have each group write six sentences about the activity, using a different stem-changing verb in each.

**Pairs** Ask students to write incomplete dehydrated sentences (only subjects and infinitives) about people and groups at the university. Ex: **el equipo de béisbol / perder / ¿?** Then have them exchange papers with a classmate, who will form a complete sentence by conjugating the verb and inventing an appropriate ending. Ask volunteers to write sentences on the board.

# (4.3) Stem-changing verbs: e→i

**ANTE TODO** You've already seen that many verbs in Spanish change their stem vowel when conjugated. There is a third kind of stem-vowel change in some verbs, such as **pedir** (*to ask for; to request*). In these verbs, the stressed vowel in the stem changes from **e** to **i**, as shown in the diagram.

| INFINITIVE | VERB STEM | STEM CHANGE | CONJUGATED FORM |
|:---:|:---:|:---:|:---:|
| pedir | p**e**d- | p**i**d- | p**i**do |

▶ As with other stem-changing verbs you have learned, there is no stem change in the **nosotros/as** or **vosotros/as** forms in the present tense.

## The verb pedir (e:i) (*to ask for; to request*)

| Singular forms | | Plural forms | |
|:---:|:---:|:---:|:---:|
| yo | p**i**do | nosotros/as | pedimos |
| tú | p**i**des | vosotros/as | pedís |
| Ud./él/ella | p**i**de | Uds./ellos/ellas | p**i**den |

▶ To help you identify verbs with the **e:i** stem change, they will appear as follows throughout the text:

**pedir (e:i)**

▶ These are the most common **e:i** stem-changing verbs:

| **conseguir** | **decir** | **repetir** | **seguir** |
|---|---|---|---|
| *to get; to obtain* | *to say;*<br>*to tell* | *to repeat* | *to follow; to continue;*<br>*to keep (doing something)* |

**Pido** favores cuando es necesario.
*I ask for favors when it's necessary.*

Javier **dice** la verdad.
*Javier is telling the truth.*

**Sigue** con su trabajo.
*He continues with his job.*

**Consiguen** ver buenas películas.
*They get to see good movies.*

▶ **¡Atención!** The verb **decir** is irregular in its **yo** form: **yo digo.**

▶ The **yo** forms of **seguir** and **conseguir** have a spelling change as well as the stem change **e→i**.

**Sigo** su plan.
*I'm following their plan.*

**Consigo** novelas en la librería.
*I get novels at the bookstore.*

**¡INTÉNTALO!** Provide the correct forms of the verbs.

| repetir (e:i) | decir (e:i) | seguir (e: i) |
|---|---|---|
| 1. Arturo y Eva _repiten_. | 1. Yo _digo_. | 1. Yo _sigo_. |
| 2. Yo _repito_. | 2. Él _dice_. | 2. Nosotros _seguimos_. |
| 3. Nosotros _repetimos_. | 3. Tú _dices_. | 3. Tú _sigües_. |
| 4. Julia _repite_. | 4. Usted _dice_. | 4. Los chicos _siguen_. |
| 5. Sofía y yo _repetimos_. | 5. Ellas _dicen_. | 5. Usted _sigue_. |

## TEACHING OPTIONS

**Game** Divide the class into two teams. Name an infinitive and a subject pronoun (Ex: **decir / yo**). Have the first member of team A give the appropriate conjugated form of the verb. If the team member answers correctly, team A gets one point. If not, give the first member of team B the same example. If he or she does not know the answer, give the correct verb form and move on. The team with the most points at the end wins.

**Extra Practice** Add a visual aspect to this grammar presentation. Bring in magazine pictures or photos of parks and city centers where people are doing fun activities. In small groups, have students describe the photos using as many stem-changing verbs from **Estructura 4.2** and **4.3** as they can. Give points for the groups who use the most stem-changing verbs. Repeat the activity orally using additional infinitives, such as **conseguir, impedir, pedir,** and **servir.**

---

### Section Goal

In **Estructura 4.3**, students will learn the present tense of stem-changing verbs: **e → i**.

**Instructional Resources**
**Supersite:** Lab MP3 Audio Files
**Lección 4**
**Supersite/IRCD:** *PowerPoints*
(**Lección 4 Estructura** Presentation); *IRM* (Lab Audio Script, WBs/VM/LM Answer Key)
**WebSAM**
**Workbook,** pp. 43–44
**Lab Manual,** p. 23
***Cuaderno para hispanohablantes***

**Teaching Tips**
• Take a survey of students' habits. Ask questions like: **¿Quiénes piden Coca-Cola?** Make a chart on the board. Then form sentences based on the chart.
• Ask volunteers to answer questions using **conseguir, decir, pedir, repetir,** and **seguir.**
• Reiterate that the personal endings for the present tense of all the verbs listed are the same as those for the present tense of regular –ir verbs.
• Point out the spelling changes in the **yo** forms of **seguir** and **conseguir.**
• Prepare dehydrated sentences and write them on the board one at a time. Ex: **1. tú / pedir / café 2. ustedes / repetir / la pregunta 3. nosotros / decir / la respuesta** Have students form complete sentences based on the cues.
• For additional drills with stem-changing verbs, do the **¡Inténtalo!** activity orally using other infinitives, such as **conseguir, impedir, pedir,** and **servir.** Keep a brisk pace.

**Note:** Students will learn more about **decir** with indirect object pronouns in **Estructura 6.2.**

# Práctica

**1 Completar** Complete these sentences with the correct form of the verb provided.

1. Cuando mi familia pasea por la ciudad, mi madre siempre (*always*) va al café y ___pide___ (pedir) una soda.
2. Pero mi padre ___dice___ (decir) que perdemos mucho tiempo. Tiene prisa por llegar al bosque de Chapultepec.
3. Mi padre tiene suerte, porque él siempre ___consigue___ (conseguir) lo que (*that which*) desea.
4. Cuando llegamos al parque, mis hermanos y yo ___seguimos___ (seguir) conversando (*talking*) con nuestros padres.
5. Mis padres siempre ___repiten___ (repetir) la misma cosa: "Nosotros tomamos el sol aquí sin ustedes."
6. Yo siempre ___pido___ (pedir) permiso para volver a casa un poco más tarde porque me gusta mucho el parque.

**NOTA CULTURAL**

A popular weekend destination for residents and tourists, **El bosque de Chapultepec** is a beautiful park located in Mexico City. It occupies over 1.5 square miles and includes lakes, wooded areas, several museums, and a botanical garden.

**2 Combinar** Combine words from the columns to create sentences about yourself and people you know. Answers will vary.

| A | B |
|---|---|
| yo | (no) pedir muchos favores |
| mi compañero/a de cuarto | nunca (*never*) pedir perdón |
| mi mejor (*best*) amigo/a | nunca seguir las instrucciones |
| mi familia | siempre seguir las instrucciones |
| mis amigos/as | conseguir libros en Internet |
| mis amigos y yo | repetir el vocabulario |
| mis padres | |
| mi hermano/a | |
| mi profesor(a) de español | |

**3 Opiniones** Work in pairs to guess how your partner completed the sentences from **Actividad 2**. If you guess incorrectly, your partner must supply the correct answer. Switch roles. Answers will vary.

**modelo**

**Estudiante 1:** En mi opinión, tus padres consiguen libros en Internet.
**Estudiante 2:** ¡No! Mi hermana consigue libros en Internet.

**CONSULTA**

To review possessive adjectives, see **Estructura 3.2**, p. 85.

---

**1 Expansion** Have students use **conseguir, decir, pedir, repetir,** and **seguir** to write original sentences, using their own family members as subjects. Then have them exchange papers with a partner for peer editing.

**Nota cultural** Have students research **El bosque de Chapultepec** in the library or on the Internet and bring a photo of the park to class. Ask them to share one new fact they learned about the park.

**2 Teaching Tip** Before beginning the activity, ask students to brainstorm their choices for the sentences. Then model the activity. Ex: **Mis amigos piden muchos favores.**

**2 Expansion** In pairs, have students create three or four true-false statements based on this activity, using stem-changing verbs from **Estructura 4.2** and **4.3**. Then have pairs share their statements with another pair, who must decide if they are true or false.

**3 Teaching Tip** Ask students to keep a record of their partner's responses. Survey the class to see how many students guessed their partner's statements correctly.

---

**TEACHING OPTIONS**

**Pairs** Ask students to write four simple statements using **e:i** verbs. Then have them read their sentences to a partner, who will guess where the situation takes place. Ex: **Consigo libros para las clases. (Estás en la biblioteca.)** Then reverse the activity, allowing them to answer with verbs from **Estructura 4.2**.

**Small Groups** Explain to students that movie titles for English-language films are frequently not directly translated into Spanish and that titles may vary from country to country. Bring in a list of movie titles in Spanish. Ex: ***Colega, ¿dónde está mi coche?*** (*Dude, Where's My Car?*); ***Lo que el viento se llevó*** (*Gone with the Wind*). In groups, have students guess the movies based on the Spanish titles. Then ask them to state which movies they prefer to watch.

# Comunicación

**4** **Las películas** Use these questions to interview a classmate. Answers will vary.

1. ¿Prefieres las películas románticas, las películas de acción o las películas de horror? ¿Por qué?
2. ¿Dónde consigues información sobre *(about)* una película?
3. ¿Dónde consigues las entradas *(tickets)* para una película?
4. Para decidir qué películas vas a ver, ¿sigues las recomendaciones de los críticos? ¿Qué dicen los críticos en general?
5. ¿Qué cines en tu comunidad muestran las mejores *(best)* películas?
6. ¿Vas a ver una película esta semana? ¿A qué hora empieza la película?

# Síntesis

**5** **El cine** In pairs, first scan the ad and jot down all the stem-changing verbs. Then answer the questions. Be prepared to share your answers with the class. Answers will vary.

1. ¿Qué palabras indican que *Un mundo azul oscuro (Dark Blue World)* es una película dramática?
2. ¿Cuántas personas hay en el póster?
3. ¿Cómo son las personas del póster? ¿Qué relación tienen?
4. ¿Te gustan las películas como ésta *(this one)*?
5. Describe tu película favorita con los verbos de la **Lección 4.**

---

---

**4 Teaching Tips**
• Have students report to the class what their partner said. After the presentation, encourage them to ask each other questions.
• Take a class poll to find out students' film genre and local movie theater preferences.

**4 Expansion** To challenge students, write some key movie-related words on the board, such as **actor, actriz, argumento,** and **efectos especiales.** Explain how to use **mejor** and **peor** as adjectives. Have student pairs say which movies this year they think should win Oscars. Model by telling them: **Pienso que____ es la mejor película del año. Debe ganar porque...** Then ask students to nominate the year's worst. Have them share their opinions with the class.

**5 Teaching Tips**
• Write the stem-changing verbs from the ad on the board. Have students conjugate the verbs using different subjects.
• In pairs, have students use the verbs from the ad to write a dramatic dialogue.
• Go over student responses to item 5.

**5 Expansion** Tell students the gist of the love triangle in *Dark Blue World*: it is the story of two Czech pilots (Franta and Karel) who fight for the British during World War II and whose friendship is tested when they both fall in love with Susan, an Englishwoman. Ask student pairs to write a short, melodramatic dialogue between two of the characters, using verbs from this lesson. Then have them role-play the scene for the class. You may want to have the class vote for an "Oscar" for the best presentation.

# 4.4 Verbs with irregular **yo** forms

**ANTE TODO** In Spanish, several verbs have irregular **yo** forms in the present tense. You have already seen three verbs with the **–go** ending in the **yo** form: **decir → digo, tener → tengo,** and **venir → vengo.**

▶ Here are some common expressions with **decir.**

| | |
|---|---|
| **decir la verdad** | **decir mentiras** |
| *to tell the truth* | *to tell lies* |
| **decir que** | **decir la respuesta** |
| *to say that* | *to say the answer* |

▶ The verb **hacer** is often used to ask questions about what someone does. Note that, when answering, **hacer** is frequently replaced with another, more specific, action verb.

### Verbs with irregular yo forms

| | hacer (to do; to make) | poner (to put; to place) | salir (to leave) | suponer (to suppose) | traer (to bring) |
|---|---|---|---|---|---|
| **SINGULAR FORMS** | **hago** | **pongo** | **salgo** | **supongo** | **traigo** |
| | haces | pones | sales | supones | traes |
| | hace | pone | sale | supone | trae |
| **PLURAL FORMS** | hacemos | ponemos | salimos | suponemos | traemos |
| | hacéis | ponéis | salís | suponéis | traéis |
| | hacen | ponen | salen | suponen | traen |

¿Qué haces los fines de semana?

Salgo con mis amigos y practico deportes.

Yo no salgo, prefiero poner la televisión y ver películas.

▶ **Poner** can also mean *to turn on* a household appliance.

Carlos **pone** la radio.
*Carlos turns on the radio.*

María **pone** la televisión.
*María turns on the television.*

▶ **Salir de** is used to indicate that someone is leaving a particular place.

Hoy **salgo del** hospital.
*Today I leave the hospital.*

**Sale de** la clase a las cuatro.
*He leaves class at four.*

▶ **Salir para** is used to indicate someone's destination.

Mañana **salgo para** México.
*Tomorrow I leave for Mexico.*

Hoy **salen para** España.
*Today they leave for Spain.*

▶ **Salir con** means *to leave with someone* or *something*, or *to date someone.*

Alberto **sale con** su mochila.
*Alberto is leaving with his backpack.*

Margarita **sale con** Guillermo.
*Margarita is going out with Guillermo.*

## The verbs ver and oír

▶ The verb **ver** (*to see*) has an irregular **yo** form. The other forms of **ver** are regular.

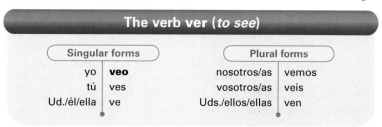

### The verb ver (*to see*)

| Singular forms | | Plural forms | |
|---|---|---|---|
| yo | **veo** | nosotros/as | vemos |
| tú | ves | vosotros/as | veis |
| Ud./él/ella | ve | Uds./ellos/ellas | ven |

▶ The verb **oír** (*to hear*) has an irregular **yo** form and the spelling change i→y in the **tú, usted, él, ella, ustedes, ellos,** and **ellas** forms. The **nosotros/as** and **vosotros/as** forms have an accent mark.

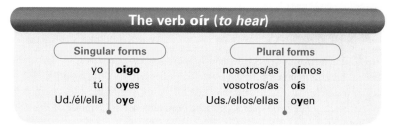

### The verb oír (*to hear*)

| Singular forms | | Plural forms | |
|---|---|---|---|
| yo | **oigo** | nosotros/as | oímos |
| tú | oyes | vosotros/as | oís |
| Ud./él/ella | oye | Uds./ellos/ellas | oyen |

▶ While most commonly translated as *to hear*, **oír** is also used in contexts where English would use *to listen.*

**Oigo** a unas personas en la otra sala.
*I hear some people in the other room.*

¿**Oyes** la radio por la mañana?
*Do you listen to the radio in the morning?*

**¡INTÉNTALO!** Provide the appropriate forms of these verbs. The first item has been done for you.

1. salir      Isabel ____sale____.      Nosotros ____salimos____.      Yo ____salgo____.
2. ver        Yo ____veo____.           Uds. ____ven____.              Tú ____ves____.
3. poner      Rita y yo ____ponemos____.   Yo ____pongo____.           Los niños ____ponen____.
4. hacer      Yo ____hago____.          Tú ____haces____.             Ud. ____hace____.
5. oír        Él ____oye____.           Nosotros ____oímos____.        Yo ____oigo____.
6. traer      Ellas ____traen____.      Yo ____traigo____.            Tú ____traes____.
7. suponer    Yo ____supongo____.       Mi amigo ____supone____.      Nosotras ____suponemos____.

---

**TEACHING OPTIONS**

**Extra Practice** To add an auditory aspect to this grammar practice, call out subject pronouns and have students respond with the correct form of **ver** or **oír**. Reverse the drill by calling out verb forms and having students provide the subject pronouns.

**Pairs** Have student pairs create questions and ask each other about their habits. Ex: **¿Sales a comer a restaurantes con tus amigos? ¿Ves la televisión en español? ¿Supones que una clase de matemáticas es muy difícil?** Have students record their partner's answers and be prepared to share the information with the class.

---

**Teaching Tips**

- Point out that **oír** is irregular in all forms. Write a model sentence on the board. Ex: **Ustedes oyen el programa de radio todos los viernes.** Then change the subject, and have students give the new sentence. Ex: **tú (Tú oyes el programa de radio todos los viernes.)**
- Call out different forms of the verbs in **Estructura 4.4** and have volunteers say the infinitive. Ex: **oyen (oír).** Keep a brisk pace.
- Do a chain drill. Start by writing **¿Qué haces los sábados?** on the board. Model an appropriate answer, such as **Salgo con mis amigos.** Ask one student to respond (Ex: **Veo una película.**). The next student you call on should repeat what the first does and add on (Ex: **Cindy ve una película y yo salgo con…**). Continue until the chain becomes too long; then start with a new question. Keep a brisk pace.
- Write these phrases on the board: **ver la tele, traer un sándwich a la universidad, salir con amigos,** and **hacer yoga.** Model the question and possible answers for each phrase. Then elicit follow-up questions (Ex: **¿Dónde ves la tele?**). Have student pairs take turns asking and answering the questions. They should be prepared to report to the class about their partners' habits.
- Explain to students that the i → y spelling change strengthens the i sound between vowels, which clarifies to the ear that the verb is **oír.**
- Explain the difference between **escuchar** (*to listen*) and **oír** (*to hear*). Ex: **Escucho la radio. No oigo el perro.**

# Práctica (SUPERSITE)

**1** **Completar** Complete this conversation with the appropriate forms of the verbs. Then act it out with a partner.

**ERNESTO** David, ¿qué (1)_____haces_____ (hacer) hoy?

**DAVID** Ahora estudio biología, pero esta noche (2)_____salgo_____ (salir) con Luisa. Vamos al cine. Los críticos (3)_____dicen_____ (decir) que la nueva (*new*) película de Almodóvar es buena.

**ERNESTO** ¿Y Diana? ¿Qué (4)_____hace_____ (hacer) ella?

**DAVID** (5)_____Sale_____ (Salir) a comer con sus padres.

**ERNESTO** ¿Qué (6)_____hacen_____ (hacer) Andrés y Javier?

**DAVID** Tienen que (7)_____hacer_____ (hacer) las maletas. (8)_____Salen_____ (Salir) para Monterrey mañana.

**ERNESTO** Pues, ¿qué (9)_____hago_____ (hacer) yo?

**DAVID** (10)_____Supongo_____ (Suponer) que puedes estudiar o (11)_____ver_____ (ver) la televisión.

**ERNESTO** No quiero estudiar. Mejor (12)_____pongo_____ (poner) la televisión. Mi programa favorito empieza en unos minutos.

**2** **Oraciones** Form sentences using the cues provided and verbs from **Estructura 4.4**.

> **modelo**
> tú / _____ / cosas / en / su lugar / antes de (*before*) / salir
> *Tú pones las cosas en su lugar antes de salir.*

1. mis amigos / _____ / conmigo / centro   Mis amigos salen conmigo al centro.
2. tú / _____ / verdad   Tú dices la verdad.
3. Alberto / _____ / música del café Pasatiempos   Alberto oye la música del café Pasatiempos.
4. yo / no / _____ / muchas películas   Yo no veo muchas películas.
5. domingo / nosotros / _____ / mucha / tarea   El domingo, nosotros hacemos mucha tarea.
6. si / yo _____ / que / yo / querer / ir / cine / mis amigos / ir / también   Si yo digo que quiero ir al cine, mis amigos van también.

**3** **Describir** Use a verb from **Estructura 4.4** to describe what these people are doing.

1. Fernán   Fernán pone la mochila en el escritorio.

2. los aficionados   Los aficionados salen del estadio.

3. yo   Yo traigo una cámara.

4. nosotros   Nosotros vemos el monumento.

5. la señora Vargas   La señora Vargas no oye bien.

6. el estudiante   El estudiante hace su tarea.

---

**1** **Teaching Tip** Quickly review the new verbs with irregular **yo** forms. Then, ask pairs to complete and role-play the conversation.

**1** **Expansion** Ask questions about the conversation. Ex: **¿Qué hace David hoy? ¿Qué hace Diana? ¿Por qué tienen que hacer las maletas Andrés y Javier? ¿Por qué pone Ernesto la televisión?**

**2** **Teaching Tips**
• Model the activity by completing the **modelo** orally. Ask volunteers to say aloud each complete sentence.
• To simplify, lead the class to identify key words in each sentence. Then have students choose the infinitive that best fits with the key words and name any missing words for each item. After students complete the activity individually, have volunteers write the sentences on the board.

**2** **Expansion**
• Change the subjects of the dehydrated sentences in the activity and have students write or say aloud the new sentences.
• Ask students to form questions that would elicit the statements in **Actividad 2**. Ex: **¿Qué hago antes de salir?**
• Have students write three sentences, each using a verb from **Estructura 4.4**. Then ask them to copy their sentences onto a sheet of paper in dehydrated form, following the model of **Actividad 2**. Students should exchange papers with a partner, who writes the complete sentences. Finally, have partners check each other's work.

**3** **Expansion** Use magazine pictures which elicit the target verbs to extend the activity. Encourage students to add further descriptions if they can.

---

**TEACHING OPTIONS**

**Game** Have students use five of the target verbs from **Estructura 4.4** to write unusual sentences about themselves. Four of the sentences should be true and one should be fictional. In small groups, have students take turns reading their sentences aloud. The first group member to guess which sentence is untrue wins a point. The player with the most points wins.

**Extra Practice** Have students use five of the target verbs from **Estructura 4.4** to write sentences about their habits that others may find somewhat unusual. Ex: **Traigo doce bolígrafos en la mochila. Hago la tarea en un café del centro. No pongo la televisión hasta las diez de la noche.**

# Comunicación

**4** **Preguntas** Get together with a classmate and ask each other these questions. Answers will vary.

1. ¿Qué traes a clase?
2. ¿Quiénes traen un diccionario a clase? ¿Por qué traen un diccionario?
3. ¿A qué hora sales de tu residencia estudiantil o de tu casa por la mañana? ¿A qué hora sale tu compañero/a de cuarto o tu esposo/a?
4. ¿Dónde pones tus libros cuando regresas de clase? ¿Siempre (*Always*) pones tus cosas en su lugar?
5. ¿Pones fotos de tu familia en tu casa? ¿Quiénes son las personas que están en las fotos?
6. ¿Oyes la radio cuando estudias?
7. ¿En qué circunstancias dices mentiras?
8. ¿Haces mucha tarea los fines de semana?
9. ¿Sales con tus amigos los fines de semana? ¿A qué hora? ¿Qué hacen?
10. ¿Te gusta ver deportes en la televisión o prefieres ver otros programas? ¿Cuáles?

**5** **Charadas** In groups, play a game of charades. Each person should think of two phrases using the verbs **hacer, oír, poner, salir, traer,** or **ver**. The first person to guess correctly acts out the next charade. Answers will vary.

**6** **Entrevista** You are doing a market research report on lifestyles. Interview a classmate to find out when he or she goes out with the following people and what they do for entertainment. Answers will vary.

► los amigos
► el/la novio/a
► el/la esposo/a
► la familia

# Síntesis

**7** **Situación** Imagine that you are speaking with your roommate. With a partner, prepare a conversation using these cues. Answers will vary.

| Estudiante 1 | Estudiante 2 |
|---|---|
| Ask your partner what he or she is doing. | → Tell your partner that you are watching TV. |
| Say what you suppose he or she is watching. | → Say that you like the show _____. Ask if he or she wants to watch. |
| Say no, because you are going out with friends and tell where you are going. | → Say you think it's a good idea, and ask what your partner and his or her friends are doing there. |
| Say what you are going to do, and ask your partner whether he or she wants to come along. | → Say no and tell your partner what you prefer to do. |

---

**TEACHING OPTIONS**

**Pairs** Have pairs of students role-play the perfect date. Students should write their script first, then present it to the class. Encourage students to use descriptive adjectives as well as the new verbs learned in **Estructura 4.4**.

**Heritage Speakers** Ask heritage speakers to make a brief oral presentation to the class about a social custom in their cultural community. Remind them to use familiar vocabulary and simple sentences.

---

*Right margin sidebar:*

**4** **Teaching Tip** Model the activity by having volunteers answer the first two items.

**4** **Expansion** Ask students about their classmate's responses. Ex: **¿Tu compañera trae un diccionario a clase? ¿Por qué?**

**5** **Teaching Tips**
• Model the activity by doing a charade for the class to guess. Ex: **Pongo un lápiz en la mesa.** Then divide the class into groups of five to seven students.
• Ask each group to choose the best **charada**. Then have students present them to the class, who will guess the activities.

**6** **Teaching Tip** Model the activity by giving a report on your lifestyle. Ex: **Salgo al cine con mis amigas. Me gusta comer en restaurantes con mi esposo. En familia vemos deportes en la televisión.** Remind students that a market researcher and the interviewee would address each other with the **usted** form of verbs.

**7** **Possible Conversation**
E1: **¿Qué haces?**
E2: **Veo la tele.**
E1: **Supongo que ves el programa *Los Simpson*.**
E2: **Sí. Me gusta el programa. ¿Quieres ver la tele conmigo?**
E1: **No puedo. Salgo con mis amigos a la plaza.**
E2: **Buena idea. ¿Qué hacen en la plaza?**
E1: **Vamos a escuchar música y a pasear. ¿Quieres venir?**
E2: **No. Prefiero descansar.**

## Section Goal

In **Recapitulación**, students will review the grammar concepts from this lesson.

---

**Instructional Resource**
**Supersite**

---

**1** **Teaching Tips**
- To simplify, before students begin the activity, have them identify the stem change (if any) in each row.
- Complete this activity orally as a class.

**1** **Expansion** Ask students to provide the remaining forms of the verbs.

**2** **Teaching Tip** To challenge students, ask them to provide alternative verbs for the blanks. Ex: **1. vemos/miramos** Then ask: Why can't **ir** be used for item 4? (needs **a**)

**2** **Expansion**
- Ask questions about **Cecilia's** typical day. Have students answer with complete sentences. **¿Qué hace Cecilia a las siete y media? ¿Por qué le gusta llegar temprano?**
- Write on the board the verb phrases about **Cecilia's** day. Ex: **ver la televisión por la mañana, almorzar a las 12:30, jugar al vóleibol por la tarde.** Brainstorm a few more entries (Ex: **hacer la tarea por la noche**). Ask students to make a two-column chart, labeled **yo** and **compañero/a**. They should initial each activity they perform. Then have them interview a partner and report back to the class.

---

# Recapitulación

**SUPERSITE** For self-scoring and diagnostics, go to **panorama.vhlcentral.com**.

Review the grammar concepts you have learned in this lesson by completing these activities.

**1** **Completar** Complete the chart with the correct verb forms. `15 pts.`

| Infinitive | yo | nosotros/as | ellos/as |
|---|---|---|---|
| volver | **vuelvo** | volvemos | vuelven |
| **comenzar** | comienzo | **comenzamos** | comienzan |
| hacer | hago | **hacemos** | **hacen** |
| **ir** | voy | vamos | van |
| jugar | **juego** | jugamos | juegan |
| **repetir** | repito | repetimos | **repiten** |

**2** **Un día típico** Complete the paragraph with the appropriate forms of the verbs in the word list. Not all verbs will be used. Some may be used more than once. `10 pts.`

| | | |
|---|---|---|
| almorzar | ir | salir |
| cerrar | jugar | seguir |
| empezar | mostrar | ver |
| hacer | querer | volver |

¡Hola! Me llamo Cecilia y vivo en Puerto Vallarta, México. ¿Cómo es un día típico en mi vida (*life*)? Por la mañana bebo café con mis padres y juntos (*together*) (1)_____vemos_____ las noticias (*news*) en la televisión. A las siete y media, (yo) (2)_____salgo_____ de mi casa y tomo el autobús. Me gusta llegar temprano (*early*) a la universidad porque siempre (*always*) (3)_____veo_____ a mis amigos en la cafetería. Tomamos café y planeamos lo que (4)_____queremos_____ hacer cada (*each*) día. A las ocho y cuarto, mi amiga Sandra y yo (5)_____vamos_____ al laboratorio de lenguas. La clase de francés (6)_____empieza_____ a las ocho y media. ¡Es mi clase favorita! A las doce y media (yo) (7)_____almuerzo_____ en la cafetería con mis amigos. Después (*Afterwards*), yo (8)_____sigo_____ con mis clases. Por las tardes, mis amigos (9)_____vuelven_____ a sus casas, pero yo (10)_____juego_____ al vóleibol con mi amigo Tomás.

---

**RESUMEN GRAMATICAL**

**4.1** **Present tense of ir** *p. 118*

| yo | voy | nos. | vamos |
|---|---|---|---|
| tú | vas | vos. | vais |
| él | va | ellas | van |

▶ **ir a +** [*infinitive*] = *to be going to* + [*infinitive*]
▶ **a + el = al**
▶ **vamos a +** [*infinitive*] = *let's* (*do something*)

**4.2** **Stem-changing verbs e:ie, o:ue, u:ue** *pp. 121–?*

| | empezar | volver | jugar |
|---|---|---|---|
| yo | empiezo | vuelvo | juego |
| tú | empiezas | vuelves | juegas |
| él | empieza | vuelve | juega |
| nos. | empezamos | volvemos | jugamos |
| vos. | empezáis | volvéis | jugáis |
| ellas | empiezan | vuelven | juegan |

▶ Other e:ie verbs: **cerrar, comenzar, entender, pensar, perder, preferir, querer**
▶ Other o:ue verbs: **almorzar, contar, dormir, encontrar, mostrar, poder, recordar**

**4.3** **Stem-changing verbs e:i** *p. 125*

| | pedir | | |
|---|---|---|---|
| yo | pido | nos. | pedimos |
| tú | pides | vos. | pedís |
| él | pide | ellas | piden |

▶ Other e:i verbs: **conseguir, decir, repetir, seguir**

**4.4** **Verbs with irregular yo forms** *pp. 128–129*

| hacer | poner | salir | suponer | traer |
|---|---|---|---|---|
| hago | pongo | salgo | supongo | traigo |

▶ **ver:** veo, ves, ve, vemos, veis, ven
▶ **oír:** oigo, oyes, oye, oímos, oís, oyen

---

**TEACHING OPTIONS**

**Pairs** Pair weaker students with more advanced students. Give each pair a numbered list of the target verbs from **Resumen gramatical** and a small plastic bag containing subject pronouns written on paper strips. Model the first verb for students by drawing out a subject pronoun at random and conjugating the verb on the board. Ask: **¿Correcto o incorrecto?** Have students take turns and correct each other's work. Keep a brisk pace.

**Extra Practice** Introduce the word **nunca** and have students use verbs from this lesson to write five sentences about things they never do. Ex: **Nunca veo películas románticas.** Collect the descriptions and read them aloud. Have the class guess which student is being described.

**3** **Oraciones** Arrange the cues provided in the correct order to form complete sentences. Make all necessary changes. `14 pts.`

1. tarea / los / hacer / sábados / nosotros / la
   Los sábados nosotros hacemos la tarea./Nosotros hacemos la tarea los sábados.

2. en / pizza / Andrés / una / restaurante / el / pedir
   Andrés pide una pizza en el restaurante.

3. a / ? / museo / ir / ¿ / el / (tú)
   ¿(Tú) Vas al museo?

4. de / oír / amigos / bien / los / no / Elena
   Los amigos de Elena no oyen bien.

5. libros / traer / yo / clase / mis / a
   Yo traigo mis libros a clase.

6. película / ver / en / Jorge y Carlos / pensar / cine / una / el
   Jorge y Carlos piensan ver una película en el cine.

7. unos / escribir / Mariana / electrónicos / querer / mensajes
   Mariana quiere escribir unos mensajes electrónicos.

**4** **Escribir** Write a short paragraph about what you do on a typical day. Use at least six of the verbs you have learned in this lesson. You can use the paragraph on the opposite page (**Actividad 2**) as a model. `11 pts.`  Answers will vary.

> *Un día típico*
>
> Hola, me llamo Julia y vivo
> en Vancouver, Canadá. Por la
> mañana, yo...

**5** **Rima** Write the missing verbs to solve the rhyme. `2 EXTRA points!`

*"Si no ___puedes___ dormir
y el sueño deseas,
lo vas a conseguir
si ___cuentas___ ovejas°."*

ovejas *sheep*

---

**3** **Teaching Tip** To simplify, provide the first word for each sentence.

**3** **Expansion** Give students these sentences as items 8–11: **8. la / ? / ustedes / cerrar / ventana / ¿ / poder (¿Pueden ustedes cerrar la ventana?) 9. cine / de / tú / las / salir / once / el / a (Tú sales del cine a las once.) 10. el / conmigo / a / en / ellos / tenis / el / jugar / parque (Ellos juegan al tenis conmigo en el parque.) 11. que / partido / mañana / un / decir / hay / Javier (Javier dice que hay un partido mañana.)**

**4** **Teaching Tips**
• To simplify, ask students to make a three-column chart with the headings **Por la mañana, Por la tarde,** and **Por la noche**. Have them brainstorm at least three verbs or verb phrases for each column and circle any stem-changing or irregular **yo** verbs.
• Have students exchange paragraphs with a classmate for peer editing. Ask them to underline grammatical and spelling errors.

**5** **Expansion** Ask students if they ever have trouble sleeping. Have volunteers share with the class what they do when they cannot sleep.

---

**TEACHING OPTIONS**

**Game** Make a Bingo card of places at school or around town, such as dorm names, libraries, cafeterias, movie theaters, and cafés. Give each student a card and model possible questions (Ex: for a cafeteria, **¿Almuerzas en _____?/¿Dónde almuerzas?**). Encourage them to circulate around the room, asking only one question per person; if they get an affirmative answer, they should write that person's name in the square. The first student

to complete a horizontal, vertical, or diagonal row and yell **¡Bingo!** is the winner.

**Heritage Speakers** Ask heritage speakers if counting sheep is common advice for sleeplessness in their families. What other insomnia remedies have they heard of or practiced?

## Section Goals

In **Lectura**, students will:
- learn the strategy of predicting content by surveying the graphic elements in reading matter
- read a magazine article containing graphs and charts

**Instructional Resources**
**Supersite**
*Cuaderno para hispanohablantes*

**Estrategia** Tell students that they can infer a great deal of information about the content of an article by surveying the graphic elements included in it. When students survey an article for its graphic elements, they should look for such things as:
- headlines or headings
- bylines
- photos
- photo captions
- graphs and tables

**Examinar el texto** Give students two minutes to take a look at the visual clues in the article and write down all the ideas the clues suggest.

**Contestar** Ask the class the questions. 1. **María Úrsula Echevarría** is the author of the article. 2. The article is about sports in the Hispanic world. 3. The most popular sports 4. Hispanic countries in world soccer championships

# Lectura

## Antes de leer

### Estrategia
**Predicting content from visuals**

When you are reading in Spanish, be sure to look for visual clues that will orient you as to the content and purpose of what you are reading. Photos and illustrations, for example, will often give you a good idea of the main points that the reading covers. You may also encounter very helpful visuals that are used to summarize large amounts of data in a way that is easy to comprehend; these include bar graphs, pie charts, flow charts, lists of percentages, and other sorts of diagrams.

**Examinar el texto**
Take a quick look at the visual elements of the magazine article in order to generate a list of ideas about its content. Then compare your list with a classmate's. Are your lists the same or are they different? Discuss your lists and make any changes needed to produce a final list of ideas.

**Contestar**
Read the list of ideas you wrote in **Examinar el texto,** and look again at the visual elements of the magazine article. Then answer these questions:

1. Who is the woman in the photo, and what is her role?
2. What is the article about?
3. What is the subject of the pie chart?
4. What is the subject of the bar graph?

### por María Úrsula Echevarría

El fútbol es el deporte más popular en el mundo° hispano, según° una encuesta° reciente realizada entre jóvenes universitarios. Mucha gente practica este deporte y tiene un equipo de fútbol favorito. Cada cuatro años se realiza la Copa Mundial°. Argentina y Uruguay han ganado° este campeonato° más de una vez°. Los aficionados siguen los partidos de fútbol en casa por tele y en muchos otros lugares como los bares, los restaurantes, los estadios y los clubes deportivos. Los jóvenes juegan al fútbol con sus amigos en parques y gimnasios.

**Países hispanos en campeonatos mundiales de fútbol (1930–2002)**

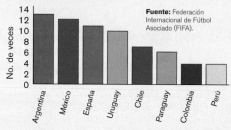

**Fuente:** Federación Internacional de Fútbol Asociado (FIFA).

Pero, por supuesto°, en los países de habla hispana también hay otros deportes populares. ¿Qué deporte sigue al fútbol en estos países? Bueno, ¡depende del país y de otros factores!

## Después de leer
### Evaluación y predicción

Which of the following sports events would be most popular among the college students surveyed? Rate them from one (most popular) to five (least popular). Which would be the most popular at your college or university?
Answers will vary.

_____  1. La Copa Mundial de Fútbol
_____  2. Los Juegos Olímpicos
_____  3. El torneo de tenis de Wimbledon
_____  4. La Serie Mundial de Béisbol
_____  5. El Tour de Francia

---

**TEACHING OPTIONS**

**Variación léxica** Remind students that **fútbol** means *soccer;* the game called *football* in the U.S. and Canada is **el fútbol americano**. You may wish to point out that in other English-speaking countries, soccer is called *football* as well.

**Extra Practice** Ask questions that require students to refer to the article. Model the use of the definite article with percentages. ¿Qué porcentaje prefiere el fútbol? (el 69 por ciento) ¿Qué porcentaje prefiere el vóleibol? (el 2 por ciento)

# No sólo el fútbol

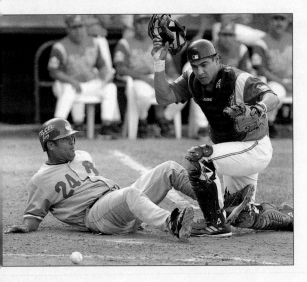

En Colombia, por ejemplo, el béisbol es muy popular después del fútbol, aunque° esto varía según la región del país. En la costa del norte de Colombia, el béisbol es una pasión. Y el ciclismo también es un deporte que los colombianos siguen con mucho interés.

## Donde el béisbol es más popular

En los países del Caribe, el béisbol es el deporte predominante. Éste es el caso en Puerto Rico, Cuba y la República Dominicana. Los niños empiezan a jugar cuando son muy pequeños. En Puerto Rico y la República Dominicana, la gente también quiere participar en otros deportes, como el baloncesto, o ver los partidos en la tele. Y para los espectadores aficionados del Caribe, el boxeo es número dos.

**Deportes más populares**

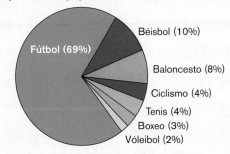

- Béisbol (10%)
- Fútbol (69%)
- Baloncesto (8%)
- Ciclismo (4%)
- Tenis (4%)
- Boxeo (3%)
- Vóleibol (2%)

## Donde el fútbol es más popular

En México el béisbol es el segundo° deporte más popular después° del fútbol. Pero en Argentina, después del fútbol, el rugby tiene mucha importancia. En Perú a la gente le gusta mucho ver partidos de vóleibol. ¿Y en España? Mucha gente prefiere el baloncesto, el tenis y el ciclismo.

mundo *world* según *according to* encuesta *survey* se realiza la Copa Mundial *the World Cup is held* han ganado *have won* campeonato *championship* más de una vez *more than once* por supuesto *of course* segundo *second* después *after* aunque *although*

## ¿Cierto o falso? 🖊

Indicate whether each sentence is **cierto** or **falso,** then correct the false statements.

| | Cierto | Falso |
|---|---|---|
| 1. El vóleibol es el segundo deporte más popular en México. Es el béisbol. | ○ | ☑ |
| 2. En España a la gente le gustan varios deportes como el baloncesto y el ciclismo. | ☑ | ○ |
| 3. En la costa del norte de Colombia, el tenis es una pasión. El béisbol es una pasión. | ○ | ☑ |
| 4. En el Caribe el deporte más popular es el béisbol. | ☑ | ○ |

## Preguntas

Answer these questions in Spanish. Answers will vary.

1. ¿Dónde ven los aficionados el fútbol? Y tú, ¿cómo ves tus deportes favoritos?
2. ¿Te gusta el fútbol? ¿Por qué?
3. ¿Miras la Copa Mundial en la televisión?
4. ¿Qué deportes miras en la televisión?
5. En tu opinión, ¿cuáles son los tres deportes más populares en tu universidad? ¿En tu comunidad? ¿En los Estados Unidos?
6. ¿Qué haces en tus ratos libres?

**Evaluación y predicción** Write two headings on the board: **Entre los jóvenes del mundo hispano** and **Entre los jóvenes de nuestra universidad**. Ask for a show of hands to respond to your questions about the ranking of each sporting event. Tally the reponses as you proceed. Ask: **¿Quiénes creen que entre los jóvenes hispanos la Copa Mundial de Fútbol es el evento más popular? ¿Quiénes creen que los Juegos Olímpicos son el evento más popular?** Then ask: **Entre los jóvenes de nuestra universidad, ¿quiénes de ustedes creen que la Copa Mundial de Fútbol es el evento más popular?** Briefly discuss the differences indicated by student responses.

**¿Cierto o falso?** After completing the activity, ask students to write an additional sentence about sports in each country or region mentioned. Ex: **El fútbol es el deporte más popular en México.**

**Preguntas** Give students these questions as items 7–10: **7. ¿Cuál es el deporte más popular en el mundo hispano? (el fútbol) 8. ¿En qué países es el béisbol el deporte más popular? (en los países del Caribe) 9. ¿Pueden nombrar algunos jugadores de béisbol hispanos en los Estados Unidos? (Answers will vary.) 10. ¿Participan muchos países hispanos en campeonatos mundiales de fútbol? (sí)**

---

**TEACHING OPTIONS**

**Pairs** In pairs, have students read the article aloud and write three questions about it. Then, ask students to exchange their questions with another pair. Alternatively, you can ask pairs to read their questions to the class.

**Heritage Speakers** Ask heritage speakers to prepare a short presentation about soccer in their families' home countries. Encourage them to include how popular the sport is, what the principal teams are, and whether their country has participated in a World Cup.

## México

NATIONAL connections cultures STANDARDS

### El país en cifras

▶ **Área:** 1.972.550 km$^2$ (761.603 millas$^2$), casi° tres veces° el área de Texas

*La situación geográfica de México, al sur° de los Estados Unidos, ha influido en° la economía y la sociedad de los dos países. Una de las consecuencias es la emigración de la población mexicana al país vecino°. Hoy día, más de 20 millones de personas de ascendencia mexicana viven en los Estados Unidos.*

▶ **Población:** 113.271.000
▶ **Capital:** México, D.F.—20.688.000
▶ **Ciudades principales:** Guadalajara—4.237.000, Monterrey—3.914.000, Ciudad Juárez—1.841.000, Puebla—1.801.000

SOURCE: Population Division, UN Secretariat

▶ **Moneda:** peso mexicano
▶ **Idiomas:** español (oficial), náhuatl, otras lenguas indígenas

Bandera de México

### Mexicanos célebres

▶ **Benito Juárez,** héroe nacional (1806–1872)
▶ **Octavio Paz,** poeta (1914–1998)
▶ **Elena Poniatowska,** periodista y escritora (1933– )
▶ **Julio César Chávez,** boxeador (1962– )

casi *almost* veces *times* sur *south* ha influido en *has influenced* vecino *neighboring* se llenan de luz *get filled with light* flores *flowers* Muertos *Dead* se ríen *laugh* muerte *death* lo cual se refleja *which is reflected* calaveras de azúcar *sugar skulls* pan *bread* huesos *bones*

**recursos**

WB pp. 47–48    VM pp. 231–232    SUPERSITE panorama.vhlcentral.com Lección 4

ESTADOS UNIDOS

Un delfín en Baja California

Ciudad Juárez

Golfo de California

Baja California

Sierra Madre Oriental

Sierra Madre Occidental

Río Bravo del Norte

Río Grande

Monterr

Autorretrato con mono (*Self-portrait with monkey*), 1938, Frida Kahlo

ESTADOS UNIDOS
MÉXICO
OCÉANO PACÍFICO
OCÉANO ATLÁNTICO
AMÉRICA DEL SUR

Océano Pacífico

Puerto Vallarta

Ciudad de México

Guadalajara

Pue

Acapulco

Ruinas aztecas en México D.F.

Saltador en Acapulco

### ¡Increíble pero cierto!

Cada dos de noviembre los cementerios de México se llenan de luz°, música y flores°. El Día de Muertos° no es un evento triste; es una fiesta en honor a las personas muertas. En ese día, los mexicanos se ríen° de la muerte°, lo cual se refleja° en detalles como las calaveras de azúcar° y el pan° de muerto —pan en forma de huesos°.

### Ciudades • **México, D.F.**

La Ciudad de México, fundada° en 1525, también se llama el D.F. o Distrito Federal. Muchos turistas e inmigrantes vienen a la ciudad porque es el centro cultural y económico del país. El crecimiento° de la población es de los más altos° del mundo. El D.F. tiene una población mayor que las de Nueva York, Madrid o París.

### Artes • **Diego Rivera y Frida Kahlo**

Frida Kahlo y Diego Rivera eran° artistas mexicanos muy famosos. Casados° en 1929, los dos se interesaron° en las condiciones sociales de la gente indígena de su país. Puedes ver algunas° de sus obras° en el Museo de Arte Moderno de la Ciudad de México.

### Historia • **Los aztecas**

Los aztecas dominaron° en México del siglo° XIV hasta el siglo XVI. Sus canales, puentes° y pirámides con templos religiosos eran muy importantes. El imperio azteca terminó° cuando llegaron° los españoles en 1519, pero la presencia azteca sigue hoy. La Ciudad de México está situada en la capital azteca de Tenochtitlán, y muchos turistas van a visitar sus ruinas.

### Economía • **La plata**

México es el mayor productor de plata° del mundo°. Estados como Zacatecas y Durango tienen ciudades fundadas cerca de los más grandes yacimientos° de plata del país. Estas ciudades fueron° en la época colonial unas de las más ricas e importantes. Hoy en día, aún° conservan mucho de su encanto° y esplendor.

Golfo de México

Península de Yucatán

Mérida

Bahía de Campeche

Cancún

uz

Istmo de huantepec

**BELICE**

**GUATEMALA**

 **¿Qué aprendiste?** Responde a cada pregunta con una oración completa.

1. ¿Qué lenguas hablan los mexicanos? Los mexicanos hablan español y lenguas indígenas.

2. ¿Cómo es la población del D.F. en comparación a otras ciudades? La población del D.F. es mayor.

3. ¿En qué se interesaron Frida Kahlo y Diego Rivera? Se interesaron en las condiciones sociales de la gente indígena de su país.

4. Nombra algunas de las estructuras de la arquitectura azteca. Hay canales, puentes y pirámides con templos religiosos.

5. ¿Dónde está situada la capital de México? Está situada en la capital azteca de Tenochtitlán.

6. ¿Qué estados de México tienen los mayores yacimientos de plata? Zacatecas y Durango tienen los mayores yacimientos de plata.

 **Conexión Internet** Investiga estos temas en **panorama.vhlcentral.com.**

1. Busca información sobre dos lugares de México. ¿Te gustaría (*Would you like*) vivir allí? ¿Por qué?

2. Busca información sobre dos artistas mexicanos. ¿Cómo se llaman sus obras más famosas?

..................

**fundada** *founded* **crecimiento** *growth* **más altos** *highest* **eran** *were* **Casados** *Married* **se interesaron** *were interested in* **algunas** *some* **obras** *works* **dominaron** *dominated* **siglo** *century* **puentes** *bridges* **terminó** *ended* **llegaron** *arrived* **plata** *silver* **mundo** *world* **yacimientos** *deposits* **fueron** *were* **aún** *still* **encanto** *charm*

---

**TEACHING OPTIONS**

**Variación léxica** Over 52 languages are spoken by indigenous communities in Mexico today; of these, Mayan languages are the most prevalent. Also, **náhuatl**, the language of the Aztecs, is spoken by a significant part of the population. Some **náhuatl** words have entered Mexican Spanish, such as **aguacate** (*avocado*), **guajolote** (*turkey*), **cacahuate** (*peanut*), **ejote**

(*green bean*), **chile** (*chili pepper*), and **elote** (*corn*). Two **náhuatl** words now used in world languages are *tomato* and *chocolate*, which are native to Mexico and were brought to Europe in the sixteenth century.

---

**Instructional Resources**
**Supersite:** Textbook &
Vocabulary MP3 Audio Files
**Lección 4**
**Supersite/IRCD:** *IRM* (WBs/
VM/LM Answer Key); *Testing
Program* (**Lección 4 Pruebas,**
Test Generator, Testing
Program MP3 Audio Files)
**WebSAM**
**Lab Manual,** p. 24

## Pasatiempos

| | |
|---|---|
| **andar en patineta** | *to skateboard* |
| **bucear** | *to scuba dive* |
| **escalar montañas** **(f. pl.)** | *to climb mountains* |
| **escribir una carta** | *to write a letter* |
| **escribir un mensaje** **electrónico** | *to write an e-mail message* |
| **esquiar** | *to ski* |
| **ganar** | *to win* |
| **ir de excursión** | *to go on a hike* |
| **leer correo** **electrónico** | *to read e-mail* |
| **leer un periódico** | *to read a newspaper* |
| **leer una revista** | *to read a magazine* |
| **nadar** | *to swim* |
| **pasear** | *to take a walk; to stroll* |
| **pasear en bicicleta** | *to ride a bicycle* |
| **patinar (en línea)** | *to (in-line) skate* |
| **practicar deportes** **(m. pl.)** | *to play sports* |
| **tomar el sol** | *to sunbathe* |
| **ver películas (f. pl.)** | *to see movies* |
| **visitar monumentos** **(m. pl.)** | *to visit monuments* |
| **la diversión** | *fun activity; entertainment; recreation* |
| **el fin de semana** | *weekend* |
| **el pasatiempo** | *pastime; hobby* |
| **los ratos libres** | *spare (free) time* |
| **el videojuego** | *video game* |

## Deportes

| | |
|---|---|
| **el baloncesto** | *basketball* |
| **el béisbol** | *baseball* |
| **el ciclismo** | *cycling* |
| **el equipo** | *team* |
| **el esquí (acuático)** | *(water) skiing* |
| **el fútbol** | *soccer* |
| **el fútbol americano** | *football* |
| **el golf** | *golf* |
| **el hockey** | *hockey* |
| **el/la jugador(a)** | *player* |
| **la natación** | *swimming* |
| **el partido** | *game; match* |
| **la pelota** | *ball* |
| **el tenis** | *tennis* |
| **el vóleibol** | *volleyball* |

## Adjetivos

| | |
|---|---|
| **deportivo/a** | *sports-related* |
| **favorito/a** | *favorite* |

## Lugares

| | |
|---|---|
| **el café** | *café* |
| **el centro** | *downtown* |
| **el cine** | *movie theater* |
| **el gimnasio** | *gymnasium* |
| **la iglesia** | *church* |
| **el lugar** | *place* |
| **el museo** | *museum* |
| **el parque** | *park* |
| **la piscina** | *swimming pool* |
| **la plaza** | *city or town square* |
| **el restaurante** | *restaurant* |

## Verbos

| | |
|---|---|
| **almorzar (o:ue)** | *to have lunch* |
| **cerrar (e:ie)** | *to close* |
| **comenzar (e:ie)** | *to begin* |
| **conseguir (e:i)** | *to get; to obtain* |
| **contar (o:ue)** | *to count; to tell* |
| **decir (e:i)** | *to say; to tell* |
| **dormir (o:ue)** | *to sleep* |
| **empezar (e:ie)** | *to begin* |
| **encontrar (o:ue)** | *to find* |
| **entender (e:ie)** | *to understand* |
| **hacer** | *to do; to make* |
| **ir** | *to go* |
| **jugar (u:ue)** | *to play* |
| **mostrar (o:ue)** | *to show* |
| **oír** | *to hear* |
| **pedir (e:i)** | *to ask for; to request* |
| **pensar (e:ie)** | *to think* |
| **pensar (+ inf.)** | *to intend* |
| **pensar en** | *to think about* |
| **perder (e:ie)** | *to lose; to miss* |
| **poder (o:ue)** | *to be able to; can* |
| **poner** | *to put; to place* |
| **preferir (e:ie)** | *to prefer* |
| **querer (e:ie)** | *to want; to love* |
| **recordar (o:ue)** | *to remember* |
| **repetir (e:i)** | *to repeat* |
| **salir** | *to leave* |
| **seguir (e:i)** | *to follow; to continue* |
| **suponer** | *to suppose* |
| **traer** | *to bring* |
| **ver** | *to see* |
| **volver (o:ue)** | *to return* |

| | |
|---|---|
| ***Decir* expressions** | *See page 128.* |
| **Expresiones útiles** | *See page 113.* |

**recursos**

LM
p. 24

panorama.vhlcentral.com
Lección 4

# Las vacaciones

## 5

## Communicative Goals

**You will learn how to:**
- Discuss and plan a vacation
- Describe a hotel
- Talk about how you feel
- Talk about the seasons and the weather

**A PRIMERA VISTA**
- ¿Dónde están ellos: en una montaña o en una ciudad?
- ¿Son viejos o jóvenes?
- ¿Pasean o ven una película?

**Lesson Goals**
In **Lección 5**, students will be introduced to the following:
- terms for traveling and vacations
- seasons and months of the year
- weather expressions
- ordinal numbers (1st–10th)
- the **Camino Inca**
- Punta del Este, Uruguay
- **estar** with conditions and emotions
- adjectives for conditions and emotions
- present progressive of regular and irregular verbs
- comparison of the uses of **ser** and **estar**
- direct object nouns and pronouns
- personal **a**
- scanning to find specific information
- cultural, geographic, and historical information about Puerto Rico

**A primera vista** Here are some additional questions you can ask based on the photo: **¿Dónde te gusta pasar tus ratos libres? ¿Qué haces en tus ratos libres? ¿Te gusta explorar otras culturas? ¿Te gusta viajar a otros países? ¿Adónde quieres ir en las próximas vacaciones?**

**INSTRUCTIONAL RESOURCES**

**MAESTRO™ SUPERSITE (panorama.vhlcentral.com)**
Textbook, Vocabulary, & Lab MP3 Audio Files
Additional Practice
Learning Management System (Assignment Task Manager, Gradebook)
*Also on DVD*
  **Fotonovela**

*Flash cultura*
*Panorama cultural*
*Also on Instructor's Resource CD-ROM*
*PowerPoints* (**Contextos** & **Estructura** Presentations, Overheads)
*Instructor's Resource Manual* (Handouts, Textbook Answer Key, WBs/VM/LM Answer Key,

Audioscripts, Videoscripts & Translations)
*Testing Program* (**Pruebas,** Test Generator, MP3s)
**WebSAM** (Workbook/Video Manual/Lab Manual)
**Workbook/Video Manual**
*Cuaderno para hispanohablantes*
**Lab Manual**

# Las vacaciones

## Más vocabulario

| | |
|---|---|
| la cama | bed |
| la habitación individual, doble | single, double room |
| el piso | floor (of a building) |
| la planta baja | ground floor |
| el campo | countryside |
| el paisaje | landscape |
| el equipaje | luggage |
| la estación de autobuses, del metro, de tren | bus, subway, train station |
| la llegada | arrival |
| el pasaje (de ida y vuelta) | (round-trip) ticket |
| la salida | departure; exit |
| acampar | to camp |
| estar de vacaciones | to be on vacation |
| hacer las maletas | to pack (one's suitcases) |
| hacer un viaje | to take a trip |
| ir de compras | to go shopping |
| ir de vacaciones | to go on vacation |
| ir en autobús (m.), auto(móvil) (m.), motocicleta (f.), taxi (m.) | to go by bus, car, motorcycle, taxi |

## Variación léxica

automóvil ⟷ coche (*Esp.*), carro (*Amér. L.*)
autobús ⟷ camión (*Méx.*), guagua (*P. Rico*)
motocicleta ⟷ moto (*coloquial*)

recursos

WB pp. 49–50 | LM p. 25 | panorama.vhlcentral.com Lección 5

la agente de viajes

el pasaporte

Confirma una reservación. (confirmar)

**En la agencia de viajes**

el ascensor

la habitación

el empleado

la llave

el botones

la huésped

el huésped

**En el hotel**

aca/Toma fotos.
(sacar, tomar)

BIENVENIDOS

el avión

la inspectora
de aduanas

## En el aeropuerto

Pesca.
(pescar)

Monta a caballo.
(montar)

Va en barco.
(ir)

mar

Juegan a las
cartas. (jugar)

la playa

## En la playa

# Práctica

**1** **Escuchar** Indicate who would probably make each statement you hear. Each answer is used twice.

a. el agente de viajes    1. ___a___    4. ___b___
b. la inspectora de aduanas    2. ___a___    5. ___c___
c. un empleado del hotel    3. ___c___    6. ___b___

**2** **¿Cierto o falso?** Mario and his wife, Natalia, are planning their next vacation with a travel agent. Indicate whether each statement is **cierto** or **falso** according to what you hear in the conversation.

|  | Cierto | Falso |
|---|---|---|
| 1. Mario y Natalia están en Puerto Rico. | ○ | ⊘ |
| 2. Mario y Natalia quieren hacer un viaje a Puerto Rico. | ⊘ | ○ |
| 3. Natalia prefiere ir a una montaña. | ○ | ⊘ |
| 4. Mario quiere pescar en Puerto Rico. | ⊘ | ○ |
| 5. La agente de viajes va a confirmar la reservación. | ⊘ | ○ |

**3** **Escoger** Choose the best answer for each sentence.

1. Un huésped es una persona que ___b___.
   a. toma fotos    b. está en un hotel    c. pesca en el mar
2. Abrimos la puerta con ___a___.
   a. una llave    b. un caballo    c. una llegada
3. Enrique tiene ___a___ porque va a viajar a otro (*another*) país.
   a. un pasaporte    b. una foto    c. una llegada
4. Antes de (*Before*) ir de vacaciones hay que ___c___.
   a. pescar    b. ir en tren    c. hacer las maletas
5. Nosotros vamos en ___a___ al aeropuerto.
   a. autobús    b. pasaje    c. viajero
6. Me gusta mucho ir al campo. El ___a___ es increíble.
   a. paisaje    b. pasaje    c. equipaje

**4** **Analogías** Complete the analogies using the words below. Two words will not be used.

| auto | huésped | mar | sacar |
|---|---|---|---|
| botones | llegada | pasaporte | tren |

1. acampar → campo ⊜ pescar → mar
2. agencia de viajes → agente ⊜ hotel → botones
3. llave → habitación ⊜ pasaje → tren
4. estudiante → libro ⊜ turista → pasaporte
5. aeropuerto → viajero ⊜ hotel → huésped
6. maleta → hacer ⊜ foto → ~~sacar~~ *TOMAR*

**1** **Teaching Tip** Have students check their answers as you go over **Actividad 1** with the class.

**1** **Script** 1. ¡Deben ir a Puerto Rico! Allí hay unas playas muy hermosas y pueden acampar. 2. Deben llamarme el lunes para confirmar la reservación. *Script continues on page 142.*

**2** **Expansion** To challenge students, give them these true-false statements as items 6–9: **6. Mario prefiere una habitación doble. (Cierto.) 7. Natalia no quiere ir a la playa. (Falso.) 8. El hotel está en la playa. (Cierto.) 9. Mario va a montar a caballo. (Falso.)**

**2** **Script** MARIO: Queremos ir de vacaciones a Puerto Rico. AGENTE: ¿Desean hacer un viaje al campo? NATALIA: Yo quiero ir a la playa. M: Pues, yo prefiero una habitación doble en un hotel con un buen paisaje. A: Puedo reservar para ustedes una habitación en el hotel San Juan que está en la playa. M: Es una buena idea, así yo voy a pescar y tú vas a montar a caballo. N: Muy bien, ¿puede confirmar la reservación? A: Claro que sí. *Textbook MP3s*

**3** **Expansion** Ask a volunteer to help you model making statements similar to item 1. Say: **Un turista es una persona que… (va de vacaciones).** Then ask volunteers to do the same with **una agente de viajes, un botones, una inspectora de aduanas, un empleado de hotel.**

**4** **Teaching Tip** Present these items using the following formula: *Acampar* **tiene la misma relación con** *campo* **que** *pescar* **tiene con… (*mar*).**

---

**TEACHING OPTIONS**

**Small Groups** Have students work in groups of three to write a riddle about one of the people or objects in the **Contextos** illustrations. The group must come up with at least three descriptions of their subject. Then one of the group members reads the description to the class and asks ¿Qué soy? Ex: **Soy un pequeño libro. Tengo una foto de una persona. Soy necesario si un viajero quiere viajar a otro país. ¿Qué soy? (Soy un pasaporte.)**

**Large Groups** Split the class into two evenly-numbered groups. Hand out cards at random to the members of each group. One type of card should contain a verb or verb phrase (Ex: **confirmar una reservación**). The other will contain a related noun (Ex: **el agente de viajes**). The people within the groups must find their partners.

**Teaching Tips**
- Point out that the names of months are not capitalized.
- Show *Overhead PowerPoint #23* and have students look over the seasons and months of the year. Call out the names of holidays or campus events and ask students to say when they occur.
- Show *Overhead PowerPoint #24* and use magazine pictures to cover as many weather conditions as possible from this page. Begin describing one of the pictures. Then, ask volunteers questions to elicit other weather expressions. Point out the use of **mucho/a** before nouns and **muy** before adjectives.
- Drill months by calling out a month and having students name the two that follow. Ex: **abril (mayo, junio)**.
- Point out the use of **primero** for the first day of the month.
- Ask volunteers to associate seasons (or months) and general weather patterns. Ex: **En invierno, hace frío/nieva. En marzo, hace viento.**
- Review the shortened forms **buen** and **mal** before **tiempo**.
- Point out that **Llueve** and **Nieva** can also mean *It rains* and *It snows*. **Está lloviendo** and **Está nevando** emphasize *at this moment*. Students will learn more about this concept in **Estructura 5.2**.

**Successful Language Learning** Remind students that weather expressions are used often in conversation and that they should make a special effort to learn them.

## Las estaciones y los meses del año

el invierno: **diciembre, enero, febrero**

la primavera: **marzo, abril, mayo**

el verano: **junio, julio, agosto**

el otoño: **septiembre, octubre, noviembre**

—¿Cuál es la fecha de hoy?　　*What is today's date?*
—Es el primero de octubre.　　*It's the first of October.*
—Es el dos de marzo.　　*It's March 2nd.*
—Es el diez de noviembre.　　*It's November 10th.*

## El tiempo

—¿Qué tiempo hace?　　*How's the weather?*
—Hace buen/mal tiempo.　　*The weather is good/bad.*

**Hace (mucho) calor.**
*It's (very) hot.*

**Hace (mucho) frío.**
*It's (very) cold.*

**Llueve. (llover o:ue)**
*It's raining.*
**Está lloviendo.**
*It's raining.*

**Nieva. (nevar e:ie)**
*It's snowing.*
**Está nevando.**
*It's snowing.*

**Más vocabulario**

| | |
|---|---|
| Está (muy) nublado. | *It's (very) cloudy.* |
| Hace fresco. | *It's cool.* |
| Hace (mucho) sol. | *It's (very) sunny.* |
| Hace (mucho) viento. | *It's (very) windy.* |

**TEACHING OPTIONS**

**Pairs** Have pairs of students create sentences for each of the drawings on this page. Ask one student to write sentences for the first four drawings and the other to write sentences for the next four. When finished, ask them to check their partner's work.
**TPR** Introduce the question **¿Cuándo es tu cumpleaños?** and the phrase **Mi cumpleaños es…** Have students ask questions and line up according to their birthdays. Allow them five minutes to form the line.
**Extra Practice** Create a series of cloze sentences about the weather in a certain place. Ex: **En Puerto Rico ____ mucho calor. (hace) No ____ muy nublado cuando ____ sol. (está; hace) No ____ frío pero a veces ____ fresco. (hace; hace) Cuando ____ mal tiempo, ____ y ____ viento pero nunca ____. (hace; llueve; hace; nieva)**

**5** **El Hotel Regis** Label the floors of the hotel.

### Números ordinales

| | |
|---|---|
| **primer** (before a masculine singular noun), **primero/a** | first |
| **segundo/a** | second |
| **tercer** (before a masculine singular noun), **tercero/a** | third |
| **cuarto/a** | fourth |
| **quinto/a** | fifth |
| **sexto/a** | sixth |
| **séptimo/a** | seventh |
| **octavo/a** | eighth |
| **noveno/a** | ninth |
| **décimo/a** | tenth |

a. __séptimo__ piso
b. __sexto__ piso
c. __quinto__ piso
d. __cuarto__ piso
e. __tercer__ piso
f. __segundo__ piso
g. __primer__ piso
h. __planta__ baja

**6** **Contestar** Look at the illustrations of the months and seasons on the previous page and answer these questions in pairs.

> **modelo**
> **Estudiante 1:** *¿Cuál es el primer mes de la primavera?*
> **Estudiante 2:** *marzo*

1. ¿Cuál es el primer mes del invierno?  diciembre
2. ¿Cuál es el segundo mes de la primavera?  abril
3. ¿Cuál es el tercer mes del otoño?  noviembre
4. ¿Cuál es el primer mes del año?  enero
5. ¿Cuál es el quinto mes del año?  mayo
6. ¿Cuál es el octavo mes del año?  agosto
7. ¿Cuál es el décimo mes del año?  octubre
8. ¿Cuál es el segundo mes del verano?  julio
9. ¿Cuál es el tercer mes del invierno?  febrero
10. ¿Cuál es la cuarta estación del año?  el otoño

**7** **Las estaciones** Name the season that applies to the description.  Some answers may vary.

1. Las clases terminan. la primavera
2. Vamos a la playa. el verano
3. Acampamos. el verano
4. Nieva mucho. el invierno
5. Las clases empiezan. el otoño
6. Hace mucho calor. el verano
7. Llueve mucho. la primavera
8. Esquiamos. el invierno
9. El entrenamiento (*training*) de béisbol  la primavera
10. Día de Acción de Gracias (*Thanksgiving*) el otoño

**8** **¿Cuál es la fecha?** Give the dates for these holidays.

> **modelo**
> el día de San Valentín   *14 de febrero*

1. el día de San Patricio 17 de marzo
2. el día de Halloween 31 de octubre
3. el primer día de verano 20–23 de junio
4. el Año Nuevo  primero de enero
5. mi cumpleaños (*birthday*)  Answers will vary.
6. mi fiesta favorita  Answers will vary.

**5** **Teaching Tips**
- Point out that for numbers greater than ten, Spanish speakers tend to use cardinal numbers instead: **Está en el piso veintiuno.**
- Add a visual aspect to this vocabulary presentation. Write each ordinal number on a separate sheet of paper and distribute them at random among ten students. Ask them to go to the front of the class, hold up their signs, and stand in the correct order.

**5** **Expansion** Ask students questions about their lives, using ordinal numbers. Ex: **¿En qué piso vives? ¿En qué piso está mi oficina?**

**6** **Teaching Tip** Review seasons and months of the year. Have students close their books while you ask questions. Ex: **¿Qué estación tiene los meses de junio, julio y agosto?**

**6** **Expansion** Ask a student which month his or her birthday is in. Ask another student to give the season the first student's birthday falls in.

**7** **Teaching Tip** Ask volunteers to name or describe events, situations, or holidays that are important to them or their families. Have the class name the season that applies.

**8** **Teaching Tip** Bring in a Spanish-language calendar, such as an academic calendar. Ask students to name the important events and their scheduled dates.

**8** **Expansion**
- Give these holidays to students as items 7–10: **7. Independencia de los EE.UU. (4 de julio) 8. Navidad (25 de diciembre) 9. Día de Acción de Gracias (cuarto jueves de noviembre) 10. Día de los Inocentes (primero de abril)**
- Ask heritage speakers to provide other important holidays, such as saint's days.

**9** **Seleccionar** Paco is talking about his family and friends. Choose the word or phrase that best completes each sentence.

1. A mis padres les gusta ir a Cancún porque (hace sol, nieva). hace sol
2. Mi primo de Kansas dice que durante (*during*) un tornado, hace mucho (sol, viento). viento
3. Mis amigos van a esquiar si (nieva, está nublado). nieva
4. Tomo el sol cuando (hace calor, llueve). hace calor
5. Nosotros vamos a ver una película si hace (buen, mal) tiempo. mal
6. Mi hermana prefiere correr cuando (hace mucho calor, hace fresco). hace fresco
7. Mis tíos van de excursión si hace (buen, mal) tiempo. buen
8. Mi padre no quiere jugar al golf si (hace fresco, llueve). llueve
9. Cuando hace mucho (sol, frío) no salgo de casa y tomo chocolate caliente (*hot*). frío
10. Hoy mi sobrino va al parque porque (está lloviendo, hace buen tiempo). hace buen tiempo

**10** **El clima** With a partner, take turns asking and answering questions about the weather and temperatures in these cities. Answers will vary.

> **modelo**
>
> **Estudiante 1:** ¿Qué tiempo hace hoy en Nueva York?
> **Estudiante 2:** Hace frío y hace viento.
> **Estudiante 1:** ¿Cuál es la temperatura máxima?
> **Estudiante 2:** Treinta y un grados (*degrees*).
> **Estudiante 1:** ¿Y la temperatura mínima?
> **Estudiante 2:** Diez grados.

soleado · lluvia · nieve · nublado · viento

| Nueva York | Miami | Chicago | París | Madrid | Tokio |
|---|---|---|---|---|---|
| Máx. 31° | Máx. 84° | Máx. 23° | Máx. 38° | Máx. 42° | Máx. 49° |
| Mín. 10° | Mín. 62° | Mín. 5° | Mín. 26° | Mín. 27° | Mín. 34° |

| Montreal | México D.F. | Cozumel | Caracas | Quito | Buenos Aires |
|---|---|---|---|---|---|
| Máx. 18° | Máx. 76° | Máx. 91° | Máx. 80° | Máx. 60° | Máx. 85° |
| Mín. 2° | Mín. 41° | Mín. 73° | Mín. 72° | Mín. 51° | Mín. 59° |

**11** **Completar** Complete these sentences with your own ideas. Answers will vary.

1. Cuando hace sol, yo…
2. Cuando llueve, mis amigos y yo…
3. Cuando hace calor, mi familia…
4. Cuando hace viento, la gente…
5. Cuando hace frío, yo…
6. Cuando hace mal tiempo, mis amigos…
7. Cuando nieva, muchas personas…
8. Cuando está nublado, mis amigos y yo…
9. Cuando hace fresco, mis padres…
10. Cuando hace buen tiempo, mis amigos…

# Comunicación

**12** **Preguntas personales** In pairs, ask each other these questions. Answers will vary.

1. ¿Cuál es la fecha de hoy?
2. ¿Qué estación es?
3. ¿Te gusta esta estación? ¿Por qué?
4. ¿Qué estación prefieres? ¿Por qué?
5. ¿Prefieres el mar o las montañas? ¿La playa o el campo? ¿Por qué?
6. Cuando estás de vacaciones, ¿qué haces?
7. Cuando haces un viaje, ¿qué te gusta hacer y ver?
8. ¿Piensas ir de vacaciones este verano? ¿Adónde quieres ir? ¿Por qué?
9. ¿Qué deseas ver y qué lugares quieres visitar?
10. ¿Cómo te gusta viajar? ¿En avión? ¿En motocicleta...?

**13** **Encuesta** Your instructor will give you a worksheet. How does the weather affect what you do? Walk around the class and ask your classmates what they prefer or like to do in the weather conditions given. Note their responses on your worksheet. Make sure to personalize your survey by adding a few original questions to the list. Be prepared to report your findings to the class.

Answers will vary.

**CONSULTA**

**Calor** and **frío** can apply to both weather and people. Use **hacer** to describe weather conditions or climate.
(**Hace frío en Santiago.** *It's cold in Santiago.*)
Use **tener** to refer to people.
(**El viajero tiene frío.** *The traveler is cold.*)
See **Estructura 3.4** p. 93.

| Tiempo | Actividades |
|--------|-------------|
| 1. Hace mucho calor. | |
| 2. Nieva. | |
| 3. Hace buen tiempo. | |
| 4. Hace fresco. | |
| 5. Llueve. | |
| 6. Está nublado. | |
| 7. Hace mucho frío. | |

**14** **Minidrama** With two or three classmates, prepare a skit about people who are on vacation or are planning a vacation. The skit should take place in one of these areas. Answers will vary.

1. una agencia de viajes
2. una casa
3. un aeropuerto, una estación de tren o una estación de autobuses
4. un hotel
5. el campo o la playa

# Síntesis

**15** **Un viaje** You are planning a trip to Mexico and have many questions about your itinerary on which your partner, a travel agent, will advise you. Your instructor will give you and your partner each a sheet with different instructions for acting out the roles. Answers will vary.

---

**TEACHING OPTIONS**

**Pairs** Tell students they are part of a scientific expedition to Antarctica (**la Antártida**). Have them write a letter back home about the weather conditions and their activities there. Begin the letter for them by writing **Queridos amigos** on the board.
**Game** Have each student create a Bingo card with 25 squares (five rows of five). Tell them to write **GRATIS** (*FREE*) in the center square and the name of a different city in each of the other

squares. Have them exchange cards. Call out different weather expressions with their corresponding months. Ex: **Hace viento.** Students who think this description fits a city or cities on their card should mark the square with the weather condition. In order to win, a student must have marked five squares in a row and be able to give the weather condition for each one. Ex: **Hace mucho viento en Chicago.**

---

**12 Expansion** Have students write the answers to questions 3–10 on a sheet of paper anonymously. Collect the papers, shuffle them, and redistribute them for pairs to guess who wrote what.

**13 Teaching Tip** Model the activity by asking volunteers what they enjoy doing in hot weather. Ex: **Cuando hace calor, ¿qué haces? (Nado.)** Then distribute the *Hojas de actividades* (Supersite/IRCD).

**14 Teaching Tip** To simplify, ask the class to brainstorm a list of people and topics that may be encountered in each situation. Write the lists on the board.

**14 Expansion** Have students judge the skits in categories such as most original, funniest, most realistic, etc.

**15 Teaching Tip** Divide the class into pairs and distribute the handouts from the Information Gap Activities (Supersite/IRCD) that correspond to this activity. Give students ten minutes to complete the activity.

**15 Expansion** Have pairs put together the ideal itinerary for someone else traveling to Mexico, like a classmate, a relative, someone famous, or **el/la profesor(a).**

# Tenemos una reservación.

Don Francisco y los estudiantes llegan al hotel.

## Section Goals

## Section Goals

In **Fotonovela**, students will:
• receive comprehensible input from free-flowing discourse
• learn functional phrases for talking to hotel personnel and describing a hotel room

---

**Instructional Resources**
**Supersite/DVD:** *Fotonovela*
**Supersite/IRCD:** *IRM*
(*Fotonovela* Videoscript & Translation, WBs/VM/LM Answer Key)
**WebSAM**
**Video Manual,** pp. 203–204

---

## Video Recap: Lección 4

Before doing this **Fotonovela** section, review the previous one with this activity.

1. ¿Qué van a hacer Inés y Javier en su hora libre? (Van a pasear por la ciudad.) 2. ¿Adónde van Maite y Álex? (Van al parque.) 3. ¿Por qué no quiere Maite jugar al fútbol? (Prefiere escribir unas postales.) 4. ¿Qué van a hacer Maite y Álex a las seis? (Van a correr.)

## Video Synopsis
The travelers check in at a hotel. **Álex** and **Javier** drop by the girls' cabin. **Inés** and **Javier** decide to explore the city further. **Álex** and **Maite** decide to stay behind. **Maite** notices that **Javier** and **Inés** spend a lot of time together.

## Teaching Tips
• Have the class glance over the **Fotonovela** captions and list words and phrases related to tourism and invitations.
• Ask individuals how they are today, using **cansado/a** and **aburrido/a**.
• Ask the class to describe the perfect hotel. Ex: **¿Cómo es una habitación de hotel perfecta?**

**PERSONAJES**

**MAITE**

**INÉS**

**DON FRANCISCO**

**ÁLEX**

**JAVIER**

**EMPLEADA**

**BOTONES**

**EMPLEADA** ¿En qué puedo servirles?

**DON FRANCISCO** Mire, yo soy Francisco Castillo Moreno y tenemos una reservación a mi nombre.

**EMPLEADA** Mmm... no veo su nombre aquí. No está.

**DON FRANCISCO** ¿Está segura, señorita? Quizás la reservación está a nombre de la agencia de viajes, Ecuatur.

**EMPLEADA** Pues sí, aquí está... dos habitaciones dobles y una individual, de la ciento uno a la ciento tres,... todas en las primeras cabañas.

**DON FRANCISCO** Gracias, señorita. Muy amable.

**BOTONES** Bueno, la habitación ciento dos... Por favor.

**INÉS** Oigan, yo estoy aburrida. ¿Quieren hacer algo?

**JAVIER** ¿Por qué no vamos a explorar la ciudad un poco más?

**INÉS** ¡Excelente idea! ¡Vamos!

**MAITE** No, yo no voy. Estoy cansada y quiero descansar un poco porque a las seis voy a correr con Álex.

**ÁLEX** Y yo quiero escribir un mensaje electrónico antes de ir a correr.

**JAVIER** Pues nosotros estamos listos, ¿verdad, Inés?

**INÉS** Sí, vamos.

**MAITE** Adiós.

**INÉS Y JAVIER** ¡Chau!

**recursos**

VM
pp. 203–204

panorama.vhlcentral.com
Lección 5

---

**TEACHING OPTIONS**

**Video Tips** General suggestions for using video clips in the classroom can be found on page IAE-12 of this Instructor's Annotated Edition.

**Tenemos una reservación** Before viewing the **Tenemos una reservación** segment of the *Fotonovela*, ask students to brainstorm a list of things that might happen in an episode

in which the characters check into a hotel and decide how to spend the rest of the day. Then play the **Tenemos una reservación** segment once without sound and have the class create a plot summary based on visual clues. Finally, show the video segment with sound and have the class correct any mistaken guesses and fill in any gaps.

**Teaching Tip** Work through the scenes that correspond to video stills 1–3 with the class, asking volunteers to play each part. Have students work together in groups of four to read scenes 4–10 aloud.

**Expresiones útiles** Remind students that **estoy**, **está**, and **están** are present-tense forms of the verb **estar**, which is often used with adjectives that describe conditions and emotions. Remind students that **es** and **son** are present-tense forms of the verb **ser**, which is often used to describe the characteristics of people and things and to make generalizations. Draw students' attention to video still 4 of the **Fotonovela**. Point out that **están haciendo** and **estamos descansando** are examples of the present progressive, which is used to emphasize an action in progress. Tell students that they will learn more about these concepts in **Estructura**.

**ÁLEX** Hola, chicas. ¿Qué están haciendo?

**MAITE** Estamos descansando.

**JAVIER** Oigan, no están nada mal las cabañas, ¿verdad?

**INÉS** Y todo está muy limpio y ordenado.

**ÁLEX** Sí, es excelente.

**MAITE** Y las camas son tan cómodas.

**ÁLEX** Bueno, nos vemos a las seis.

**MAITE** Sí, hasta luego.

**ÁLEX** Adiós.

**MAITE** ¿Inés y Javier? Juntos otra vez.

## Expresiones útiles

### Talking with hotel personnel

- **¿En qué puedo servirles?**
  *How can I help you?*
  **Tenemos una reservación a mi nombre.**
  *We have a reservation in my name.*
- **Mmm… no veo su nombre. No está.**
  *I don't see your name. It's not here.*
  **¿Está seguro/a? Quizás/Tal vez está a nombre de Ecuatur.**
  *Are you sure? Maybe it's under the name of Ecuatur.*
- **Aquí está… dos habitaciones dobles y una individual.**
  *Here it is, two double rooms and one single.*
- **Aquí tienen las llaves.**
  *Here are your keys.*
  **Gracias, señorita. Muy amable.**
  *Thank you, miss. You're very kind.*
- **¿Dónde pongo las maletas?**
  *Where do I put the suitcases?*
  **Allí, encima de la cama.**
  *There, on the bed.*

### Describing a hotel

- **No están nada mal las cabañas.**
  *The cabins aren't bad at all.*
- **Todo está muy limpio y ordenado.**
  *Everything is very clean and orderly.*
- **Es excelente/estupendo/ fabuloso/fenomenal.**
  *It's excellent/stupendous/ fabulous/great.*
- **Es increíble/magnífico/ maravilloso/perfecto.**
  *It's incredible/magnificent/ marvelous/perfect.*
- **Las camas son tan cómodas.**
  *The beds are so comfortable.*

### Talking about how you feel

- **Estoy un poco aburrido/a/ cansado/a.**
  *I'm a little bored/tired.*

**TEACHING OPTIONS**

**Pairs** Ask pairs to write five true-false statements based on the **Tenemos una reservación** captions. Then have them exchange papers with another pair, who will complete the activity and correct the false statements. Ask volunteers to read a few statements for the class, who will then answer and point out the caption that contains the information.

**Extra Practice** Ask volunteers to ad-lib the **Tenemos una reservación** segment for the class. Assure them that it is not necessary to memorize the episode or to stick strictly to its content. Allow them time to prepare. You may want to assign this activity as homework and have students present it in the next class period for review.

# ¿Qué pasó?

**1 Completar** Complete these sentences with the correct term from the word bank.

| | | |
|---|---|---|
| aburrida | cansada | habitaciones individuales |
| la agencia de viajes | descansar | hacer las maletas |
| las camas | habitaciones dobles | las maletas |

1. La reservación para el hotel está a nombre de __la agencia de viajes__.
2. Los estudiantes tienen dos __habitaciones dobles__.
3. Maite va a __descansar__ porque está __cansada__.
4. El botones lleva __las maletas__ a las habitaciones.
5. Las habitaciones son buenas y __las camas__ son cómodas.

**2 Identificar** Identify the person who would make each statement.

**EMPLEADA**　　**ÁLEX**　　**DON FRANCISCO**　　**JAVIER**　　**INÉS**

1. Antes de (*Before*) correr, voy a trabajar en la computadora un poco. Álex
2. Estoy aburrido. Tengo ganas de explorar la ciudad. ¿Vienes tú también? Javier
3. Lo siento mucho, señor, pero su nombre no está en la lista. empleada
4. Creo que la reservación está a mi nombre, señorita. don Francisco
5. Oye, el hotel es maravilloso, ¿no? Las habitaciones están muy limpias. Inés

**3 Ordenar** Place these events in the correct order.

__3__ a. Las chicas descansan en su habitación.
__5__ b. Javier e Inés deciden ir a explorar la ciudad.
__1__ c. Don Francisco habla con la empleada del hotel.
__4__ d. Javier, Maite, Inés y Álex hablan en la habitación de las chicas.
__2__ e. El botones pone las maletas en la cama.

**4 Conversar** With a partner, use these cues to create a conversation between a bellhop and a hotel guest in Spain. *Answers will vary.*

| **Huésped** | **Botones** |
|---|---|
| Ask the bellhop to carry your suitcases to your room. | → Say "yes, sir/ma'am/miss." |
| Comment that the hotel is excellent and that everything is very clean. | → Agree, then point out the guest's room, a single room on the sixth floor. |
| Ask if the bellhop is sure. You think you have room 86. | → Confirm that the guest has room 68. Ask where you should put the suitcases. |
| Tell the bellhop to put them on the bed and thank him or her. | → Say "you're welcome" and "goodbye." |

# Pronunciación

## Spanish b and v

| bueno | vóleibol | biblioteca | vivir |
|---|---|---|---|

There is no difference in pronunciation between the Spanish letters **b** and **v**. However, each letter can be pronounced two different ways, depending on which letters appear next to them.

| bonito | viajar | también | investigar |
|---|---|---|---|

**B** and **v** are pronounced like the English hard *b* when they appear either as the first letter of a word, at the beginning of a phrase, or after **m** or **n**.

| deber | novio | abril | cerveza |
|---|---|---|---|

In all other positions, **b** and **v** have a softer pronunciation, which has no equivalent in English. Unlike the hard **b**, which is produced by tightly closing the lips and stopping the flow of air, the soft **b** is produced by keeping the lips slightly open.

| bola | vela | Caribe | declive |
|---|---|---|---|

In both pronunciations, there is no difference in sound between **b** and **v**. The English *v* sound, produced by friction between the upper teeth and lower lip, does not exist in Spanish. Instead, the soft **b** comes from friction between the two lips.

### Verónica y su esposo cantan boleros.

When **b** or **v** begins a word, its pronunciation depends on the previous word. At the beginning of a phrase or after a word that ends in **m** or **n**, it is pronounced as a hard **b**.

### Benito   es de Boquerón   pero vive   en Victoria.

Words that begin with **b** or **v** are pronounced with a soft **b** if they appear immediately after a word that ends in a vowel or any consonant other than **m** or **n**.

**Práctica** Read these words aloud to practice the **b** and the **v**.

1. hablamos
2. trabajar
3. botones
4. van
5. contabilidad
6. bien
7. doble
8. novia
9. béisbol
10. cabaña
11. llave
12. invierno

No hay mal que por bien no venga.[1]

**Oraciones** Read these sentences aloud to practice the **b** and the **v**.

1. Vamos a Guaynabo en autobús.
2. Voy de vacaciones a la Isla Culebra.
3. Tengo una habitación individual en el octavo piso.
4. Víctor y Eva van en avión al Caribe.
5. La planta baja es bonita también.
6. ¿Qué vamos a ver en Bayamón?
7. Beatriz, la novia de Víctor, es de Arecibo, Puerto Rico.

Hombre prevenido vale por dos.[2]

**Refranes** Read these sayings aloud to practice the **b** and the **v**.

recursos

LM p. 26

panorama.vhlcentral.com Lección 5

[2] *An ounce of prevention equals a pound of cure.*
[1] *Every cloud has a silver lining.*

**Section Goal**

In **Pronunciación**, students will be introduced to the pronunciation of **b** and **v**.

**Instructional Resources**
**Supersite:** Textbook & Lab MP3 Audio Files **Lección 5**
**Supersite/IRCD:** *IRM* (Textbook Audio Script, Lab Audio Script, WBs/VM/LM Answer Key)
**WebSAM**
**Lab Manual**, p. 26
***Cuaderno para hispanohablantes***

**Teaching Tips**
- Emphasize that **b (alta/grande)** and **v (baja/chica)** are pronounced identically in Spanish, but that, depending on the letter's position in a word, each can be pronounced two ways. Pronounce **vóleibol** and **vivir** several times, asking students to listen for the difference between the initial and medial sounds represented by **b** and **v**.
- Explain the cases in which **b** and **v** are pronounced like English *b* in *boy* and model the pronunciation of **bonito**, **viajar**, **también**, and **investigar**.
- You may want to point out that before **b** or **v**, **n** is usually pronounced **m**.
- Explain that in all other positions, **b** and **v** are fricatives. Pronounce **deber**, **novio**, **abril**, and **cerveza** and stress that the friction is between the two lips.
- Remind the class that Spanish has no sound like the English **v**. Pronounce **vida**, **vacaciones**, **avión**, **automóvil**.
- Explain that the same rules apply in connected speech. Practice with phrases like **de vacaciones**, **de ida y vuelta**.

**Práctica/Oraciones/Refranes**
These exercises are recorded in the *Textbook MP3s*. You may want to play the audio so that students practice the pronunciation point by listening to Spanish spoken by speakers other than yourself.

## EN DETALLE

# El Camino Inca

**Early in the morning,** Larry rises, packs up his campsite, fills his water bottle in a stream, eats a quick breakfast, and begins his day. By tonight, the seven miles he and his group hiked yesterday to a height of 9,700 feet will seem easy; today the hikers will cover seven miles to a height of almost 14,000 feet, all the while carrying fifty-pound backpacks.

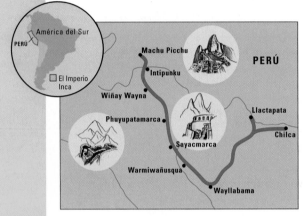

**Ruta de cuatro días**

While not everyone is cut out for such a rigorous trip, Larry is on the journey of a lifetime: el **Camino Inca**. Between 1438 and 1533, when the vast and powerful **Imperio Incaico** (*Incan Empire*) was at its height, the Incas built an elaborate network of **caminos** (*trails*) that traversed the Andes Mountains and converged on the empire's capital, Cuzco. Today, hundreds of thousands of tourists come to Peru annually to walk the surviving

**caminos** and enjoy the spectacular landscapes. The most popular trail, **el Camino Inca**, leads from Cuzco to the ancient mountain city of Machu Picchu. Many trekkers opt for a guided four-day itinerary, starting at a suspension bridge over the Urubamba River, and ending at **Intipunku** (*Sun Gate*), the entrance to Machu Picchu. Guides organize campsites and meals for travelers, as well as one night in a hostel en route.

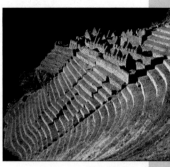

**Wiñay Wayna**

To preserve **el Camino Inca**, the National Cultural Institute of Peru limits the number of hikers to five hundred per day. Those that make the trip must book in advance and should be in good physical condition in order to endure altitude sickness and the terrain.

### Sitios en el Camino Inca

**Highlights of a four-day hike along the Inca Trail:**

**Warmiwañusqua** (*Dead Woman's Pass*), at 13,800 feet, hiker's first taste of the Andes' extreme sun and wind

**Sayacmarca** (*Inaccessible Town*), fortress ruins set on a sheer cliff

**Phuyupatamarca** (*Town in the Clouds*), an ancient town with stone baths, probably used for water worship

**Wiñay Wayna** (*Forever Young*), a town named for the pink orchid native to the area, famous for its innovative agricultural terraces which transformed the mountainside into arable land

### ACTIVIDADES

**1** **¿Cierto o falso?** Indicate whether these statements are **cierto** or **falso**. Correct the false statements.

1. **El Imperio Incaico** reached its height between 1438 and 1533. **Cierto.**
2. Lima was the capital of the Incan Empire. **Falso.** Cuzco was the capital of the Incan Empire.
3. Hikers on **el Camino Inca** must camp out every night. **Falso.** Hikers camp out and also stay in hostels.
4. The Incas invented a series of terraces to make the rough mountain landscape suitable for farming. **Cierto.**
5. Along **el Camino Inca**, one can see village ruins, native orchids, and agricultural terraces. **Cierto.**
6. Altitude sickness is one of the challenges faced by hikers on **el Camino Inca**. **Cierto.**
7. At Sayacmarca, hikers can see Incan pyramids set on a sheer cliff. **Falso.** Hikers can see fortress ruins set on a sheer cliff.
8. Travelers can complete **el Camino Inca** on their own at any time. **Falso.** Travelers hike with a guide and must reserve in advance.

## ASÍ SE DICE

### Viajes y turismo

| | |
|---|---|
| el asiento del medio, del pasillo, de la ventanilla | center, aisle, window seat |
| el itinerario | itinerary |
| media pensión | breakfast and one meal included |
| el ómnibus (Perú) | el autobús |
| pensión completa | all meals included |
| el puente | long weekend (lit., bridge) |

## EL MUNDO HISPANO

### Destinos populares

○ **Las playas del Parque Nacional Manuel Antonio** (Costa Rica) ofrecen° la oportunidad de nadar y luego caminar por el bosque tropical°.

○ **Teotihuacán** (México) Desde la época° de los aztecas, aquí se celebra el equinoccio de primavera en la Pirámide del Sol.

○ **Puerto Chicama** (Perú), con sus olas° de cuatro kilómetros de largo°, es un destino para surfistas expertos.

○ **Tikal** (Guatemala) Aquí puedes ver las maravillas de la selva° y ruinas de la civilización maya.

○ **Las playas de Rincón** (Puerto Rico) Son ideales para descansar y observar a las ballenas°.

ofrecen *offer* bosque tropical *rainforest* Desde la época *Since the time* olas *waves* de largo *in length* selva *jungle* ballenas *whales*

## PERFIL

# Punta del Este

One of South America's largest and most fashionable beach resort towns is Uruguay's **Punta del Este**, a narrow strip of land containing twenty miles of pristine beaches. Its peninsular shape gives it two very different seascapes. **La Playa Mansa**, facing the bay and therefore the more protected side, has calm waters. Here, people practice water sports like swimming, water skiing, windsurfing, and diving. **La Playa Brava**, facing the east, receives the Atlantic Ocean's powerful, wave-producing winds, making it popular for surfing, body boarding, and kite surfing. Besides the beaches, posh shopping, and world-famous nightlife, **Punta** offers its 600,000 yearly visitors yacht and fishing clubs, golf courses, and excursions to observe sea lions at the **Isla de Lobos** nature reserve.

**SUPERSITE** **Conexión Internet**

¿Cuáles son los sitios más populares para el turismo en Puerto Rico?

Go to panorama.vhlcentral.com to find more cultural information related to this **Cultura** section.

## ACTIVIDADES

**2** **Comprensión** Complete the sentences.

1. En las playas de Rincón puedes ver _____ballenas_____.
2. Cerca de 600.000 turistas visitan _Punta del Este_ cada año.
3. En el avión pides un _asiento de la ventanilla_ si te gusta ver el paisaje.
4. En Punta del Este, la gente prefiere nadar en la Playa _Mansa_.
5. El _____ómnibus_____ es un medio de transporte en el Perú.

**3** **De vacaciones** Spring break is coming up, and you want to go on a short vacation with some friends. Working in a small group, decide which of the locations featured on these pages best suits the group's likes and interests. Come to an agreement about how you will get there, where you prefer to stay and for how long, and what each of you will do during free time. Present your trip to the class.
Answers will vary.

**recursos**

**SUPERSITE**

panorama.vhlcentral.com
Lección 5

## TEACHING OPTIONS

**Cultural Comparison** For homework, ask student pairs to use the Internet to research a famous beach from the U.S. or Canada and one from the Spanish-speaking world. Ask them to make a list of **similitudes** and **diferencias** about the beaches, including the types of activities available, visitors, the high and low season, and local accommodations. Have pairs present their comparisons to the class.

**Heritage Speakers** Ask heritage speakers to describe some popular beaches, ruins, or historical sites in their families' countries of origin. If possible, ask them to bring in a map or pictures of the locations.

**Así se dice**

• To challenge students, add these airport-related words to the list: **el/la auxiliar de vuelo** (*flight attendant*), **aterrizar** (*to land*), **el bolso de mano** (*carry-on bag*), **despegar** (*to take off*), **facturar** (*to check*), **hacer escala** (*to stopover*), **el retraso** (*delay*), **la tarjeta de embarque** (*boarding pass*).

• To practice vocabulary from the list, survey the class about their travel habits. Ex: **¿Prefieres el asiento de la ventanilla, del medio o del pasillo? ¿Por qué?**

**Perfil** Punta del Este is located 80 miles east of Uruguay's capital, Montevideo, on a small peninsula that separates the Atlantic Ocean and the **Río de la Plata** estuary. At the beginning of the nineteenth century, Punta was nearly deserted and only visited by fishermen and sailors. Its glamorous hotels, dining, nightlife, and beaches have earned it the nickname "the St. Tropez of South America."

**El mundo hispano**

• Add a visual aspect to this list by using a map to point out the locations of the different **destinos populares**.

• Ask students which destination interests them the most and why.

**2** **Expansion** Ask students to write two additional cloze statements about the information on this page. Then have them exchange papers with a partner and complete the sentences.

**3** **Teaching Tip** To simplify, make a list on the board of the vacation destinations mentioned on this spread. As a class, brainstorm a few tourist activities in Spanish for each location.

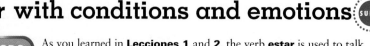

## 5.1 Estar with conditions and emotions

**ANTE TODO** As you learned in **Lecciones 1** and **2**, the verb **estar** is used to talk about how you feel and to say where people, places, and things are located. **Estar** is also used with adjectives to talk about certain emotional and physical conditions.

▶ Use **estar** with adjectives to describe the physical condition of places and things.

La habitación **está** sucia.
*The room is dirty.*

La puerta **está** cerrada.
*The door is closed.*

▶ Use **estar** with adjectives to describe how people feel, both mentally and physically.

Estoy aburrida. ¿Quieren hacer algo?

No, estoy cansada.

▶ **¡Atención!** Two important expressions with **estar** that you can use to talk about conditions and emotions are **estar de buen humor** (*to be in a good mood*) and **estar de mal humor** (*to be in a bad mood*).

### Adjectives that describe emotions and conditions

| | | | | | |
|---|---|---|---|---|---|
| **abierto/a** | open | **contento/a** | happy; content | **listo/a** | ready |
| **aburrido/a** | bored | **desordenado/a** | disorderly | **nervioso/a** | nervous |
| **alegre** | happy; joyful | **enamorado/a (de)** | in love (with) | **ocupado/a** | busy |
| **avergonzado/a** | embarrassed | | | **ordenado/a** | orderly |
| **cansado/a** | tired | **enojado/a** | mad; angry | **preocupado/a (por)** | worried (about) |
| **cerrado/a** | closed | **equivocado/a** | wrong | **seguro/a** | sure |
| **cómodo/a** | comfortable | **feliz** | happy | **sucio/a** | dirty |
| **confundido/a** | confused | **limpio/a** | clean | **triste** | sad |

**¡INTÉNTALO!**  Provide the present tense forms of **estar**, and choose which adjective best completes the sentence. The first item has been done for you.

1. La biblioteca ___está___ (cerrada / nerviosa) los domingos por la noche. *cerrada*
2. Nosotros ___estamos___ muy (ocupados / equivocados) todos los lunes. *ocupados*
3. Ellas ___están___ (alegres / confundidas) porque tienen vacaciones. *alegres*
4. Javier ___está___ (enamorado / ordenado) de Maribel. *enamorado*
5. Diana ___está___ (enojada / limpia) con su novio. *enojada*
6. Yo ___estoy___ (nerviosa / abierta) por el viaje. *nerviosa*
7. La habitación siempre ___está___ (ordenada / segura) cuando vienen sus padres. *ordenada*
8. Ustedes no comprenden; ___están___ (equivocados / tristes). *equivocados*

**CONSULTA**

To review the present tense of **ser**, see **Estructura 1.3**, p. 20.

• • •

To review the present tense of **estar**, see **Estructura 2.3**, p. 55.

**recursos**

WB
pp. 51–52

LM
p. 27

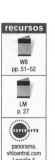
panorama.
vhlcentral.com
Lección 5

---

**Section Goals**

In **Estructura 5.1**, students will learn:

• to use **estar** to describe conditions and emotions
• adjectives that describe conditions and emotions

**Instructional Resources**
**Supersite:** Lab MP3 Audio Files **Lección 5**
**Supersite/IRCD:** *PowerPoints* (**Lección 5 Estructura** Presentation); *IRM* (Lab Audio Script, WBs/VM/LM Answer Key)
**WebSAM**
**Workbook**, pp. 51–52
**Lab Manual**, p. 27
*Cuaderno para hispanohablantes*

**Teaching Tips**

• Ask students to find examples of **estar** used with adjectives in the **Fotonovela**. Draw attention to video still 5 on page 147 and compare the use of **estar** in the first two sentences with the use of **ser** in the third.
• Remind students that adjectives agree in number and gender with the nouns they modify.
• Add a visual aspect to this grammar presentation. Bring in personal or magazine photos of people with varying facial expressions. Hold up each one and state the person's emotion. Ex: **Mi esposa y yo estamos contentos.**
• Point to objects and people and have volunteers supply the correct form of **estar** + [*adjective*]. Ex: Point to windows. (**Están abiertas.**)
• Use TPR to practice the adjectives. Have the class stand and signal a student. Say: ____, **estás enojado/a.** (Student will make an angry face.) Vary by indicating more than one student.
• Point out the use of **de** with **enamorado/a** and **por** with **preocupado/a**. Write cloze sentences on the board and have students complete them. Ex: **María Shriver está ____ Arnold Schwarzenegger. (enamorada de)**

**TEACHING OPTIONS**

**TPR** Call out a sentence using an adjective and have students mime the emotion or show the condition. Ex: **Sus libros están abiertos.** (Students show their open books.) **Ustedes están alegres.** (Students act happy.) Next, call on volunteers to act out an emotion or condition and have the class tell what is going on. Ex: A student pretends to cry. (**Carlos está triste.**)

**Video** Replay the *Fotonovela* episode and ask comprehension questions using **estar** and adjectives expressing emotions or conditions. Ex: **¿Cómo está la cabaña? (Todo está muy limpio y ordenado.) ¿Está cansado Javier? (No, no está cansado.) ¿Quién está cansado? (Maite está cansada.)**

# Práctica (SUPERSITE)

**1** **¿Cómo están?** Complete Martín's statements about how he and other people are feeling. In the first blank, fill in the correct form of **estar**. In the second blank, fill in the adjective that best fits the context. Some answers may vary.

1. Yo ___estoy___ un poco ___nervioso___ porque tengo un examen mañana.
2. Mi hermana Patricia ___está___ muy ___contenta___ porque mañana va a hacer una excursión al campo.
3. Mis hermanos Juan y José salen de la casa a las cinco de la mañana. Por la noche, siempre ___están___ muy ___cansados___.
4. Mi amigo Ramiro ___está___ ___enamorado___; su novia se llama Adela.
5. Mi papá y sus colegas ___están___ muy ___ocupados___ hoy. ¡Hay mucho trabajo!
6. Patricia y yo ___estamos___ un poco ___preocupados___ por ellos porque trabajan mucho.
7. Mi amiga Mónica ___está___ un poco ___triste/enojada___ porque su novio no puede salir esta noche.
8. Esta clase no es muy interesante. ¿Tú ___estás___ ___aburrido/a___ también?

**2** **Describir** Describe these people and places. Answers will vary.

1. Anabela
Está contenta.

2. Juan y Luisa
Están enojados.

3. la habitación de Teresa
Está ordenada/limpia.

4. la habitación de César
Está desordenada/sucia.

# Comunicación

**3** **Situaciones** With a partner, use **estar** to talk about how you feel in these situations.
Answers will vary.
1. Cuando hace sol…
2. Cuando tomas un examen…
3. Cuando estás de vacaciones…
4. Cuando tienes mucho trabajo…
5. Cuando viajas en avión…
6. Cuando estás con la familia…
7. Cuando estás en la clase de español…
8. Cuando ves una película con tu actor/actriz favorito/a…

## Section Goals

In **Estructura 5.2**, students will learn:
- the present progressive of regular and irregular verbs
- the present progressive versus the simple present tense in Spanish

**Instructional Resources**
**Supersite:** Lab MP3 Audio Files **Lección 5**
**Supersite/IRCD:** *PowerPoints*
(**Lección 5 Estructura** Presentation, Overhead #25); *IRM*
(Information Gap Activities, Lab Audio Script, WBs/VM/LM Answer Key)
**WebSAM**
**Workbook,** p. 53
**Lab Manual,** p. 28
*Cuaderno para hispanohablantes*

## Teaching Tips

- Have students read the caption under video still 4 on page 147. Focus attention on **estar** + [*present participle*] to express what is going on at that moment. Then have students describe what is happening in the rest of the episode.
- Use regular verbs to ask questions about things students are not doing. Ex: **¿Estás comiendo pizza? (No, no estoy comiendo pizza.)**
- Explain the formation of the present progressive, writing examples on the board.
- Add a visual aspect to this grammar presentation. Use photos to elicit sentences with the present progressive. Ex: **¿Qué está haciendo el hombre alto? (Está sacando fotos.)** Include present participles ending in **–yendo** as well as those with stem changes.
- Point out that the present progressive is rarely used with the verbs **ir, poder,** and **venir** since they already imply an action in progress.

### 5.2 The present progressive

**ANTE TODO** Both Spanish and English use the present progressive, which consists of the present tense of the verb *to be* and the present participle (the *-ing* form in English).

Hola, chicas. ¿Qué están haciendo?

Estamos descansando.

▶ Form the present progressive with the present tense of **estar** and a present participle.

| FORM OF ESTAR | + PRESENT PARTICIPLE | | FORM OF ESTAR | + PRESENT PARTICIPLE |
|---|---|---|---|---|
| **Estoy** | **pescando.** | | **Estamos** | **comiendo.** |
| *I am* | *fishing.* | | *We are* | *eating.* |

▶ The present participle of regular **–ar, –er,** and **–ir** verbs is formed as follows:

| INFINITIVE | STEM | ENDING | PRESENT PARTICIPLE |
|---|---|---|---|
| hablar | habl- | **-ando** | habl**ando** |
| comer | com- | **-iendo** | com**iendo** |
| escribir | escrib- | **-iendo** | escrib**iendo** |

▶ **¡Atención!** When the stem of an **–er** or **–ir** verb ends in a vowel, the present participle ends in **–yendo**.

| INFINITIVE | STEM | ENDING | PRESENT PARTICIPLE |
|---|---|---|---|
| leer | le- | **-yendo** | le**yendo** |
| oír | o- | **-yendo** | o**yendo** |
| traer | tra- | **-yendo** | tra**yendo** |

▶ **Ir, poder,** and **venir** have irregular present participles (**yendo, pudiendo, viniendo**). Several other verbs have irregular present participles that you will need to learn.

▶ **–Ir** stem-changing verbs have a stem change in the present participle.

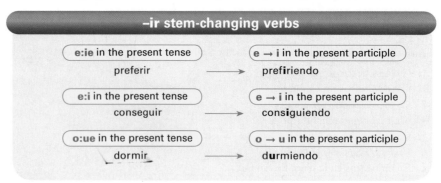

**–ir stem-changing verbs**

| e:ie in the present tense | e → i in the present participle |
|---|---|
| preferir | prefi**r**iendo |

| e:i in the present tense | e → i in the present participle |
|---|---|
| conseguir | consig**u**iendo |

| o:ue in the present tense | o → u in the present participle |
|---|---|
| dormir | d**u**rmiendo |

**TEACHING OPTIONS**

**TPR** Divide the class into three groups. Appoint leaders and give them a list of verbs. Leaders call out a verb and a subject (Ex: **seguir/yo**), then toss a foam or paper ball to someone in the group. That student says the appropriate present progressive form of the verb (Ex: **estoy siguiendo**) and tosses the ball back. Leaders should call out all verbs on the list and toss the ball to every member of the group.

**TPR** Play charades. In groups of four, have students take turns miming actions for the rest of the group to guess. Ex: Student pretends to read a newspaper. (**Estás leyendo el periódico.**) For incorrect guesses, the student should respond negatively. Ex: **No, no estoy estudiando.**

## COMPARE & CONTRAST

The use of the present progressive is much more restricted in Spanish than in English. In Spanish, the present progressive is mainly used to emphasize that an action is in progress at the time of speaking.

Inés **está escuchando** música latina **ahora mismo**.
*Inés is listening to Latin music right now.*

Álex y su amigo **todavía están jugando** al fútbol.
*Álex and his friend are still playing soccer.*

In English, the present progressive is often used to talk about situations and actions that occur over an extended period of time or in the future. In Spanish, the simple present tense is often used instead.

Javier **estudia** computación este semestre.
*Javier is studying computer science this semester.*

Inés y Maite **salen** mañana para los Estados Unidos.
*Inés and Maite are leaving tomorrow for the United States.*

Estamos pensando en lo mismo:

su **F**uturo

Su asesor para ganar
**FIDU**COLOMBIA
Sociedad Fiduciaria S.A.

**¡INTÉNTALO!** Create complete sentences by putting the verbs in the present progressive. The first item has been done for you.

1. mis amigos / descansar en la playa _Mis amigos están descansando en la playa._
2. nosotros / practicar deportes _Estamos practicando deportes._
3. Carmen / comer en casa _Carmen está comiendo en casa._
4. nuestro equipo / ganar el partido _Nuestro equipo está ganando el partido._
5. yo / leer el periódico _Estoy leyendo el periódico._
6. él / pensar comprar una bicicleta _Está pensando comprar una bicicleta._
7. ustedes / jugar a las cartas _Ustedes están jugando a las cartas._
8. José y Francisco / dormir _José y Francisco están durmiendo._
9. Marisa / leer correo electrónico _Marisa está leyendo correo electrónico._
10. yo / preparar sándwiches _Estoy preparando sándwiches._
11. Carlos / tomar fotos _Carlos está tomando fotos._
12. ¿dormir / tú? _¿Estás durmiendo?_

**recursos**

WB
p. 53

LM
p. 28

SUPERSITE
panorama.
vhlcentral.com
Lección 5

**Teaching Tips**
• Discuss each point in the **Compare & Contrast** box.
• Write these statements on the board. Ask students if they would use the present or the present progressive in Spanish for each item. 1. I'm going on vacation tomorrow. 2. She's packing her suitcase right now. 3. They are fishing in Puerto Rico this week. 4. Roberto is still working. Then ask students to translate the items. (**1. Voy de vacaciones mañana. 2. Está haciendo la maleta ahora mismo. 3. Pescan en Puerto Rico esta semana. 4. Roberto todavía está trabajando.**)
• In this lesson, students learn **todavía** to mean *still* in the present progressive tense. You may want to point out that **todavía** also means *yet*. They will be able to use that meaning in later lessons as they learn the past tenses.
• Have students rewrite the sentences in the **¡Inténtalo!** activity using the simple present. Ask volunteers to explain how the sentences change depending on whether the verb is in the present progressive or the simple present.

## TEACHING OPTIONS

**Pairs** Have students write eight sentences in Spanish modeled after the examples in the **Compare & Contrast** box. There should be two sentences modeled after each example. Ask students to replace the verbs with blanks. Then, have students exchange papers with a partner and complete the sentences.

**Extra Practice** For homework, ask students to find five photos from a magazine or create five simple drawings of people performing different activities. For each image, have them write one sentence telling what the people are doing and one describing how they feel. Ex: **Juan está trabajando. Está cansado.**

# Práctica

**1** **Completar** Alfredo's Spanish class is preparing to travel to Puerto Rico. Use the present progressive of the verb in parentheses to complete Alfredo's description of what everyone is doing.

1. Yo __estoy investigando__ (investigar) la situación política de la isla (*island*).
2. La esposa del profesor __está haciendo__ (hacer) las maletas.
3. Marta y José Luis __están buscando__ (buscar) información sobre San Juan en Internet.
4. Enrique y yo __estamos leyendo__ (leer) un correo electrónico de nuestro amigo puertorriqueño.
5. Javier __está aprendiendo__ (aprender) mucho sobre la cultura puertorriqueña.
6. Y tú __estás practicando__ (practicar) el español, ¿verdad?

**2** **¿Qué están haciendo?** María and her friends are vacationing at a resort in San Juan, Puerto Rico. Complete her description of what everyone is doing right now.

◄ **CONSULTA**
For more information about Puerto Rico, see **Panorama**, pp. 170–171.

1. Yo
estoy escribiendo una carta.

2. Javier
está buceando en el mar.

3. Alejandro y Rebeca
están jugando a las cartas.

4. Celia y yo
estamos tomando el sol.

5. Samuel
está escuchando música.

6. Lorenzo
está durmiendo.

**3** **Personajes famosos** Say what these celebrities are doing right now, using the cues provided. ◄
Answers will vary.

**AYUDA**
John Grisham: **novelas**
Martha Stewart: **televisión, negocios** (*business*)
James Cameron: **cine**
Venus y Serena Williams: **tenis**
Tiger Woods: **golf**
Avril Lavigne: **canciones**
Bode Miller: **esquí**
Las New York Rockettes: **baile**

**modelo**
Celine Dion
*Celine Dion está cantando una canción ahora mismo.*

| A | | B | |
|---|---|---|---|
| John Grisham | Avril Lavigne | bailar | hablar |
| Martha Stewart | Bode Miller | cantar | hacer |
| James Cameron | Las New York Rockettes | correr | jugar |
| Venus y Serena | ¿? | escribir | ¿? |
| Williams | ¿? | esquiar | ¿? |
| Tiger Woods | | | |

**TEACHING OPTIONS**

**Pairs** Have students bring in personal photos (or magazine photos) from a vacation. Ask them to describe the photos to a partner. Students should explain what the weather is like, who is in the photo, what they are doing, and where they are.
**Game** Have the class form a circle. Appoint one student to be the starter, who will begin play by miming an action (Ex: eating) and saying what he or she is doing (Ex: **Estoy comiendo.**). In a

clockwise direction around the circle, the next student mimes the same action, says what that person is doing (_____ **está comiendo.**), and then mimes and states a different action (Ex: sleeping/**Estoy durmiendo.**). Have students continue the chain until it breaks, in which case the starter changes the direction to counterclockwise. Have students see how long the chain can get in three minutes.

# Comunicación

**4** **Preguntar** With a partner, take turns asking each other what you are doing at this times.

*Answers will vary.*

> **modelo**
> 8:00 a.m.
> **Estudiante 1:** ¡Hola, Andrés! Son las ocho de la mañana. ¿Qué estás haciendo?
> **Estudiante 2:** Estoy desayunando.

| | | | |
|---|---|---|---|
| 1. 5:00 a.m. | 3. 11:00 a.m. | 5. 2:00 p.m. | 7. 9:00 p.m. |
| 2. 9:30 a.m. | 4. 12:00 p.m. | 6. 5:00 p.m. | 8. 11:30 p.m. |

**5** **Describir** Work with a partner and use the present progressive to describe what is going on in this Spanish beach scene. *Answers will vary.*

**6** **Conversar** Imagine that you and a classmate are each babysitting a group of children. With a partner, prepare a telephone conversation using these cues. Be creative and add further comments. *Answers will vary.*

| **Estudiante 1** | **Estudiante 2** |
|---|---|
| Say hello and ask what the kids are doing. | → Say hello and tell your partner that two of your kids are doing their homework. Then ask what the kids at his/her house are doing. |
| Tell your partner that two of your kids are running and dancing in the house. | → Tell your partner that one of the kids is reading. |
| Tell your partner that you are tired and that two of your kids are watching TV and eating pizza. | → Tell your partner that one of the kids is sleeping. |
| Tell your partner you have to go; the kids are playing soccer in the house. | → Say goodbye and good luck (**¡Buena suerte!**). |

# Síntesis

**7** **¿Qué están haciendo?** A group of classmates is traveling to San Juan, Puerto Rico for a week-long Spanish immersion program. The participants are running late before the flight, and you and your partner must locate them. Your instructor will give you and your partner different handouts that will help you do this. *Answers will vary.*

---

**TEACHING OPTIONS**

**Video** Show the *Fotonovela* episode again, pausing after each exchange. Ask students to describe what each person in the shot is doing at that moment.
**TPR** Write sentences with the present progressive on strips of paper. Call on volunteers to draw papers out of a hat to act out. The class should guess what the sentences are. Ex: **Yo estoy durmiendo en la cama.**

**Pairs** Add an auditory aspect to this grammar practice. Ask students to write five sentences using the present progressive. Students should try to make their sentences as complex as possible. Have students dictate their sentences to a partner. After pairs have finished dictating their sentences, have them exchange papers to check for accuracy. Circulate around the room and look over students' work.

---

**4** **Teaching Tips**
- To simplify, first have students outline their daily activities and what time they do them.
- Remind students to use **a la(s)** when expressing time.

**5** **Teaching Tip** Show *Overhead PowerPoint #25* and have students do the activity with their books closed.

**5** **Expansion** In pairs, have students write a conversation between two or more of the people in the drawing. Conversations should consist of at least three exchanges.

**6** **Teaching Tip** To simplify, before beginning their conversation, have students prepare for their roles by brainstorming two lists: one with verbs that describe what the children are doing at home and the other with adjectives that describe how the babysitter feels.

**6** **Expansion** Ask pairs to tell each other what the parents of the two sets of children are doing. Ex: **Los padres de los niños buenos están visitando el museo. Los padres de los niños malos están en una fiesta.**

**7** **Teaching Tip** Divide the class into pairs and distribute the handouts from the Information Gap Activities (Supersite/IRCD) that correspond to this activity. Give students ten minutes to complete the activity.

**7** **Expansion** Have students work in pairs to say what each program participant is doing in flight. Ex: **Pedro está leyendo una novela.**

## Section Goal

In **Estructura 5.3**, students will review and compare the uses of **ser** and **estar**.

**Instructional Resources**
**Supersite:** Lab MP3 Audio Files **Lección 5**
**Supersite/IRCD:** *PowerPoints* (Lección 5 Estructura Presentation, Overhead #26); *IRM* (Lab Audio Script, WBs/VM/LM Answer Key)
**WebSAM**
**Workbook,** pp. 54–55
**Lab Manual,** p. 29
*Cuaderno para hispanohablantes*

### Teaching Tips

• Have pairs brainstorm as many uses of **ser** with examples as they can. Compile a list on the board, and repeat for **estar**.

• Divide the board or an overhead transparency into two columns. In column one, write sentences using **ser** and **estar** in random order (Ex: **Álex es de México.**). In column two, write the uses of **ser** and **estar** taught so far, also in random order (Ex: place of origin). Ask volunteers to match the sentence with its corresponding use.

• Write cloze sentences on the board. Ask students to supply the correct form of **ser** or **estar.** Ex: **Mi casa ____ lejos de aquí.** (estar, location; **está**) If either **ser** or **estar** could be used, ask students to explain how the meaning of the sentence would change.

• Contrast uses of **ser** and **estar** by talking about celebrities. Ex: **Nelly Furtado es canadiense y su familia es de origen portugués. Es bonita y delgada. Es cantante. Ella está en los Estados Unidos ahora. Está haciendo una gira de conciertos. Tiene un concierto hoy; es a las ocho. El concierto es en un estadio. El estadio está en Miami.** Pause after each sentence and have students identify the use(s). Then have volunteers create sentences about other famous people.

---

### 5.3 Ser and estar  SUPERSITE

**ANTE TODO** You have already learned that **ser** and **estar** both mean *to be* but are used for different purposes. These charts summarize the key differences in usage between **ser** and **estar.**

#### Uses of ser

1. **Nationality and place of origin** — Martín **es** argentino. / **Es** de Buenos Aires.
2. **Profession or occupation** — Adela **es** agente de viajes. / Francisco **es** médico.
3. **Characteristics of people and things** — José y Clara **son** simpáticos. / El clima de Puerto Rico **es** agradable.
4. **Generalizations** — ¡**Es** fabuloso viajar! / **Es** difícil estudiar a la una de la mañana.
5. **Possession** — **Es** la pluma de Maite. / **Son** las llaves de don Francisco.
6. **What something is made of** — La bicicleta **es** de metal. / Los pasajes **son** de papel.
7. **Time and date** — Hoy **es** martes. **Son** las dos. / Hoy **es** el primero de julio.
8. **Where or when an event takes place** — El partido **es** en el estadio Santa Fe. / La conferencia **es** a las siete.

*Soy Francisco Castillo Moreno. Yo soy de la agencia Ecuatur.*

*Su nombre no está en mi lista.*

#### Uses of estar

1. **Location or spatial relationships** — El aeropuerto **está** lejos de la ciudad. / Tu habitación **está** en el tercer piso.
2. **Health** — ¿Cómo **estás**? / **Estoy** bien, gracias.
3. **Physical states and conditions** — El profesor **está** ocupado. / Las ventanas **están** abiertas.
4. **Emotional states** — Marisa **está** feliz hoy. / **Estoy** muy enojado con Javier.
5. **Certain weather expressions** — **Está** lloviendo. / **Está** nublado.
6. **Ongoing actions (progressive tenses)** — **Estamos** estudiando para un examen. / Ana **está** leyendo una novela.

**¡ATENCIÓN!**
Note that **de** is generally used after **ser** to express not only origin (**Es de Buenos Aires.**) and possession (**Es la pluma de Maite.**), but also what material something is made of (**La bicicleta es de metal.**).

---

**TEACHING OPTIONS**

**Extra Practice** Add an auditory aspect to this grammar presentation. Call out sentences containing forms of **ser** or **estar**. Ask students to identify the use of the verb.
**Heritage Speakers** Ask heritage speakers to write a postcard to a friend or family member about a vacation in Puerto Rico, incorporating as many of the uses of **ser** and **estar** as they can.

**TPR** Divide the class into two teams. Call out a use of **ser** or **estar**. The first member of each team runs to the board and writes a sample sentence. The first student to finish a sentence correctly earns a point for his or her team. Practice all uses of each verb and make sure each team member has at least two turns. Then tally the points to see which team wins.

# Ser and estar with adjectives

▶ With many descriptive adjectives, **ser** and **estar** can both be used, but the meaning will change.

Juan **es** delgado.
*Juan is thin.*

Juan **está** más delgado hoy.
*Juan looks thinner today.*

Ana **es** nerviosa.
*Ana is a nervous person.*

Ana **está** nerviosa por el examen.
*Ana is nervous because of the exam.*

▶ In the examples above, the statements with **ser** are general observations about the inherent qualities of Juan and Ana. The statements with **estar** describe conditions that are variable.

▶ Here are some adjectives that change in meaning when used with **ser** and **estar**.

| With ser | With estar |
|---|---|
| El chico **es listo**. | El chico **está listo**. |
| *The boy is smart.* | *The boy is ready.* |
| La profesora **es mala**. | La profesora **está mala**. |
| *The professor is bad.* | *The professor is sick.* |
| Jaime **es aburrido**. | Jaime **está aburrido**. |
| *Jaime is boring.* | *Jaime is bored.* |
| Las peras **son verdes**. | Las peras **están verdes**. |
| *The pears are green.* | *The pears are not ripe.* |
| El gato **es muy vivo**. | El gato **está vivo**. |
| *The cat is very lively.* | *The cat is alive.* |
| Él **es muy seguro**. | Él no **está seguro**. |
| *He is very confident.* | *He's not sure.* |

**¡ATENCIÓN!**

When referring to objects, **ser seguro** means *to be safe.*
**El puente es seguro.**
*The bridge is safe.*

---

**¡INTÉNTALO!**  Form complete sentences by using the correct form of **ser** or **estar** and making any other necessary changes. The first item has been done for you.

1. Alejandra / cansado
   Alejandra *está cansada.*

2. ellos / pelirrojo
   Ellos son pelirrojos.

3. Carmen / alto
   Carmen es alta.

4. yo / la clase de español
   Estoy en la clase de español.

5. película / a las once
   La película es a las once.

6. hoy / viernes
   Hoy es viernes.

7. nosotras / enojado
   Nosotras estamos enojadas.

8. Antonio / médico
   Antonio es médico.

9. Romeo y Julieta / enamorado
   Romeo y Julieta están enamorados.

10. libros / de Ana
    Los libros son de Ana.

11. Marisa y Juan / estudiando
    Marisa y Juan están estudiando.

12. partido de baloncesto / gimnasio
    El partido de baloncesto es en el gimnasio.

**recursos**

WB
pp. 54–55

LM
p. 29

panorama.
vhlcentral.com
Lección 5

**Teaching Tips**

• Ask students if they notice any context clues in the examples that would help them choose between **ser** and **estar**.

• Write sentences like these on the board: 1. **Pilar** is worried because she has a quiz tomorrow. (**Pilar está preocupada porque tiene una prueba mañana.**) 2. The bell-hop is very busy right now. (**El botones está muy ocupado ahora.**) 3. The beach is pretty. (**La playa es bonita.**) 4. Juan is/looks very handsome today. (**Juan está muy guapo hoy.**) Have students translate the sentences into Spanish and ask them why they chose either **ser** or **estar** for their translation.

• Ask students questions like these to practice the different meanings of adjectives, depending on whether they are used with **ser** or **estar**. 1. **Manuel es un muchacho muy inteligente. ¿Está listo o es listo? 2. No me gusta la clase de física. ¿Está aburrida o es aburrida? 3. No sé si Carlos tiene 50 ó 51 años. ¿No estoy seguro/a o no soy seguro/a? 4. ¿El color del taxi es verde o está verde? 5. El profesor no enseña muy bien. ¿Está malo o es malo?**

• Note that some heritage speakers may use **ser vivo/a** to mean *astute* or *sharp/clever.*

**The Affective Dimension**
If students feel anxious that Spanish has two verbs that mean *to be*, reassure them that they will soon feel more comfortable with this concept as they read more examples and complete more practice activities. Point out that **ser** and **estar** express rich shades of meaning.

---

**TEACHING OPTIONS**

**Extra Practice** Ask students to write sentences illustrating the contrasting meanings of adjectives used with **ser** or **estar**. Have students exchange papers for peer editing before going over them with the class.
**Video** Show the *Fotonovela* episode again. Have students jot down the forms of **ser** or **estar**. Discuss each use of **ser** and **estar**.

**Pairs** Tell students to imagine that they are going to interview a celebrity visiting their hometown. Ask them to write questions with at least ten different uses of **ser** and **estar**. Next, have them interview a partner and record the answers. Have students write a summary of their interviews.

# Práctica SUPERSITE

**1** **¿Ser o estar?** Indicate whether each adjective takes **ser** or **estar**. **¡Ojo!** Three of them can take both verbs.

| | ser | estar | | | ser | estar |
|---|---|---|---|---|---|---|
| 1. delgada | ● | ● | 5. seguro | ● | ● |
| 2. canadiense | ● | ○ | 6. enojada | ○ | ● |
| 3. enamorado | ○ | ● | 7. importante | ● | ○ |
| 4. lista | ● | ● | 8. avergonzada | ○ | ● |

**2** **Completar** Complete this conversation with the appropriate forms of **ser** and **estar**.

**EDUARDO** ¡Hola, Ceci! ¿Cómo (1)___estás___?

**CECILIA** Hola, Eduardo. Bien, gracias. ¡Qué guapo (2)___estás___ hoy!

**EDUARDO** Gracias. (3)___Eres___ muy amable. Oye, ¿qué (4)___estás___ haciendo? (5)¿___Estás___ ocupada?

**CECILIA** No, sólo le (6)___estoy___ escribiendo una carta a mi prima Pilar.

**EDUARDO** ¿De dónde (7)___es___ ella?

**CECILIA** Pilar (8)___es___ del Ecuador. Su papá (9)___es___ médico en Quito. Pero ahora Pilar y su familia (10)___están___ de vacaciones en Ponce, Puerto Rico.

**EDUARDO** Y... ¿cómo (11)___es___ Pilar?

**CECILIA** (12)___Es___ muy lista. Y también (13)___es___ alta, rubia y muy bonita.

**3** **Describir** With a partner, describe the people in the drawing. Your descriptions should answer the questions provided. *Answers will vary.*

1. ¿Quiénes son las personas?
2. ¿Dónde están?
3. ¿Cómo son?
4. ¿Cómo están?
5. ¿Qué están haciendo?
6. ¿Qué estación es?
7. ¿Qué tiempo hace?
8. ¿Quiénes están de vacaciones?

# Comunicación

**4** **Describir** With a classmate, take turns describing these people. First mention where each person is from. Then describe what each person is like, how each person is feeling, and what he or she is doing right now. *Answers will vary.*

> **modelo**
> tu compañero/a de cuarto
> *Mi compañera de cuarto es de San Juan, Puerto Rico. Es muy inteligente. Está cansada pero está estudiando porque tiene un examen.*

1. tu mejor (*best*) amigo/a
2. tus padres
3. tu profesor(a) favorito/a
4. tu novio/a o esposo/a
5. tu primo/a favorito/a
6. tus abuelos

**5** **Adivinar** Get together with a partner and describe a celebrity to him or her using these questions as a guide. Don't mention the celebrity's name. Can your partner guess who you are describing? *Answers will vary.*

1. ¿Cómo es?
2. ¿Cómo está?
3. ¿De dónde es?
4. ¿Dónde está?
5. ¿Qué está haciendo?
6. ¿Cuál es su profesión?

**6** **En el aeropuerto** In small groups, take turns using **ser** and **estar** to describe this scene at Luis Muñoz Marín International Airport. What do the people in the picture look like? How are they feeling? What are they doing? *Answers will vary.*

**NOTA CULTURAL**
**Luis Muñoz Marín International Airport** in San Juan, Puerto Rico, is a major transportation hub of the Caribbean. It is named after Puerto Rico's first elected governor.

# Síntesis

**7** **Conversación** You and your partner are two of the characters in the drawing in **Actividad 6**. After boarding, you discover that you are sitting next to each other and must make conversation. Act out what you would say to your fellow passenger. Choose one of the pairs below or pick your own. *Answers will vary.*

1. Señor Villa y Elena
2. Señorita Esquivel y la señora Limón
3. Señora Villa y Luz
4. Emilio y Elena

---

**4** **Expansion** Have pairs select two descriptions to present to the class.

**5** **Teaching Tip** Model the activity for the class. In order to create ambiguity, you may want to tell students to use **una persona** to answer items 1, 2, and 6. Ex: **Es una persona alta…**

**6** **Teaching Tip** Ask groups to choose a leader to moderate the activity, a secretary to record the group's description, and a proofreader to check that the written description is accurate. Then show *Overhead PowerPoint #26*. All students should take turns adding one sentence at a time to the group's description.

**6** **Expansion** Have students pick one of the individuals pictured and write a one-paragraph description, employing as many different uses of **ser** and **estar** as possible.

**7** **Teaching Tips**
• To simplify, first have students create a character description for the person they will be playing. Then, as a class, brainstorm topics of conversation.
• Make sure that students use **ser** and **estar**, the present progressive, and stem-changing verbs in their conversation, as well as vacation-, pastime-, and family-related vocabulary.

**The Affective Dimension** Encourage students to consider pair and group activities as a cooperative venture in which group members support and motivate each other.

---

**TEACHING OPTIONS**

**Heritage Speakers** Have heritage speakers write a television commercial for a vacation resort in the Spanish-speaking world. Ask them to employ as many uses of **ser** and **estar** as they can. If possible, after they have written the commercial, have them videotape it to show to the class.

**TPR** Call on a volunteer and whisper the name of a celebrity in his or her ear. The volunteer mimes actions, acts out characteristics, and uses props to elicit descriptions from the class. Ex: The volunteer points to the U.S. on a map. (**Es de los Estados Unidos.**) He or she then indicates a short, thin man. (**Es un hombre bajo y delgado.**) He or she mimes riding a bicycle. (**Está paseando en bicicleta. ¿Es Lance Armstrong?**)

## Section Goals

In **Estructura 5.4**, students will study:

• direct object nouns
• the personal **a**
• direct object pronouns

**Instructional Resources**
**Supersite:** Lab MP3 Audio Files **Lección 5**
**Supersite/IRCD:** *PowerPoints* (**Lección 5 Estructura** Presentation); *IRM* (Lab Audio Script, WBs/VM/LM Answer Key)
**WebSAM**
**Workbook,** p. 56
**Lab Manual,** p. 30
*Cuaderno para hispanohablantes*

**Teaching Tips**

• Write these sentences on the board: —¿Quién tiene el pasaporte? —Juan lo tiene. Underline **pasaporte** and explain that it is a direct object noun. Then underline **lo** and explain that it is the masculine singular direct object pronoun. Translate both sentences. Continue with: —¿Quién saca fotos? —Simón las saca. —¿Quién tiene la llave? —Pilar la tiene.

• Read this exchange aloud: —¿Haces las maletas? —No, no hago las maletas. —¿Por qué no haces las maletas? —No hago las maletas porque las maletas no están aquí. Ask students if the exchange sounds natural to them. Then write it on the board and ask students to use direct object pronouns to avoid repetition. If students try to say **no las están** in the last sentence, point out that direct object pronouns cannot replace the subject of a verb. The only option is to eliminate the subject: **no están.**

• Ask individuals questions to elicit the personal **a**: ¿Visitas a tu abuela los fines de semana? ¿Llamas a tu padre los sábados?

• Ask questions to elicit third-person direct object pronouns. Ex: ¿Quién ve el lápiz de Marcos? ¿Quién quiere este diccionario?

---

## 5.4 Direct object nouns and pronouns

| SUBJECT | VERB | DIRECT OBJECT NOUN |
|---|---|---|
| Álex y Javier | están tomando | fotos. |
| *Álex and Javier* | *are taking* | *photos.* |

▶ A direct object noun receives the action of the verb directly and generally follows the verb. In the example above, the direct object noun answers the question *What are Álex and Javier taking?*

▶ When a direct object noun in Spanish is a person or a pet, it is preceded by the word **a**. This is called the personal **a**; there is no English equivalent for this construction.

Don Francisco visita **a** la señora Ramos.    Don Francisco visita el Hotel Prado.
*Don Francisco is visiting Mrs. Ramos.*          *Don Francisco is visiting the Hotel Prado.*

▶ In the first sentence above, the personal **a** is required because the direct object is a person. In the second sentence, the personal **a** is not required because the direct object is a place, not a person.

¿Dónde pongo las maletas?

Puede ponerlas encima de la cama.

Hay muchos lugares interesantes por aquí. ¿Quieren ir a verlos?

### Direct object pronouns

| SINGULAR | | PLURAL | |
|---|---|---|---|
| **me** | *me* | **nos** | *us* |
| **te** | *you* (fam.) | **os** | *you* (fam.) |
| **lo** | *you* (m., form.) | **los** | *you* (m., form.) |
| | *him; it* (m.) | | *them* (m.) |
| **la** | *you* (f., form.) | **las** | *you* (f., form.) |
| | *her; it* (f.) | | *them* (f.) |

▶ Direct object pronouns are words that replace direct object nouns. Like English, Spanish sometimes uses a direct object pronoun to avoid repeating a noun already mentioned.

| | DIRECT OBJECT | | DIRECT OBJECT PRONOUN |
|---|---|---|---|
| Maribel hace | las maletas. | Maribel | las hace. |
| Felipe compra | el sombrero. | Felipe | lo compra. |
| Vicky tiene | la llave. | Vicky | la tiene. |

---

**TEACHING OPTIONS**

**TPR** Call out a series of sentences with direct object nouns, some of which require the personal **a** and some of which do not. Ex: **Visito muchos museos. Visito a mis tíos.** Have students raise their hands if the personal **a** is used.

**Extra Practice** Write six sentences on the board that have direct object nouns. Use two verbs in the simple present tense, two in the present progressive, and two using **ir a** + [*infinitive*]. Draw a line through the direct objects as students call them out. Have students state which pronouns to write to replace them. Then, draw an arrow from each pronoun to where it goes in the sentence, as indicated by students.

▶ In affirmative sentences, direct object pronouns generally appear before the conjugated verb. In negative sentences, the pronoun is placed between the word **no** and the verb.

Adela practica **el tenis**.
Adela **lo** practica.

Carmen compra **los pasajes**.
Carmen **los** compra.

Gabriela no tiene **las llaves**.
Gabriela **no las** tiene.

Diego no hace **las maletas**.
Diego **no las** hace.

▶ When the verb is an infinitive construction, such as **ir a** + [*infinitive*], the direct object pronoun can be placed before the conjugated form or attached to the infinitive.

Ellos van a escribir **unas postales**.
⎰ Ellos **las** van a escribir.
⎱ Ellos van a escribir**las**.

Lidia quiere ver **una película**.
⎰ Lidia **la** quiere ver.
⎱ Lidia quiere ver**la**.

▶ When the verb is in the present progressive, the direct object pronoun can be placed before the conjugated form or attached to the present participle. **¡Atención!** When a direct object pronoun is attached to the present participle, an accent mark is added to maintain the proper stress.

Gerardo está leyendo **la lección**.
⎰ Gerardo **la** está leyendo.
⎱ Gerardo está leyéndo**la**.

Toni está mirando **el partido**.
⎰ Toni **lo** está mirando.
⎱ Toni está mirándo**lo**.

**CONSULTA**

To learn more about accents, see **Lección 4, Pronunciación**, p. 115, **Lección 10, Ortografía**, p. 315, and **Lección 11, Ortografía**, p. 349.

 **¡INTÉNTALO!** Choose the correct direct object pronoun for each sentence. The first one has been done for you.

1. Tienes el libro de español. *c*
   a. La tienes.           b. Los tienes.           c. Lo tienes.
2. Voy a ver el partido de baloncesto. *a*
   a. Voy a verlo.         b. Voy a verte.          c. Voy a vernos.
3. El artista quiere dibujar a Luisa con su mamá. *c*
   a. Quiere dibujarme.    b. Quiere dibujarla.     c. Quiere dibujarlas.
4. Marcos busca la llave. *b*
   a. Me busca.            b. La busca.             c. Las busca.
5. Rita me lleva al aeropuerto y también lleva a Tomás. *a*
   a. Nos lleva.           b. Las lleva.            c. Te lleva.
6. Puedo oír a Gerardo y a Miguel. *b*
   a. Puedo oírte.         b. Puedo oírlos.         c. Puedo oírlo.
7. Quieren estudiar la gramática. *c*
   a. Quieren estudiarnos. b. Quieren estudiarlo.   c. Quieren estudiarla.
8. ¿Practicas los verbos irregulares? *a*
   a. ¿Los practicas?      b. ¿Las practicas?       c. ¿Lo practicas?
9. Ignacio ve la película. *a*
   a. La ve.               b. Lo ve.                c. Las ve.
10. Sandra va a invitar a Mario a la excursión. También me va a invitar a mí. *c*
   a. Los va a invitar.    b. Lo va a invitar.      c. Nos va a invitar.

**recursos**

WB
p. 56

LM
p. 30

SUPERSITE
panorama.
vhlcentral.com
Lección 5

**Teaching Tips**
• Elicit first- and second-person direct object pronouns by asking questions first of individual students and then groups of students. Ex: **¿Quién te invita a bailar con frecuencia? (Mi novio me invita a bailar con frecuencia.) ¿Quién te comprende? (Mi amigo me comprende.)**
• Ask questions directed at the class as a whole to elicit first-person plural direct object pronouns. Ex: **¿Quiénes los llaman los fines de semana? (Nuestros padres nos llaman.) ¿Quiénes los esperan después de la clase? (Los amigos nos esperan.)**
• Add a visual aspect to this grammar presentation. Use magazine pictures to practice the third-person direct object pronouns with infinitives and the present progressive. Ex: **¿Quién está practicando tenis? (Roger Federer lo está practicando. / Roger Federer está practicándolo.) ¿Quién va a mirar la televisión? (El hombre pelirrojo la va a mirar. / El hombre pelirrojo va a mirarla.)**
• Point out that the direct object pronoun **los** refers to both masculine and mixed groups. **Las** refers only to feminine groups.

**TEACHING OPTIONS**

**Large Group** Make a list of 20 questions requiring direct object pronouns in the answer. Arrange students in two concentric circles. Students in the center circle ask questions from the list to those in the outer circle until you say stop (**¡Paren!**). The outer circle moves one person to the right and the questions begin again. Continue for five minutes, then have the students in the outer circle ask the questions.

**Pairs** Have students write ten sentences using direct object nouns. Their sentences should also include a mixture of verbs in the present progressive, simple present, and **ir a** + [*infinitive*]. Ask students to exchange their sentences with a partner, who will rewrite them using direct object pronouns. Students should check their partner's work.

# Práctica ⬤ SUPERSITE

**1** **Teaching Tip** To simplify, ask individual students to identify the direct object in each sentence before beginning the activity.

**1** **Sustitución** Professor Vega's class is planning a trip to Costa Rica. Describe their preparations by changing the direct object nouns into direct object pronouns.

> **modelo**
>
> La profesora Vega tiene su pasaporte.
> *La profesora Vega lo tiene.*

1. Gustavo y Héctor confirman las reservaciones. Gustavo y Héctor las confirman.
2. Nosotros leemos los folletos (*brochures*). Nosotros los leemos.
3. Ana María estudia el mapa. Ana María lo estudia.
4. Yo aprendo los nombres de los monumentos de San José. Yo los aprendo.
5. Alicia escucha a la profesora. Alicia la escucha.
6. Miguel escribe las direcciones para ir al hotel. Miguel las escribe.
7. Esteban busca el pasaje. Esteban lo busca.
8. Nosotros planeamos una excursión. Nosotros la planeamos.

**¡LENGUA VIVA!**

There are many Spanish words that correspond to *ticket*. **Billete** and **pasaje** usually refer to a ticket for travel, such as an airplane ticket. **Entrada** refers to a ticket to an event, such as a concert or a movie. **Boleto** can be used in either case.

**2** **Expansion** Ask questions (using direct objects) about the people in the activity to elicit **Sí/No** answers. Ex: **¿Tiene Ramón reservaciones en el hotel? (Sí, las tiene.) ¿Tiene su mochila? (No, no la tiene.)**

**2** **Vacaciones** Ramón is going to San Juan, Puerto Rico with his friends, Javier and Marcos. Express his thoughts more succinctly using direct object pronouns.

> **modelo**
>
> Quiero hacer una excursión.
> *Quiero hacerla./La quiero hacer.*

1. Voy a hacer mi maleta. Voy a hacerla./La voy a hacer.
2. Necesitamos llevar los pasaportes. Necesitamos llevarlos./Los necesitamos llevar.
3. Marcos está pidiendo el folleto turístico. Marcos está pidiéndolo./Marcos lo está pidiendo.
4. Javier debe llamar a sus padres. Javier debe llamarlos./Javier los debe llamar.
5. Ellos esperan visitar el Viejo San Juan. Ellos esperan visitarlo./Ellos lo esperan visitar.
6. Puedo llamar a Javier por la mañana. Puedo llamarlo./Lo puedo llamar.
7. Prefiero llevar mi cámara. Prefiero llevarla./La prefiero llevar.
8. No queremos perder nuestras reservaciones de hotel. No queremos perderlas./No las queremos perder.

**NOTA CULTURAL**

Because Puerto Rico is a U.S. territory, passengers traveling there from the U.S. mainland do not need passports or visas. Passengers traveling to Puerto Rico from a foreign country, however, must meet travel requirements identical to those required for travel to the U.S. mainland. Puerto Ricans are U.S. citizens and can therefore travel to the U.S. mainland without any travel documents.

**3** **Expansion**
- Ask students questions about who does what in the activity. Ex: **¿La señora Garza busca la cámara? (No, María la busca.)**
- Ask additional questions about the family's preparations, allowing students to decide who does what. Ex: **¿Quién compra una revista para leer en el avión? ¿Quién llama al taxi? ¿Quién practica el español?**

**3** **¿Quién?** The Garza family is preparing to go on a vacation to Puerto Rico. Based on the clues, answer the questions. Use direct object pronouns in your answers.

> **modelo**
>
> ¿Quién hace las reservaciones para el hotel? (el Sr. Garza)
> *El Sr. Garza las hace.*

1. ¿Quién compra los pasajes para el vuelo (*flight*)? (la Sra. Garza)
   La Sra. Garza los compra.
2. ¿Quién tiene que hacer las maletas de los niños? (María)
   María tiene que hacerlas./María las tiene que hacer.
3. ¿Quiénes buscan los pasaportes? (Antonio y María)
   Antonio y María los buscan.
4. ¿Quién va a confirmar las reservaciones para el hotel? (la Sra. Garza)
   La Sra. Garza va a confirmarlas./La Sra. Garza las va a confirmar.
5. ¿Quién busca la cámara? (María)
   María la busca.
6. ¿Quién compra un mapa de Puerto Rico? (Antonio) Antonio lo compra.

---

**TEACHING OPTIONS**

**Pairs** Have students take turns asking each other who does these activities: **leer revistas, practicar el ciclismo, ganar siempre los partidos, visitar a sus padres durante las vacaciones, leer el periódico, escribir cartas, escuchar a sus profesores, practicar la natación.** Ex: **—¿Quién lee revistas? —Yo las leo.**

**Heritage Speakers** Pair heritage speakers with other students. Ask the pairs to create a dialogue between a travel agent and client. Assign the role of traveler to the heritage speaker, who would like to travel to his or her family's home country. Encourage both students to draw on their experiences from past vacations and trips to Spanish speaking countries. Have students role-play their dialogues for the class.

# Comunicación

**4** **Entrevista** Interview a classmate using these questions. Be sure to use direct object pronouns in your responses. Answers will vary.

1. ¿Ves mucho la televisión?
2. ¿Cuándo vas a ver tu programa favorito?
3. ¿Quién prepara la comida (*food*) en tu casa?
4. ¿Te visita mucho tu familia?
5. ¿Visitas mucho a tus abuelos?
6. ¿Nos entienden nuestros padres a nosotros?
7. ¿Cuándo ves a tus amigos/as?
8. ¿Cuándo te llaman tus amigos/as?

**5** **En el aeropuerto** Get together with a partner and take turns asking each other questions about the drawing. Use the word bank and direct object pronouns. Answers will vary.

> **modelo**
>
> **Estudiante 1:** ¿Quién está leyendo el libro?
> **Estudiante 2:** Susana lo está leyendo./Susana está leyéndolo.

| buscar | confirmar | escribir | leer | tener | vender |
|--------|-----------|----------|------|-------|--------|
| comprar | encontrar | escuchar | llevar | traer | ¿? |

Sra. Sánchez · Orlando · Sr. López

Marta · Sr. Sánchez · Susana · Miguelito

# Síntesis

**6** **Adivinanzas** Play a guessing game in which you describe a person, place, or thing and your partner guesses who or what it is. Then switch roles. Each of you should give at least five descriptions. Answers will vary.

> **modelo**
>
> **Estudiante 1:** Lo uso para (*I use it to*) escribir en mi cuaderno.
>                   No es muy grande y tiene borrador. ¿Qué es?
> **Estudiante 2:** ¿Es un lápiz?
> **Estudiante 1:** ¡Sí!

---

**4** **Teaching Tip** Ask students to record their partner's answers. After the interviews, have students review answers in groups and report the most common responses to the class.

**4** **Expansion** Have students write five additional questions, then continue their interviews.

**5** **Teaching Tip** To simplify, before assigning the activity, ask individual students to identify different objects in the picture that might be used as direct objects in questions and answers.

**5** **Expansion**
• Reverse the activity by having students say what the people are doing for a partner to guess. Ex: **Está escribiendo en su cuaderno. (Es Miguelito.)**
• Have students use **ser** and **estar** to describe the people in the drawing.

**6** **Teaching Tip** To simplify, first have students write out their descriptions.

**6** **Expansion** Have pairs write out five additional riddles. Have them read their riddles aloud for the rest of the class to answer.

---

**TEACHING OPTIONS**

**Game** Play a game of **20 Preguntas**. Divide the class into two teams. Think of an object in the room and alternate calling on teams to ask questions. Once a team knows the answer, the team captain should raise his or her hand. If right, the team gets a point. If wrong, the team loses a point. Play until one team has earned five points.

**Pairs** Have students create five questions that include the direct object pronouns **me, te,** and **nos.** Then have them ask their partners the questions on their list. Ex: —¿Quién te llama **mucho? —Mi novia me llama mucho. —¿Quién nos escucha cuando hacemos preguntas en español? —El/La profesor(a) y los estudiantes nos escuchan.**

## Section Goal

In **Recapitulación**, students will review the grammar concepts from this lesson.

**Instructional Resource**
**Supersite**

**1 Expansion** Create a list of present participles and have students supply the infinitive. Ex: **durmiendo** (**dormir**)

**2 Teaching Tip** Ask students to explain why they chose **ser** or **estar** for each item.

**2 Expansion** Have students use **ser** and **estar** to write a brief paragraph describing **Julia's** first few days in Paris.

**3 Teaching Tip** To simplify, have students begin by underlining the direct object nouns and identifying the corresponding direct object pronouns.

# Recapitulación

**SUPERSITE** For self-scoring and diagnostics, go to **panorama.vhlcentral.com**.

Review the grammar concepts you have learned in this lesson by completing these activities.

**1** **Completar** Complete the chart with the correct present participle of these verbs. **8 pts.**

| INFINITIVE | PRESENT PARTICIPLE | INFINITIVE | PRESENT PARTICIPLE |
|---|---|---|---|
| **hacer** | haciendo | **estar** | estando |
| **acampar** | acampando | **ser** | siendo |
| **tener** | teniendo | **vivir** | viviendo |
| **venir** | viniendo | **estudiar** | estudiando |

**2** **Vacaciones en París** Complete this paragraph about Julia's trip to Paris with the correct form of **ser** or **estar**. **12 pts.**

Hoy (1) __es__ (es/está) el 3 de julio y voy a París por tres semanas. (Yo) (2) __Estoy__ (Soy/Estoy) muy feliz porque voy a ver a mi mejor amiga. Ella (3) __es__ (es/está) de Puerto Rico, pero ahora (4) __está__ (es/está) viviendo en París. También (yo) (5) __estoy__ (soy/estoy) un poco nerviosa porque (6) __es__ (es/está) mi primer viaje a Francia. El vuelo (*flight*) (7) __es__ (es/está) hoy por la tarde pero ahora (8) __está__ (es/está) lloviendo. Por eso (9) __estamos__ (somos/estamos) preocupadas, porque probablemente el avión va a salir tarde. Mi equipaje ya (10) __está__ (es/está) listo. (11) __Es__ (Es/Está) tarde y me tengo que ir. ¡Va a (12) __ser__ (ser/estar) un viaje fenomenal!

**3** **¿Qué hacen?** Respond to these questions by indicating what people do with the items mentioned. Use direct object pronouns. **5 pts.**

> **modelo**
> ¿Qué hacen los viajeros con las vacaciones? (planear)
> Las planean.

1. ¿Qué haces tú con el libro de viajes? (leer) __Lo leo.__
2. ¿Qué hacen los turistas en la ciudad? (explorar) __La exploran.__
3. ¿Qué hace el botones con el equipaje? (llevar) __Lo lleva (a la habitación).__
4. ¿Qué hace la agente con las reservaciones? (confirmar) __Las confirma.__
5. ¿Qué hacen ustedes con los pasaportes? (mostrar) __Los mostramos.__

### RESUMEN GRAMATICAL

**5.1 Estar with conditions and emotions**  *p. 152*

► Yo est**oy** aburrido/a, feliz, nervioso/a.
► El cuarto est**á** desordenado, limpio, ordenado.
► Estos libros est**án** abiertos, cerrados, sucios.

**5.2 The present progressive**  *pp. 154–155*

► The present progressive is formed with the present tense of **estar** plus the present participle.

**Forming the present participle**

| infinitive | stem | ending | present participle |
|---|---|---|---|
| hablar | habl- | -ando | habl**ando** |
| comer | com- | -iendo | com**iendo** |
| escribir | escrib- | -iendo | escrib**iendo** |

**-ir stem-changing verbs**

| | infinitive | present participle |
|---|---|---|
| e:ie | preferir | **prefiriendo** |
| e:i | conseguir | **consiguiendo** |
| o:ue | dormir | **d**u**rmiendo** |

► Irregular present participles: **yendo (ir), pudiendo (poder), viniendo (venir)**

**5.3 Ser and estar**  *pp. 158–159*

► Uses of **ser**: nationality, origin, profession or occupation, characteristics, generalizations, possession, what something is made of, time and date, time and place of events
► Uses of **estar**: location, health, physical states and conditions, emotional states, weather expressions, ongoing actions
► **Ser** and **estar** can both be used with many adjectives, but the meaning will change.

Juan **es** delgado.    Juan **está** más delgado hoy.
*Juan is thin.*    *Juan looks thinner today.*

---

**TEACHING OPTIONS**

**Extra Practice** Add an auditory aspect to this grammar review. Go around the room and read a sentence with a direct object. Each student must repeat the sentence using a direct object pronoun. Ex: **María y Jennifer están comprando sus libros para la clase. (María y Jennifer los están comprando./María y Jennifer están comprándolos.)**

**TPR** Divide the board into two columns, with the heads **ser** and **estar**. Ask two volunteers to stand in front of each verb. The rest of the class should take turns calling out a use of **ser** or **estar**. The volunteer standing in front of the correct verb should step forward and give an example sentence. Ex: nationality or origin (**Soy norteamericano/a.**)

**4 Opuestos** Complete these sentences with the appropriate form of the verb **estar** and an adjective with the opposite meaning of the underlined adjective. `5 pts.`

> **modelo**
>
> Mis respuestas están <u>bien</u>, pero las de Susana **están mal**.

1. Las tiendas están <u>abiertas</u>, pero la agencia de viajes **está** **cerrada**.
2. No me gustan las habitaciones <u>desordenadas</u>. Incluso (*Even*) mi habitación de hotel **está** **ordenada**.
3. Nosotras estamos <u>tristes</u> cuando trabajamos. Hoy comienzan las vacaciones y **estamos** **contentas/alegres/felices**
4. En esta ciudad los autobuses están <u>sucios</u>, pero los taxis **están** **limpios**.
5. —El avión sale a las 5:30, ¿verdad? —No, estás <u>confundida</u>. Yo **estoy** **seguro/a** de que el avión sale a las 5:00.

**5.4 Direct object nouns and pronouns** *pp. 162–163*

**Direct object pronouns**

| Singular | | Plural | |
|---|---|---|---|
| me | lo | nos | los |
| te | la | os | las |

In affirmative sentences:
Adela practica **el tenis**. → Adela **lo** practica.

In negative sentences: Adela **no lo** practica.

With an infinitive:
Adela **lo** va a practicar./Adela va a practicar**lo**.

With the present progressive:
Adela **lo** está practicando./Adela está practicándo**lo**.

**5 En la playa** Describe what these people are doing. Complete the sentences using the present progressive tense. `8 pts.`

1. El Sr. Camacho **está pescando** .
2. Felicia **está yendo/paseando en barco**
3. Leo **está montando a caballo** .
4. Nosotros **estamos jugando a las cartas** .

**6 Antes del viaje** Write a paragraph of at least six sentences describing the time right before you go on a trip. Say how you feel and what you are doing. You can use **Actividad 2** as a model. `12 pts.` Answers will vary.

> **modelo**
>
> Hoy es viernes, 27 de octubre. Estoy en mi habitación...

**7 Refrán** Complete this Spanish saying. Refer to the translation and the drawing. `2 EXTRA points!`

¡LA CIUDAD ESTÁ MUY SUCIA!

❝ Se consigue más

**haciendo** que

**diciendo** . ❞

(*You can accomplish more by doing than by saying.*)

**4 Expansion** Have students create three sentences about their own lives, using opposite adjectives. Ex: **Mi hermano es desordenado, pero yo soy muy ordenado.**

**5 Expansion** To challenge students, have them imagine these people are in a hotel. Ask students to say what they are doing. Ex: **Leo está mirando un programa sobre los caballos.**

**6 Teaching Tips**
• Have students exchange papers with a partner for peer editing.
• To make this activity more challenging, require students to include at least two examples each of **ser, estar,** and direct object pronouns.

**7 Teaching Tip** Explain the use of the impersonal **se** and explain that **Se consigue** means *You can* (as in the translation) or *One can*. Students will learn the impersonal **se** in **Estructura 10.3**.

**7 Expansion** To challenge students, have them work in pairs to create a short dialogue that ends with this saying. Encourage them to be creative.

**TEACHING OPTIONS**

**TPR** Prepare five anonymous descriptions of easily recognizable people, using **ser** and **estar**. Write each name on a separate card and give each student a set of cards. Read the descriptions aloud and have students hold up the corresponding name. Ex: **Es cantante y autora de libros infantiles. Es rubia y delgada. No es muy joven, pero no es vieja. Es de Michigan, pero ahora está en Inglaterra. Está enamorada de Guy Ritchie. (Madonna)**

**Extra Practice** Give students these items to make sentences with the present progressive. **1.** con / madre / hablar / yo / mi / estar (**Yo estoy hablando con mi madre.**) **2.** nuestro / equipaje / buscar / nosotros / estar (**Nosotros estamos buscando nuestro equipaje.**) **3.** ¿ / llover / playa / la / estar / en / ? (**¿Está lloviendo en la playa?**) **4.** el / Nueva York / pasaje / ella / para / comprar / estar (**Ella está comprando el pasaje para Nueva York.**)

## Section Goals

In **Lectura**, students will:
- learn the strategy of scanning to find specific information in reading matter
- read a brochure about eco-tourism in Puerto Rico

---

**Instructional Resources**
**Supersite**
*Cuaderno para hispanohablantes*

---

**Estrategia** Explain to students that a good way to get an idea of what an article or other text is about is to scan it before reading. Scanning means running one's eyes over a text in search of specific information that can be used to infer the content of the text. Explain that scanning a text before reading it is a good way to improve Spanish reading comprehension.

**The Affective Dimension**
Point out to students that becoming familiar with cognates will help them feel less overwhelmed when they encounter new Spanish texts.

**Examinar el texto** Do the activity orally as a class. Some cognates that give a clue to the content of the text are: **turismo ecológico, hotel, aire acondicionado, perfecto, Parque Nacional Foresta, Museo de Arte Nativo, Reserva, Biosfera, Santuario**. These clues should tell a reader scanning the text that it is about a hotel promoting ecotourism.

**Preguntas** Ask the questions orally of the class. Possible responses: 1. travel brochure 2. Puerto Rico 3. photos of beautiful tropical beaches, bays, and forests; the document is trying to attract the reader 4. **Hotel La Cabaña** in Lajas, Puerto Rico; attract guests

# Lectura

## Antes de leer

### Estrategia
**Scanning**

Scanning involves glancing over a document in search of specific information. For example, you can scan a document to identify its format, to find cognates, to locate visual clues about the document's content, or to find specific facts. Scanning allows you to learn a great deal about a text without having to read it word for word.

### Examinar el texto
Scan the reading selection for cognates and write a few of them down. Answers will vary.

1. _____  4. _____
2. _____  5. _____
3. _____  6. _____

Based on the cognates you found, what do you think this document is about?

_____

### Preguntas
Read these questions. Then scan the document again to look for answers. Answers will vary.

1. What is the format of the reading selection?
   _____

2. Which place is the document about?
   _____

3. What are some of the visual cues this document provides? What do they tell you about the content of the document?
   _____

4. Who produced the document, and what do you think it is for?
   _____

**recursos**

panorama.vhlcentral.com
Lección 5

---

# Turismo ecológico en Puerto Rico

## Hotel La Cabaña
~ *Lajas, Puerto Rico* ~

### Habitaciones

- 40 individuales
- 15 dobles
- Teléfono / TV / Cable
- Aire acondicionado

- Restaurante (Bar)
- Piscina
- Área de juegos
- Cajero automático°

*E*l hotel está situado en Playa Grande, un pequeño pueblo de pescadores del mar Caribe. Es el lugar perfecto para el viajero que viene de vacaciones. Las playas son seguras y limpias, ideales para tomar el sol, descansar, tomar fotografías y nadar. Está abierto los 365 días del año. Hay una rebaja° especial para estudiantes universitarios.

DIRECCIÓN: Playa Grande 406, Lajas, PR 00667, cerca del Parque Nacional Foresta.

Cajero automático *ATM* rebaja *discount*

---

### TEACHING OPTIONS

**Heritage Speakers** Ask heritage speakers of Puerto Rican descent who have lived on or visited the island to prepare a short presentation about the climate, geography, or people of Puerto Rico. Ask them to illustrate their presentations with photos they have taken or illustrations from magazines, if possible.

**Small Groups** Have students work in groups of five to brainstorm a list of what would constitute an ideal tropical vacation for them. Each student should contribute at least one idea. Ask the group to designate one student to take notes and another to present the information to the class. When each group has its list, ask the designated presenter to share the information with the rest of the class. How do the groups differ? How are they similar?

## Atracciones cercanas

**Playa Grande** ¿Busca la playa perfecta? Playa Grande es la playa que está buscando. Usted puede pescar, sacar fotos, nadar y pasear en bicicleta. Playa Grande es un paraíso para el turista que quiere practicar deportes acuáticos. El lugar es bonito e interesante y usted tiene muchas oportunidades para descansar y disfrutar en familia.

**Valle Niebla** Ir de excursión, tomar café, montar a caballo, caminar, acampar, hacer picnic. Más de 100 lugares para acampar.

**Bahía Fosforescente** Sacar fotos, salidas de noche, excursión en barco. Una maravillosa experiencia con pecesº fosforescentes.

**Arrecifes de Coral** Sacar fotos, bucear, explorar. Es un lugar único en el Caribe.

**Playa Vieja** Tomar el sol, pasear en bicicleta, jugar a las cartas, escuchar música. Ideal para la familia.

**Parque Nacional Foresta** Sacar fotos, visitar el Museo de Arte Nativo. Reserva Mundial de la Biosfera.

**Santuario de las Aves** Sacar fotos, observar avesº, seguir rutas de excursión.

peces *fish*   aves *birds*

---

# Después de leer

### Listas

Which of the amenities of the Hotel La Cabaña would most interest these potential guests? Explain your choices. Answers will vary.

1. dos padres con un hijo de seis años y una hija de ocho años

   _____

2. un hombre y una mujer en su luna de miel (*honeymoon*)

   _____

3. una persona en un viaje de negocios (*business trip*)

   _____

### Conversaciones

With a partner, take turns asking each other these questions. Answers will vary.

1. ¿Quieres visitar el Hotel La Cabaña? ¿Por qué?
2. Tienes tiempo de visitar sólo tres de las atracciones turísticas que están cerca del hotel. ¿Cuáles vas a visitar? ¿Por qué?
3. ¿Qué prefieres hacer en Valle Niebla? ¿En Playa Vieja? ¿En el Parque Nacional Foresta?

### Situaciones

You have just arrived at the Hotel La Cabaña. Your classmate is the concierge. Use the phrases below to express your interests and ask for suggestions about where to go. Answers will vary.

1. montar a caballo
2. bucear
3. pasear en bicicleta
4. pescar
5. observar aves

### Contestar

Answer these questions. Answers will vary.

1. ¿Quieres visitar Puerto Rico? Explica tu respuesta.

   _____

2. ¿Adónde quieres ir de vacaciones el verano que viene? Explica tu respuesta.

   _____

---

**Listas**
- Ask these comprehension questions. 1. **¿El Hotel La Cabaña está situado cerca de qué mar?** (el mar Caribe) 2. **¿Qué playa es un paraíso para el turista?** (la Playa Grande) 3. **¿Dónde puedes ver peces fosforescentes?** (en la Bahía Fosforescente)
- Encourage discussion on each of the items by asking questions such as: **En tu opinión, ¿qué tipo de atracciones buscan los padres con hijos de seis y ocho años? ¿Qué esperan de un hotel? Y una pareja en su luna de miel, ¿qué tipo de atracciones espera encontrar en un hotel? En tu opinión, ¿qué busca una persona en un viaje de negocios?**

**Conversaciones** Ask individuals about what their partners said. Ex: **¿Por qué (no) quiere _____ visitar el Hotel La Cabaña? ¿Qué atracciones quiere ver?** Ask other students: **Y tú, ¿quieres visitar el Parque Nacional Foresta o prefieres visitar otro lugar?**

**Situaciones** Give students a couple of minutes to review **Más vocabulario** on page 140 and **Expresiones útiles** on page 147. Add to the list activities such as **sacar fotos, correr, nadar,** and **ir de excursión.**

**Contestar** Have volunteers explain how the reading selection might influence their choice of vacation destination for next summer.

---

**Pairs** Have pairs of students work together to read the brochure aloud and write three questions about it. After they have finished, ask pairs to exchange papers with another pair, who will work together to answer them. Alternatively, you might pick pairs to read their questions to the class. Ask volunteers to answer them.

**Small Groups** To practice scanning written material to infer its content, bring in short, simple Spanish-language magazine or newspaper articles you have read. Have small groups scan the articles to determine what they are about. Have them write down all the clues that help them. When each group has come to a decision, ask it to present its findings to the class. Confirm the accuracy of the inferences.

## Section Goal

In **Panorama**, students will read about the geography, history, and culture of Puerto Rico.

**Instructional Resources**
**Supersite/DVD:** *Panorama cultural*
**Supersite/IRCD:** *PowerPoints* (Overheads #3, #4, #27); *IRM* (*Panorama cultural* Videoscript & Translation, WBs/VM/LM Answer Key)
**WebSAM**
**Workbook,** pp. 57–58
**Video Manual,** pp. 233–234

**Teaching Tip** Have students look at the map of Puerto Rico or show *Overhead PowerPoint #27*. Discuss Puerto Rico's location in relation to the U.S. mainland and the other Caribbean islands. Encourage students to describe what they see in the photos on this page.

**El país en cifras** After reading **Puertorriqueños célebres**, ask volunteers who are familiar with these individuals to tell a little more about each. **Rita Moreno** is the only female performer to have won an Oscar, a Tony, an Emmy, and a Grammy. You might also mention novelist **Rosario Ferré,** whose *House on the Lagoon (La casa de la laguna)* gives a fictional portrait of a large part of Puerto Rican history.

**¡Increíble pero cierto!** The **río Camuy** caves are actually a series of karstic sinkholes, formed by water sinking into and eroding limestone. Another significant cave in this system is Clara Cave, located in the **río Camuy** Cave Park. The entrance of the 170-foot-high cave resembles the façade of a cathedral.

# Puerto Rico

*NATIONAL STANDARDS — connections cultures*

## El país en cifras

▶ **Área:** 8.959 km$^2$ (3.459 millas$^2$) menor° que el área de Connecticut
▶ **Población:** 4.060.000
*Puerto Rico es una de las islas más densamente pobladas° del mundo. Más de la tercera parte de la población vive en San Juan, la capital.*
▶ **Capital:** San Juan—2.758.000

SOURCE: Population Division, UN Secretariat

▶ **Ciudades principales:** Arecibo, Bayamón, Fajardo, Mayagüez, Ponce
▶ **Moneda:** dólar estadounidense
▶ **Idiomas:** español (oficial); inglés (oficial)
*Aproximadamente la cuarta parte de la población puertorriqueña habla inglés. Pero, en las zonas turísticas este porcentaje es mucho más alto. El uso del inglés es obligatorio para documentos federales.*

Bandera de Puerto Rico

### Puertorriqueños célebres

▶ **Raúl Juliá,** actor (1940–1994)
▶ **Roberto Clemente,** beisbolista (1934–1972)
▶ **Julia de Burgos,** escritora (1914–1953)
▶ **Ricky Martin,** cantante° y actor (1971– )
▶ **Rita Moreno,** actriz, cantante, bailarina (1931– )

menor *less* pobladas *populated* cantante *singer* río subterráneo *underground river* más largo *longest* cuevas *caves* bóveda *vault* fortaleza *fort* caber *fit*

**recursos**

| | | |
|---|---|---|
| WB pp. 57–58 | VM pp. 233–234 | SUPERSITE panorama.vhlcentral.com Lección 5 |

Hoteles en El Condado, San Juan

Plaza de Arecibo

Océano Atlántico

Arecibo

San Juan

Bayamón

Río Grande de Añasco

Mayagüez

Cordillera Central

Ponce

Sierra de Cay

Mar Caribe

Parque de Bombas, Ponce

Pescadores en Mayagüez

OCÉANO ATLÁNTICO

PUERTO R

OCÉANO PACÍFICO

### ¡Increíble pero cierto!

El río Camuy es el tercer río subterráneo° más largo° del mundo y tiene el sistema de cuevas° más grande en el hemisferio occidental. La Cueva de los Tres Pueblos es una gigantesca bóveda°, tan grande que toda la fortaleza° del Morro puede caber° en su interior.

**TEACHING OPTIONS**

**Heritage Speakers** Encourage heritage speakers of Puerto Rican descent who have lived on the island or visited it to write a short description of their impressions. Ask them to describe people they knew or met, places they saw, and experiences they had. Ask them to think about what the most important thing they would tell a person unfamiliar with the island would be and to try to express it.

**El béisbol** Baseball is a popular sport in Puerto Rico, home of the Winter League. **Roberto Clemente**, a player with the Pittsburgh Pirates who died tragically in a plane crash, was the first Latino to be inducted into the Baseball Hall of Fame. He is venerated all over the island with buildings and monuments.

### Lugares • El Morro

El Morro es una fortaleza que se construyó para proteger° la bahía° de San Juan desde principios del siglo° XVI hasta principios del siglo XX. Hoy día muchos turistas visitan este lugar, convertido en un museo. Es el sitio más fotografiado de Puerto Rico. La arquitectura de la fortaleza es impresionante. Tiene misteriosos túneles, oscuras mazmorras° y vistas fabulosas de la bahía.

### Artes • Salsa

La salsa, este estilo musical de origen puertorriqueño y cubano, nació° en el barrio latino de la ciudad de Nueva York. Dos de los músicos de salsa más famosos son Tito Puente y Willie Colón, los dos de Nueva York. Las estrellas° de la salsa en Puerto Rico son Felipe Rodríguez y Héctor Lavoe. Hoy en día, Puerto Rico es el centro internacional de la salsa. El Gran Combo de Puerto Rico es una de las orquestas de salsa más famosas del mundo°.

Isla de Culebra

Fajardo

Isla de Vieques

### Ciencias • El Observatorio de Arecibo

El Observatorio de Arecibo tiene uno de los radiotelescopios más grandes del mundo. Gracias a este telescopio, los científicos° pueden estudiar las propiedades de la Tierra°, la Luna° y otros cuerpos celestes. También pueden analizar fenómenos celestiales como los quasares y pulsares, y detectar emisiones de radio de otras galaxias, en busca de inteligencia extraterrestre.

### Historia • Relación con los Estados Unidos

Puerto Rico pasó a ser° parte de los Estados Unidos después de° la guerra° de 1898 y se hizo° un estado libre asociado en 1952. Los puertorriqueños, ciudadanos° estadounidenses desde° 1917, tienen representación política en el Congreso pero no votan en las elecciones presidenciales y no pagan impuestos° federales. Hay un debate entre los puertorriqueños: ¿debe la isla seguir como estado libre asociado, hacerse un estado como los otros° o volverse° independiente?

**¿Qué aprendiste?** Responde a las preguntas con una oración completa.
1. ¿Cuál es la moneda de Puerto Rico? La moneda de Puerto Rico es el dólar estadounidense.
2. ¿Qué idiomas se hablan (*are spoken*) en Puerto Rico? Se hablan español e inglés en Puerto Rico.
3. ¿Cuál es el sitio más fotografiado de Puerto Rico? El Morro es el sitio más fotografiado de Puerto Rico.
4. ¿Qué es el Gran Combo? Es una orquesta de Puerto Rico.
5. ¿Qué hacen los científicos en el Observatorio de Arecibo? Los científicos estudian la atmósfera de la Tierra y la Luna y escuchan emisiones de otras galaxias.

**Conexión Internet** Investiga estos temas en **panorama.vhlcentral.com**.
1. Describe a dos puertorriqueños famosos. ¿Cómo son? ¿Qué hacen? ¿Dónde viven? ¿Por qué son célebres?
2. Busca información sobre lugares buenos para el ecoturismo en Puerto Rico. Luego presenta un informe a la clase.

..............................................................................................

proteger *protect* bahía *bay* siglo *century* mazmorras *dungeons* nació *was born* estrellas *stars* mundo *world* científicos *scientists* Tierra *Earth* Luna *Moon* pasó a ser *became* después de *after* guerra *war* se hizo *became* ciudadanos *citizens* desde *since* pagan impuestos *pay taxes* debería *should* otros *others* volverse *to become*

**El Morro**
- Remind students that at the time **El Morro** was built, piracy was a major concern for Spain and its Caribbean colonies. If possible, show other photos of **El Morro**, San Juan Bay, and **Viejo San Juan**.
- For additional information about **El Morro** and **Viejo San Juan**, you may want to play the *Panorama cultural* video footage for this lesson.

**Salsa** With students, listen to **salsa** or **merengue** from the Dominican Republic, and **rumba** or **mambo** from Cuba. Encourage them to identify common elements in the music (strong percussion patterns rooted in African traditions, alternating structure of soloist and ensemble, incorporation of Western instruments and musical vocabulary). Then, have them point out contrasts.

**El Observatorio de Arecibo** The Arecibo Ionospheric Observatory has the world's most sensitive radio telescope. It can detect objects up to 13 billion light years away. The telescope dish is 1,000 feet in diameter and covers 20 acres. The dish is made of about 40,000 aluminum mesh panels.

**Relación con los Estados Unidos** Point out that only Puerto Ricans living on the island vote in plebiscites (or referenda) on the question of the island's political relationship with the United States.

**Conexión Internet** Students will find supporting Internet activities and links at **panorama.vhlcentral.com**.

**TEACHING OPTIONS**

**Variación léxica** When the first Spanish colonists arrived on the island they were to name Puerto Rico, they found it inhabited by the Taínos, who called the island **Boriquen**. Puerto Ricans still use **Borinquén** to refer to the island, and they frequently call themselves **boricuas**. The Puerto Rican national anthem is *La borinqueña*. Some other Taíno words that have entered Spanish (and English) are **huracán**, **hamaca**, **canoa**, and **iguana**. **Juracán** was the name of the Taíno god of the winds whose anger stirred up the great storms that periodically devastated the island. The hammock, of course, was the device the Taínos slept in, and canoes were the boats made of great hollowed-out logs with which they paddled between islands. The Taíno language also survives in many Puerto Rican place names: **Arecibo, Bayamón, Guayama, Sierra de Cayey, Yauco,** and **Coamo**.

**Instructional Resources**
**Supersite:** Textbook &
Vocabulary MP3 Audio Files
**Lección 5**
**Supersite/IRCD:** *IRM* (WBs/
VM/LM Answer Key); *Testing
Program* (**Lección 5 Pruebas,**
Test Generator, Testing
Program MP3 Audio Files)
**WebSAM**
**Lab Manual,** p. 30

## Los viajes y las vacaciones

| | |
|---|---|
| acampar | *to camp* |
| confirmar una reservación | *to confirm a reservation* |
| estar de vacaciones (*f. pl.*) | *to be on vacation* |
| hacer las maletas | *to pack (one's suitcases)* |
| hacer un viaje | *to take a trip* |
| ir de compras (*f. pl.*) | *to go shopping* |
| ir de vacaciones | *to go on vacation* |
| ir en autobús (*m.*), auto(móvil) (*m.*), avión (*m.*), barco (*m.*), moto(cicleta) (*f.*), taxi (*m.*) | *to go by bus, car, plane, boat, motorcycle, taxi* |
| jugar a las cartas | *to play cards* |
| montar a caballo (*m.*) | *to ride a horse* |
| pescar | *to fish* |
| sacar/tomar fotos (*f. pl.*) | *to take photos* |
| el/la agente de viajes | *travel agent* |
| el/la inspector(a) de aduanas | *customs inspector* |
| el/la viajero/a | *traveler* |
| el aeropuerto | *airport* |
| la agencia de viajes | *travel agency* |
| la cabaña | *cabin* |
| el campo | *countryside* |
| el equipaje | *luggage* |
| la estación de autobuses, del metro, de tren | *bus, subway, train station* |
| la llegada | *arrival* |
| el mar | *sea* |
| el paisaje | *landscape* |
| el pasaje (de ida y vuelta) | *(round-trip) ticket* |
| el pasaporte | *passport* |
| la playa | *beach* |
| la salida | *departure; exit* |

## El hotel

| | |
|---|---|
| el ascensor | *elevator* |
| el/la botones | *bellhop* |
| la cama | *bed* |
| el/la empleado/a | *employee* |
| la habitación individual, doble | *single, double room* |
| el hotel | *hotel* |
| el/la huésped | *guest* |
| la llave | *key* |
| el piso | *floor (of a building)* |
| la planta baja | *ground floor* |

## Adjetivos

| | |
|---|---|
| abierto/a | *open* |
| aburrido/a | *bored; boring* |
| alegre | *happy; joyful* |
| amable | *nice; friendly* |
| avergonzado/a | *embarrassed* |
| cansado/a | *tired* |
| cerrado/a | *closed* |
| cómodo/a | *comfortable* |
| confundido/a | *confused* |
| contento/a | *happy; content* |
| desordenado/a | *disorderly* |
| enamorado/a (de) | *in love (with)* |
| enojado/a | *mad; angry* |
| equivocado/a | *wrong* |
| feliz | *happy* |
| limpio/a | *clean* |
| listo/a | *ready; smart* |
| nervioso/a | *nervous* |
| ocupado/a | *busy* |
| ordenado/a | *orderly* |
| preocupado/a (por) | *worried (about)* |
| seguro/a | *sure; safe* |
| sucio/a | *dirty* |
| triste | *sad* |

## Los números ordinales

| | |
|---|---|
| primer, primero/a | *first* |
| segundo/a | *second* |
| tercer, tercero/a | *third* |
| cuarto/a | *fourth* |
| quinto/a | *fifth* |
| sexto/a | *sixth* |
| séptimo/a | *seventh* |
| octavo/a | *eighth* |
| noveno/a | *ninth* |
| décimo/a | *tenth* |

## Palabras adicionales

| | |
|---|---|
| ahora mismo | *right now* |
| el año | *year* |
| ¿Cuál es la fecha (de hoy)? | *What is the date (today)?* |
| de buen/mal humor | *in a good/bad mood* |
| la estación | *season* |
| el mes | *month* |
| todavía | *yet; still* |

| | |
|---|---|
| Seasons, months, and dates | *See page 142.* |
| Weather expressions | *See page 142.* |
| Direct object pronouns | *See page 162.* |
| Expresiones útiles | *See page 147.* |

**recursos**

LM
p. 30

panorama.vhlcentral.com
Lección 5

# ¡De compras!

## 6

### Communicative Goals

*You will learn how to:*
- Talk about and describe clothing
- Express preferences in a store
- Negotiate and pay for items you buy

## Lesson Goals

In **Lección 6**, students will be introduced to the following:
- terms for clothing and shopping
- colors
- open-air markets
- Venezuelan clothing designer **Carolina Herrera**
- the verbs **saber** and **conocer**
- indirect object pronouns
- preterite tense of regular verbs
- demonstrative adjectives and pronouns
- skimming a text
- how to report an interview
- writing a report
- listening for linguistic cues
- a television commercial for **Galerías**, a Spanish department store
- Cuban singer **Celia Cruz**
- cultural, geographic, economic, and historical information about Cuba

**A primera vista** Here are some additional questions you can ask based on the photo: **¿Te gusta ir de compras? ¿Por qué? ¿Estás de buen humor cuando vas de compras? ¿Estás pensando ir de compras este fin de semana? ¿Dónde? ¿Qué compras cuando estás de vacaciones?**

### A PRIMERA VISTA
- ¿Está comprando algo la mujer?
- ¿Está buscando una maleta?
- ¿Está contenta o enojada?
- ¿Cómo es la mujer?

### INSTRUCTIONAL RESOURCES

*MAESTRO*™ **SUPERSITE (panorama.vhlcentral.com)**
Textbook, Vocabulary, & Lab MP3 Audio Files
Additional Practice
Learning Management System (Assignment Task Manager, Gradebook)
*Also on DVD*
   *Fotonovela*

*Flash cultura*
*Panorama cultural*
*Also on Instructor's Resource CD-ROM*
*PowerPoints* (**Contextos** & **Estructura** Presentations, Overheads)
*Instructor's Resource Manual* (Handouts, Textbook Answer Key, WBs/VM/LM Answer Key,

Audioscripts, Videoscripts & Translations)
*Testing Program* (**Pruebas**, Test Generator, MP3s)
**Vista Higher Learning** *Cancionero*
**WebSAM** (Workbook/Video Manual/Lab Manual)
**Workbook/Video Manual**
*Cuaderno para hispanohablantes*
**Lab Manual**

## ¡De compras!

### Más vocabulario

| | |
|---|---|
| el abrigo | coat |
| los calcetines (el calcetín) | sock(s) |
| el cinturón | belt |
| las gafas (de sol) | (sun)glasses |
| los guantes | gloves |
| el impermeable | raincoat |
| la ropa | clothing; clothes |
| la ropa interior | underwear |
| las sandalias | sandals |
| el traje | suit |
| el vestido | dress |
| los zapatos de tenis | tennis shoes; sneakers |
| el regalo | gift |
| el almacén | department store |
| el centro comercial | shopping mall |
| el mercado (al aire libre) | (open-air) market |
| el precio (fijo) | (fixed; set) price |
| la rebaja | sale |
| la tienda | shop; store |
| costar (o:ue) | to cost |
| gastar | to spend (money) |
| pagar | to pay |
| regatear | to bargain |
| vender | to sell |
| hacer juego (con) | to match (with) |
| llevar | to wear; to take |
| usar | to wear; to use |

### Variación léxica

| | | |
|---|---|---|
| calcetines | ⟷ | medias (*Amér. L.*) |
| cinturón | ⟷ | correa (*Col., Venez.*) |
| gafas/lentes | ⟷ | espejuelos (*Cuba, P.R.*), anteojos (*Arg., Chile*) |
| zapatos de tenis | ⟷ | zapatillas de deporte (*Esp.*), zapatillas (*Arg., Perú*) |

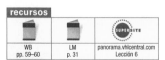

recursos

| WB pp. 59–60 | LM p. 31 | panorama.vhlcentral.com Lección 6 |

los pantalones cortos
el traje de baño
los pantalones
la camiseta
el dependiente/el vendedor
la camisa
la clienta
el dinero en efectivo
la blusa
el suéter
la bolsa
las medias
la falda

Damas

# Práctica

el sombrero

Caballeros

un par de zapatos

los zapatos

chaqueta

la caja

la cartera

la dependienta/la vendedora

la corbata

la tarjeta de crédito

los bluejeans

la bota

SUPERSITE

**1** **Escuchar** Listen to Juanita and Vicente talk about what they're packing for their vacations. Indicate who is packing each item. If both are packing an item, write both names. If neither is packing an item, write an X.

1. abrigo ___Vicente___
2. zapatos de tenis ___Juanita, Vicente___
3. impermeable ___X___
4. chaqueta ___Vicente___
5. sandalias ___Juanita___
6. bluejeans ___Juanita, Vicente___
7. gafas de sol ___Vicente___
8. camisetas ___Juanita, Vicente___
9. traje de baño ___Juanita___
10. botas ___Vicente___
11. pantalones cortos ___Juanita___
12. suéter ___Vicente___

**2** **Lógico o ilógico** Listen to Guillermo and Ana talk about vacation destinations. Indicate whether each statement is **lógico** or **ilógico**.

1. ___ilógico___
2. ___lógico___
3. ___ilógico___
4. ___lógico___

**3** **Completar** Anita is talking about going shopping. Complete each sentence with the correct word(s), adding definite or indefinite articles when necessary.

| | | |
|---|---|---|
| caja | medias | tarjeta de crédito |
| centro comercial | par | traje de baño |
| dependientas | ropa | vendedores |

1. Hoy voy a ir de compras al ___centro comercial___.
2. Voy a ir a la tienda de ropa para mujeres. Siempre hay muchas rebajas y las ___dependientas___ son muy simpáticas.
3. Necesito comprar ___un par___ de zapatos.
4. Y tengo que comprar ___un traje de baño___ porque el sábado voy a la playa con mis amigos.
5. También voy a comprar unas ___medias___ para mi mamá.
6. Voy a pagar todo (*everything*) en ___la caja___.
7. Pero hoy no tengo dinero. Voy a tener que usar mi ___tarjeta de crédito___.
8. Mañana voy al mercado al aire libre. Me gusta regatear con los ___vendedores___.

**4** **Escoger** Choose the item in each group that does not belong.

1. almacén • centro comercial • mercado • (sombrero)
2. camisa • camiseta • blusa • (botas)
3. bluejeans • (bolsa) • falda • pantalones
4. abrigo • suéter • (corbata) • chaqueta
5. mercado • tienda • almacén • (cartera)
6. (pagar) • llevar • hacer juego (con) • usar
7. botas • sandalias • zapatos • (traje)
8. vender • regatear • (ropa interior) • gastar

**1** **Script** JUANITA: Hola. Me llamo Juanita. Mi familia y yo salimos de vacaciones mañana y estoy haciendo mis maletas. Para nuestra excursión al campo ya tengo bluejeans, camisetas y zapatos de tenis. También vamos a la playa… ¡no puedo esperar! *Script continues on page 176.*

**1** **Teaching Tip** Have students check their answers by going over **Actividad 1** with the class.

**2** **Teaching Tip** You may want to do this activity as a TPR exercise. Have students raise their right hands if they hear a logical statement and their left hands if they hear an illogical statement.

**2** **Script** 1. Este verano quiero ir de vacaciones a un lugar caliente, con playas y mucho, mucho sol; por eso, necesito comprar un abrigo y botas. 2. A mí me gustaría visitar Costa Rica en la estación de lluvias. Hace mucho calor, pero llueve muchísimo. Voy a necesitar mi impermeable todo el tiempo. 3. Mi lugar favorito para ir de vacaciones es Argentina en invierno. Me gusta esquiar en las montañas. No puedo ir sin mis sandalias ni mi traje de baño. 4. En mi opinión, el lugar ideal para ir de vacaciones es mi club. Allí juego mi deporte favorito, el tenis y también asisto a fiestas elegantes. Por eso siempre llevo mis zapatos de tenis y a veces traje y corbata. *Textbook MP3s*

**3** **Expansion** Ask students to write three additional fill-in-the-blank sentences for a partner to complete.

**4** **Expansion** Go over the answers quickly in class. After each answer, indicate why a particular item does not belong. Ex: **1. Un sombrero no es un lugar donde compras cosas.**

**1 Script (continued)**
Para ir a la playa necesito un traje de baño, pantalones cortos y sandalias. ¿Qué más necesito? Creo que es todo. VICENTE: Buenos días. Soy Vicente. Estoy haciendo mis maletas porque mi familia y yo vamos a las montañas a esquiar. Los primeros dos días vamos a hacer una excursión por las montañas. Necesito zapatos de tenis, camisetas, una chaqueta y bluejeans. El tercer día vamos a esquiar. Necesito un abrigo, un suéter y botas… y gafas de sol. *Textbook MP3s*

**Teaching Tips**
• Show *Overhead PowerPoint #29* and go through the color words. Point to each drawing and ask: **¿De qué color es esta camiseta?** Ask about combinations. Ex: **Si combino rojo y azul, ¿qué color resulta? (morado)**
• Point to objects in the classroom and clothes you and students are wearing to elicit color words.
• Give dates and have students name the colors that they associate with each one. Ex: **el 14 de febrero (rojo, rosado); el 31 de octubre (negro, anaranjado)** You may want to repeat the process with brand names. Ex: **FedEx (anaranjado, morado, blanco)**
• Point out that color words are adjectives and agree in number and gender with the nouns they modify.

**5 Expansion** Add a visual aspect to this activity. Show magazine pictures of various products (cars, computers, etc.) and ask questions. Ex: **¿Es cara o barata esta computadora? (Es barata.)**

**6 Expansion** Point to students and ask others what color of clothing each is wearing. Ex: _____, ¿de qué color es la falda de _____? (Es _____.)

## Los colores

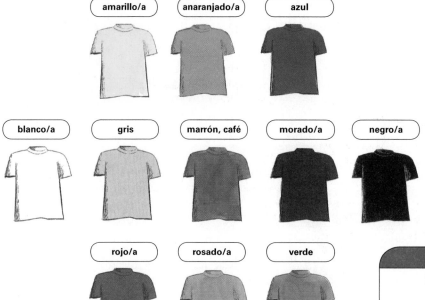

amarillo/a · anaranjado/a · azul

blanco/a · gris · marrón, café · morado/a · negro/a

rojo/a · rosado/a · verde

SUPERSITE

**¡LENGUA VIVA!**
The names of colors vary throughout the Spanish-speaking world. For example, in some countries, **anaranjado/a** may be referred to as **naranja**, **morado/a** as **púrpura**, and **rojo/a** as **colorado/a**.
Other terms that will prove helpful include **claro** (*light*) and **oscuro** (*dark*): **azul claro**, **azul oscuro**.

### Adjetivos

| | |
|---|---|
| barato/a | cheap |
| bueno/a | good |
| cada | each |
| caro/a | expensive |
| corto/a | short (in length) |
| elegante | elegant |
| hermoso/a | beautiful |
| largo/a | long |
| loco/a | crazy |
| nuevo/a | new |
| otro/a | other; another |
| pobre | poor |
| rico/a | rich |

**5 Contrastes** Complete each phrase with the opposite of the underlined word.

1. una corbata <u>barata</u> • unas camisas… caras
2. unas vendedoras <u>malas</u> • unos dependientes… buenos
3. un vestido <u>corto</u> • una falda… larga
4. un hombre muy <u>pobre</u> • una mujer muy… rica
5. una cartera <u>nueva</u> • un cinturón… viejo
6. unos trajes <u>hermosos</u> • unos bluejeans… feos
7. un impermeable <u>caro</u> • unos suéteres… baratos
8. unos calcetines <u>blancos</u> • unas medias… negras

**CONSULTA**
Like other adjectives you have seen, colors must agree in gender and number with the nouns they modify. Ex: **las camisas verdes, el vestido amarillo.** For a review of descriptive adjectives, see **Estructura 3.1**, pp. 80–81.

**6 Preguntas** Answer these questions with a classmate.

1. ¿De qué color es la rosa de Texas? Es amarilla.
2. ¿De qué color es la bandera (*flag*) de Canadá? Es roja y blanca.
3. ¿De qué color es la casa donde vive el presidente de los EE.UU.? Es blanca.
4. ¿De qué color es el océano Atlántico? Es azul.
5. ¿De qué color es la nieve? Es blanca.
6. ¿De qué color es el café? Es marrón./Es café.
7. ¿De qué color es el dólar de los EE.UU.? Es verde y blanco.
8. ¿De qué color es la cebra (*zebra*)? Es negra y blanca.

---

**TEACHING OPTIONS**

**Pairs** Ask student pairs to write a physical description of a well-known TV or cartoon character. Then have them read their descriptions for the rest of the class to guess. Ex: **Soy bajo y un poco gordo. Llevo pantalones cortos azules y una camiseta anaranjada. Tengo el pelo amarillo. También soy amarillo. ¿Quién soy? (Bart Simpson)**
**Game** Add a visual aspect to this vocabulary practice by playing

**Concentración**. On eight cards, write descriptions of clothing, including colors. Ex: **unos pantalones negros**. On another eight cards, draw pictures that match the descriptions. Shuffle the cards and place them face-down in four rows of four. In pairs, students select two cards. If the cards match, the pair keeps them. If the cards do not match, students replace them in their original position. The pair with the most cards at the end wins.

# Comunicación

**7** **Las maletas** With a classmate, answer these questions about the drawings.

1. ¿Qué ropa hay al lado de la maleta de Carmela?
   Hay una camiseta, unos pantalones cortos y un traje de baño.
2. ¿Qué hay en la maleta?
   Hay un sombrero y un par de sandalias.
3. ¿De qué color son las sandalias?
   Las sandalias son rojas.
4. ¿Adónde va Carmela?
   Va a la playa.

**CONSULTA**

To review weather, see **Lección 5, Contextos,** p. 142.

▶ 5. ¿Qué tiempo va a hacer?
   Va a hacer sol./ Va a hacer calor.
6. ¿Qué hay al lado de la maleta de Pepe?
   Hay un par de calcetines, un par de guantes, un suéter y una chaqueta.

**NOTA CULTURAL**

**Bariloche** is a popular resort for skiing in South America. Located in Argentina's Patagonia region, the town is also known for its chocolate factories and its beautiful lakes, mountains, and forests.

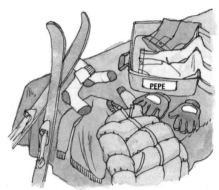

7. ¿Qué hay en la maleta?
   Hay dos pantalones.
8. ¿De qué color es el suéter?
   El suéter es rosado.
▶ 9. ¿Qué va a hacer Pepe en Bariloche?
   Va a esquiar.
10. ¿Qué tiempo va a hacer?
   Va a hacer frío./ Va a nevar.

**8** **¿Adónde van?** Imagine that you are going on a vacation with two classmates. Get together with your classmates and decide where you are going. Then draw three suitcases and write in each one what clothing each person is taking. Present your drawings to the rest of the class, answering these questions. Answers will vary.

- ¿Adónde van?
- ¿Qué tiempo va a hacer allí?
- ¿Qué van a hacer allí?
- ¿Qué hay en sus maletas?
- ¿De qué color es la ropa que llevan?

**9** **Preferencias** Use these questions to interview a classmate. Then switch roles. Answers will vary.

1. ¿Adónde vas a comprar ropa? ¿Por qué?
2. ¿Qué tipo de ropa prefieres? ¿Por qué?
3. ¿Cuáles son tus colores favoritos?
4. En tu opinión, ¿es importante comprar ropa nueva frecuentemente? ¿Por qué?
5. ¿Gastas mucho dinero en ropa cada mes? ¿Buscas rebajas?
6. ¿Regateas cuando compras ropa? ¿Usas una tarjeta de crédito?

**7** **Expansion** Ask volunteers what kind of clothing they take with them when they visit these places at these times: **Seattle en la primavera, la Florida en el verano, Minnesota en el invierno, San Francisco en el otoño.**

**8** **Teaching Tip** One class period before doing this activity, assign groups and have them discuss where they are going.

**8** **Expansion** Have students guess where the groups are going, based on the content of the suitcases. Facilitate guessing by asking questions 2–5.

**9** **Expansion**
- Ask students to report the findings of their interviews to the class. Ex: _____ **va a The Gap para comprar ropa porque allí la ropa no es cara. Prefiere ropa informal...**
- Have different pairs choose two famous people and explain their clothing preferences, using the questions from **Actividad 9.**

**TEACHING OPTIONS**

**Pairs** Have students form pairs and tell them they are going on a shopping spree. On paper strips, write varying dollar amounts, from ten dollars to three thousand, and distribute them. Have pairs tell what they will buy. Encourage creativity. Ex: **Tenemos quince dólares y vamos a Old Navy. Ella va a comprar medias amarillas y yo voy a comprar un sombrero en rebaja.**
**Extra Practice** Add an auditory aspect to this vocabulary

practice. Ask students to write an anonymous description of the article of clothing or outfit that best defines them. Collect the papers, shuffle them, and read the descriptions aloud for the class to guess.
**Pairs** Have pairs take turns describing classmates' clothing and guessing the person. Ex: **Esta persona usa bluejeans y una blusa marrón. Lleva sandalias blancas. (Es _____.)**

# ¡Qué ropa más bonita!

Javier e Inés van de compras al mercado.

## Section Goals

In **Fotonovela**, students will:
- receive comprehensible input from free-flowing discourse
- learn functional phrases involving clothing and how much things cost

**Instructional Resources**
**Supersite/DVD:** *Fotonovela*
**Supersite/IRCD:** *IRM*
(*Fotonovela* Videoscript & Translation, WBs/VM/LM Answer Key)
**WebSAM**
**Video Manual,** pp. 205–206

### Video Recap: Lección 5

Before doing this **Fotonovela** section, review the previous one with this activity.
1. ¿Qué pasa cuando llegan al hotel? (La empleada no encuentra la reservación.) 2. ¿Qué piensan Javier, Inés, Maite y Álex de las cabañas? (No están nada mal; están muy limpias y ordenadas.) 3. ¿Por qué quiere descansar Maite? (A las seis va a correr con Álex.) 4. ¿Qué está pensando Maite cuando los otros salen de la habitación? (Inés y Javier están juntos otra vez.)

### Video Synopsis

**Inés** and **Javier** go to an open-air market. **Inés** browses the market and eventually buys a purse for her sister, as well as a shirt and a hat for herself. **Javier** buys a sweater for the hike in the mountains.

### Teaching Tips

- Have students scan the **Fotonovela** captions for vocabulary related to clothing or colors.
- Point out the clothing that a few individual students are wearing and ask them some questions about it. Ex: **Me gusta esa camisa azul. ¿Es de algodón? ¿Dónde la compraste?**
- Point out that in September 2000 the U.S. dollar became the official currency of Ecuador.

**PERSONAJES**

**INÉS**

**JAVIER**

**EL VENDEDOR**

**1**

**INÉS** Javier, ¡qué ropa más bonita! A mí me gusta esa camisa blanca y azul. Debe ser de algodón. ¿Te gusta?

**JAVIER** Yo prefiero la camisa de la izquierda... la gris con rayas rojas. Hace juego con mis botas marrones.

**2**

**INÉS** Está bien, Javier. Mira, necesito comprarle un regalo a mi hermana Graciela. Acaba de empezar un nuevo trabajo...

**JAVIER** ¿Tal vez una bolsa?

**3**

**VENDEDOR** Esas bolsas son típicas de las montañas. ¿Le gusta?

**INÉS** Sí. Quiero comprarle una a mi hermana.

**6**

**VENDEDOR** Buenas tardes, joven. ¿Le puedo servir en algo?

**JAVIER** Sí. Voy a ir de excursión a las montañas y necesito un buen suéter.

**VENDEDOR** ¿Qué talla usa usted?

**JAVIER** Uso talla grande.

**7**

**VENDEDOR** Éstos son de talla grande.

**JAVIER** ¿Qué precio tiene ése?

**VENDEDOR** ¿Le gusta este suéter? Le cuesta ciento cincuenta mil sucres.

**JAVIER** Quiero comprarlo, pero, señor, no soy rico. ¿Ciento veinte mil sucres?

**8**

**VENDEDOR** Bueno, para usted... sólo ciento treinta mil sucres.

**JAVIER** Está bien, señor.

**recursos**

VM
pp. 205–206

SUPERSITE
panorama.vhlcentral.com
Lección 6

---

**Video Tips** General suggestions for using video clips in the classroom can be found on page IAE-12 of this Instructor's Annotated Edition.

**¡Qué ropa más bonita!** Photocopy the **Fotonovela** Videoscript (Supersite/IRCD) and white out 7–10 words in order to create a master for a cloze activity. Distribute photocopies of the master and have students fill in the missing words as they watch the **¡Qué ropa más bonita!** segment. You may want students to work in small groups and help each other fill in any gaps.

**INÉS** Me gusta aquélla. ¿Cuánto cuesta?

**VENDEDOR** Ésa cuesta ciento sesenta mil sucres. ¡Es de muy buena calidad!

**INÉS** Uy, demasiado cara. Quizás otro día.

**JAVIER** Acabo de comprarme un suéter. Y tú, ¿qué compraste?

**INÉS** Compré esta bolsa para mi hermana.

**INÉS** También compré una camisa y un sombrero. ¿Qué tal me veo?

**JAVIER** ¡Guapa, muy guapa!

## Expresiones útiles

### Talking about clothing

- **¡Qué ropa más bonita!**
  *What nice clothing!*
- **Me gusta esta/esa camisa blanca de rayas negras.**
  *I like this/that white shirt with black stripes.*
- **Está de moda.**
  *It's in fashion.*
- **Debe ser de algodón/lana/seda.**
  *It must be cotton/wool/silk.*
- **Es de cuadros/lunares/rayas.**
  *It's plaid/polka-dotted/striped.*
- **Me gusta este/ese suéter.**
  *I like this/that sweater.*
- **Es de muy buena calidad.**
  *It's very good quality.*
- **¿Qué talla lleva/usa usted?**
  *What size do you (form.) wear?*
  **Llevo/Uso talla grande.**
  *I wear a large.*
- **¿Qué número calza usted?**
  *What (shoe) size do you (form.) wear?*
  **Calzo el treinta y seis.**
  *I wear a size thirty-six.*

### Talking about how much things cost

- **¿Cuánto cuesta?**
  *How much does it cost?*
  **Sólo cuesta noventa mil sucres.**
  *It only costs ninety thousand sucres.*
  **Demasiado caro/a.**
  *Too expensive.*
  **Es una ganga.**
  *It's a bargain.*

### Saying what you bought

- **¿Qué compró Ud./él/ella?**
  *What did you (form.)/he/she buy?*
  **Compré esta bolsa para mi hermana.**
  *I bought this purse for my sister.*
- **¿Qué compraste?**
  *What did you (fam.) buy?*
  **Acabo de comprarme un sombrero.**
  *I have just bought myself a hat.*

**Teaching Tip** Have students work in pairs to read the parts of **Inés** and **Javier** as they arrive at the market (captions 1–2), **Inés** bargaining with the vendor (captions 3–5), and **Javier** bargaining with the vendor (captions 6–8). Ask for volunteers to read their segment for the class.

**Expresiones útiles**
- Point out the verb forms **compré, compraste,** and **compró.** Tell the class that these are forms of the verb **comprar** in the preterite tense, which is used to tell what happened in the past. Tell the class that **este, esta, ese,** and **esa** are examples of demonstrative adjectives, which are used to single out particular nouns. Also point out that the **me** in **Acabo de comprarme un sombrero** is an indirect object pronoun, used to tell for whom the hat was bought. Tell students that they will learn more about these concepts in **Estructura.**
- Help students with adjective placement and agreement when talking about clothing. Ask them to translate phrases such as these:
1. a white tie with gray and brown stripes (**una corbata blanca con rayas grises y marrones**) 2. black wool pants (**unos pantalones negros de lana**) 3. a yellow cotton shirt with purple polka dots (**una camisa amarilla de algodón de lunares morados**) 4. an elegant, blue plaid suit (**un traje azul elegante de cuadros**) 5. a red silk dress (**un vestido rojo de seda**) Discuss different possibilities for adjective placement and how it affects agreement.
Ex: **Un vestido rojo de seda** versus **Un vestido de seda roja.**

**TEACHING OPTIONS**

**TPR** Ask students to write **clientes** and **vendedores** on separate sheets on paper. Read aloud phrases from **Expresiones útiles** and have them hold up the paper(s) that correspond(s) to the people that would say that expression. Ex: **¿Qué número calza usted? (vendedores)**

**Small Groups** Have the class work in small groups to write statements about the **Fotonovela.** Ask each group to exchange its statements with another group. Each group will then write out the question that would have elicited each statement. Ex: **G1: Graciela acaba de empezar un nuevo trabajo. G2: ¿Quién acaba de empezar un nuevo trabajo?**

# ¿Qué pasó? SUPERSITE

## 1 ¿Cierto o falso? Indicate whether each sentence is **cierto** or **falso**. Correct the false statements.

|  | Cierto | Falso |
|---|---|---|
| 1. A Inés le gusta la camisa verde y amarilla. | ○ | ⊘ A Inés le gusta la camisa blanca y azul. |
| 2. Javier necesita comprarle un regalo a su hermana. | ○ | ⊘ Inés necesita comprarle un regalo a su hermana. |
| 3. Las bolsas en el mercado son típicas de las montañas. | ⊘ | ○ |
| 4. Javier busca un traje de baño. | ○ | ⊘ Javier busca un suéter. |

## 2 Identificar Provide the first initial of the person who would make each statement.

I 1. ¿Te gusta el sombrero que compré?
V 2. Estos suéteres son de talla grande. ¿Qué talla usa usted?
J 3. ¿Por qué no compras una bolsa para Graciela?
J 4. Creo que mis botas hacen juego con la camisa.
V 5. Estas bolsas son excelentes, de muy buena calidad.
I 6. Creo que las blusas aquí son de algodón.

**INÉS**

**JAVIER**

**EL VENDEDOR**

## 3 Completar Answer the questions using the information in the **Fotonovela**.

1. Inés quiere comprarle un regalo a su hermana. ¿Por qué? Porque su hermana acaba de empezar un nuevo trabajo.
2. ¿Cuánto cuesta la bolsa de las montañas? Cuesta ciento sesenta mil sucres.
3. ¿Por qué necesita Javier un buen suéter? Porque va de excursión a las montañas.
4. ¿Cuál es el precio final del suéter? El precio final del suéter es ciento treinta mil sucres.
5. ¿Qué compra Inés en el mercado? Inés compra una bolsa, una camisa y un sombrero.

## 4 Conversar With a partner, role-play a conversation between a customer and a salesperson in an open-air market. Use these expressions and also look at **Expresiones útiles** on the previous page.
Answers will vary.

| ¿Qué desea? | Estoy buscando... | Prefiero el/la rojo/a. |
|---|---|---|
| *What would you like?* | *I'm looking for...* | *I prefer the red one.* |

| **Cliente/a** | **Vendedor(a)** |
|---|---|
| Say good afternoon. | Greet the customer and ask what he/she would like. |
| Explain that you are looking for a particular item of clothing. | Show him/her some items and ask what he/she prefers. |
| Discuss colors and sizes. | Discuss colors and sizes. |
| Ask for the price and begin bargaining. | Tell him/her a price. Negotiate a price. |
| Settle on a price and purchase the item. | Accept a price and say thank you. |

NATIONAL communication STANDARDS

# Pronunciación

## The consonants **d** and **t**

**¿Dónde?**  **vender**  **nadar**  **verdad**

Like **b** and **v**, the Spanish **d** can also have a hard sound or a soft sound, depending on which letters appear next to it.

**Don**  **dinero**  **tienda**  **falda**

At the beginning of a phrase and after **n** or **l**, the letter **d** is pronounced with a hard sound. This sound is similar to the English *d* in *dog*, but a little softer and duller. The tongue should touch the back of the upper teeth, not the roof of the mouth.

**medias**  **verde**  **vestido**  **huésped**

In all other positions, **d** has a soft sound. It is similar to the English *th* in *there*, but a little softer.

**Don Diego no tiene el diccionario.**

When **d** begins a word, its pronunciation depends on the previous word. At the beginning of a phrase or after a word that ends in **n** or **l**, it is pronounced as a hard **d**.

**Doña Dolores es de la capital.**

Words that begin with **d** are pronounced with a soft **d** if they appear immediately after a word that ends in a vowel or any consonant other than **n** or **l**.

**traje**  **pantalones**  **tarjeta**  **tienda**

When pronouncing the Spanish **t**, the tongue should touch the back of the upper teeth, not the roof of the mouth. Unlike the English *t*, no air is expelled from the mouth.

**Práctica** Read these phrases aloud to practice the **d** and the **t**.

1. Hasta pronto.
2. De nada.
3. Mucho gusto.
4. Lo siento.
5. No hay de qué.
6. ¿De dónde es usted?
7. ¡Todos a bordo!
8. No puedo.
9. Es estupendo.
10. No tengo computadora.
11. ¿Cuándo vienen?
12. Son las tres y media.

**Oraciones** Read these sentences aloud to practice the **d** and the **t**.

1. Don Teodoro tiene una tienda en un almacén en La Habana.
2. Don Teodoro vende muchos trajes, vestidos y zapatos todos los días.
3. Un día un turista, Federico Machado, entra en la tienda para comprar un par de botas.
4. Federico regatea con don Teodoro y compra las botas y también un par de sandalias.

**Refranes** Read these sayings aloud to practice the **d** and the **t**.

> En la variedad está el gusto.[1]

> Aunque la mona se vista de seda, mona se queda.[2]

[1] *Variety is the spice of life.* [2] *You can't make a silk purse out of a sow's ear.*

**Section Goal**

In **Pronunciación**, students will be introduced to the pronunciation of the letters **d** and **t**.

**Instructional Resources**
**Supersite:** Textbook & Lab MP3 Audio Files **Lección 6**
**Supersite/IRCD:** *IRM* (Textbook Audio Script, Lab Audio Script, WBs/VM/LM Answer Key)
**WebSAM**
**Lab Manual,** p. 32
*Cuaderno para hispanohablantes*

**Teaching Tips**
- Explain that **d** has a hard sound at the beginning of a phrase or after **n** or **l**. Write **don, dinero, tienda,** and **falda** on the board and have the class pronounce them.
- Explain that **d** has a soft sound in all other positions. Pronounce **medias, verde, vestido,** and **huésped** and have the class repeat.
- Point out that within phrases, **d** at the beginning of a word has a hard or soft sound depending on the last sound of the preceding word. Read the examples aloud and have the class repeat.
- Explain that **t** is pronounced with the tongue at the back of the upper teeth and that, unlike English, no air is expelled from the mouth. Pronounce **traje, pantalones, tarjeta,** and **tienda** and have the class repeat. Then pronounce pairs of similar-sounding Spanish and English words, having students focus on the difference between the **t** sounds: **ti***/tea*; **tal***/tall*; **todo***/toad*; **tema***/tame*; **tela***/tell.*

**Práctica/Oraciones/ Refranes** These exercises are recorded in the *Textbook MP3s*. You may want to play the audio so that students practice the pronunciation point by listening to Spanish spoken by speakers other than yourself.

**Extra Practice** Write some additional proverbs on the board and have the class practice saying each one. Ex: **De tal padre, tal hijo.** (*Like father, like son.*) **El que tiene tejado de cristal no tira piedras al vecino.** (*People who live in glass houses shouldn't throw stones.*) **Cuatro ojos ven más que dos.** (*Two heads are better than one.*)

**Extra Practice** Write on the board the names of these famous Cuban literary figures: **José Martí, Julián del Casal, Gertrudis Gómez de Avellaneda,** and **Dulce María Loynaz.** Say the names aloud and have the class repeat. Then ask volunteers to explain the pronunciation of each **d** and **t** in these names.

---

**EN DETALLE**

# Los mercados al aire libre

**El Rastro**

**Daily or weekly mercados al aire libre** in the Spanish-speaking world are an important part of commerce and culture, where locals, tourists, and vendors interact. People come to the marketplace to shop, socialize, taste local foods, and watch street performers. One can simply wander from one **puesto** (*stand*) to the next, browsing through fresh fruits and vegetables, clothing, CDs and DVDs, jewelry, tapestries, pottery, and crafts (**artesanías**). Used merchandise—such as antiques, clothing, and books—can also be found at markets.

When shoppers see an item they like, they can bargain with the vendor. Friendly bargaining is an expected ritual and usually results in lowering the price by about twenty-five percent. Occasionally vendors may give the customer a little extra quantity of the item they purchase; this free addition is known as **la ñapa**.

Many open-air markets are also tourist attractions. The market in Otavalo, Ecuador, is world-famous and has taken place every Saturday since pre-Incan times. This market is well-known for the colorful textiles woven by the **otavaleños**, the indigenous people of the area. One can also find leather goods and wood carvings from nearby towns. Another popular market is **El Rastro**, held every Sunday in Madrid, Spain. Sellers set up **puestos** along the streets to display their wares, which range from local artwork and antiques to inexpensive clothing and electronics.

**Mercado de Otavalo**

### Otros mercados famosos

| Mercado | Lugar | Productos |
|---|---|---|
| Feria Artesanal de Recoleta | Buenos Aires, Argentina | artesanías |
| Mercado Central | Santiago, Chile | mariscos°, pescado°, frutas, verduras° |
| Tianguis Cultural del Chopo | Ciudad de México, México | ropa, música, revistas, libros, arte, artesanías |
| El mercado de Chichicastenango | Chichicastenango, Guatemala | frutas y verduras, flores°, cerámica, textiles |

mariscos *seafood* pescado *fish* verduras *vegetables*
flores *flowers*

---

**ACTIVIDADES**

**1 ¿Cierto o falso?** Indicate whether these statements are **cierto** or **falso**. Correct the false statements.

1. Generally, open-air markets specialize in one type of goods. **Falso.** They sell a variety of goods.
2. Bargaining is commonplace at outdoor markets. **Cierto.**
3. Only new goods can be found at open-air markets. **Falso.** They sell both new and used goods.
4. A Spaniard in search of antiques could search at **El Rastro**. **Cierto.**
5. If you are in Guatemala and want to buy ceramics, you can go to Chichicastenango. **Cierto.**
6. A **ñapa** is a tax on open-air market goods. **Falso.** A **ñapa** is a free addition sometimes given to customers.
7. The **otavaleños** weave colorful textiles to sell on Saturdays. **Cierto.**
8. Santiago's **Mercado Central** is known for books and music. **Falso.** It's known for seafood, fish, fruits, and vegetables.

---

## ASÍ SE DICE

### La ropa

| | |
|---|---|
| la chamarra (Méx.) | la chaqueta |
| de manga corta/larga | *short/long-sleeved* |
| los mahones (P. Rico); el pantalón de mezclilla (Méx.); los tejanos (Esp.); los vaqueros (Arg., Cuba, Esp., Uru.) | los bluejeans |
| la marca | *brand* |
| la playera (Méx.); la remera (Arg.) | la camiseta |

## EL MUNDO HISPANO

### Diseñadores de moda

○ **Adolfo Domínguez** (España) Su ropa tiene un estilo minimalista y práctico. Usa telas° naturales y cómodas en sus diseños.

○ **Silvia Tcherassi** (Colombia) Los colores vivos y líneas asimétricas de sus vestidos y trajes muestran influencias tropicales.

○ **Óscar de la Renta** (República Dominicana) Diseña ropa opulenta para la mujer clásica.

○ **Narciso Rodríguez** (EE.UU.) En sus diseños delicados y finos predominan los colores blanco y negro. Hizo° el vestido de boda° de Carolyn Bessette Kennedy.

telas *fabrics* Hizo *He made* boda *wedding*

## PERFIL

# Carolina Herrera

In 1980, at the urging of some friends, **Carolina Herrera** created a fashion collection as a "test." The Venezuelan designer received such a favorable response that within one year she moved her family from Caracas to New York City and created her own label, Carolina Herrera, Ltd.

"I love elegance and intricacy, but whether it is in a piece of clothing or a fragrance, the intricacy must appear as simplicity," Herrera once stated. She quickly found that many sophisticated women agreed; from the start, her sleek and glamorous

designs have been in constant demand. Over the years, Herrera has grown her brand into a veritable fashion empire that encompasses her fashion and bridal collections, cosmetics, perfume, and accessories that are sold around the globe.

### SUPERSITE Conexión Internet

¿Qué marcas de ropa son populares en el mundo hispano?

Go to **panorama.vhlcentral.com** to find more cultural information related to this **Cultura** section.

## ACTIVIDADES

**2 Comprensión** Complete these sentences.

1. Adolfo Domínguez usa telas <u>naturales</u> y <u>cómodas</u> en su ropa.
2. Si hace fresco en el D.F., puedes llevar una <u>chamarra</u>.
3. La diseñadora <u>Carolina Herrera</u> hace ropa, perfumes y más.
4. La ropa de <u>Silvia Tcherassi</u> muestra influencias tropicales.
5. Los <u>mahones</u> son una ropa casual en Puerto Rico.

**3 Mi ropa favorita** Write a brief description of your favorite article of clothing. Mention what store it is from, the brand, colors, fabric, style, and any other information. Then get together with a small group, collect the descriptions, and take turns reading them aloud at random. Can the rest of the group guess whose favorite piece of clothing is being described? Answers will vary.

**recursos**

panorama.vhlcentral.com
Lección 6

## Section Goals

In **Estructura 6.1**, students will learn:
- the uses of **saber** and **conocer**
- more uses of the personal **a**
- other verbs conjugated like **conocer**

---

**Instructional Resources**
**Supersite:** Lab MP3 Audio Files **Lección 6**
**Supersite/IRCD:** *PowerPoints* (**Lección 6 Estructura** Presentation); *IRM* (Lab Audio Script, WBs/VM/LM Answer Key)
**WebSAM**
**Workbook,** p. 61
**Lab Manual,** p. 33
*Cuaderno para hispanohablantes*

---

## Teaching Tips

- Point out the irregular **yo** forms of **saber** and **conocer**.
- Divide the board or an overhead transparency into two columns with the headings **saber** and **conocer**. In the first column, write the uses of **saber** and model them by asking individuals what they know how to do and what factual information they know. Ex: _____, ¿**sabes bailar salsa? ¿Sabes mi número de teléfono?** In the second column, write the uses of **conocer** and model them by asking individuals about people and places they know. Ex: _____, ¿**conoces Cuba? ¿Conoces a Anier García?**
- Further distinguish the uses of **saber** and **conocer** by making statements such as: **Sé quién es el presidente de este país, pero no lo conozco.**
- Point out that the verbs listed under **¡Atención!** are conjugated like **conocer**. Ask volunteers to provide the **yo** form of each verb.

---

### 6.1 Saber and conocer ⬤SUPERSITE

**ANTE TODO** Spanish has two verbs that mean *to know*: **saber** and **conocer**. They cannot be used interchangeably. Note the irregular **yo** forms.

#### The verbs saber and conocer

| | | saber *(to know)* | conocer *(to know)* |
|---|---|---|---|
| **SINGULAR FORMS** | yo | sé | conozco |
| | tú | sabes | conoces |
| | Ud./él/ella | sabe | conoce |
| **PLURAL FORMS** | nosotros/as | sabemos | conocemos |
| | vosotros/as | sabéis | conocéis |
| | Uds./ellos/ellas | saben | conocen |

▶ **Saber** means *to know a fact or piece(s) of information* or *to know how to do something.*

No **sé** tu número de teléfono.
*I don't know your telephone number.*

Mi hermana **sabe** hablar francés.
*My sister knows how to speak French.*

▶ **Conocer** means *to know* or *be familiar/acquainted* with a person, place, or thing.

¿**Conoces** la ciudad de Nueva York?
*Do you know New York City?*

No **conozco** a tu amigo Esteban.
*I don't know your friend Esteban.*

▶ When the direct object of **conocer** is a person or pet, the personal **a** is used.

¿Conoces La Habana?     *but*     ¿Conoces **a** Celia Cruz?
*Do you know Havana?*          *Do you know Celia Cruz?*

▶ **¡Atención!** These verbs are also conjugated like **conocer**.

| conducir | parecer | ofrecer | traducir |
|---|---|---|---|
| *to drive* | *to seem* | *to offer* | *to translate* |

*(handwritten)* A SAbe + adjective = TASTES like
ex: SAbe A AJO = IT TASTES like gArlic

---

**¡INTÉNTALO!** Provide the appropriate forms of these verbs. The first item in each column has been done for you.

**saber**

1. José no ___sabe___ la hora.
2. Sara y yo ___sabemos___ jugar al tenis.
3. ¿Por qué no ___sabes___ tú estos verbos?
4. Mis padres ___saben___ hablar japonés.
5. Yo ___sé___ a qué hora es la clase.
6. Usted no ___sabe___ dónde vivo.
7. Mi hermano no ___sabe___ nadar.
8. Nosotros ___sabemos___ muchas cosas.

**conocer**

1. Usted y yo ___conocemos___ bien Miami.
2. ¿Tú ___conoces___ a mi amigo Manuel?
3. Sergio y Taydé ___conocen___ mi pueblo.
4. Emiliano ___conoce___ a mis padres.
5. Yo ___conozco___ muy bien el centro.
6. ¿Ustedes ___conocen___ la tienda Gigante?
7. Nosotras ___conocemos___ una playa hermosa.
8. ¿Usted ___conoce___ a mi profesora?

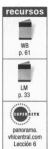

**recursos**

WB p. 61

LM p. 33

SUPERSITE
panorama. vhlcentral.com
Lección 6

---

**TEACHING OPTIONS**

**TPR** Divide the class into two teams, **saber** and **conocer**, and have them line up. Indicate the first member of each team and call out a sentence in English that uses *to know* (Ex: We know the answer.). The team member whose verb corresponds to the English sentence has five seconds to step forward and provide the Spanish translation.

**Extra Practice** Ask students to jot down three things they know how to do well (**saber** + *[infinitive]* + **bien**). Collect the papers, shuffle them, and read the sentences aloud. Have the rest of the class guess who wrote the sentences.

# Práctica y Comunicación

**1** **Completar** Indicate the correct verb for each sentence.

1. Mis hermanos (conocen/**saben**) conducir, pero yo no (**sé**/conozco).
2. —¿(Conocen/**Saben**) ustedes dónde está el estadio? —No, no (conocemos/**sabemos**).
3. —¿(**Conoces**/Sabes) a Cher? —Bueno, (**sé**/conozco) quién es, pero no la (**conozco**/sé).
4. Mi profesora (sabe/**conoce**) Cuba y también (conoce/**sabe**) bailar salsa.

**2** **Combinar** Combine elements from each column to create sentences. *Answers will vary.*

| A | B | C |
|---|---|---|
| Shakira | (no) conocer | Jessica Simpson |
| los Yankees | (no) saber | cantar y bailar |
| el primer ministro | | La Habana Vieja |
| de Canadá | | muchas personas importantes |
| mis amigos y yo | | hablar dos lenguas extranjeras |
| tú | | jugar al béisbol |

**3** **Preguntas** In pairs, ask each other these questions. Answer with complete sentences.
*Answers will vary.*

1. ¿Conoces a un(a) cantante famoso/a? ¿Te gusta cómo canta?
2. En tu familia, ¿quién sabe cantar? ¿Tu opinión es objetiva?
3. Y tú, ¿conduces bien o mal? ¿Y tus amigos?
4. Si un(a) amigo/a no conduce muy bien, ¿le ofreces crítica constructiva?
5. ¿Cómo parece estar el/la profesor(a) hoy? ¿Y tus compañeros de clase?

**4** **Entrevista** Jot down three things you know how to do, three people you know, and three places you are familiar with. Then, in a small group, find out what you have in common. *Answers will vary.*

> **modelo**
>
> **Estudiante 1:** ¿Conocen ustedes a David Lomas?
> **Estudiante 2:** Sí, conozco a David. Vivimos en la misma residencia estudiantil.
> **Estudiante 3:** No, no lo conozco. ¿Cómo es?

**5** **Anuncio** In groups, read the ad and answer the questions. *Answers will vary.*

1. Busquen ejemplos de los verbos **saber** y **conocer**.
2. ¿Qué saben del Centro Comercial Oviedo?
3. ¿Qué pueden hacer en el Centro Comercial Oviedo?
4. ¿Conocen otros centros comerciales similares? ¿Cómo se llaman? ¿Dónde están?
5. ¿Conocen un centro comercial en otro país? ¿Cómo es?

Él sabe dónde comer
lo que más le gusta

Él sabe cómo jugar
cuatro horas seguidas

Él sabe dónde
está su regalo
de cumpleaños

Él sabe dónde divertirse

... y usted sabe dónde puede
encontrar un poco de todo.
¿Conoce algún otro lugar como éste?

**Oviedo**
Centro Comercial
Sabe lo que te gusta

---

**TEACHING OPTIONS**

**Extra Practice** Use the Internet to research advertising slogans that use verbs from **Estructura 6.1**. In groups, have students guess the company or product for each slogan. Ex: **Sabemos por qué vuelas. (American Airlines), No es lo mismo conducir que conducir. (BMW), Necesitas saber siempre. (CNN)**
**Small Groups** Ask students to write down four sentences (two true, two false) using **saber** and **conocer**. In groups of three,

have them read their sentences aloud. The rest of the group should guess if the person is lying or telling the truth.
**Large Group** Ask students to write down six things they know how to do. Have them circulate around the room to find out who else knows how to do those things, jotting down the names of those that answer **sí**. Have students report back to the class. Ex: **Keisha y yo sabemos tocar el piano.**

---

**Side column:**

**1** **Teaching Tip** To challenge students, write this activity on the board as cloze sentences.

**1** **Expansion** Give students these sentences as items 5–8:
**5. No (sé/conozco) a qué hora es el examen. (sé) 6. (Conoces/Sabes) las ruinas de Machu Picchu, ¿verdad? (Conoces) 7. ¿Quieren (saber/conocer) dónde va a ser la fiesta? (saber) 8. Esta noche voy a salir con mi novia, pero mis padres no lo (conocen/saben). Todavía no la (conocen/saben)… ¡no (conocen/saben) quién es ella! (saben, conocen, saben)**

**2** **Teaching Tip** To simplify, before beginning the activity, read through column C and have students determine whether each item takes the verb **saber** or **conocer**.

**2** **Expansion**
- Add more elements to column A (Ex: **yo, mis padres, mi profesor(a) de español**) and continue the activity.
- Ask students questions about what certain celebrities know how to do or whom they know. Ex: **Brad Pitt, ¿conoce a Angelina Jolie? (Sí, la conoce.) David Ortiz, ¿sabe jugar al béisbol? (Sí, sabe jugarlo.)**

**3** **Expansion** In pairs, have students create three additional questions using the verbs **conducir, ofrecer,** and **traducir**. Then have students form groups of four to ask and answer their questions.

**4** **Teaching Tip** To simplify, have students divide a sheet of paper into three columns with the headings **Sé, Conozco a,** and **Conozco**. Then have them complete their lists.

**5** **Expansion** Ask each group to create an advertisement using two examples each of **saber** and **conocer**.

**Section Goals**

**Section Goals**

In **Estructura 6.2**, students will learn:

- to identify an indirect object noun
- how to use indirect object pronouns

---

**Instructional Resources**

**Supersite:** Lab MP3 Audio Files **Lección 6**

**Supersite/IRCD:** *PowerPoints* (**Lección 6 Estructura** Presentation); *IRM* (Lab Audio Script, WBs/VM/LM Answer Key)

**WebSAM**

**Workbook,** pp. 62–63

**Lab Manual,** p. 34

***Cuaderno para hispanohablantes***

---

**Teaching Tips**

- Write on the board: **Mi novio me escribe un mensaje electrónico.** Ask students what the direct object of the verb is. Then tell them that an indirect object answers the questions *to whom* or *for whom*.

- Write the indirect object pronouns on the board. Ask how their forms differ from those of direct object pronouns.

- Ask volunteers to read aloud the video-still captions, and have the class identify the indirect object pronoun in each. Have students identify the two indirect object nouns to which the pronouns refer.

- Point out that the redundant use of both an indirect object pronoun and an indirect object noun is common in Spanish and that, unlike in English, it is the indirect object noun that is optional, not the pronoun. Ex: **Ella le vende la ropa** is possible but **Ella vende la ropa a Elena** is less common.

---

## (6.2) Indirect object pronouns

**ANTE TODO** In **Lección 5**, you learned that a direct object receives the action of the verb directly. In contrast, an indirect object receives the action of the verb indirectly.

| SUBJECT | I.O. PRONOUN | VERB | DIRECT OBJECT | INDIRECT OBJECT |
|---------|--------------|------|---------------|-----------------|
| Roberto | **le** | presta | cien pesos | **a Luisa**. |
| *Roberto* | | *lends* | *100 pesos* | *to Luisa*. |

An indirect object is a noun or pronoun that answers the question *to whom* or *for whom* an action is done. In the preceding example, the indirect object answers this question:

**¿A quién le presta Roberto cien pesos?** *To whom does Roberto lend 100 pesos?*

### Indirect object pronouns

| Singular forms | | Plural forms | |
|----------------|--|--------------|--|
| **me** | (to, for) *me* | **nos** | (to, for) *us* |
| **te** | (to, for) *you* (fam.) | **os** | (to, for) *you* (fam.) |
| **le** | (to, for) *you* (form.) (to, for) *him; her* | **les** | (to, for) *you* (form.) (to, for) *them* |

▶ **¡Atención!** The forms of indirect object pronouns for the first and second persons (**me, te, nos, os**) are the same as the direct object pronouns. Indirect object pronouns agree in number with the corresponding nouns, but not in gender.

*Buenas tardes. ¿Le puedo servir en algo?*

*Quiero comprarle una a mi hermana.*

## Using indirect object pronouns

▶ Spanish speakers commonly use both an indirect object pronoun and the noun to which it refers in the same sentence. This is done to emphasize and clarify to whom the pronoun refers.

| I.O. PRONOUN | | INDIRECT OBJECT | I.O. PRONOUN | | INDIRECT OBJECT |
|--------------|--|-----------------|--------------|--|-----------------|

Ella **le** vende la ropa **a Elena**.        **Les** prestamos el dinero **a Inés y a Álex**.

▶ Indirect object pronouns are also used without the indirect object noun when the person for whom the action is being done is known.

Ana **le** presta la falda **a Elena**.          También **le** presta unos bluejeans.
*Ana lends her skirt to Elena.*            *She also lends her a pair of blue jeans.*

---

---

**TEACHING OPTIONS**

**Extra Practice** Write sentences like these on the board: **1. Ana te prepara unos tacos. 2. Pablo no me escribe. 3. Le presto dinero a Luisa. 4. Les compramos unos regalos a los niños. 5. María nos habla.** Ask students to come to the board and underline the direct objects and circle the indirect objects. If the indirect object is implied, have them write *Impl.* next to the sentence.

**Small Groups** Have students work in groups of three. Have Student A "lend" an object to Student B and say: **Te presto mi...** Student B responds: **Me prestas tu...** Student C says: _____ **le presta a** _____ **su...** Have groups practice until each member has begun the chain twice. Practice plural pronouns by having two groups join together and two students "lend" something to two other students.

▶ Indirect object pronouns are usually placed before the conjugated form of the verb. In negative sentences the pronoun is placed between **no** and the conjugated verb.

> Martín **me** compra un regalo.          Eva **no me** escribe cartas.
> *Martín buys me a gift.*                *Eva doesn't write me letters.*

**CONSULTA**

For more information on accents, see **Lección 4, Pronunciación**, p. 115, **Lección 10, Ortografía**, p. 315, and **Lección 11, Ortografía**, p. 349.

▶ When a conjugated verb is followed by an infinitive or the present progressive, the indirect object pronoun may be placed before the conjugated verb or attached to the infinitive or present participle. **¡Atención!** When an indirect object pronoun is attached to a present participle, an accent mark is added to maintain the proper stress.

> Él no quiere **pagarte**./          Él está **escribiéndole** una postal a ella./
> Él no **te** quiere pagar.           Él **le** está escribiendo una postal a ella.
> *He does not want to pay you.*     *He is writing a postcard to her.*

▶ Because the indirect object pronouns **le** and **les** have multiple meanings, Spanish speakers often clarify to whom the pronouns refer with the preposition **a** + [*pronoun*] or **a** + [*noun*].

UNCLARIFIED STATEMENTS         CLARIFIED STATEMENTS

Yo **le** compro un abrigo.          Yo **le** compro un abrigo **a usted/él/ella.**

Ella **le** describe un libro.        Ella **le** describe un libro **a Juan.**

UNCLARIFIED STATEMENTS         CLARIFIED STATEMENTS

Él **les** vende unos sombreros.     Él **les** vende unos sombreros **a ustedes/ellos/ellas.**

Ellos **les** hablan muy claro.      Ellos **les** hablan muy claro **a los clientes.**

▶ The irregular verbs **dar** (*to give*) and **decir** are often used with direct and indirect object pronouns.

### The verb dar (*to give*)

| Singular forms | | Plural forms | |
|---|---|---|---|
| yo | **doy** | nosotros/as | **damos** |
| tú | **das** | vosotros/as | **dais** |
| Ud./él/ella | **da** | Uds./ellos/ellas | **dan** |

**CONSULTA**

Remember that **decir** is a stem-changing verb (**e:i**) with an irregular **yo** form: **digo**. To review the present tense of **decir**, see **Estructura 4.3**, p. 125.

**Me dan** una fiesta cada año.       **Te digo** la verdad.
*They give (throw) me a party every year.*   *I'm telling you the truth.*

Voy a **darle** consejos.           No **les digo** mentiras a mis padres.
*I'm going to give her advice.*      *I don't tell lies to my parents.*

**recursos**

WB pp. 62–63

LM p. 34

panorama. vhlcentral.com Lección 6

**¡INTÉNTALO!**   Use the cues in parentheses to provide the indirect object pronoun for the sentence. The first item has been done for you.

1. Juan ___le___ quiere dar un regalo. (*to Elena*)
2. María ___nos___ prepara un café. (*for us*)
3. Beatriz y Felipe ___me___ escriben desde (*from*) Cuba. (*to me*)
4. Marta y yo ___les___ compramos unos guantes. (*for them*)
5. Los vendedores ___te___ venden ropa. (*to you, fam. sing.*)
6. La dependienta ___nos___ muestra los guantes. (*to us*)

---

**Teaching Tips**

- Point out that the position of indirect object pronouns in a sentence is the same as that of direct object pronouns.
- Ask individuals questions using indirect object pronouns. Ex: **¿A quién le ofreces ayuda? ¿Les das consejos a tus amigos? ¿Qué te dicen tus padres que no debes hacer? ¿Les dices mentiras a tus padres? ¿Cuándo vas a escribirles a tus abuelos?**
- After going over the **¡Inténtalo!** orally with the class, ask students which items might require clarification (items 1 and 4). Ask them what they would add to each sentence in order to clarify **le** or **les**.
- As a comprehension check, have students write answers to these questions: 1. **Es el cumpleaños de tu mejor amigo. ¿Qué vas a comprarle? 2. ¿A quiénes les hablas todos los días? 3. ¿Quién te presta dinero cuando lo necesitas? 4. ¿Quién les está enseñando español a ustedes?**

**TEACHING OPTIONS**

**Video** Replay the *Fotonovela*. Ask students to note each time an indirect object pronoun is used. Point out that the pronouns used with **gustar** are indirect objects because they answer the question (*is pleasing*) *to whom*. Then, have students find each use of **le** and **les** and state to whom the pronouns refer.
**Game** Give each student an envelope and a sheet of paper. Ask them to write a sentence using an indirect object pronoun, cut the paper into strips (one word per strip), shuffle them, and place them in the envelope. Then have students pass their envelopes to the person sitting behind them. Allow thirty seconds for them to decipher the sentence and write it down, before placing the shuffled strips back into the envelope and passing it on. After three minutes, the row with the most correctly deciphered sentences wins.

# Práctica

**1 Teaching Tip** Have students find the indirect object in each sentence and circle it.

**1 Expansion** Have students write four sentences about themselves, leaving out the indirect object pronoun. Ex: **Yo ____ doy un regalo a mis padres. Mi tío ____ compra a mí una moto.** Then have them exchange papers with a classmate and complete the sentences.

**2 Teaching Tip** Have students describe to a partner what they see in the photos. Ask them to describe not only the action, but also each person's physical appearance and clothing.

**2 Expansion** Divide the class into groups of four. Have each student pick a photo to present to the group as a verbal portrait, including an introductory sentence that sets the scene, followed by a body and conclusion. The verbal portrait should answer the questions *who, what, where, when,* and *why* with regard to what is seen in the photo. After each group member has presented his or her photo, the group chooses one to present to the class.

**3 Expansion** Have students convert three of their statements into questions, using **¿Quién?, ¿A quién?,** and **¿Qué?** Have pairs take turns asking and answering their questions. Ex: **¿Quién les vende la ropa? (el dependiente) ¿A quiénes les das regalos? (a mis primos) ¿Qué te explican tus padres? (los problemas)**

**1  Completar** Fill in the correct pronouns to complete Mónica's description of her family's holiday shopping.

1. Juan y yo ___le___ damos una blusa a nuestra hermana Gisela.
2. Mi tía ___nos___ da a nosotros una mesa para la casa.
3. Gisela ___le___ da dos corbatas a su novio.
4. A mi mamá yo ___le___ doy un par de guantes negros.
5. A mi profesora ___le___ doy dos libros de José Martí.
6. Juan ___les___ da un regalo a mis padres.
7. Mis padres ___me___ dan a mí un traje nuevo.
8. Y a ti, yo ___te___ doy un regalo también. ¿Quieres verlo?

**NOTA CULTURAL**

Cuban writer and patriot **José Martí** (1853–1895) was born in **La Habana Vieja**, the old colonial center of Havana. Founded by Spanish explorers in the early 1500s, Havana, along with San Juan, Puerto Rico, served as a major stopping point for Spaniards traveling to Mexico and South America.

**2  Describir** Describe what is happening in these photos based on the cues provided.

1. escribir / mensaje electrónico Álex le escribe un mensaje electrónico (a Ricardo).

2. mostrar / fotos Javier les muestra fotos (a Inés y a Maite).

3. dar / documentos La Sra. Ramos le da los documentos (a Maite).

4. pedir / llaves Don Francisco le pide las llaves (a la empleada).

5. vender / suéter El vendedor le vende un suéter (a Javier).

6. comprar / bolsa Inés le compra una bolsa (a su hermana).

**NOTA CULTURAL**

Javier and Inés are shopping in the open-air market in Otavalo, Ecuador. **La Habana Vieja**, Cuba, is the site of another well-known outdoor market. Located in the **Plaza de la Catedral**, it is a place where Cuban painters, artists, and sculptors sell their work, and other vendors offer handmade crafts and clothing.

**3  Combinar** Use an item from each column and an indirect object pronoun to create logical sentences. Answers will vary.

> **modelo**
>
> Mis padres les dan regalos a mis primos.

| A | B | C | D |
|---|---|---|---|
| yo | comprar | correo electrónico | mí |
| el dependiente | dar | corbata | ustedes |
| el profesor Arce | decir | dinero en efectivo | clienta |
| la vendedora | escribir | ejercicio | novia |
| mis padres | explicar | problemas | primos |
| tú | pagar | regalos | ti |
| nosotros/as | prestar | ropa | nosotros |
| ¿? | vender | ¿? | ¿? |

**TEACHING OPTIONS**

**Heritage Speakers** Ask heritage speakers to create a radio commercial for their favorite clothing store. Have them tell customers what they can buy, for whom, and at what price.
**Pairs** Ask students to write five questions that elicit indirect object pronouns. In pairs, have students ask their questions and write down their partner's answers. Then ask pairs to review the questions and answers for accuracy.

**Pairs** Brainstorm on the board a list of things that parents tell high school-age or college-age children they should or should not do. Ex: **Los padres les dicen a sus hijos que no deben tomar mucho café.** Then have pairs ask each other if their parents tell them these things and summarize their findings for the class. Ex: **Nuestros padres nos dicen que no debemos tomar mucho café.**

# Comunicación

**4** **Entrevista** Take turns with a classmate asking and answering questions using the word bank. *Answers will vary.*

> **modelo**
>
> escribir mensajes electrónicos
> **Estudiante 1:** ¿A quién le escribes mensajes electrónicos?
> **Estudiante 2:** Le escribo mensajes electrónicos a mi hermano.

| | |
|---|---|
| cantar canciones de amor (*love songs*) | escribir mensajes electrónicos |
| comprar ropa | mostrar fotos de un viaje |
| dar una fiesta | pedir dinero |
| decir mentiras | preparar comida (*food*) mexicana |

**5** **¡Somos ricos!** You and your classmates chipped in on a lottery ticket and you won! Now you want to spend money on your loved ones. In groups of three, discuss what each person is buying for family and friends. *Answers will vary.*

> **modelo**
>
> **Estudiante 1:** Quiero comprarle un vestido de Carolina Herrera a mi madre.
> **Estudiante 2:** Y yo voy a darles un automóvil nuevo a mis padres.
> **Estudiante 3:** Voy a comprarles una casa a mis padres, pero a mis amigos no les voy a dar nada.

**6** **Entrevista** Use these questions to interview a classmate. *Answers will vary.*

1. ¿Qué tiendas, almacenes o centros comerciales prefieres?
2. ¿A quién le compras regalos cuando hay rebajas?
3. ¿A quién le prestas dinero cuando lo necesita?
4. Quiero ir de compras. ¿Cuánto dinero me puedes prestar?
5. ¿Te dan tus padres su tarjeta de crédito cuando vas de compras?

# Síntesis

**7** **Minidrama** With two classmates, take turns playing the roles of two shoppers and a clerk in a clothing store. The shoppers should take turns talking about the articles of clothing they are looking for and for whom they are buying the clothes. The clerk should recommend several items based on the shoppers' descriptions. Use these expressions and also look at **Expresiones útiles** on page 179. *Answers will vary.*

> Me queda grande/pequeño.
> *It's big/small on me.*
> ¿Tiene otro color?
> *Do you have another color?*
> ¿Está en rebaja?
> *Is it on sale?*

**4 Teaching Tips**
• Have two volunteers read the model aloud. Then go through the phrases in the word bank and model question formation.
• To challenge students, have them ask follow-up questions for each item. Ex: **¿A quién le compras ropa? ¿Qué ropa le compras? ¿Dónde la compras?**

**4 Expansion** In groups of three, give students five minutes to brainstorm as many questions as they can using different forms of the verbs in the word bank. Invite two groups to come to the front of the class. Each group takes a turn asking the other its questions.

**5 Teaching Tip** Give each group a different lottery payout. Remind students they have to split it equally amongst the group members.

**5 Expansion** Have students research information about national lotteries in Spanish-speaking countries.

**6 Expansion** Take a class survey of the answers and write the results on the board.

**7 Teaching Tips**
• To simplify, have students begin by brainstorming phrases for their role. Remind them that, except for dialogue *between* the two shoppers, they should use **usted** in their conversation.
• Have students rehearse their mini-dramas.
• Videotape the scenes in or outside of class.

**TEACHING OPTIONS**

**Small Groups** Have students write a conversation. One friend tries to convince the other to go shopping with him or her this weekend. The other friend explains that he or she cannot and lists all the things he or she is going to do. Students should include as many different indirect object pronouns as possible. **Pairs** Ask students to imagine that they are going on an extended trip. Have them make a list of five things they are going to do (e.g., things they are going to buy for themselves or others) before leaving. Ex: **Voy a comprarme unos zapatos.**

**Extra Practice** Add a visual aspect to this grammar practice. Bring in personal or magazine photos that elicit statements with indirect object pronouns. Have students describe what is happening in each image. Encourage creativity. Ex: **La mujer está diciéndole a su hijo que tiene que comer el brócoli.**

## 6.3 Preterite tense of regular verbs

**ANTE TODO** In order to talk about events in the past, Spanish uses two simple tenses: the preterite and the imperfect. In this lesson, you will learn how to form the preterite tense, which is used to express actions or states completed in the past.

### Preterite of regular -ar, -er, and -ir verbs

| | | -ar verbs<br>**comprar** | -er verbs<br>**vender** | -ir verbs<br>**escribir** |
|---|---|---|---|---|
| **SINGULAR FORMS** | yo | compr**é** *I bought* | vend**í** *I sold* | escrib**í** *I wrote* |
| | tú | compr**aste** | vend**iste** | escrib**iste** |
| | Ud./él/ella | compr**ó** | vend**ió** | escrib**ió** |
| **PLURAL FORMS** | nosotros/as | compr**amos** | vend**imos** | escrib**imos** |
| | vosotros/as | compr**asteis** | vend**isteis** | escrib**isteis** |
| | Uds./ellos/ellas | compr**aron** | vend**ieron** | escrib**ieron** |

▶ **¡Atención!** The **yo** and **Ud./él/ella** forms of all three conjugations have written accents on the last syllable to show that it is stressed.

▶ As the chart shows, the endings for regular **-er** and **-ir** verbs are identical in the preterite.

¿Qué compraste?

Compré esta bolsa.

▶ Note that the **nosotros/as** forms of regular **-ar** and **-ir** verbs in the preterite are identical to the present tense forms. Context will help you determine which tense is being used.

En invierno **compramos** ropa.
*In the winter, we buy clothing.*

Anoche **compramos** unos zapatos.
*Last night we bought some shoes.*

▶ **-Ar** and **-er** verbs that have a stem change in the present tense are regular in the preterite. They do *not* have a stem change.

| | PRESENT | PRETERITE |
|---|---|---|
| **cerrar** (e:ie) | La tienda **cierra** a las seis. | La tienda **cerró** a las seis. |
| **volver** (o:ue) | Carlitos **vuelve** tarde. | Carlitos **volvió** tarde. |
| **jugar** (u:ue) | Él **juega** al fútbol. | Él **jugó** al fútbol. |

▶ **¡Atención!** **-Ir** verbs that have a stem change in the present tense also have a stem change in the preterite.

**CONSULTA**

You will learn about stem-changing verbs in **Estructura 8.1**, p. 254.

▶ Verbs that end in **-car**, **-gar**, and **-zar** have a spelling change in the first person singular (**yo** form) in the preterite.

| bus**car** | | busc- | | **qu-** | | yo bus**qu**é |
| lle**gar** | | lleg- | | **gu-** | | yo lle**gu**é |
| empe**zar** | | empez- | | **c-** | | yo empe**c**é |

▶ Except for the **yo** form, all other forms of **-car**, **-gar**, and **-zar** verbs are regular in the preterite.

▶ Three other verbs—**creer**, **leer**, and **oír**—have spelling changes in the preterite. The **i** of the verb endings of **creer**, **leer**, and **oír** carries an accent in the **yo, tú, nosotros/as,** and **vosotros/as** forms, and changes to **y** in the **Ud./él/ella** and **Uds./ellos/ellas** forms.

| creer | | cre- | | cre**í**, cre**í**ste, cre**y**ó, cre**í**mos, cre**í**steis, cre**y**eron |
| leer | | le- | | le**í**, le**í**ste, le**y**ó, le**í**mos, le**í**steis, le**y**eron |
| oír | | o- | | o**í**, o**í**ste, o**y**ó, o**í**mos, o**í**steis, o**y**eron |

▶ **Ver** is regular in the preterite, but none of its forms has an accent.

**ver** ⟶ vi, viste, vio, vimos, visteis, vieron

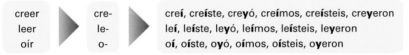

### Words commonly used with the preterite

| | | | |
|---|---|---|---|
| **anoche** | *last night* | **pasado/a** (*adj.*) | *last; past* |
| **anteayer** | *the day before yesterday* | **el año pasado** | *last year* |
| | | **la semana pasada** | *last week* |
| **ayer** | *yesterday* | **una vez** | *once; one time* |
| **de repente** | *suddenly* | **dos veces** | *twice; two times* |
| **desde... hasta...** | *from... until...* | **ya** | *already* |

**Ayer** llegué a Santiago de Cuba.      **Anoche** oí un ruido extraño.
*Yesterday I arrived in Santiago de Cuba.*    *Last night I heard a strange noise.*

▶ **Acabar de** + [*infinitive*] is used to say that something has just occurred. Note that **acabar** is in the present tense in this construction.

**Acabo de comprar** una falda.      **Acabas de ir** de compras.
*I just bought a skirt.*        *You just went shopping.*

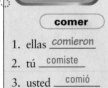
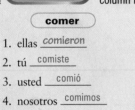

**¡INTÉNTALO!**   Provide the appropriate preterite forms of the verbs. The first item in each column has been done for you.

| | **comer** | **salir** | **comenzar** | **leer** |
|---|---|---|---|---|
| 1. ellas | *comieron* | *salieron* | *comenzaron* | *leyeron* |
| 2. tú | comiste | saliste | comenzaste | leíste |
| 3. usted | comió | salió | comenzó | leyó |
| 4. nosotros | comimos | salimos | comenzamos | leímos |
| 5. yo | comí | salí | comencé | leí |

**recursos**

WB
pp. 64–65

LM
p. 35

SUPERSITE
panorama.
vhlcentral.com
Lección 6

---

**Teaching Tips**
• Point out that verbs ending in -car and -gar are regular and have logical spelling changes in the **yo** form in order to preserve the hard **c** and **g** sounds.
• Students will learn the preterite of **dar** in **Estructura 9.1**. If you wish to present it for recognition only at this point, you can tell them that the endings are identical to **ver** in the preterite.
• Provide sentence starters using the present indicative and have students complete them in a logical manner. Ex: **Todos los días los estudiantes llegan temprano, pero anteayer… (llegaron tarde.)**
• Practice verbs with spelling changes in the preterite by asking students about things they read, heard, and saw yesterday. Ex: **¿Leíste el periódico ayer? ¿Quiénes vieron el pronóstico del tiempo? Yo oí que va a llover hoy. ¿Qué oyeron ustedes?**
• Add a visual aspect to this grammar presentation. Use magazine pictures to demonstrate **acabar de**. Ex: **¿Quién acaba de ganar? (Tiger Woods acaba de ganar.) ¿Qué acaban de ver ellos? (Acaban de ver una película.)**

# Práctica

**1 Completar** Andrea is talking about what happened last weekend. Complete each sentence by choosing the correct verb and putting it in the preterite.

1. El sábado a las diez de la mañana, la profesora Mora ___asistió___ (asistir, costar, usar) a una reunión (*meeting*) de profesores.
2. A la una, yo ___llegué___ (llegar, bucear, llevar) a la tienda con mis amigos.
3. Mis amigos y yo ___compramos___ (comprar, regatear, gastar) dos o tres cosas.
4. Yo ___compré___ (costar, comprar, escribir) unos pantalones negros y mi amigo Mateo ___compró___ (gastar, pasear, comprar) una camisa azul.
5. Después, nosotros ___comimos___ (llevar, vivir, comer) cerca de un mercado.
6. A las tres, Pepe ___habló___ (hablar, pasear, nadar) con su novia por teléfono.
7. El sábado por la tarde, mi mamá ___escribió___ (escribir, beber, vivir) una carta.
8. El domingo mi tía ___decidió___ (decidir, salir, escribir) comprarme un traje.
9. A las cuatro de la tarde, mi tía ___encontró___ (beber, salir, encontrar) el traje y después nosotras ___vimos___ (acabar, ver, salir) una película.

**2 Preguntas** Imagine that you have a pesky friend who keeps asking you questions. Respond that you already did or have just done what he/she asks.

> **modelo**
>
> leer la lección
> **Estudiante 1:** ¿Leíste la lección?
> **Estudiante 2:** Sí, ya la leí./Sí, acabo de leerla.

1. escribir el correo electrónico
2. lavar (*to wash*) la ropa
3. oír las noticias (*news*)
4. comprar pantalones cortos
5. practicar los verbos
6. pagar la cuenta (*bill*)
7. empezar la composición
8. ver la película *Diarios de motocicleta*

1. E1: ¿Escribiste el correo electrónico?
   E2: Sí, ya lo escribí./Acabo de escribirlo.
2. E1: ¿Lavaste la ropa?
   E2: Sí, ya la lavé./Acabo de lavarla.
3. E1: ¿Oíste las noticias?
   E2: Sí, ya las oí./Acabo de oírlas.
4. E1: ¿Compraste pantalones cortos?
   E2: Sí, ya los compré./Acabo de comprarlos.
5. E1: ¿Practicaste los verbos?
   E2: Sí, ya los practiqué./Acabo de practicarlos.
6. E1: ¿Pagaste la cuenta?
   E2: Sí, ya la pagué./Acabo de pagarla.
7. E1: ¿Empezaste la composición?
   E2: Sí, ya la empecé./Acabo de empezarla.
8. E1: ¿Viste la película *Diarios de motocicleta*?
   E2: Sí, ya la vi./Acabo de verla.

**NOTA CULTURAL**

Based on Ernesto "Che" Guevara's diaries, *Diarios de motocicleta* (2004) traces the road trip of Che (played by Gael García Bernal) with his friend Alberto Granado (played by Rodrigo de la Serna) through Argentina, Chile, Peru, Colombia, and Venezuela.

**3 ¿Cuándo?** Use the time expressions from the word bank to talk about when you and others did the activities listed. Answers will vary.

| | | | |
|---|---|---|---|
| anoche | anteayer | el mes pasado | una vez |
| ayer | la semana pasada | el año pasado | dos veces |

1. mi compañero/a de cuarto: llegar tarde a clase
2. mi mejor (*best*) amigo/a: salir con un(a) chico/a guapo/a
3. mis padres: ver una película
4. yo: llevar un traje/vestido
5. el presidente de los EE.UU.: asistir a una conferencia internacional
6. mis amigos y yo: comer en un restaurante
7. ¿?: comprar algo (*something*) bueno, bonito y barato

# Comunicación

**4** **Las vacaciones** Imagine that you took these photos on a vacation with friends. Get together with a partner and use the pictures to tell him or her about your trip. Answers will vary.

**5** **El fin de semana** Your instructor will give you and your partner different incomplete charts about what four employees at **Almacén Gigante** did last weekend. After you fill out the chart based on each other's information, you will fill out the final column about your partner.
Answers will vary.

# Síntesis

**6** **Conversación** Get together with a partner and have a conversation about what you did last week using verbs from the word bank. Don't forget to include school activities, shopping, and pastimes. Answers will vary.

| | | | |
|---|---|---|---|
| acampar | comer | gastar | tomar |
| asistir | comprar | hablar | trabajar |
| bailar | correr | jugar | vender |
| beber | escribir | leer | ver |
| buscar | estudiar | oír | viajar |

**4** **Teaching Tip** Have students first state where they traveled and when. Then have them identify the people in the photos, stating their names and their relationship to them and describing their personalities. Finally, students should tell what everyone did on the trip.

**4** **Expansion** After completing the activity orally, have students write a paragraph about their vacation, basing their account on the photos.

**5** **Teaching Tip** Divide the class into pairs and distribute the handouts from the Information Gap Activities (Supersite/IRCD) that correspond to this activity. Give students ten minutes to complete the activity.

**5** **Expansion** Have students tell the class about any activities that both their partner and one of the **Almacén Gigante** employees did. Ex: **La señora Zapata leyó un libro y _____ también. Los dos leyeron un libro.**

**6** **Teaching Tip** Have volunteers rehearse their conversation, then present it to the class.

**6** **Expansion** Have volunteers report to the class what their partners did last week.

## TEACHING OPTIONS

**Large Group** Have students stand up. Tell them to create a story chain about a student who had a very bad day. Begin the story by saying: **Ayer, Rigoberto pasó un día desastroso.** In order to sit down, students must contribute to the story. Call on a student to tell how **Rigoberto** began his day. The second person tells what happened next, and so on, until only one student remains. That person must conclude the story.

**Extra Practice** For homework, have students make a "to do" list at the beginning of their day. Then, ask students to return to their lists at the end of the day and write sentences stating which activities they completed. Ex: **limpiar mi habitación; No, no limpié mi habitación.**

**Section Goal**

In **Estructura 6.4**, students will learn to use demonstrative adjectives and pronouns.

---

**Instructional Resources**
**Supersite:** Lab MP3 Audio Files **Lección 6**
**Supersite/IRCD:** *PowerPoints* (**Lección 6 Estructura** Presentation); *IRM* (Information Gap Activities, Lab Audio Script, WBs/VM/LM Answer Key)
**WebSAM**
Workbook, pp. 66–68
Lab Manual, p. 36
*Cuaderno para hispanohablantes*

**Teaching Tips**
- Point to the book on your desk. Say: **Este libro está en la mesa.** Point to a book on a student's desk. Say: **Ese libro está encima del escritorio de _____.** Then point to a book on the window ledge. Say: **Aquel libro está cerca de la ventana.** Repeat the procedure with **tiza, papeles,** and **plumas.**
- Point out that although the masculine singular forms **este** and **ese** do not end in **–o,** their plural forms end in **–os: estos, esos.**
- Hold up or point to objects and have students give the plural: **este libro, esta mochila, este traje, este zapato.** Repeat with forms of **ese** and **aquel** with other nouns.
- You may want to have students associate **este** with **aquí, ese** with **allí,** and **aquel** with **allá.**

## 6.4 Demonstrative adjectives and pronouns

### Demonstrative adjectives

**ANTE TODO**   In Spanish, as in English, demonstrative adjectives are words that "demonstrate" or "point out" nouns. Demonstrative adjectives precede the nouns they modify and, like other Spanish adjectives you have studied, agree with them in gender and number. Observe these, then study the following chart.

| **esta** camisa | **ese** vendedor | **aquellos** zapatos |
|---|---|---|
| *this shirt* | *that salesman* | *those shoes (over there)* |

| Demonstrative adjectives | | | | |
|---|---|---|---|---|
| **Singular** | | **Plural** | | |
| MASCULINE | FEMININE | MASCULINE | FEMININE | |
| **este** | **esta** | **estos** | **estas** | *this; these* |
| **ese** | **esa** | **esos** | **esas** | *that; those* |
| **aquel** | **aquella** | **aquellos** | **aquellas** | *that; those (over there)* |

▶ There are three sets of demonstrative adjectives. To determine which one to use, you must establish the relationship between the speaker and the noun(s) being pointed out.

▶ The demonstrative adjectives **este, esta, estos,** and **estas** are used to point out nouns that are close to the speaker and the listener.

Me gustan estos zapatos.

▶ The demonstrative adjectives **ese, esa, esos,** and **esas** are used to point out nouns that are not close in space and time to the speaker. They may, however, be close to the listener.

Prefiero esos zapatos.

---

**TEACHING OPTIONS**

**Extra Practice** Hold up one or two items of clothing or classroom objects. Have students write all three forms of the demonstrative pronouns that would apply. Ex: **estos zapatos, esos zapatos, aquellos zapatos.**

**Pairs** Refer students to **Contextos** illustration on pages 174–175. Have them work with a partner to comment on the articles of clothing pictured. Ex: **Este suéter es bonito, ¿no? (No, ese suéter no es bonito. Es feo.) Aquella camiseta es muy cara. (Sí, aquella camiseta es cara.)**

▶ The demonstrative adjectives **aquel, aquella, aquellos,** and **aquellas** are used to point out nouns that are far away from the speaker and the listener.

> *Aquel auto es de mi hermana.*

## Demonstrative pronouns

▶ Demonstrative pronouns are identical to their corresponding demonstrative adjectives, with the exception that traditionally they carry an accent mark on the stressed vowel.

—¿Quieres comprar **este suéter**?
*Do you want to buy this sweater?*

—No, no quiero **éste**. Quiero **ése**.
*No, I don't want this one. I want that one.*

—¿Vas a leer **estas revistas**?
*Are you going to read these magazines?*

—Sí, voy a leer **éstas**. También voy a leer **aquéllas**.
*Yes, I'm going to read these. I'll also read those (over there).*

### Demonstrative pronouns

| Singular | | Plural | |
|---|---|---|---|
| MASCULINE | FEMININE | MASCULINE | FEMININE |
| **éste** | **ésta** | **éstos** | **éstas** |
| **ése** | **ésa** | **ésos** | **ésas** |
| **aquél** | **aquélla** | **aquéllos** | **aquéllas** |

▶ **¡Atención!** Like demonstrative adjectives, demonstrative pronouns agree in gender and number with the corresponding noun.

**Este libro** es de Pablito.       **Éstos** son de Juana.

▶ There are three neuter demonstrative pronouns: **esto, eso,** and **aquello**. These forms refer to unidentified or unspecified nouns, situations, ideas, and concepts. They do not change in gender or number and never carry an accent mark.

¿Qué es **esto**?
*What's this?*

**Eso** es interesante.
*That's interesting.*

**Aquello** es bonito.
*That's pretty.*

**recursos**

WB
pp. 66–68

LM
p. 36

SUPERSITE
panorama.
vhlcentral.com
Lección 6

---

**¡INTÉNTALO!**   Provide the correct form of the demonstrative adjective for these nouns. The first item has been done for you.

1. la falda / este   _esta falda_
2. los estudiantes / este   _estos estudiantes_
3. los países / aquel   _aquellos países_
4. la ventana / ese   _esa ventana_
5. los periodistas / ese   _esos periodistas_
6. el chico / aquel   _aquel chico_
7. las sandalias / este   _estas sandalias_
8. las chicas / aquel   _aquellas chicas_

---

**TEACHING OPTIONS**

**Small Groups** Ask students to bring in fashion magazines. Have students work in groups of three to give their opinions about the clothing they see in the magazines. Students should tell which items they like and which they do not, using demonstrative adjectives and pronouns.

**Video** Have students listen for the use of demonstrative pronouns as you replay the ***Fotonovela***. Ask students to write each pronoun and the noun it refers to. Then, have students look at a copy of the ***Fotonovela*** Videoscript (Supersite/IRCD) to see if they were correct.

**Teaching Tips**

• Have a volunteer stand next to you in front of the class. Place one book close to you and two more at varying distances. Say: **Necesito un libro.** Depending on the book the student hands to you, respond: **No, [éste] no. Quiero [ése].** Then place several books at each location. Say: **Necesito unos libros.** If needed, prompt the student to ask: **¿Cuáles? ¿Éstos?** Say: **No, quiero [aquéllos].** Repeat the process with pens (**plumas**) to elicit feminine forms.

• Engage students in short conversations about classroom objects and items of clothing. Ex: Pick up a student's backpack and ask him or her: **¿Es ésta mi mochila? (No, ésta es mi mochila.)** Turn to another student and ask about the same backpack: **¿Es ésa mi mochila? (No, ésa es la mochila de _____.)** Point to a student's pencil you have placed on the windowsill. Ask: **¿Es aquél tu lápiz? (No, aquél es su lápiz.)**

• Note that, since the **Real Academia Española** has determined that accents on demonstrative pronouns are only needed for clarification (Ex: **Esta mañana vendrá** versus **Ésta mañana vendrá**), students may see them without accents in some publications.

• To practice the neuter forms, write these expressions on the board: **¡Eso es fenomenal!, ¡Esto es horrible!, ¡Esto es estupendo!,** and **¿Qué es esto?** Then state situations and have students respond with one of the expressions. Ex: **1. Voy a cancelar el próximo examen. 2. La cafetería va a cerrar los lunes, miércoles y viernes. 3. Aquí te tengo un regalo.**

• Redo the **¡Inténtalo!** activity, using demonstrative pronouns.

# Práctica (SUPERSITE)

**1 Expansion** To challenge students, ask them to expand each sentence with a phrase that includes a demonstrative pronoun. Ex: **Aquellos sombreros son muy elegantes, pero éstos son más baratos.**

**1** **Cambiar** Make the singular sentences plural and the plural sentences singular.

> **modelo**
> Estas camisas son blancas.
> Esta camisa es blanca.

1. Aquellos sombreros son muy elegantes.   Aquel sombrero es muy elegante.
2. Ese abrigo es muy caro.   Esos abrigos son muy caros.
3. Estos cinturones son hermosos.   Este cinturón es hermoso.
4. Esos precios son muy buenos.   Ese precio es muy bueno.
5. Estas faldas son muy cortas.   Esta falda es muy corta.
6. ¿Quieres ir a aquel almacén?   ¿Quieres ir a aquellos almacenes?
7. Esas blusas son baratas.   Esa blusa es barata.
8. Esta corbata hace juego con mi traje.   Estas corbatas hacen juego con mi traje.

**2 Teaching Tips**
• To simplify, have students underline the nouns to which the demonstrative pronouns will refer.
• As you go over the activity, write each demonstrative pronoun on the board so students may verify that they have placed the accent marks correctly.

**2** **Completar** Here are some things people might say while shopping. Complete the sentences with the correct demonstrative pronouns.

1. No me gustan esos zapatos. Voy a comprar _____éstos_____. (*these*)
2. ¿Vas a comprar ese traje o ___éste___? (*this one*)
3. Esta guayabera es bonita, pero prefiero ___ésa___. (*that one*)
4. Estas corbatas rojas son muy bonitas, pero ___ésas___ son fabulosas. (*those*)
5. Estos cinturones cuestan demasiado. Prefiero ___aquéllos___. (*those over there*)
6. ¿Te gustan esas botas o ___éstas___? (*these*)
7. Esa bolsa roja es bonita, pero prefiero ___aquélla___. (*that one over there*)
8. No voy a comprar estas botas; voy a comprar ___aquéllas___. (*those over there*)
9. Sé que gasté demasiado dinero en zapatos, pero no quiero hablar de ___eso / esto___. (*that*)
10. Me gusta este vestido, pero voy a comprar ___ése___. (*that one*)
11. Me gusta ese almacén, pero ___aquél___ es mejor (*better*). (*that one over there*)
12. Esa blusa es bonita pero cuesta demasiado. Voy a comprar ___ésta___. (*this one*)

◄ **NOTA CULTURAL**

The **guayabera** is a men's shirt typically worn in some parts of the Caribbean. Never tucked in, it is casual wear, but variations exist for more formal occasions, such as weddings, parties, or the office.

**3 Expansion** Ask students to find a photo featuring different articles of clothing or to draw several articles of clothing. Have them write five statements like that of the **Estudiante 1** model in part one of this activity. Then have students exchange their statements and photo/drawing with a partner to write responses like that of the **Estudiante 2** model.

**3** **Describir** With your partner, look for two items in the classroom that are one of these colors: **amarillo, azul, blanco, marrón, negro, verde, rojo.** Take turns pointing them out to each other, first using demonstrative adjectives, and then demonstrative pronouns.   Answers will vary.

> **modelo**
> azul
> **Estudiante 1:** Esta silla es azul. Aquella mochila es azul.
> **Estudiante 2:** Ésta es azul. Aquélla es azul.

Now use demonstrative adjectives and pronouns to discuss the colors of your classmates' clothing. One of you can ask a question about an article of clothing, using the wrong color. Your partner will correct you and point out that color somewhere else in the room.

> **modelo**
> **Estudiante 1:** ¿Esa camisa es negra?
> **Estudiante 2:** No, ésa es azul. Aquélla es negra.

---

**TEACHING OPTIONS**

**Heritage Speakers** Have heritage speakers role-play a dialogue between friends shopping for clothes. Student A tries to convince the friend that the clothes he or she wants to buy are not attractive. Student A suggests other items of clothing, but the friend does not agree. Students should use as many demonstrative adjectives and pronouns as possible.
**Game** Divide the class into two teams. Post pictures of different

versions of the same object (Ex: sedan, sports car, all-terrain vehicle) on the board. Assign each a dollar figure, but do not share the prices with the class. Team A guesses the price of each object, using demonstrative adjectives and pronouns. Team B either agrees or guesses a higher or lower price. The team that guesses the closest price, wins. Ex: **Este carro cuesta $20.000, ése cuesta $35.000 y aquél cuesta $18.000.**

# Comunicación

**4** **Conversación** With a classmate, use demonstrative adjectives and pronouns to ask each other questions about the people around you. Use expressions from the word bank and/or your own ideas.
Answers will vary.

| | |
|---|---|
| ¿Cómo se llama…? | ¿Cuántos años tiene(n)…? |
| ¿Cómo es/son…? | ¿A qué hora…? |
| ¿De quién es/son…? | ¿Cuándo…? |
| ¿De dónde es/son…? | ¿Qué clases toma(n)…? |

**modelo**

**Estudiante 1:** ¿Cómo se llama esa chica?
**Estudiante 2:** Se llama Rebeca.
**Estudiante 1:** ¿A qué hora llegó aquel chico a la clase?
**Estudiante 2:** A las nueve.

**5** **En una tienda** Imagine that you and a classmate are in Madrid shopping at Zara. Study the floor plan, then have a conversation about your surroundings. Use demonstrative adjectives and pronouns.
Answers will vary.

**modelo**

**Estudiante 1:** Me gusta este suéter azul.
**Estudiante 2:** Yo prefiero aquella chaqueta.

**NOTA CULTURAL**

**Zara** is an international company based in Spain. It manufactures clothing and accessories for men, women, and children and also markets a popular fragrance line. While Zara makes both casual and sophisticated clothing, it is better known for its trendy, classy style that appeals to young professional women.

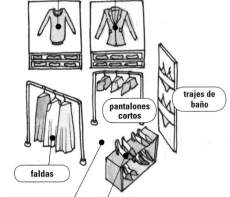

chaquetas   suéteres   blusas   chaquetas

camisas

pantalones cortos   pantalones cortos

trajes de baño   trajes de baño

botas   pantalones   faldas   zapatos

**Estudiante 1**   **Estudiante 2**

# Síntesis

**6** **Diferencias** Your instructor will give you and a partner each a drawing of a store. They are almost identical, but not quite. Use demonstrative adjectives and pronouns to find seven differences.
Answers will vary.

**modelo**

**Estudiante 1:** Aquellas gafas de sol son feas, ¿verdad?
**Estudiante 2:** No. Aquellas gafas de sol son hermosas.

---

**4 Teaching Tip** To challenge students, have both partners ask a question for each item in the word bank and at least one other question using an interrogative expression that is not included.

**5 Expansion** Divide students into groups of three to role-play a scene between a sales-person and two customers. The customers should ask about the different items of clothing pictured and the sales-person will answer. They talk about how the items fit and their cost. The customers then express their preferences and decide which items to buy.

**6 Teaching Tip** Divide the class into pairs and distribute the handouts from the Information Gap Activities (Supersite/IRCD) that correspond to this activity. Give students ten minutes to complete the activity.

**6 Expansion** Have pairs work together with another pair to compare the seven responses that confirmed the seven differences. Ex: **No. Aquellas gafas de sol no son feas. Aquéllas son hermosas.** Ask a few groups to share some of the sentences with the class.

---

**TEACHING OPTIONS**

**Pairs** Ask students to write a conversation between two people sitting at a busy sidewalk café in the city. They are watching the people who walk by, asking each other questions about what the passersby are doing, and making comments on their clothing. Students should use as many demonstrative adjectives and pronouns as possible in their conversations. Invite several pairs to present their conversation to the class.

**Small Groups** Ask students to bring in pictures of their families, a sports team, a group of friends, etc. Have them take turns asking about and identifying the people in the pictures.
Ex: —**¿Quién es aquella mujer? (¿Cuál?)**
—**Aquélla con la camiseta roja. (Es mi…)**

## Section Goal

In **Recapitulación**, students will review the grammar concepts from this lesson.

**Instructional Resource**
**Supersite**

**1 Teaching Tips**
• Before beginning the activity, ask students which preterite forms usually require accent marks.
• Ask a volunteer to identify which verbs have a spelling change in the preterite (**pagar, leer**).

**1 Expansion** Ask students to provide the **tú** and **nosotros** forms for these verbs.

**2 Teaching Tip** To simplify this activity, have students start by identifying each blank as a spot for an adjective or pronoun. If the blank requires an adjective, have them underline the corresponding noun. If the blank calls for a pronoun, have them identify the noun it replaces.

**2 Expansion** Have two volunteers role-play the dialogue for the class.

# Recapitulación

 For self-scoring and diagnostics, go to **panorama.vhlcentral.com**.

Review the grammar concepts you have learned in this lesson by completing these activities.

**1 Completar** Complete the chart with the correct preterite or infinitive form of the verbs. **15 pts.**

| Infinitive | yo | ella | ellos |
|---|---|---|---|
| tomar | tomé | tomó | **tomaron** |
| abrir | abrí | **abrió** | abrieron |
| **comprender** | comprendí | comprendió | comprendieron |
| leer | **leí** | leyó | leyeron |
| **pagar** | pagué | pagó | pagaron |

**2 En la tienda** Look at the drawing and complete the conversation with demonstrative adjectives and pronouns. **7 pts.**

**CLIENTE** Buenos días, señorita. Deseo comprar (1) ___esta___ corbata.

**VENDEDORA** Muy bien, señor. ¿No le interesa mirar (2) ___aquellos___ trajes que están allá? Hay unos que hacen juego con la corbata.

**CLIENTE** (3) ___Aquéllos___ de allá son de lana, ¿no? Prefiero ver (4) ___ese___ traje marrón que está detrás de usted.

**VENDEDORA** Estupendo. Como puede ver, es de seda. Cuesta ciento ochenta dólares.

**CLIENTE** Ah… eh… no, creo que sólo voy a comprar la corbata, gracias.

**VENDEDORA** Bueno… si busca algo más económico, hay rebaja en (5) ___aquellos___ sombreros. Cuestan sólo treinta dólares.

**CLIENTE** ¡Magnífico! Me gusta (6) ___aquél___, el blanco que está arriba. Y quiero pagar todo con (7) ___esta___ tarjeta.

**VENDEDORA** Sí, señor. Ahora mismo le traigo el sombrero.

**RESUMEN GRAMATICAL**

**6.1 Saber and conocer** *p. 184*

| saber | conocer |
|---|---|
| sé | conozco |
| sabes | conoces |
| sabe | conoce |
| sabemos | conocemos |
| sabéis | conocéis |
| saben | conocen |

▶ **saber** = to know facts/how to do something
▶ **conocer** = to know a person, place, or thing

**6.2 Indirect object pronouns** *pp. 186–187*

**Indirect object pronouns**

| Singular | Plural |
|---|---|
| me | nos |
| te | os |
| le | les |

▶ **dar** = doy, das, da, damos, dais, dan

**6.3 Preterite tense of regular verbs** *pp. 190–191*

| comprar | vender | escribir |
|---|---|---|
| compré | vendí | escribí |
| compraste | vendiste | escribiste |
| compró | vendió | escribió |
| compramos | vendimos | escribimos |
| comprasteis | vendisteis | escribisteis |
| compraron | vendieron | escribieron |

**Verbs with spelling changes in the preterite**

▶ **-car:** buscar → yo busqué
▶ **-gar:** llegar → yo llegué
▶ **-zar:** empezar → yo empecé
▶ **creer:** creí, creíste, creyó, creímos, creísteis, creyeron
▶ **leer:** leí, leíste, leyó, leímos, leísteis, leyeron
▶ **oír:** oí, oíste, oyó, oímos, oísteis, oyeron
▶ **ver:** vi, viste, vio, vimos, visteis, vieron

**TEACHING OPTIONS**

**Game** Divide the class into two teams. Indicate a team member. Give an infinitive and a subject, and have the team member supply the correct preterite form. Award one point for each correct answer. Award a bonus point for correctly writing the verb on the board. The team with the most points wins.
**TPR** Write **presente** and **pretérito** on the board and have a volunteer stand in front of each word. Call out sentences using the present or the preterite. The student whose tense corresponds to the sentence has three seconds to step forward.
Ex: **Compramos una chaqueta anteayer. (pretérito)**
**Small Groups** Ask students to write a description of a famous person, using **saber, conocer,** and one verb in the preterite. In small groups, have students read their descriptions aloud for the group to guess.

**3** **¿Saber o conocer?** Complete each dialogue with the correct form of **saber** or **conocer**. **10 pts.**

1. —¿Qué __sabes__ hacer tú?
   —(Yo) __Sé__ jugar al fútbol.
2. —¿__Conoces__ tú esta tienda de ropa?
   —No, (yo) no la __conozco__. ¿Es buena?
3. —¿Tus padres no __conocen__ a tu novio?
   —No, ¡ellos no __saben__ que tengo novio!
4. —Mi compañero de cuarto todavía no me __conoce__ bien.
   —Y tú, ¿lo quieres __conocer__ a él?
5. —¿__Saben__ ustedes dónde está el mercado?
   —No, nosotros no __conocemos__ bien esta ciudad.

**4** **Oraciones** Form complete sentences using the information provided. Use indirect object pronouns and the present tense of the verbs. **10 pts.**

1. Javier / prestar / el abrigo / a Maripili
   Javier le presta el abrigo a Maripili.
2. nosotros / vender / ropa / a los clientes
   Nosotros les vendemos ropa a los clientes.
3. el vendedor / traer / las camisetas / a mis amigos y a mí
   El vendedor nos trae las camisetas (a mis amigos y a mí).
4. yo / querer dar / consejos / a ti
   Yo quiero darte consejos (a ti)./Yo te quiero dar consejos (a ti).
5. ¿tú / ir a comprar / un regalo / a mí?
   ¿Tú vas a comprarme un regalo (a mí)?/¿Tú me vas a comprar un regalo (a mí)?

**5** **Mi última compra** Write a short paragraph describing the last time you went shopping. Use at least four verbs in the preterite tense. **8 pts.** Answers will vary.

> **modelo**
> El viernes pasado, busqué unos zapatos en el centro comercial...

**6** **Poema** Write the missing words to complete the excerpt from the poem *Romance sonámbulo* by Federico García Lorca. **2 EXTRA points!**

❝Verde que __te__ quiero verde.
Verde viento. Verdes ramas°.
El barco sobre la mar
y el caballo en la montaña, [...]
Verde que te quiero __verde__ (*green*).❞

ramas *branches*

---

**6.4** **Demonstrative adjectives and pronouns** *pp. 194–195*

**Demonstrative adjectives**

| Singular | | Plural | |
|---|---|---|---|
| **Masc.** | **Fem.** | **Masc.** | **Fem.** |
| este | esta | estos | estas |
| ese | esa | esos | esas |
| aquel | aquella | aquellos | aquellas |

**Demonstrative pronouns**

| Singular | | Plural | |
|---|---|---|---|
| **Masc.** | **Fem.** | **Masc.** | **Fem.** |
| éste | ésta | éstos | éstas |
| ése | ésa | ésos | ésas |
| aquél | aquélla | aquéllos | aquéllas |

---

**3** Teaching Tip Ask students to explain why they chose **saber** or **conocer** in each case.

**3** Expansion Have students choose one dialogue from this activity and write a continuation. Encourage them to use at least one more example of **saber** and **conocer**.

**4** Teaching Tips
• Ask a volunteer to model the first sentence for the class.
• Before forming sentences, have students circle the indirect object in each item.
• Remind students of the possible placements of indirect object pronouns when using an infinitive.

**4** Expansion
• Ask students to create three dehydrated sentences similar to those in **Actividad 4**. Have them exchange papers with a classmate and form complete sentences.
• For items 1–4, have students write questions that would elicit these statements. Ex: **1. ¿A quién le presta el abrigo Javier?/¿Qué le presta Javier a Maripili?** For item 5, have them write a response.

**5** Teaching Tip To add a visual aspect to this activity, have students create a time line of what they did when they went shopping.

**6** Teaching Tips
• Tell students to read through the whole excerpt before filling in the blanks.
• Have a volunteer read the excerpt aloud.

---

**TEACHING OPTIONS**

**Extra Practice** Add an auditory aspect to this grammar review. Read each of these sentences twice, pausing after the second time for students to write: **1. Ayer empecé a leer sobre los diseñadores hispanos. 2. Ellas buscaron unas bolsas en el mercado al aire libre. 3. El dependiente vendió cinco camisetas. 4. Nosotras oímos una explosión. 5. El joven le leyó el libro a su hermanito. 6. Raúl vio una película anoche.**

**Game** Divide the class into two teams. Indicate a member of each team and call out a color. The first student to find an object or article of clothing in the room, point to it, and use the correct form of a demonstrative adjective to express it earns a point for their team. Ex: **¡Aquella camiseta es morada!** The team with the most points at the end wins.

# Lectura

**Antes de leer**

## Estrategia

### Skimming

Skimming involves quickly reading through a document to absorb its general meaning. This allows you to understand the main ideas without having to read word for word. When you skim a text, you might want to look at its title and subtitles. You might also want to read the first sentence of each paragraph.

### Examinar el texto

Look at the format of the reading selection. How is it organized? What does the organization of the document tell you about its content?

### Buscar cognados

Scan the reading selection to locate at least five cognates. Based on the cognates, what do you think the reading selection is about? Answers will vary.

1. _____    4. _____
2. _____    5. _____
3. _____

The reading selection is about _____.

### Impresiones generales

Now skim the reading selection to understand its general meaning. Jot down your impressions. What new information did you learn about the document by skimming it? Based on all the information you now have, answer these questions in Spanish.

1. Who produced this document? un almacén
2. What is its purpose? vender ropa
3. Who is its intended audience? gente que quiere comprar ropa

**recursos**

panorama.vhlcentral.com
Lección 6

---

## ¡Real° Liquidación en Corona

### ¡Grandes rebajas!
### ¡La rebaja está de moda en Corona!

| SEÑORAS | CABALLEROS° |
|---|---|
| **Falda larga** **ROPA BONITA** Algodón. De cuadros y rayas Talla mediana <br> Precio especial: $8.000 | **Pantalones** **OCÉANO** Colores blanco, azul y café Ahora: $11.550 <br> 30% de rebaja |
| **Blusas de seda** **BAMBÚ** Seda. De cuadros y de lunares Ahora: $21.000 <br> 40% de rebaja | **Zapatos** **COLOR** Italianos y franceses Números del 40 al 45 <br> Sólo $20.000 el par |
| **Sandalias de playa** **GINO** Números del 35 al 38 Ahora: $12.000 el par <br> 50% de rebaja | **Chaqueta** **CASINO** Microfibra. Colores negro, blanco y gris Tallas P-M-G-XG <br> Ahora: $22.500 |
| **Carteras** **ELEGANCIA** Colores anaranjado, blanco, rosado y amarillo Ahora: $15.000 <br> 50% de rebaja | **Traje inglés** **GALES** Modelos originales Ahora: $105.000 <br> 30% de rebaja |
| **Vestido de algodón** **PANAMÁ** Colores blanco, azul y verde Ahora: $18.000 <br> 30% de rebaja | **Ropa interior** **ATLÁNTICO** Talla mediana Colores blanco, negro, gris <br> 40% de rebaja |

**Lunes a sábado de 9 a 21 horas.**
**Domingo de 10 a 14 horas.**

---

# Despúes de leer

## Completar

Complete this paragraph about the reading selection with the correct forms of the words from the word bank.

| | | |
|---|---|---|
| almacén | hacer juego | tarjeta de crédito |
| caro | increíble | tienda |
| dinero | pantalones | verano |
| falda | rebaja | zapato |

En este anuncio de periódico el ___almacén___ Corona anuncia la liquidación de ___verano___ con grandes ___rebajas___ en todos los departamentos. Con muy poco ___dinero___ usted puede equipar a toda su familia. Si no tiene dinero en efectivo, puede utilizar su ___tarjeta de crédito___ y pagar luego. Para el caballero con gustos refinados, hay ___zapatos___ importados de París y Roma. La señora elegante puede encontrar blusas de seda que ___hacen juego___ con todo tipo de ___faldas/pantalones___ o ___pantalones/faldas___. Los precios de esta liquidación son realmente ___increíbles___.

## ¿Cierto o falso?

Indicate whether each statement is **cierto** or **falso**. Correct the false statements.

1. Hay ropa de algodón para jóvenes. Cierto.
2. La ropa interior tiene una rebaja del 30%. Falso. Tiene una rebaja del 40%.
3. El almacén Corona tiene un departamento de zapatos. Cierto.
4. Normalmente las sandalias cuestan $22.000 el par. Falso. Normalmente cuestan $24.000.
5. Cuando gastas $3.000 en la tienda, llevas un regalo gratis. Falso. Cuando gastas $40.000 en la tienda, llevas un regalo gratis.
6. Tienen carteras amarillas. Cierto.

## Preguntas

Answer these questions in Spanish. Answers will vary.

1. Imagina que vas a ir a la tienda Corona. ¿Qué departamentos vas a visitar? ¿El departamento de ropa para señoras, el departamento de ropa para caballeros…?
2. ¿Qué vas a buscar en Corona?
3. ¿Hay tiendas similares a la tienda Corona en tu pueblo o ciudad? ¿Cómo se llaman? ¿Tienen muchas gangas?

---

**Left advertisement panel:**

Corona tiene las ofertas más locas el verano!

**30%  40%  50%**

a tienda más elegante de la ciudad on precios increíbles y con la tarjeta e crédito más conveniente del mercado.

| JÓVENES | NIÑOS |
|---|---|
| Huejeans chicos y chicas | **Vestido de niña** |
| **PACOS** | **GIRASOL** |
| mericanos. Tradicional | Tallas de la 2 a la 12. De cuadros y rayas |
| hora: $9.000 el par | Ahora: $8.625 |
| 0% de rebaja | 30% de rebaja |
| **Suéteres** | **Pantalón deportivo de niño** |
| **CARAMELO** | **MILÁN** |
| lgodón y lana. olores blanco, gris y negro ntes: $10.500 | Tallas de la 4 a la 16 Ahora: $13.500 |
| Ahora: $6.825 | 30% de rebaja |
| **Bolsas** | **Zapatos de tenis** |
| **LA MODERNA** | **ACUARIO** |
| mericanas. stilos variados ntes: $15.000 | Números del 20 al 25 Ahora: $15.000 el par |
| Ahora $10.000 | 30% de rebaja |
| **rajes de baño chicos chicas** | **Pantalones cortos** |
| **SUBMARINO** | **MACARENA** |
| licrofibra. Todas las tallas hora: $12.500 | Talla mediana Ahora: $15.000 |
| 0% de rebaja | 30% de rebaja |
| **Gafas de sol** | **Camisetas de algodón** |
| **VISIÓN** | **POLO** |
| rigen canadiense ntes: $23.000 | Antes: $15.000 Ahora: $7.500 |
| Ahora: $14.950 | 50% de rebaja |

or la compra de $40.000, puede llevar un regalo gratis.
- Un hermoso cinturón de señora
- Un par de calcetines
- Una corbata de seda
- Una bolsa para la playa
- Una mochila
- Unas medias

al *Royal* Liquidación *Clearance sale* caballeros *gentlemen* Antes *Before*

---

---

## Section Goals

In **Escritura**, students will:
• conduct an interview
• integrate vocabulary and structures taught in **Lección 6** into a written report
• report on an interview

---

**Instructional Resources**
**Supersite**
*Cuaderno para hispanohablantes*

---

**Estrategia** Model an interview for students by asking a volunteer a few of the questions on this page. Then model how to report on an interview by transcribing verbatim a section of the dialogue on the board. Then give an example each of summarizing and summarizing but quoting occasionally.

**Tema** Tell students that they may interview another member of their class or they may interview a Spanish-speaking student they know. Encourage them to take notes as they conduct the interview or tape record it. They might want to work with a classmate they are not going to interview to brainstorm additional questions. Introduce terms such as **entrevista, entrevistar, diálogo,** and **citas** as you present the activity.

# Escritura

### Estrategia

**How to report an interview**

There are several ways to prepare a written report about an interview. For example, you can transcribe the interview verbatim, you can simply summarize it, or you can summarize it but quote the speakers occasionally. In any event, the report should begin with an interesting title and a brief introduction, which may include the five Ws (*who, what, where, when, why*) and the H (*how*) of the interview. The report should end with an interesting conclusion. Note that when you transcribe dialogue in Spanish, you should pay careful attention to format and punctuation.

**Writing dialogue in Spanish**

• If you need to transcribe an interview verbatim, you can use speakers' names to indicate a change of speaker.

| | |
|---|---|
| CARMELA | ¿Qué compraste? ¿Encontraste muchas gangas? |
| ROBERTO | Sí, muchas. Compré un suéter, una camisa y dos corbatas. Y tú, ¿qué compraste? |
| CARMELA | Una blusa y una falda muy bonitas. ¿Cuánto costó tu camisa? |
| ROBERTO | Sólo diez dólares. ¿Cuánto costó tu blusa? |
| CARMELA | Veinte dólares. |

• You can also use a dash (*raya*) to mark the beginning of each speaker's words.

— ¿Qué compraste?
— Un suéter y una camisa muy bonitos. Y tú, ¿encontraste muchas gangas?
— Sí... compré dos blusas, tres camisetas y un par de zapatos.
— ¡A ver!

**recursos**

panorama.vhlcentral.com
Lección 6

## Tema

**Escribe un informe**

Write a report for the school newspaper about an interview you conducted with a student about his or her shopping habits and clothing preferences. First, brainstorm a list of interview questions. Then conduct the interview using the questions below as a guide, but feel free to ask other questions as they occur to you.

Examples of questions:

▶ ¿Cuándo vas de compras?

▶ ¿Adónde vas de compras?

▶ ¿Con quién vas de compras?

▶ ¿Qué tiendas, almacenes o centros comerciales prefieres?

▶ ¿Compras ropa de catálogos o por Internet?

▶ ¿Prefieres comprar ropa cara o barata? ¿Por qué? ¿Te gusta buscar gangas?

▶ ¿Qué ropa llevas cuando vas a clase?

▶ ¿Qué ropa llevas cuando sales a bailar?

▶ ¿Qué ropa llevas cuando practicas un deporte?

▶ ¿Cuáles son tus colores favoritos? ¿Compras mucha ropa de esos colores?

▶ ¿Les das ropa a tu familia o a tus amigos/as?

---

**EVALUATION: Informe**

| Criteria | Scale |
|---|---|
| Content | 1 2 3 4 5 |
| Organization | 1 2 3 4 5 |
| Accuracy | 1 2 3 4 5 |
| Creativity | 1 2 3 4 5 |

| Scoring | |
|---|---|
| Excellent | 18–20 points |
| Good | 14–17 points |
| Satisfactory | 10–13 points |
| Unsatisfactory | < 10 points |

# Escuchar

## Estrategia

### Listening for linguistic cues

You can enhance your listening comprehension by listening for specific linguistic cues. For example, if you listen for the endings of conjugated verbs, or for familiar constructions, such as **acabar de** + [*infinitive*] or **ir a** + [*infinitive*], you can find out whether an event already took place, is taking place now, or will take place in the future. Verb endings also give clues about who is participating in the action.

 To practice listening for linguistic cues, you will now listen to four sentences. As you listen, note whether each sentence refers to a past, present, or future action. Also jot down the subject of each sentence.

## Preparación

Based on the photograph, what do you think Marisol has recently done? What do you think Marisol and Alicia are talking about? What else can you guess about their conversation from the visual clues in the photograph?

## Ahora escucha 🎧

Now you are going to hear Marisol and Alicia's conversation. Make a list of the clothing items that each person mentions. Then put a check mark after the item if the person actually purchased it.

| Marisol | |
|---|---|
| 1. | pantalones ✓ |
| 2. | blusa ✓ |
| 3. | |
| 4. | |

| Alicia | |
|---|---|
| 1. | falda |
| 2. | blusa |
| 3. | zapatos |
| 4. | cinturón |

**recursos**

panorama.vhlcentral.com
Lección 6

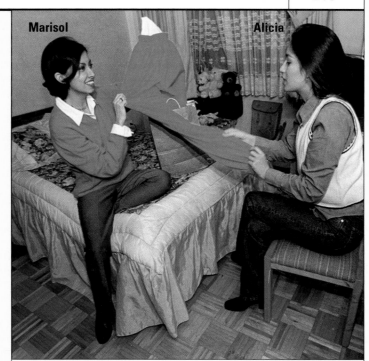

Marisol         Alicia

## Comprensión

### ¿Cierto o falso?

Indicate whether each statement is **cierto** or **falso**. Then correct the false statements.

1. Marisol y Alicia acaban de ir de compras juntas (*together*). Falso. Marisol acaba de ir de compras.
2. Marisol va a comprar unos pantalones y una blusa mañana. Falso. Marisol ya los compró.
3. Marisol compró una blusa de cuadros. Cierto.
4. Alicia compró unos zapatos nuevos hoy. Falso. Alicia va a comprar unos zapatos nuevos.
5. Alicia y Marisol van a ir al café. Cierto.
6. Marisol gastó todo el dinero de la semana en ropa nueva. Cierto.

### Preguntas

Discuss the following questions with a classmate. Be sure to explain your answers. Answers will vary.

1. ¿Crees que Alicia y Marisol son buenas amigas? ¿Por qué?
2. ¿Cuál de las dos estudiantes es más ahorradora (*frugal*)? ¿Por qué?
3. ¿Crees que a Alicia le gusta la ropa que Marisol compró?
4. ¿Crees que la moda es importante para Alicia? ¿Para Marisol? ¿Por qué?
5. ¿Es importante para ti estar a la moda? ¿Por qué?

NATIONAL communication STANDARDS

## Section Goals

In **Escuchar**, students will:
• listen for specific linguistic cues in oral sentences
• answer questions based on a recorded conversation

**Instructional Resources**
**Supersite:** Textbook MP3 Audio Files
**Supersite/IRCD:** *IRM* (Textbook Audio Script)

**Estrategia**
**Script** 1. Acabamos de pasear por la ciudad y encontramos unos monumentos fenomenales. 2. Estoy haciendo las maletas. 3. Carmen y Alejandro decidieron ir a un restaurante. 4. Mi familia y yo vamos a ir a la playa.

**Teaching Tip** Ask students to look at the photo of **Marisol** and **Alicia** and predict what they are talking about.

**Ahora escucha**
**Script** MARISOL: Oye, Alicia, ¿qué estás haciendo?
ALICIA: Estudiando no más. ¿Qué hay de nuevo?
M: Acabo de comprarme esos pantalones que andaba buscando.
A: ¿Los encontraste en el centro comercial? ¿Y cuánto te costaron?
M: Míralos. ¿Te gustan? En el almacén Melo tienen tremenda rebaja. Como estaban baratos me compré una blusa también. Es de cuadros pero creo que hace juego con los pantalones por el color rojo. ¿Qué piensas?
A: Es de los mismos colores que la falda y la blusa que llevaste cuando fuimos al cine anoche. La verdad es que te quedan muy bien esos colores. ¿No encontraste unos zapatos y un cinturón para completar el juego?
M: No lo digas ni de chiste. Mi tarjeta de crédito está que

*(Script continues at far left in the bottom panels.)*

# En pantalla

In Spain, during Francisco Franco's dictatorship (1939–1975), students in public schools were required to wear uniforms. After the fall of Franco's regime and the establishment of democracy, educational authorities rejected this former policy and decided it should no longer be obligatory to wear uniforms in public schools. Today, only some private schools in Spain enforce the use of uniforms; even Catholic schools do not have anything more than a basic dress code.

### Vocabulario útil

| | |
|---|---|
| anoraks | anoraks (Spain) |
| anchas | loose-fitting |
| vaqueros | jeans (Spain) |
| trencas | duffel coats (Spain) |
| lavables | washable |
| carteras | book bags (Spain) |
| chándals | tracksuits (Spain) |
| resiste | withstands |
| tanto como | as much as |

### Identificar

Check off each word that you hear in the ad.

_____ 1. camisetas  ✔ 5. chaquetas
✔ 2. hijos  _____ 6. clientas
✔ 3. zapatos  ✔ 7. lana
_____ 4. algodón  _____ 8. precio

 ### Conversar

Work with a classmate to ask each other these questions. Use as much Spanish as you can. Answers will vary.

1. ¿Qué ropa llevas normalmente cuando vienes a la universidad?
2. ¿Y los fines de semana?
3. ¿Tienes una prenda (*garment*) favorita? ¿Cómo es?
4. ¿Qué tipo de ropa no te gusta usar? ¿Por qué?

próximo *next* Tejidos *Fabrics* resistentes *strong, tough*

## Anuncio de tiendas Galerías

**Presentamos la moda para el próximo° curso.**

**Formas geométricas y colores vivos.**

**Tejidos° resistentes°.**

**recursos**

panorama.vhlcentral.com
Lección 6

 **Conexión Internet**

Go to **panorama.vhlcentral.com** to watch the TV clip featured in this **En pantalla** section.

# Oye cómo va

## Celia Cruz

nown as the Queen of Salsa, **Úrsula Hilaria
Celia Caridad Cruz Alfonso (Celia Cruz)** was
born in Havana, Cuba, on October 21, 1924. She
began singing at an early age and studied music
at Havana's **Conservatorio Musical.** For many
years Celia sang with the Sonora Matancera
ensemble, recording over 150 songs. Then, on
July 15, 1960, she left Cuba, never to return.
After a stay in Mexico, Celia settled in New York
City, where she recorded over fifty solo albums.
Celia formed an engaging stage presence, with
eccentric outfits, colorful wigs, and her popular
catchword, **¡Azúcar!** (*Sugar!*) Throughout her
long and prolific career, Celia received numerous
awards and recognitions, such as the National
Endowment for the Arts, in 1994. After her
cancer-related death on July 16, 2003, Celia
Cruz's life was celebrated with public funerals in
Miami and New York.

Your instructor will play the song. Listen and then
complete these activities.

### Usted abusó

Usted abusó°.
Sacó provecho° de mí, abusó.
Sacó partido° de mí, abusó.
De mi cariño° usted abusó.

**Cierto o falso?**

ndicate whether each statement is **cierto** or **falso.**

|  | Cierto | Falso |
|---|---|---|
| 1. Celia Cruz es cubana. | ☑ | ○ |
| 2. Ella comenzó a cantar a los 35 años. | ○ | ☑ |
| 3. Cantó con la Sonora Matancera. | ☑ | ○ |
| 4. Usó ropa tradicional. | ○ | ☑ |

**Preguntas**

Work with a partner to answer these questions.
*Answers will vary.*

1. ¿Creen que estos versos de la canción son ciertos?
   ¿Por qué?

   "Yo sólo sé que en esta vida
   el amor todo es mentira".

2. ¿Es posible estar enamorado/a de una persona y a
   la vez odiarla (*hate them*)? ¿Conocen a una persona
   en una situación como ésa?

**abusó** *took advantage* **Sacó provecho** *You took advantage* **Sacó partido**
*You took advantage* **cariño** *love*

**Celia y la moda**
Celia Cruz created a unique
personal style to match her
lively spirit. On stage, she
favored large wigs in bright
colors, over-the-top dresses,
and glittery platform shoes.

**recursos**

SUPERSITE

panorama.vhlcentral.com
Lección 6

**SUPERSITE Conexión Internet**
Go to **panorama.vhlcentral.com** to learn more about
the artist featured in this **Oye cómo va** section.

### Section Goals
In **Oye cómo va**, students will:
• read about **Celia Cruz**
• listen to a song by **Celia Cruz**

**Instructional Resources
Supersite
Vista Higher Learning**
*Cancionero*

**Antes de escuchar**
• Have students read the title
of the song and scan the
lyrics for examples of the
preterite tense. Tell them
to write down any other
examples they hear as they
listen to the song.
• Ask students to predict what
type of song this is, based on
the lyrics.

**¿Cierto o falso?** Give
students these true-false
statements as items 5–7:
**5. Celia vivió en Nueva York por
muchos años. (Cierto.) 6. Murió
en La Habana, Cuba. (Falso.)
7. Recibió muchos premios**
(*awards*). **(Cierto.)**

**Preguntas** Ask additional
questions such as these:
**¿Conocen otras canciones
que tienen el mismo tema que
esta canción? ¿Creen que
hay esperanza** (*hope*) **en esta
canción? ¿Por qué?**

**TEACHING OPTIONS**

**Worth Noting Celia's** inimitable trademark word, **¡Azúcar!**,
animated audiences and became inextricably linked with her
lively spirit. In an interview, she explained how she came up
with it. She was at a restaurant in Miami once, and she ordered
a Cuban coffee. The waiter asked if she wanted sugar in it. She
replied, "Of course I want sugar in it! Isn't that how we Cubans
always drink our coffee? **¡Azúcar!**"

**Small Groups** Have students work in groups of three. For homework, have them do research on the Internet to find a photo of
**Celia Cruz** during one of her performances. Have them research the
performance as well. Have them write a short paragraph describing
where the concert took place, when, what **Celia** sang and what she
wore, using vocabulary and grammar from this lesson. Have groups
present their photos and descriptions to the class.

# Cuba

connections cultures NATIONAL STANDARDS

## El país en cifras

‣ **Área:** 110.860 km$^2$ (42.803 millas$^2$), *aproximadamente el área de Pensilvania*

‣ **Población:** 11.379.000

‣ **Capital:** La Habana—2.159.000

*La Habana Vieja fue declarada° Patrimonio° Cultural de la Humanidad por la UNESCO en 1982. Este distrito es uno de los lugares más fascinantes de Cuba. En La Plaza de Armas, se puede visitar el majestuoso Palacio de Capitanes Generales, que ahora es un museo. En la calle° Obispo, frecuentada por el autor Ernest Hemingway, hay hermosos cafés, clubes nocturnos y tiendas elegantes.*

‣ **Ciudades principales:** Santiago de Cuba; Camagüey; Holguín; Guantánamo
SOURCE: Population Division, UN Secretariat

‣ **Moneda:** peso cubano

‣ **Idiomas:** español (oficial)

Bandera de Cuba

**Cubanos célebres**

‣ **Carlos Finlay,** doctor y científico (1833–1915)

‣ **José Martí,** político y poeta (1853–1895)

‣ **Fidel Castro,** primer ministro, comandante en jefe° de las fuerzas armadas (1926– )

‣ **Zoé Valdés,** escritora (1959– )

‣ **Ibrahim Ferrer,** músico (1927–2005)

fue declarada *was declared* Patrimonio *Heritage* calle *street* comandante en jefe *commander in chief* liviano *light* colibrí abeja *hummingbird bee* ave *bird* mundo *world* miden *measure* pesan *weigh*

Fortaleza El Morro

Golfo de México

ESTADOS UNIDOS

Playa en Santiago de Cuba

Océano Atlántico

Cabaret Tropicana, famoso club de La Habana

La Habana

Cordillera de los Órganos

ESTADOS UNIDOS
CUBA OCÉANO ATLÁNTICO
OCÉANO PACÍFICO
AMÉRICA DEL SUR

Isla de la Juventud

Mar Caribe

Camagüe

Vista aérea de campos de caña de azúcar

**recursos**

WB pp. 69–70

VM pp. 235–236

SUPERSITE panorama.vhlcentral.com Lección 6

### ¡Increíble pero cierto!

Pequeño y liviano°, el colibrí abeja° de Cuba es una de las 320 especies de colibrí, y es también el ave° más pequeña del mundo°. Menores que muchos insectos, estas aves minúsculas miden° 5 centímetros y pesan° sólo 1,95 gramos.

---

---

## Baile • Ballet Nacional de Cuba

La bailarina Alicia Alonso fundó el Ballet Nacional de Cuba en 1948, después de° convertirse en una estrella° internacional en el Ballet de Nueva York y en Broadway. El Ballet Nacional de Cuba es famoso en todo el mundo por su creatividad y perfección técnica.

## Economía • La caña de azúcar y el tabaco

La caña de azúcar° es el producto agrícola° que más se cultiva en la isla y su exportación es muy importante para la economía del país. El tabaco, que se usa para fabricar los famosos puros° cubanos, es otro cultivo de mucha importancia.

## Historia • Los taínos

Los taínos eran° una de las tres tribus indígenas que vivían° en Cuba cuando llegaron los españoles en el siglo XV. Los taínos también vivían en Puerto Rico, la República Dominicana, Haití, Trinidad, Jamaica y en partes de las Bahamas y la Florida.

## Música • Buena Vista Social Club

En 1997 nace° el fenómeno musical conocido como *Buena Vista Social Club*. Este proyecto reúne° a un grupo de importantes músicos de Cuba, la mayoría ya mayores, con una larga trayectoria interpretando canciones clásicas del son° cubano. Ese mismo año ganaron un *Grammy*. Hoy en día estos músicos son conocidos en todo el mundo, y personas de todas las edades bailan al ritmo° de su música.

Holguín

Santiago de Cuba
Guantánamo

rra Maestra

 **¿Qué aprendiste?** Responde a las preguntas con una oración completa.

1. ¿En qué año nació la escritora cubana Zoé Valdés? Zoé Valdés nació en 1959.
2. ¿Qué autor está asociado con la Habana Vieja? Ernest Hemingway está asociado con la Habana Vieja.
3. ¿Por qué es famoso el Ballet Nacional de Cuba? Es famoso por su creatividad y perfección técnica.
4. ¿Cuáles son los dos cultivos más importantes para la economía cubana? Los cultivos más importantes son la caña de azúcar y el tabaco.
5. ¿Qué fabrican los cubanos con la planta del tabaco? Los cubanos fabrican puros.
6. ¿Quiénes son los taínos? Son una tribu indígena.
7. ¿En qué año ganó un *Grammy* el disco *Buena Vista Social Club*? Ganó un *Grammy* en 1997.

 **Conexión Internet** Investiga estos temas en **panorama.vhlcentral.com.**

1. Busca información sobre un(a) cubano/a célebre. ¿Por qué es célebre? ¿Qué hace? ¿Todavía vive en Cuba?
2. Busca información sobre una de las ciudades principales de Cuba. ¿Qué atracciones hay en esta ciudad?

................................................................................................................................

después de *after*  estrella *star*  caña de azúcar *sugar cane*  agrícola *farming*  puros *cigars*  eran *were*  vivían *lived*
nace *is born*  reúne *gets together*  son *Cuban musical genre*  ritmo *rhythm*

---

**Ballet Nacional de Cuba**
Although the **Ballet Nacional de Cuba** specializes in classical dance, Cuban popular dances (**habanera, mambo, rumba**) have gained worldwide popularity. Students can interview grandparents or other adults to see what they remember about Cuban dances.

**La caña de azúcar y el tabaco**
With the collapse of the Soviet bloc and the end of subsidies, Cuba's economy suffered. In 1990, Cuba entered **el período especial en tiempo de paz**. Government planners have developed tourism, which formerly was seen as bourgeois and corrupting, as a means of gaining badly-needed foreign currency.

**Los taínos** The Taínos had a deep understanding of the use of native plants for medicinal purposes. Traditional Taíno healing arts have been preserved and handed down across generations in Cuba. Today, ethno-botanists are exploring this traditional knowledge as they search for modern medical resources.

**Buena Vista Social Club**
If students are not familiar with the film or the music of **Buena Vista Social Club,** bring in some songs from the sound track for students to hear. Read some song titles and have students make predictions about the music before they listen.

**Conexión Internet** Students will find supporting Internet activities and links at **panorama.vhlcentral.com.**

**Teaching Tip** You may want to wrap up this section by playing the *Panorama cultural* video footage for this lesson.

---

**TEACHING OPTIONS**

**Language Notes** Some Cuban songs mention beings with names that do not sound Spanish, such as **Obatalá, Elegguá,** and **Babaluayé**. These are divinities (**orichas**) of the Afro-Cuban religion, which has its origins in Yoruba-speaking West Africa. Forcibly converted to Catholicism upon their arrival in Cuba, Africans developed a syncretized religion in which they worshiped the gods they had brought from Africa in the form of Catholic saints. **Babaluayé,** for instance, is worshiped as **San Lázaro. Obatalá** is **Nuestra Señora de las Mercedes.** Cuban popular music is deeply rooted in the songs and dances with which Afro-Cubans expressed their devotion to the **orichas.**

**Instructional Resources**
**Supersite:** Textbook & Vocabulary MP3 Audio Files
**Lección 6**
**Supersite/IRCD:** *IRM* (WBs/ VM/LM Answer Key); *Testing Program* (**Lección 6 Pruebas,** Test Generator, Testing Program MP3 Audio Files)
**WebSAM**
**Lab Manual,** p. 36

## La ropa

| | |
|---|---|
| el abrigo | coat |
| los bluejeans | jeans |
| la blusa | blouse |
| la bolsa | purse; bag |
| la bota | boot |
| los calcetines (el calcetín) | sock(s) |
| la camisa | shirt |
| la camiseta | t-shirt |
| la cartera | wallet |
| la chaqueta | jacket |
| el cinturón | belt |
| la corbata | tie |
| la falda | skirt |
| las gafas (de sol) | (sun)glasses |
| los guantes | gloves |
| el impermeable | raincoat |
| las medias | pantyhose; stockings |
| los pantalones | pants |
| los pantalones cortos | shorts |
| la ropa | clothing; clothes |
| la ropa interior | underwear |
| las sandalias | sandals |
| el sombrero | hat |
| el suéter | sweater |
| el traje | suit |
| el traje de baño | bathing suit |
| el vestido | dress |
| los zapatos de tenis | tennis shoes, sneakers |

## Verbos

| | |
|---|---|
| conducir | to drive |
| conocer | to know; to be acquainted with |
| ofrecer | to offer |
| parecer | to seem |
| saber | to know; to know how |
| traducir | to translate |

## Ir de compras

| | |
|---|---|
| el almacén | department store |
| la caja | cash register |
| el centro comercial | shopping mall |
| el/la cliente/a | customer |
| el/la dependiente/a | clerk |
| el dinero | money |
| (en) efectivo | cash |
| el mercado (al aire libre) | (open-air) market |
| un par (de zapatos) | a pair (of shoes) |
| el precio (fijo) | (fixed; set) price |
| la rebaja | sale |
| el regalo | gift |
| la tarjeta de crédito | credit card |
| la tienda | shop; store |
| el/la vendedor(a) | salesperson |
| costar (o:ue) | to cost |
| gastar | to spend (money) |
| hacer juego (con) | to match (with) |
| llevar | to wear; to take |
| pagar | to pay |
| regatear | to bargain |
| usar | to wear; to use |
| vender | to sell |

## Adjetivos

| | |
|---|---|
| barato/a | cheap |
| bueno/a | good |
| cada | each |
| caro/a | expensive |
| corto/a | short (in length) |
| elegante | elegant |
| hermoso/a | beautiful |
| largo/a | long |
| loco/a | crazy |
| nuevo/a | new |
| otro/a | other; another |
| pobre | poor |
| rico/a | rich |

## Los colores

| | |
|---|---|
| el color | color |
| amarillo/a | yellow |
| anaranjado/a | orange |
| azul | blue |
| blanco/a | white |
| gris | gray |
| marrón, café | brown |
| morado/a | purple |
| negro/a | black |
| rojo/a | red |
| rosado/a | pink |
| verde | green |

## Palabras adicionales

| | |
|---|---|
| acabar de (+ *inf.*) | to have just done something |
| anoche | last night |
| anteayer | the day before yesterday |
| ayer | yesterday |
| de repente | suddenly |
| desde | from |
| dos veces | twice; two times |
| hasta | until |
| pasado/a (*adj.*) | last; past |
| el año pasado | last year |
| la semana pasada | last week |
| prestar | to lend; to loan |
| una vez | once; one time |
| ya | already |

| | |
|---|---|
| Indirect object pronouns | See page 186. |
| Demonstrative adjectives and pronouns | See page 194. |
| Expresiones útiles | See page 179. |

recursos

LM p. 36 | panorama.vhlcentral.com Lección 6

# La rutina diaria

## Communicative Goals

**You will learn how to:**

- **Describe your daily routine**
- **Talk about personal hygiene**
- **Reassure someone**

## Lesson Goals

In **Lección 7**, students will be introduced to the following:

- terms for daily routines
- reflexive verbs
- adverbs of time
- the custom of **la siesta**
- **ir de tapas** as part of a daily routine
- indefinite and negative words
- preterite of **ser** and **ir**
- verbs like **gustar**
- predicting content from the title
- cultural, geographic, and historical information about Peru

**A primera vista** Here are some additional questions you can ask based on the photo: **¿Con quién vives? ¿Qué le dices antes de salir de casa? ¿Qué tipo de ropa llevas para ir a tus clases? ¿Les prestas esta ropa a tus amigos/as? ¿Qué ropa usaste en el verano? ¿Y en el invierno?**

### A PRIMERA VISTA

- ¿Está él en casa o en una tienda?
- ¿Está contento o enojado?
- ¿Cómo es él?
- ¿Qué colores hay en la foto?

---

**INSTRUCTIONAL RESOURCES**

*MAESTRO™* SUPERSITE (panorama.vhlcentral.com)
  Textbook, Vocabulary, & Lab MP3 Audio Files
  Additional Practice
  Learning Management System (Assignment Task
  Manager, Gradebook)
  *Also on DVD*
    **Fotonovela**

*Flash cultura*
*Panorama cultural*
*Also on Instructor's Resource CD-ROM*
  *PowerPoints* (**Contextos** & **Estructura** Presentations,
  Overheads)
  *Instructor's Resource Manual* (Handouts,
  Textbook Answer Key, WBs/VM/LM Answer Key,

Audioscripts, Videoscripts & Translations)
  *Testing Program* (**Pruebas,** Test Generator, MP3s)
**WebSAM** (Workbook/Video Manual/Lab Manual)
**Workbook/Video Manual**
*Cuaderno para hispanohablantes*
**Lab Manual**

## Section Goals

In **Contextos**, students will learn and practice:
- vocabulary to talk about daily routines
- reflexive verbs to talk about daily routines
- adverbs of time

### Instructional Resources

**Supersite:** Textbook, Vocabulary, & Lab MP3 Audio Files **Lección 7**
**Supersite/IRCD:** *PowerPoints* (**Lección 7 Contextos** Presentation, Overhead #31); *IRM* (**Vocabulario adicional,** Textbook Audio Script, Lab Audio Script, WBs/VM/LM Answer Key)
**WebSAM**
**Workbook,** pp. 73–74
**Lab Manual,** p. 37
*Cuaderno para hispanohablantes*

### Teaching Tips

- Write **levantarse por la mañana** on the board and explain that it means *to get up in the morning.* Ask: **¿A qué hora te levantas por la mañana los lunes?** Ask another student: **¿A qué hora se levanta _____ ?** Then ask about Saturdays. Write **acostarse (o:ue)** on the board and explain that it means *to go to bed.* Follow the same procedure as for **levantarse.**
- Reflexives will only be used in the infinitive and third-person forms until **Estructura 7.1.**
- Show *Overhead PowerPoint #31* and have students refer to the scenes as you make true-false statements about them. Have them correct false statements. Ex: **Hay una chica que se peina por la noche en la habitación. (Cierto.)**
- If students ask, explain that **el pelo** is never used with **peinarse,** only with **cepillarse.**

**Note:** At this point you may want to present *Vocabulario adicional: Más vocabulario para la vida diaria,* from the Supersite/IRCD.

# La rutina diaria

## Más vocabulario

| | |
|---|---|
| el baño, el cuarto de baño | bathroom |
| el inodoro | toilet |
| el jabón | soap |
| el despertador | alarm clock |
| el maquillaje | makeup |
| la rutina diaria | daily routine |
| bañarse | to bathe; to take a bath |
| cepillarse el pelo | to brush one's hair |
| dormirse (o:ue) | to go to sleep; to fall asleep |
| lavarse la cara | to wash one's face |
| levantarse | to get up |
| maquillarse | to put on makeup |
| antes (de) | before |
| después | afterwards; then |
| después (de) | after |
| durante | during |
| entonces | then |
| luego | then |
| más tarde | later |
| por la mañana | in the morning |
| por la noche | at night |
| por la tarde | in the afternoon; in the evening |
| por último | finally |

## Variación léxica

| | | |
|---|---|---|
| afeitarse | ⟷ | rasurarse *(Méx., Amér. C.)* |
| ducha | ⟷ | regadera *(Col., Méx., Venez.)* |
| ducharse | ⟷ | bañarse *(Amér. L.)* |
| pantuflas | ⟷ | chancletas *(Méx., Col.);* zapatillas *(Esp.)* |

**recursos**

| WB pp. 73–74 | LM p. 37 | panorama.vhlcentral.com Lección 7 |

### En la habitación por la mañana

Se viste. (vestirse)

Se despierta. (despertarse)

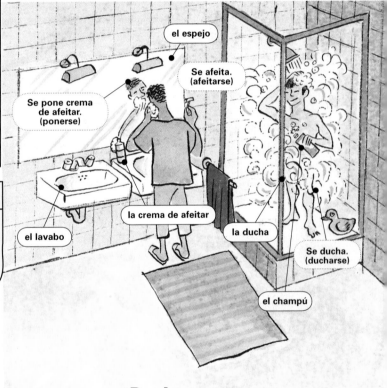

el espejo

Se afeita. (afeitarse)

Se pone crema de afeitar. (ponerse)

el lavabo

la crema de afeitar

la ducha

Se ducha. (ducharse)

el champú

### Por la mañana

## TEACHING OPTIONS

**TPR** In groups of three, have students take turns miming actions involving daily routines. The other group members should guess the verb or verb phrase. You may want to have students use only the infinitive form at this point. Ex: A student mimes washing their hands (**lavarse las manos**).

**Variación léxica** Ask heritage speakers if they use any of the words in **Variación léxica** and if they know of other words used to describe daily routines (Ex: **lavarse la boca/los dientes**). You may want to point out that other words for *bedroom* include **la alcoba, el aposento, el cuarto, el dormitorio,** and **la recámara.**

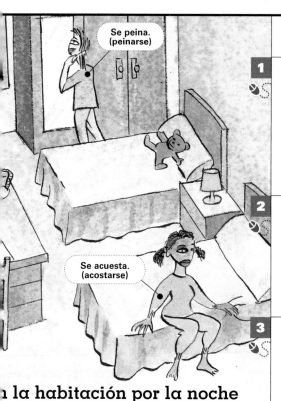

Se peina.
(peinarse)

Se acuesta.
(acostarse)

la habitación por la noche

Se lava las manos.
(lavarse las manos)

Se cepilla los dientes.
(cepillarse los dientes)

la toalla

la pasta
de dientes

tuflas

Por la noche

# Práctica

**1** **Escuchar** 🎧 Escucha las oraciones e indica si cada oración es **cierta** o **falsa**, según el dibujo.

1. _falsa_
2. _cierta_
3. _falsa_
4. _cierta_
5. _falsa_
6. _falsa_
7. _falsa_
8. _cierta_
9. _falsa_
10. _cierta_

**2** **Ordenar** 🎧 Escucha la rutina diaria de Marta. Después ordena los verbos según lo que escuchaste.

_5_ a. almorzar
_2_ b. ducharse
_4_ c. peinarse
_7_ d. ver la televisión
_3_ e. desayunar
_8_ f. dormirse
_1_ g. despertarse
_6_ h. estudiar en la biblioteca

**3** **Seleccionar** Selecciona la palabra que no está relacionada con cada grupo.

1. lavabo • toalla • despertador • jabón ___despertador___
2. manos • antes de • después de • por último ___manos___
3. acostarse • jabón • despertarse • dormirse ___jabón___
4. espejo • lavabo • despertador • entonces ___entonces___
5. dormirse • toalla • vestirse • levantarse ___toalla___
6. pelo • cara • manos • inodoro ___inodoro___
7. espejo • champú • jabón • pasta de dientes ___espejo___
8. maquillarse • vestirse • peinarse • dientes ___dientes___
9. baño • dormirse • despertador • acostarse ___baño___
10. ducharse • luego • bañarse • lavarse ___luego___

**4** **Identificar** Con un(a) compañero/a, identifica las cosas que cada persona necesita. Sigue el modelo. Some answers will vary.

> **modelo**
> Jorge / lavarse la cara
> **Estudiante 1:** ¿Qué necesita Jorge para lavarse la cara?
> **Estudiante 2:** Necesita jabón y una toalla.

1. Mariana / maquillarse  maquillaje y un espejo
2. Gerardo / despertarse  un despertador
3. Celia / bañarse  jabón y una toalla
4. Gabriel / ducharse  una ducha, una toalla y jabón
5. Roberto / afeitarse  crema de afeitar
6. Sonia / lavarse el pelo  champú y una toalla
7. Vanesa / lavarse las manos  jabón y una toalla
8. Manuel / vestirse  su ropa/una camiseta/unos pantalones/etc.
9. Simón / acostarse  una cama
10. Daniela / cepillarse los dientes  pasta de dientes

---

**TEACHING OPTIONS**

**Pairs** Have students write out three daily routine activities without showing them to their partner. The partner will ask questions that contain adverbs of time in order to guess the action.
Ex: —¿Es antes o después de ducharse? —Antes de ducharse.
—¿Es levantarse? —Sí.

**Small Groups** Write verbs and verb phrases used to describe daily routines on separate note cards. Divide the class into small groups and give each group a set of cards. Have them work together to place them in the most logical order in which the actions occur.

**1** **Teaching Tip** Go over **Actividad 1** with the class. Then, have volunteers correct the false statements.

**1** **Script** 1. Hay dos despertadores en la habitación de las chicas. 2. Un chico se pone crema de afeitar en la cara. 3. Una de las chicas se ducha. 4. Uno de los chicos se afeita. 5. Hay una toalla en la habitación de las chicas. 6. Una de las chicas se maquilla. 7. Las chicas están en el baño. 8. Uno de los chicos se cepilla los dientes en el baño. 9. Uno de los chicos se viste. 10. Una de las chicas se despierta.
*Textbook MP3s*

**2** **Teaching Tip** To simplify, point out that the verbs in the list are in the infinitive form and tell students that they will hear them in conjugated (third-person singular) form. Before listening, have volunteers provide the third-person singular form of each verb.

**2** **Script** Normalmente, Marta por la mañana se despierta a las siete, pero no puede levantarse hasta las siete y media. Se ducha y después se viste. Luego desayuna y se cepilla los dientes. Después, se peina y se maquilla. Entonces sale para sus clases. Después de las clases almuerza con sus amigos y por la tarde estudia en la biblioteca. Regresa a casa, cena y ve un poco la televisión. Por la noche, generalmente se acuesta a las diez y por último, se duerme.
*Textbook MP3s*

**3** **Expansion** Go over the answers and indicate why a particular item does not belong. Ex: **El lavabo, la toalla y el jabón son para lavarse. El despertador es para despertarse.**

**4** **Expansion** Have students make statements about the people's actions, then ask a question. Ex: **Jorge se lava la cara. ¿Qué necesita?**

**5 Teaching Tip** To simplify, have students begin by identifying the adverbs of time in the sentences. Then have them read through all the items before attempting to put them in order.

**5 Expansion** Ask students if **Andrés's** schedule represents that of a "typical" student. Ask: **Un estudiante típico, ¿se despierta normalmente a las seis y media de la mañana? ¿A qué hora se despiertan ustedes?**

**6 Expansion**
- Ask brief comprehension questions about the actions in the drawings. Ex: **¿Quién se maquilla? (Lupe) ¿Quién se cepilla el pelo? (Ángel)**
- If students ask, point out that in drawing number 7, **Ángel se mira en el espejo.** Reflexive pronouns and verbs will be formally presented in **Estructura 7.1.** For now it is enough just to explain that *he is looking at himself*, hence the use of the pronoun **se**.

---

**5** **La rutina de Andrés** Ordena esta rutina de una manera lógica.

a. Se afeita después de cepillarse los dientes. __4__
b. Se acuesta a las once y media de la noche. __9__
c. Por último, se duerme. __10__
d. Después de afeitarse, sale para las clases. __5__
e. Asiste a todas sus clases y vuelve a su casa. __6__
f. Andrés se despierta a las seis y media de la mañana. __1__
g. Después de volver a casa, come un poco. Luego estudia en su habitación. __7__
h. Se viste y entonces se cepilla los dientes. __3__
i. Se cepilla los dientes antes de acostarse. __8__
j. Se ducha antes de vestirse. __2__

**6** **La rutina diaria** Con un(a) compañero/a, mira los dibujos y describe lo que hacen Ángel y Lupe.
Some answers may vary.

1.

Ángel se afeita y mira la televisión.

2.

Lupe se maquilla y escucha la radio.

3.

Ángel se ducha y canta.

4.

Lupe se baña y lee.

5.

Ángel se lava la cara con jabón.

6.

Lupe se lava el pelo con champú en la ducha.

7.

Ángel se cepilla el pelo.

8.

Lupe se cepilla los dientes.

---

**TEACHING OPTIONS**

**Extra Practice** Name daily routine activities and have students list all the words that they associate with each activity, such as things, places, and parts of the body. Ex: **lavarse las manos: el jabón, el cuarto de baño, el agua, la toalla**. How many associations can the class make for each activity?

**Small Groups** In groups of three or four, students think of a famous person or character and describe his or her daily routine. In their descriptions, students may use names of friends or family of the famous person or character. Have groups read their descriptions aloud for the rest of the class to guess.

# Comunicación

**7** **La farmacia** Lee el anuncio y responde a las preguntas con un(a) compañero/a.
Answers will vary.

**LA FARMACIA NUEVO SOL** tiene todo
lo que necesitas para la vida diaria.

**Esta semana tenemos grandes rebajas.**

Por poco dinero puedes comprar lo que necesitas para el
cuarto de baño ideal.

**Para los hombres ofrecemos…**
Buenas cremas de afeitar
de Guapo y Máximo

**Para las mujeres ofrecemos…**
Nuevos maquillajes de Marisol y
jabones de baño Ilusiones y Belleza

Y para todos tenemos los mejores jabones, pastas de dientes
y cepillos de dientes.

¡Visita **LA FARMACIA NUEVO SOL**!
Te ofrecemos los mejores precios. Tenemos una tienda cerca de tu casa.

1. ¿Qué tipo de tienda es?  Es una farmacia.
2. ¿Qué productos ofrecen para las mujeres?  maquillajes, jabones de baño
3. ¿Qué productos ofrecen para los hombres?  cremas de afeitar
4. Haz (*Make*) una lista de los verbos que asocias con los productos del anuncio.
5. ¿Dónde compras tus productos de higiene?  Answers will vary.
6. ¿Tienes una tienda favorita? ¿Cuál es?  Answers will vary.

Suggested answers:
afeitarse, maquillarse,
cepillarse los dientes

**8** **Rutinas diarias** Trabajen en parejas para describir la rutina diaria de dos o tres
de estas personas. Pueden usar palabras de la lista.  Answers will vary.

| antes (de) | entonces | primero |
|---|---|---|
| después (de) | luego | tarde |
| durante el día | por último | temprano |

- un(a) profesor(a) de la universidad
- un(a) turista
- un hombre o una mujer de negocios (*businessman/woman*)
- un vigilante (*night watchman*)
- un(a) jubilado/a (*retired person*)
- el presidente de los Estados Unidos
- un niño de cuatro años
▶ - Daniel Espinosa

**NOTA CULTURAL**

**Daniel Espinosa**
(México, 1961) es un
famoso diseñador
de joyería (*jewelry*).
Su trabajo es
vanguardista (*avant-
garde*), arriesgado
(*risky*) e innovador.
Su material favorito
es la plata (*silver*).
Entre sus clientes
están Nelly Furtado,
Eva Longoria, Salma
Hayek, Lindsay Lohan
y Daisy Fuentes.

**7** **Expansion** Ask small
groups to write a competing
ad for another pharmacy. Have
each group present its ad to
the class, who will vote for the
most persuasive one.

**8** **Expansion** Ask volunteers
to read their descriptions
aloud. Ask other pairs who
chose the same people if their
descriptions are similar and
how they differ.

**TEACHING OPTIONS**

**Small Groups** In groups of three or four, have students act out
a brief skit. The situation: they are roommates who are trying
to get ready for their morning classes at the same time. The
problem: there is only one bathroom in the house or apartment.
Have the class vote for the most original or funniest skit.

**Heritage Speakers** Ask heritage speakers to write paragraphs
describing their daily routine when living with their families.
Remind them to use the present tense and several expressions
of time from **Contextos** (**por la mañana, antes, durante,** etc.).
Have students read their paragraphs to the class, then verify
comprehension by calling on volunteers to describe their
classmates' routines.

## Section Goals

In **Fotonovela**, students will:
- receive comprehensible input from free-flowing discourse
- learn functional phrases that preview lesson grammatical structures

---

**Instructional Resources**
**Supersite/DVD:** *Fotonovela*
**Supersite/IRCD:** *IRM*
(*Fotonovela* Videoscript & Translation, WBs/VM/LM Answer Key)
**WebSAM**
**Video Manual,** pp. 207–208

---

### Video Recap: Lección 6
Before doing this **Fotonovela** section, review the previous one with this activity.

1. ¿Qué está buscando Inés en el mercado? (un regalo para su hermana Graciela) 2. ¿Qué necesita Javier para su excursión a las montañas? (un suéter) 3. ¿Por qué le da el vendedor un buen precio a Javier? (Javier regatea.) 4. ¿Qué compró Inés en el mercado? (una bolsa, una camisa y un sombrero)

### Video Synopsis
**Javier** returns from the market and shows **Álex** the sweater he bought. Since they have to get up early the next day, **Álex** agrees to wake up **Javier** after his morning run. **Don Francisco** comes by to remind them that the bus will leave at 8:30 a.m.

### Teaching Tip
Have students skim the **Fotonovela** captions for the gist and write down their impressions. Ask a few volunteers to share their impressions with the class.

---

# ¡Jamás me levanto temprano!

Álex y Javier hablan de sus rutinas diarias.

**PERSONAJES**

**DON FRANCISCO**

**ÁLEX**

**JAVIER**

**JAVIER** Hola, Álex. ¿Qué estás haciendo?

**ÁLEX** Nada… sólo estoy leyendo mi correo electrónico. ¿Adónde fueron?

**JAVIER** Inés y yo fuimos a un mercado. Fue muy divertido. Mira, compré este suéter. Me encanta. No fue barato pero es chévere, ¿no?

**ÁLEX** Sí, es ideal para las montañas.

**JAVIER** ¡Qué interesantes son los mercados al aire libre! Me gustaría volver pero ya es tarde. Oye, Álex, sabes que mañana tenemos que levantarnos temprano.

**ÁLEX** Ningún problema.

**JAVIER** ¡Increíble! ¡Álex, el superhombre!

**ÁLEX** Oye, Javier, ¿por qué no puedes levantarte temprano?

**JAVIER** Es que por la noche no quiero dormir, sino dibujar y escuchar música. Por eso es difícil despertarme por la mañana.

**JAVIER** El autobús no sale hasta las ocho y media. ¿Vas a levantarte mañana a las seis también?

**ÁLEX** No, pero tengo que levantarme a las siete menos cuarto porque voy a correr.

**JAVIER** Ah, ya… ¿Puedes despertarme después de correr?

**ÁLEX** Éste es el plan para mañana. Me levanto a las siete menos cuarto y corro por treinta minutos. Vuelvo, me ducho, me visto y a las siete y media te despierto. ¿De acuerdo?

**JAVIER** ¡Absolutamente ninguna objeción!

**recursos**

VM
pp. 207–208

panorama.vhlcentral.com
Lección 7

---

**JAVIER** ¿Seguro? Pues yo jamás me levanto temprano. Nunca oigo el despertador cuando estoy en casa y mi mamá se enoja mucho.

**ÁLEX** Tranquilo, Javier. Yo tengo una solución.

**ÁLEX** Cuando estoy en casa en la Ciudad de México, siempre me despierto a las seis en punto. Me ducho en cinco minutos y luego me cepillo los dientes. Después me afeito, me visto y ¡listo! ¡Me voy!

**DON FRANCISCO** Hola, chicos. Mañana salimos temprano, a las ocho y media... ni un minuto antes ni un minuto después.

**ÁLEX** No se preocupe, don Francisco. Todo está bajo control.

**DON FRANCISCO** Bueno, pues, hasta mañana.

**DON FRANCISCO** ¡Ay, los estudiantes! Siempre se acuestan tarde. ¡Qué vida!

## Expresiones útiles

### Telling where you went

- **¿Adónde fuiste/fue usted?**
  *Where did you go?*
  **Fui a un mercado.**
  *I went to a market.*
- **¿Adónde fueron ustedes?**
  *Where did you go?*
  **Fuimos a un mercado. Fue divertido.**
  *We went to a market. It was fun.*

### Talking about morning routines

- **(Jamás) me levanto temprano/tarde.**
  *I (never) get up early/late.*
- **Nunca oigo el despertador.**
  *I never hear the alarm clock.*
- **Es difícil/fácil despertarme.**
  *It's hard/easy to wake up.*
- **Cuando estoy en casa, siempre me despierto a las seis en punto.**
  *When I'm home, I always wake up at six on the dot.*
- **Me ducho y luego me cepillo los dientes.**
  *I take a shower and then I brush my teeth.*
- **Después me afeito y me visto.**
  *Afterwards, I shave and get dressed.*

### Reassuring someone

- **No hay problema.**
  *No problem.*
- **No te/se preocupes/preocupe.**
  *Don't worry. (fam.)/(form.)*
- **Tranquilo.**
  *Don't worry.; Be cool.*

### Additional vocabulary

- **sino**
  *but (rather)*
- **Me encanta este suéter.**
  *I love this sweater.*
- **Me fascinó la película.**
  *I liked the movie a lot.*

**Teaching Tip** Have students get together in groups of three to role-play the episode. Have one or two groups present it to the class.

**Expresiones útiles** Draw attention to preterite forms of **ser** and **ir** in the captions for video stills 1 and 2. Ask volunteers to use context to determine which verb is used in each example. Point out first- and second-person reflexive verb forms and call on students to provide the infinitive form of each verb. Explain that **siempre**, **nunca**, and **jamás** are examples of indefinite and negative words. Tell students they will learn more about these concepts in **Estructura**.

---

**TEACHING OPTIONS**

**TPR** Ask students to write **Javier** and **Álex** on separate pieces of paper. Read aloud statements about the characters' daily routines and have students hold up the corresponding name. Ex: **No me gusta levantarme temprano. (Javier)** Then repeat the process for tomorrow's plan. Ex: **Mañana me ducho después de correr. (Álex)**

**Extra Practice** Ask students to write a short description about what they think **don Francisco's** daily routine is like. Then have them get together with a classmate to find similarities and differences in their descriptions.

**Pairs** Ask pairs of students to work together to create six true-false sentences about the **Fotonovela**. Have pairs exchange papers and complete the activity.

# ¿Qué pasó?

**1** ¿Cierto o falso? Indica si lo que dicen estas oraciones es **cierto** o **falso**. Corrige las oraciones falsas.

1. Álex está mirando la televisión.
   Falso. Álex está leyendo su correo electrónico.
2. El suéter que Javier acaba de comprar es caro pero es muy bonito.
   Cierto.
3. Javier cree que el mercado es aburrido y no quiere volver.
   Falso. Javier piensa que el mercado es muy interesante.
4. El autobús va a salir mañana a las siete y media en punto.
   Falso. El autobús sale mañana a las ocho y media en punto.
5. A Javier le gusta mucho dibujar y escuchar música por la noche.
   Cierto.

**¡LENGUA VIVA!**

Remember that **en punto** means *on the dot*. If the group were instead leaving at *around seven thirty*, you would say **a eso de las siete y media**.

**2** Identificar Identifica quién puede decir estas oraciones. Puedes usar cada nombre más de una vez.

1. ¡Ay, los estudiantes nunca se acuestan temprano!
   _don Francisco_
2. ¿El despertador? ¡Jamás lo oigo por la mañana!
   _Javier_
3. Es fácil despertarme temprano. Y sólo necesito cinco minutos para ducharme. ___Álex___
4. Mañana vamos a salir a las ocho y media.
   _Javier, don Francisco_
5. Acabo de ir a un mercado fabuloso. ___Javier___
6. No se preocupe. Tenemos todo bajo control para mañana. ___Álex___

**DON FRANCISCO**

**JAVIER**

**ÁLEX**

**3** Ordenar Ordena correctamente los planes que tiene Álex.

- _5_ a. Me visto.
- _2_ b. Corro por media hora.
- _6_ c. Despierto a Javier a las siete y media.
- _3_ d. Vuelvo a la habitación.
- _1_ e. Me levanto a las siete menos cuarto.
- _4_ f. Me ducho.

**4** Mi rutina En parejas, hablen de sus rutinas de la mañana y de la noche. Indiquen a qué horas hacen las actividades más importantes. Answers will vary.

**CONSULTA**

To review telling time in Spanish, see **Estructura 1.4**, pp. 24–25.

**modelo**

**Estudiante 1:** ¿Prefieres levantarte temprano o tarde?
**Estudiante 2:** Prefiero levantarme tarde… muy tarde.

**Estudiante 1:** ¿A qué hora te levantas durante la semana?
**Estudiante 2:** A las once. ¿Y tú?

---

**1** **Expansion** Give students these true-false statements as items 6–8: **6. Javier siempre se despierta temprano. (Falso. Álex siempre se despierta temprano.) 7. Don Francisco cree que los estudiantes siempre se acuestan temprano. (Falso. Don Francisco cree que los estudiantes siempre se acuestan tarde.) 8. Álex va a despertar a Javier después de ducharse. (Cierto.)**

**2** **Expansion** Give students these sentences as items 7–8: **7. Quiero volver al mercado, pero no hay tiempo. (Javier) 8. Cuando estoy en casa, siempre me despierto muy temprano. (Álex)**

**3** **Teaching Tip** Before doing this activity, have students quickly glance over the caption for video still 8, page 214.

**3** **Expansion** Ask pairs to imagine another character's plans for the following day and list them using the **yo** form of the verbs, as in the activity. Then have pairs share their lists with the class.

**4** **Teaching Tip** Encourage students to use as many reflexive infinitives from **Contextos** as they can.

**4** **Possible Conversation**
E1: ¿Prefieres levantarte tarde o temprano?
E2: Prefiero levantarme tarde… muy tarde.
E1: ¿A qué hora te levantas durante la semana?
E2: A las once. ¿Y tú?
E1: Siempre me levanto muy temprano… a las cinco y media.
E2: Y, ¿a qué hora te acuestas?
E1: Siempre me acuesto temprano, a las diez o a las once. ¿Y tú?
E2: Yo prefiero acostarme a las doce.

---

**TEACHING OPTIONS**

**Extra Practice** Add an auditory aspect to this vocabulary practice. Ask students to close their books. Then read aloud the sentences from **Actividad 3**, in the correct order. Read each sentence twice slowly to give students an opportunity to write. Then read them again at normal speed, without pausing, to allow students to check for accuracy or fill in any gaps.

**Small Groups** Have students get together in groups of three to discuss and compare their daily routines. Have them use as many of the words and expressions from this lesson as they can. Then ask for a few volunteers to describe the daily routine of one of their group members.

# Pronunciación
## The consonant r

| ropa | rutina | rico | Ramón |
|---|---|---|---|

In Spanish, **r** has a strong trilled sound at the beginning of a word. No English words have a trill, but English speakers often produce a trill when they imitate the sound of a motor.

| gustar | durante | primero | crema |
|---|---|---|---|

In any other position, **r** has a weak sound similar to the English *tt* in *better* or the English *dd* in *ladder*. In contrast to English, the tongue touches the roof of the mouth behind the teeth.

| pizarra | corro | marrón | aburrido |
|---|---|---|---|

The letter combination **rr**, which only appears between vowels, always has a strong trilled sound.

| caro | carro | pero | perro |
|---|---|---|---|

Between vowels, the difference between the strong trilled **rr** and the weak **r** is very important, as a mispronunciation could lead to confusion between two different words.

**Práctica** Lee las palabras en voz alta, prestando (*paying*) atención a la pronunciación de la **r** y la **rr**.

1. Perú
2. Rosa
3. borrador
4. madre
5. comprar
6. favor
7. rubio
8. reloj
9. Arequipa
10. tarde
11. cerrar
12. despertador

**Oraciones** Lee las oraciones en voz alta, prestando atención a la pronunciación de la **r** y la **rr**.

1. Ramón Robles Ruiz es programador. Su esposa Rosaura es artista.
2. A Rosaura Robles le encanta regatear en el mercado.
3. Ramón nunca regatea… le aburre regatear.
4. Rosaura siempre compra cosas baratas.
5. Ramón no es rico pero prefiere comprar cosas muy caras.
6. ¡El martes Ramón compró un carro nuevo!

**Refranes** Lee en voz alta los refranes, prestando atención a la **r** y la **rr**.

Perro que ladra no muerde.[1]

No se ganó Zamora en una hora.[2]

[1] A dog's bark is worse than its bite.
[2] Rome wasn't built in a day.

| recursos |
|---|
| LM p. 38 |
| panorama.vhlcentral.com Lección 7 |

**Section Goal**

In **Pronunciación**, students will be introduced to the pronunciation of the consonant **r** and the letter combination **rr**.

**Instructional Resources**
**Supersite:** Textbook & Lab MP3 Audio Files **Lección 7**
**Supersite/IRCD:** *IRM* (Textbook Audio Script, Lab Audio Script, WB/VM/LM Answer Key)
**WebSAM**
**Lab Manual,** p. 38
*Cuaderno para hispanohablantes*

**Teaching Tips**
• Before students repeat the sample words, ask the class to imitate the sound of a motorcycle. To avoid frustration, remind students that most native English speakers have difficulty with the trilled **r** sound and that their ability to pronounce it will improve with practice.
• Explain that **r** is trilled at the beginning of a word, and that there are no words that have a trill in American English. Model the pronunciation of **ropa, rutina, rico,** and **Ramón** and have the class repeat.
• Point out that in any other position, **r** is pronounced like the *tt* in American English *better*. Write the words **gustar, durante, primero,** and **crema** on the board and ask a volunteer to pronounce each word.
• Point out that **rr** always has a strong trilled sound and that it only appears between vowels. Pronounce the words **pizarra, corro, marrón,** and **aburrido** and have the class repeat.
• To help students discriminate between **r** and **rr**, write on the board the pairs **caro/carro** and **pero/perro**. Then pronounce each pair several times in random order, pausing after each for students to repeat. Ex: **caro, carro, caro, carro, caro, carro**

**Práctica/Oraciones/Refranes** These exercises are recorded in the *Textbook MP3s.* You may want to play the audio so that students practice the pronunciation point by listening to Spanish spoken by speakers other than yourself.

**TEACHING OPTIONS**

**Extra Practice** Write the names of a few Peruvian cities on the board and ask for a volunteer to pronounce each name. Ex: **Huaraz, Cajamarca, Trujillo, Puerto Maldonado, Cerro de Pasco, Piura.** Then write the names of a few Peruvian literary figures on the board and repeat the process. Ex: **Ricardo Palma, Ciro Alegría, Mario Vargas Llosa, César Vallejo.**

**Small Groups** Have students work in small groups and take turns reading aloud sentences from the **Fotonovela** on pages 214–215, focusing on the correct pronunciation of **r** and **rr**.
**Extra Practice** Write this rhyme on the board and have students practice trilling: **Erre con erre, cigarro, erre con erre, barril, rápido corren los carros, sobre los rieles del ferrocarril.**

## Section Goals

In **Cultura**, students will:
- read about the custom of **la siesta**
- learn terms related to personal hygiene
- read about how **ir de tapas** is part of a daily routine
- read about special customs in Mexico, El Salvador, Costa Rica, and Argentina

---

**Instructional Resources**
**Supersite:** *Flash cultura*
Videoscript & Translation
**Supersite/DVD:** *Flash cultura*
***Cuaderno para hispanohablantes***

---

**En detalle**
**Antes de leer** Ask students about their sleep habits.
**¿Cuántas horas duermes al día? ¿Tu horario te permite volver a casa y descansar al mediodía? Si no duermes bien durante la noche, ¿te duermes en clase?**

**Lectura**
- Point out that observance of the **siesta** is not universal. For example, when Spain entered the European Union, businesspeople began to adjust their work schedules to mirror those of their counterparts in other European countries.
- Explain that, as a result of the midday rest, a typical workday might end at 7 or 8 p.m.

**Después de leer**
- Have students share what facts in this reading are new or surprising to them.
- Ask students if they think the **siesta** should be incorporated into academic and business schedules in the United States or Canada. What sort of impact would this have?

**1** **Expansion** Ask students to create questions related to the corrected statements. Ex: **1. ¿Dónde empezó la costumbre de la siesta?**

---

**EN DETALLE**

# La siesta

**¿Sientes cansancio° después de comer?** ¿Te cuesta° volver al trabajo° o a clase después del almuerzo? Estas sensaciones son normales. A muchas personas les gusta relajarse° después de almorzar. Este momento de descanso es **la siesta**. La siesta es popular en los países hispanos y viene de una antigua costumbre° del área del Mediterráneo. La palabra *siesta* viene del latín; es una forma corta de decir "sexta hora". La sexta hora del día es después del mediodía, el momento de más calor. Debido al° calor y al cansancio, los habitantes de España, Italia, Grecia e incluso Portugal, tienen la costumbre de dormir la siesta desde hace° más de° dos mil años. Los españoles y los portugueses llevaron la costumbre a los países americanos.

La siesta es muy importante en la cultura hispana. Muchas oficinas° y tiendas cierran dos o tres horas después del mediodía. Los empleados van a su casa, almuerzan, duermen la siesta y regresan al trabajo entre las 2:30 y las 4:30 de la tarde. Esto ocurre especialmente en Suramérica, México y España.

Los estudios científicos explican que una siesta corta después de almorzar ayuda° a trabajar más y mejor° durante la tarde. Pero, ¡cuidado! Esta siesta debe durar° sólo entre veinte y cuarenta minutos. Si dormimos más, entramos en la fase de sueño profundo y es difícil despertarse.

Hoy día, algunas empresas° de los Estados Unidos, Canadá, Japón, Inglaterra y Alemania tienen salas° especiales en las que los empleados pueden dormir la siesta.

**¿Dónde duermen la siesta?**

■ Costumbre antigua
■ Costumbre nueva

**En los lugares donde la siesta es una costumbre antigua, las personas la duermen en su casa. En los países donde la siesta es una costumbre nueva, la gente duerme en sus lugares de trabajo o en centros de siesta.**

Sientes cansancio *Do you feel tired* Te cuesta *Is it hard for you* trabajo *work* relajarse *to relax* antigua costumbre *old custom* Debido al *Because (of)* desde hace *for* más de *more than* oficinas *offices* ayuda *helps* mejor *better* durar *last* algunas empresas *some businesses* salas *rooms*

---

**ACTIVIDADES**

**1**  **¿Cierto o falso?** Indica si lo que dicen las oraciones es **cierto** o **falso**. Corrige la información falsa.

1. La costumbre de la siesta empezó en Asia. Falso. La costumbre de la siesta empezó en el área del Mediterráneo.
2. La palabra *siesta* está relacionada con la sexta hora del día. Cierto.
3. Los españoles y los portugueses llevaron la costumbre de la siesta a Latinoamérica. Cierto.
4. La siesta ayuda a trabajar más y mejor durante la tarde. Cierto.
5. Los horarios de trabajo de los países hispanos son los mismos que los de los Estados Unidos. Falso. En muchos países hispanos las oficinas y las tiendas cierran dos o tres horas después del mediodía.
6. Una siesta larga siempre es mejor que una siesta corta. Falso. La siesta sólo debe durar entre veinte y cuarenta minutos.
7. En los Estados Unidos, los empleados de algunas empresas pueden dormir la siesta en el trabajo. Cierto.
8. Es fácil despertar de un sueño profundo. Falso. Es difícil despertar de un sueño profundo.

---

**TEACHING OPTIONS**

**Small Groups** Have students work in groups of three to invent an original product related to the **siesta**. Then have them present an ad for their product to the class. Encourage creativity. Ex: **¿Tienes problemas para despertarte después de la siesta? Necesitas el nuevo despertador "AguaSiestas". Si no quieres entrar en la fase de sueño profundo, sólo pones el despertador y a los veinte minutos, se convierte en una mini-ducha de agua** **fría.** Have the class vote for the products they would most likely buy.
**Cultural Comparison** Divide the class into two groups. Have students debate the advantages and disadvantages of the **siesta** in the workplace and university life. Allow each group time to prepare their arguments, and provide additional vocabulary as needed.

## ASÍ SE DICE

### El cuidado personal

| | |
|---|---|
| el aseo; el excusado; el servicio; el váter (Esp.) | el baño |
| el cortaúñas | *nail clippers* |
| el desodorante | *deodorant* |
| el enjuague bucal | *mouthwash* |
| el hilo dental/la seda dental | *dental floss* |
| la máquina de afeitar/ de rasurar (Méx.) | *electric razor* |

## EL MUNDO HISPANO

### Costumbres especiales

○ **México y El Salvador** Los vendedores pasan por las calles gritando° su mercancía°: tanques de gas y flores° en México; pan y tortillas en El Salvador.

○ **Costa Rica** Para encontrar las direcciones° los costarricenses usan referencias a anécdotas, lugares o características geográficas. Por ejemplo: *200 metros norte de la Iglesia Católica, frente al° Supermercado Mi Mega.*

○ **Argentina** En El Tigre, una ciudad en una isla del Río° de la Plata, la gente usa barcos particulares°, colectivos° y barcos-taxi para ir de un lugar a otro. Todas las mañanas, un barco colectivo recoge° a los niños y los lleva a la escuela.

gritando *shouting* mercancía *merchandise* flores *flowers* direcciones *addresses* frente al *opposite* río *river* particulares *private* colectivos *collective* recoge *picks up*

## PERFIL

### Ir de tapas

En España, **las tapas** son pequeños platos°. **Ir de tapas** es una costumbre que consiste en comer estos platillos en bares, cafés y restaurantes. Dos tapas muy populares son la tortilla de patatas° y los calamares°. La historia de las tapas empezó cuando los dueños° de las tabernas tuvieron° la idea de servir el vaso de vino° tapado° con una rodaja° de pan°. La comida era° la "tapa"° del vaso; de ahí viene el nombre. Con la tapa, los insectos no podían° entrar en el vaso. Más tarde los dueños de las tabernas pusieron° la

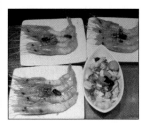

tapa al lado del vaso. Luego, empezaron a servir también pequeñas porciones de platos tradicionales.

Para muchos españoles, ir de tapas con los amigos después del trabajo es una rutina diaria.

platos *dishes* tortilla de patatas *potato omelet* calamares *squid* dueños *owners* tuvieron *had* vaso de vino *glass of wine* tapado *covered* rodaja *slice* pan *bread* era *was* tapa *lid* no podían *couldn't* pusieron *put*

### SUPERSITE Conexión Internet

¿Qué costumbres son populares en los países hispanos?

Go to **panorama.vhlcentral.com** to find more cultural information related to this **Cultura** section.

## ACTIVIDADES

**2** **Comprensión** Completa las oraciones.
1. Uso ___el hilo dental/la seda dental___ para limpiar (*to clean*) entre los dientes.
2. En ___El Salvador___ las personas compran pan y tortillas a los vendedores que pasan por la calle.
3. Muchos españoles ___van de tapas___ después del trabajo.
4. En Costa Rica usan anécdotas y lugares para dar ___direcciones___.

**3** **¿Qué costumbres tienes?** Escribe cuatro oraciones sobre una costumbre que compartes con tus amigos o con tu familia (por ejemplo: ir al cine, ir a eventos deportivos, leer, comer juntos, etc.). Explica qué haces, cuándo lo haces y con quién. Answers will vary.

**recursos**

SUPERSITE
panorama.vhlcentral.com
Lección 7

**Así se dice**
- Point out that **cortaúñas** is a compound word and explain its formation.
- To challenge students, add these hygiene-related words to the list: **el acondicionador, el suavizante (Esp.)** (*conditioner*); **la bañera, la tina** (*bathtub*); **el cabello** (*hair*); **la crema (hidrante), la loción** (*lotion*); **el dentífrico, la crema dental (Col.), la pasta dental (Perú, P. Rico)** (*toothpaste*); **las pinzas** (*tweezers*).
- Ask volunteers to create sentences using words from the list. Ex: **El aseo de mujeres está lejos de la sala de clase.**

**Perfil**
- Point out the photo of **tapas** dishes lining the bar. Explain that a **tapa** would consist of a few bites of one of these dishes. Explain that, in some parts of Spain, a drink order might be accompanied by a complimentary **pincho**, which tends to be smaller than a **tapa**. Give students additional examples of typical **tapas** (Ex: **la ensaladilla rusa, las gambas al ajillo, el jamón serrano**).
- Ask students if they know of any **tapas** restaurants in your community and if they have eaten there.

**El mundo hispano**
Ask students to create three true-false statements based on the information in **El mundo hispano**. Have pairs exchange papers and complete the activity.

**2** **Expansion** Give students these sentences as items 5–6: **5. Venden ___ y ___ en las calles de México. (tanques de gas, flores) 6. ___ y ___ son dos tapas muy populares. (La tortilla de patatas, los calamares)**

**3** **Teaching Tip** To simplify, write time expressions on the board that students can use in their descriptions (Ex: **siempre, todos los años, cada mes**).

## TEACHING OPTIONS

**TPR** On slips of paper, write phrases related to daily routines and hygiene from **Así se dice** and **Contextos** (Ex: **usar desodorante, usar enjuague bucal, afeitarse con una máquina de afeitar**). Divide the class into two teams. Have a member of team A draw out a slip of paper and mime the activity for team B to guess. Have teams alternate miming activities. Give one point for each correct answer.
**Heritage Speakers** Ask heritage speakers to describe customs from their cultural communities that have since changed or been adapted for U.S./Canadian culture.
**Cultural Activity** Ask pairs to choose a country not mentioned in **Perfil** or **El mundo hispano** and use the Internet to research a custom or tradition that affects daily life (Ex: **las medias nueves** and **las onces**, the routine of eating morning and afternoon snacks in Colombia). Have pairs present the custom to the class.

## Section Goals

In **Estructura 7.1**, students will learn:
- the conjugation of reflexive verbs
- common reflexive verbs

### Instructional Resources
**Supersite:** Lab MP3 Audio Files
**Lección 7**
**Supersite/IRCD:** *PowerPoints*
(Lección 7 Estructura
Presentation); *IRM* (Information
Gap Activities, Lab Audio Script,
WBs/VM/LM Answer Key)
**WebSAM**
**Workbook,** pp. 75–76
**Lab Manual,** p. 39
*Cuaderno para hispanohablantes*

### Teaching Tips
- Model the first-person reflexive by talking about yourself. Ex: **Me levanto a las cinco de la mañana.** Then model the second person by asking questions. Ex: **Y tú, _____, ¿a qué hora te levantas?** Use follow-up questions to introduce the third person. Ex: **¿A qué hora se levanta _____?**
- Introduce the third person by making statements and asking questions about what a student has told you. Ex: **_____ se levanta muy tarde, ¿no? (Sí, se levanta muy tarde.)**
- Add a visual aspect to this grammar presentation. Use magazine pictures to clarify meanings between third-person singular and third-person plural forms. Ex: **Se lava las manos** and **Se lavan las manos.**
- On the board or an overhead, summarize the three possible positions for reflexive pronouns. You may want to show this visually by using an **X** to represent the reflexive pronoun: **X verbo conjugado, infinitivoX, gerundioX.** Remind students that they have already learned these positions for direct and indirect object pronouns.

## 7.1 Reflexive verbs

**ANTE TODO**  A reflexive verb is used to indicate that the subject does something to or for himself or herself. In other words, it "reflects" the action of the verb back to the subject. Reflexive verbs always use reflexive pronouns.

SUBJECT    REFLEXIVE VERB

Joaquín    **se ducha** por la mañana.

### The verb lavarse (*to wash oneself*)

| SINGULAR FORMS | | | |
|---|---|---|---|
| | yo | **me lavo** | *I wash (myself)* |
| | tú | **te lavas** | *you wash (yourself)* |
| | Ud. | **se lava** | *you wash (yourself)* |
| | él/ella | **se lava** | *he/she washes (himself/herself)* |

| PLURAL FORMS | | | |
|---|---|---|---|
| | nosotros/as | **nos lavamos** | *we wash (ourselves)* |
| | vosotros/as | **os laváis** | *you wash (yourselves)* |
| | Uds. | **se lavan** | *you wash (yourselves)* |
| | ellos/ellas | **se lavan** | *they wash (themselves)* |

▶ The pronoun **se** attached to an infinitive identifies the verb as reflexive: **lavarse.**

▶ When a reflexive verb is conjugated, the reflexive pronoun agrees with the subject.

**Me afeito.**

**Te despiertas** a las siete.

*Me ducho, me cepillo los dientes, me visto y ¡listo!*

*¡Ay, los estudiantes! Siempre se acuestan tarde.*

**AYUDA**
Except for **se**, reflexive pronouns have the same forms as direct and indirect object pronouns.

•••

**Se** is used for both singular and plural subjects—there is no individual plural form:
Pablo **se** lava.
Ellos **se** lavan.

▶ Like object pronouns, reflexive pronouns generally appear before a conjugated verb. With infinitives and present participles, they may be placed before the conjugated verb or attached to the infinitive or present participle.

Ellos **se** van a vestir.
Ellos van a vestir**se**.
*They are going to get dressed.*

**Nos** estamos lavando las manos.
Estamos lavándo**nos** las manos.
*We are washing our hands.*

▶ **¡Atención!** When a reflexive pronoun is attached to a present participle, an accent mark is added to maintain the original stress.

bañando ⟶ bañ**á**ndo**se**

durmiendo ⟶ durmi**é**ndo**se**

---

### TEACHING OPTIONS

**Extra Practice**  To provide oral practice with reflexive verbs, create sentences that follow the pattern of the sentences in the examples. Say the sentence, have students repeat it, then say a different subject, varying the gender and number. Have students then say the sentence with the new subject, changing pronouns and verbs as necessary.

**Heritage Speakers**  Have heritage speakers describe daily routines in their families. Encourage them to use their own linguistic variation of words presented in this lesson. Ex: **regarse (e:ie), pintarse.** Have heritage speakers work together to compare and contrast activities as well as lexical variations.

## Common reflexive verbs

| | | | |
|---|---|---|---|
| **acordarse (de)** (o:ue) | *to remember* | **llamarse** | *to be called; to be named* |
| **acostarse** (o:ue) | *to go to bed* | | |
| **afeitarse** | *to shave* | **maquillarse** | *to put on makeup* |
| **bañarse** | *to bathe; to take a bath* | **peinarse** | *to comb one's hair* |
| **cepillarse** | *to brush* | **ponerse** | *to put on* |
| **despedirse (de)** (e:i) | *to say goodbye (to)* | **ponerse (+ adj.)** | *to become (+ adj.)* |
| **despertarse** (e:ie) | *to wake up* | **preocuparse (por)** | *to worry (about)* |
| **dormirse** (o:ue) | *to go to sleep; to fall asleep* | **probarse** (o:ue) | *to try on* |
| | | **quedarse** | *to stay; to remain* |
| **ducharse** | *to shower; to take a shower* | **quitarse** | *to take off* |
| | | **secarse** | *to dry (oneself)* |
| **enojarse (con)** | *to get angry (with)* | **sentarse** (e:ie) | *to sit down* |
| **irse** | *to go away; to leave* | **sentirse** (e:ie) | *to feel* |
| **lavarse** | *to wash (oneself)* | **vestirse** (e:i) | *to get dressed* |
| **levantarse** | *to get up* | | |

### COMPARE & CONTRAST

Unlike English, a number of verbs in Spanish can be reflexive or non-reflexive. If the verb acts upon the subject, the reflexive form is used. If the verb acts upon something other than the subject, the non-reflexive form is used. Compare these sentences.

Lola **lava** los platos.

Lola **se lava** la cara.

As the preceding sentences show, reflexive verbs sometimes have different meanings than their non-reflexive counterparts. For example, **lavar** means *to wash*, while **lavarse** means *to wash oneself, to wash up.*

▶ **¡Atención!** Parts of the body or clothing are generally not referred to with possessives, but with the definite article.

La niña se quitó **los** zapatos.     Necesito cepillarme **los** dientes.

**¡INTÉNTALO!** Indica el presente de estos verbos reflexivos. El primero de cada columna ya está conjugado.

**despertarse**

1. Mis hermanos _se despiertan_ tarde.
2. Tú _te despiertas_ tarde.
3. Nosotros _nos despertamos_ tarde.
4. Benito _se despierta_ tarde.
5. Yo _me despierto_ tarde.

**ponerse**

1. Él _se pone_ una chaqueta.
2. Yo _me pongo_ una chaqueta.
3. Usted _se pone_ una chaqueta.
4. Nosotras _nos ponemos_ una chaqueta.
5. Las niñas _se ponen_ una chaqueta.

# Práctica

## 1  Nuestra rutina
La familia de Blanca sigue la misma rutina todos los días. Según Blanca, ¿qué hacen ellos?

> **modelo**
> mamá / despertarse a las 5:00
> *Mamá se despierta a las cinco.*

1. Roberto y yo / levantarse a las 7:00  Roberto y yo nos levantamos a las siete.
2. papá / ducharse primero y / luego afeitarse  Papá se ducha primero y luego se afeita.
3. yo / lavarse la cara y / vestirse antes de tomar café  Yo me lavo la cara y me visto antes de tomar café.
4. mamá / peinarse y / luego maquillarse  Mamá se peina y luego se maquilla.
5. todos (nosotros) / sentarse a la mesa para comer  Todos nos sentamos a la mesa para comer.
6. Roberto / cepillarse los dientes después de comer  Roberto se cepilla los dientes después de comer.
7. yo / ponerse el abrigo antes de salir  Yo me pongo el abrigo antes de salir.
8. nosotros / despedirse de mamá  Nosotros nos despedimos de mamá.

## 2  La fiesta elegante
Selecciona el verbo apropiado y completa las oraciones con la forma correcta.

1. Tú ___lavas___ (lavar / lavarse) el auto antes de ir a la fiesta.
2. Nosotros no ___nos acordamos___ (acordar / acordarse) de comprar regalos.
3. Para llegar a tiempo, Raúl y Marta ___acuestan___ (acostar / acostarse) a los niños antes de irse.
4. Yo ___me siento___ (sentir / sentirse) bien hoy.
5. Mis amigos siempre ___se visten___ (vestir / vestirse) con ropa muy cara.
6. ¿___Se prueban___ (Probar / Probarse) ustedes la ropa antes de comprarla?
7. Usted ___se preocupa___ (preocupar / preocuparse) mucho por sus amigos, ¿no?
8. En general, ___me afeito___ (afeitar / afeitarse) yo mismo, pero hoy el barbero (*barber*) me ___afeita___ (afeitar / afeitarse).

## 3  Describir
Mira los dibujos y describe lo que estas personas hacen.  Some answers may vary.

1. el joven  El joven se quita los zapatos.

2. Carmen  Carmen se duerme.

3. Juan  Juan se pone la camiseta.

4. ellos  Ellos se despiden.

5. Estrella  Estrella se maquilla.

6. Toni  Toni se enoja con el perro.

---

### Left margin notes

**1 Teaching Tip** Before assigning the activity, review reflexive verbs by comparing and contrasting weekday and weekend routines. Ex: **¿Te levantas tarde o temprano los sábados? ¿Te acuestas tarde o temprano los domingos?**

**1 Expansion** To practice the formal register, describe situations and have students tell you what you are going to do. Ex: **Hace frío y nieva, pero necesito salir. (Usted va a ponerse el abrigo.) Acabo de levantarme. (Usted se va a lavar la cara.)**

**2 Teaching Tip** Before assigning the activity, review reflexive and non-reflexive verbs by asking questions using both forms. Ex: **¿Cuándo nos lavamos? (Nos lavamos todos los días.) ¿Cuándo lavamos el coche? (Lavamos el coche los fines de semana.)**

**2 Expansion** Ask students to write five sentence pairs contrasting reflexive and non-reflexive forms. Ex: **Me despierto a las siete. Despierto a mi compañero de cuarto a las ocho.**

**3 Expansion**
- Repeat the activity as a pattern drill, supplying different subjects for each drawing. Ex: **Número uno, yo. (Me quito los zapatos.) Número cinco, nosotras. (Nosotras nos maquillamos.)**
- Repeat the activity using the present progressive. Ask students to provide both possible sentences. Ex: **1. El joven se está quitando los zapatos./ El joven está quitándose los zapatos.**

### Right margin notes

**NOTA CULTURAL**

Como en los EE.UU., **tomar café** en el desayuno es muy común en los países hispanos.

En muchas familias, los niños toman café con leche (*milk*) en el desayuno antes de ir a la escuela.

El café en los países hispanos generalmente es más fuerte que en los EE.UU., y el descafeinado no es muy popular.

**¡LENGUA VIVA!**

In Spain a car is called a **coche**, while in many parts of Latin America it is known as a **carro**. Although you'll be understood using any of these terms, using **auto (automóvil)** will surely get you where you want to go.

---

**TEACHING OPTIONS**

**Extra Practice** Have students figure out the morning schedule of the **Ramírez** family. Say: **El señor Ramírez se afeita antes que Alberto, pero después que Rafael. La señora Ramírez es la primera en ducharse y Montse es la última. Lolita se peina cuando su padre sale del cuarto de baño y antes que uno de sus hermanos. Nuria se maquilla después que Lolita, pero no inmediatamente después. (Primero se ducha la señora Ramírez.**

**Después se afeita Rafael seguido por el señor Ramírez. Después se peina Lolita. Alberto se afeita y después Nuria se maquilla. Finalmente Montse se ducha.)**

# Comunicación

**4**

**Preguntas personales** En parejas, túrnense para hacerse estas preguntas. Answers will vary.

1. ¿A qué hora te levantas durante la semana?
2. ¿A qué hora te levantas los fines de semana?
3. ¿Prefieres levantarte tarde o temprano? ¿Por qué?
4. ¿Te enojas frecuentemente con tus amigos?
5. ¿Te preocupas fácilmente? ¿Qué te preocupa?
6. ¿Qué te pone contento/a?
7. ¿Qué haces cuando te sientes triste?
8. ¿Y cuando te sientes alegre?
9. ¿Te acuestas tarde o temprano durante la semana?
10. ¿A qué hora te acuestas los fines de semana?

**5**

**Charadas** En grupos, jueguen a las charadas. Cada persona debe pensar en dos frases con verbos reflexivos. La primera persona que adivina la charada dramatiza la siguiente. Answers will vary.

**6**

**Debate** En grupos, discutan este tema: ¿Quiénes necesitan más tiempo para arreglarse (*to get ready*) antes de salir, los hombres o las mujeres? Hagan una lista de las razones (*reasons*) que tienen para defender sus ideas e informen a la clase. Answers will vary.

# Síntesis

**7**

**La familia ocupada** Tú y tu compañero/a asisten a un programa de verano en Lima, Perú. Viven con la familia Ramos. Tu profesor(a) te va a dar la rutina incompleta que la familia sigue en las mañanas. Trabaja con tu compañero/a para completarla. Answers will vary.

> **modelo**
> **Estudiante 1:** ¿Qué hace el señor Ramos a las seis y cuarto?
> **Estudiante 2:** El señor Ramos se levanta.

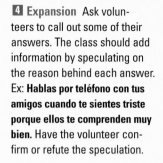

## Section Goals

In **Estructura 7.2**, students will learn:
• high-frequency indefinite and negative words
• the placement and use of indefinite and negative words

---

**Instructional Resources**
**Supersite:** Lab MP3 Audio Files **Lección 7**
**Supersite/IRCD:** *PowerPoints* (**Lección 7 Estructura** Presentation); *IRM* (**Hojas de actividades,** Lab Audio Script, WBs/VM/LM Answer Key)
**WebSAM**
**Workbook,** pp. 77–78
**Lab Manual,** p. 40
***Cuaderno para hispanohablantes***

---

## Teaching Tips

• Write **alguien** and **nadie** on the board and ask questions about what students are wearing. Ex: **Hoy alguien lleva una camiseta verde. ¿Quién es? ¿Alguien lleva pantalones anaranjados?**

• Present negative words by complaining dramatically in a whining tone. Ex: **Nadie me llama por teléfono. Jamás recibo un correo electrónico de ningún estudiante. Ni mi esposo ni mis hijos se acuerdan de mi cumpleaños.** Then smile radiantly and state the opposite. Ex: **Alguien me llama por teléfono.**

• Add a visual aspect to this grammar presentation. Use magazine pictures to compare and contrast indefinite and negative words. Ex: **La señora tiene algo en las manos. ¿El señor tiene algo también? No, el señor no tiene nada.**

• Have students say they do the opposite of what you do. Ex: **Yo siempre canto en la ducha. (Nosotros no cantamos nunca en la ducha.)**

• Point out that **uno/a(s)** can be used as an indefinite pronoun. Ex: **¿Tienes un lápiz? Sí, tengo uno.**

---

## **7.2** Indefinite and negative words **SUPERSITE**

**ANTE TODO** Indefinite words refer to people and things that are not specific, for example, *someone* or *something*. Negative words deny the existence of people and things or contradict statements, for instance, *no one* or *nothing*. Spanish indefinite words have corresponding negative words, which are opposite in meaning.

### Indefinite and negative words

| Indefinite words | | Negative words | |
|---|---|---|---|
| **algo** | something; anything | **nada** | nothing; not anything |
| **alguien** | someone; somebody; anyone | **nadie** | no one; nobody; not anyone |
| **alguno/a(s), algún** | some; any | **ninguno/a, ningún** | no; none; not any |
| **o... o** | either... or | **ni... ni** | neither... nor |
| **siempre** | always | **nunca, jamás** | never, not ever |
| **también** | also; too | **tampoco** | neither; not either |

▶ There are two ways to form negative sentences in Spanish. You can place the negative word before the verb, or you can place **no** before the verb and the negative word after.

**Nadie se levanta** temprano.
*No one gets up early.*

**No se levanta nadie** temprano.
*No one gets up early.*

Ellos **nunca gritan**.
*They never shout.*

Ellos **no gritan nunca**.
*They never shout.*

Yo siempre me despierto a las seis en punto. ¿Y tú?

Pues yo jamás me levanto temprano. Nunca oigo el despertador.

▶ Because they refer to people, **alguien** and **nadie** are often used with the personal **a**. The personal **a** is also used before **alguno/a, algunos/as,** and **ninguno/a** when these words refer to people and they are the direct object of the verb.

—Perdón, señor, ¿busca usted **a alguien**?
—No, gracias, señorita, no busco **a nadie**.

—Tomás, ¿buscas **a alguno** de tus hermanos?
—No, mamá, no busco **a ninguno**.

▶ **¡Atención!** Before a masculine, singular noun, **alguno** and **ninguno** are shortened to **algún** and **ningún**.

—¿Tienen ustedes **algún** amigo peruano?

—No, no tenemos **ningún** amigo peruano.

---

**AYUDA**

**Alguno/a, algunos/as** are not always used in the same way English uses *some* or *any*. Often, **algún** is used where *a* would be used in English.

**¿Tienes algún libro que hable de los incas?**
*Do you have a book that talks about the Incas?*

Note that **ninguno/a** is rarely used in the plural.

—¿Visitaste algunos museos?
—No, no visité ninguno.

---

**NATIONAL STANDARDS** comparisons

---

**TEACHING OPTIONS**

**Extra Practice** Write cloze sentences on the board and have the students complete them with an indefinite or negative word. Ex: **Los vegetarianos no comen hamburguesas ____. (nunca) Las madres ____ se preocupan por sus hijos. (siempre) En las fiestas ella no es sociable, ____ baila ____ habla con ____. (ni, ni, nadie)**

**Pairs** Have students take turns giving one-word indefinite and negative word prompts and having the other respond in complete sentences. Ex: E1: **siempre** E2: **Siempre le mando un mensaje electrónico a mi madre por la mañana.** E1: **tampoco** E2: **Yo no me levanto temprano tampoco.**

### COMPARE & CONTRAST

In English, it is incorrect to use more than one negative word in a sentence. In Spanish, however, sentences frequently contain two or more negative words. Compare these Spanish and English sentences.

> **Nunca** le escribo a **nadie**.
> *I never write to anyone.*

> **No** me preocupo por **nada nunca**.
> *I do not ever worry about anything.*

As the preceding sentences show, once an English sentence contains one negative word (for example, *not* or *never*), no other negative word may be used. Instead, indefinite (or affirmative) words are used. In Spanish, however, once a sentence is negative, no other affirmative (that is, indefinite) word may be used. Instead, all indefinite ideas must be expressed in the negative.

▶ Although in Spanish **pero** and **sino** both mean *but*, they are not interchangeable. **Sino** is used when the first part of a sentence is negative and the second part contradicts it. In this context, **sino** means *but rather* or *on the contrary*. In all other cases, **pero** is used to mean *but*.

> Los estudiantes no se acuestan temprano **sino** tarde.
> *The students don't go to bed early, but rather late.*

> Las toallas son caras, **pero** bonitas.
> *The towels are expensive, but beautiful.*

> María no habla francés **sino** español.
> *María doesn't speak French, but rather Spanish.*

> José es inteligente, **pero** no saca buenas notas.
> *José is intelligent but doesn't get good grades.*

 **¡INTÉNTALO!** Cambia las oraciones para que sean negativas. La primera se da como ejemplo.

1. Siempre se viste bien.
   <u>Nunca</u> se viste bien.
   <u>No</u> se viste bien <u>nunca</u>.
2. Alguien se ducha.
   <u>Nadie</u> se ducha.
   <u>No</u> se ducha <u>nadie</u>.
3. Ellas van también.
   Ellas <u>tampoco</u> van.
   Ellas <u>no</u> van <u>tampoco</u>.
4. Alguien se pone nervioso.
   <u>Nadie</u> se pone nervioso.
   <u>No</u> se pone nervioso <u>nadie</u>.
5. Tú siempre te lavas las manos.
   Tú <u>nunca / jamás</u> te lavas las manos.
   Tú <u>no</u> te lavas las manos <u>nunca / jamás</u>.
6. Voy a traer algo.
   <u>No</u> voy a traer <u>nada</u>.
7. Juan se afeita también.
   Juan <u>tampoco</u> se afeita.
   Juan <u>no</u> se afeita <u>tampoco</u>.
8. Mis amigos viven en una residencia o en casa.
   Mis amigos <u>no</u> viven <u>ni</u> en una residencia <u>ni</u> en casa.
9. La profesora hace algo en su escritorio.
   La profesora <u>no</u> hace <u>nada</u> en su escritorio.
10. Tú y yo vamos al mercado.
    <u>Ni</u> tú <u>ni</u> yo vamos al mercado.
11. Tienen un espejo en su casa.
    <u>No</u> tienen <u>ningún</u> espejo en su casa.
12. Algunos niños se ponen el abrigo.
    <u>Ningún</u> niño se pone el abrigo.

**recursos**

WB
pp. 77–78

LM
p. 40

SUPERSITE
panorama.
vhlcentral.com
Lección 7

**Teaching Tips**
- Emphasize that there is no limit to the number of negative words that can be strung together in a sentence in Spanish. Ex: **No hablo con nadie nunca de ningún problema, ni con mi familia ni con mis amigos.**
- Ask volunteers questions about their activities since the last class, reiterating the answers. Ex: **¿Quién compró algo nuevo? Sólo dos personas. Nadie más compró algo nuevo. Yo no compré nada nuevo tampoco.**
- Elicit negative responses by asking questions whose answers will clearly be negative. Ex: **¿Alguien lleva zapatos de lunares? (No, nadie lleva zapatos de lunares.) ¿Piensas comprar un barco mañana? (No, no pienso comprar ninguno/ningún barco.) ¿Tienes nietos? (No, no tengo ninguno/ningún nieto.)**
- Give examples of **pero** and **sino** using the seating of the students. Ex: _____ **se sienta al lado de** _____**, pero no al lado de** _____**. No se sienta a la izquierda de** _____**, sino a la derecha.** _____ **no se sienta al lado de la ventana, pero está cerca de la puerta.**

### TEACHING OPTIONS

**Video** Show the *Fotonovela* again to give students more input containing indefinite and negative words. Stop the video where appropriate to discuss how these words are used.
**Pairs** Have pairs create sentences about your community using affirmative and negative words. Ex: **En nuestra ciudad no hay ningún mercado al aire libre. Hay algunos restaurantes de tapas. El equipo de béisbol juega bien, pero no gana muchos partidos.**

**Small Groups** Give small groups five minutes to write a description of **un señor muy, pero muy antipático**. Tell them to use as many indefinite and negative words as possible to describe what makes this person so unpleasant. Encourage exaggeration and creativity.

# Práctica SUPERSITE

**1** **¿Pero o sino?** Forma oraciones sobre estas personas usando **pero** o **sino**.

> **modelo**
>
> muchos estudiantes viven en residencias estudiantiles / muchos de ellos quieren vivir fuera del *(off)* campus
> *Muchos estudiantes viven en residencias estudiantiles, pero muchos de ellos quieren vivir fuera del campus.*

1. Marcos nunca se despierta temprano / siempre llega puntual a clase
   Marcos nunca se despierta temprano, pero siempre llega puntual a clase.
2. Lisa y Katarina no se acuestan temprano / muy tarde
   Lisa y Katarina no se acuestan temprano sino muy tarde.
3. Alfonso es inteligente / algunas veces es antipático
   Alfonso es inteligente, pero algunas veces es antipático.
4. los directores de la residencia no son ecuatorianos / peruanos
   Los directores de la residencia no son ecuatorianos sino peruanos.
5. no nos acordamos de comprar champú / compramos jabón
   No nos acordamos de comprar champú, pero compramos jabón.
6. Emilia no es estudiante / profesora
   Emilia no es estudiante sino profesora.
7. no quiero levantarme / tengo que ir a clase
   No quiero levantarme, pero tengo que ir a clase.
8. Miguel no se afeita por la mañana / por la noche
   Miguel no se afeita por la mañana sino por la noche.

**2** **Completar** Completa esta conversación. Usa expresiones negativas en tus respuestas. Luego, dramatiza la conversación con un(a) compañero/a.    Answers will vary.

**AURELIO**    Ana María, ¿encontraste algún regalo para Eliana?

**ANA MARÍA** (1)_____ No, no encontré ningún regalo/nada para Eliana. _____

**AURELIO**    ¿Viste a alguna amiga en el centro comercial?

**ANA MARÍA** (2)_____ No, no vi a ninguna amiga/ninguna/nadie en el centro comercial. _____

**AURELIO**    ¿Me llamó alguien?

**ANA MARÍA** (3)_____ No, nadie te llamó./No, no te llamó nadie. _____

**AURELIO**    ¿Quieres ir al teatro o al cine esta noche?

**ANA MARÍA** (4)_____ No, no quiero ir ni al teatro ni al cine. _____

**AURELIO**    ¿No quieres salir a comer?

**ANA MARÍA** (5)_____ No, no quiero salir a comer (tampoco). _____

**AURELIO**    ¿Hay algo interesante en la televisión esta noche?

**ANA MARÍA** (6)_____ No, no hay nada interesante en la televisión. _____

**AURELIO**    ¿Tienes algún problema?

**ANA MARÍA** (7)_____ No, no tengo ningún problema/ninguno. _____

# Comunicación

**3** Opiniones Completa estas oraciones de una manera lógica. Luego, compara tus respuestas con las de un(a) compañero/a.  *Answers will vary.*

1. Mi habitación es _____ pero _____.
2. Por la noche me gusta _____ pero _____.
3. Un(a) profesor(a) ideal no es _____ sino _____.
4. Mis amigos son _____ pero _____.

**4** En el campus En parejas, háganse preguntas para ver qué hay en su universidad: residencias bonitas, departamento de ingeniería, cines, librerías baratas, estudiantes guapos, equipo de fútbol, playa, clases fáciles, museo, profesores estrictos. Sigan el modelo. *Answers will vary.*

> **modelo**
> **Estudiante 1:** ¿Hay algunas residencias bonitas?
> **Estudiante 2:** Sí, hay una/algunas. Está(n) detrás del estadio.
> **Estudiante 1:** ¿Hay algún museo?
> **Estudiante 2:** No, no hay ninguno.

**5** Quejas (*Complaints*) En parejas, hagan una lista de cinco quejas comunes que tienen los estudiantes. Usen expresiones negativas. *Answers will vary.*

> **modelo**
> Nadie me entiende.

Ahora hagan una lista de cinco quejas que los padres tienen de sus hijos.

> **modelo**
> Nunca limpian sus habitaciones.

**6** Anuncios En parejas, lean el anuncio y contesten las preguntas. *Some answers will vary.*

1. ¿Es el anuncio positivo o negativo? ¿Por qué? *Answers will vary.*
2. ¿Qué palabras indefinidas hay? *algún, siempre, algo*
3. Escriban el texto del anuncio cambiando todo por expresiones negativas. *¿No buscas ningún producto especial? ¡Nunca hay nada para nadie en las tiendas García!*
4. Ahora preparen su propio (*own*) anuncio usando expresiones afirmativas y negativas.

¿Buscas algún producto especial?

¡Siempre hay algo para todos en las tiendas García!

# Síntesis

**7** Encuesta Tu profesor(a) te va a dar una hoja de actividades para hacer una encuesta. Circula por la clase y pídeles a tus compañeros que comparen las actividades que hacen durante la semana con las que hacen durante los fines de semana. Escribe las respuestas. *Answers will vary.*

---

**3 Teaching Tip** Use personal examples to preview the activity. Ex: **Mi hijo es inteligente, pero no le gusta estudiar. Mi amiga no es norteamericana, sino española.**

**3 Expansion** Give students these sentences as items 5–6: **5. Mis padres no son ____ sino ____. 6. Mi compañero/a de cuarto es ____ pero ____.**

**4 Teaching Tip** To simplify, before beginning the activity, practice question formation for each item as a class.

**4 Expansion** Have pairs of students create two additional sentences about your school.

**5 Expansion** Divide the class into all-male and all-female groups. Then have each group make two different lists: **Quejas que tienen los hombres de las mujeres** and **Quejas que tienen las mujeres de los hombres.** After five minutes, compare and contrast the answers and perceptions.

**6 Expansion** Have pairs work with another pair to combine the best aspects of each of their individual ads. Then have them present the "fused" ads to the class.

**7 Teaching Tip** Distribute the *Hojas de actividades* from the Supersite/IRCD that correspond to this activity.

**7 Expansion** Have students write five sentences using the information obtained through the **encuesta.** Ex: **1. Nadie va a la biblioteca durante el fin de semana, pero muchos vamos durante la semana. 2. No estudiamos los sábados sino los domingos.**

---

**TEACHING OPTIONS**

**Large Groups** Write the names of four vacation spots on four slips of paper and post them in different corners of the room. Ask students to pick their vacation preference by going to one of the corners. Then, have each group produce five reasons for their choice as well as one complaint about each of the other places.

**Extra Practice** Have students complete this cloze activity using **pero, sino,** and **tampoco:** Yo me levanto temprano y hago mi tarea, ____ mi compañera de apartamento prefiere hacerla por la noche y acostarse muy tarde. (pero) Ella no tiene exámenes este semestre ____ proyectos. (sino) Yo no tengo exámenes ____. (tampoco) Sólo tengo mucha, mucha tarea.

**7.3** ## Preterite of **ser** and **ir**

**ANTE TODO**　In **Lección 6**, you learned how to form the preterite tense of regular -**ar**, -**er**, and -**ir** verbs. The following chart contains the preterite forms of **ser** (*to be*) and **ir** (*to go*). Since these forms are irregular, you will need to memorize them.

| Preterite of **ser** and **ir** | | |
| --- | --- | --- |
| | **ser** (*to be*) | **ir** (*to go*) |
| **SINGULAR FORMS** | | |
| yo | **fui** | **fui** |
| tú | **fuiste** | **fuiste** |
| Ud./él/ella | **fue** | **fue** |
| **PLURAL FORMS** | | |
| nosotros/as | **fuimos** | **fuimos** |
| vosotros/as | **fuisteis** | **fuisteis** |
| Uds./ellos/ellas | **fueron** | **fueron** |

**AYUDA**

Note that, whereas regular -**er** and -**ir** verbs have accent marks in the **yo** and **Ud./él/ella** forms of the preterite, **ser** and **ir** do not.

▶ Since the preterite forms of **ser** and **ir** are identical, context clarifies which of the two verbs is being used.

Él **fue** a comprar champú y jabón.
*He went to buy shampoo and soap.*

¿Cómo **fue** la película anoche?
*How was the movie last night?*

¿Adónde fueron ustedes?

Inés y yo fuimos a un mercado. Fue muy divertido.

**¡INTÉNTALO!**　Completa las oraciones usando el pretérito de **ser** e **ir**. La primera oración de cada columna se da como ejemplo.

**ir**

1. Los viajeros __fueron__ a Perú.
2. Patricia __fue__ a Cuzco.
3. Tú __fuiste__ a Iquitos.
4. Gregorio y yo __fuimos__ a Lima.
5. Yo __fui__ a Trujillo.
6. Ustedes __fueron__ a Arequipa.
7. Mi padre __fue__ a Lima.
8. Nosotras __fuimos__ a Cuzco.
9. Él __fue__ a Machu Picchu.
10. Usted __fue__ a Nazca.

**ser**

1. Usted __fue__ muy amable.
2. Yo __fui__ muy cordial.
3. Ellos __fueron__ simpáticos.
4. Nosotros __fuimos__ muy tontos.
5. Ella __fue__ antipática.
6. Tú __fuiste__ muy generoso.
7. Ustedes __fueron__ cordiales.
8. La gente __fue__ amable.
9. Tomás y yo __fuimos__ muy felices.
10. Los profesores __fueron__ buenos.

recursos

WB
p. 79

LM
p. 41

panorama.
vhlcentral.com
Lección 7

# Práctica

### 1

**Completar** Completa estas conversaciones con la forma correcta del pretérito de **ser** o **ir**. Indica el infinitivo de cada forma verbal.

**NOTA CULTURAL**

La ciudad peruana de **El Callao**, fundada en 1537, fue por muchos años el puerto (*port*) más activo de la costa del Pacífico en Suramérica. En el siglo XVIII, se construyó (*was built*) una fortaleza allí para proteger (*protect*) la ciudad de los ataques de piratas y bucaneros.

#### Conversación 1

**RAÚL** ¿Adónde (1)_____fueron_____ ustedes de vacaciones? _____ir_____

**PILAR** (2)_____Fuimos_____ al Perú. _____ir_____

**RAÚL** ¿Cómo (3)_____fue_____ el viaje? _____ser_____

▶ **PILAR** ¡(4)_____Fue_____ estupendo! Machu Picchu y El Callao son increíbles. _____ser_____

**RAÚL** ¿(5)_____Fue_____ caro el viaje? _____ser_____

**PILAR** No, el precio (6)_____fue_____ muy bajo. Sólo costó tres mil dólares. _____ser_____

#### Conversación 2

**ISABEL** Tina y Vicente (7)_____fueron_____ novios, ¿no? _____ser_____

**LUCÍA** Sí, pero ahora no. Anoche Tina (8)_____fue_____ a comer con Gregorio y la semana pasada ellos (9)_____fueron_____ al partido de fútbol. _____ir_____ _____ir_____

**ISABEL** ¿Ah sí? Javier y yo (10)_____fuimos_____ al partido y no los vimos. _____ir_____

### 2

**Descripciones** Forma oraciones con estos elementos. Usa el pretérito. *Answers will vary.*

| A | B | C | D |
|---|---|---|---|
| yo | (no) ir | a un restaurante | ayer |
| tú | (no) ser | en autobús | anoche |
| mi compañero/a | | estudiante | anteayer |
| nosotros | | muy simpático/a | la semana pasada |
| mis amigos | | a la playa | el año pasado |
| ustedes | | dependiente/a en una tienda | |

# Comunicación

### 3

**Preguntas** En parejas, túrnense para hacerse estas preguntas. *Answers will vary.*

1. ¿Adónde fuiste de vacaciones el año pasado? ¿Con quién fuiste?
2. ¿Cómo fueron tus vacaciones?
3. ¿Fuiste de compras la semana pasada? ¿Adónde? ¿Qué compraste?
4. ¿Fuiste al cine la semana pasada? ¿Qué película viste? ¿Cómo fue?
5. ¿Fuiste a la cafetería hoy? ¿A qué hora?
6. ¿Adónde fuiste durante el fin de semana? ¿Por qué?
7. ¿Quién fue tu profesor(a) favorito/a el semestre pasado? ¿Por qué?

### 4

**El viaje** En parejas, escriban un diálogo de un(a) viajero/a hablando con el/la agente de viajes sobre un viaje que tomó recientemente. Usen el pretérito de **ser** e **ir**. *Answers will vary.*

*modelo*
**Agente:** ¿Cómo fue el viaje?
**Viajero:** El viaje fue maravilloso/horrible...

**1 Teaching Tip** Before assigning the activity, write cloze sentences on the board and ask volunteers to fill in the blanks. Ex: **¿Cómo ____ los guías turísticos durante tu viaje? (fueron) ¿Quién ____ con Marcela al baile? (fue)**

**1 Expansion** Ask small groups to write four questions based on the conversations. Have groups exchange papers and answer the questions they receive. Then have them confirm their answers with the group who wrote the questions.

**2 Expansion** Ask a volunteer to say one of his or her sentences aloud. Point to another student, and call out an interrogative word in order to cue a question. Ex: **E1: No fui a un restaurante anoche.** Say: **¿Adónde? E2: ¿Adónde fuiste? E1: Fui al cine.**

**3 Expansión** Have pairs team up to form groups of four. Each student should report three things about his or her partner to the group.

**4 Expansion** Ask pairs to write a similar conversation within a different context (Ex: **Un día horrible**).

**TEACHING OPTIONS**

**Small Groups** Have small groups of students prepare and perform a TV interview with astronauts who have just returned from a long stay on Mars. Review previous vocabulary as needed. Students should include three uses each of **ser** and **ir** in the preterite.

**TPR** Read aloud a series of sentences using **ser** and **ir** in the preterite. Have students raise their right hand if the verb is **ser**, and their left hand for **ir**. Ex: **Yo fui camarero a los dieciocho años.** (right hand)

## 7.4 Verbs like gustar (supersite)

**ANTE TODO** In **Lección 2**, you learned how to express preferences with **gustar**. You will now learn more about the verb **gustar** and other similar verbs. Observe these examples.

**Me gusta** ese champú.

> **ENGLISH EQUIVALENT**
> *I like that shampoo.*
> **LITERAL MEANING**
> *That shampoo is pleasing to me.*

**¿Te gustaron** las clases?

> **ENGLISH EQUIVALENT**
> *Did you like the classes?*
> **LITERAL MEANING**
> *Were the classes pleasing to you?*

▶ As the examples show, constructions with **gustar** do not have a direct equivalent in English. The literal meaning of this construction is *to be pleasing to (someone)*, and it requires the use of an indirect object pronoun.

| INDIRECT OBJECT PRONOUN | | SUBJECT | SUBJECT | | DIRECT OBJECT |
|---|---|---|---|---|---|
| **Me** | **gusta** | ese champú. | *I* | *like* | *that shampoo.* |

▶ In the diagram above, observe how in the Spanish sentence the object being liked **(ese champú)** is really the subject of the sentence. The person who likes the object, in turn, is an indirect object because it answers the question: *To whom is the shampoo pleasing?*

¿No te gustan las computadoras?

Me gustan mucho los parques.

▶ Other verbs in Spanish are used in the same way as **gustar**. Here is a list of the most common ones.

### Verbs like gustar

| | | | |
|---|---|---|---|
| **aburrir** | to bore | **importar** | to be important to; to matter |
| **encantar** | to like very much; to love (inanimate objects) | **interesar** | to be interesting to; to interest |
| **faltar** | to lack; to need | **molestar** | to bother; to annoy |
| **fascinar** | to fascinate; to like very much | **quedar** | to be left over; to fit (clothing) |

> **¡ATENCIÓN!**
>
> **Faltar** expresses what is lacking or missing.
> **Me falta una página.**
> *I'm missing one page.*
> **Quedar** expresses how much of something is left.
> **Nos quedan tres pesos.**
> *We have three pesos left.*
>
> • • •
>
> **Quedar** means *to fit.* It's also used to tell how something looks (on someone).
> **Estos zapatos me quedan bien.** *These shoes fit me well.*
> **Esa camisa te queda muy bien.** *That shirt looks good on you.*

**Teaching Tips**
- Write a model sentence on the board such as those found in the examples. Ex: **A Carlos le encanta la pasta dental Crest.** Then change the noun and ask volunteers to say the new sentence. Ex: **A nosotros (A nosotros nos encanta la pasta dental Crest.)**
- Ask students about their preferences, using verbs that follow the pattern of **gustar**. Ex: **A mí me encantan las lenguas, pero me aburren las matemáticas. ¿Qué les interesa a ustedes? ¿Qué les aburre?**

▶ The forms most commonly used with **gustar** and similar verbs are the third person (singular and plural). When the object or person being liked is singular, the singular form (**gusta/molesta**, etc.) is used. When two or more objects or persons are being liked, the plural form (**gustan/molestan**, etc.) is used. Observe the following diagram:

| | | | |
|---|---|---|---|
| SINGULAR | me, te, le | encanta / interesó | la película / el concierto |
| PLURAL | nos, os, les | importan / fascinaron | las vacaciones / los museos de Lima |

▶ To express what someone likes or does not like to do, use an appropriate verb followed by an infinitive. The singular form is used even if there is more than one infinitive.

**Nos molesta comer** a las nueve.
*It bothers us to eat at nine o'clock.*

**Les encanta cantar** y **bailar** en las fiestas.
*They love to sing and dance at parties.*

▶ As you learned in **Lección 2**, the construction **a** + [*pronoun*] (**a mí, a ti, a usted, a él,** etc.) is used to clarify or to emphasize who is pleased, bored, etc. The construction **a** + [*noun*] can also be used before the indirect object pronoun to clarify or to emphasize who is pleased.

**A los turistas** les gustó mucho Machu Picchu.
*The tourists liked Machu Picchu a lot.*

**A ti** te gusta cenar en casa, pero **a mí** me aburre.
*You like to eat dinner at home, but I get bored.*

▶ **¡Atención! Mí** (*me*) has an accent mark to distinguish it from the possessive adjective **mi** (*my*).

**AYUDA**

Note that the **a** must be repeated if there is more than one person. **A Armando** y **a Cinta** les molesta levantarse temprano.

---

 **¡INTÉNTALO!**  Indica el pronombre del objeto indirecto y la forma del tiempo presente adecuados en cada oración. La primera oración de cada columna se da como ejemplo.

**fascinar**

1. A él _le fascina_ viajar.
2. A mí _me fascina_ bailar.
3. A nosotras _nos fascina_ cantar.
4. A ustedes _les fascina_ leer.
5. A ti _te fascina_ correr.
6. A Pedro _le fascina_ gritar.
7. A mis padres _les fascina_ caminar.
8. A usted _le fascina_ jugar al tenis.
9. A mi esposo y a mí _nos fascina_ dormir.
10. A Alberto _le fascina_ dibujar.
11. A todos _nos/les fascina_ opinar.
12. A Pili _le fascina_ ir de compras.

**aburrir**

1. A ellos _les aburren_ los deportes.
2. A ti _te aburren_ las películas.
3. A usted _le aburren_ los viajes.
4. A mí _me aburren_ las revistas.
5. A Jorge y a Luis _les aburren_ los perros.
6. A nosotros _nos aburren_ las vacaciones.
7. A ustedes _les aburren_ las fiestas.
8. A Marcela _le aburren_ los libros.
9. A mis amigos _les aburren_ los museos.
10. A ella _le aburre_ el ciclismo.
11. A Omar _le aburre_ el Internet.
12. A ti y a mí _nos aburre_ el baile.

**recursos**

WB pp. 80–82

LM p. 42

panorama. vhlcentral.com Lección 7

---

**TEACHING OPTIONS**

**Large Group** Have the class sit in a circle. Student A begins by saying **Me encanta** and an activity he or she enjoys. Ex: **Me encanta correr.** Student B reports what student A said and adds his or her own favorite activity. **A Frank le encanta correr. A mí me fascina bailar.** Student C reports the preferences of the first two students and adds his or her own, and so forth. This activity may be used with any verb that follows the pattern of **gustar**.

**Extra Practice** Add an auditory aspect to this grammar presentation. Read a series of sentences aloud, pausing to allow students to write. Ex: **1. A todos en mi familia nos encanta viajar. 2. Nos gusta viajar en avión, pero nos molestan los aviones pequeños. 3. A mi hijo le interesan las culturas latinoamericanas, a mi esposo le encantan los países de Asia y a mí me fascina Europa. 4. Todavía nos quedan muchos lugares por visitar y nos falta el tiempo necesario.**

# Práctica (SUPERSITE)

**1** **Teaching Tip** To simplify, have students underline the subject in each sentence before filling in the blanks.

**1** **Expansion** Have students use the verbs in the activity to write a paragraph describing their own musical tastes.

**2** **Expansion** Repeat the activity using the preterite. Invite students to provide additional details. Ex: **1. A Ramón le molestó el despertador ayer. 2. A nosotros nos encantó esquiar en Vail.**

**3** **Expansion** Ask students to create two additional sentences using verbs from column B. Have students read their sentences aloud. After everyone has had a turn, ask the class how many similar or identical sentences they heard and what they were.

**1** **Completar** Completa las oraciones con todos los elementos necesarios.

1. _____A_____ Adela __le encanta__ (encantar) la música de Enrique Iglesias.
2. A __mí__ me __interesa__ (interesar) la música de otros países.
3. A mis amigos __les encantan__ (encantar) las canciones (*songs*) de Maná.
4. A Juan y __a__ Rafael no les __molesta__ (molestar) la música alta (*loud*).
5. _____A_____ nosotros __nos fascinan__ (fascinar) los grupos de pop latino.
6. __Al__ señor Ruiz __le interesa__ (interesar) más la música clásica.
7. A __mí__ me __aburre__ (aburrir) la música clásica.
8. ¿A __ti__ te __falta__ (faltar) dinero para el concierto de Carlos Santana?
9. Sí. Sólo __me quedan__ (quedar) cinco dólares.
10. ¿Cuánto dinero te __queda__ (quedar) a __ti__?

**NOTA CULTURAL**

Hoy día, la música latina es popular en los EE.UU. gracias a artistas como **Shakira**, de nacionalidad colombiana, y **Enrique Iglesias**, español. Otros artistas, como **Carlos Santana** y **Gloria Estefan**, difundieron (*spread*) la música latina en los años 60, 70, 80 y 90.

**2** **Describir** Mira los dibujos y describe lo que está pasando. Usa los verbos de la lista.
Some answers will vary.

| aburrir | faltar | molestar |
| encantar | interesar | quedar |

1. a Ramón   A Ramón le molesta despertarse temprano.

2. a nosotros   A nosotros nos encanta esquiar.

3. a ti   A ti no te queda bien este vestido. A ti te queda mal/grande este vestido.

LIBROS DE ARTE MODERNO

4. a Sara   A Sara le interesan los libros de arte moderno.

**3** **Gustos** Forma oraciones con los elementos de las tres columnas. Answers will vary.

> **modelo**
> A ti te interesan las ruinas de Machu Picchu.

| A | B | C |
|---|---|---|
| yo | aburrir | despertarse temprano |
| tú | encantar | mirarse en el espejo |
| mi mejor amigo/a | faltar | la música rock |
| mis amigos y yo | fascinar | las pantuflas rosadas |
| Bart y Homero Simpson | interesar | la pasta de dientes con menta (*mint*) |
| Shakira | molestar | las ruinas de Machu Picchu |
| Antonio Banderas | | los zapatos caros |

**TEACHING OPTIONS**

**TPR** Have students stand and form a circle. Begin by tossing a foam or paper ball to a student, who should state a complaint using a verb like **gustar** (Ex: **Me falta dinero para comprar los libros**) and then toss the ball to another student. The next student should offer advice (Ex: **Debes pedirle dinero a tus padres**) and throw the ball to another person, who will air another complaint. Repeat the activity with positive statements (**Me fascinan las**

películas cómicas) and advice (**Debes ver las películas de Will Ferrel**).

**Extra Practice** Write sentences like these on the board. Have students copy them and draw faces (☺/☹) to indicate the feelings expressed. Ex: **1. Me encantan las enchiladas verdes. 2. Me aburren las matemáticas. 3. Me fascina la ópera italiana. 4. No me falta dinero para comprar un auto. 5. Me queda pequeño el sombrero.**

# Comunicación

**4** **Preguntas** En parejas, túrnense para hacer y contestar estas preguntas. *Answers will vary.*

1. ¿Te gusta levantarte temprano o tarde? ¿Por qué? ¿Y a tu compañero/a de cuarto?
2. ¿Te gusta acostarte temprano o tarde? ¿Y a tu compañero/a de cuarto?
3. ¿Te gusta dormir la siesta?
4. ¿Te encanta acampar o prefieres quedarte en un hotel cuando estás de vacaciones?
5. ¿Qué te gusta hacer en el verano?
6. ¿Qué te fascina de esta universidad? ¿Qué te molesta?
7. ¿Te interesan más las ciencias o las humanidades? ¿Por qué?
8. ¿Qué cosas te molestan?

**5** **Completar** Completa estas frases de una manera lógica. *Answers will vary.*

1. A mi novio/a le fascina(n)…
2. A mi mejor (*best*) amigo/a no le interesa(n)…
3. A mis padres les importa(n)…
4. A nosotros nos molesta(n)…
5. A mis hermanos les aburre(n)…
6. A mi compañero/a de cuarto le aburre(n)…
7. A los turistas les interesa(n)…
8. A los jugadores profesionales les encanta(n)…
9. A nuestro/a profesor(a) le molesta(n)…
10. A mí me importa(n)…

**6** **La residencia** Tú y tu compañero/a de clase son los directores de una residencia estudiantil en Perú. Su profesor(a) les va a dar a cada uno de ustedes las descripciones de cinco estudiantes. Con la información tienen que escoger quiénes van a ser compañeros de cuarto. Después, completen la lista. *Answers will vary.*

# Síntesis

**7** **Situación** Trabajen en parejas para representar los papeles de un(a) cliente/a y un(a) dependiente/a en una tienda de ropa. Usen las instrucciones como guía. *Answers will vary.*

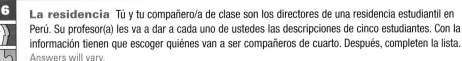

**Dependiente/a**

- Saluda al/a la cliente/a y pregúntale en qué le puedes servir.
- Pregúntale si le interesan los estilos modernos y empieza a mostrarle la ropa.
- Habla de los gustos del/de la cliente/a.
- Da opiniones favorables al/a la cliente/a (las botas te quedan fantásticas…).

**Cliente/a**

- Saluda al/a la dependiente/a y dile (*tell him/her*) qué quieres comprar y qué colores prefieres.
- Explícale que los estilos modernos te interesan. Escoge las cosas que te interesan.
- Habla de la ropa (me queda(n) bien/mal, me encanta(n)…).
- Decide cuáles son las cosas que te gustan y qué vas a comprar.

**4 Expansion** Take a class survey of the answers and write the results on the board. Ask volunteers to use verbs like **gustar** to summarize them.

**5 Teaching Tip** For items that start with **A mi(s)…**, have pairs compare their answers and then report to the class: first answers in common, then answers that differed. Ex: **A mis padres les importan los estudios, pero a los padres de _____ les importa más el dinero.**

**6 Teaching Tip** Divide the class into pairs and distribute the handouts from the Information Gap Activities (Supersite/IRCD) that correspond to this activity. Give students ten minutes to complete this activity.

**6 Expansion**
- Have pairs compare their matches by circulating around the classroom until they have all compared their answers with one another.
- Have pairs choose one of the students and write his or her want ad looking for a suitable roommate.

**7 Teaching Tip** To simplify, have students prepare for their roles by brainstorming a list of words and phrases. Remind students to use the formal register in this conversation.

**7 Expansion** Ask pairs to perform their conversation for the class or have them videotape it.

**TEACHING OPTIONS**

**Pairs** Have pairs prepare short TV commercials in which they use the target verbs presented in **Estructura 7.4** to sell a particular product. Group three pairs together to present their skits.
**Extra Practice** Add a visual aspect to this grammar practice. Bring in magazine pictures of people enjoying or not enjoying what they are doing. Have them create sentences with verbs like **gustar**. Ex: **A los chicos no les interesa estudiar biología.**

**Game** Give groups of students five minutes to write a description of social life during a specific historical period, such as the French Revolution or prehistoric times, using as many of the target verbs presented in **Estructura 7.4** as possible. When finished, ask groups how many of these verbs they used in their descriptions. Have the top three read their descriptions for the class, who vote for their favorite description.

# Recapitulación

**SUPERSITE** For self-scoring and diagnostics, go to **panorama.vhlcentral.com**.

Completa estas actividades para repasar los conceptos de gramática que aprendiste en esta lección.

**1 Completar** Completa la tabla con la forma correcta de los verbos. **6 pts.**

| yo | tú | nosotros | ellas |
|---|---|---|---|
| **me levanto** | te levantas | nos levantamos | se levantan |
| me afeito | **te afeitas** | nos afeitamos | se afeitan |
| me visto | te vistes | **nos vestimos** | se visten |
| me seco | te secas | nos secamos | **se secan** |

**2 Hoy y ayer** Cambia los verbos del presente al pretérito. **5 pts.**

1. Vamos de compras hoy. ____Fuimos____ de compras hoy.
2. Por último, voy a poner el despertador. Por último, ____fui____ a poner el despertador.
3. Lalo es el primero en levantarse. Lalo ____fue____ el primero en levantarse.
4. ¿Vas a tu habitación? ¿____Fuiste____ a tu habitación?
5. Ustedes son profesores. Ustedes ____fueron____ profesores.

**3 Reflexivos** Completa cada conversación con la forma correcta del presente del verbo reflexivo. **11 pts.**

**TOMÁS** Yo siempre (1) ____me baño____ (bañarse) antes de (2) ____acostarme____ (acostarse). Esto me relaja porque no (3) ____me duermo____ (dormirse) fácilmente. Y así puedo (4) ____levantarme____ (levantarse) más tarde. Y tú, ¿cuándo (5) ____te duchas____ (ducharse)?

**LETI** Pues por la mañana, para poder (6) ____despertarme____ (despertarse).

**DAVID** ¿Cómo (7) ____se siente____ (sentirse) Pepa hoy?

**MARÍA** Todavía está enojada.

**DAVID** ¿De verdad? Ella nunca (8) ____se enoja____ (enojarse) con nadie.

**BETO** ¿(Nosotros) (9) ____Nos vamos____ (Irse) de esta tienda? Estoy cansado.

**SARA** Pero antes vamos a (10) ____probarnos____ (probarse) estos sombreros. Si quieres, después (nosotros) (11) ____nos sentamos____ (sentarse) un rato.

## RESUMEN GRAMATICAL

**7.1 Reflexive verbs** *pp. 220–221*

| lavarse | |
|---|---|
| me lavo | nos lavamos |
| te lavas | os laváis |
| se lava | se lavan |

**7.2 Indefinite and negative words** *pp. 224–225*

| Indefinite words | Negative words |
|---|---|
| algo | nada |
| alguien | nadie |
| alguno/a(s), algún | ninguno/a, ningún |
| o... o | ni... ni |
| siempre | nunca, jamás |
| también | tampoco |

**7.3 Preterite of ser and ir** *p. 228*

► The preterite of **ser** and **ir** are identical. Context will determine the meaning.

| ser and ir | |
|---|---|
| fui | fuimos |
| fuiste | fuisteis |
| fue | fueron |

**7.4 Verbs like gustar** *pp. 230–231*

| aburrir | importar |
|---|---|
| encantar | interesar |
| faltar | molestar |
| fascinar | quedar |

**SINGULAR** me, te, le
**PLURAL** nos, os, les

encanta / interesó → la película / el concierto

importan / fascinaron → las vacaciones / los museos

► Use the construction a + [*noun/pronoun*] to clarify the person in question.

**A mí me encanta ver películas, ¿y a ti?**

**4** **Conversaciones** Completa cada conversación de manera lógica con palabras de la lista. No tienes que usar todas las palabras. **8 pts.**

| algo | nada | ningún | siempre |
|------|------|--------|---------|
| alguien | nadie | nunca | también |
| algún | ni... ni | o... o | tampoco |

1. —¿Tienes _algún_ plan para esta noche?

   —No, prefiero quedarme en casa. Hoy no quiero ver a _nadie_.

   —Yo _también_ me quedo. Estoy muy cansado.

2. —¿Puedo entrar? ¿Hay _alguien_ en el cuarto de baño?

   —Sí. Ahora mismo salgo.

3. —¿Puedes prestarme _algo_ para peinarme? No encuentro _ni_ mi cepillo _ni_ mi peine.

   —Lo siento, yo _tampoco_ encuentro los míos (*mine*).

4. —¿Me prestas tu maquillaje?

   —Lo siento, no tengo. _Nunca_ me maquillo.

**5** **Oraciones** Forma oraciones completas con los elementos dados (*given*). Usa el presente de los verbos. **8 pts.**

1. David y Juan / molestar / levantarse temprano  A David y a Juan les molesta levantarse temprano.
2. Lucía / encantar / las películas de terror  A Lucía le encantan las películas de terror.
3. todos (nosotros) / importar / la educación  A todos nos importa la educación.
4. tú / aburrir / ver / la televisión  A ti te aburre ver la televisión.

**6** **Rutinas** Escribe seis oraciones describiendo las rutinas de dos personas que conoces. **12 pts.**
Answers will vary.

> **modelo**
> Mi tía se despierta temprano, pero mi primo...

**7** **Adivinanza** Completa la adivinanza con las palabras que faltan y adivina la respuesta. **¡2 puntos EXTRA!**

“ Cuanto más° _te seca_ (*it dries you*),
más se moja°. ”
¿Qué es? _La toalla_

Cuanto más *The more* se moja *it gets wet*

**4** **Expansion** Have students create four additional sentences using the remaining indefinite and negative words from the word bank.

**5** **Teaching Tip** Remind students to use the personal **a** in their answers.

**5** **Expansion** Give students these sentences as items 5–8: 5. yo / faltar / dinero (A mí me falta dinero.) 6. Pedro y yo / fascinar / cantar y bailar (A Pedro y a mí nos fascina cantar y bailar.) 7. usted / quedar / muy bien / esas gafas de sol (A usted le quedan muy bien esas gafas de sol.) 8. ¿ / ustedes / interesar / conocer / otros países / ? (¿A ustedes les interesa conocer otros países?)

**6** **Expansion** Have volunteers share their sentences with the class. Encourage classmates to ask them follow-up questions. Ex: **¿Por qué se despierta temprano tu tía?**

**7** **Expansion** To challenge students, have them work in small groups to create a riddle using grammar and/or vocabulary from this lesson. Have groups share their riddles with the class.

**TEACHING OPTIONS**

**Game** Play a game of **Diez Preguntas**. Ask a volunteer to think of a person in the class. Other students get one chance each to ask a question using indefinite and negative words. Ex: **¿Es alguien que siempre llega temprano a clase?**

**Extra Practice** Have students imagine they are a famous singer or actor. Then have them write eight sentences from the point of view of that person using verbs like **gustar** and indefinite and negative words. Ex: **Jennifer López: Me encanta la música pop pero me aburre la música clásica. Tampoco me interesa la música *country*.** Ask volunteers to share some of their sentences and see if the rest of the class agrees with their statements.

## Section Goals

In **Lectura**, students will:
• learn the strategy of predicting content from the title
• read an e-mail in Spanish

**Instructional Resources**
**Supersite**
*Cuaderno para hispanohablantes*

**Estrategia** Tell students that they can often predict the content of a newspaper article from its headline. Display or make up several cognate-rich headlines from Spanish newspapers. Ex: **Decenas de miles recuerdan la explosión atómica en Hiroshima; Lanzamiento de musicahoy.net, sitio para profesionales y aficionados a la música; Científicos anuncian que Plutón ya no es planeta**. Ask students to predict the content of each article.

**Examinar el texto** Survey the class to find out the most common predictions. Were most of them about a positive or negative experience?

**Compartir** Have students discuss how they are able to tell what the content will be by looking at the format of the text.

**Cognados** Discuss how scanning the text for cognates can help predict the content.

# Lectura  communication cultures NATIONAL STANDARDS

## Antes de leer

### Estrategia

**Predicting content from the title**

Prediction is an invaluable strategy in reading for comprehension. For example, we can usually predict the content of a newspaper article from its headline. We often decide whether to read the article based on its headline. Predicting content from the title will help you increase your reading comprehension in Spanish.

### Examinar el texto

Lee el título de la lectura y haz tres predicciones sobre el contenido. Escribe tus predicciones en una hoja de papel.

### Compartir

Comparte tus ideas con un(a) compañero/a de clase.

### Cognados

Haz una lista de seis cognados que encuentres en la lectura. Answers will vary.

1. _____
2. _____
3. _____
4. _____
5. _____
6. _____

¿Qué te dicen los cognados sobre el tema de la lectura?

recursos
SUPERSITE
panorama.vhlcentral.com
Lección 7

## ¡Qué día!

Anterior ▼ ⬇Siguiente ▼ 🔼 Responder 🔼 Respon[der] a todos

Fecha: Lunes, 10 de mayo
De: Guillermo Zamora
Asunto: ¡Qué día!
Para: Lupe; Marcos; Sandra; Jorge

### Hola, chicos:

La semana pasada me di cuenta° de que necesito organizar mejor° mi rutina... pero especialmente necesito prepararme mejor para los exámenes. Me falta mucha disciplina, me molesta no tener control de mi tiempo y nunca deseo repetir los eventos de la semana pasada.

El miércoles pasé todo el día y toda la noche estudiando para el examen de biología del jueves por la mañana. Me aburre la biología y no empecé a estudiar hasta el día antes del examen. El jueves a las 8, después de no dormir en toda la noche, fui exhausto al examen. Fue difícil, pero afortunadamente° me acordé de todo el material. Esa noche me acosté temprano y dormí mucho.

Me desperté a las 7, y fue extraño° ver a mi compañero de cuarto, Andrés, preparándose para ir a dormir. Como° siempre se enferma° y nunca

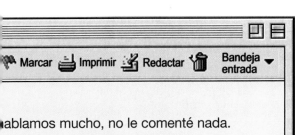

ablamos mucho, no le comenté nada.
ui al baño a cepillarme los dientes
para ir a clase. ¿Y Andrés? Él se
acostó. "Debe estar enfermo°,
otra vez!", pensé.

Mi clase es a las 8, y fue
necesario hacer las cosas rápido. Todo
empezó a ir mal... eso pasa siempre
cuando uno tiene prisa. Cuando
busqué mis cosas para el baño, no
las encontré. Entonces me duché sin
abón, me cepillé los dientes sin cepillo
de dientes y me peiné con las manos.
Tampoco encontré ropa limpia, y usé
a sucia. Rápido, tomé mis libros. ¿Y
Andrés? Roncando°... ¡a las 7:50!

Cuando salí corriendo para la clase,
a prisa no me permitió ver el campus
desierto. Cuando llegué a la clase, no
vi a nadie. No vi al profesor ni a los
estudiantes. Por último miré mi reloj,
v vi la hora. Las 8 en punto... ¡de la
noche!

Dormí 24 horas!

Guillermo

me di cuenta *I realized* mejor *better* afortunadamente *fortunately*
extraño *strange* Como *Since* se enferma *he gets sick* enfermo *sick*
Roncando *Snoring*

# Después de leer

## Seleccionar

Selecciona la respuesta correcta.

1. ¿Quién es el/la narrador(a)? **c**
   a. Andrés
   b. una profesora
   c. Guillermo
2. ¿Qué le molesta al narrador? **b**
   a. Le molestan los exámenes de biología.
   b. Le molesta no tener control de su tiempo.
   c. Le molesta mucho organizar su rutina.
3. ¿Por qué está exhausto? **c**
   a. Porque fue a una fiesta la noche anterior.
   b. Porque no le gusta la biología.
   c. Porque pasó la noche anterior estudiando.
4. ¿Por qué no hay nadie en clase? **a**
   a. Porque es de noche.
   b. Porque todos están de vacaciones.
   c. Porque el profesor canceló la clase.
5. ¿Cómo es la relación de Guillermo y Andrés? **b**
   a. Son buenos amigos.
   b. No hablan mucho.
   c. Tienen una buena relación.

## Ordenar

Ordena los sucesos de la narración. Utiliza los
números del 1 al 9.

a. Toma el examen de biología. __2__
b. No encuentra sus cosas para el baño. __5__
c. Andrés se duerme. __7__
d. Pasa todo el día y toda la noche estudiando
   para un examen. __1__
e. Se ducha sin jabón. __6__
f. Se acuesta temprano. __3__
g. Vuelve a su cuarto a las 8 de la noche. __9__
h. Se despierta a las 7 y su compañero de cuarto se
   prepara para dormir. __4__
i. Va a clase y no hay nadie. __8__

## Contestar

Contesta estas preguntas. Answers will vary.

1. ¿Cómo es tu rutina diaria? ¿Muy organizada?
2. ¿Cuándo empiezas a estudiar para los exámenes?
3. ¿Tienes compañero/a de cuarto? ¿Son amigos/as?
4. Para comunicarte con tus amigos/as, ¿prefieres
   el teléfono o el correo electrónico? ¿Por qué?

# Perú

## El país en cifras

- **Área:** 1.285.220 km² (496.224 millas²), *un poco menos que el área de Alaska*
- **Población:** 30.063.000
- **Capital:** Lima —7.590.000
- **Ciudades principales:** Arequipa —915.000, Trujillo, Chiclayo, Callao, Iquitos

SOURCE: Population Division, UN Secretariat

*Iquitos es un puerto muy importante en el río Amazonas. Desde Iquitos se envían° muchos productos a otros lugares, incluyendo goma°, nueces°, madera°, arroz°, café y tabaco. Iquitos es también un destino popular para los ecoturistas que visitan la selva°.*

- **Moneda:** nuevo sol
- **Idiomas:** español (oficial), quechua (oficial), aimará

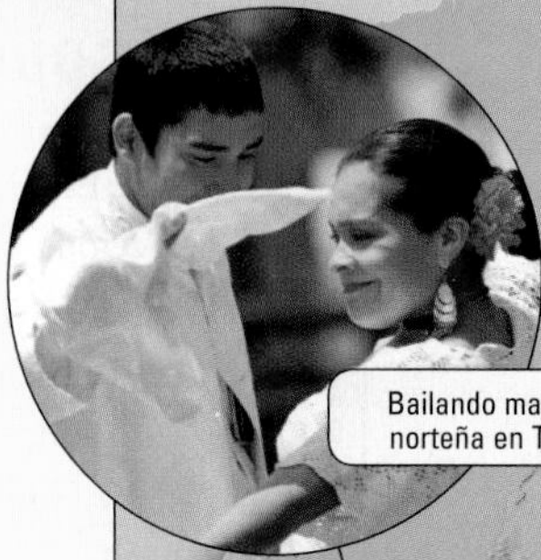

Bandera del Perú

### Peruanos célebres

- **Clorinda Matto de Turner,** escritora (1854–1901)
- **César Vallejo,** poeta (1892–1938)
- **Javier Pérez de Cuéllar,** diplomático (1920– )
- **Mario Vargas Llosa,** escritor (1936– )

Mario Vargas Llosa

se envían *are shipped* goma *rubber* nueces *nuts* madera *timber* arroz *rice* selva *jungle* Hace más de *More than... ago* grabó *engraved* tamaño *size*

### ¡Increíble pero cierto!

Hace más de° dos mil años la civilización nazca de Perú grabó° más de 2.000 kilómetros de líneas en el desierto. Los dibujos sólo son descifrables desde el aire. Uno de ellos es un cóndor del tamaño° de un estadio. Las Líneas de Nazca son uno de los grandes misterios de la humanidad.

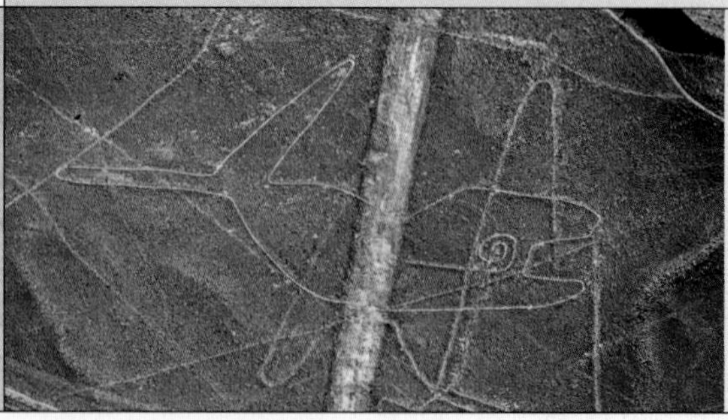

---

## Section Goal

In **Panorama**, students will read about the geography, culture, and history of Peru.

**Instructional Resources**
**Supersite/DVD:** *Panorama cultural*
**Supersite/IRCD:** *PowerPoints* (Overheads #5, #6, #32); *IRM* (*Panorama cultural* Videoscript & Translation, WBs/VM/LM Answer Key)
**WebSAM**
**Workbook,** pp. 83–84
**Video Manual,** pp. 237–238

**Teaching Tip** Have students look at the map of Peru or show *Overhead PowerPoint #32*. Ask them to find the **Río Amazonas** and the **Cordillera de los Andes**, and to speculate about the types of climate found in Peru. As a mountainous country near the equator, climate varies according to elevation, and ranges from tropical to arctic. Point out that well over half of the territory of Peru lies within the Amazon Basin. Encourage students to share what they know about Peru.

**El país en cifras** After each section, pause to ask students questions about the content. Point out that Iquitos, Peru's port city on the Amazon River, is a destination for ships that travel 2,300 miles up the Amazon from the Atlantic Ocean.

**¡Increíble pero cierto!** In recent years, the **El Niño** weather phenomenon has caused flooding in the deserts of southern Peru. The Peruvian government is working to preserve the **Líneas de Nazca** from further deterioration in the hope that someday scientists will discover more about their origins and meaning.

---

**recursos** — WB pp. 83–84 | VM pp. 237–238 | panorama.vhlcentral.com Lección 7

Map labels: ECUADOR, COLOMBIA, Río Putumayo, Río Napo, Río Tigre, Río Amazonas, Iquitos, Río Pastaza, Río Marañón, Río Huallaga, Río Ucayali, Río Urubamba, Chiclayo, Trujillo, Cordillera Oriental de los Andes, Cordillera Central de los Andes, Cordillera Occidental de los Andes, Callao, Lima, Océano Pacífico, Machu Picchu, Cuzco, Arequipa, La Titicaca

Captions: Bailando marinera norteña en Trujillo; Calle en la ciudad de Iquitos; Fuente de la Justicia en Lima; Mercado indígena en Cuzco

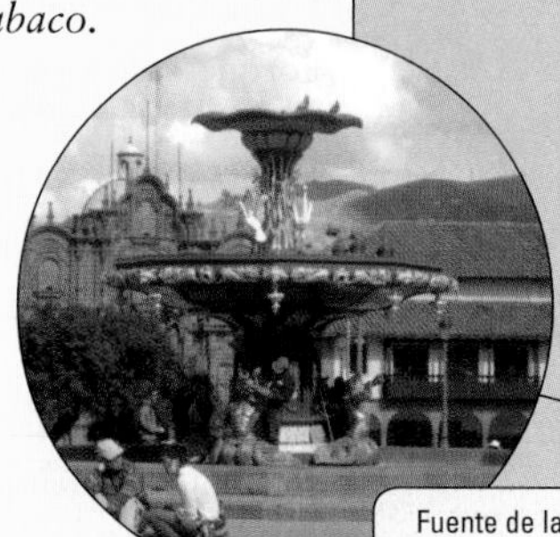

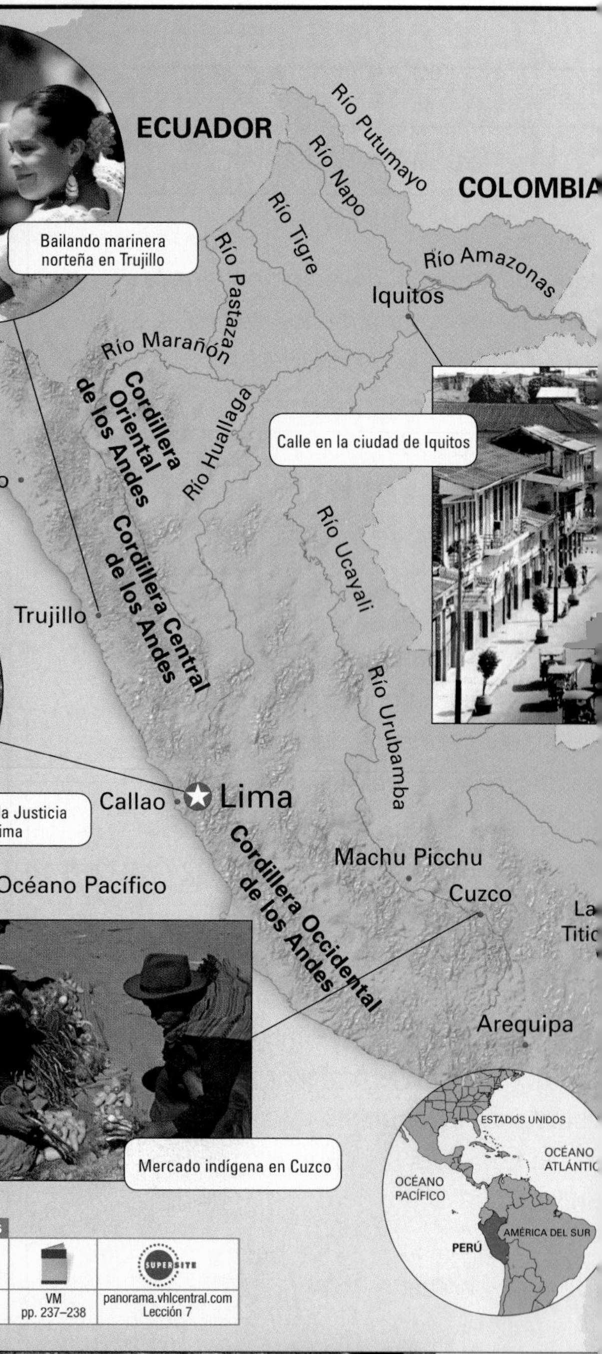

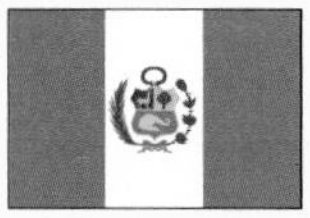

### TEACHING OPTIONS

**Heritage Speakers** Ask heritage speakers of Peruvian origin or students who have visited Peru to make a short presentation to the class about their impressions. Encourage them to speak of the region they are from or have visited and how it differs from other regions in this vast country. If they have photographs, ask them to bring them to class to illustrate their talk.

**TPR** Invite students to take turns guiding the class on tours of Peru's waterways: one student gives directions, and the others follow by tracing the route on their map of Peru. For example: **Comenzamos en el río Amazonas, pasando por Iquitos hasta llegar al río Ucayali.**

## Lugares • Lima

Lima es una ciudad moderna y antigua° a la vez°. La Iglesia de San Francisco es notable por la influencia de la arquitectura barroca colonial. También son fascinantes las exhibiciones sobre los incas en el Museo Oro del Perú y en el Museo Nacional de Antropología y Arqueología. Barranco, el barrio° bohemio de la ciudad, es famoso por su ambiente cultural y sus bares y restaurantes.

## Historia • Machu Picchu

A 80 kilómetros al noroeste de Cuzco está Machu Picchu, una ciudad antigua del imperio inca. Está a una altitud de 2.350 metros (7.710 pies), entre dos cimas° de los Andes. Cuando los españoles llegaron al Perú, nunca encontraron Machu Picchu. En 1911, el arqueólogo norteamericano Hiram Bingham la descubrió. Todavía no se sabe ni cómo se construyó° una ciudad a esa altura, ni por qué los incas la abandonaron. Sin embargo°, esta ciudad situada en desniveles° naturales es el ejemplo más conocido de la arquitectura inca.

## Artes • La música andina

Machu Picchu aún no existía° cuando se originó la música cautivadora° de las antiguas culturas indígenas de los Andes. La influencia española y la música africana contribuyeron a la creación de los ritmos actuales de la música andina. Dos tipos de flauta°, la quena y la antara, producen esta música tan particular. En las décadas de los sesenta y los setenta se popularizó un movimiento para preservar la música andina, y hasta° Simon y Garfunkel la incorporaron en su repertorio con la canción *El cóndor pasa*.

## Economía • Llamas y alpacas

El Perú se conoce por sus llamas, alpacas, guanacos y vicuñas, todos ellos animales mamíferos° parientes del camello. Estos animales todavía tienen una enorme importancia en la economía del país. Dan lana para hacer ropa, mantas°, bolsas y artículos para turistas. La llama se usa también para la carga y el transporte.

**¿Qué aprendiste?**  Responde a cada pregunta con una oración completa.

1. ¿Qué productos envía Iquitos a otros lugares? Iquitos envía goma, nueces, madera, arroz, café y tabaco.
2. ¿Cuáles son las lenguas oficiales del Perú? Las lenguas oficiales del Perú son el español y el quechua.
3. ¿Por qué es notable la Iglesia de San Francisco en Lima? Es notable por la influencia de la arquitectura barroca colonial.
4. ¿Qué información sobre Machu Picchu no se sabe todavía? No se sabe ni cómo se construyó ni por qué la abandonaron.
5. ¿Qué son la quena y la antara? Son dos tipos de flauta.
6. ¿Qué hacen los peruanos con la lana de sus llamas y alpacas? Hacen ropa, mantas, bolsas y artículos para turistas.

**Conexión Internet**  Investiga estos temas en **panorama.vhlcentral.com**.

1. Investiga la cultura incaica. ¿Cuáles son algunos de los aspectos interesantes de su cultura?
2. Busca información sobre dos artistas, escritores o músicos peruanos y presenta un breve informe a tu clase.

antigua *old*  a la vez *at the same time*  barrio *neighborhood*  cimas *summits*  se construyó *was built*  Sin embargo *However* desniveles *uneven pieces of land*  aún no existía *didn't exist yet*  cautivadora *captivating*  flauta *flute*  hasta *even* mamíferos *mammalian*  mantas *blankets*

---

**Lima**  Lima, rich in colonial architecture, is also the home of the **Universidad de San Marcos,** established in 1551, the oldest university in South America.

**Los incas**  Another invention of the Incas were the **quipus,** clusters of knotted strings that were a means of keeping records and sending messages. A **quipu** consisted of a series of small, knotted cords attached to a larger cord. Each cord's color, place, size, and the knots it contained all had significance.

**La música andina**  Ancient tombs belonging to pre-Columbian cultures like the Nasca and Moche have yielded instruments and other artifacts indicating that the precursors of Andean music go back at least two millenia.

**Llamas y alpacas**  Of the camel-like animals of the Andes, only the sturdy **llama** has been domesticated as a pack animal. Its long, thick coat also provides fiber that is woven into a coarser grade of cloth. The more delicate **alpaca** and **vicuña** are raised only for their beautiful coats, used to create extremely high-quality cloth. The **guanaco** has never been domesticated.

**Conexión Internet**  Students will find supporting Internet activities and links at **panorama.vhlcentral.com**.

**Teaching Tip**  You may want to wrap up this section by playing the *Panorama cultural* video footage for this lesson.

---

**TEACHING OPTIONS**

**Variación léxica**  Some of the most familiar words to have entered Spanish from the Quechua language are the names of animals native to the Andean region, such as **el cóndor, la llama, el puma,** and **la vicuña**. These words later passed from Spanish to a number of European languages, including English. **La alpaca** comes not from Quechua, (the language of the Incas and their descendants, who inhabit most of the Andean region), but from Aymara, the language of indigenous people who live near Lake Titicaca on the Peruvian-Bolivian border. Some students may be familiar with the traditional Quechua tune, *El cóndor pasa*, which was popularized in a version by Simon and Garfunkel.

**Instructional Resources**
**Supersite:** Textbook &
Vocabulary MP3 Audio Files
**Lección 7**
**Supersite/IRCD:** *IRM* (WBs/
VM/LM Answer Key); *Testing
Program* (**Lección 7 Pruebas**,
Test Generator, Testing
Program MP3 Audio Files)
**WebSAM**
**Lab Manual,** p. 42

## Los verbos reflexivos

| | |
|---|---|
| **acordarse (de) (o:ue)** | to remember |
| **acostarse (o:ue)** | to go to bed |
| **afeitarse** | to shave |
| **bañarse** | to bathe; to take a bath |
| **cepillarse el pelo** | to brush one's hair |
| **cepillarse los dientes** | to brush one's teeth |
| **despedirse (de) (e:i)** | to say goodbye (to) |
| **despertarse (e:ie)** | to wake up |
| **dormirse (o:ue)** | to go to sleep; to fall asleep |
| **ducharse** | to shower; to take a shower |
| **enojarse (con)** | to get angry (with) |
| **irse** | to go away; to leave |
| **lavarse la cara** | to wash one's face |
| **lavarse las manos** | to wash one's hands |
| **levantarse** | to get up |
| **llamarse** | to be called; to be named |
| **maquillarse** | to put on makeup |
| **peinarse** | to comb one's hair |
| **ponerse** | to put on |
| **ponerse (+ *adj.*)** | to become (+ adj.) |
| **preocuparse (por)** | to worry (about) |
| **probarse (o:ue)** | to try on |
| **quedarse** | to stay; to remain |
| **quitarse** | to take off |
| **secarse** | to dry oneself |
| **sentarse (e:ie)** | to sit down |
| **sentirse (e:ie)** | to feel |
| **vestirse (e:i)** | to get dressed |

## Palabras de secuencia

| | |
|---|---|
| **antes (de)** | before |
| **después** | afterwards; then |
| **después (de)** | after |
| **durante** | during |
| **entonces** | then |
| **luego** | then |
| **más tarde** | later (on) |
| **por último** | finally |

## Palabras afirmativas y negativas

| | |
|---|---|
| **algo** | something; anything |
| **alguien** | someone; somebody; anyone |
| **alguno/a(s), algún** | some; any |
| **jamás** | never; not ever |
| **nada** | nothing; not anything |
| **nadie** | no one; nobody; not anyone |
| **ni… ni** | neither… nor |
| **ninguno/a, ningún** | no; none; not any |
| **nunca** | never; not ever |
| **o… o** | either… or |
| **siempre** | always |
| **también** | also; too |
| **tampoco** | neither; not either |

## En el baño

| | |
|---|---|
| **el baño, el cuarto de baño** | bathroom |
| **el champú** | shampoo |
| **la crema de afeitar** | shaving cream |
| **la ducha** | shower |
| **el espejo** | mirror |
| **el inodoro** | toilet |
| **el jabón** | soap |
| **el lavabo** | sink |
| **el maquillaje** | makeup |
| **la pasta de dientes** | toothpaste |
| **la toalla** | towel |

## Verbos similares a gustar

| | |
|---|---|
| **aburrir** | to bore |
| **encantar** | to like very much; to love (inanimate objects) |
| **faltar** | to lack; to need |
| **fascinar** | to fascinate; to like very much |
| **importar** | to be important to; to matter |
| **interesar** | to be interesting to; to interest |
| **molestar** | to bother; to annoy |
| **quedar** | to be left over; to fit (clothing) |

## Palabras adicionales

| | |
|---|---|
| **el despertador** | alarm clock |
| **las pantuflas** | slippers |
| **la rutina diaria** | daily routine |
| **por la mañana** | in the morning |
| **por la noche** | at night |
| **por la tarde** | in the afternoon; in the evening |

| | |
|---|---|
| **Expresiones útiles** | See page 215. |

**recursos**

LM p. 42

panorama.vhlcentral.com Lección 7

# La comida

## 8

## Lesson Goals

In **Lección 8**, students will be introduced to the following:
- food terms
- meal-related words
- fruits and vegetables native to the Americas
- Spanish chef **Ferrán Adrià**
- preterite of stem-changing verbs
- double object pronouns
- converting **le** and **les** to **se** with double object pronouns
- comparatives
- superlatives
- reading for the main idea
- cultural, geographic, and historical information about Guatemala

**A primera vista** Here are some additional questions you can ask based on the photo: **¿Dónde te encanta comer? ¿Por qué? ¿Fuiste a algún lugar especial para comer la semana pasada? ¿Compras comida? ¿Dónde? ¿Quién prepara la comida en tu casa?**

## A PRIMERA VISTA
- ¿Dónde está ella?
- ¿Qué hace?
- ¿Es parte de su rutina diaria?
- ¿Qué colores hay en la foto?

**INSTRUCTIONAL RESOURCES**

*MAESTRO*™ **SUPERSITE (panorama.vhlcentral.com)**
Textbook, Vocabulary, & Lab MP3 Audio Files
Additional Practice
Learning Management System (Assignment Task Manager, Gradebook)
*Also on DVD*
  **Fotonovela**

*Flash cultura*
*Panorama cultural*
*Also on Instructor's Resource CD-ROM*
*PowerPoints* (**Contextos** & **Estructura** Presentations, Overheads)
*Instructor's Resource Manual* (Handouts, Textbook Answer Key, WBs/VM/LM Answer Key,

Audioscripts, Videoscripts & Translations)
*Testing Program* (**Pruebas,** Test Generator, MP3s)
**WebSAM** (Workbook/Video Manual/Lab Manual)
**Workbook/Video Manual**
*Cuaderno para hispanohablantes*
**Lab Manual**

# La comida

## Section Goals

In **Contextos**, students will learn and practice:
• food names
• meal-related vocabulary

**Instructional Resources**
**Supersite:** Textbook, Vocabulary, & Lab MP3 Audio Files **Lección 8**
**Supersite/IRCD:** *PowerPoints* (**Lección 8 Contextos** Presentation, Overheads #33, #34); *IRM* (**Vocabulario adicional,** Textbook Audio Script, Information Gap Activities, Lab Audio Script, WBs/VM/LM Answer Key)
**WebSAM**
**Workbook,** pp. 85–86
**Lab Manual,** p. 43
*Cuaderno para hispanohablantes*

## Teaching Tips
• Tell what you are going to have for lunch, writing food vocabulary on the board. Ex: **Tengo hambre y voy a preparar una hamburguesa. ¿Qué ingredientes necesito? Pues, carne de res, queso, tomates, lechuga y mayonesa. También voy a preparar una ensalada. ¿Con qué ingredientes preparo la ensalada? A ver, lechuga, tomates, zanahorias,…**
• Show *Overhead PowerPoint #33.* Ask: **¿Sí o no? ¿Hay bananas en el mercado? (Sí.) ¿Qué otras frutas hay? Y, ¿hay cerveza? (No.)** Then mention typical dishes and ask students to tell what ingredients are used to make them. Ex: **una ensalada mixta, una ensalada de fruta, un sándwich.**
• Ask students what some of their favorite foods are. Ex: **Y a ti, _____, ¿qué te gusta comer?**

### Más vocabulario

| | |
|---|---|
| el/la camarero/a | waiter/waitress |
| la comida | food; meal |
| el/la dueño/a | owner; landlord |
| los entremeses | hors d'oeuvres; appetizers |
| el menú | menu |
| el plato (principal) | (main) dish |
| la sección de (no) fumar | (non) smoking section |
| el agua (mineral) | (mineral) water |
| la bebida | drink |
| la cerveza | beer |
| la leche | milk |
| el refresco | soft drink |
| el ajo | garlic |
| las arvejas | peas |
| los cereales | cereal; grain |
| los frijoles | beans |
| el melocotón | peach |
| el pollo (asado) | (roast) chicken |
| el queso | cheese |
| el sándwich | sandwich |
| el yogur | yogurt |
| el aceite | oil |
| la margarina | margarine |
| la mayonesa | mayonnaise |
| el vinagre | vinegar |
| delicioso/a | delicious |
| sabroso/a | tasty; delicious |
| saber | to taste; to know |
| saber a | to taste like |

### Variación léxica

camarones ⟷ gambas (*Esp.*)
camarero ⟷ mesero (*Amér. L.*), mesonero (*Ven.*), mozo (*Arg., Chile, Urug., Perú*)
refresco ⟷ gaseosa (*Amér. C., Amér. S.*)

Las frutas — la pera, la banana, las uvas, la naranja, el limón, el maíz, la cebolla, la lechuga, el champiñón, la zanahoria, el tomate

Las verduras

**recursos**
WB pp. 85–86
LM p. 43
SUPERSITE
panorama.vhlcentral.com Lección 8

---

**TEACHING OPTIONS**

**Extra Practice** To review vocabulary for colors, ask students what colors these food items are: **las bananas (amarillas), las uvas (verdes o moradas), las zanahorias (anaranjadas), los tomates (rojos), los frijoles (blancos, marrones, rojos o negros), la lechuga (verde), las cebollas (blancas).**

**Heritage Speakers** Point out that food vocabulary varies from region to region in the Spanish-speaking world. Ask heritage speakers to share food-related terms they are familiar with and where the terms are used. Possible responses: **el guisante, el chícaro, el banano, el guineo, el cambur, el plátano, el hongo, la habichuela, el choclo, el elote, la patata, el jitomate.**

# Práctica

LAS CARNES

el pollo
el pavo
el jamón
la carne de res
la chuleta (de cerdo)
el atún
el salmón
los camarones (el camarón)
la langosta

Pescados y mariscos

**1 Escuchar** Indica si las oraciones que vas a escuchar son **ciertas** o **falsas**, según el dibujo. Después, corrige las falsas.

1. Cierta
2. Falsa. El hombre compra una naranja.
3. Cierta
4. Falsa. El pollo es una carne y la zanahoria es una verdura.
5. Cierta
6. Falsa. El hombre y la mujer no compran vinagre.
7. Falsa. La naranja es una fruta.
8. Falsa. La chuleta de cerdo es una carne.
9. Falsa. El limón es una fruta y el jamón es una carne.
10. Cierta

**2 Seleccionar** Paulino y Pilar van a cenar a un restaurante. Escucha la conversación y selecciona la respuesta que mejor completa cada oración.

1. Paulino le pide el ___menú___ (menú / plato) al camarero.
2. El plato del día es (atún / salmón) ___atún___.
3. Pilar ordena ___agua mineral___ (leche / agua mineral) para beber.
4. Paulino quiere un refresco de ___naranja___ (naranja / limón).
5. Paulino hoy prefiere ___la chuleta___ (el salmón / la chuleta).
6. Dicen que la carne en ese restaurante es muy ___sabrosa___ (sabrosa / mal).
7. Pilar come salmón con ___zanahorias___ (zanahorias / champiñones).

**3 Identificar** Identifica la palabra que no está relacionada con cada grupo.

1. champiñón • cebolla • (banana) • zanahoria
2. camarones • (ajo) • atún • salmón
3. (aceite) • leche • refresco • agua mineral
4. jamón • chuleta de cerdo • (vinagre) • carne de res
5. (cerveza) • lechuga • arvejas • frijoles
6. carne • pescado • mariscos • (camarero)
7. (pollo) • naranja • limón • melocotón
8. maíz • (queso) • tomate • champiñón

**4 Completar** Completa las oraciones con las palabras más lógicas.

1. ¡Me gusta mucho este plato! Sabe __b__.
   a. feo   b. delicioso   c. antipático
2. Camarero, ¿puedo ver el __c__, por favor?
   a. aceite   b. maíz   c. menú
3. Carlos y yo bebemos siempre agua __b__.
   a. cómoda   b. mineral   c. principal
4. El plato del día es __a__.
   a. el pollo asado   b. la mayonesa   c. el ajo
5. Margarita es vegetariana. Ella come __a__.
   a. frijoles   b. chuletas   c. jamón
6. Mi hermana le da __c__ a su niña.
   a. ajo   b. vinagre   c. yogur

SUPERSITE

**Teaching Tips**
- Involve the class in a conversation about meals. Say: **Por lo general, desayuno sólo café con leche y pan tostado, pero cuando tengo mucha hambre desayuno dos huevos y una salchicha también. _____, ¿qué desayunas tú?**
- Show *Overhead PowerPoint #34.* Say: **Mira el desayuno aquí. ¿Qué desayuna esta persona?** Then continue to **el almuerzo** and **la cena.** Have students identify the food items and talk about their eating habits. Get them to talk about what, when, and where they eat. Say: **Yo siempre desayuno en casa, pero casi nunca almuerzo en casa. ¿A qué hora almuerzan ustedes por lo general?**
- Ask students to tell you their favorite foods to eat for each of the three meals. Ex: _____, **¿qué te gusta desayunar?** Introduce additional items such as **los espaguetis, la pasta, la pizza.**

**Nota cultural** Point out that in Spanish-speaking countries, **el almuerzo,** also called **la comida,** usually is the main meal of the day, consists of several courses, and is enjoyed at a leisurely pace. **La cena** is typically much lighter than **el almuerzo.**

**Note:** At this point you may want to present *Vocabulario adicional: Más vocabulario relacionado con la comida,* from the Supersite/IRCD.

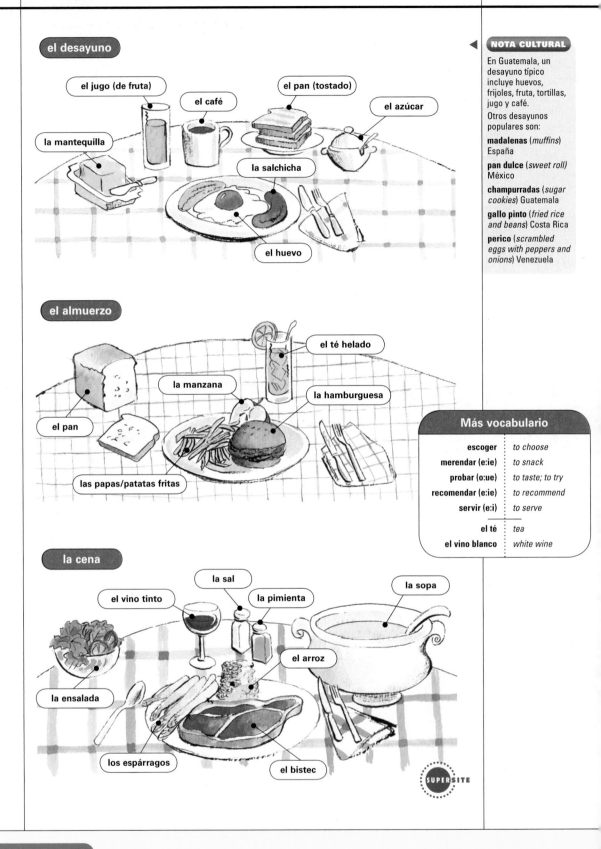

el desayuno

- el jugo (de fruta)
- el café
- el pan (tostado)
- el azúcar
- la mantequilla
- la salchicha
- el huevo

el almuerzo

- el té helado
- la manzana
- la hamburguesa
- el pan
- las papas/patatas fritas

la cena

- la sal
- el vino tinto
- la pimienta
- la sopa
- el arroz
- la ensalada
- los espárragos
- el bistec

**NOTA CULTURAL**

En Guatemala, un desayuno típico incluye huevos, frijoles, fruta, tortillas, jugo y café.
Otros desayunos populares son:

**madalenas** (*muffins*) España

**pan dulce** (*sweet roll*) México

**champurradas** (*sugar cookies*) Guatemala

**gallo pinto** (*fried rice and beans*) Costa Rica

**perico** (*scrambled eggs with peppers and onions*) Venezuela

**Más vocabulario**

| | |
|---|---|
| **escoger** | *to choose* |
| **merendar (e:ie)** | *to snack* |
| **probar (o:ue)** | *to taste; to try* |
| **recomendar (e:ie)** | *to recommend* |
| **servir (e:i)** | *to serve* |
| **el té** | *tea* |
| **el vino blanco** | *white wine* |

**TEACHING OPTIONS**

**Small Groups** In groups of three or four, have students create a menu for a special occasion. Ask them to describe what they are going to serve for **el entremés, el plato principal,** and **bebidas.** Write **el postre** on the board and explain that it means *dessert.* Explain that in Spanish-speaking countries fresh fruit and cheese are common as dessert, but you may also want to give **el pastel** (*pie, cake*) and **el helado** (*ice cream*). Have

groups present their menus to the class.
**Extra Practice** Add an auditory aspect to this vocabulary presentation. Prepare descriptions of five to seven different meals, with a mix of breakfasts, lunches, and dinners. As you read each description aloud, have students write down what you say as a dictation and then guess the meal it describes.

# Comunicación

**9** **Conversación** En grupos, contesten estas preguntas. Answers will vary.

1. ¿Meriendas mucho durante el día? ¿Qué comes? ¿A qué hora?
2. ¿Qué comidas te gustan más para la cena?
3. ¿A qué hora, dónde y con quién almuerzas?
4. ¿Cuáles son las comidas más (*most*) típicas de tu almuerzo?
5. ¿Desayunas? ¿Qué comes y bebes por la mañana?
6. ¿Qué comida deseas probar?
7. ¿Comes cada día comidas de los diferentes grupos de la pirámide alimenticia? ¿Cuáles son las comidas y bebidas más frecuentes en tu dieta?
8. ¿Qué comida recomiendas a tus amigos? ¿Por qué?
9. ¿Eres vegetariano/a? ¿Crees que ser vegetariano/a es una buena idea? ¿Por qué?
10. ¿Te gusta cocinar (*to cook*)? ¿Qué comidas preparas para tus amigos? ¿Para tu familia?

**10** **Describir** Con dos compañeros/as de clase, describe las dos fotos, contestando estas preguntas.
Answers will vary.

▶ ¿Quiénes están en las fotos?

▶ ¿Dónde están?

▶ ¿Qué hora es?

▶ ¿Qué comen y qué beben?

**11** **Crucigrama (*Crossword puzzle*)** Tu profesor(a) les va a dar a ti y a tu compañero/a un crucigrama incompleto. Tú tienes las palabras que necesita tu compañero/a y él/ella tiene las palabras que tú necesitas. Tienen que darse pistas (*clues*) para completarlo. No pueden decir la palabra necesaria; deben utilizar definiciones, ejemplos y frases. Answers will vary.

> **modelo**
> **6 vertical:** Es un condimento que normalmente viene con la sal.
> **2 horizontal:** Es una fruta amarilla.

**9 Expansion** Ask the same questions of individual students. Ask other students to restate what their classmates answered.

**10 Expansion** Repeat the activity with additional photos of people in eating situations.

**11 Teaching Tip** Divide the class into pairs and distribute the handouts from the Information Gap Activities (Supersite/IRCD) that correspond to this activity. Give students ten minutes to complete this activity.

**11 Expansion** Have groups create another type of word puzzle, such as a word-find, to share with the class. It should contain additional food- and meal-related vocabulary.

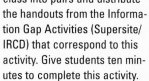

---

**TEACHING OPTIONS**

**Small Groups** In groups of two to four, ask students to prepare brief skits related to food. The skits may involve being in a market, in a restaurant, in a café, inviting people over for dinner, and so forth. Allow groups time to rehearse before performing their skits for the class, who will vote for the most creative one.

**Game** Play a game of continuous narration. One student begins with: **Voy a preparar** (*name of dish*) **y voy al mercado. Necesito comprar...** and names one food item. The next student then repeats the entire narration, adding another food item. Continue on with various students. When the possibilities for that particular dish are used up, have another student begin with another dish.

# ¿Qué tal la comida?

communication cultures
NATIONAL STANDARDS

**Don Francisco y los estudiantes van al restaurante El Cráter.**

**PERSONAJES**

MAITE

INÉS

DON FRANCISCO

ÁLEX

JAVIER

DOÑA RITA

CAMARERO

**JAVIER** ¿Sabes dónde estamos?
**INÉS** Mmm, no sé. Oiga, don Francisco, ¿sabe usted dónde estamos?
**DON FRANCISCO** Estamos cerca de Cotacachi.

**ÁLEX** ¿Dónde vamos a almorzar, don Francisco? ¿Conoce un buen restaurante en Cotacachi?
**DON FRANCISCO** Pues, conozco a doña Rita Perales, la dueña del mejor restaurante de la ciudad, el restaurante El Cráter.

**DOÑA RITA** Hombre, don Paco, ¿usted por aquí?
**DON FRANCISCO** Sí, doña Rita... y hoy le traigo clientes. Le presento a Maite, Inés, Álex y Javier. Los llevo a las montañas para ir de excursión.

**MAITE** Voy a tomar un caldo de patas y un lomo a la plancha.
**JAVIER** Para mí las tortillas de maíz y el ceviche de camarón.
**ÁLEX** Yo también quisiera las tortillas de maíz y el ceviche.
**INÉS** Voy a pedir caldo de patas y lomo a la plancha.

**DON FRANCISCO** Yo quiero tortillas de maíz y una fuente de fritada, por favor.
**DOÑA RITA** Y de tomar, les recomiendo el jugo de piña, frutilla y mora. ¿Se lo traigo a todos?
**TODOS** Sí, perfecto.

**CAMARERO** ¿Qué plato pidió usted?
**MAITE** Un caldo de patas y lomo a la plancha.

**recursos**

VM
pp. 209–210

panorama.vhlcentral.com
Lección 8

---

**DOÑA RITA** ¡Bienvenidos al restaurante El Cráter! Están en muy buenas manos... don Francisco es el mejor conductor del país. Y no hay nada más bonito que nuestras montañas. Pero si van a ir de excursión deben comer bien. Vengan chicos, por aquí.

**JAVIER** ¿Qué nos recomienda usted?

**DOÑA RITA** Bueno, las tortillas de maíz son riquísimas. La especialidad de la casa es el caldo de patas... ¡tienen que probarlo! El lomo a la plancha es un poquito más caro que el caldo pero es sabrosísimo. También les recomiendo el ceviche y la fuente de fritada.

**DOÑA RITA** ¿Qué tal la comida? ¿Rica?

**JAVIER** Rica, no. ¡Riquísima!

**ÁLEX** Sí. ¡Y nos la sirvieron tan rápidamente!

**MAITE** Una comida deliciosa, gracias.

**DON FRANCISCO** Hoy es el cumpleaños de Maite...

**DOÑA RITA** ¡Ah! Tenemos unos pasteles que están como para chuparse los dedos...

## Expresiones útiles

### Finding out where you are

- **¿Sabe usted/Sabes dónde estamos?**
  *Do you know where we are?*
  **Estamos cerca de Cotacachi.**
  *We're near Cotacachi.*

### Talking about people and places you're familiar with

- **¿Conoce usted/Conoces un buen restaurante en Cotacachi?**
  *Do you know a good restaurant in Cotacachi?*
  **Sí, conozco varios.**
  *Yes, I know several.*
- **¿Conoce/Conoces a doña Rita?**
  *Do you know Doña Rita?*

### Ordering food

- **¿Qué le puedo traer?**
  *What can I bring you?*
  **Voy a tomar/pedir un caldo de patas y un lomo a la plancha.**
  *I am going to have/to order the beef soup and grilled flank steak.*
  **Para mí, las tortillas de maíz y el ceviche de camarón, por favor.**
  *Corn tortillas and lemon-marinated shrimp for me, please.*
  **Yo también quisiera...**
  *I also would like...*
  **Y de tomar, el jugo de piña, frutilla y mora.**
  *And pineapple/strawberry/blackberry juice to drink.*
- **¿Qué plato pidió usted?**
  *What did you order?*
  **Yo pedí un caldo de patas.**
  *I ordered the beef soup.*

### Talking about the food at a restaurant

- **¿Qué tal la comida?**
  *How is the food?*
  **Muy rica, gracias.**
  *Very tasty, thanks.*
  **¡Riquísima!**
  *Extremely delicious!*

**Teaching Tip** Have the class read through the entire **Fotonovela**, with volunteers playing the parts of **don Francisco, Javier, Inés, Álex, Maite, doña Rita**, and the **Camarero**. Have students take turns playing the roles so that more students participate.

**Expresiones útiles** Draw attention to the verb **pidió** and explain that **pedir** has a stem change in the preterite. Have the class read the captions for video stills 5 and 9. Point out that **más** + [*adjective*] + **que** is used to make comparisons, and that **nos la** is an example of an indirect object pronoun and a direct object pronoun used together. Tell students that they will learn more about these concepts in **Estructura**.

---

**TEACHING OPTIONS**

**Pairs** Have students work in pairs to create original mini-dialogues, using sentences in **Expresiones útiles** with other words and expressions they know. Ex: —**¿Qué tal la hamburguesa? —Perdón, pero no sabe a nada. Quisiera pedir otro plato.**

**Extra Practice** Photocopy the **Fotonovela** Videoscript (Supersite/IRCD) and white out words related to food, meals, and other key vocabulary in order to create a master for a cloze activity. Distribute the photocopies and have students fill in the target words as they watch the episode.

# ¿Qué pasó?

**1** **Escoger** Escoge la respuesta que completa mejor cada oración.

1. Don Francisco lleva a los estudiantes a ___c___ al restaurante de una amiga.
   a. cenar   b. desayunar   c. almorzar
2. Doña Rita es ___b___.
   a. la hermana de don Francisco   b. la dueña del restaurante
   c. una camarera que trabaja en El Cráter
3. Doña Rita les recomienda a los viajeros ___a___.
   a. el caldo de patas y el lomo a la plancha
   b. el bistec, las verduras frescas y el vino tinto   c. unos pasteles (*cakes*)
4. Inés va a pedir ___c___.
   a. las tortillas de maíz y una fuente de fritada (*mixed grill*)
   b. el ceviche de camarón y el caldo de patas
   c. el caldo de patas y el lomo a la plancha

**2** **Identificar** Indica quién puede decir estas oraciones.

1. No me gusta esperar en los restaurantes.
   ¡Qué bueno que nos sirvieron rápidamente! Álex
2. Les recomiendo la especialidad de la casa. doña Rita
3. ¡Maite y yo pedimos los mismos platos! Inés
4. Disculpe, señora… ¿qué platos recomienda usted? Javier
5. Yo conozco a una señora que tiene un restaurante excelente. Les va a gustar mucho. don Francisco
6. Hoy es mi cumpleaños (*birthday*). Maite

**INÉS**

**ÁLEX**

**DOÑA RITA**

**MAITE**

**DON FRANCISCO**

**JAVIER**

**3** **Preguntas** Contesta estas preguntas sobre la **Fotonovela**.

1. ¿Dónde comieron don Francisco y los estudiantes?
   Comieron en el restaurante de doña Rita/El Cráter.
2. ¿Cuál es la especialidad de El Cráter?
   La especialidad de la casa es el caldo de patas.
3. ¿Qué pidió Javier? ¿Y Álex? ¿Qué tomaron todos? Javier pidió tortillas de maíz y el ceviche. Álex también pidió las tortillas de maíz y el ceviche. Todos tomaron jugo.
4. ¿Cómo son los pasteles en El Cráter?
   Los pasteles en El Cráter son sabrosísimos.

**4** **En el restaurante** Answers will vary.

1. Prepara con un(a) compañero/a una conversación en la que le preguntas si conoce algún buen restaurante en tu comunidad. Tu compañero/a responde que él/ella sí conoce un restaurante que sirve una comida deliciosa. Lo/La invitas a cenar y tu compañero/a acepta. Determinan la hora para verse en el restaurante y se despiden.

2. Trabaja con un(a) compañero/a para representar los papeles de un(a) cliente/a y un(a) camarero/a en un restaurante. El/La camarero/a te pregunta qué te puede servir y tú preguntas cuál es la especialidad de la casa. El/La camarero/a te dice cuál es la especialidad y te recomienda algunos platos del menú. Tú pides entremeses, un plato principal y escoges una bebida. El/La camarero/a te sirve la comida y tú le das las gracias.

**CONSULTA**
To review indefinite words like **algún**, see **Estructura 7.2**, p. 224.

---

**TEACHING OPTIONS**

**Extra Practice** Ask students questions about the **Fotonovela** episode. Ex: **1. ¿En qué ciudad está el restaurante El Cráter? (Cotacachi) 2. ¿Qué pidió Javier en el restaurante? (tortillas de maíz, ceviche de camarón) 3. ¿Qué pidió don Francisco? (tortillas de maíz, fuente de fritada) 4. ¿Cuándo es el cumpleaños de Maite? (hoy)**

**Large Groups** Have students work in groups of five or six to prepare a skit in which a family goes to a restaurant, is seated by a waitperson, examines the menu, and orders dinner. Each family member should ask a few questions about the menu and then order an entree and a drink. Have one or two groups perform the skit in front of the class.

# Pronunciación

## ll, ñ, c, and z

| pollo | llave | ella | cebolla |
|---|---|---|---|

Most Spanish speakers pronounce the letter **ll** like the *y* in *yes*.

| mañana | señor | baño | niña |
|---|---|---|---|

The letter **ñ** is pronounced much like the *ny* in *canyon*.

| café | colombiano | cuando | rico |
|---|---|---|---|

Before **a**, **o**, or **u**, the Spanish **c** is pronounced like the *c* in *car*.

| cereales | delicioso | conducir | conocer |
|---|---|---|---|

Before **e** or **i**, the Spanish **c** is pronounced like the *s* in *sit*. (In parts of Spain, **c** before **e** or **i** is pronounced like the *th* in *think*.)

| zeta | zanahoria | almuerzo | cerveza |
|---|---|---|---|

The Spanish **z** is pronounced like the *s* in *sit*. (In parts of Spain, **z** is pronounced like the *th* in *think*.)

**Práctica** Lee las palabras en voz alta.

1. mantequilla
2. cuñada
3. aceite
4. manzana
5. español
6. cepillo
7. zapato
8. azúcar
9. quince
10. compañera
11. almorzar
12. calle

**Oraciones** Lee las oraciones en voz alta.

1. Mi compañero de cuarto se llama Toño Núñez. Su familia es de la ciudad de Guatemala y de Quetzaltenango.
2. Dice que la comida de su mamá es deliciosa, especialmente su pollo al champiñón y sus tortillas de maíz.
3. Creo que Toño tiene razón porque hoy cené en su casa y quiero volver mañana para cenar allí otra vez.

**Refranes** Lee los refranes en voz alta.

Panza llena, corazón contento.[2]

Las apariencias engañan.[1]

1 Looks can be deceiving.
2 A full belly makes a happy heart.

| recursos |
|---|
| LM p. 44 — panorama.vhlcentral.com Lección 8 |

## Section Goal

In **Pronunciación**, students will be introduced to the pronunciation of the letter combination **ll** and the letters **ñ**, **c**, and **z**.

**Instructional Resources**
**Supersite:** Textbook & Lab MP3 Audio Files **Lección 8**
**Supersite/IRCD:** *IRM* (Textbook Audio Script, Lab Audio Script, WB/VM/LM Answer Key)
**WebSAM**
**Lab Manual**, p. 44
*Cuaderno para hispanohablantes*

**Teaching Tips**
- Point out that the Spanish letter combination **ll** is usually pronounced like the English *y* in *you*.
- Ask the class how the letter **ñ** is pronounced (like the *ny* in *canyon*).
- Tell the class that **c** is pronounced like the English *c* in *car* before **a**, **o**, or **u**.
- Ask the class how most Spanish speakers pronounce the letter **c** when it appears before **e** or **i** (like the English *s* in *sit*). Then point out that **c** before **e** or **i** is pronounced like the English *th* in *think* in some parts of Spain.
- Explain that the Spanish **z** is usually pronounced like the English *s* in *some*. Mention that in parts of Spain, **z** is pronounced like the English *th* in *think*.
- As you explain the pronunciation of these sounds, write a few of the example words on the board and have students pronounce them.

**Práctica/Oraciones/Refranes** These exercises are recorded in the *Textbook MP3s*. You may want to play the audio so that students practice the pronunciation point by listening to Spanish spoken by speakers other than yourself.

---

**TEACHING OPTIONS**

**Extra Practice** Write the names of a few distinguished Guatemalans on the board and ask for a volunteer to pronounce each one. Ex: **Luis Cardoza y Aragón** (writer), **Carlos Mérida** (painter), **Enrique Gómez Carrillo** (writer), **José Milla** (writer), **Alonso de la Paz** (sculptor). Repeat the process with a few city names: **Villanueva, Zacapa, Escuintla, Cobán.**

**Pairs** Have the class work in pairs to practice the pronunciation of the sentences given in **Actividad 2 (Identificar)** on page 250. Encourage students to help their partner if he or she has trouble pronouncing a particular word. Circulate around the class and model correct pronunciation as needed, focusing on the letter combination **ll** and the letters **ñ, c,** and **z.**

**EN DETALLE**

# Frutas y verduras de las Américas

**Imagínate una pizza sin salsa° de tomate** o una hamburguesa sin papas fritas. Ahora piensa que quieres ver una película, pero las palomitas de maíz° y el chocolate no existen. ¡Qué mundo° tan insípido°! Muchas de las comidas más populares del mundo tienen ingredientes esenciales que son originarios de las Américas. Estas frutas y verduras no fueron introducidas en Europa sino hasta° el siglo° XVI.

El tomate, por ejemplo, era° usado como planta ornamental cuando llegó por primera vez a Europa porque pensaron que era venenoso°. El maíz, por su parte, era ya la base de la comida de muchos países latinoamericanos muchos siglos antes de la llegada de los españoles.

La papa fue un alimento° básico para los incas. Incluso consiguieron deshidratarlas para almacenarlas° durante mucho tiempo. El cacao (planta con la que se hace el chocolate) fue muy importante para los aztecas y los mayas. Ellos usaron sus semillas° como moneda° y como ingrediente de diversas salsas. También las molían° para preparar una bebida, mezclándolas° con agua ¡y con chile!

El aguacate°, la guayaba°, la papaya, la piña y el maracuyá (o fruta de la pasión) son sólo algunos ejemplos de frutas originarias de las Américas que son hoy día conocidas en todo el mundo.

**Mole**

---

**¿En qué alimentos encontramos estas frutas y verduras?**

**Tomate:** pizza, ketchup, salsa de tomate, sopa de tomate
**Maíz:** palomitas de maíz, tamales, tortillas, arepas (Colombia y Venezuela), pan
**Papa:** papas fritas, frituras de papa°, puré de papas°, sopa de papas, tortilla de patatas (España)
**Cacao:** salsa mole (México), chocolatinas°, cereales, helados°, tartas°
**Aguacate:** guacamole (México), cóctel de camarones, sopa de aguacate, nachos, enchiladas hondureñas

---

salsa *sauce* palomitas de maíz *popcorn* mundo *world* insípido *flavorless* hasta *until* siglo *century* era *was* venenoso *poisonous* alimento *food* almacenarlas *to store them* semillas *seeds* moneda *currency* las molían *they used to grind them* mezclándolas *mixing them* aguacate *avocado* guayaba *guava* frituras de papa *chips* puré de papas *mashed potatoes* chocolatinas *chocolate bars* helados *ice cream* tartas *cakes*

---

**ACTIVIDADES**

**1** **¿Cierto o falso?** Indica si lo que dicen estas oraciones es **cierto** o **falso.** Corrige la información falsa.

1. El tomate se introdujo a Europa como planta ornamental. Cierto.
2. Los aztecas y los mayas usaron las papas como moneda. Falso. Los aztecas y los mayas usaron las semillas de cacao como moneda.
3. Los incas sólo consiguieron almacenar las papas por poco tiempo. Falso. Los incas pudieron almacenar las papas por mucho tiempo.
4. En México se hace una salsa con chocolate. Cierto.
5. El aguacate, la guayaba, la papaya, la piña y el maracuyá son originarios de las Américas. Cierto.
6. Las arepas se hacen con cacao. Falso. Las arepas se hacen con maíz.
7. El aguacate es un ingrediente del cóctel de camarones. Cierto.
8. En España hacen una tortilla con papas. Cierto.

## ASÍ SE DICE

### La comida

| | |
|---|---|
| el banano (Col.), el cambur (Ven.), el guineo (Nic.), el plátano (Amér. L., Esp.) | la banana |
| el choclo (Amér. S.), el elote (Méx.), el jojoto (Ven.), la mazorca (Esp.) | *corncob* |
| las caraotas (Ven.), los porotos (Amér. S.), las habichuelas | los frijoles |
| el durazno | el melocotón |
| el jitomate (Méx.) | el tomate |

## EL MUNDO HISPANO

### Algunos platos típicos

○ **Ceviche peruano:** Es un plato de pescado crudo° que se marina° en jugo de limón, con sal, pimienta, cebolla y ají°. Se sirve con lechuga, maíz, camote° y papa amarilla.

○ **Gazpacho andaluz:** Es una sopa fría típica del sur de España. Se hace con verduras crudas y molidas°: tomate, ají, pepino° y ajo. También lleva pan, sal, aceite y vinagre.

○ **Sancocho colombiano:** Es una sopa de pollo o de carne con plátano, maíz, zanahoria, yuca, papas, cebolla y ajo. Se sirve con arroz blanco.

crudo *raw* se marina *gets marinated* ají *pepper* camote *sweet potato* molidas *mashed* pepino *cucumber*

## PERFIL

### Ferrán Adrià: arte en la cocina°

¿Qué haces si un amigo te invita a comer croquetas líquidas o paella de Kellogg's? ¿Piensas que es una broma°? ¡Cuidado! Puedes estar perdiendo la oportunidad de cenar en el restaurante más innovador de España: **El Bulli**.

**Ferrán Adrià**, el dueño de El Bulli, está entre los mejores° chefs del mundo. Su éxito° se basa en su creatividad. Adrià modifica combinaciones de ingredientes y juega con contrastes de gustos y sensaciones: frío-caliente, crudo-cocido°, dulce°-salado°... Sus platos son sorprendentes° y divertidos: cócteles en forma de espuma°, salsas servidas en tubos y sorbetes salados.

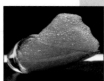

**Aire de zanahorias**

Adrià también creó **Fast Good** (un restaurante de comida rápida de calidad), escribe libros de cocina y participa en programas de televisión.

cocina *kitchen* broma *joke* mejores *best* éxito *success* cocido *cooked* dulce *sweet* salado *savory* sorprendentes *surprising* espuma *foam*

### Conexión Internet

**¿Qué platos comen los hispanos en los Estados Unidos?**

Go to **panorama.vhlcentral.com** to find more cultural information related to this **Cultura** section.

## ACTIVIDADES

**2** **Comprensión** Empareja cada palabra con su definición.

1. fruta amarilla d
2. sopa típica de Colombia c
3. ingrediente del ceviche e
4. restaurante español b

a. gazpacho
b. El Bulli
c. sancocho
d. guineo
e. pescado

**3** **¿Qué plato especial hay en tu región?** Escribe cuatro oraciones sobre un plato típico de tu región. Explica los ingredientes que contiene y cómo se sirve. Answers will vary.

recursos
panorama.vhlcentral.com
Lección 8

## Section Goal

In **Estructura 8.1**, students will be introduced to the preterite of stem-changing verbs.

---

**Instructional Resources**
**Supersite:** Lab MP3 Audio Files **Lección 8**
**Supersite/IRCD:** *PowerPoints* (**Lección 8 Estructura** Presentation); *IRM* (Lab Audio Script, WBs/VM/LM Answer Key)
**WebSAM**
**Workbook,** pp. 87–88
**Lab Manual,** p. 45
*Cuaderno para hispanohablantes*

---

## Teaching Tips

- Review present-tense forms of –**ir** stem-changing verbs like **pedir** and **dormir**. Also review formation of the preterite of regular –**ir** verbs using **escribir** and **recibir**.

- Give model sentences that use these verbs in the preterite, emphasizing stem-changing forms. Ex: **Me dormí temprano anoche, pero mi compañero de cuarto se durmió muy tarde.**

- Ask students questions using stem-changing –**ir** verbs in the preterite. Ex: **¿Cuántas horas dormiste anoche?** Then have other students summarize the answers. Ex: _____ **durmió seis horas, pero** _____ **durmió ocho.** _____ **y** _____ **durmieron cinco horas.**

- Point out that **morir** means *to die* and offer sample sentences using stem-changing preterite forms of the verb. Ex: **No tengo bisabuelos. Ya murieron.**

- Other –**ir** verbs that change their stem vowel in the preterite are **conseguir, despedirse, divertirse, pedir, preferir, repetir, seguir, sentir, sugerir,** and **vestirse.**

---

**8.1** **Preterite of stem-changing verbs**  SUPERSITE

**ANTE TODO** As you learned in **Lección 6**, –**ar** and –**er** stem-changing verbs have no stem change in the preterite. –**Ir** stem-changing verbs, however, do have a stem change. Study the following chart and observe where the stem changes occur.

### Preterite of –ir stem-changing verbs

| | | **servir** *(to serve)* | **dormir** *(to sleep)* |
|---|---|---|---|
| **SINGULAR FORMS** | yo | serví | dormí |
| | tú | serviste | dormiste |
| | Ud./él/ella | si**r**vió | du**r**mió |
| **PLURAL FORMS** | nosotros/as | servimos | dormimos |
| | vosotros/as | servisteis | dormisteis |
| | Uds./ellos/ellas | si**r**vieron | du**r**mieron |

▶ Stem-changing –**ir** verbs, in the preterite only, have a stem change in the third-person singular and plural forms. The stem change consists of either **e** to **i** or **o** to **u**.

(e → i) pedir: **pi**dió, **pi**dieron      (o → u) morir (*to die*): **mu**rió, **mu**rieron

*Perdón, ¿quiénes pidieron las tortillas de maíz?*

*¿Y qué plato pidió usted?*

---

**¡INTÉNTALO!** Cambia cada infinitivo al pretérito.

1. Yo ___serví___. (servir, dormir, pedir, preferir, repetir, seguir)
   dormí, pedí, preferí, repetí, seguí

2. Usted _____. (morir, conseguir, pedir, sentirse, despedirse, vestirse)
   murió, consiguió, pidió, se sintió, se despidió, se vistió

3. Tú _____. (conseguir, servir, morir, pedir, dormir, repetir)
   conseguiste, serviste, moriste, pediste, dormiste, repetiste

4. Ellas _____. (repetir, dormir, seguir, preferir, morir, servir)
   repitieron, durmieron, siguieron, prefirieron, murieron, sirvieron

5. Nosotros _____. (seguir, preferir, servir, vestirse, despedirse, dormirse)
   seguimos, preferimos, servimos, nos vestimos, nos despedimos, nos dormimos

6. Ustedes _____. (sentirse, vestirse, conseguir, pedir, despedirse, dormirse)
   se sintieron, se vistieron, consiguieron, pidieron, se despidieron, se durmieron

7. Él _____. (dormir, morir, preferir, repetir, seguir, pedir)
   durmió, murió, prefirió, repitió, siguió, pidió

**recursos**

WB
pp. 87–88

LM
p. 45

SUPERSITE
panorama.
vhlcentral.com
Lección 8

---

**TEACHING OPTIONS**

**TPR** Have the class stand and form a circle. Call out a name or subject pronoun and an infinitive that has a stem change in the preterite (Ex: **Miguel/seguir**). Toss a foam or paper ball to a student, who will say the correct form (Ex: **siguió**) and toss the ball back to you. Then name another pronoun and infinitive and throw the ball to another student. To challenge students, include some infinitives without a stem change in the preterite.

**Pairs** Ask students to work in pairs to come up with ten original sentences in which they use the **Ud./él/ella** and **Uds./ellos/ellas** preterite forms of stem-changing –**ir** verbs. Point out that students should try to use vocabulary items from **Contextos** in their sentences. Ask pairs to share their sentences with the class.

# Práctica ⬤SUPERSITE

**1** **Completar** Completa estas oraciones para describir lo que pasó anoche en el restaurante El Famoso.

▶ 1. Paula y Humberto Suárez llegaron al restaurante El Famoso a las ocho y ____siguieron____ (seguir) al camarero a una mesa en la sección de no fumar.

2. El señor Suárez ____pidió____ (pedir) una chuleta de cerdo.

3. La señora Suárez ____prefirió____ (preferir) probar los camarones.

4. De tomar, los dos ____pidieron____ (pedir) vino tinto.

5. El camarero ____repitió____ (repetir) el pedido (*the order*) para confirmarlo.

6. La comida tardó mucho (*took a long time*) en llegar y los señores Suárez ____se durmieron____ (dormirse) esperando la comida.

7. A las nueve y media el camarero les ____sirvió____ (servir) la comida.

8. Después de comer la chuleta, el señor Suárez ____se sintió____ (sentirse) muy mal.

9. Pobre señor Suárez… ¿por qué no ____pidió____ (pedir) los camarones?

**2** **El camarero loco** En el restaurante La Hermosa trabaja un camarero muy loco que siempre comete muchos errores. Indica lo que los clientes pidieron y lo que el camarero les sirvió.

**modelo**

Armando / papas fritas
Armando pidió papas fritas, pero el camarero le sirvió maíz.

1. nosotros / jugo de naranja Nosotros pedimos jugo de naranja, pero el camarero nos sirvió papas.

2. Beatriz / queso Beatriz pidió queso, pero el camarero le sirvió uvas.

3. tú / arroz Tú pediste arroz, pero el camarero te sirvió arvejas/sopa.

4. Elena y Alejandro / atún Elena y Alejandro pidieron atún, pero el camarero les sirvió camarones (mariscos).

5. usted / agua mineral Usted pidió agua mineral, pero el camarero le sirvió vino tinto.

6. yo / hamburguesa Yo pedí una hamburguesa, pero el camarero me sirvió zanahorias.

# Comunicación

**3**

**El almuerzo** Trabajen en parejas. Túrnense para completar las oraciones de César de una manera lógica. Answers will vary.

> **modelo**
>
> Mi compañero de cuarto se despertó temprano, pero yo...
> Mi compañero de cuarto se despertó temprano, pero yo me desperté tarde.

1. Yo llegué al restaurante a tiempo, pero mis amigos...
2. Beatriz pidió la ensalada de frutas, pero yo...
3. Yolanda les recomendó el bistec, pero Eva y Paco...
4. Nosotros preferimos las papas fritas, pero Yolanda...
5. El camarero sirvió la carne, pero yo...
6. Beatriz y yo pedimos café, pero Yolanda y Paco...
7. Eva se sintió enferma, pero Paco y yo...
8. Nosotros repetimos el postre (*dessert*), pero Eva...
9. Ellos salieron tarde, pero yo...
10. Yo me dormí temprano, pero mi compañero de cuarto...

**4**

**Entrevista** Trabajen en parejas y túrnense para entrevistar a su compañero/a. Answers will vary.

1. ¿Te acostaste tarde o temprano anoche? ¿A qué hora te dormiste? ¿Dormiste bien?
2. ¿A qué hora te despertaste esta mañana? Y ¿a qué hora te levantaste?
3. ¿A qué hora vas a acostarte esta noche?
4. ¿Qué almorzaste ayer? ¿Quién te sirvió el almuerzo?
5. ¿Qué cenaste ayer?
6. ¿Cenaste en un restaurante recientemente? ¿Con quién?
7. ¿Qué pediste en el restaurante? ¿Qué pidieron los demás?
8. ¿Se durmió alguien en alguna de tus clases la semana pasada? ¿En qué clase?

# Síntesis

**5**

**Describir** En grupos, estudien la foto y las preguntas. Luego, describan la cena romántica de Eduardo y Rosa. Answers will vary.

▶ ¿Adónde salieron a cenar?

▶ ¿Qué pidieron?

▶ ¿Les sirvieron la comida rápidamente?

▶ ¿Les gustó la comida?

▶ ¿Cuánto costó?

▶ ¿Van a volver a este restaurante en el futuro?

▶ ¿Recomiendas el restaurante?

---

**3 Expansion** Have students share their sentences with the class. Ask other students comprehension questions based on what was said.

**4 Expansion** To practice the formal register, have students ask you the same questions.

**5 Expansion** Have groups present their description to the class in the form of a narration.

**Consulta** In addition to pointing out words and expressions that may signal the preterite, remind students about transition words that help to move the flow of a narration (Ex: **primero, después, luego, también**).

---

**Pairs** In pairs, have students take turns telling each other about a memorable experience in a restaurant, whether it was a date, dinner with family or friends, and so forth. Encourage students to take notes as their partners narrate. Then have students reveal what their partners told them.

**Extra Practice** Add a visual aspect to this grammar practice. As you hold up magazine pictures that show restaurant scenes, have students describe them in the past tense, using the preterite. You may want to write on the board some stem-changing –**ir** verbs that might apply to what is going on in the pictures.

# 8.2 Double object pronouns

**comparisons**
**NATIONAL STANDARDS**

**ANTE TODO**   In **Lecciones 5** and **6**, you learned that direct and indirect object pronouns replace nouns and that they often refer to nouns that have already been referenced. You will now learn how to use direct and indirect object pronouns together. Observe the following diagram.

|  Indirect Object Pronouns  |  |  |  Direct Object Pronouns  |  |
|---|---|---|---|---|
| me | nos |  | lo | los |
| te | os | **+** |  |  |
| le (se) | les (se) |  | la | las |

▶ When direct and indirect object pronouns are used together, the indirect object pronoun always precedes the direct object pronoun.

| I.O.  D.O. | | DOUBLE OBJECT PRONOUNS |
|---|---|---|
| El camarero **me** muestra **el menú**. | → | El camarero **me lo** muestra. |
| *The waiter shows me the menu.* | | *The waiter shows it to me.* |

| I.O.  D.O. | | DOUBLE OBJECT PRONOUNS |
|---|---|---|
| **Nos** sirven **los platos**. | → | **Nos los** sirven. |
| *They serve us the dishes.* | | *They serve them to us.* |

| I.O.  D.O. | | DOUBLE OBJECT PRONOUNS |
|---|---|---|
| Maribel **te** pidió **una hamburguesa**. | → | Maribel **te la** pidió. |
| *Maribel ordered a hamburger for you.* | | *Maribel ordered it for you.* |

*Y de tomar, les recomiendo el jugo de piña... ¿Se lo traigo a todos?*

*Sí, perfecto.*

▶ In Spanish, two pronouns that begin with the letter **l** cannot be used together. Therefore, the indirect object pronouns **le** and **les** always change to **se** when they are used with **lo, los, la,** and **las.**

| I.O.  D.O. | | DOUBLE OBJECT PRONOUNS |
|---|---|---|
| **Le** escribí **la carta**. | → | **Se la** escribí. |
| *I wrote him the letter.* | | *I wrote it to him.* |

| I.O.  D.O. | | DOUBLE OBJECT PRONOUNS |
|---|---|---|
| **Les** sirvió **los sándwiches**. | → | **Se los** sirvió. |
| *He served them the sandwiches.* | | *He served them to them.* |

---

## Section Goals

In **Estructura 8.2**, students will be introduced to:
- the use of double object pronouns
- converting **le** and **les** into **se** when used with direct object pronouns **lo, la, los,** and **las**

**Instructional Resources**
**Supersite:** Lab MP3 Audio Files **Lección 8**
**Supersite/IRCD:** *PowerPoints* (**Lección 8 Estructura** Presentation); *IRM* (Information Gap Activities, Lab Audio Script, WBs/VM/LM Answer Key)
**WebSAM**
**Workbook**, pp. 89–90
**Lab Manual**, p. 46
***Cuaderno para hispanohablantes***

## Teaching Tips
- Briefly review direct and indirect object pronouns (**Estructura 5.4, 6.2**). Give sentences and have students convert objects into object pronouns. Ex: **Sara escribió la carta. (Sara la escribió.) Mis padres escribieron una carta. (yo) (Mis padres me escribieron una carta.)**
- Model additional examples for students, asking them to make the conversion with **se**. Ex: **Le pedí papas fritas. (Se las pedí.) Les servimos café. (Se lo servimos.)**
- Emphasize that, with double object pronouns, the indirect object pronoun always precedes the direct object pronoun.

---

**TEACHING OPTIONS**

**Extra Practice** Write six sentences on the board for students to restate using double object pronouns. Ex: **Rita les sirvió la cena a los viajeros. (Rita se la sirvió.)**
**Pairs** In pairs, ask students to write five sentences that contain both direct and indirect objects (not pronouns). Have them exchange papers with another pair, who will restate the sentences using double object pronouns.

**Video** Show the *Fotonovela* again to give students more input containing double object pronouns. Stop the video where appropriate to discuss how double object pronouns were used and to ask comprehension questions.

**Teaching Tips**
- Ask questions to elicit third-person double object pronouns. Ex: **¿Le recomiendas el restaurante Acapulco a ___?** (Sí, se lo recomiendo.) **¿Le traes sándwiches a tus compañeros?** (No, no se los traigo.)
- Practice pronoun placement with infinitives and present participles by giving sentences that show one method of pronoun placement and asking students to restate them another way. Ex: **Se lo voy a mandar.** (Voy a mandárselo.)

▶ Because **se** has multiple meanings, Spanish speakers often clarify to whom the pronoun refers by adding **a usted, a él, a ella, a ustedes, a ellos,** or **a ellas.**

¿El sombrero? Carlos **se** lo vendió **a ella.**
*The hat? Carlos sold it to her.*

¿Las verduras? Ellos **se** las compran **a usted.**
*The vegetables? They buy them for you.*

▶ Double object pronouns are placed before a conjugated verb. With infinitives and present participles, they may be placed before the conjugated verb or attached to the end of the infinitive or present participle.

DOUBLE OBJECT PRONOUNS
**Te lo** voy a mostrar.

DOUBLE OBJECT PRONOUNS
Voy a mostrár**telo**.

DOUBLE OBJECT PRONOUNS
**Nos las** están sirviendo.

DOUBLE OBJECT PRONOUNS
Están sirviéndo**noslas**.

¿Qué tal la comida, rica?

Sí. ¡Y nos la sirvieron tan rápidamente!

▶ As you can see above, when double object pronouns are attached to an infinitive or a present participle, an accent mark is added to maintain the original stress.

**¡INTÉNTALO!**    Escribe el pronombre de objeto directo o indirecto que falta en cada oración.

### Objeto directo

1. ¿La ensalada? El camarero nos ___la___ sirvió.
2. ¿El salmón? La dueña me ___lo___ recomienda.
3. ¿La comida? Voy a prepárarte___la___.
4. ¿Las bebidas? Estamos pidiéndose___las___.
5. ¿Los refrescos? Te ___los___ puedo traer ahora.
6. ¿Los platos de arroz? Van a servírnos___los___ después.

### Objeto indirecto

1. ¿Puedes traerme tu plato? No, no ___te___ lo puedo traer.
2. ¿Quieres mostrarle la carta? Sí, voy a mostrár___se___la ahora.
3. ¿Les serviste la carne? No, no ___se___ la serví.
4. ¿Vas a leerle el menú? No, no ___se___ lo voy a leer.
5. ¿Me recomiendas la langosta? Sí, ___te___ la recomiendo.
6. ¿Cuándo vas a prepararnos la cena? ___Se___ la voy a preparar en una hora.

**recursos**

WB pp. 89–90

LM p. 46

SUPERSITE
panorama.
vhlcentral.com
Lección 8

---

**TEACHING OPTIONS**

**Pairs** Have students create five dehydrated sentences for their partner to complete. They should include the following elements: subject / action / direct object / indirect object (name or pronoun). Ex: **Carlos / escribe / carta / Marta** Their partners should "hydrate" the sentences using double object pronouns. Ex: **Carlos se la escribe (a Marta).**

**Large Groups** Split the class into two groups. Give cards that contain verbs that can take a direct object to one group. The other group gets cards containing nouns. Then select one member from each group to stand up and show his or her card. Another student converts the two elements into a sentence using double object pronouns. Ex: **mostrar / el libro →** [Name of student] **se lo va a mostrar.**

# Práctica

**1** **Responder** Imagínate que trabajas de camarero/a en un restaurante. Responde a las órdenes de estos clientes usando pronombres.

> **modelo**
>
> Sra. Gómez: Una ensalada, por favor.
> Sí, señora. Enseguida *(Right away)* se la traigo.

1. Sres. López: La mantequilla, por favor. Sí, señores. Enseguida se la traigo.
2. Srta. Rivas: Los camarones, por favor. Sí, señorita. Enseguida se los traigo.
3. Sra. Lugones: El pollo asado, por favor. Sí, señora. Enseguida se lo traigo.
4. Tus compañeros/as de cuarto: Café, por favor. Sí, chicos. Enseguida se lo traigo.
5. Tu profesor(a) de español: Papas fritas, por favor. Sí, profesor(a). Enseguida se las traigo.
6. Dra. González: La chuleta de cerdo, por favor. Sí, doctora. Enseguida se la traigo.
7. Tu padre: Los champiñones, por favor. Sí, papá. Enseguida te los traigo.
8. Dr. Torres: La cuenta *(check)*, por favor. Sí, doctor. Enseguida se la traigo.

**2** **¿Quién?** La señora Cevallos está planeando una cena. Se pregunta cómo va a resolver ciertas situaciones. En parejas, túrnense para decir lo que ella está pensando. Cambien los sustantivos subrayados por pronombres de objeto directo y hagan los otros cambios necesarios.

> **modelo**
>
> ¡No tengo carne! ¿Quién va a traerme <u>la carne</u> del supermercado? (mi esposo)
> Mi *esposo va a traérmela./Mi esposo me la va a traer.*

1. ¡Las invitaciones! ¿Quién les manda <u>las invitaciones</u> a los invitados *(guests)*? (mi hija) Mi hija se las manda.
2. No tengo tiempo de ir a la bodega. ¿Quién me puede comprar <u>el vino</u>? (mi hijo) Mi hijo puede comprármelo./Mi hijo me lo puede comprar.
3. ¡Ay! No tengo suficientes platos *(plates)*. ¿Quién puede prestarme <u>los platos</u> que necesito? (mi mamá) Mi mamá puede prestármelos./Mi mamá me los puede prestar.
4. Nos falta mantequilla. ¿Quién nos trae <u>la mantequilla</u>? (mi cuñada) Mi cuñada nos la trae.
5. ¡Los entremeses! ¿Quién está preparándonos <u>los entremeses</u>? (Silvia y Renata) Silvia y Renata están preparándonoslos./Silvia y Renata nos los están preparando.
6. No hay suficientes sillas. ¿Quién nos trae <u>las sillas</u> que faltan? (Héctor y Lorena) Héctor y Lorena nos las traen.
7. No tengo tiempo de pedirle el aceite a Mónica. ¿Quién puede pedirle <u>el aceite</u>? (mi hijo) Mi hijo puede pedírselo./Mi hijo se lo puede pedir.
8. ¿Quién va a servirles la cena a los invitados? (mis hijos) Mis hijos van a servírsela./Mis hijos se la van a servir.
9. Quiero poner buena música de fondo *(background)*. ¿Quién me va a recomendar <u>la música</u>? (mi esposo) Mi esposo va a recomendármela./Mi esposo me la va a recomendar.
10. ¡Los postres! ¿Quién va a preparar los postres para los invitados? (Sra. Villalba) La señora Villalba va a preparárselos./La señora Villalba se los va a preparar.

---

**AYUDA**

Here are some other useful expressions:

**ahora mismo**
*right now*

**inmediatamente**
*immediately*

**¡A la orden!**
*At your service!*

**¡Ya voy!**
*I'm on my way!*

---

**NOTA CULTURAL**

Los vinos de Chile son conocidos internacionalmente. **Concha y Toro** es el productor y exportador más grande de vinos de Chile. Las zonas más productivas de vino están al norte de Santiago, en el Valle Central.

---

**1** **Teaching Tip** Do the activity with the class, selecting two students for each exchange. Encourage them to vary their responses with the phrases in the sidebar.

**Ayuda** Model the helpful phrases in sentences. Point out that **Ahora mismo, Inmediatamente,** and **Ya** can replace **Enseguida** in the **modelo** for **Actividad 1**.

**2** **Expansion**
• For each item, change the subject in parentheses so that students practice different forms of the verbs.
• Add a visual aspect to this activity. Hold up magazine pictures and ask students who is doing what to or for whom. Ex: **La señora les muestra la casa a los jóvenes. Se la muestra a los jóvenes.**

---

**TEACHING OPTIONS**

**Heritage Speakers** Ask heritage speakers to talk about a favorite gift they received. Write **regalar** on the board and explain that it means *to give (a gift)*. Have students talk about what they received, who gave it to them (**regalar**), and why. Ask the rest of the class comprehension questions.
**Game** Play **Concentración**. Write sentences that use double object pronouns on each of eight cards. Ex: **Óscar se las**

**muestra.** On another eight cards, draw or paste a picture that matches each sentence. Ex: A photo of a boy showing photos to his grandparents. Place the cards face-down in four rows of four. In pairs, students select two cards. If the two cards match, the pair keeps them. If they do not match, students replace them in their original position. The pair with the most cards at the end wins.

# Comunicación

**3** **Teaching Tips**
- To simplify, begin by having students read through each item. Guide them in choosing **¿quién?** or **¿cuándo?** for each one.
- Continue the **modelo** exchange by asking: **¿Cuándo nos lo enseña? (Nos lo enseña los lunes, miércoles, jueves y viernes.)**
- To challenge students, have them ask follow-up questions using other interrogative words.

**3** **Expansion** Ask questions of individual students. Then ask them why they answered as they did. Students answer using double object pronouns. Ex: **¿Quién te enseña español? (Usted me lo enseña.) ¿Por qué? (Usted me lo enseña porque es profesor(a) de español.)**

**4** **Expansion** Ask the questions of individual students. Then verify class comprehension by asking other students to repeat the information given.

**3**

**Contestar** Trabajen en parejas. Túrnense para hacer preguntas y para responderlas usando las palabras interrogativas **¿Quién?** o **¿Cuándo?** Sigan el modelo. *Answers will vary.*

> **modelo**
> nos enseña español
> **Estudiante 1:** ¿Quién nos enseña español?
> **Estudiante 2:** La profesora Camacho nos lo enseña.

1. te puede explicar (*explain*) la tarea cuando no la entiendes
2. les vende el almuerzo a los estudiantes
3. vas a comprarme boletos (*tickets*) para un concierto
4. te escribe mensajes electrónicos
5. nos prepara los entremeses
6. me vas a prestar tu computadora
7. te compró esa bebida
8. nos va a recomendar el menú de la cafetería
9. le enseñó español al/a la profesor(a)
10. me vas a mostrar tu casa o apartamento

**4**

**Preguntas** Hazle estas preguntas a un(a) compañero/a. *Answers will vary.*

> **modelo**
> **Estudiante 1:** ¿Les prestas tu casa a tus amigos? ¿Por qué?
> **Estudiante 2:** No, no se la presto a mis amigos porque no son muy responsables.

1. ¿Me prestas tu auto? ¿Ya le prestaste tu auto a otro/a amigo/a?
2. ¿Quién te presta dinero cuando lo necesitas?
3. ¿Les prestas dinero a tus amigos? ¿Por qué?
4. ¿Nos compras el almuerzo a mí y a los otros compañeros de clase?
5. ¿Les mandas correo electrónico a tus amigos? ¿Y a tu familia?
6. ¿Les das regalos a tus amigos? ¿Cuándo?
7. ¿Quién te va a preparar la cena esta noche?
8. ¿Quién te va a preparar el desayuno mañana?

# Síntesis

**5** **Teaching Tip** Divide the class into pairs and distribute the handouts from the Information Gap Activities (Supersite/IRCD) that correspond to this activity. Give students ten minutes to complete this activity.

**5** **Expansion** With a different partner, ask pairs to make a list of the gifts they each received for their last birthday or other occasion. Then have them point to each item on their list and, using double object pronouns, tell their partner who bought it for them. Ex: **zapatos nuevos (Me los compró mi prima.)**

**5**

**Regalos de Navidad** (*Christmas gifts*) Tu profesor(a) te va a dar a ti y a un(a) compañero/a una parte de la lista de los regalos de Navidad que Berta pidió y los regalos que sus parientes le compraron. Conversen para completar sus listas. *Answers will vary.*

> **modelo**
> **Estudiante 1:** ¿Qué le pidió Berta a su mamá?
> **Estudiante 2:** Le pidió una computadora. ¿Se la compró?
> **Estudiante 1:** Sí, se la compró.

**NOTA CULTURAL**

Las fiestas navideñas (*Christmas season*) en los países hispanos duran hasta enero. En muchos lugares celebran **la Navidad** (*Christmas*), pero no se dan los regalos hasta el seis de enero, **el Día de los Reyes Magos** (*Three Kings' Day/The Feast of the Epiphany*).

---

**TEACHING OPTIONS**

**Heritage Speakers** Ask heritage speakers if they or their families celebrate **el Día de los Reyes Magos** (The Feast of the Epiphany, January 6). Ask them to expand on the information given in the **Nota cultural** box and to tell whether **el Día de los Reyes** is more important for them than **la Navidad**.

**Large Groups** Divide the class into two groups. Give each member of the first group a strip of paper with a question on it. Ex: **¿Te compró ese suéter tu novia?** Give each member of the second group the answer to one of the questions. Ex: **Sí, ella me lo compró.** Students must find their partners. Take care not to create sentences that can have more than one match.

# 8.3 Comparisons

**ANTE TODO** Spanish and English use comparisons to indicate which of two people or things has a lesser, equal, or greater degree of a quality.

( Comparisons )

| **menos interesante** | **más grande** | **tan sabroso como** |
|---|---|---|
| *less interesting* | *bigger* | *as delicious as* |

## Comparisons of inequality

▶ Comparisons of inequality are formed by placing **más** (*more*) or **menos** (*less*) before adjectives, adverbs, and nouns and **que** (*than*) after them.

$$\textbf{más/menos} + \begin{bmatrix} adjective \\ adverb \\ noun \end{bmatrix} + \textbf{que}$$

▶ **¡Atención!** Note that while English has a comparative form for short adjectives (*taller*), such forms do not exist in Spanish (**más** alto).

( adjectives )

| Los bistecs son **más caros que** el pollo. | Estas uvas son **menos ricas que** esa pera. |
|---|---|
| *Steaks are more expensive than chicken.* | *These grapes are less tasty than that pear.* |

( adverbs )

| Me acuesto **más tarde que** tú. | Luis se despierta **menos temprano que** yo. |
|---|---|
| *I go to bed later than you (do).* | *Luis wakes up less early than I (do).* |

( nouns )

| Juan prepara **más platos que** José. | Susana come **menos carne que** Enrique. |
|---|---|
| *Juan prepares more dishes than José (does).* | *Susana eats less meat than Enrique (does).* |

*Tengo más hambre que un elefante.*

*El lomo a la plancha es un poquito más caro pero es sabrosísimo.*

▶ When the comparison involves a numerical expression, **de** is used before the number instead of **que**.

| Hay más **de** cincuenta naranjas. | Llego en menos **de** diez minutos. |
|---|---|
| *There are more than fifty oranges.* | *I'll be there in less than ten minutes.* |

▶ With verbs, this construction is used to make comparisons of inequality.

$$\begin{bmatrix} verb \end{bmatrix} + \textbf{más/menos que}$$

| Mis hermanos **comen más que** yo. | Arturo **duerme menos que** su padre. |
|---|---|
| *My brothers eat more than I (do).* | *Arturo sleeps less than his father (does).* |

---

## Section Goals

In **Estructura 8.3**, students will be introduced to:
- comparisons of inequality
- comparisons of equality
- irregular comparative words

**Instructional Resources**
**Supersite:** Lab MP3 Audio Files
**Lección 8**
**Supersite/IRCD:** *PowerPoints* (Lección 8 Estructura Presentation); *IRM* (Lab Audio Script, WBs/VM/LM Answer Key)
**WebSAM**
**Workbook,** pp. 91–92
**Lab Manual,** p. 47
***Cuaderno para hispanohablantes***

**Teaching Tips**
- Write **más** + [*adjective*] + **que** and **menos** + [*adjective*] + **que** on the board, explaining their meaning. Illustrate with examples. Ex: **Esta clase es más grande que la clase de la tarde. La clase de la tarde es menos trabajadora que ésta.**
- Practice the structures by asking volunteers questions about classroom objects. **El lápiz de ____, ¿es más largo que el lápiz de ____?** (**No, es menos largo que el lápiz de ____.**)
- Point out that **que** and what follows it are optional if the items being compared are evident. Ex: **Los bistecs son más caros (que el pollo).**

---

**Teaching Tips**
- Ask the class questions to elicit comparisons of equality. Ex: **¿Quién es tan guapa como Jennifer López? ¿Quién tiene tanto dinero como Tiger Woods?**
- Ask questions that involve comparisons with yourself. Ex: **¿Quién es tan alto/a como yo? ¿Quién se acostó tan tarde como yo?**
- Involve the class in a conversation about themselves and classroom objects. Ex: **____, ¿por qué tienes tantas plumas? ____, ¡tu mochila es tan grande! Puedes llevar muchos libros, ¿no? ¿Quién más tiene una mochila tan grande?**

## Comparisons of equality

▶ This construction is used to make comparisons of equality.

¿Qué tal tu ceviche?

La comida es tan buena como en España.

▶ **¡Atención!** Note that **tanto** acts as an adjective and therefore agrees in number and gender with the noun it modifies.

| | |
|---|---|
| Este plato es **tan rico como** aquél. *This dish is as tasty as that one (is).* | Yo probé **tantos platos como** él. *I tried as many dishes as he did.* |

▶ **Tan** and **tanto** can also be used for emphasis, rather than to compare, with these meanings: **tan** *so*, **tanto** *so much*, **tantos/as** *so many*.

| | |
|---|---|
| ¡Tu almuerzo es **tan** grande! *Your lunch is so big!* | ¡Comes **tantas** manzanas! *You eat so many apples!* |
| ¡Comes **tanto**! *You eat so much!* | ¡Preparan **tantos** platos! *They prepare so many dishes!* |

▶ Comparisons of equality with verbs are formed by placing **tanto como** after the verb. Note that in this construction **tanto** does not change in number or gender.

$$\boxed{verb} + \textbf{tanto como}$$

| | |
|---|---|
| Tú viajas **tanto como** mi tía. *You travel as much as my aunt (does).* | Ellos hablan **tanto como** mis hermanas. *They talk as much as my sisters.* |

**Estudiamos tanto como** ustedes.
*We study as much as you (do).*

No **descanso tanto como** Felipe.
*I don't rest as much as Felipe (does).*

---

**TEACHING OPTIONS**

**Extra Practice** Have students write three original comparative sentences that describe themselves. Ex: **Soy tan bajo como Danny DeVito**. Then collect the papers, shuffle them, and read the sentences aloud. See if the rest of the class can guess who wrote each description.

**Game** Divide the class into two teams, A and B. Place the names of twenty famous people into a hat. Select a member from each team to draw a name. The student from team A then has ten seconds to compare those two famous people. If the student has made a logical comparison, team A gets a point. Then it is team B's turn to make a different comparison. The team with the most points at the end wins.

# Irregular comparisons

▶ Some adjectives have irregular comparative forms.

## Irregular comparative forms

| Adjective | | Comparative form | |
|---|---|---|---|
| **bueno/a** | good | **mejor** | better |
| **malo/a** | bad | **peor** | worse |
| **grande** | big | **mayor** | bigger |
| **pequeño/a** | small | **menor** | smaller |
| **joven** | young | **menor** | younger |
| **viejo/a** | old | **mayor** | older |

▶ When **grande** and **pequeño/a** refer to age, the irregular comparative forms, **mayor** and **menor**, are used. However, when these adjectives refer to size, the regular forms, **más grande** and **más pequeño/a**, are used.

Yo soy **menor** que tú.
*I'm younger than you.*

Pedí un plato **más pequeño**.
*I ordered a smaller dish.*

El médico es **mayor** que Isabel.
*The doctor is older than Isabel.*

La ensalada de Inés es **más grande** que ésa.
*Inés's salad is bigger than that one.*

▶ The adverbs **bien** and **mal** have the same irregular comparative forms as the adjectives **bueno/a** and **malo/a**.

Julio nada **mejor** que los otros chicos.
*Julio swims better than the other boys.*

Ellas cantan **peor** que las otras chicas.
*They sing worse than the other girls.*

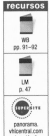

**¡INTÉNTALO!**    Escribe el equivalente de las palabras en inglés.

1. Ernesto mira más televisión ___que___ (*than*) Alberto.
2. Tú eres ___menos___ (*less*) simpático que Federico.
3. La camarera sirve ___tanta___ (*as much*) carne como pescado.
4. Conozco ___más___ (*more*) restaurantes que tú.
5. No estudio ___tanto como___ (*as much as*) tú.
6. ¿Sabes jugar al tenis tan bien ___como___ (*as*) tu hermana?
7. ¿Puedes beber ___tantos___ (*as many*) refrescos como yo?
8. Mis amigos parecen ___tan___ (*as*) simpáticos como ustedes.

# Práctica SUPERSITE

**1** **Escoger** Escoge la palabra correcta para comparar a dos hermanas muy diferentes. Haz los cambios necesarios.

1. Lucila es más alta y más bonita ___que___ Tita. (de, más, menos, que)
2. Tita es más delgada porque come ___más___ verduras que su hermana. (de, más, menos, que)
3. Lucila es más ___simpática___ que Tita porque es alegre. (listo, simpático, bajo)
4. A Tita le gusta comer en casa. Va a ___menos___ restaurantes que su hermana. (más, menos, que) Es tímida, pero activa. Hace ___más___ ejercicio (*exercise*) que su hermana. (más, tanto, menos) Todos los días toma más ___de___ cinco vasos (*glasses*) de agua mineral. (que, tan, de)
5. Lucila come muchas papas fritas y se preocupa ___menos___ que Tita por comer frutas. (de, más, menos) Son ___tan___ diferentes, pero se llevan (*they get along*) bien. (como, tan, tanto)

**2** **Emparejar** Completa las oraciones de la columna A con información de la columna B para comparar a Mario y a Luis, los novios de Lucila y Tita.

| A | B |
|---|---|
| 1. Mario es ___tan interesante___ como Luis. | tantas |
| 2. Mario viaja tanto ___como___ Luis. | diferencia |
| 3. Luis toma ___tantas___ clases de cocina (*cooking*) como Mario. | tan interesante |
| 4. Luis habla ___francés___ tan bien como Mario. | amigos extranjeros |
| 5. Mario tiene tantos ___amigos extranjeros___ como Luis. | como |
| 6. ¡Qué casualidad (*coincidence*)! Mario y Luis también son hermanos, pero no hay tanta ___diferencia___ entre ellos como entre Lucila y Tita. | francés |

**3** **Oraciones** Combina elementos de las columnas A, B y C para hacer comparaciones. Usa oraciones completas. Answers will vary.

**modelo**
Arnold Schwarzenegger tiene tantos autos como Jennifer Aniston.
Jennifer Aniston es menos musculosa que Arnold Schwarzenegger.

| A | B | C |
|---|---|---|
| la comida japonesa | costar | la gente de Los Ángeles |
| el fútbol | saber | la música *country* |
| Arnold Schwarzenegger | ser | el brócoli |
| el pollo | tener | el presidente de los EE.UU. |
| la gente de Nueva York | ¿? | la comida italiana |
| la primera dama (*lady*) de los EE.UU. | | el hockey |
| las universidades privadas | | Jennifer Aniston |
| las espinacas | | las universidades públicas |
| la música rap | | la carne de res |

# Comunicación

**4**  **Intercambiar** En parejas, hagan comparaciones sobre diferentes cosas. Pueden usar las
sugerencias de la lista u otras ideas.  Answers will vary.

**AYUDA**

You can use these
adjectives in your
comparisons:

**bonito/a**
**caro/a**
**elegante**
**interesante**
**inteligente**

> **modelo**
>
> **Estudiante 1:** Los pollos de *Pollitos del Corral* son muy ricos.
> **Estudiante 2:** Pues yo creo que los pollos de *Rostipollos* son tan
> buenos como los pollos de *Pollitos del Corral*.
> **Estudiante 1:** Mmm… no tienen tanta mantequilla como
> los pollos de *Pollitos del Corral*. Tienes razón.
> Son muy sabrosos.

restaurantes en tu ciudad/pueblo
cafés en tu comunidad
tiendas en tu ciudad/pueblo

periódicos en tu ciudad/pueblo
revistas favoritas
libros favoritos

comidas favoritas
los profesores
los cursos que toman

**5**  **Conversar** En grupos, túrnense para hacer comparaciones entre ustedes mismos (*yourselves*) y
una persona de cada categoría de la lista.  Answers will vary.

▶ una persona de tu familia
▶ un(a) amigo/a especial
▶ una persona famosa

# Síntesis

**6**  **La familia López** En grupos, túrnense para hablar de Sara, Sabrina, Cristina, Ricardo y David
y hacer comparaciones entre ellos.  Answers will vary.

Sara   Sabrina   Ricardo   David   Cristina

> **modelo**
>
> **Estudiante 1:** Sara es tan alta como Sabrina.
> **Estudiante 2:** Sí, pero David es más alto que ellas.
> **Estudiante 3:** En mi opinión, él es guapo también.

**4 Expansion** Ask pairs of
volunteers to present one of
their conversations to the
class. Then survey the class to
see with which of the students
the class agrees more.

**5 Teaching Tip** Model the
activity by making a few comparisons between yourself and
a celebrity.

**5 Expansion** Ask a volunteer
to share his or her comparisons. Then make comparisons
between yourself and the
student or yourself and the
person the student mentioned.
Continue to do this with different students, asking them to
make similar comparisons
as well.

**6 Expansion** Have students
create a drawing of a family
similar to the one on this page.
Tell them not to let anyone
see their drawings. Then pair
students up and have them
describe their drawings to one
another. Each student must
draw the family described by
his or her partner.

## 8.4 Superlatives

**ANTE TODO** Both English and Spanish use superlatives to express the highest or lowest degree of a quality.

| el/la mejor | el/la peor | la más alta |
|---|---|---|
| *the best* | *the worst* | *the tallest* |

▶ This construction is used to form superlatives. Note that the noun is always preceded by a definite article and that **de** is equivalent to the English *in* or *of*.

> **el/la/los/las** + [ *noun* ] + **más/menos** + [ *adjective* ] + **de**

▶ The noun can be omitted if the person, place, or thing referred to is clear.

¿El restaurante El Cráter?
Es **el más elegante** de la ciudad.
*The El Cráter restaurant?*
*It's the most elegant (one) in the city.*

Recomiendo el pollo asado.
Es **el más sabroso** del menú.
*I recommend the roast chicken.*
*It's the most delicious on the menu.*

▶ Here are some irregular superlative forms.

### Irregular superlatives

| Adjective | | Superlative form | |
|---|---|---|---|
| bueno/a | good | el/la mejor | (the) best |
| malo/a | bad | el/la peor | (the) worst |
| grande | big | el/la mayor | (the) biggest |
| pequeño/a | small | el/la menor | (the) smallest |
| joven | young | el/la menor | (the) youngest |
| viejo/a | old | el/la mayor | (the) eldest |

▶ The absolute superlative is equivalent to *extremely, super,* or *very*. To form the absolute superlative of most adjectives and adverbs, drop the final vowel, if there is one, and add **-ísimo/a(s).**

malo → mal- → **malísimo**          mucho → much- → **muchísimo**
¡El bistec está **malísimo**!          Comes **muchísimo**.

▶ Note these spelling changes.

rico → **riquísimo**    largo → **larguísimo**    feliz → **felicísimo**
fácil → **facilísimo**    joven → **jovencísimo**    trabajador → **trabajadorcísimo**

**¡INTÉNTALO!** Escribe el equivalente de las palabras en inglés.

1. Marisa es <u>la más inteligente</u> (*the most intelligent*) de todas.
2. Ricardo y Tomás son <u>los menos aburridos</u> (*the least boring*) de la fiesta.
3. Miguel y Antonio son <u>los peores</u> (*the worst*) estudiantes de la clase.
4. Mi profesor de biología es <u>el mayor</u> (*the oldest*) de la universidad.

# Práctica y Comunicación

**1** **El más...** Responde a las preguntas afirmativamente. Usa las palabras en paréntesis.

> **modelo**
> El cuarto está sucísimo, ¿no? (residencia)
> Sí, es el más sucio de la residencia.

1. El almacén Velasco es buenísimo, ¿no? (centro comercial)   Sí, es el mejor del centro comercial.
2. La silla de tu madre es comodísima, ¿no? (casa)   Sí, es la más cómoda de la casa.
3. Ángela y Julia están nerviosísimas por el examen, ¿no? (clase)   Sí, son las más nerviosas de la clase.
4. Jorge es jovencísimo, ¿no? (mis amigos)   Sí, es el menor de mis amigos.

**2** **Completar** Tu profesor(a) te va a dar una hoja de actividades con descripciones de José Valenzuela Carranza y Ana Orozco Hoffman. Completa las oraciones con las palabras de la lista. Answers will vary.

| | | | |
|---|---|---|---|
| altísima | del | mejor | peor |
| atlética | la | menor | periodista |
| bajo | más | guapísimo | trabajadorcísimo |
| de | mayor | Orozco | Valenzuela |

1. José tiene 22 años; es el _____menor_____ y el más _____bajo_____ de su familia. Es _____guapísimo_____ y _____trabajadorcísimo_____. Es el mejor _____periodista_____ de la ciudad y el _____peor_____ jugador de baloncesto.
2. Ana es la más _____atlética_____ y _____la_____ mejor jugadora de baloncesto del estado. Es la _____mayor_____ de sus hermanos (tiene 28 años) y es _____altísima_____. Estudió la profesión _____más_____ difícil _____de_____ todas: medicina.
3. Jorge es el _____mejor_____ jugador de videojuegos de su familia.
4. Mauricio es el menor de la familia _____Orozco_____.
5. El abuelo es el _____mayor_____ de todos los miembros de la familia Valenzuela.
6. Fifí es la perra más antipática _____del_____ mundo.

**3** **Superlativos** Trabajen en parejas para hacer comparaciones. Usen superlativos. Answers will vary.

> **modelo**
> Angelina Jolie, Bill Gates, Jimmy Carter
> **Estudiante 1:** Bill Gates es el más rico de los tres.
> **Estudiante 2:** Sí, ¡es riquísimo! Y Jimmy Carter es el mayor de los tres.

1. Guatemala, Argentina, España
2. Jaguar, Hummer, Mini Cooper
3. la comida mexicana, la comida francesa, la comida árabe
4. Paris Hilton, Meryl Streep, Katie Holmes
5. Ciudad de México, Buenos Aires, Nueva York
6. *Don Quijote de la Mancha, Cien años de soledad, Como agua para chocolate*
7. el fútbol americano, el golf, el béisbol
8. las películas románticas, las películas de acción, las películas cómicas

NATIONAL communication STANDARDS

**1 Expansion**
• Give these sentences to students as items 5–7: **5. Esas películas son malísimas, ¿no? (Hollywood) (Sí, son las peores de Hollywood.) 6. El centro comercial Galerías es grandísimo, ¿no? (ciudad) (Sí, es el mayor de la ciudad.) 7. Tus bisabuelos son viejísimos, ¿no? (familia) (Sí, son los mayores de mi familia.)**
• To challenge students, after they have completed the activity, have them repeat it by answering in the negative. Ex: **1. No, es el peor del centro comercial.**

**2 Teaching Tip** Distribute the *Hojas de actividades* (Supersite/IRCD) that correspond to this activity.

**2 Expansion** In pairs, have students select a family member or a close friend and describe him or her using comparatives and superlatives. Ask volunteers to share their description with the class.

**3 Teaching Tips**
• To simplify, read through the items with students and, in English, brainstorm points of comparison between the three people or things. For item 6, briefly describe these novels for students who are not familiar with them.
• Encourage students to create as many superlatives as they can for each item. Have volunteers share their most creative statements with the class.

**TEACHING OPTIONS**

**Extra Practice** Add an auditory aspect to this grammar practice. Prepare ten superlative sentences and read them aloud slowly, pausing about thirty seconds after each sentence to allow students to write the direct opposite. Ex: **Ernesto es el menor de la familia. (Ernesto es el mayor de la familia.)**

**Pairs** Bring in clothing catalogs and have students work in pairs to create superlative statements about the prices of different items. Ask volunteers to share some of their statements with the class. You may want to have students review clothing-related vocabulary from **Lección 6.**

## Section Goal

In **Recapitulación**, students will review the grammar concepts from this lesson.

**Instructional Resource**
**Supersite**

**1 Teaching Tip** Before beginning the activity, ask students to identify which verb forms have stem changes.

**1 Expansion** To challenge students, add columns for **tú** and **nosotros**.

**2 Expansion** Have students create questions about the dialogue. Ex: **¿Cómo se vistieron Marta y Daniel el sábado? ¿Por qué?** Call on volunteers to answer the questions.

**3 Teaching Tips**
• Remind students that indirect object pronouns always precede direct object pronouns.
• To simplify, have students underline the direct object and circle the indirect object in each question.

**3 Expansion** For additional practice, have pairs write a brief dialogue from the point of view of two of the restaurant's customers, using indirect and direct object pronouns. Then have pairs perform their dialogues for the class.

# Recapitulación

 For self-scoring and diagnostics, go to **panorama.vhlcentral.com**.

Completa estas actividades para repasar los conceptos de gramática que aprendiste en esta lección.

**1 Completar** Completa la tabla con la forma correcta del pretérito. **9 pts.**

| Infinitive | yo | usted | ellos |
|---|---|---|---|
| **dormir** | dormí | durmió | durmieron |
| **servir** | serví | sirvió | sirvieron |
| **vestirse** | me vestí | se vistió | se vistieron |

**2 La cena** Completa la conversación con el pretérito de los verbos. **7 pts.**

**PAULA** ¡Hola, Daniel! ¿Qué tal el fin de semana?

**DANIEL** Muy bien. Marta y yo (1) conseguimos (conseguir) hacer muchas cosas, pero lo mejor fue la cena del sábado.

**PAULA** Ah, ¿sí? ¿Adónde fueron?

**DANIEL** Al restaurante Vistahermosa. Es elegante, así que (nosotros) (2) nos vestimos (vestirse) bien.

**PAULA** Y, ¿qué platos (3) pidieron (pedir, ustedes)?

**DANIEL** Yo (4) pedí (pedir) camarones y Marta (5) prefirió (preferir) el pollo. Y al final, el camarero nos (6) sirvió (servir) flan.

**PAULA** ¡Qué rico!

**DANIEL** Sí. Pero después de la cena Marta no (7) se sintió (sentirse) bien.

**3 Camareros** Genaro y Úrsula son camareros en un restaurante. Completa la conversación que tienen con su jefe usando pronombres. **8 pts.**

**JEFE** Úrsula, ¿le ofreciste agua fría al cliente de la mesa 22?

**ÚRSULA** Sí, (1) se la ofrecí de inmediato.

**JEFE** Genaro, ¿los clientes de la mesa 5 te pidieron ensaladas?

**GENARO** Sí, (2) me las pidieron.

**ÚRSULA** Genaro, ¿recuerdas si ya me mostraste los vinos nuevos?

**GENARO** Sí, ya (3) te los mostré.

**JEFE** Genaro, ¿van a pagarte la cuenta (*bill*) los clientes de la mesa 5?

**GENARO** Sí, (4) me la van a pagar/ van a pagármela ahora mismo.

**RESUMEN GRAMATICAL**

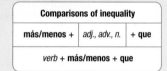

**8.1 Preterite of stem-changing verbs** *p. 254*

| servir | dormir |
|---|---|
| serví | dormí |
| serviste | dormiste |
| sirvió | durmió |
| servimos | dormimos |
| servisteis | dormisteis |
| sirvieron | durmieron |

**8.2 Double object pronouns** *pp. 257–258*

Indirect Object Pronouns: **me, te, le (se), nos, os, les (se)**

Direct Object Pronouns: **lo, la, los, las**

**Le escribí la carta. → Se la escribí.**

**Nos van a servir los platos. → Nos los van a servir./ Van a servírnoslos.**

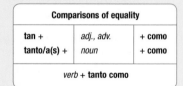

**8.3 Comparisons** *pp. 261–263*

**Comparisons of inequality**

| más/menos + | adj., adv., n. | + que |
|---|---|---|
| *verb* + más/menos + que | | |

**Comparisons of equality**

| tan + | adj., adv. | + como |
|---|---|---|
| tanto/a(s) + | noun | + como |
| *verb* + tanto como | | |

**Irregular comparative forms**

| bueno/a | mejor |
|---|---|
| malo/a | peor |
| grande | mayor |
| pequeño/a | menor |
| joven | menor |
| viejo/a | mayor |

**TEACHING OPTIONS**

**Game** Divide the class into two teams and have them line up. Name a preterite stem-changing verb in the infinitive as well as a subject pronoun (Ex: **conseguir/ustedes**). The first team member to reach the board and correctly write the subject pronoun and the conjugated verb form earns one point for their team (Ex: **consiguieron**). The team with the most points at the end wins.

**TPR** Have the class stand in a circle. Point to two students to step forward into the circle. Toss a foam or paper ball to another student, who must make a comparison between the students inside the circle. Ex: **Ian es más alto que Omar.** Have students continue tossing the ball to each other and making original comparisons, until you indicate them to pause. Then have another student join the middle of the circle and have students make superlative statements. Repeat the process by indicating two new students to stand inside the circle.

**4** **El menú** Observa el menú y sus características.
Completa las oraciones basándote en los elementos dados.
Usa comparativos y superlativos. **14 pts.**

<table>
<tr><td>*Ensaladas*</td><td>*Precio*</td><td>*Calorías*</td></tr>
<tr><td>Ensalada de tomates</td><td>$9.00</td><td>170</td></tr>
<tr><td>Ensalada de mariscos</td><td>$12.99</td><td>325</td></tr>
<tr><td>Ensalada de zanahorias</td><td>$9.00</td><td>200</td></tr>
<tr><td>*Platos principales*</td><td></td><td></td></tr>
<tr><td>Pollo con champiñones</td><td>$13.00</td><td>495</td></tr>
<tr><td>Cerdo con papas</td><td>$10.50</td><td>725</td></tr>
<tr><td>Atún con espárragos</td><td>$18.95</td><td>495</td></tr>
</table>

1. ensalada de mariscos / otras ensaladas / costar
   La ensalada de mariscos ____cuesta más que____ las otras ensaladas.
2. pollo con champiñones / cerdo con papas / calorías
   El pollo con champiñones tiene ____menos calorías que____ el cerdo con papas.
3. atún con espárragos / pollo con champiñones / calorías
   El atún con espárragos tiene ____tantas calorías como____ el pollo con champiñones.
4. ensalada de tomates / ensalada de zanahorias / caro
   La ensalada de tomates es ____tan cara como____ la ensalada de zanahorias.
5. cerdo con papas / platos principales / caro
   El cerdo con papas es ____el menos caro de____ los platos principales.
6. ensalada de zanahorias / ensalada de tomates / costar
   La ensalada de zanahorias ____cuesta tanto como____ la ensalada de tomates.
7. ensalada de mariscos / ensaladas / caro
   La ensalada de mariscos es ____la más cara de____ las ensaladas.

**5** **Dos restaurantes** ¿Cuál es el mejor restaurante que conoces? ¿Y el peor? Escribe un párrafo de
por lo menos (*at least*) seis oraciones donde expliques por qué piensas así. Puedes hablar de la calidad
de la comida, el ambiente, los precios, el servicio, etc. **12 pts.** Answers will vary.

**6** **Adivinanza** Completa la adivinanza y adivina la respuesta. **¡2 puntos EXTRA!**

" En el campo yo nací°,
mis hermanos son
los ____ajos____ (*garlic, pl.*),
y aquél que llora° por mí
me está partiendo°
en pedazos°. "
¿Quién soy? ____La cebolla____

nací *was born*  llora *cries*  partiendo *cutting*  pedazos *pieces*

recursos

SUPERSITE

panorama.vhlcentral.com
Lección 8

---

8.4 **Superlatives** *p. 266*

| el/la/ los/las + | noun | + más/ menos + | adjective | + de |
|---|---|---|---|---|

▶ Irregular superlatives follow the same pattern as
irregular comparatives.

---

**4** **Teaching Tips**
• Remind students that the
comparative **tanto/a** must
agree in gender and number
with the noun it modifies.
• To challenge students,
have pairs ask each other
questions about the menu
using comparatives and
superlatives. Ex: **¿Qué
ensalada cuesta tanto como
la ensalada de tomates?**
**(La ensalada de zanahorias
cuesta tanto como la ensalada
de tomates.)**

**5** **Teaching Tip** To help
students organize their ideas,
have them divide their paper
into two columns: **mejor** and
**peor**. Under each category,
have students list the different
reasons why their chosen
restaurants are the best
or worst.

**6** **Expansion** Have students
work in groups of three or four
to create an original riddle
related to food. Have groups
read their riddles for the class
to guess.

---

**TEACHING OPTIONS**

**TPR** Have students write a celebrity's name, a place, and a thing
on separate slips of paper. Collect the papers in three envelopes,
separated by category. Then divide the class into two teams,
**comparativos** and **superlativos**, and have them line up. Draw out
two or three slips of paper (alternate randomly) and read the terms
aloud. The corresponding team member has five seconds to step
forward and create a logical comparison or superlative statement.

**Pairs** Have pairs imagine they went to a restaurant where
the server mixed up all the orders. Call on pairs to share their
experiences, using **pedir** and **servir** as well as double object
pronouns. Ex: **Fui a un restaurante italiano. Pedí la pasta
primavera. ¡El camarero me sirvió la sopa de mariscos! ¡Y me
la sirvió fría! Mi compañero pidió langosta, pero el camarero
no se la sirvió. ¡Le sirvió una chuleta de cerdo!**

# Section Goals

In **Lectura**, students will:
• learn to identify the main idea in a text
• read a content-rich menu and restaurant review

**Instructional Resources**
**Supersite**
*Cuaderno para hispanohablantes*

**Estrategia** Tell students that recognizing the main idea of a text will help them unlock the meaning of unfamiliar words and phrases they come across while reading. Tell them first to check the title, where the main idea is often expressed. Have them read the topic sentence of each paragraph before they read the full text to get a sense of the main idea.

**Examinar el texto** First, have students scan the menu. Ask how the title and subheadings help predict the content. Ask volunteers to state the meaning of each category of food served. Then have students scan the newspaper article. Ask them how the title and the format (the box with ratings) of the text give clues to the content.

**Identificar la idea principal** Ask students to read the column heading and the title of the article and predict the subject of the article and the author's purpose. Then have students read the topic sentence of the first paragraph and state the main idea. Finally, have them read the entire paragraph.

# Lectura

## Antes de leer

### Estrategia
**Reading for the main idea**

As you know, you can learn a great deal about a reading selection by looking at the format and looking for cognates, titles, and subtitles. You can skim to get the gist of the reading selection and scan it for specific information. Reading for the main idea is another useful strategy; it involves locating the topic sentences of each paragraph to determine the author's purpose for writing a particular piece. Topic sentences can provide clues about the content of each paragraph, as well as the general organization of the reading. Your choice of which reading strategies to use will depend on the style and format of each reading selection.

### Examinar el texto

En esta sección tenemos dos textos diferentes. ¿Qué estrategias puedes usar para leer la crítica culinaria (*restaurant review*)? ¿Cuáles son las apropiadas para familiarizarte con el menú? Utiliza las estrategias más eficaces (*efficient*) para cada texto. ¿Qué tienen en común? ¿Qué tipo de comida sirven en el restaurante?

### Identificar la idea principal

Lee la primera frase de cada párrafo de la crítica culinaria del restaurante **La feria del maíz**. Apunta (*Jot down*) el tema principal de cada párrafo. Luego lee todo el primer párrafo. ¿Crees que el restaurante le gustó al autor de la crítica culinaria? ¿Por qué? Ahora lee la crítica entera. En tu opinión, ¿cuál es la idea principal de la crítica? ¿Por qué la escribió el autor? Compara tus opiniones con las de un(a) compañero/a.

recursos

panorama.vhlcentral.com
Lección 8

## MENÚ

### Entremeses
Tortilla servida con
• Ajiaceite (chile, aceite)   • Ajicomino (chile, comino)

Pan tostado servido con
• Queso frito a la pimienta   • Salsa de ajo y mayonesa

### Sopas
• Tomate   • Cebolla   • Verduras   • Pollo y huevo
• Carne de res   • Mariscos

### Entradas
Tomaticán
(tomate, papas, maíz, chile, arvejas y zanahorias)

Tamales
(maíz, azúcar, ajo, cebolla)

Frijoles enchilados
(frijoles negros, carne de cerdo o de res, arroz, chile)

Chilaquil
(tortilla de maíz, queso, hierbas y chile)

Tacos
(tortillas, pollo, verduras y salsa)

Cóctel de mariscos
(camarones, langosta, vinagre, sal, pimienta, aceite)

### Postres°
• Plátanos caribeños   • Cóctel de frutas al ron°
• Uvate (uvas, azúcar de caña y ron)   • Flan napolitano
• Helado° de piña y naranja   • Pastel° de yogur

## Después de leer

### Preguntas

En parejas, contesten estas preguntas sobre la crítica culinaria de **La feria del maíz**.

1. ¿Quién es el dueño y chef de **La feria del maíz**?
   Ernesto Sandoval
2. ¿Qué tipo de comida se sirve en el restaurante?
   tradicional
3. ¿Cuál es el problema con el servicio?
   Se necesitan más camareros.
4. ¿Cómo es el ambiente del restaurante?
   agradable
5. ¿Qué comidas probó el autor? las tortillas, el ajiaceite, la sopa de mariscos, los tamales, los tacos de pollo y los plátanos caribeños
6. ¿Quieren ir ustedes al restaurante **La feria del maíz**?
   ¿Por qué? Answers will vary.

---

**TEACHING OPTIONS**

**Small Groups** Ask groups to create a dinner menu featuring their favorite dishes, including lists of ingredients similar to those in the menu above. Have groups present their menus to the class.

**Heritage Speakers** Ask a heritage speaker of Guatemalan origin or a student who has visited Guatemala and dined in restaurants or cafés to prepare a short presentation about his or her experiences there. Of particular interest would be a comparison and contrast of city vs. small-town restaurants. If possible, the presentation should be illustrated with menus from the restaurants, advertisements, or photos of and articles about the country.

# Gastronomía

Por Eduardo Fernández

23F

## La feria del maíz

**Sobresaliente°.** En el nuevo restaurante **La feria del maíz** va a encontrar la perfecta combinación entre la comida tradicional y el encanto° de la vieja ciudad de Antigua. Ernesto Sandoval, antiguo jefe de cocina° del famoso restaurante **El fogón**, está teniendo mucho éxito° en su nueva aventura culinaria.

El gerente°, el experimentado José Sierra, controla a la perfección la calidad del servicio. El camarero que me atendió esa noche fue muy amable en todo momento. Sólo hay que comentar que,

**La feria del maíz**
**13 calle 4-41 Zona 1**
**La Antigua, Guatemala**
**2329912**

*lunes a sábado*
*10:30am-11:30pm*
*domingo 10:00am-10:00pm*

Comida ♈♈♈♈♈

Servicio ♈♈♈

Ambiente ♈♈♈♈

Precio ♈♈♈

debido al éxito inmediato de **La feria del maíz**, se necesitan más camareros para atender a los clientes de una forma más eficaz. En esta ocasión, el mesero se tomó unos veinte minutos en traerme la bebida.

Afortunadamente, no me importó mucho la espera entre plato y plato, pues el ambiente es tan agradable que me sentí como en casa. El restaurante mantiene el estilo colonial de Antigua. Por dentro°, el estilo es elegante y rústico a la vez. Cuando el tiempo lo permite, se puede comer también en el patio, donde hay muchas flores.

El servicio de camareros y el ambiente agradable del local pasan a un segundo plano cuando llega la comida, de una calidad extraordinaria. Las tortillas de casa se sirven con un ajiaceite delicioso. La sopa de mariscos es excelente, y los tamales, pues, tengo que confesar que son mejores que los de mi abuelita. También recomiendo los tacos de pollo, servidos con un mole buenísimo. De postre, don Ernesto me preparó su especialidad, unos plátanos caribeños sabrosísimos.

Los precios pueden parecer altos° para una comida tradicional, pero la calidad de los productos con que se cocinan los platos y el exquisito ambiente de **La feria del maíz** le garantizan° una experiencia inolvidable°.

*Bebidas*

• Cerveza negra  • Chilate (bebida de maíz, chile y cacao)
• Jugos de fruta  • Agua mineral  • Té helado
• Vino tinto/blanco  • Ron

Postres *Desserts*  ron *rum*  Helado *Ice cream*  Pastel *Cake*  Sobresaliente
*Outstanding*  encanto *charm*  jefe de cocina *head chef*  éxito *success*
gerente *manager*  Por dentro *Inside*  altos *high*  garantizan *guarantee*
inolvidable *unforgettable*

**Preguntas**
• Have students quickly review the article before answering the questions. Suggest that pairs take turns answering them. The student who does not answer a question should find the line of text that contains the answer.
• Give students these questions as items 7–9: **7. ¿Cómo fue el camarero que atendió al crítico? (Fue muy amable, pero estaba muy ocupado con otros clientes del restaurante.) 8. ¿Cuál fue la opinión del crítico con respecto a la comida? (La encontró toda de muy alta calidad.) 9. ¿Cómo son los precios de La feria del maíz? (Son altos, pero la calidad de la comida los justifica.)**

**Un(a) guía turístico/a** Choose an alternative food for the customer to order that would better suit his or her dietary needs.

**The Affective Dimension**
A source of discomfort in travel can be unfamiliar foods. Tell students that by learning about the foods of a country they are going to visit they can make that part of their visit even more enjoyable.

## Un(a) guía turístico/a

Tú eres un(a) guía turístico/a en Guatemala. Estás en el restaurante **La feria del maíz** con un grupo de turistas norteamericanos. Ellos no hablan español y quieren pedir de comer, pero necesitan tu ayuda. Lee nuevamente el menú e indica qué error comete cada turista.

1. La señora Johnson es diabética y no puede comer azúcar. Pide sopa de verdura y tamales. No pide nada de postre.
   No debe pedir los tamales porque tienen azúcar.

2. Los señores Petit son vegeterianos y piden sopa de tomate, frijoles enchilados y plátanos caribeños.
   No deben pedir los frijoles enchilados porque tienen carne.

3. El señor Smith, que es alérgico al chocolate, pide tortilla servida con ajiaceite, chilaquil y chilate para beber.
   No debe pedir chilate porque tiene cacao.

4. La adorable hija del señor Smith tiene sólo cuatro años y le gustan mucho las verduras y las frutas naturales. Su papá le pide tomaticán y un cóctel de frutas.
   No debe pedir el cóctel de frutas porque tiene ron.

5. La señorita Jackson está a dieta y pide uvate, flan napolitano y helado.
   No debe pedir postres porque está a dieta.

---

**TEACHING OPTIONS**

**Large Groups** Ask students to review the items in **Un(a) guía turístico/a**, write a conversation, and role-play the scene involving a tour guide eating lunch in a Guatemalan restaurant with several tourists. Have them work in groups of eight to assign the following roles: **camarero, guía turístico/a, la señora Johnson, los señores Petit, el señor Smith, la hija del señor Smith,** and **la señorita Jackson**. Have groups perform their skits for the class.

**Variación léxica** Tell students that the adjective of place or nationality for Guatemala is **guatemalteco/a**. Guatemalans often use a more colloquial term, **chapín**, as a synonym for **guatemalteco/a**.

# Guatemala

connections cultures NATIONAL STANDARDS

## El país en cifras

ESTADOS UNIDOS
OCÉANO ATLÁNTICO
**GUATEMALA**
OCÉANO PACÍFICO
AMÉRICA DEL SUR

Vista de una calle céntrica la Ciudad de Guatemala

▸ **Área:** 108.890 km² (42.042 millas²), *un poco más pequeño que Tennessee*

▸ **Población:** 14.213.000

▸ **Capital:** Ciudad de Guatemala—1.103.000

▸ **Ciudades principales:** Quetzaltenango, Escuintla, Mazatenango, Puerto Barrios

SOURCE: Population Division, UN Secretariat

▸ **Moneda:** quetzal

▸ **Idiomas:** español (oficial), lenguas mayas

*El español es la lengua de un 60 por ciento° de la población; el otro 40 por ciento tiene una de las lenguas mayas (cakchiquel, quiché y kekchícomo, entre otras) como lengua materna. Una palabra que las lenguas mayas tienen en común es* ixim, *que significa maíz, un cultivo° de mucha importancia en estas culturas.*

MÉXICO

Sierra de Lacandón
Río Usumacinta
Río de la Pasión
Lago Petén Itzá

Mujeres indígenas limpiando cebollas

Sierra Madre
Lago de Atitlán
Quetzaltenango
Sierra de las Minas
Lago Izaba
Río M...

★ **Guatemala**
Antigua Guatemala

Mazatenango

Escuintla

Iglesia de la Merced en Antigua Guatemala

EL SALVADO...

Océano Pacífico

Bandera de Guatemala

### Guatemaltecos célebres

▸ **Carlos Mérida,** pintor (1891–1984)
▸ **Miguel Ángel Asturias,** escritor (1899–1974)
▸ **Margarita Carrera,** poeta y ensayista (1929– )
▸ **Rigoberta Menchú Tum,** activista (1959– ), premio Nobel de la Paz° en 1992

**recursos**
WB pp. 95–96 | VM pp. 239–240 | SUPERSITE panorama.vhlcentral.com Lección 8

por ciento *percent* cultivo *crop* Paz *Peace* telas *fabrics* tinte *dye* aplastados *crushed* hace... destiñan *keeps the colors from running*

## ¡Increíble pero cierto!

¿Qué ingrediente secreto se encuentra en las telas° tradicionales de Guatemala? ¡El mosquito! El excepcional tinte° de estas telas es producto de una combinación de flores y de mosquitos aplastados°. El insecto hace que los colores no se destiñan°. Quizás es por esto que los artesanos representan la figura del mosquito en muchas de sus telas.

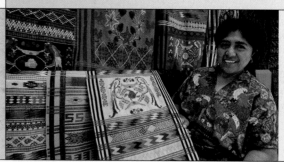

## Section Goal

In **Panorama**, students will read about the geography, history, and culture of Guatemala.

**Instructional Resources**
**Supersite/DVD:** *Panorama cultural*
**Supersite/IRCD:** *PowerPoints* (Overheads #3, #4, #35); *IRM* (*Panorama cultural* Videoscript & Translation, WBs/VM/LM Answer Key)
**WebSAM**
**Workbook,** pp. 95–96
**Video Manual,** pp. 239–240

**Teaching Tip** Have students use the map in their books or show *Overhead PowerPoint #35.* Point out that Guatemala has three main climatic regions: the tropical Pacific and Caribbean coasts, the highlands (southwest), and jungle lowlands (north). Ask volunteers to read aloud the names of the cities, mountains, and rivers of Guatemala. Point out that indigenous languages are the source of many place names.

**El país en cifras** As you read about the languages of Guatemala, you might point out that while some Guatemalans are monolingual in either Spanish or a Mayan language, many are bilingual, speaking an indigenous language and Spanish.

**¡Increíble pero cierto!** Guatemala is internationally renowned for the wealth and diversity of its textile arts. Each village has a traditional, "signature" weaving style that allows others to quickly identify where each beautiful piece comes from.

**TEACHING OPTIONS**

**Worth Noting** Although the indigenous population of Guatemala is Mayan, many place names in southwestern Guatemala are in Nahuatl, the language of the Aztecs of central Mexico. In the sixteenth century, Guatemala was conquered by Spaniards who came from the Valley of Mexico after having overthrown the Aztec rulers there. The Spanish were accompanied by large numbers of Nahuatl-speaking allies, who renamed the captured Mayan strongholds with Nahuatl names. The suffix **–tenango,** which appears in many of these names, means *place with a wall,* that is, a fortified place. **Quetzaltenango,** then, means *fortified place of the quetzal bird;* **Mazatenango** means *fortified place of the deer.*

Mar Caribe

•lfo de
•nduras

•rto
•os

**•**S
**URAS**

## Ciudades • Antigua Guatemala

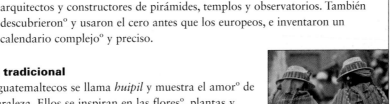

Antigua Guatemala fue fundada en 1543. Fue una capital de gran importancia hasta 1773, cuando un terremoto° la destruyó. Sin embargo, conserva el carácter original de su arquitectura y hoy es uno de los centros turísticos del país. Su celebración de la Semana Santa° es, para muchas personas, la más importante del hemisferio.

## Naturaleza • El quetzal

El quetzal simbolizó la libertad para los antiguos° mayas porque creían° que este pájaro° no podía° vivir en cautividad°. Hoy el quetzal es el símbolo nacional. El pájaro da su nombre a la moneda nacional y aparece también en los billetes° del país. Desafortunadamente, está en peligro° de extinción. Para su protección, el gobierno mantiene una reserva biológica especial.

## Historia • Los mayas

Desde 1500 a.C. hasta 900 d.C., los mayas habitaron gran parte de lo que ahora es Guatemala. Su civilización fue muy avanzada. Los mayas fueron arquitectos y constructores de pirámides, templos y observatorios. También descubrieron° y usaron el cero antes que los europeos, e inventaron un calendario complejo° y preciso.

## Artesanía • La ropa tradicional

La ropa tradicional de los guatemaltecos se llama *huipil* y muestra el amor° de la cultura maya por la naturaleza. Ellos se inspiran en las flores°, plantas y animales para crear sus diseños° de colores vivos° y formas geométricas. El diseño y los colores de cada *huipil* indican el pueblo de origen y a veces también el sexo y la edad° de la persona que lo lleva.

 **¿Qué aprendiste?** Responde a cada pregunta con una oración completa.

1. ¿Qué significa la palabra *ixim*?
   La palabra *ixim* significa maíz.
2. ¿Quién es Rigoberta Menchú?
   Rigoberta Menchú es una activista de Guatemala.
3. ¿Qué pájaro representa a Guatemala?
   El quetzal representa a Guatemala.
4. ¿Qué simbolizó el quetzal para los mayas?
   El quetzal simbolizó la libertad para los mayas.
5. ¿Cuál es la moneda nacional de Guatemala?
   La moneda nacional de Guatemala es el quetzal.
6. ¿De qué fueron arquitectos los mayas?
   Los mayas fueron arquitectos de pirámides, templos y observatorios.
7. ¿Qué celebración de la Antigua Guatemala es la más importante del hemisferio para muchas personas? La celebración de la Semana Santa de la Antigua Guatemala es la más importante del hemisferio.
8. ¿Qué descubrieron los mayas antes que los europeos? Los mayas descubrieron el cero antes que los europeos.
9. ¿Qué muestra la ropa tradicional de los guatemaltecos? La ropa muestra el amor a la naturaleza.
10. ¿Qué indica un *huipil* con su diseño y sus colores? Con su diseño y colores, un *huipil* indica el pueblo de origen, el sexo y la edad de la persona.

**Conexión Internet** Investiga estos temas en **panorama.vhlcentral.com**.

1. Busca información sobre Rigoberta Menchú. ¿De dónde es? ¿Qué libros publicó? ¿Por qué es famosa?
2. Estudia un sitio arqueológico en Guatemala para aprender más sobre los mayas, y prepara un breve informe para tu clase.

terremoto *earthquake* Semana Santa *Holy Week* antiguos *ancient* creían *they believed* pájaro *bird* no podía *couldn't* cautividad *captivity* los billetes *bills* peligro *danger* descubrieron *they discovered* complejo *complex* amor *love* flores *flowers* diseños *designs* vivos *bright* edad *age*

---

---

**Instructional Resources**
**Supersite:** Textbook & Vocabulary MP3 Audio Files
**Lección 8**
**Supersite/IRCD:** *IRM* (WBs/ VM/LM Answer Key); *Testing Program* (**Lección 8 Pruebas**, Test Generator, Testing Program MP3 Audio Files)
**WebSAM**
**Lab Manual**, p. 48

## Las comidas

| | |
|---|---|
| el/la camarero/a | *waiter/waitress* |
| la comida | *food; meal* |
| el/la dueño/a | *owner; landlord* |
| el menú | *menu* |
| la sección de (no) fumar | *(non) smoking section* |
| el almuerzo | *lunch* |
| la cena | *dinner* |
| el desayuno | *breakfast* |
| los entremeses | *hors d'oeuvres; appetizers* |
| el plato (principal) | *(main) dish* |
| delicioso/a | *delicious* |
| rico/a | *tasty; delicious* |
| sabroso/a | *tasty; delicious* |

## Las frutas

| | |
|---|---|
| la banana | *banana* |
| las frutas | *fruits* |
| el limón | *lemon* |
| la manzana | *apple* |
| el melocotón | *peach* |
| la naranja | *orange* |
| la pera | *pear* |
| la uva | *grape* |

## Las verduras

| | |
|---|---|
| las arvejas | *peas* |
| la cebolla | *onion* |
| el champiñón | *mushroom* |
| la ensalada | *salad* |
| los espárragos | *asparagus* |
| los frijoles | *beans* |
| la lechuga | *lettuce* |
| el maíz | *corn* |
| las papas/patatas (fritas) | *(fried) potatoes; French fries* |
| el tomate | *tomato* |
| las verduras | *vegetables* |
| la zanahoria | *carrot* |

## La carne y el pescado

| | |
|---|---|
| el atún | *tuna* |
| el bistec | *steak* |
| los camarones | *shrimp* |
| la carne | *meat* |
| la carne de res | *beef* |
| la chuleta (de cerdo) | *(pork) chop* |
| la hamburguesa | *hamburger* |
| el jamón | *ham* |
| la langosta | *lobster* |
| los mariscos | *shellfish* |
| el pavo | *turkey* |
| el pescado | *fish* |
| el pollo (asado) | *(roast) chicken* |
| la salchicha | *sausage* |
| el salmón | *salmon* |

## Otras comidas

| | |
|---|---|
| el aceite | *oil* |
| el ajo | *garlic* |
| el arroz | *rice* |
| el azúcar | *sugar* |
| los cereales | *cereal; grains* |
| el huevo | *egg* |
| la mantequilla | *butter* |
| la margarina | *margarine* |
| la mayonesa | *mayonnaise* |
| el pan (tostado) | *(toasted) bread* |
| la pimienta | *black pepper* |
| el queso | *cheese* |
| la sal | *salt* |
| el sándwich | *sandwich* |
| la sopa | *soup* |
| el vinagre | *vinegar* |
| el yogur | *yogurt* |

## Las bebidas

| | |
|---|---|
| el agua (mineral) | *(mineral) water* |
| la bebida | *drink* |
| el café | *coffee* |
| la cerveza | *beer* |
| el jugo (de fruta) | *(fruit) juice* |
| la leche | *milk* |
| el refresco | *soft drink* |
| el té (helado) | *(iced) tea* |
| el vino (blanco/ tinto) | *(white/red) wine* |

## Verbos

| | |
|---|---|
| escoger | *to choose* |
| merendar (e:ie) | *to snack* |
| morir (o:ue) | *to die* |
| pedir (e:i) | *to order (food)* |
| probar (o:ue) | *to taste; to try* |
| recomendar (e:ie) | *to recommend* |
| saber | *to taste; to know* |
| saber a | *to taste like* |
| servir (e:i) | *to serve* |

## Las comparaciones

| | |
|---|---|
| como | *like; as* |
| más de *(+ number)* | *more than* |
| más... que | *more ... than* |
| menos de *(+ number)* | *fewer than* |
| menos... que | *less ... than* |
| tan... como | *as ... as* |
| tantos/as... como | *as many... as* |
| tanto... como | *as much... as* |
| el/la mayor | *the eldest* |
| el/la mejor | *the best* |
| el/la menor | *the youngest* |
| el/la peor | *the worst* |
| mejor | *better* |
| peor | *worse* |

| | |
|---|---|
| **Expresiones útiles** | *See page 249.* |

**recursos**

LM
p. 48

panorama.vhlcentral.com
Lección 8

# Las fiestas

## 9

**Communicative Goals**

*You will learn how to:*
- Express congratulations
- Express gratitude
- Ask for and pay the bill at a restaurant

## Lesson Goals

In **Lección 9**, students will be introduced to the following:
- terms for parties and celebrations
- words for stages of life and interpersonal relations
- **Semana Santa** celebrations
- Chile's **Festival de Viña del Mar**
- irregular preterites
- verbs that change meaning in the preterite
- uses of ¿qué? and ¿cuál?
- pronouns after prepositions
- recognizing word families
- using a Venn diagram to organize information
- writing a comparative analysis
- using context to infer the meaning of unfamiliar words
- a television commercial for **Energizer**
- Chilean singer **Myriam Hernández**
- cultural, geographic, and economic information about Chile

**A primera vista** Here are some additional questions you can ask based on the photo: **¿Fuiste a una fiesta importante el año pasado? ¿Cuál fue la ocasión? ¿Sirvieron comida en la fiesta? ¿Qué sirvieron? En tu opinión, ¿qué fiestas son las más divertidas? ¿Por qué?**

### A PRIMERA VISTA
- ¿Se conocen ellas?
- ¿Cómo se sienten, alegres o tristes?
- ¿Está una de las chicas más contenta que la otra?
- ¿De qué color es su ropa, marrón o negra?

**INSTRUCTIONAL RESOURCES**

**MAESTRO™ SUPERSITE (panorama.vhlcentral.com)**
Textbook, Vocabulary, & Lab MP3 Audio Files
Additional Practice
Learning Management System (Assignment Task Manager, Gradebook)
*Also on DVD*
  *Fotonovela*

*Flash cultura*
**Panorama cultural**
*Also on Instructor's Resource CD-ROM*
*PowerPoints* (**Contextos** & **Estructura** Presentations, Overheads)
*Instructor's Resource Manual* (Handouts, Textbook Answer Key, WBs/VM/LM Answer Key,

Audioscripts, Videoscripts & Translations)
*Testing Program* (**Pruebas,** Test Generator, MP3s)
**Vista Higher Learning** *Cancionero*
**WebSAM** (Workbook/Video Manual/Lab Manual)
**Workbook/Video Manual**
*Cuaderno para hispanohablantes*
**Lab Manual**

# Las fiestas

## Más vocabulario

| | |
|---|---|
| la alegría | *happiness* |
| la amistad | *friendship* |
| el amor | *love* |
| el beso | *kiss* |
| la sorpresa | *surprise* |
| el aniversario (de bodas) | *(wedding) anniversary* |
| la boda | *wedding* |
| el cumpleaños | *birthday* |
| el día de fiesta | *holiday* |
| el divorcio | *divorce* |
| el matrimonio | *marriage* |
| la Navidad | *Christmas* |
| el/la recién casado/a | *newlywed* |
| la quinceañera | *young woman's fifteenth birthday celebration* |
| cambiar (de) | *to change* |
| celebrar | *to celebrate* |
| divertirse (e:ie) | *to have fun* |
| graduarse (de/en) | *to graduate (from/in)* |
| invitar | *to invite* |
| jubilarse | *to retire (from work)* |
| nacer | *to be born* |
| odiar | *to hate* |
| pasarlo bien/mal | *to have a good/bad time* |
| reírse (e:i) | *to laugh* |
| relajarse | *to relax* |
| sorprender | *to surprise* |
| sonreír (e:i) | *to smile* |
| juntos/as | *together* |

## Variación léxica

pastel ⟷ torta (*Arg., Venez.*)
comprometerse ⟷ prometerse (*Esp.*)

**recursos**

| WB pp. 97–98 | LM p. 49 | SUPERSITE panorama.vhlcentral.com Lección 9 |
|---|---|---|

la pareja
el pastel de chocolate
la botella de vino
el flan de caramelo
las galletas
los postres
el champán
los dulces

# Práctica

**brindar**

**el invitado**

**el helado**

### Relaciones personales

| | |
|---|---|
| **casarse (con)** | to get married (to) |
| **comprometerse (con)** | to get engaged (to) |
| **divorciarse (de)** | to get divorced (from) |
| **enamorarse (de)** | to fall in love (with) |
| **llevarse bien/mal (con)** | to get along well/badly (with) |
| **romper (con)** | to break up (with) |
| **salir (con)** | to go out (with); to date |
| **separarse (de)** | to separate (from) |
| **tener una cita** | to have a date; to have an appointment |

---

**1** **Escuchar** Escucha la conversación e indica si las oraciones son **ciertas** o **falsas**.

1. A Silvia no le gusta mucho el chocolate. Falsa.
2. Silvia sabe que sus amigos le van a hacer una fiesta. Falsa.
3. Los amigos de Silvia le compraron un pastel de chocolate. Cierta.
4. Los amigos brindan por Silvia con refrescos. Falsa.
5. Silvia y sus amigos van a comer helado. Cierta.
6. Los amigos de Silvia le van a servir flan y galletas. Falsa.

---

**2** **Ordenar** Escucha la narración y ordena las oraciones de acuerdo con los eventos de la vida de Beatriz.

___5___ a. Beatriz se compromete con Roberto.

___4___ b. Beatriz se gradúa.

___3___ c. Beatriz sale con Emilio.

___2___ d. Sus padres le hacen una gran fiesta.

___6___ e. La pareja se casa.

___1___ f. Beatriz nace en Montevideo.

---

**3** **Emparejar** Indica la letra de la frase que mejor completa cada oración.

| | | |
|---|---|---|
| a. cambió de | d. nos divertimos | g. se llevan bien |
| b. lo pasaron mal | e. se casaron | h. sonrió |
| c. nació | f. se jubiló | i. tenemos una cita |

1. María y sus compañeras de cuarto __g__. Son buenas amigas.
2. Pablo y yo __d__ en la fiesta. Bailamos y comimos mucho.
3. Manuel y Felipe __b__ en el cine. La película fue muy mala.
4. ¡Tengo una nueva sobrina! Ella __c__ ayer por la mañana.
5. Mi madre __a__ profesión. Ahora es artista.
6. Mi padre __f__ el año pasado. Ahora no trabaja.
7. Jorge y yo __i__ esta noche. Vamos a ir a un restaurante muy elegante.
8. Jaime y Laura __e__ el septiembre pasado. La boda fue maravillosa.

---

**4** **Definiciones** En parejas, definan las palabras y escriban una oración para cada ejemplo. Answers will vary. Suggested answers below.

**modelo**

**romper (con)** una pareja termina la relación
*Marta rompió con su novio.*

1. regalar dar un regalo
2. helado una comida fría y dulce
3. pareja dos personas enamoradas
4. invitado una persona que va a una fiesta
5. casarse ellos deciden estar juntos para siempre
6. pasarlo bien divertirse
7. sorpresa la persona no sabe lo que va a pasar
8. quinceañera la fiesta de cumpleaños de una chica de 15 años

---

---

**1** **Teaching Tip** Have students check their answers by going over **Actividad 1** with the class.

**1** **Script** E1: ¿Estamos listos, amigos? E2: Creo que sí. Aquí tenemos el pastel y el helado… E3: De chocolate, espero. Ustedes saben cómo le encanta a Silvia el chocolate… E2: Por supuesto, el chocolate para Silvia. Bueno, un pastel de chocolate, el helado… *Script continues on page 278.*

**2** **Teaching Tip** Before listening, point out that although the items are in the present tense, students will hear a mix of present indicative and preterite in the audio.

**2** **Script** Beatriz García nace en Montevideo, Uruguay. Siempre celebra su cumpleaños con pastel y helado. Para su cumpleaños número veinte, sus padres la sorprendieron y le organizaron una gran fiesta. Beatriz se divirtió muchísimo y conoció a Emilio, un chico muy simpático. Después de varias citas, Beatriz rompió con Emilio porque no fueron compatibles. Luego de dos años Beatriz conoció a Roberto en su fiesta de graduación y se enamoraron. En Navidad se comprometieron y celebraron su matrimonio un año más tarde al que asistieron más de cien invitados. Los recién casados son muy felices juntos y ya están planeando otra gran fiesta para celebrar su primer aniversario de bodas. *Textbook MP3s*

**3** **Expansion** Have students write three cloze sentences based on the drawing on pages 276–277 for a partner to complete.

**4** **Expansion** Ask students questions using verbs from the **Relaciones personales** box. Ex: **¿Con quién te llevas mal?**

# Las etapas de la vida de Sergio

el nacimiento

la niñez

la adolescencia

la juventud

la madurez

la vejez

| Más vocabulario | |
|---|---|
| la edad | age |
| el estado civil | marital status |
| las etapas de la vida | the stages of life |
| la muerte | death |
| casado/a | married |
| divorciado/a | divorced |
| separado/a | separated |
| soltero/a | single |
| viudo/a | widower/widow |

**SUPERSITE**

**5** **Las etapas de la vida** Identifica las etapas de la vida que se describen en estas oraciones.

1. Mi abuela se jubiló y se mudó (*moved*) a Viña del Mar.  la vejez
2. Mi padre trabaja para una compañía grande en Santiago.  la madurez
3. ¿Viste a mi nuevo sobrino en el hospital? Es precioso y ¡tan pequeño!  el nacimiento
4. Mi abuelo murió este año.  la muerte
5. Mi hermana se enamoró de un chico nuevo en la escuela.  la adolescencia
6. Mi hermana pequeña juega con muñecas (*dolls*).  la niñez

**6** **Cambiar** Tu hermano/a menor no entiende nada de las etapas de la vida. En parejas, túrnense para decir que las afirmaciones son falsas y corríjanlas (*correct them*) cambiando las expresiones subrayadas (*underlined*).

**modelo**
**Estudiante 1:** La *niñez* es cuando trabajamos mucho.
**Estudiante 2:** No, te equivocas (*you're wrong*). La madurez es cuando trabajamos mucho.

1. El nacimiento es el fin de la vida.  La muerte
2. La juventud es la etapa cuando nos jubilamos.  La vejez
3. A los sesenta y cinco años, muchas personas comienzan a trabajar.  se jubilan
4. Julián y nuestra prima se divorcian mañana.  se casan
5. Mamá odia a su hermana.  quiere / se lleva bien con
6. El abuelo murió, por eso la abuela es separada.  viuda
7. Cuando te gradúas de la universidad, estás en la etapa de la adolescencia.  la juventud
8. Mi tío nunca se casó; es viudo.  soltero

**NOTA CULTURAL**

**Viña del Mar** es una ciudad en la costa de Chile, situada al oeste de Santiago. Tiene playas hermosas, excelentes hoteles, casinos y buenos restaurantes. El poeta Pablo Neruda pasó muchos años allí.

**AYUDA**

Other ways to contradict someone:
**No es verdad.**
*It's not true.*
**Creo que no.**
*I don't think so.*
**¡Claro que no!**
*Of course not!*
**¡Qué va!**
*No way!*

# Comunicación

**7** **Una fiesta** Trabaja con dos compañeros/as para planear una fiesta. Recuerda incluir la siguiente información. Answers will vary.

1. ¿Qué tipo de fiesta es? ¿Dónde va a ser? ¿Cuándo va a ser?
2. ¿A quiénes van a invitar?
3. ¿Qué van a comer? ¿Quiénes van a llevar o a preparar la comida?
4. ¿Qué van a beber? ¿Quiénes van a llevar las bebidas?
5. ¿Qué van a hacer todos durante la fiesta?

**8** **Encuesta** Tu profesor(a) va a darte una hoja de actividades. Haz las preguntas de la hoja a dos o tres compañeros/as de clase para saber qué actitudes tienen en sus relaciones personales. Luego comparte los resultados de la encuesta con la clase y comenta tus conclusiones.

Answers will vary.

| Preguntas | Nombres | Actitudes |
|---|---|---|
| 1. ¿Te importa la amistad? ¿Por qué? | | |
| 2. ¿Es mejor tener un(a) buen(a) amigo/a o muchos/as amigos/as? | | |
| 3. ¿Cuáles son las características que buscas en tus amigos/as? | | |
| 4. ¿Tienes novio/a? ¿A qué edad es posible enamorarse? | | |
| 5. ¿Deben las parejas hacer todo juntos? ¿Deben tener las mismas opiniones? ¿Por qué? | | |

**¡LENGUA VIVA!**

While a **buen(a) amigo/a** is a *good friend*, the term **amigo/a íntimo/a** refers to a *close friend*, or a very good friend, without any romantic overtones.

**9** **Minidrama** En parejas, consulten la ilustración en la página 278, y luego, usando las palabras de la lista, preparen un minidrama para representar las etapas de la vida de Sergio. Pueden ser creativos e inventar más información sobre su vida. Answers will vary.

| | | | |
|---|---|---|---|
| amor | celebrar | enamorarse | romper |
| boda | comprometerse | graduarse | salir |
| cambiar | cumpleaños | jubilarse | separarse |
| casarse | divorciarse | nacer | tener una cita |

---

**7** **Teaching Tip** To simplify, create a six-column chart on the board, with the headings **Lugar, Fecha y hora, Invitados, Comida, Bebidas,** and **Actividades.** Have groups brainstorm a few items for each category.

**7** **Expansion**
• Ask volunteer groups to talk to the class about the party they have just planned.
• Have students make invitations for their party. Ask the class to judge which invitation is the cleverest, funniest, most elegant, and so forth.

**8** **Teaching Tip** Distribute the *Hojas de actividades* (Supersite/IRCD). Give students eight minutes to ask other group members the questions.

**8** **Expansion** Take a survey of the attitudes found in the entire class. Ex: ¿**Quiénes creen que es más importante tener un buen amigo que muchos amigos? ¿Quiénes creen que es más importante tener muchos amigos que un buen amigo?**

**9** **Teaching Tip** To simplify, read through the word list as a class and have students name the stage(s) of life that correspond to each word.

**9** **Expansion** After all skits have been presented, have the class vote on the most original, funniest, truest to life, and so forth.

---

**TEACHING OPTIONS**

**Extra Practice** Add a visual aspect to this vocabulary practice. Using magazine pictures, display images that pertain to parties or celebrations, stages of life, or interpersonal relations. Have students describe the pictures and make guesses about who the people are, how they are feeling, and so forth.

**Extra Practice** Add an auditory aspect to this vocabulary practice. As a listening comprehension activity, prepare short descriptions of five easily recognizable people. Use as much active lesson vocabulary as possible. Write their names on the board in random order. Then read the descriptions aloud and have students match each one to the appropriate name. Ex: **Me casé tres veces. Me divorcié dos veces y ahora estoy casada con otro cantante latino. No sólo canto, pero soy también actriz y tengo mi propia marca de perfume. (Jennifer López)**

## Section Goals

In **Fotonovela**, students will:
- receive comprehensible input from free-flowing discourse
- learn functional phrases that preview lesson grammatical structures

**Instructional Resources**
**Supersite/DVD:** *Fotonovela*
**Supersite/IRCD:** *IRM*
(*Fotonovela* Videoscript & Translation, WBs/VM/LM Answer Key)
**WebSAM**
**Video Manual,** pp. 211–212

**Video Recap: Lección 8**
Before doing this **Fotonovela** section, review the previous one with this activity.
1. ¿Quién es doña Rita Perales? (la dueña del restaurante El Cráter) 2. ¿Qué platos sirven en El Cráter? (tortillas de maíz, caldo de patas, lomo a la plancha, ceviche, fuente de fritada, pasteles) 3. ¿Qué opinión tienen los estudiantes de la comida? (Es riquísima.) 4. ¿Cuál es la ocasión especial ese día? (el cumpleaños de Maite)

**Video Synopsis** While the travelers are looking at the dessert menu, **Doña Rita** and the waiter bring in some flan, a cake, and some wine to celebrate **Maite's** birthday. The group leaves **Doña Rita** a nice tip, thanks her, and says goodbye.

**Teaching Tip** Have students read the first line of dialogue in each caption and guess what happens in this episode.

# ¡Feliz cumpleaños, Maite!

Don Francisco y los estudiantes celebran el cumpleaños de Maite en el restaurante El Cráter.

**PERSONAJES**

**MAITE**

**INÉS**

**DON FRANCISCO**

**ÁLEX**

**JAVIER**

**DOÑA RITA**

**CAMARERO**

**INÉS** A mí me encantan los dulces. Maite, ¿tú qué vas a pedir?

**MAITE** Ay, no sé. Todo parece tan delicioso. Quizás el pastel de chocolate.

**JAVIER** Para mí el pastel de chocolate con helado. Me encanta el chocolate. Y tú, Álex, ¿qué vas a pedir?

**ÁLEX** Generalmente prefiero la fruta, pero hoy creo que voy a probar el pastel de chocolate.

**DON FRANCISCO** Yo siempre tomo un flan y un café.

**DOÑA RITA** ¡Feliz cumpleaños, Maite!

**INÉS** ¿Hoy es tu cumpleaños, Maite?

**MAITE** Sí, el 22 de junio. Y parece que vamos a celebrarlo.

**TODOS MENOS MAITE** ¡Felicidades!

**ÁLEX** Yo también acabo de cumplir los veintitrés años.

**MAITE** ¿Cuándo?

**ÁLEX** El cuatro de mayo.

**DOÑA RITA** Aquí tienen un flan, pastel de chocolate con helado… y una botella de vino para dar alegría.

**MAITE** ¡Qué sorpresa! ¡No sé qué decir! Muchísimas gracias.

**DON FRANCISCO** El conductor no puede tomar vino. Doña Rita, gracias por todo. ¿Puede traernos la cuenta?

**DOÑA RITA** Enseguida, Paco.

**recursos**

VM
pp. 211–212

panorama.vhlcentral.com
Lección 9

---

**TEACHING OPTIONS**

**Video Tips** General suggestions for using video clips in the classroom can be found on page IAE-12 of this Instructor's Annotated Edition.
**¡Feliz cumpleaños, Maite!** Ask students to brainstorm a list of things that might happen during a surprise birthday party. Then play the **¡Feliz cumpleaños, Maite!** episode once, asking

students to take notes about what they see and hear. After viewing, have students use their notes to tell you what happened in this episode. Then play the segment again to allow students to refine their notes. Repeat the discussion process and guide the class to an accurate summary of the plot.

**MAITE** ¡Gracias! Pero, ¿quién le dijo que es mi cumpleaños?

**DOÑA RITA** Lo supe por don Francisco.

**ÁLEX** Ayer te lo pregunté, ¡y no quisiste decírmelo! ¿Eh? ¡Qué mala eres!

**JAVIER** ¿Cuántos años cumples?

**MAITE** Veintitrés.

**INÉS** Creo que debemos dejar una buena propina. ¿Qué les parece?

**MAITE** Sí, vamos a darle una buena propina a la señora Perales. Es simpatiquísima.

**DON FRANCISCO** Gracias una vez más. Siempre lo paso muy bien aquí.

**MAITE** Muchísimas gracias, señora Perales. Por la comida, por la sorpresa y por ser tan amable con nosotros.

## Expresiones útiles

### Celebrating a birthday party

- **¡Feliz cumpleaños!**
  *Happy birthday!*
- **¡Felicidades!/¡Felicitaciones!**
  *Congratulations!*

- **¿Quién le dijo que es mi cumpleaños?**
  *Who told you* (form.) *that it's my birthday?*
  **Lo supe por don Francisco.**
  *I found out through Don Francisco.*

- **¿Cuántos años cumples/ cumple Ud.?**
  *How old are you now?*
  **Veintitrés.**
  *Twenty-three.*

### Asking for and getting the bill

- **¿Puede traernos la cuenta?**
  *Can you bring us the bill?*
- **La cuenta, por favor.**
  *The bill, please.*
  **Enseguida, señor/señora/señorita.**
  *Right away, sir/ma'am/miss.*

### Expressing gratitude

- **¡(Muchas) gracias!**
  *Thank you (very much)!*
- **Muchísimas gracias.**
  *Thank you very, very much.*
- **Gracias por todo.**
  *Thanks for everything.*
- **Gracias una vez más.**
  *Thanks again. (lit. Thanks one more time.)*

### Leaving a tip

- **Creo que debemos dejar una buena propina. ¿Qué les parece?**
  *I think we should leave a good tip. What do you guys think?*
  **Sí, vamos a darle/dejarle una buena propina.**
  *Yes, let's give her/leave her a good tip.*

## ¿Qué pasó?

**1**

**Completar** Completa las oraciones con la información correcta, según la **Fotonovela**.

1. De postre, don Francisco siempre pide _un café y un flan_.
2. A Javier le encanta _el chocolate_.
3. Álex cumplió los _veintitrés_ años _el cuatro de mayo_.
4. Hoy Álex quiere tomar algo diferente. De postre, quiere pedir _un pastel de chocolate_.
5. Los estudiantes le van a dejar _una buena propina_ a doña Rita.

**2**

**Identificar** Identifica quién puede decir estas oraciones.

1. Gracias, doña Rita, pero no puedo tomar vino. _don Francisco_
2. ¡Qué simpática es doña Rita! Fue tan amable conmigo. _Maite_
3. A mí me encantan los dulces y los pasteles, ¡especialmente si son de chocolate! _Javier_
4. Mi amigo acaba de informarme que hoy es el cumpleaños de Maite. _doña Rita_
5. ¿Tienen algún postre de fruta? Los postres de fruta son los mejores. _Álex_
6. Me parece una buena idea dejarle una buena propina a la dueña. ¿Qué piensan ustedes? _Inés_

JAVIER    ÁLEX

INÉS    MAITE

DON FRANCISCO    DOÑA RITA

**3**

**Seleccionar** Selecciona algunas de las opciones de la lista para completar las oraciones.

| | | | |
|---|---|---|---|
| el amor | la cuenta | la galleta | la quinceañera |
| una botella de champán | día de fiesta | pedir | ¡Qué sorpresa! |
| celebrar | el divorcio | un postre | una sorpresa |

1. Maite no sabe que van a celebrar su cumpleaños porque es _una sorpresa_.
2. Cuando una pareja celebra su aniversario y quiere tomar algo especial, compra _una botella de champán_.
3. Después de una cena o un almuerzo, es normal pedir _un postre/la cuenta_.
4. Inés y Maite no saben exactamente lo que van a _pedir_ de postre.
5. Después de comer en un restaurante, tienes que pagar _la cuenta_.
6. Una pareja de enamorados nunca piensa en _el divorcio_.
7. Hoy no trabajamos porque es un _día de fiesta_.

**4**

**Un cumpleaños** Trabajen en grupos para representar una conversación en la que uno/a de ustedes está celebrando su cumpleaños en un restaurante.

- Una persona le desea feliz cumpleaños a su compañero/a y le pregunta cuántos años cumple.
- Cada persona del grupo le pide al/a la camarero/a un postre y algo de beber.
- Después de terminar los postres, una persona pide la cuenta.
- Otra persona habla de dejar una propina.
- Los amigos que no cumplen años dicen que quieren pagar la cuenta.
- El/La que cumple años les da las gracias por todo.

---

**NOTA CULTURAL**

En los países hispanos los camareros no dependen tanto de **las propinas** como en los EE.UU. Por eso, en estos países no es común dejar propina, pero siempre es buena idea dejar una buena propina cuando el grupo es grande o el servicio es excepcional.

**CONSULTA**

En algunos países hispanos, el cumpleaños número quince de una chica se celebra haciendo una **quinceañera**. Ésta es una fiesta en su honor y en la que es "presentada" a la sociedad. Para conocer más sobre este tema, ve a **Lectura**, p. 299.

---

**1 Expansion** Have students work in pairs or small groups and write questions that would have elicited these statements.

**2 Teaching Tip** Before doing this activity, ask these questions: **¿A quién le gusta mucho la fruta? (a Álex) ¿A quién le gusta muchísimo el chocolate? (a Javier) ¿Quién no puede tomar vino? (don Francisco)**

**2 Expansion** Give these sentences to students as items 7–8: **7. ¡No me lo puedo creer! ¿Pastel de chocolate y flan para mí? (Maite) 8. ¿Mi cumpleaños? Es el cuatro de mayo. (Álex)**

**3 Teaching Tip** Before doing this activity, have the class review the vocabulary on pages 276–277.

**3 Expansion** Have pairs create additional sentences with the leftover items from the word bank.

**4 Possible Conversation**
E1: ¡Feliz cumpleaños! ¿Cuántos años cumples hoy?
E2: ¡Muchas gracias! Cumplo diecinueve.
E3: Buenas noches. ¿En qué les puedo servir?
E1: Quisiera el pastel de chocolate y un café, por favor.
E2: Voy a pedir un pastel de chocolate con helado, y de tomar, un café.
[LATER...]
E1: Señorita, ¿puede traernos la cuenta?
E3: Enseguida, señor.
E2: La camarera fue muy amable. Debemos dejarle una buena propina, ¿no crees?
E1: Sí. Y yo quiero pagar la cuenta, porque es tu cumpleaños.
E2: Gracias por todo...

---

**TEACHING OPTIONS**

**Extra Practice** Ask a group of volunteers to ad-lib the **Fotonovela** episode for the class. Assure them that it is not necessary to memorize the episode or stick strictly to its content. They should try to get the general meaning across with the vocabulary and expressions they know, and they should also feel free to be creative.

**Pairs** Have students tell each other about their last birthday celebration, using new vocabulary from **Fotonovela** and **Contextos**.

# Pronunciación

## The letters h, j, and g

| helado | hombre | hola | hermosa |
|---|---|---|---|

The Spanish **h** is always silent.

| José | jubilarse | dejar | pareja |
|---|---|---|---|

The letter **j** is pronounced much like the English *h* in *his*.

| agencia | general | Gil | Gisela |
|---|---|---|---|

The letter **g** can be pronounced three different ways. Before **e** or **i**, the letter **g** is pronounced much like the English *h*.

### Gustavo, gracias por llamar el domingo.

At the beginning of a phrase or after the letter **n**, the Spanish **g** is pronounced like the English *g* in *girl*.

### Me gradué en agosto.

In any other position, the Spanish **g** has a somewhat softer sound.

| Guerra | conseguir | guantes | agua |
|---|---|---|---|

In the combinations **gue** and **gui**, the **g** has a hard sound and the **u** is silent. In the combination **gua**, the **g** has a hard sound and the **u** is pronounced like the English *w*.

**Práctica** Lee las palabras en voz alta, prestando atención a la **h**, la **j** y la **g**.

1. hamburguesa
2. jugar
3. oreja
4. guapa
5. geografía
6. magnífico
7. espejo
8. hago
9. seguir
10. gracias
11. hijo
12. galleta
13. Jorge
14. tengo
15. ahora
16. guantes

**Oraciones** Lee las oraciones en voz alta, prestando atención a la **h**, la **j** y la **g**.

1. Hola. Me llamo Gustavo Hinojosa Lugones y vivo en Santiago de Chile.
2. Tengo una familia grande; somos tres hermanos y tres hermanas.
3. Voy a graduarme en mayo.
4. Para celebrar mi graduación mis padres van a regalarme un viaje a Egipto.
5. ¡Qué generosos son!

**Refranes** Lee los refranes en voz alta, prestando atención a la **h**, la **j** y la **g**.

A la larga, lo más dulce amarga.[1]

El hábito no hace al monje.[2]

1 Too much of a good thing.
2 The clothes don't make the man.

**recursos**

LM
p. 50

SUPERSITE
panorama.vhlcentral.com
Lección 9

---

**Section Goal**

In **Pronunciación**, students will be introduced to the pronunciation of **h**, **j**, and **g**.

**Instructional Resources**
**Supersite:** Textbook & Lab MP3 Audio Files **Lección 9**
**Supersite/IRCD:** *IRM* (Textbook Audio Script, Lab Audio Script, WB/VM/LM Answer Key)
**WebSAM**
**Lab Manual**, p. 50
***Cuaderno para hispanohablantes***

**Teaching Tips**
- Ask the class how the Spanish **h** is pronounced. Ask volunteers to pronounce the example words. Contrast the pronunciations of the English *hotel* and the Spanish **hotel**.
- Explain that **j** is pronounced much like the English *h*.
- Draw attention to the fact that the letter **g** is pronounced like the English *h* before **e** or **i**. Write the example words on the board and ask volunteers to pronounce them.
- Point out that the letter **g** is pronounced like the English *g* in *good* at the beginning of a phrase or after the letter **n**.
- Explain that in any other position, particularly between vowels, **g** has a softer sound.
- Tell the class that in the combinations **gue** and **gui**, **g** has a hard sound and **u** is not pronounced. Explain that in the combinations **gua** and **guo**, the **u** sounds like the English *w*.

**Práctica/Oraciones/Refranes**
These exercises are recorded in the *Textbook MP3s*. You may want to play the audio so that students practice the pronunciation point by listening to Spanish spoken by speakers other than yourself.

---

**TEACHING OPTIONS**

**Extra Practice** Write the names of these Chilean cities on the board and ask for a volunteer to pronounce each one: **Santiago, Antofagasta, Rancagua, Coihaique.** Repeat the process with the names of these Chilean writers: **Alberto Blest Gana, Vicente Huidobro, Gabriela Mistral, Juan Modesto Castro.**
**Pairs** Have students work in pairs to read aloud the sentences in **Actividad 2, Identificar**, page 282. Encourage students to help their partners if they have trouble pronouncing a particular word.
**Heritage Speakers** Provide heritage speakers with several words and phrases containing the letter **g** and ask them to read them aloud. Have the class underline the words with a hard **g** sound, circle the words with a softer **g** sound, and put an X on words with the English *h* sound.

**EN DETALLE**

# Semana Santa:
# vacaciones y tradición

**¿Te imaginas pasar veinticuatro horas tocando un tambor°** entre miles de personas? Así es como mucha gente celebra el Viernes Santo° en el pequeño pueblo de **Calanda**, España. De todas las celebraciones hispanas, la **Semana Santa°** es una de las más espectaculares y únicas.

**Procesión en Sevilla, España**

Semana Santa es la semana antes de Pascua°, una celebración religiosa que conmemora la Pasión de Jesucristo. Generalmente, la gente tiene unos días de vacaciones en esta semana. Algunas personas aprovechan° estos días para viajar, pero otras prefieren participar en las tradicionales celebraciones religiosas en las calles. En **Antigua**, Guatemala, hacen alfombras° de flores° y altares; también organizan Vía Crucis° y danzas. En las famosas procesiones y desfiles° religiosos de **Sevilla**, España, los fieles°

sacan a las calles imágenes religiosas. Las imágenes van encima de plataformas ricamente decoradas con abundantes flores y velas°. En la procesión, los penitentes llevan túnicas y unos sombreros cónicos que les cubren° la cara°. En sus manos llevan faroles° o velas encendidas.

Si visitas algún país hispano durante la Semana Santa, debes asistir a un desfile. Las playas pueden esperar hasta la semana siguiente.

**Alfombra de flores en Antigua, Guatemala**

---

### Otras celebraciones famosas

**Ayacucho, Perú:** Además de alfombras de flores y procesiones, aquí hay una antigua tradición llamada "quema de la chamiza"°.

**Iztapalapa, Ciudad de México:** Es famoso el Vía Crucis del cerro° de la Estrella. Es una representación del recorrido° de Jesucristo con la cruz°.

**Popayán, Colombia:** En las procesiones "chiquitas" los niños llevan imágenes que son copias pequeñas de las que llevan los mayores.

---

tocando un tambor *playing a drum* Viernes Santo *Good Friday* Semana Santa *Holy Week* Pascua *Easter Sunday* aprovechan *take advantage of* alfombras *carpets* flores *flowers* Vía Crucis *Stations of the Cross* desfiles *parades* fieles *faithful* velas *candles* cubren *cover* cara *face* faroles *lamps* quema de la chamiza *burning of brushwood* cerro *hill* recorrido *route* cruz *cross*

---

**ACTIVIDADES**

**1**  **¿Cierto o falso?** Indica si lo que dicen estas oraciones es **cierto** o **falso**. Corrige la información falsa.

1. La Semana Santa se celebra después de Pascua. Falso. La Semana Santa es la semana antes de Pascua.
2. En los países hispanos, las personas tienen días libres durante la Semana Santa. Cierto.
3. En los países hispanos, todas las personas asisten a las celebraciones religiosas. Falso. Algunas personas aprovechan estos días para viajar.

4. En los países hispanos, las celebraciones se hacen en las calles. Cierto.
5. El Vía Crucis de Iztapalapa es en el interior de una iglesia. Falso. Es en el cerro de la Estrella.
6. En Antigua y en Ayacucho es típico hacer alfombras de flores en Semana Santa. Cierto.
7. Las procesiones "chiquitas" son famosas en Sevilla, España. Falso. Son famosas en Popayán, Colombia.
8. En Sevilla, sacan imágenes religiosas a las calles. Cierto.

---

## ASÍ SE DICE

### Fiestas y celebraciones

| | |
|---|---|
| la despedida de soltero/a | *bachelor(ette) party* |
| el día feriado/festivo | el día de fiesta |
| disfrutar | *to enjoy* |
| festejar | celebrar |
| los fuegos artificiales | *fireworks* |
| pasarlo en grande | divertirse mucho |
| la vela | *candle* |

## EL MUNDO HISPANO

### Celebraciones latinoamericanas

○ **Oruro, Bolivia** Durante el carnaval de Oruro se realiza la famosa Diablada, una antigua danza° que muestra la lucha° entre el bien y el mal: ángeles contra° demonios.

○ **Panchimalco, El Salvador** La primera semana de mayo, Panchimalco se cubre de flores y de color. También hacen el Desfile de las palmas° y bailan danzas antiguas.

○ **Quito, Ecuador** El mes de agosto es el Mes de las Artes. Danza, teatro, música, cine, artesanías° y otros eventos culturales inundan la ciudad.

○ **San Pedro Sula, Honduras** En junio se celebra la Feria Juniana. Hay comida típica, bailes, desfiles, conciertos, rodeos, exposiciones ganaderas° y eventos deportivos y culturales.

danza *dance* lucha *fight* contra *versus* palmas *palm leaves* artesanías *handcrafts* exposiciones ganaderas *cattle shows*

## PERFIL

# Festival de Viña del Mar

En 1959 unos estudiantes de **Viña del Mar**, Chile, celebraron una fiesta en una casa de campo conocida como la Quinta Vergara donde hubo° un espectáculo° musical. En 1960 repitieron el evento. Asistió tanta gente que muchos vieron el espectáculo parados° o sentados en el suelo°. Algunos se subieron a los árboles°.

Años después, se convirtió en el **Festival Internacional de la Canción**. Este evento se celebra en febrero, en el mismo lugar donde empezó. ¡Pero ahora nadie necesita subirse a un árbol para verlo! Hay un anfiteatro con capacidad para quince mil personas.

En el festival hay concursos° musicales y conciertos de artistas famosos como Daddy Yankee y Paulina Rubio.

**Daddy Yankee**

hubo *there was* espectáculo *show* parados *standing* suelo *floor* se subieron a los árboles *climbed trees* concursos *competitions*

**SUPERSITE** **Conexión Internet**

¿Qué celebraciones hispanas hay en los Estados Unidos y Canadá?

Go to panorama.vhlcentral.com to find more cultural information related to this **Cultura** section.

## ACTIVIDADES

**2** **Comprensión** Responde a las preguntas.

1. ¿Cuántas personas pueden asistir al Festival de Viña del Mar hoy día? quince mil
2. ¿Qué es la Diablada? Es una antigua danza que muestra la lucha entre el bien y el mal.
3. ¿Qué celebran en Quito en agosto? Celebran el Mes de las Artes.
4. Nombra dos atracciones en la Feria Juniana de San Pedro Sula. Answers will vary.
5. ¿Qué es la Quinta Vergara? una casa de campo donde empezó el Festival de Viña del Mar

**3** **¿Cuál es tu celebración favorita?** Escribe un pequeño párrafo sobre la celebración que más te gusta de tu comunidad. Explica cómo se llama, cuándo ocurre y cómo es. Answers will vary.

**recursos**

**SUPERSITE**

panorama.vhlcentral.com
Lección 9

---

## TEACHING OPTIONS

**Pairs** Have students work in pairs to research and plan a trip to a festival mentioned in the reading. Students should explain why they want to visit that particular festival, how they will get there, and present a one-day itinerary to the class.

**TPR** Divide the class into five groups: **Viña del Mar, Oruro, Panchimalco, Quito,** and **San Pedro Sula.** Call out a series of statements about the festivals without mentioning the city in which they take place. Have groups stand up when the festival refers to their city. Ex: **Su festival tiene lugar la primera semana de mayo.** (Group **Panchimalco** stands.)

---

**Así se dice**
- Explain that it is common in the Spanish-speaking world to **hacer puente** (have a four-day weekend, literally *to make a bridge*) if a **día festivo** falls on a Thursday or Tuesday.
- To challenge students, add these celebration-related words to the list: **la carroza** (*float*); **el desfile** (*parade*); **la feria** (*fair*); **pasarlo bomba** (**Esp.**) (*to have fun*).

**Perfil** **Viña del Mar,** commonly called **Viña** or **La Ciudad Jardín,** is a thriving coastal city in central Chile and, apart from the **Festival Internacional de la Canción,** it is best known for its beaches. During the six days of the **Festival,** lesser-known artists participate in musical competitions, with winners receiving the coveted statuette **La Gaviota de Plata.** International superstars of all musical genres also make special appearances.

**El mundo hispano** Ask students to compare the festivals. Ex: **¿Qué festival les parece el más interesante? ¿Creen que el carnaval de Oruro es tan divertido como el desfile de Panchimalco? ¿Por qué?**

**2** **Expansion** Give students these questions as items 6–7: **6. ¿Qué fiesta puede celebrar una mujer antes de casarse? (la despedida de soltera) 7. ¿Cuándo es el festival de Panchimalco? (la primera semana de mayo)**

**3** **Expansion** Have students exchange papers with a classmate for peer editing. When finished, have a few volunteers read their paragraphs aloud for the class.

## 9.1 Irregular preterites ⦿SUPERSITE

**ANTE TODO** You already know that the verbs **ir** and **ser** are irregular in the preterite. You will now learn other verbs whose preterite forms are also irregular.

| Preterite of tener, venir, and decir | | | |
|---|---|---|---|
| | | tener (u-stem) | venir (i-stem) | decir (j-stem) |
| SINGULAR FORMS | yo | tuve | vine | dije |
| | tú | tuviste | viniste | dijiste |
| | Ud./él/ella | tuvo | vino | dijo |
| PLURAL FORMS | nosotros/as | tuvimos | vinimos | dijimos |
| | vosotros/as | tuvisteis | vinisteis | dijisteis |
| | Uds./ellos/ellas | tuvieron | vinieron | dijeron |

▶ **¡Atención!** The endings of these verbs are the regular preterite endings of **–er/–ir** verbs, except for the **yo** and **usted** forms. Note that these two endings are unaccented.

▶ These verbs observe similar stem changes to **tener, venir,** and **decir.**

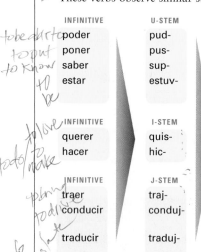

| INFINITIVE | U-STEM | PRETERITE FORMS |
|---|---|---|
| poder | pud- | pude, pudiste, pudo, pudimos, pudisteis, pudieron |
| poner | pus- | puse, pusiste, puso, pusimos, pusisteis, pusieron |
| saber | sup- | supe, supiste, supo, supimos, supisteis, supieron |
| estar | estuv- | estuve, estuviste, estuvo, estuvimos, estuvisteis, estuvieron |

| INFINITIVE | I-STEM | PRETERITE FORMS |
|---|---|---|
| querer | quis- | quise, quisiste, quiso, quisimos, quisisteis, quisieron |
| hacer | hic- | hice, hiciste, hizo, hicimos, hicisteis, hicieron |

| INFINITIVE | J-STEM | PRETERITE FORMS |
|---|---|---|
| traer | traj- | traje, trajiste, trajo, trajimos, trajisteis, trajeron |
| conducir | conduj- | conduje, condujiste, condujo, condujimos, condujisteis, condujeron |
| traducir | traduj- | traduje, tradujiste, tradujo, tradujimos, tradujisteis, tradujeron |

▶ **¡Atención!** Most verbs that end in **-cir** are **j**-stem verbs in the preterite. For example, **producir → produje, produjiste,** etc.

> **Produjimos** un documental sobre los accidentes en la casa.
> *We produced a documentary about accidents in the home.*

▶ Notice that the preterites with **j**-stems omit the letter **i** in the **ustedes/ellos/ellas** form.

> Mis amigos **trajeron** comida a la fiesta.   Ellos **dijeron** la verdad.

**Section Goal**

In **Estructura 9.1**, students will be introduced to the irregular preterites of several common verbs.

**Instructional Resources**
**Supersite:** Lab MP3 Audio Files **Lección 9**
**Supersite/IRCD:** *PowerPoints* (**Lección 9 Estructura** Presentation); *IRM* (**Hojas de actividades,** Lab Audio Script, WBs/VM/LM Answer Key)
**WebSAM**
**Workbook,** pp. 99–100
**Lab Manual,** p. 51
*Cuaderno para hispanohablantes*

**Teaching Tips**
• Quickly review the present tense of a stem-changing verb such as **pedir**. Write the paradigm on the board and ask volunteers to point out the stem-changing forms.
• Work through the preterite paradigms of **tener, venir,** and **decir,** modeling the pronunciation.
• Add a visual aspect to this grammar presentation. Use magazine pictures to ask about social events in the past. Ex: **¿Con quién vino este chico a la fiesta? (Vino con esa chica rubia.) ¿Qué se puso esta señora para ir a la boda? (Se puso un sombrero.)**
• Write the preterite paradigm for **estar** on the board. Then erase the initial **es-** for each form and point out that the preterite of **estar** and **tener** are identical except for the initial **es-**.

## The preterite of dar

| yo | d**i** | | nosotros/as | d**imos** |
|---|---|---|---|---|
| tú | d**iste** | | vosotros/as | d**isteis** |
| Ud./él/ella | d**io** | | Uds./ellos/ellas | d**ieron** |

SINGULAR FORMS *to give*     PLURAL FORMS

▶ The endings for **dar** are the same as the regular preterite endings for **–er** and **–ir** verbs, except that there are no accent marks.

La camarera me **dio** el menú.
*The waitress gave me the menu.*

Le **di** a Juan algunos consejos.
*I gave Juan some advice.*

Los invitados le **dieron** un regalo.
*The guests gave him/her a gift.*

Nosotros **dimos** una gran fiesta.
*We gave a great party.*

▶ The preterite of **hay** (*inf.* **haber**) is **hubo** (*there was; there were*).

**CONSULTA**

Note that there are other ways to say *there was* or *there were* in Spanish. See **Estructura 10.1**, p. 318.

Doña Rita les dio una botella de vino a los viajeros.

Hubo una fiesta en el restaurante El Cráter.

**¡INTÉNTALO!** Escribe la forma correcta del pretérito de cada verbo que está entre paréntesis.

1. (querer) tú _quisiste_
2. (decir) usted _dijo_
3. (hacer) nosotras _hicimos_
4. (traer) yo _traje_
5. (conducir) ellas _condujeron_
6. (estar) ella _estuvo_
7. (tener) tú _tuviste_
8. (dar) ella y yo _dimos_
9. (traducir) yo _traduje_
10. (haber) ayer _hubo_
11. (saber) usted _supo_
12. (poner) ellos _pusieron_
13. (venir) yo _vine_
14. (poder) tú _pudiste_
15. (querer) ustedes _quisieron_
16. (estar) nosotros _estuvimos_
17. (decir) tú _dijiste_
18. (saber) ellos _supieron_
19. (hacer) él _hizo_
20. (poner) yo _puse_
21. (traer) nosotras _trajimos_
22. (tener) yo _tuve_
23. (dar) tú _diste_
24. (poder) ustedes _pudieron_

**recursos**

WB pp. 99–100

LM p. 51

SUPERSITE
panorama.
vhlcentral.com
Lección 9

**Teaching Tips**

• Use the preterite forms of all these verbs by talking about what you did in the recent past and then asking students questions that involve them in a conversation about what they did in the recent past. You may want to avoid the preterite of **poder, saber,** and **querer** for the moment. Ex: **El sábado pasado tuve que ir a la fiesta de cumpleaños de mi sobrina. Cumplió siete años. Le di un bonito regalo. ____, ¿tuviste que ir a una fiesta el sábado? ¿No? Pues, ¿qué hiciste el sábado?**

• Point out that **dar** has the same preterite endings as **ver**.

• Drill the preterite of **dar** by asking students about what they gave their family members for their last birthdays or other special occasion. Ex: **¿Qué le diste a tu hermano para su cumpleaños?** Then ask what other family members gave them. Ex: **¿Qué te dio tu padre? ¿Y tu madre?**

• In a dramatically offended tone, say: **Di una fiesta el sábado. Los invité a todos ustedes y ¡no vino nadie!** Complain about all the work you did to prepare for the party. Ex: **Limpié toda la casa, preparé tortilla española, fui al supermercado y compré refrescos, puse la mesa con platos bonitos, puse música salsa…** Then write **¿Por qué no viniste a mi fiesta?** and **Lo siento, profesor(a), no pude venir a su fiesta porque tuve que…** on the board and give students ten seconds to write a creative excuse. Have volunteers read their excuses aloud. Ex: **Lo siento, profesor, no pude venir a su fiesta porque tuve que lavarme el pelo.**

**TEACHING OPTIONS**

**Video** Show the *Fotonovela* again to give students more input containing irregular preterite forms. Stop the video where appropriate to discuss how certain verbs were used and to ask comprehension questions.

**Extra Practice** Have students write down six things they brought to class today. Then have them circulate around the room, asking other students if they also brought those items (**¿Trajiste tus llaves a clase hoy?**). When they find a student that answers **sí,** they ask that student to sign his or her name next to that item (**Firma aquí, por favor.**). Can students get signatures for all the items they brought to class?

# Práctica

**1** **Completar** Completa estas oraciones con el pretérito de los verbos entre paréntesis.

1. El sábado ____hubo____ (haber) una fiesta sorpresa para Elsa en mi casa.
2. Sofía ____hizo____ (hacer) un pastel para la fiesta y Miguel ____trajo____ (traer) un flan.
3. Los amigos y parientes de Elsa ____vinieron____ (venir) y ____trajeron____ (traer) regalos.
4. El hermano de Elsa no ____vino____ (venir) porque ____tuvo____ (tener) que trabajar.
5. Su tía María Dolores tampoco ____pudo____ (poder) venir.
6. Cuando Elsa abrió la puerta, todos gritaron: "¡Feliz cumpleaños!" y su esposo le ____dio____ (dar) un beso.
7. Al final de la fiesta, todos ____dijeron____ (decir) que se divirtieron mucho.
8. La historia (*story*) le ____dio____ (dar) a Elsa tanta risa (*laughter*) que no ____pudo____ (poder) dejar de reírse (*stop laughing*) durante toda la noche.

**2** **Describir** En parejas, usen verbos de la lista para describir lo que estas personas hicieron. Deben dar por lo menos dos oraciones por cada dibujo. *Some answers will vary.*

| | | | |
|---|---|---|---|
| dar | hacer | tener | traer |
| estar | poner | traducir | venir |

1. el señor López
El señor López le dio dinero a su hijo.

2. Norma
Norma puso el pavo en la mesa.

3. anoche nosotros
Anoche nosotros tuvimos (hicimos/dimos) una fiesta de Navidad./Anoche nosotros estuvimos en una fiesta de Navidad.

4. Roberto y Elena
Roberto y Elena le trajeron/dieron un regalo a su amigo.

# Comunicación

**3** **Preguntas** En parejas, túrnense para hacerse y responder a estas preguntas. Answers will vary.

1. ¿Fuiste a una fiesta de cumpleaños el año pasado? ¿De quién?
2. ¿Quiénes fueron a la fiesta?
3. ¿Quién condujo el auto?
4. ¿Cómo estuvo la fiesta?
5. ¿Quién llevó regalos, bebidas o comida? ¿Llevaste algo especial?
6. ¿Hubo comida? ¿Quién la hizo? ¿Hubo champán?
7. ¿Qué regalo diste tú? ¿Qué otros regalos dieron los invitados?
8. ¿Cuántos invitados hubo en la fiesta?
9. ¿Qué tipo de música hubo?
10. ¿Qué dijeron los invitados de la fiesta?

**4**  **Encuesta** Tu profesor(a) va a darte una hoja de actividades. Para cada una de las actividades de la lista, encuentra a alguien que hizo esa actividad en el tiempo indicado. Answers will vary.

> **modelo**
> traer dulces a clase
> **Estudiante 1:** ¿Trajiste dulces a clase?
> **Estudiante 2:** Sí, traje galletas y helado a la fiesta del fin del semestre.

**Actividades** | **Nombres**

1. ponerse un disfraz (*costume*) de Halloween
2. traer dulces a clase
3. conducir su auto a clase
4. estar en la biblioteca ayer
5. dar un regalo a alguien ayer
6. poder levantarse temprano esta mañana
7. hacer un viaje a un país hispano en el verano
8. tener una cita anoche
9. ir a una fiesta el fin de semana pasado
10. tener que trabajar el sábado pasado

# Síntesis

**5**  **Conversación** En parejas, preparen una conversación en la que uno/a de ustedes va a visitar a su hermano/a para explicarle por qué no fue a su fiesta de graduación y para saber cómo estuvo la fiesta. Incluyan esta información en la conversación: Answers will vary.

- cuál fue el menú
- quiénes vinieron a la fiesta y quiénes no pudieron venir
- quiénes prepararon la comida o trajeron algo
- si él/ella tuvo que preparar algo
- lo que la gente hizo antes y después de comer
- cómo lo pasaron, bien o mal

**3** **Teaching Tip** Instead of having students take turns, ask them to go through all the questions with their partners, writing down the information the partners give them. Later, have them write a third-person description about their partners' experiences.

**3** **Expansion** To practice the formal register, call on different students to ask you the questions in the activity. Ex: **¿Fue usted a una fiesta de cumpleaños el año pasado? (Sí, fui a la fiesta de cumpleaños de Lisa.)**

**4** **Teaching Tip** Distribute the *Hojas de actividades* (Supersite/IRCD). Point out that to get information, students must form questions using the **tú** forms of the infinitives. Ex: **¿Trajiste dulces a clase?**

**4** **Expansion** Write items 1–10 on the board and ask for a show of hands for each item. Ex: **¿Quién trajo dulces a clase?** Write tally marks next to each item to find out which activity was the most popular.

**5** **Expansion** Have pairs work in groups of four to write a paragraph combining the most interesting or unusual aspects of each pair's conversation. Ask a group representative to read the paragraph to the class, who will vote for the most creative or funniest paragraph.

**TEACHING OPTIONS**

**Extra Practice** Ask students to write a brief composition on the *Fotonovela* from this lesson. Students should write about where the characters went, what they did, who ordered what, what they said to each other, and so forth. (Note: Students should stick to completed actions in the past [preterite]. The use of the imperfect for narrating a story will not be presented until **Lección 10.**)

**Large Groups** Divide the class into two groups. Give each member of the first group a strip of paper with a question. Ex: **¿Quién me trajo el pastel de cumpleaños?** Give each member of the second group a strip of paper with an answer. Ex: **Marta te lo trajo.** Students must find their partners.

## Section Goal

In **Estructura 9.2**, students will be introduced to verbs that change meaning in the preterite tense.

**Instructional Resources**
**Supersite:** Lab MP3 Audio Files **Lección 9**
**Supersite/IRCD:** *PowerPoints* (Lección 9 Estructura Presentation); *IRM* (Lab Audio Script, WBs/VM/LM Answer Key)
**WebSAM**
**Workbook,** p. 101
**Lab Manual,** p. 52
*Cuaderno para hispanohablantes*

**Teaching Tip**
• Introduce the preterite of **conocer**. Say: **Ahora los conozco a ustedes muy bien. Pero me acuerdo del día en que los conocí. ¿Ustedes se acuerdan del día en que nos conocimos?** Ask volunteers to compare and contrast the meanings of **conocer** in your example.
• Stress the meaning of **poder** in the preterite by giving both affirmative (*to manage; to succeed*) and negative (*to try and fail*) examples. Ex: **Pude leer todas sus composiciones anoche, pero no pude leer las composiciones de la otra clase.**
• Stress the meaning of **querer** in the preterite by giving both affirmative (*to try*) and negative (*to refuse*) examples. Ex: **Quisimos ver una película el sábado, pero no quise ver ninguna película violenta.**

## 9.2 Verbs that change meaning in the preterite

**ANTE TODO** The verbs **conocer**, **saber**, **poder**, and **querer** change meanings when used in the preterite. Because of this, each of them corresponds to more than one verb in English, depending on its tense.

### Verbs that change meaning in the preterite

| Present | Preterite |
|---|---|
| **conocer** | |
| *to know; to be acquainted with* | *to meet* |
| **Conozco** a esa pareja. | **Conocí** a esa pareja ayer. |
| *I know that couple.* | *I met that couple yesterday.* |
| **saber** | |
| *to know information; to know how to do something* | *to find out; to learn* |
| **Sabemos** la verdad. | **Supimos** la verdad anoche. |
| *We know the truth.* | *We found out (learned) the truth last night.* |
| **poder** | |
| *to be able; can* | *to manage; to succeed (could and did)* |
| **Podemos** hacerlo. | **Pudimos** hacerlo ayer. |
| *We can do it.* | *We managed to do it yesterday.* |
| **querer** | |
| *to want; to love* | *to try* |
| **Quiero** ir pero tengo que trabajar. | **Quise** evitarlo pero fue imposible. |
| *I want to go but I have to work.* | *I tried to avoid it, but it was impossible.* |

**¡ATENCIÓN!**
In the preterite, the verbs **poder** and **querer** have different meanings, depending on whether they are used in affirmative or negative sentences.
**pude** *I succeeded*
**no pude** *I failed (to)*
**quise** *I tried (to)*
**no quise** *I refused (to)*

 **¡INTÉNTALO!** Elige la respuesta más lógica.

1. Yo no hice lo que me pidieron mis padres. ¡Tengo mis principios! a
   a. No quise hacerlo.    b. No supe hacerlo.

2. Hablamos por primera vez con Nuria y Ana en la boda. a
   a. Las conocimos en la boda.    b. Las supimos en la boda.

3. Por fin hablé con mi hermano después de llamarlo siete veces. b
   a. No quise hablar con él.    b. Pude hablar con él.

4. Josefina se acostó para relajarse. Se durmió inmediatamente. a
   a. Pudo relajarse.    b. No pudo relajarse.

5. Después de mucho buscar, encontraste la definición en el diccionario. b
   a. No supiste la respuesta.    b. Supiste la respuesta.

6. Las chicas fueron a la fiesta. Cantaron y bailaron mucho. a
   a. Ellas pudieron divertirse.    b. Ellas no supieron divertirse.

**recursos**

WB p. 101

LM p. 52

panorama. vhlcentral.com Lección 9

# Práctica SUPERSITE

**1** **Carlos y Eva** Forma oraciones con los siguientes elementos. Usa el pretérito y haz todos los cambios necesarios. Al final, inventa la razón del divorcio de Carlos y Eva.

1. anoche / mi esposa y yo / saber / que / Carlos y Eva / divorciarse
   Anoche mi esposa y yo supimos que Carlos y Eva se divorciaron.
2. los / conocer / viaje / isla de Pascua.
   Los conocimos en un viaje a la isla de Pascua.
3. no / poder / hablar / mucho / con / ellos / ese día
   No pudimos hablar mucho con ellos ese día.
4. pero / ellos / ser / simpático / y / nosotros / hacer planes / vernos / con más / frecuencia
   Pero ellos fueron simpáticos y nosotros hicimos planes para vernos con más frecuencia.
5. yo / poder / encontrar / su / número / teléfono / páginas / amarillo
   Yo pude encontrar su número de teléfono en las páginas amarillas.
6. (yo) querer / llamar / les / ese día / pero / no / tener / tiempo
   Quise llamarles ese día pero no tuve tiempo.
7. cuando / los / llamar / nosotros / poder / hablar / Eva
   Cuando los llamé, nosotros pudimos hablar con Eva.
8. nosotros / saber / razón / divorcio / después / hablar / ella
   Nosotros supimos la razón del divorcio después de hablar con ella.

**NOTA CULTURAL**

**La isla de Pascua** es un remoto territorio chileno situado en el océano Pacífico Sur. Sus inmensas estatuas son uno de los mayores misterios del mundo: nadie sabe cómo o por qué se construyeron. Para más información, véase **Panorama**, p. 305.

**2** **Completar** Completa estas frases de una manera lógica. Answers will vary.

1. Ayer mi compañero/a de cuarto supo…
2. Esta mañana no pude…
3. Conocí a mi mejor amigo/a en…
4. Mis padres no quisieron…
5. Mi mejor amigo/a no pudo…
6. Mi novio/a y yo nos conocimos en…
7. La semana pasada supe…
8. Ayer mis amigos quisieron…

# Comunicación

**3** **Telenovela (*Soap opera*)** En parejas, escriban el diálogo para una escena de una telenovela. La escena trata de una situación amorosa entre tres personas: Mirta, Daniel y Raúl. Usen el pretérito de **conocer, poder, querer** y **saber** en su diálogo. Answers will vary.

PASIÓN            AVENTURA

HECHICERÍA        INQUISICIÓN

LA MUJER DOBLE

# Síntesis

**4** **Conversación** En una hoja de papel, escribe dos listas: las cosas que hiciste durante el fin de semana y las cosas que quisiste hacer pero no pudiste. Luego, compara tu lista con la de un(a) compañero/a, y expliquen por qué no pudieron hacer esas cosas. Answers will vary.

---

**TEACHING OPTIONS**

**Video** Show the *Fotonovela* again to give students more input containing verbs that change meaning in the preterite. Stop the video where appropriate to discuss how certain verbs were used and to ask comprehension questions.

**Pairs** In pairs, have students write three sentences using verbs that change meaning in the preterite. Two of the sentences should be true and the third should be false. Their partner has to guess which of the sentences is the false one.

**1** **Expansion**
- In pairs, students create five additional dehydrated sentences for their partner to complete, using the verbs **conocer, saber, poder**, and **querer**. After pairs have finished, ask volunteers to share some of their dehydrated sentences. Write them on the board and have the rest of the class "hydrate" them.
- To challenge students, have pairs use preterite forms of **conocer, saber, poder**, and **querer** to role-play **Carlos** and **Eva** explaining their separate versions of the divorce to their friends.

**2** **Teaching Tip** Before assigning the activity, share with the class some recent things you found out, tried to do but could not, or the names of people you met, inviting students to respond.

**3** **Teaching Tip** Point out that unlike their U.S. counterparts, Hispanic soap operas run for a limited period of time, like a miniseries.

**4** **Expansion** Have pairs repeat the activity, this time describing another person. Ask students to share their descriptions with the class, who will guess the person being described.

# 9.3  ¿Qué? and ¿cuál?

**ANTE TODO**  You've already learned how to use interrogative words and phrases. As you know, **¿qué?** and **¿cuál?** or **¿cuáles?** mean *what?* or *which?* However, they are not interchangeable.

▶ **¿Qué?** followed by a verb is used to ask for a definition or an explanation.

| **¿Qué** es el flan? | **¿Qué** estudias? |
|---|---|
| *What is flan?* | *What do you study?* |

▶ **¿Cuál(es)?** is used when there is a choice among several possibilities.

| **¿Cuál** de los dos prefieres, el vino o el champán? | **¿Cuáles** son tus medias, las negras o las blancas? |
|---|---|
| *Which of these (two) do you prefer, wine or champagne?* | *Which ones are your socks, the black ones or the white ones?* |

▶ **¿Cuál?** cannot be used before a noun; in this case, **¿qué?** is used.

| **¿Qué** sorpresa te dieron tus amigos? | **¿Qué** colores te gustan? |
|---|---|
| *What surprise did your friends give you?* | *What colors do you like?* |

▶ **¿Qué?** used before a noun has the same meaning as **¿cuál?**

| **¿Qué regalo** te gusta? | **¿Qué dulces** quieren ustedes? |
|---|---|
| *What (Which) gift do you like?* | *What (Which) sweets do you want?* |

### Review of interrogative words and phrases

| | | | |
|---|---|---|---|
| **¿a qué hora?** | at what time? | **¿cuánto/a?** | how much? |
| **¿adónde?** | (to) where? | **¿cuántos/as?** | how many? |
| **¿cómo?** | how? | **¿de dónde?** | from where? |
| **¿cuál(es)?** | what?; which? | **¿dónde?** | where? |
| **¿cuándo?** | when? | **¿qué?** | what?; which? |
| | | **¿quién(es)?** | who? |

**¡INTÉNTALO!**  Completa las preguntas con **¿qué?** o **¿cuál(es)?**, según el contexto.

1. ¿ _Cuál_ de los dos te gusta más?
2. ¿ _Cuál_ es tu teléfono?
3. ¿ _Qué_ tipo de pastel pediste?
4. ¿ _Qué_ es una quinceañera?
5. ¿ _Qué_ haces ahora?
6. ¿ _Cuáles_ son tus platos favoritos?
7. ¿ _Qué_ bebidas te gustan más?
8. ¿ _Qué_ es esto?
9. ¿ _Cuál_ es el mejor?
10. ¿ _Cuál_ es tu opinión?
11. ¿ _Qué_ fiestas celebras tú?
12. ¿ _Qué_ botella de vino prefieres?
13. ¿ _Cuál_ es tu helado favorito?
14. ¿ _Qué_ pones en la mesa?
15. ¿ _Qué_ restaurante prefieres?
16. ¿ _Qué_ estudiantes estudian más?
17. ¿ _Qué_ quieres comer esta noche?
18. ¿ _Cuál_ es la sorpresa mañana?
19. ¿ _Qué_ postre prefieres?
20. ¿ _Qué_ opinas?

# Práctica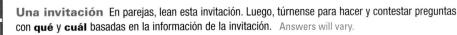

**1** **Completar** Tu clase de español va a crear un sitio web. Completa estas preguntas con alguna(s) palabra(s) interrogativa(s). Luego, con un(a) compañero/a, hagan y contesten las preguntas para obtener la información para el sitio web.

1. ¿____Cuál____ es la fecha de tu cumpleaños?
2. ¿____Dónde____ naciste?
3. ¿____Cuál____ es tu estado civil?
4. ¿__Cómo/Cuándo/Dónde__ te relajas?
5. ¿____Quién____ es tu mejor amigo/a?
6. ¿____Qué____ cosas te hacen reír?
7. ¿____Qué____ postres te gustan? ¿____Cuál____ te gusta más?
8. ¿____Qué____ problemas tuviste en la primera cita con alguien?

# Comunicación

**2** **Una invitación** En parejas, lean esta invitación. Luego, túrnense para hacer y contestar preguntas con **qué** y **cuál** basadas en la información de la invitación. *Answers will vary.*

> **modelo**
> **Estudiante 1:** ¿Cuál es el nombre del padre de la novia?
> **Estudiante 2:** Su nombre es Fernando Sandoval Valera.

> Fernando Sandoval Valera      Lorenzo Vásquez Amaral
> Isabel Arzipe de Sandoval      Elena Soto de Vásquez
>
> tienen el agrado de invitarlos
> a la boda de sus hijos
>
> María Luisa y José Antonio
>
> La ceremonia religiosa tendrá lugar
> el sábado 10 de junio a las dos de la tarde
> en el Templo de Santo Domingo
> (Calle Santo Domingo, 961).
>
> Después de la ceremonia sírvanse pasar a la recepción en el salón
> de baile del Hotel Metrópoli (Sotero del Río, 465).

**¡LENGUA VIVA!**

The word **invitar** is not always used exactly like *invite*. Sometimes, if you say **Te invito a un café**, it means that you are offering to buy that person a coffee.

**3** **Quinceañera** Trabaja con un(a) compañero/a. Uno/a de ustedes es el/la director(a) del salón de fiestas "Renacimiento". La otra persona es el padre/la madre de Ana María, quien quiere hacer la fiesta de quinceañera de su hija sin gastar más de $25 por invitado. Su profesor(a) va a darles la información necesaria para confirmar la reservación. *Answers will vary.*

> **modelo**
> **Estudiante 1:** ¿Cuánto cuestan los entremeses?
> **Estudiante 2:** Depende. Puede escoger champiñones por 50 centavos o camarones por dos dólares.
> **Estudiante 1:** ¡Uf! A mi hija le gustan los camarones, pero son muy caros.
> **Estudiante 2:** Bueno, también puede escoger quesos por un dólar por invitado.

**1** **Expansion** Conduct a conversation with the whole class to find consensus on some of the questions.

**2** **Expansion**
- Add a visual aspect to this activity. Bring in images showing a group of people at a wedding reception. Have pairs of students imagine they are sitting at a table at the reception and ask each other questions about the attendees. Encourage creativity. Ex: **¿Quién es esa mujer que baila con el señor alto y delgado? ¿Qué postres van a servir? ¿Dónde está el novio?**
- Have pairs design an invitation to a party, wedding, **quinceañera**, or other social event. Then have them answer questions from the class about their invitation without showing it. The class guesses what kind of social event is announced. Ex: **¿Dónde es el evento? (en el salón de baile "Cosmopolita") ¿A qué hora es? (a las ocho de la noche) ¿De quiénes es la invitación? (de los señores López Pujol) Es una quinceañera. (Sí.)** Finally, have pairs reveal their design to the class.

**3** **Teaching Tip** Divide the class into pairs and distribute the handouts from the Information Gap Activities (Supersite/ IRCD) that correspond to this activity. Give students ten minutes to complete this activity.

**3** **Expansion** With the same partner, have students prepare a **telenovela** skit with characters from the **quinceañera** activity. Encourage them to use interrogative words and verbs that change meaning in the preterite.

## Section Goals

In **Estructura 9.4**, students will be introduced to:
- pronouns as objects of prepositions
- the pronoun-preposition combinations **conmigo** and **contigo**

---

**Instructional Resources**
**Supersite:** Lab MP3 Audio Files **Lección 9**
**Supersite/IRCD:** *PowerPoints* (**Lección 9 Estructura** Presentation); *IRM* (Information Gap Activities, Lab Audio Script, WBs/VM/LM Answer Key)
**WebSAM**
**Workbook,** pp. 103–104
**Lab Manual,** p. 54
*Cuaderno para hispanohablantes*

---

## Teaching Tips

- Review the chart "Prepositions often used with **estar**" in **Estructura 2.3**. Use prepositional pronouns as you describe yourself and others in relation to people and things. Say:
  **¿Quién está delante de mí?**
  **Sí, _____ está delante de mí.**
  **¿Y quién está detrás de ella?**
  **Sí, _____ está detrás de ella.**

- Ask students which pronouns they recognize and which are new. Ask the class to deduce the rules for pronouns after prepositions.

- Point out that students have been using these pronouns with the preposition **a** since **Lección 2**, when they learned the verb **gustar**.

- Practice **conmigo** and **contigo** by making invitations and having students decline.
  Ex: _____, ¿quieres ir conmigo al museo? (No, no quiero ir contigo.) In a sad tone, say:
  **Nadie quiere ir conmigo a ningún lado.**

# 9.4 Pronouns after prepositions

**ANTE TODO**   In Spanish, as in English, the object of a preposition is the noun or pronoun that follows a preposition. Observe the following diagram.

| PREPOSITION | NOUN | PREPOSITION | PRONOUN |
|---|---|---|---|
| La sopa es para | Alicia | y para | él. |

### Prepositional pronouns

| | Singular | | Plural | |
|---|---|---|---|---|
| | **mí** | me | **nosotros/as** | us |
| | **ti** | you (fam.) | **vosotros/as** | you (fam.) |
| preposition + | **Ud.** | you (form.) | **Uds.** | you (form.) |
| | **él** | him | **ellos** | them (m.) |
| | **ella** | her | **ellas** | them (f.) |

▶ Note that, except for **mí** and **ti**, these pronouns are the same as the subject pronouns. **¡Atención!** **Mí** (*me*) has an accent mark to distinguish it from the possessive adjective **mi** (*my*).

▶ The preposition **con** combines with **mí** and **ti** to form **conmigo** and **contigo**, respectively.

—¿Quieres venir **conmigo** a Concepción?    —Sí, gracias, me gustaría ir **contigo**.
*Do you want to come with me to Concepción?*    *Yes, thanks, I would like to go with you.*

▶ The preposition **entre** is followed by **tú** and **yo** instead of **ti** and **mí**.

Papá va a sentarse **entre tú y yo**.
*Dad is going to sit between you and me.*

**CONSULTA**

For more prepositions, refer to **Estructura 2.3**, p. 56.

**¡INTÉNTALO!**   Completa estas oraciones con las preposiciones y los pronombres apropiados.

1. *(with him)* No quiero ir _con él_.
2. *(for her)* Las galletas son _para ella_.
3. *(for me)* Los mariscos son _para mí_.
4. *(with you, pl. form.)* Preferimos estar _con ustedes_.
5. *(with you, sing. fam.)* Me gusta salir _contigo_.
6. *(with me)* ¿Por qué no quieres tener una cita _conmigo_?
7. *(for her)* La cuenta es _para ella_.
8. *(for them, m.)* La habitación es muy pequeña _para ellos_.
9. *(with them, f.)* Anoche celebré la Navidad _con ellas_.
10. *(for you, sing. fam.)* Este beso es _para ti_.
11. *(with you, sing. fam.)* Nunca me aburro _contigo_.
12. *(with you, pl. form.)* ¡Qué bien que vamos _con ustedes_!
13. *(for you, sing. fam.)* _Para ti_ la vida es muy fácil.
14. *(for them, f.)* _Para ellas_ no hay sorpresas.

**recursos**

WB
pp. 103–104

LM
p. 54

**SUPERSITE**
panorama.
vhlcentral.com
Lección 9

---

**TEACHING OPTIONS**

**Extra Practice** Describe someone in the classroom using prepositions of location, without saying the student's name. Ex: **Esta persona está entre la ventana y _____. Y está enfrente de mí.** The rest of the class has to guess the person being described. Once students have this model, ask individuals to create similar descriptions so that their classmates may guess who is being described.

**Game** Divide the class into two teams. One student from the first team chooses an item in the classroom and writes it down. Call on five students from the other team to ask questions about the item's location. Ex: **¿Está cerca de mí?** The first student can respond with **sí, no, caliente,** or **frío.** If a team guesses the item within five tries, give them a point. If not, give the other team a point. The team with the most points wins.

# Práctica

SUPERSITE

**1**

**Completar** David sale con sus amigos a comer. Para saber quién come qué, lee el mensaje electrónico que David le envió (*sent*) a Cecilia dos días después y completa el diálogo en el restaurante con los pronombres apropiados.

*modelo*

**Camarero:** Los camarones en salsa verde, ¿para quién son?
**David:** Son para ___ella___.

| Para: Cecilia | Asunto: El menú |
|---|---|

```
Hola, Cecilia:
¿Recuerdas la comida del viernes? Quiero repetir el menú en
mi casa el miércoles. Ahora voy a escribir lo que comimos,
luego me dices si falta algún plato. Yo pedí el filete de
pescado y Maribel camarones en salsa verde. Tatiana pidió
un plato grandísimo de machas a la parmesana. Diana y Silvia
pidieron langostas, ¿te acuerdas? Y tú, ¿qué pediste? Ah, sí,
un bistec grande con papas. Héctor también pidió un bistec,
pero más pequeño. Miguel pidió pollo y vino tinto para todos.
Y la profesora comió ensalada verde porque está a dieta.
¿Falta algo? Espero tu mensaje. Hasta pronto. David.
```

**CAMARERO** El filete de pescado, ¿para quién es?
**DAVID** Es para (1) ___mí___.
**CAMARERO** Aquí está. ¿Y las machas a la parmesana y las langostas?
**DAVID** Las machas son para (2) ___ella___.
**SILVIA Y DIANA** Las langostas son para (3) ___nosotras___.
**CAMARERO** Tengo un bistec grande...
**DAVID** Cecilia, es para (4) ___ti___, ¿no es cierto? Y el bistec más pequeño es para (5) ___él___.
**CAMARERO** ¿Y la botella de vino?
**MIGUEL** Es para todos (6) ___nosotros___, y el pollo es para (7) ___mí___.
**CAMARERO** (*a la profesora*) Entonces la ensalada verde es para (8) ___usted___.

**NOTA CULTURAL**

**Las machas a la parmesana** es un plato muy típico de Chile. Se prepara con machas, un tipo de almeja (*clam*) que se encuentra en Suramérica. Las machas a la parmesana se hacen con queso parmesano, limón, sal, pimienta y mantequilla, y luego se ponen en el horno (*oven*).

NATIONAL communication STANDARDS

# Comunicación

**2**

**Compartir** Tu profesor(a) va a darte una hoja de actividades en la que hay un dibujo. En parejas, hagan preguntas para saber dónde está cada una de las personas en el dibujo. Ustedes tienen dos versiones diferentes de la ilustración. Al final deben saber dónde está cada persona. Answers will vary.

*modelo*

**Estudiante 1:** ¿Quién está al lado de Óscar?
**Estudiante 2:** Alfredo está al lado de él.

| | | | |
|---|---|---|---|
| Alfredo | Dolores | Graciela | Raúl |
| Sra. Blanco | Enrique | Leonor | Rubén |
| Carlos | Sra. Gómez | Óscar | Yolanda |

**AYUDA**

Here are some other useful prepositions: **al lado de, debajo de, a la derecha de, a la izquierda de, cerca de, lejos de, delante de, detrás de, entre.**

**1 Teaching Tips**
- Remind students that they are to fill in the blanks with prepositional pronouns, not names of the characters in the conversation.
- To simplify, have students begin by scanning the e-mail message. On the board, list the people who ate at the restaurant (starting with the sender of the e-mail and its recipient). Then guide students in matching each name with the dish ordered. Have students refer to the list as they complete the dialogue.

**1 Expansion** In small groups, have students play the roles of the people mentioned in the e-mail message. Ex: **E1: ¿Para quién son los camarones? E2: Son para mí. E1: ¿Y el bistec? E2: Es para él.**

**2 Teaching Tip** Divide the class into pairs and distribute the handouts from the Information Gap Activities (Supersite/IRCD) that correspond to this activity. Give students ten minutes to complete this activity.

**2 Expansion**
- Using both versions of the drawing as a guide, ask questions of the class to find out where the people are. Ex: **¿Quién sabe dónde está la señora Blanco?**
- Verify that all students labeled the characters correctly by suggesting changes to the drawing and using prepositions to ask about their new locations. Ex: **Yolanda y Carlos cambian de lugar. ¿Quién está al lado de Yolanda ahora? (Rubén)**

**TEACHING OPTIONS**

**Video** Show the ***Fotonovela*** again to give students more input containing prepositional pronouns. Stop the video where appropriate to discuss how certain pronouns were used and to ask comprehension questions.

**Large Groups** Divide the class into two groups. Give group A cards that contain an activity (Ex: **jugar al baloncesto**) and give group B cards that contain a place (Ex: **el gimnasio**). Have students circulate around the room to find places that match their activities. Ex: **E1: Voy a jugar al baloncesto. ¿Puedo ir contigo? E2: Pues, yo voy al museo. No puedes ir conmigo.** or **Voy al gimnasio. Sí, puedes ir conmigo.**

# Recapitulación

Completa estas actividades para repasar los conceptos de gramática que aprendiste en esta lección.

**1** **Completar** Completa la tabla con el pretérito de los verbos. **9 pts.**

| Infinitive | yo | ella | nosotros |
|---|---|---|---|
| **conducir** | conduje | condujo | condujimos |
| **hacer** | hice | hizo | hicimos |
| **saber** | supe | supo | supimos |

**2** **Mi fiesta** Completa este mensaje electrónico con el pretérito de los verbos de la lista. Vas a usar cada verbo sólo una vez. **10 pts.**

| dar | haber | tener |
|---|---|---|
| decir | hacer | traer |
| estar | poder | venir |
| | poner | |

Hola, Omar:

Como tú no (1) ___pudiste___ venir a mi fiesta de cumpleaños, quiero contarte cómo fue. El día de mi cumpleaños muy temprano por la mañana mis hermanos me (2) ___dieron___ una gran sorpresa: ellos (3) ___pusieron___ un regalo delante de la puerta de mi habitación: ¡una bicicleta roja preciosa! Mi madre nos preparó un desayuno riquísimo. Después de desayunar, mis hermanos y yo (4) ___tuvimos___ que limpiar toda la casa, así que (*therefore*) no (5) ___hubo___ más celebración hasta la tarde. A las seis y media (nosotros) (6) ___hicimos___ una barbacoa en el patio de la casa. Todos los invitados (7) ___trajeron___ bebidas y regalos. (8) ___Vinieron___ todos mis amigos, excepto tú, ¡qué pena! :-( La fiesta (9) ___estuvo___ muy animada hasta las diez de la noche, cuando mis padres (10) ___dijeron___ que los vecinos (*neighbors*) iban a (*were going to*) protestar y entonces todos se fueron a sus casas.

## RESUMEN GRAMATICAL

### 9.1 Irregular preterites pp. 286–287

| | | | |
|---|---|---|---|
| **u-stem** | estar<br>poder<br>poner<br>saber<br>tener | estuv-<br>pud-<br>pus-<br>sup-<br>tuv- | |
| **i-stem** | hacer<br>querer<br>venir | hic-<br>quis-<br>vin- | -e, -iste,<br>-o, -imos,<br>-isteis, -(i)eron |
| **j-stem** | conducir<br>decir<br>traducir<br>traer | conduj-<br>dij-<br>traduj-<br>traj- | |

► Preterite of **dar**: di, diste, dio, dimos, disteis, dieron

► Preterite of **hay** (*inf.* haber): hubo

### 9.2 Verbs that change meaning in the preterite p.

| Present | Preterite |
|---|---|
| **conocer** | |
| *to know;*<br>*to be acquainted with* | *to meet* |
| **saber** | |
| *to know info.; to know*<br>*how to do something* | *to find out; to learn* |
| **poder** | |
| *to be able; can* | *to manage; to succeed* |
| **querer** | |
| *to want; to love* | *to try* |

### 9.3 ¿Qué? and ¿cuál? p. 292

► Use **¿qué?** to ask for a definition or an explanation.

► Use **¿cuál(es)?** when there is a choice among several possibilities.

► **¿Cuál?** cannot be used before a noun; use **¿qué?** instead.

► **¿Qué?** used before a noun has the same meaning as **¿cuál?**

---

---

**TEACHING OPTIONS**

**TPR** Have students stand and form a circle. Call out an infinitive from **Resumen gramatical** and a subject pronoun (Ex: **poder/ nosotros**) and toss a foam or paper ball to a student, who will give the correct preterite form (Ex: **pudimos**). He or she then tosses the ball to another student, who must use the verb correctly in a sentence before throwing the ball back to you. Ex: **No pudimos comprar los regalos**.

**Small Groups** Tell small groups to imagine that one of them has received an anonymous birthday gift from a secret admirer. Have them create a dialogue in which friends ask questions about the gift and the potential admirer. Students must use at least two irregular preterites, two examples of **¿qué?** or **¿cuál?**, and three pronouns after prepositions.

**3** **¿Presente o pretérito?** Escoge la forma correcta de los verbos en paréntesis. **6 pts.**

1. Después de muchos intentos (*tries*), (podemos/<u>pudimos</u>) hacer una piñata.
2. —¿Conoces a Pepe?
   —Sí, lo (conozco/<u>conocí</u>) en tu fiesta.
3. Como no es de aquí, Cristina no (<u>sabe</u>/supo) mucho de las celebraciones locales.
4. Yo no (<u>quiero</u>/quise) ir a un restaurante grande, pero tú decides.
5. Ellos (quieren/<u>quisieron</u>) darme una sorpresa, pero Nina me lo dijo todo.
6. Mañana se terminan las clases; por fin (<u>podemos</u>/pudimos) divertirnos.

**4** **Preguntas** Escribe una pregunta para cada respuesta con los elementos dados. Empieza con **qué**, **cuál** o **cuáles** de acuerdo con el contexto y haz los cambios necesarios. **8 pts.**

1. —¿? / pastel / querer —Quiero el pastel de chocolate. 1. ¿Qué pastel quieres?
2. —¿? / ser / sangría —La sangría es una bebida típica española. 2. ¿Qué es la sangría?
3. —¿? / ser / restaurante favorito —Mis restaurantes favoritos son Dalí y Jaleo. 3. ¿Cuáles son tus restaurantes favoritos?
4. —¿? / ser / dirección electrónica —Mi dirección electrónica es paco@email.com. 4. ¿Cuál es tu dirección electrónica?

**5** **¿Dónde me siento?** Completa la conversación con los pronombres apropiados. **7 pts.**

**JUAN** A ver, te voy a decir dónde te vas a sentar. Manuel, ¿ves esa silla? Es para ___<u>ti</u>___. Y esa otra silla es para tu novia, que todavía no está aquí.

**MANUEL** Muy bien, yo la reservo para ___<u>ella</u>___.

**HUGO** ¿Y esta silla es para ___<u>mí</u>___?

**JUAN** No, Hugo. No es para ___<u>ti</u>___. Es para Carmina, que viene con Julio.

**HUGO** No, Carmina y Julio no pueden venir. Hablé con ___<u>ellos</u>___ y me lo dijeron.

**JUAN** Pues ellos se lo pierden (*it's their loss*). ¡Más comida para ___<u>nosotros</u>___ (*us*)!

**CAMARERO** Aquí tienen el menú. Les doy un minuto y enseguida estoy con ___<u>ustedes</u>___.

**6** **Cumpleaños feliz** Escribe cinco oraciones describiendo cómo celebraste tu último cumpleaños. Usa el pretérito y los pronombres que aprendiste en esta lección. **10 pts.** Answers will vary.

**7** **Poema** Completa este fragmento del poema *Elegía nocturna* de Carlos Pellicer con el pretérito de los verbos entre paréntesis. **¡2 puntos EXTRA!**

**" Ay de mi corazón°** que nadie ___<u>quiso</u>___ (querer)
tomar de entre mis manos desoladas.
Tú ___<u>viniste</u>___ (venir) a mirar sus llamaradas°
y le miraste arder° claro° y sereno. **"**

corazón *heart* llamaradas *flames* arder *to burn* claro *clear*

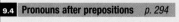

**9.4** **Pronouns after prepositions** *p. 294*

**Prepositional pronouns**

| | Singular | Plural |
|---|---|---|
| Preposition + | mí | nosotros/as |
| | ti | vosotros/as |
| | Ud. | Uds. |
| | él | ellos |
| | ella | ellas |

► Exceptions: conmigo, contigo, entre tú y yo

**3** **Teaching Tip** To challenge students, ask them to explain why they chose the preterite or present tense in each case.

**4** **Expansion** Give students these answers as items 5–8:
**5.** —¿? / libro / comprar —Voy a comprar el libro de viajes. (¿Qué libro vas a comprar?) **6.** —¿? / ser / última película / ver —Vi la película *Volver*. (¿Cuál fue la última película que viste?) **7.** —¿? / ser / número de la suerte —Mi número de la suerte es el ocho. (¿Cuál es tu número de la suerte?) **8.** —¿? / ser / nacimiento —El nacimiento es la primera etapa de la vida. (¿Qué es el nacimiento?)

**5** **Expansion** Have four volunteers role-play the dialogue for the class.

**6** **Teaching Tip** To simplify, have students make an idea map to help them organize their ideas. In the center circle, have them write **Mi último cumpleaños**. Help them brainstorm labels for the surrounding circles, such as **lugar, invitados, regalos,** etc. You also may want to provide a list of infinitives that students may use in their descriptions.

**7** **Teaching Tip** You may want to point out the example of **leísmo** in line 5 (**le miraste**). Explain that some Spanish speakers tend to use **le** or **les** as direct object pronouns. In this case, **le** replaces the direct object pronoun **lo**, which refers to **mi corazón**.

**7** **Poema** Mexican poet **Carlos Pellicer** mixes in his works the splendor of nature with the most intimate emotions. Some of his most important works are *Práctica de vuelo*, *Hora de junio*, and *Camino*. Also a museologist, he helped create the **Museo Casa de Frida Kahlo** and the **Anahuacalli**, which exhibits pre-Hispanic art donated by **Diego Rivera**.

---

**TEACHING OPTIONS**

**TPR** Divide the class into two teams and have them line up. Indicate the first member of each team and call out a sentence. Ex: **Me gusta el color gris.** The first student to reach the board and write a corresponding question using the proper interrogative form earns a point for his or her team. Ex: **¿Qué color te gusta?** or **¿Cuál es tu color preferido?** The team with the most points at the end wins.
**Pairs** Add a visual aspect to this grammar review. Have pairs choose

a photo of a person from a magazine and invent an imaginary list of the ten most important things that happened to that person in his or her lifetime. Tell them to use at least four preterites from this lesson. Ex: **Conoció al presidente de los Estados Unidos. Ganó la lotería y le dio todo el dinero a su mejor amigo.** Have pairs present their photos and lists to the class, who will ask follow-up questions. Ex: **¿Por qué le dio todo el dinero a un amigo?**

## Section Goals

In **Lectura**, students will:
- learn to use word families to infer meaning in context
- read content-rich texts

**Instructional Resources**
**Supersite**
*Cuaderno para hispanohablantes*

**Estrategia** Write **conocer** (*to know*) on the board. Next to it, write **conocimiento** and **conocido** and guide students to recognize their meanings (*knowledge* and *known*). Explain that recognizing word families will help students infer the meaning of new words.

**Examinar el texto** Have students scan the text for clues to its contents. Ask volunteers to tell what kind of text it is and how they know. Headlines (**titulares**), photos, and layout (**composición de la página**) reveal that it is the society news (**notas de sociedad**) in a newspaper.

**Raíces** Have students fill in the rest of the chart after they have read **Vida social**.

# Lectura

## Antes de leer

### Estrategia
#### Recognizing word families

Recognizing root words can help you guess the meaning of words in context, ensuring better comprehension of a reading selection. Using this strategy will enrich your Spanish vocabulary as you will see below.

### Examinar el texto

Familiarízate con el texto usando las estrategias de lectura más efectivas para ti. ¿Qué tipo de documento es? ¿De qué tratan (*What are… about?*) las cuatro secciones del documento? Explica tus respuestas.

### Raíces (*Roots*)

Completa el siguiente cuadro (*chart*) para ampliar tu vocabulario. Usa palabras de la lectura de esta lección y el vocabulario de las lecciones anteriores. ¿Qué significan las palabras que escribiste en el cuadro? Answers will vary.

| | Verbo | Sustantivos | Otras formas |
|---|---|---|---|
| 1. | agradecer | agradecimiento/ gracias | agradecido |
| 2. | estudiar | estudiante / student | estudiado / studied |
| 3. | celebrar / to celebrate | celebración / celebration | celebrado |
| 4. | bailar / to dance | baile | bailable / danceable |
| 5. | bautizar | bautismo / baptism | bautizado / baptized |

**recursos**

panorama.vhlcentral.com
Lección 9

# Vida social

## Matrimonio
### Espinoza Álvarez-Reyes Salazar

El día sábado 17 de junio de 2006 a las 19 horas, se celebró el matrimonio de Silvia Reyes y Carlos Espinoza en la catedral de Santiago. La ceremonia fue oficiada por el pastor Federico Salas y participaron los padres de los novios, el señor Jorge Espinoza y señora y el señor José Alfredo Reyes y señora. Después de la ceremonia, los padres de los recién casados ofrecieron una fiesta bailable en el restaurante La Misión.

# Bautismo

José María recibió el bautismo el 26 de junio de 2006.

Sus padres, don Roberto Lagos Moreno y doña María Angélica Sánchez, compartieron la alegría de la fiesta con todos sus parientes y amigos. La ceremonia religiosa tuvo lugar° en la catedral de Aguas Blancas. Después de la ceremonia, padres, parientes y amigos celebraron una fiesta en la residencia de la familia Lagos.

---

**Heritage Speakers** Ask heritage speakers to share with the class other terms they use to refer to various types of celebrations. Possible responses: wedding **boda, casamiento**; graduation: **graduación, promoción**; baptism: **bautizo**; birthday: **cumpleaños, día del santo**.

**Extra Practice** Here are some related words of which at least one form will be familiar to students. Guide them to recognize the relationship between words and meanings. **idea, ideal, idealismo, idealizar, idear, ideario, idealista • conservar, conservación, conserva, conservador • bueno, bondad, bondadoso, bonito • habla, hablador, hablar, hablante, hablado**

# Fiesta quinceañera

32B

El doctor don Amador Larenas Fernández y la señora Felisa Vera de Larenas celebraron los quince años de su hija Ana Ester junto a sus parientes y amigos. La quinceañera° reside en la ciudad de Valparaíso y es estudiante del Colegio Francés. La fiesta de presentación en sociedad de la señorita Ana Ester fue el día viernes 2 de mayo a las 19 horas, en el Club Español. Entre los invitados especiales asistieron el alcalde° de la ciudad, don Pedro Castedo, y su esposa. La música estuvo a cargo de la Orquesta Americana. ¡Feliz cumpleaños le deseamos a la señorita Ana Ester en su fiesta bailable!

## Expresión de gracias
### Carmen Godoy Tapia

Agradecemos° sinceramente a todas las personas que nos acompañaron en el último adiós a nuestra apreciada esposa, madre, abuela y tía, la señora Carmen Godoy Tapia. El funeral tuvo lugar el día 28 de junio de 2006 en la ciudad de Viña del Mar. La vida de Carmen Godoy fue un ejemplo de trabajo, amistad, alegría y amor para todos nosotros. La familia agradece de todo corazón° su asistencia° al funeral a todos los parientes y amigos. Su esposo, hijos y familia.

tuvo lugar *took place* quinceañera *fifteen year-old girl* alcalde *mayor*
Agradecemos *We thank* de todo corazón *sincerely* asistencia *attendance*

# Después de leer

## Corregir ✎ⓢ
Escribe estos comentarios otra vez para corregir la información errónea.

1. El alcalde y su esposa asistieron a la boda de Silvia y Carlos. El alcalde y su esposa asistieron a la fiesta de quinceañera de Ana Ester.
2. Todos los anuncios (*announcement*) describen eventos felices. Tres de los anuncios tratan de eventos felices. Uno trata de una muerte.
3. Ana Ester Larenas cumple dieciséis años. Ana Ester Larenas cumple quince años.
4. Roberto Lagos y María Angélica Sánchez son hermanos. Roberto Lagos y María Angélica Sánchez están casados/son esposos.
5. Carmen Godoy Tapia les dio las gracias a las personas que asistieron al funeral. La familia de Carmen Godoy Tapia les dio las gracias a las personas que asistieron al funeral.

## Identificar ✎ⓢ
Escribe el nombre de la(s) persona(s) descrita(s) (*described*).

1. Dejó viudo a su esposo en junio de 2006.
   Carmen Godoy Tapia
2. Sus padres y todos los invitados brindaron por él, pero él no entendió por qué.
   José María
3. El Club Español les presentó una cuenta considerable para pagar.
   don Amador Larenas Fernández y doña Felisa Vera de Larenas
4. Unió a los novios en santo matrimonio.
   el pastor Federico Salas
5. La celebración de su cumpleaños marcó el comienzo de su vida adulta.
   Ana Ester

## Un anuncio
Trabaja con dos o tres compañeros/as de clase e inventen un anuncio breve sobre una celebración importante. Esta celebración puede ser una graduación, un matrimonio o una gran fiesta en la que ustedes participan. Incluyan la siguiente información. Answers will vary.

1. nombres de los participantes
2. la fecha, la hora y el lugar
3. qué se celebra
4. otros detalles de interés

## Section Goals

In **Escritura**, students will:
- create a Venn diagram to organize information
- learn words and phrases that signal similarity and difference
- write a comparative analysis

---

**Instructional Resources**
**Supersite**
*Cuaderno para hispanohablantes*

---

**Estrategia** Explain that a graphic organizer, such as a Venn diagram, is a useful way to record information and visually organize details to be compared and contrasted in a comparative analysis. On the board, draw a Venn diagram with the headings **La boda de mi hermano, El bautismo de mi sobrina,** and the subheadings **Diferencias** and **Similitudes.** Tell students they are going to complete a Venn diagram to compare two celebrations. Discuss with the class how these events are alike and how they are different, using some of the terms to signal similarities and differences.

**Tema** Explain to students that to write a comparative analysis, they will need to use words or phrases that signal similarities **(similitudes)** and differences **(diferencias).** Model the pronunciation of the words and expressions under **Escribir una composición.** Then have volunteers use them in sentences to express the similarities and differences listed in the Venn diagram.

# Escritura SUPERSITE

## Estrategia
**Planning and writing a comparative analysis**

Writing any kind of comparative analysis requires careful planning. Venn diagrams are useful for organizing your ideas visually before comparing and contrasting people, places, objects, events, or issues. To create a Venn diagram, draw two circles that overlap and label the top of each circle. List the differences between the two elements in the outer rings of the two circles, then list their similarities where the two circles overlap. Review the following example.

**Diferencias y similitudes**

**Boda de Silvia Reyes y Carlos Espinoza**

**Diferencias:**
1. Primero hay una celebración religiosa.
2. Se celebra en un restaurante.

**Similitudes:**
1. Las dos fiestas se celebran por la noche.
2. Las dos fiestas son bailables.

**Quinceañera de Ana Ester Larenas Vera**

**Diferencias:**
1. Se celebra en un club.
2. Vienen invitados especiales.

La lista de palabras y expresiones a la derecha puede ayudarte a escribir este tipo de ensayo (*essay*).

**recursos**

panorama.vhlcentral.com
Lección 9

## Tema

**Escribir una composición**

Compara una celebración familiar (como una boda, una fiesta de cumpleaños o una graduación) a la que tú asististe recientemente, con otro tipo de celebración. Utiliza palabras y expresiones de esta lista.

**Para expresar similitudes**

| | |
|---|---|
| **además; también** | *in addition; also* |
| **al igual que** | *the same as* |
| **como** | *as; like* |
| **de la misma manera** | *in the same manner (way)* |
| **del mismo modo** | *in the same manner (way)* |
| **tan +** [*adjetivo*] **+ como** | *as +* [adjective] *+ as* |
| **tanto/a(s) +** [*sustantivo*] **+ como** | *as many/much +* [noun] *+ as* |

**Para expresar diferencias**

| | |
|---|---|
| **a diferencia de** | *unlike* |
| **a pesar de** | *in spite of* |
| **aunque** | *although* |
| **en cambio** | *on the other hand* |
| **más/menos... que** | *more/less . . . than* |
| **no obstante** | *nevertheless; however* |
| **por otro lado** | *on the other hand* |
| **por el contrario** | *on the contrary* |
| **sin embargo** | *nevertheless; however* |

---

**EVALUATION: Composición**

| Criteria | Scale |
|---|---|
| Content | 1 2 3 4 |
| Organization | 1 2 3 4 |
| Use of comparisons/contrasts | 1 2 3 4 |
| Use of vocabulary | 1 2 3 4 |
| Accuracy | 1 2 3 4 |

| Scoring | |
|---|---|
| Excellent | 18–20 points |
| Good | 14–17 points |
| Satisfactory | 10–13 points |
| Unsatisfactory | < 10 points |

# Escuchar

**Section Goals**

In **Escuchar**, students will:
- use context to infer meaning of unfamiliar words
- answer questions based on a recorded conversation

## Estrategia

**Guessing the meaning of words through context**

When you hear an unfamiliar word, you can often guess its meaning by listening to the words and phrases around it.

 To practice this strategy, you will now listen to a paragraph. Jot down the unfamiliar words that you hear. Then listen to the paragraph again and jot down the word or words that are the most useful clues to the meaning of each unfamiliar word.

## Preparación

Lee la invitación. ¿De qué crees que van a hablar Rosa y Josefina?

## Ahora escucha

Ahora escucha la conversación entre Josefina y Rosa. Cuando oigas una de las palabras de la columna A, usa el contexto para identificar el sinónimo o la definición en la columna B.

| A | B |
|---|---|
| d festejar | a. conmemoración religiosa de una muerte |
| c dicha | b. tolera |
| h bien parecido | c. suerte |
| g finge (fingir) | d. celebrar |
| b soporta (soportar) | e. me divertí |
| e yo lo disfruté (disfrutar) | f. horror |
| | g. crea una ficción |
| | h. guapo |

---

*Margarita Robles de García
y Roberto García Olmos*

*Piden su presencia en la celebración
del décimo aniversario de bodas
el día 13 de marzo de 2006
con una misa en la Iglesia Virgen del Coromoto
a las 6:30*

*seguida por cena y baile
en el restaurante El Campanero,
Calle Principal, Las Mercedes
a las 8:30*

---

## Comprensión

### ¿Cierto o falso?

Lee cada oración e indica si lo que dice es **cierto** o **falso**. Corrige las oraciones falsas.

1. No invitaron a mucha gente a la fiesta de Margarita y Roberto porque ellos no conocen a muchas personas. Falso. Fueron muchos invitados.

2. Algunos fueron a la fiesta con pareja y otros fueron sin compañero/a. Cierto.

3. Margarita y Roberto decidieron celebrar el décimo aniversario porque no tuvieron ninguna celebración en su matrimonio. Falso. Celebraron el décimo aniversario porque les gustan las fiestas.

4. A Rosa y a Josefina les parece interesante Rafael. Cierto.

5. Josefina se divirtió mucho en la fiesta porque bailó toda la noche con Rafael. Falso. Josefina se divirtió mucho pero bailó con otros, no con Rafael.

### Preguntas   Answers will vary.

1. ¿Son solteras Rosa y Josefina? ¿Cómo lo sabes?

2. ¿Tienen las chicas una amistad de mucho tiempo con la pareja que celebra su aniversario? ¿Cómo lo sabes?

---

**Estrategia**
**Script** Hoy mi sobrino Gabriel cumplió seis años. Antes de la fiesta, ayudé a mi hermana a decorar la sala con globos de todos los colores, pero ¡qué bulla después!, cuando los niños se pusieron a estallarlos todos. El pastel de cumpleaños estaba riquísimo y cuando Gabriel sopló las velas, apagó las seis. Los otros niños le regalaron un montón de juguetes, y nos divertimos mucho.

**Teaching Tip** Have students read the invitation and guess what **Rosa** and **Josefina** will be talking about in the audio.

**Ahora escucha**
**Script** JOSEFINA: Rosa, ¿te divertiste anoche en la fiesta?
ROSA: Sí, me divertí más en el aniversario que en la boda. ¡La fiesta estuvo fenomenal! Fue buena idea festejar el aniversario en un restaurante. Así todos pudieron relajarse.
J: En parte, yo lo disfruté porque son una pareja tan linda; qué dicha que estén tan enamorados después de diez años de matrimonio. Me gustaría tener una relación como la de ellos. Y también saberlo celebrar con tanta alegría. ¡Pero qué cantidad de comida y bebida!
R: Es verdad que Margarita y Roberto exageran un poco con sus fiestas, pero son de la clase de gente que le gusta celebrar los eventos de la vida. Y como tienen tantas amistades y dos familias tan grandes....

*(Script continues at far left in the bottom panels.)*

---

J: Oye, Rosa, hablando de familia, ¿llegaste a conocer al cuñado de Magali? Es soltero, ¿no? Quise bailar con él pero no me sacó a bailar.
R: Hablas de Rafael. Es muy bien parecido; ¡ese pelo...! Estuve hablando con él después del brindis. Me dijo que

no le gusta ni el champán ni el vino; él finge tomar cuando brindan porque no lo soporta. No te sacó a bailar porque él y Susana estaban juntos en la fiesta.
J: De todos modos, aun sin Rafael, bailé toda la noche. Lo pasé muy, pero muy bien.

# En pantalla

En México existe una franja° de tierra° a lo largo de° toda la costa del país que es considerada parte del territorio público federal. Esta área abarca° aproximadamente cincuenta metros a partir de° la línea del mar. Sin embargo°, existe la posibilidad de que los propietarios de la tierra que está al lado de la zona federal puedan pedir una concesión. Así pueden utilizar el área adyacente a su propiedad, por ejemplo, para hacer un festival musical o una fiesta privada. Casos similares ocurren en otros países hispanos.

> **Vocabulario útil**
>
> **conejo** | *bunny*

### Opciones

Elige la opción correcta.

1. El chico está comprando en __b__.
   a. una farmacia   b. un supermercado   c. un almacén
2. Él imagina __a__ en la playa.
   a. una fiesta      b. un examen      c. un almuerzo
3. El chico de la guitarra canta __b__.
   a. bien       b. mal       c. fabulosamente bien
4. Al final (*At the end*), el chico __a__ compra las baterías.
   a. sí          b. no          c. nunca

 **Fiesta**

Trabajen en grupos de tres. Imaginen que van a organizar una fiesta en la playa. Escriban una invitación electrónica para invitar a sus amigos a la fiesta. Describan los planes que tienen para la fiesta y díganles a sus amigos qué tiene que traer cada uno.
Answers will vary.
*franja strip* tierra *land* a lo largo de *along* abarca *covers* a partir de *from* Sin embargo *However* ¿Y si no compraras... *And what if you didn't buy...?* cómpralas *buy them*

## Anuncio de Energizer

**¿Y si no compraras° las Energizer Max?**

**Hey, no se preocupen.**

**Sí, mejor cómpralas°.**

**recursos**

**SUPERSITE**

panorama.vhlcentral.com
Lección 9

**SUPERSITE** Conexión Internet

Go to panorama.vhlcentral.com to watch the TV clip featured in this **En pantalla** section.

# Oye cómo va

## Myriam Hernández

a actriz° y cantante° **Myriam Hernández** nació
n Chile y empezó su carrera a los diez años
uando ganó un festival estudiantil. Más tarde,
rabajó en la telenovela *De cara al mañana*.
esde 1988, año en que salió a la venta° su
rimer álbum, su éxito° se extendió por toda
atinoamérica y los Estados Unidos. En 1989
a canción *El hombre que yo amo* fue incluida
n la lista *Hot Latin* de la revista *Billboard*.
ambién se ha presentado° en escenarios° como
l Madison Square Garden en Nueva York y el
estival de Viña del Mar, en Chile.

l profesor(a) va a poner la canción en la clase.
scúchala y completa las actividades.

### Emparejar

ndica qué elemento del segundo grupo está relacionado
on cada elemento del primer grupo.

_d_ 1. lugar donde nació Myriam Hernández
_f_ 2. telenovela en la que trabajó
_e_ 3. año en que salió a la venta su primer álbum
_c_ 4. canción incluida en la lista *Hot Latin*

a. Festival de Viña del Mar    d. Chile
b. 1986    e. 1988
c. *El hombre que yo amo*    f. *De cara al mañana*

### Preguntas

n parejas, respondan a las preguntas. Answers will vary.

1. ¿Creen que la cantante está triste o feliz? ¿Cómo
   lo saben?
2. ¿Es el amor el motor del universo? ¿Por qué?
3. Completen estos versos con sus propias (*your
   own*) ideas. Tomen la canción de Myriam
   Hernández como modelo.

> Quiero cantarle a _____
> en tres o cuatro versos;
> cantarle porque _____,
> porque _____.

*riz actress*   **cantante** *singer*   **salió a la venta** *was released*
**to** *success*   **se ha presentado** *she has performed*   **escenarios** *stages*
**lar** *to find*   **soledad** *loneliness*   **alma** *soul*   **volar** *fly*

communication
cultures
NATIONAL STANDARDS

## Quiero cantarle al amor

Quiero cantarle al amor
porque me supo hallar°.
Quiero cantarle al amor,
que me vino a buscar.
Se llevó mi soledad°
y a cambio me dejó
su fantasía en el alma°.
Quiero cantarle al amor,
que me dio libertad.
Quiero cantarle al amor
porque me hizo volar°.
Se llevó mi soledad
y a cambio me dejó
su fantasía en el alma.

### Discografía selecta

| | |
|---|---|
| 1990 | *Dos* |
| 1998 | *Todo el amor* |
| 2000 | *+ y más* |
| 2001 | *El amor en concierto* |
| 2004 | *Huellas* |

**recursos**

SUPERSITE
panorama.vhlcentral.com
Lección 9

**SUPERSITE Conexión Internet**
Go to **panorama.vhlcentral.com** to learn more about
the artist featured in this **Oye cómo va** section.

## Section Goals

In **Oye cómo va**, students will:
- read about **Myriam Hernández**
- listen to a song by **Myriam Hernández**

**Instructional Resources**
**Supersite**
**Vista Higher Learning** *Cancionero*

### Antes de escuchar
- Have students read the
  title of the song and scan
  the lyrics for cognates and
  familiar words.
- Ask students to predict what
  type of song this is. They
  should support their opinion
  by citing words from the lyrics.
- Tell students to listen for
  irregular preterite verb forms
  and jot them down as you
  play the song.

**Emparejar** Ask additional
comprehension questions:
**¿Cómo empezó la carrera de
Myriam Hernández?** (Ganó un
festival estudiantil a los diez
años.) **¿Tuvo éxito su primer
álbum?** (Sí, tuvo éxito en Latinoamérica y los Estados Unidos.)
**¿En qué revista se encuentra la
lista *Hot Latin*?** (Se encuentra
en la revista *Billboard*.)

**Preguntas**
- Have volunteers give examples of the different ways
  love is described in the song.
- Play the song a second time.
  Then ask: **¿A quién canta esta
  canción? ¿Cómo lo saben?
  ¿Creen que esta canción le
  da esperanza a una persona
  que está buscando pareja?
  ¿Por qué?**

---

### TEACHING OPTIONS

**Extra Practice** Have students imagine that their best friend has
just been dumped by his or her significant other. Ask students
to write an e-mail to cheer up their friend. Encourage them to
use the song lyrics as the inspiration for their message. Have
students exchange papers with a classmate for peer editing.

**Pairs** Ask pairs to think of a movie in which this song might be
featured. Pairs should support their decision by giving a movie
synopsis and the scene where they think the song should be
featured. Have pairs share their ideas with the class.

# Chile

*connections cultures NATIONAL STANDARDS*

## El país en cifras

▶ **Área:** 756.950 km² (292.259 millas²), *dos veces el área de Montana*

▶ **Población:** 17.134.000 *Aproximadamente el 80 por ciento de la población del país es urbana.*

▶ **Capital:** Santiago de Chile—5.982.000

▶ **Ciudades principales:** Concepción, Viña del Mar, Valparaíso, Temuco

SOURCE: Population Division, UN Secretariat

▶ **Moneda:** peso chileno

▶ **Idiomas:** español (oficial), mapuche

Bandera de Chile

### Chilenos célebres

▶ **Bernardo O'Higgins,** militar° y héroe nacional (1778–1842)

▶ **Gabriela Mistral,** Premio Nobel de Literatura, 1945; poeta y diplomática (1889–1957)

▶ **Pablo Neruda,** Premio Nobel de Literatura, 1971; poeta (1904–1973)

▶ **Isabel Allende,** novelista (1942– )

Pablo Neruda

militar *soldier*   terremoto *earthquake*   heridas *wounded*   hogar *home*

### ¡Increíble pero cierto!

El terremoto° de mayor intensidad registrado tuvo lugar en Chile el 22 de mayo de 1960. Registró una intensidad récord de 9.5 en la escala de Richter. Murieron 2.000 personas, 3.000 resultaron heridas° y 2.000.000 perdieron su hogar°. La geografía del país se modificó notablemente.

PERÚ

Palacio de la Moneda en Santiago

Pampa del Tamarugal

BOLIVIA

Cordillera de los Andes

Una calle de Santiago

Vista de la costa de Viña del Mar

Océano Pacífico

Viña del Mar
Valparaíso

★ Santiago de Chile

ARGENTINA

Pescadores de Valparaíso

Concepción

Temuco

Una celebración en Temuco

Lago Buenos Aires

Océano Atlántico

Punta Arenas

| recursos | | |
|---|---|---|
| WB pp. 105–106 | VM pp. 241–242 | panorama.vhlcentral.com Lección 9 |

Estrecho de Magallanes

Isla Grande de Tierra del Fuego

## Lugares • **La isla de Pascua**

La isla de Pascua° recibió ese nombre porque los exploradores holandeses° llegaron a la isla por primera vez el día de Pascua de 1722. Ahora es parte del territorio de Chile. La isla de Pascua es famosa por los *moai*, estatuas enormes que representan personas con rasgos° muy exagerados. Estas estatuas las construyeron los *rapa nui*, los antiguos habitantes de la zona. Todavía no se sabe mucho sobre los *rapa nui*, ni tampoco se sabe por qué decidieron abandonar la isla.

## Deportes • **Los deportes de invierno**

Hay muchos lugares para practicar los deportes de invierno en Chile porque las montañas nevadas de los Andes ocupan gran parte del país. El Parque Nacional de Villarrica, por ejemplo, situado al pie de un volcán y junto a° un lago, es un sitio popular para el esquí y el *snowboard*. Para los que prefieren deportes más extremos, el centro de esquí Valle Nevado organiza excursiones para practicar el heliesquí.

## Ciencias • **Astronomía**

Los observatorios chilenos, situados en los Andes, son lugares excelentes para las observaciones astronómicas. Científicos° de todo el mundo van a Chile para estudiar las estrellas° y otros cuerpos celestes. Hoy día Chile está construyendo nuevos observatorios y telescopios para mejorar las imágenes del universo.

## Economía • **El vino**

La producción de vino comenzó en Chile en el siglo° XVI. Ahora la industria del vino constituye una parte importante de la actividad agrícola del país y la exportación de sus productos está subiendo° cada vez más. Los vinos chilenos reciben el aprecio internacional por su gran variedad, sus ricos y complejos sabores° y su precio moderado. Los más conocidos internacionalmente son los vinos de Aconcagua, de Santiago y de Huasco.

 **¿Qué aprendiste?** Responde a cada pregunta con una oración completa.

1. ¿Qué porcentaje (*percentage*) de la población chilena es urbana?
   El 80 por ciento de la población chilena es urbana.
2. ¿Qué son los *moai*? ¿Dónde están? Los *moai* son estatuas enormes. Están en la isla de Pascua.
3. ¿Qué deporte extremo ofrece el centro de esquí Valle Nevado?
   Ofrece la práctica de heliesquí.

4. ¿Por qué van a Chile científicos de todo el mundo? Porque los observatorios chilenos son excelentes para las observaciones astronómicas.
5. ¿Cuándo comenzó la producción de vino en Chile?
   Comenzó en el siglo XVI.
6. ¿Por qué reciben los vinos chilenos el aprecio internacional? Lo reciben por su variedad, sus ricos y complejos sabores y su precio moderado.

 **Conexión Internet** Investiga estos temas en **panorama.vhlcentral.com.**

1. Busca información sobre Pablo Neruda e Isabel Allende. ¿Dónde y cuándo nacieron? ¿Cuáles son algunas de sus obras (*works*)? ¿Cuáles son algunos de los temas de sus obras?
2. Busca información sobre sitios donde los chilenos y los turistas practican deportes de invierno en Chile. Selecciona un sitio y descríbeselo a tu clase.

La isla de Pascua *Easter Island*   holandeses *Dutch*   rasgos *features*   junto a *beside*   Científicos *Scientists*   estrellas *stars*   siglo *century*   subiendo *increasing*   complejos sabores *complex flavors*

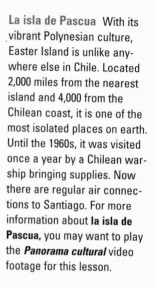

**La isla de Pascua** With its vibrant Polynesian culture, Easter Island is unlike anywhere else in Chile. Located 2,000 miles from the nearest island and 4,000 from the Chilean coast, it is one of the most isolated places on earth. Until the 1960s, it was visited once a year by a Chilean warship bringing supplies. Now there are regular air connections to Santiago. For more information about **la isla de Pascua,** you may want to play the *Panorama cultural* video footage for this lesson.

**Los deportes de invierno** Remind students that some of the highest mountains in South America lie along the border Chile shares with Argentina. In the south is the **Parque Nacional Torres del Paine,** a national park featuring ice caverns, deep glacial trenches, and other spectacular features.

**Astronomía** In 1962, the Cerro Tololo Inter-American Observatory was founded as a joint project between Chilean and American astronomers. Since that time, so many other major telescopes have been installed for research purposes that Chile is home to the highest concentration of telescopes in the world.

**El vino** Invite students to research the wine-growing regions of Chile and to compare them to wine-growing regions in California, Spain, or other wine-producing areas.

**Conexión Internet** Students will find supporting Internet activities and links at **panorama.vhlcentral.com.**

**TEACHING OPTIONS**

**Worth Noting** The native Mapuche people of southern Chile are a small minority of the Chilean population today, but have maintained a strong cultural identity since the time of their first contact with Europeans. In fact, they resisted conquest so well that it was only in the late nineteenth century that the government of Chile could assert sovereignty over the region south of the Bío-Bío River. However, the majority of Chileans are of European descent. Chilean Spanish is much less infused with indigenous lexical items than the Spanish of countries such as Guatemala and Mexico, where the larger indigenous population has made a greater impact on the language.

**Instructional Resources**
**Supersite:** Textbook &
Vocabulary MP3 Audio Files
**Lección 9**
**Supersite/IRCD:** *IRM* (WBs/
VM/LM Answer Key); *Testing
Program* (**Lección 9 Pruebas**,
Test Generator, Testing
Program MP3 Audio Files)
**WebSAM**
**Lab Manual,** p. 54

## Las celebraciones

| | |
|---|---|
| el aniversario (de bodas) | (wedding) anniversary |
| la boda | wedding |
| el cumpleaños | birthday |
| el día de fiesta | holiday |
| la fiesta | party |
| el/la invitado/a | guest |
| la Navidad | Christmas |
| la quinceañera | young woman's fifteenth birthday celebration |
| la sorpresa | surprise |
| brindar | to toast (drink) |
| celebrar | to celebrate |
| divertirse (e:ie) | to have fun |
| invitar | to invite |
| pasarlo bien/mal | to have a good/bad time |
| regalar | to give (a gift) |
| reírse (e:i) | to laugh |
| relajarse | to relax |
| sonreír (e:i) | to smile |
| sorprender | to surprise |

## Los postres y otras comidas

| | |
|---|---|
| la botella (de vino) | bottle (of wine) |
| el champán | champagne |
| los dulces | sweets; candy |
| el flan (de caramelo) | baked (caramel) custard |
| la galleta | cookie |
| el helado | ice cream |
| el pastel (de chocolate) | (chocolate) cake; pie |
| el postre | dessert |

## Las relaciones personales

| | |
|---|---|
| la amistad | friendship |
| el amor | love |
| el divorcio | divorce |
| el estado civil | marital status |
| el matrimonio | marriage |
| la pareja | (married) couple; partner |
| el/la recién casado/a | newlywed |
| casarse (con) | to get married (to) |
| comprometerse (con) | to get engaged (to) |
| divorciarse (de) | to get divorced (from) |
| enamorarse (de) | to fall in love (with) |
| llevarse bien/mal (con) | to get along well/ badly (with) |
| odiar | to hate |
| romper (con) | to break up (with) |
| salir (con) | to go out (with); to date |
| separarse (de) | to separate (from) |
| tener una cita | to have a date; to have an appointment |
| casado/a | married |
| divorciado/a | divorced |
| juntos/as | together |
| separado/a | separated |
| soltero/a | single |
| viudo/a | widower/widow |

## Las etapas de la vida

| | |
|---|---|
| la adolescencia | adolescence |
| la edad | age |
| el estado civil | marital status |
| las etapas de la vida | the stages of life |
| la juventud | youth |
| la madurez | maturity; middle age |
| la muerte | death |
| el nacimiento | birth |
| la niñez | childhood |
| la vejez | old age |
| cambiar (de) | to change |
| graduarse (de/en) | to graduate (from/in) |
| jubilarse | to retire (from work) |
| nacer | to be born |

## Palabras adicionales

| | |
|---|---|
| la alegría | happiness |
| el beso | kiss |
| conmigo | with me |
| contigo | with you |

| | |
|---|---|
| Expresiones útiles | See page 281. |

recursos

| LM p. 54 | panorama.vhlcentral.com Lección 9 |
|---|---|

# En el consultorio 10

## Communicative Goals

**You will learn how to:**

- **Describe how you feel physically**
- **Talk about health and medical conditions**

## Lesson Goals

In **Lección 10**, students will be introduced to the following:

- names of parts of the body
- health-related terms
- medical-related vocabulary
- health services in Spanish-speaking countries
- healers and shamans
- imperfect tense
- uses of the preterite and imperfect tenses
- impersonal constructions with **se**
- using **se** for unplanned events
- forming adverbs using [*adjective*] + –**mente**
- common adverbs and adverbial expressions
- activating background knowledge
- cultural, geographic, and economic information about Costa Rica
- cultural and geographic information about Nicaragua

**A primera vista** Here are some additional questions you can ask based on the photo: **¿Cuándo fue la última vez que viste a tu médico/a? ¿Vas mucho a verlo/a? ¿Estuviste en su oficina la semana pasada? ¿El año pasado? ¿Cuáles son las mejores comidas para sentirte bien? ¿Cuáles son las peores?**

### A PRIMERA VISTA

- ¿Cuál de ellas es la doctora? ¿La mujer de pelo largo o la mujer de pelo corto?
- ¿En qué etapa de la vida está la doctora, la vejez o la madurez?
- ¿Es una de ellas mayor que la otra o son aproximadamente de la misma edad?

**INSTRUCTIONAL RESOURCES**

**MAESTRO™ SUPERSITE (panorama.vhlcentral.com)**
Textbook, Vocabulary, & Lab MP3 Audio Files
Additional Practice
Learning Management System (Assignment Task Manager, Gradebook)
*Also on DVD*
  *Fotonovela*

*Flash cultura*
*Panorama cultural*
*Also on Instructor's Resource CD-ROM*
  *PowerPoints* (**Contextos** & **Estructura** Presentations, Overheads)
  *Instructor's Resource Manual* (Handouts, Textbook Answer Key, WBs/VM/LM Answer Key,

Audioscripts, Videoscripts & Translations)
  *Testing Program* (**Pruebas,** Test Generator, MP3s)
**WebSAM** (Workbook/Video Manual/Lab Manual)
**Workbook/Video Manual**
*Cuaderno para hispanohablantes*
**Lab Manual**

## Section Goals

In **Contextos**, students will learn and practice:
- names of parts of the body
- vocabulary for talking about illnesses and accidents
- vocabulary associated with medical visits

### Instructional Resources

**Supersite:** Textbook, Vocabulary, & Lab MP3 Audio Files **Lección 10**
**Supersite/IRCD:** *PowerPoints* (**Lección 10 Contextos** Presentation, Overhead #38); *IRM* (**Vocabulario adicional,** Information Gap Activities, Textbook Audio Script, Lab Audio Script, WBs/VM/LM Answer Key)
**WebSAM**
**Workbook,** pp. 109–110
**Lab Manual,** p. 55
*Cuaderno para hispanohablantes*

## Teaching Tips

- Pretend to have had an accident-filled day. Ex: **Ayer pasé un día horrible. Fui a pasear en bicicleta y me caí. Me lastimé las rodillas y los brazos. Luego, cuando llegué a casa, me di con la puerta y me lastimé el ojo. Esta mañana cerré la puerta del auto y me lastimé el dedo.** Then ask comprehension questions about what hurts. Ex: **¿Me duele la garganta? (No.)** Finally, ask students about likely treatment options.
- Show *Overhead PowerPoint #38*. Have students refer to the scene and the vocabulary boxes as you give yes-no statements about the new vocabulary. Ex: **¿Sí o no? La enfermera le toma la temperatura a la paciente. (Sí.) La doctora le pone una inyección al hombre. (No.)** Then ask volunteers to describe what is going on in the scene, using as much of the new vocabulary as possible.

# En el consultorio

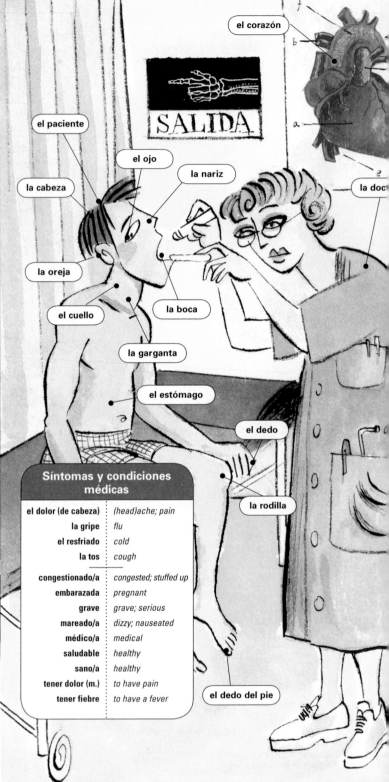

### Más vocabulario

| | |
|---|---|
| la clínica | *clinic* |
| el consultorio | *doctor's office* |
| el/la dentista | *dentist* |
| el examen médico | *physical exam* |
| la farmacia | *pharmacy* |
| el hospital | *hospital* |
| la operación | *operation* |
| la sala de emergencia(s) | *emergency room* |
| el cuerpo | *body* |
| el oído | *(sense of) hearing; inner ear* |
| el accidente | *accident* |
| la salud | *health* |
| el síntoma | *symptom* |
| caerse | *to fall (down)* |
| darse con | *to bump into; to run into* |
| doler (o:ue) | *to hurt* |
| enfermarse | *to get sick* |
| estar enfermo/a | *to be sick* |
| poner una inyección | *to give an injection* |
| recetar | *to prescribe* |
| romperse (la pierna) | *to break (one's leg)* |
| sacar(se) un diente | *to have a tooth removed* |
| sufrir una enfermedad | *to suffer an illness* |
| torcerse (o:ue) (el tobillo) | *to sprain (one's ankle)* |
| toser | *to cough* |

### Variación léxica

| | | |
|---|---|---|
| gripe | ⟷ | gripa (*Col., Gua., Méx.*) |
| resfriado | ⟷ | catarro (*Cuba, Esp., Gua.*) |
| sala de emergencia(s) | ⟷ | sala de urgencias (*Arg., Esp., Méx.*) |
| romperse | ⟷ | quebrarse (*Arg., Gua.*) |

**recursos**

WB pp. 109–110

LM p. 55

SUPERSITE panorama.vhlcentral.com Lección 10

Labels on the illustration:
el corazón, el paciente, SALIDA, el ojo, la nariz, la cabeza, la oreja, el cuello, la boca, la garganta, el estómago, el dedo, la rodilla, el dedo del pie, la doctora

### Síntomas y condiciones médicas

| | |
|---|---|
| el dolor (de cabeza) | *(head)ache; pain* |
| la gripe | *flu* |
| el resfriado | *cold* |
| la tos | *cough* |
| congestionado/a | *congested; stuffed up* |
| embarazada | *pregnant* |
| grave | *grave; serious* |
| mareado/a | *dizzy; nauseated* |
| médico/a | *medical* |
| saludable | *healthy* |
| sano/a | *healthy* |
| tener dolor (m.) | *to have pain* |
| tener fiebre | *to have a fever* |

---

**TEACHING OPTIONS**

**TPR** Play a game of **Simón dice.** Write **señalen** on the board and explain that it means *point.* Start by saying: **Simón dice... señalen la nariz.** Students are to touch their noses and keep their hands there until instructed to do otherwise. Work through various parts of the body. Be sure to give instructions occasionally without saying **Simón dice...**

**Variación léxica** Point out differences in health-related vocabulary, as well as some false cognates. **Embarazada** means *pregnant,* not *embarrassed.* You may also want to present **constipado/a** and explain that it does not mean *constipated,* but rather *congested* or *stuffed up.* Point out that, whereas in English people have ten fingers and ten toes, in Spanish people have twenty **dedos: diez dedos de las manos y diez de los pies.**

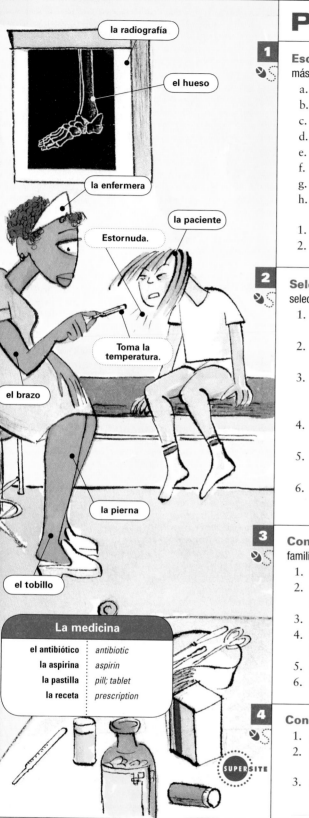

la radiografía

el hueso

la enfermera

Estornuda.

la paciente

Toma la temperatura.

el brazo

la pierna

el tobillo

### La medicina

| | |
|---|---|
| **el antibiótico** | *antibiotic* |
| **la aspirina** | *aspirin* |
| **la pastilla** | *pill; tablet* |
| **la receta** | *prescription* |

# Práctica

**1** **Escuchar** 🎧 Escucha las preguntas y selecciona la respuesta más adecuada.

a. Tengo dolor de cabeza y fiebre.
b. No fui a la clase porque estaba (*I was*) enfermo.
c. Me caí la semana pasada jugando al tenis.
d. Debes ir a la farmacia.
e. Porque tengo gripe.
f. Sí, tengo mucha tos por las noches.
g. Lo llevaron directamente a la sala de emergencia.
h. No sé. Todavía tienen que tomarme la temperatura.

1. __c__   3. __g__   5. __f__   7. __a__
2. __e__   4. __d__   6. __h__   8. __b__

**2** **Seleccionar** 🎧 Escucha la conversación entre Daniel y su doctor y selecciona la respuesta que mejor complete cada oración.

1. Daniel cree que tiene __a__.
   a. gripe     b. un resfriado     c. la temperatura alta
2. A Daniel le duele la cabeza, estornuda, tose y __c__.
   a. se cae     b. tiene fiebre     c. está congestionado
3. El doctor le __b__.
   a. pone una inyección     b. toma la temperatura
   c. mira el oído
4. A Daniel no le gustan __a__.
   a. las inyecciones   b. los antibióticos   c. las visitas al doctor
5. El doctor dice que Daniel tiene __b__.
   a. gripe     b. un resfriado     c. fiebre
6. Después de la consulta Daniel va a __c__.
   a. la sala de emergencia     b. la clínica     c. la farmacia

**3** **Completar** Completa las oraciones con una palabra de la misma familia de la palabra subrayada. Usa la forma correcta de cada palabra.

1. Cuando <u>oyes</u> algo, usas el __oído__.
2. Cuando te <u>enfermas</u>, te sientes __enfermo/a__ y necesitas ir al consultorio para ver a la __enfermera__.
3. ¿Alguien __estornudó__? Creo que oí un <u>estornudo</u> (*sneeze*).
4. No puedo <u>arrodillarme</u> (*kneel down*) porque me lastimé la __rodilla__ en un accidente de coche.
5. ¿Vas al __consultorio__ para <u>consultar</u> al médico?
6. Si te rompes un <u>diente</u>, vas al __dentista__.

**4** **Contestar** Mira el dibujo y contesta las preguntas. Answers will vary.

1. ¿Qué hace la doctora?
2. ¿Qué hay en la pared (*wall*)?
3. ¿Qué hace la enfermera?
4. ¿Qué hace el paciente?
5. ¿A quién le duele la garganta?
6. ¿Qué tiene la paciente?

SUPERSITE

310
Instr...

**5 Teaching Tip** Point out that there are several parts of the body that may be associated with each activity. Encourage students to list as many as they can.

**5 Expansion** Name parts of the body and ask students to associate them with as many activities as they can.

**6 Expansion**
- Ask for a show of hands for those who fall into the different health levels based on point totals. Analyze the trends of the class—are your students healthy or unhealthy?
- Ask for volunteers from each of the three groups to explain whether they think the results of the survey are accurate or not. Ask them to give examples based on their own eating, exercise, and other health habits.
- You may want to have students brainstorm a few additional health-related questions and responses, and adjust the point totals accordingly. Ex: **¿Con qué frecuencia te lavas las manos? ¿Con qué frecuencia usas seda dental? ¿Tomas el sol sin bloqueador solar? ¿Comes comida rápida (McDonald's, etc.)? ¿Fumas cigarros? ¿Consumes mucha cafeína?**

**Note:** At this point you may want to present *Vocabulario adicional: Más vocabulario para el consultorio,* from the Supersite/IRCD.

---

**5**

**Asociaciones** Trabajen en parejas para identificar las partes del cuerpo que ustedes asocian con estas actividades. Sigan el modelo. Answers will vary.

> **modelo**
> nadar
> **Estudiante 1:** Usamos los brazos para nadar.
> **Estudiante 2:** Usamos las piernas también.

1. hablar por teléfono
2. tocar el piano
3. correr en el parque
4. escuchar música
5. ver una película
6. toser
7. llevar zapatos
8. comprar perfume
9. estudiar biología
10. comer lomo a la plancha

**6**

**Cuestionario** Contesta el cuestionario seleccionando las respuestas que reflejen mejor tus experiencias. Suma (*Add*) los puntos de cada respuesta y anota el resultado. Después, con el resto de la clase, compara y analiza los resultados del cuestionario y comenta lo que dicen de la salud y de los hábitos de todo el grupo. Answers will vary.

# ¿Tienes buena salud?

| | |
|---|---|
| **27–30 puntos** | Salud y hábitos excelentes |
| **23–26 puntos** | Salud y hábitos buenos |
| **22 puntos o menos** | Salud y hábitos problemáticos |

1. **¿Con qué frecuencia te enfermas? (resfriados, gripe, etc.)**
   Cuatro veces por año o más. (1 punto)
   Dos o tres veces por año. (2 puntos)
   Casi nunca. (3 puntos)

2. **¿Con qué frecuencia tienes dolores de estómago o problemas digestivos?**
   Con mucha frecuencia. (1 punto)
   A veces. (2 puntos)
   Casi nunca. (3 puntos)

3. **¿Con qué frecuencia sufres de dolores de cabeza?**
   Frecuentemente. (1 punto)
   A veces. (2 puntos)
   Casi nunca. (3 puntos)

4. **¿Comes verduras y frutas?**
   No, casi nunca como verduras ni frutas. (1 punto)
   Sí, a veces. (2 puntos)
   Sí, todos los días. (3 puntos)

5. **¿Eres alérgico/a a algo?**
   Sí, a muchas cosas. (1 punto)
   Sí, a algunas cosas. (2 puntos)
   No. (3 puntos)

6. **¿Haces ejercicios aeróbicos?**
   No, casi nunca hago ejercicios aeróbicos. (1 punto)
   Sí, a veces. (2 puntos)
   Sí, con frecuencia. (3 puntos)

7. **¿Con qué frecuencia te haces un examen médico?**
   Nunca o casi nunca. (1 punto)
   Cada dos años. (2 puntos)
   Cada año y/o antes de practicar un deporte. (3 puntos)

8. **¿Con qué frecuencia vas al dentista?**
   Nunca voy al dentista. (1 punto)
   Sólo cuando me duele un diente. (2 puntos)
   Por lo menos una vez por año. (3 puntos)

9. **¿Qué comes normalmente por la mañana?**
   No como nada por la mañana. (1 punto)
   Tomo una bebida dietética. (2 puntos)
   Como cereal y fruta. (3 puntos)

10. **¿Con qué frecuencia te sientes mareado/a?**
    Frecuentemente. (1 punto)
    A veces. (2 puntos)
    Casi nunca. (3 puntos)

---

**TEACHING OPTIONS**

**Small Groups** On the board, write popular expressions related to parts of the body and guide students in guessing their meanings. Ex: **tomarle el pelo (a alguien), no tener pelos en la lengua, salvarse por un pelo, costar un ojo de la cara, no tener dos dedos de frente, ponerle los pelos de punta, hablar hasta por los codos**. In small groups, have students create a sentence about a famous person or classmate for each expression.

Ex: **El presidente no tiene pelos en la lengua.**
**Game** Play a modified version of **20 Preguntas.** Ask a volunteer to think of a part of the body. Other students get one chance each to ask a yes-no question until someone guesses the correct body part. Limit attempts to ten questions per item. Encourage students to guess by associating activities with various parts of the body.

# Comunicación

**7** **¿Qué le pasó?** Trabajen en un grupo de dos o tres personas. Hablen de lo que les pasó y de cómo se sienten las personas que aparecen en los dibujos. *Answers will vary.*

1. Adela

2. Francisco

3. Pilar

4. Pedro

5. Cristina

6. Félix

**8** **Un accidente** Cuéntale a la clase de un accidente o una enfermedad que tuviste. Incluye información que conteste estas preguntas. *Answers will vary.*

- ✓ ¿Qué ocurrió?
- ✓ ¿Dónde ocurrió?
- ✓ ¿Cuándo ocurrió?
- ✓ ¿Cómo ocurrió?
- ✓ ¿Quién te ayudó y cómo?
- ✓ ¿Tuviste algún problema después del accidente o después de la enfermedad?
- ✓ ¿Cuánto tiempo tuviste el problema?

**9** **Crucigrama (*Crossword*)** Tu profesor(a) les va a dar a ti y a tu compañero/a un crucigrama incompleto. Tú tienes las palabras que necesita tu compañero/a y él/ella tiene las palabras que tú necesitas. Tienen que darse pistas para completarlo. No pueden decir la palabra necesaria; deben utilizar definiciones, ejemplos y frases. *Answers will vary.*

> **modelo**
> **10 horizontal:** La usamos para hablar.
> **14 vertical:** Es el médico que examina los dientes.

---

### TEACHING OPTIONS

**Pairs** For homework, ask students to draw an alien or other fantastic being. In the next class period, have students describe the alien to a classmate, who will draw it according to the description. Ex: **Tiene una cabeza grande y tres piernas delgadas con pelo en las rodillas. Encima de la cabeza tiene ocho ojos pequeños y uno grande...** Then have students compare the drawings for accuracy.

**Extra Practice** Write **Mido ____ pies y ____ pulgadas** on the board and explain what it means. Then have students write physical descriptions of themselves using as much vocabulary from this lesson as they can. Collect the papers, shuffle them, and read the descriptions aloud. The rest of the class has to guess who is being described.

**Section Goals**

In **Fotonovela**, students will:
• receive comprehensible input from free-flowing discourse
• learn functional phrases that preview lesson grammatical structures

**Instructional Resources**
**Supersite/DVD:** *Fotonovela*
**Supersite/IRCD:** *IRM*
(*Fotonovela* Videoscript & Translation, WBs/VM/LM Answer Key)
**WebSAM**
**Video Manual,** pp. 213–214

**Video Recap: Lección 9**
Before doing this **Fotonovela** section, review the previous one with this activity.
**1. ¿De quién fue el cumpleaños?** (de Maite) **2. ¿Cómo supo doña Rita del cumpleaños?** (Se lo dijo don Francisco.) **3. ¿Qué trajo doña Rita de comer para celebrar el cumpleaños?** (flan, pastel de chocolate con helado y vino) **4. ¿Quién no tomó vino? ¿Por qué no?** (don Francisco; porque es el conductor)

**Video Synopsis** While on the bus, **Javier** injures his ankle. **Don Francisco** takes him to the clinic of his friend, **Doctora Márquez**. **Doctora Márquez** determines that **Javier** has twisted his ankle. She prescribes some pain medication and sends them on their way.

**Teaching Tips**
• Have students scan the **Fotonovela** for words and expressions related to health care. Then have them predict what will happen in this episode.
• Review the predictions and ask a few questions to guide students in summarizing this episode.

# ¡Uf! ¡Qué dolor!

Don Francisco y Javier van a la clínica de la doctora Márquez.

**PERSONAJES**

INÉS

DON FRANCISCO

JAVIER

DRA. MÁRQUEZ

**JAVIER** Estoy aburrido... tengo ganas de dibujar. Con permiso.

**INÉS** ¡Javier! ¿Qué te pasó?
**JAVIER** ¡Ay! ¡Uf! ¡Qué dolor! ¡Creo que me rompí el tobillo!

**DON FRANCISCO** No te preocupes, Javier. Estamos cerca de la clínica donde trabaja la doctora Márquez, mi amiga.

**DRA. MÁRQUEZ** ¿Cuánto tiempo hace que se cayó?
**JAVIER** Ya se me olvidó... déjeme ver... este... eran más o menos las dos o dos y media cuando me caí... o sea hace más de una hora. ¡Me duele mucho!
**DRA. MÁRQUEZ** Bueno, vamos a sacarle una radiografía.

**DON FRANCISCO** Sabes, Javier, cuando era chico yo les tenía mucho miedo a los médicos. Visitaba mucho al doctor porque me enfermaba con mucha frecuencia y tenía muchas infecciones de la garganta. No me gustaban las inyecciones ni las pastillas. Una vez me rompí la pierna jugando al fútbol...

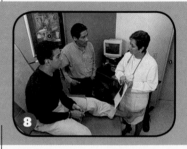

**JAVIER** ¡Doctora! ¿Qué dice? ¿Está roto el tobillo?
**DRA. MÁRQUEZ** Tranquilo, le tengo buenas noticias, Javier. No está roto el tobillo. Apenas está torcido.

**recursos**

VM
pp. 213–214

panorama.vhlcentral.com
Lección 10

JAVIER ¿Tengo dolor? Sí, mucho. ¿Dónde? En el tobillo. ¿Tengo fiebre? No lo creo. ¿Estoy mareado? Un poco. ¿Soy alérgico a algún medicamento? No. ¿Embarazada? Definitivamente NO.

DRA. MÁRQUEZ ¿Cómo se lastimó el pie?

JAVIER Me caí cuando estaba en el autobús.

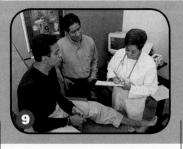

JAVIER Pero, ¿voy a poder ir de excursión con mis amigos?

DRA. MÁRQUEZ Creo que sí. Pero debe descansar y no caminar mucho durante un par de días. Le receto unas pastillas para el dolor.

DRA. MÁRQUEZ Adiós, Francisco. Adiós, Javier. ¡Cuidado! ¡Buena suerte en las montañas!

## Expresiones útiles

### Discussing medical conditions

- **¿Cómo se lastimó el pie? (lastimarse)**
  *How did you hurt your foot?*
  **Me caí en el autobús.**
  *I fell when I was on the bus.*

- **¿Te duele el tobillo?**
  *Does your ankle hurt? (fam.)*
- **¿Le duele el tobillo?**
  *Does your ankle hurt? (form.)*
  **Sí, (me duele) mucho.**
  *Yes, (it hurts) a lot.*

- **¿Es usted alérgico/a a algún medicamento?**
  *Are you allergic to any medication?*
  **Sí, soy alérgico/a a la penicilina.**
  *Yes, I'm allergic to penicillin.*

- **¿Está roto el tobillo?**
  *Is my ankle broken?*
  **No está roto. Apenas está torcido.**
  *It's not broken. It's just twisted.*

- **¿Te enfermabas frecuentemente?**
  *Did you get sick frequently? (fam.)*
  **Sí, me enfermaba frecuentemente.**
  *Yes, I used to get sick frequently.*
  **Tenía muchas infecciones.**
  *I used to get a lot of infections.*

### Other expressions

- **hace +** [*period of time*] **+ que +** [*present tense*]:
- **¿Cuánto tiempo hace que te duele?**
  *How long has it been hurting?*
  **Hace una hora que me duele.**
  *It's been hurting for an hour.*

- **hace +** [*period of time*] **+ que +** [*preterite*]:
- **¿Cuánto tiempo hace que se cayó?**
  *How long ago did you fall?*
  **Me caí hace más de una hora./ Hace más de una hora que me caí.**
  *I fell more than an hour ago.*

# ¿Qué pasó?

**1** ¿Cierto o falso? Decide si lo que dicen estas oraciones sobre Javier es **cierto** o **falso**. Corrige las oraciones falsas.

|  | Cierto | Falso |
|---|---|---|
| 1. Está aburrido y tiene ganas de hacer algo creativo. | ☑ | ○ |
| 2. Cree que se rompió la rodilla. | ○ | ☑   Cree que se rompió el tobillo. |
| 3. Se lastimó cuando se cayó en el autobús. | ☑ | ○ |
| 4. Es alérgico a dos medicamentos. | ○ | ☑   No es alérgico a ningún medicamento. |
| 5. No está mareado pero sí tiene un poco de fiebre. | ○ | ☑   Está un poco mareado pero no tiene fiebre. |

**2** Identificar Identifica quién puede decir estas oraciones.

1. Hace años me rompí la pierna cuando estaba jugando al fútbol. don Francisco
2. Hace más de una hora que me lastimé el pie. Me duele muchísimo. Javier
3. Tengo que sacarle una radiografía. No sé si se rompió uno de los huesos del pie. Dra. Márquez
4. No hay problema, vamos a ver a mi amiga, la doctora Márquez. don Francisco
5. Bueno, parece que el tobillo no está roto. Qué bueno, ¿no? Dra. Márquez
6. No sé si voy a poder ir de excursión con el grupo. Javier

**DRA. MÁRQUEZ**

**DON FRANCISCO**

**JAVIER**

**3** Ordenar Pon estos eventos en el orden correcto.

a. La doctora le saca una radiografía. ___4___
b. La doctora le receta unas pastillas para el dolor. ___6___
c. Javier se lastima el tobillo en el autobús. ___2___
d. Don Francisco le habla a Javier de cuando era chico. ___5___
e. Javier quiere dibujar un rato (a while). ___1___
f. Don Francisco lo lleva a una clínica. ___3___

**4** En el consultorio Trabajen en parejas para representar los papeles de un(a) médico/a y su paciente. Usen las instrucciones como guía.

| El/La médico/a | El/La paciente |
|---|---|
| Pregúntale al/a la paciente si le duele. → | Te caíste en casa. Describe tu dolor. |
| Pregúntale cuánto tiempo hace que se cayó. → | Describe la situación. Piensas que te rompiste el dedo. |
| Mira el dedo. Debes recomendar un tratamiento (treatment) al/a la paciente. → | Debes hacer preguntas al/a la médico/a sobre el tratamiento (treatment). |

NATIONAL communication STANDARDS

**AYUDA**

Here are some useful expressions:

¿Cómo se lastimó...?
¿Le duele...?
¿Cuánto tiempo hace que...?
Tengo...
Estoy...
¿Es usted alérgico/a a algún medicamento?
Usted debe...

---

**TEACHING OPTIONS**

**Heritage Speakers** Ask heritage speakers to prepare a poster about the health-care system of their families' countries of origin or other Spanish-speaking countries they have visited. Have them present their posters to the class, who can ask questions about the information.

**Extra Practice** Ask students questions about the **Fotonovela**. Ex: 1. ¿Quién se lastimó en el autobús? (Javier) 2. ¿Cómo se llama la amiga de don Francisco? (Dra. Márquez) 3. ¿Adónde lleva don Francisco a Javier? (a la clínica de la doctora Márquez) 4. ¿Quién tenía muchas infecciones de la garganta? (don Francisco)

# Ortografía  SUPERSITE
## El acento y las sílabas fuertes

In Spanish, written accent marks are used on many words. Here is a review of some of the principles governing word stress and the use of written accents.

**as-pi-ri-na    gri-pe      to-man      an-tes**

In Spanish, when a word ends in a vowel, **-n**, or **-s**, the spoken stress usually falls on the next-to-last syllable. Words of this type are very common and do not need a written accent.

**a-sí      in-glés      in-fec-ción      hé-ro-e**

When a word ends in a vowel, **-n**, or **-s**, and the spoken stress does *not* fall on the next-to-last syllable, then a written accent is needed.

**hos-pi-tal    na-riz      re-ce-tar      to-ser**

When a word ends in any consonant *other* than **-n** or **-s**, the spoken stress usually falls on the last syllable. Words of this type are very common and do not need a written accent.

**lá-piz      fút-bol      hués-ped      sué-ter**

When a word ends in any consonant *other* than **-n** or **-s** and the spoken stress does *not* fall on the last syllable, then a written accent is needed.

**far-ma-cia    bio-lo-gí-a    su-cio      frí-o**

Diphthongs (two weak vowels or a strong and weak vowel together) are normally pronounced as a single syllable. A written accent is needed when a diphthong is broken into two syllables.

**sol      pan      mar      tos**

Spanish words of only one syllable do not usually carry a written accent (unless it is to distinguish meaning: **se** and **sé**.)

> **CONSULTA**
>
> In Spanish, **a**, **e**, and **o** are considered strong vowels while **i** and **u** are weak vowels. To review this concept, see **Lección 3**, **Pronunciación**, p. 77.

**Práctica** Busca las palabras que necesitan acento escrito y escribe su forma correcta.

1. sal-mon  salmón
2. ins-pec-tor
3. nu-me-ro  número
4. fa-cil  fácil
5. ju-go
6. a-bri-go
7. ra-pi-do  rápido
8. sa-ba-do  sábado
9. vez
10. me-nu  menú
11. o-pe-ra-cion  operación
12. im-per-me-a-ble
13. a-de-mas  además
14. re-ga-te-ar
15. an-ti-pa-ti-co  antipático
16. far-ma-cia
17. es-qui  esquí
18. pen-sion  pensión
19. pa-is  país
20. per-don  perdón

**El ahorcado** (*Hangman*) Juega al ahorcado para adivinar las palabras.

1. _ l _ _ _ _ _ a      Vas allí cuando estás enfermo.  clínica
2. _ _ _ _ e _ c _ _ n      Se usa para poner una vacuna (*vaccination*).  inyección
3. _ _ d _ o _ _ _ _ _ a      Ves los huesos.  radiografía
4. _ _ _ _ i _ o      Trabaja en un hospital.  médico
5. a _ _ _ b _ _ _ _ _ _      Es una medicina.  antibiótico

> **recursos**
>
> LM p. 56    SUPERSITE panorama.vhlcentral.com Lección 10

**Section Goals**

In **Ortografía**, students will review:
• word stress
• the use of written accent marks

**Instructional Resources**
**Supersite:** Lab MP3 Audio Files **Lección 10**
**Supersite/IRCD:** *IRM* (Lab Audio Script, WBs/VM/LM Answer Key)
**WebSAM**
**Lab Manual,** p. 56
*Cuaderno para hispanohablantes*

**Teaching Tips**
• You may want to explain that all words in which the spoken stress falls on the antepenultimate syllable or one before will carry a written accent, regardless of the letter they end in.
• As you go through each point in the explanation, write the example words on the board, pronounce them, and have students repeat. Then, ask students to provide words they learned in previous lessons that exemplify each point.
• For additional auditory practice, read several words aloud and have students raise their hand if the word has a written accent mark. Ask volunteers to write the words on the board.
• Point out that **Ortografía** replaces **Pronunciación** in the Student Edition for **Lecciones 10–15**, but not in the Lab Manual. The **Recursos** box references the **Pronunciación** sections found in all lessons of the Lab Manual.

> **TEACHING OPTIONS**
>
> **Extra Practice** Add an auditory aspect to this **Ortografía** section. Have students close their books. Then read aloud the sentences in **Actividad 1, ¿Cierto o falso?**, page 314. Say each sentence twice slowly and once at normal speed to give students enough time to write. Then have them open their books and check their work.
>
> **Pairs** Ask students to work in pairs and explain why each word in the **Práctica** activity does or does not have a written accent mark. The same process can be followed with the words in the **El ahorcado** activity.

SUPERSITE | Flash CULTURA

## Section Goals

In **Cultura**, students will:
- read about health services in Spanish-speaking countries
- learn health-related terms
- read about **curanderos** and **chamanes**
- read about home remedies and medicinal plants

---

**Instructional Resources**
**Supersite:** *Flash cultura*
Videoscript & Translation
**Supersite/DVD:** *Flash cultura*
*Cuaderno para hispanohablantes*

---

**En detalle**
**Antes de leer** Ask students about their experiences with health care while traveling.
Ex: **¿Alguna vez te enfermaste durante un viaje? ¿Dónde? ¿Fuiste al hospital o al médico? ¿Quién lo pagó?**

**Lectura**
- Point out that many over-the-counter health-care products in the U.S. are available by request at pharmacies in Spanish-speaking countries (e.g. face cleansers, sun block, contact solution).
- Tell students that most pharmacies are closed on Sundays.
- While traditional pharmacies are privately owned and consist of a small counter and retail space, large chain pharmacies are entering the market, especially in Latin America.

**Después de leer**
- Ask students what facts in this reading are new or surprising to them.

**1 Expansion** Give students these true-false statements as items 9–10: **9. El sistema de salud en Cuba no es muy desarrollado. (Falso. Es muy desarrollado.) 10. Las farmacias generalmente tienen un horario comercial. (Cierto.)**

---

**EN DETALLE**

# Servicios de salud

**¿Pensaste alguna vez en visitar un país hispano?** Si lo haces, vas a encontrar algunas diferencias respecto a la vida en los Estados Unidos. Una de ellas está en los servicios de salud.

En la mayor parte de los países hispanos, el gobierno ofrece servicios médicos muy baratos o gratuitos° a sus ciudadanos°. Los turistas y extranjeros también pueden tener acceso a los servicios médicos a bajo° costo. La Seguridad Social y organizaciones similares son las responsables de gestionar° estos servicios.

Naturalmente, esto no funciona igual° en todos los países. En Colombia, Ecuador, México y Perú, la situación varía según las regiones. Los habitantes de las ciudades y pueblos grandes tienen acceso a más servicios médicos, mientras que quienes viven en pueblos remotos sólo cuentan con° pequeñas clínicas.

**Cruz verde de farmacia en Madrid, España**

Por su parte, Argentina, Costa Rica, Cuba, Uruguay y España tienen sistemas de salud muy desarrollados°. Toda la población tiene acceso a ellos y en muchos casos son completamente gratuitos. Costa Rica ofrece servicios gratuitos también a los extranjeros.

¡Así que ya lo sabes! Si vas a viajar a otro país, antes de ir debes obtener información sobre los servicios médicos en el lugar de destino°. Prepara todos los documentos necesarios. ¡Y disfruta° tu estadía° en el extranjero sin problemas!

**Consulta médica en la República Dominicana**

### Las farmacias

**Farmacia de guardia:** Las farmacias generalmente tienen un horario comercial. Sin embargo°, en cada barrio° hay una farmacia de guardia que abre las veinticuatro horas del día.

**Productos farmacéuticos:** Todavía hay muchas farmacias tradicionales que están más especializadas en medicinas y productos farmacéuticos. No venden una gran variedad de productos.

**Recetas:** Muchos medicamentos se venden sin receta médica. Los farmacéuticos aconsejan° a las personas sobre problemas de salud y les dan las medicinas.

**Cruz° verde:** En muchos países, las farmacias tienen el signo de una cruz verde. Cuando la cruz verde está encendida°, la farmacia está abierta.

gratuitos *free (of charge)* ciudadanos *citizens* bajo *low* gestionar *to manage* igual *in the same way* cuentan con *have* desarrollados *developed* destino *destination* disfruta *enjoy* estadía *stay* Sin embargo *However* barrio *neighborhood* aconsejan *advise* Cruz *Cross* encendida *lit (up)*

---

**ACTIVIDADES**

**1**  **¿Cierto o falso?** Indica si lo que dicen las oraciones es **cierto** o **falso**. Corrige la información falsa.

1. En los países hispanos los gobiernos ofrecen servicios de salud accesibles a sus ciudadanos. Cierto.

2. En los países hispanos los extranjeros tienen que pagar mucho dinero por los servicios médicos. Falso. Los extranjeros tienen acceso a los servicios médicos a bajo costo.

3. En Costa Rica los extranjeros pueden recibir servicios médicos gratuitos. Cierto.

4. Las farmacias de guardia abren sólo los sábados y domingos. Falso. Las farmacias de guardia abren las 24 horas del día.

5. En los países hispanos las farmacias venden una gran variedad de productos. Falso. En los países hispanos las farmacias están más especializadas en medicinas y productos farmacéuticos.

6. Los farmacéuticos de los países hispanos aconsejan a los enfermos y venden algunas medicinas sin necesidad de receta. Cierto.

7. En México y otros países, los pueblos remotos cuentan con grandes centros médicos. Falso. Cuentan con pequeñas clínicas.

8. Muchas farmacias usan una cruz verde como símbolo. Cierto.

---

**TEACHING OPTIONS**

**Cultural Comparison** Ask students to write a short paragraph in which they compare the health-care systems in the U.S. or Canada with those of different Spanish-speaking countries. You may want to have students review comparisons (**Estructura 8.3**) before writing.

**Pairs** Ask pairs to write a dialogue in which a foreign tourist in Costa Rica goes to the emergency room due to an injury. Have them use vocabulary from **Contextos** and **Expresiones útiles**. Have students role-play their dialogues for the class.

## ASÍ SE DICE

### La salud

| | |
|---|---|
| el chequeo (Esp., Méx.) | el examen médico |
| la droguería (Col.) | la farmacia |
| la herida | *injury; wound* |
| la píldora | la pastilla |
| los primeros auxilios | *first aid* |
| la sangre | *blood* |

## EL MUNDO HISPANO

### Remedios caseros° y plantas medicinales

○ **Achiote°** En Suramérica se usa para curar inflamaciones de garganta. Las hojas° de achiote se cuecen° en agua, se cuelan° y se hacen gargarismos° con esa agua.

○ **Ají** En Perú se usan cataplasmas° de las semillas° de ají para aliviar los dolores reumáticos y la tortícolis°.

○ **Azúcar** En Nicaragua y otros países centroamericanos se usa el azúcar para detener° la sangre en pequeñas heridas.

○ **Sábila (aloe vera)** En Latinoamérica, el jugo de las hojas de sábila se usa para reducir cicatrices°. Se recomienda aplicarlo sobre la cicatriz dos veces al día, durante varios meses.

Remedios caseros *Home remedies* Achiote *Annatto* hojas *leaves* se cuecen *are cooked* se cuelan *they are drained* gargarismos *gargles* cataplasmas *pastes* semillas *seeds* tortícolis *stiff neck* detener *to stop* cicatrices *scars*

## PERFILES

### Curanderos° y chamanes

¿Quieres ser doctor(a), juez(a)°, político/a o psicólogo/a? En algunas sociedades de las Américas **los curanderos** y **los chamanes** no tienen que escoger entre estas profesiones porque ellos son mediadores de conflictos y dan consejos a la comunidad. Su opinión es muy respetada.

**Códice Florentino, México, siglo XVI**

Desde las culturas antiguas° de las Américas muchas personas piensan que la salud del cuerpo y de la mente sólo puede existir si hay un equilibrio entre el ser humano y la naturaleza. Los curanderos y los chamanes son quienes cuidan este equilibrio.

Los curanderos se especializan más en enfermedades físicas, mientras que los chamanes están más

relacionados con los males° de la mente y el alma°. Ambos° usan plantas, masajes y rituales, y sus conocimientos se basan en la tradición, la experiencia, la observación y la intuición.

**Cuzco, Perú**

Curanderos *Healers* juez(a) *judge* antiguas *ancient* males *illnesses* alma *soul* Ambos *Both*

**SUPERSITE** ⁀ Conexión Internet

¿Cuáles son algunos hospitales importantes del mundo hispano? | Go to panorama.vhlcentral.com to find more cultural information related to this **Cultura** section.

## ACTIVIDADES

**2** **Comprensión** Responde a las preguntas.

1. ¿Cómo se les llama a las farmacias en Colombia? droguerías
2. ¿Qué parte del achiote se usa para curar la garganta? las hojas
3. ¿Cómo se aplica la sábila para reducir cicatrices? Se aplica sobre la cicatriz dos veces al día.
4. En algunas partes de las Américas, ¿quiénes mantienen el equilibrio entre el ser humano y la naturaleza? los chamanes y curanderos
5. ¿Qué usan los curanderos y chamanes para curar? Usan plantas, masajes y rituales.

**3** **¿Qué haces cuando tienes gripe?** Escribe cuatro oraciones sobre las cosas que haces cuando tienes gripe. Explica si vas al médico, si tomas medicamentos o si sigues alguna dieta especial. Después, comparte tu texto con un(a) compañero/a. Answers will vary.

**recursos**

**SUPERSITE**

panorama.vhlcentral.com
Lección 10

## TEACHING OPTIONS

**TPR** Divide the class into two teams, **remedios naturales** and **medicina moderna**, and have them stand at opposite sides of the room. Indicate the first member of each team and describe a situation. The student whose team corresponds to the situation has five seconds to step forward. Ex: **1. Juan tiene dolor de cabeza. Decide comprar vitamina B2.** (remedios naturales) **2. María tiene mucha ansiedad. Toma pastillas calmantes.** (medicina moderna)

**Small Groups** Have students work in small groups to create a television commercial for a new natural product. Encourage students to include a testimonial from a satisfied customer about how long he or she has had these symptoms (**hace** + [*time period*] + **que** + [*present*]), when he or she started using the product (**hace** + [*time period*] + **que** + [*preterite*]), and how he or she feels now.

## Section Goal

In **Estructura 10.1**, students will learn the imperfect tense.

---

**Instructional Resources**
**Supersite:** Lab MP3 Audio Files **Lección 10**
**Supersite/IRCD:** *PowerPoints* (Lección 10 Estructura Presentation); *IRM* (Information Gap Activities, Lab Audio Script, WBs/VM/LM Answer Key)
**WebSAM**
**Workbook,** pp. 111–112
**Lab Manual,** p. 57
*Cuaderno para hispanohablantes*

---

## Teaching Tips

• Explain to students that they can already express the past with the preterite tense, and now they are learning the imperfect tense, which expresses the past in a different way.

• As you work through the discussion of the imperfect, test comprehension by asking volunteers to supply the correct form of verbs for the subjects you name. Ex: **romper/nosotros (rompíamos)**

• Point out that **había** is impersonal and can be followed by a singular or plural noun. Ex: **Había una enfermera. Había muchos pacientes.**

**¡Atención!** To demonstrate that the accents on **–er** and **–ir** verbs break diphthongs, write **farmacia** and **vendia** on the board. Ask volunteers to pronounce each word, and have the class identify which needs a written accent to break the diphthong (**vendía**).

---

**10.1** **The imperfect tense** ·SUPERSITE·

NATIONAL comparisons STANDARDS

**ANTE TODO** In **Lecciones 6–9,** you learned the preterite tense. You will now learn the imperfect, which describes past activities in a different way.

### The imperfect of regular verbs

| | | cantar | beber | escribir |
|---|---|---|---|---|
| SINGULAR FORMS | yo | cant**aba** | beb**ía** | escrib**ía** |
| | tú | cant**abas** | beb**ías** | escrib**ías** |
| | Ud./él/ella | cant**aba** | beb**ía** | escrib**ía** |
| PLURAL FORMS | nosotros/as | cant**ábamos** | beb**íamos** | escrib**íamos** |
| | vosotros/as | cant**abais** | beb**íais** | escrib**íais** |
| | Uds./ellos/ellas | cant**aban** | beb**ían** | escrib**ían** |

**¡ATENCIÓN!**

Note that the imperfect endings of **–er** and **–ir** verbs are the same. Also note that the **nosotros** form of **–ar** verbs always carries an accent mark on the first **a** of the ending. All forms of **–er** and **–ir** verbs in the imperfect carry an accent on the first **i** of the ending.

▶ There are no stem changes in the imperfect.

| | |
|---|---|
| **entender** (e:ie) | **Entendíamos** japonés. *We used to understand Japanese.* |
| **servir** (e:i) | El camarero les **servía** el café. *The waiter was serving them coffee.* |
| **doler** (o:ue) | A Javier le **dolía** el tobillo. *Javier's ankle was hurting.* |

▶ The imperfect form of **hay** is **había** *(there was; there were; there used to be).*

▶ **¡Atención!** **Ir, ser,** and **ver** are the only verbs that are irregular in the imperfect.

**AYUDA**

Like **hay**, **había** can be followed by a singular or plural noun.
**Había** un solo médico en la sala.
**Había** dos pacientes allí.

### The imperfect of irregular verbs

| | | ir | ser | ver |
|---|---|---|---|---|
| SINGULAR FORMS | yo | ib**a** | era | ve**ía** |
| | tú | ib**as** | eras | ve**ías** |
| | Ud./él/ella | ib**a** | era | ve**ía** |
| PLURAL FORMS | nosotros/as | íb**amos** | ér**amos** | ve**íamos** |
| | vosotros/as | ib**ais** | erais | ve**íais** |
| | Uds./ellos/ellas | ib**an** | eran | ve**ían** |

---

**TEACHING OPTIONS**

**Extra Practice** To provide oral practice with the imperfect tense, change the subjects in **¡Inténtalo!** on page 319.
**Large Group** Write a list of activities on the board. Ex: **1. tenerle miedo a la oscuridad 2. ir a la escuela en autobús 3. llevar el almuerzo a la escuela 4. comer brócoli 5. ser atrevido/a en clase 6. creer en Santa Claus** Have students copy the list on a sheet of paper and check off the items that they used to do

when they were in the second grade. Then have them circulate around the room and find other students that used to do the same activities. Ex: **¿Le tenías miedo a la oscuridad?** When they find a student who used to do the same activity, have them write that student's name next to the item. Then have students report back to the class. Ex: **Mark y yo creíamos en Santa Claus.**

# Uses of the imperfect

▶ As a general rule, the imperfect is used to describe actions which are seen by the speaker as incomplete or "continuing," while the preterite is used to describe actions which have been completed. The imperfect expresses what was happening at a certain time or how things used to be. The preterite, in contrast, expresses a completed action.

—¿Qué te **pasó**?
*What happened to you?*

—Me **torcí** el tobillo.
*I sprained my ankle.*

—¿Dónde **vivías** de niño?
*Where did you live as a child?*

—**Vivía** en San José.
*I lived in San José.*

▶ These expressions are often used with the imperfect because they express habitual or repeated actions: **de niño/a** (*as a child*), **todos los días** (*every day*), **mientras** (*while*).

### Uses of the imperfect

| | |
|---|---|
| 1. Habitual or repeated actions . . . . . . . | **Íbamos** al parque los domingos. *We used to go to the park on Sundays.* |
| 2. Events or actions that were in progress | Yo **leía** mientras él **estudiaba**. *I was reading while he was studying.* |
| 3. Physical characteristics . . . . . . . . . . . | **Era** alto y guapo. *He was tall and handsome.* |
| 4. Mental or emotional states . . . . . . . . | **Quería** mucho a su familia. *He loved his family very much.* |
| 5. Telling time . . . . . . . . . . . . . . . . . . . . | **Eran** las tres y media. *It was 3:30.* |
| 6. Age . . . . . . . . . . . . . . . . . . . . . . . . . . | Los niños **tenían** seis años. *The children were six years old.* |

**CONSULTA**

You will learn more about the contrast between the preterite and the imperfect in **Estructura 10.2,** pp. 322–323.

 **¡INTÉNTALO!** Indica la forma correcta de cada verbo en el imperfecto.

1. Mis hermanos _____ *veían* _____ (ver) la televisión.
2. Yo _____ *viajaba* _____ (viajar) a la playa.
3. ¿Dónde _____ *vivía* _____ (vivir) Samuel de niño?
4. Tú _____ *hablabas* _____ (hablar) con Javier.
5. Leonardo y yo _____ *corríamos* _____ (correr) por el parque.
6. Ustedes _____ *iban* _____ (ir) a la clínica.
7. Nadia _____ *bailaba* _____ (bailar) merengue.
8. ¿Cuándo _____ *asistías* _____ (asistir) tú a clase de español?
9. Yo _____ *era* _____ (ser) muy feliz.
10. Nosotras _____ *comprendíamos* _____ (comprender) las preguntas.

**recursos**

WB
pp. 111–112

LM
p. 57

panorama.
vhlcentral.com
Lección 10

**TEACHING OPTIONS**

**Extra Practice** Add an auditory aspect to this grammar presentation. Prepare a list of sentences in the present tense. Ex: **Todos los días jugamos al tenis.** Read each sentence twice, pausing to allow students to convert the present tense to the imperfect. Ex: **Todos los días jugábamos al tenis.**
**Extra Practice** Ask students to write a description of their first-grade classroom and teacher, using the imperfect. Ex: **En la sala**

de clases había... La maestra se llamaba... Ella era... Have students share their descriptions with a classmate.
**TPR** Have the class stand and form a circle. Call out a name or subject pronoun and an infinitive (Ex: **ellas/ver**). Toss a foam or paper ball to a student, who will say the correct imperfect form (Ex: **veían**). He or she should then name another subject and infinitive and throw the ball to another student.

**Teaching Tips**
• Ask students to compare and contrast a home video with a family picture. Then call their attention to the description of uses of the imperfect. Which actions would be best captured by a home video? (Continuing actions; incomplete actions; what was happening; how things used to be.) Which actions are best captured in a snapshot? (A completed action.)
• Ask students to answer questions about themselves in the past. Ex: **Y tú, _____ , ¿ibas al parque los domingos cuando eras niño/a? ¿Qué hacías mientras tu madre preparaba la comida? ¿Cómo eras de niño/a?**
• Ask questions about the **Fotonovela** characters using the imperfect.

**Successful Language Learning** Ask students to think about what they used to do when they were younger and practice saying it in Spanish. This is good practice for real-life conversations because people often talk about their childhood when making new friends.

# Práctica SUPERSITE

**1 Teaching Tips**
- Before assigning the activity, review the forms of the imperfect by calling out an infinitive and a series of subject pronouns. Ask volunteers to give the corresponding forms. Ex: **querer: usted (quería); yo (quería); nosotras (queríamos).** Include irregular verbs.
- As a model, write these sentences on the board and have volunteers supply the verb forms and then reorder the sentences. **No ____ (dormir) bien. (dormía/1) ____ (Ser) la una de la mañana cuando llamé al doctor. (Era/3) Me desperté a las once porque ____ (sentirse) mal. (me sentía/2)**

**1 Expansion** Have students write a conversation between **Miguelito** and his friends in which he relates what happened after the accident.

**2 Expansion** To challenge students, ask them to identify the reason the imperfect was necessary in each sentence.

**3 Expansion** Write these sentences on the board, and have students complete them in pairs. **1. Fui al doctor porque ____. 2. Tuvo que ir al dentista porque ____. 3. El médico le dio unas pastillas porque ____. 4. La enfermera le tomó la temperatura porque ____.**

**1** **Completar** Primero, completa las oraciones con el imperfecto de los verbos. Luego, pon las oraciones en orden lógico y compáralas con las de un(a) compañero/a.

7 a. El doctor dijo que no **era** (ser) nada grave.
6 b. El doctor **quería** (querer) ver la nariz del niño.
3 c. Su mamá **estaba** (estar) dibujando cuando Miguelito entró llorando.
4 d. Miguelito **tenía** (tener) la nariz hinchada (*swollen*). Fueron al hospital.
8 e. Miguelito no **iba** (ir) a jugar más. Ahora quería ir a casa a descansar.
2 f. Miguelito y sus amigos **jugaban** (jugar) al béisbol en el patio.
1 g. **Eran** (Ser) las dos de la tarde.
5 h. Miguelito le dijo a la enfermera que **le dolía** (dolerle) la nariz.

**2** **Transformar** Forma oraciones completas para describir lo que hacían Julieta y César. Usa las formas correctas del imperfecto y añade todas las palabras necesarias.

1. Julieta y César / ser / paramédicos
   Julieta y César eran paramédicos.
2. trabajar / juntos y / llevarse / muy bien
   Trabajaban juntos y se llevaban muy bien.
3. cuando / haber / accidente, / siempre / analizar / situación / con cuidado
   Cuando había un accidente, siempre analizaban la situación con cuidado.
4. preocuparse / mucho / por / pacientes
   Se preocupaban mucho por los pacientes.
5. si / paciente / tener / mucho / dolor, / ponerle / inyección
   Si el paciente tenía mucho dolor, le ponían una inyección.

**3** **En la escuela de medicina** Usa los verbos de la lista para completar las oraciones con las formas correctas del imperfecto. Algunos verbos se usan más de una vez. Some answers will vary.

| caerse | enfermarse | ir | querer | tener |
|---|---|---|---|---|
| comprender | estornudar | pensar | sentirse | tomar |
| doler | hacer | poder | ser | toser |

1. Cuando Javier y Victoria **eran** estudiantes de medicina, siempre **tenían** que ir al médico.
2. Cada vez que él **tomaba** un examen, a Javier le **dolía** mucho la cabeza.
3. Cuando Victoria **hacía** ejercicios aeróbicos, siempre **se sentía** mareada.
4. Todas las primaveras, Javier **estornudaba/tosía** mucho porque es alérgico al polen.
5. Victoria también **se caía** de su bicicleta en camino a clase.
6. Después de comer en la cafetería, a Victoria siempre le **dolía** el estómago.
7. Javier **quería/pensaba** ser médico para ayudar a los demás.
8. Pero no **comprendía** por qué él **se enfermaba** con tanta frecuencia.
9. Cuando Victoria **tenía** fiebre, no **podía** ni leer el termómetro.
10. A Javier **le dolían** los dientes, pero nunca **quería** ir al dentista.
11. Victoria **tosía/estornudaba** mucho cuando **se sentía** congestionada.
12. Javier y Victoria **pensaban** que nunca **iban** a graduarse.

**TEACHING OPTIONS**

**TPR** Model gestures for physical or emotional states using the imperfect. Ex: **Me dolía la cabeza.** (Furrow your brow and rub your forehead.) **Tenía fiebre.** (Fan yourself.) Have students stand. Say an expression at random (Ex: **Estornudabas**) and signal a student to perform the appropriate gesture. Keep a brisk pace. Vary by pointing to multiple students (Ex: **Ustedes se enfermaban.**).

**Small Groups** Ask students to write about a favorite or disliked doctor or dentist from the past. They should use at least five verbs in the imperfect. Then have them read, compare, and discuss the descriptions in groups of four.
**Extra Practice** If possible, have students bring in video clips from popular movies. Choose three or four clips and have the students describe the events after viewing each one.

# Comunicación

**4**  **Entrevista** Trabajen en parejas. Un(a) estudiante usa estas preguntas para entrevistar a su compañero/a. Luego compartan los resultados de la entrevista con la clase. Answers will vary.

1. Cuando eras estudiante de primaria, ¿te gustaban tus profesores/as?
2. ¿Veías mucha televisión cuando eras niño/a?
3. Cuando tenías diez años, ¿cuál era tu programa de televisión favorito?
4. Cuando eras niño/a, ¿qué hacía tu familia durante las vacaciones?
5. ¿Cuántos años tenías en 2000?
6. Cuando estabas en el quinto año escolar, ¿qué hacías con tus amigos/as?
7. Cuando tenías once años, ¿cuál era tu grupo musical favorito?
8. Antes de tomar esta clase, ¿sabías hablar español?

**5**  **Describir** En parejas, túrnense para describir cómo eran sus vidas cuando eran niños. Pueden usar las sugerencias de la lista u otras ideas. Luego informen a la clase sobre la vida de su compañero/a. Answers will vary.

**NOTA CULTURAL**

**El Parque Nacional Tortuguero** está en la costa del Caribe, al norte de la ciudad de Limón, en Costa Rica. Varias especies de tortuga (*turtle*) utilizan las playas del parque para poner (*lay*) sus huevos. Esto ocurre de noche, y hay guías que llevan pequeños grupos de turistas a observar este fenómeno biológico.

> **modelo**
>
> Cuando yo era niña, mi familia y yo siempre íbamos a Tortuguero. Tomábamos un barco desde Limón, y por las noches mirábamos las tortugas (*turtles*) en la playa. Algunas veces teníamos suerte, porque las tortugas venían a poner (*lay*) huevos. Otras veces, volvíamos al hotel sin ver ninguna tortuga.

- las vacaciones
- ocasiones especiales
- qué hacías durante el verano
- celebraciones con tus amigos/as
- celebraciones con tu familia

- cómo era tu escuela
- cómo eran tus amigos/as
- los viajes que hacías
- a qué jugabas
- qué hacías cuando te sentías enfermo/a

# Síntesis

**6**  **En el consultorio** Tu profesor(a) te va a dar una lista incompleta con los pacientes que fueron al consultorio del doctor Donoso ayer. En parejas, conversen para completar sus listas y saber a qué hora llegaron las personas al consultorio y cuáles eran sus problemas. Answers will vary.

**4** **Teaching Tip** To simplify, have students record the results of their interviews in a Venn diagram, which they can use to present the information to the class.

**5** **Teaching Tips**
- Before students report to the class, divide the class into groups of four. After each report, the groups decide on a question for the presenter. Then have the groups take turns asking the student about his or her experience.
- You may want to assign this activity as a short written composition.

**6** **Teaching Tip** Divide the class into pairs and distribute the handouts from the Information Gap Activities (Supersite/ IRCD) that correspond to this activity. Give students ten minutes to complete this activity.

**6** **Expansion** Have pairs write **Dr. Donoso's** advice for three of the patients. Then have them read the advice to the class and compare it with what other pairs wrote for the same patients.

**TEACHING OPTIONS**

**Large Groups** Label the four corners of the room **La Revolución Americana, Tiempos prehistóricos, El Imperio Romano,** and **El Japón de los samurai.** Have students go to the corner that best represents the historical period they would visit if they could. Each group should then discuss their reasons for choosing that period using the imperfect tense. A spokesperson will summarize the group response to the rest of the class.

**Game** Divide the class into teams of three. Each team should choose a historical or fictional villain. When it is their turn, they will give the class one hint. The other teams are allowed three questions, which must be answered truthfully. At the end of the question/answer session, teams must guess the identity. Award one point for each correct guess and two to any team able to stump the class.

## 10.2 The preterite and the imperfect

**ANTE TODO**  Now that you have learned the forms of the preterite and the imperfect, you will learn more about how they are used. The preterite and the imperfect are not interchangeable. In Spanish, the choice between these two tenses depends on the context and on the point of view of the speaker.

*Me caí cuando estaba en el autobús.*

*De niño jugaba mucho al fútbol. Una vez me rompí la pierna.*

### COMPARE & CONTRAST

**Use the preterite to...**

1. Express actions that are viewed by the speaker as completed
   Don Francisco **se rompió** la pierna.
   *Don Francisco broke his leg.*

   **Fueron** a Buenos Aires ayer.
   *They went to Buenos Aires yesterday.*

2. Express the beginning or end of a past action
   La película **empezó** a las nueve.
   *The movie began at nine o'clock.*

   Ayer **terminé** el proyecto para la clase de química.
   *Yesterday I finished the project for chemistry class.*

3. Narrate a series of past actions or events
   La doctora me **miró** los oídos, me **hizo** unas preguntas y **escribió** la receta.
   *The doctor looked in my ears, asked me some questions, and wrote the prescription.*

   **Me di** con la mesa, **me caí** y **me lastimé** el pie.
   *I bumped into the table, I fell, and I injured my foot.*

**Use the imperfect to...**

1. Describe an ongoing past action with no reference to its beginning or end
   Don Francisco **esperaba** a Javier.
   *Don Francisco was waiting for Javier.*

   El médico **se preocupaba** por sus pacientes.
   *The doctor worried about his patients.*

2. Express habitual past actions and events
   Cuando **era** joven, **jugaba** al tenis.
   *When I was young, I used to play tennis.*

   De niño, don Francisco **se enfermaba** con mucha frecuencia.
   *As a child, Don Francisco used to get sick very frequently.*

3. Describe physical and emotional states or characteristics
   La chica **quería** descansar. **Se sentía** mal y **tenía** dolor de cabeza.
   *The girl wanted to rest. She felt ill and had a headache.*

   Ellos **eran** altos y **tenían** ojos verdes.
   *They were tall and had green eyes.*

   **Estábamos** felices de ver a la familia.
   *We were happy to see the family.*

**AYUDA**

These words and expressions, as well as similar ones, commonly occur with the preterite: **ayer, anteayer, una vez, dos veces, tres veces, el año pasado, de repente.**
They usually imply that an action has happened at a specific point in time. For a review, see **Estructura 6.3,** p. 191.

**AYUDA**

These words and expressions, as well as similar ones, commonly occur with the imperfect: **de niño/a, todos los días, mientras, siempre, con frecuencia, todas las semanas.** They usually express habitual or repeated actions in the past.

▶ The preterite and the imperfect often appear in the same sentence. In such cases the imperfect describes what *was happening*, while the preterite describes the action that "interrupted" the ongoing activity.

**Miraba** la tele cuando **sonó** el teléfono.
*I was watching TV when the phone rang.*

Maite **leía** el periódico cuando **llegó** Álex.
*Maite was reading the newspaper when Álex arrived.*

▶ You will also see the preterite and the imperfect together in narratives such as fiction, news, and retelling of events. The imperfect provides background information, such as time, weather, and location, while the preterite indicates the specific events that occurred.

**Eran** las dos de la mañana y el detective ya no **podía** mantenerse despierto. **Se bajó** lentamente del coche, **estiró** las piernas y **levantó** los brazos hacia el cielo oscuro.
*It was two in the morning, and the detective could no longer stay awake. He slowly stepped out of the car, stretched his legs, and raised his arms toward the dark sky.*

La luna **estaba** llena y no **había** en el cielo ni una sola nube. De repente, el detective **escuchó** un grito espeluznante proveniente del parque.
*The moon was full and there wasn't a single cloud in the sky. Suddenly, the detective heard a piercing scream coming from the park.*

## Un médico colombiano descubrió la vacuna contra la malaria

**El doctor colombiano Manuel Elkin Patarroyo** descubrió una vacuna contra la malaria. Esta enfermedad se erradicó hace décadas en muchas partes del mundo. Sin embargo, los casos de malaria empezaban a aumentar otra vez, justo cuando salió la vacuna de Patarroyo. En mayo de 1993, el doctor Patarroyo donó la vacuna, a nombre de Colombia, a la Organización Mundial de la Salud. Los grandes laboratorios farmacéuticos presionaron a la OMS porque querían la vacuna. Pero en 1995 las dos partes, el doctor Patarroyo y la OMS, ratificaron el pacto original.

 **¡INTÉNTALO!**    Elige el pretérito o el imperfecto para completar la historia. Explica por qué se usa ese tiempo verbal en cada ocasión.

1. ___Eran___ (Fueron/Eran) las doce.
2. ___Había___ (Hubo/Había) mucha gente en la calle.
3. A las doce y media, Tomás y yo ___entramos___ (entramos/entrábamos) en el restaurante Tárcoles.
4. Todos los días yo ___almorzaba___ (almorcé/almorzaba) con Tomás al mediodía.
5. El camarero ___llegó___ (llegó/llegaba) inmediatamente, para darnos el menú.
6. Nosotros ___empezamos___ (empezamos/empezábamos) a leerlo.
7. Yo ___pedí___ (pedí/pedía) el pescado.
8. De repente, el camarero ___volvió___ (volvió/volvía) a nuestra mesa.
9. Y nos ___dio___ (dio/daba) una mala noticia.
10. Desafortunadamente, no ___tenían___ (tuvieron/tenían) más pescado.
11. Por eso Tomás y yo ___decidimos___ (decidimos/decidíamos) comer en otro lugar.
12. ___Llovía___ (Llovió/Llovía) mucho cuando ___salimos___ (salimos/salíamos) del restaurante.
13. Así que ___regresamos___ (regresamos/regresábamos) al restaurante Tárcoles.
14. Esta vez, ___pedí___ (pedí/pedía) el arroz con pollo.

**recursos**

WB
pp. 113–116

LM
p. 58

SUPERSITE
panorama.
vhlcentral.com
Lección 10

**Teaching Tips**
• Give further examples from your own experience that contrast the imperfect and the preterite. Ex: **Quería ver la nueva película ____, pero anoche sólo pude ir a las diez de la noche. La película fue buena, pero terminó muy tarde. Era la una cuando llegué a casa. Me acosté muy tarde y esta mañana, cuando me levanté, estaba cansadísimo/a.**
• Have students find the example of an interrupted action in the realia.
• Create a two-layer overhead of a simple narration in Spanish, in such a way that the first layer shows only the sentences with imperfect verbs and the second layer has only the preterite. Project the first transparency and read it aloud. Ask students what tense is used (imperfect) and if they know what happened and why not (no, it only sets the scene). Remove the first transparency and show the second. After reading through the sentences, ask students the tense (preterite), if they know what happened (yes), and if this is an interesting story (no). Then layer the transparencies together and read through the complete narration. Explain that, now that students have learned both the imperfect and the preterite, they are able to communicate in a more complete, interesting way.
• After completing ¡Inténtalo!, have students explain why the preterite or imperfect was used in each case. Then call on different students to create other sentences illustrating the same uses.

**TEACHING OPTIONS**

**Pairs** Ask students to narrate the most interesting, embarrassing, exciting, or annoying thing that has happened to them recently. Tell them to describe what happened and how they felt, using preterite and imperfect verbs.
**Video** Show the *Fotonovela* again to give students more input about the use of the imperfect. Stop the video at appropriate moments to contrast the use of preterite and imperfect tenses.

**Heritage Speakers** Have heritage speakers work with other students in pairs to write a simple summary of this lesson's **Fotonovela**. First, as a class, briefly summarize the episode in English and, in a two-column chart on the board, write which verbs would be in imperfect or preterite. Then have pairs write their paragraphs. Tell them they should set the scene, and describe where the characters were, what they were doing, and what happened.

# Práctica SUPERSITE

**1 Teaching Tip** To simplify, begin by reading through the items as a class. Have students label each blank with an *I* for *imperfect* or *P* for *preterite*.

**1 Expansion** Have volunteers explain why they chose the preterite or imperfect in each case. Ask them to point out any words or expressions that triggered one tense or the other.

**2 Expansion** Ask comprehension questions about the article. Ex: **¿Qué pasó ayer? (Hubo un accidente.) ¿Dónde hubo un accidente? (en el centro de San José) ¿Qué tiempo hacía? (Estaba muy nublado y llovía.) ¿Qué le pasó a la mujer que manejaba? (Murió al instante.) ¿Y a su pasajero? (Sufrió varias fracturas.) ¿Qué hizo el conductor del autobús? (Intentó dar un viraje brusco y perdió control del autobús.) ¿Qué les pasó a los pasajeros del autobús? (Nada; no se lastimó ninguno.)**

**3 Expansion**
- After students have compared their sentences, ask them to report to the class the most interesting things their partners said.
- To challenge students, ask them to expand on one of their sentences, creating a paragraph about an imaginary or actual past experience.

**1** **Seleccionar** Utiliza el tiempo verbal adecuado, según el contexto.

1. La semana pasada, Manolo y Aurora __querían__ (querer) dar una fiesta. __Decidieron__ (Decidir) invitar a seis amigos y servirles mucha comida.
2. Manolo y Aurora __estaban__ (estar) preparando la comida cuando Elena __llamó__ (llamar). Como siempre, __tenía__ (tener) que estudiar para un examen.
3. A las seis, __volvió__ (volver) a sonar el teléfono. Su amigo Francisco tampoco __podía__ (poder) ir a la fiesta, porque __tenía__ (tener) fiebre. Manolo y Aurora __se sentían__ (sentirse) muy tristes, pero __tenían__ (tener) que preparar la comida.
4. Después de otros 15 minutos, __sonó__ (sonar) el teléfono. Sus amigos, los señores Vega, __estaban__ (estar) en camino (*en route*) al hospital: a su hijo le __dolía__ (doler) mucho el estómago. Sólo dos de los amigos __podían__ (poder) ir a la cena.
5. Por supuesto, __iban__ (ir) a tener demasiada comida. Finalmente, cinco minutos antes de las ocho, __llamaron__ (llamar) Ramón y Javier. Ellos __pensaban__ (pensar) que la fiesta __era__ (ser) la próxima semana.
6. Tristes, Manolo y Aurora __se sentaron__ (sentarse) a comer solos. Mientras __comían__ (comer), pronto __llegaron__ (llegar) a la conclusión de que __era__ (ser) mejor estar solos: ¡La comida __estaba__ (estar) malísima!

**2** **En el periódico** Completa esta noticia con la forma correcta del pretérito o el imperfecto.

## Un accidente trágico

Ayer temprano por la mañana (1)__hubo__ (haber) un trágico accidente en el centro de San José cuando el conductor de un autobús no (2)__vio__ (ver) venir un carro. La mujer que (3)__manejaba__ (manejar) el carro (4)__murió__ (morir) al instante y los paramédicos (5)__tuvieron__ (tener) que llevar al pasajero al hospital porque (6)__sufrió__ (sufrir) varias fracturas. El conductor del autobús (7)__dijo__ (decir) que no (8)__vio__ (ver) el carro hasta el último momento porque (9)__estaba__ (estar) muy nublado y (10)__llovía__ (llover). Él (11)__intentó__ (intentar) (*to attempt*) dar un viraje brusco (*to swerve*), pero (12)__perdió__ (perder) el control del autobús y no (13)__pudo__ (poder) evitar (*to avoid*) el accidente. Según nos informaron, no (14)__se lastimó__ (lastimarse) ningún pasajero del autobús.

**AYUDA**

Reading Spanish-language newspapers is a good way to practice verb tenses. You will find that both the imperfect and the preterite occur with great regularity. Many newsstands carry international papers, and many Spanish-language newspapers (such as Spain's *El País*, Mexico's *Reforma,* and Argentina's *Clarín*) are on the Web.

**3** **Completar** Completa las frases de una manera lógica. Usa el pretérito o el imperfecto. En parejas, comparen sus respuestas. Answers will vary.

1. De niño/a, yo...
2. Yo conducía el auto mientras...
3. Anoche mi novio/a...
4. Ayer el/la profesor(a)...
5. La semana pasada un(a) amigo/a...
6. Con frecuencia mis padres...
7. Esta mañana en la cafetería...
8. Hablábamos con el doctor cuando...

**TEACHING OPTIONS**

**Small Groups** In groups of four, have students write a short article about an imaginary trip they took last summer. Students should use the imperfect to set the scene and the preterite to narrate the events. Each student should contribute three sentences to the article. When finished, have students read their articles to the class.

**Heritage Speakers** Ask heritage speakers to write a brief narration of a well-known fairy tale, such as *Little Red Riding Hood* (**Caperucita Roja**). Allow them to change details as they see fit, modernizing the story or setting it in another country, for example, but tell them to pay special attention to the use of preterite and imperfect verbs. Have them share their retellings with the class.

# Comunicación

**4** **Entrevista** Usa estas preguntas para entrevistar a un(a) compañero/a acerca de su primer(a) novio/a. Si quieres, puedes añadir otras preguntas. Answers will vary.

1. ¿Quién fue tu primer(a) novio/a?
2. ¿Cuántos años tenían ustedes cuando se conocieron?
3. ¿Cómo era él/ella?
4. ¿Qué le gustaba hacer? ¿Le interesaban los deportes?
5. ¿Por cuánto tiempo salieron ustedes?
6. ¿Qué hacían ustedes cuando salían?
7. ¿Pensaban casarse?
8. ¿Cuándo y por qué rompieron ustedes?

**5**  **La sala de emergencias** En parejas, miren la lista e inventen qué les pasó a estas personas que están en la sala de emergencias. Answers will vary.

> **modelo**
> Eran las tres de la tarde. Como todos los días, Pablo jugaba al fútbol con sus amigos. Estaba muy contento. De repente, se cayó y se rompió el brazo. Después fue a la sala de emergencias.

| Paciente | Edad | Hora | Condición |
|---|---|---|---|
| 1. Pablo Romero | 9 años | 15:20 | hueso roto (el brazo) |
| 2. Estela Rodríguez | 45 años | 15:25 | tobillo torcido |
| 3. Lupe Quintana | 29 años | 15:37 | embarazada, dolores |
| 4. Manuel López | 52 años | 15:45 | infección de garganta |
| 5. Marta Díaz | 3 años | 16:00 | temperatura muy alta, fiebre |
| 6. Roberto Salazar | 32 años | 16:06 | dolor de oído |
| 7. Marco Brito | 18 años | 16:18 | daño en el cuello, posible fractura |
| 8. Ana María Ortiz | 66 años | 16:29 | reacción alérgica a un medicamento |

**6**  **Situación** Anoche alguien robó (*stole*) el examen de la **Lección 10** de la oficina de tu profesor(a) y tú tienes que averiguar quién lo hizo. Pregúntales a tres compañeros dónde estaban, con quién estaban y qué hicieron entre las ocho y las doce de la noche. Answers will vary.

# Síntesis

**7**  **La primera vez** En grupos, cuéntense cómo fue la primera vez que les pusieron una inyección, se rompieron un hueso, pasaron la noche en un hospital, estuvieron mareados/as, etc. Incluyan estos puntos en su conversación: una descripción del tiempo que hacía, sus edades, qué pasó y cómo se sentían. Answers will vary.

---

---

**4** **Teaching Tip** To simplify, have students prepare a few notes to help them in their responses.

**4** **Expansion** Have students write a summary of their partners' responses, omitting all names. Collect the summaries, then read them to the class. Have students guess who had the relationship described in the summary.

**5** **Teaching Tip** Remind students that the 24-hour clock is often used for schedules. Go through a few of the times and ask volunteers to provide the equivalent in the 12-hour clock.

**5** **Expansion** Have pairs share their answers with the class, but without mentioning the patient's name. The class must guess who is being described.

**6** **Expansion** Have students decide who in their group would be the most likely thief based on his or her responses. Ask the group to prepare a police report explaining why they believe their suspect is the culprit.

**7** **Teaching Tip** To simplify, before assigning groups, have students list information they can include in their descriptions, such as their age, the time, the date, what the weather was like, and so forth. Then have them list the events of the day in the order they happened.

**7** **Expansion** Have students decide who in their group is most accident prone on the basis of his or her responses. Ask the group to prepare a doctor's account of his or her treatments.

## [10.3] Constructions with **se**

> **ANTE TODO**  In **Lección 7**, you learned how to use **se** as the third person reflexive pronoun (**Él se despierta. Ellos se visten. Ella se baña.**). **Se** can also be used to form constructions in which the person performing the action is not expressed or is de-emphasized.

### Impersonal constructions with se

▶ In Spanish, verbs that are not reflexive can be used with **se** to form impersonal constructions. These are statements in which the person performing the action is not defined.

| | |
|---|---|
| **Se habla** español en Costa Rica. | **Se puede leer** en la sala de espera. |
| *Spanish is spoken in Costa Rica.* | *You can read in the waiting room.* |
| **Se hacen** operaciones aquí. | **Se necesitan** medicinas enseguida. |
| *They perform operations here.* | *They need medicine right away.* |

▶ **¡Atención!** Note that the third person singular verb form is used with singular nouns and the third person plural form is used with plural nouns.

| | |
|---|---|
| **Se vende** ropa. | **Se venden** camisas. |

▶ You often see the impersonal **se** in signs, advertisements, and directions.

 SE PROHÍBE NADAR

 **Se necesitan programadores** GRUPO TECNO Tel. 778-34-34

 ENTRADA  Se entra por la izquierda

### Se for unplanned events

¿Cuánto tiempo hace que se cayó?

Ya se me olvidó.

Bueno, vamos a sacarle una radiografía para ver si se le rompió el hueso.

▶ **Se** also describes accidental or unplanned events. In this construction, the person who performs the action is de-emphasized, implying that the accident or unplanned event is not his or her direct responsibility. Note this construction.

$$\textbf{se} + \begin{bmatrix} \text{INDIRECT} \\ \text{OBJECT} \\ \text{PRONOUN} \end{bmatrix} + \begin{bmatrix} \text{VERB} \end{bmatrix} + \begin{bmatrix} \text{SUBJECT} \end{bmatrix}$$

|  |  |  |  |
|---|---|---|---|
| **Se** | me | cayó | la pluma. |

---

**Section Goals**

In **Estructura 10.3**, students will be introduced to:
- impersonal constructions with **se**
- using **se** for unplanned events

**Instructional Resources**
**Supersite:** Lab MP3 Audio Files **Lección 10**
**Supersite/IRCD:** *PowerPoints* (**Lección 10 Estructura** Presentation); *IRM* (Lab Audio Script, WBs/VM/LM Answer Key)
**WebSAM**
**Workbook,** pp. 117–118
**Lab Manual,** p. 59
*Cuaderno para hispanohablantes*

**Teaching Tips**
- Emphasize that this construction has no exact equivalent in English. Have students examine the model sentences and make up some of their own in order to get a feel for how **se** is used to describe unplanned events.
- Test comprehension by asking questions based on similar **se** constructions. Ex: **¿Se habla español en Inglaterra? (No, se habla inglés.) ¿Dónde se hacen las películas norteamericanas? (Se hacen en Hollywood.)**
- Divide the board into two columns, labeled **Sí** and **No**. Ask volunteers to describe what is and is not allowed in Spanish class, using impersonal constructions with **se**. Ex: **Se debe hablar español. Se prohíben las gafas de sol.**

---

**TEACHING OPTIONS**

**TPR** Use impersonal constructions with **se** to have students draw what you say. Ex: You say: **Se prohíbe entrar,** and students draw a door with a diagonal line through it. Other possible expressions could be: **Se sale por la derecha. Se permiten perros. Se prohíben botellas.**

**Extra Practice** For homework, have students search the Internet for common icons or international signs. Then pair students to write directions using **se** for each of the icons and signs. Ex: **Se prohíbe pasear en bicicleta. Se prohíbe pasar. Se habla español.**

**TPR** Mime activities and have students state what happened, using **se.** Ex: Leave your keys out on the table, wave goodbye, and head for the door. (**Se le olvidaron/quedaron las llaves.**) Mime turning a key in the ignition, but the car does not start. (**Se le dañó el auto.**)

▶ In this type of construction, what would normally be the direct object of the sentence becomes the subject, and it agrees with the verb, not with the indirect object pronoun.

| I.O. PRONOUN | VERB | | SUBJECT |
|---|---|---|---|
| | quedó | | la receta. |
| me, te, le | cayó | SINGULAR | la taza. |
| Se | dañó | | el radio. |
| | rompieron | | las botellas. |
| nos, os, les | olvidaron | PLURAL | las pastillas. |
| | perdieron | | las llaves. |

▶ These verbs are the ones most frequently used with **se** to describe unplanned events.

### Verbs commonly used with se

| | | | |
|---|---|---|---|
| **caer** | to fall; to drop | **perder (e:ie)** | to lose |
| **dañar** | to damage; to break down | **quedar** | to be left behind |
| **olvidar** | to forget | **romper** | to break |

**Se me perdió** el teléfono de la farmacia.
*I lost the pharmacy's phone number.*

**Se nos olvidaron** los pasajes.
*We forgot the tickets.*

▶ **¡Atención!** While Spanish has a verb for *to fall* (**caer**), there is no direct translation for *to drop*. **Dejar caer** (*To let fall*) or a **se** construction is often used to mean *to drop*.

El médico **dejó caer** la aspirina.
*The doctor dropped the aspirin.*

A mí **se me cayeron** los cuadernos.
*I dropped the notebooks.*

**CONSULTA**

For an explanation of prepositional pronouns, refer to **Estructura 9.4**, p. 294.

▶ To clarify or emphasize who the person involved in the action is, this construction commonly begins with the preposition **a** + [*noun*] or **a** + [*prepositional pronoun*].

**Al paciente** se le perdió la receta.
*The patient lost his prescription.*

**A ustedes** se les quedaron los libros en casa.
*You left the books at home.*

---

**¡INTÉNTALO!**   Completa las oraciones con **se** impersonal y los verbos en presente.

#### A

1. <u>Se enseñan</u> (enseñar) cinco lenguas en esta universidad.
2. <u>Se come</u> (comer) muy bien en El Cráter.
3. <u>Se venden</u> (vender) muchas camisetas allí.
4. <u>Se sirven</u> (servir) platos exquisitos cada noche.

Completa las oraciones con **se** y los verbos en pretérito.

#### B

1. <u>Se me rompieron</u> (*I broke*) las gafas.
2. <u>Se te cayeron</u> (*You* (fam., sing.) *dropped*) las pastillas.
3. <u>Se les perdió</u> (*They lost*) la receta.
4. <u>Se le quedó</u> (*You* (form., sing.) *left*) aquí la radiografía.

**Teaching Tips**
• Test comprehension by asking volunteers to change sentences from plural to singular and vice versa. Ex: **Se me perdieron las llaves.** (**Se me perdió la llave.**)
• Have students finish sentences using a construction with **se** to express an unplanned event. Ex: **1. Al doctor ____. (se le cayó el termómetro) 2. A la profesora ____. (se le quedaron los papeles en casa)**
• Involve students in a conversation about unplanned events that happened to them recently. Say: **Se me olvidaron las gafas de sol esta mañana. Y a ti, ____, ¿se te olvidó algo esta mañana? ¿Qué se te olvidó?** Continue with other verbs. Ex: **¿A quién se le perdió algo importante esta semana? ¿Qué se te perdió?**

**Successful Language Learning** Tell students that this construction has no exact equivalent in English. Tell them to examine the examples in the textbook and make up some of their own in order to get a feel for how this construction works.

---

**TEACHING OPTIONS**

**Video** Show the *Fotonovela* again to give students more input containing constructions with **se**. Have students write down as many of the examples as they can. After viewing, have students edit their lists and cross out any reflexive verbs that they mistakenly understood to be constructions with **se**.
**Heritage Speakers** Ask heritage speakers to write a fictional or true account of a day in which everything went wrong. Ask them to include as many constructions with **se** as possible. Have them read their accounts aloud to the class, who will summarize the events.
**Extra Practice** Have students use **se** constructions to make excuses in different situations. Ex: You did not bring in a composition to class. (**Se me dañó la computadora.**)

# Práctica

**1** **¿Cierto o falso?** Lee estas oraciones sobre la vida en 1901. Indica si lo que dice cada oración es **cierto** o **falso**. Luego corrige las oraciones falsas.

1. Se veía mucha televisión. Falso. No se veía televisión. Se leía mucho.
2. Se escribían muchos libros. Cierto.
3. Se viajaba mucho en tren. Cierto.
4. Se montaba a caballo. Cierto.
5. Se mandaba mucho correo electrónico. Falso. No se mandaba correo electrónico. Se mandaban muchas cartas y postales.
6. Se preparaban muchas comidas en casa. Cierto.
7. Se llevaban minifaldas. Falso. No se llevaban minifaldas. Se llevaban faldas largas.
8. Se pasaba mucho tiempo con la familia. Cierto.

**2** **Traducir** Traduce estos letreros *(signs)* y anuncios al español.

1. Nurses needed   Se necesitan enfermeros/as
2. Eating and drinking prohibited   Se prohíbe comer y beber
3. Programmers sought   Se buscan programadores
4. English is spoken   Se habla inglés
5. Computers sold   Se venden computadoras
6. No talking   Se prohíbe hablar
7. Teacher needed   Se necesita profesor(a)
8. Books sold   Se venden libros
9. Do not enter   Se prohíbe entrar
10. Spanish is spoken   Se habla español

**3** **¿Qué pasó?** Mira los dibujos e indica lo que pasó en cada uno. Some answers will vary.

1. camarero / pastel

Al camarero se le cayó el pastel.

2. Sr. Álvarez / espejo

Al señor Álvarez se le rompió el espejo.

3. Arturo / tarea

A Arturo se le olvidó la tarea.

4. Sra. Domínguez / llaves

A la Sra. Domínguez se le perdieron las llaves.

5. Carla y Lupe / botellas de vino

A Carla y a Lupe se les rompieron dos botellas de vino.

6. Juana / platos

A Juana se le rompieron los platos.

---

---

**TEACHING OPTIONS**

**Extra Practice** Have students imagine that they have just seen a movie about the future. In groups have them prepare a description of the way of life portrayed in the movie using the imperfect tense and constructions with **se**. Ex: **No se necesitaba trabajar. Se usaban robots para hacer todo. Se viajaba por telepatía. No se comía nada sino en los fines de semana.**

**Game** Divide the class into teams of four. Have each team think of a famous place or public building and compose four signs that could be found on the premises. Teams will take turns reading their signs aloud. Each team that correctly identifies the place or building receives one point. The team with the most points wins.

# Comunicación

**4** **Preguntas** Trabajen en parejas y usen estas preguntas para entrevistarse. *Answers will vary.*

1. ¿Qué comidas se sirven en tu restaurante favorito?
2. ¿Se te olvidó invitar a alguien a tu última fiesta o comida? ¿A quién?
3. ¿A qué hora se abre la cafetería de tu universidad?
4. ¿Alguna vez se te quedó algo importante en la casa? ¿Qué?
5. ¿Alguna vez se te perdió algo importante durante un viaje? ¿Qué?
6. ¿Qué se vende en una farmacia?
7. ¿Sabes si en la farmacia se aceptan cheques?
8. ¿Alguna vez se te rompió algo muy caro? ¿Qué?

**5** **Opiniones** En parejas, terminen cada oración con ideas originales. Después, comparen los resultados con la clase para ver qué pareja tuvo las mejores ideas. *Answers will vary.*

1. No se tiene que dejar propina cuando…
2. Antes de viajar, se debe…
3. Si se come bien,…
4. Para tener una vida sana, se debe…
5. Se sirve la mejor comida en…
6. Se hablan muchas lenguas en…

# Síntesis

**6** **Anuncios** En grupos, preparen dos anuncios de televisión para presentar a la clase. Usen el imperfecto y por lo menos dos construcciones con **se** en cada uno. *Answers will vary.*

> **modelo**
>
> Se me cayeron unos libros en el pie y me dolía mucho. Pero ahora no, gracias a SuperAspirina 500. ¡Dos pastillas y se me fue el dolor! Se puede comprar SuperAspirina 500 en todas las farmacias Recetamax.

---

**4** **Teaching Tip** Model a detailed answer by choosing among questions 4, 5, and 8, providing as many details as possible. Ex: **Una vez cuando era adolescente se me rompió un plato muy caro de mi abuela. Pero ella no se enojó. Me dijo: No te preocupes por el plato. ¿Te lastimaste?**

**4** **Expansion** Have each pair decide on the most unusual answer to the questions. Ask the student who gave it to describe the event to the class.

**5** **Expansion** Ask pairs to write similar beginnings to three different statements using **se** constructions. Have pairs exchange papers and finish each other's sentences.

**6** **Expansion** After all the groups have presented their ads, have each group write a letter of complaint. Their letter should be directed to one of the other groups, claiming false advertising.

---

**Extra Practice** Write these sentence fragments on the board and ask students to supply several logical endings using a construction with **se**. **1. Cuando ella subía al avión, \_\_\_\_. (se le cayó la maleta; se le torció el pie) 2. Una vez, cuando yo comía en un restaurante elegante, \_\_\_\_. (se me rompió un vaso; se me perdió la tarjeta de crédito) 3. Ayer cuando yo venía a clase,** \_\_\_\_. **(se me dañó la bicicleta; me caí y se me rompió el brazo) 4. Cuando era niño/a, siempre \_\_\_\_. (se me olvidaban las cosas; se me perdían las cosas) 5. El otro día cuando yo lavaba los platos, \_\_\_\_. (se me rompieron tres vasos; se me terminó el detergente)**

## Section Goals

In **Estructura 10.4**, students will learn:

- the formation of adverbs using [*adjective*] + **–mente**
- common adverbs and adverbial expressions

---

**Instructional Resources**

**Supersite:** Lab MP3 Audio Files **Lección 10**
**Supersite/IRCD:** *PowerPoints* (**Lección 10 Estructura** Presentation); *IRM* (Lab Audio Script, WBs/VM/LM Answer Key)
**WebSAM**
**Workbook,** pp. 119–120
**Lab Manual,** p. 60
*Cuaderno para hispanohablantes*

---

## Teaching Tips

- Add a visual aspect to this grammar presentation. Use magazine pictures to review known adverbs. Ex: **Miren la foto que tengo *aquí*. *Hoy* esta chica se siente *bien*, pero *ayer* se sentía *mal*.** Write the adverbs on the board as you proceed.
- After presenting the formation of adverbs that end in **–mente**, ask volunteers to convert known adjectives into adverbs and then use them in a sentence. Ex: **cómodo/cómodamente: Alberto se sentó cómodamente en la silla.**
- Name celebrities and have students create sentences about them, using adverbs. Ex: **Shakira (Shakira baila maravillosamente.)**

---

## 10.4 Adverbs

**ANTE TODO** Adverbs are words that describe how, when, and where actions take place. They can modify verbs, adjectives, and even other adverbs. In previous lessons, you have already learned many Spanish adverbs, such as the ones below.

| | | |
|---|---|---|
| aquí | hoy | nunca |
| ayer | mal | siempre |
| bien | muy | temprano |

▸ The most common adverbs end in **–mente**, equivalent to the English ending *-ly*.

**verdaderamente** *truly, really*   **generalmente** *generally*   **simplemente** *simply*

▸ To form these adverbs, add **–mente** to the feminine form of the adjective. If the adjective does not have a special feminine form, just add **–mente** to the standard form. **¡Atención!** Adjectives do not lose their accents when adding **–mente**.

| ADJECTIVE | FEMININE FORM | SUFFIX | ADVERB |
|---|---|---|---|
| seguro | segura | -mente | seguramente |
| fabuloso | fabulosa | -mente | fabulosamente |
| enorme | | -mente | enormemente |
| fácil | | -mente | fácilmente |

▸ Adverbs that end in **–mente** generally follow the verb, while adverbs that modify an adjective or another adverb precede the word they modify.

Javier dibuja **maravillosamente**.
*Javier draws wonderfully.*

Inés está **casi siempre** ocupada.
*Inés is almost always busy.*

### Common adverbs and adverbial expressions

| | | | | | |
|---|---|---|---|---|---|
| **a menudo** | *often* | **así** | *like this; so* | **menos** | *less* |
| **a tiempo** | *on time* | **bastante** | *enough; rather* | **muchas veces** | *a lot; many times* |
| **a veces** | *sometimes* | **casi** | *almost* | | |
| **además (de)** | *furthermore; besides* | **con frecuencia** | *frequently* | **poco** | *little* |
| | | | | **por lo menos** | *at least* |
| **apenas** | *hardly; scarcely* | **de vez en cuando** | *from time to time* | **pronto** | *soon* |
| | | **despacio** | *slowly* | **rápido** | *quickly* |

**¡INTÉNTALO!** Transforma los adjetivos en adverbios.

1. alegre _alegremente_
2. constante _constantemente_
3. gradual _gradualmente_
4. perfecto _perfectamente_
5. real _realmente_
6. frecuente _frecuentemente_
7. tranquilo _tranquilamente_
8. regular _regularmente_
9. maravilloso _maravillosamente_
10. normal _normalmente_
11. básico _básicamente_
12. afortunado _afortunadamente_

---

**¡ATENCIÓN!**

When a sentence contains two or more adverbs in sequence, the suffix **–mente** is dropped from all but the last adverb.
Ex: **El médico nos habló simple y abiertamente.** *The doctor spoke to us simply and openly.*

---

**¡ATENCIÓN!**

**Rápido** functions as an adjective (**Ella tiene una computadora rápida.**) as well as an adverb (**Ella corre rápido.**). Note that as an adverb, **rápido** does not need to agree with any other word in the sentence. You can also use the adverb **rápidamente** (**Ella corre rápidamente**).

---

**recursos**

WB
pp. 119–120

LM
p. 60

panorama.
vhlcentral.com
Lección 10

---

**TEACHING OPTIONS**

**Heritage Speakers** Have heritage speakers interview an older friend or family member about daily life when he or she was a young adult. Students should write a summary of the information, using at least eight of the common adverbs and adverbial expressions listed.

**Extra Practice** Have pairs of students write sentences using adverbs such as **nunca, hoy, lentamente,** and so forth. When they have finished, ask volunteers to dictate their sentences to you to write on the board. After you have written a sentence and checked for accuracy, ask a volunteer to create a sentence that uses the antonym of the adverb.

## Práctica

**1**

**Escoger** Completa las oraciones con los adverbios adecuados.

1. La cita era a las dos, pero llegamos _____tarde_____. (mientras, nunca, tarde)
2. El problema fue que _____ayer_____ se nos dañó el despertador. (aquí, ayer, despacio)
3. La recepcionista no se enojó porque sabe que normalmente llego _____a tiempo_____. (a veces, a tiempo, poco)
4. _____Por lo menos_____ el doctor estaba listo. (Por lo menos, Muchas veces, Casi)
5. _____Apenas_____ tuvimos que esperar cinco minutos. (Así, Además, Apenas)
6. El doctor dijo que nuestra hija Irene necesitaba cambiar su rutina diaria _____inmediatamente_____. (temprano, menos, inmediatamente)
▶ 7. El doctor nos explicó _____bien_____ las recomendaciones del Cirujano General (*Surgeon General*) sobre la salud de los jóvenes. (de vez en cuando, bien, apenas)
8. _____Afortunadamente_____ nos dijo que Irene estaba bien, pero tenía que hacer más ejercicio y comer mejor. (Bastante, Afortunadamente, A menudo)

## Comunicación

**2**

**Aspirina** Lee el anuncio y responde a las preguntas con un(a) compañero/a.    Answers will vary.

No Hay Tiempo Para el Dolor de Cabeza

Si tienes prisa, o simplemente quieres que tu dolor de cabeza se vaya muy pronto, piensa en Bayer. Se asimila mejor y actúa rápidamente. Ya no se puede perder tiempo por un dolor de cabeza.

ASPIRINA

Bayer
Siempre a tu lado.

1. ¿Cuáles son los adverbios que aparecen en el anuncio?
2. Según el anuncio, ¿cuáles son las ventajas (*advantages*) de este tipo de aspirina?
3. ¿Tienen ustedes muchos dolores de cabeza? ¿Qué toman para curarlos?
4. ¿Qué medicamentos ven con frecuencia en los anuncios de televisión? Escriban descripciones de varios de estos anuncios. Usen adverbios en sus descripciones.

## Section Goal

In **Recapitulación**, students will review the grammar concepts from this lesson.

**Instructional Resource**
**Supersite**

**1** **Teaching Tip** Ask students to identify the infinitive for each row.

**1** **Expansion** Ask students to provide the forms for **ir, ver,** and **doler**.

**2** **Expansion**

• To challenge students, have them create sentences to express the opposite meaning for each item. Ex: **1. Pablito se cae muy poco.**

• Ask students to write a paragraph in which they use at least five of the listed adverbs. Then have them exchange papers with a partner for peer editing.

# Recapitulación

For self-scoring and diagnostics, go to panorama.vhlcentral.com.

Completa estas actividades para repasar los conceptos de gramática que aprendiste en esta lección.

**1** **Completar** Completa el cuadro con la forma correspondiente del imperfecto. **12 pts.**

| yo/Ud./él/ella | tú | nosotros | Uds./ellos/ellas |
|---|---|---|---|
| **era** | eras | éramos | eran |
| cantaba | **cantabas** | cantábamos | cantaban |
| venía | venías | **veníamos** | venían |
| quería | querías | queríamos | **querían** |

**2** **Adverbios** Escoge el adverbio correcto de la lista para completar estas oraciones. Lee con cuidado las oraciones; los adverbios sólo se usan una vez. No vas a usar uno de los adverbios. **8 pts.**

| | | |
|---|---|---|
| a menudo | apenas | fácilmente |
| a tiempo | casi | maravillosamente |
| además | despacio | por lo menos |

1. Pablito se cae __a menudo__; cuatro veces por semana en promedio (*average*).

2. No me duele nada y no sufro de ninguna enfermedad; me siento __maravillosamente__ bien.

3. —Doctor, ¿cómo supo que tuve una operación de garganta?
   —Muy __fácilmente__, lo leí en su historial médico.

4. ¿Le duele mucho la espalda? Entonces tiene que levantarse __despacio__.

5. Ya te sientes mucho mejor, ¿verdad? Mañana puedes volver al trabajo; tu temperatura es __casi__ normal.

6. Es importante hacer ejercicio con regularidad, __por lo menos__ tres veces a la semana.

7. El examen médico no comenzó ni tarde ni temprano. Comenzó __a tiempo__, a las tres de la tarde.

8. Parece que ya te estás curando del resfriado. __Apenas__ estás congestionada.

---

**RESUMEN GRAMATICAL**

**10.1** **The imperfect tense** *pp. 318–319*

**The imperfect of regular verbs**

| cantar | beber | escribir |
|---|---|---|
| cantaba | bebía | escribía |
| cantabas | bebías | escribías |
| cantaba | bebía | escribía |
| cantábamos | bebíamos | escribíamos |
| cantabais | bebíais | escribíais |
| cantaban | bebían | escribían |

► There are no stem changes in the imperfect: entender (e:ie) → entendía; servir (e:i) → servía; doler (o:ue) → dolía

► The imperfect of **hay** is **había**.

► Only three verbs are irregular in the imperfect.
ir: iba, ibas, iba, íbamos, ibais, iban
ser: era, eras, era, éramos, erais, eran
ver: veía, veías, veía, veíamos, veíais, veían

**10.2** **The preterite and the imperfect** *pp. 322–323*

| Preterite | Imperfect |
|---|---|
| 1. Completed actions | 1. Ongoing past action |
| **Fueron** a Buenos Aires el mes pasado. | De niño, usted jugaba al fútbol. |
| 2. Beginning or end of past action | 2. Habitual past actions |
| La película **empezó** a las nueve. | **Todos los días yo jugaba** al tenis. |
| 3. Series of past actions or events | 3. Description of states or characteristics |
| Me **caí** y me **lastimé** el pie. | Ella **era** alta. Quería descansar. |

**10.3** **Constructions with se** *pp. 326–327*

**Impersonal constructions with se**

| | |
|---|---|
| | prohíbe fumar. |
| Se | habla español. |
| | hablan varios idiomas. |

---

**TEACHING OPTIONS**

**TPR** Divide the class into three groups: **-ar** verbs, **-er** verbs, and **-ir** verbs. Read a series of sentences that contain the imperfect tense. Have groups stand up when their verb form is used. Ex: **Mi escuela primaria tenía un patio grande.** (-er verb group stands)

**Extra Practice** Ask students to use the preterite and imperfect to write a paragraph about a celebrity's imaginary injury and trip to the emergency room. Have students describe the person's age, where he or she was, the weather, the time, what he or she was doing when the accident occurred, and what happened at the hospital. Ask volunteers to read their paragraphs aloud.

**3** **Un accidente** Escoge el imperfecto o el pretérito según el contexto para completar esta conversación. **10 pts.**

**NURIA** Hola, Felipe. ¿Estás bien? ¿Qué es eso? ¿(1) (**Te lastimaste**/Te lastimabas) el pie?

**FELIPE** Ayer (2) (**tuve**/tenía) un pequeño accidente.

**NURIA** Cuéntame. ¿Cómo (3) (**pasó**/pasaba)?

**FELIPE** Bueno, (4) (**fueron**/eran) las cinco de la tarde y (5) (llovió/**llovía**) mucho cuando (6) (**salí**/salía) de la casa en mi bicicleta. No (7) (**vi**/veía) a una chica que (8) (caminó/**caminaba**) en mi dirección, y los dos (9) (**nos caímos**/nos caíamos) al suelo (*ground*).

**NURIA** Y la chica, ¿está bien ella?

**FELIPE** Sí. Cuando llegamos al hospital, ella sólo (10) (tuvo/**tenía**) dolor de cabeza.

---

**Se for unplanned events**

| Se | me, te, le, nos, os, les | cayó la taza. |
| --- | --- | --- |
| | | dañó el radio. |
| | | rompieron las botellas. |
| | | olvidaron las llaves. |

**10.4 Adverbs** *p. 330*

**Formation of adverbs**

| fácil | → | fácilmente |
| --- | --- | --- |
| seguro | → | seguramente |
| verdadero | → | verdaderamente |

---

**4** **Oraciones** Escribe oraciones con **se** a partir de los elementos dados (*given*). Usa el tiempo especificado entre paréntesis y añade pronombres cuando sea necesario. **10 pts.**

> **modelo**
> Carlos / quedar / la tarea en casa (pretérito)
> A Carlos se le quedó la tarea en casa.

1. en la farmacia / vender / medicamentos (presente) En la farmacia se venden medicamentos.

2. ¿(tú) / olvidar / las llaves / otra vez? (pretérito) ¿Se te olvidaron las llaves otra vez?

3. (yo) / dañar / la computadora (pretérito) Se me dañó la computadora.

4. en esta clase / prohibir / hablar inglés (presente) En esta clase se prohíbe hablar inglés.

5. ellos / romper / las gafas / en el accidente (pretérito) A ellos se les rompieron las gafas en el accidente.

**5** **En la consulta** Escribe al menos cinco oraciones describiendo tu última visita al médico. Incluye cinco verbos en pretérito y cinco en imperfecto. Habla de qué te pasó, cómo te sentías, cómo era el/la doctor(a), qué te dijo, etc. Usa tu imaginación. **10 pts.**    Answers will vary.

**6** **Refrán** Completa el refrán con las palabras que faltan. **¡2 puntos EXTRA!**

66 Lo que ___bien___ (*well*) se aprende,
nunca ___se___ pierde. 99

**3** **Teaching Tip** To challenge students, have them explain why they used the preterite and imperfect in each case and how the meaning might change if the other tense were used.

**4** **Teaching Tip** For items 2, 3, and 5, have volunteers rewrite the sentences on the board using other subjects. Ex: **2. (nosotros) ¿Se nos olvidaron las llaves otra vez?**

**4** **Expansion** Give students these additional items: **6. (yo) / caer / el vaso de cristal (pretérito) (Se me cayó el vaso de cristal.) 7. (ustedes) / quedar / las maletas en el aeropuerto (pretérito) (A ustedes se les quedaron las maletas en el aeropuerto.) 8. en esta tienda / hablar / español e italiano (presente) (En esta tienda se hablan español e italiano.)**

**5** **Teaching Tip** After writing their paragraphs, have students work in pairs and ask each other follow-up questions about their visits.

**6** **Teaching Tips**
• Have volunteers give additional examples of situations in which one might say this expression.
• Ask students to give the English equivalent of this phrase.

---

**TEACHING OPTIONS**

**Extra Practice** Write questions on the board that elicit the impersonal **se**. Have pairs write two responses for each question. Ex: **¿Qué se hace para mantener la salud? ¿Dónde se come bien en esta ciudad? ¿Cuándo se dan fiestas en esta universidad? ¿Dónde se consiguen los bluejeans más baratos?**

**Game** Divide the class into two teams and have them line up. Point to the first member of each team and call out an adjective that can be changed into an adverb (Ex: **lento**). The first student to reach the board and correctly write the adverb (**lentamente**) earns a point for his or her team. If the student can also write an "opposite" adverb (Ex: **rápidamente**), he or she earns a bonus point. The team with the most points at the end wins.

## Section Goals

In **Lectura**, students will:
- learn to activate background knowledge to understand a reading selection
- read a content-rich text on health care while traveling

---

**Instructional Resources**
**Supersite**
*Cuaderno para hispanohablantes*

---

**Estrategia** Tell students that they will find it easier to understand the content of a reading selection on a particular topic by reviewing what they know about the subject before reading. Then ask students to brainstorm ways to stay healthy while traveling. Possible responses: do not drink the water, do not eat raw fruit or vegetables, pack personal medical supplies that may not be available at the destination.

**Examinar el texto** Students should mention that the text is an interview (**entrevista**) by a journalist (**periodista**) of an author (**autora**) whose book is about health care while traveling.

**Conocimiento previo** Have small groups write a paragraph summarizing ways to safeguard health while traveling. Their recommendations should be based on their collective experiences. Encourage them to draw on the experiences of people they know if no one in the group can relate personally to one of the situations mentioned in the items. Have groups share their paragraphs with the class.

**The Affective Dimension** Remind students that they will probably feel less anxious about reading in Spanish if they follow the suggestions in the **Estrategia** sections, which are designed to reinforce and increase reading comprehension skills.

# Lectura

## Antes de leer

### Estrategia
**Activating background knowledge**

Using what you already know about a particular subject will often help you better understand a reading selection. For example, if you read an article about a recent medical discovery, you might think about what you already know about health in order to understand unfamiliar words or concepts.

### Examinar el texto

Utiliza las estrategias de lectura que tú consideras más efectivas para hacer unas observaciones preliminares acerca del texto. Después trabajen en parejas para comparar sus observaciones acerca del texto. Luego contesten estas preguntas:

- Analicen el formato del texto. ¿Qué tipo de texto es? ¿Dónde creen que se publicó este artículo?
- ¿Quiénes son Carla Baron y Tomás Monterrey?
- Miren la foto del libro. ¿Qué sugiere el título del libro sobre su contenido?

### Conocimiento previo (*Background Knowledge*)

Ahora piensen en su conocimiento previo sobre el cuidado de la salud en los viajes. Consideren estas preguntas:

- ¿Viajaron alguna vez a otro estado o a otro país?
- ¿Tuvieron algunos problemas durante sus viajes con el agua, la comida o el clima del lugar?
- ¿Olvidaron poner en su maleta algún medicamento que después necesitaron?
- Imaginen que su amigo/a se va de viaje. Díganle por lo menos cinco cosas que debe hacer para prevenir cualquier problema de salud.

**recursos**
SUPERSITE
panorama.vhlcentral.com
Lección 10

## Libro de la semana

**Cómo hacer un viaje saludable y feliz**

Carla Baron

## Después de leer

### Correspondencias

Busca las correspondencias entre los problemas y las recomendaciones.

**Problemas**

1. el agua __b__
2. el sol __d__
3. la comida __a__
4. la identificación __e__
5. el clima __c__

**Recomendaciones**

a. Hay que adaptarse a los ingredientes no familiares.
b. Toma sólo productos purificados (*purified*).
c. Es importante llevar ropa adecuada cuando viajas.
d. Lleva loción o crema con alta protección solar.
e. Lleva tu pasaporte.

---

**TEACHING OPTIONS**

**Heritage Speakers** Ask heritage speakers to state consequences for a tourist who does not follow the recommendations in **Correspondencias**. Ex: **a. La persona prueba una comida picante y le da dolor de estómago.** After each consequence is stated, have volunteers suggest an appropriate course of action or treatment. Ex: **Debe ir a una farmacia y comprar unas pastillas, como Tums.**

**Small Groups** Have groups of three select a country they would like to visit. Ask students to research what food and beverage precautions should be taken (**precauciones que se deben tomar**) by visitors to that country. Students should mention precautions such as not eating undercooked meat, uncooked seafood or vegetables, unwashed fruits, or unpasteurized dairy products, and not drinking tap water or drinks with ice or mixed with water.

**Correspondencias** Ask students to work together in pairs and use cognates or context clues to match **Problemas** with **Recomendaciones**.

**Seleccionar**
- Have students check their work by locating the sections in the text where the answers can be found.
- Ask the class the questions. Have volunteers answer orally or to write their answers on the board.

# Entrevista a Carla Baron

**por Tomás Monterrey**

**Tomás:** ¿Por qué escribió su libro *Cómo hacer un viaje saludable y feliz?*

**Carla:** Me encanta viajar, conocer otras culturas y escribir. Mi primer viaje lo hice cuando era estudiante universitaria. Todavía recuerdo el día en que llegamos a San Juan, Puerto Rico. Era el panorama ideal para unas vacaciones maravillosas, pero al llegar a la habitación del hotel, bebí mucha agua de la llave° y luego pedí un jugo de frutas con mucho hielo°. El clima en San Juan es tropical y yo tenía mucha sed y calor. Los síntomas llegaron en menos de media hora: pasé dos días con dolor de estómago y corriendo al cuarto de baño cada diez minutos. Desde entonces, siempre que viajo sólo bebo agua mineral y llevo un pequeño bolso con medicinas necesarias como pastillas para el dolor y también bloqueador solar, una crema repelente de mosquitos y un desinfectante.

**Tomás:** ¿Son reales° las situaciones que se narran en su libro?

**Carla:** Sí, son reales y son mis propias° historias°. A menudo los autores crean caricaturas divertidas de un turista en dificultades. ¡En mi libro la turista en dificultades soy yo!

**Tomás:** ¿Qué recomendaciones puede encontrar el lector en su libro?

**Carla:** Bueno, mi libro es anecdótico y humorístico, pero el tema de la salud se trata° de manera seria. En general, se dan recomendaciones sobre ropa adecuada para cada sitio, consejos para protegerse del sol, y comidas y bebidas adecuadas para el turista que viaja al Caribe o Suramérica.

**Tomás:** ¿Tiene algún consejo para las personas que se enferman cuando viajan?

**Carla:** Muchas veces los turistas toman el avión sin saber nada acerca del país que van a visitar. Ponen toda su ropa en la maleta, toman el pasaporte, la cámara fotográfica y ¡a volar°! Es necesario tomar precauciones porque nuestro cuerpo necesita adaptarse al clima, al sol, a la humedad, al agua y a la comida. Se trata de° viajar, admirar las maravillas del mundo y regresar a casa con hermosos recuerdos. En resumen, el secreto es "prevenir en vez de° curar".

llave *faucet*  hielo *ice*  reales *true*  propias *own*  historias *stories*
se trata *is treated*  ¡a volar! *Off they go!*  Se trata de *It's a question of*
en vez de *instead of*

## Seleccionar

Selecciona la respuesta correcta.

1. El tema principal de este libro es ___d___.
   a. Puerto Rico  b. la salud y el agua  c. otras culturas
   d. el cuidado de la salud en los viajes
2. Las situaciones narradas en el libro son ___a___.
   a. autobiográficas  b. inventadas  c. ficticias
   d. imaginarias
3. ¿Qué recomendaciones no vas a encontrar en este libro? ___d___
   a. cómo vestirse adecuadamente
   b. cómo prevenir las quemaduras solares
   c. consejos sobre la comida y la bebida
   d. cómo dar propina en los países del Caribe o de Suramérica

4. En opinión de la señorita Baron, ___b___.
   a. es bueno tomar agua de la llave y beber jugo de frutas con mucho hielo
   b. es mejor tomar solamente agua embotellada (*bottled*)
   c. los minerales son buenos para el dolor abdominal
   d. es importante visitar el cuarto de baño cada diez minutos
5. ¿Cuál de estos productos no lleva la autora cuando viaja a otros países? ___c___
   a. desinfectante
   b. crema repelente
   c. detergente
   d. pastillas medicinales

---

**TEACHING OPTIONS**

**Pairs** Ask pairs to use the items in **Correspondencias** on page 334 as a model. Have them work together to write additional possibilities for **Problemas** and **Recomendaciones**. Ex: **Problema: el dinero; Recomendación: Lleva cheques de viajero o una tarjeta de crédito internacional**. When pairs have completed five more items, have them exchange their items with another pair, who will match them.

**Heritage Speakers** Ask heritage speakers to prepare a short presentation of health tips for traveling in their families' countries of origin. Students should include information on any immunizations that may be required; appropriate clothing, particularly for countries in which the seasons are opposite ours; spicy regional foods or dishes that may cause digestive problems; and so forth.

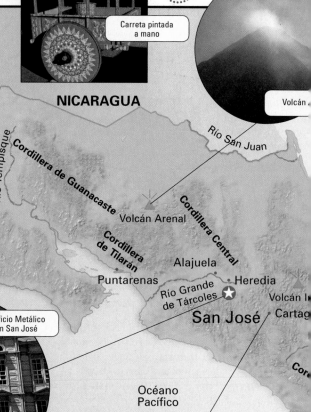

Carreta pintada a mano

Volcán...

**NICARAGUA**

## Costa Rica

NATIONAL STANDARDS — connections cultures

### El país en cifras

▸ **Área:** 51.100 km² (19.730 millas²), *aproximadamente el área de Virginia Occidental°*

▸ **Población:** 4.665.000
*Costa Rica es el país de Centroamérica con la población más homogénea. El 98% de sus habitantes es blanco y mestizo°. Más del 50% de la población es de ascendencia° española y un alto porcentaje tiene sus orígenes en otros países europeos.*

▸ **Capital:** San José —1.374.000

▸ **Ciudades principales:** Alajuela, Cartago, Puntarenas, Heredia

SOURCE: Population Division, UN Secretariat

▸ **Moneda:** colón costarricense°

▸ **Idioma:** español (oficial)

Bandera de Costa Rica

### Costarricenses célebres

▸ **Carmen Lyra,** escritora (1888–1949)
▸ **Chavela Vargas,** cantante° (1919– )
▸ **Óscar Arias Sánchez,** presidente de Costa Rica (1949– )
▸ **Claudia Poll,** nadadora° olímpica (1972– )

Óscar Arias recibió el Premio Nobel de la Paz en 1987.

**Virginia Occidental** *West Virginia* **mestizo** *of indigenous and white parentage* **ascendencia** *descent* **costarricense** *Costa Rican* **cantante** *singer* **nadadora** *swimmer* **ejército** *army* **gastos** *expenditures* **invertir** *to invest* **cuartel** *barracks*

Río Tempisque
Cordillera de Guanacaste
Río San Juan
Cordillera Central
Volcán Arenal
Cordillera de Tilarán
Alajuela
Puntarenas
Heredia
Río Grande de Tárcoles
Volcán I...
**San José** / Cartag...
Cor...

Edificio Metálico en San José

Océano Pacífico

ESTADOS UNIDOS
OCÉANO ATLÁNTICO
**COSTA RICA**
OCÉANO PACÍFICO
AMÉRICA DEL SUR

Basílica de Nuestra Señor... de los Ángeles en Cartag...

**recursos**

| | | |
|---|---|---|
| WB pp. 121–122 | VM pp. 243–244 | panorama.vhlcentral.com Lección 10 |

### ¡Increíble pero cierto!

Costa Rica es el único país latinoamericano que no tiene ejército°. Sin gastos° militares, el gobierno puede invertir° más dinero en la educación y las artes. En la foto aparece el Museo Nacional de Costa Rica, antiguo cuartel° del ejército.

MUSEO NACIONA...

**Section Goal**
In **Panorama**, students will read about the geography, culture, and economy of Costa Rica.

**Instructional Resources**
**Supersite/DVD:** *Panorama cultural*
**Supersite/IRCD:** *PowerPoints* (Overheads #3, #4, #39); *IRM* (*Panorama cultural* Videoscript & Translation, WBs/VM/LM Answer Key)
**WebSAM**
**Workbook,** pp. 121–122
**Video Manual,** pp. 243–244

**Teaching Tip** Have students look at the map of Costa Rica or show *Overhead PowerPoint #39.* Encourage them to mention the physical features that they notice. Discuss the images in the call-out photos.

**El país en cifras** After each section, ask students questions about the content. Ex: **¿Entre qué masas de agua está Costa Rica? Las ciudades principales, ¿en qué lado de la cordillera Central están?** When reading about Costa Rica's population, point out that the country has over a 90% literacy rate, the best in Latin America. Point out that **Óscar Arias** received the Nobel Peace Prize for his work in resolving civil wars in the other Central American countries during the 1970s.

**¡Increíble pero cierto!** Costa Rica has one of the most long-standing democratic traditions in America. Although it has no army, it does have a national police force and a rural guard.

---

**TEACHING OPTIONS**

**Heritage Speakers** Invite students of Costa Rican background or whose families are from other countries of Central America to share information about the national nicknames that Central Americans use for each other. Costa Ricans are called **ticos,** Nicaraguans are called **nicas,** and Guatemalans are called **chapines.**

**Variación léxica** Tell students that if they visit Costa Rica, they may hear a few interesting colloquialisms such as these. **Pulpería** is the word for the *corner grocery store.* A gas station is called a **bomba,** literally a *pump.* A city block is called **cien metros,** literally *a hundred meters.*

## Lugares • **Los parques nacionales**

El sistema de parques nacionales de Costa Rica ocupa el 9,3% de su territorio y fue establecido° para la protección de su biodiversidad. En los parques, los ecoturistas pueden admirar montañas, cataratas° y una gran variedad de plantas exóticas. Algunos ofrecen también la oportunidad de ver quetzales°, monos°, jaguares, armadillos y serpientes° en su hábitat natural.

Caribe

## Economía • **Las plantaciones de café**

Costa Rica fue el primer país centroamericano en desarrollar° la industria del café. En el siglo° XIX, los costarricenses empezaron a exportar esta semilla a Inglaterra°, lo que significó una contribución importante a la economía de la nación. Actualmente, más de 50.000 costarricenses trabajan en el cultivo del café. Este producto representa cerca del 15% de sus exportaciones anuales.

ón

## Sociedad • **Una nación progresista**

Costa Rica es un país progresista. Tiene un nivel de alfabetización° del 96%, uno de los más altos de Latinoamérica. En 1870, esta nación centroamericana abolió la pena de muerte° y en 1948 eliminó el ejército e hizo obligatoria y gratuita° la educación para todos sus ciudadanos.

**PANAMÁ**

**¿Qué aprendiste?** Responde a cada pregunta con una oración completa.

1. ¿Cómo se llama la capital de Costa Rica? La capital de Costa Rica se llama San José.
2. ¿Quién es Claudia Poll? Claudia Poll es una nadadora olímpica.
3. ¿Qué porcentaje del territorio de Costa Rica ocupan los parques nacionales? Los parques nacionales ocupan el 9,3% del territorio de Costa Rica.
4. ¿Para qué se establecen los parques nacionales? Los parques nacionales se establecen para proteger los ecosistemas de la región y su biodiversidad.
5. ¿Qué pueden ver los turistas en los parques nacionales? En los parques nacionales, los turistas pueden ver cataratas, montañas y muchas plantas exóticas.
6. ¿Cuántos costarricenses trabajan en las plantaciones de café hoy día? Más de 50.000 costarricenses trabajan en las plantaciones de café hoy día.
7. ¿Cuándo eliminó Costa Rica la pena de muerte? Costa Rica eliminó la pena de muerte en 1870.

Bañistas en Limón

**Conexión Internet** Investiga estos temas en **panorama.vhlcentral.com**.

1. Busca información sobre Óscar Arias Sánchez. ¿Quién es? ¿Por qué se le considera (*is he considered*) un costarricense célebre?
2. Busca información sobre los artistas de Costa Rica. ¿Qué artista, escritor o cantante te interesa más? ¿Por qué?

........................................................................

establecido *established*  cataratas *waterfalls*  quetzales *type of tropical bird*  monos *monkeys*  serpientes *snakes*
en desarrollar *to develop*  siglo *century*  Inglaterra *England*  nivel de alfabetización *literacy rate*  pena de muerte *death penalty*  gratuita *free*

## Section Goal

In **Panorama**, students will read about the geography, history, and culture of Nicaragua.

---

**Instructional Resources**
**Supersite/DVD:** *Panorama cultural*
**Supersite/IRCD:** *PowerPoints* (Overheads #3, #4, #40); *IRM* (**Panorama cultural** Videoscript & Translation, WBs/VM/LM Answer Key)
**WebSAM**
**Workbook,** pp. 123–124
**Video Manual,** pp. 245–246

---

**Teaching Tip** Have students look at the map of Nicaragua or show *Overhead Power-Point #40* and talk about the geographical features of the country. Point out the concentration of cities along the country's Pacific Coast, and note the sparse settlement in the eastern part of the country and along the Caribbean coast. Tell students that, nearly 100 years after construction of the Panama Canal, plans are underway for a new interoceanic canal, utilizing the San Juan River and Lake Nicaragua.

**El país en cifras** After reading about the country's varied terrain and many volcanoes, tell students that Nicaragua's national slogan is **"El país de lagos y volcanes."** After students read about the capital, ask: **¿Qué porcentaje de nicaragüenses vive en Managua? (el 20%)** Tell students that one reason so many Nicaraguans live in the capital is due to the devastation experienced in much of the rest of the country over the past two decades due to war and natural disasters, such as Hurricane Mitch in 1998, and earthquakes and volcanic eruptions in 1999.

**¡Increíble pero cierto!** Lake Nicaragua is the largest lake in Central America. Over forty rivers drain into the lake.

---

# Nicaragua

NATIONAL / connections cultures / STANDARDS

## El país en cifras

▶ **Área:** 129.494 km² (49.998 millas²), *aproximadamente el área de Nueva York. Nicaragua es el país más grande de Centroamérica. Su terreno es muy variado e incluye bosques tropicales, montañas, sabanasº y marismasº, además de unos 40 volcanes.*

▶ **Población:** 6.066.000
▶ **Capital:** Managua—1.312.000
*Managua está en una región de una notable inestabilidad geográfica, con muchos volcanes y terremotosº. En décadas recientes, los nicaragüenses han decidido que no vale la penaº construir rascacielosº porque no resisten los terremotos.*

▶ **Ciudades principales:** León, Masaya, Granada
SOURCE: Population Division, UN Secretariat

▶ **Moneda:** córdoba
▶ **Idiomas:** español (oficial), misquito, inglés

Bandera de Nicaragua

### Nicaragüenses célebres

▶ **Rubén Darío,** poeta (1867–1916)
▶ **Violeta Barrios de Chamorro,** política y ex-presidenta (1930– )
▶ **Daniel Ortega,** político y ex-presidente (1945– )
▶ **Gioconda Belli,** poeta (1948– )

sabanas *grasslands* marismas *marshes* Pintada *Political graffiti*
terremotos *earthquakes* no vale la pena *it's not worthwhile*
rascacielos *skyscrapers* tiburón *shark* agua dulce *freshwater*
bahía *bay* fue cercada *was closed off* atunes *tuna*

Pintadaº en una pared de Managua

Típico hogar misquit en la costa atlántica

HONDURAS
Río Coco
Cordillera Isabelia
Chachagón · Saslaya · Piu
Río Tuma
Río Grande
Cordillera Dariense
León ·
Sierra Madre
Océano Pacífico
Lago de Managua
Managua ☆
Lago Nicaragua
Masaya · · Granada
Isla Zapatera
Concepción
Maderas · Isla Ometepe
Archipiélago Solentiname
Río San Juan
COSTA RICA

Violeta Barrios de Chamorro

ESTADOS UNIDOS
OCÉANO ATLÁNTICO
NICARAGUA
OCÉANO PACÍFICO
AMÉRICA DEL SUR

**recursos**

| WB pp. 123–124 | VM pp. 245–246 | panorama.vhlcentral.com Lección 10 |

---

### ¡Increíble pero cierto!

En el lago Nicaragua está la única especie de tiburónº de agua dulceº del mundo. Los científicos creen que el lago fue antes una enorme bahíaº que luego fue cercadaº por erupciones volcánicas. Esta teoría explicaría la presencia de tiburones, atunesº y otras especies de peces que normalmente sólo viven en mares y océanos.

---

### TEACHING OPTIONS

**Worth Noting** Managua is a city that has been destroyed and rebuilt multiple times due to wars and natural disasters. This has contributed to the unusual method used for listing street addresses in this capital city. Many places do not have an address that includes an actual building number and street name. Instead, the address includes a reference to a local landmark, and its relationship to other permanent features of the landscape, such as Lake Managua. Here is a typical Managua address: **De la Clínica Don Bosco, 2 cuadras al norte, 3 al sur.**
**Extra Practice** Invite students to compare the romantic poetry of **Rubén Darío** to the contemporary work of **Ernesto Cardenal** and **Gioconda Belli.** Students can choose several poems to read aloud to the class, and then comment on differences in style and content.

## Historia • Las huellasº de Acahualinca

La región de Managua se caracteriza por tener un gran número de sitios prehistóricos. Las huellas de Acahualinca son uno de los restosº más famosos y antiguosº. Se formaron hace más de 6.000 años, a orillasº del lago Managua. Las huellas, tanto de humanos como de animales, se dirigenº hacia una misma dirección. Esto hace pensar a los expertos que corrían hacia el lago para escapar de una erupción volcánica.

## Artes • Ernesto Cardenal (1925– )

Ernesto Cardenal, poeta, escultor y sacerdoteº católico, es uno de los escritores más famosos de Nicaragua, país conocido por sus grandes poetas. Ha escritoº más de 35 libros y se le considera uno de los principales autores de Latinoamérica. Desde joven creyó en el poderº de la poesíaº. En los años 60, Cardenal organizó la comunidad artística del archipiélago Solentiname en el lago Nicaragua. Fue ministro de cultura del país desde 1979 hasta 1988, y también fue vicepresidente de Casa de los Tres Mundos, una organización creada para el intercambio cultural internacional.

## Naturaleza • El lago Nicaragua

El lago Nicaragua, con un área de más de 8.000 km$^2$ (3.100 millas$^2$), es el lago más grande de Centroamérica. Tiene más de 370 islasº, formadas por las erupciones del volcán Mombacho. La isla Zapatera, casi deshabitada ahora, fue un cementerioº indígena donde todavía se encuentran estatuas prehistóricas. En el lago también encontramos muchos peces exóticos.

 **¿Qué aprendiste?** Responde a cada pregunta con una oración completa.

1. ¿Por qué no hay muchos rascacielos en Managua?
   No hay muchos rascacielos en Managua porque no resisten los terremotos.
2. Nombra dos ex-presidentes de Nicaragua.
   Violeta Barrios de Chamorro y Daniel Ortega son dos ex-presidentes de Nicaragua.
3. ¿Qué especie única vive en el lago Nicaragua?
   La única especie de tiburón de agua dulce vive en el lago Nicaragua.
4. ¿Cuál es una de las teorías sobre la formación de las huellas de Acahualinca?
   Una teoría dice que las personas y los animales corrían para escapar de la erupción del volcán.
5. ¿Por qué es famoso el archipiélago Solentiname?
   El archipiélago Solentiname es famoso porque es el sitio de la comunidad artística organizada por Cardenal.
6. ¿Quién es Ernesto Cardenal?
   Es un poeta, escultor y sacerdote de Nicaragua.
7. ¿Cómo se formaron las islas del lago Nicaragua?
   Las islas se formaron por erupciones volcánicas.
8. ¿Qué hay de interés arqueológico en la isla Zapatera?
   En la isla Zapatera existió un cementerio indígena en que todavía se encuentran estatuas prehistóricas.

**Conexión Internet** Investiga estos temas en **panorama.vhlcentral.com.**

1. ¿Dónde se habla inglés en Nicaragua y por qué?
2. ¿Qué información hay ahora sobre la economía y/o los derechos humanos en Nicaragua?

........................................................................

huellas *footprints* restos *remains* antiguos *ancient* orillas *shores* se dirigen *are headed* sacerdote *priest*
Ha escrito *He has written* poder *power* poesía *poetry* islas *islands* cementerio *cemetery*

**Las huellas de Acahualinca**
The **huellas de Acahualinca** were preserved in soft mud that was then covered with volcanic ash which became petrified, preserving the prints of bison, otter, deer, lizards, and birds—as well as humans.

**Ernesto Cardenal** After completing undergraduate courses in Nicaragua, **Ernesto Cardenal** studied in Mexico and in the United States, where he worked with the religious poet Thomas Merton at the Trappist seminary in Kentucky. He later studied theology in Colombia and was ordained in Nicaragua in 1965. Shortly after that, **Cardenal** founded the faith-based community of artists on the Solentiname Islands of Lake Nicaragua.

**El lago Nicaragua** Environmental groups in Nicaragua have been concerned about the recent introduction of a variety of **tilapia** into Lake Nicaragua. Although **tilapia** are native to the lake, this variety is a more prolific species. Environmentalists are concerned that the Nicaraguan-Norwegian joint venture responsible for this initiative has not done an adequate environmental impact study, and that the delicate and unique ecology of the lake may be negatively impacted.

**Conexión Internet** Students will find supporting Internet activities and links at **panorama.vhlcentral.com.**

**Teaching Tip** You may want to wrap up this section by playing the *Panorama cultural* video footage for this lesson.

**TEACHING OPTIONS**

**Worth Noting** On July 19, 1979, the **FSLN (Frente Sandinista de Liberación Nacional),** known as the **Sandinistas,** came to power in Nicaragua after winning a revolutionary struggle against the dictatorship of **Anastasio Somoza.** The **Sandinistas** began a program of economic and social reform that threatened the power of Nicaragua's traditional elite, leading to a civil war known as the **Contra** war. The United States became enmeshed in this conflict, illegally providing funding and arms to the **Contras,** who fought to oust the **Sandinistas.** The **Sandinistas** were ultimately voted out of power in 1990.

## El cuerpo

| | |
|---|---|
| la boca | mouth |
| el brazo | arm |
| la cabeza | head |
| el corazón | heart |
| el cuello | neck |
| el cuerpo | body |
| el dedo | finger |
| el dedo del pie | toe |
| el estómago | stomach |
| la garganta | throat |
| el hueso | bone |
| la nariz | nose |
| el oído | (sense of) hearing; inner ear |
| el ojo | eye |
| la oreja | (outer) ear |
| el pie | foot |
| la pierna | leg |
| la rodilla | knee |
| el tobillo | ankle |

## La salud

| | |
|---|---|
| el accidente | accident |
| el antibiótico | antibiotic |
| la aspirina | aspirin |
| la clínica | clinic |
| el consultorio | doctor's office |
| el/la dentista | dentist |
| el/la doctor(a) | doctor |
| el dolor (de cabeza) | (head)ache; pain |
| el/la enfermero/a | nurse |
| el examen médico | physical exam |
| la farmacia | pharmacy |
| la gripe | flu |
| el hospital | hospital |
| la infección | infection |
| el medicamento | medication |
| la medicina | medicine |
| la operación | operation |
| el/la paciente | patient |
| la pastilla | pill; tablet |
| la radiografía | X-ray |
| la receta | prescription |
| el resfriado | cold (illness) |
| la sala de emergencia(s) | emergency room |
| la salud | health |
| el síntoma | symptom |
| la tos | cough |

## Verbos

| | |
|---|---|
| caerse | to fall (down) |
| dañar | to damage; to break down |
| darse con | to bump into; to run into |
| doler (o:ue) | to hurt |
| enfermarse | to get sick |
| estar enfermo/a | to be sick |
| estornudar | to sneeze |
| lastimarse (el pie) | to injure (one's foot) |
| olvidar | to forget |
| poner una inyección | to give an injection |
| prohibir | to prohibit |
| recetar | to prescribe |
| romper | to break |
| romperse (la pierna) | to break (one's leg) |
| sacar(se) un diente | to have a tooth removed |
| ser alérgico/a (a) | to be allergic (to) |
| sufrir una enfermedad | to suffer an illness |
| tener dolor (m.) | to have a pain |
| tener fiebre | to have a fever |
| tomar la temperatura | to take someone's temperature |
| torcerse (o:ue) (el tobillo) | to sprain (one's ankle) |
| toser | to cough |

## Adjetivos

| | |
|---|---|
| congestionado/a | congested; stuffed-up |
| embarazada | pregnant |
| grave | grave; serious |
| mareado/a | dizzy; nauseated |
| médico/a | medical |
| saludable | healthy |
| sano/a | healthy |

## Adverbios

| | |
|---|---|
| a menudo | often |
| a tiempo | on time |
| a veces | sometimes |
| además (de) | furthermore; besides |
| apenas | hardly; scarcely |
| así | like this; so |
| bastante | enough; rather |
| casi | almost |
| con frecuencia | frequently |
| de niño/a | as a child |
| de vez en cuando | from time to time |
| despacio | slowly |
| menos | less |
| mientras | while |
| muchas veces | a lot; many times |
| poco | little |
| por lo menos | at least |
| pronto | soon |
| rápido | quickly |
| todos los días | every day |

| | |
|---|---|
| **Expresiones útiles** | *See page 313.* |

**recursos**

LM p. 60

panorama.vhlcentral.com Lección 10

# La tecnología

# 11

## Communicative Goals

### You will learn how to:

- **Talk about using technology and electronic products**
- **Use common expressions on the telephone**
- **Talk about car trouble**

contextos

### pages 342–345

- Home electronics
- Computers and the Internet
- The car and its accessories

fotonovela

### pages 346–349

Inés and Javier tease Álex about his obsession with computers. Don Francisco asks everyone to get off the bus because of mechanical problems. Inés and Álex come to the rescue.

cultura

### pages 350–351

- Cell phones in the Spanish-speaking world
- Cybercafés in Latin America

estructura

### pages 352–367

- Familiar commands
- **Por** and **para**
- Reciprocal reflexives
- Stressed possessive adjectives and pronouns
- **Recapitulación**

adelante

### pages 368–373

**Lectura:** An article about artificial intelligence
**Panorama:** Argentina y Uruguay

## A PRIMERA VISTA

- ¿Se llevan ellos bien o mal?
- ¿Crees que hace mucho tiempo que se conocen?
- ¿Son saludables?
- ¿Qué partes del cuerpo se ven en la foto?

## Lesson Goals

In **Lección 11**, students will be introduced to the following:

- terms related to home electronics and the Internet
- terms related to cars and their accessories
- cell phone use in Spanish-speaking countries
- cybercafés in Latin America
- familiar (**tú**) commands
- uses of **por** and **para**
- reciprocal reflexive verbs
- stressed possessive adjectives and pronouns
- recognizing borrowed words
- cultural, geographic, and historical information about Argentina
- cultural and geographic information about Uruguay

**A primera vista** Here are some additional questions you can ask based on the photo: **¿Te gustan las computadoras? ¿Para qué usas el correo electrónico? ¿Cómo se escribían tus abuelos cuando no existía el correo electrónico? ¿Cuánto tiempo hace que sabes conducir? ¿Tienes auto?**

## INSTRUCTIONAL RESOURCES

**MAESTRO™ SUPERSITE (panorama.vhlcentral.com)**
Textbook, Vocabulary, & Lab MP3 Audio Files
Additional Practice
Learning Management System (Assignment Task Manager, Gradebook)
*Also on DVD*
  **Fotonovela**

*Flash cultura*
*Panorama cultural*
*Also on Instructor's Resource CD-ROM*
  *PowerPoints* (**Contextos** & **Estructura** Presentations, Overheads)
  *Instructor's Resource Manual* (Handouts, Textbook Answer Key, WBs/VM/LM Answer Key,

Audioscripts, Videoscripts & Translations)
  *Testing Program* (**Pruebas,** Test Generator, MP3s)
**WebSAM** (Workbook/Video Manual/Lab Manual)
**Workbook/Video Manual**
*Cuaderno para hispanohablantes*
**Lab Manual**

# La tecnología

## Más vocabulario

| | |
|---|---|
| la calculadora | calculator |
| la cámara de video, digital | video, digital camera |
| el canal | (TV) channel |
| la contestadora | answering machine |
| el estéreo | stereo |
| el fax | fax (machine) |
| la televisión por cable | cable television |
| el tocadiscos compacto | compact disc player |
| el video(casete) | video(cassette) |
| el archivo | file |
| arroba | @ symbol |
| la dirección electrónica | e-mail address |
| Internet | Internet |
| el mensaje de texto | text message |
| la página principal | home page |
| el programa de computación | software |
| la red | network; Web |
| el sitio web | website |
| apagar | to turn off |
| borrar | to erase |
| descargar | to download |
| funcionar | to work |
| grabar | to record |
| guardar | to save |
| imprimir | to print |
| llamar | to call |
| navegar (en Internet) | to surf (the Internet) |
| poner, prender | to turn on |
| quemar | to burn (a CD) |
| sonar (o:ue) | to ring |
| descompuesto/a | not working; out of order |
| lento/a | slow |
| lleno/a | full |

## Variación léxica

computadora ←→ ordenador (*Esp.*), computador (*Col.*)
descargar ←→ bajar (*Esp., Col., Arg., Ven.*)

Labels on illustration: el televisor · la pantalla · el reproductor de DVD · la videocasetera · la impresora · la computadora (portátil) · el monitor · el (teléfono) celular · el ratón · el teclado · el cederrón

# Práctica

**1** **Escuchar** 🎧 Escucha la conversación entre dos amigas. Después completa las oraciones.

1. María y Ana están en ___b___.
   a. una tienda   b. un cibercafé   c. un restaurante
2. A María le encantan ___b___.
   a. los celulares   b. las cámaras digitales   c. los cibercafés
3. Ana prefiere guardar las fotos en ___c___.
   a. la pantalla   b. un archivo   c. un cederrón
4. María quiere tomar un café y ___c___.
   a. poner la computadora   b. sacar fotos digitales
   c. navegar en Internet
5. Ana paga por el café y ___a___.
   a. el uso de Internet   b. la impresora   c. el cederrón

**2** **¿Cierto o falso?** 🎧 Escucha las oraciones e indica si lo que dice cada una es **cierto** o **falso**, según el dibujo.

| | | | |
|---|---|---|---|
| 1 | cierto | 5. | cierto |
| 2. | falso | 6. | falso |
| 3. | falso | 7. | cierto |
| 4. | cierto | 8. | falso |

**3** **Oraciones** Escribe oraciones usando estos elementos. Usa el pretérito y añade las palabras necesarias.

1. yo / descargar / fotos digitales / Internet
   Yo descargué las fotos digitales por Internet.
2. tú / apagar / televisor / diez / noche
   Tú apagaste el televisor a las diez de la noche.
3. Daniel y su esposa / comprar / computadora portátil / ayer
   Daniel y su esposa compraron una computadora portátil ayer.
4. Sara y yo / ir / cibercafé / para / navegar en Internet
   Sara y yo fuimos al cibercafé para navegar en Internet.
5. Jaime / decidir / comprar / reproductor de MP3
   Jaime decidió comprar un reproductor de MP3.
6. teléfono celular / sonar / pero / yo / no contestar
   El teléfono celular sonó, pero yo no contesté.

**4** **Preguntas** Mira el dibujo y contesta las preguntas. Answers will vary.

1. ¿Qué tipo de café es?
2. ¿Cuántas impresoras hay? ¿Cuántos ratones?
3. ¿Por qué vinieron estas personas al café?
4. ¿Qué hace el camarero?
5. ¿Qué hace la mujer en la computadora? ¿Y el hombre?
6. ¿Qué máquinas están cerca del televisor?
7. ¿Dónde hay un cibercafé en tu comunidad?
8. ¿Por qué puedes tú necesitar un cibercafé?

Cibercafé CORRIENTES

el control remoto

el reproductor de MP3

el disco compacto

SUPERSITE

**1** **Teaching Tip** Have students check their answers by going over **Actividad 1** with the class.

**1** **Script** ANA: ¿María? ¿Qué haces aquí en el cibercafé? ¿No tienes Internet en casa? MARÍA: Pues, sí, pero la computadora está descompuesta. Tengo que esperar unos días más. A: Te entiendo. Me pasó lo mismo con la computadora portátil hace poco. Todavía no funciona bien … por eso vine aquí. M: ¿Recibiste algún mensaje interesante? A: Sí. Mi hijo está de vacaciones con unos amigos en Argentina. Tiene una cámara digital y me mandó unas fotos digitales. M: ¡Qué bien! Me encantan las cámaras digitales. Normalmente imprimimos las fotos con nuestra impresora y no tenemos que ir a ninguna tienda. Es muy conveniente. *Script continues on page 344.*

**2** **Teaching Tip** To challenge students, have them provide the correct information.

**2** **Script** 1. Hay dos personas navegando en Internet. 2. El camarero está hablando por su teléfono celular. 3. Dos señoras están mirando la televisión por cable. 4. En la pantalla del televisor se puede ver un partido de fútbol. 5. Un hombre habla por teléfono mientras navega en la red. 6. Hay cuatro computadoras portátiles en el cibercafé. 7. Hay dos discos compactos encima de una mesa. 8. El cibercafé tiene videocasetera pero no tiene reproductor de DVD. *Textbook MP3s*

**3** **Expansion** Have students create three dehydrated sentences for a partner to complete.

**4** **Expansion** For item 8, survey the class for overall trends.

---

**TEACHING OPTIONS**

**Pairs** Have pairs of students role-play one of these situations in a cybercafé. 1. One student plays an irate customer who claims to have been overcharged for brief Internet use. The second plays the employee, who insists on being paid the full amount, claiming that the customer spent quite a bit of time online. 2. One student plays a customer who has been waiting over an hour to use a computer and must ask another customer to log off and give him

or her a chance. The second customer becomes annoyed at the request and the two must sort it out.
**Heritage Speakers** Ask heritage speakers to describe their experiences with Spanish-language Web applications, such as e-mail or websites. Do they or their families regularly visit Spanish-language websites? Which ones?

**En la gasolinera**

### Más vocabulario

| | |
|---|---|
| la autopista, la carretera | highway |
| la calle | street |
| la circulación, el tráfico | traffic |
| el garaje, el taller (mecánico) | (mechanic's) garage; repair shop |
| la licencia de conducir | driver's license |
| el/la mecánico/a | mechanic |
| la policía | police (force) |
| la velocidad máxima | speed limit |
| arrancar | to start |
| arreglar | to fix; to arrange |
| bajar(se) de | to get off of/out of (a vehicle) |
| conducir, manejar | to drive |
| estacionar | to park |
| parar | to stop |
| subir(se) a | to get on/into (a vehicle) |

**5** **Completar** Completa estas oraciones con las palabras correctas.

1. Para poder conducir legalmente, necesitas… *una licencia de conducir.*
2. Puedes poner las maletas en… *el baúl.*
3. Si tu carro no funciona, debes llevarlo a… *un mecánico/taller.*
4. Para llenar el tanque de tu coche, necesitas ir a… *la gasolinera.*
5. Antes de un viaje largo, es importante revisar… *el aceite.*
6. Otra palabra para autopista es… *carretera.*
7. Mientras hablas por teléfono celular, no es buena idea… *manejar/conducir.*
8. Otra palabra para coche es… *carro.*

**¡LENGUA VIVA!**

Aunque **carro** es el término que se usa en la mayoría de países hispanos, no es el único. En España, por ejemplo, se dice **coche**, y en Argentina, Chile y Uruguay se dice **auto**.

**6** **Conversación** Completa la conversación con las palabras de la lista.

| el aceite | la gasolina | llenar | revisar | el taller |
|---|---|---|---|---|
| el baúl | las llantas | manejar | el parabrisas | el volante |

**EMPLEADO** Bienvenido al (1)___taller___ mecánico Óscar. ¿En qué le puedo servir?

**JUAN** Buenos días. Quiero (2)___llenar___ el tanque y revisar (3)___el aceite___, por favor.

**EMPLEADO** Con mucho gusto. Si quiere, también le limpio (4)___el parabrisas___.

**JUAN** Sí, gracias. Está un poquito sucio. La próxima semana tengo que (5)___manejar___ hasta Buenos Aires. ¿Puede cambiar (6)___las llantas___? Están gastadas *(worn).*

**EMPLEADO** Claro que sí, pero voy a tardar *(it will take me)* un par de horas.

**JUAN** Mejor regreso mañana. Ahora no tengo tiempo. ¿Cuánto le debo por (7)___la gasolina___?

**EMPLEADO** Sesenta pesos. Y veinticinco por (8)___revisar___ y cambiar el aceite.

**CONSULTA**

For more information about **Buenos Aires,** see **Panorama,** p. 370.

# Comunicación

**7** **Preguntas** Trabajen en grupos para contestar estas preguntas. Después compartan sus respuestas con la clase. *Answers will vary.*

1. a. ¿Tienes un teléfono celular? ¿Para qué lo usas?
   b. ¿Qué utilizas más: el teléfono o el correo electrónico? ¿Por qué?
   c. En tu opinión, ¿cuáles son las ventajas (*advantages*) y desventajas de los diferentes modos de comunicación?
2. a. ¿Con qué frecuencia usas la computadora?
   b. ¿Para qué usas Internet?
   c. ¿Tienes tu propio sitio web? ¿Cómo es?
3. a. ¿Miras la televisión con frecuencia? ¿Qué programas ves?
   b. ¿Tienes televisión por cable? ¿Por qué?
   c. ¿Tienes una videocasetera? ¿Un reproductor de DVD? ¿Un reproductor de DVD en la computadora?
   d. ¿A través de (*By*) qué medio escuchas música? ¿Radio, estéreo, tocadiscos compacto, reproductor de MP3 o computadora?
4. a. ¿Tienes licencia de conducir?
   b. ¿Cuánto tiempo hace que la conseguiste?
   c. ¿Tienes carro? Descríbelo.
   d. ¿Llevas tu carro al taller? ¿Para qué?

**NOTA CULTURAL**

Algunos sitios web utilizan códigos para identificar su país de origen. Éstos son los códigos para algunos países hispanohablantes.

| Argentina | .ar |
|-----------|-----|
| Colombia | .co |
| España | .es |
| México | .mx |
| Venezuela | .ve |

**CONSULTA**

To review expressions like **hace…que**, see **Lección 10, Expresiones útiles**, p. 313.

**8** **Postal** En parejas, lean la tarjeta postal. Después contesten las preguntas. *Answers will vary.*

*19 julio de 1979*

*Hola, Paco:*

*¡Saludos! Estamos de viaje por unas semanas. La Costa del Sol es muy bonita. No hemos encontrado (we haven't found) a tus amigos porque nunca están en casa cuando llamamos. El teléfono suena y suena y nadie contesta. Vamos a seguir llamando.*

*Sacamos muchas fotos muy divertidas. Cuando regresemos y las revelemos (get them developed), te las voy a enseñar. Las playas son preciosas. Hasta ahora el único problema fue que la oficina en la cual reservamos un carro perdió nuestros papeles y tuvimos que esperar mucho tiempo.*

*También tuvimos un pequeño problema con el hotel. La agencia de viajes nos reservó una habitación en un hotel que está muy lejos de todo. No podemos cambiarla, pero no me importa mucho. A pesar de eso, estamos contentos.*

*Tu hermana, Gabriela*

EUROPA 12
ESPAÑA

*Francisco Jiménez*
*San Lorenzo 3250*
*Rosario, Argentina 2000*

1. ¿Cuáles son los problemas que ocurren en el viaje de Gabriela?
2. Con la tecnología de hoy, ¿existen los mismos problemas cuando se viaja? ¿Por qué?
3. Hagan una comparación entre la tecnología de los años 70 y 80 y la de hoy.
4. Imaginen que la hija de Gabriela escribe un correo electrónico sobre el mismo tema con fecha de hoy. Escriban ese correo, incorporando la tecnología de hoy (teléfonos celulares, Internet, cámaras digitales, etc.). Inventen nuevos problemas.

---

**7** **Expansion** Write names of electronic communication devices on the board (Ex: **teléfono celular**, *fax*, **computadora**). Then survey the class to find out how many people own or use these items. Analyze the trends of the class.

**8** **Teaching Tip** Possible answers: **1. Gabriela no encuentra a los amigos de Paco porque nunca están en casa, tuvo que esperar mucho por el carro y su hotel estaba muy lejos de todo. 2. No existen los mismos problemas porque existen las contestadoras y los teléfonos celulares, se puede reservar un carro en Internet y se puede buscar información sobre un hotel en la red antes del viaje.**

**8** **Expansion** Ask groups to write a postcard in which the problems are a direct result of the existence of technology, not its absence.

**Note:** At this point you may want to present *Vocabulario adicional: Más vocabulario para el carro y la tecnología,* from the Supersite/IRCD.

---

**TEACHING OPTIONS**

**Extra Practice** For homework, have students do an Internet research project on technology and technology terminology in the Spanish-speaking world. Suggest possible topics and websites where students may look for information. Have students write out their reports and present them to the class.

**Large Groups** Stage a debate about the role of technology in today's world. Divide the class into two groups and assign each side a position. Propose this debate topic: **La tecnología: ¿beneficio o no?** Allow groups time to plan their arguments before staging the debate.

**SUPERSITE**

# Tecnohombre, ¡mi héroe!

communication
cultures
NATIONAL
STANDARDS

El autobús se daña.

## Section Goals

In **Fotonovela**, students will:
- receive comprehensible input from free-flowing discourse
- learn functional phrases that preview lesson grammatical structures

**Instructional Resources**
**Supersite/DVD:** *Fotonovela*
**Supersite/IRCD:** *IRM*
(*Fotonovela* Videoscript & Translation, WBs/VM/LM Answer Key)
**WebSAM**
**Video Manual,** pp. 215-216

**Video Recap: Lección 10**
Before doing this **Fotonovela** section, review the previous one with this activity.
**1. ¿Qué le pasó a Javier en el autobús? (Se lastimó el tobillo.)**
**2. ¿Adónde llevó don Francisco a Javier? (a ver a su amiga, la doctora Márquez) 3. ¿Qué mostró la radiografía? (El tobillo de Javier estaba torcido.) 4. ¿Qué le recetó la doctora a Javier? (unas pastillas para el dolor)**

**Video Synopsis** On the way to Ibarra, the bus breaks down. **Don Francisco** cannot locate the problem, but **Inés**, an experienced mechanic, diagnoses it as a burned-out alternator. **Álex** uses his cell phone to call **Don Francisco's** friend, **Sr. Fonseca,** who is a mechanic. **Maite** and **Don Francisco** praise **Inés** and **Álex** for saving the day.

**Teaching Tips**
- Have students predict the content of this episode based on the video stills only.
- Quickly review the predictions and ask students a few questions to guide them in summarizing this episode.

**PERSONAJES**

MAITE

INÉS

DON FRANCISCO

ÁLEX

JAVIER

SR. FONSECA

**1**

**ÁLEX** ¿Bueno? ... Con él habla... Ah, ¿cómo estás? ... Aquí, yo muy bien. Vamos para Ibarra. ¿Sabes lo que pasó? Esta tarde íbamos para Ibarra cuando Javier tuvo un accidente en el autobús. Se cayó y tuvimos que llevarlo a una clínica.

**2**

**JAVIER** Episodio veintiuno: Tecnohombre y los superamigos suyos salvan el mundo una vez más.

**INÉS** Oh, Tecnohombre, ¡mi héroe!

**MAITE** ¡Qué cómicos! Un día de éstos, ya van a ver...

**3**

**ÁLEX** Van a ver quién es realmente Tecnohombre. Mis superamigos y yo nos hablamos todos los días por el teléfono Internet, trabajando para salvar el mundo. Pero ahora, con su permiso, quiero escribirle un mensaje electrónico a mi mamá y navegar en la red un ratito.

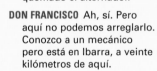
**6**

**INÉS** Pues... no sé... creo que es el alternador. A ver... sí... Mire, don Francisco... está quemado el alternador.

**DON FRANCISCO** Ah, sí. Pero aquí no podemos arreglarlo. Conozco a un mecánico pero está en Ibarra, a veinte kilómetros de aquí.

**7**

**ÁLEX** ¡Tecnohombre, a sus órdenes!

**DON FRANCISCO** ¡Eres la salvación, Álex! Llama al Sr. Fonseca al cinco, treinta y dos, cuarenta y siete, noventa y uno. Nos conocemos muy bien. Seguro que nos ayuda.

**8**

**ÁLEX** Buenas tardes. ¿Con el Sr. Fonseca por favor? ... Soy Álex Morales, cliente de Ecuatur. Le hablo de parte del señor Francisco Castillo... Es que íbamos para Ibarra y se nos dañó el autobús. ... Pensamos que es el... el alternador... Estamos a veinte kilómetros de la ciudad...

**recursos**

VM
pp. 215–216

**SUPERSITE**
panorama.vhlcentral.com
Lección 11

## TEACHING OPTIONS

**Video Tips** General suggestions for using video clips in the classroom can be found on page IAE-12 of this Instructor's Annotated Edition.

**Tecnohombre, ¡mi héroe!** Show the **Tecnohombre, ¡mi héroe!** episode once without sound and have the class create a plot summary based on the visual cues. Then show the episode with sound and have the class make corrections and fill in any gaps in the plot summary.

**DON FRANCISCO** Chicos, creo que tenemos un problema con el autobús. ¿Por qué no se bajan?

**DON FRANCISCO** Mmm, no veo el problema.

**INÉS** Cuando estaba en la escuela secundaria, trabajé en el taller de mi tío. Me enseñó mucho sobre mecánica. Por suerte, arreglé unos autobuses como éste.

**DON FRANCISCO** ¡No me digas!

**SR. FONSECA** Creo que va a ser mejor arreglar el autobús allí mismo. Tranquilo, enseguida salgo.

**ÁLEX** Buenas noticias. El señor Fonseca viene enseguida. Piensa que puede arreglar el autobús aquí mismo.

**MAITE** ¡La Mujer Mecánica y Tecnohombre, mis héroes!

**DON FRANCISCO** ¡Y los míos también!

## Expresiones útiles

### Talking on the telephone
- **Aló./¿Bueno?/Diga.** *Hello.*
- **¿Quién habla?** *Who is speaking?*
- **¿De parte de quién?** *Who is calling?*
  **Con él/ella habla.** *This is he/she.*
  **Le hablo de parte de Francisco Castillo.** *I'm speaking to you on behalf of Francisco Castillo.*
- **¿Puedo dejar un recado?** *May I leave a message?*
  **Está bien. Llamo más tarde.** *That's fine. I'll call later.*

### Talking about bus or car problems
- **¿Qué pasó?** *What happened?*
  **Se nos dañó el autobús.** *The bus broke down.*
  **Se nos pinchó una llanta.** *We had a flat tire.*
  **Está quemado el alternador.** *The alternator is burned out.*

### Saying how far away things are
- **Está a veinte kilómetros de aquí.** *It's twenty kilometers from here.*
- **Estamos a veinte millas de la ciudad.** *We're twenty miles from the city.*

### Expressing surprise
- **¡No me digas!** *You don't say! (fam.)*
- **¡No me diga!** *You don't say! (form.)*

### Offering assistance
- **A sus órdenes.** *At your service.*

### Additional vocabulary
- **aquí mismo** *right here*

### TEACHING OPTIONS

**Extra Practice** Make a photocopy of the **Fotonovela** Videoscript (Supersite/IRCD) and white out key words to create a master for a cloze activity. Hand out photocopies of the master to students and have them fill in the missing words as they watch the **Tecnohombre, ¡mi héroe!** episode. You may have students share their answers in small groups and help each other fill in any gaps.
**Pairs** Write some phone call scenarios on the board. Ex: **1. Llamas a la casa de tu mejor amigo/a, pero no está. 2. Llamas a tu profesor(a) de español para explicarle por qué no fuiste a clase.** Ask students to sit or stand in twos, back-to-back and have them role-play the conversations, using phrases from **Expresiones útiles**. To simplify, you may want to have students brainstorm phrases for each situation. If nearly all students have cell phones, have them use the phones as props for this activity.

# ¿Qué pasó?

**1**

**Seleccionar** Selecciona las respuestas que completan correctamente estas oraciones.

1. Álex quiere __b__.
   a. llamar a su mamá por teléfono celular   b. escribirle a su mamá y navegar en la red
   c. hablar por teléfono Internet y navegar en la red
2. Se les dañó el autobús. Inés dice que __a__.
   a. el alternador está quemado   b. se pinchó una llanta   c. el taller está lejos
3. Álex llama al mecánico, el señor __c__.
   a. Castillo   b. Ibarra   c. Fonseca
4. Maite llama a Inés la "Mujer Mecánica" porque antes __a__.
   a. trabajaba en el taller de su tío   b. arreglaba computadoras
   c. conocía a muchos mecánicos
5. El grupo está a __c__ de la ciudad.
   a. veinte millas   b. veinte grados centígrados   c. veinte kilómetros

**2**

**Identificar** Identifica quién puede decir estas oraciones.

1. Gracias a mi tío tengo un poco de experiencia arreglando autobuses. Inés
2. Sé manejar un autobús pero no sé arreglarlo. ¿Por qué no llamamos a mi amigo? don Francisco
3. Sabes, admiro mucho a la Mujer Mecánica y a Tecnohombre. Maite
4. Aló... Sí, ¿de parte de quién? Álex
5. El nombre de Tecnohombre fue idea mía. ¡Qué cómico!, ¿no? Javier

 JAVIER
 ÁLEX
MAITE
INÉS
 DON FRANCISCO

**3**

**Problema mecánico** Trabajen en parejas para representar los papeles de un(a) mecánico/a y un(a) cliente/a que está llamando al taller porque su carro está descompuesto. Usen las instrucciones como guía. Answers will vary.

 communication

| Mecánico/a | Cliente/a |
|---|---|
| Contesta el teléfono con un saludo y el nombre del taller. → | Saluda y explica que tu carro está descompuesto. |
| Pregunta qué tipo de problema tiene exactamente. → | Explica que tu carro no arranca cuando hace frío. |
| Di que debe traer el carro al taller. → | Pregunta cuándo puedes llevarlo. |
| Ofrece una hora para revisar el carro. → | Acepta la hora que ofrece el/la mecánico/a. |
| Da las gracias y despídete. → | Despídete y cuelga (*hang up*) el teléfono. |

Ahora cambien los papeles y representen otra conversación. Ustedes son un(a) técnico/a y un(a) cliente/a. Usen estas ideas:

> el celular no guarda mensajes          la impresora imprime muy lentamente
> la computadora no descarga fotos       el reproductor de DVD está descompuesto

# Ortografía

## La acentuación de palabras similares

Although accent marks usually indicate which syllable in a word is stressed, they are also used to distinguish between words that have the same or similar spellings.

**Él** maneja **el** coche.     **Sí**, voy **si** quieres.

Although one-syllable words do not usually carry written accents, some *do* have accent marks to distinguish them from words that have the same spelling but different meanings.

**Sé** cocinar.    **Se** baña.     ¿Tomas **té**?    **Te** duermes.

**Sé** (*I know*) and **té** (*tea*) have accent marks to distinguish them from the pronouns **se** and **te**.

para **mí**     **mi** cámara     **Tú** lees.     **tu** estéreo

**Mí** (*Me*) and **tú** (*you*) have accent marks to distinguish them from the possessive adjectives **mi** and **tu**.

¿**Por qué** vas?     Voy **porque** quiero.

Several words of more than one syllable also have accent marks to distinguish them from words that have the same or similar spellings.

**Éste** es rápido.     **Este** módem es rápido.

Demonstrative pronouns have accent marks to distinguish them from demonstrative adjectives.

¿**Cuándo** fuiste?     Fui **cuando** me llamó.

¿**Dónde** trabajas?     Voy al taller **donde** trabajo.

Adverbs have accent marks when they are used to convey a question.

**Práctica** Marca los acentos en las palabras que los necesitan.

**ANA** Alo, soy Ana. ¿Que tal?   Aló/¿Qué?

**JUAN** Hola, pero... ¿por que me llamas tan tarde?   ¿por qué?

**ANA** Porque mañana tienes que llevarme a la universidad. Mi auto esta dañado.   está

**JUAN** ¿Como se daño?   ¿Cómo?/dañó

**ANA** Se daño el sabado. Un vecino (*neighbor*) choco con (*crashed into*) el.   dañó/sábado/chocó/él

**Crucigrama** Utiliza las siguientes pistas (*clues*) para completar el crucigrama. ¡Ojo con los acentos!

**Horizontales**

1. Él _____ levanta.
4. No voy _____ no puedo.
7. Tú _____ acuestas.
9. ¿_____ es el examen?
10. Quiero este video y _____.

**Verticales**

2. ¿Cómo _____ usted?
3. Eres _____ mi hermano.
5. ¿_____ tal?
6. Me gusta _____ suéter.
8. Navego _____ la red.

| ¹S | ²E | | ³C | | | |
| | S | ⁴P | O | R | ⁵Q | U | ⁶E |
| | ⁷T | ⁸E | M | | U | | S |
| ⁹C | U | Á | N | D | O | ¹⁰É | S | E |

**recursos**

LM p. 62    panorama.vhlcentral.com Lección 11

**Section Goal**

In **Ortografía**, students will learn about the use of accent marks to distinguish between words that have the same or similar spellings.

**Instructional Resources**
**Supersite:** Lab MP3 Audio Files
**Lección 11**
**Supersite/IRCD:** *IRM* (Lab Audio Script, WBs/VM/LM Answer Key)
**WebSAM**
**Lab Manual,** p. 62
*Cuaderno para hispanohablantes***

**Teaching Tips**
- As you go through each point in the explanation, pronounce the example sentences, as well as some of your own, and have students write them on the board.
- Write the example sentences, as well as some of your own, on the board without accent marks. Ask students where the written accents should go.
- Emphasize the difference in stress between **por qué** and **porque**.
- Ask students to provide words they learned in previous lessons that exemplify each point. Have them make a two-column chart of words they know. Ex: **mi/mí, tu/tú, te/té, el/él, si/sí, se/sé**, etc.
- Point out that **Ortografía** replaces **Pronunciación** in the Student Edition for **Lecciones 10–15**, but not in the Lab Manual. The **Recursos** box references the **Pronunciación** sections found in all lessons of the Lab Manual.

---

**TEACHING OPTIONS**

**Small Groups** Have students work in groups to explain which words in the **Práctica** activity need written accents and why. If necessary, have them quickly review the information about accents in the **Ortografía** section of **Lección 10**, page 315.
**Extra Practice** Add an auditory aspect to this **Ortografía** section. Prepare a series of mini-dialogues. Slowly read each one aloud, pausing to allow students to write. Then, in pairs,

have students check their work. Ex: **1.** —¿**Ésta** es tu cámara? —**Sí**, papá lo trajo de Japón para **mí**. **2.** —¿**Dónde** encontraste mi mochila? —¡Pues, **donde** la dejaste! **3.** —¿**Cuándo** visitó Buenos Aires Mario? —Yo **sé** que Laura fue allí el año pasado, ¿pero **cuándo** fue **él**? ¡Ni idea! **4.** —¿Me quieres explicar por **qué** llegas tarde? —**Porque** mi carro está descompuesto.

---

**EN DETALLE**

# El teléfono
# **celular**

**¿Cómo te comunicas con tus amigos y familia?** En países como Argentina y España, el servicio de teléfono común° es bastante caro, por lo que **el teléfono celular**, más accesible y barato, es el favorito de mucha gente.

El servicio más popular entre los jóvenes es el sistema de tarjetas prepagadas°, porque no requiere de un contrato ni de cuotas° extras. En muchas ciudades puedes encontrar estas tarjetas en cualquier° tienda. Para tener un servicio todavía más económico, mucha gente usa el mensaje de texto en sus teléfonos celulares. Un mensaje típico de un joven frugal podría° ser, por ejemplo: **N LLMS X TL. ¡S MY KRO!** (No llames por teléfono. ¡Es muy caro!)

Los celulares de la década de 1980 eran grandes e incómodos, y estaban limitados al uso de la voz°. Los celulares de hoy tienen muchas funciones más. Se pueden usar como despertadores, como cámara de fotos y hasta para leer y escribir correo electrónico. Sin embargo°, la función favorita de muchos jóvenes es la de poder descargar música de Internet en sus teléfonos para poder escucharla cuando lo deseen°, es decir, ¡casi todo el tiempo!

| Mensajes de texto en español | | | |
|---|---|---|---|
| **¿K TL?** | ¿Qué tal? | **CONT, XFA** | Contesta, por favor. |
| **STY S3A2** | Estoy estresado°. | **TB** | también |
| **TQ MXO.** | Te quiero mucho. | **¿A K ORA S** | ¿A qué hora es |
| **A2** | Adiós. | **L FSTA?** | la fiesta? |
| **¿XQ?** | ¿Por qué? | **M DBS $** | Me debes dinero. |
| **GNL** | genial | **5MNTRIOS** | Sin comentarios. |
| **¡K RSA!** | ¡Qué risa!° | **¿K ACS?** | ¿Qué haces? |
| **¡QT 1 BD!** | ¡Que tengas un | **STY N L BBLIOTK** | Estoy en la biblioteca. |
| | buen día!° | **1 BSO** | Un beso. |
| **SALU2, PP** | Saludos, Pepe. | **NS VMS + TRD** | Nos vemos más tarde. |

común *ordinary* prepagadas *prepaid* cuotas *fees* cualquier *any* podría *could* voz *voice* Sin embargo *However* cuando lo deseen *whenever they wish* estresado *stressed out* ¡Qué risa! *So funny!* ¡Que tengas un buen día! *Have a nice day!*

**ACTIVIDADES**

**1**  **¿Cierto o falso?** Indica si lo que dicen estas oraciones es **cierto** o **falso**. Corrige la información falsa.

1. El teléfono común es un servicio caro en Argentina. Cierto.
2. Muchas personas usan más el teléfono celular que el teléfono común. Cierto.
3. Es difícil encontrar tarjetas prepagadas en las ciudades hispanas. Falso. Puedes encontrar tarjetas prepagadas en cualquier tienda.

4. Los jóvenes suelen (*tend to*) usar el mensaje de texto para pagar menos por el servicio de teléfono celular. Cierto.
5. Los primeros teléfonos celulares eran muy cómodos y pequeños. Falso. Los primeros teléfonos celulares eran incómodos y grandes.
6. En la década de 1980, los teléfonos celulares tenían muchas funciones. Falso. En la década de 1980, los celulares estaban limitados al uso de la voz.
7. **STY S3A2** significa "Te quiero mucho". Falso. **STY S3A2** significa "Estoy estresado".

## ASÍ SE DICE

### La tecnología

| | |
|---|---|
| los audífonos (Méx., Col.), los auriculares (Arg.), los cascos (Esp.) | headset; earphones |
| el móvil (Esp.) | el celular |
| (teléfono) deslizable | slider (phone) |
| inalámbrico/a | cordless; wireless |
| el manos libres (Amér. S.) | free-hands system |
| (teléfono) plegable | flip (phone) |

## EL MUNDO HISPANO

### Las bicimotos

○ **Argentina** El ciclomotor se usa mayormente° para repartir a domicilio° comidas y medicinas.

○ **Perú** La motito se usa mucho para el reparto a domicilio de pan fresco todos los días.

○ **México** La *Vespa* se usa para evitar° el tráfico en grandes ciudades.

○ **España** La población usa el *Vespino* para ir y volver al trabajo cada día.

○ **Puerto Rico** Una *scooter* es el medio de transporte favorito en las zonas rurales.

○ **República Dominicana** Las moto-taxis son el medio de transporte más económico, ¡pero no olvides el casco°!

mayormente *mainly* repartir a domicilio *home delivery of* evitar *to avoid* casco *helmet*

## PERFIL

# Los cibercafés

Hoy día, en casi cualquier ciudad grande latinoamericana te puedes encontrar en cada esquina° un nuevo tipo de café: **el cibercafé**. Allí uno puede disfrutar de° un refresco o un café mientras navega en Internet, escribe correo electrónico o chatea° en múltiples foros virtuales.

De hecho°, el negocio° del cibercafé está mucho más desarrollado° en Latinoamérica que en los Estados Unidos. En una ciudad hispana, es común ver varios en una misma cuadra°. Los extranjeros piensan que no puede haber suficientes clientes para todos, pero los cibercafés ofrecen servicios especializados que permiten su coexistencia. Por ejemplo, mientras que el cibercafé Videomax atrae° a los niños con videojuegos, el Conécta-T ofrece servicio de chat con cámara para jóvenes, y el Mundo° Ejecutivo atrae a profesionales, todo en la misma calle.

esquina *corner* disfrutar de *enjoy* chatea *chat (from the English verb to chat)* De hecho *In fact* negocio *business* desarrollado *developed* cuadra *(city) block* atrae *attracts* Mundo *World*

### Conexión Internet

¿Qué sitios web son populares entre los jóvenes hispanos?

Go to panorama.vhlcentral.com to find more cultural information related to this Cultura section.

## ACTIVIDADES

**2 Comprensión** Responde a las preguntas.

1. ¿Cuáles son tres formas de decir *headset*? los audífonos, los auriculares, los cascos
2. ¿Para qué se usan las bicimotos en Argentina? para repartir a domicilio comidas y medicinas
3. ¿Qué puedes hacer mientras tomas un refresco en un cibercafé? Puedes navegar en Internet, escribir correo electrónico o chatear.
4. ¿Qué tienen de especial los cibercafés en Latinoamérica? Ofrecen servicios especializados.

**3 ¿Cómo te comunicas?** Escribe un párrafo breve en donde expliques qué utilizas para comunicarte con tus amigos/as (correo electrónico, teléfono, etc.) y de qué hablan cuando se llaman por teléfono. Answers will vary.

recursos
panorama.vhlcentral.com
Lección 11

## Section Goals

In **Estructura 11.1**, students will learn:
- affirmative **tú** commands
- negative **tú** commands

---

**Instructional Resources**
**Supersite:** Lab MP3 Audio Files **Lección 11**
**Supersite/IRCD:** *PowerPoints* (**Lección 11 Estructura** Presentation); *IRM* (Information Gap Activities, Lab Audio Script, WBs/VM/LM Answer Key)
**WebSAM**
**Workbook,** pp. 127–128
**Lab Manual,** p. 63
***Cuaderno para hispanohablantes***

---

**Teaching Tips**
- Model the use of informal commands with simple examples using TPR and gestures. Ex: Point to a student and say: _____ , **levántate. Gracias, ahora siéntate.** Give other commands using **camina, vuelve, toca,** and **corre.**
- Help students recognize that the affirmative **tú** command forms of regular verbs are the same as the third-person singular forms.

## 11.1 Familiar commands

**ANTE TODO**  In Spanish, the command forms are used to give orders or advice. You use **tú** commands (**mandatos familiares**) when you want to give an order or advice to someone you normally address with the familiar **tú**.

### Affirmative tú commands

| Infinitive | Present tense él/ella form | Affirmative tú command |
|---|---|---|
| hablar | habla | **habla** (tú) |
| guardar | guarda | **guarda** (tú) |
| prender | prende | **prende** (tú) |
| volver | vuelve | **vuelve** (tú) |
| pedir | pide | **pide** (tú) |
| imprimir | imprime | **imprime** (tú) |

▶ Affirmative **tú** commands usually have the same form as the **él/ella** form of the present indicative.

**Guarda** el documento antes de cerrarlo.
*Save the document before closing it.*

**Imprime** tu tarea para la clase de inglés.
*Print your homework for English class.*

▶ There are eight irregular affirmative **tú** commands.

### Irregular affirmative tú commands

| decir | **di** | salir | **sal** |
|---|---|---|---|
| hacer | **haz** | ser | **sé** |
| ir | **ve** | tener | **ten** |
| poner | **pon** | venir | **ven** |

**¡Sal** de aquí ahora mismo!
*Leave here at once!*

**Haz** los ejercicios.
*Do the exercises.*

▶ Since **ir** and **ver** have the same **tú** command (**ve**), context will determine the meaning.

**Ve** al cibercafé con Yolanda.
*Go to the cybercafé with Yolanda.*

**Ve** ese programa… es muy interesante.
*See that program… it's very interesting.*

Apaga ese walkman y contesta el teléfono.

¡No me digas!

---

**TEACHING OPTIONS**

**TPR** Ask individual students to comply with a series of commands requiring them to perform actions or move around the room. While the student follows the command, the class writes it down as a volunteer writes it on the board. Be sure to use both affirmative and negative commands. Ex: **Recoge ese papel. Ponlo en la basura. Regresa a tu escritorio. No te sientes. Siéntate ahora.**

**Pairs** Ask students to imagine they are starting a computer club. Have them make a list of five things to do in order to get ready for the first meeting and five things not to do to make sure everything runs smoothly, using infinitives. Then have students take turns telling partners what to do or not do.

## Negative tú commands

| Infinitive | Present tense yo form | Negative tú command |
|------------|----------------------|---------------------|
| hablar | hablo | **no hables** (tú) |
| guardar | guardo | **no guardes** (tú) |
| prender | prendo | **no prendas** (tú) |
| volver | vuelvo | **no vuelvas** (tú) |
| pedir | pido | **no pidas** (tú) |

▶ The negative **tú** commands are formed by dropping the final **-o** of the **yo** form of the present tense. For **-ar** verbs, add **-es**. For **-er** and **-ir** verbs, add **-as**.

> Héctor, **no pares** el carro aquí.
> *Héctor, don't stop the car here.*

> **No prendas** la computadora todavía.
> *Don't turn on the computer yet.*

▶ Verbs with irregular **yo** forms maintain the same irregularity in their negative **tú** commands. These verbs include **conducir, conocer, decir, hacer, ofrecer, oír, poner, salir, tener, traducir, traer, venir,** and **ver.**

> **No pongas** el cederrón en la computadora.
> *Don't put the CD-ROM in the computer.*

> **No conduzcas** tan rápido.
> *Don't drive so fast.*

▶ Note also that stem-changing verbs keep their stem changes in negative **tú** commands.

> No p**ie**rdas tu celular.
> *Don't lose your cell phone.*

> No v**ue**lvas a esa gasolinera.
> *Don't go back to that gas station.*

> No rep**i**tas las instrucciones.
> *Don't repeat the instructions.*

▶ Verbs ending in **-car, -gar,** and **-zar** have a spelling change in the negative **tú** commands.

| sa**car** | c ⟶ **qu** | no sa**qu**es |
|-----------|------------|---------------|
| apa**gar** | g ⟶ **gu** | no apa**gu**es |
| almor**zar** | z ⟶ **c** | no almuer**c**es |

▶ The following verbs have irregular negative **tú** commands.

### Irregular negative tú commands

| dar | no des |
|-----|--------|
| estar | no estés |
| ir | no vayas |
| saber | no sepas |
| ser | no seas |

### ¡ATENCIÓN!

In affirmative commands, reflexive, indirect, and direct object pronouns are always attached to the end of the verb. In negative commands, these pronouns always precede the verb.

**Bórralos./No los borres.**

**Escríbeles** un correo electrónico./**No les escribas** un correo electrónico.

•••

When a pronoun is attached to an affirmative command that has two or more syllables, an accent mark is added to maintain the original stress:

**borra** → **bórralos**

**prende** → **préndela**

**imprime** → **imprímelo**

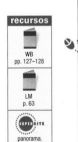
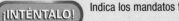

**¡INTÉNTALO!**  Indica los mandatos familiares afirmativos y negativos de estos verbos.

1. correr — _Corre_ más rápido. — No _corras_ más rápido.
2. llenar — _Llena_ el tanque. — No _llenes_ el tanque.
3. salir — _Sal_ ahora. — No _salgas_ ahora.
4. descargar — _Descarga_ ese documento. — No _descargues_ ese documento.
5. levantarse — _Levántate_ temprano. — No _te levantes_ temprano.
6. hacerlo — _Hazlo_ ya. — No _lo hagas_ ahora.

### Teaching Tips

• Contrast the negative forms of **tú** commands by giving an affirmative command followed by a negative command. Ex: _____ , camina a la puerta. **No camines rápidamente.** Write the examples on the board as you go along.

• Test comprehension and practice negative **tú** commands by calling out the infinitives of a variety of regular verbs the students already know and asking individual students to convert them into negative commands. Ex: **toser: no tosas; pedir: no pidas; pensar: no pienses.**

• Ask volunteers to convert affirmative **tú** commands with reflexive and object pronouns into negative forms. Ex: **Imprímelo. (No lo imprimas.) Vete. (No te vayas.)**

### TEACHING OPTIONS

**Heritage Speakers** Ask heritage speakers to look for an advertisement in a Spanish-language magazine or newspaper in which they find informal commands used. Have students bring a copy of the ad to class. Ask them to share it with the class and explain why they think informal commands were used instead of formal ones.

**Pairs** Have pairs imagine that they are in charge of a computer lab at a university in a Spanish-speaking country. Have them make a handout of four things students must do and four things they must not do while in the lab. Instruct them to use **tú** commands throughout. Then, write **Mandatos afirmativos** and **Mandatos negativos** on the board and ask individuals to write one of their commands in the appropriate column.

# Práctica SUPERSITE

**1** **Expansion** Continue this
activity orally with the class,
using regular verbs. Call out a
negative command and designate individuals to make corresponding affirmative commands.
Ex: **No sirvas la comida ahora.**
**(Sirve la comida ahora./Sírvela**
**ahora.)**

**1** **Completar** Tu mejor amigo no entiende nada de tecnología y te pide ayuda. Completa los comentarios de tu amigo con el mandato de cada verbo.

1. No ____vengas____ en una hora. ____Ven____ ahora mismo. (venir)
2. ____Haz____ tu tarea después. No la ____hagas____ ahora. (hacer)
3. No ____vayas____ a la tienda a comprar papel para la impresora. ____Ve____ a la cafetería a comprarme algo de comer. (ir)
4. No ____me digas____ que no puedes abrir un archivo. ____Dime____ que el programa de computación funciona sin problemas. (decirme)
5. ____Sé____ generoso con tu tiempo, y no ____seas____ antipático si no entiendo fácilmente. (ser)
6. ____Ten____ mucha paciencia y no ____tengas____ prisa. (tener)
7. ____Apaga____ tu teléfono celular, pero no ____apagues____ la computadora. (apagar)

**2** **Expansion** Ask volunteers
to role-play the exchanges
between **Pedro** and **Marina**.

**2** **Cambiar** Pedro y Marina no pueden ponerse de acuerdo (*agree*) cuando viajan en su carro. Cuando Pedro dice que algo es necesario, Marina expresa una opinión diferente. Usa la información entre paréntesis para formar las órdenes que Marina le da a Pedro.

> **modelo**
>
> **Pedro:** Necesito revisar el aceite del carro. (seguir hasta el próximo pueblo)
> **Marina:** No revises el aceite del carro. Sigue hasta el próximo pueblo.

1. Necesito conducir más rápido. (parar el carro) No conduzcas más rápido. Para el carro.
2. Necesito poner el radio. (hablarme) No pongas el radio. Háblame.
3. Necesito almorzar ahora. (comer más tarde) No almuerces ahora. Come más tarde.
4. Necesito sacar los discos compactos. (manejar con cuidado) No saques… Maneja…
5. Necesito estacionar el carro en esta calle. (pensar en otra opción) No estaciones… Piensa…
6. Necesito volver a esa gasolinera. (arreglar el carro en un taller) No vuelvas… Arregla…
7. Necesito leer el mapa. (pedirle ayuda a aquella señora) No leas… Pídele…
8. Necesito dormir en el carro. (acostarse en una cama) No duermas… Acuéstate…

**3** **Teaching Tip** To simplify,
review the vocabulary in the
word bank by asking students
to make associations with each
word. Ex: **imprimir (documento),**
**descargar (programa)**

**3** **Problemas** Tú y tu compañero/a trabajan en el centro de computadoras de la universidad. Muchos estudiantes están llamando con problemas. Denles órdenes para ayudarlos a resolverlos.
Answers will vary. Suggested answers:

> **modelo**
>
> **Problema:** No veo nada en la pantalla.
> **Tu respuesta:** Prende la pantalla de tu computadora.

| apagar… | descargar… | grabar… | imprimir… | prender… |
|---------|-----------|---------|-----------|----------|
| borrar… | funcionar… | guardar… | navegar… | quemar… |

1. No me gusta este programa de computación. Descarga otro.
2. Tengo miedo de perder mi documento. Guárdalo.
3. Prefiero leer este sitio web en papel. Imprímelo.
4. Mi correo electrónico funciona muy lentamente. Borra los mensajes más viejos.
5. Busco información sobre los gauchos de Argentina. Navega en Internet.
6. Tengo demasiados archivos en mi computadora. Borra algunos archivos.
7. Mi computadora se congeló (*froze*). Apaga la computadora y luego préndela.
8. Quiero ver las fotos del cumpleaños de mi hermana. Descárgalas.

**NOTA CULTURAL**

**Los gauchos**
(*nomadic cowboys*),
conocidos por su
habilidad (*skill*) para
montar caballos y
utilizar lazos, viven
en la región más
extensa de Argentina,
la Patagonia. Esta
región ocupa casi
la mitad (*half*) de la
superficie (*land area*)
del país.

**TEACHING OPTIONS**

**TPR** Have pairs of students brainstorm a list of actions that can be mimed. Then have them give each other **tú** commands based on the actions. Call on several pairs to demonstrate their actions for the class. When a repertoire of mimable actions is established, do rapid-fire TPR with the whole class using these commands/actions.

**Pairs** Have students create three questions about what they should do with electronic equipment, then work with a partner to ask and respond to the questions with affirmative and negative commands. If a student responds with a negative command, he or she must follow it with an affirmative command. Ex: **¿Debo apagar la computadora todos los días antes de acostarme? (No, no la apagues. Pero guarda todos tus documentos.)**

# Comunicación

**4**   **Órdenes** Circula por la clase e intercambia mandatos negativos y afirmativos con tus compañeros/as. Debes seguir las órdenes que ellos te dan o reaccionar apropiadamente. Answers will vary.

> **modelo**
>
> **Estudiante 1:** Dame todo tu dinero.
> **Estudiante 2:** No, no quiero dártelo. Muéstrame tu cuaderno.
> **Estudiante 1:** Aquí está.
> **Estudiante 3:** Ve a la pizarra y escribe tu nombre.
> **Estudiante 4:** No quiero. Hazlo tú.

**5**   **Anuncios** Miren este anuncio. Luego, en grupos pequeños, preparen tres anuncios adicionales para tres escuelas que compiten (*compete*) con ésta. Answers will vary.

**INFORMÁTICA ARGENTINA**

Toma nuestros cursos y aprende a usar la computadora

abre y lee tus archivos

imprime tus documentos

entra al campo de la tecnología

¡Ponte en contacto con nosotros llamando al **11-4-129-1508** HOY!

# Síntesis

**6**   **¡Tanto que hacer!** Tu profesor(a) te va a dar una lista de diligencias (*errands*). Algunas las hiciste tú y algunas las hizo tu compañero/a. Las diligencias que ya hicieron tienen esta marca ✔. Pero quedan cuatro diligencias por hacer. Dale mandatos a tu compañero/a, y él/ella responde para confirmar si hay que hacerla o si ya la hizo. Answers will vary.

> **modelo**
>
> **Estudiante 1:** Llena el tanque.
> **Estudiante 2:** Ya llené el tanque. / ¡Ay, no! Tenemos que llenar el tanque.

## Section Goal

In **Estructura 11.2**, students will learn when to use **por** and **para**.

**Instructional Resources**
**Supersite:** Lab MP3 Audio Files **Lección 11**
**Supersite/IRCD:** *PowerPoints* (**Lección 11 Estructura** Presentation); *IRM* (Lab Audio Script, WBs/VM/LM Answer Key)
**WebSAM**
**Workbook,** pp. 129–130
**Lab Manual,** p. 64
*Cuaderno para hispanohablantes*

## Teaching Tips

• Have a volunteer read the caption of video still 3 on page 346. Focus on **...nos hablamos todos los días por el teléfono Internet, trabajando para salvar el mundo.** Point out the uses of **por** and **para**.

• Ask students to translate phrases requiring **por**. Ex: *talk by phone, send information by e-mail, walk across campus, walk along Bécquer Street, arrive in the afternoon/in the morning, be worried about the accident/about your friend, drive 30 miles per hour, study for four hours.*

### 11.2 Por and para SUPERSITE

**ANTE TODO** Unlike English, Spanish has two words that mean *for*: **por** and **para**. These two prepositions are not interchangeable. Study the following charts to see how they are used.

Es para usted. Es un cliente de don Paco.

Álex habla por teléfono.

**Por is used to indicate...**

1. **Motion or a general location** . . . . . . . .
   *(around, through, along, by)*

   La excursión nos llevó **por** el centro.
   *The tour took us through downtown.*

   Pasamos **por** el parque y **por** el río.
   *We passed by the park and along the river.*

2. **Duration of an action** . . . . . . . . . . . . . .
   *(for, during, in)*

   Estuve en la Patagonia **por** un mes.
   *I was in Patagonia for a month.*

   Ana navegó la red **por** la tarde.
   *Ana surfed the net in the afternoon.*

3. **Reason or motive for an action** . . . . . . .
   *(because of, on account of, on behalf of)*

   Lo hizo **por** su familia.
   *She did it on behalf of her family.*

   Papá llegó a casa tarde **por** el tráfico.
   *Dad arrived home late because of the traffic.*

4. **Object of a search** . . . . . . . . . . . . . . . . .
   *(for, in search of)*

   Vengo **por** ti a las ocho.
   *I'm coming for you at eight.*

   Javier fue **por** su cámara digital.
   *Javier went in search of his digital camera.*

5. **Means by which something is done** . . .
   *(by, by way of, by means of)*

   Ellos viajan **por** la autopista.
   *They travel by (by way of) the highway.*

   ¿Hablaste con la policía **por** teléfono?
   *Did you talk to the police by (on the) phone?*

6. **Exchange or substitution** . . . . . . . . . . .
   *(for, in exchange for)*

   Le di dinero **por** la videocasetera.
   *I gave him money for the VCR.*

   Muchas gracias **por** el cederrón.
   *Thank you very much for the CD-ROM.*

7. **Unit of measure** . . . . . . . . . . . . . . . . . .
   *(per, by)*

   José manejaba a 120 kilómetros **por** hora.
   *José was driving 120 kilometers per hour.*

**¡ATENCIÓN!**

**Por** is also used in several idiomatic expressions, including:
**por aquí** *around here*
**por ejemplo** *for example*
**por eso** *that's why; therefore*
**por fin** *finally*

**AYUDA**

Remember that when giving an exact time, **de** is used instead of **por** before **la mañana, la tarde,** or **la noche.**
La clase empieza a las nueve **de** la mañana.

• • •

In addition to **por, durante** is also commonly used to mean *for* when referring to time.
Esperé al mecánico **durante** cincuenta minutos.

### TEACHING OPTIONS

**TPR** Label one half of the classroom **por**, the other half **para**. Write a sentence on the board, omitting the preposition, and ask students to go to the appropriate half of the classroom. Ex: **Tengo que leer el capítulo 11 _____ mañana. (para); Jimena trabaja _____ la noche. (por)** Avoid cases where either **por** or **para** could be used.

**Game** Divide the class into four or five teams. Call out a use of either **por** or **para**. Teams have one minute to write as many sentences as they can, employing that use. Check answers by having a volunteer read his or her team's sentences. Give one point for each correct sentence. Keep score on the board. The team with the most correct sentences wins.

---

### Para is used to indicate...

| | |
|---|---|
| **1. Destination** . . . . . . . . . . . . . . . . . . . . . . . <br>(*toward, in the direction of*) | Salimos **para** Córdoba el sábado. <br>*We are leaving for Córdoba on Saturday.* |
| **2. Deadline or a specific time in the future** . . . <br>(*by, for*) | Él va a arreglar el carro **para** el viernes. <br>*He will fix the car by Friday.* |
| **3. Purpose or goal** + [*infinitive*] . . . . . . . . . <br>(*in order to*) | Juan estudia **para** (ser) mecánico. <br>*Juan is studying to be a mechanic.* |
| **4. Purpose** + [*noun*] . . . . . . . . . . . . . . . . . . . <br>(*for, used for*) | Es una llanta **para** el carro. <br>*It's a tire for the car.* |
| **5. The recipient of something** . . . . . . . . . . <br>(*for*) | Compré una impresora **para** mi hijo. <br>*I bought a printer for my son.* |
| **6. Comparison with others or an opinion** . . <br>(*for, considering*) | **Para** un joven, es demasiado serio. <br>*For a young person, he is too serious.* <br><br>**Para** mí, esta lección no es difícil. <br>*For me, this lesson isn't difficult.* |
| **7. In the employ of** . . . . . . . . . . . . . . . . . . . <br>(*for*) | Sara trabaja **para** Telecom Argentina. <br>*Sara works for Telecom Argentina.* |

▶ In many cases it is grammatically correct to use either **por** or **para** in a sentence. The meaning of the sentence is different, however, depending on which preposition is used.

| | |
|---|---|
| Caminé **por** el parque. <br>*I walked through the park.* | Caminé **para** el parque. <br>*I walked to (toward) the park.* |
| Trabajó **por** su padre. <br>*He worked for (in place of) his father.* | Trabajó **para** su padre. <br>*He worked for his father('s company).* |

---

**¡INTÉNTALO!**    Completa estas oraciones con las preposiciones **por** o **para**.

1. Fuimos al cibercafé __por__ la tarde.
2. Necesitas un módem __para__ navegar en la red.
3. Entraron __por__ la puerta.
4. Quiero un pasaje __para__ Buenos Aires.
5. __Para__ arrancar el carro, necesito la llave.
6. Arreglé el televisor __para__ mi amigo.
7. Estuvieron nerviosos __por__ el examen.
8. ¿No hay una gasolinera __por__ aquí?
9. El reproductor de MP3 es __para__ usted.
10. Juan está enfermo. Tengo que trabajar __por__ él.
11. Estuvimos en Canadá __por__ dos meses.
12. __Para__ mí, el español es fácil.
13. Tengo que estudiar la lección __para__ el lunes.
14. Voy a ir __por__ la carretera.
15. Compré dulces __para__ mi novia.
16. Compramos el auto __por__ un buen precio.

---

**Teaching Tips**

• Create a matching activity for the uses of **para**. Write sentences exemplifying each use of **para** listed, but not in the order they are given in the text. Ex: **1. El señor López compró el Ferrari para Mariana. 2. Este autobús va para Corrientes. 3. Para don Francisco, conducir un autobús no es nada difícil. 4. Don Francisco trabaja para Ecuatur. 5. Estudia para llegar a ser ingeniero. 6. El baúl es para las maletas. 7. Tengo que pagar la multa para el lunes.** Call on individual students to match each sentence with its usage.

• Have students make two flashcards. On one they write **por** and on the other **para**. Call out one of the uses for either word. Students show the appropriate card. Then call on a volunteer to write a sentence illustrating that use on the board. The class determines whether the sentence is correct or not.

• Add a visual aspect to this grammar presentation. Use magazine pictures to practice sentences demonstrating the uses of **por** and **para**. Ex: **Este señor hace la cena para su esposa. Los novios montan a caballo por el campo.**

---

**TEACHING OPTIONS**

**Large Group** Give each student in the class a strip of paper on which you have written one of the uses of **por** or **para**, or a sentence that is an example of one of the uses. Have students circulate around the room until they find the person who has the match for their use or sentence. After everyone has found a partner, the pairs read their sentences and uses to the class.

**Game** Play **Concentración**. Create one card for each use of **por** and **para**, and one card with a sentence illustrating each use, for a total of 28 cards. Shuffle the cards and lay them face down. Then, taking turns, students uncover two cards at a time, trying to match a use to a sentence. The student with the most matches wins.

# Práctica

**1 Completar** Completa este párrafo con las preposiciones **por** o **para**.

El mes pasado mi esposo y yo hicimos un viaje a Buenos Aires y sólo pagamos dos mil dólares (1)___por___ los pasajes. Estuvimos en Buenos Aires (2)___por___ una semana y paseamos por toda la ciudad. Durante el día caminamos (3)___por___ la plaza San Martín, el microcentro y el barrio de La Boca, donde viven muchos artistas. (4)___Por___ la noche fuimos a una tanguería, que es una especie de teatro, (5)___para___ mirar a la gente bailar tango. Dos días después decidimos hacer una excursión (6)___por___ las pampas (7)___para___ ver el paisaje y un rodeo con gauchos. Alquilamos (*We rented*) un carro y manejamos (8)___por___ todas partes y pasamos unos días muy agradables. El último día que estuvimos en Buenos Aires fuimos a Galerías Pacífico (9)___para___ comprar recuerdos (*souvenirs*) (10)___para___ nuestros hijos y nietos. Compramos tantos regalos que tuvimos que pagar impuestos (*duties*) en la aduana al regresar.

**2 Oraciones** Crea oraciones originales con los elementos de las columnas. Une los elementos usando **por** o **para**. Answers will vary.

> **modelo**
> Fuimos a Mar del Plata por razones de salud para visitar a un especialista. ◄

| (no) fuimos al mercado | por/para | comprar frutas | por/para | ¿? |
| (no) fuimos a las montañas | por/para | tres días | por/para | ¿? |
| (no) fuiste a Mar del Plata | por/para | razones de salud | por/para | ¿? |
| (no) fueron a Buenos Aires | por/para | tomar el sol | por/para | ¿? |

**3 Describir** Usa **por** o **para** y el tiempo presente para describir estos dibujos. Answers will vary.

1. _____ 2. _____ 3. _____

4. _____ 5. _____ 6. _____

---

---

# Comunicación

**4** **Descripciones** Usa **por** o **para** y completa estas frases de manera lógica. Luego, compara tus respuestas con las de un(a) compañero/a. Answers will vary.

1. En casa, hablo con mis amigos…
2. Mi padre/madre trabaja…
3. Ayer fui al taller…
4. Los miércoles tengo clases…
5. A veces voy a la biblioteca…
6. Esta noche tengo que estudiar…
7. Necesito… dólares…
8. Compré un regalo…
9. Mi mejor amigo/a estudia…
10. Necesito hacer la tarea…

**5** **Situación** En parejas, dramaticen esta situación. Utilicen muchos ejemplos de **por** y **para**.
Answers will vary.

| **Hijo/a** | **Padre/Madre** |
|---|---|
| Pídele dinero a tu padre/madre. | → Pregúntale a tu hijo/a para qué lo necesita. |
| Dile que quieres comprar un carro. | → Pregúntale por qué necesita un carro. |
| Explica tres razones por las que necesitas un carro. | → Explica por qué sus razones son buenas o malas. |
| Dile que por no tener un carro tu vida es muy difícil. | → Decide si vas a darle el dinero y explica por qué. |

# Síntesis

**6** **Una subasta** (*auction*) Cada estudiante debe traer a la clase un objeto o una foto del objeto para vender. En grupos, túrnense para ser el/la vendedor(a) y los postores (*bidders*). Para empezar, el/la vendedor(a) describe el objeto y explica para qué se usa y por qué alguien debe comprarlo.
Answers will vary.

> **modelo**
>
> **Vendedora:** Aquí tengo una videocasetera Sony. Pueden usar esta videocasetera para ver películas en su casa o para grabar sus programas favoritos. Sólo hace un año que la compré y todavía funciona perfectamente. ¿Quién ofrece $1.500 para empezar?
>
> **Postor(a) 1:** Pero las videocaseteras son anticuadas y no tienen buena imagen. Te doy $5,00.
>
> **Vendedora:** Ah, pero ésta es muy especial porque viene con el video de mi fiesta de quinceañera.
>
> **Postor(a) 2:** ¡Yo te doy $2.000!

**4** **Teaching Tip** Model the activity by completing one of the sentence starters in two different ways.

**4** **Expansion** Have students create new sentences, employing additional uses of **por** and **para**.

**5** **Teaching Tip** Ask students about the car in the picture. Ex: **¿Te gusta este carro? ¿Cuánto se paga por un carro así? ¿A cuántas millas por hora corre este carro?**

**5** **Expansion**
• Ask volunteers to role-play their conversation for the class.
• Show a picture of an old used car and ask students to create a new conversation. The parents are offering to buy their son/daughter this car instead of the one shown in the activity.

**6** **Teaching Tips**
• Before the bidding begins, display the items to be auctioned off and name them. Invite students to walk around with their group members and discuss what the items are, their purposes, and how much they will pay for them.
• Have groups prepare the opening statements for the items their members brought. Students then take turns opening up the bidding for the entire class. Non-group members may bid on each item. Group members should place bids to keep the bidding alive.

**TEACHING OPTIONS**

**Small Groups** Have students create a television advertisement for a car or piece of technological equipment. Students should: describe the item, why the customer should buy it, and how much it costs; explain that the item is on sale only until a certain date; and detail any possible trade-ins. Students should use **por** and **para** when possible in their ad.

**Extra Practice** For students still having trouble distinguishing between **por** and **para**, have them create a mnemonic device, like a story or chant, for remembering the different uses. Ex: **Vine por la tarde y busqué por el parque, por el río y por el centro. Busqué por horas. Viajé por carro, por tren y por avión.** Do the same for **para**.

## 11.3 Reciprocal reflexives

**ANTE TODO** In **Lección 7**, you learned that reflexive verbs indicate that the subject of a sentence does the action to itself. Reciprocal reflexives, on the other hand, express a shared or reciprocal action between two or more people or things. In this context, the pronoun means *(to) each other* or *(to) one another*.

Luis y Marta **se** miran en el espejo.
*Luis and Marta look at themselves in the mirror.*

Luis y Marta **se** miran.
*Luis and Marta look at each other.*

▶ Only the plural forms of the reflexive pronouns (**nos, os, se**) are used to express reciprocal actions because the action must involve more than one person or thing.

Cuando **nos vimos** en la calle, **nos abrazamos**.
*When we saw each other on the street, we hugged one another.*

**Nos ayudamos** cuando usamos la computadora.
*We help each other when we use the computer.*

Ustedes **se** van a **encontrar** en el cibercafé, ¿no?
*You are meeting each other at the cybercafé, right?*

Las amigas **se saludaron** y **se besaron**.
*The friends greeted each other and kissed one another.*

**¡ATENCIÓN!**

Here is a list of common verbs that can express reciprocal actions:

**abrazar(se)** *to hug; to embrace (each other)*

**ayudar(se)** *to help (each other)*

**besar(se)** *to kiss (each other)*

**encontrar(se)** *to meet (each other); to run into (each other)*

**saludar(se)** *to greet (each other)*

**¡INTÉNTALO!** Indica el reflexivo recíproco adecuado y el presente o el pretérito de estos verbos.

**presente**

1. (escribir) Los novios _se escriben_.
   Nosotros _nos escribimos_.
   Ana y Ernesto _se escriben_.
2. (escuchar) Mis tíos _se escuchan_.
   Nosotros _nos escuchamos_.
   Ellos _se escuchan_.
3. (ver) Nosotros _nos vemos_.
   Fernando y Tomás _se ven_.
   Ustedes _se ven_.
4. (llamar) Ellas _se llaman_.
   Mis hermanos _se llaman_.
   Pepa y yo _nos llamamos_.

**pretérito**

1. (saludar) Nicolás y tú _se saludaron_.
   Nuestros vecinos _se saludaron_.
   Nosotros _nos saludamos_.
2. (hablar) Los amigos _se hablaron_.
   Elena y yo _nos hablamos_.
   Nosotras _nos hablamos_.
3. (conocer) Alberto y yo _nos conocimos_.
   Ustedes _se conocieron_.
   Ellos _se conocieron_.
4. (encontrar) Ana y Javier _se encontraron_.
   Los primos _se encontraron_.
   Mi hermana y yo _nos encontramos_.

**recursos**

WB
pp. 131–132

LM
p. 65

panorama.
vhlcentral.com
Lección 11

---

# Práctica SUPERSITE

**1** **Un amor recíproco** Describe a Laura y a Elián usando los verbos recíprocos.

> **modelo**
>
> Laura veía a Elián todos los días. Elián veía a Laura todos los días.
> *Laura y Elián se veían todos los días.*

1. Laura conocía bien a Elián. Elián conocía bien a Laura.
   *Laura y Elián se conocían bien.*
2. Laura miraba a Elián con amor. Elián la miraba con amor también.
   *Laura y Elián se miraban con amor.*
3. Laura entendía bien a Elián. Elián entendía bien a Laura.
   *Laura y Elián se entendían bien.*
4. Laura hablaba con Elián todas las noches por teléfono. Elián hablaba con Laura todas las noches por teléfono.
   *Laura y Elián se hablaban todas las noches por teléfono.*
5. Laura ayudaba a Elián con sus problemas. Elián la ayudaba también con sus problemas.
   *Laura y Elián se ayudaban con sus problemas.*

**2** **Describir** Mira los dibujos y describe lo que estas personas hicieron.

1. Las hermanas ___se abrazaron___.     2. Ellos ___se besaron___.

3. Gilberto y Mercedes ___no se miraron___ / ___no se hablaron___ / ___se enojaron___.

4. Tú y yo ___nos saludamos___ / ___nos encontramos en la calle___.

# Comunicación

**3** **Preguntas** En parejas, túrnense para hacerse estas preguntas. Answers will vary.

1. ¿Se vieron tú y tu mejor amigo/a ayer? ¿Cuándo se ven ustedes normalmente?
2. ¿Dónde se encuentran tú y tus amigos?
3. ¿Se ayudan tú y tu mejor amigo/a con sus problemas?
4. ¿Se entienden bien tú y tu novio/a?
5. ¿Dónde se conocieron tú y tu novio/a? ¿Cuánto tiempo hace que se conocen ustedes?
6. ¿Cuándo se dan regalos tú y tu novio/a?
7. ¿Se escriben tú y tus amigos mensajes de texto o prefieren llamarse por teléfono?
8. ¿Siempre se llevan bien tú y tu compañero/a de cuarto? Explica.

---

## 11.4 Stressed possessive adjectives and pronouns

**ANTE TODO** Spanish has two types of possessive adjectives: the unstressed (or short) forms you learned in **Lección 3** and the stressed (or long) forms. The stressed forms are used for emphasis or to express *of mine, of yours,* and so on.

### Stressed possessive adjectives

| Masculine singular | Feminine singular | Masculine plural | Feminine plural | |
|---|---|---|---|---|
| mío | mía | míos | mías | *my; (of) mine* |
| tuyo | tuya | tuyos | tuyas | *your; (of) yours* (fam.) |
| suyo | suya | suyos | suyas | *your; (of) yours* (form.); *his; (of) his; her; (of) hers; its* |
| nuestro | nuestra | nuestros | nuestras | *our; (of) ours* |
| vuestro | vuestra | vuestros | vuestras | *your; (of) yours* (fam.) |
| suyo | suya | suyos | suyas | *your; (of) yours* (form.); *their; (of) theirs* |

▶ **¡Atención!** Used with **un/una**, these possessives are similar in meaning to the English expression *of mine/yours/etc.*

> **Juancho es un amigo mío.**
> *Juancho is a friend of mine.*

> **Ella es una compañera nuestra.**
> *She is a classmate of ours.*

▶ Stressed possessive adjectives agree in gender and number with the nouns they modify. Stressed possessive adjectives are placed after the noun they modify, while unstressed possessive adjectives are placed before the noun.

> **su** impresora
> *her printer*

> la impresora **suya**
> *her printer*

> **nuestros** televisores
> *our television sets*

> los televisores **nuestros**
> *our television sets*

▶ A definite article, an indefinite article, or a demonstrative adjective usually precedes a noun modified by a stressed possessive adjective.

Me encantan
- **unos** discos compactos **tuyos**. *I love some of your CDs.*
- **los** discos compactos **tuyos**. *I love your CDs.*
- **estos** discos compactos **tuyos**. *I love these CDs of yours.*

▶ Since **suyo, suya, suyos,** and **suyas** have more than one meaning, you can avoid confusion by using the construction: *[article] + [noun] +* **de** *+ [subject pronoun].*

> **el** teclado **suyo**
> el teclado **de él/ella** *his/her keyboard*
> el teclado **de ustedes** *your keyboard*

**CONSULTA**

This is the same construction you learned in **Lección 3** for clarifying **su** and **sus**. To review unstressed possessive adjectives, see **Estructura 3.2**, p. 85.

---

# Possessive pronouns

▶ Possessive pronouns are used to replace a noun + [*possessive adjective*]. In Spanish, the possessive pronouns have the same forms as the stressed possessive adjectives, and they are preceded by a definite article.

| | |
|---|---|
| **la** calculadora **nuestra** | **la nuestra** |
| **el** *fax* **tuyo** | **el tuyo** |
| **los** archivos **suyos** | **los suyos** |

▶ A possessive pronoun agrees in number and gender with the noun it replaces.

—Aquí está **mi coche**. ¿Dónde está **el tuyo**?
*Here's my car. Where is yours?*

—¿Tienes **las revistas** de Carlos?
*Do you have Carlos' magazines?*

—**El mío** está en el taller de mi hermano.
*Mine is at my brother's garage.*

—No, pero tengo **las nuestras**.
*No, but I have ours.*

*Episodio veintiuno: Tecnohombre y los superamigos suyos salvan el mundo una vez más.*

*La Mujer Mecánica y Tecnohombre, ¡mis héroes!*

*¡Y los míos también!*

**¡INTÉNTALO!**    Indica las formas tónicas (*stressed*) de estos adjetivos posesivos y los pronombres posesivos correspondientes.

| | | **adjetivos** | **pronombres** |
|---|---|---|---|
| 1. | su videocasetera | la videocasetera suya | la suya |
| 2. | mi televisor | el televisor mío | el mío |
| 3. | nuestros discos compactos | los discos compactos nuestros | los nuestros |
| 4. | tus calculadoras | las calculadoras tuyas | las tuyas |
| 5. | su monitor | el monitor suyo | el suyo |
| 6. | mis videos | los videos míos | los míos |
| 7. | nuestra impresora | la impresora nuestra | la nuestra |
| 8. | tu estéreo | el estéreo tuyo | el tuyo |
| 9. | nuestro cederrón | el cederrón nuestro | el nuestro |
| 10. | mi computadora | la computadora mía | la mía |

**Teaching Tips**
• Ask students questions using unstressed possessive adjectives or the [*article*] + [*noun*] + **de** construction before a name, having them answer with a possessive pronoun. Ex: **Es tu cuaderno, ¿verdad? (Sí, es el mío.) Clase, ¿son éstos sus exámenes? (Sí, son los nuestros.) Ésta es la mochila negra de ____, ¿no? (No, no es la suya. La mochila roja es la suya.)**
• Point out that the function of the stressed possessives is to give emphasis. They are often used to point out contrasts. Ex: **¿Tu carro es azul? Pues, el carro mío es rojo. ¿Tu cámara digital no es buena? La mía es excelente.**

**TEACHING OPTIONS**

**Video** Replay the *Fotonovela*, having students listen for each use of an unstressed possessive adjective and write down the sentence in which it occurs. Next, have students rewrite those sentences using a stressed possessive adjective. Then, discuss how the use of stressed possessive adjectives affected the meaning or fluidity of the sentences.

**Pairs** Tell students that their laundry has gotten mixed up with their roommate's and since they are the same size and have the same tastes in clothing, they cannot tell what belongs to whom. Have them ask each other questions about different articles of clothing. Ex: —¿**Son tuyos estos pantalones de rayas? —Sí, son míos. —Y, ¿estos calcetines rojos son tuyos? —Sí, son míos, pero esta camisa grandísima no es mía.**

# Práctica

**1**

**Oraciones** Forma oraciones con estas palabras. Usa el presente y haz los cambios necesarios.

1. un / amiga / suyo / vivir / Mendoza   Una amiga suya vive en Mendoza.
2. ¿me / prestar / calculadora / tuyo?   ¿Me prestas la calculadora tuya?
3. el / coche / suyo / nunca / funcionar / bien   El coche suyo nunca funciona bien.
4. no / nos / interesar / problemas / suyo   No nos interesan los problemas suyos.
5. yo / querer / cámara digital / mío / ahora mismo   Yo quiero la cámara digital mía ahora mismo.
6. un / amigos / nuestro / manejar / como / loco   Unos amigos nuestros manejan como locos.

**2**

**¿Es suyo?** Un policía ha capturado (*has captured*) al hombre que robó (*robbed*) en tu casa. Ahora quiere saber qué cosas son tuyas. Túrnate con un(a) compañero/a para hacer el papel del policía y usa las pistas para contestar las preguntas.

> **modelo**
>
> no/viejo
> **Policía:** Esta calculadora, ¿es suya?
> **Estudiante:** No, no es mía. La mía era más vieja.

1. sí   Este estéreo, ¿es suyo?/Sí, es mío.

2. sí   Esta computadora portátil, ¿es suya?/Sí, es mía.

3. sí   Este radio, ¿es suyo?/Sí, es mío.

4. no/grande   Este televisor, ¿es suyo?/ No, no es mío. El mío era más grande.

5. no/pequeño   Esta cámara de video, ¿es suya?/ No, no es mía. La mía era más pequeña.

6. no/de Shakira   Estos discos compactos, ¿son suyos?/ No, no son míos. Los míos eran de Shakira.

**3**

**Conversaciones** Completa estas conversaciones con las formas adecuadas de los pronombres posesivos.

1. —La casa de ellos estaba en la Avenida Borges. ¿Dónde estaba la casa de ustedes?
   —__La nuestra__ estaba en la calle Bolívar.
2. —A Carmen le encanta su monitor nuevo.
   —¿Sí? A José no le gusta __el suyo__.
3. —Puse mis discos aquí. ¿Dónde pusiste __los tuyos__, Alfonso?
   —Puse __los míos__ en el escritorio.
4. —Se me olvidó traer mis llaves. ¿Trajeron ustedes __las suyas__?
   —No, dejamos __las nuestras__ en casa.
5. —Yo compré mi computadora en una tienda y Marta compró __la suya__ en Internet. Y __la tuya__, ¿dónde la compraste?
   —__La mía__ es de Cíbermax.

# Comunicación

**4** **Identificar** Trabajen en grupos. Cada estudiante da tres objetos. Pongan todos los objetos juntos. Luego, un(a) estudiante escoge uno o dos objetos y le pregunta a otro/a si esos objetos son suyos. Usen los adjetivos posesivos en sus preguntas. Answers will vary.

> **modelo**
>
> **Estudiante 1:** Felipe, ¿son tuyos estos discos compactos?
> **Estudiante 2:** Sí, son míos.
> No, no son míos. Son los discos compactos de Bárbara.

**5** **Comparar** Trabaja con un(a) compañero/a. Intenta (*Try to*) convencerlo/la de que algo que tú tienes es mejor que el que él/ella tiene. Pueden hablar de sus carros, estéreos, discos compactos, clases, horarios o trabajos. Answers will vary.

> **modelo**
>
> **Estudiante 1:** Mi computadora tiene una pantalla de quince pulgadas (*inches*). ¿Y la tuya?
> **Estudiante 2:** La mía es mejor porque tiene una pantalla de diecisiete pulgadas.
> **Estudiante 1:** Pues la mía…

# Síntesis

**6** **Inventos locos** En grupos pequeños, lean la descripción de este invento fantástico. Después diseñen su propio invento y expliquen por qué es mejor que el de los demás grupos. Utilicen los posesivos, **por** y **para** y el vocabulario de **Contextos**. Answers will vary.

**Nuestro celular tiene conexión a Internet, ¿y el tuyo?**

**Este teléfono celular es mucho mejor que el tuyo por estas razones:**

- El nuestro tiene capacidad para guardar un millón de mensajes electrónicos.
- El celular nuestro toma video.
- Da la temperatura.
- Funciona como control remoto para la tele.
- También arranca el coche y tiene reproductor de MP3.

**Sirve para todo.**

Oferta: $45 dólares por mes (con un contrato mínimo de dos años)

Para más información, llama al 607-362-1990 o visita nuestro sitio web www.telefonoloco.com

---

**4 Teaching Tip** If students cannot bring in three objects, have them either find photos of objects or draw them. Students should find one feminine, one masculine, and one plural object to do the activity.

**5 Teaching Tip** Before beginning the activity, have students make a list of objects to compare. Then have them brainstorm as many different qualities or features of those objects as they can. Finally, have them list adjectives that they might use to compare the objects they have chosen.

**5 Expansion** Have pairs who had a heated discussion perform it for the class.

**6 Expansion** To challenge students, have them modify their ad for television or radio.

**Teaching Tip** See the Information Gap Activities (Supersite/IRCD) for an additional activity to practice the material presented in this section.

---

**Section Goal**

In **Recapitulación**, students will review the grammar concepts from this lesson.

**Instructional Resource**
**Supersite**

**1 Teaching Tip** Remind students that the **–s** ending is only present in negative familiar commands.

**1 Expansion** To challenge students, have them write mini-dialogues that include these command forms.

**2 Teaching Tip** Ask students to identify the use of **por** or **para** in each sentence.

**2 Expansion** Ask questions using **por** and **para**. Ex: *¿Hablan mucho por el messenger? ¿Para qué clase estudian más, la clase de español o la clase de matemáticas?*

**3 Expansion** Change the number of the noun in each question and have students repeat the activity. Ex: 1. *¿Éstos son mis bolígrafos? (Sí, son los tuyos.)*

# Recapitulación

**RESUMEN GRAMATICAL**

For self-scoring and diagnostics, go to **panorama.vhlcentral.com**.

Completa estas actividades para repasar los conceptos de gramática que aprendiste en esta lección.

**1** **Completar** Completa la tabla con las formas de los mandatos familiares. `8 pts.`

| Infinitivo | Mandato | |
|---|---|---|
| | **Afirmativo** | **Negativo** |
| **comer** | **come** | **no comas** |
| **hacer** | haz | no hagas |
| **sacar** | saca | no saques |
| **venir** | ven | no vengas |
| **ir** | ve | no vayas |

**2** **Por y para** Completa el diálogo con **por** o **para**. `10 pts.`

**MARIO** Hola, yo trabajo (1) ___para___ el periódico de la universidad. ¿Puedo hacerte unas preguntas?

**INÉS** Sí, claro.

**MARIO** ¿Navegas mucho (2) ___por___ la red?

**INÉS** Sí, todos los días me conecto a Internet (3) ___para___ leer mi correo y navego (4) ___por___ una hora. También me gusta hablar (5) ___por___ el *messenger* con mis amigos. Es barato y, (6) ___para___ mí, es divertido.

**MARIO** ¿Y qué piensas sobre hacer la tarea en la computadora?

**INÉS** En general, me parece bien, pero (7) ___por___ ejemplo, anoche hice unos ejercicios (8) ___para___ la clase de álgebra y al final me dolieron los ojos. (9) ___Por___ eso a veces prefiero hacer la tarea a mano.

**MARIO** Muy bien. Muchas gracias (10) ___por___ tu ayuda.

**3** **Posesivos** Completa las oraciones y confirma de quién son las cosas. `6 pts.`

1. —¿Éste es mi bolígrafo? —Sí, es el ___tuyo___ (*fam.*).

2. —¿Ésta es la cámara de tu papá? —Sí, es la ___suya___.

3. —¿Ese teléfono es de Pilar? —Sí, es el ___suyo___.

4. —¿Éstos son los cederrones de ustedes? —No, no son ___nuestros___.

5. —¿Ésta es tu computadora portátil? —No, no es ___mía___.

6. —¿Ésas son mis calculadoras? —Sí, son las ___suyas___ (*form.*).

**RESUMEN GRAMATICAL**

**11.1** **Familiar commands** *pp. 352–353*

| tú commands | | |
|---|---|---|
| **Infinitive** | **Affirmative** | **Negative** |
| guardar | **guarda** | no guardes |
| volver | **vuelve** | no vuelvas |
| imprimir | **imprime** | no imprimas |

Irregular **tú** command forms

| | |
|---|---|
| dar → no des | saber → no sepas |
| decir → di | salir → sal |
| estar → no estés | ser → sé, no seas |
| hacer → haz | tener → ten |
| ir → ve, no vayas | venir → ven |
| poner → pon | |

▶ Verbs ending in **-car, -gar, -zar** have a spelling change in the negative **tú** commands:

sa**car** → no sa**ques**
apa**gar** → no apa**gues**
almor**zar** → no almuer**ces**

**11.2** **Por and para** *pp. 356–357*

▶ Uses of **por**:

motion or general location; duration; reason or motive; object of a search; means by which something is done; exchange or substitution; unit of measure

▶ Uses of **para**:

destination; deadline; purpose or goal; recipient of something; comparison or opinion; in the employ of

**11.3** **Reciprocal reflexives** *p. 360*

▶ Reciprocal reflexives express a shared or reciprocal action between two or more people or things. Only the plural forms (**nos, os, se**) are used.

Cuando **nos vimos** en la calle, **nos abrazamos**.

▶ Common verbs that can express reciprocal actions:

**abrazar(se), ayudar(se), besar(se), conocer(se), encontrar(se), escribir(se), escuchar(se), hablar(se), llamar(se), mirar(se), saludar(se), ver(se)**

**TEACHING OPTIONS**

**Pairs** Have pairs create a short survey about technology use. Encourage them to use **por** and **para**, as well as adverbs like **a menudo, normalmente**, etc. Then have them exchange their surveys with another pair and complete them. Ask volunteers to share their survey results with the class.

**Extra Practice** Tell students that you are a new student in class who likes to take people's things. Go around the room and gather students' belongings (books, pens, bags, etc.). In each case, insist that the item is yours. Ex: **Esta mochila es mía.** Have students protest and take their item back. Ex: **Esta mochila no es tuya, es mía.** Have other students contribute by asking, **¿Esta mochila es suya o es mía?**

**4** **Ángel y diablito** A Juan le gusta pedir consejos a su ángel y a su diablito imaginarios. Completa las respuestas con mandatos familiares desde las dos perspectivas. **8 pts.**

1. Estoy manejando. ¿Voy más rápido?
   **Á** No, no ___vayas___ más rápido.
   **D** Sí, ___ve___ más rápido.
2. Es el disco compacto favorito de mi hermana. ¿Lo pongo en mi mochila?
   **Á** No, no ___lo pongas___ en tu mochila.
   **D** Sí, ___ponlo___ en tu mochila.
3. Necesito estirar (*to stretch*) las piernas. ¿Doy un paseo?
   **Á** Sí, ___da___ un paseo.
   **D** No, no ___des___ un paseo.
4. Mi amigo necesita imprimir algo. ¿Apago la impresora?
   **Á** No, no ___apagues___ la impresora.
   **D** Sí, ___apaga___ la impresora.

**11.4** **Stressed possessive adjectives and pronouns** *pp. 362–363*

| Stressed possessive adjectives | |
|---|---|
| **Masculine** | **Feminine** |
| mío(s) | mía(s) |
| tuyo(s) | tuya(s) |
| suyo(s) | suya(s) |
| nuestro(s) | nuestra(s) |
| vuestro(s) | vuestra(s) |
| suyo(s) | suya(s) |

la impresora **suya** → la **suya**
las llaves **mías** → las **mías**

**5** **Oraciones** Forma oraciones para expresar acciones recíprocas con el tiempo indicado. **6 pts.**

> **modelo**
> tú y yo / conocer / bien (presente) *Tú y yo nos conocemos bien.*

1. José y Paco / llamar / una vez por semana (imperfecto)
   José y Paco se llamaban una vez por semana.
2. mi novia y yo / ver / todos los días (presente)
   Mi novia y yo nos vemos todos los días.
3. los compañeros de clase / ayudar / con la tarea (pretérito)
   Los compañeros de clase se ayudaron con la tarea.
4. tú y tu mamá / escribir / por correo electrónico / cada semana (imperfecto)
   Tú y tu mamá se escribían por correo electrónico cada semana.
5. mis hermanas y yo / entender / perfectamente (presente)
   Mis hermanas y yo nos entendemos perfectamente.
6. los profesores / saludar / con mucho respeto (pretérito)
   Los profesores se saludaron con mucho respeto.

**6** **La tecnología** Escribe al menos seis oraciones diciéndole a un(a) amigo/a qué hacer para tener "una buena relación" con la tecnología. Usa mandatos familiares afirmativos y negativos. **12 pts.**
Answers will vary.

**7** **Saber compartir** Completa la expresión con los dos pronombres posesivos que faltan.
**¡2 puntos EXTRA!**

❝ Lo que° es ___mío___ es ___tuyo___. ❞

Lo que *What*

---

**4** **Teaching Tip** Have volunteers role-play each exchange for the class.

**4** **Expansion** Give students these situations as items 5–8:
**5. Mi amigo tiene las respuestas del examen final de historia. ¿Se las pido?** (No, no se las pidas.; Sí, pídeselas.) **6. Es el cumpleaños de mi compañero de cuarto. ¿Le compro algo?** (Sí, cómprale algo.; No, no le compres nada.) **7. Rompí la computadora portátil de mi padre. ¿Se lo digo?** (Sí, díselo.; No, no se lo digas.) **8. No tengo nada de dinero. ¿Busco trabajo?** (Sí, búscalo.; No, no lo busques.)

**5** **Expansion** Have students create two additional dehydrated sentences. Then have them exchange papers with a classmate and complete the exercise.

**6** **Teaching Tip** To challenge students, have them first write a letter from the point of view of the friend who needs help with technology. Then have students write their suggestions according to the problems outlined in the letter.

**7** **Teaching Tip** Explain that this expression takes the masculine possessive form because it does not refer to anything specific, as denoted by **lo que**.

---

**TEACHING OPTIONS**

**TPR** Divide the class into two groups, **por** and **para**, and have them line up. Indicate the first member of each team and say an English sentence using an equivalent of **por** or **para**. Ex: Yesterday I got sick and my brother worked for me. The student whose team corresponds to the correct Spanish equivalent has five seconds to step forward and give the Spanish translation. Ex: **Ayer me enfermé y mi hermano trabajó por mí.**

**Small Groups** As a class, brainstorm a list of infinitives that can be made reciprocal (**llamar, abrazar, conocer,** etc.) and write them on the board. In small groups, have students create a dialogue using at least six of these infinitives. Then have students act out their dialogues for the class. Encourage students to use lesson vocabulary.

# Lectura

## Antes de leer

### Estrategia
**Recognizing borrowed words**

One way languages grow is by borrowing words from each other. English words that relate to technology often are borrowed by Spanish and other languages throughout the world. Sometimes the words are modified slightly to fit the sounds of the languages that borrow them. When reading in Spanish, you can often increase your understanding by looking for words borrowed from English or other languages you know.

### Examinar el texto
Mira brevemente (*briefly*) la selección. ¿De qué trata (*What is it about?*)? ¿Cómo lo sabes? Answers will vary.

### Buscar
Esta lectura contiene varias palabras tomadas (*taken*) del inglés. Trabaja con un(a) compañero/a para encontrarlas. Internet, fax, Deep Blue

### Predecir
Trabaja con un(a) compañero/a para contestar estas preguntas. Answers will vary.

1. En la foto, ¿quiénes participan en el juego?
2. ¿Jugabas en una computadora cuando eras niño/a? ¿Juegas ahora?
3. ¿Cómo cambiaron las computadoras y la tecnología en los años 80? ¿En los años 90? ¿En los principios del siglo XXI?
4. ¿Qué tipo de "inteligencia" tiene una computadora?
5. ¿Qué significa "inteligencia artificial" para ti?

**recursos**
panorama.vhlcentral.com
Lección 11

## Inteligencia y memoria: la inteligencia artificial por Alfonso Santamaría

Una de las principales características de la película de ciencia ficción *2001: una odisea del espacio*, es la gran inteligencia de su protagonista no humano, la computadora HAL-9000. Para muchas personas, la genial película de Stanley Kubrick es una reflexión sobre la evolución de la inteligencia, desde que el hombre utilizó por primera vez un hueso como herramienta° hasta la llegada de la inteligencia artificial (I.A.).

Ahora que vivimos en el siglo XXI, un mundo en el que Internet y el *fax* son ya comunes, podemos preguntarnos: ¿consiguieron los científicos especialistas en I.A. crear una computadora como HAL? La respuesta es no. Hoy día no existe una computadora con las capacidades intelectuales de HAL porque todavía no existen *inteligencias*

herramienta *tool*

## Después de leer

### ¿Cierto o falso?
Indica si cada oración es **cierta** o **falsa**. Corrige las falsas.

| | | |
|---|---|---|
| Cierta | 1. | La computadora HAL-9000 era muy inteligente. |
| Falsa | 2. | Deep Blue es un buen ejemplo de la inteligencia artificial general. Deep Blue es un buen ejemplo de la inteligencia artificial especializada. |
| Falsa | 3. | El maestro de ajedrez Garry Kasparov le ganó a Deep Blue en 1997. Deep Blue le ganó a Garry Kasparov en 1997. |
| Cierta | 4. | Las computadoras no tienen la creatividad de Mozart o Picasso. |
| Falsa | 5. | Hoy hay computadoras como HAL-9000. Las computadoras con la inteligencia de HAL-9000 son pura ciencia ficción. |

¿Cierto o falso? If students have difficulty with any item, have them work in pairs to locate the source of that information in the text.

**Preguntas** As you go over the items with the class, have students jot down the correct answers in complete sentences. Then, assign each answer to a small group, who will use it as a topic sentence for a short paragraph that elaborates on the answer based on the reading. This elaboration can be done orally and groups should later share their discussions with the class.

**Conversar** Ask students how the views expressed in the article might have influenced their answers to these questions.

Thomas J. Watson de Nueva York para desarrollar Deep Blue, la computadora que en 1997 derrotó° al campeón mundial de ajedrez, Garry Kasparov. Esta extraordinaria computadora pudo ganarle al maestro ruso de ajedrez porque estaba diseñada para procesar 200 millones de jugadas° por segundo. Además, Deep Blue guardaba en su memoria una recopilación de los movimientos de ajedrez más brillantes de toda la historia, entre ellos los que Kasparov efectuó en sus competiciones anteriores.

Para muchas personas, la victoria de Deep Blue sobre Kasparov simbolizó la victoria de la inteligencia artificial sobre la del ser humano°. Debemos reconocer los grandes avances científicos en el área de las computadoras y las ventajas° que pueden traernos en un futuro, pero también tenemos que entender sus limitaciones. Las computadoras generan nuevos modelos con conocimientos° muy definidos, pero todavía no tienen sentido común: una computadora como Deep Blue puede ganar una partida° de ajedrez, pero no puede explicar la diferencia entre una reina° y un peón°. Tampoco puede crear algo nuevo y original a partir de lo establecido, como hicieron Mozart o Picasso.

*artificiales generales* que demuestren lo que llamamos "sentido común"°. Sin embargo, la I.A. está progresando mucho en el desarrollo° de las inteligencias especializadas. El ejemplo más famoso es Deep Blue, la computadora de IBM especializada en jugar al ajedrez°.

La idea de crear una máquina con capacidad para jugar al ajedrez se originó en 1950. En esa década, el científico Claude Shannon desarrolló una teoría que se convirtió en realidad en 1967, cuando apareció el primer programa que permitió a una computadora competir, aunque sin éxito°, en un campeonato° de ajedrez. Más de veinte años después, un grupo de expertos en I.A. fue al centro de investigación

Las inteligencias artificiales especializadas son una realidad. ¿Pero una inteligencia como la de HAL-9000? Pura ciencia ficción. ∎

*sentido común* *common sense* **desarrollo** *development* **ajedrez** *chess* **éxito** *success* **campeonato** *championship* **derrotó** *defeated* **jugadas** *moves* **la del ser humano** *that of the human being* **ventajas** *advantages* **conocimientos** *knowledge* **partida** *match* **reina** *queen* **peón** *pawn*

---

## Preguntas

Contesta las preguntas.

1. ¿Qué tipo de inteligencia se relaciona con HAL-9000?
   La inteligencia artificial general se relaciona con HAL-9000.

2. ¿Qué tipo de inteligencia tienen las computadoras como Deep Blue? Las computadoras como Deep Blue tienen una inteligencia especializada.

3. ¿Cuándo se originó la idea de crear una máquina para jugar al ajedrez? La idea de crear una máquina para jugar al ajedrez se originó en 1950.

4. ¿Qué compañía inventó Deep Blue? IBM inventó Deep Blue.

5. ¿Por qué Deep Blue le pudo ganar a Garry Kasparov? Deep Blue le ganó a Garry Kasparov porque podía procesar 200 millones de jugadas por segundo.

## Conversar

En grupos pequeños, hablen de estos temas.
Answers will vary.

1. ¿Son las computadoras más inteligentes que los seres humanos?

2. ¿Para qué cosas son mejores las computadoras, y para qué cosas son mejores los seres humanos? ¿Por qué?

3. En el futuro, ¿van a tener las computadoras la inteligencia de los seres humanos? ¿Cuándo?

---

**TEACHING OPTIONS**

**Large Groups** Ask students to work in groups of six. Tell them to improvise and create a humorous story as a group. Ask one person in the group to start it off by giving an introductory sentence, such as: **Ayer estuvimos en el coche y ocurrió algo muy raro.** Others add sentences with additional details to complete the story. Encourage students to be creative and make the story as long as they wish.

**Pairs** Ask students to work together to create answers and corresponding questions. Have one partner create the answers to questions about artificial intelligence. The other partner develops the questions that relate to the answers. Then partners switch roles.

Gaucho

## Section Goal

In **Panorama**, students will read about the geography, history, and culture of Argentina.

**Instructional Resources**
**Supersite/DVD:** *Panorama cultural*
**Supersite/IRCD:** *PowerPoints* (Overheads #5, #6, #43); *IRM* (*Panorama cultural* Videoscript & Translation, WBs/VM/LM Answer Key)
**WebSAM**
**Workbook,** pp. 135-136
**Video Manual,** pp. 247-248

### Teaching Tips

• Have students look at the map of Argentina or show *Overhead PowerPoint #43.* Guide students to recognize Argentina's great size and the variety of topographical features, such as mountains (**los Andes**), vast plains (**las pampas**), and large rivers.

• Point out that Argentina is one of the largest beef producers in the world and that **gauchos** have played an important role in the culture of the country. Bariloche is an important winter recreation area. Remind students that June–August is winter in the southern hemisphere.

**El país en cifras** Patagonia is very sparsely populated, but Buenos Aires is a metropolis about the size of New York City. Invite students to mention anything they know about Argentina.

**¡Increíble pero cierto!** Under the leadership of **General José de San Martín**, Argentina won its independence from Spain on July 9, 1816. Like **Simón Bolívar, San Martín** is venerated as one of the great heroes of Latin America.

# Argentina

NATIONAL STANDARDS connections cultures

## El país en cifras

▶ **Área:** 2.780.400 km² (1.074.000 millas²)
*Argentina es el país de habla española más grande del mundo. Su territorio es dos veces el tamaño° de Alaska.*

▶ **Población:** 40.738.000

▶ **Capital:** Buenos Aires —13.067.000
*En Buenos Aires vive más del treinta por ciento de la población total del país. La ciudad es conocida° como el "París de Suramérica" por el estilo parisino° de muchas de sus calles y edificios.*

Buenos Aires

▶ **Ciudades principales:** Córdoba —1.492.000, Rosario —1.231.000, Mendoza —917.000

SOURCE: Population Division, UN Secretariat

▶ **Moneda:** peso argentino

▶ **Idiomas:** español (oficial), guaraní

Bandera de Argentina

### Argentinos célebres

▶ **Jorge Luis Borges,** escritor (1899–1986)
▶ **María Eva Duarte de Perón ("Evita"),** primera dama° (1919–1952)
▶ **Mercedes Sosa,** cantante (1935– )
▶ **Gato Barbieri,** saxofonista (1935– )

tamaño *size* conocida *known* parisino *Parisian* primera dama *First Lady* ancha *wide* mide *it measures* campo *field*

### ¡Increíble pero cierto!

La Avenida 9 de Julio en Buenos Aires es la calle más ancha° del mundo. De lado a lado mide° cerca de 140 metros, lo que es equivalente a un campo° y medio de fútbol. Su nombre conmemora el Día de la Independencia de Argentina.

ESTADOS UNIDOS
OCÉANO ATLÁNTICO
OCÉANO PACÍFICO
AMÉRICA DEL SUR
ARGENTINA

BOLIVIA
PARAGUAY
Las c de
San Miguel de Tucumán
La Cordillera de los Andes
Córdoba
URUG
Aconcagua
Rosario
Río Paraná
Mendoza
CHILE
Buenos Aires
Mar del P
La Pampa
San Carlos de Bariloche
Océano Atlántico
Montañas de Patagonia
Patagonia
Vista de San Carlos de Bariloche

**recursos**
WB pp. 135–136 | VM pp. 247–248 | panorama.vhlcentral.com Lección 11

Tierra del Fuego

### TEACHING OPTIONS

**Worth Noting** The Argentinian cowboy, the **gaucho**, has played as significant a role in the folklore of Argentina as the cowboy of the Old West has played in that of the United States. Two classic works of Argentinian literature focus on the **gaucho**. *El gaucho Martín Fierro*, an epic poem by **José Hernández** (1834–1886), celebrates the **gaucho's** fiercely independent way of life, whereas **Domingo Sarmiento's** (1811–1888) biography,

*Facundo: Civilización y barbarie*, describes the nomadic, uneducated **gauchos** as hindrances in Argentina's pursuit of economic, social, and political progress.
**Extra Practice** Have students listen to a song on one of the many recordings by singer **Mercedes Sosa**. Then, have pairs work together to transcribe the lyrics. Invite volunteers to share their work with the class.

### Historia • Inmigración europea

Se dice que Argentina es el país más "europeo" de toda Latinoamérica. Después del año 1880, inmigrantes italianos, alemanes, españoles e ingleses llegaron para establecerse en esta nación. Esta diversidad cultural ha dejado° una profunda huella° en la música, el cine y la arquitectura argentinos.

### Artes • El tango

El tango es uno de los símbolos culturales más importantes de Argentina. Este género° musical es una mezcla de ritmos de origen africano, italiano y español, y se originó a finales del siglo XIX entre los porteños°. Poco después se hizo popular entre el resto de los argentinos y su fama llegó hasta París. Como baile, el tango en un principio° era provocativo y violento, pero se hizo más romántico durante los años 30. Hoy día, este estilo musical es popular en muchas partes del mundo°.

### Lugares • Las cataratas de Iguazú

Las famosas cataratas° de Iguazú se encuentran entre las fronteras de Argentina, Paraguay y Brasil, al norte de Buenos Aires. Cerca de ellas confluyen° los ríos Iguazú y Paraná. Estas extensas caídas de agua tienen unos 70 metros (230 pies) de altura° y en época° de lluvias llegan a medir 4 kilómetros (2,5 millas) de ancho. Situadas en el Parque Nacional Iguazú, las cataratas son un destino° turístico muy visitado.

**¿Qué aprendiste?** Responde a cada pregunta con una oración completa.

1. ¿Qué porcentaje de la población de Argentina vive en la capital?
   Más del treinta por ciento de la población de Argentina vive en la capital.
2. ¿Quién es Mercedes Sosa?
   Mercedes Sosa es una cantante argentina.
3. Se dice que Argentina es el país más europeo de Latinoamérica. ¿Por qué? Se dice que Argentina es el país más europeo de Latinoamérica porque muchos inmigrantes europeos se establecieron allí.
4. ¿Qué tipo de baile es uno de los símbolos culturales más importantes de Argentina?
   El tango es uno de los símbolos culturales más importantes de Argentina.
5. ¿Dónde y cuándo se originó el tango?
   El tango se originó entre los porteños en la década de 1880.
6. ¿Cómo era el tango originalmente?
   El tango era un baile provocativo y violento.
7. ¿En qué parque nacional están las cataratas de Iguazú?
   Las cataratas de Iguazú están en el Parque Nacional Iguazú.

**Conexión Internet** Investiga estos temas en **panorama.vhlcentral.com**.

1. Busca información sobre el tango. ¿Te gustan los ritmos y sonidos del tango? ¿Por qué? ¿Se baila el tango en tu comunidad?
2. ¿Quiénes fueron Juan y Eva Perón y qué importancia tienen en la historia de Argentina?

ha dejado *has left* huella *mark* género *genre* porteños *people of Buenos Aires* en un principio *at first* mundo *world* cataratas *waterfalls* confluyen *converge* altura *height* época *season* destino *destination*

Artesano en Buenos Aires

**Inmigración europea** Among the European immigrants who arrived in waves on Argentina's shores were thousands of Jews. An interesting chapter in the history of the **pampas** features Jewish **gauchos**. A generous, pre-Zionist philanthropist purchased land for Jews who settled on the Argentine grasslands. At one time, the number of Yiddish-language newspapers in Argentina was second only to that in New York City.

**El tango** Carlos Gardel (1890–1935) is considered the great classic interpreter of **tango**. If possible, bring in a recording of his version of a **tango** such as *Cuesta abajo* or *Volver*. **Astor Piazzola** (1921–1992) was a modern exponent of **tango**. His **tango nuevo** has found interpreters such as cellist Yo-Yo Ma and the Kronos Quartet. For more information about **el tango**, you may want to play the *Panorama cultural* video footage for this lesson.

**Las cataratas de Iguazú** In the **guaraní** language, **Iguazú** means "big water." The falls are three times wider than Niagara and have been declared a World Heritage Site by UNESCO. **Iguazú** National Park was established in 1934 to protect and preserve this natural treasure.

**Conexión Internet** Students will find supporting Internet activities and links at **panorama.vhlcentral.com**.

BRASIL

# Uruguay

## El país en cifras

▶ **Área:** 176.220 km² (68.039 millas²), *el tamaño° del estado de Washington*
▶ **Población:** 3.575.000
▶ **Capital:** Montevideo—1.260.000

*Casi la mitad° de la población de Uruguay vive en Montevideo. Situada en la desembocadura° del famoso Río de la Plata, esta ciudad cosmopolita e intelectual es también un destino popular para las vacaciones, debido a sus numerosas playas de arena° blanca que se extienden hasta la ciudad de Punta del Este.*

▶ **Ciudades principales:** Salto, Paysandú, Las Piedras, Rivera
SOURCE: Population Division, UN Secretariat

▶ **Moneda:** peso uruguayo
▶ **Idiomas:** español (oficial)

Bandera de Uruguay

### Uruguayos célebres

▶ **Horacio Quiroga,** escritor (1878–1937)
▶ **Juana de Ibarbourou,** escritora (1895–1979)
▶ **Mario Benedetti,** escritor (1920– )
▶ **Cristina Peri Rossi,** escritora y profesora (1941– )

tamaño *size* mitad *half* desembocadura *mouth* arena *sand*
avestruz *ostrich* no voladora *flightless* medir *measure* cotizado *valued*

Gaucho uruguayo

**BRASIL**

Río Arapey · Rivera
· Salto
Río Uruguay
Cuchilla de Haedo
· Paysandú
Río Negro
Embalse del Río Negro
Río Negro
Cuchilla Grande
Laguna Merín
Río Yí
**Cuchilla Grande Inferior**
· Colonia
Río de la Plata
Las Piedras
· Punta del Este
★ **Montevideo**

Entrada a la Ciudad Vieja, Colonia del Sacramento

**recursos**
WB pp. 137–138 | VM pp. 249–250 | panorama.vhlcentral.com Lección 11

ESTADOS UNIDOS
OCÉANO PACÍFICO
OCÉANO ATLÁNTICO
AMÉRICA DEL SUR
URUGUAY

## ¡Increíble pero cierto!

En Uruguay hay muchos animales curiosos, entre ellos el ñandú. De la misma familia del avestruz°, el ñandú es el ave no voladora° más grande del hemisferio occidental. Puede llegar a medir° dos metros. Normalmente, va en grupos de veinte o treinta y vive en el campo. Es muy cotizado° por su carne, sus plumas y sus huevos.

### TEACHING OPTIONS

**Variación léxica** Montevideo looks out across the wide estuary of the **Río de la Plata** at Buenos Aires, Argentina, and the Spanish of Uruguay's major city has much in common with the **porteño** Spanish of its neighbor. When speaking, Uruguayans tend to use **vos** as frequently as **tú,** as well as the corresponding verb forms. The plural of both forms is **ustedes,** as in the rest of Latin America. In the northern part of Uruguay, along the border with Brazil, the majority of residents are bilingual in Portuguese and Spanish.

## Costumbres • La carne y el mate

En Uruguay y Argentina, la carne es un elemento esencial de la dieta diaria. Algunos platillos representativos de estas naciones son el asado°, la parrillada° y el chivito°. El mate, una infusión similar al té, también es típico de la región. Esta bebida de origen indígena está muy presente en la vida social y familiar de estos países aunque, curiosamente, no se puede consumir en bares o restaurante.

## Deportes • El fútbol

El fútbol es el deporte nacional de Uruguay. El primer equipo de balompié° uruguayo se formó en 1891 y en 1930 el país suramericano fue la sede° de la primera Copa Mundial de esta disciplina. El equipo nacional ha conseguido° grandes éxitos a lo largo de los años: dos campeonatos olímpicos, en 1923 y 1928, y dos campeonatos mundiales, en 1930 y 1950. De hecho, los uruguayos están trabajando para que la Copa Mundial de Fútbol de 2030 se celebre en su país.

## Costumbres • El Carnaval

El Carnaval de Montevideo es el de mayor duración en el mundo. A lo largo de 40 días, los uruguayos disfrutan° de los desfiles° y la música que inundan las calles de su capital. La celebración más conocida es el Desfile de las Llamadas, en el que participan bailarines al ritmo del candombe, una danza° de tradición africana.

**La carne y el mate** A legend from the **guaraní** people of Uruguay says that **yerba mate** was a gift from the god **Pa'i Shume**. Traditionally, the **yerba mate** leaves are packed into a **mate**—a cup made from a gourd—and hot water is poured over them. The infusion is sipped through a **bombilla**—a metal straw with a built-in tea strainer. The **mate** is refilled and drained several times, passing from hand to hand among a group of friends or family. For more information on **mate**, you may want to play the *Panorama cultural* video footage for this lesson.

**El fútbol** Uruguayan women have begun to make their mark in soccer. Although the International Federation of Football Association (FIFA) established a women's league in 1982, it was not until 1985 that the first women's league—from Brazil—was formally established. The women's league of Uruguay now participates in international soccer play.

**El Carnaval** Like the rest of Latin America, Uruguay also imported slaves from Africa during the colonial period. The music of the African-influenced **candombe** culture is popular with Uruguayans from all sectors of society.

**Conexión Internet** Students will find supporting Internet activities and links at **panorama.vhlcentral.com**.

 **¿Qué aprendiste?** Responde a cada pregunta con una oración completa.

1. ¿Qué tienen en común los uruguayos célebres mencionados en la página 372?
   Son escritores.
2. ¿Cuál es el elemento esencial de la dieta uruguaya?
   La carne es esencial en la dieta uruguaya.
3. ¿En qué países es importante la producción ganadera?
   La producción ganadera es importante en Uruguay y Argentina.
4. ¿Qué es el mate?
   El mate es una bebida indígena que es similar al té.
5. ¿Cuándo se formó el primer equipo uruguayo de fútbol?
   En 1891 se formó el primer equipo de fútbol uruguayo.
6. ¿Cuándo se celebró la primera Copa Mundial de fútbol?
   La primera Copa Mundial se celebró en 1930.
7. ¿Cómo se llama la celebración más conocida del Carnaval de Montevideo?
   La celebración más conocida del Carnaval de Montevideo se llama el Desfile de las Llamadas.
8. ¿De qué origen es el candombe?
   El candombe es de origen africano.

Edificio del Parlamento en Montevideo

**Conexión Internet** Investiga estos temas en **panorama.vhlcentral.com**.

1. Uruguay es conocido como un país de muchos escritores. Busca información sobre uno de ellos y escribe una biografía.
2. Investiga cuáles son las comidas y bebidas favoritas de los uruguayos. Descríbelas e indica cuáles te gustaría probar y por qué.

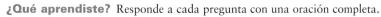

asado *barbecued beef*   parrillada *barbecue*   chivito *goat*   balompié *soccer*   sede *site*   ha conseguido *has achieved*
disfrutan *enjoy*   desfiles *parades*   danza *dance*

**Instructional Resources**
**Supersite:** Textbook &
Vocabulary MP3 Audio Files
**Lección 11**
**Supersite/IRCD:** *IRM* (WBs/
VM/LM Answer Key); *Testing
Program* (**Lección 11 Pruebas**,
Test Generator, Testing
Program MP3 Audio Files)
**WebSAM**
**Lab Manual**, p. 66

## La tecnología

| | |
|---|---|
| la calculadora | *calculator* |
| la cámara digital, de video | *digital, video camera* |
| el canal | *(TV) channel* |
| el cibercafé | *cybercafé* |
| la contestadora | *answering machine* |
| el control remoto | *remote control* |
| el disco compacto | *compact disc* |
| el estéreo | *stereo* |
| el *fax* | *fax (machine)* |
| el radio | *radio (set)* |
| el reproductor de MP3 | *MP3 player* |
| el (teléfono) celular | *(cell) telephone* |
| la televisión por cable | *cable television* |
| el televisor | *televison set* |
| el tocadiscos compacto | *compact disc player* |
| el video(casete) | *video(cassette)* |
| la videocasetera | *VCR* |
| apagar | *to turn off* |
| funcionar | *to work* |
| llamar | *to call* |
| poner, prender | *to turn on* |
| sonar (o:ue) | *to ring* |
| descompuesto/a | *not working; out of order* |
| lento/a | *slow* |
| lleno/a | *full* |

## La computadora

| | |
|---|---|
| el archivo | *file* |
| arroba | *@ symbol* |
| el cederrón | *CD-ROM* |
| la computadora (portátil) | *(portable) computer; (laptop)* |
| la dirección electrónica | *e-mail address* |
| el disco compacto | *compact disc* |
| la impresora | *printer* |
| Internet | *Internet* |
| el mensaje de texto | *text message* |
| el monitor | *(computer) monitor* |
| la página principal | *home page* |
| la pantalla | *screen* |
| el programa de computación | *software* |
| el ratón | *mouse* |
| la red | *network; Web* |
| el reproductor de DVD | *DVD player* |
| el sitio web | *website* |
| el teclado | *keyboard* |
| borrar | *to erase* |
| descargar | *to download* |
| grabar | *to record* |
| guardar | *to save* |
| imprimir | *to print* |
| navegar (en Internet) | *to surf (the Internet)* |
| quemar | *to burn (a CD)* |

## El carro

| | |
|---|---|
| la autopista, la carretera | *highway* |
| el baúl | *trunk* |
| la calle | *street* |
| el capó, el cofre | *hood* |
| el carro, el coche | *car* |
| la circulación, el tráfico | *traffic* |
| el garaje, el taller (mecánico) | *garage; (mechanic's) repair shop* |
| la gasolina | *gasoline* |
| la gasolinera | *gas station* |
| la licencia de conducir | *driver's license* |
| la llanta | *tire* |
| el/la mecánico/a | *mechanic* |
| el parabrisas | *windshield* |
| la policía | *police (force)* |
| la velocidad máxima | *speed limit* |
| el volante | *steering wheel* |
| arrancar | *to start* |
| arreglar | *to fix; to arrange* |
| bajar(se) de | *to get off of/out of (a vehicle)* |
| conducir, manejar | *to drive* |
| estacionar | *to park* |
| llenar (el tanque) | *to fill (the tank)* |
| parar | *to stop* |
| revisar (el aceite) | *to check (the oil)* |
| subir(se) a | *to get on/into (a vehicle)* |

## Verbos

| | |
|---|---|
| abrazar(se) | *to hug; to embrace (each other)* |
| ayudar(se) | *to help (each other)* |
| besar(se) | *to kiss (each other)* |
| encontrar(se) (o:ue) | *to meet (each other); to run into (each other)* |
| saludar(se) | *to greet (each other)* |

## Otras palabras y expresiones

| | |
|---|---|
| por aquí | *around here* |
| por ejemplo | *for example* |
| por eso | *that's why; therefore* |
| por fin | *finally* |

| | |
|---|---|
| **Por** and **para** | *See pages 356–357.* |
| **Stressed possessive adjectives and pronouns** | *See pages 362–363.* |
| **Expresiones útiles** | *See page 347.* |

**recursos**

| LM p. 66 | panorama.vhlcentral.com Lección 11 |
|---|---|

# La vivienda

## Communicative Goals

**You will learn how to:**
- Welcome people to your home
- Describe your house or apartment
- Talk about household chores
- Give instructions

## Lesson Goals

In **Lección 12**, students will be introduced to the following:
- terms for parts of a house
- names of common household objects
- terms for household chores
- central patios
- floating islands in Lake Titicaca
- relative pronouns
- formal commands
- object pronouns with formal commands
- present subjunctive
- subjunctive with verbs and expressions of will and influence
- locating the main parts of a sentence
- using linking words
- writing a lease agreement
- using visual cues while listening
- a television commercial for **Balay**, a Spanish appliance brand
- Panamanian singer **Rubén Blades**
- cultural and geographic information about Panama
- cultural and geographic information about El Salvador

**A primera vista** Here are some additional questions you can ask based on the photo: **¿Dónde vives? ¿Con quién vives? ¿Cómo es la casa tuya? ¿Qué haces en casa por la noche? ¿Qué haces los fines de semana? ¿Tienes una computadora en casa? ¿Qué otros productos tecnológicos tienes?**

### contextos
**pages 376–379**
- Parts of a house
- Household chores
- Table settings

### fotonovela
**pages 380–383**
The students arrive at the home where they will stay in Ibarra. After welcoming them, Sra. Vives, the housekeeper, shows them the house and assigns the bedrooms. Don Francisco reminds the students of their early start in the morning.

### cultura
**pages 384–385**
- The central patio
- The floating islands of Lake Titicaca

### estructura
**pages 386–403**
- Relative pronouns
- Formal commands
- The present subjunctive
- Subjunctive with verbs of will and influence
- **Recapitulación**

### adelante
**pages 404–413**
**Lectura:** The **Palacio de las Garzas**
**Escritura:** A rental agreement
**Escuchar:** A conversation about finding a home
**En pantalla**
**Oye cómo va**
**Panorama:** Panamá y El Salvador

### A PRIMERA VISTA
- ¿Están los chicos en casa?
- ¿Viven en una casa o en un apartamento?
- ¿Ya comieron o van a comer?
- ¿Están ellos de buen humor o de mal humor?

## INSTRUCTIONAL RESOURCES

**MAESTRO™ SUPERSITE (panorama.vhlcentral.com)**
Textbook, Vocabulary, & Lab MP3 Audio Files
Additional Practice
Learning Management System (Assignment Task Manager, Gradebook)
*Also on DVD*
  **Fotonovela**

**Flash cultura**
**Panorama cultural**
*Also on Instructor's Resource CD-ROM*
*PowerPoints* (**Contextos** & **Estructura** Presentations, Overheads)
*Instructor's Resource Manual* (Handouts, Textbook Answer Key, WBs/VM/LM Answer Key,

Audioscripts, Videoscripts & Translations)
*Testing Program* (**Pruebas,** Test Generator, MP3s)
**Vista Higher Learning Cancionero**
**WebSAM** (Workbook/Video Manual/Lab Manual)
**Workbook/Video Manual**
*Cuaderno para hispanohablantes*
**Lab Manual**

# La vivienda

## Más vocabulario

| | |
|---|---|
| las afueras | suburbs; outskirts |
| el alquiler | rent (payment) |
| el ama (m., f.) de casa | housekeeper; caretaker |
| el barrio | neighborhood |
| el edificio de apartamentos | apartment building |
| el/la vecino/a | neighbor |
| la vivienda | housing |
| el balcón | balcony |
| la entrada | entrance |
| la escalera | stairs; stairway |
| el garaje | garage |
| el jardín | garden; yard |
| el patio | patio; yard |
| el sótano | basement; cellar |
| la cafetera | coffee maker |
| el electrodoméstico | electrical appliance |
| el horno (de microondas) | (microwave) oven |
| la lavadora | washing machine |
| la luz | light; electricity |
| la secadora | clothes dryer |
| la tostadora | toaster |
| el cartel | poster |
| la mesita de noche | night stand |
| los muebles | furniture |
| alquilar | to rent |
| mudarse | to move (from one house to another) |

## Variación léxica

dormitorio ⟷ aposento (*Rep. Dom.*); recámara (*Méx.*)

apartamento ⟷ departamento (*Arg., Chile*); piso (*Esp.*)

lavar los platos ⟷ lavar/fregar los trastes (*Amér. C., Rep. Dom.*)

**recursos**

| WB pp. 139–140 | LM p. 67 | SUPERSITE panorama.vhlcentral.com Lección 12 |

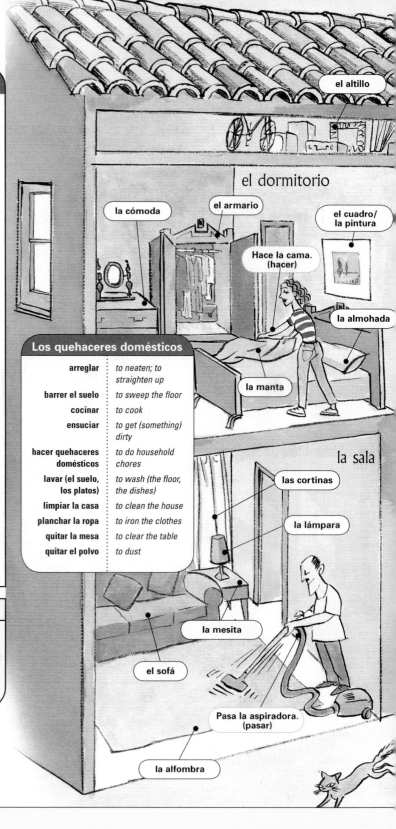

## Los quehaceres domésticos

| | |
|---|---|
| arreglar | to neaten; to straighten up |
| barrer el suelo | to sweep the floor |
| cocinar | to cook |
| ensuciar | to get (something) dirty |
| hacer quehaceres domésticos | to do household chores |
| lavar (el suelo, los platos) | to wash (the floor, the dishes) |
| limpiar la casa | to clean the house |
| planchar la ropa | to iron the clothes |
| quitar la mesa | to clear the table |
| quitar el polvo | to dust |

el altillo

el dormitorio

la cómoda

el armario

el cuadro/ la pintura

Hace la cama. (hacer)

la almohada

la manta

la sala

las cortinas

la lámpara

la mesita

el sofá

Pasa la aspiradora. (pasar)

la alfombra

# Práctica

la oficina

el sillón

la pared

el estante

cude los muebles.
(sacudir)

la cocina

el refrigerador

el congelador

la cocina, la estufa

el horno

el lavaplatos

Saca la basura.
(sacar)

SUPERSITE

**1** **Escuchar** 🎧 Escucha la conversación y completa las oraciones.

1. Pedro va a limpiar primero ___la sala___.
2. Paula va a comenzar en ___la cocina___.
3. Pedro va a ___planchar la ropa___ en el sótano.
4. Pedro también va a limpiar ___la oficina___.
5. Ellos están limpiando la casa porque
   ___la madre de Pedro viene a visitarlos___.

**2** **Respuestas** 🎧 Escucha las preguntas y selecciona la respuesta más adecuada. Una respuesta no se va a usar.

___3___ a. Sí, la alfombra estaba muy sucia.
___5___ b. No, porque todavía se están mudando.
___1___ c. Sí, sacudí la mesa y el estante.
___ ___ d. Sí, puse el pollo en el horno.
___2___ e. Hice la cama, pero no limpié los muebles.
___4___ f. Sí, después de sacarla de la secadora.

**3** **Escoger** Escoge la letra de la respuesta correcta.

1. Cuando quieres tener una lámpara y un despertador cerca de tu cama, puedes ponerlos en ___c___.
   a. el barrio   b. el cuadro   c. la mesita de noche
2. Si no quieres vivir en el centro de la ciudad, puedes mudarte ___b___.
   a. al alquiler   b. a las afueras   c. a la vivienda
3. Guardamos (*We keep*) los pantalones, las camisas y los zapatos en ___b___.
   a. la secadora   b. el armario   c. el patio
4. Para subir de la planta baja al primer piso, usamos ___c___.
   a. la entrada   b. el cartel   c. la escalera
5. Ponemos cuadros y pinturas en ___a___.
   a. las paredes   b. los quehaceres   c. los jardines

**4** **Definiciones** En parejas, identifiquen cada cosa que se describe. Luego inventen sus propias descripciones de algunas palabras y expresiones de **Contextos**.

> **modelo**
> **Estudiante 1:** Es donde pones los libros.
> **Estudiante 2:** el estante

1. Es donde pones la cabeza cuando duermes. una almohada
2. Es el quehacer doméstico que haces después de comer. lavar los platos/quitar la mesa
3. Algunos de ellos son las cómodas y los sillones. los muebles
4. Son las personas que viven en tu barrio. los vecinos

SUPERSITE

- Show *Overhead PowerPoint #46* and ask volunteers to name the items on the table. Then talk about the uses of the silverware (**cubiertos**), glassware (**cristalería**), and china (**vajilla**) pictured. Ex: **La copa sirve para tomar vino, pero la taza es para el café o el té**.

- Add a visual aspect to this vocabulary presentation. Bring in silverware, plates, and glasses. As you hold up each item, have students name it and guide you in setting the table. Ex: **¿Dónde pongo el tenedor, a la derecha o a la izquierda del plato?** Then model table manners common to many Spanish-speaking countries but different from those in the U.S. Ex: resting wrists (never elbows!) on the table, rather than placing one hand in your lap

**5 Expansion**

- Ask volunteers to answer questions modeled on the sentence starters in **Actividad 5**. Ex: **¿Qué se necesita para comer la carne?**

- Add a visual aspect to this activity. Using magazine pictures, ask students what utensils are needed. Ex: **¿Qué se necesita para comer este plato de espaguetis? (un tenedor y una cuchara)**

**6 Teaching Tip** Before breaking the class into groups, model the activity using your own situation. Ex: **En casa, mi esposa siempre pasa la aspiradora, pero yo sacudo los muebles. Mi hijo…**

el comedor

---

**5** **Completar** Completa estas frases con la palabra más adecuada.

1. Para tomar vino necesitas… una copa
2. Para comer una ensalada necesitas… un tenedor/un plato
3. Para tomar café necesitas… una taza
4. Para poner la comida en la mesa necesitas… un plato/poner la mesa
5. Para limpiarte la boca después de comer necesitas… una servilleta
6. Para cortar (*to cut*) un bistec necesitas… un cuchillo (y un tenedor)
7. Para tomar agua necesitas… un vaso/una copa
8. Para tomar sopa necesitas… una cuchara/un plato

**6** **Los quehaceres** Trabajen en grupos para indicar quién hace estos quehaceres domésticos en sus casas. Luego contesten las preguntas. Answers will vary.

**modelo**

**Estudiante 1:** ¿Quién pasa la aspiradora en tu casa?
**Estudiante 2:** Mi hermano y yo pasamos la aspiradora.

| | | |
|---|---|---|
| barrer el suelo | lavar los platos | planchar la ropa |
| cocinar | lavar la ropa | sacar la basura |
| hacer las camas | pasar la aspiradora | sacudir los muebles |

1. ¿Quién hace más quehaceres, tú o tus compañeros/as?
2. ¿Quiénes hacen la mayoría de los quehaceres, los hombres o las mujeres?
3. ¿Piensas que debes hacer más quehaceres? ¿Por qué?

---

# Comunicación

**7**   **La vida doméstica** En parejas, describan las habitaciones que ven en estas fotos. Identifiquen y describan cinco muebles o adornos (*accessories*) de cada foto y digan dos quehaceres que se pueden hacer en cada habitación. Answers will vary.

**8**   **Mi apartamento** Dibuja el plano (*floor plan*) de un apartamento amueblado (*furnished*) imaginario y escribe los nombres de las habitaciones y de los muebles. En parejas, pónganse espalda contra espalda (*sit back to back*). Uno/a de ustedes describe su apartamento mientras su compañero/a lo dibuja según la descripción. Cuando terminen, miren el segundo dibujo. ¿Es similar al dibujo original? Hablen de los cambios que se necesitan hacer para mejorar el dibujo. Repitan la actividad intercambiando los papeles. Answers will vary.

**CONSULTA**

To review bathroom-related vocabulary, see **Lección 7, Contextos,** p. 210.

**9**   **¡Corre, corre!** Tu profesor(a) va a darte una serie incompleta de dibujos que forman una historia. Tú y tu compañero/a tienen dos series diferentes. Descríbanse los dibujos para completar la historia. Answers will vary.

> **modelo**
> **Estudiante 1:** Marta quita la mesa.
> **Estudiante 2:** Francisco...

---

**TEACHING OPTIONS**

**Extra Practice** Have students complete this cloze activity.
**La vida doméstica de un estudiante universitario puede ser un desastre, ¿no? Nunca hay tiempo para hacer los _____ (quehaceres) domésticos. Sólo _____ (pasa) la aspiradora una vez al semestre y nunca _____ (sacude) los muebles. Los _____ (platos) sucios se acumulan en la _____ (cocina). Saca la ropa de la _____ (secadora) y se la pone sin _____ (planchar). Y,**

**¿por qué hacer la _____ (cama)? Se va a acostar en ella de nuevo este mismo día, ¿no?**

**Game** Have students bring in real estate ads. Ask teams of three to write a description of a property. Teams then take turns reading their descriptions aloud. Other teams guess the price. The team that guesses the amount closest to the real price without going over scores one point.

## Teaching sidebar

**7 Teaching Tips**
- Model the activity using a magazine picture. Ex: **¡Qué comedor más desordenado! ¡Es un desastre! Alguien debe quitar los platos sucios de la mesa. También es necesario sacudir los muebles y pasar la aspiradora. La mesa y las sillas son muy bonitas, pero el comedor está muy sucio.**
- To simplify, give students three minutes to look at the pictures and brainstorm possible answers.

**8 Teaching Tips**
- Draw a floor plan of a three-room apartment on the board. Ask volunteers to describe it.
- Have students draw their floor plans before you assign pairs. Make sure they understand the activity so that their floor plans do not become too complicated.

**8 Expansion**
- Have students make the suggested changes on their floor plans and repeat the activity again with a different partner.
- Have pairs repeat the activity, drawing floor plans of their real homes or apartments.

**9 Teaching Tip** Divide the class into pairs and distribute the handouts from the Information Gap Activities (Supersite/IRCD) that correspond to this activity. Give students ten minutes to complete this activity.

**9 Expansion** Have pairs tell each other about an occasion when they have had to clean up their home for a particular reason. Ask them to share their stories with the class.

# ¡Les va a encantar la casa!

**Don Francisco y los estudiantes llegan a Ibarra.**

### Section Goals

In **Fotonovela**, students will:
- receive comprehensible input from free-flowing discourse
- learn functional phrases that preview lesson grammatical structures

**Instructional Resources**
**Supersite/DVD:** *Fotonovela*
**Supersite/IRCD:** *IRM*
(*Fotonovela* Videoscript & Translation, WBs/VM/LM Answer Key)
**WebSAM**
**Video Manual,** pp. 217–218

### Video Recap: Lección 11

Before doing this **Fotonovela** section, review the previous one with this activity.

**1. ¿Qué hace Álex con sus amigos todos los días? (Hablan por teléfono Internet.) 2. ¿Por qué sabe Inés mucho de mecánica? (Trabajó en el taller de su tío.) 3. ¿Qué problema tiene el autobús? (El alternador está quemado.) 4. ¿Quién es el señor Fonseca? (Es un mecánico de Ibarra, amigo de don Francisco.) 5. ¿Cómo va a ayudar el señor Fonseca? (Va a arreglar el autobús allí mismo.)**

### Video Synopsis

**Don Francisco** and the students go to the house where they will stay before their hike. The housekeeper shows the students around the house. **Don Francisco** tells the students to help with the chores, and he advises them that their guide for the hike will arrive at seven the next morning.

### Teaching Tips

- Have students predict the content of this episode, based on its title and the video stills.
- Ask the class if this episode was what they expected, based on the predictions they made.

**PERSONAJES**

**INÉS**

**DON FRANCISCO**

**ÁLEX**

**JAVIER**

**SRA. VIVES**

**SRA. VIVES** ¡Hola, bienvenidos!
**DON FRANCISCO** Señora Vives, le presento a los chicos. Chicos, ésta es la señora Vives, el ama de casa.

**SRA. VIVES** Encantada. Síganme que quiero mostrarles la casa. ¡Les va a encantar!

**SRA. VIVES** Esta alcoba es para los chicos. Tienen dos camas, una mesita de noche, una cómoda… En el armario hay más mantas y almohadas por si las necesitan.

**SRA. VIVES** Ésta es la sala. El sofá y los sillones son muy cómodos. Pero, por favor, ¡no los ensucien!

**SRA. VIVES** Allí están la cocina y el comedor. Al fondo del pasillo hay un baño.

**DON FRANCISCO** Chicos, a ver… ¡atención! La señora Vives les va a preparar las comidas. Pero quiero que ustedes la ayuden con los quehaceres domésticos. Quiero que arreglen sus alcobas, que hagan las camas, que pongan la mesa… ¿entendido?

**JAVIER** No se preocupe… la vamos a ayudar en todo lo posible.

**ÁLEX** Sí, cuente con nosotros.

**recursos**
VM pp. 217-218
panorama.vhlcentral.com Lección 12

---

**Video Tips** General suggestions for using video clips in the classroom can be found on page IAE-12 of this Instructor's Annotated Edition.
**¡Les va a encantar la casa!** Play the last half of the **¡Les va a encantar la casa!** episode, except the **Resumen** segment. Have students summarize what they see and hear. Then, have the class predict what will happen in the first half of the episode, based on their observations. Write their predictions on the board. Then play the entire episode, including the **Resumen**, and, through discussion, guide the class to a correct summary of the plot.

**SRA. VIVES** Javier, no ponga las maletas en la cama. Póngalas en el piso, por favor.

**SRA. VIVES** Tomen ustedes esta alcoba, chicas.

**INÉS** Insistimos en que nos deje ayudarla a preparar la comida.

**SRA. VIVES** No, chicos, no es para tanto, pero gracias por la oferta. Descansen un rato que seguramente están cansados.

**ÁLEX** Gracias. A mí me gustaría pasear por la ciudad.

**INÉS** Perdone, don Francisco, ¿a qué hora viene el guía mañana?

**DON FRANCISCO** ¿Martín? Viene temprano, a las siete de la mañana. Les aconsejo que se acuesten temprano esta noche. ¡Nada de televisión ni de conversaciones largas!

**ESTUDIANTES** ¡Ay, don Francisco!

## Expresiones útiles

### Welcoming people
- **¡Bienvenido(s)/a(s)!**
  *Welcome!*

### Showing people around the house
- **Síganme... que quiero mostrarles la casa.**
  *Follow me... I want to show you the house.*
- **Esta alcoba es para los chicos.**
  *This bedroom is for the guys.*
- **Ésta es la sala.**
  *This is the living room.*
- **Allí están la cocina y el comedor.**
  *The kitchen and dining room are over there.*
- **Al fondo del pasillo hay un baño.**
  *At the end of the hall there is a bathroom.*

### Telling people what to do
- **Quiero que la ayude(n) con los quehaceres domésticos.**
  *I want you to help her with the household chores.*
- **Quiero que arregle(n) su(s) alcoba(s).**
  *I want you to straighten your room(s).*
- **Quiero que haga(n) las camas.**
  *I want you to make the beds.*
- **Quiero que ponga(n) la mesa.**
  *I want you to set the table.*
- **Cuente con nosotros.**
  *(You can) count on us.*
- **Insistimos en que nos deje ayudarla a preparar la comida.**
  *We insist that you let us help you make the food.*
- **Le (Les) aconsejo que se acueste(n) temprano.**
  *I recommend that you go to bed early.*

### Other expressions
- **No es para tanto.**
  *It's not a big deal.*
- **Gracias por la oferta.**
  *Thanks for the offer.*

**Teaching Tips** Have the class read through the entire **Fotonovela**, with volunteers playing the various parts. You may want to point out the form **gustaría** in the caption under video still 9. Explain to students that it is the conditional of **gustar** and that they will learn more about it in **Estructura 15.1**. Tell them that **me gustaría** means *I would like.*

**Expresiones útiles** Point out that the verbs **Síganme** and **Cuente** are formal command forms. Have the class guess which is an **usted** command and which is an **ustedes** command. Then point out the sentences that begin with **Quiero que...** , **Insistimos en que...** , and **Le(s) aconsejo que....** Explain that these sentences are examples of the present subjunctive with verbs of will or influence. Write two or three of these sentences on the board. Point out that the main clause in each sentence contains a verb of will or influence, while the subordinate clause contains a verb in the present subjunctive. Tell students that they will learn more about these concepts in **Estructura**.

**The Affective Dimension** Tell students that travelers in a foreign country may feel culture shock for a while. These feelings are normal and tend to diminish with time.

**TEACHING OPTIONS**

**Extra Practice** Photocopy the **Fotonovela** Videoscript (Supersite/IRCD) and white out words related to houses and household chores. Have students fill in the missing words as they watch the episode.

**Pairs** Ask students to imagine this house is for sale and create a brief conversation between the real estate agent and a prospective buyer.

## ¿Qué pasó?

**1** **¿Cierto o falso?** Indica si lo que dicen estas oraciones es **cierto** o **falso**. Corrige las oraciones falsas.

| | Cierto | Falso |
|---|---|---|
| 1. Las alcobas de los estudiantes tienen dos camas, dos mesitas de noche y una cómoda.  Tienen sólo una mesita de noche. | ○ | ⦿ |
| 2. La señora Vives no quiere que Javier ponga las maletas en la cama. | ⦿ | ○ |
| 3. El sofá y los sillones están en la sala. | ⦿ | ○ |
| 4. Los estudiantes tienen que sacudir los muebles y sacar la basura.  Tienen que arreglar las alcobas, hacer las camas y poner la mesa. | ○ | ⦿ |
| 5. Los estudiantes van a preparar las comidas.  La señora Vives va a preparar las comidas. | ○ | ⦿ |

**2** **Identificar** Identifica quién puede decir estas oraciones.

1. Nos gustaría preparar la comida esta noche. ¿Le parece bien a usted? Inés
2. Miren, si quieren otra almohada o manta, hay más en el armario. Sra. Vives
3. Tranquilo, tranquilo, que nosotros vamos a ayudarla muchísimo. Javier
4. Tengo ganas de caminar un poco por la ciudad. Álex
5. No quiero que nadie mire la televisión esta noche. ¡Tenemos que levantarnos temprano mañana! don Francisco

**ÁLEX**    **JAVIER**    **INÉS**    **DON FRANCISCO**    **SRA. VIVES**

**3** **Completar** Los estudiantes y la señora Vives están haciendo los quehaceres. Adivina en qué cuarto está cada uno de ellos.

1. Inés limpia el congelador. Inés está en __la cocina__.
2. Javier limpia el escritorio. Javier está en __la oficina__.
3. Álex pasa la aspiradora debajo de la mesa y las sillas. Álex está en __el comedor__.
4. La señora Vives sacude el sillón. La señora Vives está en __la sala__.
5. Don Francisco no está haciendo nada. Él está dormido en __el dormitorio/ la alcoba__.

**4** **Mi casa** Dibuja el plano de una casa o de un apartamento. Puede ser el plano de la casa o del apartamento donde vives o de donde te gustaría (*you would like*) vivir. Después, trabajen en parejas y describan lo que se hace en cuatro de las habitaciones. Para terminar, pídanse (*ask for*) ayuda para hacer dos quehaceres domésticos. Pueden usar estas frases en su conversación. Answers will vary.

| | |
|---|---|
| Quiero mostrarte... | Al fondo hay... |
| Ésta es (la cocina). | Quiero que me ayudes a (sacar la basura). |
| Allí yo (preparo la comida). | Por favor, ayúdame con... |

---

**TEACHING OPTIONS**

**Small Groups** Have the class label various parts of the classroom with the names of rooms one would typically find in a house. Then have groups of three perform a skit in which the owner of the house is showing it to two inquisitive exchange students who are going to be spending the semester there. Give the groups time to prepare.

**Game** Have students write a few sentences that one of the characters in this **Fotonovela** episode would say. They can look at the **Fotonovela** captions for ideas, but they should not copy sentences from it word for word. Then have students read their sentences to the class. The class will guess which character would say those sentences.

# Ortografía

SUPERSITE

## Mayúsculas y minúsculas

Here are some of the rules that govern the use of capital letters (**mayúsculas**) and lowercase letters (**minúsculas**) in Spanish.

**Los estudiantes llegaron al aeropuerto a las dos. Luego fueron al hotel.**

In both Spanish and English, the first letter of every sentence is capitalized.

---

**Rubén Blades      Panamá      Colón      los Andes**

The first letter of all proper nouns (names of people, countries, cities, geographical features, etc.) is capitalized.

---

*Cien años de soledad        Don Quijote de la Mancha*
*El País                      Muy Interesante*

The first letter of the first word in titles of books, films, and works of art is generally capitalized, as well as the first letter of any proper names. In newspaper and magazine titles, as well as other short titles, the initial letter of each word is often capitalized.

---

**la señora Ramos             don Francisco**
**el presidente               Sra. Vives**

Titles associated with people are *not* capitalized unless they appear as the first word in a sentence. Note, however, that the first letter of an abbreviated title is capitalized.

---

**Último        Álex        MENÚ        PERDÓN**

Accent marks should be retained on capital letters. In practice, however, this rule is often ignored.

---

**lunes        viernes        marzo        primavera**

The first letter of days, months, and seasons is <u>not</u> capitalized.

---

**español        estadounidense        japonés        panameños**

The first letter of nationalities and languages is <u>not</u> capitalized.

---

**Práctica** Corrige las mayúsculas y minúsculas incorrectas.

1. soy lourdes romero. Soy Colombiana.
   Soy Lourdes Romero. Soy colombiana.
2. éste Es mi Hermano álex.
   Éste es mi hermano Álex.
3. somos De panamá. Somos de Panamá.
4. ¿es ud. La sra. benavides?
   ¿Es Ud. la Sra. Benavides?
5. ud. Llegó el Lunes, ¿no?
   Ud. llegó el lunes, ¿no?

**Palabras desordenadas** Lee el diálogo de las serpientes. Ordena las letras para saber de qué palabras se trata. Después escribe las letras indicadas para descubrir por qué llora Pepito.

m n a a P á   ⬭ _ _ _ _ _ _

s t e m r a   ⬭ _ _ _ _ _ _

i g s l é n   _ _ ⬭ _ _ _

y a U r u g u   _ _ _ ⬭ _ _ _

r o ñ e s a   _ _ _ _ _ ⬭

¡ _⬭ orque _⬭ e acabo de morder° la _⬭ en _⬭ u _⬭ !

*¡Porque me acabo de morder la lengua!*
*Respuestas: Panamá, martes, inglés, Uruguay, señora.*

venenosas *venomous*   morder *to bite*

Herrera, que somos osas°?

Sí, Pepito. ¿Por qué lloras?

**recursos**

LM
p. 68

SUPERSITE
panorama.vhlcentral.com
Lección 12

---

### Section Goal

In **Ortografía**, students will learn about the rules for capitalization in Spanish.

**Instructional Resources**
**Supersite:** Lab MP3 Audio Files
**Lección 12**
**Supersite/IRCD:** *IRM* (Lab Audio Script, WBs/VM/LM Answer Key)
**WebSAM**
**Lab Manual,** p. 68
***Cuaderno para hispanohablantes***

**Teaching Tips**

- Explain that in a few Spanish city and country names, the definite article is considered part of the name, and is thus capitalized. Ex: **La Habana, La Coruña, La Haya, El Salvador**.

- Spanish treatment of titles of books, film, and works of art differs from English. In Spanish, only the first word and any proper noun gets an initial capital. Spanish treatment of the names of newspapers and magazines is the same as in English. Tell students that *El País* is a newspaper and *Muy Interesante* is a magazine. All the items mentioned are italicized in print.

- After going through the explanation, write example titles, names, sentences, etc., all in lower-case on the board. Then, ask pairs to decide which letters should be capitalized.

- Point out that **Ortografía** replaces **Pronunciación** in the Student Edition for **Lecciones 10–15**, but not in the Lab Manual. The **Recursos** box references the **Pronunciación** sections found in all lessons of the Lab Manual.

---

**TEACHING OPTIONS**

**Extra Practice** Have students scan the reading on the next page. Have them circle all the capital letters and explain why each is capitalized. Then point out the words **árabe, españoles,** and **islámica** and have volunteers explain why they are not capitalized.

**Extra Practice** Add an auditory aspect to this **Ortografía** section. Read this sentence aloud for students to write down: **El doctor Guzmán, el amigo panameño de la señorita Rivera, llegó a Quito el lunes, doce de mayo.** To allow students time to write, read the sentence twice slowly and once at full speed. Tell the class to abbreviate all titles.

# Section Goals

In **Cultura**, students will:
- read about central patios and courtyards in Spanish and colonial architecture
- learn terms related to the home
- read about the floating islands of Lake Titicaca
- read about unique furniture pieces

**Instructional Resources**
**Supersite:** *Flash cultura*
Videoscript & Translation
**Supersite/DVD:** *Flash cultura*
*Cuaderno para hispanohablantes*

## En detalle

**Antes de leer** Have students look at the photos and predict the content of this reading. Ask students if they have seen similar architecture in North America or abroad.

### Lectura
- Explain that Spanish homes with central patios are most common in the southern region of the country.
- Point out that university and administrative buildings often have central patios as well.
- As students read, have them make a list of characteristics of central patios.

**Después de leer** Ask students to give possible reasons why this architecture is not as common in the U.S. and Canada. Have heritage speakers share whether courtyards are popular in their families' home countries.

**1 Expansion** Give students these true-false statements as items 8–10: **8. Los patios centrales son comunes en las casas de México, España y Colombia. (Cierto.) 9. Las habitaciones privadas se encuentran en la planta baja. (Falso. Se encuentran en los pisos superiores.) 10. Nunca se decora el patio central. (Falso. La decoración se cuida mucho.)**

---

**EN DETALLE**

# El patio central

En las tardes cálidas° de Oaxaca, México; Córdoba, España, o Popayán, Colombia, es un placer sentarse en **el patio central** de una casa y tomar un refresco disfrutando de° una buena conversación. De influencia árabe, esta característica arquitectónica° fue traída° a las Américas por los españoles. En la época° colonial, se construyeron casas, palacios, monasterios, hospitales y escuelas con patio central. Éste es un espacio privado e íntimo en donde se puede disfrutar del sol y de la brisa° estando aislado° de la calle.

El centro del patio es un espacio abierto. Alrededor de° él, separado por columnas, hay un pasillo cubierto°. Así, en el patio hay zonas de sol y de sombra°. El patio es una parte importante de la vivienda familiar y su decoración se cuida° mucho. En el centro del patio muchas veces hay una fuente°, plantas e incluso árboles°. El agua es un elemento muy importante en la ideología islámica porque simboliza la purificación del cuerpo y del alma°. Por esta razón y para disminuir° la temperatura, el agua en estas construcciones es muy importante. El agua y la vegetación ayudan a mantener la temperatura fresca y el patio proporciona° luz y ventilación a todas las habitaciones.

### La distribución

Las casas con patio central eran usualmente las viviendas de familias adineradas°. Son casas de dos o tres pisos. Los cuartos de la planta baja son las áreas comunes: cocina, comedor, sala, etc., y tienen puertas al patio. En los pisos superiores están las habitaciones privadas de la familia.

cálidas *hot* disfrutando de *enjoying* arquitectónica *architectural* traída *brought* época *era* brisa *breeze* aislado *isolated* Alrededor de *Surrounding* cubierto *covered* sombra *shade* se cuida *is looked after* fuente *fountain* árboles *trees* alma *soul* disminuir *lower* proporciona *provides* adineradas *wealthy*

---

**ACTIVIDADES**

**1**  **¿Cierto o falso?** Indica si lo que dicen estas oraciones es **cierto** o **falso**. Corrige la información falsa.

1. Los patios centrales de Latinoamérica tienen su origen en la tradición indígena. Falso. Los patios tienen su origen en la arquitectura árabe.
2. En la época colonial las casas eran las únicas construcciones con patio central. Falso. Se construyeron casas, palacios, monasterios, hospitales y escuelas.
3. El patio es una parte importante en estas construcciones. Cierto.
4. El patio central es un lugar de descanso que da luz y ventilación a las habitaciones. Cierto.
5. Las casas con patio central eran para personas adineradas. Cierto.
6. Los cuartos de la planta baja son privados. Falso. Los cuartos de la planta baja son las áreas comunes.
7. Las fuentes en los patios tienen importancia por razones ideológicas y porque bajan la temperatura. Cierto.

---

**TEACHING OPTIONS**

**Cultural Comparison** Discuss other features of homes in Spanish-speaking countries. For example, in Spain, washing machines are typically the front-loading type and are located in the kitchen. Dryers are not commonly found in homes, and therefore most families hang their clothing to air-dry on a balcony or patio. Also, in Spain, it is very uncommon to see **armarios empotrados** (built-in closets); most people store their clothing in wardrobes. Have students describe how their lives would be different if they lived in homes with these features.

**Small Groups** Have students work in groups of three and compare a house with a central patio to a house with a backyard. Tell them to make a list of **similitudes** and **diferencias**. After completing their charts, have two groups get together and compare their lists.

## ASÍ SE DICE

### La vivienda

| | |
|---|---|
| el ático, el desván | el altillo |
| la cobija (Méx.), la frazada (Arg., Cuba, Ven.) | la manta |
| el escaparate (Cuba, Ven.), el ropero (Méx.) | el armario |
| el fregadero | *kitchen sink* |
| el frigidaire (Perú); el frigorífico (Esp.), la nevera | el refrigerador |
| el lavavajillas (Arg., Esp., Méx.) | el lavaplatos |

## EL MUNDO HISPANO

### Los muebles

○ **Mecedora°** La mecedora es un mueble típico de Latinoamérica, especialmente de la zona del Caribe. A las personas les gusta relajarse mientras se mecen° en el patio.

○ **Mesa camilla** Era un mueble popular en España hasta hace algunos años. Es una mesa con un bastidor° en la parte inferior° para poner un brasero°. En invierno, las personas se sentaban alrededor de la mesa camilla para conversar, jugar a las cartas o tomar café.

○ **Hamaca** Se cree que los taínos hicieron las primeras hamacas con fibras vegetales. Su uso es muy popular en toda Latinoamérica para dormir y descansar.

**Mecedora** *Rocking chair* **se mecen** *they rock themselves* **bastidor** *frame* **inferior** *bottom* **brasero** *container for hot coals*

## PERFIL

## Las islas flotantes del lago Titicaca

Bolivia y Perú comparten **el lago Titicaca**, donde viven **los uros**, uno de los pueblos indígenas más antiguos de América. Hace muchos años, los uros fueron a vivir al lago escapando de **los incas**. Hoy en día, siguen viviendo allí en cuarenta **islas flotantes** que ellos mismos hacen con unos juncos° llamados **totora**. Primero tejen° grandes plataformas. Luego, con el mismo material, construyen sus casas sobre las plataformas. La totora es resistente, pero con el tiempo el agua la pudre°. Los habitantes de las islas

necesitan renovar continuamente las plataformas y las casas. Sus muebles y sus barcos también están hechos° de juncos. Los uros viven de la pesca y del turismo; en las islas hay unas tiendas donde venden artesanías° hechas con totora.

**PERÚ**

**Lago Titicaca** → **BOLIVIA**

**juncos** *reeds* **tejen** *they weave* **la pudre** *rots it* **hechos** *made* **artesanías** *handcrafts*

**SUPERSITE** **Conexión Internet**

¿Cómo son las casas modernas en los países hispanos?

Go to **panorama.vhlcentral.com** to find more cultural information related to this **Cultura** section.

## ACTIVIDADES

**2 Comprensión** Responde a las preguntas.

1. Tu amigo mexicano te dice: "La **cobija** azul está en el **ropero**". ¿Qué quiere decir? La manta azul está en en el armario.

2. ¿Quiénes hicieron las primeras hamacas? ¿Qué material usaron? los taínos; fibras vegetales

3. ¿Qué grupo indígena vive en el lago Titicaca? Los uros viven en el lago Titicaca.

4. ¿Qué pueden comprar los turistas en las islas flotantes del lago Titicaca? Pueden comprar artesanías hechas con totora.

**3 Viviendas tradicionales** Escribe cuatro oraciones sobre una vivienda tradicional que conoces. Explica en qué lugar se encuentra, de qué materiales está hecha y cómo es.
Answers will vary.

**recursos**

**SUPERSITE**
panorama.vhlcentral.com
Lección 12

## Así se dice

- Model the pronunciation of each term and have students repeat it.
- Explain that compound words like **lavavajillas** are often masculine: **el lavavajillas, los lavavajillas**.
- To challenge students, add these household-related words to the list: **arrendar (Chi., Col.), rentar (Cuba, Méx, P. Rico)** (*to rent*); **la chimenea** (*fireplace*); **el corredor** (*hallway*); **el gavetero (Cuba, Pan., P. Rico)** (*dresser, bureau*); **la licuadora, la batidora (Cuba, Esp., Rep. Dom., Ven.)** (*blender*); **las persianas** (*blinds*); **el plato hondo, el tazón** (*bowl*); **el tragaluz, la claraboya** (*skylight*).

## Perfil

- Have students share any facts from the reading that are new or surprising to them.
- Ask students: **¿Les interesa visitar estas islas? ¿Cuáles son las ventajas y desventajas de vivir en un sitio así?**

## El mundo hispano

- If possible, bring in photos of the three pieces of furniture.
- Ask students if they have similar furniture in their homes.

**2 Expansion** Give students these questions as items 5–8:
**5. ¿Por qué los uros se fueron a vivir al lago Titicaca?** (Se escaparon de los incas.)
**6. ¿Cuántas islas flotantes hay entre Bolivia y Perú?** (cuarenta)
**7. ¿Cómo se hace la base de las casas flotantes?** (Se tejen con totora.) **8. ¿Por qué se usaba una mesa camilla en invierno y no en verano?** (Daba calor a los pies.)

**3 Teaching Tip** To add a visual aspect to this activity, have students find a photo of a traditional dwelling and use the photo as a basis for their written description.

## 12.1 Relative pronouns

**Section Goal**
In **Estructura 12.1**, students will learn the relative pronouns **que, quien(es), lo que** and their uses.

**Instructional Resources**
**Supersite:** Lab MP3 Audio Files **Lección 12**
**Supersite/IRCD:** *PowerPoints*
(Lección 12 Estructura Presentation); *IRM* (Lab Audio Script, WBs/VM/LM Answer Key)
**WebSAM**
**Workbook,** pp. 141–142
**Lab Manual,** p. 69
*Cuaderno para hispanohablantes*

**Teaching Tips**
• Have students open to the **Fotonovela** on pages 380–381. Ask open-ended questions about the situation and then rephrase the students' short answers into sentences using relative pronouns. Write your sentences on the board and underline the relative pronouns. Ex: **1. ¿Quién va a preparar la comida? (la Sra. Vives) Sí, ella es la persona que va a preparar la comida. 2. ¿Qué cuarto tiene un sofá y sillones cómodos? (la sala) Sí, la sala es el cuarto que tiene un sofá y sillones cómodos.**
• Compare and contrast the use of **que** and **quien** by writing some examples on the board. Ex: **Es la chica que vino con Carlos a mi fiesta. Es la chica a quien conocí en mi fiesta.** Have students deduce the rule.

**ANTE TODO** In both English and Spanish, relative pronouns are used to combine two sentences or clauses that share a common element, such as a noun or pronoun. Study this diagram.

Mis padres me regalaron **la aspiradora**.
*My parents gave me the vacuum cleaner.*

**La aspiradora** funciona muy bien.
*The vacuum cleaner works really well.*

La aspiradora **que** me regalaron mis padres funciona muy bien.
*The vacuum cleaner that my parents gave me works really well.*

**Lourdes** es muy inteligente.
*Lourdes is very intelligent.*

**Lourdes** estudia español.
*Lourdes is studying Spanish.*

Lourdes, **quien** estudia español, es muy inteligente.
*Lourdes, who studies Spanish, is very intelligent.*

*Pueden usar las almohadas que están en el armario.*

*Chicos, ésta es la señora Vives, quien les va a mostrar la casa.*

▶ Spanish has three frequently-used relative pronouns. **¡Atención!** Interrogative words (**qué, quién**, etc.) always carry an accent. Relative pronouns, however, never carry a written accent.

| que | that; which; who |
|---|---|
| quien(es) | who; whom; that |
| lo que | that which; what |

▶ **Que** is the most frequently used relative pronoun. It can refer to things or to people. Unlike its English counterpart, *that*, **que** is never omitted.

¿Dónde está la cafetera **que** compré?
*Where is the coffee maker (that) I bought?*

El hombre **que** limpia es Pedro.
*The man who is cleaning is Pedro.*

▶ The relative pronoun **quien** refers only to people, and is often used after a preposition or the personal **a. Quien** has only two forms: **quien** (singular) and **quienes** (plural).

¿Son las chicas **de quienes** me hablaste la semana pasada?
*Are they the girls (that) you told me about last week?*

Eva, **a quien** conocí anoche, es mi nueva vecina.
*Eva, whom I met last night, is my new neighbor.*

**¡LENGUA VIVA!**
When the relative pronoun refers to a person and is in the direct object position, either **que** or **a quien** can be used. Notice that the personal **a** is used only with **quien**.
**La señorita que conocí anoche es la hermana de Raquel.**
**La señorita a quien conocí anoche es la hermana de Raquel.**

**TEACHING OPTIONS**

**Extra Practice** Write these sentences on the board, and have students supply the correct relative pronoun.
1. Hay una escalera _____ sube al primer piso. (que)
2. Elena es la muchacha a _____ le presté la aspiradora. (quien)
3. ¿Dónde pusiste la ropa _____ acabas de quitarte? (que)
4. ¿Cuál es el señor a _____ le alquilas tu casa? (quien)

5. La cómoda _____ compramos la semana pasada está en el dormitorio de mi hermana. (que)
**Heritage Speakers** Have heritage speakers create descriptions of favorite gathering places in their families' home communities using complex sentences with relative pronouns. Possible sites might be the local parish, the town square, or a favorite park.

▶ **Quien(es)** is occasionally used in written Spanish instead of **que** in clauses set off by commas.

> Lola, **quien** es cubana, es médica.
> *Lola, who is Cuban, is a doctor.*

> Su tía, **que** es alemana, ya llegó.
> *His aunt, who is German, already arrived.*

▶ Unlike **que** and **quien(es)**, **lo que** doesn't refer to a specific noun. It refers to a specified or unspecified object, idea, situation, or past event and means *what*, *that which*, or *the thing that*.

*Este mercado tiene todo lo que Inés necesita.*

*A la señora Vives no le gustó lo que hizo Javier.*

> **Lo que** me molesta es el calor.
> *What bothers me is the heat.*

> **Lo que** quiero es una casa.
> *What I want is a house.*

**¡INTÉNTALO!**    Completa estas oraciones con pronombres relativos.

1. Voy a utilizar los platos ___que___ me regaló mi abuela.
2. Ana comparte un apartamento con la chica a ___quien___ conocimos en la fiesta de Jorge.
3. Esta oficina tiene todo ___lo que___ necesitamos.
4. Puedes estudiar en el dormitorio ___que___ está a la derecha de la cocina.
5. Los señores ___que___ viven en esa casa acaban de llegar de Centroamérica.
6. Los niños a ___quienes___ viste en nuestro jardín son mis sobrinos.
7. La piscina ___que___ ves desde la ventana es la piscina de mis vecinos.
8. Fue Úrsula ___que/quien___ ayudó a mamá a limpiar el refrigerador.
9. Ya te dije que fue mi padre ___que/quien___ alquiló el apartamento.
10. ___Lo que___ te dijo Pablo no es cierto.
11. Tengo que sacudir los muebles ___que___ están en el altillo una vez al mes.
12. No entiendo por qué no lavaste los vasos ___que___ te dije.
13. La mujer a ___quien___ saludaste vive en las afueras.
14. ¿Sabes ___lo que___ necesita este dormitorio? ¡Unas cortinas!
15. No quiero volver a hacer ___lo que___ hice ayer.
16. No me gusta vivir con personas a ___quienes___ no conozco.

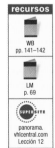

# Práctica

**1** **Combinar** Combina elementos de la columna A y la columna B para formar oraciones lógicas.

| A | B |
|---|---|
| 1. Ése es el hombre ___d___. | a. con quien bailaba es mi vecina |
| 2. Rubén Blades, ___c___. | b. que te compró Cecilia |
| 3. No traje ___e___. | c. quien es de Panamá, es un cantante muy bueno |
| 4. ¿Te gusta la manta ___b___? | d. que arregló mi lavadora |
| 5. ¿Cómo se llama el programa ___g___? | e. lo que necesito para la clase de matemáticas |
| 6. La mujer ___a___. | f. que comiste en el restaurante |
| | g. que escuchaste en la radio anoche |

**2** **Completar** Completa la historia sobre la casa que Jaime y Tina quieren comprar, usando los pronombres relativos **que, quien, quienes** o **lo que**.

1. Jaime y Tina son los chicos a ___quienes___ conocí la semana pasada.
2. Quieren comprar una casa ___que___ está en las afueras de la ciudad.
3. Es una casa ___que___ era de una artista famosa.
4. La artista, a ___quien___ yo conocía, murió el año pasado y no tenía hijos.
5. Ahora se vende la casa con todos los muebles ___que___ ella tenía.
6. La sala tiene una alfombra ___que___ ella trajo de Kuwait.
7. La casa tiene muchos estantes, ___lo que___ a Tina le encanta.

**3** **Oraciones** Javier y Ana acaban de casarse y han comprado (*they have bought*) una casa y muchas otras cosas. Combina sus declaraciones para formar una sola oración con los pronombres relativos **que, quien(es)** y **lo que**.

> **modelo**
>
> Vamos a usar los vasos nuevos mañana. Los pusimos en el comedor.
> *Mañana vamos a usar los vasos nuevos que pusimos en el comedor.*

1. Tenemos una cafetera nueva. Mi prima nos la regaló.
   Tenemos una cafetera nueva que mi prima nos regaló.
2. Tenemos una cómoda nueva. Es bueno porque no hay espacio en el armario.
   Tenemos una cómoda nueva, lo que es bueno porque no hay espacio en el armario.
3. Esos platos no nos costaron mucho. Están encima del horno.
   Esos platos que están encima del horno no nos costaron mucho.
4. Esas copas me las regaló mi amiga Amalia. Ella viene a visitarme mañana.
   Esas copas me las regaló mi amiga Amalia, quien viene a visitarme mañana.
5. La lavadora está casi nueva. Nos la regalaron mis suegros.
   La lavadora que nos regalaron mis suegros está casi nueva.
6. La vecina nos dio una manta de lana. Ella la compró en México.
   La vecina nos dio una manta de lana que compró en México.

# Comunicación

**4**   **Entrevista** En parejas, túrnense para hacerse estas preguntas. Answers will vary.

1. ¿Qué es lo que más te gusta de vivir en las afueras o en la ciudad?
2. ¿Cómo son las personas que viven en tu barrio?
3. ¿Cuál es el quehacer doméstico que menos te gusta? ¿Y el que más te gusta?
4. ¿Quién es la persona que hace los quehaceres domésticos en tu casa?
5. ¿Quiénes son las personas con quienes más sales los fines de semana? ¿Quién es la persona a quien más llamas por teléfono?
6. ¿Cuál es el deporte que más te gusta? ¿Cuál es el que menos te gusta?
7. ¿Cuál es el barrio de tu ciudad que más te gusta y por qué?
8. ¿Quién es la persona a quien más llamas cuando tienes problemas?
9. ¿Quién es la persona a quien más admiras? ¿Por qué?
10. ¿Qué es lo que más te gusta de tu casa?
11. ¿Qué es lo que más te molesta de tus amigos?
12. ¿Qué es lo que menos te gusta de tu barrio?

**5**   **Adivinanza** En grupos, túrnense para describir distintas partes de una vivienda usando pronombres relativos. Los demás compañeros tienen que hacer preguntas hasta que adivinen la palabra. Answers will vary.

> **modelo**
>
> **Estudiante 1:** Es lo que tenemos en el dormitorio.
> **Estudiante 2:** ¿Es el mueble que usamos para dormir?
> **Estudiante 1:** No. Es lo que usamos para guardar la ropa.
> **Estudiante 3:** Lo sé. Es la cómoda.

# Síntesis

**6**   **Definir** En parejas, definan las palabras. Usen los pronombres relativos **que, quien(es)** y **lo que.** Luego compartan sus definiciones con la clase. Answers will vary.

> **modelo**
>
> lavadora   Es lo que se usa para lavar la ropa.
> pastel   Es un postre que comes en tu cumpleaños.

| | | | |
|---|---|---|---|
| alquiler | flan | patio | tenedor |
| amigos | guantes | postre | termómetro |
| aspiradora | jabón | sillón | vaso |
| enfermera | manta | sótano | vecino |

---

**4 Teaching Tip** Have students take notes on the answers provided by their partners to use in expansion activities.

**4 Expansion**
• Have pairs team up to form groups of four. Each student will report on his or her partner, using the information obtained in the interview.
• Have pairs of students write four additional questions. Ask pairs to exchange their questions with another pair.

**5 Expansion** Have groups choose their three best **adivinanzas** and present them to the class.

**6 Expansion** Have pairs choose one of the items listed in the activity and develop a magazine ad. Their ad should include three sentences with relative pronouns.

---

## 12.2 Formal commands

**ANTE TODO** As you learned in **Lección 11**, the command forms are used to give orders or advice. Formal commands are used with people you address as **usted** or **ustedes**. Observe these examples, then study the chart.

**Hable** con ellos, don Francisco.
*Talk with them, Don Francisco.*

**Laven** los platos ahora mismo.
*Wash the dishes right now.*

**Coma** frutas y verduras.
*Eat fruits and vegetables.*

**Beban** menos té y café.
*Drink less tea and coffee.*

### Formal commands (Ud. and Uds.)

| Infinitive | Present tense **yo** form | Ud. command | Uds. command |
|---|---|---|---|
| limpiar | limpi**o** | limpi**e** | limpi**en** |
| barrer | barr**o** | barr**a** | barr**an** |
| sacudir | sacud**o** | sacud**a** | sacud**an** |
| decir (e:i) | dig**o** | dig**a** | dig**an** |
| pensar (e:ie) | piens**o** | piens**e** | piens**en** |
| volver (o:ue) | vuelv**o** | vuelv**a** | vuelv**an** |
| servir (e:i) | sirv**o** | sirv**a** | sirv**an** |

▶ The **usted** and **ustedes** commands, like the negative **tú** commands, are formed by dropping the final **-o** of the **yo** form of the present tense. For **-ar** verbs, add **-e** or **-en**. For **-er** and **-ir** verbs, add **-a** or **-an**.

*No se preocupe… La vamos a ayudar en todo lo posible.*

*Sí, cuente con nosotros.*

▶ Verbs with irregular **yo** forms maintain the same irregularity in their formal commands. These verbs include **conducir, conocer, decir, hacer, ofrecer, oír, poner, salir, tener, traducir, traer, venir,** and **ver.**

**Oiga,** don Francisco…
*Listen, Don Francisco…*

**Ponga** la mesa, por favor.
*Set the table, please.*

**¡Salga** inmediatamente!
*Leave immediately!*

**Hagan** la cama antes de salir.
*Make the bed before leaving.*

▶ Note also that verbs maintain their stem changes in **usted** and **ustedes** commands.

| e:ie | o:ue | e:i |
|---|---|---|
| No **pierda** la llave. | **Vuelva** temprano, joven. | **Sirva** la sopa, por favor. |
| **Cierren** la puerta. | **Duerman** bien, chicos. | **Repitan** las frases. |

**AYUDA**

These spelling changes are necessary to ensure that the words are pronounced correctly. See **Lección 8, Pronunciación,** p. 251, and **Lección 9, Pronunciación,** p.283.

• • •

It may help you to study the following five series of syllables. Note that, within each series, the consonant sound doesn't change.

**ca que qui co cu**

**za ce ci zo zu**

**ga gue gui go gu**

**ja ge gi jo ju**

▶ Verbs ending in **-car, -gar,** and **-zar** have a spelling change in the command forms.

sa**car**   c ⟶ **qu**   sa**qu**e, sa**qu**en

ju**gar**   g ⟶ **gu**   jue**gu**e, jue**gu**en

almor**zar**   z ⟶ **c**   almuer**c**e, almuer**c**en

▶ These verbs have irregular formal commands.

| Infinitive | Ud. command | Uds. command |
|---|---|---|
| dar | **dé** | **den** |
| estar | **esté** | **estén** |
| ir | **vaya** | **vayan** |
| saber | **sepa** | **sepan** |
| ser | **sea** | **sean** |

▶ To make a formal command negative, simply place **no** before the verb.

**No ponga** las maletas en la cama.   **No ensucien** los sillones.
*Don't put the suitcases on the bed.*   *Don't dirty the armchairs.*

▶ In affirmative commands, reflexive, indirect and direct object pronouns are always attached to the end of the verb.

Siénten**se**, por favor.   Acuésten**se** ahora.
Síga**me**, Laura.   Póngan**las** en el suelo, por favor.

▶ **¡Atención!** When a pronoun is attached to an affirmative command that has two or more syllables, an accent mark is added to maintain the original stress.

limpie ⟶ **límpielo**   lean ⟶ **léanlo**
diga ⟶ **dígamelo**   sacudan ⟶ **sacúdanlos**

▶ In negative commands, these pronouns always precede the verb.

No **se** preocupe.   No **los** ensucien.
No **me lo** dé.   No **nos las** traigan.

▶ **Usted** and **ustedes** can be used with the command forms to strike a more formal tone. In such instances they follow the command form.

**Muéstrele usted** la foto a su amigo.   **Tomen ustedes** esta alcoba.
*Show the photo to your friend.*   *Take this bedroom.*

**recursos**

WB
pp. 143–144

LM
p. 70

panorama.
vhlcentral.com
Lección 12

**¡INTÉNTALO!**   Indica los mandatos (*commands*) afirmativos y negativos correspondientes.

1. escucharlo (Ud.) ___*Escúchelo*___ . ___*No lo escuche*___ .
2. decírmelo (Uds.) ___*Díganmelo*___ . ___*No me lo digan*___ .
3. salir (Ud.) ___*Salga*___ . ___*No salga*___ .
4. servírnoslo (Uds.) ___*Sírvannoslo*___ . ___*No nos lo sirvan*___ .
5. barrerla (Ud.) ___*Bárrala*___ . ___*No la barra*___ .
6. hacerlo (Ud.) ___*Hágalo*___ . ___*No lo haga*___ .

**Teaching Tips**

• Ask volunteers to write formal command forms of other verbs with spelling changes on the board. Ex: **empezar (empiece); comenzar (comience); buscar (busque); pagar (pague); llegar (llegue).**

• Test comprehension as you proceed by asking volunteers to supply the correct form of other infinitives you name.

• Point out that the written accent mark on **dé** serves to distinguish the verb form from the preposition **de**.

• Point out that the affirmative answer for item 4 of **¡Inténtalo!** is spelled with a double n: **Sírvannoslo.**

**TEACHING OPTIONS**

**Extra Practice** Write a list of situations on the board using singular and plural forms. Ex: **La cocina está sucia. Mis amigos y yo tenemos hambre. Tenemos miedo.** Then have students write responses in the form of commands. Ex: **Límpiela. Hagan la cena. No tengan miedo.**

**Heritage Speakers** Ask heritage speakers to make a list of ten commands they would hear in their cultural communities that may not be heard elsewhere. Ex: **Sírvale el café al niño. Acuéstese después de almorzar.**

# Práctica

**1** **Completar** La señora González quiere mudarse de casa. Ayúdala a organizarse. Indica el mandato formal de cada verbo.

1. ___Lea___ los anuncios del periódico y ___guárdelos___. (Leer, guardarlos)
2. ___Vaya___ personalmente y ___vea___ las casas usted misma. (Ir, ver)
3. Decida qué casa quiere y ___llame___ al agente. ___Pídale___ un contrato de alquiler. (llamar, Pedirle)
4. ___Contrate___ un camión *(truck)* para ese día y ___pregúnteles___ la hora exacta de llegada. (Contratar, preguntarles)
5. El día de la mudanza *(On moving day)* ___esté___ tranquila. ___Vuelva___ a revisar su lista para completar todo lo que tiene que hacer. (estar, Volver)
6. Primero, ___dígales___ a todos en casa que usted va a estar ocupada. No ___les diga___ que usted va a hacerlo todo. (decirles, decirles)
7. ___Saque___ tiempo para hacer las maletas tranquilamente. No ___les haga___ las maletas a los niños más grandes. (Sacar, hacerles)
8. No ___se preocupe___. ___Sepa___ que todo va a salir bien. (preocuparse, Saber)

**2** **¿Qué dicen?** Mira los dibujos y escribe un mandato lógico para cada uno. Usa palabras que aprendiste en **Contextos**. Answers will vary. Suggested answers:

1. _____ Abran sus libros, por favor. _____

2. _____ Cierre la puerta. ¡Hace frío! _____

3. _____ Traiga usted la cuenta, por favor. _____

4. La cocina está sucia. Bárranla, por favor.

5. _____ Duerma bien, niña. _____

6. Arreglen el cuarto, por favor. Está desordenado.

# Comunicación

**3** **Solucionar** Trabajen en parejas para presentar estos problemas. Un(a) estudiante presenta los problemas de la columna A y el/la otro/a los de la columna B. Usen mandatos formales y túrnense para ofrecer soluciones. Answers will vary.

>
> **Estudiante 1:** Vilma se torció un tobillo jugando al tenis. Es la tercera vez.
> **Estudiante 2:** *No juegue más al tenis. / Vaya a ver a un especialista.*

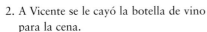

| A | B |
|---|---|
| 1. Se me perdió el libro de español con todas mis notas. | 1. Mis hijas no se levantan temprano. Siempre llegan tarde a la escuela. |
| 2. A Vicente se le cayó la botella de vino para la cena. | 2. A mi abuela le robaron (*stole*) las maletas. Era su primer día de vacaciones. |
| 3. ¿Cómo? ¿Se le olvidó traer el traje de baño a la playa? | 3. Nuestra casa es demasiado pequeña para nuestra familia. |
| 4. Se nos quedaron los boletos en la casa. El avión sale en una hora. | 4. Me preocupo constantemente por Roberto. Trabaja demasiado. |

**4** **Conversaciones** En parejas, escojan dos situaciones y preparen conversaciones para presentar a la clase. Usen mandatos formales. Answers will vary.

>
> **Lupita:** Señor Ramírez, siento mucho llegar tan tarde. Mi niño se enfermó. ¿Qué debo hacer?
> **Sr. Ramírez:** *No se preocupe. Siéntese y descanse un poco.*

**SITUACIÓN 1** Profesor Rosado, no vine la semana pasada porque el equipo jugaba en Boquete. ¿Qué debo hacer para ponerme al día *(catch up)*?

**SITUACIÓN 2** Los invitados de la boda llegan a las cuatro de la tarde, las mesas están sin poner y el champán sin servir. Los camareros apenas están llegando. ¿Qué deben hacer los camareros?

**SITUACIÓN 3** Mi novio es un poco aburrido. No le gustan ni el cine, ni los deportes, ni salir a comer. Tampoco habla mucho. ¿Qué puedo hacer?

▶ **SITUACIÓN 4** Tengo que preparar una presentación para mañana sobre el Canal de Panamá. ¿Por dónde comienzo?

**NOTA CULTURAL**

El 31 de diciembre de 1999, los Estados Unidos cedió el control del **Canal de Panamá** al gobierno de Panamá, terminando así con casi 100 años de administración estadounidense.

# Síntesis

**5** **Presentar** En grupos, preparen un anuncio de televisión para presentar a la clase. El anuncio debe tratar de un detergente, un electrodoméstico o una agencia inmobiliaria *(real estate agency)*. Usen mandatos, los pronombres relativos (**que, quien(es)** o **lo que**) y el **se** impersonal. Answers will vary.

>
> *Compre el lavaplatos Siglo XXI. Tiene todo lo que usted desea. Es el lavaplatos que mejor funciona. Venga a verlo ahora mismo... No pierda ni un minuto más. Se aceptan tarjetas de crédito.*

---

# 12.3 The present subjunctive

**ANTE TODO**  With the exception of commands, all the verb forms you have been using have been in the indicative mood. The indicative is used to state facts and to express actions or states that the speaker considers to be real and definite. In contrast, the subjunctive mood expresses the speaker's attitudes toward events, as well as actions or states the speaker views as uncertain or hypothetical.

*Quiero que ustedes ayuden con los quehaceres domésticos.*

*Insistimos en que nos deje ayudarla a preparar la comida.*

### Present subjunctive of regular verbs

| | | hablar | comer | escribir |
|---|---|---|---|---|
| SINGULAR FORMS | yo | habl**e** | com**a** | escrib**a** |
| | tú | habl**es** | com**as** | escrib**as** |
| | Ud./él/ella | habl**e** | com**a** | escrib**a** |
| PLURAL FORMS | nosotros/as | habl**emos** | com**amos** | escrib**amos** |
| | vosotros/as | habl**éis** | com**áis** | escrib**áis** |
| | Uds./ellos/ellas | habl**en** | com**an** | escrib**an** |

▶ The present subjunctive is formed very much like **usted** and **ustedes** and *negative* **tú** commands. From the **yo** form of the present indicative, drop the **-o** ending, and replace it with the subjunctive endings.

| INFINITIVE | PRESENT INDICATIVE | VERB STEM | PRESENT SUBJUNCTIVE |
|---|---|---|---|
| hablar | **hablo** | **habl-** | **hable** |
| comer | **como** | **com-** | **coma** |
| escribir | **escribo** | **escrib-** | **escriba** |

▶ The present subjunctive endings are:

| **-ar verbs** | |
|---|---|
| -e | -emos |
| -es | -éis |
| -e | -en |

| **-er and -ir verbs** | |
|---|---|
| -a | -amos |
| -as | -áis |
| -a | -an |

**¡LENGUA VIVA!**

You may think that English has no subjunctive, but it does! While once common, it now survives mostly in set expressions such as *if I were you* and *be that as it may.*

**AYUDA**

Note that, in the present subjunctive, **-ar** verbs use endings normally associated with present tense **-er** and **-ir** verbs. Likewise, **-er** and **-ir** verbs in the present subjunctive use endings normally associated with **-ar** verbs in the present tense. Note also that, in the present subjunctive, the **yo** form is the same as the **Ud./él/ella** form.

▶ Verbs with irregular **yo** forms show the same irregularity in all forms of the present subjunctive.

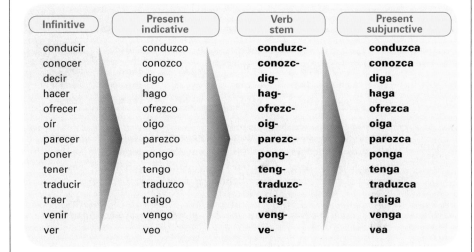

| Infinitive | Present indicative | Verb stem | Present subjunctive |
|---|---|---|---|
| conducir | conduzco | **conduzc-** | **conduzca** |
| conocer | conozco | **conozc-** | **conozca** |
| decir | digo | **dig-** | **diga** |
| hacer | hago | **hag-** | **haga** |
| ofrecer | ofrezco | **ofrezc-** | **ofrezca** |
| oír | oigo | **oig-** | **oiga** |
| parecer | parezco | **parezc-** | **parezca** |
| poner | pongo | **pong-** | **ponga** |
| tener | tengo | **teng-** | **tenga** |
| traducir | traduzco | **traduzc-** | **traduzca** |
| traer | traigo | **traig-** | **traiga** |
| venir | vengo | **veng-** | **venga** |
| ver | veo | **ve-** | **vea** |

▶ To maintain the **-c, -g,** and **-z** sounds, verbs ending in **-car, -gar,** and **-zar** have a spelling change in all forms of the present subjunctive.

> **sacar:** sa**qu**e, sa**qu**es, sa**qu**e, sa**qu**emos, sa**qu**éis, sa**qu**en
>
> **jugar:** jue**gu**e, jue**gu**es, jue**gu**e, ju**gu**emos, ju**gu**éis, jue**gu**en
>
> **almorzar:** almuer**c**e, almuer**c**es, almuer**c**e, almor**c**emos, almor**c**éis, almuer**c**en

## Present subjunctive of stem-changing verbs

**AYUDA**

Note that stem-changing verbs and verbs that have a spelling change have the same ending as regular verbs in the present subjunctive.

▶ **-Ar** and **-er** stem-changing verbs have the same stem changes in the subjunctive as they do in the present indicative.

> **pensar (e:ie):** p**ie**nse, p**ie**nses, p**ie**nse, pensemos, penséis, p**ie**nsen
>
> **mostrar (o:ue):** m**ue**stre, m**ue**stres, m**ue**stre, mostremos, mostréis, m**ue**stren
>
> **entender (e:ie):** ent**ie**nda, ent**ie**ndas, ent**ie**nda, entendamos, entendáis, ent**ie**ndan
>
> **volver (o:ue):** v**ue**lva, v**ue**lvas, v**ue**lva, volvamos, volváis, v**ue**lvan

▶ **-Ir** stem-changing verbs have the same stem changes in the subjunctive as they do in the present indicative, but in addition, the **nosotros/as** and **vosotros/as** forms undergo a stem change. The unstressed **e** changes to **i,** while the unstressed **o** changes to **u.**

> **pedir (e:i):** p**i**da, p**i**das, p**i**da, p**i**damos, p**i**dáis, p**i**dan
>
> **sentir (e:ie):** s**ie**nta, s**ie**ntas, s**ie**nta, s**i**ntamos, s**i**ntáis, s**ie**ntan
>
> **dormir (o:ue):** d**ue**rma, d**ue**rmas, d**ue**rma, d**u**rmamos, d**u**rmáis, d**ue**rman

**Teaching Tips**

• It may be helpful for students to be aware how English uses the subjunctive mood. Ex: *I wish she were here. I insist that he take notes. I suggest you be there tomorrow. If it were me, I would be happy. Be that as it may…*

• Emphasize the stem changes that occur in the **nosotros/as** and **vosotros/as** forms of **–ir** stem-changing verbs.

**TEACHING OPTIONS**

**Pairs** Have pairs of students role-play landlord/landlady and new resident. Students should refer to the **Fotonovela** as a model. Give pairs sufficient time to plan and practice. When all pairs have completed the activity, ask a few of them to introduce their characters and perform the conversation for the class.

**Extra Practice** Ask students to compare family members' attitudes toward domestic life using the subjunctive. Ex: **Los padres quieren que los hijos... Los hijos insisten en que...**

## Irregular verbs in the present subjunctive

▶ These five verbs are irregular in the present subjunctive.

### Irregular verbs in the present subjunctive

| | | dar | estar | ir | saber | ser |
|---|---|---|---|---|---|---|
| SINGULAR FORMS | yo | dé | esté | vaya | sepa | sea |
| | tú | des | estés | vayas | sepas | seas |
| | Ud./él/ella | dé | esté | vaya | sepa | sea |
| PLURAL FORMS | nosotros/as | demos | estemos | vayamos | sepamos | seamos |
| | vosotros/as | deis | estéis | vayáis | sepáis | seáis |
| | Uds./ellos/ellas | den | estén | vayan | sepan | sean |

▶ **¡Atención!** The subjunctive form of **hay** (_there is, there are_) is also irregular: **haya**.

## General uses of the subjunctive

▶ The subjunctive is mainly used to express: 1) will and influence, 2) emotion, 3) doubt, disbelief, and denial, and 4) indefiniteness and nonexistence.

▶ The subjunctive is most often used in sentences that consist of a main clause and a subordinate clause. The main clause contains a verb or expression that triggers the use of the subjunctive. The conjunction **que** connects the subordinate clause to the main clause.

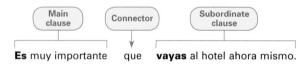

( Main clause )      ( Connector )      ( Subordinate clause )

**Es** muy importante      que      **vayas** al hotel ahora mismo.

▶ These impersonal expressions are always followed by clauses in the subjunctive:

| **Es bueno que...** | **Es mejor que...** | **Es malo que...** |
|---|---|---|
| _It's good that..._ | _It's better that..._ | _It's bad that..._ |
| **Es importante que...** | **Es necesario que...** | **Es urgente que...** |
| _It's important that..._ | _It's necessary that..._ | _It's urgent that..._ |

 **¡INTÉNTALO!**   Indica el presente de subjuntivo de estos verbos.

1. (alquilar, beber, vivir)   que yo ___ alquile, beba, viva
2. (estudiar, aprender, asistir)   que tú ___ estudies, aprendas, asistas
3. (encontrar, poder, dormir)   que él ___ encuentre, pueda, duerma
4. (hacer, tener, venir)   que nosotras ___ hagamos, tengamos, vengamos
5. (dar, hablar, escribir)   que ellos ___ den, hablen, escriban
6. (pagar, empezar, buscar)   que ustedes ___ paguen, empiecen, busquen
7. (ser, ir, saber)   que yo ___ sea, vaya, sepa
8. (estar, dar, oír)   que tú ___ estés, des, oigas

**recursos**

WB
pp. 145–146

LM
p. 71

SUPERSITE
panorama.
vhlcentral.com
Lección 12

# Práctica  SUPERSITE

**1** **Completar** Completa las oraciones con el presente de subjuntivo de los verbos entre paréntesis. Luego empareja las oraciones del primer grupo con las del segundo grupo.

### A

1. Es mejor que <u>cenemos</u> en casa. (nosotros, cenar) b
2. Es importante que <u>visites</u> las casas colgantes de Cuenca. (tú, visitar) c
3. Señora, es urgente que le <u>saque</u> el diente. Tiene una infección. (yo, sacar) e
4. Es malo que Ana les <u>dé</u> tantos dulces a los niños. (dar) a
5. Es necesario que <u>lleguen</u> a la una de la tarde. (ustedes, llegar) f
6. Es importante que <u>nos acostemos</u> temprano. (nosotros, acostarse) d

### B

a. Es importante que <u>coman</u> más verduras. (ellos, comer)
b. No, es mejor que <u>salgamos</u> a comer. (nosotros, salir)
c. Y yo creo que es bueno que <u>vaya</u> a Madrid después. (yo, ir)
d. En mi opinión, no es necesario que <u>durmamos</u> tanto. (nosotros, dormir)
e. ¿Ah, sí? ¿Es necesario que me <u>tome</u> un antibiótico también? (yo, tomar)
f. Para llegar a tiempo, es necesario que <u>almorcemos</u> temprano. (nosotros, almorzar)

**NOTA CULTURAL**

**Las casas colgantes** (*hanging*) de Cuenca, España, son muy famosas. Situadas en un acantilado (*cliff*), forman parte del paisaje de la ciudad.

# Comunicación

**2** **Minidiálogos** En parejas, completen los minidiálogos con expresiones impersonales de una manera lógica. Answers will vary.

**modelo**

**Miguelito:**    Mamá, no quiero arreglar mi cuarto.
**Sra. Casas:**   *Es necesario que lo arregles. Y es importante que sacudas los muebles también.*

1. **MIGUELITO**   Mamá, no quiero estudiar. Quiero salir a jugar con mis amigos.
   **SRA. CASAS** _____

2. **MIGUELITO**   Mamá, es que no me gustan las verduras. Prefiero comer pasteles.
   **SRA. CASAS** _____

3. **MIGUELITO**   ¿Tengo que poner la mesa, mamá?
   **SRA. CASAS** _____

4. **MIGUELITO**   No me siento bien, mamá. Me duele todo el cuerpo y tengo fiebre.
   **SRA. CASAS** _____

**3** **Entrevista** Trabajen en parejas. Entrevístense usando estas preguntas. Expliquen sus respuestas. Answers will vary.

1. ¿Es importante que los niños ayuden con los quehaceres domésticos?
2. ¿Es urgente que los norteamericanos aprendan otras lenguas?
3. Si un(a) norteamericano/a quiere aprender francés, ¿es mejor que lo aprenda en Francia?
4. En su universidad, ¿es necesario que los estudiantes vivan en residencias estudiantiles?
5. ¿Es importante que todas las personas asistan a la universidad?

---

**1 Expansion** After students have paired the sentences from each group, have them continue a couple of the short conversations with two more sentences using the subjunctive. Ex: **No es posible que encontremos un restaurante con mesas disponibles a las siete. Es mejor que salgamos ahora mismo para no tener ese problema.**

**2 Teaching Tip** To simplify, before assigning the activity, have students brainstorm impersonal expressions that a mother would say to her young son.

**2 Expansion**
• Ask volunteers to share their mini-dialogues with the rest of the class.
• Ask questions about **Miguelito** and **señora Casas** to elicit the subjunctive. Ex: **¿En qué insiste la señora Casas? (Insiste en que Miguelito arregle su cuarto, que coma verduras y que ponga la mesa.) ¿Qué quiere Miguelito? (Quiere salir a jugar y comer pasteles.)**

**3 Expansion** Ask students to report on their partner's answers using complete sentences and explanations. Ex: **¿Qué opina _____ sobre los quehaceres de los niños? ¿Cree que es importante que ayuden?**

---

**TEACHING OPTIONS**

**Heritage Speakers** Have heritage speakers write five sentences comparing mainstream social practices with those of their cultural communities. Ex: **Aquí, es necesario que llames antes de ir a visitar a un amigo. En nuestra cultura, es normal que lleguemos sin llamar a la casa de un amigo.**

**Small Groups** Divide the class into groups of four. Assign each group one of these personal characteristics: **apariencia física, dinero, inteligencia, personalidad.** Have groups use the subjunctive to write sentences about the importance or unimportance of this trait for certain individuals. Ex: **Para ser presidente es importante que la persona sea inteligente.**

## 12.4 Subjunctive with verbs of will and influence

**ANTE TODO** You will now learn how to use the subjunctive with verbs and expressions of will and influence.

Quiero que tengas dientes más blancos.

▶ Verbs of will and influence are often used when someone wants to affect the actions or behavior of other people.

> Enrique **quiere** que salgamos a cenar.
> *Enrique wants us to go out to dinner.*

> Paola **prefiere** que cenemos en casa.
> *Paola prefers that we have dinner at home.*

▶ Here is a list of widely used verbs of will and influence.

### Verbs of will and influence

| | | | |
|---|---|---|---|
| **aconsejar** | *to advise* | **pedir** (e:i) | *to ask (for)* |
| **desear** | *to wish; to desire* | **preferir** (e:ie) | *to prefer* |
| **importar** | *to be important; to matter* | **prohibir** | *to prohibit* |
| | | **querer** (e:ie) | *to want* |
| **insistir (en)** | *to insist (on)* | **recomendar** (e:ie) | *to recommend* |
| **mandar** | *to order* | **rogar** (o:ue) | *to beg; to plead* |
| **necesitar** | *to need* | **sugerir** (e:ie) | *to suggest* |

▶ Some impersonal expressions, such as **es necesario que, es importante que, es mejor que,** and **es urgente que,** are considered expressions of will or influence.

▶ When the main clause contains an expression of will or influence, the subjunctive is required in the subordinate clause, provided that the two clauses have different subjects.

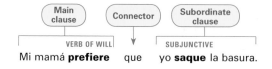

Main clause — Connector — Subordinate clause

VERB OF WILL → SUBJUNCTIVE

Mi mamá **prefiere** que yo **saque** la basura.

---

---

*Quiero que arreglen sus alcobas, que hagan las camas, que pongan la mesa…*

*…y les aconsejo que se acuesten temprano esta noche.*

▶ Indirect object pronouns are often used with the verbs **aconsejar, importar, mandar, pedir, prohibir, recomendar, rogar,** and **sugerir.**

**Te** aconsejo que estudies.
*I advise you to study.*

**Le** sugiero que vaya a casa.
*I suggest that he go home.*

**Les** recomiendo que barran el suelo.
*I recommend that you sweep the floor.*

**Le** ruego que no venga.
*I beg him not to come.*

▶ Note that all the forms of **prohibir** in the present tense carry a written accent, except for the **nosotros/as** form: **prohíbo, prohíbes, prohíbe, prohibimos, prohibís, prohíben.**

Ella les **prohíbe** que miren la televisión.
*She prohibits them from watching television.*

Nos **prohíben** que nademos en la piscina.
*They prohibit that we swim in the swimming pool.*

▶ The infinitive is used with words or expressions of will and influence, if there is no change of subject in the sentence.

No quiero **sacudir** los muebles.
*I don't want to dust the furniture.*

Paco prefiere **descansar.**
*Paco prefers to rest.*

Es importante **sacar** la basura.
*It's important to take out the trash.*

No es necesario **quitar** la mesa.
*It's not necessary to clear the table.*

---

**¡INTÉNTALO!**    Completa cada oración con la forma correcta del verbo entre paréntesis.

1. Te sugiero que _____vayas_____ (ir) con ella al supermercado.
2. Él necesita que yo le _____preste_____ (prestar) dinero.
3. No queremos que tú _____hagas_____ (hacer) nada especial para nosotros.
4. Mis papás quieren que yo _____limpie_____ (limpiar) mi cuarto.
5. Nos piden que la _____ayudemos_____ (ayudar) a preparar la comida.
6. Quieren que tú _____saques_____ (sacar) la basura todos los días.
7. Quiero _____descansar_____ (descansar) esta noche.
8. Es importante que ustedes _____limpien_____ (limpiar) los estantes.
9. Su tía les manda que _____pongan_____ (poner) la mesa.
10. Te aconsejo que no _____salgas_____ (salir) con él.
11. Mi tío insiste en que mi prima _____haga_____ (hacer) la cama.
12. Prefiero _____ir_____ (ir) al cine.
13. Es necesario _____estudiar_____ (estudiar).
14. Recomiendo que ustedes _____pasen_____ (pasar) la aspiradora.

**recursos**

WB
pp. 147–148

LM
p. 72

panorama.
vhlcentral.com
Lección 12

**Teaching Tips**
• Have a volunteer read aloud the captions to the video stills. Point out that in each example the subject of the verb in the main clause is different from the subject of the verb in the subordinate clause.
• Elicit indirect object pronouns with verbs of influence by making statements that give advice and asking students for advice. Ex: **Yo siempre les aconsejo a mis estudiantes que estudien mucho. ¿Qué me recomiendan ustedes a mí?** Continue: **1. Mi coche no arranca cuando hace mucho frío. ¿Qué me recomiendas, _____? 2. Mi apartamento está siempre desordenado. ¿Qué me aconsejan? 3. Voy a tener huéspedes este fin de semana. ¿Qué nos sugieren que hagamos?**
• Write these sentences on the board: **Quiero que almuerces en la cafetería. Quiero almorzar en la cafetería.** Ask a volunteer to explain why an infinitive is used in the second sentence instead of the subjunctive.

---

**TEACHING OPTIONS**

**Extra Practice** Create sentences that follow the pattern of the sentences in **¡Inténtalo!** Say the sentence, have students repeat it, then give a different subject pronoun for the subordinate clause, varying the person and number. Have students then say the sentence with the new subject, changing pronouns and verbs as necessary.

**TPR** Have students stand. At random, call out implied commands using statements with verbs of will or influence and actions that can be mimed. Ex: **Quiero que laves los platos. Insisto en que hagas la cama.** When you make a statement, point to a student to mime the action. Also use plural statements and point to more than one student. When you use negative statements, indicated students should do nothing. Keep a brisk pace.

# Práctica

**1**

**Completar** Completa el diálogo con palabras de la lista.

| cocina | haga | quiere | sea |
|--------|------|--------|-----|
| comas | ponga | saber | ser |
| diga | prohíbe | sé | vaya |

**IRENE** Tengo problemas con Vilma. Sé que debo hablar con ella. ¿Qué me recomiendas que le (1)___diga___?

**JULIA** Pues, necesito (2)___saber___ más antes de darte consejos.

**IRENE** Bueno, para empezar me (3)___prohíbe___ que traiga dulces a la casa.

**JULIA** Pero chica, tiene razón. Es mejor que tú no (4)___comas___ cosas dulces.

**IRENE** Sí, ya lo sé. Pero quiero que (5)___sea___ más flexible. Además, insiste en que yo (6)___haga___ todo en la casa.

**JULIA** Yo (7)___sé___ que Vilma (8)___cocina___ y hace los quehaceres todos los días.

**IRENE** Sí, pero siempre que hay fiesta me pide que (9)___ponga___ los cubiertos y las copas en la mesa y que (10)___vaya___ al sótano por las servilletas y los platos. ¡Es lo que más odio: ir al sótano!

**JULIA** Mujer, ¡Vilma sólo (11)___quiere___ que ayudes en la casa!

**2**

**Aconsejar** En parejas, lean lo que dice cada persona. Luego den consejos lógicos usando verbos como **aconsejar, recomendar** y **prohibir.** Sus consejos deben ser diferentes de lo que la persona quiere hacer. Answers will vary.

> **modelo**
>
> **Isabel:** Quiero conseguir un comedor con los muebles más caros del mundo.
>
> **Consejo:** *Te aconsejamos que consigas unos muebles menos caros.*

1. **DAVID** Pienso poner el cuadro del lago de Maracaibo en la cocina.
2. **SARA** Voy a ir a la gasolinera para comprar unas copas de cristal elegantes.
3. **SR. ALARCÓN** Insisto en comenzar a arreglar el jardín en marzo.
4. **SRA. VILLA** Quiero ver las tazas y los platos de la tienda El Ama de Casa Feliz.
5. **DOLORES** Voy a poner servilletas de tela (*cloth*) para los cuarenta invitados.
6. **SR. PARDO** Pienso poner todos mis muebles nuevos en el altillo.
7. **SRA. GONZÁLEZ** Hay una fiesta en casa esta noche pero no quiero limpiarla.
8. **CARLITOS** Hoy no tengo ganas de hacer las camas ni de quitar la mesa.

**NOTA CULTURAL**

En el **lago de Maracaibo,** en Venezuela, hay casas suspendidas sobre el agua que se llaman palafitos. Los palafitos son reminiscencias de Venecia, Italia, de donde viene el nombre "Venezuela", que significa "pequeña Venecia".

**3**

**Preguntas** En parejas, túrnense para contestar las preguntas. Usen el subjuntivo. Answers will vary.

1. ¿Te dan consejos tus amigos/as? ¿Qué te aconsejan? ¿Aceptas sus consejos? ¿Por qué?
2. ¿Qué te sugieren tus profesores que hagas antes de terminar los cursos que tomas?
3. ¿Insisten tus amigos/as en que salgas mucho con ellos?
4. ¿Qué quieres que te regalen tu familia y tus amigos/as en tu cumpleaños?
5. ¿Qué le recomiendas tú a un(a) amigo/a que no quiere salir los sábados con su novio/a?
6. ¿Qué les aconsejas a los nuevos estudiantes de tu universidad?

# Comunicación

**4** **Inventar** En parejas, preparen una lista de seis personas famosas. Un(a) estudiante da el nombre de una persona famosa y el/la otro/a le da un consejo. Answers will vary.

> **modelo**
>
> **Estudiante 1:** *Judge Judy.*
> **Estudiante 2:** *Le recomiendo que sea más simpática con la gente.*
> **Estudiante 2:** *Orlando Bloom.*
> **Estudiante 1:** *Le aconsejo que haga más películas.*

**5** **Hablar** En parejas, miren la ilustración. Imaginen que Gerardo es su hermano y necesita ayuda para arreglar su casa y resolver sus problemas románticos y económicos. Usen expresiones impersonales y verbos como **aconsejar, sugerir** y **recomendar**. Answers will vary.

> **modelo**
>
> *Es mejor que arregles el apartamento más a menudo.*
> *Te aconsejo que no dejes para mañana lo que puedes hacer hoy.*

# Síntesis

**6** **La doctora Salvamórez** Hernán tiene problemas con su novia y le escribe a la doctora Salvamórez, columnista del periódico *Panamá y su gente*. Ella responde a las cartas de personas con problemas románticos. En parejas, lean la carta de Hernán y después usen el subjuntivo para escribir los consejos de la doctora. Answers will vary.

> Estimada doctora Salvamórez:
>
> Mi novia nunca quiere que yo salga de casa. No le molesta que vengan mis amigos a visitarme. Pero insiste en que nosotros sólo miremos los programas de televisión que ella quiere. Necesita saber dónde estoy en cada momento, y yo necesito que ella me dé un poco de independencia. ¿Qué hago?
>
> Hernán

**4** **Teaching Tip** Ask volunteers to read the **modelo** aloud and provide other suggestions for Judge Judy and Orlando Bloom.

**4** **Expansion** Ask each pair to pick its favorite response and share it with the class, who will vote for the most clever, shocking, or humorous suggestion.

**5** **Teaching Tip** Before beginning the activity, show *Overhead PowerPoint #47* and ask volunteers to describe the drawing, naming everything they see and all the chores that need to be done.

**5** **Expansion** Have students change partners and take turns playing the roles of **Gerardo** and one sibling giving him advice. Ex: **Te sugiero que pongas la pizza en la basura.**

**6** **Expansion**
- Have pairs compare their responses in groups of four. Ask groups to choose which among all of the suggestions are the most likely to work for **Hernán** and have them share these with the class.
- Have pairs choose a famous couple in history or fiction. Ex: Romeo and Juliet or Napoleon and Josephine. Then have them write a letter from one of the couples to **doctora Salvamórez**. Finally, have them exchange their letters with another pair and write the corresponding responses from the doctor.

---

**TEACHING OPTIONS**

**Heritage Speakers** Have heritage speakers write a list of five suggestions for other class members participating in an exchange program in their cultural communities. Their suggestions should focus on participating in daily life in their host family's home.

**Large Group** Write the names of famous historical figures on individual sticky notes and place them on the students' backs. Have students circulate around the room, giving each other advice that will help them guess their "identity."

## Recapitulación

**SUPERSITE** For self-scoring and diagnostics, go to panorama.vhlcentral.com.

Completa estas actividades para repasar los conceptos de gramática que aprendiste en esta lección.

**1 Completar** Completa el cuadro con la forma correspondiente del presente de subjuntivo. **12 pts.**

| yo/él/ella | tú | nosotros/as | Uds./ellos/ellas |
|---|---|---|---|
| **limpie** | limpies | limpiemos | limpien |
| venga | **vengas** | vengamos | vengan |
| quiera | quieras | **queramos** | quieran |
| ofrezca | ofrezcas | ofrezcamos | **ofrezcan** |

**2 El apartamento ideal** Completa este folleto (*brochure*) informativo con las formas correctas del presente de subjuntivo. **8 pts.**

> *A los jóvenes que buscan su primera vivienda, les ofrecemos estos consejos:*
>
> ■ Te sugiero que primero (tú) (1) __escribas__ (escribir) una lista de las cosas que quieres en un apartamento.
>
> ■ Quiero que después (2) __pienses__ (pensar) muy bien cuáles son tus prioridades. Es necesario que cada persona (3) __tenga__ (tener) sus prioridades claras, porque el hogar (*home*) perfecto no existe.
>
> ■ Antes de decidir en qué área quieren vivir, les aconsejo a ti y a tu futuro/a compañero/a de apartamento que (4) __salgan__ (salir) a ver la ciudad y que (5) __conozcan__ (conocer) los distintos barrios y las afueras.
>
> ■ Pidan que el agente les (6) __muestre__ (mostrar) todas las partes de cada casa.
>
> ■ Finalmente, como consumidores, es importante que nosotros (7) __sepamos__ (saber) bien nuestros derechos (*rights*); por eso, deben insistir en que todos los puntos del contrato (8) __estén__ (estar) muy claros antes de firmarlo (*signing it*).
>
> *¡Buena suerte!*

**RESUMEN GRAMATICAL**

**12.1 Relative pronouns** *pp. 386–387*

| Relative pronouns | |
|---|---|
| que | that; which; who |
| quien(es) | who; whom; that |
| lo que | that which; what |

**12.2 Formal commands** *pp. 390–391*

| Formal commands (Ud. and Uds.) | | |
|---|---|---|
| Infinitive | Present tense yo form | Ud(s). command |
| limpiar | limpio | limpie(n) |
| barrer | barro | barra(n) |
| sacudir | sacudo | sacuda(n) |

▶ Verbs with stem changes or irregular yo forms maintain the same irregularity in the formal commands:

hacer: yo **hago** → **Hagan** la cama.

| Irregular formal commands | |
|---|---|
| dar | dé (Ud.); den (Uds.) |
| estar | esté(n) |
| ir | vaya(n) |
| saber | sepa(n) |
| ser | sea(n) |

**12.3 The present subjunctive** *pp. 394–396*

| Present subjunctive of regular verbs | | |
|---|---|---|
| hablar | comer | escribir |
| hable | coma | escriba |
| hables | comas | escribas |
| hable | coma | escriba |
| hablemos | comamos | escribamos |
| habléis | comáis | escribáis |
| hablen | coman | escriban |

---

**Section Goal**

In **Recapitulación**, students will review the grammar concepts from this lesson.

**Instructional Resource**
**Supersite**

**1 Expansion** Give students additional verbs to conjugate in the subjunctive. Ex: **comer, dar, estar, saber, traer.**

**2 Expansion**
• Have volunteers take turns reading the brochure aloud.
• To challenge students, ask them to work in pairs to write four pieces of advice for a real estate agent, using impersonal expressions. Ex: **Es importante que sea honesto.** Have a few pairs read their sentences for the class.

---

**TEACHING OPTIONS**

**TPR** Add an auditory aspect to this grammar review. Have students imagine they are landlords with students as tenants. Prepare statements about the tenants, using impersonal expressions. As you read each statement, have students give a thumbs-up if they like what they hear or a thumbs-down if they do not. Ex: **Es importante que los estudiantes mantengan el apartamento limpio.** (thumbs-up) **Es urgente que den fiestas todos los sábados.** (thumbs-down)

**Extra Practice** Call out verbs and have volunteers give the singular and plural command forms. Ex: **barrer (barra, barran)** Repeat the drill with the subjunctive, varying the subject pronouns. Ex: **dormir/nosotros (que nosotros durmamos)**

**3**  **Relativos** Completa las oraciones con **lo que**, **que** o **quien**. ( **8 pts.** )

1. Me encanta la alfombra ___que___ está en el comedor.
2. Mi amiga Tere, con ___quien___ trabajo, me regaló ese cuadro.
3. Todas las cosas ___que___ tenemos vienen de la casa de mis abuelos.
4. Hija, no compres más cosas. ___Lo que___ debes hacer ahora es organizarlo todo.
5. La agencia de decoración de ___que___ le hablé se llama Casabella.
6. Esas flores las dejaron en la puerta mis nuevos vecinos, a ___quienes___ aún (*yet*) no conozco.
7. Leonor no compró nada, porque ___lo que___ le gustaba era muy caro.
8. Mi amigo Aldo, a ___quien___ visité ayer, es un cocinero excelente.

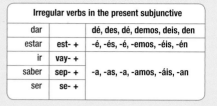

| Irregular verbs in the present subjunctive | | |
|---|---|---|
| dar | | dé, des, dé, demos, deis, den |
| estar | est- + | -é, -és, -é, -emos, -éis, -én |
| ir | vay- + | |
| saber | sep- + | -a, -as, -a, -amos, -áis, -an |
| ser | se- + | |

**12.4**   **Subjunctive with verbs of will and influence**

*pp. 398–399*

▶ Verbs of will and influence: **aconsejar, desear, importar, insistir (en), mandar, necesitar, pedir** (e:i), **preferir** (e:ie), **prohibir, querer** (e:ie), **recomendar** (e:ie), **rogar** (o:ue), **sugerir** (e:ie)

**4**  **Preparando la casa** Martín y Ángela van a hacer un curso de verano en Costa Rica y una vecina va a cuidarles (*take care of*) la casa mientras ellos no están. Completa las instrucciones de la vecina con mandatos formales. Usa cada verbo una sola vez y agrega pronombres de objeto directo o indirecto si es necesario. ( **10 pts.** )

| | | | | |
|---|---|---|---|---|
| arreglar | dejar | hacer | pedir | sacudir |
| barrer | ensuciar | limpiar | poner | tener |

Primero, (1) ___hagan___ ustedes las maletas. Las cosas que no se llevan a Costa Rica, (2) ___pónganlas___ en el altillo. Ángela, (3) ___arregle/limpie___ las habitaciones y Martín, (4) ___limpie/ arregle___ usted la cocina y el baño. Después, los dos (5) ___barran___ el suelo y (6) ___sacudan___ los muebles de toda la casa. Ángela, no (7) ___deje___ sus joyas (*jewelry*) en el apartamento. (8) ___Tengan___ cuidado ¡y (9) ___no ensucien___ nada antes de irse! Por último, (10) ___pídanle___ a alguien que recoja (*pick up*) su correo.

**5**  **Los quehaceres** A tu compañero/a de cuarto no le gusta ayudar con los quehaceres. Escribe al menos seis oraciones dándole consejos para hacer los quehaceres más divertidos. ( **12 pts.** )
Answers will vary.

> **modelo**
> *Pon música mientras lavas los platos....*

**6**  **El circo** (*circus*) Completa esta famosa frase que tiene su origen en el circo. ( **¡2 puntos EXTRA!** )

“ ¡___Pasen___ (Pasar) ustedes y ___vean___ (ver)! El espectáculo va a comenzar. ”

**3** Teaching Tip Have students circle the noun or idea to which each relative pronoun refers.

**3** Expansion
• Ask volunteers to give the corresponding questions for each item. Ex: **1. ¿Qué alfombra te encanta?**
• Have students work in pairs to create four additional sentences using relative pronouns.

**4** Teaching Tips
• To simplify, have students begin by scanning the paragraph and identifying which blanks call for **usted** commands and which call for **ustedes** commands.
• Tell students that some answers will contain object pronouns (items 2 and 10).

**5** Teaching Tip Before beginning this activity, have pairs discuss their own habits regarding chores.

**5** Expansion Have students imagine they have two room-mates and ask them to rewrite their sentences using **ustedes** commands.

**6** Expansion
• To challenge students, ask them to write two **ustedes** commands for people attending a circus and one **usted** command for the master of ceremonies.
• Ask heritage speakers to think of other popular phrases or quotes that use formal command forms. Have them write the phrases on the board, leaving blanks for classmates to guess the commands.

**TEACHING OPTIONS**

**Extra Practice** Call out formal commands. Ex: **Sacudan los muebles.** Have students respond by naming the infinitive and subject. Ex: **sacudir, ustedes.** Reverse the drill by calling out verb phrases and either **usted** or **ustedes.** Have students give the command form.
**TPR** Review present subjunctive and vocabulary from previous lessons. Divide the class into two teams and have them line

up. Name a person or group of people. Ex: **estudiantes de informática, Hilary Duff, un niño en su primer día de la escuela primaria.** Then point to the first member of team A, who has three seconds to create a piece of advice. Ex: **Quiero que apaguen las computadoras.** Then the first member of team B has to give another sentence. Continue until the chain is broken, then name a new person.

## Section Goals

In **Lectura**, students will:
- learn to locate the main parts of a sentence
- read a content-rich text with long sentences

---

**Instructional Resources**
**Supersite**
*Cuaderno para hispanohablantes*

---

**Estrategia** Tell students that if they have trouble reading long sentences in Spanish, they should pause to identify the main verb of the sentence and its subject. They should then reread the entire sentence.

**Examinar el texto** Students should see from the layout (cover page with title, photo, and phone numbers; interior pages with an introduction and several headings followed by short paragraphs) that this is a brochure. Revealing cognates are: **información** (cover) and **residencia oficial del Presidente de Panamá** (introduction).

**¿Probable o improbable?** Ask volunteers to read aloud each item and give the answer. Have a volunteer rephrase the improbable statement so that it is probable.

**Oraciones largas** Ask pairs to create a couple of long sentences. Have them point out the main verb and subject.

# Lectura

communication cultures NATIONAL STANDARDS

## Antes de leer

### Estrategia
**Locating the main parts of a sentence**

Did you know that a text written in Spanish is an average of 15% longer than the same text written in English? Because the Spanish language tends to use more words to express ideas, you will often encounter long sentences when reading in Spanish. Of course, the length of sentences varies with genre and with authors' individual styles. To help you understand long sentences, identify the main parts of the sentence before trying to read it in its entirety. First locate the main verb of the sentence, along with its subject, ignoring any words or phrases set off by commas. Then reread the sentence, adding details like direct and indirect objects, transitional words, and prepositional phrases.

### Examinar el texto

Mira el formato de la lectura. ¿Qué tipo de documento es? ¿Qué cognados encuentras en la lectura? ¿Qué te dicen sobre el tema de la selección?

### ¿Probable o improbable?

Mira brevemente el texto e indica si estas oraciones son probables o improbables.

1. Este folleto (*brochure*) es de interés turístico.  probable
2. Describe un edificio moderno cubano. improbable
3. Incluye algunas explicaciones de arquitectura.  probable
4. Espera atraer (*to attract*) a visitantes al lugar.  probable

### Oraciones largas

Mira el texto y busca algunas oraciones largas. Con un(a) compañero/a, identifiquen las partes principales de la oración y después examinen las descripciones adicionales. ¿Qué significan las oraciones?

**recursos**

 SUPERSITE

panorama.vhlcentral.com
Lección 12

---

*Bienvenidos al Palacio de Las Garzas*

**El palacio está abierto de martes a domingo.
Para más información,
llame al teléfono 507-226-7000.
También puede solicitar° un folleto
a la casilla° 3467,
Ciudad de Panamá, Panamá.**

---

## Después de leer
### Ordenar

Pon estos eventos en el orden cronológico adecuado.

_3_ El palacio se convirtió en residencia presidencial.

_2_ Durante diferentes épocas (*time periods*), maestros, médicos y banqueros practicaron su profesión en el palacio.

_4_ El Dr. Belisario Porras ocupó el palacio por primera vez.

_1_ Los españoles construyeron el palacio.

_5_ Se renovó el palacio.

_6_ Los turistas pueden visitar el palacio de martes a domingo.

---

**TEACHING OPTIONS**

**Heritage Speakers** Ask heritage speakers to give a brief presentation about the official residence of the president of their parents' home country. Tell them to include in their description recommendations to visitors about what rooms and objects are particularly noteworthy and should not be missed. If possible, they should illustrate their presentation with photographs or brochures.

**Extra Practice** Ask students to write ten statements using the subjunctive to describe their dream house (**la casa de mis sueños**). Ex: **Para mí es importante que haya una piscina de tamaño olímpico en la casa de mis sueños. Recomiendo que la cocina sea grande porque me gusta cocinar. Es necesario que tenga varios dormitorios porque siempre tengo huéspedes.** Have students share their sentences with a partner.

El Palacio de Las Garzas° es la residencia oficial del Presidente de Panamá desde 1903. Fue construido en 1673 para ser la casa de un gobernador español. Con el paso de los años fue almacén, escuela, hospital, aduana, banco y por último, palacio presidencial.

En la actualidad el edificio tiene tres pisos, pero los planos originales muestran una construcción de un piso con un gran patio en el centro. La restauración del palacio comenzó en el año 1922 y los trabajos fueron realizados por el arquitecto Villanueva-Myers y el pintor Roberto Lewis. El palacio, un monumento al estilo colonial, todavía conserva su elegancia y buen gusto, y es una de las principales atracciones turísticas del barrio Casco Viejo°.

## Planta baja

### EL PATIO DE LAS GARZAS

Una antigua puerta de hierro° recibe a los visitantes. El patio interior todavía conserva los elementos originales de la construcción: piso de mármol°, columnas cubiertas° de nácar° y una magnífica fuente° de agua en el centro. Aquí están las nueve garzas que le dan el nombre al palacio y que representan las nueve provincias de Panamá.

## Primer piso

### EL SALÓN AMARILLO

Aquí el turista puede visitar una galería de cuarenta y un retratos° de gobernadores y personajes ilustres de Panamá. La principal atracción de este salón es el sillón presidencial, que se usa especialmente cuando hay cambio de presidente. Otros atractivos de esta área son el comedor de Los Tamarindos, que se destaca° por la elegancia de sus muebles y sus lámparas de cristal, y el patio andaluz, con sus coloridos mosaicos que representan la unión de la cultura indígena y la española.

### EL SALÓN DR. BELISARIO PORRAS

Este elegante y majestuoso salón es uno de los lugares más importantes del Palacio de Las Garzas. Lleva su nombre en honor al Dr. Belisario Porras, quien fue tres veces presidente de Panamá (1912–1916, 1918–1920 y 1920–1924).

## Segundo piso

Es el área residencial del palacio y el visitante no tiene acceso a ella. Los armarios, las cómodas y los espejos de la alcoba fueron comprados en Italia y Francia por el presidente Porras, mientras que las alfombras, cortinas y frazadas° son originarias de España.

solicitar *request* casilla *post office box* Garzas *Herons* Casco Viejo *Old Quarter* hierro *iron* mármol *marble* cubiertas *covered* nácar *mother-of-pearl* fuente *fountain* retratos *portraits* se destaca *stands out* frazadas *blankets*

## Preguntas

Contesta las preguntas.

1. ¿Qué sala es notable por sus muebles elegantes y sus lámparas de cristal? el comedor de Los Tamarindos
2. ¿En qué parte del palacio se encuentra la residencia del presidente? en el segundo piso
3. ¿Dónde empiezan los turistas su visita al palacio? en el patio de las Garzas
4. ¿En qué lugar se representa artísticamente la rica herencia cultural de Panamá? en el patio andaluz
5. ¿Qué salón honra la memoria de un gran panameño? el salón Dr. Belisario Porras
6. ¿Qué partes del palacio te gustaría (*would you like*) más visitar? ¿Por qué? Explica tu respuesta. Answers will vary.

## Conversación

En grupos de tres o cuatro estudiantes, hablen sobre lo siguiente: Answers will vary.

1. ¿Qué tiene en común el Palacio de Las Garzas con otras residencias presidenciales u otras casas muy grandes?
2. ¿Te gustaría vivir en el Palacio de Las Garzas? ¿Por qué?
3. Imagina que puedes diseñar tu palacio ideal. Describe los planos para cada piso del palacio.

**Ordenar** Quickly go over the correct order by asking a volunteer to read the sentence he or she believes should be first, another volunteer to read the sentence that should be second, and so forth.

**Preguntas**
• Go over the answers as a class.
• To add a visual aspect to this reading, have students work in pairs to create a detailed floor plan of the **Palacio de Las Garzas.** Then have volunteers use **usted** commands to tell you how to draw the floor plan on the board. Ex: **Dibuje la planta baja. Ponga una fuente de agua en el centro.**

**Conversación** After groups have finished their conversations, encourage the class to discuss the three questions. Ask additional questions, such as: **¿En qué difiere el Palacio de Las Garzas de otras casas? ¿A quién no le gustaría vivir en el Palacio de Las Garzas? ¿Por qué? ¿Quién está de acuerdo?**

---

**TEACHING OPTIONS**

**Variación léxica** Point out that **piso** may mean *floor, flooring; apartment, flat;* or *story* (of a building). In Spanish, the **planta baja** of a building is its ground floor. The second story is called the **primer piso**; the third story is called the **segundo piso**, and so forth. The top floor in a building is called the **planta alta**. In the **Palacio de Las Garzas**, the **segundo piso** is also the **planta alta**.

**Large Groups** Ask students to work in groups of five to role-play a guided tour of the **Palacio de Las Garzas.** One group member plays the guide and the others play tourists. Encourage the guide to develop a script and the tourists to ask questions about the residence and its occupants. Give each group time to prepare and practice before performing its skit for the class.

## Section Goals

In **Escritura**, students will:
- learn to use linking words
- integrate **Lección 12** vocabulary and structures
- write a lease agreement

**Instructional Resources**
**Supersite**
*Cuaderno para hispanohablantes*

**Estrategia** Review the linking words. Point out that they are all words with which students are familiar. Ask volunteers to use a few of them in sentences.

**Tema**
- Review with students the details suggested for inclusion in the lease agreement. You may wish to present the following terms students can use in their agreements: **arrendatario** (*tenant*); **arrendador** (*landlord*); **propietario** (*owner*); **estipulaciones** (*stipulations*); **parte** (*party*); **de anticipación, de antelación** (*in advance*).
- Provide students with samples of legal documents in Spanish. (Many legal forms are downloadable from the Internet.) Go over the format of these documents with students, clarifying legal terminology as necessary.

# Escritura

## Estrategia

### Using linking words

You can make your writing sound more sophisticated by using linking words to connect simple sentences or ideas and create more complex sentences. Consider these passages, which illustrate this effect:

**( Without linking words )**

En la actualidad el edificio tiene tres pisos. Los planos originales muestran una construcción de un piso con un gran patio en el centro. La restauración del palacio comenzó en el año 1922. Los trabajos fueron realizados por el arquitecto Villanueva-Myers y el pintor Roberto Lewis.

**( With linking words )**

En la actualidad el edificio tiene tres pisos, pero los planos originales muestran una construcción de un piso con un gran patio en el centro. La restauración del palacio comenzó en el año 1922 y los trabajos fueron realizados por el arquitecto Villanueva-Myers y el pintor Roberto Lewis.

**( Linking words )**

| | |
|---|---|
| **cuando** | *when* |
| **mientras** | *while* |
| **o** | *or* |
| **pero** | *but* |
| **porque** | *because* |
| **pues** | *since* |
| **que** | *that; who; which* |
| **quien** | *who* |
| **sino** | *but (rather)* |
| **y** | *and* |

## Tema

### Escribir un contrato de arrendamiento°

Eres el/la administrador(a)° de un edificio de apartamentos. Prepara un contrato de arrendamiento para los nuevos inquilinos°. El contrato debe incluir estos detalles:

▶ la dirección° del apartamento y del/de la administrador(a)

▶ las fechas del contrato

▶ el precio del alquiler y el día que se debe pagar

▶ el precio del depósito

▶ información y reglas° acerca de:
  la basura
  el correo
  los animales domésticos
  el ruido°
  los servicios de electricidad y agua
  el uso de electrodomésticos

▶ otros aspectos importantes de la vida comunitaria

**recursos**

panorama.vhlcentral.com
Lección 12

contrato de arrendamiento *lease*   administrador(a) *manager*   inquilinos *tenants*
dirección *address*   reglas *rules*   ruido *noise*

## EVALUATION: Contrato

| Criteria | Scale |
|---|---|
| Content | 1 2 3 4 |
| Organization | 1 2 3 4 |
| Use of vocabulary | 1 2 3 4 |
| Use of linking words | 1 2 3 4 |
| Grammatical accuracy | 1 2 3 4 |

| Scoring | |
|---|---|
| Excellent | 18–20 points |
| Good | 14–17 points |
| Satisfactory | 10–13 points |
| Unsatisfactory | < 10 points |

# Escuchar

## Estrategia
**Using visual cues**

Visual cues like illustrations and headings provide useful clues about what you will hear.

 To practice this strategy, you will listen to a passage related to the following photo. Jot down the clues the photo gives you as you listen.

## Preparación

Mira el dibujo. ¿Qué pistas te da para comprender la conversación que vas a escuchar? ¿Qué significa *bienes raíces*?

## Ahora escucha

Mira los anuncios de esta página y escucha la conversación entre el señor Núñez, Adriana y Felipe. Luego indica si cada descripción se refiere a la casa ideal de Adriana y Felipe, a la casa del anuncio o al apartamento del anuncio.

| Frases | La casa ideal | La casa del anuncio | El apartamento del anuncio |
|---|---|---|---|
| Es barato. | ___ | ___ | ✔ |
| Tiene cuatro alcobas. | ___ | ✔ | ___ |
| Tiene una oficina. | ✔ | ___ | ___ |
| Tiene un balcón. | ___ | ___ | ✔ |
| Tiene una cocina moderna. | ___ | ✔ | ___ |
| Tiene un jardín muy grande. | ___ | ✔ | ___ |
| Tiene un patio. | ✔ | ___ | ___ |

---

**18G**

## Bienes raíces

Se vende.
4 alcobas, 3 baños, cocina moderna, jardín con árboles frutales.
B/. 225.000

Se alquila.
2 alcobas, 1 baño. Balcón. Urbanización Las Brisas. B/. 525

## Comprensión

**Preguntas**

1. ¿Cuál es la relación entre el señor Núñez, Adriana y Felipe? ¿Cómo lo sabes? El Sr. Núñez es el padre de Adriana y Felipe es su esposo.
2. ¿Qué diferencia de opinión hay entre Adriana y Felipe sobre dónde quieren vivir? Felipe prefiere vivir en la ciudad, pero Adriana quiere vivir en las afueras.
3. Usa la información de los dibujos y la conversación para entender lo que dice Adriana al final. ¿Qué significa "todo a su debido tiempo"? Answers will vary.

**Conversación** En parejas, túrnense para hacer y responder a las preguntas. Answers will vary.

1. ¿Qué tienen en común el apartamento y la casa del anuncio con el lugar donde tú vives?
2. ¿Qué piensas de la recomendación del señor Núñez?
3. ¿Qué tipo de sugerencias te da tu familia sobre dónde vivir?
4. ¿Dónde prefieres vivir tú, en un apartamento o en una casa? Explica por qué.

**recursos**
panorama.vhlcentral.com
Lección 12

*NATIONAL communication STANDARDS*

---

## Section Goals

In **Escuchar**, students will:
• use visual clues to help them understand an oral passage
• answer questions based on the content of a recorded conversation

**Instructional Resources**
**Supersite:** Textbook MP3 Audio Files
**Supersite/IRCD:** *IRM* (Textbook Audio Script)

**Estrategia**
**Script** En mi niñez lo pasé muy bien. Vivíamos en una pequeña casa en la isla Colón con vistas al mar. Pasaba las horas buceando alrededor de los arrecifes de coral. A veces me iba a pasear por las plantaciones de bananos o a visitar el pueblo de los indios guayamí. Otros días iba con mi hermano al mar en una pequeña lancha para pescar. Era una vida feliz y tranquila. Ahora vivo en la ciudad de Panamá. ¡Qué diferencia!

**Ahora escucha**
**Script** ADRIANA: Mira, papá, tienen una sección especial de bienes raíces en el periódico. Felipe, mira esta casa... tiene un jardín enorme.
FELIPE: ¡Qué linda! ¡Uy, qué cara! ¿Qué piensa usted? ¿Debemos buscar una casa o un apartamento?
SR. NÚÑEZ: Bueno, hijos, hay muchas cosas que deben considerar. Primero, ¿les gustaría vivir en las afueras o en el centro de la ciudad?
F: Pues, señor Núñez, yo prefiero vivir en la ciudad. Así tenemos el teatro, los parques, los centros comerciales... todo cerca de casa. Sé que Adriana quiere vivir en las afueras porque es más tranquilo.
S: De todos modos van a necesitar un mínimo de dos alcobas, un baño, una sala grande... ¿Qué más?
A: Es importante que tengamos

---

una oficina para mí y un patio para las plantas.
S: Como no tienen mucho dinero ahorrado, es mejor que alquilen un apartamento pequeño por un tiempo. Así pueden ahorrar su dinero para comprar la casa ideal. Miren este apartamento. Tiene un balcón precioso y está en un barrio muy seguro y

bonito. Y el alquiler es muy razonable.
F: Adriana, me parece que tu padre tiene razón. Con un alquiler tan barato, podemos comprar muebles y también ahorrar dinero cada mes.
A: ¡Ay!, quiero mi casa. Pero, bueno, ¡todo a su debido tiempo!

*(Script continues at far left in the bottom panels.)*

# En pantalla

En los países hispanos el costo del servicio de electricidad y de los electrodomésticos es muy caro. Es por esto que no es muy común tener muchos electrodomésticos. Por ejemplo, en los lugares donde hace mucho calor, mucha gente no tiene aire acondicionado°; utiliza los ventiladores°, que usan menos electricidad. Muchas personas lavan los platos a mano o barren el suelo en vez de usar un lavaplatos o una aspiradora.

| Vocabulario útil | |
|---|---|
| fabrica | *manufactures* |
| lavavajillas | lavaplatos |
| aislante | *insulation* |
| campanas | *hoods* |

### Identificar
Indica lo que veas en el anuncio.
- ✔ 1. llaves
- ___ 2. sofá
- ✔ 3. puerta
- ✔ 4. oficina
- ✔ 5. bebé (*baby*)
- ✔ 6. calle
- ✔ 7. despertador
- ___ 8. altillo

### El apartamento
Trabajen en grupos pequeños. Imaginen que terminaron la universidad, consiguieron el trabajo (*job*) de sus sueños (*dreams*) y comparten un apartamento en el centro de una gran ciudad. Describan el apartamento, los muebles y los electrodomésticos y digan qué quehaceres hace cada quien. Answers will vary.

aire acondicionado *air conditioning*  ventiladores *fans*
se agradece *it's appreciated*

**Anuncio de Balay**

**Sabemos lo mucho que se agradece°...**

**...en algunos momentos...**

**...un poco de silencio.**

**recursos**

panorama.vhlcentral.com
Lección 12

**Conexión Internet**
Go to **panorama.vhlcentral.com** to watch the TV clip featured in this **En pantalla** section.

# Oye cómo va

## Rubén Blades

**Rubén Blades** es uno de los vocalistas con más éxito° en la historia de la música panameña. En 1974 se graduó en Derecho° en la Universidad Nacional de Panamá y diez años más tarde hizo un máster de Derecho en la Universidad de Harvard. Ha sido compositor, cantante y también actor de cine. Ha grabado° más de veinte álbumes y ha actuado° en más de treinta películas. En sus canciones expresa su amor por la literatura y la política. En el año 2000 fue nombrado° embajador mundial° contra° el racismo por las Naciones Unidas. Desde el año 2004 es ministro del Instituto Panameño de Turismo.

Tu profesor(a) va a poner la canción en la clase. Escúchala y completa las actividades.

### Completar

Completa las oraciones con la opción correcta.

1. En __b__, Rubén Blades se graduó en Derecho.
   a. 1979　　b. 1974　　c. 1971
2. Le interesan la literatura y __a__.
   a. la política　b. los deportes　c. la tecnología
3. Desde __c__ es ministro de Turismo de Panamá.
   a. 2002　　b. 2003　　c. 2004
4. Trabajó en la película __b__.
   a. *Brick*　　b. *Spin*　　c. *Elf*

### Preguntas

En parejas, respondan a las preguntas. Answers will vary.

1. ¿Esta canción tiene un mensaje positivo o negativo? ¿Cómo lo saben?
2. ¿Qué actitud creen que se debe tomar al final de una etapa (*phase*) o en una despedida importante?
3. ¿Cuáles son las seis cosas más importantes que se van a llevar con ustedes cuando se gradúen?

éxito° *success* Derecho *Law* Ha grabado *He has recorded* ha actuado *he has acted* nombrado *appointed* embajador mundial *world ambassador* contra *against* ciudadanos *citizens* se acabó lo que se daba *what was being given has come to an end* trago *sip* mundo *world* ha participado *has taken part*

## La canción del final del mundo

communication
cultures

Prepárense ciudadanos°:
se acabó lo que se daba°;
a darse el último trago°.
No se me pueden quejar;
el *show* fue bueno y barato.
Ante el dolor, buen humor es esencial.
Por eso saca a tu pareja y ponte a bailar
la canción del final del mundo°;
la canción del final del mundo.

### Rubén Blades en el cine

Una de las facetas artísticas de Rubén Blades es la de actor de cine y televisión en varios países. Algunas de las películas en las que ha participado° son *All the Pretty Horses* (2000), *Once Upon a Time in Mexico* (2003, véase la foto), *Imagining Argentina* (2003) y *Spin* (2005), entre muchas otras.

recursos

panorama.vhlcentral.com
Lección 12

**SUPERSITE Conexión Internet**
Go to **panorama.vhlcentral.com** to learn more about the artist featured in this **Oye cómo va** section.

SUPERSITE

# Panamá

NATIONAL connections cultures STANDARDS

## El país en cifras

▶ **Área:** 78.200 km² (30.193 millas²), *aproximadamente el área de Carolina del Sur*
▶ **Población:** 3.509.000
▶ **Capital:** La Ciudad de Panamá —1.379.000
▶ **Ciudades principales:** Colón, David

SOURCE: Population Division, UN Secretariat

▶ **Moneda:** balboa; Es equivalente al dólar estadounidense.
*En Panamá circulan los billetes de dólar estadounidense. El país centroamericano, sin embargo, acuña° sus propias monedas. "El peso" es una moneda grande equivalente a cincuenta centavos°. La moneda de cinco centavos es llamada frecuentemente "real".*
▶ **Idiomas:** español (oficial), chibcha, inglés
*La mayoría de los panameños es bilingüe. La lengua materna del 14% de los panameños es el inglés.*

Bandera de Panamá

### Panameños célebres

▶ **Rod Carew,** beisbolista (1945– )
▶ **Mireya Moscoso,** política (1947– )
▶ **Rubén Blades,** músico y político (1948– )

acuña *mints* centavos *cents*
Actualmente *Currently*
peaje *toll* promedio *average*

**recursos**
WB pp. 149–150 | VM pp. 251–252 | SUPERSITE panorama.vhlcentral.com Lección 12

Mujer kuna lavando una mola

Un turista disfruta del bosque tropical colgado de un cable.

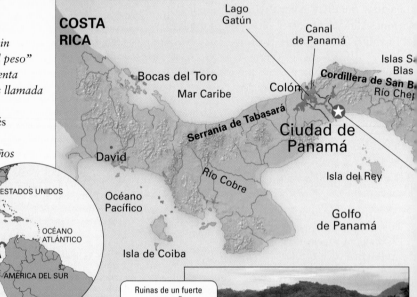
COSTA RICA · Lago Gatún · Canal de Panamá · Bocas del Toro · Mar Caribe · Colón · Cordillera de San Blas · Islas S. Blas · Río Che. · Serranía de Tabasará · Ciudad de Panamá · David · Río Cobre · Isla del Rey · Océano Pacífico · Golfo de Panamá · Isla de Coiba · ESTADOS UNIDOS · OCÉANO ATLÁNTICO · PANAMÁ · AMÉRICA DEL SUR

Ruinas de un fuerte panameño

### ¡Increíble pero cierto!

¿Conocías estos datos sobre el Canal de Panamá?
• Gracias al Canal de Panamá, el viaje en barco de Nueva York a Tokio es 3.000 millas más corto.
• Su construcción costó 639 millones de dólares.
• Actualmente° lo usan 38 barcos al día.
• El peaje° promedio° cuesta 40.000 dólares.

Tokio · Nueva York · PANAMÁ

**TEACHING OPTIONS**

## Lugares • **El Canal de Panamá**

El Canal de Panamá conecta el océano Pacífico con el océano Atlántico. La construcción de este cauce° artificial empezó en 1903 y concluyó diez años después. Es la fuente° principal de ingresos° del país, gracias al dinero que aportan los más de 12.000 buques° que transitan anualmente por esta ruta.

## Artes • **La mola**

La mola es una forma de arte textil de los kunas, una tribu indígena que vive en las islas San Blas. Esta pieza artesanal se confecciona con fragmentos de tela° de colores vivos. Algunos de sus diseños son abstractos, inspirados en las formas del coral, y otros son geométricos, como en las molas más tradicionales. Antiguamente, estos tejidos se usaban como ropa, pero hoy día también sirven para decorar las casas.

## Naturaleza • **El mar**

Panamá, cuyo° nombre significa "lugar de muchos peces°", es un país muy frecuentado por los aficionados del buceo y la pesca. El territorio panameño cuenta con una gran variedad de playas en los dos lados del istmo°, con el mar Caribe a un lado y el océano Pacífico al otro. Algunas de las zonas costeras de esta nación están destinadas al turismo y otras son protegidas por la diversidad de su fauna marina, en la que abundan los arrecifes° de coral. En la playa Bluff, por ejemplo, se pueden observar cuatro especies de tortugas° en peligro° de extinción.

**COLOMBIA**

Vista de la Ciudad de Panamá

 **¿Qué aprendiste?** Responde a cada pregunta con una oración completa.

1. ¿Cuál es la lengua materna del catorce por ciento de los panameños?
   El inglés es la lengua materna del catorce por ciento de los panameños.
2. ¿A qué unidad monetaria (*monetary unit*) es equivalente el balboa?
   El balboa es equivalente al dólar estadounidense.
3. ¿Qué océanos une el Canal de Panamá?
   El Canal de Panamá une los océanos Atlántico y Pacífico.
4. ¿Quién es Rod Carew?
   Rod Carew es un beisbolista panameño.
5. ¿Qué son las molas?
   Las molas son una forma de arte textil común entre los kunas.
6. ¿Cómo son los diseños de las molas?
   Sus diseños son abstractos.
7. ¿Para qué se usaban las molas antes?
   Las molas se usaban como ropa.
8. ¿Cómo son las playas de Panamá?
   Son muy variadas; unas están destinadas al turismo, otras tienen valor ecológico.
9. ¿Qué significa "Panamá"?
   "Panamá" significa "lugar de muchos peces".

 **Conexión Internet** Investiga estos temas en **panorama.vhlcentral.com.**

1. Investiga la historia de las relaciones entre Panamá y los Estados Unidos y la decisión de devolver (*give back*) el Canal de Panamá. ¿Estás de acuerdo con la decisión? Explica tu opinión.
2. Investiga sobre los kunas u otro grupo indígena de Panamá. ¿En qué partes del país viven? ¿Qué lenguas hablan? ¿Cómo es su cultura?

..................................................................................................................

cauce *channel*  fuente *source*  ingresos *income*  buques *ships*  tela *fabric*  cuyo *whose*  peces *fish*  istmo *isthmus*
arrecifes *reefs*  tortugas *turtles*  peligro *danger*

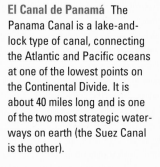

**El Canal de Panamá** The Panama Canal is a lake-and-lock type of canal, connecting the Atlantic and Pacific oceans at one of the lowest points on the Continental Divide. It is about 40 miles long and is one of the two most strategic waterways on earth (the Suez Canal is the other).

**La mola** The Kuna people originally lived on mainland Panama, but preferred to move to the San Blas Islands, where they could maintain their way of life. Elaborate traditions accompany every life-cycle event in Kuna culture, and many of these ceremonies are depicted on the elaborate appliqué **molas**.

**El mar** An excellent place for diving in Panama is the **Parque Nacional Bastimentos**, in the **Archipiélago de Bocas del Toro**. In this nature reserve, turtles nest on some of the beaches. Its coral reefs are home to more than 200 species of tropical fish, in addition to lobsters, manatees, and other marine life. The park is also known for its mangroves, which offer snorkelers another aquatic experience. For more information about **el buceo** and other ocean sports, you may want to show the *Panorama cultural* video footage for this lesson.

**Conexión Internet** Students will find supporting Internet activities and links at **panorama.vhlcentral.com**.

**TEACHING OPTIONS**

**Worth Noting** The Kuna people have a strong, rich oral tradition. During regular community meetings, ritual forms of speaking, including storytelling and speeches, are presented by community elders. It is only over the past decade that a written form of the Kuna language has been developed by outsiders. However, as Spanish—and even English—begin to encroach more into **Kuna Yala** (the Kuna name for their homeland), linguistic anthropologists have highlighted the urgency of recording and preserving the rich Kuna oral tradition, fearing that the traditional Kuna language and culture will begin to be diluted by outside influences.

# El Salvador

## El país en cifras

▸ **Área:** 21.040 km$^2$ (8.124 millas$^2$), el tamaño° de Massachusetts
▸ **Población:** 7.461.000

*El Salvador es el país centroamericano más pequeño y el más densamente° poblado. Su población, al igual que la de Honduras, es muy homogénea: casi el 95 por ciento de la población es mestiza.*

▸ **Capital:** San Salvador—1.662.000
▸ **Ciudades principales:** Soyapango, Santa Ana, San Miguel, Mejicanos

SOURCE: Population Division, UN Secretariat

▸ **Moneda:** dólar estadounidense
▸ **Idiomas:** español (oficial), náhuatl, lenca

Bandera de El Salvador

### Salvadoreños célebres

▸ **Óscar Romero,** arzobispo° y activista por los derechos humanos° (1917–1980)
▸ **Claribel Alegría,** poeta, novelista y cuentista (1924– )
▸ **Roque Dalton,** poeta, ensayista y novelista (1935–1975)
▸ **María Eugenia Brizuela,** política (1956– )

Óscar Romero

tamaño *size* densamente *densely* arzobispo *archbishop* derechos humanos *human rights* laguna *lagoon* sirena *mermaid*

Ruinas de Tazumal

Salvadoreña secando hamacas (*hammocks*)

GUATEMALA

Lago de Guija
Río de la Paz
Santa Ana
Volcán de San Salvador
Río Lempa
Mejicanos · Ilobasco
San Salvador
Soyapango
Volcán de San Vicente
Océano Pacífico
La Libertad
Volcán de San Miguel
San Miguel
Río Torola
Río Goascorán
HONDURAS
Río Lempa
Golfo de Fons

Aeropuerto Ilopango en San Salvador

ESTADOS UNIDOS
OCÉANO ATLÁNTICO
EL SALVADOR
OCÉANO PACÍFICO
AMÉRICA DEL SUR

**recursos**

| WB pp. 151–152 | VM pp. 253–254 | SUPERSITE panorama.vhlcentral.com Lección 12 |

## ¡Increíble pero cierto!

El rico folklore salvadoreño se basa sobre todo en sus extraordinarios recursos naturales. Por ejemplo, según una leyenda, las muertes que se producen en la laguna° de Alegría tienen su explicación en la existencia de una sirena° solitaria que vive en el lago y captura a los jóvenes atractivos.

---

## Deportes • El surfing

El Salvador es uno de los destinos favoritos en Latinoamérica para la práctica del surfing. Cuenta con 300 kilómetros de costa a lo largo del océano Pacífico y sus olas° altas son ideales para quienes practican este deporte. De sus playas, La Libertad es la más visitada por surfistas de todo el mundo, gracias a que está muy cerca de la capital salvadoreña. Sin embargo°, los fines de semana muchos visitantes prefieren viajar a la Costa del Bálsamo, donde se concentra menos gente.

## Naturaleza • El Parque Nacional Montecristo

El Parque Nacional Montecristo se encuentra en la región norte del país. Se le conoce también como El Trifinio porque se ubica° en el punto donde se unen° Guatemala, Honduras y El Salvador. En este bosque hay muchas especies vegetales y animales, como orquídeas, monos araña°, pumas, quetzales y tucanes. Además, las copas de sus enormes árboles forman una bóveda° que impide° el paso de la luz solar. Este espacio natural se encuentra a una altitud de 2.400 metros (7.900 pies) sobre el nivel del mar y recibe 200 centímetros (80 pulgadas°) de lluvia al año.

## Artes • La artesanía de Ilobasco

Ilobasco es un pueblo conocido por sus artesanías°. En él se elaboran objetos con arcilla° y cerámica pintada a mano, como juguetes°, adornos° y utensilios de cocina. Además, son famosas sus "sorpresas", que son pequeñas piezas° de cerámica en cuyo interior se representan escenas de la vida diaria. Los turistas realizan excursiones para conocer paso a paso° la fabricación de estos productos.

 **¿Qué aprendiste?** Responde a cada pregunta con una oración completa.

1. ¿Qué tienen en común las poblaciones de El Salvador y Honduras?
   Las poblaciones de los dos países son muy homogéneas.

2. ¿Qué es el náhuatl?
   El náhuatl es un idioma que se habla en El Salvador.

3. ¿Quién es María Eugenia Brizuela?
   Es una política salvadoreña.

4. Hay muchos lugares ideales para el surfing en El Salvador. ¿Por qué? Porque El Salvador recibe algunas de las mejores olas del océano Pacífico.

5. ¿A qué altitud se encuentra el Parque Nacional Montecristo? Se encuentra a una altitud de 2.400 metros.

6. ¿Cuáles son algunos de los animales y las plantas que viven en este parque?
   Hay orquídeas, hongos, monos araña, pumas, quetzales y tucanes.

7. ¿Por qué al Parque Nacional Montecristo se le llama también El Trifinio? Porque es el punto donde se unen Guatemala, Honduras y El Salvador.

8. ¿Por qué es famoso el pueblo de Ilobasco? Es famoso por los objetos de arcilla y por la cerámica pintada a mano.

9. ¿Qué se puede ver en un viaje a Ilobasco? Se puede ver la fabricación de los artículos de cerámica paso a paso.

10. ¿Qué son las "sorpresas" de Ilobasco? Las "sorpresas" son pequeñas piezas de cerámica con escenas de la vida diaria en su interior.

 **Conexión Internet** Investiga estos temas en **panorama.vhlcentral.com**.

1. El Parque Nacional Montecristo es una reserva natural; busca información sobre otros parques o zonas protegidas en El Salvador. ¿Cómo son estos lugares? ¿Qué tipos de plantas y animales se encuentran allí?

2. Busca información sobre museos u otros lugares turísticos en San Salvador (u otra ciudad de El Salvador).

olas *waves*  Sin embargo *However*  se ubica *it is located*  se unen *come together*  monos araña *spider monkeys*  bóveda *canopy*  impide *blocks*  pulgadas *inches*  artesanías *crafts*  arcilla *clay*  juguetes *toys*  adornos *ornaments*  piezas *pieces*  paso a paso *step by step*

**Instructional Resources**
**Supersite:** Textbook &
Vocabulary MP3 Audio Files
**Lección 12**
**Supersite/IRCD:** *IRM* (WBs/
VM/LM Answer Key); *Testing
Program* (**Lección 12 Pruebas,**
Test Generator, Testing
Program MP3 Audio Files)
**WebSAM**
**Lab Manual,** p. 72

## Las viviendas

| | |
|---|---|
| las afueras | suburbs; outskirts |
| el alquiler | rent (payment) |
| el ama (m., f.) de casa | housekeeper; caretaker |
| el barrio | neighborhood |
| el edificio de apartamentos | apartment building |
| el/la vecino/a | neighbor |
| la vivienda | housing |
| alquilar | to rent |
| mudarse | to move (from one house to another) |

## Los cuartos y otros lugares

| | |
|---|---|
| el altillo | attic |
| el balcón | balcony |
| la cocina | kitchen |
| el comedor | dining room |
| el dormitorio | bedroom |
| la entrada | entrance |
| la escalera | stairs; stairway |
| el garaje | garage |
| el jardín | garden; yard |
| la oficina | office |
| el pasillo | hallway |
| el patio | patio; yard |
| la sala | living room |
| el sótano | basement; cellar |

## Los muebles y otras cosas

| | |
|---|---|
| la alfombra | carpet; rug |
| la almohada | pillow |
| el armario | closet |
| el cartel | poster |
| la cómoda | chest of drawers |
| las cortinas | curtains |
| el cuadro | picture |
| el estante | bookcase; bookshelves |
| la lámpara | lamp |
| la luz | light; electricity |
| la manta | blanket |
| la mesita | end table |
| la mesita de noche | night stand |
| los muebles | furniture |
| la pared | wall |
| la pintura | painting; picture |
| el sillón | armchair |
| el sofá | couch; sofa |

## Los electrodomésticos

| | |
|---|---|
| la cafetera | coffee maker |
| la cocina, la estufa | stove |
| el congelador | freezer |
| el electrodoméstico | electric appliance |
| el horno (de microondas) | (microwave) oven |
| la lavadora | washing machine |
| el lavaplatos | dishwasher |
| el refrigerador | refrigerator |
| la secadora | clothes dryer |
| la tostadora | toaster |

## La mesa

| | |
|---|---|
| la copa | wineglass; goblet |
| la cuchara | (table or large) spoon |
| el cuchillo | knife |
| el plato | plate |
| la servilleta | napkin |
| la taza | cup |
| el tenedor | fork |
| el vaso | glass |

## Los quehaceres domésticos

| | |
|---|---|
| arreglar | to neaten; to straighten up |
| barrer el suelo | to sweep the floor |
| cocinar | to cook |
| ensuciar | to get (something) dirty |
| hacer la cama | to make the bed |
| hacer quehaceres domésticos | to do household chores |
| lavar (el suelo, los platos) | to wash (the floor, the dishes) |
| limpiar la casa | to clean the house |
| pasar la aspiradora | to vacuum |
| planchar la ropa | to iron the clothes |
| poner la mesa | to set the table |
| quitar la mesa | to clear the table |
| quitar el polvo | to dust |
| sacar la basura | to take out the trash |
| sacudir los muebles | to dust the furniture |

## Verbos y expresiones verbales

| | |
|---|---|
| aconsejar | to advise |
| insistir (en) | to insist (on) |
| mandar | to order |
| recomendar (e:ie) | to recommend |
| rogar (o:ue) | to beg; to plead |
| sugerir (e:ie) | to suggest |
| Es bueno que... | It's good that... |
| Es importante que... | It's important that... |
| Es malo que... | It's bad that... |
| Es mejor que... | It's better that... |
| Es necesario que... | It's necessary that... |
| Es urgente que... | It's urgent that... |

| | |
|---|---|
| **Expresiones útiles** | See page 381. |
| **Relative pronouns** | See page 386. |

recursos

LM
p. 72

panorama.vhlcentral.com
Lección 12

# La naturaleza

## 13

**Lesson Goals**

In **Lección 13**, students will be introduced to the following:
- terms to describe nature and the environment
- conservation and recycling terms
- the Andes mountain range
- Colombia's Santa Marta mountain range
- subjunctive with verbs and expressions of emotion
- subjunctive with verbs and expressions of doubt, disbelief, and denial
- expressions of certainty
- subjunctive with conjunctions
- when the infinitive follows a conjunction
- forming regular past participles
- irregular past participles
- past participles used as adjectives
- recognizing the purpose of a text
- cultural, geographic, and historical information about Colombia
- cultural and geographic information about Honduras

**A primera vista** Here are some additional questions you can ask based on the photo: **¿Vives en la ciudad? ¿En las afueras? ¿En el campo? ¿Te gusta pasar tiempo fuera de la casa? ¿Por qué? ¿Escalas montañas? ¿Te gusta acampar? ¿Dónde puedes hacer estas actividades?**

**A PRIMERA VISTA**
- ¿Son estas personas excursionistas?
- ¿Es importante que usen zapatos deportivos?
- ¿Se llevan bien o mal?
- ¿Se divierten o no?

---

**INSTRUCTIONAL RESOURCES**

**MAESTRO™ SUPERSITE (panorama.vhlcentral.com)**
Textbook, Vocabulary, & Lab MP3 Audio Files
Additional Practice
Learning Management System (Assignment Task Manager, Gradebook)
*Also on DVD*
  **Fotonovela**

*Flash cultura*
*Panorama cultural*
*Also on Instructor's Resource CD-ROM*
*PowerPoints* (**Contextos** & **Estructura** Presentations, Overheads)
*Instructor's Resource Manual* (Handouts, Textbook Answer Key, WBs/VM/LM Answer Key,

Audioscripts, Videoscripts & Translations)
*Testing Program* (**Pruebas,** Test Generator, MP3s)
**WebSAM** (Workbook/Video Manual/Lab Manual)
**Workbook/Video Manual**
*Cuaderno para hispanohablantes*
**Lab Manual**

# La naturaleza

## Más vocabulario

| | |
|---|---|
| el animal | *animal* |
| el bosque (tropical) | *(tropical; rain) forest* |
| el desierto | *desert* |
| la naturaleza | *nature* |
| la planta | *plant* |
| la selva, la jungla | *jungle* |
| la tierra | *land; soil* |
| el cielo | *sky* |
| la estrella | *star* |
| la luna | *moon* |
| la conservación | *conservation* |
| la contaminación (del aire; del agua) | *(air; water) pollution* |
| la deforestación | *deforestation* |
| la ecología | *ecology* |
| el ecoturismo | *ecotourism* |
| la energía (nuclear; solar) | *(nuclear; solar) energy* |
| la extinción | *extinction* |
| la lluvia (ácida) | *(acid) rain* |
| el medio ambiente | *environment* |
| el peligro | *danger* |
| el recurso natural | *natural resource* |
| la solución | *solution* |
| el gobierno | *government* |
| la ley | *law* |
| la población | *population* |
| puro/a | *pure* |

### Variación léxica

hierba ⟷ pasto (*Perú*); grama (*Venez., Col.*); zacate (*Méx.*)

**recursos**

| WB pp. 155-156 | LM p. 73 | SUPERSITE panorama.vhlcentral.com Lección 13 |

el ave, el pájaro — el cráter — el volcán — el pez — la vaca — el árbol — la hierba — el perro — el gato

- la nube
- el sol
- el valle
- el sendero
- el lago
- la piedra
- el río
- la flor

# Práctica

**1** **Escuchar** Mientras escuchas estas oraciones, anota los sustantivos (*nouns*) que se refieren a las plantas, los animales, la tierra y el cielo.

| Plantas | Animales | Tierra | Cielo |
|---------|----------|--------|-------|
| flores | perro | valle | sol |
| hierba | gatos | volcán | nubes |
| árboles | vacas | bosques tropicales | estrellas |

**2** **¿Cierto o falso?** Escucha las oraciones e indica si lo que dice cada una es **cierto** o **falso**, según el dibujo.

1. cierto
2. falso
3. falso
4. cierto
5. cierto
6. falso

**3** **Seleccionar** Selecciona la palabra que no está relacionada.

1. estrella • gobierno • luna • sol   gobierno
2. lago • río • mar • peligro   peligro
3. vaca • gato • pájaro • población   población
4. cielo • cráter • aire • nube   cráter
5. desierto • solución • selva • bosque   solución
6. flor • hierba • sendero • árbol   sendero

**4** **Definir** Trabaja con un(a) compañero/a para definir o describir cada palabra. Sigue el modelo. Answers will vary.

> **modelo**
> **Estudiante 1:** ¿Qué es el cielo?
> **Estudiante 2:** El cielo está sobre la tierra y tiene nubes.

1. la población
2. un valle
3. la lluvia
4. la naturaleza
5. un desierto
6. la extinción
7. la ecología
8. un sendero

**5** **Describir** Trabajen en parejas para describir estas fotos. Answers will vary.

**1** Teaching Tip Check the answers orally as a class.

**1** Script 1. Mi novio siempre me compra flores para nuestro aniversario. 2. Cuando era pequeño, jugaba con mi perro todo el tiempo. 3. Javier prefiere jugar al fútbol norteamericano sobre hierba natural. 4. Antes de las vacaciones, los estudiantes tomaban el sol en el parque. 5. No puedo visitarte porque soy alérgico a los gatos. *Script continues on page 418.*

**2** Teaching Tip To challenge students, have them correct the false statements.

**2** Script 1. Hay un gato jugando con un perro. 2. La vaca está en un sendero de la montaña. 3. No hay nubes sobre el valle. 4. La vaca está comiendo hierba. 5. Una pareja come sobre la hierba. 6. Las piedras están lejos del río. *Textbook MP3s*

**3** Teaching Tip Have students give answers and state a category for each group. Ex: **1. cosas que están en el cielo**

**4** Expansion Have pairs read their definitions aloud in random order for the class to guess which term is being described.

**5** Teaching Tip To simplify, give students these guidelines to help them prepare their descriptions: objects in the photos, colors, what the weather is like, the time of day, the country where the photo was taken.

**5** Expansion For each photo, ask students to describe objects, colors, weather, time of day, and the country where the photo may have been taken.

---

**TEACHING OPTIONS**

**TPR** Make a series of true-false statements related to the lesson theme using the vocabulary. Tell students to remain seated if a statement is true and to stand if it is false. Ex: **A los gatos les gusta nadar en los lagos.** (Students stand.) **Los carros son responsables en parte de la contaminación del aire.** (Students remain seated.)

**Game** Have students fold a sheet of paper into sixteen squares (four folds in half) and choose one vocabulary word to write in each square. Call out definitions for the vocabulary words. If students have the defined word, they mark their paper. The first student to mark four words in a row (across, down, or diagonally) calls out ¡**Loto!** Have the student read aloud his or her words to check if the definitions have been given.

**1 Script (continued)**

6. Durante la tormenta, las nubes grises cubrían toda la ciudad. 7. Cerca de la casa de mi hermana hay un valle donde siempre hay muchas vacas. 8. Algunas noches vamos al campo para ver las estrellas. 9. El Puracé es un volcán activo en los Andes colombianos. 10. Los árboles de los bosques tropicales contienen las curas para muchas enfermedades.
*Textbook MP3s*

**Teaching Tip** Involve students in a discussion about recycling and conservation. Show *Overhead PowerPoint #51* and ask volunteers to describe what is happening in the drawing. Ask: **¿Qué hace la señora de la izquierda? (Recicla una lata de aluminio.)** Cover the active vocabulary, then ask about students' own experiences and opinions. Ex: **¿Tiene un buen programa de reciclaje nuestra ciudad? ¿Qué hacen ustedes para reducir la contaminación del medio ambiente? ¿Qué hace la universidad? ¿Cómo estamos afectados por la contaminación en nuestra ciudad/región? ¿Cuál es el mayor problema ecológico de nuestra región? ¿Qué evitan ustedes por razones ecológicas?**

**6 Expansion**
- Ask questions that require students to recycle the activity vocabulary. Ex: **¿Qué debemos hacer para mantener las calles limpias de basura? ¿Para qué trabajan los científicos? ¿Por qué es necesario que trabajemos para proteger el medio ambiente?**
- Have students write five additional sentences, using different forms of the verbs. Ask volunteers to share their sentences with the class.

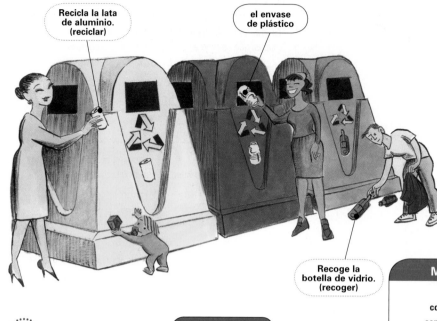

El reciclaje

Recicla la lata de aluminio. (reciclar)

el envase de plástico

Recoge la botella de vidrio. (recoger)

**Más vocabulario**

| | |
|---|---|
| cazar | *to hunt* |
| conservar | *to conserve* |
| contaminar | *to pollute* |
| controlar | *to control* |
| cuidar | *to take care of* |
| dejar de (+ *inf.*) | *to stop (doing something)* |
| desarrollar | *to develop* |
| descubrir | *to discover* |
| destruir | *to destroy* |
| estar afectado/a (por) | *to be affected (by)* |
| estar contaminado/a | *to be polluted* |
| evitar | *to avoid* |
| mejorar | *to improve* |
| proteger | *to protect* |
| reducir | *to reduce* |
| resolver (o:ue) | *to resolve; to solve* |
| respirar | *to breathe* |

**6** **Completar** Selecciona la palabra o la expresión adecuada para completar cada oración.

| | | |
|---|---|---|
| contaminar | destruyen | reciclamos |
| controlan | están afectadas | recoger |
| cuidan | mejoramos | resolver |
| descubrir | proteger | se desarrollaron |

1. Si vemos basura en las calles, la debemos ____recoger____.
2. Los científicos trabajan para ____descubrir____ nuevas soluciones.
3. Es necesario que todos trabajemos juntos para ____resolver____ los problemas del medio ambiente.
4. Debemos ____proteger____ el medio ambiente porque hoy día está en peligro.
5. Muchas leyes nuevas ____controlan____ el número de árboles que se puede cortar (*cut down*).
6. Las primeras civilizaciones ____se desarrollaron____ cerca de los ríos y los mares.
7. Todas las personas ____están afectadas____ por la contaminación.
8. Los turistas deben tener cuidado de no ____contaminar____ los lugares que visitan.
9. Podemos conservar los recursos si ____reciclamos____ el aluminio, el vidrio y el plástico.
10. La lluvia ácida, la contaminación y la deforestación ____destruyen____ el medio ambiente.

---

**TEACHING OPTIONS**

**Pairs** Have pairs of students write each vocabulary word from this page on index cards. Pairs then shuffle the cards and take turns drawing from the stack. The student who draws a card then must make a comment about conservation or the environment, using the word he or she has drawn. One partner writes down the other's comment. After students finish the stack, call on volunteers to share their comments.

**Small Groups** Divide the class into groups of three or four. Have each group make a list of eight environmental problems in the region. Ask groups to trade lists. Have them write solutions to the problems on the list they receive, and then give the lists back to the original group. After reading the solutions, the original groups should give reasons why the solutions are viable or not.

# Comunicación

**7** **¿Es importante?** Lee este párrafo y, en parejas, contesta las preguntas. *Some answers will vary.*

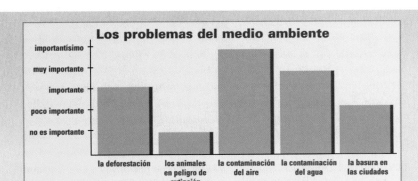

**Los problemas del medio ambiente**

importantísimo
muy importante
importante
poco importante
no es importante

la deforestación | los animales en peligro de extinción | la contaminación del aire | la contaminación del agua | la basura en las ciudades

**Para celebrar El día de la tierra**, una estación de radio colombiana hizo una pequeña encuesta entre estudiantes universitarios, donde les preguntaron sobre los problemas del medio ambiente. Se les preguntó cuáles creían que eran los cinco problemas más importantes del medio ambiente. Ellos también tenían que decidir el orden de importancia de estos problemas, del uno al cinco.

Los resultados probaron (*proved*) que la mayoría de los estudiantes están preocupados por la contaminación del aire. Muchos mencionaron que no hay aire puro en las ciudades. El problema número dos para los estudiantes es que los ríos y los lagos están afectados por la contaminación. La deforestación quedó como el problema número tres, la basura en las ciudades como el número cuatro y los animales en peligro de extinción como el número cinco.

1. ¿Según la encuesta, qué problema consideran más grave? ¿Qué problema consideran menos grave? la contaminación del aire; los animales en peligro de extinción

2. ¿Cómo creen que se puede evitar o resolver el problema más importante?

3. ¿Es necesario resolver el problema menos importante? ¿Por qué?

4. ¿Consideran ustedes que existen los mismos problemas en su comunidad? Den algunos ejemplos.

**8** **Situaciones** Trabajen en grupos pequeños para representar estas situaciones. *Answers will vary.*

1. Unos/as representantes de una agencia ambiental (*environmental*) hablan con el/la presidente/a de una compañía industrial que está contaminando un río o el aire.

2. Un(a) guía de ecoturismo habla con un grupo sobre cómo disfrutar (*enjoy*) de la naturaleza y conservar el medio ambiente.

3. Un(a) representante de la universidad habla con un grupo de nuevos estudiantes sobre la campaña (*campaign*) ambiental de la universidad y trata de reclutar (*tries to recruit*) miembros para un club que trabaja para la protección del medio ambiente.

**9** **Escribir una carta** Trabajen en parejas para escribir una carta a una empresa real o imaginaria que esté contaminando el medio ambiente. Expliquen las consecuencias que sus acciones van a tener para el medio ambiente. Sugiéranle algunas ideas para que solucione el problema. Utilicen por lo menos diez palabras de **Contextos**. *Answers will vary.*

---

**7** **Expansion** Divide the class into groups of five to discuss questions 2–4. Groups should reach a consensus for each question, then report to the class.

**8** **Teaching Tip** Divide the class into groups of three or four. Have each group choose a situation, but make sure that all situations are covered. Have students take turns playing each role. After groups have had time to prepare their situations, invite some of them to present them to the class.

**9** **Teaching Tips**
• Remind students that a business letter in Spanish begins with a salutation, such as **Estimado(s) señor(es)**, and ends with a closing such as **Atentamente**.
• With the class, brainstorm a list of agencies or companies that are known to be environmentally conscious. Ask the class to categorize the companies by the steps they take to protect the environment. Then divide the class into pairs and have them choose a company for the activity.

---

**TEACHING OPTIONS**

**Heritage Speakers** Ask heritage speakers to interview family members or people in their community about the environmental challenges in their families' countries of origin. Encourage them to find out how the problems affect the land and the people. Have students report their findings to the class.
**Large Group** Prepare two sets of index cards, one with environmental problems and the other with possible solutions.

Ex: **la destrucción de los bosques – reducir las áreas de deforestación; la contaminación de los ríos – controlar el tipo de sustancias que hay en el agua**. Shuffle the two sets of cards and distribute them. Have students with problem cards circulate around the room, asking their classmates questions until they find a viable solution.

# ¡Qué paisaje más hermoso!

**Martín y los estudiantes visitan el sendero en las montañas.**

**PERSONAJES**

**MAITE**

**INÉS**

**DON FRANCISCO**

**ÁLEX**

**JAVIER**

**MARTÍN**

**DON FRANCISCO** Chicos, les presento a Martín Dávalos, el guía de la excursión. Martín, nuestros pasajeros: Maite, Javier, Inés y Álex.

**MARTÍN** Mucho gusto. Voy a llevarlos al área donde vamos a ir de excursión mañana. ¿Qué les parece?

**ESTUDIANTES** ¡Sí! ¡Vamos!

**MAITE** ¡Qué paisaje más hermoso!

**INÉS** No creo que haya lugares más bonitos en el mundo.

**JAVIER** Entiendo que mañana vamos a cruzar un río. ¿Está contaminado?

**MARTÍN** En las montañas el río no parece estar afectado por la contaminación. Cerca de las ciudades, sin embargo, el río tiene bastante contaminación.

**ÁLEX** ¡Qué aire tan puro se respira aquí! No es como en la Ciudad de México... Tenemos un problema gravísimo de contaminación.

**MARTÍN** A menos que resuelvan ese problema, los habitantes van a sufrir muchas enfermedades en el futuro.

**INÉS** Creo que todos debemos hacer algo para proteger el medio ambiente.

**MAITE** Yo creo que todos los países deben establecer leyes que controlen el uso de automóviles.

**recursos**

VM
pp. 219–220

panorama.vhlcentral.com
Lección 13

---

**MARTÍN** Esperamos que ustedes se diviertan mucho, pero es necesario que cuiden la naturaleza.

**JAVIER** Se pueden tomar fotos, ¿verdad?

**MARTÍN** Sí, con tal de que no toques las flores o las plantas.

**ÁLEX** ¿Hay problemas de contaminación en esta región?

**MARTÍN** La contaminación es un problema en todo el mundo. Pero aquí tenemos un programa de reciclaje. Si ves por el sendero botellas, papeles o latas, recógelos.

**JAVIER** Pero Maite, ¿tú vas a dejar de usar tu carro en Madrid?

**MAITE** Pues voy a tener que usar el metro... Pero tú sabes que mi coche es tan pequeñito... casi no contamina nada.

**INÉS** ¡Ven, Javier!

**JAVIER** ¡¡Ya voy!!

## Expresiones útiles

### Talking about the environment

- ¿Hay problemas de contaminación en esta región?
  *Are there problems with pollution in this region/area?*
  **La contaminación es un problema en todo el mundo.**
  *Pollution is a problem throughout the world.*

- ¿Está contaminado el río?
  *Is the river polluted?*
  **En las montañas el río no parece estar afectado por la contaminación.**
  *In the mountains, the river does not seem to be affected by pollution.*
  **Cerca de las ciudades el río tiene bastante contaminación.**
  *Near the cities, the river is pretty polluted.*

- ¡Qué aire tan puro se respira aquí!
  *The air you breathe here is so pure!*

- Puedes tomar fotos, con tal de que no toques las plantas.
  *You can take pictures, provided that you don't touch the plants.*

- Es necesario que cuiden la naturaleza.
  *It's necessary that you take care of nature/respect the environment.*

- Tenemos un problema gravísimo de contaminación.
  *We have an extremely serious problem with pollution.*

- A menos que resuelvan el problema, los habitantes van a sufrir muchas enfermedades.
  *Unless they solve the problem, the inhabitants are going to suffer many illnesses.*

- Tenemos un programa de reciclaje.
  *We have a recycling program.*

- Si ves por el sendero botellas, papeles o latas, recógelos.
  *If you see bottles, papers, or cans along the trail, pick them up.*

# ¿Qué pasó?

**1** **Seleccionar** Selecciona la respuesta más lógica para completar cada oración.

1. Martín va a llevar a los estudiantes al lugar donde van a _____c_____.
   a. contaminar el río  b. bailar  c. ir de excursión

2. El río está más afectado por la contaminación _____b_____.
   a. cerca de los bosques  b. en las ciudades  c. en las montañas

3. Martín quiere que los estudiantes _____a_____.
   a. limpien los senderos  b. descubran nuevos senderos  c. no usen sus autos

4. La naturaleza está formada por _____c_____.
   a. los ríos, las montañas y las leyes  b. los animales, las latas y los ríos
   c. los lagos, los animales y las plantas

5. La contaminación del aire puede producir _____b_____.
   a. problemas del estómago  b. enfermedades respiratorias  c. enfermedades mentales

**2** **Identificar** Identifica quién puede decir estas oraciones. Puedes usar algunos nombres más de una vez.

1. Es necesario que hagamos algo por el medio ambiente, ¿pero qué? Inés
2. En mi ciudad es imposible respirar aire limpio. ¡Está muy contaminado! Álex
3. En el futuro, a causa del problema de la contaminación, las personas van a tener problemas de salud. Martín
4. El metro es una excelente alternativa al coche. Maite
5. ¿Está limpio o contaminado el río? Javier
6. Es importante reciclar latas y botellas. Martín
7. De todos los lugares del mundo, me parece que éste es el mejor. Inés
8. Como todo el mundo usa automóviles, debemos establecer leyes para controlar cómo y cuándo usarlos. Maite

**ÁLEX**  **INÉS**  **MAITE**  **MARTÍN**  **JAVIER**

**3** **Preguntas** Responde a estas preguntas usando la información de **Fotonovela**.

1. Según Martín, ¿qué es necesario que hagan los estudiantes? ¿Qué no pueden hacer?
   Es necesario que cuiden la naturaleza. No pueden tocar las plantas ni las flores.
2. ¿Qué problemas del medio ambiente mencionan Martín y los estudiantes?
   Hay problemas de contaminación del aire y de los ríos.
3. ¿Qué cree Maite que deben hacer los países?
   Los países deben establecer leyes que controlen el uso de los automóviles.
4. ¿Qué cosas se pueden reciclar? Menciona tres.
   Se pueden reciclar las botellas, los papeles y las latas.
5. ¿Qué otro medio de transporte importante dice Maite que hay en Madrid?
   Dice que el metro es importante.

**4** **El medio ambiente** En parejas, discutan algunos problemas ambientales y sus posibles soluciones. Usen estas preguntas y frases en su conversación.
Answers will vary.

- ¿Hay problemas de contaminación donde vives?
- Tenemos un problema muy grave de contaminación de...
- ¿Cómo podemos resolver los problemas de la contaminación?

# Ortografía

## Los signos de puntuación

In Spanish, as in English, punctuation marks are important because they help you express your ideas in a clear, organized way.

> **No podía ver las llaves. Las buscó por los estantes, las mesas, las sillas, el suelo; minutos después, decidió mirar por la ventana. Allí estaban…**

The **punto y coma** (;), the **tres puntos** (…), and the **punto** (.) are used in very similar ways in Spanish and English.

> **Argentina, Brasil, Paraguay y Uruguay son miembros de Mercosur.**

In Spanish, the **coma** (,) is not used before **y** or **o** in a series.

| 13,5% | 29,2° | 3.000.000 | $2.999,99 |
|---|---|---|---|

In numbers, Spanish uses a **coma** where English uses a decimal point and a **punto** where English uses a comma.

 **Cómo te llamas**    **¿Dónde está?**    **¡Ven aquí!**    **Hola**

Questions in Spanish are preceded and followed by **signos de interrogación** (¿ ?), and exclamations are preceded and followed by **signos de exclamación** (¡ !).

**Práctica** Lee el párrafo e indica los signos de puntuación necesarios. *Answers will vary.*

Ayer recibí la invitación de boda de Marta mi amiga colombiana inmediatamente empecé a pensar en un posible regalo fui al almacén donde Marta y su novio tenían una lista de regalos había de todo copas cafeteras tostadoras finalmente decidí regalarles un perro ya sé que es un regalo extraño pero espero que les guste a los dos

**¿Palabras de amor?** El siguiente diálogo tiene diferentes significados (*meanings*) dependiendo de los signos de puntuación que utilices y el lugar donde los pongas. Intenta encontrar los diferentes significados.
*Answers will vary.*

| | |
|---|---|
| **JULIÁN** | me quieres |
| **MARISOL** | no puedo vivir sin ti |
| **JULIÁN** | me quieres dejar |
| **MARISOL** | no me parece mala idea |
| **JULIÁN** | no eres feliz conmigo |
| **MARISOL** | no soy feliz |

**recursos**

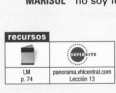

LM p. 74    panorama.vhlcentral.com Lección 13

---

## Section Goal

In **Ortografía**, students will learn the use of punctuation marks in Spanish.

**Instructional Resources**
**Supersite:** Lab MP3 Audio Files
**Lección 13**
**Supersite/IRCD:** *IRM* (Lab Audio Script, WBs/VM/LM Answer Key)
**WebSAM**
**Lab Manual,** p. 74
*Cuaderno para hispanohablantes*

## Teaching Tips

- Explain that there is no space before or between ellipsis marks in Spanish. There is, however, a space after them.
- Model reading the numerical examples. Ex: **13,5% = trece coma cinco por ciento.** Write numbers on the board for translations into Spanish. Ex: 89.3%; 5,020,307; $13.50.
- Explain that the inverted question mark or exclamation point does not always come at the beginning of a sentence, but where the question or exclamation begins. Ex:
  —**¿Cómo estás, Mirta?**
  —**¡Bien! Y tú, ¿cómo estás?**
  —**¡Ay, me duele la cabeza!**
- Point out that **Ortografía** replaces **Pronunciación** in the Student Edition for **Lecciones 10–15**, but not in the Lab Manual. The **Recursos** box references the **Pronunciación** sections found in all lessons of the Lab Manual.

**¿Palabras de amor?** Two possibilities for punctuation:

J: ¿Me quieres?
M: ¡No puedo vivir sin ti!
J: ¿Me quieres dejar?
M: No. Me parece mala idea.
J: ¿No eres feliz conmigo?
M: No. Soy feliz.

J: ¿Me quieres?
M: No. Puedo vivir sin ti.
J: ¡Me quieres dejar!
M: No me parece mala idea.
J: ¿No eres feliz conmigo?
M: No soy feliz.

---

**TEACHING OPTIONS**

**Pairs** Have pairs write example sentences for each of the four punctuation rules explained in **Ortografía**. Ask volunteers to write their sentences on the board and have the class identify the rules.
**Video** Photocopy the *Fotonovela* Videoscript (Supersite/IRCD) and white out the punctuation in order to make a master for a cloze activity. Distribute the photocopies and, as you replay the

episode, have students mark the punctuation.
**Extra Practice** To simplify the **¿Palabras de amor?** activity, go over the dialogue and point out how it can be punctuated in different ways to express opposite meanings. Reinforce this by having students work in pairs to dramatize the dialogue in both ways. Ask a few pairs to role-play the contrasting dialogues for the class.

## Section Goals

In **Cultura**, students will:
- read about the Andes mountain range
- learn nature-related terms
- read about Colombia's **Sierra Nevada de Santa Marta**
- read about important lakes in Latin America

---

**Instructional Resources**
**Supersite:** *IRM* (*Flash cultura* Videoscript & Translation)
**Supersite/DVD:** *Flash cultura*
*Cuaderno para hispanohablantes*

---

**En detalle**

**Antes de leer** Preview the reading by asking these questions: **¿Qué montañas conocen? ¿Qué les parece más interesante, pasar tiempo en la playa o en las montañas? ¿Por qué?**

**Lectura**
- Point out that the Andes pass through seven different countries.
- Tell students that the highest area of the Andes is known as the **altiplano**, where farmers raise sheep, llamas, alpacas, and vicuñas. They use these animals' wool to make clothing and blankets.
- Add a visual aspect to this reading. Bring in topographic maps of Spain, Central America, and South America and indicate other important mountain ranges in Spanish-speaking countries, such as **los Pirineos** (Spain), or **la Sierra Madre Occidental** and **Oriental** (Mexico).

**Después de leer** Ask students what facts from this reading are new or surprising to them.

**1 Teaching Tip** To challenge students, rephrase the items as comprehension questions. Ex: **1. ¿Qué es "la espina dorsal de Suramérica"?**

---

**EN DETALLE**

# ¡Los Andes se mueven!

**Los Andes,** la cadena° de montañas más extensa de las Américas, son conocidos como "la espina dorsal° de Suramérica". Sus 7.240 kilómetros (4.500 millas) van desde el norte° de la región entre Venezuela y Colombia, hasta el extremo sur°, entre Argentina y Chile, y pasan por casi todos los países suramericanos. La cordillera° de los Andes, formada hace 27 millones de años, es la segunda más alta del mundo, después de los Himalayas (aunque° ésta última es mucho más "joven", ya que se formó hace apenas cinco millones de años).

Para poder atravesar° de un lado a otro de los Andes, existen varios pasos o puertos° de montaña. Situados a grandes alturas°, son generalmente estrechos° y peligrosos. En algunos de ellos hay, también, vías ferroviarias°.

De acuerdo con° varias instituciones científicas, la cordillera de los Andes se eleva° y se hace más angosta° cada año. La capital de Chile se acerca° a la capital de Argentina a un ritmo° de 19,4 milímetros por año. Si ese ritmo se mantiene°, Santiago y Buenos Aires podrían unirse° en unos... ¡63 millones de años, casi el mismo tiempo que ha transcurrido° desde la extinción de los dinosaurios!

**cadena** *range* **espina dorsal** *spine* **norte** *north* **sur** *south* **cordillera** *mountain range* **aunque** *although* **atravesar** *to cross* **puertos** *passes* **alturas** *heights* **estrechos** *narrow* **vías ferroviarias** *railroad tracks* **De acuerdo con** *According to* **se eleva** *rises* **angosta** *narrow* **se acerca** *gets closer* **ritmo** *rate* **se mantiene** *keeps going* **podrían unirse** *could join together* **ha transcurrido** *has gone by* **A.C.** *Before Christ* **desarrollo** *development* **pico** *peak*

**Arequipa, Perú**

### Los Andes en números

**3** Cordilleras que forman los Andes: Las cordilleras Central, Occidental y Oriental

**900** (A.C.°) Año aproximado en que empezó el desarrollo° de la cultura chavín, en los Andes peruanos

**600** Número aproximado de volcanes que hay en los Andes

**6.960** Metros (22.835 pies) de altura del Aconcagua (Argentina), el pico° más alto de los Andes

---

**ACTIVIDADES**

**1**  **Escoger** Escoge la opción que completa mejor cada oración.

1. "La espina dorsal de Suramérica" es...
   a. los Andes. b. los Himalayas. c. el Aconcagua.

2. La cordillera de los Andes se extiende…
   a. de este a oeste. b. de sur a oeste. c. de norte a sur.

3. Los Himalayas y los Andes tienen…
   a. diferente altura. b. la misma altura. c. el mismo color.

4. Los Andes es la cadena montañosa más extensa del...
   a. mundo. b. continente americano. c. hemisferio norte.

5. En 63 millones de años, Buenos Aires y Santiago podrían...
   a. separarse. b. desarrollarse. c. unirse.

6. El Aconcagua es...
   a. una montaña. b. un grupo indígena. c. un volcán.

7. En algunos de los puertos de montaña de los Andes hay…
   a. puertas. b. vías ferroviarias. c. cordilleras.

---

## ASÍ SE DICE

### La naturaleza

| | |
|---|---|
| el arco iris | rainbow |
| la cascada; la catarata | waterfall |
| el cerro; la colina; la loma | hill, hillock |
| la cima; la cumbre; el tope (Col.) | summit; mountain top |
| la maleza; los rastrojos (Col.); la yerba mala (Cuba); los hierbajos (Méx.); los yuyos (Arg.) | weeds |
| la niebla | fog |

## EL MUNDO HISPANO

### Lagos importantes

○ **Lago de Maracaibo** es el único lago de agua dulce° en el mundo que tiene una conexión directa y natural con el mar. Además, es el lago más grande de Suramérica.

○ **Lago Titicaca** es el lago navegable más alto del mundo. Se encuentra a más de 3.000 metros de altitud.

○ **Lago de Nicaragua** tiene los únicos tiburones° de agua dulce del mundo y es el mayor lago de Centroamérica.

agua dulce *fresh water* tiburones *sharks*

## PERFIL

# La Sierra Nevada de Santa Marta

**La Sierra Nevada de Santa Marta** es una cadena de montañas en la costa norte de Colombia. Se eleva abruptamente desde las costas del mar Caribe y en apenas 42 kilómetros llega a una altura de 5.775 metros (18.947 pies) en sus picos nevados°. Tiene las montañas más altas de Colombia y es la formación montañosa costera° más alta del mundo.

Los pueblos indígenas que habitan esta zona lograron° mantener los frágiles ecosistemas de estas montañas a través de° un sofisticado sistema de terrazas° y senderos

empedrados° que permitieron° el control de las aguas en una región de muchas lluvias, evitando° así la erosión de la tierra.

nevados *snowcapped* costera *coastal* lograron *managed* a través de *by means of* terrazas *terraces* empedrados *cobblestone* permitieron *allowed* evitando *avoiding*

### SUPERSITE Conexión Internet

¿Dónde se puede hacer ecoturismo en Latinoamérica?

Go to **panorama.vhlcentral.com** to find more cultural information related to this **Cultura** section.

## ACTIVIDADES

**2 Comprensión** Indica si lo que dice cada oración es **cierto** o **falso**. Corrige la información falsa.

1. En Colombia, *weeds* se dice hierbajos. Falso. Se dice rastrojos.
2. El lago Titicaca es el más grande del mundo. Falso. Es el lago navegable más alto del mundo.
3. La Sierra Nevada de Santa Marta es la formación montañosa costera más alta del mundo. Cierto.
4. Los indígenas destruyeron el ecosistema de Santa Marta. Falso. Lograron mantener los ecosistemas de las montañas.

**3 Maravillas de la naturaleza** Escribe un párrafo breve donde describas alguna maravilla de la naturaleza que has (*you have*) visitado y que te impresionó. Puede ser cualquier (*any*) sitio natural: un río, una montaña, una selva, etc. Answers will vary.

**recursos**

SUPERSITE
panorama.vhlcentral.com
Lección 13

## Section Goals

In **Estructura 13.1**, students will learn:

- to use the subjunctive with verbs and expressions of emotion
- common verbs and expressions of emotion

### Instructional Resources

**Supersite:** Lab MP3 Audio Files **Lección 13**
**Supersite/IRCD:** *PowerPoints* (**Lección 13 Estructura** Presentation); *IRM* (Information Gap Activities, Lab Audio Script, WBs/VM/LM Answer Key)
**WebSAM**
**Workbook,** pp. 157–158
**Lab Manual,** p. 75
*Cuaderno para hispanohablantes*

### Teaching Tips

- Before beginning this grammar presentation, review the conjugation of regular **-ar, -er,** and **-ir** verbs in the subjunctive (see **Estructura 12.3**). Ask students to call out verbs and expressions of will and influence that trigger the subjunctive, then have volunteers use them in sentences.
- Model the use of some common verbs and expressions of emotion. Ex: **Me molesta mucho que recojan la basura sólo una vez a la semana. Me sorprende que alguna gente no se interese por cuestiones del medio ambiente. Es ridículo que echemos tanto en la basura.** Then ask volunteers to use other verbs and expressions in sentences.

### 13.1 The subjunctive with verbs of emotion

**ANTE TODO** In the previous lesson, you learned how to use the subjunctive with expressions of will and influence. You will now learn how to use the subjunctive with verbs and expressions of emotion.

| Main clause | | Subordinate clause |
| --- | --- | --- |

Marta **espera** (que) yo **vaya** al lago este fin de semana.

▶ When the verb in the main clause of a sentence expresses an emotion or feeling such as hope, fear, joy, pity, surprise, etc., the subjunctive is required in the subordinate clause.

**Nos alegramos de** que te **gusten** las flores.
*We are happy that you like the flowers.*

**Siento** que tú no **puedas** venir mañana.
*I'm sorry that you can't come tomorrow.*

**Temo** que Ana no **pueda** ir mañana con nosotros.
*I'm afraid that Ana won't be able to go with us tomorrow.*

Le **sorprende** que Juan **sea** tan joven.
*It surprises him that Juan is so young.*

Esperamos que ustedes se diviertan mucho en la excursión.

Es triste que tengamos un problema grave de contaminación en la Ciudad de México.

### Common verbs and expressions of emotion

| | | | |
| --- | --- | --- | --- |
| **alegrarse (de)** | *to be happy* | **tener miedo (de)** | *to be afraid (of)* |
| **esperar** | *to hope; to wish* | **es extraño** | *it's strange* |
| **gustar** | *to be pleasing; to like* | **es una lástima** | *it's a shame* |
| **molestar** | *to bother* | **es ridículo** | *it's ridiculous* |
| **sentir (e:ie)** | *to be sorry; to regret* | **es terrible** | *it's terrible* |
| **sorprender** | *to surprise* | **es triste** | *it's sad* |
| **temer** | *to be afraid; to fear* | **ojalá (que)** | *I hope (that); I wish (that)* |

**CONSULTA**

Certain verbs of emotion, like **gustar, molestar,** and **sorprender,** require indirect object pronouns. For more examples, see **Estructura 7.4,** pp. 230–231.

**Me molesta** que la gente no **recicle** el plástico.
*It bothers me that people don't recycle plastic.*

**Es triste** que **tengamos** problemas con la deforestación.
*It's sad that we have problems with deforestation.*

---

**TEACHING OPTIONS**

**Large Group** Have students circulate around the room, interviewing classmates about their hopes and fears for the future. Ex: **Temo que destruyamos nuestro medio ambiente.**

**Extra Practice** Ask students to imagine that they have just finished watching a documentary about the effects of pollution. Have them write five responses to what they saw and heard, using different verbs or expressions of emotion in each sentence. Ex: **Me sorprende que el río esté contaminado.**

▶ As with expressions of will and influence, the infinitive, not the subjunctive, is used after an expression of emotion when there is no change of subject from the main clause to the subordinate clause. Compare these sentences.

Temo **llegar** tarde.
*I'm afraid I'll arrive late.*

Temo que mi novio **llegue** tarde.
*I'm afraid my boyfriend will arrive late.*

▶ The expression **ojalá (que)** means *I hope* or *I wish*, and it is always followed by the subjunctive. Note that the use of **que** with this expression is optional.

**Ojalá (que) se conserven** nuestros recursos naturales.
*I hope (that) our natural resources will be conserved.*

**Ojalá (que) recojan** la basura hoy.
*I hope (that) they collect the garbage today.*

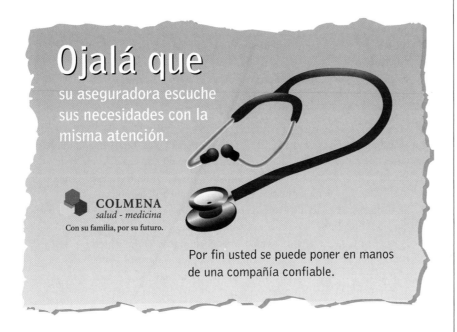

# Ojalá que
su aseguradora escuche sus necesidades con la misma atención.

**COLMENA**
*salud - medicina*
Con su familia, por su futuro.

Por fin usted se puede poner en manos de una compañía confiable.

**Teaching Tip** Compare and contrast the use of the infinitive and the subjunctive with examples like these: **Juan espera hacer algo para aliviar el problema de la contaminación ambiental. Juan espera que el gobierno haga algo para aliviar el problema de la contaminación ambiental.** Then ask: **¿Es terrible no reciclar? ¿Es terrible que yo no recicle? ¿Les molesta sentarse aquí? ¿Les molesta que nos sentemos aquí?**

**The Affective Dimension** Reassure students that they will feel more comfortable with the subjunctive as they continue studying Spanish.

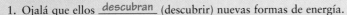

**¡INTÉNTALO!** Completa las oraciones con las formas correctas de los verbos.

1. Ojalá que ellos __descubran__ (descubrir) nuevas formas de energía.
2. Espero que Ana nos __ayude__ (ayudar) a recoger la basura en la carretera.
3. Es una lástima que la gente no __recicle__ (reciclar) más.
4. Esperamos __proteger__ (proteger) el aire de nuestra comunidad.
5. Me alegro de que mis amigos __quieran__ (querer) conservar la naturaleza.
6. Espero que tú __vengas__ (venir) a la reunión (*meeting*) del Club de Ecología.
7. Es malo __contaminar__ (contaminar) el medio ambiente.
8. A mis padres les gusta que nosotros __participemos__ (participar) en las reuniones.
9. Siento que nuestras ciudades __estén__ (estar) afectadas por la contaminación.
10. Ojalá que yo __pueda__ (poder) hacer algo para reducir la contaminación.

**recursos**

WB
pp. 157-158

LM
p. 75

SUPERSITE
panorama.
vhlcentral.com
Lección 13

**TEACHING OPTIONS**

**Extra Practice** Have students look at the drawing for **Contextos** on pages 416–417. Ask them to imagine they are one of the people pictured. Then have them write five sentences about how they feel from the point of view of that person. Ex: **Ojalá Gustavo no pierda las llaves del carro esta vez.**
**Pairs** Have students tell a partner three things that bother him or her and three things he or she is happy about.

**TPR** Expand the **¡Inténtalo!** activity. Read the beginning of one of the sentences (stop just before the blank) and throw a foam or paper ball to a student. He or she must complete the sentence in an original manner, using the correct subjunctive form or an infinitive.

# Práctica SUPERSITE

**1** **Completar** Completa el diálogo con palabras de la lista. Compara tus respuestas con las de un(a) compañero/a.

Bogotá, Colombia

| | | |
|---|---|---|
| alegro | molesta | salga |
| encuentren | ojalá | tengo miedo de |
| estén | puedan | vayan |
| lleguen | reduzcan | visitar |

**OLGA** Me alegro de que Adriana y Raquel (1)___vayan___ a Colombia. ¿Van a estudiar?

**SARA** Sí. Es una lástima que (2)___lleguen___ una semana tarde. Ojalá que la universidad las ayude a buscar casa. (3)___Tengo miedo de___ que no consigan dónde vivir.

**OLGA** Me (4)___molesta___ que seas tan pesimista, pero sí, yo también espero que (5)___encuentren___ gente simpática y que hablen mucho español.

**SARA** Sí, ojalá. Van a hacer un estudio sobre la deforestación en las costas. Es triste que en tantos países los recursos naturales (6)___estén___ en peligro.

**OLGA** Pues, me (7)___alegro___ de que no se queden mucho en la capital por la contaminación. (8)___Ojalá___ tengan tiempo de viajar por el país.

**SARA** Sí, espero que (9)___puedan___ por lo menos ir a la costa. Sé que también esperan (10)___visitar___ la Catedral de Sal de Zipaquirá.

**2** **Transformar** Transforma estos elementos en oraciones completas para formar un diálogo entre Juan y la madre de Raquel. Añade palabras si es necesario. Luego, con un(a) compañero/a, presenta el diálogo a la clase.

1. Juan, / esperar / (tú) escribirle / Raquel. / Ser / tu / novia. / Ojalá / no / sentirse / sola   Juan, espero que (tú) le escribas a Raquel. Es tu novia. Ojalá (que) no se sienta sola.

2. molestarme / (usted) decirme / lo que / tener / hacer. / Ahora / mismo / le / estar / escribiendo   Me molesta que (Ud.) me diga lo que tengo que hacer. Ahora mismo le estoy escribiendo.

3. alegrarme / oírte / decir / eso. / Ser / terrible / estar / lejos / cuando / nadie / recordarte   Me alegra oírte decir eso. Es terrible estar lejos cuando nadie te recuerda.

4. señora, / ¡yo / tener / miedo / (ella) no recordarme / mí! / Ser / triste / estar / sin / novia   Señora, ¡yo tengo miedo que (ella) no me recuerde a mí! Es triste estar sin novia.

5. ser / ridículo / (tú) sentirte / así. / Tú / saber / ella / querer / casarse / contigo   Es ridículo que te sientas así. Tú sabes que ella quiere casarse contigo.

6. ridículo / o / no, / sorprenderme / (todos) preocuparse / ella / y / (nadie) acordarse / mí   Ridículo o no, me sorprende que todos se preocupen por ella y nadie se acuerde de mí.

# Comunicación

**3**   **Comentar** En parejas, túrnense para formar oraciones sobre su ciudad, sus clases, su gobierno o algún otro tema, usando expresiones como **me alegro de que, temo que** y **es extraño que.** Luego reaccionen a los comentarios de su compañero/a. Answers will vary.

> **modelo**
> **Estudiante 1:** *Me alegro de que vayan a limpiar el río.*
> **Estudiante 2:** *Yo también. Me preocupa que el agua del río esté tan sucia.*

**4**   **Contestar** Lee el mensaje electrónico que Raquel le escribió a su novio Juan. Luego, en parejas, contesten el mensaje usando expresiones como **me sorprende que, me molesta que** y **es una lástima que.** Answers will vary.

---

↩ Para: Juan  |  De: Raquel

Hola, Juan:

Mi amor, siento no escribirte más frecuentemente. La verdad es que estoy muy ocupada todo el tiempo. No sabes cuánto me estoy divirtiendo en Colombia. Me sorprende haber podido adaptarme tan bien. Es bueno tener tanto trabajo. Aprendo mucho más aquí que en el laboratorio de la universidad. Me encanta que me den responsabilidades y que compartan sus muchos conocimientos conmigo. Ay, pero pienso mucho en ti. Qué triste es que no podamos estar juntos por tanto tiempo. Ojalá que los días pasen rápido. Bueno, querido, es todo por ahora. Escríbeme pronto.

Te quiero y te extraño mucho,

Raquel

---

**AYUDA**

**Echar de menos (a alguien)** and **extrañar (a alguien)** are two ways of saying *to miss (someone).*

# Síntesis

**5**   **No te preocupes** Estás muy preocupado/a por los problemas del medio ambiente y le comentas a tu compañero/a todas tus preocupaciones. Él/Ella va a darte la solución adecuada para tus preocupaciones. Su profesor(a) les va a dar una hoja distinta a cada uno/a con la información necesaria para completar la actividad. Answers will vary.

> **modelo**
> **Estudiante 1:** *Me molesta que las personas tiren basura en las calles.*
> **Estudiante 2:** *Por eso es muy importante que los políticos hagan leyes para conservar las ciudades limpias.*

---

**3 Teaching Tips**
- To simplify, have students divide a sheet of paper into four columns, with these headings: **Nuestra ciudad, Las clases, El gobierno**, and another subject of their choosing. Ask them to brainstorm topics or issues for each column.
- Have groups write statements about these issues and then give them to another group for its reactions. The second group should write down their comments and exchange them with the first group.

**4 Expansion** In pairs, have students tell each other about a memorable e-mail that they have written. Using verbs and expressions of emotion, partners must respond to the e-mail as if they had received it. Wherever applicable, ask pairs to compare their partners' responses with the one they actually received from the real recipients.

**5 Teaching Tip** Divide the class into pairs and distribute the handouts from the Information Gap Activities (Supersite/ IRCD) that correspond to this activity. Give students ten minutes to complete the activity.

**5 Expansion** Have students work in groups of three to create a public service announcement. Groups should choose one of the ecological problems they mentioned in the activity, and include the proposed solutions for that problem in their announcement.

---

**TEACHING OPTIONS**

**Small Groups** Divide students into groups of three. Have students write three predictions about the future on separate pieces of paper and put them in a sack. Students take turns drawing predictions and reading them to the group. Group members respond with an appropriate expression of emotion. Ex: **Voy a ganar millones de dólares algún día. (Me alegro que vayas a ganar millones de dólares.)**

**Extra Practice** Ask students to imagine that they are world leaders speaking at an environmental summit. Have them deliver a short speech to the class about some of the world's environmental problems and how they hope to solve them. Students should include three verbs of will and influence and three verbs or expressions of emotion, followed by the subjunctive.

**13.2** # The subjunctive with doubt, disbelief, and denial

**ANTE TODO** Just as the subjunctive is required with expressions of emotion, influence, and will, it is also used with expressions of doubt, disbelief, and denial.

| Main clause | | Subordinate clause |
|---|---|---|
| **Dudan** | que | su hijo les **diga** la verdad. |

▶ The subjunctive is always used in a subordinate clause when there is a change of subject and the expression in the main clause implies negation or uncertainty.

*No creo que haya lugares más bonitos en el mundo.*

*Dudo que el río esté contaminado aquí en las montañas.*

▶ Here is a list of some common expressions of doubt, disbelief, or denial.

### Expressions of doubt, disbelief, or denial

| | | | |
|---|---|---|---|
| **dudar** | to doubt | **no es seguro** | it's not certain |
| **negar (e:ie)** | to deny | **no es verdad** | it's not true |
| **no creer** | not to believe | **es imposible** | it's impossible |
| **no estar seguro/a (de)** | not to be sure | **es improbable** | it's improbable |
| **no es cierto** | it's not true; it's not certain | **(no) es posible** | it's (not) possible |
| | | **(no) es probable** | it's (not) probable |

El gobierno **niega** que el agua **esté** contaminada.
*The government denies that the water is contaminated.*

**Dudo** que el gobierno **resuelva** el problema.
*I doubt that the government will solve the problem.*

**Es probable** que **haya** menos bosques y selvas en el futuro.
*It's probable that there will be fewer forests and jungles in the future.*

**No es verdad** que mi hermano **estudie** ecología.
*It's not true that my brother studies ecology.*

**¡LENGUA VIVA!**

In English, the expression *it is probable* indicates a fairly high degree of certainty. In Spanish, however, **es probable** implies uncertainty and therefore triggers the subjunctive in the subordinate clause: **Es muy probable que venga Elena.**

▶ The indicative is used in a subordinate clause when there is no doubt or uncertainty in the main clause. Here is a list of some expressions of certainty.

### Expressions of certainty

| no dudar | not to doubt | estar seguro/a (de) | to be sure |
|---|---|---|---|
| no cabe duda de | there is no doubt | es cierto | it's true; it's certain |
| no hay duda de | there is no doubt | es seguro | it's certain |
| no negar (e:ie) | not to deny | es verdad | it's true |
| creer | to believe | es obvio | it's obvious |

**No negamos** que **hay** demasiados carros en las carreteras.
*We don't deny that there are too many cars on the highways.*

**No hay duda de** que el Amazonas **es** uno de los ríos más largos.
*There is no doubt that the Amazon is one of the longest rivers.*

**Es verdad** que Colombia **es** un país bonito.
*It's true that Colombia is a beautiful country.*

**Es obvio** que los tigres **están** en peligro de extinción.
*It's obvious that tigers are in danger of extinction.*

▶ In affirmative sentences, the verb **creer** expresses belief or certainty, so it is followed by the indicative. In negative sentences, however, when doubt is implied, **creer** is followed by the subjunctive.

**No creo** que **haya** vida en el planeta Marte.
*I don't believe that there is life on the planet Mars.*

**Creo** que **debemos** usar exclusivamente la energía solar.
*I believe we should use solar energy exclusively.*

▶ The expressions **quizás** and **tal vez** are usually followed by the subjunctive because they imply doubt about something.

**Quizás haga** sol mañana.
*Perhaps it will be sunny tomorrow.*

**Tal vez veamos** la luna esta noche.
*Perhaps we will see the moon tonight.*

---

**¡INTÉNTALO!** Completa estas oraciones con la forma correcta del verbo.

1. Dudo que ellos __trabajen__ (trabajar).
2. Es cierto que él __come__ (comer) mucho.
3. Es imposible que ellos __salgan__ (salir).
4. Es probable que ustedes __ganen__ (ganar).
5. No creo que ella __vuelva__ (volver).
6. Es posible que nosotros __vayamos__ (ir).
7. Dudamos que tú __recicles__ (reciclar).
8. Creo que ellos __juegan__ (jugar) al fútbol.
9. No niego que ustedes __estudian__ (estudiar).
10. Es posible que ella no __venga__ (venir) a casa.
11. Es probable que Lucio y Carmen __duerman__ (dormir).
12. Es posible que mi prima Marta __llame__ (llamar).
13. Tal vez Juan no nos __oiga__ (oír).
14. No es cierto que Paco y Daniel nos __ayuden__ (ayudar).

**recursos**

WB
pp. 159-160

LM
p. 76

SUPERSITE
panorama.
vhlcentral.com
Lección 13

**Teaching Tips**
- Have students respond to statements that elicit expressions of doubt, disbelief, or denial and expressions of certainty. Ex: **Terminan la nueva residencia antes del próximo año. (Es seguro que la terminan antes del próximo año.) La universidad va a tener un nuevo presidente pronto. (No es verdad que la universidad vaya a tener un nuevo presidente pronto.)**
- Have students change the items in **¡Inténtalo!**, making the affirmative verbs in the main clauses negative, and the negative ones affirmative, and making all corresponding changes. Ex: **1. No dudo que ellos trabajan.**
- Point out that **ojalá, quizás,** and **tal vez** are exceptions to the general rule that **que** is used before verbs in the subjunctive.

---

### TEACHING OPTIONS

**TPR** Call out a series of sentences, using either an expression of certainty or an expression of doubt, disbelief, or denial. Have students stand if they hear an expression of certainty or remain seated if they hear an expression of doubt. Ex: **Es cierto que algunos pájaros hablan.** (Students stand.)
**Heritage Speakers** Ask heritage speakers to jot down a few statements about things unique to their cultural communities.

Ex: **Como chiles en el desayuno.** Have the class react using expressions of doubt, disbelief, denial, or certainty. Ex: **Dudo que comas chiles en el desayuno.**
**Extra Practice** Ask students to write sentences about three things of which they are certain and three things they doubt or cannot believe. Have students share some of their sentences with the class.

**1 Expansion** Have pairs prepare another conversation between **Raúl** and his father using expressions of doubt, disbelief, and denial, as well as expressions of certainty. This time, **Raúl** is explaining the advantages of the Internet to his reluctant father and trying to persuade him to use it. Have pairs role-play their conversations for the class.

# Práctica 🔵 SUPERSITE

**1**

**Escoger** Escoge las respuestas correctas para completar el diálogo. Luego dramatiza el diálogo con un(a) compañero/a.

**RAÚL** Ustedes dudan que yo realmente (1)___estudie___ (estudio/estudie). No niego que a veces me (2)___divierto___ (divierto/divierta) demasiado, pero no cabe duda de que (3)___tomo___ (tomo/tome) mis estudios en serio. Estoy seguro de que cuando me vean graduarme van a pensar de manera diferente. Creo que no (4)___tienen___ (tienen/tengan) razón con sus críticas.

**PAPÁ** Es posible que tu mamá y yo no (5)___tengamos___ (tenemos/tengamos) razón. Es cierto que a veces (6)___dudamos___ (dudamos/dudemos) de ti. Pero no hay duda de que te (7)___pasas___ (pasas/pases) toda la noche en Internet y oyendo música. No es nada seguro que (8)___estés___ (estás/estés) estudiando.

**RAÚL** Es verdad que (9)___uso___ (uso/use) mucho la computadora pero, ¡piensen! ¿No es posible que (10)___sea___ (es/sea) para buscar información para mis clases? ¡No hay duda de que Internet (11)___es___ (es/sea) el mejor recurso del mundo! Es obvio que ustedes (12)___piensan___ (piensan/piensen) que no hago nada, pero no es cierto.

**PAPÁ** No dudo que esta conversación nos (13)___va___ (va/vaya) a ayudar. Pero tal vez esta noche (14)___puedas___ (puedes/puedas) trabajar sin música. ¿Está bien?

**2 Expansion** Continue the activity by making other false statements. Ex: **Voy a hacer una excursión a la Patagonia mañana. Mi abuela sólo come pasteles y cebollas.**

**2**

**Dudas** Carolina es una chica que siempre miente. Expresa tus dudas sobre lo que Carolina está diciendo ahora. Usa las expresiones entre paréntesis para tus respuestas.

> **modelo**
> El próximo año Marta y yo vamos de vacaciones por diez meses. (dudar)
> ¡Ja! Dudo que vayan de vacaciones por ese tiempo. ¡Ustedes no son ricas!

1. Estoy escribiendo una novela en español. (no creer)
   No creo que estés escribiendo una novela en español.
2. Mi tía es la directora del *Sierra Club*. (no ser verdad)
   No es verdad que tu tía sea la directora del *Sierra Club*.
3. Dos profesores míos juegan para los Osos *(Bears)* de Chicago. (ser imposible)
   Es imposible que dos profesores tuyos jueguen para los Osos de Chicago.
4. Mi mejor amiga conoce al chef Emeril. (no ser cierto)
   No es cierto que tu mejor amiga conozca al chef Emeril.
5. Mi padre es dueño del Centro Rockefeller. (no ser posible)
   No es posible que tu padre sea dueño del Centro Rockefeller.
6. Yo ya tengo un doctorado *(doctorate)* en lenguas. (ser improbable)
   Es improbable que ya tengas un doctorado en lenguas.

**TEACHING OPTIONS**

**Large Groups** Divide the class into groups of six to stage an environmental debate. Some groups should play the role of environmental advocates while others represent industrialists and big business. Have students take turns presenting a policy platform for the group they represent. When they are finished, opposing groups express their doubts, disbeliefs, and denials.

**Heritage Speakers** Ask heritage speakers to write a brief editorial about a current event or political issue in their cultural community. In the body of their essay, students should include expressions of certainty as well as expressions of doubt, disbelief, or denial.

# Comunicación

**3**

**Entrevista** En parejas, imaginen que trabajan para un periódico y que tienen que hacerle una entrevista a la conservacionista Mary Axtmann, quien colaboró en la fundación del programa Ciudadanos Pro Bosque San Patricio, en Puerto Rico. Escriban seis preguntas para la entrevista después de leer las declaraciones de Mary Axtmann. Al final, inventen las respuestas de Axtmann. Answers will vary.

**NOTA CULTURAL**

La asociación de **Mary Axtmann** trabaja para la conservación del bosque San Patricio. También ofrece conferencias sobre temas ambientales, hace un censo anual de pájaros y tiene un grupo de guías voluntarios. La comunidad hace todo el trabajo; la asociación no recibe ninguna ayuda del gobierno.

## Declaraciones de Mary Axtmann:

"...que el bosque es un recurso ecológico educativo para la comunidad."

"El bosque San Patricio es un pulmón (*lung*) que produce oxígeno para la ciudad."

"El bosque San Patricio está en medio de la ciudad de San Juan. Por eso digo que este bosque es una esmeralda (*emerald*) en un mar de concreto."

"El bosque pertenece (*belongs*) a la comunidad."

"Nosotros salvamos este bosque mediante la propuesta (*proposal*) y no la protesta."

**4**

**Adivinar** Escribe cinco oraciones sobre tu vida presente y futura. Cuatro deben ser falsas y sólo una debe ser cierta. Presenta tus oraciones al grupo. El grupo adivina cuál es la oración cierta y expresa sus dudas sobre las oraciones falsas. Answers will vary.

**AYUDA**

Here are some useful verbs for talking about plans.

**esperar** → to hope
**querer** → to want
**pretender** → to intend
**pensar** → to plan

Note that **pretender** and *pretend* are false cognates. To express *to pretend*, use the verb **fingir**.

**modelo**

**Estudiante 1:** *Quiero irme un año a la selva a trabajar.*
**Estudiante 2:** *Dudo que te guste vivir en la selva.*
**Estudiante 3:** *En cinco años voy a ser presidente de los Estados Unidos.*
**Estudiante 2:** *No creo que seas presidente de los Estados Unidos en cinco años. ¡Tal vez en treinta!*

# Síntesis

**5**

**Intercambiar** En grupos, escriban un párrafo sobre los problemas del medio ambiente en su estado o en su comunidad. Compartan su párrafo con otro grupo, que va a ofrecer opiniones y soluciones. Luego presenten su párrafo, con las opiniones y soluciones del otro grupo, a la clase. Answers will vary.

---

**3 Teaching Tip** Before starting, have the class brainstorm different topics that might be discussed with Mary Axtmann.

**3 Expansion** Ask pairs to role-play their interviews for the class.

**4 Teaching Tip** Ask students to choose a secretary to write down the group members' true statements to present to the class.

**5 Teaching Tip** Assign students to groups of four. Ask group members to appoint a mediator to lead the discussion, a secretary to write the paragraph, a checker to proofread what was written, and a stenographer to take notes on the opinions and solutions of the other group.

**5 Expansion** Have students create a poster illustrating the environmental problems in their community and proposing possible solutions.

---

**TEACHING OPTIONS**

**Small Groups** Assign scenarios to groups of three. Have students take turns playing a reporter interviewing the other two about what is happening in each situation. The interviewees should use expressions of certainty or doubt, disbelief, and denial when responding to the reporter's questions. Possible scenarios: protest in favor of animal rights, a volcano about to erupt, a local ecological problem, a vacation in the mountains.

**Game** Divide the class into two teams. Team A writes sentences with expressions of certainty while team B writes sentences with expressions of doubt, disbelief, or denial. Put all the sentences in a hat. Students take turns drawing sentences for their team and stating the opposite of what the sentence says. The team with the most sentences using the correct mood wins.

## Section Goals

In **Estructura 13.3**, students will learn:
- conjunctions that require the subjunctive
- when the infinitive follows a conjunction
- conjunctions followed by the subjunctive or the indicative

### Instructional Resources

**Supersite:** Lab MP3 Audio Files **Lección 13**
**Supersite/IRCD:** *PowerPoints* (**Lección 13 Estructura** Presentation); *IRM* (Information Gap Activities, Lab Audio Script, WBs/VM/LM Answer Key)
**WebSAM**
**Workbook,** pp. 161–162
**Lab Manual,** p. 77
*Cuaderno para hispanohablantes*

### Teaching Tips

- To introduce conjunctions that require the subjunctive, make a few statements about yourself. Ex: **Nunca llego a clase tarde a menos que tenga un problema con mi carro. Siempre leo mis mensajes electrónicos antes de que empiece mi primera clase. Camino a clase con tal de que no llueva.** Write each conjunction on the board as you go.
- Have volunteers identify the conjunctions and subjunctive verbs in the captions to the video stills.

# 13.3 The subjunctive with conjunctions

**ANTE TODO** Conjunctions are words or phrases that connect other words and clauses in sentences. Certain conjunctions commonly introduce adverbial clauses, which describe *how, why, when,* and *where* an action takes place.

| Main clause | Conjunction | Adverbial clause |
|---|---|---|
| Vamos a visitar a Carlos | **antes de que** | **regrese** a California. |

*Se pueden tomar fotos, ¿verdad?*

*Sí, con tal de que no toques ni las flores ni las plantas.*

*A menos que resuelvan el problema de la contaminación, los habitantes van a sufrir muchas enfermedades en el futuro.*

▶ The subjunctive is used to express a hypothetical situation, uncertainty as to whether an action or event will take place, or a condition that may or may not be fulfilled.

Voy a dejar un recado **en caso de que Gustavo me llame.**
*I'm going to leave a message in case Gustavo calls me.*

Voy al supermercado **para que tengas** algo de comer.
*I'm going to the store so that you'll have something to eat.*

▶ Here is a list of the conjunctions that always require the subjunctive.

### Conjunctions that require the subjunctive

| **a menos que** | unless | **en caso (de) que** | in case (that) |
|---|---|---|---|
| **antes (de) que** | before | **para que** | so that |
| **con tal (de) que** | provided that | **sin que** | without |

Algunos animales van a morir **a menos que** haya leyes para protegerlos.
*Some animals are going to die unless there are laws to protect them.*

Ellos nos llevan a la selva **para que** veamos las plantas tropicales.
*They are taking us to the jungle so that we may see the tropical plants.*

▶ The infinitive is used after the prepositions **antes de, para,** and **sin** when there is no change of subject; the subjunctive is used when there is. **¡Atención!** Note that, while you may use a present participle with the English equivalent of these conjunctions, in Spanish you cannot.

Te llamamos **antes de salir** de la casa.
*We will call you before leaving the house.*

Te llamamos mañana **antes de que salgas.**
*We will call you tomorrow before you leave.*

### TEACHING OPTIONS

**Extra Practice** Write these partial sentences on the board. Have students complete them with true or invented information about their own lives. **1. Voy a terminar los estudios con tal de que..., 2. Necesito $500 en caso de que..., 3. Puedo salir este sábado a menos que..., 4. El mundo cambia sin que..., 5. Debo... antes de que..., 6. Mis padres... para que yo...**

**Video** Have students divide a sheet of paper into four columns, labeling them **Voluntad, Emoción, Duda,** and **Conjunción.** Replay the *Fotonovela* episode. Have them listen for each use of the subjunctive, marking the example they hear in the appropriate column. Play the episode again, then have students write a short summary that includes each use of the subjunctive.

# Conjunctions with subjunctive or indicative

> Voy a formar un club de ecología tan pronto como vuelva a España.

> Cuando veo basura, la recojo.

## Conjunctions used with subjunctive or indicative

| | | | |
|---|---|---|---|
| **cuando** | *when* | **hasta que** | *until* |
| **después de que** | *after* | **tan pronto como** | *as soon as* |
| **en cuanto** | *as soon as* | | |

▶ With the conjunctions above, use the subjunctive in the subordinate clause if the main clause expresses a future action or command.

Vamos a resolver el problema **cuando desarrollemos** nuevas tecnologías.
*We are going to solve the problem when we develop new technologies.*

**Después de que** ustedes **tomen** sus refrescos, reciclen las botellas.
*After you drink your soft drinks, recycle the bottles.*

▶ With these conjunctions, the indicative is used in the subordinate clause if the verb in the main clause expresses an action that habitually happens, or that happened in the past.

Contaminan los ríos **cuando construyen** nuevos edificios.
*They pollute the rivers when they build new buildings.*

Contaminaron el río **cuando construyeron** ese edificio.
*They polluted the river when they built that building.*

---

**¡INTÉNTALO!**    Completa las oraciones con las formas correctas de los verbos.

1. Voy a estudiar ecología cuando ___vuelva___ (volver) a la universidad.
2. No podemos evitar la lluvia ácida a menos que todos ___trabajemos___ (trabajar) juntos.
3. No podemos conducir sin ___contaminar___ (contaminar) el aire.
4. Siempre recogemos mucha basura cuando ___vamos___ (ir) al parque.
5. Elisa habló con el presidente del Club de Ecología después de que ___terminó___ (terminar) la reunión.
6. Vamos de excursión para ___observar___ (observar) los animales y las plantas.
7. La contaminación va a ser un problema muy serio hasta que nosotros ___cambiemos___ (cambiar) nuestros sistemas de producción y transporte.
8. El gobierno debe crear más parques nacionales antes de que los bosques y ríos ___estén___ (estar) completamente contaminados.
9. La gente recicla con tal de que no ___sea___ (ser) díficil.

**recursos**

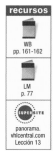

WB
pp. 161-162

LM
p. 77

**SUPERSITE**
panorama.
vhlcentral.com
Lección 13

# Práctica

**1 Completar** La señora Montero habla de una excursión que quiere hacer con su familia. Completa las oraciones con la forma correcta de cada verbo.

1. Voy a llevar a mis hijos al parque para que aprendan (aprender) sobre la naturaleza.
2. Voy a pasar todo el día allí a menos que haga (hacer) mucho frío.
3. En bicicleta podemos explorar el parque sin caminar (caminar) demasiado.
4. Vamos a bajar al cráter con tal de que no se prohíba (prohibir).
5. Siempre llevamos al perro cuando vamos (ir) al parque.
6. No pensamos ir muy lejos en caso de que llueva (llover).
7. Vamos a almorzar a la orilla (*shore*) del río cuando nosotros terminemos (terminar) de preparar la comida.
8. Mis hijos van a dejar todo limpio antes de salir (salir) del parque.

**2 Frases** Completa estas frases de una manera lógica. Answers will vary.

1. No podemos controlar la contaminación del aire a menos que…
2. Voy a reciclar los productos de papel y de vidrio en cuanto…
3. Debemos comprar coches eléctricos tan pronto como…
4. Protegemos los animales en peligro de extinción para que…
5. Mis amigos y yo vamos a recoger la basura de la universidad después de que…
6. No podemos desarrollar nuevas fuentes *(sources)* de energía sin…
7. Hay que eliminar la contaminación del agua para…
8. No podemos proteger la naturaleza sin que…

**3 Organizaciones** En parejas, lean las descripciones de las organizaciones de conservación. Luego expresen en sus propias (*own*) palabras las opiniones de cada organización. Answers will vary.

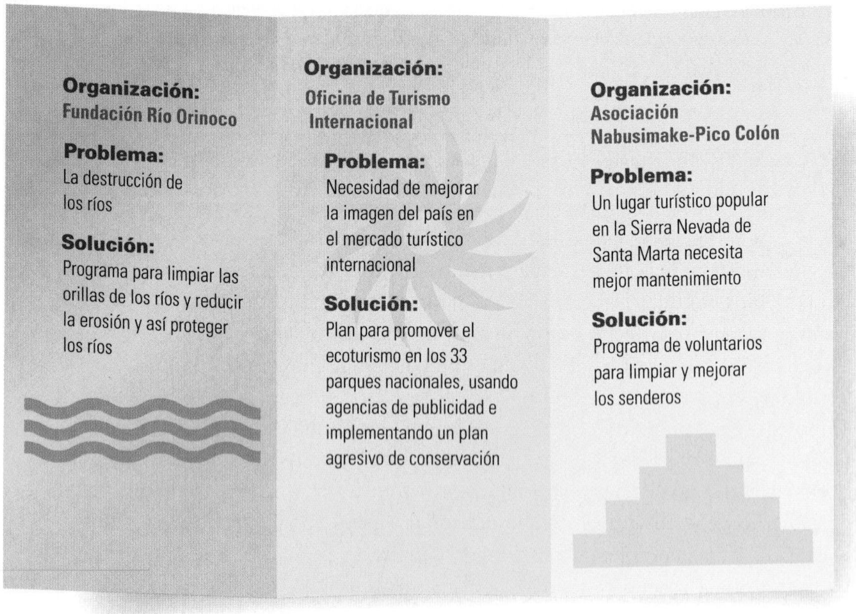
Organización:
Fundación Río Orinoco
Problema:
La destrucción de los ríos
Solución:
Programa para limpiar las orillas de los ríos y reducir la erosión y así proteger los ríos
Organización:
Oficina de Turismo Internacional
Problema:
Necesidad de mejorar la imagen del país en el mercado turístico internacional
Solución:
Plan para promover el ecoturismo en los 33 parques nacionales, usando agencias de publicidad e implementando un plan agresivo de conservación
Organización:
Asociación Nabusimake-Pico Colón
Problema:
Un lugar turístico popular en la Sierra Nevada de Santa Marta necesita mejor mantenimiento
Solución:
Programa de voluntarios para limpiar y mejorar los senderos

**AYUDA**

Here are some expressions you can use as you complete **Actividad 3.**

**Se puede evitar… con tal de que…**
**Es necesario… para que…**
**Debemos prohibir… antes de que…**
**No es posible… sin que…**
**Vamos a… tan pronto como…**
**A menos que… no vamos a…**

**1 Expansion**
- Ask students to write new endings for each sentence. Ex: **Voy a llevar a mis hijos al parque para que… (hagan más ejercicio/jueguen con sus amigos/pasen más tiempo fuera de la casa).**
- Ask pairs to write six original sentences about a trip they plan to take. Have them use one conjunction that requires the subjunctive in each sentence.

**2 Teaching Tip** As you go through the items, ask students which conjunctions require the subjunctive and which could be followed by the subjunctive or the indicative. For those that could take both, discuss which one students used and why.

**3 Expansion**
- Ask students to identify the natural resources and environmental problems mentioned in the reading.
- Have students create a newspaper advertisement for an environmental agency that protects one of the natural resources mentioned in the reading. Students should state the name and goals of the agency, how these goals serve public interest, and where and how donations can be made.

**TEACHING OPTIONS**

**Pairs** Ask students to imagine that, unless some dramatic actions are taken, the world as we know it will end in five days. It is their responsibility as community leaders to give a speech warning people what will happen unless everyone takes action. Have students work with a partner to prepare a three-minute presentation for the class, using as many different conjunctions that require the subjunctive as possible.

**Small Groups** Divide the class into groups of four. The first student begins a sentence, the second picks a conjunction, and the third student finishes the sentence. The fourth student writes the sentence down. Students should take turns playing the different roles until they have created eight sentences.

# Comunicación

**4** **Preguntas** En parejas, túrnense para hacerse estas preguntas.   Answers will vary.

1. ¿Qué haces cada noche antes de acostarte?
2. ¿Qué haces después de salir de la universidad?
3. ¿Qué hace tu familia para que puedas asistir a la universidad?
4. ¿Qué piensas hacer tan pronto como te gradúes?
5. ¿Qué quieres hacer mañana, a menos que haga mal tiempo?
6. ¿Qué haces en tus clases sin que los profesores lo sepan?

**5** **Comparar** En parejas, comparen una actividad rutinaria que ustedes hacen con algo que van a hacer en el futuro. Usen palabras de la lista.   Answers will vary.

| | | | |
|---|---|---|---|
| antes de | después de que | hasta que | sin (que) |
| antes de que | en caso de que | para (que) | tan pronto como |

> **modelo**
>
> **Estudiante 1:** El sábado vamos al lago. Tan pronto como volvamos, vamos a estudiar para el examen.
> **Estudiante 2:** Todos los sábados llevo a mi primo al parque para que juegue. Pero el sábado que viene, con tal de que no llueva, lo voy a llevar a las montañas.

# Síntesis

**6** **Tres en raya (*Tic-Tac-Toe*)** Formen dos equipos. Una persona comienza una frase y otra persona de su equipo la termina usando palabras de la gráfica. El primer equipo que forme tres oraciones seguidas *(in a row)* gana el tres en raya. Hay que usar la conjunción o la preposición y el verbo correctamente. Si no, ¡no cuenta!   Answers will vary.

**¡LENGUA VIVA!**

*Tic-Tac-Toe* has various names in the Spanish-speaking world, including **tres en raya, tres en línea, ta-te-ti, gato, la vieja,** and **triqui-triqui.**

> **modelo**
>
> *Equipo 1*
> **Estudiante 1:** *Dudo que podamos eliminar la deforestación...*
> **Estudiante 2:** *sin que nos ayude el gobierno.*
> *Equipo 2*
> **Estudiante 1:** *Creo que podemos conservar nuestros recursos naturales...*
> **Estudiante 2:** *con tal de que todos hagamos algo para ayudar.*

| cuando | con tal de que | para que |
|---|---|---|
| antes de que | para | sin que |
| hasta que | en caso de que | antes de |

---

**4** **Expansion** When pairs have finished asking and answering the questions, work with the whole class, asking several individuals each of the questions and asking other students to react to their responses. Ex: ____ **hace aeróbicos antes de acostarse. ¿Quién más hace ejercicio? ¡Uf! Hacer ejercicio me parece excesivo. ¿Quiénes ven la tele? ¿Nadie lee un libro antes de acostarse?**

**5** **Teaching Tip** Have partners compare the routines of other people they know and what they are going to do in the future. Have them do the same with celebrities, making guesses about their routines.

**6** **Teaching Tip** Have groups prepare Tic-Tac-Toe cards like the one shown in the activity.

**6** **Expansion** Regroup the students to do a second round of Tic-Tac-Toe.

**Teaching Tip** See the Information Gap Activities (Supersite/IRCD) for an additional activity to practice the material presented in this section.

---

**TEACHING OPTIONS**

**Heritage Speakers** Ask heritage speakers if they played Tic-Tac-Toe when growing up. What did they call it? Was it one of the names listed in **¡Lengua viva!**? Ask them the names of other childhood games they played and to describe them. Are the games similar to those played by other students in the class?

**Pairs** Ask partners to interview each other about what they must do today for their future goals to become a reality. Students should state what their goals are, the necessary conditions to achieve them, and talk about obstacles they may encounter. Students should use as many conjunctions as possible in their interviews. Have pairs present their interviews to the class.

# 13.4 Past participles used as adjectives

**ANTE TODO** In **Lección 5**, you learned about present participles (**estudiando**). Both Spanish and English have past participles. The past participles of English verbs often end in **–ed** (*to turn* → *turned*), but many are also irregular (*to buy* → *bought*; *to drive* → *driven*).

▶ In Spanish, regular **–ar** verbs form the past participle with **–ado**. Regular **–er** and **–ir** verbs form the past participle with **–ido**.

| INFINITIVE | STEM | PAST PARTICIPLE |
|---|---|---|
| bailar | bail- | **bailado** |
| comer | com- | **comido** |
| vivir | viv- | **vivido** |

▶ **¡Atención!** The past participles of **–er** and **–ir** verbs whose stems end in **–a, –e,** or **–o** carry a written accent mark on the **i** of the **–ido** ending.

| | | | | |
|---|---|---|---|---|
| caer | **caído** | reír | **reído** | |
| creer | **creído** | sonreír | **sonreído** | |
| leer | **leído** | traer | **traído** | |
| oír | **oído** | | | |

### Irregular past participles

| | | | | |
|---|---|---|---|---|
| abrir | **abierto** | morir | **muerto** | |
| decir | **dicho** | poner | **puesto** | |
| describir | **descrito** | resolver | **resuelto** | |
| descubrir | **descubierto** | romper | **roto** | |
| escribir | **escrito** | ver | **visto** | |
| hacer | **hecho** | volver | **vuelto** | |

▶ In Spanish, as in English, past participles can be used as adjectives. They are often used with the verb **estar** to describe a condition or state that results from an action. Like other Spanish adjectives, they must agree in gender and number with the nouns they modify.

Me gusta usar papel **reciclado.**
*I like to use recycled paper.*

Tenemos la mesa **puesta** y la cena **hecha.**
*We have the table set and dinner made.*

**¡INTÉNTALO!** Indica la forma correcta del participio pasado de estos verbos.

1. hablar ___hablado___
2. beber ___bebido___
3. decidir ___decidido___
4. romper ___roto___
5. escribir ___escrito___
6. cantar ___cantado___
7. oír ___oído___
8. traer ___traído___
9. correr ___corrido___
10. leer ___leído___
11. ver ___visto___
12. hacer ___hecho___

# Práctica

**1**

**Completar** Completa las oraciones con la forma adecuada del participio pasado del verbo que está entre paréntesis.

▶ 1. Nuestra excursión a la selva ya está __preparada__ (preparar).
2. Todos los detalles están __escritos__ (escribir) en español.
3. Tenemos que comprar los pasajes, pero Sara no encuentra el mapa. ¡Oh no! Creo que estamos __perdidos__ (perder).
4. Sabemos que la agencia de viajes está en una plaza muy __conocida__ (conocer), la Plaza Bolívar. Está __abierta__ (abrir) de nueve a tres.
5. El nombre de la agencia está __escrito__ (escribir) en el letrero y en la acera (*sidewalk*).
6. Pero ya son las tres y diez.... que mala suerte. Seguramente la oficina ya está __cerrada__ (cerrar).

**2**

**Preparativos** Tú y tu compañero/a van a hacer un viaje. Túrnense para hacerse estas preguntas sobre los preparativos (*preparations*). Usen el participio pasado en sus respuestas.

> **modelo**
>
> **Estudiante 1:** ¿Compraste los pasajes del avión?
> **Estudiante 2:** Sí, los pasajes ya están comprados.

1. ¿Hiciste las maletas?
   Sí, las maletas ya están hechas.
2. ¿Confirmaste las reservaciones para el hotel?
   Sí, las reservaciones ya están confirmadas.
3. ¿Compraste tus medicinas?
   Sí, las medicinas ya están compradas.
4. ¿Lavaste la ropa?
   Sí, la ropa ya está lavada.
5. ¿Apagaste todas las luces?
   Sí, las luces ya están apagadas.
6. ¿Cerraste bien la puerta?
   Sí, la puerta ya está cerrada.

# Comunicación

**3**

**Describir** Tú y un(a) compañero/a son agentes de policía y tienen que investigar un crimen. Miren el dibujo y describan lo que encontraron en la habitación del señor Villalonga. Usen el participio pasado en la descripción. Luego, comparen su descripción con la de otra pareja. Answers will vary.

> **modelo**
>
> La puerta del baño no estaba cerrada.

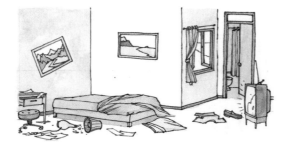

# Recapitulación

**SUPERSITE** For self-scoring and diagnostics, go to **panorama.vhlcentral.com**.

Completa estas actividades para repasar los conceptos de gramática que aprendiste en esta lección.

**1 Completar** Completa la tabla con la forma correcta de los verbos. **6 pts.**

| Infinitivo | Participio (f.) | Infinitivo | Participio (m.) |
|---|---|---|---|
| completar | completada | hacer | hecho |
| cubrir | cubierta | pagar | pagado |
| decir | dicha | perder | perdido |
| escribir | escrita | poner | puesto |

**2 Subjuntivo con conjunciones** Escoge la forma correcta del verbo para completar las oraciones. **6 pts.**

1. En cuanto (empiecen/empiezan) las vacaciones, vamos a viajar.
2. Por favor, llámeme a las siete y media en caso de que no (me despierto/me despierte).
3. Toni va a usar su bicicleta hasta que los coches híbridos (cuesten/cuestan) menos dinero.
4. Estudiantes, pueden entrar al parque natural con tal de que (van/vayan) todos juntos.
5. Debemos conservar el agua antes de que no (queda/quede) nada para beber.
6. Siempre quiero vender mi coche cuando (yo) (piense/pienso) en la contaminación.

**3 Creer o no creer** Completa esta conversación con la forma correcta del presente de indicativo o de subjuntivo, según el contexto. **6 pts.**

**CAROLA** Creo que (1) _____debemos_____ (nosotras, deber) escribir nuestra presentación sobre el reciclaje.

**MÓNICA** Hmm, no estoy segura de que el reciclaje (2) _____sea_____ (ser) un buen tema. No hay duda de que la gente ya (3) _____sabe_____ (saber) reciclar.

**CAROLA** Sí, pero dudo que todos lo (4) _____practiquen_____ (practicar).

**MÓNICA** ¿Sabes, Néstor? El sábado vamos a ir a limpiar la playa con un grupo de voluntarios. ¿Quieres venir?

**NÉSTOR** No creo que (5) _____pueda_____ (yo, poder) ir, tengo que estudiar.

**CAROLA** ¿Estás seguro? ¡Es imposible que (6) _____vayas_____ (tú, ir) a estudiar todo el fin de semana!

**NÉSTOR** Bueno, sí, tengo un par de horas en la tarde para ir a la playa...

**4** **Oraciones** Escribe oraciones con estos elementos. Usa el subjuntivo y el participio de pasado cuando sea necesario. **20 pts.**

1. ser ridículo / los coches / contaminar tanto
Es ridículo que los coches contaminen tanto.

2. el gobierno / ir a proteger / las ciudades / afectar / por la lluvia ácida  El gobierno va a proteger las ciudades afectadas por la lluvia ácida.

3. no caber duda de / tú y yo / poder / hacer mucho más
No cabe duda de que tú y yo podemos hacer mucho más.

4. los ecologistas / temer / los recursos naturales / desaparecer / poco a poco  Los ecologistas temen que los recursos naturales desaparezcan poco a poco.

5. (yo) no estar seguro / los niños / poder ir / porque / el parque / estar / cerrar  No estoy seguro de que los niños puedan ir porque el parque está cerrado.

6. (yo) alegrarse de / en mi ciudad / reciclarse / el plástico y el vidrio  Me alegro de que en mi ciudad se reciclen el plástico y el vidrio.

7. (nosotros) no creer que / la casa / estar / abrir
No creemos que la casa esté abierta.

8. estar prohibido / tocar o dar de comer a / estos animales / proteger  Está prohibido tocar o dar de comer a estos animales protegidos.

9. es improbable / existir / leyes / contra la deforestación
Es improbable que existan leyes contra la deforestación.

10. ojalá que / la situación / mejorar / día a día
Ojalá que la situación mejore día a día.

**5** **Escribir** Escribe un diálogo de al menos seis oraciones en el que un(a) amigo/a hace comentarios pesimistas sobre la situación del medio ambiente en tu ciudad o región y tú respondes con comentarios y reacciones optimistas. Usa verbos y expresiones de esta lección. **12 pts.** Answers will vary.

**6** **Canción** Completa estos versos de una canción de Juan Luis Guerra. **¡2 puntos EXTRA!**

❝ Ojalá que \_\_\_\_llueva\_\_\_\_ (llover)
café en el campo.
Pa'° que todos los niños
\_\_\_\_canten\_\_\_\_ (cantar) en el campo. ❞

Pa' *short for* Para

---

▶ The infinitive is used after the prepositions **antes de**, **para**, and **sin** when there is no change of subject.

Te llamamos **antes de salir** de casa.

Te llamamos mañana **antes de que salgas**.

| Conjunctions used with subjunctive or indicative | |
|---|---|
| cuando | hasta que |
| después de que | tan pronto como |
| en cuanto | |

**13.4** **Past participles used as adjectives**    *p. 438*

| Past participles | | |
|---|---|---|
| Infinitive | Stem | Past participle |
| bailar | bail- | **bail**ado |
| comer | com- | **com**ido |
| vivir | viv- | **viv**ido |

| Irregular past participles | | | |
|---|---|---|---|
| abrir | **abierto** | morir | **muerto** |
| decir | **dicho** | poner | **puesto** |
| describir | **descrito** | resolver | **resuelto** |
| descubrir | **descubierto** | romper | **roto** |
| escribir | **escrito** | ver | **visto** |
| hacer | **hecho** | volver | **vuelto** |

▶ Like common adjectives, past participles must agree with the noun they modify.

Hay unos letreros **escritos** en español.

---

**4** **Expansion** Ask students to create three additional dehydrated sentences. Then have them exchange papers with a classmate and hydrate the sentences.

**5** **Teaching Tip** Remind students that there must be a change of subject in order to use the subjunctive.

**6** **Expansion** Have students create their own song verse by replacing **llueva café** and **canten** with other verbs in the subjunctive.

---

**TEACHING OPTIONS**

**Game** Have students make Bingo cards of different verbs, expressions, and conjunctions that require the subjunctive. Read aloud sentences using the subjunctive. If students have the verb, expression, or phrase on their card, they should cover the space. The first student to complete a horizontal, vertical, or diagonal row is the winner.

**Pairs** Ask students to write down two true sentences and two false ones. Encourage them to write sentences that are all very likely. In pairs, have students take turns reading their sentences. Their partner should react, using expressions of doubt, disbelief, denial, or certainty. The student who stumps his or her partner with all four statements wins. Have pairs share their most challenging sentences with the class.

## Section Goals

In **Lectura**, students will:
• learn that recognizing the purpose of a text can help them to understand it
• read two fables

**Instructional Resources**
**Supersite**
*Cuaderno para hispanohablantes*

**Estrategia** Tell students that recognizing the writer's purpose will help them comprehend an unfamiliar text.

**Examinar los textos** Have students scan the texts, using the reading strategies they have learned to determine the authors' purposes. Then have them work with a partner to answer the questions. Students should recognize that the texts are fables because the characters are animals.

**Predicciones**
• Tell pairs that where their predictions differ they should refer back to the texts for resolution.
• Give students these additional predictions: **5. Los textos son infantiles. 6. Se trata de una historia romántica.**

**Determinar el propósito**
• Tell students to take notes about the characters as they read. Remind students that they should be able to retell the stories in their own words.
• Ask about who reads fables. Ex: **Por lo general, ¿las fábulas se escriben para niños, adultos o ambos? Expliquen sus respuestas.**

# Lectura

## Antes de leer

### Estrategia

**Recognizing the purpose of a text**

When you are faced with an unfamiliar text, it is important to determine the writer's purpose. If you are reading an editorial in a newspaper, for example, you know that the journalist's objective is to persuade you of his or her point of view. Identifying the purpose of a text will help you better comprehend its meaning.

### Examinar los textos

Primero, utiliza la estrategia de lectura para familiarizarte con los textos. Después contesta estas preguntas y compara tus respuestas con las de un(a) compañero/a. Answers will vary.
• ¿De qué tratan los textos (*What are the texts about?*)?
• ¿Son fábulas (*fables*), poemas, artículos de periódico…?
• ¿Cómo lo sabes?

### Predicciones

Lee estas predicciones sobre la lectura e indica si estás de acuerdo (*you agree*) con ellas. Después compara tus opiniones con las de un(a) compañero/a.
1. Los textos son del género (*genre*) de ficción.
2. Los personajes son animales.
3. La acción de los textos tiene lugar en un zoológico.
4. Hay alguna moraleja (*moral*).

### Determinar el propósito

Con un(a) compañero/a, hablen de los posibles propósitos (*purposes*) de los textos. Consideren estas preguntas:
• ¿Qué te dice el género de los textos sobre los posibles propósitos de los textos?
• ¿Piensas que los textos pueden tener más de un propósito? ¿Por qué?

## Sobre los autores

**Félix María Samaniego** (1745–1801) nació en España y escribió las *Fábulas morales* que ilustran de manera humorística el carácter humano. Los protagonistas de muchas de sus fábulas son animales que hablan.

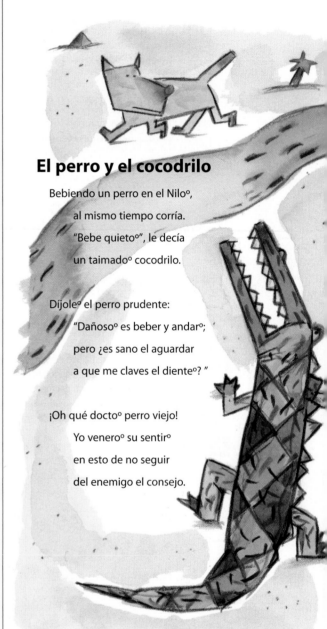

## El perro y el cocodrilo

Bebiendo un perro en el Nilo°,
al mismo tiempo corría.
"Bebe quieto°", le decía
un taimado° cocodrilo.

Díjole° el perro prudente:
"Dañoso° es beber y andar°;
pero ¿es sano el aguardar
a que me claves el diente°? "

¡Oh qué docto° perro viejo!
Yo venero° su sentir°
en esto de no seguir
del enemigo el consejo.

**Tomás de Iriarte** (1750–1791) nació en las islas Canarias y tuvo gran éxito° con su libro *Fábulas literarias*. Su tendencia a representar la lógica a través de° símbolos de la naturaleza fue de gran influencia para muchos autores de su época°.

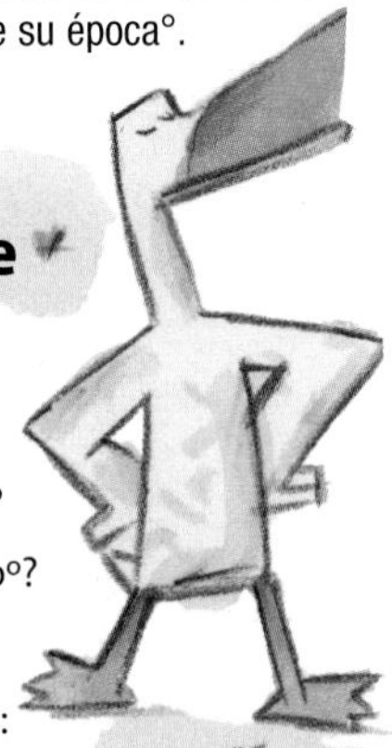

## El pato° y la serpiente

A orillas° de un estanque°,
diciendo estaba un pato:
"¿A qué animal dio el cielo°
los dones que me ha dado°?

"Soy de agua, tierra y aire:
cuando de andar me canso°,
si se me antoja, vuelo°;
si se me antoja, nado".

Una serpiente astuta
que le estaba escuchando,
le llamó con un silbo°,
y le dijo "¡Seo° guapo!

"No hay que echar tantas plantas°;
pues ni anda como el gamo°,
ni vuela como el sacre°,
ni nada como el barbo°;

"y así tenga sabido
que lo importante y raro°
no es entender de todo,
sino ser diestro° en algo".

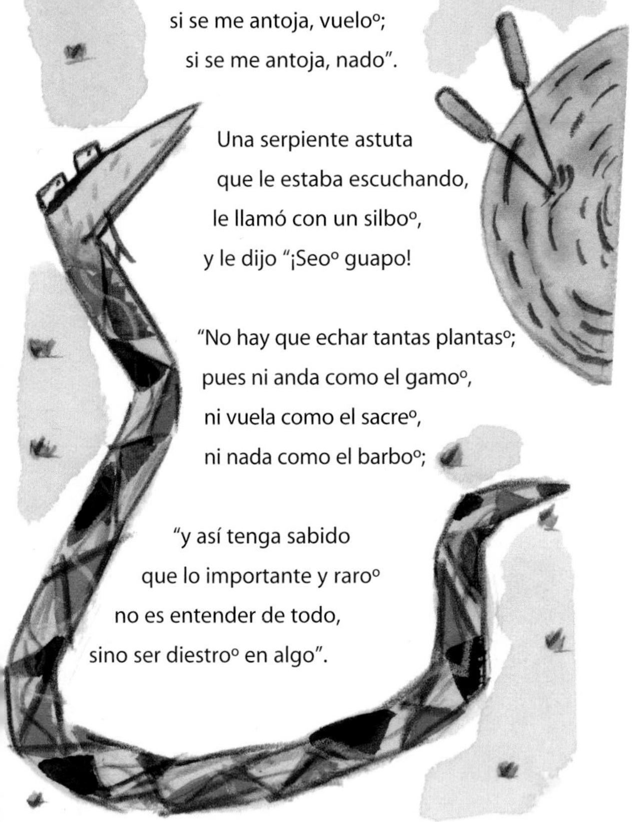

Nilo *Nile* quieto *in peace* taimado *sly* Díjole *Said to him* Dañoso *Harmful* andar *to walk* ¿es sano... diente? *Is it good for me to wait for you to sink your teeth into me?* docto *wise* venero *revere* sentir *wisdom* éxito *success* a través de *through* época *time* pato *duck* orillas *banks* estanque *pond* cielo *heaven* los dones... dado *the gifts that it has given me* me canso *I get tired* si se... vuelo *if I feel like it, I fly* silbo *hiss* Seo *Señor* No hay... plantas *There's no reason to boast* gamo *deer* sacre *falcon* barbo *barbel (a type of fish)* raro *rare* diestro *skillful*

# Después de leer

### Comprensión

Escoge la mejor opción para completar cada oración.

1. El cocodrilo ____ perro.
   a. está preocupado por el  b. quiere comerse al
   c. tiene miedo del
2. El perro ____ cocodrilo.
   a. tiene miedo del  b. es amigo del
   c. quiere quedarse con el
3. El pato cree que es un animal ____.
   a. muy famoso  b. muy hermoso
   c. de muchos talentos
4. La serpiente cree que el pato es ____.
   a. muy inteligente  b. muy tonto  c. muy feo

### Preguntas

Responde a las preguntas. Answers will vary.

1. ¿Qué representa el cocodrilo?
2. ¿Qué representa el pato?
3. ¿Cuál es la moraleja (*moral*) de "El perro y el cocodrilo"?
4. ¿Cuál es la moraleja de "El pato y la serpiente"?

### Coméntalo

En parejas, túrnense para hacerse estas preguntas. ¿Estás de acuerdo con las moralejas de estas fábulas? ¿Por qué? ¿Cuál de estas fábulas te gusta más? ¿Por qué? ¿Conoces otras fábulas? ¿Cuál es su propósito? Answers will vary.

### Escribir

Escribe una fábula para compartir con la clase. Puedes escoger algunos animales de la lista o escoger tus propios (*own*). ¿Qué características deben tener estos animales? Answers will vary.

- una abeja (*bee*)
- un gato
- un burro
- un perro
- un águila (*eagle*)
- un pavo real (*peacock*)

**Comprensión**
- To simplify, before beginning the activity, call on volunteers to explain the fables in their own words.
- Encourage students to justify their answers by citing the text.

**Preguntas** For items 1 and 2, have the class brainstorm a list of adjectives to describe each animal.

**Coméntalo** For additional discussion, have students imagine they must rewrite fables with the same morals, but using other animals as the protagonists. **¿Qué animales escogen para sustituir a estos animales? ¿Cómo cambia la historia?**

**Escribir** Before writing, encourage students to outline their fables. Have them include the characters, the setting, the basic plot, and the moral in their outlines.

**TEACHING OPTIONS**

**Extra Practice** To challenge students, have them write a story from the viewpoint of the dog, the crocodile, the duck, or the snake, in which they explain their encounter with another animal and what they learned from the experience. You may want to review the imperfect and preterite tenses before assigning this activity.

**Small Groups** If time and resources permit, bring in other fables in Spanish, such as **Samaniego's *El herrero y el perro*** or ***La abeja haragana*** by **Horacio Quiroga**. Have students work in small groups to analyze one fable in terms of its characters and moral. Then have one representative from each group summarize the analysis for the class.

## Section Goal

In **Panorama**, students will read about the geography, history, and culture of Colombia.

**Instructional Resources**
**Supersite/DVD:** *Panorama cultural*
**Supersite/IRCD:** *PowerPoints* (Overheads #5, #6, #52); *IRM* (*Panorama cultural* Videoscript & Translation, WBs/VM/LM Answer Key)
**WebSAM**
**Workbook,** pp. 165–166
**Video Manual,** pp. 255–256

**Teaching Tip** Have students look at the map of Colombia or show *Overhead PowerPoint #52* and talk about the physical features of the country. Point out the three parallel ranges of the Andes in the west, and the Amazon Basin in the east and south. After students look at the call-out photos and read the captions, point out that there are no major cities in the eastern half of the country. Ask students to suggest reasons for the lack of population in that area.

**El país en cifras** After reading the **Población** section, ask students what the impact might be of having 55% of the nation's territory unpopulated, and the sort of problems this might create for a national government. Point out that, although Spanish is the official language, some indigenous peoples speak **chibcha** and **araucano**.

**¡Increíble pero cierto!** In their desperation to uncover the gold from Lake Guatavita, Spaniards made several attempts to drain the lake. Around 1545, **Hernán Pérez de Quesada** set up a bucket brigade that lowered the water level by several meters, allowing gold to be gathered.

# Colombia

NATIONAL STANDARDS connections cultures

## El país en cifras

▶ **Área:** 1.138.910 km² (439.734 millas²), *tres veces el área de Montana*
▶ **Población:** 48.930.000
*De todos los países de habla hispana, sólo México tiene más habitantes que Colombia. Casi toda la población colombiana vive en las áreas montañosas y la costa occidental° del país. Aproximadamente el 55% de la superficie° del país está sin poblar°.*
▶ **Capital:** Santa Fe de Bogotá —8.416.000
▶ **Ciudades principales:** Medellín —3.304.000, Cali —2.767.000, Barranquilla —2.042.000, Cartagena —1.067.000

SOURCE: Population Division, UN Secretariat

Medellín

▶ **Moneda:** peso colombiano
▶ **Idiomas:** español (oficial)

Bandera de Colombia

### Colombianos célebres

▶ **Edgar Negret,** escultor°, pintor (1920– )
▶ **Gabriel García Márquez,** escritor (1928– )
▶ **Juan Pablo Montoya,** automovilista (1975– )
▶ **Fernando Botero,** pintor, escultor (1932– )
▶ **Shakira,** cantante (1977– )

occidental *western* superficie *surface* sin poblar *unpopulated* escultor *sculptor* dioses *gods* arrojaban *threw* oro *gold* cacique *chief* llevó *led*

### ¡Increíble pero cierto!

En el siglo XVI los exploradores españoles oyeron la leyenda de El Dorado. Esta leyenda cuenta que los indios, como parte de un ritual en honor a los dioses°, arrojaban° oro° a la laguna de Guatavita y el cacique° se sumergía en sus aguas cubierto de oro. Aunque esto era cierto, muy pronto la exageración llevó° al mito de una ciudad de oro.

Plaza Bolívar, Bogotá

Baile típico de Barranquilla

PANAMÁ

Barranquilla
Cartagena
Mar Caribe

Sierra Nevada de Santa Marta

VENEZUEL

ESTADOS UNIDOS
OCÉANO ATLÁNTICO
COLOMBIA
OCÉANO PACÍFICO
AMÉRICA DEL SUR

Río Magdalena

Medellín

Cordillera Occidental de los Andes
Cordillera Central de los Andes

Río Meta

Cali

Volcán Nevado del Huíla

Bogotá

Cordillera Oriental de los Andes

Océano Pacífico

Cultivo de caña de azúcar cerca de Cali

ECUADOR

PERÚ

**recursos**
WB pp. 165–166
VM pp. 255–256
SUPERSITE panorama.vhlcentral.com Lección 13

Laguna de Guatavita

---

**TEACHING OPTIONS**

**La música** One of Colombia's contributions to Latin popular music is the dance called the **cumbia**. The **cumbia** was born out of the fusion of musical elements contributed by each of Colombia's three main ethnic groups: indigenous Andeans, Africans, and Europeans. According to ethnomusicologists, the flutes and wind instruments characteristically used in the **cumbia** derive from indigenous Andean music, the rhythms have their origin in African music, and the melodies are shaped by Spanish popular melodies. **Cumbias** are popular outside of Colombia, particularly in Mexico. Another Colombian dance, native to the Caribbean coast, is the **vallenato**, a fusion of African and European elements. If possible, bring in examples of **cumbias** and **vallenatos** for the class to listen to and compare and contrast.

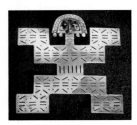

### Lugares • **El Museo del Oro**

El famoso Museo del Oro del Banco de la República fue fundado° en Bogotá en 1939 para preservar las piezas de orfebrería° de la época precolombina. En el museo, que tiene más de 30.000 piezas de oro, se pueden ver joyas°, ornamentos religiosos y figuras que sirvieron de ídolos. El cuidado con el que se hicieron los objetos de oro refleja la creencia° de las tribus indígenas de que el oro era la expresión física de la energía creadora° de los dioses.

### Literatura • **Gabriel García Márquez (1928– )**

Gabriel García Márquez, ganador del Premio Nobel de Literatura en 1982, es uno de los escritores contemporáneos más importantes del mundo. García Márquez publicó su primer cuento° en 1947, cuando era estudiante universitario. Su libro más conocido, *Cien años de soledad*, está escrito en el estilo° literario llamado "realismo mágico", un estilo que mezcla° la realidad con lo irreal y lo mítico°.

### Historia • **Cartagena de Indias**

Los españoles fundaron la ciudad de Cartagena de Indias en 1533 y construyeron a su lado la fortaleza° más grande de las Américas, el Castillo de San Felipe de Barajas. En la ciudad de Cartagena se conservan muchos edificios de la época colonial, como iglesias, monasterios, palacios y mansiones. Cartagena es conocida también por el Festival de Música del Caribe y su prestigioso Festival Internacional de Cine.

### Costumbres • **El Carnaval**

Durante el Carnaval de Barranquilla, la ciudad vive casi exclusivamente para esta fiesta. Este festival es una fusión de las culturas que han llegado° a las costas caribeñas de Colombia y de sus grupos autóctonos°. El evento más importante es la Batalla° de las Flores, un desfile° de carrozas° decoradas con flores. En 2003, la UNESCO declaró este carnaval como Patrimonio de la Humanidad°.

**¿Qué aprendiste?** Responde a cada pregunta con una oración completa.
1. ¿Cuáles son las principales ciudades de Colombia? Santa Fe de Bogotá, Cali, Medellín y Barranquilla son las ciudades principales de Colombia.
2. ¿Qué país de habla hispana tiene más habitantes que Colombia? México tiene más habitantes que Colombia.
3. ¿Quién es Edgar Negret? Edgar Negret es un escultor y pintor colombiano.
4. ¿Cuándo oyeron los españoles la leyenda de El Dorado? En el siglo XVI los españoles oyeron la leyenda.
5. ¿Para qué fue fundado el Museo del Oro? El museo fue fundado para preservar las piezas de orfebrería de la época precolombina.
6. ¿Quién ganó el Premio Nobel de Literatura en 1982? Gabriel García Márquez lo ganó.
7. ¿Qué construyeron los españoles al lado de la ciudad de Cartagena de Indias? Construyeron el Castillo de San Felipe de Barajas.
8. ¿Cuál es el evento más importante del Carnaval de Barranquilla? El evento más importante es la Batalla de las Flores.

**Conexión Internet** Investiga estos temas en **panorama.vhlcentral.com**.

1. Busca información sobre las ciudades más grandes de Colombia. ¿Qué lugares de interés hay en estas ciudades? ¿Qué puede hacer un(a) turista en estas ciudades?
2. Busca información sobre pintores y escultores colombianos como Edgar Negret, Débora Arango o Fernando Botero. ¿Cuáles son algunas de sus obras más conocidas? ¿Cuáles son sus temas?

................................................................

fundado *founded* orfebrería *goldsmithing* joyas *jewels* creencia *belief* creadora *creative* cuento *story* estilo *style* mezcla *mixes* mítico *mythical* fortaleza *fortress* han llegado *have arrived* autóctonos *indigenous* Batalla *Battle* desfile *parade* carrozas *floats* Patrimonio de la Humanidad *World Heritage*

---

**El Museo del Oro** In pre-Columbian times, the native peoples from different regions of Colombia developed distinct styles of working with gold. Some preferred to melt copper into the metal before working it, some pounded the gold, while others poured it into molds. If possible, bring photos of pre-Columbian gold-work for the class to look at.

**Gabriel García Márquez (1928– )** **García Márquez** was raised primarily by his maternal grandparents, who made a profound impression upon his life and literature. His grandfather was a man of strong ideals and a military hero. His grandmother, who held many superstitious beliefs, regaled the young **García Márquez** with fantastical stories.

**Cartagena de Indias** Because Cartagena de Indias was the point of departure for shipments of Andean gold to Spain, it was the frequent target of pirate attacks from the sixteenth through the eighteenth centuries. The most famous siege was led by the English pirate Sir Francis Drake, in 1586. He held the city for 100 days, until the residents surrendered to him some 100,000 pieces of gold.

**El Carnaval** The many events that make up the **Carnaval de Barranquilla** are spread out over about a month. Although the carnival queen is crowned at the beginning of the month, the real opening act is the **Guacherna**, which is a nighttime street parade involving **comparsas** (live bands) and costumed dancers. The **Carnaval's** official slogan is **¡Quien lo vive es quien lo goza!**

**Conexión Internet** Students will find supporting Internet activities and links at **panorama.vhlcentral.com**.

---

## Section Goal

In **Panorama**, students will read about the georgraphy, economy, and culture of Honduras.

**Instructional Resources**
**Supersite/DVD:** *Panorama cultural*
**Supersite/IRCD:** *PowerPoints* (Overheads #3, #4, #53); *IRM* (*Panorama cultural* Videoscript & Translation, WBs/VM/LM Answer Key)
**WebSAM**
**Workbook,** pp. 167–168
**Video Manual,** pp. 257–258

**Teaching Tip** Have students look at the map of Honduras or show *Overhead PowerPoint #53* and talk about the geographical features of the country. Hills and mountains cover three quarters of Honduras, with lowlands found only along coastal areas and in major river valleys. Deforestation is a major environmental challenge in Honduras. If deforestation continues at the current rate of 300 square kilometers per year, the country will have no trees left by 2020.

**El país en cifras** After reading about the indigenous populations of Honduras, tell students that the **miskito** people are also found along the Caribbean coast of Nicaragua. After students read about **Idiomas**, point out that **garífuna** speakers are descendants of indigenous Caribs who intermarried with African slaves following a shipwreck some 300 years ago.

**¡Increíble pero cierto!** Although the Honduran justice system is not known for its fairness, the case of the artisan prisoners at the **Penitenciaría Central de Tegucigalpa** is a surprising example of business ethics. All profits from the sale of the crafts go directly to the creators: the prisoners themselves.

# Honduras

NATIONAL STANDARDS connections cultures

## El país en cifras

▶ **Área:** 112.492 km$^2$ (43.870 millas$^2$), *un poco más grande que Tennessee*

▶ **Población:** 7.997.000

*Cerca del 90 por ciento de la población de Honduras es mestiza. Todavía hay pequeños grupos indígenas como los jicaque, los miskito y los paya, que han mantenido su cultura sin influencias exteriores y que no hablan español.*

▶ **Capital:** Tegucigalpa—1.075.000

Tegucigalpa

▶ **Ciudades principales:** San Pedro Sula, El Progreso, La Ceiba

SOURCE: Population Division, UN Secretariat

▶ **Moneda:** lempira

▶ **Idiomas:** español (oficial), miskito, garífuna

Bandera de Honduras

**Hondureños célebres**

▶ **José Antonio Velásquez,** pintor (1906–1983)
▶ **Argentina Díaz Lozano,** escritora (1917–1999)
▶ **Carlos Roberto Reina,** juez° y presidente del país (1926–2003)
▶ **Roberto Sosa,** escritor (1930– )

juez *judge* presos *prisoners* madera *wood* hamacas *hammocks* artesanías *crafts*

Guacamayo

Hombres garífuna en Santa Fe

Islas de la Bahía    Mar Caribe

Golfo de Honduras

**GUATEMALA**    La Ceiba    Santa Fe

San Pedro Sula    Río Ulúa    Sierra Rijol    Sierra de Payas    Laguna de Carataso

**Sierra Espíritu Santo**    Sierra Grita    El Progreso    Río Patuca

Lago de Yojoa    Sierra Villasanta    Río Guyambre    Montañas de Colón

**Tegucigalpa**    Río Coco

**EL SALVADOR**    Río Choluteca

Océano Pacífico    **NICARAGUA**

Niños pescando en el lago de Yojoa

ESTADOS UNIDOS

OCÉANO ATLÁNTICO

**HONDURAS**

OCÉANO PACÍFICO    AMÉRICA DEL SUR

**recursos**

WB pp. 167–168

VM pp. 257–258

SUPERSITE panorama.vhlcentral.com Lección 13

### ¡Increíble pero cierto!

Los presos° de la Penitenciaría Central de Tegucigalpa hacen objetos de madera°, hamacas° y hasta instrumentos musicales. Sus artesanías° son tan populares que los funcionarios de la prisión han abierto una pequeña tienda donde los turistas pueden regatear con este especial grupo de artesanos.

**TEACHING OPTIONS**

**Worth Noting** It was in Honduras, on his fourth voyage of discovery, that Christopher Columbus first set foot on the mainland of the continent that would become known as the Americas. On August 14, 1502, the navigator landed at a site near the town of Trujillo and named the country **Honduras** (*Depths*) because of the deep waters along the northern Caribbean coast.

**Extra Practice** Have students choose one of the people listed in **Hondureños célebres** and find out more about his or her work. They should report their findings to the class.

### Lugares • **Copán**

Copán es una zona arqueológica muy importante de Honduras. Fue construida por los mayas y se calcula que en el año 400 d.C. albergaba a° una ciudad con más de 150 edificios y una gran cantidad de plazas, patios, templos y canchas° para el juego de pelota°. Las ruinas más famosas del lugar son los edificios adornados con esculturas pintadas a mano, los cetros° ceremoniales de piedra y el templo Rosalila.

### Economía • **Las plantaciones de bananas**

Desde hace más de cien años, las bananas son la exportación principal de Honduras y han tenido un papel fundamental en su historia. En 1889, la Standard Fruit Company empezó a exportar bananas del país centroamericano hacia Nueva Orleans. Esta fruta resultó tan popular en los Estados Unidos que generó grandes beneficios° para esta compañía y para la United Fruit Company, otra empresa norteamericana. Estas trasnacionales intervinieron muchas veces en la política hondureña gracias al enorme poder° económico que alcanzaron° en la nación.

### Artes • **José Antonio Velásquez (1906–1983)**

*San Antonio de Oriente,* 1957,
José Antonio Velásquez

José Antonio Velásquez fue un famoso pintor hondureño. Es catalogado como primitivista° porque sus obras° representan aspectos de la vida cotidiana. En la pintura° de Velásquez es notorio el énfasis en los detalles°, la falta casi total de los juegos de perspectiva y la pureza en el uso del color. Por todo ello, el artista ha sido comparado con importantes pintores europeos del mismo género° como Paul Gauguin o Emil Nolde.

**¿Qué aprendiste?** Responde a cada pregunta con una oración completa.

1. ¿Qué es el lempira?
   El lempira es la moneda nacional de Honduras.

2. ¿Por qué es famoso Copán?
   Porque es el sitio arqueológico más importante de Honduras.

3. ¿Dónde está el templo Rosalila?
   El templo Rosalila está en Copán.

4. ¿Cuál es la exportación principal de Honduras?
   Las bananas son la exportación principal de Honduras.

5. ¿Qué es la Standard Fruit Company? La Standard Fruit Company es una compañía norteamericana
   que exportaba bananas de Honduras e intervino muchas veces en la política hondureña.

6. ¿Cómo es el estilo de José Antonio Velásquez?
   El estilo de Velásquez es primitivista.

**Conexión Internet** Investiga estos temas en **panorama.vhlcentral.com.**

1. ¿Cuáles son algunas de las exportaciones principales de Honduras, además de las bananas?
   ¿A qué países exporta Honduras sus productos?

2. Busca información sobre Copán u otro sitio arqueológico en Honduras. En tu opinión,
   ¿cuáles son los aspectos más interesantes del sitio?

......................................................................................................................

albergaba a *was home for*   canchas *courts*   juego de pelota *pre-Columbian ceremonial ball game*   cetros *scepters*   beneficios
*profits*   poder *power*   alcanzaron *reached*   primitivista *primitivist*   obras *works*   pintura *painting*   detalles *details*   género *genre*

**Copán** Recent archaeological studies have focused on the abrupt disappearance of the Mayans from Copán around the ninth century C.E. Findings indicate that the Mayan dynasty suffered a sudden collapse that left the Copán valley virtually depopulated within a century. For more information about Copán, you may want to play the *Panorama cultural* video footage for this lesson.

**Las plantaciones de bananas** When Hurricane Mitch struck Central America in November 1998, it not only wiped out much of the infrastructure of Honduras, but also destroyed 60% of the projected agricultural exports. Instead of the 33 million boxes of bananas projected for export in 1999, only 4 million boxes were exported.

**José Antonio Velásquez** The primitive style established by **José Antonio Velásquez** is now being carried on by his son, **Tulio Velásquez. Tulio,** who was taught by his father, had his first exhibition in 1959. Since then, his primitive art has been exhibited throughout the Americas, in Europe, and in Asia. Have students view works by each artist and then write a brief comparison of their styles.

**Conexión Internet** Students will find supporting Internet activities and links at **panorama.vhlcentral.com.**

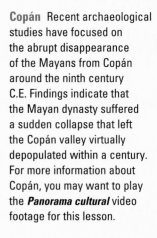

---

**TEACHING OPTIONS**

**Worth Noting** Honduras was among the hardest hit of the Central American nations when Hurricane Mitch struck in late October 1998. Major roadways and bridges were destroyed, entire communities were covered in mud, and an air of hopelessness and desperation pervaded the country. With one of the lowest per capita income levels and one of the highest illiteracy rates in Central America, Hondurans were already struggling

before the devastation of the hurricane. Despite international aid, reconstruction was slow and the level of desperation in Honduras was reflected in the increase in violent crime.
**Heritage Speakers** Ask heritage speakers to research one of the Honduran topics mentioned in **Panorama** and write a three-paragraph essay about it. They may then present their findings orally to the class.

## La naturaleza

| | |
|---|---|
| el árbol | tree |
| el bosque (tropical) | (tropical; rain) forest |
| el cielo | sky |
| el cráter | crater |
| el desierto | desert |
| la estrella | star |
| la flor | flower |
| la hierba | grass |
| el lago | lake |
| la luna | moon |
| la naturaleza | nature |
| la nube | cloud |
| la piedra | stone |
| la planta | plant |
| el río | river |
| la selva, la jungla | jungle |
| el sendero | trail; trailhead |
| el sol | sun |
| la tierra | land; soil |
| el valle | valley |
| el volcán | volcano |

## Los animales

| | |
|---|---|
| el animal | animal |
| el ave, el pájaro | bird |
| el gato | cat |
| el perro | dog |
| el pez | fish |
| la vaca | cow |

## El medio ambiente

| | |
|---|---|
| la conservación | conservation |
| la contaminación (del aire; del agua) | (air; water) pollution |
| la deforestación | deforestation |
| la ecología | ecology |
| el ecoturismo | ecotourism |
| la energía (nuclear, solar) | (nuclear, solar) energy |
| el envase | container |
| la extinción | extinction |
| el gobierno | government |
| la lata | (tin) can |
| la ley | law |
| la lluvia (ácida) | (acid) rain |
| el medio ambiente | environment |
| el peligro | danger |
| la población | population |
| el reciclaje | recycling |
| el recurso natural | natural resource |
| la solución | solution |
| cazar | to hunt |
| conservar | to conserve |
| contaminar | to pollute |
| controlar | to control |
| cuidar | to take care of |
| dejar de (+ *inf.*) | to stop (doing something) |
| desarrollar | to develop |
| descubrir | to discover |
| destruir | to destroy |
| estar afectado/a (por) | to be affected (by) |
| estar contaminado/a | to be polluted |
| evitar | to avoid |
| mejorar | to improve |
| proteger | to protect |
| reciclar | to recycle |
| recoger | to pick up |
| reducir | to reduce |
| resolver (o:ue) | to resolve; to solve |
| respirar | to breathe |
| de aluminio | (made) of aluminum |
| de plástico | (made) of plastic |
| de vidrio | (made) of glass |
| puro/a | pure |

## Las emociones

| | |
|---|---|
| alegrarse (de) | to be happy |
| esperar | to hope; to wish |
| sentir (e:ie) | to be sorry; to regret |
| temer | to fear |
| es extraño | it's strange |
| es una lástima | it's a shame |
| es ridículo | it's ridiculous |
| es terrible | it's terrible |
| es triste | it's sad |
| ojalá (que) | I hope (that); I wish (that) |

## Las dudas y certezas

| | |
|---|---|
| (no) creer | (not) to believe |
| (no) dudar | (not) to doubt |
| (no) negar (e:ie) | (not) to deny |
| es imposible | it's impossible |
| es improbable | it's improbable |
| es obvio | it's obvious |
| No cabe duda de | There is no doubt that… |
| No hay duda de | There is no doubt that… |
| (no) es cierto | it's (not) certain |
| (no) es posible | it's (not) possible |
| (no) es probable | it's (not) probable |
| (no) es seguro | it's (not) certain |
| (no) es verdad | it's (not) true |

## Conjunciones

| | |
|---|---|
| a menos que | unless |
| antes (de) que | before |
| con tal (de) que | provided (that) |
| cuando | when |
| después de que | after |
| en caso (de) que | in case (that) |
| en cuanto | as soon as |
| hasta que | until |
| para que | so that |
| sin que | without |
| tan pronto como | as soon as |

| | |
|---|---|
| **Expresiones útiles** | See page 421. |
| **Past participles used as adjectives** | See page 438. |

recursos

LM
p. 78

panorama.vhlcentral.com
Lección 13

# En la ciudad

## 14

### Lesson Goals

In **Lección 14**, students will be introduced to the following:

- names of commercial establishments
- banking terminology
- citing locations
- means of transportation
- Mexican architect **Luis Barragán**
- subjunctive in adjective clauses
- **nosotros/as** commands
- future tense
- irregular future tense verbs
- identifying a narrator's point of view
- geographic, economic, and historical information about Venezuela
- cultural and geographic information about the Dominican Republic

**A primera vista**  Here are some additional questions you can ask based on the photo: **¿Cómo es la vida en la ciudad? ¿Y en el campo? ¿Dónde prefieres vivir? ¿Por qué? ¿Es posible que no haya contaminación en una ciudad? ¿Cómo? ¿Qué responsabilidades tienen las personas que viven en una ciudad para proteger el medio ambiente?**

### A PRIMERA VISTA

- ¿Viven estas personas en un bosque, un pueblo o una ciudad?
- ¿Dónde están, en una calle o en un sendero?
- ¿Es posible que estén afectadas por la contaminación?
- ¿Está limpio o sucio el lugar donde están?

**INSTRUCTIONAL RESOURCES**

**MAESTRO™ SUPERSITE (panorama.vhlcentral.com)**
Textbook, Vocabulary, & Lab MP3 Audio Files
Additional Practice
Learning Management System (Assignment Task Manager, Gradebook)
*Also on DVD*
**Fotonovela**

*Flash cultura*
*Panorama cultural*
*Also on Instructor's Resource CD-ROM*
*PowerPoints* (**Contextos** & **Estructura** Presentations, Overheads)
*Instructor's Resource Manual* (Handouts, Textbook Answer Key, WBs/VM/LM Answer Key,

Audioscripts, Videoscripts & Translations)
*Testing Program* (**Pruebas**, Test Generator, MP3s)
**WebSAM** (Workbook/Video Manual/Lab Manual)
**Workbook/Video Manual**
*Cuaderno para hispanohablantes*
**Lab Manual**

## Section Goals

In **Contextos**, students will learn and practice:
- names of commercial establishments
- banking terminology
- citing locations

### Instructional Resources

**Supersite:** Textbook, Vocabulary, & Lab MP3 Audio Files **Lección 14**
**Supersite/IRCD:** *PowerPoints* (**Lección 14 Contextos** Presentation, Overheads #54, #55); *IRM* (**Vocabulario adicional,** Textbook Audio Script, Lab Audio Script, WBs/VM/LM Answer Key)
**WebSAM**
**Workbook,** pp. 169–170
**Lab Manual,** p. 79
*Cuaderno para hispanohablantes*

### Teaching Tips

- Using realia or magazine pictures, ask volunteers to identify the items. Ex: **carne, zapato, pan.** As students give their answers, write the names of corresponding establishments on the board (**carnicería, zapatería, panadería**). Then present banking vocabulary by miming common transactions. Ex: **Cuando necesito dinero, voy al banco. Escribo un cheque y lo cobro.**

- Show *Overhead PowerPoint #54.* Have students refer to the scene to answer your questions about it. Ex: **¿Qué tienda queda entre la lavandería y la carnicería? Las dos señoras frente a la estatua, ¿de qué hablan? ¿Qué tipo de transacciones pueden hacerse en un banco?**

### Successful Language Learning

Ask students to imagine how they would use this vocabulary when traveling.

**Note:** At this point you may want to present *Vocabulario adicional: Más vocabulario para la ciudad,* from the Supersite/IRCD.

# En la ciudad

la peluquería, el salón de belleza

el banco

el supermercado

la panadería

la joyería

el cajero automático

Da direcciones. (dar)

Está perdida. (estar)

## Más vocabulario

| | |
|---|---|
| la frutería | fruit store |
| la heladería | ice cream shop |
| la pastelería | pastry shop |
| la pescadería | fish market |
| la cuadra | (city) block |
| la dirección | address |
| la esquina | corner |
| el estacionamiento | parking lot |
| derecho | straight (ahead) |
| enfrente de | opposite; facing |
| hacia | toward |
| cruzar | to cross |
| doblar | to turn |
| hacer diligencias | to run errands |
| quedar | to be located |
| el cheque (de viajero) | (traveler's) check |
| la cuenta corriente | checking account |
| la cuenta de ahorros | savings account |
| ahorrar | to save (money) |
| cobrar | to cash (a check) |
| depositar | to deposit |
| firmar | to sign |
| llenar (un formulario) | to fill out (a form) |
| pagar a plazos | to pay in installments |
| pagar al contado, en efectivo | to pay in cash |
| pedir prestado/a | to borrow |
| pedir un préstamo | to apply for a loan |
| ser gratis | to be free of charge |

## Variación léxica

cuadra ←→ manzana (*Esp.*)
direcciones ←→ indicaciones (*Esp.*)
doblar ←→ girar; virar; voltear
hacer diligencias ←→ hacer mandados

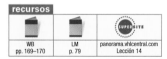

**recursos**

| WB pp. 169–170 | LM p. 79 | SUPERSITE panorama.vhlcentral.com Lección 14 |

### TEACHING OPTIONS

**Extra Practice** Add an auditory aspect to this vocabulary presentation. Prepare a series of mini-dialogues. Read each exchange aloud and have students name the place or activity. Ex: —**Señorita, ¿no tienen un número más grande? —Sí, creo que un 42 le queda bien. (la zapatería) —Perdón, ¿cómo llego a la carnicería? —Cruzas la plaza y está allá, en la esquina. (dar direcciones)**

**Pairs** Have students individually draw schematic maps of a couple of blocks around a city square, labeling every establishment and naming the streets. Then have them each write a description of the location of each establishment and exchange it with a partner. Have each student use the partner's description to recreate the city map. Finally, have partners compare the two sets of maps to check for accuracy.

# Práctica

**el letrero**

**la carnicería**

**la zapatería**

**la lavandería**

**1 Escuchar** 🎧 Mira el dibujo. Luego escucha las oraciones e indica si lo que dice cada una es **cierto** o **falso**.

| | Cierto | Falso | | | Cierto | Falso |
|---|---|---|---|---|---|---|
| 1. | ○ | ⊘ | | 6. | ⊘ | ○ |
| 2. | ⊘ | ○ | | 7. | ⊘ | ○ |
| 3. | ○ | ⊘ | | 8. | ○ | ⊘ |
| 4. | ⊘ | ○ | | 9. | ○ | ⊘ |
| 5. | ○ | ⊘ | | 10. | ⊘ | ○ |

**2 ¿Quién la hizo?** 🎧 Escucha la conversación entre Telma y Armando. Escribe el nombre de la persona que hizo cada diligencia o una **X** si nadie la hizo. Una diligencia la hicieron los dos.

1. abrir una cuenta corriente  Armando
2. abrir una cuenta de ahorros  Telma
3. ir al banco  Armando, Telma
4. ir a la panadería  X
5. ir a la peluquería  Telma
6. ir al supermercado  Armando

**3 Seleccionar** Selecciona los lugares de la lista en los que haces estas diligencias.

| | | |
|---|---|---|
| banco | joyería | pescadería |
| carnicería | lavandería | salón de belleza |
| frutería | pastelería | zapatería |

1. comprar galletas  pastelería
2. comprar manzanas  frutería
3. lavar la ropa  lavandería
4. comprar mariscos  pescadería
5. comprar pollo  carnicería
6. comprar sandalias  zapatería

**4 Completar** Completa las oraciones con las palabras más adecuadas.

1. El banco me regaló un reloj. Fue ___gratis___.
2. Me gusta ___ahorrar___ dinero, pero no me molesta gastarlo.
3. La cajera me dijo que tenía que ___firmar___ el cheque en el dorso (*on the back*) para cobrarlo.
4. Para pagar con un cheque, necesito tener dinero en mi ___cuenta corriente___.
5. Mi madre va a un cajero ___automático___ para obtener dinero en efectivo cuando el banco está cerrado.
6. Cada viernes, Julio lleva su cheque al banco y lo ___cobra___ para tener dinero en efectivo.
7. Ana ___deposita___ su cheque en su cuenta de ahorros.
8. Cuando viajas, es buena idea llevar cheques ___de viajero___.

---

**1 Teaching Tip** Have students check their answers by reading each statement in the script to the class and asking volunteers to say whether it is true or false. To challenge students, have them correct the false statements.

**1 Script** 1. El supermercado queda al este de la plaza, al lado de la joyería. 2. La zapatería está al lado de la carnicería. 3. El banco queda al sur de la plaza. 4. Cuando sales de la zapatería, la lavandería está a su lado. 5. La carnicería está al lado del banco. *Script continues on page 452.*

**2 Teaching Tip** Do this listening exercise as a TPR activity. Have students raise their right hand if **Armando** did the errand, their left hand if it was **Telma**, or both hands if both people did it.

**2 Script** TELMA: Hola, Armando, ¿qué tal? ARMANDO: Pues bien. Acabo de hacer unas diligencias. Fui a la carnicería y al supermercado. ¿Y tú? Estás muy guapa. ¿Fuiste a la peluquería? T: Sí, fui al nuevo salón de belleza que está enfrente de la panadería. También fui al banco. A: ¿A qué banco fuiste? T: Fui al banco Mercantil. Está aquí en la esquina. A: Ah, ¿sí? Yo abrí una cuenta corriente ayer, ¡y fue gratis! T: Sí, yo abrí una cuenta de ahorros esta mañana y no me cobraron nada. *Textbook MP3s*

**3 Expansion** After students finish, ask them what else can be bought in the establishments. Ex: ¿Qué más podemos comprar en la pastelería?

**4 Expansion** Ask students to compare and contrast aspects of banking. Ex: ATM vs. traditional tellers; credit card vs. check; savings account vs. checking account. Have them work in groups of three to make a list of **Ventajas** and **Desventajas**.

---

**TEACHING OPTIONS**

**Game** Add a visual aspect to this vocabulary presentation by playing **Concentración**. On eight cards, write names of types of commercial establishments. On another eight cards, draw or paste a picture that matches each commercial establishment. Place the cards facedown in four rows of four. In pairs, students select two cards. If the cards match, the pair keeps them. If the cards do not match, students replace them in their original posi-

tion. The pair with the most cards at the end wins.
**Pairs** Have each student write a shopping list with ten items. Have students include items found in different stores. Then have them exchange their shopping list with a partner. Each student tells his or her partner where to go to get each item. Ex: **unas botas (Para comprar unas botas, tienes que ir a la zapatería que queda en la calle ___.)**

Manda/Envía un paquete. (mandar, enviar)

la estampilla, el sello

Hacen cola. (hacer)

Echa una carta al buzón. (echar)

el sobre

el cartero

el correo

**En el correo**

---

**5**   **Conversación** Completa la conversación entre Juanita y el cartero con las palabras más adecuadas.

**CARTERO**   Buenas tardes, ¿es usted la señorita Ramírez? Le traigo un (1) ___paquete___.

**JUANITA**   Sí, soy yo. ¿Quién lo envía?

**CARTERO**   La señora Ramírez. Y también tiene dos (2) ___cartas___.

**JUANITA**   Ay, pero ¡ninguna es de mi novio! ¿No llegó nada de Manuel Fuentes?

**CARTERO**   Sí, pero él echó la carta al (3) ___buzón___ sin poner un (4) ___sello___ en el sobre.

**JUANITA**   Entonces, ¿qué recomienda usted que haga?

**CARTERO**   Sugiero que vaya al (5) ___correo___. Con tal de que pague el costo del sello, se le puede dar la carta sin ningún problema.

**JUANITA**   Uy, otra diligencia, y no tengo mucho tiempo esta tarde para (6) ___hacer___ cola en el correo, pero voy enseguida. ¡Ojalá que sea una carta de amor!

**6**   **En el banco** Tú eres un(a) empleado/a de banco y tu compañero/a es un(a) estudiante universitario/a que necesita abrir una cuenta corriente. En parejas, hagan una lista de las palabras que pueden necesitar para la conversación. Después lean estas situaciones y modifiquen su lista original según la situación. Answers will vary.

• una pareja de recién casados quiere pedir un préstamo para comprar una casa
• una persona quiere información de los servicios que ofrece el banco
• un(a) estudiante va a estudiar al extranjero (*abroad*) y quiere saber qué tiene que hacer para llevar su dinero de una forma segura
• una persona acaba de ganar 50 millones de dólares en la lotería y quiere saber cómo invertirlos (*invest it*)

Ahora, escojan una de las cuatro situaciones y represéntenla para la clase.

---

# Comunicación

**7** **Diligencias** En parejas, decidan quién va a hacer cada diligencia y cuál es la manera más rápida de llegar a los diferentes lugares desde el campus. Answers will vary.

> **modelo**
>
> cobrar unos cheques
> **Estudiante 1:** *Yo voy a cobrar unos cheques. ¿Cómo llego al banco?*
> **Estudiante 2:** *Conduce hacia el norte hasta cruzar la calle Oak.*
> *El banco queda en la esquina a la izquierda.*

1. enviar un paquete
2. comprar botas nuevas
3. comprar un pastel de cumpleaños
4. lavar unas camisas
5. comprar helado
6. cortarte (*to cut*) el pelo

**8** **El Hatillo** Trabajen en parejas para representar los papeles de un(a) turista que está perdido/a en El Hatillo y de un(a) residente de la ciudad que quiere ayudarlo/la. Answers will vary.

Plaza Bolívar
Plaza Sucre
banco
Casa de la Cultura
farmacia
iglesia
terminal
escuela
estacionamiento
joyería
zapatería
café Primavera

**El Hatillo**

> **modelo**
>
> Plaza Sucre, café Primavera
> **Estudiante 1:** *Perdón, ¿por dónde queda la Plaza Sucre?*
> **Estudiante 2:** *Del café Primavera, camine derecho por la calle Sucre*
> *hasta cruzar la calle Comercio...*

1. Plaza Bolívar, farmacia
2. Casa de la Cultura, Plaza Sucre
3. banco, terminal
4. estacionamiento (este), escuela
5. Plaza Sucre, estacionamiento (oeste)
6. joyería, banco
7. farmacia, joyería
8. zapatería, iglesia

**9** **Direcciones** En grupos, escriban un minidrama en el que unos/as turistas están preguntando cómo llegar a diferentes sitios de la comunidad en la que ustedes viven.
Answers will vary.

---

# Estamos perdidos.

Maite y Álex hacen diligencias en el centro.

## Section Goals

In **Fotonovela**, students will:
• receive comprehensible input from free-flowing discourse
• learn functional phrases that preview lesson grammatical structures

**Instructional Resources**
**Supersite/DVD:** *Fotonovela*
**Supersite/IRCD:** *IRM*
(***Fotonovela*** Videoscript & Translation, WBs/VM/LM Answer Key)
**WebSAM**
**Video Manual,** pp. 221–222

**Video Recap: Lección 13**
Before doing this **Fotonovela** section, review the previous one with this activity.
**1. ¿Adónde lleva Martín a los chicos? (al área donde van a ir de excursión) 2. ¿Qué dice él de la contaminación en la región? (Es un problema en todo el mundo; tienen un programa de reciclaje.) 3. ¿Qué dice Martín de la contaminación del río? (En las montañas no está contaminado; cerca de las ciudades tiene bastante contaminación.) 4. ¿Qué va a hacer Maite para proteger el medio ambiente? (Va a usar el metro.)**

**Video Synopsis** **Don Francisco** and **Martín** advise the students about things they need for the hike. **Álex** and **Maite** decide to go to the supermarket, the bank, and the post office. They get lost downtown, but a young man gives them directions. After finishing their errands, **Álex** and **Maite** return to the house.

**Teaching Tip** Ask students to predict what they would see and hear in an episode in which the main characters get lost while running errands. Then, ask them a few questions to help them summarize this episode.

**PERSONAJES**

**MAITE**

**INÉS**

**DON FRANCISCO**

**ÁLEX**

**JAVIER**

**MARTÍN**

**JOVEN**

**MARTÍN Y DON FRANCISCO** Buenas tardes.
**JAVIER** Hola. ¿Qué tal? Estamos conversando sobre la excursión de mañana.

**DON FRANCISCO** ¿Ya tienen todo lo que necesitan? A todos los excursionistas yo siempre les recomiendo llevar zapatos cómodos, una mochila, gafas oscuras y un suéter por si hace frío.
**JAVIER** Todo listo, don Francisco.

**MARTÍN** Les aconsejo que traigan algo de comer.
**ÁLEX** Mmm… no pensamos en eso.
**MAITE** ¡Deja de preocuparte tanto, Álex! Podemos comprar algo en el supermercado ahora mismo. ¿Vamos?

**JOVEN** ¡Hola! ¿Puedo ayudarte en algo?
**MAITE** Sí, estamos perdidos. ¿Hay un banco por aquí con cajero automático?
**JOVEN** Mmm… no hay ningún banco en esta calle que tenga cajero automático.

**JOVEN** Pero conozco uno en la calle Pedro Moncayo que sí tiene cajero automático. Cruzas esta calle y luego doblas a la izquierda. Sigues todo derecho y antes de que lleguen a la Joyería Crespo van a ver un letrero grande del Banco del Pacífico.

**MAITE** También buscamos un supermercado.
**JOVEN** Pues, allí mismo enfrente del banco hay un supermercado pequeño. Fácil, ¿no?
**MAITE** Creo que sí. Muchas gracias por su ayuda.

**recursos**

VM pp. 221–222

**SUPERSITE**
panorama.vhlcentral.com
Lección 14

---

**TEACHING OPTIONS**

**Video Tips** General suggestions for using video clips in the classroom can be found on page IAE-12 of this Instructor's Annotated Edition.

**Estamos perdidos** Play the **Resumen** segment of the episode first, without sound. Ask the class to summarize what they see, then to predict the content of the main episode. Write their predictions on the board, then play the entire episode with sound and have students revise their predictions as necessary.

**ÁLEX** ¡Excelente idea! En cuanto termine mi café te acompaño.

**MAITE** Necesito pasar por el banco y por el correo para mandar unas cartas.

**ÁLEX** Está bien.

**ÁLEX** ¿Necesitan algo del centro?

**INÉS** ¡Sí! Cuando vayan al correo, ¿pueden echar estas postales al buzón? Además necesito unas estampillas.

**ÁLEX** Por supuesto.

**MAITE** Ten, guapa, tus sellos.

**INÉS** Gracias, Maite. ¿Qué tal les fue en el centro?

**MAITE** ¡Súper bien! Fuimos al banco y al correo. Luego en el supermercado compramos comida para la excursión. Y antes de regresar, paramos en una heladería.

**MAITE** ¡Ah! Y otra cosa. Cuando llegamos al centro conocimos a un joven muy simpático que nos dio direcciones. Era muy amable... ¡y muy guapo!

## Expresiones útiles

### Giving advice

- **Les recomiendo/Hay que llevar zapatos cómodos.**
  *I recommend that you/It's necessary to wear comfortable shoes.*
- **Les aconsejo que traigan algo de comer.**
  *I advise you to bring something to eat.*

### Talking about errands

- **Necesito pasar por el banco.**
  *I need to go by the bank.*
  **En cuanto termine mi café te acompaño.**
  *As soon as I finish my coffee, I'll go with you.*

### Getting directions

- **Estamos perdidos.**
  *We're lost.*

- **¿Hay un banco por aquí con cajero automático?**
  *Is there a bank around here with an ATM?*
  **Crucen esta calle y luego doblen a la izquierda/derecha.**
  *Cross this street and then turn to the left/right.*
  **Sigan todo derecho.**
  *Go straight ahead.*
  **Antes de que lleguen a la joyería van a ver un letrero grande.**
  *Before you get to the jewelry store, you're going to see a big sign.*

- **¿Por dónde queda el supermercado?**
  *Where is the supermarket?*
  **Está a dos cuadras de aquí.**
  *It's two blocks from here.*
  **Queda en la calle Flores.**
  *It's on Flores Street.*
  **Pues, allí mismo enfrente del banco hay un supermercado.**
  *Well, right in front of the bank there is a supermarket.*

## ¿Qué pasó?

**1 ¿Cierto o falso?** Decide si lo que dicen estas oraciones es **cierto** o **falso**. Corrige las oraciones falsas.

| | Cierto | Falso | |
|---|---|---|---|
| 1. Don Francisco insiste en que los chicos lleven una cámara. | ○ | ☑ | Don Francisco recomienda que los chicos lleven zapatos cómodos, una mochila, gafas oscuras y un suéter. |
| 2. Inés escribió unas postales y ahora necesita mandarlas por correo. | ☑ | ○ | |
| 3. El joven dice que el Banco del Atlántico tiene un cajero automático. | ○ | ☑ | El Banco del Pacífico tiene un cajero automático. |
| 4. Enfrente del banco hay una heladería. | ○ | ☑ | Enfrente del banco hay un supermercado pequeño. |

> **CONSULTA**
> To review the use of verbs like **insistir**, see **Estructura 12.4**, p. 398.

**2 Ordenar** Pon los eventos de la **Fotonovela** en el orden correcto.

a. Un joven ayuda a Álex y a Maite a encontrar el banco porque están perdidos. __3__
b. Álex y Maite comen un helado. __6__
c. Inés les da unas postales a Maite y a Álex para echar al buzón. __2__
d. Maite y Álex van al banco y al correo. __4__
e. Álex termina su café. __1__
f. Maite y Álex van al supermercado y compran comida. __5__

**3 Otras diligencias** En parejas, hagan una lista de las diligencias que Maite, Álex, Inés y Javier necesitan hacer para completar estas actividades. Answers will vary.

1. ir de excursión
2. pedir una beca (*scholarship*)
3. visitar una nueva ciudad
4. abrir una cuenta corriente
5. celebrar el cumpleaños de Maite
6. comprar una nueva computadora portátil

JAVIER

MAITE

ÁLEX

INÉS

**4 Conversación** Un(a) compañero/a y tú son vecinos/as. Uno/a de ustedes acaba de mudarse y necesita ayuda porque no conoce la ciudad. Los/Las dos tienen que hacer algunas diligencias y deciden hacerlas juntos/as. Preparen una conversación breve incluyendo planes para ir a estos lugares.
Answers will vary.

> **modelo**
> **Estudiante 1:** Necesito lavar mi ropa. ¿Sabes dónde queda una lavandería?
> **Estudiante 2:** Sí. Aquí a dos cuadras hay una. También tengo que lavar mi ropa. ¿Qué te parece si vamos juntos?

▶ un banco
▶ una lavandería
▶ un supermercado
▶ una heladería
▶ una panadería

> **AYUDA**
> **primero** *first*
> **luego** *then*
> **¿Sabes dónde queda…?**
> *Do you know where…is?*
>
> **¿Qué te parece?**
> *What do you think?*
>
> **¡Cómo no!**
> *But of course!*

NATIONAL communication STANDARDS

---

**TEACHING OPTIONS**

**Extra Practice** Add an auditory aspect to this vocabulary practice. Prepare several sets of directions that explain how to get to well-known places on campus or in your community, without mentioning the destinations by name. Read each set of directions aloud and ask the class to tell you where they would end up if they followed your directions.

**Pairs** Ask pairs to create a skit in which a tourist asks for directions in a Spanish-speaking country. Give the class sufficient time to prepare and rehearse the skits, then ask a few volunteers to role-play their skits for the class.

# Ortografía SUPERSITE
## Las abreviaturas

In Spanish, as in English, abbreviations are often used in order to save space and time while writing. Here are some of the most commonly used abbreviations in Spanish.

| | |
|---|---|
| usted ⟶ Ud. | ustedes ⟶ Uds. |

As you have already learned, the subject pronouns **usted** and **ustedes** are often abbreviated.

| | | |
|---|---|---|
| don ⟶ D. | doña ⟶ Dña. | doctor(a) ⟶ Dr(a). |
| señor ⟶ Sr. | señora ⟶ Sra. | señorita ⟶ Srta. |

These titles are frequently abbreviated.

| | | |
|---|---|---|
| centímetro ⟶ cm | metro ⟶ m | kilómetro ⟶ km |
| litro ⟶ l | gramo ⟶ g, gr | kilogramo ⟶ kg |

The abbreviations for these units of measurement are often used, but without periods.

| | |
|---|---|
| por ejemplo ⟶ p. ej. | página(s) ⟶ pág(s). |

These abbreviations are often seen in books.

| | |
|---|---|
| derecha ⟶ dcha. | izquierda ⟶ izq., izqda. |
| código postal ⟶ C.P. | número ⟶ n.° |

These abbreviations are often used in mailing addresses.

> Sra. Emilia F. Bazán
> Cía. Romero, S.A.
> 3396
> Calle Lozano, n.° 37
> Caracas, Venezuela

| | |
|---|---|
| Banco ⟶ Bco. | Compañía ⟶ Cía. |
| cuenta corriente ⟶ c/c. | Sociedad Anónima (*Inc.*) ⟶ S.A. |

These abbreviations are frequently used in the business world.

**Práctica**  Escribe otra vez esta información usando las abreviaturas adecuadas.

1. doña María Dña.
2. señora Pérez Sra.
3. Compañía Mexicana de Inversiones Cía.
4. usted Ud.
5. Banco de Santander Bco.
6. doctor Medina Dr.
7. Código Postal 03697 C.P.
8. cuenta corriente número 20-453 c/c., n.º

**Emparejar**  En la tabla hay nueve abreviaturas. Empareja los cuadros necesarios para formarlas. S.A., Bco., cm, Dña., c/c., dcha., Srta., C.P., Ud.

| S. | c. | C. | c | co. | U |
|---|---|---|---|---|---|
| B | c/ | Sr | A. | D | dc |
| ta. | P. | ña. | ha. | m | d. |

**recursos**

| | |
|---|---|
| LM p. 80 | panorama.vhlcentral.com Lección 14 |

---

## Section Goal

In **Ortografía**, students will learn some common Spanish abbreviations.

**Instructional Resources**
**Supersite:** Lab MP3 Audio Files
**Lección 14**
**Supersite/IRCD:** *IRM* (Lab Audio Script, WBs/VM/LM Answer Key)
**WebSAM**
**Lab Manual**, p. 80
*Cuaderno para hispanohablantes*

## Teaching Tips
- Point out that the abbreviations **Ud.** and **Uds.** begin with a capital letter, though the spelled-out forms do not.
- Write **D., Dña., Dr., Dra., Sr., Sra.,** and **Srta.** on the board. Again, point out that the abbreviations begin with a capital letter, though the spelled-out forms do not.
- Explain that **codigó postal** means *zip code*.
- Point out that the period in **n.°** does not appear at the end of the abbreviation.
- Point out that **Ortografía** replaces **Pronunciación** in the Student Edition for **Lecciones 10–15**, but not in the Lab Manual. The **Recursos** box references the **Pronunciación** sections found in all lessons of the Lab Manual.

## Successful Language Learning
Tell students that the ability to recognize common abbreviations will make it easier for them to interpret written information in a Spanish-speaking country.

---

### TEACHING OPTIONS

**Pairs**  In pairs, have students write an imaginary address with as many abbreviations as possible. Then write their work on the board and have volunteers read the addresses aloud.
**Extra Practice**  Write a list of abbreviations on the board; each abbreviation should have one letter missing. Have the class fill in the missing letters and tell you what each abbreviation stands for. Ex: **U__., D__a., g__, Bc__., d__ha., p__gs., __zq., S.__.**

**Heritage Speakers**  Ask heritage speakers if they are familiar with any additional abbreviations in Spanish (Ex: **a.C., d.C., etc., Lic., tel.**). Have them write abbreviations on the board and ask classmates to guess what each abbreviation stands for.

**EN DETALLE**

# Paseando en metro

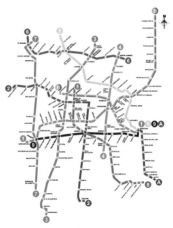

**Hoy es el primer día de Teresa en la Ciudad de México.** Debe tomar el metro para ir del centro de la ciudad a Coyoacán, en el sur. Llega a la estación Zócalo y compra un pasaje por el equivalente a dieciocho centavos° de dólar, ¡qué ganga! Con este pasaje puede ir a cualquier° parte de la ciudad o del área metropolitana.

No sólo en México, sino también en ciudades de Venezuela, Chile, Argentina y España, hay sistemas de transporte público eficientes y muy económicos. También suele haber° varios tipos de transporte: autobús, metro, tranvía°, microbús y tren. Generalmente se pueden comprar abonos° de uno o varios días para un determinado tipo de transporte.

**Metro de Barcelona**

En algunas ciudades también existen abonos de transporte combinados que permiten usar, por ejemplo, el metro y el autobús o el autobús y el tren. En estas ciudades, los metros, autobuses y trenes pasan con mucha frecuencia. Las paradas° y estaciones están bien señalizadas°.

Vaya°, Teresa ya está llegando a Coyoacán. Con lo que ahorró en el pasaje del metro, puede comprarse un helado de mango y unos esquites° en el jardín Centenario.

### El metro

El primer metro de Suramérica que se abrió al público fue el de Buenos Aires, Argentina (1° de diciembre de 1913); el último, el de Valparaíso, Chile (23 de noviembre de 2005).

| Ciudad | Pasajeros/Día (aprox.) |
|---|---|
| México D.F., México | 4.406.300 |
| Madrid, España | 2.400.000 |
| Buenos Aires, Argentina | 1.500.000 |
| Santiago, Chile | 1.500.000 |
| Caracas, Venezuela | 1.400.000 |
| Medellín, Colombia | 350.000 |
| Guadalajara, México | 161.910 |

centavos *cents* cualquier *any* suele haber *there usually are* tranvía *streetcar* abonos *passes* paradas *stops* señalizadas *labeled* Vaya *Well* esquites *toasted corn kernels*

**ACTIVIDADES**

**1** **¿Cierto o falso?** Indica si lo que dice cada oración es **cierto** o **falso**. Corrige la información falsa.

1. En la Ciudad de México, el pasaje de metro cuesta 18 dólares. Falso. Cuesta 18 centavos de dólar.
2. En México, un pasaje se puede usar sólo para ir al centro de la ciudad. Falso. Se puede usar para ir a cualquier parte de la ciudad y el área metropolitana.
3. Los trenes, autobuses y metros pasan con mucha frecuencia. Cierto.
4. En Venezuela, Chile, Argentina y España hay varios tipos de transporte. Cierto.

5. En ningún caso los abonos de transporte sirven para más de un tipo de transporte. Falso. Hay abonos combinados que permiten usar distintos tipos de transporte.
6. Hay pocos letreros en las paradas y estaciones. Falso. Las paradas y estaciones están bien señalizadas.
7. Los dos metros en los que viaja más gente cada día están en México y España. Cierto.
8. El metro que lleva menos tiempo en servicio es el de Medellín, Colombia. Falso. Es el de Valparaíso, Chile.

## ASÍ SE DICE

### En la ciudad

| | |
|---|---|
| el aparcamiento (Esp.); el parqueadero (Col., Pan.); el parqueo (Bol., Cuba, Amér. C.) | el estacionamiento |
| dar un aventón (Méx.); dar botella (Cuba); dar un chance (Col.) | to give (someone) a ride |
| el subterráneo, el subte (Arg.) | el metro |

## EL MUNDO HISPANO

### Apodos° de ciudades

Así como Nueva York es la Gran Manzana, muchas ciudades hispanas tienen un apodo.

○ **La tacita de plata°** A Cádiz, España, se le llama así por sus edificios blancos de estilo árabe.

○ **Ciudad de la eterna primavera** Arica, Chile; Cuernavaca, México, y Medellín, Colombia, llevan este sobrenombre por su clima templado° durante todo el año.

○ **La docta°** Así se conoce a la ciudad argentina de Córdoba por su gran tradición universitaria.

○ **La ciudad de los reyes** Así se conoce Lima, Perú, porque fue la capital del Virreinato° del Perú y allí vivían los virreyes°.

○ **Curramba la Bella** A Barranquilla, Colombia, se le llama así por su gente alegre y espíritu carnavalesco.

Apodos *Nicknames* plata *silver* templado *mild* docta *erudite* Virreinato *Viceroyalty* virreyes *viceroys*

## PERFIL

# Luis Barragán: arquitectura y emoción

Para el arquitecto mexicano **Luis Barragán** (1902–1988) los sentimientos° y emociones que despiertan sus diseños eran muy importantes. Afirmaba° que la arquitectura tiene una dimensión espiritual. Para él, era belleza, inspiración, magia°, serenidad, misterio, silencio, privacidad, asombro°...

Las obras de Barragán muestran un suave° equilibrio entre la naturaleza y la creación humana. Su estilo también combina características de la arquitectura tradicional mexicana con conceptos modernos. Una característica de sus casas son las paredes envolventes° de diferentes colores con muy pocas ventanas.

En 1980, Barragán obtuvo° el Premio Pritzker, algo así como el Premio Nobel de Arquitectura. Está claro que este artista logró° que sus casas transmitieran sentimientos especiales.

**Casa Barragán, Ciudad de México, 1947-1948**

sentimientos *feelings* Afirmaba *He stated* magia *magic* asombro *amazement* suave *smooth* envolventes *enveloping* obtuvo *received* logró *managed*

### SUPERSITE Conexión Internet

**¿Qué otros arquitectos combinan las construcciones con la naturaleza?**

Go to **panorama.vhlcentral.com** to find more cultural information related to this **Cultura** section.

## ACTIVIDADES

**2 Comprensión** Responde a las preguntas.

1. ¿En qué país estás si te dicen "Dame un chance al parqueadero"? *en Colombia*
2. ¿Qué ciudades tienen clima templado todo el año? *Arica, Chile; Cuernavaca, México, y Medellín, Colombia*
3. ¿Qué es más importante en los diseños de Barragán: la naturaleza o la creación humana? *Son igual de importantes.*
4. ¿Qué premio obtuvo Barragán y cuándo? *Barragán obtuvo el Premio Pritzker en 1980.*

**3 ¿Qué ciudad te gusta?** Escribe un párrafo breve sobre el sentimiento que despiertan las construcciones que hay en una ciudad o un pueblo que te guste mucho. Explica cómo es el lugar y cómo te sientes cuando estás allí. Inventa un apodo para este lugar. *Answers will vary.*

**recursos**

panorama.vhlcentral.com
Lección 14

---

---

## TEACHING OPTIONS

## Section Goal

In **Estructura 14.1**, students will learn the use of the subjunctive in adjective clauses.

**Instructional Resources**
**Supersite:** Lab MP3 Audio
Files **Lección 14**
**Supersite/IRCD:** *PowerPoints*
(**Lección 14 Estructura**
Presentation); *IRM* (**Hojas de actividades,** Information Gap
Activities, Lab Audio Script,
WBs/VM/LM Answer Key)
**WebSAM**
**Workbook,** pp. 171–172
**Lab Manual,** p. 81
*Cuaderno para hispanohablantes*

## Teaching Tips

• Add a visual aspect to this grammar presentation. Use magazine pictures to compare and contrast the uses of the indicative and subjunctive in adjective clauses. Ex: **Esta casa tiene una fuente en el jardín. Yo busco una casa que tenga piscina. Este señor come insectos vivos. ¿Conocen a alguien que coma insectos vivos?**

• Ask volunteers to answer questions that describe their wishes. Ex: **¿Qué buscas en una casa? ¿Qué buscas en un(a) compañero/a de cuarto?**

• Ask volunteers to read the captions to the video stills and point out the subordinate adjective clause and its antecedent, then indicate the verb in the present subjunctive.

## 14.1 The subjunctive in adjective clauses

**ANTE TODO** In **Lección 13**, you learned that the subjunctive is used in adverbial clauses after certain conjunctions. You will now learn how the subjunctive can be used in adjective clauses to express that the existence of someone or something is uncertain or indefinite.

¿Hay un banco por aquí que tenga cajero automático?

No hay ningún banco en esta calle que tenga cajero automático.

▶ The subjunctive is used in an adjective (or subordinate) clause that refers to a person, place, thing, or idea that either does not exist or whose existence is uncertain or indefinite. In the examples below, compare the differences in meaning between the statements using the indicative and those using the subjunctive.

**¡ATENCIÓN!**

Adjective clauses are subordinate clauses that modify a noun or pronoun in the main clause of a sentence. That noun or pronoun is called the *antecedent*.

| Indicative | Subjunctive |
|---|---|
| Necesito **el libro** que **tiene** información sobre Venezuela. | Necesito **un libro** que **tenga** información sobre Venezuela. |
| *I need the book that has information about Venezuela.* | *I need a book that has information about Venezuela.* |
| Quiero vivir en **esta casa** que **tiene** jardín. | Quiero vivir en **una casa** que **tenga** jardín. |
| *I want to live in this house that has a garden.* | *I want to live in a house that has a garden.* |
| En mi barrio, hay **una heladería** que **vende** helado de mango. | En mi barrio no hay **ninguna heladería** que **venda** helado de mango. |
| *In my neighborhood, there's an ice cream store that sells mango ice cream.* | *In my neighborhood, there are no ice cream stores that sell mango ice cream.* |

▶ When the adjective clause refers to a person, place, thing, or idea that is clearly known, certain, or definite, the indicative is used.

Quiero ir **al supermercado** que **vende** productos venezolanos.
*I want to go to the supermarket that sells Venezuelan products.*

Conozco **a alguien** que **va** a esa peluquería.
*I know someone who goes to that beauty salon.*

Busco **al profesor** que **enseña** japonés.
*I'm looking for the professor who teaches Japanese.*

Tengo **un amigo** que **vive** cerca de mi casa.
*I have a friend who lives near my house.*

**TEACHING OPTIONS**

**Extra Practice** To provide oral practice with adjective clauses in the subjunctive and indicative, create sentences that follow the pattern of the sentences in the examples. Say a sentence, have students repeat it, then change the main clause. Have students then say the sentence with the new clause, changing the subordinate clause as necessary. **Conozco una tienda donde venden helados riquísimos. (Busco una tienda donde…)**

**Heritage Speakers** Ask heritage speakers to compare and contrast business establishments in their cultural communities and communities outside it. They should use both the indicative and the subjunctive, varying the verbs in the main clause as much as possible.

▶ The personal **a** is not used with direct objects that are hypothetical people. However, as you learned in **Lección 7**, **alguien** and **nadie** are always preceded by the personal **a** when they function as direct objects.

Necesitamos **un empleado** que
**sepa** usar computadoras.
*We need an employee who knows
how to use computers.*

Necesitamos **al empleado** que
**sabe** usar computadoras.
*We need the employee who knows how
to use computers.*

Buscamos **a alguien** que
**pueda** cocinar.
*We're looking for someone who
can cook.*

No conocemos **a nadie** que
**pueda** cocinar.
*We don't know anyone who
can cook.*

▶ The subjunctive is commonly used in questions with adjective clauses when the speaker is trying to find out information about which he or she is uncertain. However, if the person who responds to the question knows the information, the indicative is used.

—¿Hay un parque que **esté** cerca de
nuestro hotel?
*Is there a park that's near our hotel?*

—Sí, hay un parque que **está** muy
cerca del hotel.
*Yes, there's a park that's very near the hotel.*

▶ **¡Atención!** Here are some verbs which are commonly followed by adjective clauses in the subjunctive:

### Words commonly used with subjunctive

| | |
|---|---|
| buscar | haber |
| conocer | necesitar |
| encontrar | querer |

**SECCIÓN AMARILLA**
Busque cualquier
información que
necesite.

**recursos**

WB
pp. 171–172

LM
p. 81

panorama.
vhlcentral.com
Lección 14

 **¡INTÉNTALO!** Escoge entre el subjuntivo y el indicativo para completar cada oración.

1. Necesito una persona que **pueda** (puede/pueda) cantar bien.
2. Buscamos a alguien que **tenga** (tiene/tenga) paciencia.
3. ¿Hay restaurantes aquí que **sirvan** (sirven/sirvan) comida japonesa?
4. Tengo una amiga que **saca** (saca/saque) fotografías muy bonitas.
5. Hay una carnicería que **está** (está/esté) cerca de aquí.
6. No vemos ningún apartamento que nos **interese** (interesa/interese).
7. Conozco a un estudiante que **come** (come/coma) hamburguesas todos los días.
8. ¿Hay alguien que **diga** (dice/diga) la verdad?

**TEACHING OPTIONS**

**Pairs** Ask pairs to rewrite the sentences in the **¡Inténtalo!** activity with the unused verbs (**puede, tiene, sirven, saque, esté, interesa, coma, dice**) and change the main clauses accordingly.
**Extra Practice** Ask students to describe the ideal community. Their descriptions should include only sentences in the subjunctive. Refer them to the verbs in the list to help them develop their descriptions.

**Extra Practice** Also, to provide oral practice, create additional sample sentences with adjective clauses. Say a sentence aloud and have students repeat. Ex: **Conozco una tienda que vende helados riquísimos.** Then change the main clause and have students repeat again, changing the verb form in the adjective clause. Ex: **Busco una tienda que... (venda helados riquísimos.)**

# Práctica SUPERSITE

**1 Completar** Completa estas oraciones con la forma correcta del indicativo o del subjuntivo de los verbos entre paréntesis.

1. Buscamos un hotel que ___tenga___ (tener) piscina.
2. ¿Sabe usted dónde ___queda___ (quedar) el Correo Central?
3. ¿Hay algún buzón por aquí donde yo ___pueda___ (poder) echar una carta?
4. Ana quiere ir a la carnicería que ___está___ (estar) en la avenida Lecuna.
5. Encontramos un restaurante que ___sirve___ (servir) comida venezolana típica.
6. ¿Conoces a alguien que ___sepa___ (saber) mandar un *fax* por computadora?
7. Necesitas al empleado que ___entiende___ (entender) este nuevo programa de computación.
8. No hay nada en este mundo que ___sea___ (ser) gratis.

**2 Oraciones** Marta está haciendo diligencias en Caracas con una amiga. Forma oraciones con estos elementos, usando el presente del indicativo o del subjuntivo. Haz los cambios que sean necesarios.

1. yo / conocer / un / panadería / que / vender / pan / cubano
 Yo conozco una panadería que vende pan cubano.
2. ¿hay / alguien / que / saber / dirección / de / un / buen / carnicería?
 ¿Hay alguien que sepa la dirección de una buena carnicería?
3. yo / querer / comprarle / mi / hija / un / zapatos / que / gustar
 Yo quiero comprarle a mi hija unos zapatos que le gusten.
4. ella / no / encontrar / nada / que / gustar / en / ese / zapatería
 Ella no encuentra nada que le guste en esa zapatería.
5. ¿tener / dependientas / algo / que / ser / más / barato?
 ¿Tienen las dependientas algo que sea más barato?
6. ¿conocer / tú / alguno / banco / que / ofrecer / cuentas / corrientes / gratis?
 ¿Conoces tú algún banco que ofrezca cuentas corrientes gratis?
7. nosotras / no / conocer / nadie / que / hacer / tanto / diligencias / como / nosotras
 Nosotras no conocemos a nadie que haga tantas diligencias como nosotras.
8. nosotras / necesitar / un / línea / de / metro / que / nos / llevar / a / casa
 Nosotras necesitamos una línea de metro que nos lleve a casa.

**3 Anuncios clasificados** En parejas, lean estos anuncios y luego describan el tipo de persona u objeto que se busca. Answers will vary.

**CLASIFICADOS**

**VENDEDOR(A)** Se necesita persona dinámica y responsable con buena presencia. Experiencia mínima de un año. Horario de trabajo flexible. Llamar a Joyería Aurora de 10 a 13h y de 16 a 18h. Tel: 263-7553

**PELUQUERÍA UNISEX** Se busca persona con experiencia en peluquería y maquillaje para trabajar tiempo completo. Llamar de 9 a 13:30h. Tel: 261-3548

**COMPARTIR APARTAMENTO** Se necesita compañera para compartir apartamento de 2 alcobas en el Chaco. Alquiler $500 por mes. No fumar. Llamar al 951-3642 entre 19 y 22h.

**CLASES DE INGLÉS** Profesor de Inglaterra con diez años de experiencia ofrece clases para grupos o instrucción privada para individuos. Llamar al 933-4110 de 16:30 a 18:30.

**SE BUSCA CONDOMINIO** Se busca condominio en Sabana Grande con 3 alcobas, 2 baños, sala, comedor y aire acondicionado. Tel: 977-2018.

**EJECUTIVO DE CUENTAS** Se requiere joven profesional con al menos dos años de experiencia en el sector financiero. Se ofrecen beneficios excelentes. Enviar currículum vitae al Banco Unión, Avda. Urdaneta 263, Caracas.

# Comunicación

**4**   **Subjuntivo** Completa estas frases de una manera lógica. Luego, compara tus respuestas con las de un(a) compañero/a. *Answers will vary.*

1. Deseo un trabajo (*job*) que…
2. Algún día espero tener un apartamento (una casa) que…
3. Mis padres buscan un carro que…, pero yo quiero un carro que…
4. Tengo un(a) novio/a que…
5. Un(a) consejero/a (*advisor*) debe ser una persona que…
6. Me gustaría (*I would like*) conocer a alguien que…
7. En esta clase no hay nadie que…
8. No tengo ningún profesor que…

**5**   **Encuesta** Tu profesor(a) va a darte una hoja de actividades. Circula por la clase y pregúntales a tus compañeros/as si conocen a alguien que haga cada actividad de la lista. Si responden que sí, pregúntales quién es y anota sus respuestas. Luego informa a la clase de los resultados de tu encuesta.

*Answers will vary.*

**modelo**

trabajar en un supermercado

**Estudiante 1:** ¿Conoces a alguien que trabaje en un supermercado?

**Estudiante 2:** Sí, conozco a alguien que trabaja en un supermercado. Es mi hermano menor.

| Actividades | Nombres | Respuestas |
|---|---|---|
| 1. dar direcciones buenas | | |
| 2. hablar japonés | | |
| 3. graduarse este año | | |
| 4. necesitar un préstamo | | |
| 5. pedir prestado un carro | | |
| 6. odiar ir de compras | | |
| 7. ser venezolano/a | | |
| 8. manejar una motocicleta | | |
| 9. trabajar en una zapatería | | |
| 10. no tener tarjeta de crédito | | |

# Síntesis

**6**   **Busca los cuatro** Tu profesor(a) te va a dar una hoja con ocho anuncios clasificados y a tu compañero/a otra hoja con ocho anuncios distintos a los tuyos. Háganse preguntas para encontrar los cuatro anuncios de cada hoja que tienen su respuesta en la otra. *Answers will vary.*

**modelo**

**Estudiante 1:** ¿Hay alguien que necesite una alfombra?

**Estudiante 2:** No, no hay nadie que necesite una alfombra.

---

**TEACHING OPTIONS**

**Video** Show the ***Fotonovela*** episode again to give students more input on the use of the subjunctive in adjective clauses. Stop the video where appropriate to discuss why the subjunctive or indicative was used.

**Small Groups** Ask students to bring in travel brochures or tourist information from the Internet. Divide the class into groups of four and have them write a short radio spot for one of the tourist locations using only the subjunctive and formal commands.

---

**4** **Teaching Tip** Model the activity by giving a personal example. Write, for example, **No conozco ningún restaurante cercano que…** on the board, then complete the sentence. Ex: **No conozco ningún restaurante cercano que sirva comida venezolana. No conozco ningún restaurante cercano que tenga un patio grande.**

**4** **Expansion** Assign students to groups of six. Have each student compare his or her responses with those of the rest of the group. Then ask the group to pick two responses and make a visual representation of them. Designate a student from each group to show the visual for the class to guess what the response was. Guesses should include an adjective clause.

**5** **Teaching Tip** Distribute the ***Hojas de actividades*** (Supersite/IRCD) that correspond to this activity.

**5** **Expansion** Have pairs write six original sentences with adjective clauses based on the answers of the **encuesta**. Three sentences should have subordinate clauses in the subjunctive and three in the indicative.

**6** **Teaching Tip** Divide the class into pairs and distribute the handouts from the Information Gap Activities (Supersite/IRCD) that correspond to this activity. Give students ten minutes to complete the activity.

**6** **Expansion** Have pairs write counterparts for two of the ads that do not have them. One ad should be for someone wanting to buy something and the other for someone wanting to sell something.

# 14.2 Nosotros/as commands

**ANTE TODO** You have already learned familiar (**tú**) commands and formal (**usted/ustedes**) commands. You will now learn **nosotros/as** commands, which are used to give orders or suggestions that include yourself and other people.

▶ **Nosotros/as** commands correspond to the English *Let's*.

### Nosotros/as commands

| Infinitive | Nosotros/as form of present subjunctive | Nosotros/as command |
|---|---|---|
| cruzar | crucemos | **(no) crucemos** |
| comer | comamos | **(no) comamos** |
| escribir | escribamos | **(no) escribamos** |
| pedir | pidamos | **(no) pidamos** |
| salir | salgamos | **(no) salgamos** |
| volver | volvamos | **(no) volvamos** |

▶ As the chart shows, both affirmative and negative **nosotros/as** commands are generally formed by using the first-person plural form of the present subjunctive.

**Crucemos** la calle.
*Let's cross the street.*

**No crucemos** la calle.
*Let's not cross the street.*

▶ The affirmative *Let's* + [*verb*] command may also be expressed with **vamos a** + [*infinitive*]. Remember, however, that **vamos a** + [*infinitive*] can also mean *we are going to (do something).* Context and tone of voice determine which meaning is being expressed.

**Vamos a cruzar** la calle.
*Let's cross the street.*

**Vamos a trabajar** mucho.
*We're going to work a lot.*

▶ To express *Let's go*, the present indicative form of **ir** (**vamos**) is used, not the subjunctive. For the negative command, however, the subjunctive is used.

**Vamos** a la pescadería.
*Let's go to the fishmarket.*

No **vayamos** a la pescadería.
*Let's not go to the fish market.*

> **CONSULTA**
>
> Remember that stem-changing –**ir** verbs have an additional stem change in the **nosotros/as** and **vosotros/as** forms of the present subjunctive. To review these forms, see **Estructura 12.3,** p. 395.

¿Quieres ir al supermercado?

¡Excelente idea! ¡Vamos!

▶ Object pronouns are always attached to affirmative **nosotros/as** commands. A written accent is added to maintain the original stress.

**Firmemos** el cheque. ——————▶ **Firmémoslo.**
*Let's sign the check.*                        *Let's sign it.*

**Escribamos** a Ana y Raúl. ——————▶ **Escribámosles.**
*Let's write Ana and Raúl.*                    *Let's write them.*

▶ Object pronouns are placed in front of negative **nosotros/as** commands.

No **les paguemos** el préstamo.               No **se lo digamos** a ellos.
*Let's not pay them the loan.*                 *Let's not tell them.*

No **lo compremos.**                           No **se la presentemos.**
*Let's not buy it.*                            *Let's not introduce her.*

▶ When **nos** or **se** is attached to an affirmative **nosotros/as** command, the final **–s** is dropped from the verb ending.

**Sentémonos** allí.                           **Démoselo** a ella.
*Let's sit there.*                             *Let's give it to her.*

▶ The **nosotros/as** command form of **irse** (*to go away*) is **vámonos**. Its negative form is **no nos vayamos**.

¡**Vámonos** de vacaciones!                    **No nos vayamos** de aquí.
*Let's go away on vacation!*                   *Let's not go away from here.*

**Teaching Tips**
• Call out affirmative commands and point to individuals to convert them into negative commands (and vice versa).
• Call out commands with object nouns and ask volunteers to repeat the commands with the appropriate pronouns.

**recursos**

WB
pp. 173–174

LM
p. 82

SUPERSITE
panorama.
vhlcentral.com
Lección 14

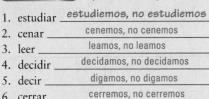

**¡INTÉNTALO!**  Indica los mandatos afirmativos y negativos de la primera persona del plural (**nosotros/as**) de estos verbos.

1. estudiar  *estudiemos, no estudiemos*
2. cenar  *cenemos, no cenemos*
3. leer  *leamos, no leamos*
4. decidir  *decidamos, no decidamos*
5. decir  *digamos, no digamos*
6. cerrar  *cerremos, no cerremos*

7. levantarse  *levantémonos, no nos levantemos*
8. irse  *vámonos, no nos vayamos*
9. depositar  *depositemos, no depositemos*
10. quedarse  *quedémonos, no nos quedemos*
11. pedir  *pidamos, no pidamos*
12. vestirse  *vistámonos, no nos vistamos*

**TEACHING OPTIONS**

**Pairs** Have pairs create an ad similar to the one on this page, using **nosotros/as** commands. Then have them exchange their ads with another pair who corrects them. Finally, have some pairs share their ads with the class.

**Small Groups** Divide the class into groups of three. Student A writes a sentence that contains a **nosotros/as** command with direct or indirect objects. Ex: **Firmemos el cheque.** Student B must rewrite the sentence using pronouns. Ex: **Firmémoslo.** Then, student C must express the statement negatively. Ex: **No lo firmemos.** Have them switch roles and continue writing sentences until each has played student A twice.

**1 Expansion**
- Encourage pairs performing in front of the class to ad-lib additional material as they see fit.
- For additional practice, have pairs convert the affirmative commands into negative commands and vice versa.

**2 Expansion** To challenge students, have pairs create another logical **nosotros/as** command for each item. Ex: **1. Vamos a levantarnos a las seis. (Sí, levantémonos a las seis. Y acostémonos temprano por la noche.)**

# Práctica SUPERSITE

**1**

**Completar** Completa esta conversación con mandatos usando **nosotros/as.** Luego, representa la conversación con un(a) compañero/a.

**MARÍA** Sergio, ¿quieres hacer diligencias ahora o por la tarde?

**SERGIO** No (1)___las dejemos___ (dejarlas) para más tarde. (2)___Hagámoslas___ (Hacerlas) ahora. ¿Qué tenemos que hacer?

**MARÍA** Necesito comprar sellos.

**SERGIO** Yo también. (3)___Vamos___ (Ir) al correo.

**MARÍA** Pues, antes de ir al correo, necesito sacar dinero de mi cuenta corriente.

**SERGIO** Bueno, (4)___busquemos___ (buscar) un cajero automático.

**MARÍA** ¿Tienes hambre?

**SERGIO** Sí. (5)___Crucemos___ (Cruzar) la calle y (6)___entremos___ (entrar) en ese café.

**MARÍA** Buena idea.

**SERGIO** ¿Nos sentamos aquí?

**MARÍA** No, no (7)___nos sentemos___ (sentarse) aquí; (8)___sentémonos___ (sentarse) enfrente de la ventana.

**SERGIO** ¿Qué pedimos?

**MARÍA** (9)___Pidamos___ (Pedir) café y pan dulce.

**2**

**Responder** Responde a cada mandato usando **nosotros/as** según las indicaciones. Sustituye los sustantivos por los objetos directos e indirectos.

> **modelo**
> Vamos a vender el carro.
> Sí, vendámoslo.
> No, no los vendamos.

1. Vamos a levantarnos a las seis. (Sí)
   Sí, levantémonos a las seis.
2. Vamos a enviar los paquetes. (No)
   No, no los enviemos.
3. Vamos a depositar el cheque. (Sí)
   Sí, depositémoslo.
4. Vamos al supermercado. (No)
   No, no vayamos al supermercado.
5. Vamos a mandar esta tarjeta postal a nuestros amigos. (No)
   No, no se la mandemos.
6. Vamos a limpiar la habitación. (Sí)
   Sí, limpiémosla.
7. Vamos a mirar la televisión. (No)
   No, no la miremos.
8. Vamos a bailar. (Sí)
   Sí, bailemos.
9. Vamos a pintar la sala. (No)
   No, no la pintemos.
10. Vamos a comprar estampillas. (Sí)
    Sí, comprémoslas.

**TEACHING OPTIONS**

**Heritage Speakers** Ask heritage speakers to write a conversation using **nosotros/as** commands. The topic of the conversation should be typical errands run in their home communities. Have them read their conversations to the class, making sure to note any new vocabulary on the board.

**Game** Divide the class into teams of three. Teams will take turns responding to your cues with a **nosotros/as** command. Ex: **Necesitamos pan. (Vamos a la panadería.)** Give the cue. Allow the team members to confer and come up with a team answer, and then call on a team. Each correct answer earns one point. The team with the most points at the end wins.

# Comunicación

**3** **Preguntar** Tú y tu compañero/a están de vacaciones en Caracas y se hacen sugerencias para resolver las situaciones que se presentan. Inventen mandatos afirmativos o negativos de **nosotros/as**.
Answers will vary.

 *modelo*

> Se nos olvidaron las tarjetas de crédito.
> *Paguemos en efectivo./No compremos más regalos.*

| **A** | **B** |
|---|---|
| 1. El museo está a sólo una cuadra de aquí. | 1. Tenemos muchos cheques de viajero. |
| 2. Tenemos hambre. | 2. Tenemos prisa para llegar al cine. |
| 3. Hay mucha cola en el cine. | 3. Estamos cansados y queremos dormir. |

**4** **Decisiones** Trabajen en grupos pequeños. Ustedes están en Caracas por dos días. Lean esta página de una guía turística sobre la ciudad y decidan qué van a hacer hoy por la mañana, por la tarde y por la noche. Hagan oraciones con mandatos afirmativos o negativos de **nosotros/as.**
Answers will vary.

 *modelo*

> Visitemos el Museo de Arte Contemporáneo Sofía Imber
> esta tarde. Quiero ver las esculturas de Jesús Rafael Soto.

---

**GUÍA DE Caracas**

**MUSEOS**
- **Museo de Arte Colonial** Avenida Panteón
- **Museo de Arte Contemporáneo Sofía Imber** Parque Central. Esculturas de Jesús Rafael Soto y pinturas de Miró, Chagall y Picasso.
- **Galería de Arte Nacional** Parque Central. Colección de más de 4000 obras de arte venezolano.

**SITIOS DE INTERÉS**
- **Plaza Bolívar**
- **Jardín Botánico** Avenida Interna UCV. De 8:00 a 5:00.
- **Parque del Este** Avenida Francisco de Miranda Parque más grande de la ciudad con terrario.
- **Casa Natal de Simón Bolívar** Esquina de Sociedad de la avenida Universitaria. Casa colonial donde nació El Libertador.

**RESTAURANTES**
- **El Barquero** Avenida Luis Roche
- **Restaurante El Coyuco** Avenida Urdaneta
- **Restaurante Sorrento** Avenida Francisco Solano
- **Café Tonino** Avenida Andrés Bello

---

# Síntesis

**5** **Situación** Tú y un(a) compañero/a viven juntos/as en un apartamento y tienen problemas económicos. Describan los problemas y sugieran algunas soluciones. Hagan oraciones con mandatos afirmativos o negativos de **nosotros/as.** Answers will vary.

 *modelo*

> Es importante que reduzcamos nuestros gastos (*expenses*).
> *Hagamos un presupuesto (budget).*

---

**TEACHING OPTIONS**

**Heritage Speakers** Ask heritage speakers to write a conversation using **nosotros/as** commands. The topic of the conversation should be typical errands run in their communities. Have them read their conversations to the class, making sure to note any new vocabulary on the board.
**Pairs** Working in pairs, have students create a guide of their favorite city, based on the **Guía de Caracas** in **Actividad 4**. Have

them exchange their guides with another pair. That pair should decide what places they will and will not visit, using **nosotros/as** commands.
**Pairs** Have students create a dialogue in which two friends are deciding at which local restaurant to have dinner. Students should use **nosotros/as** commands as much as possible. Have pairs perform their role-plays for the class.

---

**3** **Expansion** To challenge students, ask them to expand their answers with a reason for their choice. Ex: **Paguemos en efectivo. Tenemos bastante dinero.**

**4** **Expansion** Have groups bring in tourist information for another city in the Spanish-speaking world and repeat the activity. Encourage them to make copies of this information for the class. They should then present to the class their suggestions for what to do, using **nosotros/as** commands.

**5** **Teaching Tip** To simplify, have students brainstorm different financial problems and solutions encountered by roommates sharing an apartment. Write their responses on the board.

**5** **Expansion** Call on pairs to perform their **Situación** for the class.

**Teaching Tip** See the Information Gap Activities (Supersite/IRCD) for an additional activity to practice the material presented in this section.

# 14.3 The future

**ANTE TODO** You have already learned ways of expressing the near future in Spanish. You will now learn how to form and use the future tense. Compare the different ways of expressing the future in Spanish and English.

| Present indicative |
| --- |
| **Voy** al cine mañana. |
| *I'm going to the movies tomorrow.* |

| Present subjunctive |
| --- |
| Ojalá **vaya al cine** mañana. |
| *I hope I will go to the movies tomorrow.* |

| ir a + [*infinitive*] |
| --- |
| **Voy a ir** al cine. |
| *I'm going to go to the movies.* |

| Future |
| --- |
| **Iré** al cine. |
| *I will go to the movies.* |

**CONSULTA**

To review **ir a** + [*infinitive*], see **Estructura 4.1**, p. 118.

### Future tense

| | | estudiar | aprender | recibir |
| --- | --- | --- | --- | --- |
| **SINGULAR FORMS** | yo | estudiar**é** | aprender**é** | recibir**é** |
| | tú | estudiar**ás** | aprender**ás** | recibir**ás** |
| | Ud./él/ella | estudiar**á** | aprender**á** | recibir**á** |
| **PLURAL FORMS** | nosotros/as | estudiar**emos** | aprender**emos** | recibir**emos** |
| | vosotros/as | estudiar**éis** | aprender**éis** | recibir**éis** |
| | Uds./ellos/ellas | estudiar**án** | aprender**án** | recibir**án** |

▶ In Spanish, the future is a simple tense that consists of one word, whereas in English it is made up of the auxiliary verb *will* or *shall*, and the main verb. **¡Atención!** Note that all of the future endings have a written accent except the **nosotros/as** form.

¿Cuándo **recibirás** la carta?
*When will you receive the letter?*

Mañana **aprenderemos** más.
*Tomorrow we will learn more.*

▶ The future endings are the same for regular and irregular verbs. For regular verbs, simply add the endings to the infinitive. For irregular verbs, add the endings to the irregular stem.

### Irregular verbs in the future

| INFINITIVE | STEM | FUTURE FORMS |
| --- | --- | --- |
| decir | dir- | dir**é** |
| hacer | har- | har**é** |
| poder | podr- | podr**é** |
| poner | pondr- | pondr**é** |
| querer | querr- | querr**é** |
| saber | sabr- | sabr**é** |
| salir | saldr- | saldr**é** |
| tener | tendr- | tendr**é** |
| venir | vendr- | vendr**é** |

▶ The future of **hay** (*inf.* **haber**) is **habrá** (*there will be*).

La próxima semana **habrá**          **Habrá** más formularios en
un nuevo director.                   el correo.
*Next week there will be*            *There will be more forms at*
*a new director.*                    *the post office.*

▶ Although the English word *will* can refer to future time, it also refers to someone's willingness to do something. In this case, Spanish uses **querer** + [*infinitive*], not the future tense.

**¿Quieres llamarme,**               **¿Quieren ustedes escucharnos,**
por favor?                           por favor?
*Will you please call me?*           *Will you please listen to us?*

**COMPARE & CONTRAST**

In Spanish, the future tense has an additional use: expressing conjecture or probability. English sentences involving expressions such as *I wonder, I bet, must be, may, might,* and *probably* are often translated into Spanish using the *future of probability*.

—¿Dónde **estarán** mis llaves?          —¿Qué hora **será**?
*I wonder where my keys are.*             *What time can it be? (I wonder*
                                          *what time it is.)*

—**Estarán** en la cocina.                —**Serán** las once o las doce.
*They're probably in the kitchen.*        *It must be (It's probably) eleven*
                                          *or twelve.*

Note that although the future tense is used, these verbs express conjecture about *present* conditions, events, or actions.

**CONSULTA**

To review these conjunctions of time, see **Estructura 13.3,** p. 435.

▶ The future may also be used in the main clause of sentences in which the present subjunctive follows a conjunction of time such as **cuando, después (de) que, en cuanto, hasta que,** and **tan pronto como.**

**Cuando llegues** a casa,               **Nos verás en cuanto entres**
**hablaremos.**                          en la cafetería.
*When you get home,*                     *You'll see us as soon as you enter*
*we will talk.*                          *the cafeteria.*

**recursos**

WB
pp. 175–176

LM
p. 83

**SUPERSITE**
panorama.
vhlcentral.com
Lección 14

**¡INTÉNTALO!**  Conjuga los verbos entre paréntesis en futuro.

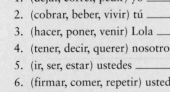

1. (dejar, correr, pedir) yo ___ dejaré, correré, pediré ___
2. (cobrar, beber, vivir) tú ___ cobrarás, beberás, vivirás ___
3. (hacer, poner, venir) Lola ___ hará, pondrá, vendrá ___
4. (tener, decir, querer) nosotros ___ tendremos, diremos, querremos ___
5. (ir, ser, estar) ustedes ___ irán, serán, estarán ___
6. (firmar, comer, repetir) usted ___ firmará, comerá, repetirá ___
7. (saber, salir, poder) yo ___ sabré, saldré, podré ___
8. (encontrar, jugar, servir) tú ___ encontrarás, jugarás, servirás ___

**Teaching Tips**
• Go over the future of **haber**. Remind students that **hay/habrá** has only one form and does not agree with any element in a sentence.
• Go over the explanation of **querer** + [*infinitive*].
• Explain the use of the future for expressing conjecture, which English generally expresses with the present tense. Add a visual aspect to this grammar presentation. Use magazine pictures to get students to speculate about what people are thinking or going to do. Ex: **¿Qué estará pensando la mujer que hace cola en el banco? (Estará pensando en su cita en el salón de belleza.)**
• Go over the use of the future in the main clause of sentences in which the present subjunctive follows a conjunction of time. Check for understanding by asking individuals to supply the main clause to prompts of present subjunctive clauses. Ex: **En cuanto pueda…; Tan pronto como me lo digas…**
• Ask students to answer questions about the future of the **Fotonovela** characters. Ex: **¿Quién tendrá la profesión más interesante? ¿Por qué? ¿Quién será más feliz?**

**TEACHING OPTIONS**

**Pairs** Ask students to write ten academic resolutions for the upcoming semester, using the future. Ex: **Haré dos o tres borradores de cada composición. Practicaré el español con los estudiantes hispanos.** Have students share their resolutions with a partner, who will then report back to the class. Ex: ___ **hará dos o tres borradores de cada composición.**

**Extra Practice** Ask students to finish these sentences logically: **1. Tan pronto como termine mis estudios,… 2. El día que gane la lotería,… 3. Cuando lleguen las vacaciones,… 4. Hasta que tenga mi propio (*own*) apartamento,…**

# Práctica

**1** **Planes** Celia está hablando de sus planes. Repite lo que dice, usando el tiempo futuro.

> **modelo**
>
> Hoy voy a hacer unas compras.
> Hoy haré unas compras.

1. Voy a pasar por el banco a cobrar un cheque. Pasaré por el banco a cobrar un cheque.
2. Mi hermana va a venir conmigo al supermercado. Mi hermana vendrá conmigo al supermercado.
3. Vamos a buscar las mejores rebajas. Buscaremos las mejores rebajas.
4. Voy a comprarme unas botas. Me compraré unas botas.
5. Después voy a volver a casa y me voy a duchar. Después volveré a casa y me ducharé.
6. Seguramente mis amigos me van a llamar para salir esta noche. Seguramente mis amigos me llamarán para salir esta noche.

**2** **¿Quién será?** En parejas, imaginen que están en un café y ven entrar a un hombre o una mujer. Imaginen cómo será su vida y utilicen el futuro de probabilidad en su conversación. Usen estas preguntas como guía y después lean su conversación delante de la clase. Answers will vary.

> **modelo**
>
> **Estudiante 1:** ¿Será simpático?
> **Estudiante 2:** Creo que no, está muy serio. Será antipático.

- ¿Estará soltero/a?
- ¿Cuántos años tendrá?
- ¿Vivirá por aquí cerca?
- ¿Será famoso/a?

- ¿Será de otro país?
- ¿Con quién vivirá?
- ¿Estará esperando a alguien? ¿A quién?

**3** **¿Qué pasará?** Imagina que tienes que adivinar (to predict) el futuro de tu compañero/a. En parejas, túrnense para hablar sobre cada una de estas categorías usando el futuro. Answers will vary.

> **modelo**
>
> **Estudiante 1:** ¿Seré rico? ¿Tendré una casa grande?
> **Estudiante 2:** Mmm... tendrás muy poco dinero durante los próximos cinco años, pero después serás muy, muy rico con una casa enorme. Luego te mudarás a una isla desierta (deserted) donde conocerás a...

▶ Amor
▶ Dinero
▶ Salud
▶ Trabajo
▶ Vivienda

# Comunicación

**4** **Conversar** Tú y tu compañero/a viajarán a la República Dominicana por siete días. En parejas, indiquen lo que harán y no harán. Digan dónde, cómo, con quién o en qué fechas lo harán, usando el anuncio (ad) como guía. Pueden usar sus propias ideas también. Answers will vary.

> **modelo**
>
> **Estudiante 1:** ¿Qué haremos el martes?
> **Estudiante 2:** Visitaremos el Jardín Botánico.
> **Estudiante 1:** Pues, tú visitarás el Jardín Botánico y yo
> caminaré por el Mercado Modelo.

### ¡Bienvenido a la República Dominicana!

Se divertirá desde el momento en que llegue al **Aeropuerto Internacional de las Américas.**

• Visite la ciudad colonial de **Santo Domingo** con su interesante arquitectura.

• Vaya al **Jardín Botánico** y disfrute de nuestra abundante naturaleza.

• En el **Mercado Modelo** no va a poder resistir la tentación de comprar artesanías.

• No deje de escalar la montaña del **Pico Duarte** (se recomiendan 3 días).

• ¿Le gusta bucear? **Cabarete** tiene todo el equipo que usted necesita.

• ¿Desea nadar? **Punta Cana** le ofrece hermosas playas.

**5** **Planear** En grupos pequeños, imaginen que están haciendo planes para empezar un negocio (*business*). Elijan una de las opciones y usen las preguntas como guía. Finalmente, presenten su plan a la clase. Answers will vary.

> un supermercado    un salón de belleza    una heladería

1. ¿Cómo se llamará?
2. ¿Cuánta gente trabajará en este lugar? ¿Qué hará cada persona?
3. ¿En qué parte de la ciudad estará? ¿Cómo llegará la gente?
4. ¿Quién será el/la director(a)? ¿Por qué?
5. ¿Van a necesitar un préstamo? ¿Cómo lo pedirán?
6. Este supermercado / salón de belleza / heladería será el/la mejor de la ciudad porque...

# Síntesis

**6** **El futuro de Cristina** Tu profesor(a) va a darte una serie incompleta de dibujos sobre el futuro de Cristina. Tú y tu compañero/a tienen dos series diferentes. Háganse preguntas y respondan de acuerdo a los dibujos para completar la historia. Answers will vary.

> **modelo**
>
> **Estudiante 1:** ¿Qué hará Cristina en el año 2015?
> **Estudiante 2:** Ella se graduará en el año 2015.

**4** **Teaching Tips**
• Encourage pairs to read the ad before they complete the activity.
• If you have any students of Dominican heritage in your class, or if any of your students have visited the Dominican Republic, ask them to share what they know about the places named in the ad.

**4** **Expansion** Have several pairs present their conversations to the class.

**5** **Expansion** Have groups develop visual aids to accompany their presentation.

**6** **Teaching Tip** Divide the class into pairs and distribute the handouts from the Information Gap Activities (Supersite/IRCD) that correspond to this activity. Give students ten minutes to complete the activity.

**6** **Expansion**
• Have students change partners, and have the new pairs use the future to retell the story without looking at the drawings. Later, ask students if the second version of the story differed from the first one.
• Have pairs pick a person who is currently in the news and write predictions about his or her future. Ask pairs to share their predictions with the class.

---

**TEACHING OPTIONS**

**Game** Use a ball (or balled-up piece of paper) to practice the simple future forms. Say an infinitive of a known verb followed by a subject pronoun. Ex: **tener (Uds.)** Toss the ball to a student who must give the simple future of the verb in the indicated form. **(tendrán)** When the student has given the appropriate form, he or she tosses the ball back to you. Include verbs from all conjugation and those that have irregular futures. Keep the pace rapid.

**Large Groups** Assign a century to each corner of the room. Ex: 23rd century. Tell students they are going to go into the future in a time machine (**máquina de transporte a través del tiempo**). They should pick which year they would like to visit and go to that corner. Once assembled, each group should develop a summary of life in their century. After groups have finished, call on a spokesperson in each group to report to the class.

## Section Goal

In **Recapitulación**, students will review the grammar concepts from this lesson.

---

**Instructional Resource**
**Supersite**

---

**1 Teaching Tip** Complete this activity orally as a class.

**1 Expansion** To challenge students, add the verbs **saber**, **tener**, and **hacer** to the chart.

**2 Teaching Tip** Have students begin by identifying which commands are negative. Call on a volunteer to explain the difference in the formation of affirmative and negative **nosotros/as** commands.

**2 Expansion** Have students work in pairs to create an original dialogue using **nosotros/as** commands.

---

# Recapitulación

**SUPERSITE**   For self-scoring and diagnostics, go to **panorama.vhlcentral.com**.

Completa estas actividades para repasar los conceptos de gramática que aprendiste en esta lección.

**1** **Completar** Completa el cuadro con la forma correspondiente del futuro.
**10 pts.**

| Infinitive | yo | ella | nosotros |
|---|---|---|---|
| **ahorrar** | **ahorraré** | ahorrará | ahorraremos |
| **decir** | diré | **dirá** | diremos |
| **poner** | pondré | pondrá | **pondremos** |
| **querer** | **querré** | querrá | querremos |
| **salir** | saldré | **saldrá** | saldremos |

**2** **Los novios** Completa este diálogo entre dos novios con mandatos en la forma de **nosotros/as**. **10 pts.**

**SIMÓN** ¿Quieres ir al cine mañana?

**CARLA** Sí, ¡qué buena idea! (1) _Compremos_ (Comprar) los boletos (*tickets*) por teléfono.

**SIMÓN** No, mejor (2) _pidámoselos_ (pedírselos) gratis a mi prima, quien trabaja en el cine.

**CARLA** ¡Fantástico!

**SIMÓN** Y también quiero visitar la nueva galería de arte el fin de semana que viene.

**CARLA** ¿Por qué esperar? (3) _Visitémosla_ (Visitarla) esta tarde.

**SIMÓN** Bueno, pero primero tengo que limpiar mi apartamento.

**CARLA** No hay problema. (4) _Limpiémoslo_ (Limpiarlo) juntos.

**SIMÓN** Muy bien. ¿Y tú no tienes que hacer diligencias hoy? (5) _Hagámoslas_ (Hacerlas) también.

**CARLA** Sí, tengo que ir al correo y al banco. (6) _Vamos_ (Ir) al banco hoy, pero no (7) _vayamos_ (ir) al correo todavía. Antes tengo que escribir una carta.

**SIMÓN** ¿Una carta misteriosa? (8) _Escribámosla_ (Escribirla) ahora.

**CARLA** No, mejor no (9) _la escribamos_ (escribirla) hasta que regresemos de la galería donde venden un papel reciclado muy lindo (*cute*).

**SIMÓN** ¿Papel lindo? ¿Pues para quién es la carta?

**CARLA** No importa. (10) _Empecemos_ (Empezar) a limpiar.

---

### RESUMEN GRAMATICAL

**14.1** **The subjunctive in adjective clauses**
*pp. 460–461*

▶ When adjective clauses refer to something that is known, certain, or definite, the indicative is used.

Necesito **el libro** que **tiene** fotos.

▶ When adjective clauses refer to something that is uncertain or indefinite, the subjunctive is used.

Necesito **un libro** que **tenga** fotos.

**14.2** **Nosotros/as commands** *pp. 464–465*

▶ Same as **nosotros/as** form of present subjunctive.

| Affirmative | Negative |
|---|---|
| **Démosle** un libro a Lola. | **No le demos** un libro a Lola. |
| **Démoselo.** | **No se lo demos.** |

▶ While the subjunctive form of the verb **ir** is used for the negative **nosotros/as** command, the indicative is used for the affirmative command.

**Vamos** a la plaza.     No **vayamos** a la plaza.

**14.3** **The future** *pp. 468–469*

| Future tense of **estudiar*** | |
|---|---|
| **estudiaré** | **estudiaremos** |
| **estudiarás** | **estudiaréis** |
| **estudiará** | **estudiarán** |

*Same ending for **-ar**, **-er**, and **-ir** verbs.

▶ The future of **hay** is **habrá** (*there will be*).

▶ The future can also express conjecture or probability.

---

**TEACHING OPTIONS**

**TPR** Have students stand and form a circle. Have one student step forward and name a situation. Ex: **Tenemos un examen mañana.** The student to the right should step forward and propose a solution, using a **nosotros/as** command form. Ex: **Estudiemos el subjuntivo.** Continue around the circle until each student has had a turn forming commands.

**Large Groups** Divide the class into two groups. Give one group cards with situations. Ex: **El profesor canceló la clase.** Give the other group cards with statements using the future to express conjecture or probability. Ex: **Llegaré a clase y no habrá nadie.** Students must find their partners.

**3** **Frases** Escribe oraciones con los elementos que se dan. Usa el tiempo futuro. **10 pts.**

1. Lorenzo y yo / ir / al banco / mañana / y / pedir / un préstamo  *Lorenzo y yo iremos al banco mañana y pediremos un préstamo.*

2. la empleada del banco / hacernos / muchas preguntas / y / también / darnos / un formulario  *La empleada del banco nos hará muchas preguntas y también nos dará un formulario.*

3. Lorenzo / llenar / el formulario / y / yo / firmarlo  *Lorenzo llenará el formulario y yo lo firmaré.*

4. nosotros / salir / del banco / contentos / porque el dinero / llegar / a nuestra cuenta / muy pronto  *Nosotros saldremos del banco contentos porque el dinero llegará a nuestra cuenta muy pronto.*

5. los dos / tener / que trabajar mucho / para pagar el préstamo / pero nuestros padres / ayudarnos  *Los dos tendremos que trabajar mucho para pagar el préstamo, pero nuestros padres nos ayudarán.*

| Irregular verbs in the future | | |
|---|---|---|
| **Infinitive** | **Stem** | **Future forms** |
| decir | dir- | diré |
| hacer | har- | haré |
| poder | podr- | podré |
| poner | pondr- | pondré |
| querer | querr- | querré |
| saber | sabr- | sabré |
| salir | saldr- | saldré |
| tener | tendr- | tendré |
| venir | vendr- | vendré |

**4** **Verbos** Escribe los verbos en el presente de indicativo o de subjuntivo. **10 pts.**

1. —¿Sabes dónde hay un restaurante donde nosotros (1) _podamos_ (poder) comer paella valenciana? —No, no conozco ninguno que (2) _sirva_ (servir) paella, pero conozco uno que (3) _se especializa_ (especializarse) en tapas españolas.

2. Busco vendedores que (4) _sean_ (ser) educados. No estoy seguro de conocer a alguien que (5) _tenga_ (tener) esa característica. Pero ahora que lo pienso, ¡sí! Tengo dos amigos que (6) _trabajan_ (trabajar) en el almacén Excelencia. Los voy a llamar. Y debo decirles que necesitamos que (ellos) (7) _sepan_ (saber) hablar inglés.

3. Se busca apartamento que (8) _esté_ (estar) bien situado, que (9) _cueste_ (costar) menos de $800 al mes y que (10) _permita_ (permitir) tener perros.

**5** **La ciudad ideal** Escribe un párrafo de al menos cinco oraciones describiendo cómo es la comunidad ideal donde te gustaría (*you would like*) vivir en el futuro y compárala con la comunidad donde vives ahora. Usa cláusulas adjetivas y el vocabulario de esta lección. **10 pts.** Answers will vary.

**6** **Adivinanza** Completa la adivinanza y adivina la respuesta. **¡2 puntos EXTRA!**

❝ Me llegan las cartas
y no sé _leer_ (*to read*)
y, aunque° me las como,
no mancho° el papel. ❞
¿Quién soy? _el buzón_

**aunque** *although* **no mancho** *I don't stain*

**recursos**
panorama.vhlcentral.com
Lección 14

## Section Goals

In **Lectura**, students will:
- learn the strategy of identifying a narrator's point of view
- read an authentic narrative in Spanish

**Instructional Resources**
**Supersite**
*Cuaderno para hispanohablantes*

**Estrategia** Tell students that recognizing the point of view from which a narrative is told will help them comprehend it. Write examples of first-person and omniscient narratives on the board and ask students to identify the point of view in each.

**Examinar el texto** Ask students to read the first two paragraphs of *Nada* and determine whether the narrative is written from the first- or third-person point of view. Call on a volunteer to explain what clues in the text help reveal the narrator. Ask what words indicate that the narrator is a woman (**sola, asustada**).

**Seleccionar** Have students do this activity in pairs. If a student has difficulty answering an item, suggest that his or her partner read aloud the corresponding portions of the text.

**Teaching Tips**
- Explain that *Nada* was published during the early years of **Francisco Franco's** dictatorship (1939–1975), a time in which literature was heavily censored. It is one of the few books from this era that is considered a classic of twentieth-century Spanish literature. **Carmen Laforet** was only in her early twenties when she wrote the novel.
- Add a visual aspect to this reading. Bring in maps of Barcelona and photos of the places mentioned in the excerpt. Have students trace the protagonist's arrival.

# Lectura

*connections cultures*
*NATIONAL STANDARDS*

## Antes de leer

### Estrategia
**Identifying point of view**

You can understand a narrative more completely if you identify the point of view of the narrator. You can do this by simply asking yourself from whose perspective the story is being told. Some stories are narrated in the first person. That is, the narrator is a character in the story, and everything you read is filtered through that person's thoughts, emotions, and opinions. Other stories have an omniscient narrator who is not one of the story's characters and who reports the thoughts and actions of all the characters.

### Examinar el texto

Lee brevemente el texto. ¿De qué trata (*What is it about?*)? ¿Cómo lo sabes? ¿Se narra en primera persona o tiene un narrador omnisciente? ¿Cómo lo sabes?

### Seleccionar

Completa cada oración con la opción correcta.
1. La narradora de *Nada* es ___b___.
   a. una abuela   b. una joven   c. una doctora
2. La protagonista describe su llegada a ___c___.
   a. Madrid      b. Francia      c. Barcelona
3. Ella viajó ___b___.
   a. en avión    b. en tren      c. en barco
4. Su maleta es pesada (*heavy*) porque lleva muchos ___a___.
   a. libros      b. zapatos      c. pantalones
5. Ella se va a quedar en Barcelona con ___a___.
   a. unos parientes   b. una amiga
   c. sus compañeras de clase

**recursos**

panorama.vhlcentral.com
Lección 14

# *Nada* (fragmento)

*Carmen Laforet*

Carmen Laforet nació en Barcelona en 1921. Estudió Filosofía y Letras° y Derecho°. Escribió novelas, relatos y ensayos. Vivió apartada° de las letras las últimas décadas de su vida y murió en el año 2004 tras una larga enfermedad. Aquí presentamos un fragmento de su novela *Nada*, que en 1944 ganó el Premio Nadal, el más importante y antiguo° de España.

Por dificultades en el último momento para adquirir billetes°, llegué a Barcelona a medianoche, en un tren distinto del que había anunciado, y no me esperaba nadie.

Era la primera noche que viajaba sola°, pero no estaba asustada°; por el contrario, […] parecía una aventura agradable° y excitante aquella profunda libertad en la noche. La sangre°, después del viaje largo y cansado, me empezaba a circular en las piernas entumecidas° y con una sonrisa de asombro° miraba la gran estación de Francia y los grupos que estaban aguardando el expreso y los que llegábamos con tres horas de retraso°.

El olor° especial, el gran rumor de la gente, las luces siempre tristes, tenían para mí un gran encanto, ya que envolvía° todas mis impresiones en la maravilla de haber llegado por fin a una ciudad grande, adorada en mis ensueños° por desconocida°.

Empecé a seguir —una gota° entre la corriente°— el rumbo° de la masa humana que, cargada de maletas, se volcaba en° la salida. Mi equipaje era un maletón muy pesado —porque estaba casi lleno de libros— y lo llevaba yo misma con toda la fuerza° de mi juventud y de mi ansiosa expectativa.

## Después de leer

**Completar** ✎

Completa cada oración con la información adecuada.
1. La protagonista llega a Barcelona a las __doce__ de la noche.
2. Ella llegó a la __estación__ de Francia.
3. Siguió a la gente hacia la __salida__.
4. Las personas tomaban taxis, __tranvías__ y coches de caballos.
5. El __coche__ que ella tomó era viejo.
6. Sus parientes vivían en la calle de __Aribau__.

---

**TEACHING OPTIONS**

**Pairs** Have pairs of students reread the excerpt from *Nada* and write four discussion questions about the selection. When they have finished, have them exchange questions with another pair, who can work together to answer them.

**Cultural Comparison** Ask students to think of other stories in the *bildungsroman* (or "novel of formation") genre, such as *The Adventures of Tom Sawyer* or *The Catcher in the Rye*. Have students compare and contrast how the protagonist starts out to **Andrea's** arrival to Barcelona in *Nada*.

Un aire marino, pesado y fresco, entró en mis pulmones° con la primera sensación confusa de la ciudad: una masa de casas dormidas; de establecimientos cerrados; de faroles° como centinelas borrachos de soledad°. Una respiración grande, dificultosa, venía con el cuchicheo° de la madrugada°. Muy cerca, a mi espalda°, enfrente de las callejuelas misteriosas que conducen al Borne, sobre mi corazón excitado, estaba el mar.

Debía parecer una figura extraña con mi aspecto risueño° y mi viejo abrigo que, a impulsos de la brisa, me azotaba° las piernas, defendiendo mi maleta, desconfiada° de los obsequiosos «camàlics»°.

Recuerdo que, en pocos minutos, me quedé sola en la gran acera°, porque la gente corría a coger los escasos taxis o luchaba por arracimarse° en el tranvía°.

Uno de esos viejos coches de caballos que han vuelto a surgir después de la guerra° se detuvo° delante de mí y lo tomé sin titubear°, causando la envidia de un señor que se lanzaba° detrás de él desesperado, agitando° el sombrero.

Corrí aquella noche, en el desvencijado° vehículo, por anchas calles vacías° y atravesé° el corazón de la ciudad lleno de luz a toda hora, como yo quería que estuviese, en un viaje que me pareció corto y que para mí se cargaba de° belleza.

El coche dio vuelta a la plaza de la Universidad y recuerdo que el bello edificio me conmovió° como un grave saludo de bienvenida.

Enfilamos° la calle de Aribau, donde vivían mis parientes, con sus plátanos llenos aquel octubre de espeso verdor° y su silencio vívido de la respiración de mil almas° detrás de los balcones apagados. Las ruedas del coche levantaban una estela° de ruido°, que repercutía° en mi cerebro°. De improviso° sentí crujir° y balancearse todo el armatoste°. Luego quedó inmóvil.

—Aquí es —dijo el cochero.

Filosofía y Letras *Arts* Derecho *Law* apartada *isolated* antiguo *old* adquirir billetes *buy tickets* sola *alone* asustada *afraid* agradable *pleasant* sangre *blood* entumecidas *stiff* asombro *astonishment* retraso *delay* olor *smell* envolvía *it encompassed* ensueños *fantasies* desconocida *unknown* gota *drop* corriente *current* rumbo *direction* se volcaba en *was throwing itself towards* fuerza *strength* pulmones *lungs* faroles *streetlights* borrachos de soledad *drunk with loneliness* cuchicheo *whispering* madrugada *dawn* espalda *back* risueño *smiling* azotaba *was lashing* desconfiada *distrustful* camàlics *porters (in Catalan)* acera *sidewalk* arracimarse *cluster together* tranvía *streetcar* guerra *war* se detuvo *stopped* titubear *hesitating* se lanzaba *was throwing himself* agitando *waving* desvencijado *beat-up* vacías *empty* atravesé *I crossed* se cargaba de *was full of* me conmovió *moved me* Enfilamos *We took* espeso verdor *thick greenery* almas *souls* estela *trail* ruido *noise* repercutía *reverberated* cerebro *brain* De improviso *Unexpectedly* crujir *creak* armatoste *bulky thing*

## Interpretación

Responde a las preguntas. Answers will vary.

1. ¿Cómo se siente la protagonista cuando descubre que nadie fue a recogerla a la estación? Busca algunas palabras que describan las sensaciones de ella.

2. Sabiendo que la protagonista es una chica joven, ¿qué significado pueden tener las palabras "aventura agradable" y "profunda libertad" en este contexto?

3. ¿Qué impresión crees que siente ella ante la gran ciudad y qué expectativas tiene para el futuro?

4. ¿Qué significa la expresión "una gota entre la corriente" en el cuarto párrafo? ¿Qué idea nos da esto del individuo ante la "masa humana" de la gran ciudad?

5. ¿Qué edificio le gustó especialmente a la protagonista y qué tiene que ver esto con su viaje?

## Sensaciones

Trabaja con un(a) compañero/a. Descríbele tus sensaciones, ideas e impresiones de la primera vez que llegaste a un lugar desconocido. Comparen sus experiencias. Answers will vary.

## Debate

Trabajen en grupos. La mitad (*half*) del grupo debe defender los beneficios (*benefits*) de vivir en una gran ciudad y la otra mitad debe exponer sus inconvenientes. Answers will vary.

# Venezuela

## El país en cifras

▸ **Área:** 912.050 km$^2$ (352.144 millas$^2$), *aproximadamente dos veces el área de California*

▸ **Población:** 29.076.000

▸ **Capital:** Caracas —2.988.000

▸ **Ciudades principales:** Valencia —3.090.000, Maracaibo —2.639.000, Maracay —1.333.000, Barquisimeto —1.143.000

SOURCE: Population Division, UN Secretariat

▸ **Moneda:** bolívar

▸ **Idiomas:** español (oficial), arahuaco, caribe
*El yanomami es uno de los idiomas indígenas que se habla en Venezuela. La cultura de los yanomami tiene su centro en el sur de Venezuela, en el bosque tropical. Son cazadores° y agricultores y viven en comunidades de hasta 400 miembros.*

Bandera de Venezuela

**Venezolanos célebres**

▸ **Teresa Carreño,** compositora° y pianista (1853–1917)

▸ **Rómulo Gallegos,** escritor y político (1884–1979)

▸ **Andrés Eloy Blanco,** poeta (1897–1955)

▸ **Baruj Benacerraf,** científico (1920– )
*En 1980, Baruj Benacerraf, junto con dos de sus colegas, recibió el Premio Nobel por sus investigaciones en el campo° de la inmunología y las enfermedades autoinmunes. Nacido en Caracas, Benacerraf también vivió en París y reside ahora en los Estados Unidos.*

cazadores *hunters* compositora *composer* campo *field*
caída *drop* Salto Ángel *Angel Falls* catarata *waterfall*

---

### ¡Increíble pero cierto!

Con una caída° de 979 metros (3.212 pies) desde la meseta de Auyan Tepuy, Salto Ángel°, en Venezuela, es la catarata° más alta del mundo, ¡diecisiete veces más alta que las cataratas del Niágara! James C. Angel la descubrió en 1935. Los indígenas de la zona la denominan Churún Merú.

---

Vista central de Caracas

Maracaibo •

★ Caracas
Valencia •
**Cordillera Central de la Costa**
Lago de
Maracaibo

Río Orinoco

**COLOMBIA**

**Macizo de las Guayanas**

GU

Río Orinoco

**BRASIL**

Llanero de la zona central de Venezuela

Una piragua

ESTADOS UNIDOS
OCÉANO ATLÁNTICO
OCÉANO PACÍFICO
**VENEZUELA**

**recursos**

| WB pp. 177–178 | VM pp. 259–260 | panorama.vhlcentral.com Lección 14 |

---

## Economía • El petróleo

La industria petrolera° es muy importante para la economía venezolana. La mayor concentración de petróleo del país se encuentra debajo del lago Maracaibo. En 1976 se nacionalizaron las empresas° petroleras y pasaron a ser propiedad° del estado con el nombre de *Petróleos de Venezuela*. Este producto representa más del 70% de las exportaciones del país, siendo los Estados Unidos su principal comprador°.

## Actualidades • Caracas

El *boom* petrolero de los años cincuenta transformó a Caracas en una ciudad cosmopolita. Sus rascacielos° y excelentes sistemas de transporte la hacen una de las ciudades más modernas de Latinoamérica. El metro, construido en 1983, es uno de los más modernos del mundo y sus extensas carreteras y autopistas conectan la ciudad con el interior del país. El corazón de la ciudad es el Parque Central, una zona de centros comerciales, tiendas, restaurantes y clubes.

## Historia • Simón Bolívar (1783–1830)

A finales del siglo° XVIII, Venezuela, al igual que otros países suramericanos, todavía estaba bajo el dominio de la corona° española. El general Simón Bolívar, nacido en Caracas, es llamado "El Libertador" porque fue el líder del movimiento independentista suramericano en el área que hoy es Venezuela, Colombia, Ecuador, Perú y Bolivia.

 **¿Qué aprendiste?** Responde a cada pregunta con una oración completa.

1. ¿Cuál es la moneda de Venezuela?
   La moneda de Venezuela es el bolívar.
2. ¿Quién fue Rómulo Gallegos?
   Rómulo Gallegos fue un escritor y político venezolano.
3. ¿Cuándo fue descubierto el Salto Ángel?
   El Salto Ángel fue descubierto en 1935.
4. ¿Cuál es el producto más exportado de Venezuela?
   El producto más exportado de Venezuela es el petróleo.
5. ¿Qué ocurrió en 1976 con las empresas petroleras?
   En 1976 las empresas petroleras se nacionalizaron.
6. ¿Cómo se llama la capital de Venezuela?
   La capital de Venezuela se llama Caracas.
7. ¿Qué hay en el Parque Central de Caracas?
   Hay centros comerciales, tiendas, restaurantes y clubes.
8. ¿Por qué es conocido Simón Bolívar como "El Libertador"?
   Simón Bolívar es conocido como "El Libertador" porque fue el líder del movimiento independentista suramericano.

Tejedor° en Los Aleros, aldea° en los Andes de Venezuela

**Conexión Internet** Investiga estos temas en **panorama.vhlcentral.com**.

1. Busca información sobre Simón Bolívar. ¿Cuáles son algunos de los episodios más importantes de su vida? ¿Crees que Bolívar fue un estadista (*statesman*) de primera categoría? ¿Por qué?
2. Prepara un plan para un viaje de ecoturismo por el Orinoco. ¿Qué quieres ver y hacer durante la excursión? ¿Por qué?

....................................................................

**industria petrolera** *oil industry* **empresas** *companies* **propiedad** *property* **comprador** *buyer* **rascacielos** *skyscrapers*
**siglo** *century* **corona** *crown* **Tejedor** *Weaver* **aldea** *village*

**Teaching Tip** Have students look at the map of the Dominican Republic or show *Overhead PowerPoint #57* and talk about geographical features of the country. Have students note that the majority of cities are located along the coast or close to it and that there are few cities in the center of the island. Point out that there are rugged mountains through the center of the country, with fertile valleys interspersed.

**El país en cifras** After reading **Población,** point out to students that the neighboring country of Haiti is the poorest in the western hemisphere. Ask students to speculate about how that might impact the Dominican Republic. After reading **Idiomas,** the information that Haitian Creole is widely spoken should confirm that there is a major Haitian presence in the Dominican Republic.

**¡Increíble pero cierto!** The actual whereabouts of the remains of Christopher Columbus are a matter of dispute. While Santo Domingo claims to house them, the navigator died in Spain and there is an elaborate tomb said to be his in the cathedral of Seville.

# La República Dominicana

## El país en cifras

▶ **Área:** 48.730 km$^2$ (18.815 millas$^2$), *el área combinada de New Hampshire y Vermont*

▶ **Población:** 9.522.000

*La isla La Española, llamada así tras° el primer viaje de Cristóbal Colón, estuvo bajo el completo dominio de la corona° española hasta 1697, cuando la parte oeste de la isla pasó a ser propiedad° francesa. Hoy día está dividida políticamente en dos países, la República Dominicana en la zona este y Haití en el oeste.*

SOURCE: Population Division, UN Secretariat

▶ **Capital:** Santo Domingo—2.240.000

▶ **Ciudades principales:** Santiago de los Caballeros, La Vega, Puerto Plata, San Pedro de Macorís

▶ **Moneda:** peso dominicano

▶ **Idiomas:** español (oficial)

Bandera de la República Dominicana

### Dominicanos célebres

▶ **Juan Pablo Duarte,** político y padre de la patria° (1808–1876)

▶ **Celeste Woss y Gil,** pintora (1891–1985)

▶ **Juan Luis Guerra,** compositor y cantante de merengue (1956– )

tras *after* corona *crown* propiedad *property* padre de la patria *founding father* fortaleza *fortress* se construyó *was built* naufragó *was shipwrecked* Aunque *Although* enterrado *buried*

Catedral de Santa María la Menor

Hombres tocando los palos en una misa en Nochebuena

Océano Atlántico

La Española

Puerto Plata

Santiago · Bahía Escocesa

Pico Duarte · Río Yuna

**HAITÍ** · La Vega

Cordillera Central

Río San Juan

Sierra de Neiba · San Pedro de Macorís

★ Santo Domingo

Sierra de Baoruco · Bahía de Ocoa

Mar Caribe

ESTADOS UNIDOS
**LA REPÚBLICA DOMINICANA**
OCÉANO PACÍFICO · OCÉANO ATLÁNTICO
AMÉRICA DEL SUR

Trabajadores del campo recogen la cosecha de ajos

**recursos**

| | | |
|---|---|---|
| WB pp. 179–180 | VM pp. 261–262 | panorama.vhlcentral.com Lección 14 |

### ¡Increíble pero cierto!

La primera fortaleza° del Nuevo Mundo se construyó° en la República Dominicana en 1492 cuando la Santa María, uno de los tres barcos de Cristóbal Colón, naufragó° allí. Aunque° la fortaleza, hecha con los restos del barco, fue destruida por tribus indígenas, el amor de Colón por la isla nunca murió. Colón insistió en ser enterrado° allí.

---

### TEACHING OPTIONS

**Language Notes** Although the Arawak and Taíno people who were indigenous to Hispaniola were virtually eliminated following the European conquest, Caribbean Spanish continues to be marked by lexical items from these cultures. Point out these words of Native American origin that have entered Spanish: **ají, cacique, canoa, hamaca, huracán** *(chili pepper, political leader, canoe, hammock, hurricane).*

**Extra Practice** Bring in recordings by **Juan Luis Guerra,** such as his 1998 release *Ni es lo mismo ni es igual.* Invite students to follow the printed lyrics as they listen to a track such as *Mi PC*. Then, have students work together to create an English translation of the song.

### Ciudades • **Santo Domingo**

La zona colonial de Santo Domingo, fundada en 1496, posee° algunas de las construcciones más antiguas del hemisferio. Gracias a las restauraciones°, la arquitectura de la ciudad es famosa no sólo por su belleza sino también por el buen estado de sus edificios. Entre sus sitios más visitados se cuentan° la Calle de las Damas, llamada así porque allí paseaban las señoras de la corte del Virrey; el Alcázar de Colón, un palacio construido en 1509 por Diego Colón, hijo de Cristóbal; y la Fortaleza Ozama, la más vieja de las Américas, construida en 1503.

### Deportes • **El béisbol**

El béisbol es un deporte muy practicado en el Caribe. Los primeros países hispanos en tener una liga fueron Cuba y México, donde se empezó a jugar al béisbol en el siglo° XIX. Hoy día este deporte es una afición° nacional en la República Dominicana. Pedro Martínez (foto, derecha) y David Ortiz son sólo dos de los muchísimos beisbolistas dominicanos que han alcanzado° enorme éxito° e inmensa popularidad entre los aficionados.

### Artes • **El merengue**

El merengue, un ritmo originario de la República Dominicana, tiene sus raíces° en el campo. Tradicionalmente las canciones° hablaban de los problemas sociales de los campesinos°. Sus instrumentos eran el acordeón, el saxofón, el bajo°, el guayano° y la tambora, un tambor° característico del lugar. Entre 1930 y 1960, el merengue se popularizó en las ciudades y adoptó un tono más urbano. En este período empezaron a formarse grandes orquestas°. Uno de los cantantes y compositores de merengue más famosos es Juan Luis Guerra.

 **¿Qué aprendiste?** Responde a cada pregunta con una oración completa.

1. ¿Cuál es la moneda de la República Dominicana?
   La moneda de la República Dominicana es el peso dominicano.
2. ¿Cuándo se fundó la ciudad de Santo Domingo?
   Santo Domingo se fundó en 1496.
3. ¿Qué es el Alcázar de Colón?
   El Alcázar de Colón es un palacio construido en 1509 por Diego Colón, hijo de Cristóbal.
4. Nombra dos beisbolistas famosos de la República Dominicana.
   Dos beisbolistas famosos de la República Dominicana son Pedro Martínez y David Ortiz.
5. ¿De qué hablaban las canciones de merengue tradicionales?
   Las canciones de merengue tradicionales hablaban de los problemas sociales de los campesinos.
6. ¿Qué instrumentos se utilizaban para tocar (play) el merengue?
   Se utilizaban el acordeón, el saxofón, el bajo, el guayano y/o la tambora.
7. ¿Cuándo se transformó el merengue en un estilo urbano?
   El merengue se transformó en un estilo urbano entre los años 1930 y 1960.
8. ¿Quién es Juan Luis Guerra?
   Juan Luis Guerra es un compositor y cantante de merengue.

 **Conexión Internet** Investiga estos temas en **panorama.vhlcentral.com**.

1. Busca más información sobre la isla La Española. ¿Cómo son las relaciones entre la República Dominicana y Haití?
2. Busca más información sobre la zona colonial de Santo Domingo: la Catedral de Santa María, la Casa de Bastidas o el Panteón Nacional. ¿Cómo son estos edificios? ¿Te gustan? Explica tus respuestas.

......................................................................................................

posee *possesses*　restauraciones *restorations*　se cuentan *are included*　siglo *century*　afición *love*　han alcanzado *have reached*　éxito *success*　raíces *roots*　canciones *songs*　campesinos *rural people*　bajo *bass*　guayano *metal scraper*　tambor *drum*　orquestas *orchestras*

---

**Santo Domingo** UNESCO has declared Santo Domingo a World Heritage site because of the abundance of historical architecture. Efforts are being made to restore buildings to their original grandeur, and to "correct" restorations made in the past that were not true to original architectural styles.

**El béisbol** Like many other Dominicans, baseball player **Sammy Sosa's** first baseball glove was a milk carton, his bat was a stick, and the ball was a rolled-up sock wound with tape. **Sosa** has not forgotten the difficult conditions experienced by most Dominicans. After a devastating hurricane swept the island, **Sosa's** charitable foundation raised $700,000 for reconstruction.

**El merengue** The **merengue** synthesizes elements of the cultures that make up the Dominican Republic's heritage. The gourd scraper—or **güiro**—comes from the Arawak people, the **tambora**—a drum unique to the Dominican Republic—is part of the nation's African legacy, the stringed instruments were adapted from the Spanish guitar, and the accordion was introduced by German merchants. Once students hear this quick-paced music, they will understand how it came to be named after meringue—a dessert made by furiously beating egg whites! For more information about **merengue,** you may want to play the ***Panorama cultural*** video footage for this lesson.

**Conexión Internet** Students will find supporting Internet activities and links at **panorama.vhlcentral.com**.

---

## En la ciudad

| | |
|---|---|
| el banco | bank |
| la carnicería | butcher shop |
| el correo | post office |
| el estacionamiento | parking lot |
| la frutería | fruit store |
| la heladería | ice cream shop |
| la joyería | jewelry store |
| la lavandería | laundromat |
| la panadería | bakery |
| la pastelería | pastry shop |
| la peluquería, el salón de belleza | beauty salon |
| la pescadería | fish market |
| el supermercado | supermarket |
| la zapatería | shoe store |
| hacer cola | to stand in line |
| hacer diligencias | to run errands |

## En el banco

| | |
|---|---|
| el cajero automático | ATM |
| el cheque (de viajero) | (traveler's) check |
| la cuenta corriente | checking account |
| la cuenta de ahorros | savings account |
| ahorrar | to save (money) |
| cobrar | to cash (a check) |
| depositar | to deposit |
| firmar | to sign |
| llenar (un formulario) | to fill out (a form) |
| pagar a plazos | to pay in installments |
| pagar al contado, en efectivo | to pay in cash |
| pedir prestado/a | to borrow |
| pedir un préstamo | to apply for a loan |
| ser gratis | to be free of charge |

## Las direcciones

| | |
|---|---|
| la cuadra | (city) block |
| la dirección | address |
| la esquina | corner |
| el letrero | sign |
| cruzar | to cross |
| dar direcciones | to give directions |
| doblar | to turn |
| estar perdido/a | to be lost |
| quedar | to be located |
| (al) este | (to the) east |
| (al) norte | (to the) north |
| (al) oeste | (to the) west |
| (al) sur | (to the) south |
| derecho | straight (ahead) |
| enfrente de | opposite; facing |
| hacia | toward |

| | |
|---|---|
| **Expresiones útiles** | See page 455. |

## En el correo

| | |
|---|---|
| el cartero | mail carrier |
| el correo | mail/post office |
| el paquete | package |
| la estampilla, el sello | stamp |
| el sobre | envelope |
| echar (una carta) al buzón | to put (a letter) in the mailbox; to mail |
| enviar, mandar | to send; to mail |

**recursos**

LM
p. 83

panorama.vhlcentral.com
Lección 14

# El bienestar

## Communicative Goals

**You will learn how to:**

- Talk about health, well-being, and nutrition
- Talk about physical activities

### Lesson Goals

In **Lección 15**, students will be introduced to the following:
- terms for health and exercise
- nutrition terms
- natural spas
- fruits and health
- conditional tense
- present perfect
- past perfect
- making inferences
- organizing information logically when writing
- writing a personal wellness plan
- listening for the gist and for cognates
- a news report about swimming
- Bolivian musical group **Los Kjarkas**
- cultural, geographic, and historical information about Bolivia
- cultural and geographic information about Paraguay

**A primera vista** Here are some additional questions you can ask based on the photo: **¿Crees que tienes buena salud? ¿Vas al gimnasio regularmente? ¿Usas tu carro para hacer diligencias, o caminas? ¿Qué haces cuando te sientes nervioso/a o cansado/a? ¿Es importante que desayunes todas las mañanas? ¿Cuántas horas duermes cada noche?**

## A PRIMERA VISTA

- ¿Está la chica en un gimnasio o en un lugar al aire libre?
- ¿Practica ella deportes frecuentemente?
- ¿Es activa o sedentaria?
- ¿Es probable que le importe su salud?

# El bienestar

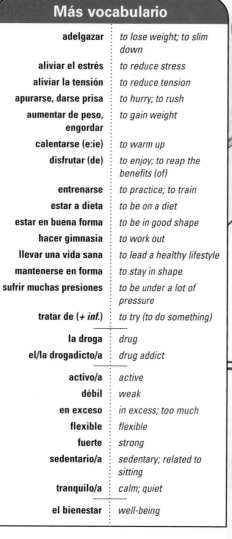

## Más vocabulario

| | |
|---|---|
| adelgazar | to lose weight; to slim down |
| aliviar el estrés | to reduce stress |
| aliviar la tensión | to reduce tension |
| apurarse, darse prisa | to hurry; to rush |
| aumentar de peso, engordar | to gain weight |
| calentarse (e:ie) | to warm up |
| disfrutar (de) | to enjoy; to reap the benefits (of) |
| entrenarse | to practice; to train |
| estar a dieta | to be on a diet |
| estar en buena forma | to be in good shape |
| hacer gimnasia | to work out |
| llevar una vida sana | to lead a healthy lifestyle |
| mantenerse en forma | to stay in shape |
| sufrir muchas presiones | to be under a lot of pressure |
| tratar de (+ *inf.*) | to try (to do something) |
| la droga | drug |
| el/la drogadicto/a | drug addict |
| activo/a | active |
| débil | weak |
| en exceso | in excess; too much |
| flexible | flexible |
| fuerte | strong |
| sedentario/a | sedentary; related to sitting |
| tranquilo/a | calm; quiet |
| el bienestar | well-being |

## Variación léxica

hacer ejercicios aeróbicos ⟷ hacer aeróbic *(Esp.)*

entrenador ⟷ monitor

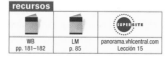

**recursos**

WB pp. 181–182 | LM p. 85 | SUPERSITE panorama.vhlcentral.com Lección 15

**el teleadicto**

**Hace ejercicios de estiramiento.** (hacer)

**la clase de ejercicios aeróbicos**

**Suda.** (sudar)

**Hace ejercicio.** (hacer)

**el entrenador**

**el músculo**

**la cinta caminadora**

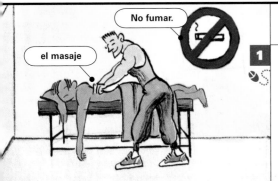

No fumar.

el masaje

Hacen ejercicios aeróbicos.
(hacer)

Levanta pesas.
(levantar)

# Práctica

**1** **Escuchar** Mira el dibujo. Luego escucha las oraciones e indica si lo que se dice en cada oración es **cierto** o **falso**.

| | Cierto | Falso | | Cierto | Falso |
|---|---|---|---|---|---|
| 1. | ○ | ☑ | 6. | ○ | ☑ |
| 2. | ○ | ☑ | 7. | ○ | ☑ |
| 3. | ☑ | ○ | 8. | ☑ | ○ |
| 4. | ☑ | ○ | 9. | ○ | ☑ |
| 5. | ☑ | ○ | 10. | ○ | ☑ |

**2** **Seleccionar** 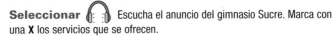 Escucha el anuncio del gimnasio Sucre. Marca con una **X** los servicios que se ofrecen.

__X__ 1. dietas para adelgazar

_____ 2. programa para aumentar de peso

__X__ 3. clases de gimnasia

__X__ 4. entrenador personal

__X__ 5. masajes

_____ 6. programa para dejar de fumar

**3** **Identificar** Identifica el opuesto (*opposite*) de cada palabra.

| | |
|---|---|
| apurarse | fuerte |
| disfrutar | mantenerse en forma |
| engordar | sedentario |
| estar enfermo | sufrir muchas presiones |
| flexible | tranquilo |

1. activo  sedentario
2. adelgazar  engordar
3. aliviar el estrés  sufrir muchas presiones
4. débil  fuerte
5. ir despacio  apurarse
6. estar sano  estar enfermo
7. nervioso  tranquilo
8. ser teleadicto  mantenerse en forma

**4** **Combinar** Combina palabras de cada columna para formar ocho oraciones lógicas sobre el bienestar.

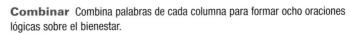

1. David levanta pesas  h
2. Estás en buena forma  d
3. Felipe se lastimó  f
4. José y Rafael  e
5. Mi hermano  a
6. Sara hace ejercicios de  b
7. Mis primas están a dieta  c
8. Para llevar una vida sana,  g

a. aumentó de peso.
b. estiramiento.
c. porque quieren adelgazar.
d. porque haces ejercicio.
e. sudan mucho en el gimnasio.
f. un músculo de la pierna.
g. no se debe fumar.
h. y corre mucho.

**1** **Teaching Tip** Check answers by reading each statement and asking volunteers to say whether it is true or false. To challenge students, have them correct the false information.

**1** **Script** 1. Se puede fumar dentro del gimnasio. 2. El teleadicto está en buena forma. 3. Los músculos del entrenador son grandes. 4. La mujer que está corriendo también está sudando.
*Script continues on page 484.*

**2** **Teaching Tip** For this exercise, tell students not to look at the drawing, rather only to listen to the audio.

**2** **Script** Si quieres estar en buena forma, aliviar el estrés o adelgazar, el gimnasio Sucre te ofrece una serie de programas que se adaptarán a tus gustos. Tenemos un equipo de entrenadores que te pueden ayudar a mantenerte en forma con las clases de ejercicios aeróbicos y de gimnasia. Si sufres muchas presiones y lo que necesitas es un servicio más especial, puedes trabajar con un entrenador personal en nuestros programas privados de pesas, masajes y dietas para adelgazar.
*Textbook MP3s*

**3** **Expansion** Have students use each pair of opposite terms in sentences. Ex: **José está muy nervioso porque no estudió para el examen. Roberto estudió por dos horas; por eso está tranquilo.**

**4** **Expansion** Have students create original endings for the sentence starters in the left column.

**Note:** At this point you may want to present *Vocabulario adicional: Más vocabulario para el bienestar*, from the Supersite/IRCD.

**TEACHING OPTIONS**

**Pairs** Have pairs of students interview each other about what they do to stay in shape. Interviewers should also find out how often their partner does these things and when he or she did them over the past week. Ask students to write a brief report summarizing the interview.

**Game** Divide the class into teams of three. Ask a team to leave the room while the class chooses a vocabulary word or expression. When the team returns, they must try to guess it by asking the class yes-no questions. If the team guesses the word within ten questions, they get a point. Ex: **¿Es un lugar? ¿Describe a una persona? ¿Es una acción? ¿Es algo que haces para estar en buena forma?**

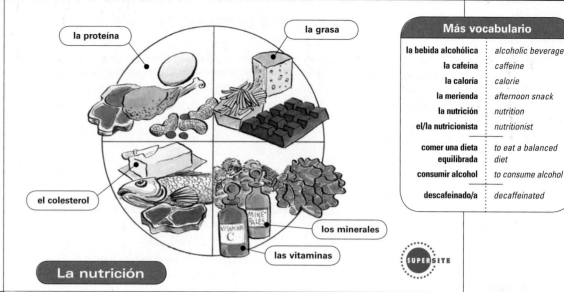

**Más vocabulario**

| | |
|---|---|
| la bebida alcohólica | alcoholic beverage |
| la cafeína | caffeine |
| la caloría | calorie |
| la merienda | afternoon snack |
| la nutrición | nutrition |
| el/la nutricionista | nutritionist |
| comer una dieta equilibrada | to eat a balanced diet |
| consumir alcohol | to consume alcohol |
| descafeinado/a | decaffeinated |

**La nutrición**

**5** **Completar** Completa cada oración con la palabra adecuada.

1. Después de hacer ejercicio, como pollo o bistec porque contienen ___b___.
   a. drogas  b. proteínas  c. grasa
2. Para ___c___, es necesario consumir comidas de todos los grupos alimenticios (*nutrition groups*).
   a. aliviar el estrés  b. correr  c. comer una dieta equilibrada
3. Mis primas ___a___ una buena comida.
   a. disfrutan de  b. tratan de  c. sudan
4. Mi entrenador no come chocolate ni papas fritas porque contienen ___c___.
   a. dietas  b. vitaminas  c. mucha grasa
5. Mi padre no come mantequilla porque él necesita reducir ___b___.
   a. la nutrición  b. el colesterol  c. el bienestar
6. Mi novio cuenta ___c___ porque está a dieta.
   a. las pesas  b. los músculos  c. las calorías

**CONSULTA**
To review what you have learned about nutrition and food groups, see **Contextos, Lección 8**, pp. 242–245.

**6** **La nutrición** En parejas, hablen de los tipos de comida que comen y las consecuencias que tienen para su salud. Luego compartan la información con la clase. Answers will vary.

1. ¿Cuántas comidas con mucha grasa comes regularmente? ¿Piensas que debes comer menos comidas de este tipo? ¿Por qué?
2. ¿Compras comidas con muchos minerales y vitaminas? ¿Necesitas consumir más comidas que los contienen? ¿Por qué?
3. ¿Tiene algún miembro de tu familia problemas con el colesterol? ¿Qué haces para evitar problemas con el colesterol?
4. ¿Eres vegetariano/a? ¿Conoces a alguien que sea vegetariano/a? ¿Qué piensas de la idea de no comer carne u otros productos animales? ¿Es posible comer una dieta equilibrada sin comer carne? Explica.
5. ¿Tomas cafeína en exceso? ¿Qué ventajas (*advantages*) y desventajas tiene la cafeína? Da ejemplos de productos que contienen cafeína y de productos descafeinados.
6. ¿Llevas una vida sana? ¿Y tus amigos? ¿Crees que, en general, los estudiantes llevan una vida sana? ¿Por qué?

**AYUDA**
Some useful words:
**sano = saludable**
**en general = por lo general**
**estricto**
**normalmente**
**muchas veces**
**a veces**
**de vez en cuando**

---

**TEACHING OPTIONS**

**TPR** Add an auditory aspect to this vocabulary practice. Have students write **bueno** on one piece of paper and **malo** on another. Prepare a series of statements about healthy and unhealthy habits. As you read each statement, have students hold up the corresponding paper. Ex: **Antes de hacer ejercicio, siempre como comidas con mucha grasa. (malo) Consumo muy poco alcohol. (bueno)**

**Small groups** In groups of three or four, have students take turns miming actions involving fitness, health, and well-being. The other group members should guess the verb or verb phrase. Ex: A student mimes lifting weights (**Estás levantando pesas.**).

# Comunicación

**7** **Un anuncio** En grupos de cuatro, imaginen que son dueños/as de un gimnasio con un equipo (*equipment*) moderno, entrenadores calificados y un(a) nutricionista. Preparen y presenten un anuncio para la televisión que hable del gimnasio y atraiga (*attracts*) a una gran variedad de nuevos clientes. No se olviden de presentar esta información: Answers will vary.

▶ las ventajas de estar en buena forma
▶ el equipo que tienen
▶ los servicios y clases que ofrecen
▶ las características únicas del gimnasio
▶ la dirección y el teléfono del gimnasio
▶ el precio para los socios (*members*) del gimnasio

**8** **Recomendaciones para la salud** En parejas, imaginen que están preocupados/as por los malos hábitos de un(a) amigo/a que no está bien últimamente (*lately*). Escriban y representen una conversación en la cual hablen de lo que está pasando en la vida de su amigo/a y los cambios que necesita hacer para llevar una vida sana. Answers will vary.

**9** **El teleadicto** Con un(a) compañero/a, representen los papeles de un(a) nutricionista y un(a) teleadicto/a. La persona sedentaria habla de sus malos hábitos en las comidas y de que no hace ejercicio. También dice que toma demasiado café y que siente mucho estrés. El/La nutricionista le sugiere una dieta equilibrada con bebidas descafeinadas y una rutina para mantenerse en buena forma. El/La teleadicto/a le da las gracias por su ayuda. Answers will vary.

**10** **El gimnasio perfecto** Tú y tu compañero/a quieren encontrar el gimnasio perfecto. Tú tienes el anuncio del gimnasio Bienestar y tu compañero/a tiene el del gimnasio Músculos. Hazle preguntas a tu compañero/a sobre las actividades que se ofrecen en el otro gimnasio. Tu profesor(a) le va a dar a cada uno de ustedes una hoja distinta con la información necesaria para completar la actividad. Answers will vary.

> **modelo**
> **Estudiante 1:** ¿Se ofrecen clases para levantar pesas?
> **Estudiante 2:** Sí, para levantar pesas se ofrecen clases todos los lunes a las seis de la tarde.

---

**TEACHING OPTIONS**

**Pairs** Tell students to imagine that they are personal wellness consultants. Have them give their partner a set of ten guidelines on how to begin a comprehensive health program. Suggestions should be made regarding diet, aerobic exercise, strength training, flexibility training, and stress management. Have students switch roles.

**Extra Practice** Ask students to write down five personal goals for achieving or maintaining a healthy lifestyle. Then have them write a brief paragraph explaining why they want to attain these goals and how they plan to achieve them. Call on volunteers to share their goals with the class.

**7 Teaching Tips**
• If possible, have students visit health clubs in your area to gather advertising brochures and/or fitness magazines to help them brainstorm ideas for their commercials.
• Have groups write their advertisement so that each student gets to speak for an equal amount of time.

**8 Teaching Tips**
• Ask students to include uses of the subjunctive after verbs and expressions of will and influence; emotion; and doubt, disbelief, or denial. For review, refer students to pages 398-399, pages 426-427, and pages 430-431.
• Have students discuss at least five bad habits their friend has, explain why he or she has them, and what he or she did unsuccessfully to overcome them. Then, have students discuss ways of successfully overcoming each habit.

**9 Teaching Tip** Before doing this activity, review the verbs and expressions of will and influence on pages 398–399.

**9 Expansion** Have students conduct a follow-up interview which takes place one month after the initial meeting.

**10 Teaching Tip** Divide the class into pairs and distribute the handouts from the Information Gap Activities (Supersite/IRCD) that correspond to this activity. Give students ten minutes to complete the activity.

**10 Expansion**
• Have pairs work in groups to discuss which gym they would join and why.
• Have groups compare the gyms described in the activity with your campus gym and share their comparisons with the class.

# ¡Qué buena excursión!

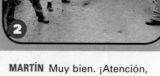

Martín y los estudiantes van de excursión a las montañas.

## Section Goals

In **Fotonovela**, students will:
• receive comprehensible input from free-flowing discourse
• learn functional phrases that preview lesson grammatical structures

**Instructional Resources**
**Supersite/DVD:** *Fotonovela*
**Supersite/IRCD:** *IRM*
(*Fotonovela* Videoscript & Translation, WBs/VM/LM Answer Key)
**WebSAM**
**Video Manual,** pp. 223–224

**Video Recap: Lección 14**
Before doing this **Fotonovela** section, review the previous one with this activity.
**1. ¿Qué recomienda don Francisco que lleven todos los excursionistas?** (zapatos cómodos, una mochila, gafas oscuras y un suéter) **2. ¿Qué quiere Inés que Álex y Maite le compren en el centro?** (unas estampillas/unos sellos) **3. ¿Por qué hablaron Maite y Álex con un joven?** (porque estaban perdidos) **4. ¿Dónde estaba el supermercado?** (enfrente del banco)

**Video Synopsis Martín** leads the students in some warm-up stretches before the hike. During the hike, the students chat, take pictures, and admire their surroundings. Afterward, they talk about the wonderful time they had. **Don Francisco** tells the group that it is time to go back for dinner.

**Teaching Tip** Ask students to read only the first statement in each caption. Then have them predict the content of the episode, based only on those sentences. After viewing the episode, have students summarize the plot and correct their original predictions as necessary.

**PERSONAJES**

 MAITE

 INÉS

 DON FRANCISCO

 ÁLEX

 JAVIER

 MARTÍN

**MARTÍN** Buenos días, don Francisco.
**DON FRANCISCO** ¡Hola, Martín!
**MARTÍN** Ya veo que han traído lo que necesitan. ¡Todos han venido muy bien equipados!

**MARTÍN** Muy bien. ¡Atención, chicos! Primero hagamos algunos ejercicios de estiramiento…

**MARTÍN** Es bueno que se hayan mantenido en buena forma. Entonces, jóvenes, ¿ya están listos?
**JAVIER** ¡Sí, listísimos! No puedo creer que finalmente haya llegado el gran día.

**DON FRANCISCO** ¡Hola! ¡Qué alegría verlos! ¿Cómo les fue en la excursión?
**JAVIER** Increíble, don Efe. Nunca había visto un paisaje tan espectacular. Es un lugar estupendo. Saqué mil fotos y tengo montones de escenas para dibujar.

**MAITE** Nunca había hecho una excursión. ¡Me encantó! Cuando vuelva a España, voy a tener mucho que contarle a mi familia.

**INÉS** Ha sido la mejor excursión de mi vida. Amigos, Martín, don Efe, mil gracias.

**recursos**
 VM pp. 223–224 | panorama.vhlcentral.com Lección 15

**TEACHING OPTIONS**

**Video Tips** General suggestions for using video clips in the classroom can be found on page IAE-12 of this Instructor's Annotated Edition.
**¡Qué buena excursión!** To introduce the class to this video episode, play only the **Resumen** segment and have students tell you what they saw and heard. Then play the entire episode and have students jot down notes about the plot. Next, have the class work in small groups to compare notes and prepare summaries of the episode. Ask one or two groups to read their summaries to the class. Finally, discuss the plot with the class and check for accuracy.

**MARTÍN** ¡Fabuloso! ¡En marcha, pues!

**DON FRANCISCO** ¡Adiós! ¡Cuídense!

*Martín y los estudiantes pasan ocho horas caminando en las montañas. Hablan, sacan fotos y disfrutan del paisaje. Se divierten muchísimo.*

**ÁLEX** Sí, gracias, Martín. Gracias por todo.

**MARTÍN** No hay de qué. Ha sido un placer.

**DON FRANCISCO** Chicos, pues, es hora de volver. Creo que la señora Vives nos ha preparado una cena muy especial.

## Expresiones útiles

### Getting ready to start a hike

- **Ya veo que han traído lo que necesitan.**
  *I see that you have brought what you need.*
- **¡Todos han venido muy bien equipados!**
  *Everyone has come very well equipped!*
- **Primero hagamos algunos ejercicios de estiramiento.**
  *First let's do some stretching exercises.*
- **No puedo creer que finalmente haya llegado el gran día.**
  *I can't believe that the big day has finally arrived.*
- **¿(Están) listos?**
  *(Are you) ready?*
  **¡En marcha, pues!**
  *Let's get going, then!*

### Talking about a hike

- **¿Cómo les fue en la excursión?**
  *How did the hike go?*
- **Nunca había visto un paisaje tan espectacular.**
  *I had never seen such spectacular scenery.*
- **Nunca había hecho una excursión. ¡Me encantó!**
  *I had never gone on a hike before. I loved it!*
- **Ha sido la mejor excursión de mi vida.**
  *It's been the best hike of my life.*

### Courtesy expressions

- **Gracias por todo.**
  *Thanks for everything.*
- **Ha sido un placer.**
  *It's been a pleasure.*
- **¡Cuídense!**
  *Take care!*

**Teaching Tip** Have the class read through the entire **Fotonovela**, with volunteers playing the various parts.

**Expresiones útiles** Draw attention to the verbs **han traído, han venido, ha sido, había visto, había hecho,** and **haya llegado.** Point out their English equivalents and briefly explain that the past participle can be used with forms of the verb **haber** to form the present perfect, the past perfect, and the present perfect subjunctive. Finally, draw attention to the sentence **No puedo creer que finalmente haya llegado el gran día.** Tell students that **haya llegado** is an example of the present perfect subjunctive, which combines a present subjunctive form of **haber** with a past participle. Tell students that they will learn more about these concepts in **Estructura**.

---

**TEACHING OPTIONS**

**Pairs** Have students work in pairs to write five true-false statements about the **¡Qué buena excursión!** episode. Then, have pairs exchange papers with another pair, who will work together to complete the activity and correct the false information.

**Extra Practice** Photocopy the **Fotonovela** Videoscript (Supersite/IRCD) and white out key vocabulary in order to make a master for a cloze activity. Distribute the copies and, as you play the **¡Qué buena excursión!** episode, have students fill in the blanks.

# ¿Qué pasó?

**1 Expansion** Have the class work in pairs or small groups to write a question that would elicit each statement.

**1** **Seleccionar** Selecciona la respuesta que mejor completa cada oración.

1. Antes de salir, Martín les recomienda a los estudiantes que hagan _____ a _____.
   a. ejercicios de estiramiento  b. ejercicios aeróbicos  c. gimnasia
2. Los excursionistas hablaron, _____ c _____ en las montañas.
   a. levantaron pesas y se divirtieron  b. caminaron y dibujaron
   c. sacaron fotos y disfrutaron del paisaje
3. Inés dice que ha sido la mejor excursión _____ c _____.
   a. del viaje  b. del año  c. de su vida
4. Cuando Maite vuelva a España, va a _____ b _____.
   a. tener montones de escenas para dibujar  b. tener mucho que contarle a su familia
   c. tener muchas fotos que enseñarle a su familia
5. La señora Vives les ha preparado _____ a _____.
   a. una cena especial  b. un día en las montañas muy especial
   c. una excursión espectacular

**2 Expansion**
- Give the class these statements as items 7–8: **7. Bueno, chicos… hay que hacer unos ejercicios antes de empezar. (Martín)** 8. **¿Qué tal les fue en la excursión? (don Francisco)**
- Add an auditory aspect to this activity. Have students close their books, then give them these sentences as a dictation. Read each sentence twice slowly and then once at regular speed so that students will have time to write.

**2** **Identificar** Identifica quién puede decir estas oraciones.

1. Oye, muchísimas gracias por el mejor día de mi vida. ¡Fue divertidísimo! Inés
2. Parece que están todos preparados, ¿no? ¡Perfecto! Bueno, ¡vamos! Martín
3. Cuando vea a mis papás y a mis hermanos voy a tener mucho que contarles. Maite
4. Debemos volver ahora para comer. ¡Vamos a tener una cena especial! don Francisco
5. El lugar fue fenomenal, uno de los más bonitos que he visto. ¡Qué bueno que traje mi cámara! Javier
6. ¡Gracias por todo, Martín! Álex/Maite/Inés/Javier

 JAVIER

 INÉS

 ÁLEX

DON FRANCISCO

 MAITE

MARTÍN

**3 Teaching Tip** Ask students a few questions using words from the list. Ex: **¿Comes mucha grasa? ¿Qué es un teleadicto? ¿Cómo te mantienes en forma?**

**3 Expansion** Have pairs write sentences using any left-over words from the word bank. Ask volunteers to share their sentences with the class.

**3**  **Inventar** En parejas, hagan descripciones de los personajes de la **Fotonovela**. Utilicen las oraciones, la lista de palabras y otras expresiones que sepan. Answers will vary.

| | | |
|---|---|---|
| aliviar el estrés | hacer ejercicios de estiramiento | masaje |
| bienestar | llevar una vida sana | teleadicto/a |
| grasa | mantenerse en forma | vitamina |

**modelo**

**Estudiante 1:** *Martín es activo, flexible y fuerte.*
**Estudiante 2:** *Martín siempre hace ejercicios de estiramiento. Está en buena forma y lleva una vida muy sana…*

1. A Javier le duelen los músculos después de hacer gimnasia.
2. Don Francisco a veces sufre presiones y estrés en su trabajo.
3. A Inés le encanta salir con amigos o leer un buen libro.
4. Álex trata de comer una dieta equilibrada.
5. Maite no es muy flexible.

**TEACHING OPTIONS**

**Extra Practice** Ask the class a few additional questions about the **Fotonovela**. Ex: **¿Qué hicieron Martín y los chicos antes de empezar la excursión? (Hicieron unos ejercicios de estiramiento.) ¿Qué hicieron los estudiantes durante la excursión? (Caminaron, hablaron, sacaron fotos y miraron el paisaje.)**

**Pairs** Have pairs prepare a television program in which a traveler is interviewed about a recent hiking trip. Give them time to prepare and rehearse; then ask volunteers to present their programs to the class. Alternately, you may want the students to videotape their programs and play them for the class.

# Ortografía SUPERSITE

## Las letras **b** y **v**

Since there is no difference in pronunciation between the Spanish letters **b** and **v**, spelling words that contain these letters can be tricky. Here are some tips.

| | | | |
|---|---|---|---|
| no**mb**re | **bl**usa | a**bs**oluto | descu**br**ir |

The letter **b** is always used before consonants.

| | | | |
|---|---|---|---|
| **bon**ita | **bot**ella | **bus**car | **bien**estar |

At the beginning of words, the letter **b** is usually used when it is followed by the letter combinations **-on, -or, -ot, -u, -ur, -us, -ien,** and **-ene.**

| | | | |
|---|---|---|---|
| adelgaza**ba** | disfruta**ban** | i**bas** | í**bamos** |

The letter **b** is used in the verb endings of the imperfect tense for **-ar** verbs and the verb **ir.**

| | | | |
|---|---|---|---|
| **v**oy | **v**amos | estu**v**o | tu**v**ieron |

The letter **v** is used in the present tense forms of **ir** and in the preterite forms of **estar** and **tener.**

| | | | |
|---|---|---|---|
| oct**avo** | hu**evo** | act**iva** | gr**ave** |

The letter **v** is used in these noun and adjective endings: **-avo/a, -evo/a, -ivo/a, -ave, -eve.**

**Práctica** Completa las palabras con las letras **b** o **v.**

1. Una _v_ez me lastimé el _b_razo cuando esta_b_a _b_uceando.
2. Manuela se ol_v_idó sus li_b_ros en el auto_b_ús.
3. Ernesto tomó el _b_orrador y se puso todo _b_lanco de tiza.
4. Para tener una _v_ida sana y saluda_b_le, necesitas tomar _v_itaminas.
5. En mi pue_b_lo hay un _b_ule_v_ar que tiene muchos ár_b_oles.

**El ahorcado** (*Hangman*) Juega al ahorcado para adivinar las palabras.

1. _n_ _u_ _b_ _e_ _s_     Están en el cielo. nubes
2. _b_ _u_ _z_ _ó_ _n_     Relacionado con el correo buzón
3. _b_ _o_ _t_ _e_ _l_ _l_ _a_     Está llena de líquido. botella
4. _n_ _i_ _e_ _v_ _e_     Fenómeno meteorológico nieve
5. _v_ _e_ _n_ _t_ _a_ _n_ _a_ _s_     Los "ojos" de la casa ventanas

**recursos**

| | |
|---|---|
| LM p. 86 | panorama.vhlcentral.com Lección 15 |

**Section Goal**

In **Ortografía**, students will learn about the spelling of words that contain **b** and **v**.

**Instructional Resources**
**Supersite:** Lab MP3 Audio Files
**Lección 15**
**Supersite/IRCD:** *IRM* (Lab Audio Script, WBs/VM/LM Answer Key)
**WebSAM**
**Lab Manual,** p. 86
*Cuaderno para hispanohablantes*

**Teaching Tips**
• Ask the class if **b** or **v** is used before a consonant. Then say the words **nombre, blusa, absoluto,** and **descubrir** and have volunteers write them on the board.
• Write the words **bonita, botella, buscar,** and **bienestar** on the board. Ask the class to explain why these words are spelled with **b**.
• Ask the class if **b** or **v** is used in the endings of **-ar** verbs and the verb **ir** in the imperfect tense. Then say the words **adelgazaba, disfrutaban, ibas,** and **íbamos** and ask volunteers to write them on the board.
• Ask why the words **voy, vamos, estuvo,** and **tuvieron** are spelled with **v** and have volunteers write them on the board.
• Write the words **octavo, huevo, activa,** and **grave** on the board and ask the class to explain why these words are spelled with **v**.
• Point out that **Ortografía** replaces **Pronunciación** in the Student Edition for **Lecciones 10–15,** but not in the Lab Manual. The **Recursos** box references the **Pronunciación** sections found in all lessons of the Lab Manual.

---

**TEACHING OPTIONS**

**Extra Practice** Add an auditory aspect to this **Ortografía** presentation. Prepare a dictation exercise with words containing **b** and **v**. Slowly read each sentence twice, allowing time for students to write. Ex: **1. Doña Victoria era muy activa y llevaba una vida muy sana. 2. Siempre almorzaba verduras y nunca tomaba vino ni refrescos. 3. Nunca fumaba e iba al gimnasio todos los sábados para tomar clases aeróbicos.**

**Pairs** In pairs, have students use **Vocabulario** at the back of the book to help them write five additional sentences using as many words with **b** and **v** as possible. Then have students exchange with another pair and fill in the blanks with **b** or **v**.

**EN DETALLE**

# Spas naturales

**¿Hay algo mejor que un buen baño° para descansar y aliviar la tensión?** Y si el baño se toma en una terma°, el beneficio° es mayor. Los tratamientos con agua y lodo° para mejorar la salud y el bienestar son populares en las Américas desde hace muchos siglos°. Las termas son manantiales° naturales de agua caliente. La temperatura facilita la absorción de minerales y otros elementos que el agua contiene y que son buenos para la salud. El agua de las termas se usa en piscinas, baños y duchas o en el sitio natural en el que surge° el agua: pozas°, estanques° o cuevas°.

**Ecotermales en Arenal, Costa Rica**

**Volcán de lodo El Totumo, Colombia**

En Baños de San Vicente, en Ecuador, son muy populares los tratamientos° con lodo volcánico. El lodo caliente se extiende por el cuerpo; así la piel° absorbe los minerales beneficiosos para la salud; también se usa para dar masajes. La lodoterapia es útil para tratar varias enfermedades, además hace que la piel se vea radiante.

En Costa Rica, la actividad volcánica también ha dado° origen a fuentes° y pozas termales. Si te gusta cuidarte y amas la naturaleza, recuerda estos nombres: Las Hornillas y Las Pailas. Son pozas naturales de aguas termales que están cerca del volcán Rincón de la Vieja. ¡Un baño termal en medio de un paisaje tan hermoso es una experiencia única!

**Otros balnearios°**

Todos ofrecen piscinas, baños, pozas y duchas de aguas termales y además...

| Lugar | Servicios |
|---|---|
| El Edén y Yanasara, Curgos (Perú) | cascadas° de aguas termales |
| Montbrió del Camp, Tarragona (España) | baños de algas° |
| Puyuhuapi (Chile) | duchas de agua de mar; baños de algas |
| Termas de Río Hondo, Santiago del Estero (Argentina) | baños de lodo |
| Tepoztlán, Morelos (México) | temazcales° aztecas |
| Uyuni, Potosí (Bolivia) | baños de sal |

baño *bath* terma *hot spring* beneficio *benefit* lodo *mud* siglos *centuries* manantiales *springs* surge *springs forth* pozas *small pools* estanques *ponds* cuevas *caves* tratamientos *treatments* piel *skin* ha dado *has given* fuentes *springs* balnearios *spas* cascadas *waterfalls* algas *seaweed* temazcales *steam and medicinal herb baths*

**ACTIVIDADES**

**1**

**1** **¿Cierto o falso?** Indica si lo que dice cada oración es **cierto** o **falso**. Corrige la información falsa.

1. Los tratamientos con agua y lodo se conocen sólo desde hace pocos años. Falso. Son populares desde hace muchos siglos.

2. Las termas son manantiales naturales de agua caliente. Cierto.

3. La temperatura de las aguas termales no afecta la absorción de los minerales. Falso. Facilita la absorción de minerales y otros elementos.

4. Las Hornillas y Las Pailas son pozas de aguas termales en Costa Rica. Cierto.

5. Mucha gente va a Baños de San Vicente, Ecuador, por sus playas. Falso. Mucha gente va por los tratamientos de lodo.

6. Montbrió del Camp ofrece baños de sal. Falso. Montbrió del Camp ofrece baños de algas.

7. Es posible ver aguas termales en forma de cascadas. Cierto.

8. Tepoztlán ofrece temazcales aztecas. Cierto.

## ASÍ SE DICE

### El ejercicio

| | |
|---|---|
| los abdominales | *sit-ups* |
| la bicicleta estática | *stationary bicycle* |
| el calambre muscular | *(muscular) cramp* |
| el (fisi)culturismo; la musculación (Esp.) | *bodybuilding* |
| las flexiones de pecho; las lagartijas (Méx.); las planchas (Esp.) | *push-ups* |
| la (cinta) trotadora (Arg.; Chile) | la cinta caminadora |

## EL MUNDO HISPANO

### Creencias° sobre la salud

○ **Colombia** Como algunos suelos son de baldosas°, se cree que si uno anda descalzo° se enfrían° los pies y esto puede causar un resfriado o artritis.

○ **Cuba** Por la mañana, muchas madres sacan a sus bebés a los patios y a las puertas de las casas. La creencia es que unos cinco minutos de sol ayudan a fijar° el calcio en los huesos y aumentan la inmunidad contra las enfermedades.

○ **México** Muchas personas tienen la costumbre de tomar a diario un vaso de jugo del cactus conocido como nopal. Se dice que es bueno para reducir el colesterol y el azúcar en la sangre y que ayuda a adelgazar.

**Creencias** *Beliefs* **baldosas** *tiles* **anda descalzo** *walks barefoot* **se enfrían** *get cold* **fijar** *to set*

## PERFIL

### Las frutas y la salud

Desde hace muchos años se conocen las propiedades de la papaya para tratar problemas digestivos. Esta fruta contiene una enzima, la papaína, que actúa de forma semejante° a como lo hacen los jugos gástricos. Una porción de papaya o un vaso de jugo de esta fruta ayuda a la digestión. La papaya también es rica en vitaminas A y C.

Otra fruta buena para la digestión es la piña°. La piña contiene bromelina, una enzima que, como la papaína, ayuda a digerir° las proteínas. Esta deliciosa fruta

**Papayas**

contiene también ácido cítrico, vitaminas y minerales. Además, tiene efectos diuréticos y antiinflamatorios que pueden aliviar las enfermedades reumáticas. La piña ofrece una ayuda fácil y sabrosa para perder peso por su contenido en fibra y su efecto diurético. Una rodaja°

de piña fresca o un vaso de jugo antes de comer puede ayudar en cualquier° dieta para adelgazar.

**semejante** *similar* **piña** *pineapple* **digerir** *to digest* **rodaja** *slice* **cualquier** *any*

### SUPERSITE Conexión Internet

**¿Qué sistemas de ejercicio son más populares entre los hispanos?**

Go to **panorama.vhlcentral.com** to find more cultural information related to this **Cultura** section.

## ACTIVIDADES

**2** **Comprensión** Responde a las preguntas.
1. Una argentina te dice: "Voy a usar la trotadora." ¿Qué va a hacer?
   Va a usar la cinta caminadora.
2. Según los colombianos, ¿qué efectos negativos tiene el no usar zapatos en casa? Puede causar un resfriado o artritis.
3. ¿Cómo se llama la enzima de la papaya que ayuda a la digestión?
   la papaína
4. ¿Cómo se aconseja consumir la piña en dietas de adelgazamiento?
   una rodaja de piña fresca o un vaso de jugo antes de comer

**3**  **Para sentirte mejor** Entrevista a un(a) compañero/a sobre las cosas que hace todos los días, las cosas que hace al menos una o dos veces a la semana y lo que le ayuda a sentirse mejor. Hablen sobre actividades deportivas, la alimentación y lo que hacen en sus ratos libres.
Answers will vary.

**recursos**

SUPERSITE

panorama.vhlcentral.com
Lección 15

## TEACHING OPTIONS

**Heritage Speakers** Ask heritage speakers to talk about popular health beliefs or foods with healing properties that they have encountered in their families or communities.
**Pairs** Divide the class into pairs. Have students take turns quizzing each other about the health beliefs and practices mentioned on these pages. Write a question on the board for students to use as a model. Ex: **¿Para qué sirve la lodoterapia?**

**Game** Play a *Jeopardy*-style game. Divide the class into three teams and have one member from each team stand up. Read a definition. Ex: **Es una enzima de la papaya.** The first student to raise his or her hand must answer in the form of a question. Ex: **¿Qué es la papaína?** Each correct answer earns one point. The team with the most points wins.

## Section Goals

In **Estructura 15.1** students will learn:
• to use the conditional
• to make polite requests and hypothesize about past conditions

**Instructional Resources**
**Supersite:** Lab MP3 Audio Files **Lección 15**
**Supersite/IRCD:** *PowerPoints* (**Lección 15 Estructura** Presentation); *IRM* (**Hojas de actividades,** Lab Audio Script, WBs/VM/LM Answer Key)
**WebSAM**
**Workbook,** pp. 183–184
**Lab Manual,** p. 87
*Cuaderno para hispanohablantes*

## Teaching Tips

• Ask students to imagine they are on the trip with the **Fotonovela** characters. Ask them what they would like to do there. Ex: **¿Qué te gustaría hacer o ver en Ecuador? A mí me gustaría ir de excursión. ¿Y a ti?** Tell students that **gustaría** is a polite form of **gustar** that they already know. The conditional is used to make polite requests.
• Ask volunteers to read the captions to the video stills and indicate which verbs are in the conditional.
• Point out that, as in the future, there is only one set of endings in the conditional.
• Check for understanding by citing an infinitive and a subject pronoun while pointing to a specific student. The student should respond with the conditional form. Ex: **decir / nosotros (diríamos); venir / tú (vendrías)**
• Ask students what the future form of **hay** is. Then ask them what they would expect the conditional form to be.

---

**15.1**
## 15.1 The conditional

**ANTE TODO**  The conditional tense in Spanish expresses what you *would do* or what *would happen* under certain circumstances.

### The conditional tense

| | | visitar | comer | escribir |
|---|---|---|---|---|
| SINGULAR FORMS | yo | visitaría | comería | escribiría |
| | tú | visitarías | comerías | escribirías |
| | Ud./él/ella | visitaría | comería | escribiría |
| PLURAL FORMS | nosotros/as | visitaríamos | comeríamos | escribiríamos |
| | vosotros/as | visitaríais | comeríais | escribiríais |
| | Uds./ellos/ellas | visitarían | comerían | escribirían |

*¿Volverías a este lugar?*

*Sí, me gustaría volver pronto a este lugar.*

▶ The conditional tense is formed much like the future tense. The endings are the same for all verbs, both regular and irregular. For regular verbs, you simply add the appropriate endings to the infinitive. **¡Atención!** All forms of the conditional have an accent mark.

▶ For irregular verbs, add the conditional endings to the irregular stems.

| INFINITIVE | STEM | CONDITIONAL | | INFINITIVE | STEM | CONDITIONAL |
|---|---|---|---|---|---|---|
| decir | dir- | diría | | querer | querr- | querría |
| hacer | har- | haría | | saber | sabr- | sabría |
| poder | podr- | podría | | salir | saldr- | saldría |
| poner | pondr- | pondría | | tener | tendr- | tendría |
| haber | habr- | habría | | venir | vendr- | vendría |

▶ While in English the conditional is a compound verb form made up of the auxiliary verb *would* and a main verb, in Spanish it is a simple verb form that consists of one word.

Yo no **iría** a ese gimnasio.
*I would not go to that gym.*

**¿Vendrías** conmigo a la clase de yoga?
*Would you go with me to yoga class?*

**¡ATENCIÓN!**

The polite expressions **Me gustaría...** (*I would like...*) and **Te gustaría** (*You would like...*) are commonly used examples of the conditional.

**AYUDA**

The infinitive of **hay** is **haber**, so its conditional form is **habría**.

---

**TEACHING OPTIONS**

**TPR** Line students up in teams of six several feet from the board. Call out an infinitive. The first team members race to the board and write the **yo** form of the verb in the conditional, then pass the chalk to the next team members, who write the **tú** form, and so on. The team that finishes first and has all the forms correct wins the round.

**Extra Practice** Ask students what they would or would not do over the next six months if they could do anything their hearts desired and money and time were no object. Ex: **Yo viajaría por todo el mundo.** Call on volunteers to read their sentences, then ask the class comprehension questions about what was said. Ex: **¿Qué harían _____ y ____?**

▶ The conditional is commonly used to make polite requests.

**¿Podrías** abrir la ventana, por favor?
*Would you open the window, please?*

**¿Sería** tan amable de venir a mi oficina?
*Would you be so kind as to come to my office?*

▶ In Spanish, as in English, the conditional expresses the future in relation to a past action or state of being. In other words, the future indicates what *will happen* whereas the conditional indicates what *would happen*.

**Creo** que mañana **hará** sol.
*I think it will be sunny tomorrow.*

**Creía** que hoy **haría** sol.
*I thought it would be sunny today.*

▶ The English *would* is often used with a verb to express the conditional, but it can also mean *used to*, in the sense of past habitual action. To express past habitual actions, Spanish uses the imperfect, not the conditional.

**Íbamos** al parque los sábados.
*We would go to the park on Saturdays.*

De adolescente, **entrenaba** todos los días.
*As teenager, I used to work out every day.*

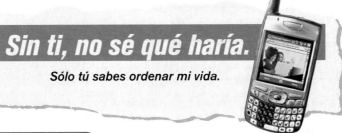

**Sin ti, no sé qué haría.**

*Sólo tú sabes ordenar mi vida.*

**COMPARE & CONTRAST**

In **Lección 14**, you learned the *future of probability*. Spanish also has the *conditional of probability*, which expresses conjecture or probability about a past condition, event, or action. Compare these Spanish and English sentences.

**Serían** las once de la noche cuando Elvira me llamó.
*It must have been (It was probably) 11 p.m. when Elvira called me.*

Sonó el teléfono. ¿**Llamaría** Emilio para cancelar nuestra cita?
*The phone rang. I wondered if it was Emilio calling to cancel our date.*

Note that English conveys conjecture or probability with phrases such as *I wondered if*, *probably*, and *must have been*. In contrast, Spanish gets these same ideas across with conditional forms.

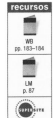

**recursos**

WB
pp. 183–184

LM
p. 87

panorama.
vhlcentral.com
Lección 15

**¡INTÉNTALO!** Indica la forma apropiada del condicional de los verbos.

1. Yo ___escucharía, leería, me apuraría___ (escuchar, leer, apurarse)
2. Tú ___te mantendrías, comprenderías, compartirías___ (mantenerse, comprender, compartir)
3. Marcos ___pondría, vendría, querría___ (poner, venir, querer)
4. Nosotras ___seríamos, sabríamos, iríamos___ (ser, saber, ir)
5. Ustedes ___adelgazarían, deberían, sufrirían___ (adelgazar, deber, sufrir)
6. Ella ___saldría, podría, haría___ (salir, poder, hacer)
7. Yo ___tendría, trataría, fumaría___ (tener, tratar, fumar)
8. Tú ___dirías, verías, engordarías___ (decir, ver, engordar)

# Práctica ⓈUPERSITE

**1** **Preparándose para el verano** Un grupo de amigos está pensando en las vacaciones. En las siguientes oraciones nos cuentan sus planes. Complétalas con el condicional del verbo entre paréntesis.

1. Antes de las vacaciones Guillermo ____debería____ (deber) adelgazar un poco porque está bastante gordo. ____Sería____ (ser) muy bueno para su salud comer una dieta más equilibrada.

2. Juan, sin embargo, está muy delgado porque es muy activo. Él ____disfrutaría____ (disfrutar) mucho de un fin de semana tranquilo en el campo y ____tendría____ (tener) tiempo para practicar su pasatiempo favorito: pescar.

3. A mí ____me gustaría____ (gustarme) pasar un fin de semana en el Salar de Uyuni para relajarme. Estoy seguro/a de que me ____aliviaría____ (aliviar) el estrés de estos últimos meses. También (ellos) me ____darían____ (dar) un buen masaje.

4. Susana y Marta ____irían____ (ir) a la playa. A ellas les ____encantaría____ (encantar) tomar un poco el sol.

> **NOTA CULTURAL**
>
> **El Salar de Uyuni** es un lago de sal muy conocido en Bolivia por ser un lugar de descanso y por sus efectos beneficiosos para la salud. En este lugar se pueden visitar los característicos hoteles de la región con paredes y muebles de sal.

**2** **¿Qué harías?** En parejas, pregúntense qué harían en las siguientes situaciones. Answers will vary.

> **modelo**
>
> Haría todo para ir a los premios Ariel. Primero, iría al médico y tomaría medicina para sentirme mejor. También, dormiría, descansaría y comería comida muy sana para estar bien el día de los premios.

Estás invitado a los premios Ariel. Es posible que te vayan a dar un premio (award), pero ese día estás muy enfermo/a.

Vas al banco a depositar un cheque y te das cuenta de (you realize) que en tu cuenta hay por error un millón de dólares que no es tuyo.

Estás manejando por el desierto y te quedas sin gasolina.

Vuelves a tu apartamento después de tus clases y tu ex novio/a no te deja entrar.

> **NOTA CULTURAL**
>
> **Los Premios Ariel** de México son el equivalente a los Premios (Awards) Oscar en los Estados Unidos. Cada año los entrega (presents) la Academia Mexicana de Ciencias y Artes Cinematográficas. Algunas películas que han ganado un premio Ariel son *Amores perros* y *El laberinto del fauno*.

**3** **Presidente por un día** Imagina que eres el/la presidente/a de tu universidad por un día. Escribe ocho cosas que harías en esa situación. Usa el condicional. Luego compara tus ideas con las de un(a) compañero/a. Answers will vary.

> **modelo**
>
> Si yo fuera presidente, tendría un jet privado para mis viajes.

| | | |
|---|---|---|
| conocer | hacer | poner |
| dar | invertir en | sufrir |
| disfrutar | mejorar | tener |

---

**TEACHING OPTIONS**

**Pairs** Have students take turns asking each other for favors, using the conditional for courtesy. Partners respond by saying whether they will do the favor. If partners cannot do it, they should make up an excuse. Ex: **¿Me podrías recoger del gimnasio a las cinco de la tarde?** (Lo siento, pero no puedo. Tengo una clase de química hasta las cinco y media.)

**Large Groups** Ask students to think about what they would do if they were training for the Olympics. Have them pick an event and a Spanish-speaking country to represent. Ex: **Sería de Paraguay. Nadaría los 200 metros.** Then go around asking each student to read his or her sentence aloud, but have them listen carefully to their classmates so they can first restate what their classmates said.

# Comunicación

**4**

**Conversaciones** Tu profesor(a) te dará una hoja de actividades. En ella se presentan dos listas con diferentes problemas que supuestamente tienen los estudiantes. En parejas, túrnense para explicar los problemas de su lista; uno/a cuenta lo que le pasa y el/la otro/a dice lo que haría en esa situación usando la frase "Yo en tu lugar..." (*If I were you...*)　Answers will vary.

**AYUDA**

Here are two ways of saying *If I were you:*
**Si yo fuera tú...**
**Yo en tu lugar...**

> **modelo**
>
> **Estudiante 1:** ¡Qué problema! Mi novio/a no me habla desde el domingo.
> **Estudiante 2:** Yo en tu lugar, no le diría nada por unos días para ver qué pasa.

**5**

**Roberto en el gimnasio** Roberto es una persona muy sedentaria. El médico le dice que tiene que adelgazar para mejorar su salud. Dile ocho cosas que tú harías si fueras él. Usa el condicional. Después, compara tus sugerencias con las del resto de la clase.　Answers will vary.

> **modelo**
>
> Si yo fuera tú, vería menos la televisión e iría a una clase de ejercicios aeróbicos.

# Síntesis

**6**

**Encuesta** Tu profesor(a) te dará una hoja de actividades. Circula por la clase y pregúntales a tres compañeros/as qué actividad(es) de las que se describen les gustaría realizar. Usa el condicional de los verbos. Anota las respuestas e informa a la clase de los resultados de la encuesta.　Answers will vary.

> **modelo**
>
> **Estudiante 1:** ¿Dejarías de fumar?
> **Estudiante 2:** Claro que sí. Sería difícil al principio, pero podría hacerlo.

| Actividades | Nombre de tu compañero/a y su respuesta | Nombre de tu compañero/a y su respuesta | Nombre de tu compañero/a y su respuesta |
|---|---|---|---|
| 1. escribir poesía | | | |
| 2. bailar en un festival | | | |
| 3. tocar en una banda | | | |
| 4. hacer el papel principal en un drama | | | |
| 5. participar en un concurso en la televisión | | | |
| 6. cantar en un musical | | | |

**4 Teaching Tip** Distribute the *Hojas de actividades* (Supersite/IRCD) that correspond to this activity.

**4 Expansion** Working as a class, name a problem from one of the lists and ask several volunteers to share the suggestions they received. Encourage other students to comment on the suggestions.

**5 Teaching Tip** Go over the directions with the class. Work with the class to brainstorm a list of Roberto's problems. Write them on the board. Then give students time to write eight pieces of advice.

**5 Suggestion** Point out that/Remind students that **y** changes to **e** in front of a word starting with **i**, as seen in the model.

**6 Teaching Tip** Distribute the *Hojas de actividades* (Supersite/IRCD) that correspond to this activity.

**6 Expansion** Encourage students to add two more activities to their list.

**TEACHING OPTIONS**

**Game** Have students each write down the name of a well-known person. Then, have them read it aloud to the student at their left. That student has to say what he or she would do if he or she were that person. Ex: **E1: Salma Hayek E2: Si yo fuera Salma Hayek, haría una película con Orlando Bloom.**

**Extra Practice** Ask students to write a short paragraph answering this question: **¿Qué harías para cambiar tu vida?** Call on volunteers to write their paragraphs on the board. Ask the class to check the paragraphs for accuracy.

## Section Goal

In **Estructura 15.2**, students will learn the use of the past perfect tense.

**Instructional Resources**

**Supersite:** Lab MP3 Audio Files **Lección 15**
**Supersite/IRCD:** *PowerPoints* (**Lección 15 Estructura** Presentation); *IRM* (Lab Audio Script, WBs/VM/LM Answer Key)
**WebSAM**
**Workbook,** pp. 185–186
**Lab Manual,** p. 88
*Cuaderno para hispanohablantes*

## Teaching Tips

• Have students read the **Fotonovela** captions again and underline the past participles. Ask if they are used as adjectives or as parts of verbs.

• Model the present perfect by making statements about what you and others in the class have done, or by asking students questions. Ex: **Yo he preparado una lección. Ustedes han leído la sección de Estructura, ¿verdad? ¿Quién no la ha leído?**

**Consulta** Tell students that while the present perfect is generally used in Spanish just as it is in English, the expression *to have just done something* is expressed in Spanish by **acabar de** + [*infinitive*]. Write these sentences on the board and contrast them:
**Acabo de venir del gimnasio.**
**He venido del gimnasio.**

---

## 15.2 The present perfect SUPERSITE

**ANTE TODO** In **Lección 13**, you learned how to form past participles. You will now learn how to form the present perfect indicative (**el pretérito perfecto de indicativo**), a compound tense that uses the past participle. The present perfect is used to talk about what someone *has done*. In Spanish, it is formed with the present tense of the auxiliary verb **haber** and a past participle.

Ya veo que han traído todo lo que necesitan.

Todos han venido muy bien equipados.

### Present indicative of **haber**

| Singular forms | | Plural forms | |
|---|---|---|---|
| yo | **he** | nosotros/as | **hemos** |
| tú | **has** | vosotros/as | **habéis** |
| Ud./él/ella | **ha** | Uds./ellos/ellas | **han** |

Tú no **has aumentado** de peso.
*You haven't gained weight.*

Yo ya **he leído** esos libros.
*I've already read those books.*

¿**Ha asistido** Juan a la clase de yoga?
*Has Juan attended the yoga class?*

**Hemos conocido** al entrenador.
*We have met the trainer.*

▶ The past participle does not change in form when it is part of the present perfect tense; it only changes in form when it is used as an adjective.

Clara **ha abierto** las ventanas.
*Clara has opened the windows.*

Yo **he cerrado** la puerta del gimnasio.
*I've closed the door to the gym.*

Las ventanas están **abiertas.**
*The windows are open.*

La puerta del gimnasio está **cerrada.**
*The door to the gym is closed.*

▶ In Spanish, the present perfect indicative generally is used just as in English: to talk about what someone has done or what has occurred. It usually refers to the recent past.

**He trabajado** cuarenta horas esta semana.
*I have worked forty hours this week.*

¿Cuál es el último libro que **has leído**?
*What is the last book that you have read?*

**CONSULTA**

To review what you have learned about participles, see **Estructura 13.4**, p. 438.

**¡LENGUA VIVA!**

Words like **ya, aún,** and **todavía** are very commonly used with the present perfect.

**CONSULTA**

Remember that the Spanish equivalent of the English *to have just* (done something) is **acabar de** + [infinitive]. Do not use the present perfect to express that English structure.
**Juan acaba de llegar.**
Juan has just arrived.
See **Estructura 6.3**, p. 191.

---

**TEACHING OPTIONS**

**Extra Practice** Ask students what they have done over the past week to lead a healthy lifestyle. Ask follow-up questions to elicit a variety of different conjugations of the present perfect. Ex: **¿Qué han hecho esta semana para llevar una vida sana? Y tú, _____, ¿qué has hecho? ¿Qué ha hecho _____ esta semana?**
**Pairs** Ask students to tell their partners five things they have done in the past to stay in shape. Partners repeat back what the

person has said, using the **tú** form of the present perfect. Ex: **He levantado pesas. (Muy bien. Has levantado pesas.)**
**TPR** Have the class stand in a circle. Call out a subject pronoun and an infinitive. Ex: **yo/sufrir.** Toss a foam or paper ball to a student, who will say the correct present perfect form (Ex: **yo he sufrido**) and toss the ball to another student, who will use the verb in a sentence.

▶ In English, the auxiliary verb and the past participle are often separated. In Spanish, however, these two elements—**haber** and the past participle—cannot be separated by any word.

Siempre **hemos vivido** en Bolivia.
*We have always lived in Bolivia.*

Usted nunca **ha venido** a mi oficina.
*You have never come to my office.*

*Creo que la señora Vives nos ha preparado una cena muy especial.*

*Gracias, Martín.*

*No hay de qué. Ha sido un placer.*

▶ The word **no** and any object or reflexive pronouns are placed immediately before **haber.**

Yo **no he comido** la merienda.
*I haven't eaten the snack.*

¿Por qué **no la has comido**?
*Why haven't you eaten it?*

Susana ya **se ha entrenado**.
*Susana has already practiced.*

Ellos **no lo han terminado**.
*They haven't finished it.*

▶ Note that *to have* can be either a main verb or an auxiliary verb in English. As a main verb, it corresponds to **tener,** while as an auxiliary, it corresponds to **haber.**

**Tengo** muchos amigos.
*I have a lot of friends.*

**He tenido** mucho éxito.
*I have had a lot of success.*

▶ To form the present perfect of **hay,** use the third-person singular of **haber (ha) + habido.**

**Ha habido** muchos problemas con el nuevo profesor.
*There have been a lot of problems with the new professor.*

**Ha habido** un accidente en la calle Central.
*There has been an accident on Central Street.*

---

**¡INTÉNTALO!**   Indica el pretérito perfecto de indicativo de estos verbos.

1. (disfrutar, comer, vivir) yo _he disfrutado, he comido, he vivido_
2. (traer, adelgazar, compartir) tú _has traído, has adelgazado, has compartido_
3. (venir, estar, correr) usted _ha venido, ha estado, ha corrido_
4. (leer, resolver, poner) ella _ha leído, ha resuelto, ha puesto_
5. (decir, romper, hacer) ellos _han dicho, han roto, han hecho_
6. (mantenerse, dormirse) nosotros _nos hemos mantenido, nos hemos dormido_
7. (estar, escribir, ver) yo _he estado, he escrito, he visto_
8. (vivir, correr, morir) él _ha vivido, ha corrido, ha muerto_

**recursos**

WB
pp. 185–186

LM
p. 88

panorama.
vhlcentral.com
Lección 15

**Teaching Tips**
- Ask students questions in the present perfect with indirect and direct objects. Ex: _____, ¿has estudiado bien la lección? (Sí, la he estudiado bien.) _____, ¿has entendido todo lo que te he dicho? (No, no lo he entendido todo.) ¿Todos me han entregado el trabajo de hoy? (Sí, todos se lo hemos entregado.)
- Explain that, although an adverb can never appear between **haber** and its past participle, it may appear in other positions in the sentence to change emphasis. Ex: **Hemos vivido siempre en Bolivia. Siempre hemos vivido en Bolivia.**
- Practice adverb placement by supplying an adverb for each item in the **¡Inténtalo!** activity. Ex: **siempre (Siempre he disfrutado./He disfrutado siempre.)**
- Tell the students that the present perfect used with **alguna vez** means *ever*. Ex: ¿Alguna vez has corrido un maratón? ¿Has ido alguna vez a la India?

---

**TEACHING OPTIONS**

**Large Groups** Divide the class into three groups. Have students write down five physical activities. Then have them ask each of their group members if they have ever done those activities and record their answers. Ex: **¿Has hecho ejercicios de estiramiento alguna vez? ¿Has levantado pesas? ¿Has hecho ejercicio en un gimnasio?**

**Extra Practice** Add a visual aspect to this grammar presentation. Draw a time line on the board. On the far right of the line, write **el presente**. Just to the left of that point, write **el pasado muy reciente**. To the left of that, write **el pasado reciente**. Then to the far left, write **el pasado**. Make a statement using the preterite, the present perfect, or **acabar de** + [*infinitive*]. Have students indicate on the time line when the action took place.

# Práctica  SUPERSITE

**1 Completar** Estas oraciones describen el bienestar o los problemas de unos estudiantes. Completa las oraciones con el pretérito perfecto de indicativo de los verbos de la lista.

adelgazar   comer   llevar
aumentar   hacer   sufrir

1. Luisa __ha sufrido__ muchas presiones este año.
2. Juan y Raúl __han aumentado__ de peso porque no hacen ejercicio.
3. Pero María y yo __hemos adelgazado__ porque trabajamos en exceso y nos olvidamos de comer.
4. Desde siempre, yo __he llevado__ una vida muy sana.
5. Pero tú y yo no __hemos hecho__ gimnasia este semestre.

**2 ¿Qué has hecho?** Indica si has hecho lo siguiente. Answers will vary.

**modelo**
escalar una montaña
Sí, he escalado varias montañas./No, no he escalado nunca una montaña.

1. jugar al baloncesto
2. viajar a Bolivia
3. conocer a una persona famosa
4. levantar pesas
5. comer un insecto
6. recibir un masaje
7. aprender varios idiomas
8. bailar salsa
9. ver una película en español
10. escuchar música latina
11. estar despierto/a 24 horas
12. bucear

**AYUDA**
You may use some of these expressions in your answers:
**una vez** once
**un par de veces** a couple of times
**alguna vez** ever
**algunas veces** a few times
**varias veces** several times
**muchas veces** many times, often

**3 La vida sana** En parejas, túrnense para hacer preguntas sobre el tema de la vida sana. Sean creativos. Answers will vary.

**modelo**
encontrar un gimnasio
**Estudiante 1:** ¿Has encontrado un buen gimnasio cerca de tu casa?
**Estudiante 2:** Yo no he encontrado un gimnasio pero sé que debo buscar uno.

1. tratar de estar en forma
2. estar a dieta los últimos dos meses
3. dejar de tomar refrescos
4. hacerse una prueba del colesterol
5. entrenarse cinco días a la semana
6. cambiar de una vida sedentaria a una vida activa
7. tomar vitaminas por las noches y por las mañanas
8. hacer ejercicio para aliviar la tensión
9. consumir mucha proteína
10. dejar de fumar

# Comunicación

**4** **Descripción** En parejas, describan lo que han hecho y no han hecho estas personas. Usen la imaginación. Answers will vary.

1. Jorge y Raúl

2. Luisa

3. Jacobo

4. Natalia y Diego

5. Ricardo

6. Carmen

**5** **Describir** En parejas, identifiquen a una persona que lleva una vida muy sana. Puede ser una persona que conocen o un personaje que aparece en una película o programa de televisión. Entre los dos, escriban una descripción de lo que esta persona ha hecho para llevar una vida sana. Answers will vary.

**modelo**

*Pedro Penzini Fleury siempre ha hecho todo lo posible para mantenerse en forma. Él…*

**NOTA CULTURAL**

El doctor venezolano **Pedro Penzini Fleury** tiene un popular programa de radio sobre la importancia del bienestar en la vida diaria.

# Síntesis

**6** **Situación** Trabajen en parejas para representar los papeles de un(a) enfermero/a de la universidad y un(a) estudiante. El/La enfermero/a de la clínica de la universidad está conversando con el/la estudiante que no se siente nada bien. El/La enfermero/a debe averiguar de dónde viene el problema e investigar los hábitos del/de la estudiante. El/La estudiante le explica lo que ha hecho en los últimos meses y cómo se ha sentido. Luego el/la enfermero/a le da recomendaciones al/a la estudiante de cómo llevar una vida más sana. Answers will vary.

**4** **Teaching Tip** To simplify, before beginning the activity, ask volunteers to describe the people in the drawings and how they feel.

**5** **Teaching Tip** Have pairs describe eight things their chosen person has done that exemplify a healthy lifestyle. Remind them to include introductory and concluding statements in their descriptions.

**5** **Expansion** Have students choose someone who is the exact opposite of the healthy person they chose earlier and write a description of what that person has done that exemplifies an unhealthy lifestyle.

**6** **Expansion** While pairs are performing their role plays for the class, stop the action after the patient has described his or her symptoms and what he or she has done in the last few months. Ask the class to make a diagnosis. Then have the players finish their presentation.

**TEACHING OPTIONS**

**Game** Have students write three important things they have done over the past year on a slip of paper and put it in a box. Ex: **Este año he creado un sitio web.** Have students draw a paper from the box, then circulate around the room, asking students if they have done the activities listed, until they find the person who wrote the slip of paper. The first person to find a match wins.

**Heritage Speakers** Have heritage speakers interview someone who has immigrated from a Spanish-speaking country to the United States or Canada to find out how that person's life has changed since moving. Students should find out how the interviewee's physical activity and diet have changed. Have students present their findings in a brief written report.

## Section Goal

In **Estructura 15.3** students will learn the use of the past perfect tense.

**Instructional Resources**
**Supersite:** Lab MP3 Audio Files **Lección 15**
**Supersite/IRCD:** *PowerPoints* (**Lección 15 Estructura** Presentation); *IRM* (**Hojas de actividades,** Information Gap Activities, Lab Audio Script, WBs/VM/LM Answer Key)
**WebSAM**
**Workbook,** pp. 187–188
**Lab Manual,** p. 89
*Cuaderno para hispanohablantes*

**Teaching Tips**
• Introduce the past perfect tense by making statements about the past that are true for you. Write examples of the past perfect on the board as you use them. Ex: **Esta mañana vine a la universidad en la bicicleta de mi hijo. Nunca antes había venido en bicicleta. Por lo general, vengo en carro. Muchas veces antes había caminado y también había venido en autobús cuando tenía prisa, pero nunca en bicicleta.**
• Check for comprehension of **ya** by contrasting it with **nunca.** Ex: **Antes del semestre pasado, nunca había enseñado este curso, pero ya había enseñado otros cursos de español.**

**Successful Language Learning** Tell students to imagine how they might use the past perfect to tell someone about their lives.

---

### 15.3 The past perfect

**ANTE TODO** The past perfect indicative (**el pretérito pluscuamperfecto de indicativo**) is used to talk about what someone *had done* or what *had occurred* before another past action, event, or state. Like the present perfect, the past perfect uses a form of **haber**—in this case, the imperfect—plus the past participle.

*Nunca había visto un paisaje tan espectacular.*

*Nunca había hecho una excursión.*

### Past perfect indicative

| | | cerrar | perder | asistir |
|---|---|---|---|---|
| SINGULAR FORMS | yo | **había** cerrado | **había** perdido | **había** asistido |
| | tú | **habías** cerrado | **habías** perdido | **habías** asistido |
| | Ud./él/ella | **había** cerrado | **había** perdido | **había** asistido |
| PLURAL FORMS | nosotros/as | **habíamos** cerrado | **habíamos** perdido | **habíamos** asistido |
| | vosotros/as | **habíais** cerrado | **habíais** perdido | **habíais** asistido |
| | Uds./ellos/ellas | **habían** cerrado | **habían** perdido | **habían** asistido |

Antes de 2005, **había vivido** en La Paz.
*Before 2005, I had lived in La Paz.*

Cuando llegamos a casa, Luis ya **había salido.**
*When we arrived to the house, Luis had already left.*

▶ The past perfect is often used with the word **ya** (*already*) to indicate that an action, event, or state had already occurred before another. Remember that, unlike its English equivalent, **ya** cannot be placed between **haber** and the past participle.

Ella **ya había salido** cuando llamaron.
*She had already left when they called.*

Cuando llegué, Raúl **ya se había acostado.**
*When I arrived, Raúl had already gone to bed.*

**¡ATENCIÓN!**
The past perfect is often used in conjunction with **antes de** + [*noun*] or **antes de** + [*infinitive*] to describe when the action(s) occurred.

**Antes de este año, nunca había estudiado español.**
*Before this year, I had never studied Spanish.*

**Luis me había llamado antes de venir.**
*Luis had called me before he came.*

**¡INTÉNTALO!** Indica el pretérito pluscuamperfecto de indicativo de cada verbo.

1. Nosotros ya __habíamos cenado__ (cenar) cuando nos llamaron.
2. Antes de tomar esta clase, yo no __había estudiado__ (estudiar) nunca el español.
3. Antes de ir a México, ellos nunca __habían ido__ (ir) a otro país.
4. Eduardo nunca __se había entrenado__ (entrenarse) tanto en invierno.
5. Tú siempre __habías llevado__ (llevar) una vida sana antes del año pasado.
6. Antes de conocerte, yo ya te __había visto__ (ver) muchas veces.

**recursos**

WB
pp. 187–188

LM
p. 89

SUPERSITE
panorama.
vhlcentral.com
Lección 15

---

**TEACHING OPTIONS**

**Extra Practice** Have students write sentences, using the past perfect and each of the following twice: **antes de** + [*noun*], **antes de** + [*infinitive*], the preterite, and the imperfect. Have students peer edit their work before sharing their sentences with the class. Ex: **Nuestros bisabuelos ya habían muerto cuando éramos niños.**

**TPR** Make a series of statements about the past, using two different verbs. After making a statement, call out the infinitive of one of the verbs. If that action occurred first, have students raise one finger. If it occurred second, have them raise two fingers. Ex: **Tomás ya había bajado de la montaña cuando empezó a nevar. Empezar.** (two fingers)

# Práctica

**1** **Completar** Completa los minidiálogos con las formas correctas del pretérito pluscuamperfecto de indicativo.

1. **SARA** Antes de cumplir los 15 años, ¿____habías estudiado____ (estudiar) tú otra lengua?
   **JOSÉ** Sí, ____había tomado____ (tomar) clases de inglés y de italiano.

▶ 2. **DOLORES** Antes de ir a Argentina, ¿____habían probado____ (probar) tú y tu familia el mate?
   **TOMÁS** Sí, ya ____habíamos tomado____ (tomar) mate muchas veces.

3. **ANTONIO** Antes de este año, ¿____había corrido____ (correr) usted en un maratón?
   **SRA. VERA** No, nunca lo ____había hecho____ (hacer).

4. **SOFÍA** Antes de su enfermedad, ¿____había sufrido____ (sufrir) muchas presiones tu tío?
   **IRENE** Sí... y él nunca ____se había mantenido____ (mantenerse) en buena forma.

**2** **Tu vida** Indica si ya habías hecho estas cosas antes de cumplir los 16 años. Answers will vary.

1. hacer un viaje en avión
2. escribir un poema
3. enamorarte
4. tomar clases de aeróbicos
5. montar a caballo
6. escalar una montaña
7. manejar un carro
8. navegar en la red
9. ir de pesca

# Comunicación

**3** **Gimnasio Olímpico** En parejas, lean el anuncio y contesten las preguntas.

Hasta el año pasado, siempre había mirado la tele sentado en el sofá durante mis ratos libres. ¡Era un sedentario y un teleadicto! Jamás había practicado ningún deporte y había aumentado mucho de peso.

Este año, he empezado a comer una dieta más sana y voy al gimnasio todos los días. He comenzado a ser una persona muy activa y he adelgazado. Disfruto de una vida sana. ¡Me siento muy feliz!

Manténgase en forma.

**¡Acabo de descubrir una nueva vida!**

**¡Venga al Gimnasio Olímpico hoy mismo!**

1. Identifiquen los elementos del pretérito pluscuamperfecto de indicativo en el anuncio. había mirado; había practicado; había aumentado
2. ¿Cómo era la vida del hombre cuando llevaba una vida sedentaria? ¿Cómo es ahora? Answers will vary.
3. ¿Se identifican ustedes con algunos de los hábitos, presentes o pasados, de este hombre? ¿Con cuáles? Answers will vary.
4. ¿Qué les recomienda el hombre del anuncio a los lectores? ¿Creen que les da buenos consejos? Answers will vary.

---

**1 Expansion**
- Have students pick one of the exchanges and expand upon it to create a conversation with six lines.
- Have students create an original conversation like the ones in the activity. Call on volunteers to perform them for the class.

**Nota cultural** Traditionally, drinking **mate** is a social custom. The leaves are steeped in a decorative gourd and the beverage is sipped through a filtering straw called a **bombilla**. The gourd may be passed from person to person.

**2 Teaching Tip** Ask students questions to elicit the answers for the activity. Ex: ¿**Quién había hecho un viaje en avión antes de cumplir los 16 años?** Ask follow-up questions to elicit other conjugations of the past perfect. Ex: **Entonces clase, ¿quiénes habían hecho un viaje en avión antes de cumplir los 16 años? (___ y ___ habían hecho...)**

**3 Teaching Tip** Before beginning the activity, survey the class to find out who exercises regularly and/or carefully watches what he or she eats. Ask these students to use the past perfect to say what they had done in their life prior to starting their fitness or diet program. Ex: **Había comido pastel de chocolate todos los días.**

**3 Expansion** Have groups use the present perfect and past perfect to create an ad for a different health-related business, such as a vegetarian restaurant or a weight-loss program.

**Teaching Tip** See the **Hojas de actividades** and Information Gap Activities (Supersite/IRCD) for additional activities to practice the material presented in this section.

---

**TEACHING OPTIONS**

**Pairs** Have students imagine they have joined a gym for the first time and are telling a friend about their new experiences. Ask students to tell their partner five things they had never done before going to a gym. Ex: **Nunca había sudado tanto antes de empezar a ir al gimnasio.**

**Large Groups** Divide the class into groups of six for a game of "one-upmanship." The first student states something he or she had done before a certain event in his or her past. The second student tells what the first one had done, then counters with something even more outrageous that he or she had done, and so on, until everyone has participated. Ex: _____ **había..., pero yo había...**

## Section Goal

In **Recapitulación**, students will review the grammar concepts from this lesson.

---

**Instructional Resource**
**Supersite**

---

**1** **Teaching Tips**
• Remind students that every verb form in the conditional carries an accent mark.
• Complete this activity orally as a class.

**1** **Expansion**
• Ask students to provide the remaining forms of the verbs.
• Add **decir, tener,** and **venir** to the chart.

**2** **Teaching Tips**
• Before beginning the activity, call on a volunteer to name the reflexive verb in the exercise. Remind students that the reflexive pronoun should appear before the conjugated verb.
• Complete this activity orally as a class.

**2** **Expansion** To challenge students, have them provide the remaining verb forms.

**3** **Teaching Tip** To simplify, have students underline the subject for each item.

**3** **Expansion**
• Have students compose questions about the conversation. Ex: **¿Nidia le dijo a Omar que Jaime y ella irían a la demostración de yoga?**
• To challenge students, ask them to identify which sentences from the conversation could be replaced by **ir a** + [*infinitive*] in the imperfect and retain the same meaning. Ex: **1. Yo creía que iba a llover, pero hizo sol.**

---

# Recapitulación

**SUPERSITE** For self-scoring and diagnostics, go to **panorama.vhlcentral.com.**

Completa estas actividades para repasar los conceptos de gramática que aprendiste en esta lección.

**1** **Verbos** Completa el cuadro con la forma correcta de los verbos. **12 pts.**

| Infinitivo | tú | nosotros | ellas |
|---|---|---|---|
| **pintar** | pintarías | **pintaríamos** | pintarían |
| querer | **querrías** | querríamos | **querrían** |
| poder | podrías | **podríamos** | podrían |
| haber | **habrías** | habríamos | **habrían** |
| **vivir** | vivirías | viviríamos | vivirían |

**2** **Completar** Completa el cuadro con el pretérito perfecto de los verbos. **6 pts.**

| Infinitivo | yo | él | ellas |
|---|---|---|---|
| **tratar** | he tratado | ha tratado | han tratado |
| **entrenarse** | me he entrenado | se ha entrenado | se han entrenado |

**3** **Diálogo** Completa la conversación con la forma adecuada del condicional de los verbos. **8 pts.**

| aconsejar | encantar | ir | poder |
|---|---|---|---|
| dejar | gustar | llover | volver |

**OMAR** ¿Sabes? La demostración de yoga al aire libre fue un éxito. Yo creía que (1) ___llovería___, pero hizo sol.

**NIDIA** Ah, me alegro. Te dije que Jaime y yo (2) ___iríamos___, pero tuvimos un imprevisto (*something came up*) y no pudimos. Y a Laura, ¿la viste allí?

**OMAR** Sí, ella vino. Al contrario que tú, al principio me dijo que ella y su marido no (3) ___podrían___ venir, pero al final aparecieron (*showed up*). Necesitaba relajarse un poco; está muy estresada con su trabajo.

**NIDIA** Yo le (4) ___aconsejaría___ que busque otra cosa. En su lugar, (5) ___dejaría___ esa compañía y (6) ___volvería___ a escribir un libro.

**OMAR** Estoy de acuerdo. Oye, esta noche voy a ir al gimnasio. ¿(7) ___Te gustaría___ venir conmigo?

**NIDIA** Sí, (8) ___me encantaría/___ . ¿A qué hora vamos?
            ___me gustaría___

**OMAR** A las siete y media.

---

**RESUMEN GRAMATICAL**

**15.1** **The conditional** *pp. 492–493*

| The conditional tense* of **disfrutar** | |
|---|---|
| disfrutaría | disfrutaríamos |
| disfrutarías | disfrutaríais |
| disfrutaría | disfrutarían |

*Same ending for **-ar, - er,** and **-ir** verbs.

▶ Verbs with irregular conditional: **decir, haber, hacer, poder, poner, querer, saber, salir, tener, venir**

**15.2** **The present perfect** *pp. 496–497*

| Present indicative of **haber** | |
|---|---|
| he | hemos |
| has | habéis |
| ha | han |

**Present perfect:** present tense of **haber** + past participle

| Present perfect indicative | |
|---|---|
| **he** empezado | **hemos** empezado |
| **has** empezado | **habéis** empezado |
| **ha** empezado | **han** empezado |

**He empezado** a ir al gimnasio con regularidad.
*I have begun to go to the gym regularly.*

**15.3** **The past perfect** *p. 500*

**Past perfect:** imperfect tense of **haber** + past participle

| Past perfect indicative | |
|---|---|
| **había** vivido | **habíamos** vivido |
| **habías** vivido | **habíais** vivido |
| **había** vivido | **habían** vivido |

Antes de 2006, yo ya **había vivido** en tres países diferen...
*Before 2006, I had already lived in three different countr...*

---

**TEACHING OPTIONS**

**Extra practice** Ask students to say which Spanish-speaking country they would visit and why. Ex: **Iría a Uruguay y visitaría Punta del Este.**
**TPR** Have students form a circle. Throw a foam or paper ball to a student and call out a time expression. Ex: **Antes de este semestre...** The student must complete the sentence using

the past perfect (Ex: **Antes de este semestre, había estudiado japonés.**) and throw the ball to another student, who should do the same. Continue through a few more students, then provide a new sentence starter. Ex: **Antes de estudiar en esta universidad...**

**4** **Preguntas** Completa las preguntas para estas respuestas usando el pretérito perfecto de indicativo. **8 pts.**

> **modelo**
>
> —¿Has llamado a tus padres? —Sí, los llamé ayer.

1. —¿Tú __has hecho__ ejercicio esta mañana en el gimnasio? —No, hice ejercicio en el parque.
2. —Y ustedes, ¿__han desayunado__ ya? —Sí, desayunamos en el hotel.
3. —Y Juan y Felipe, ¿adónde __han ido__ ? —Fueron al cine.
4. —Paco, ¿(nosotros) __hemos recibido__ la cuenta del gimnasio? —Sí, la recibimos la semana pasada.
5. —Señor Martín, ¿__ha pescado__ algo ya? —Sí, pesqué uno grande. Ya me puedo ir a casa contento.
6. —Inés, ¿__has visto__ mi pelota de fútbol? —Sí, la vi esta mañana en el coche.
7. —Yo no __he tomado__ café todavía. ¿Alguien quiere acompañarme? —No, gracias. Yo ya tomé mi café en casa.
8. —¿Ya te __ha dicho__ el doctor que puedes comer chocolate? —Sí, me lo dijo ayer.

**5** **Antes de graduarse** Di lo que cada una de estas personas ya había hecho o no había hecho todavía antes de graduarse de la universidad. Sigue el modelo. **6 pts.**

> **modelo**
>
> yo / ya conocer a muchos amigos
> *Yo ya había conocido a muchos amigos.*

1. Margarita / ya dejar de fumar
   Margarita ya había dejado de fumar.
2. tú / ya aprender a mantenerse en forma
   Tú ya habías aprendido a mantenerte en forma.
3. Julio / ya casarse
   Julio ya se había casado.
4. Mabel y yo / ya practicar yoga
   Mabel y yo ya habíamos practicado yoga.
5. los hermanos Falsero / todavía no perder un partido de voleyball
   Los hermanos Falsero todavía no habían perdido un partido de voleyball.
6. yo / ya entrenarse para el maratón
   Yo ya me había entrenado para el maratón.

**6** **Manteniéndote en forma** Escribe al menos cinco oraciones para describir cómo te has mantenido en forma este semestre. Di qué cosas han cambiado este semestre en relación con el año pasado. Por ejemplo, ¿qué cosas has hecho o practicado este semestre que nunca habías probado antes? **10 pts.** Answers will vary.

**7** **Poema** Completa este fragmento de un poema de Nezahualcóyotl con el pretérito perfecto de indicativo de los verbos. **¡2 puntos EXTRA!**

❝ __He llegado__ (Llegar) aquí,
soy Yoyontzin.
Sólo busco las flores
sobre la tierra, __he venido__ (venir)
a cortarlas. ❞

---

**TEACHING OPTIONS**

**Extra Practice** Prepare sentences that use the present perfect. Say each sentence, have students repeat it, then say a different subject, varying the number. Have students then say the sentence with the new subject, making any necessary changes.

**Game** Divide the class into teams of five and have them sit in rows. Give the first student in each row a piece of paper. Call out an infinitive and have the first team member write the past perfect **yo** form of the verb and pass the paper to the second team member, who writes the **tú** form, and so forth. The first team to complete the paradigm correctly earns a point. The team with the most points at the end wins.

---

**4 Teaching Tips**
• Call on volunteers to read the model aloud.
• To simplify, have students begin by identifying the subject and infinitive for each blank.

**4 Expansion** Have students change the response for each item to the present perfect. Ex: **1. No, he hecho ejercicio en el parque.**

**5 Expansion** Give students these sentence cues as items 7-8: **7. nosotros / ya sufrir muchas presiones (Nosotros ya habíamos sufrido muchas presiones.) 8. Óscar / ya ir al gimnasio (Óscar ya había ido al gimnasio.)**

**6 Teaching Tip** To simplify, before students begin writing, encourage them to list their ideas under two columns: **El año pasado** and **Este semestre**. Have students brainstorm a few verbs in the past perfect for the first column and in the present perfect for the second.

**7 Expansion** Have students write a personalized version of the poem fragment. Ex: **He venido aquí, soy ____ . Sólo busco ____ . He ____ a ____ .**

## Section Goals

In **Lectura**, students will:
- learn to make inferences and draw conclusions to understand a text
- read a short story and practice inferential reading

**Instructional Resources**
**Supersite**
*Cuaderno para hispanohablantes*

**Estrategia** Tell students that authors do not always spell out everything for their readers. Explain that they will need to look for clues in the story to infer information left unstated.

**El autor** Have students read the biography and list three important facts about the author.

**El título** Ask students to read the title and come up with an English equivalent for it. (*One of These Days*) Have pairs explain the different meanings this expression can convey. (revenge, hope)

**El cuento** Have students work in pairs to look up the words and answer the question. When they have finished, survey the class to see what most students think the story is about.

# Lectura

## Antes de leer

### Estrategia
**Making inferences**

For dramatic effect and to achieve a smoother writing style, authors often do not explicitly supply the reader with all the details of a story or poem. Clues in the text can help you infer those things the writer chooses not to state in a direct manner. You simply "read between the lines" to fill in the missing information and draw conclusions. To practice making inferences, read these statements:

A Liliana le encanta ir al gimnasio. Hace años que empezó a levantar pesas.

Based on this statement alone, what inferences can you draw about Liliana?

### El autor

Ve a la página 445 de tu libro y lee la biografía de Gabriel García Márquez.

### El título

Sin leer el texto del cuento (*story*), lee el título. Escribe cinco oraciones que empiecen con la frase "Un día de éstos".

### El cuento

Éstas son algunas palabras que vas a encontrar al leer *Un día de éstos*. Busca su significado en el diccionario. Según estas palabras, ¿de qué piensas que trata (*is about*) el cuento?

| | |
|---|---|
| alcalde | lágrimas |
| dentadura postiza | muela |
| displicente | pañuelo |
| enjuto | rencor |
| guerrera | teniente |

**recursos**

panorama.vhlcentral.com
Lección 15

# Un día de éstos
### Gabriel García Márquez

El lunes amaneció tibio° y sin lluvia. Don Aurelio Escovar, dentista sin título y buen madrugador°, abrió su gabinete° a las seis. Sacó de la vidriera° una dentadura postiza montada aún° en el molde de yeso° y puso sobre la mesa un puñado de instrumentos que ordenó de mayor a menor, como en una exposición. Llevaba una camisa a rayas, sin cuello, cerrada arriba con un botón dorado°, y los pantalones sostenidos con cargadores° elásticos. Era rígido, enjuto, con una mirada que raras veces correspondía a la situación, como la mirada de los sordos°.

Cuando tuvo las cosas dispuestas sobre la mesa rodó la fresa° hacia el sillón de resortes y se sentó a pulir° la dentadura postiza. Parecía no pensar en lo que hacía, pero trabajaba con obstinación, pedaleando en la fresa incluso cuando no se servía de ella.

Después de las ocho hizo una pausa para mirar el cielo por la ventana y vio dos gallinazos° pensativos que se secaban al sol en el caballete° de la casa vecina. Siguió trabajando con la idea de que antes del almuerzo volvería a llover°. La voz destemplada° de su hijo de once años lo sacó de su abstracción.

—Papá.

—Qué.

—Dice el alcalde que si le sacas una muela.

—Dile que no estoy aquí.

Estaba puliendo un diente de oro°. Lo retiró a la distancia del brazo y lo examinó con los ojos a medio cerrar. En la salita de espera volvió a gritar su hijo.

—Dice que sí estás porque te está oyendo.

El dentista siguió examinando el diente. Sólo cuando lo puso en la mesa con los trabajos terminados, dijo:

amaneció tibio *dawn broke warm* madrugador *early riser* gabinete *office* vidriera *glass cabinet* montada aún *still set* yeso *plaster* dorado *gold* sostenidos con cargadores *held by suspenders* sordos *deaf* rodó la fresa *he turned the drill* pulir *to polish* gallinazos *vultures* caballete *ridge* volvería a llover *it would rain again* voz destemplada *discordant voice* oro *gold* cajita de cartón *small cardboard box* puente *bridge* te pega un tiro *he will shoot you* Sin apresurarse *Without haste* gaveta *drawer* Hizo girar *He turned* apoyada *resting* umbral *threshold* mejilla *cheek* hinchada *swollen* barba *beard* marchitos *faded* hervían *were boiling* pomos de loza *china bottles* cancel de tela *cloth screen* se acercaba *was approaching* talones *heels* mandíbula *jaw* cautelosa *cautious* cacerola *saucepan* pinzas *pliers* escupidera *spittoon* aguamanil *washstand* cordal *wisdom tooth* gatillo *pliers* se aferró *clung* barras *arms* descargó *unloaded* vacío helado *icy hollowness* riñones *kidneys* no soltó un suspiro *he didn't let out a sigh* muñeca *wrist* amarga ternura *bitter tenderness* crujido *crunch* a través de *through* sudoroso *sweaty* jadeante *panting* se desabotonó *he unbuttoned* a tientas *blindly* bolsillo *pocket* trapo *cloth* cielorraso desfondado *ceiling with the paint sagging* telaraña polvorienta *dusty spiderweb* haga buches de *rinse your mouth out with* vaina *thing*

---

### TEACHING OPTIONS

**Pairs** Have students work in pairs to compare and contrast **don Aurelio Escovar** and **el alcalde**. Encourage them to use adjectives and descriptive phrases from the reading to make inferences about the personality of these characters. Have volunteers present their character analyses to the class.

**Small Groups** Have students work in groups of three to rewrite the story from a different point of view. Assign groups the point of view of the boy, the dentist, or the mayor. Have groups share their stories with the class for comparison and contrast.

—Mejor.

Volvió a operar la fresa. De una cajita de cartón° donde guardaba las cosas por hacer, sacó un puente° de varias piezas y empezó a pulir el oro.

—Papá.

—Qué.

Aún no había cambiado de expresión.

—Dice que si no le sacas la muela te pega un tiro°.

Sin apresurarse°, con un movimiento extremadamente tranquilo, dejó de pedalear en la fresa, la retiró del sillón y abrió por completo la gaveta° inferior de la mesa. Allí estaba el revólver.

—Bueno —dijo—. Dile que venga a pegármelo.

Hizo girar° el sillón hasta quedar de frente a la puerta, la mano apoyada° en el borde de la gaveta. El alcalde apareció en el umbral°. Se había afeitado la mejilla° izquierda, pero en la otra, hinchada° y dolorida, tenía una barba° de cinco días. El dentista vio en sus ojos marchitos° muchas noches de desesperación. Cerró la gaveta con la punta de los dedos y dijo suavemente:

—Siéntese.

—Buenos días —dijo el alcalde.

—Buenos —dijo el dentista.

Mientras hervían° los instrumentos, el alcalde apoyó el cráneo en el cabezal de la silla y se sintió mejor. Respiraba un olor glacial. Era un gabinete pobre: una vieja silla de madera, la fresa de pedal y una vidriera con pomos de loza°. Frente a la silla, una ventana con un cancel de tela° hasta la altura de un hombre. Cuando sintió que el dentista se acercaba°, el alcalde afirmó los talones° y abrió la boca.

Don Aurelio Escovar le movió la cabeza hacia la luz. Después de observar la muela dañada, ajustó la mandíbula° con una presión cautelosa° de los dedos.

—Tiene que ser sin anestesia —dijo.

—¿Por qué?

—Porque tiene un absceso.

El alcalde lo miró en los ojos.

—Está bien —dijo, y trató de sonreír. El dentista no le correspondió. Llevó a la mesa de trabajo la cacerola° con los instrumentos hervidos y los sacó del agua con unas pinzas° frías, todavía sin apresurarse. Después rodó la escupidera° con la punta del zapato y fue a lavarse las manos en el aguamanil°. Hizo todo sin mirar al alcalde. Pero el alcalde no lo perdió de vista.

Era una cordal° inferior. El dentista abrió las piernas y apretó la muela con el gatillo° caliente. El alcalde se aferró a las barras° de la silla, descargó° toda su fuerza en los pies y sintió un vacío helado° en los riñones°, pero no soltó un suspiro°. El dentista sólo movió la muñeca°. Sin rencor, más bien con una amarga ternura°, dijo:

—Aquí nos paga veinte muertos, teniente.

El alcalde sintió un crujido° de huesos en la mandíbula y sus ojos se llenaron de lágrimas. Pero no suspiró hasta que no sintió salir la muela. Entonces la vio a través de° las lágrimas. Le pareció tan extraña a su dolor, que no pudo entender la tortura de sus cinco noches anteriores. Inclinado sobre la escupidera, sudoroso°, jadeante°, se desabotonó° la guerrera y buscó a tientas° el pañuelo en el bolsillo° del pantalón. El dentista le dio un trapo° limpio.

—Séquese las lágrimas —dijo.

El alcalde lo hizo. Estaba temblando. Mientras el dentista se lavaba las manos, vio el cielorraso desfondado° y una telaraña polvorienta° con huevos de araña e insectos muertos. El dentista regresó secándose. "Acuéstese —dijo— y haga buches de° agua de sal." El alcalde se puso de pie, se despidió con un displicente saludo militar, y se dirigió a la puerta estirando las piernas, sin abotonarse la guerrera.

—Me pasa la cuenta —dijo.

—¿A usted o al municipio?

El alcalde no lo miró. Cerró la puerta, y dijo, a través de la red metálica:

—Es la misma vaina°.

# Después de leer

## Comprensión 🖊⎙

Completa las oraciones con la palabra o expresión correcta.

1. Don Aurelio Escovar es <u>dentista</u> sin título.
2. Al alcalde le duele <u>una muela</u>.
3. Aurelio Escovar y el alcalde se llevan <u>mal</u>.
4. El alcalde amenaza (*threatens*) al dentista con pegarle un <u>tiro</u>.
5. Finalmente, Aurelio Escovar <u>le saca</u> la muela al alcalde.
6. El alcalde llevaba varias noches sin <u>dormir</u>.

## Interpretación 🖊⎙

En parejas, respondan a estas preguntas. Luego comparen sus respuestas con las de otra pareja. Answers will vary.

1. ¿Cómo reacciona don Aurelio cuando escucha que el alcalde amenaza con pegarle un tiro? ¿Qué les dice esta actitud sobre las personalidades del dentista y del alcalde?
2. ¿Por qué creen que don Aurelio y el alcalde no se llevan bien?
3. ¿Creen que era realmente necesario no usar anestesia?
4. ¿Qué piensan que significa el comentario "aquí nos paga veinte muertos, teniente"? ¿Qué les dice esto del alcalde y su autoridad en el pueblo?
5. ¿Cómo se puede interpretar el saludo militar y la frase final del alcalde "es la misma vaina"?

**Teaching Tips**

- Explain that *Un día de éstos* is part of the short story collection *Los funerales de la Mamá Grande*, which **García Márquez** finished writing in 1959.

- The events of *Un día de éstos* take place during **La Violencia**, an era of intense civil conflict in Colombian history, which started in 1946 and lasted two decades. This complex conflict generally centered around supporters of liberal and conservative political parties. The liberal and communist parties organized self-defense groups and guerrilla units, both of which fought against the conservatives and amongst each other.

**Comprensión** Ask pairs to work together to complete the sentences. When they have finished, go over the answers orally with the class.

**Interpretación** Give students these questions as items 6–9 and have them identify information in the text that they used to infer their answers: 6. ¿Creen que el dentista y el alcalde habían sido amigos antes de ese día? 7. En su opinión, ¿quién tiene más poder, el dentista o el alcalde? 8. ¿Cómo creen que es la relación entre el gobierno y la gente de este pueblo? 9. ¿Qué creen que va a pasar cuando el alcalde se mejore?

# Escritura

## Estrategia
### Organizing information logically

Many times a written piece may require you to include a great deal of information. You might want to organize your information in one of three different ways:

▶ chronologically (e.g., events in the history of a country)
▶ sequentially (e.g., steps in a recipe)
▶ in order of importance

Organizing your information in this manner will make both your writing and your message clearer to your readers. If you were writing a piece on weight reduction, for example, you would need to organize your ideas about two general areas: eating right and exercise. You would need to decide which of the two is more important according to your purpose in writing the piece. If your main idea is that eating right is the key to losing weight, you might want to start your piece with a discussion of good eating habits. You might want to discuss the following aspects of eating right in order of their importance:

▶ quantities of food
▶ selecting appropriate foods from the food pyramid
▶ healthful recipes
▶ percentage of fat in each meal
▶ calorie count
▶ percentage of carbohydrates in each meal
▶ frequency of meals

You would then complete the piece by following the same process to discuss the various aspects of the importance of getting exercise.

**recursos**

panorama.vhlcentral.com
Lección 15

## Tema

**Escribir un plan personal de bienestar**

Desarrolla un plan personal para mejorar tu bienestar, tanto físico como emocional. Tu plan debe describir:

1. lo que has hecho para mejorar tu bienestar y llevar una vida sana
2. lo que no has podido hacer todavía
3. las actividades que debes hacer en los próximos meses

Considera también estas preguntas.

**La nutrición**
▶ ¿Comes una dieta equilibrada?
▶ ¿Consumes suficientes vitaminas y minerales? ¿Consumes demasiada grasa?
▶ ¿Quieres aumentar de peso o adelgazar?
▶ ¿Qué puedes hacer para mejorar tu dieta?

**El ejercicio**
▶ ¿Haces ejercicio? ¿Con qué frecuencia?
▶ ¿Vas al gimnasio? ¿Qué tipo de ejercicios haces allí?
▶ ¿Practicas algún deporte?
▶ ¿Qué puedes hacer para mejorar tu bienestar físico?

**El estrés**
▶ ¿Sufres muchas presiones?
▶ ¿Qué actividades o problemas te causan estrés?
▶ ¿Qué haces (o debes hacer) para aliviar el estrés y sentirte más tranquilo/a?
▶ ¿Qué puedes hacer para mejorar tu bienestar emocional?

---

**EVALUATION: Plan personal de bienestar**

| Criteria | Scale | | Scoring | |
|---|---|---|---|---|
| Content | 1 2 3 4 | | Excellent | 18–20 points |
| Organization | 1 2 3 4 | | Good | 14–17 points |
| Use of vocabulary | 1 2 3 4 | | Satisfactory | 10–13 points |
| Accuracy and mechanics | 1 2 3 4 | | Unsatisfactory | < 10 points |
| Creativity | 1 2 3 4 | | | |

# Escuchar

## Section Goals

In **Escuchar**, students will:
- listen for the gist and for cognates
- answer questions about a radio program

**Instructional Resources**
**Supersite:** Textbook MP3 Audio Files
**Supersite/IRCD:** *IRM* (Textbook Audio Script)

## Estrategia

**Listening for the gist/
Listening for cognates**

Combining these two strategies is an easy way to get a good sense of what you hear. When you listen for the gist, you get the general idea of what you're hearing, which allows you to interpret cognates and other words in a meaningful context. Similarly, the cognates give you information about the details of the story that you might not have understood when listening for the gist.

 To practice these strategies, you will listen to a short paragraph. Write down the gist of what you hear and jot down a few cognates. Based on the gist and the cognates, what conclusions can you draw about what you heard?

## Preparación

Mira la foto. ¿Qué pistas° te da de lo que vas a oír?

## Ahora escucha

Escucha lo que dice Ofelia Cortez de Bauer. Anota algunos de los cognados que escuchas y también la idea general del discurso°. Answers will vary.

_____
_____
_____

Idea general: _____

Ahora contesta las siguientes preguntas.

1. ¿Cuál es el género° del discurso?
2. ¿Cuál es el tema?
3. ¿Cuál es el propósito°?

**recursos**  panorama.vhlcentral.com Lección 15

pistas *clues* discurso *speech* género *genre* propósito *purpose* público *audience* debía haber incluido *should have included*

## Comprensión

**¿Cierto o falso?**
Indica si lo que dicen estas oraciones es **cierto** o **falso**. Corrige las oraciones que son falsas.

|  | Cierto | Falso |
|---|---|---|
| 1. La señora Bauer habla de la importancia de estar en buena forma y de hacer ejercicio. | ☑ | ○ |
| 2. Según ella, lo más importante es que lleves el programa sugerido por los expertos. *Lo más importante es que lleves un programa variado que te guste.* | ○ | ☑ |
| 3. La señora Bauer participa en actividades individuales y de grupo. | ☑ | ○ |
| 4. El único objetivo del tipo de programa que ella sugiere es adelgazar. *Los objetivos de su programa son: condicionar el sistema cardiopulmonar, aumentar la fuerza muscular y mejorar la flexibilidad.* | ○ | ☑ |

**Preguntas** Answers will vary.

1. Imagina que el programa de radio sigue. Según las pistas que ella dio, ¿qué vas a oír en la segunda parte?
2. ¿A qué tipo de público° le interesa el tema del que habla la señora Bauer?
3. ¿Sigues los consejos de la señora Bauer? Explica tu respuesta.
4. ¿Qué piensas de los consejos que ella da? ¿Hay otra información que ella debía haber incluido°?

**Estrategia**
**Script** Cuando nos casamos le prometí a Magdalena que no íbamos a residir con su familia por más de un año. Y si Dios quiere, ¡así va a ser! Magdalena y yo encontramos un condominio absolutamente perfecto. Hoy pasamos por el banco para pedir el préstamo hipotecario. ¡Espero que no haya problema con el chequeo del crédito!

**Teaching Tip** Have students describe what they see in the photo.

**Ahora escucha**
**Script** Buenos días, radioyentes, y bienvenidos a "Tu bienestar". Les habla Ofelia Cortez de Bauer. Hoy vamos a hablar de la importancia de estar en buena forma. Primero, quiero que entiendan que estar en buena forma no es sólo cosa de estar delgado o ser fuerte. Para mantenerse en forma deben tener tres objetivos: condicionar el sistema cardiopulmonar, aumentar la fuerza muscular y mejorar la flexibilidad. Cada persona tiene sus propios objetivos, y también sus propias limitaciones físicas, y debe diseñar su programa con un monitor de acuerdo con éstos. Pero óiganme bien, ¡lo más importante es tener una rutina variada, con ejercicios que les gusten —porque de otro modo no lo van a hacer! Mi rutina personal es la siguiente. Dos días por semana voy a la clase de ejercicios aeróbicos, claro

*(Script continues at far left in the bottom panels.)*

con un buen calentamiento al comienzo. Tres días por semana corro en el parque, o si hace mal tiempo, uso una caminadora en el gimnasio. Luego levanto pesas y termino haciendo estiramientos de los músculos. Los fines de semana me mantengo activa pero hago una variedad de cosas de acuerdo a lo que quiere hacer la familia. A veces practico la natación; otras, vamos de excursión al campo, por ejemplo. Como les había

dicho la semana pasada, como unas 1.600 calorías al día, mayormente alimentos con poca grasa y sin sal. Disfruto mucho del bienestar que estos hábitos me producen. Ahora iremos a unos anuncios de nuestros patrocinadores. Cuando regresemos, voy a contestar sus preguntas acerca del ejercicio, la dieta o el bienestar en general. El teléfono es el 43.89.76. No se vayan. Ya regresamos con mucha más información.

# En pantalla

Georgina Bardach, nacida en Córdoba, Argentina, en 1983, es una versátil nadadora° que ha triunfado a nivel° internacional. En los Juegos Olímpicos de Atenas 2004, ganó la medalla de bronce en los 400 metros combinados°. En mayo de 2006, rompió el récord suramericano en los 200 metros de espalda°. Ella, como los niños de este reportaje° de televisión, aprendió a nadar desde pequeña y comenta que para triunfar en la natación o en cualquier° actividad deportiva, en primer lugar "te tiene que gustar. El segundo papel° lo juega la familia, que te apoya°."

### Vocabulario útil

| | |
|---|---|
| cordón | cord |
| cloro | chlorine |
| por medio de | through |
| familiarizando | getting familiar |
| beneficios | benefits |
| sí mismos | themselves |
| chiquitos | little |
| reglas | rules |
| capacidad pulmonar | lung capacity |

### ¿Cierto o falso?

Indica si lo que dice cada oración es **cierto** o **falso**.

1. Algunos bebés pueden empezar a nadar antes de los cuatro meses. cierto
2. Los juegos les ayudan a familiarizarse con la tierra. falso
3. Las clases son buenas para aprender a socializar. cierto
4. También hacen a los niños menos independientes. falso
5. El entrenador debe ser un profesional certificado. cierto

 ### Entrevista

En parejas, escriban una entrevista sobre el bienestar a un(a) atleta, un(a) entrenador(a) o un(a) doctor(a). Escriban las preguntas y lo que piensan que esa persona va a responder. Answers will vary.

nadadora *swimmer* nivel *level* combinados *medley* de espalda *backstroke* reportaje *report* cualquier *any* papel *role* apoya *supports* bebés *babies* a partir de *from* juguetes *toys*

---

 ## Reportaje sobre **natación**

**La actividad acuática para bebés°** **se puede empezar...**

**...a partir de° los cuatro o** **cinco meses de edad...**

**...con canciones y juegos y** **juguetes°.**

panorama.vhlcentral.com
Lección 15

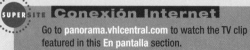 **Conexión Internet**

Go to **panorama.vhlcentral.com** to watch the TV clip featured in this **En pantalla** section.

---

---

# Oye cómo va

## Los Kjarkas

El grupo folklórico **Los Kjarkas** fue fundado en el año de 1965 por los tres hermanos Wilson, Castel y Gonzalo Hermosa, junto con Edgar Villarroel. La idea era crear° una forma nueva y original de interpretar la música andina boliviana. A través de° los años, esta agrupación musical ha cambiado de integrantes°, pero mantienen la misma filosofía. Actualmente°, este grupo es conocido en Latinoamérica, Norteamérica, Europa y Asia. Los Kjarkas han fundado tres escuelas para el estudio de la música andina y sus instrumentos musicales, una en Bolivia, otra en Perú y otra en Ecuador. Algunas de sus canciones más famosas son *El amor y la libertad, Wa ya vay, Sueño de los Andes* y el éxito internacional *Llorando se fue.*

Tu profesor(a) va a poner la canción en la clase. Escúchala y completa las actividades.

## Completar

Completa las frases.

1. Los hermanos Hermosa y Edgar Villarroel fundaron...  el grupo Los Kjarkas.
2. Los Kjarkas interpretan música...  andina boliviana.
3. Este grupo ha cambiado varias veces de...  integrantes.
4. Pero ha mantenido la misma...  filosofía.
5. La zampoña, la quena y el charango son...  instrumentos andinos.

## Preguntas

En grupos pequeños, respondan a las preguntas.  Answers will vary.
1. ¿De que habla la canción?
2. ¿Qué consejos le da el autor de la canción a la chica?
3. ¿Creen ustedes en el amor a primera vista? ¿Por qué?
4. ¿Conoce alguno/a de ustedes a una pareja que se haya enamorado a primera vista? Describe su historia a tus compañeros/as.

crear° *to create* **A través de** *Over* integrantes *members* **Actualmente** *Nowadays* labios *lips* madrugadas *dawns* golpear *knocking (on)* carmín *lipstick* tiernos *tender* camino *path* encuentro *meeting* flauta *flute* quena *reed flute* bombo *bass drum*

## El hombre equivocado

Tengo quince años y no he vivido.
En mis labios° besos nunca he sentido.
Mis ojos vieron mil madrugadas°
y pasó el amor sin golpear° mi puerta.
Mis ojos vieron mil madrugadas
y pasó el amor sin golpear mi puerta.

Un día se puso el mejor vestido
y puso carmín° en sus labios tiernos°.
Forzó el camino° de su destino.
No quiso esperar y salió al encuentro°.
Forzó el camino de su destino.
No quiso esperar y salió al encuentro.

*(NATIONAL communication cultures STANDARDS)*

### Instrumentos andinos

Los instrumentos que se utilizan en la interpretación de la música andina son la zampoña o flauta° de pan, la quena°, el arpa, el bombo°, la guitarra y el charango, que es una guitarra pequeña.

**Quena**

**recursos**

SUPERSITE

panorama.vhlcentral.com
Lección 15

**SUPERSITE Conexión Internet**

Go to **panorama.vhlcentral.com** to learn more about the artist featured in this **Oye cómo va** section.

# Bolivia

NATIONAL STANDARDS connections cultures

## El país en cifras

- ▶ **Área:** 1.098.580 km² (424.162 millas²), *equivalente al área total de Francia y España*
- ▶ **Población:** 10.031.000

*Los indígenas quechua y aimará constituyen más de la mitad° de la población de Bolivia. Estos grupos indígenas han mantenido sus culturas y lenguas tradicionales. Las personas de ascendencia° indígena y europea representan la tercera parte de la población. Los demás son de ascendencia europea nacida en Latinoamérica. Una gran mayoría de los bolivianos, más o menos el 70%, vive en el altiplano°.*

- ▶ **Capital:** La Paz, sede° del gobierno, capital administrativa—1.692.000; Sucre, sede del Tribunal Supremo, capital constitucional y judicial
- ▶ **Ciudades principales:** Santa Cruz de la Sierra—1.551.000, Cochabamba, Oruro, Potosí

SOURCE: Population Division, UN Secretariat

- ▶ **Moneda:** peso boliviano
- ▶ **Idiomas:** español (oficial), aimará (oficial), quechua (oficial)

Bandera de Bolivia

### Bolivianos célebres

- ▶ **Jesús Lara,** escritor (1898–1980)
- ▶ **Víctor Paz Estenssoro,** político y presidente (1907–2001)
- ▶ **María Luisa Pacheco,** pintora (1919–1982)
- ▶ **Matilde Casazola,** poeta (1942– )

mitad *half*  ascendencia *descent*  altiplano *high plateau*  sede *seat*
paraguas *umbrella*  cascada *waterfall*

Plaza San Francisco

Vista de la ciudad de Sucre

Mujer indígena con bebé

PERÚ

BRASIL

Río Beni
Río Mamoré
Illampu
Lago Titicaca
La Paz
Tiahuanaco
Cordillera Oriental de los Andes
Río Grande
Río Desaguadero
Cordillera Central de los Andes
Oruro
Lago Poopó
Potosí
Sucre
Cochabamba
Santa Cruz de la Sierra
Río Pilcomayo

PARAGUAY

ARGENTINA

CHILE

ESTADOS UNIDOS
OCÉANO ATLÁNTICO
OCÉANO PACÍFICO
BOLIVIA

**recursos**
WB pp. 189–190
VM pp. 263–264
panorama.vhlcentral.com Lección 15

## ¡Increíble pero cierto!

La Paz es la capital más alta del mundo. Su aeropuerto está situado a una altitud de 3.600 metros (12.000 pies). Ah, y si viajas en carro hasta La Paz, ¡no te olvides del paraguas°! En la carretera, que cruza 9.000 metros de densa selva, te encontrarás con una cascada°.

## Lugares • **El lago Titicaca**

Titicaca, situado en los Andes de Bolivia y Perú, es el lago navegable más alto del mundo, a una altitud de 3.815 metros (12.500 pies). Con un área de más de 8.000 kilómetros² (3.000 millas²), también es el segundo lago más grande de Suramérica, después del lago de Maracaibo. La mitología inca cuenta que los hijos del dios° Sol emergieron de las profundas aguas del lago Titicaca para fundar su imperio°.

**El lago Titicaca** Sitting more than two miles above sea level, Lake Titicaca is larger than the area of Delaware and Rhode Island combined. More than twenty-five rivers drain into the lake, which has forty-one islands.

## Artes • **La música andina**

La música andina, compartida por Bolivia, Perú, Ecuador, Chile y Argentina, es el aspecto más conocido de su folklore. Hay muchos conjuntos° profesionales que dan a conocer° esta música popular, de origen indígena, alrededor° del mundo. Algunos de los grupos más importantes y que llevan más de treinta años actuando en escenarios internacionales son Los Kjarkas (Bolivia), Inti Illimani (Chile), Los Chaskis (Argentina) e Illapu (Chile).

**La música andina** Andean music is characterized by its plaintive, haunting melodies, often based in a minor or pentatonic scale.

## Historia • **Tiahuanaco**

Tiahuanaco, que significa "Ciudad de los dioses", es un sitio arqueológico de ruinas preincaicas situado cerca de La Paz y del lago Titicaca. Se piensa que los antepasados° de los indígenas aimará fundaron este centro ceremonial hace unos 15.000 años. En el año 1100, la ciudad tenía unos 60.000 habitantes. En este sitio se pueden ver el Templo de Kalasasaya, el Monolito Ponce, el Templete Subterráneo, la Puerta del Sol y la Puerta de la Luna. La Puerta del Sol es un impresionante monumento que tiene tres metros de alto y cuatro metros de ancho° y que pesa unas 10 toneladas.

**Tiahuanaco** The pre-Incan civilization that flourished at **Tiahuanaco** was probably a theocracy, governed by priest-kings. The primary deity was **Viracocha**, a sky and thunder god worshipped throughout much of the Andean world. The Tiahuanacan head of state was viewed as **Viracocha's** embodiment on earth.

 **¿Qué aprendiste?** Responde a cada pregunta con una oración completa.

1. ¿Qué idiomas se hablan en Bolivia? En Bolivia se hablan español, quechua y aimará.
2. ¿Dónde vive la mayoría de los bolivianos? La mayoría de los bolivianos vive en el altiplano.
3. ¿Cuál es la capital administrativa de Bolivia? La capital administrativa de Bolivia es La Paz.
4. Según la mitología inca, ¿qué ocurrió en el lago Titicaca? Los hijos del dios Sol emergieron del lago para fundar el imperio inca.
5. ¿De qué países es la música andina? La música andina es de Bolivia, Perú, Ecuador, Chile y Argentina.
6. ¿Qué origen tiene esta música? Es música de origen indígena.
7. ¿Cómo se llama el sitio arqueológico situado cerca de La Paz y el lago Titicaca? El sitio arqueológico situado cerca de La Paz y el lago Titicaca se llama Tiahuanaco.
8. ¿Qué es la Puerta del Sol? La Puerta del Sol es un monumento que está en Tiahuanaco.

 **Conexión Internet** Investiga estos temas en **panorama.vhlcentral.com**.

1. Busca información sobre un(a) boliviano/a célebre. ¿Cuáles son algunos de los episodios más importantes de su vida? ¿Qué ha hecho esta persona? ¿Por qué es célebre?
2. Busca información sobre Tiahuanaco u otro sitio arqueológico en Bolivia. ¿Qué han descubierto los arqueólogos en ese sitio?

................................................................................

**dios** *god* **imperio** *empire* **conjuntos** *groups* **dan a conocer** *make known* **alrededor** *around* **antepasados** *ancestors* **ancho** *wide*

**Conexión Internet** Students will find supporting Internet activities and links at **panorama.vhlcentral.com**.

**Teaching Tip** You may want to wrap up this section by playing the *Panorama cultural* video footage for this lesson.

---

**TEACHING OPTIONS**

**Worth Noting** Teams of scientists have extracted sediment samples from Titicaca's lakebed to study the history of climatological change in the region. Such research helps scientists build models to analyze contemporary trends in global climate change.

**Worth Noting** Students might enjoy learning this indigenous riddle about the **armadillo**, the animal whose outer shell is used to make the **charango**, a small guitar used in Andean music.
**Vive en el cerro, lejos del mar.**
**De concha el saco sin abrochar.**
**Cuando se muere... ¡pues a cantar!**

# Paraguay

## El país en cifras

▶ **Área:** 406.750 km² (157.046 millas²), el tamaño° de California
▶ **Población:** 6.882.000
▶ **Capital:** Asunción—2.264.000
▶ **Ciudades principales:** Ciudad del Este, San Lorenzo, Lambaré, Fernando de la Mora

SOURCE: Population Division, UN Secretariat

▶ **Moneda:** guaraní
▶ **Idiomas:** español (oficial), guaraní (oficial)

*Las tribus indígenas que habitaban la zona antes de la llegada de los españoles hablaban guaraní. Ahora el 90 por ciento de los paraguayos habla esta lengua, que se usa con frecuencia en canciones, poemas, periódicos y libros. Varios institutos y asociaciones, como el Teatro Guaraní, se dedican a preservar la cultura y la lengua guaraníes.*

Bandera de Paraguay

## Paraguayos célebres

▶ **Agustín Barrios,** guitarrista y compositor (1885–1944)
▶ **Josefina Plá,** escritora y ceramista (1909–1999)
▶ **Augusto Roa Bastos,** escritor (1917–2005)
▶ **Olga Blinder,** pintora (1921– )

**recursos**

| WB pp. 191–192 | VM pp. 265–266 | SUPERSITE panorama.vhlcentral.com Lección 15 |

tamaño *size* multara *fined* ciudadanos *citizens* elecciones *election*

BOLIVIA

ESTADOS UNIDOS
OCÉANO PACÍFICO
OCÉANO ATLÁNTICO
AMÉRICA DEL SUR
PARAGUAY

Paraguayo con alfombras típicas del país

BRASIL

Río Verde

Río Negro

Concepción

ARGENTINA

Asunción
Fernando de la Mora
San Lorenzo
Lambaré
Río Tebicuary

Ciu del
Río
Cordillera d Caaguazú

Río Paraná

Agricultor indígena de la tribu maca

Itapúa

## ¡Increíble pero cierto!

¿Te imaginas qué pasaría si el gobierno multara° a los ciudadanos° que no van a votar? En Paraguay, es una obligación. Ésta es una ley nacional, que otros países también tienen, para obligar a los ciudadanos a participar en las elecciones°. En Paraguay los ciudadanos que no van a votar tienen que pagar una multa al gobierno.

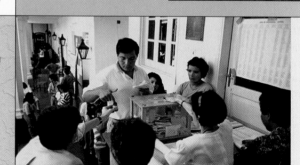

---

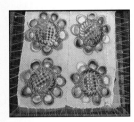

## Artesanía • El ñandutí

La artesanía° más famosa de Paraguay se llama ñandutí y es un encaje° hecho a mano originario de Itaguá. En guaraní, la palabra ñandutí significa telaraña° y esta pieza recibe ese nombre porque imita el trazado° que crean los arácnidos. Estos encajes suelen ser° blancos, pero también los hay de colores, con formas geométricas o florales.

## Ciencias • La represa Itaipú

La represa° Itaipú es una instalación hidroeléctrica que se encuentra en la frontera° entre Paraguay y Brasil. Su construcción inició en 1974 y duró 11 años. La cantidad de concreto que se utilizó durante los primeros cinco años de esta obra° fue similar a la que se necesita para construir un edificio de 350 pisos. Cien mil trabajadores paraguayos participaron en el proyecto. En 1984 se puso en funcionamiento la Central Hidroeléctrica de Itaipú y gracias a su cercanía con las famosas Cataratas de Iguazú, muchos turistas la visitan diariamente.

## Naturaleza • Los ríos Paraguay y Paraná

Los ríos Paraguay y Paraná sirven de frontera natural entre Argentina y Paraguay, y son las principales rutas de transporte de este último país. El Paraná tiene unos 3.200 kilómetros navegables, y por esta ruta pasan barcos de más de 5.000 toneladas, los cuales viajan desde el estuario° del Río de la Plata hasta la ciudad de Asunción. El río Paraguay divide el Gran Chaco de la meseta° Paraná, donde vive la mayoría de los paraguayos.

 **¿Qué aprendiste?** Responde a cada pregunta con una oración completa.

1. ¿Quién fue Augusto Roa Bastos?
   Augusto Roa Bastos fue un escritor paraguayo.
2. ¿Cómo se llama la moneda de Paraguay?
   La moneda de Paraguay se llama guaraní.
3. ¿Qué es el ñandutí?
   El ñandutí es un tipo de encaje.
4. ¿De dónde es originario el ñandutí?
   El ñandutí es originario de Itaguá.
5. ¿Qué forma imita el ñandutí?
   Imita la forma de una telaraña.
6. En total, ¿cuántos años tomó la construcción de la represa Itaipú?
   La construcción de la represa Itaipú tomó 11 años.
7. ¿A cuántos paraguayos dio trabajo la construcción de la represa?
   La construcción de la represa dio trabajo a 100.000 paraguayos.
8. ¿Qué países separan los ríos Paraguay y Paraná?
   Los ríos Paraguay y Paraná separan Argentina y Paraguay.
9. ¿Qué distancia se puede navegar por el Paraná?
   Se pueden navegar 3.200 kilómetros.

 **Conexión Internet** Investiga estos temas en **panorama.vhlcentral.com**.

1. Busca información sobre Alfredo Stroessner, el ex presidente de Paraguay. ¿Por qué se le considera un dictador?
2. Busca información sobre la historia de Paraguay. En tu opinión, ¿cuáles fueron los episodios decisivos en su historia?

................................................................................................

artesanía *crafts* encaje *lace* telaraña *spiderweb* trazado *outline; design* suelen ser *are usually* represa *dam* frontera *border*
obra *work* estuario *estuary* meseta *plateau*

**El ñandutí** In recent years, the number of traditional **ñandutí** makers has been in serious decline. The artisans of Itaguá grew tired of the low levels of compensation they received, and many have turned to other more profitable sources of income. Formal instruction in the skill of making **ñandutí** has even been incorporated in the curriculum of local handicraft schools in an effort to keep this traditional art alive.

**La represa Itaipú** The Itaipú dam project is a joint venture between Brazil and Paraguay, and has been remarkably successful. By 1995, four years after it went into production, the dam generated 25% of Brazil's energy supply, and 78% of Paraguay's. Annual electrical output continues to increase yearly.

**Los ríos Paraguay y Paraná** The Paraná River in particular was a highway for the settlement of Paraguay. Along its banks, between the sixteenth and late eighteenth centuries, the Jesuits organized their **guaraní**-speaking parishioners into small, self-supporting city-states built around mission settlements, similar to the Franciscan mission system in California during the same period.

**Conexión Internet** Students will find supporting Internet activities and links at **panorama.vhlcentral.com**.

**Teaching Tip** You may want to wrap up this section by playing the *Panorama cultural* video footage for this lesson.

**TEACHING OPTIONS**

**Worth Noting** Paraguay has eight national parks, encompassing over 11,000 square miles. In addition, there are eight ecological reserves dedicated to the preservation of endangered flora and fauna. The rich diversity of plant and animal life, and the government's commitment to preserving these natural wonders, have made Paraguay a popular destination for ecotourists. The parks cover a wide spectrum of ecology. The **Parque Nacional Defensores del Chaco** and **Parque Nacional Teniente Enciso** are located in the semi-arid Chaco. Other parks, like **Parque Nacional Caaguazú** southeast of Asunción, are covered with subtropical rainforest.

**Instructional Resources**
**Supersite:** Textbook &
Vocabulary MP3 Audio Files
**Lección 15**
**Supersite/IRCD:** *IRM* (WBs/
VM/LM Answer Key); *Testing
Program* (**Lección 15 Pruebas,**
Test Generator, Testing
Program MP3 Audio Files)
**WebSAM**
**Lab Manual,** p. 89

## El bienestar

| | |
|---|---|
| el bienestar | *well-being* |
| la droga | *drug* |
| el/la drogadicto/a | *drug addict* |
| el masaje | *massage* |
| el/la teleadicto/a | *couch potato* |
| adelgazar | *to lose weight; to slim down* |
| aliviar el estrés | *to reduce stress* |
| aliviar la tensión | *to reduce tension* |
| apurarse, darse prisa | *to hurry; to rush* |
| aumentar de peso, engordar | *to gain weight* |
| disfrutar (de) | *to enjoy; to reap the benefits (of)* |
| estar a dieta | *to be on a diet* |
| (no) fumar | *(not) to smoke* |
| llevar una vida sana | *to lead a healthy lifestyle* |
| sufrir muchas presiones | *to be under a lot of pressure* |
| tratar de (+ *inf.*) | *to try (to do something)* |
| activo/a | *active* |
| débil | *weak* |
| en exceso | *in excess; too much* |
| flexible | *flexible* |
| fuerte | *strong* |
| sedentario/a | *sedentary; related to sitting* |
| tranquilo/a | *calm; quiet* |

## En el gimnasio

| | |
|---|---|
| la cinta caminadora | *treadmill* |
| la clase de ejercicios aeróbicos | *aerobics class* |
| el/la entrenador(a) | *trainer* |
| el músculo | *muscle* |
| calentarse (e:ie) | *to warm up* |
| entrenarse | *to practice; to train* |
| estar en buena forma | *to be in good shape* |
| hacer ejercicio | *to exercise* |
| hacer ejercicios aeróbicos | *to do aerobics* |
| hacer ejercicios de estiramiento | *to do stretching exercises* |
| hacer gimnasia | *to work out* |
| levantar pesas | *to lift weights* |
| mantenerse en forma | *to stay in shape* |
| sudar | *to sweat* |

## La nutrición

| | |
|---|---|
| la bebida alcohólica | *alcoholic beverage* |
| la cafeína | *caffeine* |
| la caloría | *calorie* |
| el colesterol | *cholesterol* |
| la grasa | *fat* |
| la merienda | *afternoon snack* |
| el mineral | *mineral* |
| la nutrición | *nutrition* |
| el/la nutricionista | *nutritionist* |
| la proteína | *protein* |
| la vitamina | *vitamin* |
| comer una dieta equilibrada | *to eat a balanced diet* |
| consumir alcohol | *to consume alcohol* |
| descafeinado/a | *decaffeinated* |

| | |
|---|---|
| **Expresiones útiles** | *See page 487.* |

**recursos**

| LM p. 89 | panorama.vhlcentral.com Lección 15 |

# Plan de escritura

**1 Ideas y organización**

Begin by organizing your writing materials. If you prefer to write by hand, you may want to have a few spare pens and pencils on hand, as well as an eraser or correction fluid. If you prefer to use a word-processing program, make sure you know how to type Spanish accent marks, the **tilde,** and Spanish punctuation marks. Then make a list of the resources you can consult while writing. Finally, make a list of the basic ideas you want to cover. Beside each idea, jot down a few Spanish words and phrases you may want to use while writing.

**2 Primer borrador**

Write your first draft, using the resources and ideas you gathered in **Ideas y organización.**

**3 Comentario**

Exchange papers with a classmate and comment on each other's work, using these questions as a guide. Begin by mentioning what you like about your classmate's writing.

a. How can your classmate make his or her writing clearer, more logical, or more organized?

b. What suggestions do you have for making the writing more interesting or complete?

c. Do you see any spelling or grammatical errors?

**4 Redacción**

Revise your first draft, keeping in mind your classmate's comments. Also, incorporate any new information you may have. Before handing in the final version, review your work using these guidelines:

a. Make sure each verb agrees with its subject. Then check the gender and number of each article, noun, and adjective.

b. Check your spelling and punctuation.

c. Consult your **Anotaciones para mejorar la escritura** (see description below) to avoid repetition of previous errors.

**5 Evaluación y progreso**

You may want to share what you've written with a classmate, a small group, or the entire class. After your instructor has returned your paper, review the comments and corrections. On a separate sheet of paper, write the heading **Anotaciones para mejorar** (*Notes for improving*) **la escritura** and list your most common errors. Place this list and your corrected document in your writing portfolio (**Carpeta de trabajos**) and consult it from time to time to gauge your progress.

# Spanish Terms for Direction Lines and Classroom Use

Below is a list of useful terms that you might hear your instructor say in class. It also includes Spanish terms that appear in the direction lines of your textbook.

## En las instrucciones · *In direction lines*

| | |
|---|---|
| **Cambia/Cambien...** | *Change...* |
| **Camina/Caminen por la clase.** | *Walk around the classroom.* |
| **Ciertas o falsas** | *True or false* |
| **Cierto o falso** | *True or false* |
| **Circula/Circulen por la clase.** | *Walk around the classroom.* |
| **Completa las oraciones de una manera lógica.** | *Complete the sentences logically.* |
| **Con un(a) compañero/a...** | *With a classmate...* |
| **Contesta las preguntas.** | *Answer the questions.* |
| **Corrige las oraciones falsas.** | *Correct the false statements.* |
| **Cuenta/Cuenten...** | *Tell...* |
| **Di/Digan...** | *Say...* |
| **Discute/Discutan...** | *Discuss...* |
| **En grupos...** | *In groups...* |
| **En parejas...** | *In pairs...* |
| **Entrevista...** | *Interview...* |
| **Escúchala** | *Listen to it* |
| **Forma oraciones completas.** | *Create/Make complete sentences.* |
| **Háganse preguntas.** | *Ask each other questions.* |
| **Haz el papel de...** | *Play the role of...* |
| **Haz los cambios necesarios.** | *Make the necessary changes.* |
| **Indica/Indiquen si las oraciones...** | *Indicate if the sentences...* |
| **Intercambia/Intercambien...** | *Exchange...* |
| **Lee/Lean en voz alta.** | *Read aloud.* |
| **Pon/Pongan...** | *Put...* |
| **...que mejor completa...** | *...that best completes...* |
| **Reúnete...** | *Get together...* |
| **...se da/dan como ejemplo.** | *...is/are given as a model.* |
| **Toma nota...** | *Take note...* |
| **Tomen apuntes.** | *Take notes.* |
| **Túrnense...** | *Take turns...* |

## Palabras útiles · *Useful words*

| | |
|---|---|
| **la adivinanza** | *riddle* |
| **el anuncio** | *advertisement/ad* |
| **los apuntes** | *notes* |
| **el borrador** | *draft* |
| **la canción** | *song* |
| **la concordancia** | *agreement* |
| **el contenido** | *contents* |
| **eficaz** | *efficient* |
| **la encuesta** | *survey* |
| **el equipo** | *team* |
| **el esquema** | *outline* |
| **el folleto** | *brochure* |
| **las frases** | *statements* |
| **la hoja de actividades** | *activity sheet/handout* |
| **la hoja de papel** | *piece of paper* |
| **la información errónea** | *incorrect information* |
| **el/la lector(a)** | *reader* |
| **la lectura** | *reading* |
| **las oraciones** | *sentences* |
| **la ortografía** | *spelling* |
| **las palabras útiles** | *useful words* |
| **el papel** | *role* |
| **el párrafo** | *paragraph* |
| **el paso** | *step* |
| **la(s) persona(s) descrita(s)** | *the person (people) described* |
| **la pista** | *clue* |
| **por ejemplo** | *for example* |
| **el propósito** | *purpose* |
| **los recursos** | *resources* |
| **el reportaje** | *report* |
| **los resultados** | *results* |
| **según** | *according to* |
| **siguiente** | *following* |
| **la sugerencia** | *suggestion* |
| **el sustantivo** | *noun* |
| **el tema** | *topic* |
| **último** | *last* |
| **el último recurso** | *last resort* |

## Verbos útiles  *Useful verbs*

| | |
|---|---|
| **adivinar** | *to guess* |
| **anotar** | *to jot down* |
| **añadir** | *to add* |
| **apoyar** | *to support* |
| **averiguar** | *to find out* |
| **cambiar** | *to change* |
| **combinar** | *to combine* |
| **compartir** | *to share* |
| **comprobar (o:ue)** | *to check* |
| **corregir (e:i)** | *to correct* |
| **crear** | *to create* |
| **devolver (o:ue)** | *to return* |
| **doblar** | *to fold* |
| **dramatizar** | *to act out* |
| **elegir (e:i)** | *to choose/select* |
| **emparejar** | *to match* |
| **entrevistar** | *to interview* |
| **escoger** | *to choose* |
| **identificar** | *to identify* |
| **incluir** | *to include* |
| **informar** | *to report* |
| **intentar** | *to try* |
| **intercambiar** | *to exchange* |
| **investigar** | *to research* |
| **marcar** | *to mark* |
| **preguntar** | *to ask* |
| **recordar (o:ue)** | *to remember* |
| **responder** | *to answer* |
| **revisar** | *to revise* |
| **seguir (e:i)** | *to follow* |
| **seleccionar** | *to select* |
| **subrayar** | *to underline* |
| **traducir** | *to translate* |
| **tratar de** | *to be about* |

## Expresiones útiles  *Useful expressions*

| | |
|---|---|
| **Ahora mismo.** | *Right away.* |
| **¿Cómo no?** | *But of course.* |
| **¿Cómo se dice _____ en español?** | *How do you say _____ in Spanish?* |
| **¿Cómo se escribe _____?** | *How do you spell _____?* |
| **¿Comprende(n)?** | *Do you understand?* |
| **Con gusto.** | *With pleasure.* |
| **Con permiso.** | *Excuse me.* |
| **De acuerdo.** | *Okay.* |
| **De nada.** | *You're welcome.* |
| **¿De veras?** | *Really?* |
| **¿En qué página estamos?** | *What page are we on?* |
| **¿En serio?** | *Seriously?* |
| **Enseguida.** | *Right away.* |
| **hoy día** | *nowadays* |
| **Más despacio, por favor.** | *Slower, please.* |
| **Muchas gracias.** | *Thanks a lot.* |
| **No entiendo.** | *I don't understand.* |
| **No hay de qué.** | *Don't mention it.* |
| **No importa.** | *No problem./It doesn't matter.* |
| **¡No me digas!** | *You don't say!* |
| **No sé.** | *I don't know.* |
| **¡Ojalá!** | *Hopefully!* |
| **Perdone.** | *Pardon me.* |
| **Por favor.** | *Please.* |
| **Por supuesto.** | *Of course.* |
| **¡Qué bien!** | *Great!* |
| **¡Qué gracioso!** | *How funny!* |
| **¡Qué pena!** | *What a shame/pity!* |
| **¿Qué significa _____?** | *What does _____ mean?* |
| **Repite, por favor.** | *Please repeat.* |
| **Tengo una pregunta.** | *I have a question.* |
| **¿Tiene(n) alguna pregunta?** | *Do you have any questions?* |
| **Vaya(n) a la página dos.** | *Go to page 2.* |

# Glossary of Grammatical Terms

**ADJECTIVE** A word that modifies, or describes, a noun or pronoun.

| | |
|---|---|
| **muchos** libros | un hombre **rico** |
| *many books* | *a rich man* |

las mujeres **altas**
*the tall women*

**Demonstrative adjective** An adjective that specifies which noun a speaker is referring to.

| | |
|---|---|
| **esta** fiesta | **ese** chico |
| *this party* | *that boy* |

**aquellas** flores
*those flowers*

**Possessive adjective** An adjective that indicates ownership or possession.

| | |
|---|---|
| **mi** mejor vestido | Éste es **mi** hermano. |
| *my best dress* | *This is my brother.* |

**Stressed possessive adjective** A possessive adjective that emphasizes the owner or possessor.

Es un libro **mío**.
*It's my book./It's a book of mine.*

Es amiga **tuya**; yo no la conozco.
*She's a friend of yours; I don't know her.*

**ADVERB** A word that modifies, or describes, a verb, adjective, or other adverb.

Pancho escribe **rápidamente**.
*Pancho writes quickly.*

Este cuadro es **muy** bonito.
*This picture is very pretty.*

**ARTICLE** A word that points out a noun in either a specific or a non-specific way.

**Definite article** An article that points out a noun in a specific way.

| | |
|---|---|
| **el** libro | **la** maleta |
| *the book* | *the suitcase* |

| | |
|---|---|
| **los** diccionarios | **las** palabras |
| *the dictionaries* | *the words* |

**Indefinite article** An article that points out a noun in a general, non-specific way.

| | |
|---|---|
| **un** lápiz | **una** computadora |
| *a pencil* | *a computer* |

| | |
|---|---|
| **unos** pájaros | **unas** escuelas |
| *some birds* | *some schools* |

**CLAUSE** A group of words that contains both a conjugated verb and a subject, either expressed or implied.

**Main (or Independent) clause** A clause that can stand alone as a complete sentence.

Pienso ir a cenar pronto.
*I plan to go to dinner soon.*

**Subordinate (or Dependent) clause** A clause that does not express a complete thought and therefore cannot stand alone as a sentence.

Trabajo en la cafetería **porque necesito dinero para la escuela**.
*I work in the cafeteria because I need money for school.*

**COMPARATIVE** A construction used with an adjective or adverb to express a comparison between two people, places, or things.

Este programa es **más interesante que** el otro.
*This program is more interesting than the other one.*

Tomás no es **tan alto como** Alberto.
*Tomás is not as tall as Alberto.*

**CONJUGATION** A set of the forms of a verb for a specific tense or mood or the process by which these verb forms are presented.

Preterite conjugation of **cantar**:

| | |
|---|---|
| canté | cantamos |
| cantaste | cantasteis |
| cantó | cantaron |

**CONJUNCTION** A word used to connect words, clauses, or phrases.

Susana es de Cuba **y** Pedro es de España.
*Susana is from Cuba and Pedro is from Spain.*

No quiero estudiar **pero** tengo que hacerlo.
*I don't want to study, but I have to.*

**CONTRACTION** The joining of two words into one. The only contractions in Spanish are **al** and **del**.

Mi hermano fue **al** concierto ayer.
*My brother went **to the** concert yesterday.*

Saqué dinero **del** banco.
*I took money **from the** bank.*

**DIRECT OBJECT** A noun or pronoun that directly receives the action of the verb.

Tomás lee **el libro.**      La **pagó** ayer.
*Tomás reads **the book.**      She paid **it** yesterday.*

**GENDER** The grammatical categorizing of certain kinds of words, such as nouns and pronouns, as masculine, feminine, or neuter.

**Masculine**
*articles*  el, un
*pronouns*  él, lo, mío, éste, ése, aquél
*adjective*  simpático

**Feminine**
*articles*  la, una
*pronouns*  ella, la, mía, ésta, ésa, aquélla
*adjective*  simpática

**IMPERSONAL EXPRESSION** A third-person expression with no expressed or specific subject.

Es muy importante.      Llueve mucho.
*It's very important.      It's raining hard.*

Aquí **se habla** español.
*Spanish **is spoken** here.*

**INDIRECT OBJECT** A noun or pronoun that receives the action of the verb indirectly; the object, often a living being, to or for whom an action is performed.

Eduardo **le** dio un libro **a Linda.**
*Eduardo gave a book **to Linda.***

La profesora **me** dio una C en el examen.
*The professor gave **me** a C on the test.*

**INFINITIVE** The basic form of a verb. Infinitives in Spanish end in **-ar, -er,** or **-ir.**

hablar      correr      abrir
*to speak      to run      to open*

**INTERROGATIVE** An adjective or pronoun used to ask a question.

**¿Quién** habla?      **¿Cuántos** compraste?
*Who is speaking?      How many did you buy?*

**¿Qué** piensas hacer hoy?
*What do you plan to do today?*

**INVERSION** Changing the word order of a sentence, often to form a question.

*Statement:* Elena pagó la cuenta del restaurante.

*Inversion:* ¿Pagó Elena la cuenta del restaurante?

**MOOD** A grammatical distinction of verbs that indicates whether the verb is intended to make a statement or command or to express a doubt, emotion, or condition contrary to fact.

**Imperative mood** Verb forms used to make commands.

**Di** la verdad.      **Caminen** ustedes conmigo.
*Tell the truth.      Walk with me.*

**¡Comamos** ahora!
*Let's eat now!*

**Indicative mood** Verb forms used to state facts, actions, and states considered to be real.

Sé que **tienes** el dinero.
*I know that **you have** the money.*

**Subjunctive mood** Verb forms used principally in subordinate (dependent) clauses to express wishes, desires, emotions, doubts, and certain conditions, such as contrary-to-fact situations.

Prefieren que **hables** en español.
*They prefer that **you speak** in Spanish.*

Dudo que Luis **tenga** el dinero necesario.
*I doubt that Luis **has** the necessary money.*

**NOUN** A word that identifies people, animals, places, things, and ideas.

hombre      gato
*man*      *cat*

México      casa
*Mexico*      *house*

libertad      libro
*freedom*      *book*

**NUMBER** A grammatical term that refers to singular or plural. Nouns in Spanish and English have number. Other parts of a sentence, such as adjectives, articles, and verbs, can also have number.

| Singular | Plural |
|---|---|
| **una** cosa | **unas** cosas |
| *a thing* | *some things* |
| **el** profesor | **los** profesores |
| *the professor* | *the professors* |

**NUMBERS** Words that represent amounts.

**Cardinal numbers** Words that show specific amounts.

**cinco** minutos
*five minutes*

el año **dos mil siete**
*the year 2007*

**Ordinal numbers** Words that indicate the order of a noun in a series.

el **cuarto** jugador      la **décima** hora
*the **fourth** player*      *the **tenth** hour*

**PAST PARTICIPLE** A past form of the verb used in compound tenses. The past participle may also be used as an adjective, but it must then agree in number and gender with the word it modifies.

Han **buscado** por todas partes.
*They have **searched** everywhere.*

Yo no había **estudiado** para el examen.
*I hadn't **studied** for the exam.*

Hay una **ventana abierta** en la sala.
*There is an **open window** in the living room.*

**PERSON** The form of the verb or pronoun that indicates the speaker, the one spoken to, or the one spoken about. In Spanish, as in English, there are three persons: first, second, and third.

| Person | Singular | Plural |
|---|---|---|
| 1st | yo  *I* | nosotros/as  *we* |
| 2nd | tú, Ud.  *you* | vosotros/as, Uds.  *you* |
| 3rd | él, ella  *he, she* | ellos, ellas  *they* |

**PREPOSITION** A word or words that describe(s) the relationship, most often in time or space, between two other words.

Anita es **de** California.
*Anita is **from** California.*

La chaqueta está **en** el carro.
*The jacket is **in** the car.*

Marta se peinó **antes de** salir.
*Marta combed her hair **before** going out.*

**PRESENT PARTICIPLE** In English, a verb form that ends in *-ing*. In Spanish, the present participle ends in **-ndo**, and is often used with **estar** to form a progressive tense.

Mi hermana está **hablando** por teléfono ahora mismo.
*My sister is **talking** on the phone right now.*

**PRONOUN** A word that takes the place of a noun or nouns.

**Demonstrative pronoun** A pronoun that takes the place of a specific noun.

Quiero **ésta**.
*I want **this one**.*

¿Vas a comprar **ése**?
*Are you going to buy **that one**?*

Juan prefirió **aquéllos**.
*Juan preferred **those** (over there).*

**Object pronoun** A pronoun that functions as a direct or indirect object of the verb.

**Te** digo la verdad.
*I'm telling **you** the truth.*

**Me lo** trajo Juan.
*Juan brought **it** to **me**.*

**Reflexive pronoun** A pronoun that indicates that the action of a verb is performed by the subject on itself. These pronouns are often expressed in English with *-self: myself, yourself*, etc.

Yo **me** bañé antes de salir.
*I **bathed** (**myself**) before going out.*

Elena **se acostó** a las once y media.
*Elena **went to bed** at eleven-thirty.*

**Relative pronoun** A pronoun that connects a subordinate clause to a main clause.

El chico **que** nos escribió viene de visita mañana.
*The boy **who** wrote us is coming to visit tomorrow.*

Ya sé **lo que** tenemos que hacer.
*I already know **what** we have to do.*

**Subject pronoun** A pronoun that replaces the name or title of a person or thing, and acts as the subject of a verb.

**Tú** debes estudiar más.
***You** should study more.*

**Él** llegó primero.
***He** arrived first.*

**SUBJECT** A noun or pronoun that performs the action of a verb and is often implied by the verb.

**María** va al supermercado.
***María** goes to the supermarket.*

**(Ellos)** Trabajan mucho.
***They** work hard.*

Esos **libros** son muy caros.
*Those **books** are very expensive.*

**SUPERLATIVE** A word or construction used with an adjective or adverb to express the highest or lowest degree of a specific quality among three or more people, places, or things.

De todas mis clases, ésta es la **más interesante**.
*Of all my classes, this is the **most interesting**.*

Raúl es el **menos simpático** de los chicos.
*Raúl is the **least pleasant** of the boys.*

**TENSE** A set of verb forms that indicates the time of an action or state: past, present, or future.

**Compound tense** A two-word tense made up of an auxiliary verb and a present or past participle. In Spanish, there are two auxiliary verbs: **estar** and **haber**.

En este momento, **estoy estudiando**.
*At this time, **I am studying**.*

El paquete no **ha llegado** todavía.
*The package **has** not **arrived** yet.*

**Simple tense** A tense expressed by a single verb form.

María **estaba** mal anoche.
*María **was** ill last night.*

Juana **hablará** con su mamá mañana.
*Juana **will speak** with her mom tomorrow.*

**VERB** A word that expresses actions or states-of-being.

**Auxiliary verb** A verb used with a present or past participle to form a compound tense. **Haber** is the most commonly used auxiliary verb in Spanish.

Los chicos **han** visto los elefantes.
*The children **have** seen the elephants.*

Espero que **hayas** comido.
*I hope you **have** eaten.*

**Reflexive verb** A verb that describes an action performed by the subject on itself and is always used with a reflexive pronoun.

**Me** compré un carro nuevo.
*I bought **myself** a new car.*

Pedro y Adela **se levantan** muy temprano.
*Pedro and Adela **get (themselves) up** very early.*

**Spelling change verb** A verb that undergoes a predictable change in spelling, in order to reflect its actual pronunciation in the various conjugations.

| | | | |
|---|---|---|---|
| practicar | c→qu | practico | practiqué |
| dirigir | g→j | dirigí | dirijo |
| almorzar | z→c | almorzó | almorcé |

**Stem-changing verb** A verb whose stem vowel undergoes one or more predictable changes in the various conjugations.

| | |
|---|---|
| entender (e:ie) | entiendo |
| pedir (e:i) | piden |
| dormir (o:ue, u) | duermo, durmieron |

# Verb Conjugation Tables

### The verb lists

The list of verbs below, and the model-verb tables that start on page A-11 show you how to conjugate every verb taught in **PANORAMA**. Each verb in the list is followed by a model verb conjugated according to the same pattern. The number in parentheses indicates where in the verb tables you can find the conjugated forms of the model verb. If you want to find out how to conjugate **divertirse**, for example, look up number 33, **sentir**, the model for verbs that follow the e:ie stem-change pattern.

### How to use the verb tables

In the tables you will find the infinitive, present and past participles, and all the simple forms of each model verb. The formation of the compound tenses of any verb can be inferred from the table of compound tenses, pages A-11–12, either by combining the past participle of the verb with a conjugated form of **haber** or by combining the present participle with a conjugated form of **estar**.

**abrazar** (z:c) like cruzar (37)

**abrir** like vivir (3) *except* past participle is **abierto**

**aburrir(se)** like vivir (3)

**acabar de** like hablar (1)

**acampar** like hablar (1)

**acompañar** like hablar (1)

**aconsejar** like hablar (1)

**acordarse** (o:ue) like contar (24)

**acostarse** (o:ue) like contar (24)

**adelgazar** (z:c) like cruzar (37)

**afeitarse** like hablar (1)

**ahorrar** like hablar (1)

**alegrarse** like hablar (1)

**aliviar** like hablar (1)

**almorzar** (o:ue) like contar (24) *except* (z:c)

**alquilar** like hablar (1)

**andar** like hablar (1) *except* preterite stem is **anduv-**

**anunciar** like hablar (1)

**apagar** (g:gu) like llegar (41)

**aplaudir** like vivir (3)

**apreciar** like hablar (1)

**aprender** like comer (2)

**apurarse** like hablar (1)

**arrancar** (c:qu) like tocar (43)

**arreglar** like hablar (1)

**asistir** like vivir (3)

**aumentar** like hablar (1)

**ayudar(se)** like hablar (1)

**bailar** like hablar (1)

**bajar(se)** like hablar (1)

**bañarse** like hablar (1)

**barrer** like comer (2)

**beber** like comer (2)

**besar(se)** like hablar (1)

**borrar** like hablar (1)

**brindar** like hablar (1)

**bucear** like hablar (1)

**buscar** (c:qu) like tocar (43)

**caber** (4)

**caer(se)** (5)

**calentarse** (e:ie) like pensar (30)

**calzar** (z:c) like cruzar (37)

**cambiar** like hablar (1)

**caminar** like hablar (1)

**cantar** like hablar (1)

**casarse** like hablar (1)

**cazar** (z:c) like cruzar (37)

**celebrar** like hablar (1)

**cenar** like hablar (1)

**cepillarse** like hablar (1)

**cerrar** (e:ie) like pensar (30)

**cobrar** like hablar (1)

**cocinar** like hablar (1)

**comenzar** (e:ie) (z:c) like empezar (26)

**comer** (2)

**compartir** like vivir (3)

**comprar** like hablar (1)

**comprender** like comer (2)

**comprometerse** like comer (2)

**comunicarse** (c:qu) like tocar (43)

**conducir** (c:zc) (6)

**confirmar** like hablar (1)

**conocer** (c:zc) (35)

**conseguir** (e:i) (g:gu) like seguir (32)

**conservar** like hablar (1)

**consumir** like vivir (3)

**contaminar** like hablar (1)

**contar** (o:ue) (24)

**controlar** like hablar (1)

**correr** like comer (2)

**costar** (o:ue) like contar (24)

**creer** (y) (36)

**cruzar** (z:c) (37)

**cubrir** like vivir (3) *except* past participle is **cubierto**

**cuidar** like hablar (1)

**cumplir** like vivir (3)

**dañar** like hablar (1)

**dar** (7)

**deber** like comer (2)

**decidir** like vivir (3)

**decir** (e:i) (8)

**declarar** like hablar (1)

**dejar** like hablar (1)

**depositar** like hablar (1)

**desarrollar** like hablar (1)

**desayunar** like hablar (1)

**descansar** like hablar (1)

**descargar** like hablar (1)

**describir** like vivir (3) *except* past participle is **descrito**

**descubrir** like vivir (3) *except* past participle is **descubierto**

**desear** like hablar (1)

**despedirse** (e:i) like pedir (29)

**despertarse** (e:ie) like pensar (30)

**destruir** (y) (38)

**dibujar** like hablar (1)

**dirigir** (g:j) like vivir (3) *except* (g:j)

**disfrutar** like hablar (1)

**divertirse** (e:ie) like sentir (33)

**divorciarse** like hablar (1)

**doblar** like hablar (1)

**doler** (o:ue) like volver (34) *except* past participle is regular

**dormir(se)** (o:ue, u) (25)

**ducharse** like hablar (1)

**dudar** like hablar (1)

**durar** like hablar (1)

**echar** like hablar (1)

**elegir** (e:i) like pedir (29) *except* (g:j)

**emitir** like vivir (3)

empezar (e:ie) (z:c) (26)

enamorarse like hablar (1)

encantar like hablar (1)

encontrar(se) (o:ue) like contar (24)

enfermarse like hablar (1)

engordar like hablar (1)

enojarse like hablar (1)

enseñar like hablar (1)

ensuciar like hablar (1)

entender (e:ie) (27)

entrenarse like hablar (1)

entrevistar like hablar (1)

enviar (envío) (39)

escalar like hablar (1)

escoger (g:j) like proteger (42)

escribir like vivir (3) except past participle is escrito

escuchar like hablar (1)

esculpir like vivir (3)

esperar like hablar (1)

esquiar (esquío) like enviar (39)

establecer (c:zc) like conocer (35)

estacionar like hablar (1)

estar (9)

estornudar like hablar (1)

estudiar like hablar (1)

evitar like hablar (1)

explicar (c:qu) like tocar (43)

explorar like hablar (1)

faltar like hablar (1)

fascinar like hablar (1)

firmar like hablar (1)

fumar like hablar (1)

funcionar like hablar (1)

ganar like hablar (1)

gastar like hablar (1)

grabar like hablar (1)

graduarse (gradúo) (40)

guardar like hablar (1)

gustar like hablar (1)

haber (hay) (10)

hablar (1)

hacer (11)

importar like hablar (1)

imprimir like vivir (3)

informar like hablar (1)

insistir like vivir (3)

interesar like hablar (1)

invertir (e:ie) like sentir (33)

invitar like hablar (1)

ir(se) (12)

jubilarse like hablar (1)

jugar (u:ue) (g:gu) (28)

lastimarse like hablar (1)

lavar(se) like hablar (1)

leer (y) like creer (36)

levantar(se) like hablar (1)

limpiar like hablar (1)

llamar(se) like hablar (1)

llegar (g:gu) (41)

llenar like hablar (1)

llevar(se) like hablar (1)

llover (o:ue) like volver (34) except past participle is regular

luchar like hablar (1)

mandar like hablar (1)

manejar like hablar (1)

mantener(se) (e:ie) like tener (20)

maquillarse like hablar (1)

mejorar like hablar (1)

merendar (e:ie) like pensar (30)

mirar like hablar (1)

molestar like hablar (1)

montar like hablar (1)

morir (o:ue) like dormir (25) except past participle is muerto

mostrar (o:ue) like contar (24)

mudarse like hablar (1)

nacer (c:zc) like conocer (35)

nadar like hablar (1)

navegar (g:gu) like llegar (41)

necesitar like hablar (1)

negar (e:ie) like pensar (30) except (g:gu)

nevar (e:ie) like pensar (30)

obedecer (c:zc) like conocer (35)

obtener (e:ie) like tener (20)

ocurrir like vivir (3)

odiar like hablar (1)

ofrecer (c:zc) like conocer (35)

oír (13)

olvidar like hablar (1)

pagar (g:gu) like llegar (41)

parar like hablar (1)

parecer (c:zc) like conocer (35)

pasar like hablar (1)

pasear like hablar (1)

patinar like hablar (1)

pedir (e:i) (29)

peinarse like hablar (1)

pensar (e:ie) (30)

perder (e:ie) like entender (27)

pescar (c:qu) like tocar (43)

pintar like hablar (1)

planchar like hablar (1)

poder (o:ue) (14)

poner(se) (15)

practicar (c:qu) like tocar (43)

preferir (e:ie) like sentir (33)

preguntar like hablar (1)

preocuparse like hablar (1)

preparar like hablar (1)

presentar like hablar (1)

prestar like hablar (1)

probar(se) (o:ue) like contar (24)

prohibir like vivir (3)

proteger (g:j) (42)

publicar (c:qu) like tocar (43)

quedar(se) like hablar (1)

quemar like hablar (1)

querer (e:ie) (16)

quitar(se) like hablar (1)

recetar like hablar (1)

recibir like vivir (3)

reciclar like hablar (1)

recoger (g:j) like proteger (42)

recomendar (e:ie) like pensar (30)

recordar (o:ue) like contar (24)

reducir (c:zc) like conducir (6)

regalar like hablar (1)

regatear like hablar (1)

regresar like hablar (1)

reír(se) (e:i) (31)

relajarse like hablar (1)

renunciar like hablar (1)

repetir (e:i) like pedir (29)

resolver (o:ue) like volver (34)

respirar like hablar (1)

revisar like hablar (1)

rogar (o:ue) like contar (24)

except (g:gu)

romper(se) like comer (2) except past participle is roto

saber (17)

sacar (c:qu) like tocar (43)

sacudir like vivir (3)

salir (18)

saludar(se) like hablar (1)

secar(se) (c:qu) like tocar (43)

seguir (e:i) (32)

sentarse (e:ie) like pensar (30)

sentir(se) (e:ie) (33)

separarse like hablar (1)

ser (19)

servir (e:i) like pedir (29)

solicitar like hablar (1)

sonar (o:ue) like contar (24)

sonreír (e:i) like reír(se) (31)

sorprender like comer (2)

subir like vivir (3)

sudar like hablar (1)

sufrir like vivir (3)

sugerir (e:ie) like sentir (33)

suponer like poner (15)

temer like comer (2)

tener (e:ie) (20)

terminar like hablar (1)

tocar (c:qu) (43)

tomar like hablar (1)

torcerse (o:ue) like volver (34) except (c:z) and past participle is regular; e.g., yo tuerzo

toser like comer (2)

trabajar like hablar (1)

traducir (c:zc) like conducir (6)

traer (21)

transmitir like vivir (3)

tratar like hablar (1)

usar like hablar (1)

vender like comer (2)

venir (e:ie, i) (22)

ver (23)

vestirse (e:i) like pedir (29)

viajar like hablar (1)

visitar like hablar (1)

vivir (3)

volver (o:ue) (34)

votar like hablar (1)

# Regular verbs: simple tenses

| Infinitive | INDICATIVE Present | Imperfect | Preterite | Future | Conditional | SUBJUNCTIVE Present | Past | IMPERATIVE |
|---|---|---|---|---|---|---|---|---|
| **1** hablar | hablo | hablaba | hablé | hablaré | hablaría | hable | hablara | |
| | hablas | hablabas | hablaste | hablarás | hablarías | hables | hablaras | habla tú (no hables) |
| | habla | hablaba | habló | hablará | hablaría | hable | hablara | hable Ud. |
| **Participles:** | hablamos | hablábamos | hablamos | hablaremos | hablaríamos | hablemos | habláramos | hablemos |
| hablando | habláis | hablabais | hablasteis | hablaréis | hablaríais | habléis | hablarais | hablad (no habléis) |
| hablado | hablan | hablaban | hablaron | hablarán | hablarían | hablen | hablaran | hablen Uds. |
| **2** comer | como | comía | comí | comeré | comería | coma | comiera | |
| | comes | comías | comiste | comerás | comerías | comas | comieras | come tú (no comas) |
| | come | comía | comió | comerá | comería | coma | comiera | coma Ud. |
| **Participles:** | comemos | comíamos | comimos | comeremos | comeríamos | comamos | comiéramos | comamos |
| comiendo | coméis | comíais | comisteis | comeréis | comeríais | comáis | comierais | comed (no comáis) |
| comido | comen | comían | comieron | comerán | comerían | coman | comieran | coman Uds. |
| **3** vivir | vivo | vivía | viví | viviré | viviría | viva | viviera | |
| | vives | vivías | viviste | vivirás | vivirías | vivas | vivieras | vive tú (no vivas) |
| | vive | vivía | vivió | vivirá | viviría | viva | viviera | viva Ud. |
| **Participles:** | vivimos | vivíamos | vivimos | viviremos | viviríamos | vivamos | viviéramos | vivamos |
| viviendo | vivís | vivíais | vivisteis | viviréis | viviríais | viváis | vivierais | vivid (no viváis) |
| vivido | viven | vivían | vivieron | vivirán | vivirían | vivan | vivieran | vivan Uds. |

# All verbs: compound tenses

## PERFECT TENSES

| INDICATIVE Present Perfect | | Past Perfect | | Future Perfect | | Conditional Perfect | |
|---|---|---|---|---|---|---|---|
| he | hablado | había | hablado | habré | hablado | habría | hablado |
| has | comido | habías | comido | habrás | comido | habrías | comido |
| ha | vivido | había | vivido | habrá | vivido | habría | vivido |
| hemos | | habíamos | | habremos | | habríamos | |
| habéis | | habíais | | habréis | | habríais | |
| han | | habían | | habrán | | habrían | |

| SUBJUNCTIVE Present Perfect | | Past Perfect | |
|---|---|---|---|
| haya | hablado | hubiera | hablado |
| hayas | comido | hubieras | comido |
| haya | vivido | hubiera | vivido |
| hayamos | | hubiéramos | |
| hayáis | | hubierais | |
| hayan | | hubieran | |

## PROGRESSIVE TENSES

### INDICATIVE

| Present Progressive | Past Progressive | Future Progressive | Conditional Progressive | |
|---|---|---|---|---|
| estoy | estaba | estaré | estaría | |
| estás | estabas | estarás | estarías | |
| está | estaba | estará | estaría | hablando |
| estamos | estábamos | estaremos | estaríamos | comiendo |
| estáis | estabais | estaréis | estaríais | viviendo |
| están | estaban | estarán | estarían | |

### SUBJUNCTIVE

| Present Progressive | Past Progressive | |
|---|---|---|
| esté | estuviera | |
| estés | estuvieras | |
| esté | estuviera | hablando |
| estemos | estuviéramos | comiendo |
| estéis | estuvierais | viviendo |
| estén | estuvieran | |

## Irregular verbs

| Infinitive | INDICATIVE Present | Imperfect | Preterite | Future | Conditional | SUBJUNCTIVE Present | Past | IMPERATIVE |
|---|---|---|---|---|---|---|---|---|
| **4** caber | **quepo** | cabía | **cupe** | **cabré** | **cabría** | **quepa** | **cupiera** | |
| | cabes | cabías | **cupiste** | **cabrás** | **cabrías** | **quepas** | **cupieras** | cabe tú (no **quepas**) |
| **Participles:** | cabe | cabía | **cupo** | **cabrá** | **cabría** | **quepa** | **cupiera** | **quepa** Ud. |
| cabiendo | cabemos | cabíamos | **cupimos** | **cabremos** | **cabríamos** | **quepamos** | **cupiéramos** | **quepamos** |
| cabido | cabéis | cabíais | **cupisteis** | **cabréis** | **cabríais** | **quepáis** | **cupierais** | cabed (no **quepáis**) |
| | caben | cabían | **cupieron** | **cabrán** | **cabrían** | **quepan** | **cupieran** | **quepan** Uds. |
| **5** caer(se) | **caigo** | caía | caí | caeré | caería | **caiga** | **cayera** | |
| | caes | caías | **caíste** | caerás | caerías | **caigas** | **cayeras** | cae tú (no **caigas**) |
| **Participles:** | cae | caía | **cayó** | caerá | caería | **caiga** | **cayera** | **caiga** Ud. |
| **cayendo** | caemos | caíamos | **caímos** | caeremos | caeríamos | **caigamos** | **cayéramos** | **caigamos** |
| **caído** | caéis | caíais | **caísteis** | caeréis | caeríais | **caigáis** | **cayerais** | caed (no **caigáis**) |
| | caen | caían | **cayeron** | caerán | caerían | **caigan** | **cayeran** | **caigan** Uds. |
| **6** conducir (c:zc) | **conduzco** | conducía | **conduje** | conduciré | conduciría | **conduzca** | **condujera** | |
| | conduces | conducías | **condujiste** | conducirás | conducirías | **conduzcas** | **condujeras** | conduce tú (no **conduzcas**) |
| | conduce | conducía | **condujo** | conducirá | conduciría | **conduzca** | **condujera** | **conduzca** Ud. |
| **Participles:** | conducimos | conducíamos | **condujimos** | conduciremos | conduciríamos | **conduzcamos** | **condujéramos** | **conduzcamos** |
| conduciendo | conducís | conducíais | **condujisteis** | conduciréis | conduciríais | **conduzcáis** | **condujerais** | conducid (no **conduzcáis**) |
| conducido | conducen | conducían | **condujeron** | conducirán | conducirían | **conduzcan** | **condujeran** | **conduzcan** Uds. |

| | INDICATIVE | | | | | SUBJUNCTIVE | | IMPERATIVE |
|---|---|---|---|---|---|---|---|---|
| Infinitive | Present | Imperfect | Preterite | Future | Conditional | Present | Past | |
| **7** dar<br>Participles:<br>dando<br>dado | **doy**<br>das<br>da<br>damos<br>dais<br>dan | daba<br>dabas<br>daba<br>dábamos<br>dabais<br>daban | **di**<br>**diste**<br>**dio**<br>**dimos**<br>**disteis**<br>**dieron** | daré<br>darás<br>dará<br>daremos<br>daréis<br>darán | daría<br>darías<br>daría<br>daríamos<br>daríais<br>darían | **dé**<br>**des**<br>**dé**<br>**demos**<br>**deis**<br>**den** | **diera**<br>**dieras**<br>**diera**<br>**diéramos**<br>**dierais**<br>**dieran** | <br>da tú (no des)<br>**dé** Ud.<br>**demos**<br>dad (no **deis**)<br>**den** Uds. |
| **8** decir (e:i)<br>Participles:<br>**diciendo**<br>**dicho** | **digo**<br>**dices**<br>**dice**<br>decimos<br>decís<br>**dicen** | decía<br>decías<br>decía<br>decíamos<br>decíais<br>decían | **dije**<br>**dijiste**<br>**dijo**<br>**dijimos**<br>**dijisteis**<br>**dijeron** | **diré**<br>**dirás**<br>**dirá**<br>**diremos**<br>**diréis**<br>**dirán** | **diría**<br>**dirías**<br>**diría**<br>**diríamos**<br>**diríais**<br>**dirían** | **diga**<br>**digas**<br>**diga**<br>**digamos**<br>**digáis**<br>**digan** | **dijera**<br>**dijeras**<br>**dijera**<br>**dijéramos**<br>**dijerais**<br>**dijeran** | <br>**di** tú (no **digas**)<br>**diga** Ud.<br>**digamos**<br>decid (no **digáis**)<br>**digan** Uds. |
| **9** estar<br>Participles:<br>estando<br>estado | **estoy**<br>estás<br>está<br>estamos<br>estáis<br>están | estaba<br>estabas<br>estaba<br>estábamos<br>estabais<br>estaban | **estuve**<br>**estuviste**<br>**estuvo**<br>**estuvimos**<br>**estuvisteis**<br>**estuvieron** | estaré<br>estarás<br>estará<br>estaremos<br>estaréis<br>estarán | estaría<br>estarías<br>estaría<br>estaríamos<br>estaríais<br>estarían | esté<br>estés<br>esté<br>estemos<br>estéis<br>estén | **estuviera**<br>**estuvieras**<br>**estuviera**<br>**estuviéramos**<br>**estuvierais**<br>**estuvieran** | <br>está tú (no estés)<br>esté Ud.<br>estemos<br>estad (no estéis)<br>estén Uds. |
| **10** haber<br>Participles:<br>habiendo<br>habido | **he**<br>**has**<br>**ha**<br>**hemos**<br>**habéis**<br>**han** | había<br>habías<br>había<br>habíamos<br>habíais<br>habían | **hube**<br>**hubiste**<br>**hubo**<br>**hubimos**<br>**hubisteis**<br>**hubieron** | **habré**<br>**habrás**<br>**habrá**<br>**habremos**<br>**habréis**<br>**habrán** | **habría**<br>**habrías**<br>**habría**<br>**habríamos**<br>**habríais**<br>**habrían** | **haya**<br>**hayas**<br>**haya**<br>**hayamos**<br>**hayáis**<br>**hayan** | **hubiera**<br>**hubieras**<br>**hubiera**<br>**hubiéramos**<br>**hubierais**<br>**hubieran** | |
| **11** hacer<br>Participles:<br>haciendo<br>**hecho** | **hago**<br>haces<br>hace<br>hacemos<br>hacéis<br>hacen | hacía<br>hacías<br>hacía<br>hacíamos<br>hacíais<br>hacían | **hice**<br>**hiciste**<br>**hizo**<br>**hicimos**<br>**hicisteis**<br>**hicieron** | **haré**<br>**harás**<br>**hará**<br>**haremos**<br>**haréis**<br>**harán** | **haría**<br>**harías**<br>**haría**<br>**haríamos**<br>**haríais**<br>**harían** | **haga**<br>**hagas**<br>**haga**<br>**hagamos**<br>**hagáis**<br>**hagan** | **hiciera**<br>**hicieras**<br>**hiciera**<br>**hiciéramos**<br>**hicierais**<br>**hicieran** | <br>**haz** tú (no **hagas**)<br>**haga** Ud.<br>**hagamos**<br>haced (no **hagáis**)<br>**hagan** Uds. |
| **12** ir<br>Participles:<br>**yendo**<br>ido | **voy**<br>**vas**<br>**va**<br>**vamos**<br>**vais**<br>**van** | **iba**<br>**ibas**<br>**iba**<br>**íbamos**<br>**ibais**<br>**iban** | **fui**<br>**fuiste**<br>**fue**<br>**fuimos**<br>**fuisteis**<br>**fueron** | iré<br>irás<br>irá<br>iremos<br>iréis<br>irán | iría<br>irías<br>iría<br>iríamos<br>iríais<br>irían | **vaya**<br>**vayas**<br>**vaya**<br>**vayamos**<br>**vayáis**<br>**vayan** | **fuera**<br>**fueras**<br>**fuera**<br>**fuéramos**<br>**fuerais**<br>**fueran** | <br>**ve** tú (no **vayas**)<br>**vaya** Ud.<br>**vamos**<br>id (no **vayáis**)<br>**vayan** Uds. |
| **13** oír (y)<br>Participles:<br>**oyendo**<br>oído | **oigo**<br>**oyes**<br>**oye**<br>**oímos**<br>**oís**<br>**oyen** | oía<br>oías<br>oía<br>oíamos<br>oíais<br>oían | **oí**<br>**oíste**<br>**oyó**<br>**oímos**<br>**oísteis**<br>**oyeron** | oiré<br>oirás<br>oirá<br>oiremos<br>oiréis<br>oirán | oiría<br>oirías<br>oiría<br>oiríamos<br>oiríais<br>oirían | **oiga**<br>**oigas**<br>**oiga**<br>**oigamos**<br>**oigáis**<br>**oigan** | **oyera**<br>**oyeras**<br>**oyera**<br>**oyéramos**<br>**oyerais**<br>**oyeran** | <br>**oye** tú (no **oigas**)<br>**oiga** Ud.<br>**oigamos**<br>oíd (no **oigáis**)<br>**oigan** Uds. |

**14. poder (o:ue)**
Participles: **pudiendo**, podido

| | INDICATIVE | | | | | SUBJUNCTIVE | | IMPERATIVE |
|---|---|---|---|---|---|---|---|---|
| | Present | Imperfect | Preterite | Future | Conditional | Present | Past | |
| | **puedo** | podía | **pude** | **podré** | **podría** | **pueda** | **pudiera** | |
| | **puedes** | podías | **pudiste** | **podrás** | **podrías** | **puedas** | **pudieras** | **puede** tú (no **puedas**) |
| | **puede** | podía | **pudo** | **podrá** | **podría** | **pueda** | **pudiera** | **pueda** Ud. |
| | podemos | podíamos | **pudimos** | **podremos** | **podríamos** | podamos | **pudiéramos** | podamos |
| | podéis | podíais | **pudisteis** | **podréis** | **podríais** | podáis | **pudierais** | poded (no podáis) |
| | **pueden** | podían | **pudieron** | **podrán** | **podrían** | **puedan** | **pudieran** | **puedan** Uds. |

**15. poner**
Participles: poniendo, **puesto**

| | INDICATIVE | | | | | SUBJUNCTIVE | | IMPERATIVE |
|---|---|---|---|---|---|---|---|---|
| | Present | Imperfect | Preterite | Future | Conditional | Present | Past | |
| | **pongo** | ponía | **puse** | **pondré** | **pondría** | **ponga** | **pusiera** | |
| | pones | ponías | **pusiste** | **pondrás** | **pondrías** | **pongas** | **pusieras** | **pon** tú (no **pongas**) |
| | pone | ponía | **puso** | **pondrá** | **pondría** | **ponga** | **pusiera** | **ponga** Ud. |
| | ponemos | poníamos | **pusimos** | **pondremos** | **pondríamos** | **pongamos** | **pusiéramos** | **pongamos** |
| | ponéis | poníais | **pusisteis** | **pondréis** | **pondríais** | **pongáis** | **pusierais** | poned (no **pongáis**) |
| | ponen | ponían | **pusieron** | **pondrán** | **pondrían** | **pongan** | **pusieran** | **pongan** Uds. |

**16. querer (e:ie)**
Participles: queriendo, querido

| | INDICATIVE | | | | | SUBJUNCTIVE | | IMPERATIVE |
|---|---|---|---|---|---|---|---|---|
| | Present | Imperfect | Preterite | Future | Conditional | Present | Past | |
| | **quiero** | quería | **quise** | **querré** | **querría** | **quiera** | **quisiera** | |
| | **quieres** | querías | **quisiste** | **querrás** | **querrías** | **quieras** | **quisieras** | **quiere** tú (no **quieras**) |
| | **quiere** | quería | **quiso** | **querrá** | **querría** | **quiera** | **quisiera** | **quiera** Ud. |
| | queremos | queríamos | **quisimos** | **querremos** | **querríamos** | queramos | **quisiéramos** | **queramos** |
| | queréis | queríais | **quisisteis** | **querréis** | **querríais** | queráis | **quisierais** | quered (no queráis) |
| | **quieren** | querían | **quisieron** | **querrán** | **querrían** | **quieran** | **quisieran** | **quieran** Uds. |

**17. saber**
Participles: sabiendo, sabido

| | INDICATIVE | | | | | SUBJUNCTIVE | | IMPERATIVE |
|---|---|---|---|---|---|---|---|---|
| | Present | Imperfect | Preterite | Future | Conditional | Present | Past | |
| | **sé** | sabía | **supe** | **sabré** | **sabría** | **sepa** | **supiera** | |
| | sabes | sabías | **supiste** | **sabrás** | **sabrías** | **sepas** | **supieras** | sabe tú (no **sepas**) |
| | sabe | sabía | **supo** | **sabrá** | **sabría** | **sepa** | **supiera** | **sepa** Ud. |
| | sabemos | sabíamos | **supimos** | **sabremos** | **sabríamos** | **sepamos** | **supiéramos** | **sepamos** |
| | sabéis | sabíais | **supisteis** | **sabréis** | **sabríais** | **sepáis** | **supierais** | sabed (no **sepáis**) |
| | saben | sabían | **supieron** | **sabrán** | **sabrían** | **sepan** | **supieran** | **sepan** Uds. |

**18. salir**
Participles: saliendo, salido

| | INDICATIVE | | | | | SUBJUNCTIVE | | IMPERATIVE |
|---|---|---|---|---|---|---|---|---|
| | Present | Imperfect | Preterite | Future | Conditional | Present | Past | |
| | **salgo** | salía | salí | **saldré** | **saldría** | **salga** | saliera | |
| | sales | salías | saliste | **saldrás** | **saldrías** | **salgas** | salieras | **sal** tú (no **salgas**) |
| | sale | salía | salió | **saldrá** | **saldría** | **salga** | saliera | **salga** Ud. |
| | salimos | salíamos | salimos | **saldremos** | **saldríamos** | **salgamos** | saliéramos | **salgamos** |
| | salís | salíais | salisteis | **saldréis** | **saldríais** | **salgáis** | salierais | salid (no **salgáis**) |
| | salen | salían | salieron | **saldrán** | **saldrían** | **salgan** | salieran | **salgan** Uds. |

**19. ser**
Participles: siendo, sido

| | INDICATIVE | | | | | SUBJUNCTIVE | | IMPERATIVE |
|---|---|---|---|---|---|---|---|---|
| | Present | Imperfect | Preterite | Future | Conditional | Present | Past | |
| | **soy** | **era** | **fui** | seré | sería | **sea** | **fuera** | |
| | **eres** | **eras** | **fuiste** | serás | serías | **seas** | **fueras** | **sé** tú (no **seas**) |
| | **es** | **era** | **fue** | será | sería | **sea** | **fuera** | sea Ud. |
| | **somos** | **éramos** | **fuimos** | seremos | seríamos | **seamos** | **fuéramos** | **seamos** |
| | **sois** | **erais** | **fuisteis** | seréis | seríais | **seáis** | **fuerais** | sed (no **seáis**) |
| | **son** | **eran** | **fueron** | serán | serían | **sean** | **fueran** | **sean** Uds. |

**20. tener (e:ie)**
Participles: teniendo, tenido

| | INDICATIVE | | | | | SUBJUNCTIVE | | IMPERATIVE |
|---|---|---|---|---|---|---|---|---|
| | Present | Imperfect | Preterite | Future | Conditional | Present | Past | |
| | **tengo** | **tenía** | **tuve** | **tendré** | **tendría** | **tenga** | **tuviera** | |
| | **tienes** | **tenías** | **tuviste** | **tendrás** | **tendrías** | **tengas** | **tuvieras** | **ten** tú (no **tengas**) |
| | **tiene** | **tenía** | **tuvo** | **tendrá** | **tendría** | **tenga** | **tuviera** | **tenga** Ud. |
| | tenemos | **teníamos** | **tuvimos** | **tendremos** | **tendríamos** | **tengamos** | **tuviéramos** | **tengamos** |
| | tenéis | **teníais** | **tuvisteis** | **tendréis** | **tendríais** | **tengáis** | **tuvierais** | tened (no **tengáis**) |
| | **tienen** | **tenían** | **tuvieron** | **tendrán** | **tendrían** | **tengan** | **tuvieran** | **tengan** Uds. |

**21 traer**

Participles: trayendo, traído

| | INDICATIVE | | | | | SUBJUNCTIVE | | IMPERATIVE |
|---|---|---|---|---|---|---|---|---|
| Infinitive | Present | Imperfect | Preterite | Future | Conditional | Present | Past | |
| traer | traigo | traía | traje | traeré | traería | traiga | trajera | |
| | traes | traías | trajiste | traerás | traerías | traigas | trajeras | trae tú (no traigas) |
| | trae | traía | trajo | traerá | traería | traiga | trajera | traiga Ud. |
| | traemos | traíamos | trajimos | traeremos | traeríamos | traigamos | trajéramos | traigamos |
| | traéis | traíais | trajisteis | traeréis | traeríais | traigáis | trajerais | traed (no traigáis) |
| | traen | traían | trajeron | traerán | traerían | traigan | trajeran | traigan Uds. |

**22 venir (e:ie)**

Participles: viniendo, venido

| | INDICATIVE | | | | | SUBJUNCTIVE | | IMPERATIVE |
|---|---|---|---|---|---|---|---|---|
| Infinitive | Present | Imperfect | Preterite | Future | Conditional | Present | Past | |
| venir | vengo | venía | vine | vendré | vendría | venga | viniera | |
| | vienes | venías | viniste | vendrás | vendrías | vengas | vinieras | ven tú (no vengas) |
| | viene | venía | vino | vendrá | vendría | venga | viniera | venga Ud. |
| | venimos | veníamos | vinimos | vendremos | vendríamos | vengamos | viniéramos | vengamos |
| | venís | veníais | vinisteis | vendréis | vendríais | vengáis | vinierais | venid (no vengáis) |
| | vienen | venían | vinieron | vendrán | vendrían | vengan | vinieran | vengan Uds. |

**23 ver**

Participles: viendo, visto

| | INDICATIVE | | | | | SUBJUNCTIVE | | IMPERATIVE |
|---|---|---|---|---|---|---|---|---|
| Infinitive | Present | Imperfect | Preterite | Future | Conditional | Present | Past | |
| ver | veo | veía | vi | veré | vería | vea | viera | |
| | ves | veías | viste | verás | verías | veas | vieras | ve tú (no veas) |
| | ve | veía | vio | verá | vería | vea | viera | vea Ud. |
| | vemos | veíamos | vimos | veremos | veríamos | veamos | viéramos | veamos |
| | veis | veíais | visteis | veréis | veríais | veáis | vierais | ved (no veáis) |
| | ven | veían | vieron | verán | verían | vean | vieran | vean Uds. |

## Stem-changing verbs

**24 contar (o:ue)**

Participles: contando, contado

| | INDICATIVE | | | | | SUBJUNCTIVE | | IMPERATIVE |
|---|---|---|---|---|---|---|---|---|
| Infinitive | Present | Imperfect | Preterite | Future | Conditional | Present | Past | |
| contar | cuento | contaba | conté | contaré | contaría | cuente | contara | |
| | cuentas | contabas | contaste | contarás | contarías | cuentes | contaras | cuenta tú (no cuentes) |
| | cuenta | contaba | contó | contará | contaría | cuente | contara | cuente Ud. |
| | contamos | contábamos | contamos | contaremos | contaríamos | contemos | contáramos | contemos |
| | contáis | contabais | contasteis | contaréis | contaríais | contéis | contarais | contad (no contéis) |
| | cuentan | contaban | contaron | contarán | contarían | cuenten | contaran | cuenten Uds. |

**25 dormir (o:ue)**

Participles: durmiendo, dormido

| | INDICATIVE | | | | | SUBJUNCTIVE | | IMPERATIVE |
|---|---|---|---|---|---|---|---|---|
| Infinitive | Present | Imperfect | Preterite | Future | Conditional | Present | Past | |
| dormir | duermo | dormía | dormí | dormiré | dormiría | duerma | durmiera | |
| | duermes | dormías | dormiste | dormirás | dormirías | duermas | durmieras | duerme tú (no duermas) |
| | duerme | dormía | durmió | dormirá | dormiría | duerma | durmiera | duerma Ud. |
| | dormimos | dormíamos | dormimos | dormiremos | dormiríamos | durmamos | durmiéramos | durmamos |
| | dormís | dormíais | dormisteis | dormiréis | dormiríais | durmáis | durmierais | dormid (no durmáis) |
| | duermen | dormían | durmieron | dormirán | dormirían | duerman | durmieran | duerman Uds. |

**26 empezar (e:ie) (z:c)**

Participles: empezando, empezado

| | INDICATIVE | | | | | SUBJUNCTIVE | | IMPERATIVE |
|---|---|---|---|---|---|---|---|---|
| Infinitive | Present | Imperfect | Preterite | Future | Conditional | Present | Past | |
| empezar | empiezo | empezaba | empecé | empezaré | empezaría | empiece | empezara | |
| | empiezas | empezabas | empezaste | empezarás | empezarías | empieces | empezaras | empieza tú (no empieces) |
| | empieza | empezaba | empezó | empezará | empezaría | empiece | empezara | empiece Ud. |
| | empezamos | empezábamos | empezamos | empezaremos | empezaríamos | empecemos | empezáramos | empecemos |
| | empezáis | empezabais | empezasteis | empezaréis | empezaríais | empecéis | empezarais | empezad (no empecéis) |
| | empiezan | empezaban | empezaron | empezarán | empezarían | empiecen | empezaran | empiecen Uds. |

**27. entender (e:ie)** — Participles: entendiendo, entendido

| | INDICATIVE | | | | | SUBJUNCTIVE | | IMPERATIVE |
|---|---|---|---|---|---|---|---|---|
| | Present | Imperfect | Preterite | Future | Conditional | Present | Past | |
| | entiendo | entendía | entendí | entenderé | entendería | entienda | entendiera | |
| | entiendes | entendías | entendiste | entenderás | entenderías | entiendas | entendieras | entiende tú (no entiendas) |
| | entiende | entendía | entendió | entenderá | entendería | entienda | entendiera | entienda Ud. |
| | entendemos | entendíamos | entendimos | entenderemos | entenderíamos | entendamos | entendiéramos | entendamos |
| | entendéis | entendíais | entendisteis | entenderéis | entenderíais | entendáis | entendierais | entended (no entendáis) |
| | entienden | entendían | entendieron | entenderán | entenderían | entiendan | entendieran | entiendan Uds. |

**28. jugar (u:ue) (g:gu)** — Participles: jugando, jugado

| | INDICATIVE | | | | | SUBJUNCTIVE | | IMPERATIVE |
|---|---|---|---|---|---|---|---|---|
| | Present | Imperfect | Preterite | Future | Conditional | Present | Past | |
| | juego | jugaba | jugué | jugaré | jugaría | juegue | jugara | |
| | juegas | jugabas | jugaste | jugarás | jugarías | juegues | jugaras | juega tú (no juegues) |
| | juega | jugaba | jugó | jugará | jugaría | juegue | jugara | juegue Ud. |
| | jugamos | jugábamos | jugamos | jugaremos | jugaríamos | juguemos | jugáramos | juguemos |
| | jugáis | jugabais | jugasteis | jugaréis | jugaríais | juguéis | jugarais | jugad (no juguéis) |
| | juegan | jugaban | jugaron | jugarán | jugarían | jueguen | jugaran | jueguen Uds. |

**29. pedir (e:i)** — Participles: pidiendo, pedido

| | INDICATIVE | | | | | SUBJUNCTIVE | | IMPERATIVE |
|---|---|---|---|---|---|---|---|---|
| | Present | Imperfect | Preterite | Future | Conditional | Present | Past | |
| | pido | pedía | pedí | pediré | pediría | pida | pidiera | |
| | pides | pedías | pediste | pedirás | pedirías | pidas | pidieras | pide tú (no pidas) |
| | pide | pedía | pidió | pedirá | pediría | pida | pidiera | pida Ud. |
| | pedimos | pedíamos | pedimos | pediremos | pediríamos | pidamos | pidiéramos | pidamos |
| | pedís | pedíais | pedisteis | pediréis | pediríais | pidáis | pidierais | pedid (no pidáis) |
| | piden | pedían | pidieron | pedirán | pedirían | pidan | pidieran | pidan Uds. |

**30. pensar (e:ie)** — Participles: pensando, pensado

| | INDICATIVE | | | | | SUBJUNCTIVE | | IMPERATIVE |
|---|---|---|---|---|---|---|---|---|
| | Present | Imperfect | Preterite | Future | Conditional | Present | Past | |
| | pienso | pensaba | pensé | pensaré | pensaría | piense | pensara | |
| | piensas | pensabas | pensaste | pensarás | pensarías | pienses | pensaras | piensa tú (no pienses) |
| | piensa | pensaba | pensó | pensará | pensaría | piense | pensara | piense Ud. |
| | pensamos | pensábamos | pensamos | pensaremos | pensaríamos | pensemos | pensáramos | pensemos |
| | pensáis | pensabais | pensasteis | pensaréis | pensaríais | penséis | pensarais | pensad (no penséis) |
| | piensan | pensaban | pensaron | pensarán | pensarían | piensen | pensaran | piensen Uds. |

**31. reír(se) (e:i)** — Participles: riendo, reído

| | INDICATIVE | | | | | SUBJUNCTIVE | | IMPERATIVE |
|---|---|---|---|---|---|---|---|---|
| | Present | Imperfect | Preterite | Future | Conditional | Present | Past | |
| | río | reía | reí | reiré | reiría | ría | riera | |
| | ríes | reías | reíste | reirás | reirías | rías | rieras | ríe tú (no rías) |
| | ríe | reía | rió | reirá | reiría | ría | riera | ría Ud. |
| | reímos | reíamos | reímos | reiremos | reiríamos | riamos | riéramos | riamos |
| | reís | reíais | reísteis | reiréis | reiríais | riáis | rierais | reíd (no riáis) |
| | ríen | reían | rieron | reirán | reirían | rían | rieran | rían Uds. |

**32. seguir (e:i) (gu:g)** — Participles: siguiendo, seguido

| | INDICATIVE | | | | | SUBJUNCTIVE | | IMPERATIVE |
|---|---|---|---|---|---|---|---|---|
| | Present | Imperfect | Preterite | Future | Conditional | Present | Past | |
| | sigo | seguía | seguí | seguiré | seguiría | siga | siguiera | |
| | sigues | seguías | seguiste | seguirás | seguirías | sigas | siguieras | sigue tú (no sigas) |
| | sigue | seguía | siguió | seguirá | seguiría | siga | siguiera | siga Ud. |
| | seguimos | seguíamos | seguimos | seguiremos | seguiríamos | sigamos | siguiéramos | sigamos |
| | seguís | seguíais | seguisteis | seguiréis | seguiríais | sigáis | siguierais | seguid (no sigáis) |
| | siguen | seguían | siguieron | seguirán | seguirían | sigan | siguieran | sigan Uds. |

**33. sentir (e:ie)** — Participles: sintiendo, sentido

| | INDICATIVE | | | | | SUBJUNCTIVE | | IMPERATIVE |
|---|---|---|---|---|---|---|---|---|
| | Present | Imperfect | Preterite | Future | Conditional | Present | Past | |
| | siento | sentía | sentí | sentiré | sentiría | sienta | sintiera | |
| | sientes | sentías | sentiste | sentirás | sentirías | sientas | sintieras | siente tú (no sientas) |
| | siente | sentía | sintió | sentirá | sentiría | sienta | sintiera | sienta Ud. |
| | sentimos | sentíamos | sentimos | sentiremos | sentiríamos | sintamos | sintiéramos | sintamos |
| | sentís | sentíais | sentisteis | sentiréis | sentiríais | sintáis | sintierais | sentid (no sintáis) |
| | sienten | sentían | sintieron | sentirán | sentirían | sientan | sintieran | sientan Uds. |

**34** volver (o:ue) — Participles: volviendo, vuelto

| | INDICATIVE | | | | | SUBJUNCTIVE | | IMPERATIVE |
|---|---|---|---|---|---|---|---|---|
| Infinitive | Present | Imperfect | Preterite | Future | Conditional | Present | Past | |
| volver (o:ue) | **vuelvo** | volvía | volví | volveré | volvería | **vuelva** | volviera | |
| | **vuelves** | volvías | volviste | volverás | volverías | **vuelvas** | volvieras | **vuelve** tú (no **vuelvas**) |
| Participles: | **vuelve** | volvía | volvió | volverá | volvería | **vuelva** | volviera | **vuelva** Ud. |
| volviendo | volvemos | volvíamos | volvimos | volveremos | volveríamos | volvamos | volviéramos | volvamos |
| **vuelto** | volvéis | volvíais | volvisteis | volveréis | volveríais | volváis | volvierais | volved (no volváis) |
| | **vuelven** | volvían | volvieron | volverán | volverían | **vuelvan** | volvieran | **vuelvan** Uds. |

# Verbs with spelling changes only

**35** conocer (c:zc) — Participles: conociendo, conocido

| | INDICATIVE | | | | | SUBJUNCTIVE | | IMPERATIVE |
|---|---|---|---|---|---|---|---|---|
| Infinitive | Present | Imperfect | Preterite | Future | Conditional | Present | Past | |
| conocer (c:zc) | **conozco** | conocía | conocí | conoceré | conocería | **conozca** | conociera | |
| | conoces | conocías | conociste | conocerás | conocerías | **conozcas** | conocieras | conoce tú (no **conozcas**) |
| Participles: | conoce | conocía | conoció | conocerá | conocería | **conozca** | conociera | **conozca** Ud. |
| conociendo | conocemos | conocíamos | conocimos | conoceremos | conoceríamos | **conozcamos** | conociéramos | **conozcamos** |
| conocido | conocéis | conocíais | conocisteis | conoceréis | conoceríais | **conozcáis** | conocierais | conoced (no **conozcáis**) |
| | conocen | conocían | conocieron | conocerán | conocerían | **conozcan** | conocieran | **conozcan** Uds. |

**36** creer (y) — Participles: creyendo, creído

| | INDICATIVE | | | | | SUBJUNCTIVE | | IMPERATIVE |
|---|---|---|---|---|---|---|---|---|
| Infinitive | Present | Imperfect | Preterite | Future | Conditional | Present | Past | |
| creer (y) | creo | creía | **creí** | creeré | creería | crea | **creyera** | |
| | crees | creías | **creíste** | creerás | creerías | creas | **creyeras** | cree tú (no creas) |
| Participles: | cree | creía | **creyó** | creerá | creería | crea | **creyera** | crea Ud. |
| **creyendo** | creemos | creíamos | **creímos** | creeremos | creeríamos | creamos | **creyéramos** | creamos |
| **creído** | creéis | creíais | **creísteis** | creeréis | creeríais | creáis | **creyerais** | creed (no creáis) |
| | creen | creían | **creyeron** | creerán | creerían | crean | **creyeran** | crean Uds. |

**37** cruzar (z:c) — Participles: cruzando, cruzado

| | INDICATIVE | | | | | SUBJUNCTIVE | | IMPERATIVE |
|---|---|---|---|---|---|---|---|---|
| Infinitive | Present | Imperfect | Preterite | Future | Conditional | Present | Past | |
| cruzar (z:c) | cruzo | cruzaba | **crucé** | cruzaré | cruzaría | **cruce** | cruzara | |
| | cruzas | cruzabas | cruzaste | cruzarás | cruzarías | **cruces** | cruzaras | cruza tú (no **cruces**) |
| Participles: | cruza | cruzaba | cruzó | cruzará | cruzaría | **cruce** | cruzara | **cruce** Ud. |
| cruzando | cruzamos | cruzábamos | cruzamos | cruzaremos | cruzaríamos | **crucemos** | cruzáramos | **crucemos** |
| cruzado | cruzáis | cruzabais | cruzasteis | cruzaréis | cruzaríais | **crucéis** | cruzarais | cruzad (no **crucéis**) |
| | cruzan | cruzaban | cruzaron | cruzarán | cruzarían | **crucen** | cruzaran | **crucen** Uds. |

**38** destruir (y) — Participles: destruyendo, destruido

| | INDICATIVE | | | | | SUBJUNCTIVE | | IMPERATIVE |
|---|---|---|---|---|---|---|---|---|
| Infinitive | Present | Imperfect | Preterite | Future | Conditional | Present | Past | |
| destruir (y) | **destruyo** | destruía | destruí | destruiré | destruiría | **destruya** | **destruyera** | |
| | **destruyes** | destruías | destruiste | destruirás | destruirías | **destruyas** | **destruyeras** | **destruye** tú (no **destruyas**) |
| Participles: | **destruye** | destruía | **destruyó** | destruirá | destruiría | **destruya** | **destruyera** | **destruya** Ud. |
| **destruyendo** | destruimos | destruíamos | destruimos | destruiremos | destruiríamos | **destruyamos** | **destruyéramos** | **destruyamos** |
| destruido | destruís | destruíais | destruisteis | destruiréis | destruiríais | **destruyáis** | **destruyerais** | destruid (no **destruyáis**) |
| | **destruyen** | destruían | **destruyeron** | destruirán | destruirían | **destruyan** | **destruyeran** | **destruyan** Uds. |

**39** enviar (envío) — Participles: enviando, enviado

| | INDICATIVE | | | | | SUBJUNCTIVE | | IMPERATIVE |
|---|---|---|---|---|---|---|---|---|
| Infinitive | Present | Imperfect | Preterite | Future | Conditional | Present | Past | |
| enviar (envío) | **envío** | enviaba | envié | enviaré | enviaría | **envíe** | enviara | |
| | **envías** | enviabas | enviaste | enviarás | enviarías | **envíes** | enviaras | **envía** tú (no **envíes**) |
| Participles: | **envía** | enviaba | envió | enviará | enviaría | **envíe** | enviara | **envíe** Ud. |
| enviando | enviamos | enviábamos | enviamos | enviaremos | enviaríamos | enviemos | enviáramos | enviemos |
| enviado | enviáis | enviabais | enviasteis | enviaréis | enviaríais | enviéis | enviarais | enviad (no enviéis) |
| | **envían** | enviaban | enviaron | enviarán | enviarían | **envíen** | enviaran | **envíen** Uds. |

| Infinitive | INDICATIVE | | | | | SUBJUNCTIVE | | IMPERATIVE |
|---|---|---|---|---|---|---|---|---|
| | Present | Imperfect | Preterite | Future | Conditional | Present | Past | |
| **40** graduarse (gradúo) | gradúo | graduaba | gradué | graduaré | graduaría | gradúe | graduara | |
| | gradúas | graduabas | graduaste | graduarás | graduarías | gradúes | graduaras | gradúa tú (no gradúes) |
| | gradúa | graduaba | graduó | graduará | graduaría | gradúe | graduara | gradúe Ud. |
| **Participles:** | graduamos | graduábamos | graduamos | graduaremos | graduaríamos | graduemos | graduáramos | graduemos |
| graduando | graduáis | graduabais | graduasteis | graduaréis | graduaríais | graduéis | graduarais | graduad (no graduéis) |
| graduado | gradúan | graduaban | graduaron | graduarán | graduarían | gradúen | graduaran | gradúen Uds. |
| **41** llegar (g:gu) | llego | llegaba | llegué | llegaré | llegaría | llegue | llegara | |
| | llegas | llegabas | llegaste | llegarás | llegarías | llegues | llegaras | llega tú (no llegues) |
| | llega | llegaba | llegó | llegará | llegaría | llegue | llegara | llegue Ud. |
| **Participles:** | llegamos | llegábamos | llegamos | llegaremos | llegaríamos | lleguemos | llegáramos | lleguemos |
| llegando | llegáis | llegabais | llegasteis | llegaréis | llegaríais | lleguéis | llegarais | llegad (no lleguéis) |
| llegado | llegan | llegaban | llegaron | llegarán | llegarían | lleguen | llegaran | lleguen Uds. |
| **42** proteger (g:j) | protejo | protegía | protegí | protegeré | protegería | proteja | protegiera | |
| | proteges | protegías | protegiste | protegerás | protegerías | protejas | protegieras | protege tú (no protejas) |
| | protege | protegía | protegió | protegerá | protegería | proteja | protegiera | proteja Ud. |
| **Participles:** | protegemos | protegíamos | protegimos | protegeremos | protegeríamos | protejamos | protegiéramos | protejamos |
| protegiendo | protegéis | protegíais | protegisteis | protegeréis | protegeríais | protejáis | protegierais | proteged (no protejáis) |
| protegido | protegen | protegían | protegieron | protegerán | protegerían | protejan | protegieran | protejan Uds. |
| **43** tocar (c:qu) | toco | tocaba | toqué | tocaré | tocaría | toque | tocara | |
| | tocas | tocabas | tocaste | tocarás | tocarías | toques | tocaras | toca tú (no toques) |
| | toca | tocaba | tocó | tocará | tocaría | toque | tocara | toque Ud. |
| **Participles:** | tocamos | tocábamos | tocamos | tocaremos | tocaríamos | toquemos | tocáramos | toquemos |
| tocando | tocáis | tocabais | tocasteis | tocaréis | tocaríais | toquéis | tocarais | tocad (no toquéis) |
| tocado | tocan | tocaban | tocaron | tocarán | tocarían | toquen | tocaran | toquen Uds. |

# Guide to Vocabulary

## Note on alphabetization

For purposes of alphabetization, **ch** and **ll** are not treated as separate letters, but **ñ** follows **n**. Therefore, in this glossary you will find that **año**, for example, appears after **anuncio**.

## Abbreviations used in this glossary

| | | | | | |
|---|---|---|---|---|---|
| *adj.* | adjective | *form.* | formal | *pl.* | plural |
| *adv.* | adverb | *indef.* | indefinite | *poss.* | possessive |
| *art.* | article | *interj.* | interjection | *prep.* | preposition |
| *conj.* | conjunction | *i.o.* | indirect object | *pron.* | pronoun |
| *def.* | definite | *m.* | masculine | *ref.* | reflexive |
| *d.o.* | direct object | *n.* | noun | *sing.* | singular |
| *f.* | feminine | *obj.* | object | *sub.* | subject |
| *fam.* | familiar | *p.p.* | past participle | *v.* | verb |

## Spanish-English

### A

**a** *prep.* at; to 1
  **¿A qué hora...?** At what time...? 1
  **a bordo** aboard 1
  **a dieta** on a diet 15
  **a la derecha** to the right 2
  **a la izquierda** to the left 2
  **a la plancha** grilled 8
  **a la(s)** + *time* at + *time* 1
  **a menos que** unless 13
  **a menudo** *adv.* often 10
  **a nombre de** in the name of 5
  **a plazos** in installments 14
  **A sus órdenes.** At your service. 11
  **a tiempo** *adv.* on time 10
  **a veces** *adv.* sometimes 10
  **a ver** let's see 2
**¡Abajo!** *adv.* Down! 15
**abeja** *f.* bee
**abierto/a** *adj.* open 5, 14
**abogado/a** *m., f.* lawyer
**abrazar(se)** *v.* to hug; to embrace (each other) 11
**abrazo** *m.* hug
**abrigo** *m.* coat 6
**abril** *m.* April 5
**abrir** *v.* to open 3
**abuelo/a** *m., f.* grandfather; grandmother 3
**abuelos** *pl.* grandparents 3
**aburrido/a** *adj.* bored; boring 5
**aburrir** *v.* to bore 7
**aburrirse** *v.* to get bored
**acabar de (+ inf.)** *v.* to have just done something 6
**acampar** *v.* to camp 5
**accidente** *m.* accident 10
**acción** *f.* action

  **de acción** action (genre)
**aceite** *m.* oil 8
**ácido/a** *adj.* acid 13
**acompañar** *v.* to go with; to accompany 14
**aconsejar** *v.* to advise 12
**acontecimiento** *m.* event
**acordarse (de) (o:ue)** *v.* to remember 7
**acostarse (o:ue)** *v.* to go to bed 7
**activo/a** *adj.* active 15
**actor** *m.* actor
**actriz** *f.* actor, actress
**actualidades** *f., pl.* news; current events
**acuático/a** *adj.* aquatic 4
**adelgazar** *v.* to lose weight; to slim down 15
**además (de)** *adv.* furthermore; besides 10
**adicional** *adj.* additional
**adiós** *m.* good-bye 1
**adjetivo** *m.* adjective
**administración de empresas** *f.* business administration 2
**adolescencia** *f.* adolescence 9
**¿adónde?** *adv.* where (to)? (destination) 2
**aduana** *f.* customs 5
**aeróbico/a** *adj.* aerobic 15
**aeropuerto** *m.* airport 5
**afectado/a** *adj.* affected 13
**afeitarse** *v.* to shave 7
**aficionado/a** *adj.* fan 4
**afirmativo/a** *adj.* affirmative
**afueras** *f., pl.* suburbs; outskirts 12
**agencia de viajes** *f.* travel agency 5
**agente de viajes** *m., f.* travel agent 5
**agosto** *m.* August 5
**agradable** *adj.* pleasant
**agua** *f.* water 8

  **agua mineral** mineral water 8
**ahora** *adv.* now 2
  **ahora mismo** right now 5
**ahorrar** *v.* to save (money) 14
**ahorros** *m.* savings 14
**aire** *m.* air 5
**ajo** *m.* garlic 8
**al** (*contraction of* **a + el**) 2
  **al aire libre** open-air 6
  **al contado** in cash 14
  **(al) este** (to the) east 14
  **al fondo (de)** at the end (of) 12
  **al lado de** beside 2
  **(al) norte** (to the) north 14
  **(al) oeste** (to the) west 14
  **(al) sur** (to the) south 14
**alcoba** *f.* bedroom 12
**alcohol** *m.* alcohol 15
**alcohólico/a** *adj.* alcoholic 15
**alegrarse (de)** *v.* to be happy 13
**alegre** *adj.* happy; joyful 5
**alegría** *f.* happiness 9
**alemán, alemana** *adj.* German 3
**alérgico/a** *adj.* allergic 10
**alfombra** *f.* carpet; rug 12
**algo** *pron.* something; anything 7
**algodón** *m.* cotton 6
**alguien** *pron.* someone; somebody; anyone 7
**algún, alguno/a(s)** *adj.* any; some 7
**alimento** *m.* food
  **alimentación** *f.* diet
**aliviar** *v.* to reduce 15
  **aliviar el estrés/la tensión** to reduce stress/tension 15
**allí** *adv.* there 5
  **allí mismo** right there 14
**almacén** *m.* department store 6
**almohada** *f.* pillow 12
**almorzar (o:ue)** *v.* to have lunch 4
**almuerzo** *m.* lunch 8

**aló** *interj.* hello (*on the telephone*) **11**
**alquilar** *v.* to rent **12**
**alquiler** *m.* rent (payment) **12**
**alternador** *m.* alternator **11**
**altillo** *m.* attic **12**
**alto/a** *adj.* tall **3**
**aluminio** *m.* aluminum **13**
**ama de casa** *m., f.* housekeeper; caretaker **12**
**amable** *adj.* nice; friendly **5**
**amarillo/a** *adj.* yellow **6**
**amigo/a** *m., f.* friend **3**
**amistad** *f.* friendship **9**
**amor** *m.* love **9**
**anaranjado/a** *adj.* orange **6**
**andar** *v.* **en patineta** to skateboard **4**
**animal** *m.* animal **13**
**aniversario (de bodas)** *m.* (wedding) anniversary **9**
**anoche** *adv.* last night **6**
**anteayer** *adv.* the day before yesterday **6**
**antes** *adv.* before **7**
  **antes (de) que** *conj.* before **13**
  **antes de** *prep.* before **7**
**antibiótico** *m.* antibiotic **10**
**antipático/a** *adj.* unpleasant **3**
**anunciar** *v.* to announce; to advertise
**anuncio** *m.* advertisement
**año** *m.* year **5**
  **año pasado** last year **6**
**apagar** *v.* to turn off **11**
**aparato** *m.* appliance
**apartamento** *m.* apartment **12**
**apellido** *m.* last name **3**
**apenas** *adv.* hardly; scarcely **10**
**aplaudir** *v.* to applaud
**apreciar** *v.* to appreciate
**aprender (a + *inf.*)** *v.* to learn **3**
**apurarse** *v.* to hurry; to rush **15**
**aquel, aquella** *adj.* that; those (over there) **6**
**aquél, aquélla** *pron.* that; those (over there) **6**
**aquello** *neuter, pron.* that; that thing; that fact **6**
**aquellos/as** *pl. adj.* those (over there) **6**
**aquéllos/as** *pl. pron.* those (ones) (over there) **6**
**aquí** *adv.* here **1**
  **Aquí está...** Here it is... **5**
  **Aquí estamos en...** Here we are at/in... **2**
  **aquí mismo** right here **11**
**árbol** *m.* tree **13**
**archivo** *m.* file **11**
**armario** *m.* closet **12**
**arqueólogo/a** *m., f.* archaeologist
**arquitecto/a** *m., f.* architect
**arrancar** *v.* to start (*a car*) **11**

**arreglar** *v.* to fix; to arrange **11**; to neaten; to straighten up **12**
**arriba** *adv.* up
**arroba** *f.* @ symbol **11**
**arroz** *m.* rice **8**
**arte** *m.* art **2**
**artes** *f., pl.* arts
**artesanía** *f.* craftsmanship; crafts
**artículo** *m.* article
**artista** *m., f.* artist **3**
**artístico/a** *adj.* artistic
**arveja** *m.* pea **8**
**asado/a** *adj.* roast **8**
**ascenso** *m.* promotion
**ascensor** *m.* elevator **5**
**así** *adv.* like this; so (*in such a way*) **10**
  **así así** so so
**asistir (a)** *v.* to attend **3**
**aspiradora** *f.* vacuum cleaner **12**
**aspirante** *m., f.* candidate; applicant
**aspirina** *f.* aspirin **10**
**atún** *m.* tuna **8**
**aumentar** *v.* **de peso** to gain weight **15**
**aumento** *m.* increase
  **aumento de sueldo** pay raise
**aunque** although
**autobús** *m.* bus **1**
**automático/a** *adj.* automatic
**auto(móvil)** *m.* auto(mobile) **5**
**autopista** *f.* highway **11**
**ave** *f.* bird **13**
**avenida** *f.* avenue
**aventura** *f.* adventure
  **de aventura** adventure (genre)
**avergonzado/a** *adj.* embarrassed **5**
**avión** *m.* airplane **5**
**¡Ay!** *interj.* Oh!
  **¡Ay, qué dolor!** Oh, what pain!
**ayer** *adv.* yesterday **6**
**ayudar(se)** *v.* to help (each other) **11, 12**
**azúcar** *m.* sugar **8**
**azul** *adj. m., f.* blue **6**

**B**

**bailar** *v.* to dance **2**
**bailarín/bailarina** *m., f.* dancer
**baile** *m.* dance
**bajar(se) de** *v.* to get off of/out of (a vehicle) **11**
**bajo/a** *adj.* short (*in height*) **3**
**bajo control** under control **7**
**balcón** *m.* balcony **12**
**baloncesto** *m.* basketball **4**
**banana** *f.* banana **8**
**banco** *m.* bank **14**

**banda** *f.* band
**bandera** *f.* flag
**bañarse** *v.* to bathe; to take a bath **7**
**baño** *m.* bathroom **7**
**barato/a** *adj.* cheap **6**
**barco** *m.* boat **5**
**barrer** *v.* to sweep **12**
  **barrer el suelo** *v.* to sweep the floor **12**
**barrio** *m.* neighborhood **12**
**bastante** *adv.* enough; rather **10**; pretty **13**
**basura** *f.* trash **12**
**baúl** *m.* trunk **11**
**beber** *v.* to drink **3**
**bebida** *f.* drink **8**
  **bebida alcohólica** *f.* alcoholic beverage **15**
**béisbol** *m.* baseball **4**
**bellas artes** *f., pl.* fine arts
**belleza** *f.* beauty **14**
**beneficio** *m.* benefit
**besar(se)** *v.* to kiss (each other) **11**
**beso** *m.* kiss **9**
**biblioteca** *f.* library **2**
**bicicleta** *f.* bicycle **4**
**bien** *adj.* well **1**
**bienestar** *m.* well-being **15**
**bienvenido(s)/a(s)** *adj.* welcome **12**
**billete** *m.* paper money; ticket
**billón** *m.* trillion
**biología** *f.* biology **2**
**bisabuelo/a** *m., f.* great-grandfather/great-grandmother **3**
**bistec** *m.* steak **8**
**bizcocho** *m.* biscuit
**blanco/a** *adj.* white **6**
**bluejeans** *m., pl.* jeans **6**
**blusa** *f.* blouse **6**
**boca** *f.* mouth **10**
**boda** *f.* wedding **9**
**boleto** *m.* ticket
**bolsa** *f.* purse, bag **6**
**bombero/a** *m., f.* firefighter
**bonito/a** *adj.* pretty **3**
**borrador** *m.* eraser **2**
**borrar** *v.* to erase **11**
**bosque** *m.* forest **13**
  **bosque tropical** tropical forest; rainforest **13**
**bota** *f.* boot **6**
**botella** *f.* bottle **9**
  **botella de vino** bottle of wine **9**
**botones** *m., f. sing.* bellhop **5**
**brazo** *m.* arm **10**
**brindar** *v.* to toast (*drink*) **9**
**bucear** *v.* to scuba dive **4**
**bueno** *adv.* well **2**
**buen, bueno/a** *adj.* good **3, 6**
  **¡Buen viaje!** Have a good trip! **1**
  **buena forma** good shape (*physical*) **15**

**Buena idea.** Good idea. 4
**Buenas noches.** Good evening; Good night. 1
**Buenas tardes.** Good afternoon. 1
**buenísimo/a** extremely good
**¿Bueno?** Hello. (*on telephone*) 11
**Buenos días.** Good morning. 1
**bulevar** *m.* boulevard
**buscar** *v.* to look for 2
**buzón** *m.* mailbox 14

## C

**caballo** *m.* horse 5
**cabaña** *f.* cabin 5
**cabe: no cabe duda de** there's no doubt 13
**cabeza** *f.* head 10
**cada** *adj. m., f.* each 6
**caerse** *v.* to fall (down) 10
**café** *m.* café 4; *adj. m., f.* brown 6; *m.* coffee 8
**cafeína** *f.* caffeine 14
**cafetera** *f.* coffee maker 12
**cafetería** *f.* cafeteria 2
**caído/a** *p.p.* fallen 14
**caja** *f.* cash register 6
**cajero/a** *m., f.* cashier 14
    **cajero automático** *m.* ATM 14
**calcetín (calcetines)** *m.* sock(s) 6
**calculadora** *f.* calculator 11
**caldo** *m.* soup 8
    **caldo de patas** *m.* beef soup 8
**calentarse (e:ie)** *v.* to warm up 15
**calidad** *f.* quality 6
**calle** *f.* street 11
**calor** *m.* heat 4
**caloría** *f.* calorie 15
**calzar** *v.* to take size... shoes 6
**cama** *f.* bed 5
**cámara digital** *f.* digital camera 11
**cámara de video** *f.* video camera 11
**camarero/a** *m., f.* waiter/ waitress 8
**camarón** *m.* shrimp 8
**cambiar (de)** *v.* to change 9
**cambio** *m.* **de moneda** currency exchange
**caminar** *v.* to walk 2
**camino** *m.* road
**camión** *m.* truck; bus
**camisa** *f.* shirt 6
**camiseta** *f.* t-shirt 6
**campo** *m.* countryside 5
**canadiense** *adj.* Canadian 3
**canal** *m.* (TV) channel 11
**canción** *f.* song
**candidato/a** *m., f.* candidate
**cansado/a** *adj.* tired 5
**cantante** *m., f.* singer

**cantar** *v.* to sing 2
**capital** *f.* capital city 1
**capó** *m.* hood 11
**cara** *f.* face 7
**caramelo** *m.* caramel 9
**carne** *f.* meat 8
    **carne de res** *f.* beef 8
**carnicería** *f.* butcher shop 14
**caro/a** *adj.* expensive 6
**carpintero/a** *m., f.* carpenter
**carrera** *f.* career
**carretera** *f.* highway 11
**carro** *m.* car; automobile 11
**carta** *f.* letter 4; *(playing)* card 5
**cartel** *m.* poster 12
**cartera** *f.* wallet 6
**cartero** *m.* mail carrier 14
**casa** *f.* house; home 2
**casado/a** *adj.* married 9
**casarse (con)** *v.* to get married (to) 9
**casi** *adv.* almost 10
**catorce** *adj.* fourteen 1
**cazar** *v.* to hunt 13
**cebolla** *f.* onion 8
**cederrón** *m.* CD-ROM 11
**celebrar** *v.* to celebrate 9
**celular** *adj.* cellular 11
**cena** *f.* dinner 8
**cenar** *v.* to have dinner 2
**centro** *m.* downtown 4
    **centro comercial** shopping mall 6
**cepillarse los dientes/el pelo** *v.* to brush one's teeth/one's hair 7
**cerámica** *f.* pottery
**cerca de** *prep.* near 2
**cerdo** *m.* pork 8
**cereales** *m., pl.* cereal; grains 8
**cero** *m.* zero 1
**cerrado/a** *adj.* closed 5, 14
**cerrar (e:ie)** *v.* to close 4
**cerveza** *f.* beer 8
**césped** *m.* grass
**ceviche** *m.* marinated fish dish 8
    **ceviche de camarón** *m.* lemon-marinated shrimp 8
**chaleco** *m.* vest
**champán** *m.* champagne 9
**champiñón** *m.* mushroom 8
**champú** *m.* shampoo 7
**chaqueta** *f.* jacket 6
**chau** *fam. interj.* bye 1
**cheque** *m.* (bank) check 14
    **cheque (de viajero)** *m.* (traveler's) check 14
**chévere** *adj., fam.* terrific
**chico/a** *m., f.* boy/girl 1
**chino/a** *adj.* Chinese 3
**chocar (con)** *v.* to run into
**chocolate** *m.* chocolate 9
**choque** *m.* collision
**chuleta** *f.* chop *(food)* 8
    **chuleta de cerdo** *f.* pork chop 8

**cibercafé** *m.* cybercafé
**ciclismo** *m.* cycling 4
**cielo** *m.* sky 13
**cien(to)** one hundred 2
**ciencia** *f.* science 2
    **de ciencia ficción** *f.* science fiction (genre)
**científico/a** *m., f.* scientist
**cierto** *m.* certain 13
    **es cierto** it's certain 13
    **no es cierto** it's not certain 13
**cinco** five 1
**cincuenta** fifty 2
**cine** *m.* movie theater 4
**cinta** *f.* (audio)tape
**cinta caminadora** *f.* treadmill 15
**cinturón** *m.* belt 6
**circulación** *f.* traffic 11
**cita** *f.* date; appointment 9
**ciudad** *f.* city 4
**ciudadano/a** *m., f.* citizen
**Claro (que sí).** *fam.* Of course.
**clase** *f.* class 2
    **clase de ejercicios aeróbicos** *f.* aerobics class 15
**clásico/a** *adj.* classical
**cliente/a** *m., f.* customer 6
**clínica** *f.* clinic 10
**cobrar** *v.* to cash (a check) 14
**coche** *m.* car; automobile 11
**cocina** *f.* kitchen; stove 12
**cocinar** *v.* to cook 12
**cocinero/a** *m., f.* cook, chef
**cofre** *m.* hood 14
**cola** *f.* line 14
**colesterol** *m.* cholesterol 15
**color** *m.* color 6
**comedia** *f.* comedy; play
**comedor** *m.* dining room 12
**comenzar (e:ie)** *v.* to begin 4
**comer** *v.* to eat 3
**comercial** *adj.* commercial; business-related
**comida** *f.* food; meal 8
**como** like; as 8
**¿cómo?** what?; how? 1
    **¿Cómo es...?** What's... like? 3
    **¿Cómo está usted?** *form.* How are you? 1
    **¿Cómo estás?** *fam.* How are you? 1
    **¿Cómo les fue...?** *pl.* How did ... go for you? 15
    **¿Cómo se llama (usted)?** *(form.)* What's your name? 1
    **¿Cómo te llamas (tú)?** *(fam.)* What's your name? 1
**cómoda** *f.* chest of drawers 12
**cómodo/a** *adj.* comfortable 5
**compañero/a de clase** *m., f.* classmate 2
**compañero/a de cuarto** *m., f.* roommate 2
**compañía** *f.* company; firm
**compartir** *v.* to share 3

**completamente** *adv.* completely
**compositor(a)** *m., f.* composer
**comprar** *v.* to buy 2
**compras** *f., pl.* purchases 5
  **ir de compras** go shopping 5
**comprender** *v.* to understand 3
**comprobar** *v.* to check
**comprometerse (con)** *v.* to get engaged (to) 9
**computación** *f.* computer science 2
**computadora** *f.* computer 1
**computadora portátil** *f.* portable computer; laptop 11
**comunicación** *f.* communication
**comunicarse (con)** *v.* to communicate (with)
**comunidad** *f.* community 1
**con** *prep.* with 2
  **Con él/ella habla.** This is he/she. (*on telephone*) 11
  **con frecuencia** *adv.* frequently 10
  **Con permiso.** Pardon me; Excuse me. 1
  **con tal (de) que** provided (that) 13
**concierto** *m.* concert
**concordar** *v.* to agree
**concurso** *m.* game show; contest
**conducir** *v.* to drive 6, 11
**conductor(a)** *m., f.* driver 1
**confirmar** *v.* to confirm 5
**confirmar** *v.* **una reservación** *f.* to confirm a reservation 5
**confundido/a** *adj.* confused 5
**congelador** *m.* freezer 12
**congestionado/a** *adj.* congested; stuffed-up 10
**conmigo** *pron.* with me 4, 9
**conocer** *v.* to know; to be acquainted with 6
**conocido** *adj.; p.p.* known
**conseguir (e:i)** *v.* to get; to obtain 4
**consejero/a** *m., f.* counselor; advisor
**consejo** *m.* advice
**conservación** *f.* conservation 13
**conservar** *v.* to conserve 13
**construir** *v.* to build
**consultorio** *m.* doctor's office 10
**consumir** *v.* to consume 15
**contabilidad** *f.* accounting 2
**contador(a)** *m., f.* accountant
**contaminación** *f.* pollution 13
  **contaminación del aire/del agua** air/water pollution 13
**contaminado/a** *adj.* polluted 13
**contaminar** *v.* to pollute 13
**contar (o:ue)** *v.* to count; to tell 4
**contar (con)** *v.* to count (on) 12
**contento/a** *adj.* happy; content 5
**contestadora** *f.* answering machine 11
**contestar** *v.* to answer 2
**contigo** *fam. pron.* with you 9
**contratar** *v.* to hire
**control** *m.* control 7

**control remoto** remote control 11
**controlar** *v.* to control 13
**conversación** *f.* conversation 1
**conversar** *v.* to converse, to chat 2
**copa** *f.* wineglass; goblet 12
**corazón** *m.* heart 10
**corbata** *f.* tie 6
**corredor(a)** *m., f.* **de bolsa** stockbroker
**correo** *m.* mail; post office 14
  **correo electrónico** *m.* e-mail 4
**correr** *v.* to run 3
**cortesía** *f.* courtesy
**cortinas** *f., pl.* curtains 12
**corto/a** *adj.* short (*in length*) 6
**cosa** *f.* thing 1
**costar (o:ue)** *f.* to cost 6
**cráter** *m.* crater 13
**creer** *v.* to believe 13
  **creer (en)** *v.* to believe (in) 3
  **no creer (en)** *v.* not to believe (in) 13
**creído/a** *adj., p.p.* believed 14
**crema de afeitar** *f.* shaving cream 7
**crimen** *m.* crime; murder
**cruzar** *v.* to cross 14
**cuaderno** *m.* notebook 1
**cuadra** *f.* (city) block 14
**¿cuál(es)?** which?; which one(s)? 2
  **¿Cuál es la fecha de hoy?** What is today's date? 5
**cuadro** *m.* picture 12
**cuadros** *m., pl.* plaid 6
**cuando** when 7; 13
**¿cuándo?** when? 2
**¿cuánto(s)/a(s)?** how much/how many? 1
  **¿Cuánto cuesta...?** How much does... cost? 6
  **¿Cuántos años tienes?** How old are you? 3
**cuarenta** forty 2
**cuarto de baño** *m.* bathroom 7
**cuarto** *m.* room 2; 7
**cuarto/a** *adj.* fourth 5
  **menos cuarto** quarter to (time)
  **y cuarto** quarter after (time) 1
**cuatro** four 1
**cuatrocientos/as** four hundred 2
**cubiertos** *m., pl.* silverware
**cubierto/a** *p.p.* covered
**cubrir** *v.* to cover
**cuchara** *f.* (table or large) spoon 12
**cuchillo** *m.* knife 12
**cuello** *m.* neck 10
**cuenta** *f.* bill 9; account 14
  **cuenta corriente** *f.* checking account 14
  **cuenta de ahorros** *f.* savings account 14
**cuento** *m.* short story
**cuerpo** *m.* body 10
**cuidado** *m.* care 3
**cuidar** *v.* to take care of 13

  **¡Cuídense!** Take care! 14
**cultura** *f.* culture
**cumpleaños** *m., sing.* birthday 9
**cumplir años** *v.* to have a birthday 9
**cuñado/a** *m., f.* brother-in-law; sister-in-law 3
**currículum** *m.* résumé
**curso** *m.* course 2

## D

**danza** *f.* dance
**dañar** *v.* to damage; to break down 10
**dar** *v.* to give 6, 9
  **dar direcciones** *v.* to give directions 14
  **dar un consejo** *v.* to give advice
  **darse con** *v.* to bump into; to run into (something) 10
  **darse prisa** *v.* to hurry; to rush 15
**de** *prep.* of; from 1
  **¿De dónde eres?** *fam.* Where are you from? 1
  **¿De dónde es usted?** *form.* Where are you from? 1
  **¿De parte de quién?** Who is calling? (*on telephone*) 11
  **¿de quién...?** whose...? (*sing.*) 1
  **¿de quiénes...?** whose...? (*pl.*) 1
  **de algodón** (made) of cotton 6
  **de aluminio** (made) of aluminum 13
  **de buen humor** in a good mood 5
  **de compras** shopping 5
  **de cuadros** plaid 6
  **de excursión** hiking 4
  **de hecho** in fact
  **de ida y vuelta** roundtrip 5
  **de la mañana** in the morning; A.M. 1
  **de la noche** in the evening; at night; P.M. 1
  **de la tarde** in the afternoon; in the early evening; P.M. 1
  **de lana** (made) of wool 6
  **de lunares** polka-dotted 6
  **de mal humor** in a bad mood 5
  **de mi vida** of my life 15
  **de moda** in fashion 6
  **De nada.** You're welcome. 1
  **De ninguna manera.** No way.
  **de niño/a** as a child 10
  **de parte de** on behalf of 11
  **de plástico** (made) of plastic 13
  **de rayas** striped 6
  **de repente** suddenly 6
  **de seda** (made) of silk 6
  **de vaqueros** western (genre)
  **de vez en cuando** from time to time 10

**de vidrio** (made) of glass 13
**debajo de** *prep.* below; under 2
**deber** (+ *inf.*) *v.* should; must; ought to 3
   **Debe ser...** It must be... 6
**deber** *m.* responsibility; obligation
**debido a** due to (the fact that)
**débil** *adj.* weak 15
**decidido/a** *adj.* decided 14
**decidir** (+ *inf.*) *v.* to decide 3
**décimo/a** *adj.* tenth 5
**decir** (e:i) *v.* (**que**) to say (that); to tell (that) 4, 9
   **decir la respuesta** to say the answer 4
   **decir la verdad** to tell the truth 4
   **decir mentiras** to tell lies 4
   **decir que** to say that 4
**declarar** *v.* to declare; to say
**dedo** *m.* finger 10
**dedo del pie** *m.* toe 10
**deforestación** *f.* deforestation 13
**dejar** *v.* to let 12; to quit; to leave behind
   **dejar de** (+ *inf.*) *v.* to stop (*doing something*) 13
   **dejar una propina** *v.* to leave a tip 9
**del** (*contraction of* **de** + **el**) of the; from the
**delante de** *prep.* in front of 2
**delgado/a** *adj.* thin; slender 3
**delicioso/a** *adj.* delicious 8
**demás** *adj.* the rest
**demasiado** *adj., adv.* too much 6
**dentista** *m., f.* dentist 10
**dentro de (diez años)** within (ten years); inside
**dependiente/a** *m., f.* clerk 6
**deporte** *m.* sport 4
**deportista** *m.* sports person
**deportivo/a** *adj.* sports-related 4
**depositar** *v.* to deposit 14
**derecha** *f.* right 2
**derecho** *adj.* straight (ahead) 14
   **a la derecha de** to the right of 2
**derechos** *m., pl.* rights
**desarrollar** *v.* to develop 13
**desastre (natural)** *m.* (natural) disaster
**desayunar** *v.* to have breakfast 2
**desayuno** *m.* breakfast 8
**descafeinado/a** *adj.* decaffeinated 15
**descansar** *v.* to rest 2
**descargar** *v.* to download 11
**descompuesto/a** *adj.* not working; out of order 11
**describir** *v.* to describe 3
**descrito/a** *p.p.* described 14
**descubierto/a** *p.p.* discovered 14
**descubrir** *v.* to discover 13
**desde** *prep.* from 6
**desear** *v.* to wish; to desire 2

**desempleo** *m.* unemployment
**desierto** *m.* desert 13
**desigualdad** *f.* inequality
**desordenado/a** *adj.* disorderly 5
**despacio** *adv.* slowly 10
**despedida** *f.* farewell; good-bye
**despedir** (e:i) *v.* to fire
**despedirse (de)** (e:i) *v.* to say goodbye (to) 7
**despejado/a** *adj.* clear (*weather*)
**despertador** *m.* alarm clock 7
**despertarse** (e:ie) *v.* to wake up 7
**después** *adv.* afterwards; then 7
   **después de** after 7
   **después de que** *conj.* after 13
**destruir** *v.* to destroy 13
**detrás de** *prep.* behind 2
**día** *m.* day 1
**día de fiesta** holiday 9
**diario** *m.* diary 1; newspaper
   **diario/a** *adj.* daily 7
**dibujar** *v.* to draw 2
**dibujo** *m.* drawing
   **dibujos animados** *m., pl.* cartoons
**diccionario** *m.* dictionary 1
**dicho/a** *p.p.* said 14
**diciembre** *m.* December 5
**dictadura** *f.* dictatorship
**diecinueve** nineteen 1
**dieciocho** eighteen 1
**dieciséis** sixteen 1
**diecisiete** seventeen 1
**diente** *m.* tooth 7
**dieta** *f.* diet 15
   **comer una dieta equilibrada** to eat a balanced diet 15
**diez** ten 1
**difícil** *adj.* difficult; hard 3
**Diga.** Hello. (*on telephone*) 11
**diligencia** *f.* errand 14
**dinero** *m.* money 6
**dirección** *f.* address 14
   **dirección electrónica** *f.* e-mail address 11
**direcciones** *f., pl.* directions 14
**director(a)** *m., f.* director; (*musical*) conductor
**dirigir** *v.* to direct
**disco compacto** compact disc (CD) 11
**discriminación** *f.* discrimination
**discurso** *m.* speech
**diseñador(a)** *m., f.* designer
**diseño** *m.* design
**disfrutar (de)** *v.* to enjoy; to reap the benefits (of) 15
**diversión** *f.* fun activity; entertainment; recreation 4
**divertido/a** *adj.* fun 7
**divertirse** (e:ie) *v.* to have fun 9
**divorciado/a** *adj.* divorced 9
**divorciarse (de)** *v.* to get divorced (from) 9
**divorcio** *m.* divorce 9
**doblar** *v.* to turn 14

**doble** *adj.* double
**doce** twelve 1
**doctor(a)** *m., f.* doctor 3; 10
**documental** *m.* documentary
**documentos de viaje** *m., pl.* travel documents
**doler** (o:ue) *v.* to hurt 10
**dolor** *m.* ache; pain 10
   **dolor de cabeza** *m.* head ache 10
**doméstico/a** *adj.* domestic 12
**domingo** *m.* Sunday 2
**don/doña** *title of respect used with a person's first name* 1
**donde** *prep.* where
   **¿Dónde está...?** Where is...? 2
   **¿dónde?** where? 1
**dormir** (o:ue) *v.* to sleep 4
**dormirse** (o:ue) *v.* to go to sleep; to fall asleep 7
**dormitorio** *m.* bedroom 12
**dos** two 1
   **dos veces** *f.* twice; two times 6
**doscientos/as** two hundred 2
**drama** *m.* drama; play
**dramático/a** *adj.* dramatic
**dramaturgo/a** *m., f.* playwright
**droga** *f.* drug 15
**drogadicto/a** *adj.* drug addict 15
**ducha** *f.* shower 7
**ducharse** *v.* to shower; to take a shower 7
**duda** *f.* doubt 13
**dudar** *v.* to doubt 13
   **no dudar** *v.* not to doubt 13
**dueño/a** *m., f.* owner; landlord 8
**dulces** *m., pl.* sweets; candy 9
**durante** *prep.* during 7
**durar** *v.* to last

## E

**e** *conj.* (*used instead of* **y** *before words beginning with* **i** *and* **hi**) and 4
**echar** *v.* to throw
   **echar (una carta) al buzón** *v.* to put (a letter) in the mailbox 14; to mail 14
**ecología** *f.* ecology 13
**economía** *f.* economics 2
**ecoturismo** *m.* ecotourism 13
**Ecuador** *m.* Ecuador 1
**ecuatoriano/a** *adj.* Ecuadorian 3
**edad** *f.* age 9
**edificio** *m.* building 12
   **edificio de apartamentos** apartment building 12
**(en) efectivo** *m.* cash 6
**ejercicio** *m.* exercise 15
   **ejercicios aeróbicos** aerobic exercises 15
   **ejercicios de estiramiento** stretching exercises 15

**ejército** *m.* army
**el** *m., sing., def. art.* the 1
**él** *sub. pron.* he 1; *adj. pron.* him
**elecciones** *f., pl.* election
**electricista** *m., f.* electrician
**electrodoméstico** *m.* electric appliance 12
**elegante** *adj. m., f.* elegant 6
**elegir (e:i)** *v.* to elect
**ella** *sub. pron.* she 1; *obj. pron.* her
**ellos/as** *sub. pron.* they 1; them 1
**embarazada** *adj.* pregnant 10
**emergencia** *f.* emergency 10
**emitir** *v.* to broadcast
**emocionante** *adj. m., f.* exciting
**empezar (e:ie)** *v.* to begin 4
**empleado/a** *m., f.* employee 5
**empleo** *m.* job; employment
**empresa** *f.* company; firm
**en** *prep.* in; on; at 2
  **en casa** at home 7
  **en caso (de) que** in case (that) 13
  **en cuanto** as soon as 13
  **en efectivo** in cash 14
  **en exceso** in excess; too much 15
  **en línea** in-line 4
  **¡En marcha!** Let's get going! 15
  **en mi nombre** in my name
  **en punto** on the dot; exactly; sharp (*time*) 1
  **en qué** in what; how 2
  **¿En qué puedo servirles?** How can I help you? 5
**enamorado/a (de)** *adj.* in love (with) 5
**enamorarse (de)** *v.* to fall in love (with) 9
**encantado/a** *adj.* delighted; pleased to meet you 1
**encantar** *v.* to like very much; to love (*inanimate objects*) 7
  **¡Me encantó!** I loved it! 15
**encima de** *prep.* on top of 2
**encontrar (o:ue)** *v.* to find 4
**encontrar(se) (o:ue)** *v.* to meet (each other); to run into (each other) 11
**encuesta** *f.* poll; survey
**energía** *f.* energy 13
  **energía nuclear** nuclear energy 13
  **energía solar** solar energy 13
**enero** *m.* January 5
**enfermarse** *v.* to get sick 10
**enfermedad** *f.* illness 10
**enfermero/a** *m., f.* nurse 10
**enfermo/a** *adj.* sick 10
**enfrente de** *adv.* opposite; facing 14
**engordar** *v.* to gain weight 15
**enojado/a** *adj.* mad; angry 5
**enojarse (con)** *v.* to get angry (with) 7
**ensalada** *f.* salad 8
**enseguida** *adv.* right away 9

**enseñar** *v.* to teach 2
**ensuciar** *v.* to get (something) dirty 12
**entender (e:ie)** *v.* to understand 4
**entonces** *adv.* then 7
**entrada** *f.* entrance 12; ticket
**entre** *prep.* between; among 2
**entremeses** *m., pl.* hors d'oeuvres; appetizers 8
**entrenador(a)** *m., f.* trainer 15
**entrenarse** *v.* to practice; to train 15
**entrevista** *f.* interview
**entrevistador(a)** *m., f.* interviewer
**entrevistar** *v.* to interview
**envase** *m.* container 13
**enviar** *v.* to send; to mail 14
**equilibrado/a** *adj.* balanced 15
**equipado/a** *adj.* equipped 15
**equipaje** *m.* luggage 5
**equipo** *m.* team 4
**equivocado/a** *adj.* wrong 5
**eres** *fam.* you are 1
**es** he/she/it is 1
  **Es bueno que...** It's good that... 12
  **Es de...** He/She is from... 1
  **es extraño** it's strange 13
  **Es importante que...** It's important that... 12
  **es imposible** it's impossible 13
  **es improbable** it's improbable 13
  **Es malo que...** It's bad that... 12
  **Es mejor que...** It's better that... 12
  **Es necesario que...** It's necessary that... 12
  **es obvio** it's obvious 13
  **es ridículo** it's ridiculous 13
  **es seguro** it's sure 13
  **es terrible** it's terrible 13
  **es triste** it's sad 13
  **Es urgente que...** It's urgent that... 12
  **Es la una.** It's one o'clock. 1
  **es una lástima** it's a shame 13
  **es verdad** it's true 13
**esa(s)** *f., adj.* that; those 6
**ésa(s)** *f., pron.* that (one); those (ones) 6
**escalar** *v.* to climb 4
  **escalar montañas** *v.* to climb mountains 4
**escalera** *f.* stairs; stairway 12
**escoger** *v.* to choose 8
**escribir** *v.* to write 3
  **escribir un mensaje electrónico** to write an e-mail message 4
  **escribir una postal** to write a postcard 4
  **escribir una carta** to write a letter 4
**escrito/a** *p.p.* written 14

**escritor(a)** *m., f.* writer
**escritorio** *m.* desk 2
**escuchar** *v.* to listen to
  **escuchar la radio** to listen (to) the radio 2
  **escuchar música** to listen (to) music 2
**escuela** *f.* school 1
**esculpir** *v.* to sculpt
**escultor(a)** *m., f.* sculptor
**escultura** *f.* sculpture
**ese** *m., sing., adj.* that 6
**ése** *m., sing., pron.* that one 6
**eso** *neuter, pron.* that; that thing 6
**esos** *m., pl., adj.* those 6
**ésos** *m., pl., pron.* those (ones) 6
**España** *f.* Spain 1
**español** *m.* Spanish (*language*) 2
**español(a)** *adj. m., f.* Spanish 3
**espárragos** *m., pl.* asparagus 8
**especialización** *f.* major 2
**espectacular** *adj.* spectacular 15
**espectáculo** *m.* show
**espejo** *m.* mirror 7
**esperar** *v.* to hope; to wish 13
  **esperar (+ infin.)** *v.* to wait (for); to hope 2
**esposo/a** *m., f.* husband/wife; spouse 3
**esquí (acuático)** *m.* (water) skiing 4
**esquiar** *v.* to ski 4
**esquina** *m.* corner 14
**está** he/she/it is, you are
  **Está (muy) despejado.** It's (very) clear. (*weather*)
  **Está lloviendo.** It's raining. 5
  **Está nevando.** It's snowing. 5
  **Está (muy) nublado.** It's (very) cloudy. (*weather*) 5
  **Está bien.** That's fine. 11
**esta(s)** *f., adj.* this; these 6
  **esta noche** tonight 4
**ésta(s)** *f., pron.* this (one); these (ones) 6
  **Ésta es...** *f.* This is... (*introducing someone*) 1
**establecer** *v.* to start, to establish
**estación** *f.* station; season 5
  **estación de autobuses** bus station 5
  **estación del metro** subway station 5
  **estación de tren** train station 5
**estacionamiento** *m.* parking lot 14
**estacionar** *v.* to park 11
**estadio** *m.* stadium 2
**estado civil** *m.* marital status 9
**Estados Unidos** *m., pl.* (EE.UU.; E.U.) United States 1
**estadounidense** *adj. m., f.* from the United States 3

**estampado/a** *adj.* print
**estampilla** *f.* stamp 14
**estante** *m.* bookcase; bookshelves 12
**estar** *v.* to be 2
  **estar a (veinte kilómetros) de aquí** to be (20 kilometers) from here 11
  **estar a dieta** to be on a diet 15
  **estar aburrido/a** to be bored 5
  **estar afectado/a (por)** to be affected (by) 13
  **estar bajo control** to be under control 7
  **estar cansado/a** to be tired 5
  **estar contaminado/a** to be polluted 13
  **estar de acuerdo** to agree
    **Estoy (completamente) de acuerdo.** I agree (completely).
    **No estoy de acuerdo.** I don't agree.
  **estar de moda** to be in fashion 6
  **estar de vacaciones** *f., pl.* to be on vacation 5
  **estar en buena forma** to be in good shape 15
  **estar enfermo/a** to be sick 10
  **estar listo/a** to be ready 15
  **estar perdido/a** to be lost 14
  **estar roto/a** to be broken 10
  **estar seguro/a** to be sure 5
  **estar torcido/a** to be twisted; to be sprained 10
  **No está nada mal.** It's not bad at all. 5
**estatua** *f.* statue
**este** *m.* east 14; umm
**este** *m., sing., adj.* this 6
**éste** *m., sing., pron.* this (one) 6
  **Éste es...** *m.* This is... (*introducing someone*) 1
**estéreo** *m.* stereo 11
**estilo** *m.* style
**estiramiento** *m.* stretching 15
**esto** *neuter pron.* this; this thing 6
**estómago** *m.* stomach 10
**estornudar** *v.* to sneeze 10
**estos** *m., pl., adj.* these 6
**éstos** *m., pl., pron.* these (ones) 6
**estrella** *f.* star 13
  **estrella de cine** *m., f.* movie star
**estrés** *m.* stress 15
**estudiante** *m., f.* student 1, 2
**estudiantil** *adj. m., f.* student 2
**estudiar** *v.* to study 2
**estufa** *f.* stove 12
**estupendo/a** *adj.* stupendous 5
**etapa** *f.* stage 9
**evitar** *v.* to avoid 13
**examen** *m.* test; exam 2

**examen médico** physical exam 10
**excelente** *adj. m., f.* excellent 5
**exceso** *m.* excess; too much 15
**excursión** *f.* hike; tour; excursion
**excursionista** *m., f.* hiker
**éxito** *m.* success
**experiencia** *f.* experience
**explicar** *v.* to explain 2
**explorar** *v.* to explore
**expresión** *f.* expression
**extinción** *f.* extinction 13
**extranjero/a** *adj.* foreign
**extraño/a** *adj.* strange 13

## F

**fabuloso/a** *adj* fabulous 5
**fácil** *adj.* easy 3
**falda** *f.* skirt 6
**faltar** *v.* to lack; to need 7
**familia** *f.* family 3
**famoso/a** *adj.* famous
**farmacia** *f.* pharmacy 10
**fascinar** *v.* to fascinate 7
**favorito/a** *adj.* favorite 4
**fax** *m.* fax (machine) 11
**febrero** *m.* February 5
**fecha** *f.* date 5
**feliz** *adj.* happy 5
  **¡Felicidades!** Congratulations! (*for an event such as a birthday or anniversary*) 9
  **¡Felicitaciones!** Congratulations! (*for an event such as an engagement or a good grade on a test*) 9
  **¡Feliz cumpleaños!** Happy birthday! 9
**fenomenal** *adj.* great, phenomenal 5
**feo/a** *adj.* ugly 3
**festival** *m.* festival
**fiebre** *f.* fever 10
**fiesta** *f.* party 9
**fijo/a** *adj.* fixed, set 6
**fin** *m.* end 4
  **fin de semana** weekend 4
**finalmente** *adv.* finally 15
**firmar** *v.* to sign (*a document*) 14
**física** *f.* physics 2
**flan (de caramelo)** *m.* baked (caramel) custard 9
**flexible** *adj.* flexible 15
**flor** *f.* flower 13
**folklórico/a** *adj.* folk; folkloric
**folleto** *m.* brochure
**fondo** *m.* end 12
**forma** *f.* shape 15
**formulario** *m.* form 14
**foto(grafía)** *f.* photograph 1
**francés, francesa** *adj. m., f.* French 3
**frecuentemente** *adv.* frequently 10

**frenos** *m., pl.* brakes
**fresco/a** *adj.* cool 5
**frijoles** *m., pl.* beans 8
**frío/a** *adj.* cold 5
**frito/a** *adj.* fried 8
**fruta** *f.* fruit 8
**frutería** *f.* fruit store 14
**frutilla** *f.* strawberry 8
**fuente de fritada** *f.* platter of fried food
**fuera** *adv.* outside
**fuerte** *adj. m., f.* strong 15
**fumar** *v.* to smoke 15
  **(no) fumar** *v.* (not) to smoke 15
**funcionar** *v.* to work 11; to function
**fútbol** *m.* soccer 4
**fútbol americano** *m.* football 4
**futuro/a** *adj.* future
  **en el futuro** in the future

## G

**gafas (de sol)** *f., pl.* (sun)glasses 6
**gafas (oscuras)** *f., pl.* (sun)glasses
**galleta** *f.* cookie 9
**ganar** *v.* to win 4; to earn (money)
**ganga** *f.* bargain 6
**garaje** *m.* garage; (mechanic's) repair shop 11; garage (*in a house*) 12
**garganta** *f.* throat 10
**gasolina** *f.* gasoline 11
**gasolinera** *f.* gas station 11
**gastar** *v.* to spend (*money*) 6
**gato** *m.* cat 13
**gemelo/a** *m., f.* twin 3
**gente** *f.* people 3
**geografía** *f.* geography 2
**gerente** *m., f.* manager
**gimnasio** *m.* gymnasium 4
**gobierno** *m.* government 13
**golf** *m.* golf 4
**gordo/a** *adj.* fat 3
**grabadora** *f.* tape recorder 1
**grabar** *v.* to record 11
**gracias** *f., pl.* thank you; thanks 1
  **Gracias por todo.** Thanks for everything. 9, 15
  **Gracias una vez más.** Thanks again. 9
**graduarse (de/en)** *v.* to graduate (from/in) 9
**gran, grande** *adj.* big; large 3
**grasa** *f.* fat 15
**gratis** *adj. m., f.* free of charge 14
**grave** *adj.* grave; serious 10
**gravísimo/a** *adj.* extremely serious 13
**grillo** *m.* cricket
**gripe** *f.* flu 10
**gris** *adj. m., f.* gray 6
**gritar** *v.* to scream 7
**guantes** *m., pl.* gloves 6

**guapo/a** *adj.* handsome; good-looking 3

**guardar** *v.* to save (on a computer) 11

**guerra** *f.* war

**guía** *m., f.* guide

**gustar** *v.* to be pleasing to; to like 2
 **Me gustaría...** I would like...

**gusto** *m.* pleasure
 **El gusto es mío.** The pleasure is mine. 1
 **Gusto de verlo/la.** *(form.)* It's nice to see you.
 **Gusto de verte.** *(fam.)* It's nice to see you.
 **Mucho gusto.** Pleased to meet you. 1
 **¡Qué gusto volver a verlo/la!** *(form.)* I'm happy to see you again!
 **¡Qué gusto volver a verte!** *(fam.)* I'm happy to see you again!

### H

**haber** *(auxiliar) v.* to have (done something) 15
 **Ha sido un placer.** It's been a pleasure. 15

**habitación** *f.* room 5
 **habitación doble** double room 5
 **habitación individual** single room 5

**hablar** *v.* to talk; to speak 2

**hacer** *v.* to do; to make 4
 **Hace buen tiempo.** The weather is good. 5
 **Hace (mucho) calor.** It's (very) hot. *(weather)* 5
 **Hace fresco.** It's cool. *(weather)* 5
 **Hace (mucho) frío.** It's (very) cold. *(weather)* 5
 **Hace mal tiempo.** The weather is bad. 5
 **Hace (mucho) sol.** It's (very) sunny. *(weather)* 5
 **Hace (mucho) viento.** It's (very) windy. *(weather)* 5

**hacer cola** to stand in line 14

**hacer diligencias** to run errands 14

**hacer ejercicio** to exercise 15

**hacer ejercicios aeróbicos** to do aerobics 15

**hacer ejercicios de estiramiento** to do stretching exercises 15

**hacer el papel (de)** to play the role (of)

**hacer gimnasia** to work out 15

**hacer juego (con)** to match (with) 6

**hacer la cama** to make the bed 12

**hacer las maletas** to pack (one's) suitcases 5

**hacer quehaceres domésticos** to do household chores 12

**hacer turismo** to go sightseeing

**hacer un viaje** to take a trip 5

**hacer una excursión** to go on a hike; to go on a tour

**hacia** *prep.* toward 14

**hambre** *f.* hunger 3

**hamburguesa** *f.* hamburger 8

**hasta** *prep.* until 6; toward
 **Hasta la vista.** See you later. 1
 **Hasta luego.** See you later. 1
 **Hasta mañana.** See you tomorrow. 1
 **hasta que** until 13
 **Hasta pronto.** See you soon. 1

**hay** there is; there are 1
 **Hay (mucha) contaminación.** It's (very) smoggy.
 **Hay (mucha) niebla.** It's (very) foggy.
 **Hay que** It is necessary that 14
 **No hay duda de** There's no doubt 13
 **No hay de qué.** You're welcome. 1

**hecho/a** *p.p.* done 14

**heladería** *f.* ice cream shop 14

**helado/a** *adj.* iced 8

**helado** *m.* ice cream 9

**hermanastro/a** *m., f.* stepbrother/stepsister 3

**hermano/a** *m., f.* brother/sister 3

**hermano/a mayor/menor** *m., f.* older/younger brother/sister 3

**hermanos** *m., pl.* siblings (brothers and sisters) 3

**hermoso/a** *adj.* beautiful 6

**hierba** *f.* grass 13

**hijastro/a** *m., f.* stepson/stepdaughter 3

**hijo/a** *m., f.* son/daughter 3
 **hijo/a único/a** *m., f.* only child 3

**hijos** *m., pl.* children 3

**historia** *f.* history 2; story

**hockey** *m.* hockey 4

**hola** *interj.* hello; hi 1

**hombre** *m.* man 1
 **hombre de negocios** *m.* businessman

**hora** *f.* hour 1; the time

**horario** *m.* schedule 2

**horno** *m.* oven 12
 **horno de microondas** *m.* microwave oven 12

**horror** *m.* horror
 **de horror** horror (genre)

**hospital** *m.* hospital 10

**hotel** *m.* hotel 5

**hoy** *adv.* today 2

**hoy día** *adv.* nowadays

**Hoy es...** Today is... 2

**huelga** *f.* strike (labor)

**hueso** *m.* bone 10

**huésped** *m., f.* guest 5

**huevo** *m.* egg 8

**humanidades** *f., pl.* humanities 2

**huracán** *m.* hurricane

### I

**ida** *f.* one way (travel)

**idea** *f.* idea 4

**iglesia** *f.* church 4

**igualdad** *f.* equality

**igualmente** *adv.* likewise 1

**impermeable** *m.* raincoat 6

**importante** *adj. m., f.* important 3

**importar** *v.* to be important to; to matter 7

**imposible** *adj. m., f.* impossible 13

**impresora** *f.* printer 11

**imprimir** *v.* to print 11

**improbable** *adj. m., f.* improbable 13

**impuesto** *m.* tax

**incendio** *m.* fire

**increíble** *adj. m., f.* incredible 5

**individual** *adj.* private (room) 5

**infección** *f.* infection 10

**informar** *v.* to inform

**informe** *m.* report; paper (written work)

**ingeniero/a** *m., f.* engineer 3

**inglés** *m.* English (language) 2

**inglés, inglesa** *adj.* English 3

**inodoro** *m.* toilet 7

**insistir (en)** *v.* to insist (on) 12

**inspector(a) de aduanas** *m., f.* customs inspector 5

**inteligente** *adj. m., f.* intelligent 3

**intercambiar** *v.* to exchange

**interesante** *adj. m., f.* interesting 3

**interesar** *v.* to be interesting to; to interest 7

**internacional** *adj. m., f.* international

**Internet** Internet 11

**inundación** *f.* flood

**invertir (e:ie)** *v.* to invest

**invierno** *m.* winter 5

**invitado/a** *m., f.* guest (at a function) 9

**invitar** *v.* to invite 9

**inyección** *f.* injection 10

**ir** *v.* to go 4
 **ir a (+ inf.)** to be going to do something 4
 **ir de compras** to go shopping 5
 **ir de excursión (a las montañas)** to go for a hike (in the mountains) 4
 **ir de pesca** to go fishing

**ir de vacaciones** to go on vacation 5
**ir en autobús** to go by bus 5
**ir en auto(móvil)** to go by auto(mobile); to go by car 5
**ir en avión** to go by plane 5
**ir en barco** to go by boat 5
**ir en metro** to go by subway
**ir en motocicleta** to go by motorcycle 5
**ir en taxi** to go by taxi 5
**ir en tren** to go by train
**irse** *v.* to go away; to leave 7
**italiano/a** *adj.* Italian 3
**izquierdo/a** *adj.* left 2
**a la izquierda de** to the left of 2

## J

**jabón** *m.* soap 7
**jamás** *adv.* never; not ever 7
**jamón** *m.* ham 8
**japonés, japonesa** *adj.* Japanese 3
**jardín** *m.* garden; yard 12
**jefe, jefa** *m., f.* boss
**joven** *adj. m., f.* young 3
**joven** *m., f.* youth; young person 1
**joyería** *f.* jewelry store 14
**jubilarse** *v.* to retire (*from work*) 9
**juego** *m.* game
**jueves** *m., sing.* Thursday 2
**jugador(a)** *m., f.* player 4
**jugar (u:ue)** *v.* to play 4
**jugar a las cartas** *f., pl.* to play cards 5
**jugo** *m.* juice 8
**jugo de fruta** *m.* fruit juice 8
**julio** *m.* July 5
**jungla** *f.* jungle 13
**junio** *m.* June 5
**juntos/as** *adj.* together 9
**juventud** *f.* youth 9

## K

**kilómetro** *m.* kilometer 1

## L

**la** *f., sing., def. art.* the 1
**la** *f., sing., d.o. pron.* her, it, *form.* you 5
**laboratorio** *m.* laboratory 2
**lago** *m.* lake 13
**lámpara** *f.* lamp 12
**lana** *f.* wool 6
**langosta** *f.* lobster 8
**lápiz** *m.* pencil 1
**largo/a** *adj.* long 6
**las** *f., pl., def. art.* the 1
**las** *f., pl., d.o. pron.* them; *form.* you 5

**lástima** *f.* shame 13
**lastimarse** *v.* to injure oneself 10
**lastimarse el pie** to injure one's foot 10
**lata** *f.* (*tin*) can 13
**lavabo** *m.* sink 7
**lavadora** *f.* washing machine 12
**lavandería** *f.* laundromat 14
**lavaplatos** *m., sing.* dishwasher 12
**lavar** *v.* to wash 12
**lavar (el suelo, los platos)** to wash (the floor, the dishes) 12
**lavarse** *v.* to wash oneself 7
**lavarse la cara** to wash one's face 7
**lavarse las manos** to wash one's hands 7
**le** *sing., i.o. pron.* to/for him, her, *form.* you 6
**Le presento a…** *form.* I would like to introduce… to you. 1
**lección** *f.* lesson 1
**leche** *f.* milk 8
**lechuga** *f.* lettuce 8
**leer** *v.* to read 3
**leer correo electrónico** to read e-mail 4
**leer un periódico** to read a newspaper 4
**leer una revista** to read a magazine 4
**leído/a** *p.p.* read 14
**lejos de** *prep.* far from 2
**lengua** *f.* language 2
**lenguas extranjeras** *f., pl.* foreign languages 2
**lentes de contacto** *m., pl.* contact lenses
**lentes (de sol)** (sun)glasses
**lento/a** *adj.* slow 11
**les** *pl., i.o. pron.* to/for them, *form.* you 6
**letrero** *m.* sign 14
**levantar** *v.* to lift 15
**levantar pesas** to lift weights 15
**levantarse** *v.* to get up 7
**ley** *f.* law 13
**libertad** *f.* liberty; freedom
**libre** *adj. m., f.* free 4
**librería** *f.* bookstore 2
**libro** *m.* book 2
**licencia de conducir** *f.* driver's license 11
**limón** *m.* lemon 8
**limpiar** *v.* to clean 12
**limpiar la casa** *v.* to clean the house 12
**limpio/a** *adj.* clean 5
**línea** *f.* line 4
**listo/a** *adj.* ready; smart 5
**literatura** *f.* literature 2
**llamar** *v.* to call 11
**llamar por teléfono** to call on the phone

**llamarse** *v.* to be called; to be named 7
**llanta** *f.* tire 11
**llave** *f.* key 5
**llegada** *f.* arrival 5
**llegar** *v.* to arrive 2
**llenar** *v.* to fill 11, 14
**llenar el tanque** to fill the tank 11
**llenar (un formulario)** to fill out (a form) 14
**lleno/a** *adj.* full 11
**llevar** *v.* to carry 2; *v.* to wear; to take 6
**llevar una vida sana** to lead a healthy lifestyle 15
**llevarse bien/mal (con)** to get along well/badly (with) 9
**llover (o:ue)** *v.* to rain 5
**Llueve.** It's raining. 5
**lluvia** *f.* rain 13
**lluvia ácida** acid rain 13
**lo** *m., sing. d.o. pron.* him, it, *form.* you 5
**¡Lo hemos pasado de película!** We've had a great time!
**¡Lo hemos pasado maravillosamente!** We've had a great time!
**lo mejor** the best (thing)
**Lo pasamos muy bien.** We had a good time.
**lo peor** the worst (thing)
**lo que** that which; what 12
**Lo siento.** I'm sorry. 1
**Lo siento muchísimo.** I'm so sorry. 4
**loco/a** *adj.* crazy 6
**locutor(a)** *m., f.* (TV or radio) announcer
**lomo a la plancha** *m.* grilled flank steak 8
**los** *m., pl., def. art.* the 1
**los** *m. pl., d.o. pron.* them, *form.* you 5
**luchar (contra/por)** *v.* to fight; to struggle (against/for)
**luego** *adv.* then 7; *adv.* later 1
**lugar** *m.* place 4
**luna** *f.* moon 13
**lunares** *m.* polka dots 6
**lunes** *m., sing.* Monday 2
**luz** *f.* light; electricity 12

## M

**madrastra** *f.* stepmother 3
**madre** *f.* mother 3
**madurez** *f.* maturity; middle age 9
**maestro/a** *m., f.* teacher
**magnífico/a** *adj.* magnificent 5
**maíz** *m.* corn 8
**mal, malo/a** *adj.* bad 3
**maleta** *f.* suitcase 1

**mamá** *f.* mom 3
**mandar** *v.* to order 12; to send; to mail 14
**manejar** *v.* to drive 11
**manera** *f.* way
**mano** *f.* hand 1
**manta** *f.* blanket 12
**mantener (e:ie)** *v.* to maintain 15
  **mantenerse en forma** to stay in shape 15
**mantequilla** *f.* butter 8
**manzana** *f.* apple 8
**mañana** *f.* morning, a.m. 1; tomorrow 1
**mapa** *m.* map 2
**maquillaje** *m.* makeup 7
**maquillarse** *v.* to put on makeup 7
**mar** *m.* sea 5
**maravilloso/a** *adj.* marvelous 5
**mareado/a** *adj.* dizzy; nauseated 10
**margarina** *f.* margarine 8
**mariscos** *m., pl.* shellfish 8
**marrón** *adj. m., f.* brown 6
**martes** *m., sing.* Tuesday 2
**marzo** *m.* March 5
**más** *pron.* more 2
  **más de (+ número)** more than 8
  **más tarde** later (on) 7
  **más... que** more... than 8
**masaje** *m.* massage 15
**matemáticas** *f., pl.* mathematics 2
**materia** *f.* course 2
**matrimonio** *m.* marriage 9
**máximo/a** *adj.* maximum 11
**mayo** *m.* May 5
**mayonesa** *f.* mayonnaise 8
**mayor** *adj.* older 3
  **el/la mayor** *adj.* eldest 8; oldest
**me** *sing., d.o. pron.* me 5; *sing. i.o. pron.* to/for me 6
  **Me duele mucho.** It hurts me a lot. 10
  **Me gusta...** I like... 2
  **No me gustan nada.** I don't like them at all. 2
  **Me gustaría(n)...** I would like...
  **Me llamo...** My name is... 1
  **Me muero por...** I'm dying to (for)...
**mecánico/a** *m., f.* mechanic 11
**mediano/a** *adj.* medium
**medianoche** *f.* midnight 1
**medias** *f., pl.* pantyhose, stockings 6
**medicamento** *m.* medication 10
**medicina** *f.* medicine 10
**médico/a** *m., f.* doctor 3; *adj.* medical 10
**medio/a** *adj.* half 3
  **medio ambiente** *m.* environment 13

**medio/a hermano/a** *m., f.* half-brother/half-sister 3
**mediodía** *m.* noon 1
**medios de comunicación** *m., pl.* means of communication; media
**y media** thirty minutes past the hour (time) 1
**mejor** *adj.* better 8
  **el/la mejor** *m., f.* the best 8
**mejorar** *v.* to improve 13
**melocotón** *m.* peach 8
**menor** *adj.* younger 3
  **el/la menor** *m., f.* youngest 8
**menos** *adv.* less 10
  **menos cuarto..., menos quince...** quarter to... (time) 1
  **menos de (+ número)** fewer than 8
  **menos... que** less... than 8
**mensaje** *m.* **de texto** text message 11
**mensaje electrónico** *m.* e-mail message 4
**mentira** *f.* lie 4
**menú** *m.* menu 8
**mercado** *m.* market 6
  **mercado al aire libre** open-air market 6
**merendar (e:ie)** *v.* to snack 8; to have an afternoon snack
**merienda** *f.* afternoon snack 15
**mes** *m.* month 5
**mesa** *f.* table 2
**mesita** *f.* end table 12
  **mesita de noche** night stand 12
**metro** *m.* subway 5
**mexicano/a** *adj.* Mexican 3
**México** *m.* Mexico 1
**mí** *pron., obj. of prep.* me 8
**mi(s)** *poss. adj.* my 3
**microonda** *f.* microwave 12
  **horno de microondas** *m.* microwave oven 12
**miedo** *m.* fear 3
**mientras** *adv.* while 10
**miércoles** *m., sing.* Wednesday 2
**mil** *m.* one thousand 2
  **mil millones** billion
  **Mil perdones.** I'm so sorry. (*lit.* A thousand pardons.) 4
**milla** *f.* mile 11
**millón** *m.* million 2
**millones (de)** *m.* millions (of)
**mineral** *m.* mineral 15
**minuto** *m.* minute 1
**mío(s)/a(s)** *poss.* my; (of) mine 11
**mirar** *v.* to look (at); to watch 2
  **mirar (la) televisión** to watch television 2
**mismo/a** *adj.* same 3
**mochila** *f.* backpack 2
**moda** *f.* fashion 6
**módem** *m.* modem
**moderno/a** *adj.* modern

**molestar** *v.* to bother; to annoy 7
**monitor** *m.* (computer) monitor 11
  **monitor(a)** *m., f.* trainer
**montaña** *f.* mountain 4
**montar** *v.* **a caballo** to ride a horse 5
**monumento** *m.* monument 4
**mora** *f.* blackberry 8
**morado/a** *adj.* purple 6
**moreno/a** *adj.* brunet(te) 3
**morir (o:ue)** *v.* to die 8
**mostrar (o:ue)** *v.* to show 4
**motocicleta** *f.* motorcycle 5
**motor** *m.* motor
**muchacho/a** *m., f.* boy; girl 3
**mucho/a** *adj., adv.* a lot of; much 2; many 3
  **(Muchas) gracias.** Thank you (very much); Thanks (a lot). 1
  **muchas veces** *adv.* a lot; many times 10
  **Muchísimas gracias.** Thank you very, very much. 9
  **Mucho gusto.** Pleased to meet you. 1
**muchísimo** very much 2
**mudarse** *v.* to move (from one house to another) 12
**muebles** *m., pl.* furniture 12
**muela** *f.* tooth
**muerte** *f.* death 9
**muerto/a** *p.p.* died 14
**mujer** *f.* woman 1
  **mujer de negocios** *f.* business woman
  **mujer policía** *f.* female police officer
**multa** *f.* fine
**mundial** *adj. m., f.* worldwide
**mundo** *m.* world 13
**municipal** *adj. m., f.* municipal
**músculo** *m.* muscle 15
**museo** *m.* museum 4
**música** *f.* music 2
**musical** *adj. m., f.* musical
**músico/a** *m., f.* musician
**muy** *adv.* very 1
  **Muy amable.** That's very kind of you. 5
  **(Muy) bien, gracias.** (Very) well, thanks. 1

## N

**nacer** *v.* to be born 9
**nacimiento** *m.* birth 9
**nacional** *adj. m., f.* national
**nacionalidad** *f.* nationality 1
**nada** nothing 1; not anything 7
  **nada mal** not bad at all 5
**nadar** *v.* to swim 4
**nadie** *pron.* no one, nobody, not anyone 7
**naranja** *f.* orange 8
**nariz** *f.* nose 10
**natación** *f.* swimming 4

**natural** *adj. m., f.* natural 13
**naturaleza** *f.* nature 13
**navegar (en Internet)** *v.* to surf (the Internet) 11
**Navidad** *f.* Christmas 9
**necesario/a** *adj.* necessary 12
**necesitar (+ *inf.*)** *v.* to need 2
**negar (e:ie)** *v.* to deny 13
  **no negar (e:ie)** *v.* not to deny 13
**negativo/a** *adj.* negative
**negocios** *m., pl.* business; commerce
**negro/a** *adj.* black 6
**nervioso/a** *adj.* nervous 5
**nevar (e:ie)** *v.* to snow 5
  **Nieva.** It's snowing. 5
**ni...ni** neither... nor 7
**niebla** *f.* fog
**nieto/a** *m., f.* grandson/granddaughter 3
**nieve** *f.* snow
**ningún, ninguno/a(s)** *adj.* no; none; not any 7
**ningún problema** no problem
**niñez** *f.* childhood 9
**niño/a** *m., f.* child 3
**no** no; not 1
  **¿no?** right? 1
  **No cabe duda de...** There is no doubt... 13
  **No es así.** That's not the way it is
  **No es para tanto.** It's not a big deal. 12
  **no es seguro** it's not sure 13
  **no es verdad** it's not true 13
  **No está nada mal.** It's not bad at all. 5
  **no estar de acuerdo** to disagree
  **No estoy seguro.** I'm not sure.
  **no hay** there is not; there are not 1
  **No hay de qué.** You're welcome. 1
  **No hay duda de...** There is no doubt... 13
  **No hay problema.** No problem. 7
  **¡No me diga(s)!** You don't say! 11
  **No me gustan nada.** I don't like them at all. 2
  **no muy bien** not very well 1
  **No quiero.** I don't want to. 4
  **No sé.** I don't know.
  **No se preocupe.** (*form.*) Don't worry. 7
  **No te preocupes.** (*fam.*) Don't worry. 7
  **no tener razón** to be wrong 3
**noche** *f.* night 1
**nombre** *m.* name 1

**norte** *m.* north 14
**norteamericano/a** *adj.* (North) American 3
**nos** *pl., d.o. pron.* us 5; *pl., i.o. pron.* to/for us 6
  **Nos divertimos mucho.** We had a lot of fun.
  **Nos vemos.** See you. 1
**nosotros/as** *sub. pron.* we 1; *ob. pron.* us
**noticias** *f., pl.* news
**noticiero** *m.* newscast
**novecientos/as** nine hundred 2
**noveno/a** *adj.* ninth 5
**noventa** ninety 2
**noviembre** *m.* November 5
**novio/a** *m., f.* boyfriend/girlfriend 3
**nube** *f.* cloud 13
**nublado/a** *adj.* cloudy 5
  **Está (muy) nublado.** It's very cloudy. 5
**nuclear** *adj. m. f.* nuclear 13
**nuera** *f.* daughter-in-law 3
**nuestro(s)/a(s)** *poss. adj.* our 3; (of ours) 11
**nueve** nine 1
**nuevo/a** *adj.* new 6
**número** *m.* number 1; (shoe) size 6
**nunca** *adj.* never; not ever 7
**nutrición** *f.* nutrition 15
**nutricionista** *m., f.* nutritionist 15

**o** or 7
**o... o** ; either... or 7
**obedecer** *v.* to obey
**obra** *f.* work (*of art, literature, music, etc.*)
  **obra maestra** *f.* masterpiece
**obtener** *v.* to obtain; to get
**obvio/a** *adj.* obvious 13
**océano** *m.* ocean
**ochenta** eighty 2
**ocho** eight 1
**ochocientos/as** eight hundred 2
**octavo/a** *adj.* eighth 5
**octubre** *m.* October 5
**ocupación** *f.* occupation
**ocupado/a** *adj.* busy 5
**ocurrir** *v.* to occur; to happen
**odiar** *v.* to hate 9
**oeste** *m.* west 14
**oferta** *f.* offer 12
**oficina** *f.* office 12
**oficio** *m.* trade
**ofrecer** *v.* to offer 6
**oído** *m.* (sense of) hearing; inner ear 10
  **oído/a** *p.p.* heard 14
**oír** *v.* to hear 4

**Oiga/Oigan.** *form., sing./pl.* Listen. (*in conversation*) 1
**Oye.** *fam., sing.* Listen. (*in conversation*) 1
**ojalá (que)** *interj.* I hope (that); I wish (that) 13
**ojo** *m.* eye 10
**olvidar** *v.* to forget 10
**once** eleven 1
**ópera** *f.* opera
**operación** *f.* operation 10
**ordenado/a** *adj.* orderly 5
**ordinal** *adj.* ordinal (*number*)
**oreja** *f.* (outer) ear 10
**orquesta** *f.* orchestra
**ortografía** *f.* spelling
**ortográfico/a** *adj.* spelling
**os** *fam., pl. d.o. pron.* you 5; *fam., pl. i.o. pron.* to/for you 6
**otoño** *m.* autumn 5
**otro/a** *adj.* other; another 6
  **otra vez** again

**paciente** *m., f.* patient 10
**padrastro** *m.* stepfather 3
**padre** *m.* father 3
  **padres** *m., pl.* parents 3
**pagar** *v.* to pay 6, 9
  **pagar a plazos** to pay in installments 14
  **pagar al contado** to pay in cash 14
  **pagar en efectivo** to pay in cash 14
  **pagar la cuenta** to pay the bill 9
**página** *f.* page 11
  **página principal** *f.* home page 11
**país** *m.* country 1
**paisaje** *m.* landscape 5
**pájaro** *m.* bird 13
**palabra** *f.* word 1
**pan** *m.* bread 8
  **pan tostado** *m.* toasted bread 8
**panadería** *f.* bakery 14
**pantalla** *f.* screen 11
**pantalones** *m., pl.* pants 6
  **pantalones cortos** *m., pl.* shorts 6
**pantuflas** *f.* slippers 7
**papa** *f.* potato 8
  **papas fritas** *f., pl.* fried potatoes; French fries 8
**papá** *m.* dad 3
  **papás** *m., pl.* parents 3
**papel** *m.* paper 2; role
**papelera** *f.* wastebasket 2
**paquete** *m.* package 14
**par** *m.* pair 6
  **par de zapatos** pair of shoes 6
**para** *prep.* for; in order to; by; used for; considering 11
  **para que** so that 13

**parabrisas** *m.*, *sing.* windshield 11
**parar** *v.* to stop 11
**parecer** *v.* to seem 6
**pared** *f.* wall 12
**pareja** *f.* (married) couple; partner 9
**parientes** *m.*, *pl.* relatives 3
**parque** *m.* park 4
**párrafo** *m.* paragraph
**parte: de parte de** on behalf of 11
**partido** *m.* game; match (*sports*) 4
**pasado/a** *adj.* last; past 6
　**pasado** *p.p.* passed
**pasaje** *m.* ticket 5
　**pasaje de ida y vuelta** *m.* roundtrip ticket 5
**pasajero/a** *m.*, *f.* passenger 1
**pasaporte** *m.* passport 5
**pasar** *v.* to go through 5
　**pasar la aspiradora** to vacuum 12
　**pasar por el banco** to go by the bank 14
　**pasar por la aduana** to go through customs
　**pasar tiempo** to spend time
　**pasarlo bien/mal** to have a good/bad time 9
**pasatiempo** *m.* pastime; hobby 4
**pasear** *v.* to take a walk; to stroll 4
　**pasear en bicicleta** to ride a bicycle 4
　**pasear por** to walk around 4
**pasillo** *m.* hallway 12
**pasta** *f.* **de dientes** toothpaste 7
**pastel** *m.* cake; pie 9
　**pastel de chocolate** *m.* chocolate cake 9
　**pastel de cumpleaños** *m.* birthday cake
**pastelería** *f.* pastry shop 14
**pastilla** *f.* pill; tablet 10
**patata** *f.* potato; 8
　**patatas fritas** *f.*, *pl.* fried potatoes; French fries 8
**patinar (en línea)** *v.* to (in-line) skate 4
**patineta** *f.* skateboard 4
**patio** *m.* patio; yard 12
**pavo** *m.* turkey 8
**paz** *f.* peace
**pedir (e:i)** *v.* to ask for; to request 4; to order (*food*) 8
　**pedir prestado** *v.* to borrow 14
　**pedir un préstamo** *v.* to apply for a loan 14
**peinarse** *v.* to comb one's hair 7
**película** *f.* movie 4
**peligro** *m.* danger 13
**peligroso/a** *adj.* dangerous
**pelirrojo/a** *adj.* red-haired 3
**pelo** *m.* hair 7
**pelota** *f.* ball 4
**peluquería** *f.* beauty salon 14
**peluquero/a** *m.*, *f.* hairdresser

**penicilina** *f.* penicillin 10
**pensar (e:ie)** *v.* to think 4
　**pensar (+ inf.)** *v.* to intend to; to plan to (*do something*) 4
　**pensar en** *v.* to think about 4
**pensión** *f.* boardinghouse
**peor** *adj.* worse 8
　**el/la peor** *adj.* the worst 8
**pequeño/a** *adj.* small 3
**pera** *f.* pear 8
**perder (e:ie)** *v.* to lose; to miss 4
**perdido/a** *adj.* lost 14
**Perdón.** Pardon me.; Excuse me. 1
**perezoso/a** *adj.* lazy
**perfecto/a** *adj.* perfect 5
**periódico** *m.* newspaper 4
**periodismo** *m.* journalism 2
**periodista** *m.*, *f.* journalist 3
**permiso** *m.* permission
**pero** *conj.* but 2
**perro** *m.* dog 13
**persona** *f.* person 3
**personaje** *m.* character
　**personaje principal** *m.* main character
**pesas** *f. pl.* weights 15
**pesca** *f.* fishing
**pescadería** *f.* fish market 14
**pescado** *m.* fish (*cooked*) 8
**pescador(a)** *m.*, *f.* fisherman/ fisherwoman
**pescar** *v.* to fish 5
**peso** *m.* weight 15
**pez** *m.* fish (*live*) 13
**pie** *m.* foot 10
**piedra** *f.* stone 13
**pierna** *f.* leg 10
**pimienta** *f.* black pepper 8
**pintar** *v.* to paint
**pintor(a)** *m.*, *f.* painter
**pintura** *f.* painting; picture 12
**piña** *f.* pineapple 8
**piscina** *f.* swimming pool 4
**piso** *m.* floor (*of a building*) 5
**pizarra** *f.* blackboard 2
**placer** *m.* pleasure 15
　**Ha sido un placer.** It's been a pleasure. 15
**planchar la ropa** *v.* to iron the clothes 12
**planes** *m.*, *pl.* plans 4
**planta** *f.* plant 13
　**planta baja** *f.* ground floor 5
**plástico** *m.* plastic 13
**plato** *m.* dish (*in a meal*) 8; *m.* plate 12
　**plato principal** *m.* main dish 8
**playa** *f.* beach 5
**plaza** *f.* city or town square 4
**plazos** *m.*, *pl.* periods; time 14
**pluma** *f.* pen 2
**población** *f.* population 13
**pobre** *adj. m.*, *f.* poor 6
**pobreza** *f.* poverty
**poco/a** *adj.* little; few 5; 10
**poder (o:ue)** *v.* to be able to; can 4

**poema** *m.* poem
**poesía** *f.* poetry
**poeta** *m.*, *f.* poet
**policía** *f.* police (force) 11
**política** *f.* politics
**político/a** *m.*, *f.* politician; *adj.* political
**pollo** *m.* chicken 8
　**pollo asado** *m.* roast chicken 8
**ponchar** *v.* to go flat
**poner** *v.* to put; to place 4; *v.* to turn on (*electrical appliances*) 11
　**poner la mesa** *v.* to set the table 12
　**poner una inyección** *v.* to give an injection 10
**ponerse (+ adj.)** *v.* to become (+ *adj.*) 7; to put on 7
**por** *prep.* in exchange for; for; by; in; through; around; along; during; because of; on account of; on behalf of; in search of; by way of; by means of 11
　**por aquí** around here 11
　**por avión** by plane
　**por ejemplo** for example 11
　**por eso** that's why; therefore 11
　**por favor** please 1
　**por fin** finally 11
　**por la mañana** in the morning 7
　**por la noche** at night 7
　**por la tarde** in the afternoon 7
　**por lo menos** *adv.* at least 10
　**¿por qué?** why? 2
　**Por supuesto.** Of course.
　**por teléfono** by phone; on the phone
　**por último** finally 7
**porque** *conj.* because 2
**portátil** *m.* portable 11
**porvenir** *m.* future
　**¡Por el porvenir!** Here's to the future!
**posesivo/a** *adj.* possessive 3
**posible** *adj.* possible 13
　**es posible** it's possible 13
　**no es posible** it's not possible 13
**postal** *f.* postcard 4
**postre** *m.* dessert 9
**practicar** *v.* to practice 2
　**practicar deportes** *m.*, *pl.* to play sports 4
**precio (fijo)** *m.* (fixed; set) price 6
**preferir (e:ie)** *v.* to prefer 4
**pregunta** *f.* question
**preguntar** *v.* to ask (*a question*) 2
**premio** *m.* prize; award
**prender** *v.* to turn on 11
**prensa** *f.* press
**preocupado/a (por)** *adj.* worried (about) 5
**preocuparse (por)** *v.* to worry (about) 7

**preparar** *v.* to prepare 2
**preposición** *f.* preposition
**presentación** *f.* introduction
**presentar** *v.* to introduce; to present; to put on (*a performance*)
  **Le presento a...** I would like to introduce (name) to you... (*form.*) 1
  **Te presento a...** I would like to introduce (name) to you... (*fam.*) 1
**presiones** *f., pl.* pressures 15
**prestado/a** *adj.* borrowed
**préstamo** *m.* loan 14
**prestar** *v.* to lend; to loan 6
**primavera** *f.* spring 5
**primer, primero/a** *adj.* first 5
**primo/a** *m., f.* cousin 3
**principal** *adj. m., f.* main 8
**prisa** *f.* haste 3
  **darse prisa** *v.* to hurry; to rush 15
**probable** *adj. m., f.* probable 13
  **es probable** it's probable 13
  **no es probable** it's not probable 13
**probar (o:ue)** *v.* to taste; to try 8
**probarse (o:ue)** *v.* to try on 7
**problema** *m.* problem 1
**profesión** *f.* profession 3
**profesor(a)** *m., f.* teacher 1, 2
**programa** *m.* 1
  **programa de computación** *m.* software 11
  **programa de entrevistas** *m.* talk show
**programador(a)** *m., f.* computer programmer 3
**prohibir** *v.* to prohibit 10; to forbid
**pronombre** *m.* pronoun
**pronto** *adv.* soon 10
**propina** *f.* tip 9
**propio/a** *adj.* own
**proteger** *v.* to protect 13
**proteína** *f.* protein 15
**próximo/a** *adj.* next
**prueba** *f.* test; quiz 2
**psicología** *f.* psychology 2
**psicólogo/a** *m., f.* psychologist
**publicar** *v.* to publish
**público** *m.* audience
**pueblo** *m.* town 4
**puerta** *f.* door 2
**Puerto Rico** *m.* Puerto Rico 1
**puertorriqueño/a** *adj.* Puerto Rican 3
**pues** *conj.* well 2
**puesto** *m.* position; job
**puesto/a** *p.p.* put 14
**puro/a** *adj.* pure 13

## Q

**que** *pron.* that; which; who 12
  **¿En qué...?** In which...? 2
  **¡Qué...!** How...! 3

**¡Qué dolor!** What pain!
**¡Qué ropa más bonita!** What pretty clothes! 6
**¡Qué sorpresa!** What a surprise!
**¿qué?** what? 1
**¿Qué día es hoy?** What day is it? 2
**¿Qué hay de nuevo?** What's new? 1
**¿Qué hora es?** What time is it? 1
**¿Qué les parece?** What do you (*pl.*) think?
**¿Qué pasa?** What's happening? What's going on? 1
**¿Qué pasó?** What happened? 11
**¿Qué precio tiene?** What is the price?
**¿Qué tal...?** How are you?; How is it going? 1; How is/are...? 2
**¿Qué talla lleva/usa?** What size do you wear? 6
**¿Qué tiempo hace?** How's the weather? 5
**quedar** *v.* to be left over; to fit (*clothing*) 7; to be left behind; to be located 14
**quedarse** *v.* to stay; to remain 7
**quehaceres domésticos** *m., pl.* household chores 12
**quemado/a** *adj.* burned (out) 11
**quemar** *v.* to burn (a CD) 11
**querer (e:ie)** *v.* to want; to love 4
**queso** *m.* cheese 8
**quien(es)** *pron.* who; whom; that 12
  **¿quién(es)?** who?; whom? 1
  **¿Quién es...?** Who is...? 1
  **¿Quién habla?** Who is speaking? (*telephone*) 11
**química** *f.* chemistry 2
**quince** fifteen 1
  **menos quince** quarter to (time) 1
  **y quince** quarter after (time) 1
**quinceañera** *f.* young woman's fifteenth birthday celebration/fifteen-year-old girl 9
**quinientos/as** *adj.* five hundred 2
**quinto/a** *adj.* fifth 5
**quisiera** *v.* I would like
**quitar el polvo** *v.* to dust 12
**quitar la mesa** *v.* to clear the table 12
**quitarse** *v.* to take off 7
**quizás** *adv.* maybe 5

## R

**racismo** *m.* racism
**radio** *f.* radio (*medium*) 2; *m.* radio (set) 2
**radiografía** *f.* X-ray 10

**rápido/a** *adv.* quickly 10
**ratón** *m.* mouse 11
**ratos libres** *m., pl.* spare (free) time 4
**raya** *f.* stripe 6
**razón** *f.* reason 3
**rebaja** *f.* sale 6
**recado** *m.* (telephone) message 11
**receta** *f.* prescription 10
**recetar** *v.* to prescribe 10
**recibir** *v.* to receive 3
**reciclaje** *m.* recycling 13
**reciclar** *v.* to recycle 13
**recién casado/a** *m., f.* newly-wed 9
**recoger** *v.* to pick up 13
**recomendar (e:ie)** *v.* to recommend 8, 12
**recordar (o:ue)** *v.* to remember 4
**recorrer** *v.* to tour an area
**recurso** *m.* resource 13
  **recurso natural** *m.* natural resource 13
**red** *f.* network; Web 11
**reducir** *v.* to reduce 13
**refresco** *m.* soft drink 8
**refrigerador** *m.* refrigerator 12
**regalar** *v.* to give (a gift) 9
**regalo** *m.* gift 6
**regatear** *v.* to bargain 6
**región** *f.* region; area 13
**regresar** *v.* to return 2
**regular** *adj. m., f.* so-so.; OK 1
**reído** *p.p.* laughed 14
**reírse (e:i)** *v.* to laugh 9
**relaciones** *f., pl.* relationships
**relajarse** *v.* to relax 9
**reloj** *m.* clock; watch 2
**renunciar (a)** *v.* to resign (from)
**repetir (e:i)** *v.* to repeat 4
**reportaje** *m.* report
**reportero/a** *m., f.* reporter; journalist
**representante** *m., f.* representative
**reproductor de DVD** *m.* DVD player 11
**reproductor de MP3** *m.* MP3 player 11
**resfriado** *m.* cold (*illness*) 10
**residencia estudiantil** *f.* dormitory 2
**resolver (o:ue)** *v.* to resolve; to solve 13
**respirar** *v.* to breathe 13
**respuesta** *f.* answer
**restaurante** *m.* restaurant 4
**resuelto/a** *p.p.* resolved 14
**reunión** *f.* meeting
**revisar** *v.* to check 11
  **revisar el aceite** *v.* to check the oil 11
**revista** *f.* magazine 4
**rico/a** *adj.* rich 6; *adj.* tasty; delicious 8
**ridículo/a** *adj.* ridiculous 13
**río** *m.* river 13

**riquísimo/a** *adj.* extremely delicious 8
**rodilla** *f.* knee 10
**rogar (o:ue)** *v.* to beg; to plead 12
**rojo/a** *adj.* red 6
**romántico/a** *adj.* romantic
**romper** *v.* to break 10
  **romperse la pierna** *v.* to break one's leg 10
  **romper (con)** *v.* to break up (with) 9
**ropa** *f.* clothing; clothes 6
  **ropa interior** *f.* underwear 6
**rosado/a** *adj.* pink 6
**roto/a** *adj.* broken 10, 14
**rubio/a** *adj.* blond(e) 3
**ruso/a** *adj.* Russian 3
**rutina** *f.* routine 7
  **rutina diaria** *f.* daily routine 7

## S

**sábado** *m.* Saturday 2
**saber** *v.* to know; to know how 6; to taste 8
  **saber a** to taste like 8
**sabrosísimo/a** *adj.* extremely delicious 8
**sabroso/a** *adj.* tasty; delicious 8
**sacar** *v.* to take out
  **sacar fotos** to take photos 5
  **sacar la basura** to take out the trash 12
  **sacar(se) un diente** to have a tooth removed 10
**sacudir** *v.* to dust 12
  **sacudir los muebles** to dust the furniture 12
**sal** *f.* salt 8
**sala** *f.* living room 12; room
  **sala de emergencia(s)** emergency room 10
**salario** *m.* salary
**salchicha** *f.* sausage 8
**salida** *f.* departure; exit 5
**salir** *v.* to leave 4; to go out
  **salir (con)** to go out (with); to date 9
  **salir de** to leave from
  **salir para** to leave for (*a place*)
**salmón** *m.* salmon 8
**salón de belleza** *m.* beauty salon 14
**salud** *f.* health 10
**saludable** *adj.* healthy 10
**saludar(se)** *v.* to greet (each other) 11
**saludo** *m.* greeting 1
  **saludos a...** greetings to... 1
**sandalia** *f.* sandal 6
**sandía** *f.* watermelon
**sándwich** *m.* sandwich 8

**sano/a** *adj.* healthy 10
**se** *ref. pron.* himself, herself, itself, *form.* yourself, themselves, yourselves 7
**se** *impersonal* one 10
  **Se nos dañó...** The... broke down. 11
  **Se hizo...** He/she/it became...
  **Se nos pinchó una llanta.** We had a flat tire. 11
**secadora** *f.* clothes dryer 12
**secarse** *v.* to dry oneself 7
**sección de (no) fumar** *f.* (non) smoking section 8
**secretario/a** *m., f.* secretary
**secuencia** *f.* sequence
**sed** *f.* thirst 3
**seda** *f.* silk 6
**sedentario/a** *adj.* sedentary; related to sitting 15
**seguir (e:i)** *v.* to follow; to continue 4
**según** according to
**segundo/a** *adj.* second 5
**seguro/a** *adj.* sure; safe 5
**seis** six 1
**seiscientos/as** six hundred 2
**sello** *m.* stamp 14
**selva** *f.* jungle 13
**semana** *f.* week 2
  **fin** *m.* **de semana** weekend 4
  **semana** *f.* **pasada** last week 6
**semestre** *m.* semester 2
**sendero** *m.* trail; trailhead 13
**sentarse (e:ie)** *v.* to sit down 7
**sentir(se) (e:ie)** *v.* to feel 7; to be sorry; to regret 13
**señor (Sr.); don** *m.* Mr.; sir 1
**señora (Sra.); doña** *f.* Mrs.; ma'am 1
**señorita (Srta.)** *f.* Miss 1
**separado/a** *adj.* separated 9
**separarse (de)** *v.* to separate (from) 9
**septiembre** *m.* September 5
**séptimo/a** *adj.* seventh 5
**ser** *v.* to be 1
  **ser aficionado/a (a)** to be a fan (of) 4
  **ser alérgico/a (a)** to be allergic (to) 10
  **ser gratis** to be free of charge 14
**serio/a** *adj.* serious
**servilleta** *f.* napkin 12
**servir (e:i)** *v.* to serve 8; to help 5
**sesenta** sixty 2
**setecientos/as** *adj.* seven hundred 2
**setenta** seventy 2
**sexismo** *m.* sexism
**sexto/a** *adj.* sixth 5
**sí** *adv.* yes 1
**si** *conj.* if 4
**SIDA** *m.* AIDS

**sido** *p.p.* been 15
**siempre** *adv.* always 7
**siete** seven 1
**silla** *f.* seat 2
**sillón** *m.* armchair 12
**similar** *adj. m., f.* similar
**simpático/a** *adj.* nice; likeable 3
**sin** *prep.* without 2, 13
  **sin duda** without a doubt
  **sin embargo** however
  **sin que** *conj.* without 13
**sino** but (rather) 7
**síntoma** *m.* symptom 10
**sitio** *m.* **web;** website 11
**situado/a** *p.p.* located
**sobre** *m.* envelope 14; *prep.* on; over 2
**sobrino/a** *m., f.* nephew; niece 3
**sociología** *f.* sociology 2
**sofá** *m.* couch; sofa 12
**sol** *m.* sun 4; 5; 13
**solar** *adj. m., f.* solar 13
**soldado** *m., f.* soldier
**soleado/a** *adj.* sunny
**solicitar** *v.* to apply (*for a job*)
**solicitud (de trabajo)** *f.* (job) application
**sólo** *adv.* only 3
**solo/a** *adj.* alone
**soltero/a** *adj.* single 9
**solución** *f.* solution 13
**sombrero** *m.* hat 6
**Son las dos.** It's two o'clock. 1
**sonar (o:ue)** *v.* to ring 11
**sonreído** *p.p.* smiled 14
**sonreír (e:i)** *v.* to smile 9
**sopa** *f.* soup 8
**sorprender** *v.* to surprise 9
**sorpresa** *f.* surprise 9
**sótano** *m.* basement; cellar 12
**soy** I am 1
  **Soy de...** I'm from... 1
  **Soy yo.** That's me. 1
**su(s)** *poss. adj.* his; her; its; *form.* your; their 3
**subir(se) a** *v.* to get on/into (*a vehicle*) 11
**sucio/a** *adj.* dirty 5
**sucre** *m.* Former Ecuadorian currency 6
**sudar** *v.* to sweat 15
**suegro/a** *m., f.* father-in-law; mother-in-law 3
**sueldo** *m.* salary
**suelo** *m.* floor 12
**sueño** *m.* sleep 3
**suerte** *f.* luck 3
**suéter** *m.* sweater 6
**sufrir** *v.* to suffer 10
  **sufrir muchas presiones** to be under a lot of pressure 15
  **sufrir una enfermedad** to suffer an illness 10
**sugerir (e:ie)** *v.* to suggest 12
**supermercado** *m.* supermarket 14
**suponer** *v.* to suppose 4

**sur** *m.* south 14
**sustantivo** *m.* noun
**suyo(s)/a(s)** *poss.* (of) his/her; (of) hers; (of) its; (of) *form.* your, (of) yours, (of) their 11

## T

**tal vez** *adv.* maybe 5
**talentoso/a** *adj.* talented
**talla** *f.* size 6
   **talla grande** *f.* large 6
**taller** *m.* **mecánico** garage; mechanic's repairshop 11
**también** *adv.* also; too 2; 7
**tampoco** *adv.* neither; not either 7
**tan** *adv.* so 5
   **tan... como** as... as 8
   **tan pronto como** *conj.* as soon as 13
**tanque** *m.* tank 11
**tanto** *adv.* so much
   **tanto... como** as much... as 8
   **tantos/as... como** as many... as 8
**tarde** *adv.* late 7; *f.* afternoon; evening; P.M. 1
**tarea** *f.* homework 2
**tarjeta** *f.* (post) card
**tarjeta de crédito** *f.* credit card 6
**tarjeta postal** *f.* postcard 4
**taxi** *m.* taxi 5
**taza** *f.* cup 12
**te** *sing., fam., d.o. pron.* you 5; *sing., fam., i.o. pron.* to/for you 6
   **Te presento a...** *fam.* I would like to introduce... to you 1
   **¿Te gustaría?** Would you like to?
   **¿Te gusta(n)... ?** Do you like... ? 2
**té** *m.* tea 8
   **té helado** *m.* iced tea 8
**teatro** *m.* theater
**teclado** *m.* keyboard 11
**técnico/a** *m., f.* technician
**tejido** *m.* weaving
**teleadicto/a** *m., f.* couch potato 15
**teléfono (celular)** *m.* (cell) telephone 11
**telenovela** *f.* soap opera
**teletrabajo** *m.* telecommuting
**televisión** *f.* television 2; 11
**televisión por cable** *f.* cable television 11
**televisor** *m.* television set 11
**temer** *v.* to fear 13
**temperatura** *f.* temperature 10
**temprano** *adv.* early 7
**tenedor** *m.* fork 12
**tener** *v.* to have 3
   **tener... años** to be... years old 3

**Tengo... años.** I'm... years old. 3
**tener (mucho) calor** to be (very) hot 3
**tener (mucho) cuidado** to be (very) careful 3
**tener dolor** to have a pain 10
**tener éxito** to be successful
**tener fiebre** to have a fever 10
**tener (mucho) frío** to be (very) cold 3
**tener ganas de (+ inf.)** to feel like (*doing something*) 3
**tener (mucha) hambre** *f.* to be (very) hungry 3
**tener (mucho) miedo (de)** to be (very) afraid (of); to be (very) scared (of) 3
**tener miedo (de) que** to be afraid that
**tener planes** *m., pl.* to have plans 4
**tener (mucha) prisa** to be in a (big) hurry 3
**tener que (+ inf.)** *v.* to have to (*do something*) 3
**tener razón** *f.* to be right 3
**tener (mucha) sed** *f.* to be (very) thirsty 3
**tener (mucho) sueño** to be (very) sleepy 3
**tener (mucha) suerte** to be (very) lucky 3
**tener tiempo** to have time 4
**tener una cita** to have a date; to have an appointment 9
**tenis** *m.* tennis 4
**tensión** *f.* tension 15
**tercer, tercero/a** *adj.* third 5
**terminar** *v.* to end; to finish 2
   **terminar de (+inf.)** *v.* to finish (*doing something*) 4
**terremoto** *m.* earthquake
**terrible** *adj. m., f.* terrible 13
**ti** *prep., obj. of prep., fam.* you
**tiempo** *m.* time 4; weather 5
   **tiempo libre** free time
**tienda** *f.* shop; store 6
   **tienda de campaña** tent
**tierra** *f.* land; soil 13
**tinto/a** *adj.* red (wine) 8
**tío/a** *m., f.* uncle; aunt 3
**tíos** *m., pl.* aunts and uncles 3
**título** *m.* title
**tiza** *f.* chalk 2
**toalla** *f.* towel 7
**tobillo** *m.* ankle 10
**tocadiscos compacto** *m.* compact disc player 11
**tocar** *v.* to play (*a musical instrument*); to touch 13
**todavía** *adv.* yet; still 5
**todo** *m.* everything 5
   **en todo el mundo** throughout the world 13
   **Todo está bajo control.** Everything is under control. 7

**todo derecho** straight (ahead) 14
**todo(s)/a(s)** *adj.* all 4; whole
**todos** *m., pl.* all of us; *m., pl.* everybody; everyone
   **¡Todos a bordo!** All aboard! 1
**todos los días** *adv.* every day 10
**tomar** *v.* to take; to drink 2
   **tomar clases** *f., pl.* to take classes 2
   **tomar el sol** to sunbathe 4
   **tomar en cuenta** to take into account
   **tomar fotos** *f., pl.* to take photos 5
   **tomar la temperatura** to take someone's temperature 10
**tomate** *m.* tomato 8
**tonto/a** *adj.* silly; foolish 3
**torcerse (o:ue) (el tobillo)** *v.* to sprain (one's ankle) 10
**torcido/a** *adj.* twisted; sprained 10
**tormenta** *f.* storm
**tornado** *m.* tornado
**tortilla** *f.* tortilla 8
   **tortilla de maíz** corn tortilla 8
**tos** *f., sing.* cough 10
**toser** *v.* to cough 10
**tostado/a** *adj.* toasted 8
**tostadora** *f.* toaster 12
**trabajador(a)** *adj.* hard-working 3
**trabajar** *v.* to work 2
**trabajo** *m.* job; work
**traducir** *v.* to translate 6
**traer** *v.* to bring 4
**tráfico** *m.* traffic 11
**tragedia** *f.* tragedy
**traído/a** *p.p.* brought 14
**traje** *m.* suit 6
   **traje (de baño)** *m.* (bathing) suit 6
**tranquilo/a** *adj.* calm; quiet 15
   **Tranquilo.** Don't worry.; Be cool. 7
**transmitir** *v.* to broadcast
**tratar de (+ inf.)** *v.* to try (*to do something*) 15
**Trato hecho.** You've got a deal.
**trece** thirteen 1
**treinta** thirty 1, 2
   **y treinta** thirty minutes past the hour (time) 1
**tren** *m.* train 5
**tres** three 1
**trescientos/as** *adj.* three hundred 2
**trimestre** *m.* trimester; quarter 2
**triste** *adj.* sad 5
**tú** *fam. sub. pron.* you 1
   **Tú eres...** You are... 1
**tu(s)** *fam. poss. adj.* your 3
**turismo** *m.* tourism 5
**turista** *m., f.* tourist 1
**turístico/a** *adj.* touristic
**tuyo(s)/a(s)** *fam. poss. pron.* your; (of) yours 11

## U

**Ud.** *form. sing.* you 1
**Uds.** *form., pl.* you 1
**último/a** *adj.* last
**un, uno/a** *indef. art.* a; one 1
  **uno/a** *m., f., sing. pron.* one 1
    **a la una** at one o'clock 1
  **una vez** once; one time 6
  **una vez más** one more time 9
**único/a** *adj.* only 3
**universidad** *f.* university;
  college 2
**unos/as** *m., f., pl. indef. art.*
  some 1
  **unos/as** *pron.* some 1
**urgente** *adj.* urgent 12
**usar** *v.* to wear; to use 6
**usted (Ud.)** *form. sing.* you 1
  **ustedes (Uds.)** *form., pl.* you 1
**útil** *adj.* useful
**uva** *f.* grape 8

## V

**vaca** *f.* cow 13
**vacaciones** *f. pl.* vacation 5
**valle** *m.* valley 13
**vamos** let's go 4
**vaquero** *m.* cowboy
  **de vaqueros** *m., pl.* western
    (genre)
**varios/as** *adj. m. f., pl.* various;
  several 8
**vaso** *m.* glass 12
**veces** *f., pl.* times 6
**vecino/a** *m., f.* neighbor 12
**veinte** twenty 1
**veinticinco** twenty-five 1
**veinticuatro** twenty-four 1
**veintidós** twenty-two 1
**veintinueve** twenty-nine 1
**veintiocho** twenty-eight 1
**veintiséis** twenty-six 1
**veintisiete** twenty-seven 1
**veintitrés** twenty-three 1

**veintiún, veintiuno/a**
  twenty-one 1
**vejez** *f.* old age 9
**velocidad** *f.* speed 11
  **velocidad máxima** *f.* speed
    limit 11
**vendedor(a)** *m., f.* salesperson 6
**vender** *v.* to sell 6
**venir** *v.* to come 3
**ventana** *f.* window 2
**ver** *v.* to see 4
  **a ver** *v.* let's see 2
  **ver películas** *f., pl.* to see
    movies 4
**verano** *m.* summer 5
**verbo** *m.* verb
**verdad** *f.* truth
  **¿verdad?** right? 1
**verde** *adj., m. f.* green 6
**verduras** *pl., f.* vegetables 8
**vestido** *m.* dress 6
**vestirse (e:i)** *v.* to get dressed 7
**vez** *f.* time 6
**viajar** *v.* to travel 2
**viaje** *m.* trip 5
**viajero/a** *m., f.* traveler 5
**vida** *f.* life 9
**video** *m.* video 1
**video(casete)** *m.* video
  (cassette) 11
**videocasetera** *f.* VCR 11
**videoconferencia** *f.*
  videoconference
**videojuego** *m.* video game 4
**vidrio** *m.* glass 13
**viejo/a** *adj.* old 3
**viento** *m.* wind 5
**viernes** *m., sing.* Friday 2
**vinagre** *m.* vinegar 8
**vino** *m.* wine 8
  **vino blanco** *m.* white wine 8
  **vino tinto** *m.* red wine 8
**violencia** *f.* violence
**visitar** *v.* to visit 4
  **visitar monumentos** *m., pl.*
    to visit monuments 4
**visto/a** *p.p.* seen 14

**vitamina** *f.* vitamin 15
**viudo/a** *adj.* widower/widow 9
**vivienda** *f.* housing 12
**vivir** *v.* to live 3
**vivo/a** *adj.* bright; lively; living
**volante** *m.* steering wheel 11
**volcán** *m.* volcano 13
**vóleibol** *m.* volleyball 4
**volver (o:ue)** *v.* to return 4
**volver a ver(te, lo, la)** *v.* to see
  (you, him, her) again
**vos** *pron.* you
**vosotros/as** *form., pl.* you 1
**votar** *v.* to vote
**vuelta** *f.* return trip
**vuelto/a** *p.p.* returned 14
**vuestro(s)/a(s)** *poss. adj.* your 3;
  (of) yours *fam.* 11

## W

**walkman** *m.* walkman

## Y

**y** *conj.* and 1
  **y cuarto** quarter after (time) 1
  **y media** half-past (time) 1
  **y quince** quarter after (time) 1
  **y treinta** thirty (minutes past
    the hour) 1
  **¿Y tú?** *fam.* And you? 1
  **¿Y usted?** *form.* And you? 1
**ya** *adv.* already 6
**yerno** *m.* son-in-law 3
**yo** *sub. pron.* I 1
  **Yo soy...** I'm... 1
**yogur** *m.* yogurt 8

## Z

**zanahoria** *f.* carrot 8
**zapatería** *f.* shoe store 14
**zapatos de tenis** *m., pl.* tennis
  shoes, sneakers 6

# English-Spanish

### A

a **un/a** *m., f., sing.; indef. art.* 1
@ (*symbol*) **arroba** *f.* 11
A.M. **mañana** *f.* 1
able: be able to **poder (o:ue)**
  *v.* 4
aboard **a bordo** 1
accident **accidente** *m.* 10
accompany **acompañar** *v.* 14
account **cuenta** *f.* 14
  on account of **por** *prep.* 11
accountant **contador(a)** *m., f.*
accounting **contabilidad** *f.* 2
ache **dolor** *m.* 10
acid **ácido/a** *adj.* 13
  acid rain **lluvia ácida** 13
acquainted: be acquainted with
  **conocer** *v.* 6
action (genre) **de acción** *f.*
active **activo/a** *adj.* 15
actor **actor** *m.,* **actriz** *f.*
addict (*drug*) **drogadicto/a**
  *adj.* 15
additional **adicional** *adj.*
address **dirección** *f.* 14
adjective **adjetivo** *m.*
adolescence **adolescencia** *f.* 9
adventure (genre) **de aventura** *f.*
advertise **anunciar** *v.*
advertisement **anuncio** *m.*
advice **consejo** *m.* 6
  give advice **dar consejos** 6
advise **aconsejar** *v.* 12
advisor **consejero/a** *m., f.*
aerobic **aeróbico/a** *adj.* 15
  aerobics class **clase de**
    **ejercicios aeróbicos** 15
  to do aerobics **hacer ejercicios**
    **aeróbicos** 15
affected **afectado/a** *adj.* 13
  be affected (by) **estar** *v.*
    **afectado/a (por)** 13
affirmative **afirmativo/a** *adj.*
afraid: be (very) afraid (of) **tener**
  **(mucho) miedo (de)** 3
  be afraid that **tener miedo**
    **(de) que**
after **después de** *prep.* 7;
  **después de que** *conj.* 13
afternoon **tarde** *f.* 1
afterward **después** *adv.* 7
again **otra vez**
age **edad** *f.* 9
agree **concordar** *v.*
agree **estar** *v.* **de acuerdo**
  I agree (completely). **Estoy**
    **(completamente) de**
    **acuerdo.**
  I don't agree. **No estoy de**
    **acuerdo.**
agreement **acuerdo** *m.*
AIDS **SIDA** *m.*

air **aire** *m.* 13
  air pollution **contaminación**
    **del aire** 13
airplane **avión** *m.* 5
airport **aeropuerto** *m.* 5
alarm clock **despertador** *m.* 7
alcohol **alcohol** *m.* 15
  to consume alcohol **consumir**
    **alcohol** 15
alcoholic **alcohólico/a** *adj.* 15
all **todo(s)/a(s)** *adj.* 4
  All aboard! **¡Todos a bordo!** 1
  all of us **todos** 1
  all over the world **en todo el**
    **mundo**
allergic **alérgico/a** *adj.* 10
  be allergic (to) **ser alérgico/a**
    **(a)** 10
alleviate **aliviar** *v.*
almost **casi** *adv.* 10
alone **solo/a** *adj.*
along **por** *prep.* 11
already **ya** *adv.* 6
also **también** *adv.* 2; 7
alternator **alternador** *m.* 11
although **aunque** *conj.*
aluminum **aluminio** *m.* 13
  (made) of aluminum **de**
    **aluminio** 13
always **siempre** *adv.* 7
American (*North*)
  **norteamericano/a** *adj.* 3
among **entre** *prep.* 2
amusement **diversión** *f.*
and **y** 1, **e** (*before words beginning*
  *with* **i** *or* **hi**) 4
  And you?**¿Y tú?** *fam.* 1;
    **¿Y usted?** *form.* 1
angry **enojado/a** *adj.* 5
  get angry (with) **enojarse** *v.*
    **(con)** 7
animal **animal** *m.* 13
ankle **tobillo** *m.* 10
anniversary **aniversario** *m.* 9
  (wedding) anniversary
    **aniversario** *m.* **(de bodas)** 9
announce **anunciar** *v.*
announcer (*TV/radio*) **locutor(a)**
  *m., f.*
annoy **molestar** *v.* 7
another **otro/a** *adj.* 6
answer **contestar** *v.* 2;
  **respuesta** *f.*
answering machine **contestadora**
  *f.* 11
antibiotic **antibiótico** *m.* 10
any **algún, alguno/a(s)** *adj.* 7
anyone **alguien** *pron.* 7
anything **algo** *pron.* 7
apartment **apartamento** *m.* 12
apartment building **edificio de**
  **apartamentos** 12
appear **parecer** *v.*
appetizers **entremeses** *m., pl.* 8
applaud **aplaudir** *v.*
apple **manzana** *f.* 8

appliance (electric) **electrodo-**
  **méstico** *m.* 12
applicant **aspirante** *m., f.*
application **solicitud** *f.*
  job application **solicitud de**
    **trabajo**
apply (for a job) **solicitar** *v.*
  apply for a loan **pedir (e:ie)** *v.*
    **un préstamo** 14
appointment **cita** *f.* 9
  have an appointment **tener** *v.*
    **una cita** 9
appreciate **apreciar** *v.*
April **abril** *m.* 5
aquatic **acuático/a** *adj.*
archaeologist **arqueólogo/a**
  *m., f.*
architect **arquitecto/a** *m., f.*
area **región** *f.* 13
arm **brazo** *m.* 10
armchair **sillón** *m.* 12
army **ejército** *m.*
around **por** *prep.* 11
  around here **por aquí** 11
arrange **arreglar** *v.* 11
arrival **llegada** *f.* 5
arrive **llegar** *v.* 2
art **arte** *m.* 2
  (fine) arts **bellas artes** *f., pl.*
article *m.* **artículo**
artist **artista** *m., f.* 3
artistic **artístico/a** *adj.*
arts **artes** *f., pl.*
as **como** 8
  as a child **de niño/a** 10
  as... as **tan... como** 8
  as many... as **tantos/as...**
    **como** 8
  as much... as **tanto...**
    **como** 8
  as soon as **en cuanto** *conj.* 13;
    **tan pronto como** *conj.* 13
ask (*a question*) **preguntar** *v.* 2
  ask for **pedir (e:i)** *v.* 4
asparagus **espárragos** *m., pl.* 8
aspirin **aspirina** *f.* 10
at **a** *prep.* 1; **en** *prep.* 2
  at + *time* **a la(s)** + *time* 1
  at home **en casa** 7
  at least **por lo menos** 10
  at night **por la noche** 7
  at the end (of) **al fondo (de)** 12
  At what time...? **¿A qué**
    **hora...?** 1
  At your service. **A sus**
    **órdenes.** 11
ATM **cajero automático** *m.* 14
attend **asistir (a)** *v.* 3
attic **altillo** *m.* 12
attract **atraer** *v.* 4
audience **público** *m.*
August **agosto** *m.* 5
aunt **tía** *f.* 3
  aunts and uncles **tíos** *m., pl.* 3
automobile **automóvil** *m.* 5;
  **carro** *m.;* **coche** *m.* 11

autumn **otoño** *m.* 5
avenue **avenida** *f.*
avoid **evitar** *v.* 13
award **premio** *m.*

## B

backpack **mochila** *f.* 2
bad **mal, malo/a** *adj.* 3
  It's bad that... **Es malo
    que...** 12
  It's not at all bad. **No está
    nada mal.** 5
bag **bolsa** *f.* 6
bakery **panadería** *f.* 14
balanced **equilibrado/a** *adj.* 15
  to eat a balanced diet **comer
    una dieta equilibrada** 15
balcony **balcón** *m.* 12
ball **pelota** *f.* 4
banana **banana** *f.* 8
band **banda** *f.*
bank **banco** *m.* 14
bargain **ganga** *f.* 6; **regatear** *v.* 6
baseball (*game*) **béisbol** *m.* 4
basement **sótano** *m.* 12
basketball (*game*) **baloncesto** *m.* 4
bathe **bañarse** *v.* 7
bathing suit **traje** *m.* **de baño** 6
bathroom **baño** *m.* 7; **cuarto de
  baño** *m.* 7
be **ser** *v.* 1; **estar** *v.* 2
  be... years old **tener... años** 3
beach **playa** *f.* 5
beans **frijoles** *m., pl.* 8
beautiful **hermoso/a** *adj.* 6
beauty **belleza** *f.* 14
  beauty salon **peluquería** *f.* 14;
    **salón** *m.* **de belleza** 14
because **porque** *conj.* 2
  because of **por** *prep.* 11
become (+ *adj.*) **ponerse (+
  *adj.*)** 7; **convertirse** *v.*
bed **cama** *f.* 5
  go to bed **acostarse (o:ue)** *v.* 7
bedroom **alcoba** *f.*; **dormitorio**
  *m.* 12; **recámara** *f.*
beef **carne de res** *f.* 8
  beef soup **caldo de patas** 8
been **sido** *p.p.* 15
beer **cerveza** *f.* 8
before **antes** *adv.* 7; **antes de**
  *prep.* 7; **antes (de) que**
  *conj.* 13
beg **rogar (o:ue)** *v.* 12
begin **comenzar (e:ie)** *v.* 4;
  **empezar (e:ie)** *v.* 4
behalf: on behalf of **de parte
  de** 11
behind **detrás de** *prep.* 2
believe (in) **creer** *v.* **(en)** 3; **creer**
  *v.* 13
  not to believe **no creer** 13
believed **creído/a** *p.p.* 14
bellhop **botones** *m., f. sing.* 5

below **debajo de** *prep.* 2
belt **cinturón** *m.* 6
benefit **beneficio** *m.*
beside **al lado de** *prep.* 2
besides **además (de)** *adv.* 10
best **mejor** *adj.*
  the best **el/la mejor** *m., f.* 8;
    **lo mejor** *neuter*
better **mejor** *adj.* 8
  It's better that... **Es mejor
    que...** 12
between **entre** *prep.* 2
beverage **bebida** *f.*
  alcoholic beverage **bebida
    alcohólica** *f.* 15
bicycle **bicicleta** *f.* 4
big **gran, grande** *adj.* 3
bill **cuenta** *f.* 9
billion **mil millones**
biology **biología** *f.* 2
bird **ave** *f.* 13; **pájaro** *m.* 13
birth **nacimiento** *m.* 9
birthday **cumpleaños** *m., sing.* 9
  have a birthday **cumplir** *v.*
    **años** 9
black **negro/a** *adj.* 6
blackberry **mora** *f.* 8
blackboard **pizarra** *f.* 2
blanket **manta** *f.* 12
block (city) **cuadra** *f.* 14
blond(e) **rubio/a** *adj.* 3
blouse **blusa** *f.* 6
blue **azul** *adj. m., f.* 6
boarding house **pensión** *f.*
boat **barco** *m.* 5
body **cuerpo** *m.* 10
bone **hueso** *m.* 10
book **libro** *m.* 2
bookcase **estante** *m.* 12
bookshelves **estante** *m.* 12
bookstore **librería** *f.* 2
boot **bota** *f.* 6
bore **aburrir** *v.* 7
bored **aburrido/a** *adj.* 5
  be bored **estar** *v.* **aburrido/a** 5
  get bored **aburrirse** *v.*
boring **aburrido/a** *adj.* 5
born: be born **nacer** *v.* 9
borrow **pedir (e:ie)** *v.*
  **prestado** 14
borrowed **prestado/a** *adj.*
boss **jefe** *m.*, **jefa** *f.*
bother **molestar** *v.* 7
bottle **botella** *f.* 9
  bottle of wine **botella de
    vino** 9
bottom **fondo** *m.*
boulevard **bulevar** *m.*
boy **chico** *m.* 1; **muchacho**
  *m.* 3
boyfriend **novio** *m.* 3
brakes **frenos** *m., pl.*
bread **pan** *m.* 8
break **romper** *v.* 10
  break (one's leg) **romperse (la
    pierna)** 10

break down **dañar** *v.* 10
  The... broke down. **Se nos
    dañó el/la...** 11
  break up (with) **romper** *v.*
    **(con)** 9
breakfast **desayuno** *m.* 2, 8
  have breakfast **desayunar** *v.* 2
breathe **respirar** *v.* 13
bring **traer** *v.* 4
broadcast **transmitir** *v.*
  **emitir** *v.*
brochure **folleto** *m.*
broken **roto/a** *adj.* 10, 14
  be broken **estar roto/a** 10
brother **hermano** *m.* 3
  brother-in-law **cuñado** *m., f.* 3
  brothers and sisters **hermanos**
    *m., pl.* 3
brought **traído/a** *p.p.* 14
brown **café** *adj.* 6; **marrón** *adj.* 6
brunet(te) **moreno/a** *adj.* 3
brush **cepillar** *v.* 7
  brush one's hair **cepillarse el
    pelo** 7
  brush one's teeth **cepillarse los
    dientes** 7
build **construir** *v.* 4
building **edificio** *m.* 12
bump into (*something accidentally*) **darse con** 10; (*someone*)
  **encontrarse** *v.* 11
burn (a CD) **quemar** *v.* 11
burned (out) **quemado/a** *adj.* 11
bus **autobús** *m.* 1
  bus station **estación** *f.* **de
    autobuses** 5
business **negocios** *m. pl.*
  business administration
    **administración** *f.* **de
    empresas** 2
  business-related **comercial**
    *adj.*
businessperson **hombre** *m.* **/
  mujer** *f.* **de negocios**
busy **ocupado/a** *adj.* 5
but **pero** *conj.* 2; (rather) **sino**
  *conj.* (*in negative sentences*) 7
butcher shop **carnicería** *f.* 14
butter **mantequilla** *f.* 8
buy **comprar** *v.* 2
by **por** *prep.* 11; **para** *prep.* 11
  by means of **por** *prep.* 11
  by phone **por teléfono** 11
  by plane **en avión** 5
  by way of **por** *prep.* 11
bye **chau** *interj. fam.* 1

## C

cabin **cabaña** *f.* 5
cable television **televisión** *f.*
  **por cable** *m.* 11
café **café** *m.* 4
cafeteria **cafetería** *f.* 2
caffeine **cafeína** *f.* 15

cake **pastel** *m.* 9
   chocolate cake **pastel de chocolate** *m.* 9
calculator **calculadora** *f.* 11
call **llamar** *v.* 11
   be called **llamarse** *v.* 7
   call on the phone **llamar por teléfono**
calm **tranquilo/a** *adj.* 15
calorie **caloría** *f.* 15
camera **cámara** *f.* 11
camp **acampar** *v.* 5
can (*tin*) **lata** *f.* 13
can **poder (o:ue)** *v.* 4
Canadian **canadiense** *adj.* 3
candidate **aspirante** *m., f.*
   candidate **candidato/a** *m., f.*
candy **dulces** *m., pl.* 9
capital city **capital** *f.* 1
car **coche** *m.* 11; **carro** *m.* 11; **auto(móvil)** *m.* 5
caramel **caramelo** *m.* 9
card **tarjeta** *f.*; (*playing*) **carta** *f.* 5
care **cuidado** *m.* 3
   Take care! **¡Cuídense!** *v.* 15
   take care of **cuidar** *v.* 13
career **carrera** *f.*
careful: be (very) careful **tener** *v.* (**mucho**) **cuidado** 3
caretaker **ama** *m., f.* **de casa** 12
carpenter **carpintero/a** *m., f.*
carpet **alfombra** *f.* 12
carrot **zanahoria** *f.* 8
carry **llevar** *v.* 2
cartoons **dibujos** *m, pl.* **animados**
case: in case (that) **en caso (de) que** 13
cash (a check) **cobrar** *v.* 14; cash (**en**) **efectivo** 6
   cash register **caja** *f.* 6
   pay in cash **pagar** *v.* **al contado** 14; **pagar en efectivo** 14
cashier **cajero/a** *m., f.*
cat **gato** *m.* 13
CD-ROM **cederrón** *m.* 11
celebrate **celebrar** *v.* 9
celebration **celebración** *f.*
   young woman's fifteenth birthday celebration **quinceañera** *f.* 9
cellar **sótano** *m.* 12
cellular **celular** *adj.* 11
   cellular telephone **teléfono celular** *m.* 11
cereal **cereales** *m., pl.* 8
certain **cierto** *m.*; **seguro** *m.* 13
   it's (not) certain (**no**) **es cierto/seguro** 13
chalk **tiza** *f.* 2
champagne **champán** *m.* 9
change **cambiar** *v.* (**de**) 9
channel (*TV*) **canal** *m.* 11
character (*fictional*) **personaje** *m.* 11

(main) character *m.* **personaje** (**principal**)
chat **conversar** *v.* 2
chauffeur **conductor(a)** *m., f.* 1
cheap **barato/a** *adj.* 6
check **comprobar (o:ue)** *v.*; **revisar** *v.* 11; (*bank*) **cheque** *m.* 14
   check the oil **revisar el aceite** 11
checking account **cuenta** *f.* **corriente** 14
cheese **queso** *m.* 8
chef **cocinero/a** *m., f.*
chemistry **química** *f.* 2
chest of drawers **cómoda** *f.* 12
chicken **pollo** *m.* 8
child **niño/a** *m., f.* 3
childhood **niñez** *f.* 9
children **hijos** *m., pl.* 3
Chinese **chino/a** *adj.* 3
chocolate **chocolate** *m.* 9
   chocolate cake **pastel** *m.* **de chocolate** 9
cholesterol **colesterol** *m.* 15
choose **escoger** *v.* 8
chop (*food*) **chuleta** *f.* 8
Christmas **Navidad** *f.* 9
church **iglesia** *f.* 4
citizen **ciudadano/a** *adj.*
city **ciudad** *f.* 4
class **clase** *f.* 2
   take classes **tomar clases** 2
classical **clásico/a** *adj.*
classmate **compañero/a** *m., f.* **de clase** 2
clean **limpio/a** *adj.* 5; **limpiar** *v.* 12
   clean the house *v.* **limpiar la casa** 12
clear (*weather*) **despejado/a** *adj.*
   clear the table **quitar la mesa** 12
   It's (very) clear. (*weather*) **Está (muy) despejado.**
clerk **dependiente/a** *m., f.* 6
climb **escalar** *v.* 4
   climb mountains **escalar montañas** 4
clinic **clínica** *f.* 10
clock **reloj** *m.* 2
close **cerrar (e:ie)** *v.* 4
closed **cerrado/a** *adj.* 5
closet **armario** *m.* 12
clothes **ropa** *f.* 6
   clothes dryer **secadora** *f.* 12
clothing **ropa** *f.* 6
cloud **nube** *f.* 13
cloudy **nublado/a** *adj.* 5
   It's (very) cloudy. **Está (muy) nublado.** 5
coat **abrigo** *m.* 6
coffee **café** *m.* 8
   coffee maker **cafetera** *f.* 12
cold **frío** *m.* 5;
   (*illness*) **resfriado** *m.* 10

be (*feel*) (very) cold **tener (mucho) frío** 3
   It's (very) cold. (*weather*) **Hace (mucho) frío.** 5
college **universidad** *f.* 2
collision **choque** *m.*
color **color** *m.* 6
comb one's hair **peinarse** *v.* 7
come **venir** *v.* 3
comedy **comedia** *f.*
comfortable **cómodo/a** *adj.* 5
commerce **negocios** *m., pl.*
commercial **comercial** *adj.*
communicate (with) **comunicarse** *v.* (**con**)
communication **comunicación** *f.*
   means of communication **medios** *m. pl.* **de comunicación**
community **comunidad** *f.* 1
compact disc (CD) **disco** *m.* **compacto** 11
   compact disc player **tocadiscos** *m. sing.* **compacto** 11
company **compañía** *f.*; **empresa** *f.*
comparison **comparación** *f.*
completely **completamente** *adv.*
composer **compositor(a)** *m., f.*
computer **computadora** *f.* 1
   computer disc **disco** *m.*
   computer monitor **monitor** *m.* 11
   computer programmer **programador(a)** *m., f.* 3
   computer science **computación** *f.* 2
concert **concierto** *m.*
conductor (*musical*) **director(a)** *m., f.*
confirm **confirmar** *v.* 5
   confirm a reservation **confirmar una reservación** 5
confused **confundido/a** *adj.* 5
congested **congestionado/a** *adj.* 10
Congratulations! (*for an event such as a birthday or anniversary*) **¡Felicidades!** 9; (*for an event such as an engagement or a good grade on a test*) *f., pl.* **¡Felicitaciones!** 9
conservation **conservación** *f.* 13
conserve **conservar** *v.* 13
considering **para** *prep.* 11
consume **consumir** *v.* 15
container **envase** *m.* 13
contamination **contaminación** *f.*
content **contento/a** *adj.* 5
contest **concurso** *m.*
continue **seguir (e:i)** *v.* 4
control **control** *m.*; **controlar** *v.* 13
   be under control **estar bajo control** 7

conversation **conversación** *f.* 1
converse **conversar** *v.* 2
cook **cocinar** *v.* 12; **cocinero/a**
  *m., f.*
cookie **galleta** *f.* 9
cool **fresco/a** *adj.* 5
  Be cool. **Tranquilo.** 7
  It's cool. (*weather*) **Hace**
    **fresco.** 5
corn **maíz** *m.* 8
corner **esquina** *f.* 14
cost **costar (o:ue)** *v.* 6
cotton **algodón** *f.* 6
  (made of) cotton **de algodón** 6
couch **sofá** *m.* 12
couch potato **teleadicto/a**
  *m., f.* 15
cough **tos** *f.* 10; **toser** *v.* 10
counselor **consejero/a** *m., f.*
count (on) **contar (o:ue)** *v.*
  **(con)** 4, 12
country (*nation*) **país** *m.* 1
countryside **campo** *m.* 5
(married) couple **pareja** *f.* 9
course **curso** *m.* 2; **materia** *f.* 2
courtesy **cortesía** *f.*
cousin **primo/a** *m., f.* 3
cover **cubrir** *v.*
covered **cubierto/a** *p.p.*
cow **vaca** *f.* 13
crafts **artesanía** *f.*
craftsmanship **artesanía** *f.*
crater **cráter** *m.* 13
crazy **loco/a** *adj.* 6
create **crear** *v.*
credit **crédito** *m.* 6
  credit card **tarjeta** *f.* **de**
    **crédito** 6
crime **crimen** *m.*
cross **cruzar** *v.* 14
culture **cultura** *f.*
cup **taza** *f.* 12
currency exchange **cambio** *m.* **de**
  **moneda**
current events **actualidades** *f.*,
  *pl.*
curtains **cortinas** *f., pl.* 12
custard (*baked*) **flan** *m.* 9
custom **costumbre** *f.* 1
customer **cliente/a** *m., f.* 6
customs **aduana** *f.* 5
  customs inspector **inspector(a)**
    *m., f.* **de aduanas** 5
cybercafé **cibercafé** *m.* 11
cycling **ciclismo** *m.* 4

## D

dad **papá** *m.* 3
daily **diario/a** *adj.* 7
  daily routine **rutina** *f.* **diaria** 7
damage **dañar** *v.* 10
dance **bailar** *v.* 2; **danza** *f.*;
  **baile** *m.*
dancer **bailarín/bailarina** *m., f.*
danger **peligro** *m.* 13

dangerous **peligroso/a** *adj.*
date (*appointment*) **cita** *f.* 9; (*calendar*) **fecha** *f.* 5; (*someone*)
  **salir** *v.* **con (alguien)** 9
  have a date **tener una cita** 9
daughter **hija** *f.* 3
daughter-in-law **nuera** *f.* 3
day **día** *m.* 1
  day before yesterday
    **anteayer** *adv.* 6
deal **trato** *m.*
  It's not a big deal. **No es para**
    **tanto.** 12
  You've got a deal! **¡Trato**
    **hecho!**
death **muerte** *f.* 9
decaffeinated **descafeinado/a**
  *adj.* 15
December **diciembre** *m.* 5
decide **decidir** *v.* **(+ inf.)** 3
decided **decidido/a** *adj. p.p.* 14
declare **declarar** *v.*
deforestation **deforestación** *f.* 13
delicious **delicioso/a** *adj.* 8; **rico/**
  **a** *adj.* 8; **sabroso/a** *adj.* 8
delighted **encantado/a** *adj.* 1
dentist **dentista** *m., f.* 10
deny **negar (e:ie)** *v.* 13
  not to deny **no dudar** 13
department store **almacén** *m.* 6
departure **salida** *f.* 5
deposit **depositar** *v.* 14
describe **describir** *v.* 3
described **descrito/a** *p.p.* 14
desert **desierto** *m.* 13
design **diseño** *m.*
designer **diseñador(a)** *m., f.*
desire **desear** *v.* 2
desk **escritorio** *m.* 2
dessert **postre** *m.* 9
destroy **destruir** *v.* 13
develop **desarrollar** *v.* 13
diary **diario** *m.* 1
dictatorship **dictadura** *f.*
dictionary **diccionario** *m.* 1
die **morir (o:ue)** *v.* 8
died **muerto/a** *p.p.* 14
diet **dieta** *f.* 15; **alimentación**
  balanced diet **dieta**
    **equilibrada** 15
  be on a diet **estar a**
    **dieta** 15
difficult **difícil** *adj. m., f.* 3
digital camera **cámara** *f.*
  **digital** 11
dining room **comedor** *m.* 12
dinner **cena** *f.* 2, 8
  have dinner **cenar** *v.* 2
direct **dirigir** *v.*
directions **direcciones** *f., pl.* 14
  give directions **dar**
    **direcciones** 14
director **director(a)** *m., f.*
dirty **ensuciar** *v.*; **sucio/a** *adj.* 5
  get (something) dirty **ensuciar**
    *v.* 12
disagree **no estar de acuerdo**

disaster **desastre** *m.*
discover **descubrir** *v.* 13
discovered **descubierto/a** *p.p.* 14
discrimination **discriminación** *f.*
dish **plato** *m.* 8, 12
  main dish *m.* **plato principal** 8
dishwasher **lavaplatos** *m.*,
  *sing.* 12
disk **disco** *m.*
disorderly **desordenado/a** *adj.* 5
dive **bucear** *v.* 4
divorce **divorcio** *m.* 9
divorced **divorciado/a** *adj.* 9
  get divorced (from) **divorciarse**
    *v.* **(de)** 9
dizzy **mareado/a** *adj.* 10
do **hacer** *v.* 4
  do aerobics **hacer ejercicios**
    **aeróbicos** 15
  do household chores **hacer**
    **quehaceres domésticos** 12
  do stretching exercises **hacer**
    **ejercicios de**
    **estiramiento** 15
  (I) don't want to. **No quiero.** 4
doctor **doctor(a)** *m., f.* 3; 10;
  **médico/a** *m., f.* 3
documentary (*film*) **documental**
  *m.*
dog **perro** *m.* 13
domestic **doméstico/a** *adj.*
  domestic appliance
    **electrodoméstico** *m.*
done **hecho/a** *p.p.* 14
door **puerta** *f.* 2
dormitory **residencia** *f.*
  **estudiantil** 2
double **doble** *adj.* 5
  double room **habitación** *f.*
    **doble** 5
doubt **duda** *f.* 13; **dudar** *v.* 13
  not to doubt 13
  There is no doubt that...
    **No cabe duda de** 13;
    **No hay duda de** 13
Down with... ! **¡Abajo el/la...!**
download **descargar** *v.* 11
downtown **centro** *m.* 4
drama **drama** *m.*
dramatic **dramático/a** *adj.*
draw **dibujar** *v.* 2
drawing **dibujo** *m.*
dress **vestido** *m.* 6
  get dressed **vestirse (e:i)** *v.* 7
drink **beber** *v.* 3; **bebida** *f.* 8;
  **tomar** *v.* 2
drive **conducir** *v.* 6; **manejar**
  *v.* 11
driver **conductor(a)** *m., f.* 1
drug **droga** *f.* 15
  drug addict **drogadicto/a**
    *adj.* 15
dry oneself **secarse** *v.* 7
during **durante** *prep.* 7; **por**
  *prep.* 11
dust **sacudir** *v.* 12;
  **quitar** *v.* **el polvo** 12

dust the furniture **sacudir los muebles** 12
DVD player **reproductor** *m.* **de DVD** 11

## E

each **cada** *adj.* 6
eagle **águila** *f.*
ear (outer) **oreja** *f.* 10
early **temprano** *adv.* 7
earn **ganar** *v.*
earthquake **terremoto** *m.*
ease **aliviar** *v.*
east **este** *m.* 14
  to the east **al este** 14
easy **fácil** *adj. m., f.* 3
eat **comer** *v.* 3
ecology **ecología** *f.* 13
economics **economía** *f.* 2
ecotourism **ecoturismo** *m.* 13
Ecuador **Ecuador** *m.* 1
Ecuadorian **ecuatoriano/a** *adj.* 3
effective **eficaz** *adj. m., f.*
egg **huevo** *m.* 8
eight **ocho** 1
eight hundred **ochocientos/as** 2
eighteen **dieciocho** 1
eighth **octavo/a** 5
eighty **ochenta** 2
either... or **o... o** *conj.* 7
eldest **el/la mayor** 8
elect **elegir** *v.*
election **elecciones** *f. pl.*
electric appliance **electrodoméstico** *m.* 12
electrician **electricista** *m., f.*
electricity **luz** *f.* 12
elegant **elegante** *adj. m., f.* 6
elevator **ascensor** *m.* 5
eleven **once** 1
e-mail **correo** *m.* **electrónico** 4
e-mail address **dirrección** *f.* **electrónica** 11
  e-mail message **mensaje** *m.* **electrónico** 4
  read e-mail **leer** *v.* **el correo electrónico** 4
embarrassed **avergonzado/a** *adj.* 5 embrace (each other) **abrazar(se)** *v.* 11
emergency **emergencia** *f.* 10
  emergency room **sala** *f.* **de emergencia** 10
employee **empleado/a** *m., f.* 5
employment **empleo** *m.*
end **fin** *m.* 4; **terminar** *v.* 2
  end table **mesita** *f.* 12
energy **energía** *f.* 13
engaged: get engaged (to) **comprometerse** *v.* **(con)** 9
engineer **ingeniero/a** *m., f.* 3
English (*language*) **inglés** *m.* 2; **inglés, inglesa** *adj.* 3
enjoy **disfrutar** *v.* **(de)** 15
enough **bastante** *adv.* 10

entertainment **diversión** *f.* 4
entrance **entrada** *f.* 12
envelope **sobre** *m.* 14
environment **medio ambiente** *m.* 13
equality **igualdad** *f.*
equipped **equipado/a** *adj.* 15
erase **borrar** *v.* 11
eraser **borrador** *m.* 2
errand **diligencia** *f.* 14
establish **establecer** *v.*
evening **tarde** *f.* 1
event **acontecimiento** *m.*
every day **todos los días** 10
everybody **todos** *m., pl.*
everything **todo** *m.* 5
  Everything is under control. **Todo está bajo control.** 7
exactly **en punto** 1
exam **examen** *m.* 2
excellent **excelente** *adj.* 5
excess **exceso** *m.* 15
  in excess **en exceso** 15
exchange **intercambiar** *v.*
  in exchange for **por** 11
exciting **emocionante** *adj. m., f.*
excursion **excursión** *f.*
excuse **disculpar** *v.*
Excuse me. (*May I?*) **Con permiso.** 1; (*I beg your pardon.*) **Perdón.** 1
exercise **ejercicio** *m.* 15
  **hacer** *v.* **ejercicio** 15
exit **salida** *f.* 5
expensive **caro/a** *adj.* 6
experience **experiencia** *f.*
explain **explicar** *v.* 2
explore **explorar** *v.*
expression **expresión** *f.*
extinction **extinción** *f.* 13
extremely delicious **riquísimo/a** *adj.* 8
extremely serious **gravísimo** *adj.* 13
eye **ojo** *m.* 10

## F

fabulous **fabuloso/a** *adj.* 5
face **cara** *f.* 7
facing **enfrente de** *prep.* 14
fact: in fact **de hecho**
fall (down) **caerse** *v.* 10
  fall asleep **dormirse (o:ue)** *v.* 7
  fall in love (with) **enamorarse** *v.* **(de)** 9
fall (season) **otoño** *m.* 5
fallen **caído/a** *p.p.* 14
family **familia** *f.* 3
famous **famoso/a** *adj.*
fan **aficionado/a** *adj.* 4
  be a fan (of) **ser aficionado/a (a)** 4
far from **lejos de** *prep.* 2
farewell **despedida** *f.*

fascinate **fascinar** *v.* 7
fashion **moda** *f.* 6
  be in fashion **estar de moda** 6
fast **rápido/a** *adj.*
fat **gordo/a** *adj.* 3; **grasa** *f.* 15
father **padre** *m.* 3
father-in-law **suegro** *m.* 3
favorite **favorito/a** *adj.* 4
fax (machine) *fax* *m.* 11
fear **miedo** *m.* 3; **temer** *v.* 13
February **febrero** *m.* 5
feel **sentir(se) (e:ie)** *v.* 7
  feel like (*doing something*) **tener ganas de (+ inf.)** 3
festival **festival** *m.*
fever **fiebre** *f.* 10
  have a fever **tener** *v.* **fiebre** 10
few **pocos/as** *adj. pl.*
  fewer than **menos de (+ number)** 8
field: major field of study **especialización** *f.*
fifteen **quince** 1
  fifteen-year-old girl **quinceañera** *f.*
  young woman's fifteenth birthday celebration **quinceañera** *f.* 9
fifth **quinto/a** 5
fifty **cincuenta** 2
fight (for/against) **luchar** *v.* **(por/ contra)**
figure (*number*) **cifra** *f.*
file **archivo** *m.* 11
fill **llenar** *v.* 11
  fill out (a form) **llenar (un formulario)** 14
  fill the tank **llenar el tanque** 11
finally **finalmente** *adv.* 15; **por último** 7; **por fin** 11
find **encontrar (o:ue)** *v.* 4
  find (each other) **encontrar(se)**
fine **multa** *f.*
  That's fine. **Está bien.** 11
(fine) arts **bellas artes** *f., pl.*
finger **dedo** *m.* 10
finish **terminar** *v.* 2
  finish (*doing something*) **terminar** *v.* **de (+ inf.)** 4
fire **incendio** *m.*; **despedir (e:i)** *v.*
firefighter **bombero/a** *m., f.*
firm **compañía** *f.*; **empresa** *f.*
first **primer, primero/a** 5
fish (*food*) **pescado** *m.* 8; **pescar** *v.* 5; (*live*) **pez** *m.* 13
  fish market **pescadería** *f.* 14
fisherman **pescador** *m.*
fisherwoman **pescadora** *f.*
fishing **pesca** *f.* 5
fit (*clothing*) **quedar** *v.* 7
five **cinco** 1
five hundred **quinientos/as** 2
fix (*put in working order*) **arreglar** *v.* 11
fixed **fijo/a** *adj.* 6
flag **bandera** *f.*
flank steak **lomo** *m.* 8

flat tire: We had a flat tire. **Se nos pinchó una llanta.** 11
flexible **flexible** *adj.* 15
flood **inundación** *f.*
floor (*of a building*) **piso** *m.* 5; **suelo** *m.* 12
  ground floor **planta baja** *f.* 5
  top floor **planta** *f.* **alta**
flower **flor** *f.* 13
flu **gripe** *f.* 10
fog **niebla** *f.*
folk **folklórico/a** *adj.*
follow **seguir (e:i)** *v.* 4
food **comida** *f.* 8; **alimento**
foolish **tonto/a** *adj.* 3
foot **pie** *m.* 10
football **fútbol** *m.* **americano** 4
for **para** *prep.* 11; **por** *prep.* 11
  for example **por ejemplo** 11
  for me **para mí** 8
forbid **prohibir** *v.*
foreign **extranjero/a** *adj.*
  foreign languages **lenguas** *f., pl.* **extranjeras** 2
forest **bosque** *m.* 13
forget **olvidar** *v.* 10
fork **tenedor** *m.* 12
form **formulario** *m.* 14
forty **cuarenta** *m.* 2
four **cuatro** 1
four hundred **cuatrocientos/as** 2
fourteen **catorce** 1
fourth **cuarto/a** *m., f.* 5
free **libre** *adj. m., f.* 4
  be free (of charge) **ser gratis** 14
  free time **tiempo libre;** spare (free) time **ratos libres** 4
freedom **libertad** *f.*
freezer **congelador** *m.* 12
French **francés, francesa** *adj.* 3
  French fries **papas** *f., pl.* **fritas** 8; **patatas** *f., pl.* **fritas** 8
frequently **frecuentemente** *adv.* 10; **con frecuencia** *adv.* 10
Friday **viernes** *m., sing.* 2
fried **frito/a** *adj.* 8
  fried potatoes **papas** *f., pl.* **fritas** 8; **patatas** *f., pl.* **fritas** 8
friend **amigo/a** *m., f.* 3
friendly **amable** *adj. m., f.* 5
friendship **amistad** *f.* 9
from **de** *prep.* 1; **desde** *prep.* 6
  from the United States **estadounidense** *m., f. adj.* 3
  from time to time **de vez en cuando** 10
  He/She/It is from… **Es de…;** I'm from… **Soy de…** 1
fruit **fruta** *f.* 8
  fruit juice **jugo** *m.* **de fruta** 8
  fruit store **frutería** *f.* 14
full **lleno/a** *adj.* 11

fun **divertido/a** *adj.* 7
  fun activity **diversión** *f.* 4
  have fun **divertirse (e:ie)** *v.* 9
function **funcionar** *v.*
furniture **muebles** *m., pl.* 12
furthermore **además (de)** *adv.* 10
future **futuro** *adj.;* **porvenir** *m.*
  Here's to the future! **¡Por el porvenir!**
  in the future **en el futuro**

## G

gain weight **aumentar** *v.* **de peso** 15; **engordar** *v.* 15
game **juego** *m.;* (*match*) **partido** *m.* 4
  game show **concurso** *m.*
garage (*in a house*) **garaje** *m.* 12; **garaje** *m.* 11; **taller (mecánico)** 11
garden **jardín** *m.* 12
garlic **ajo** *m.* 8
gas station **gasolinera** *f.* 11
gasoline **gasolina** *f.* 11
geography **geografía** *f.* 2
German **alemán, alemana** *adj.* 3
get **conseguir (e:i)** *v.* 4; **obtener** *v.*
  get along well/badly (with) **llevarse bien/mal (con)** 9
  get bored **aburrirse** *v.*
  get off of (a vehicle) **bajar(se)** *v.* **de** 11
  get on/into (a vehicle) **subir(se)** *v.* **a** 11
  get out of (a vehicle) **bajar(se)** *v.* **de** 11
  get up **levantarse** *v.* 7
gift **regalo** *m.* 6
girl **chica** *f.* 1; **muchacha** *f.* 3
girlfriend **novia** *f.* 3
give **dar** *v.* 6, 9; (*as a gift*) **regalar** 9
glass (*drinking*) **vaso** *m.* 12; **vidrio** *m.* 13
  (made) of glass **de vidrio** 13
glasses **gafas** *f., pl.* 6
  sunglasses **gafas** *f., pl.* **de sol** 6
gloves **guantes** *m., pl.* 6
go **ir** *v.* 4
  go away **irse** 7
  go by boat **ir en barco** 5
  go by bus **ir en autobús** 5
  go by car **ir en auto(móvil)** 5
  go by motorcycle **ir en motocicleta** 5
  go by taxi **ir en taxi** 5
  go by the bank **pasar por el banco** 14
  go down; **bajar(se)** *v.*
  go on a hike (in the mountains)

**ir de excursión (a las montañas)** 4
  go out **salir** *v.* 9
  go out (with) **salir** *v.* **(con)** 9
  go up **subir** *v.*
  go with **acompañar** *v.* 14
  Let's go. **Vamos.** 4
goblet **copa** *f.* 12
going to: be going to (*do something*) **ir a (+ inf.)** 4
golf **golf** *m.* 4
good **buen, bueno/a** *adj.* 3, 6
  Good afternoon. **Buenas tardes.** 1
  Good evening. **Buenas noches.** 1
  Good idea. **Buena idea.** 4
  Good morning. **Buenos días.** 1
  Good night. **Buenas noches.** 1
  It's good that… **Es bueno que…** 12
goodbye **adiós** *m.* 1
  say goodbye (to) **despedirse** *v.* **(de) (e:i)** 7
good-looking **guapo/a** *adj.* 3
government **gobierno** *m.* 13
graduate (from/in) **graduarse** *v.* **(de/en)** 9
grains **cereales** *m., pl.* 8
granddaughter **nieta** *f.* 3
grandfather **abuelo** *m.* 3
grandmother **abuela** *f.* 3
grandparents **abuelos** *m., pl.* 3
grandson **nieto** *m.* 3
grape **uva** *f.* 8
grass **hierba** *f.* 13
grave **grave** *adj.* 10
gray **gris** *adj. m., f.* 6
great **fenomenal** *adj. m., f.* 5
great-grandfather **bisabuelo** *m.* 3
great-grandmother **bisabuela** *f.* 3
green **verde** *adj. m., f.* 6
greet (each other) **saludar(se)** *v.* 11
greeting **saludo** *m.* 1
  Greetings to… **Saludos a…** 1
grilled (*food*) **a la plancha** 8
  grilled flank steak **lomo a la plancha** 8
ground floor **planta baja** *f.* 5
guest (*at a house/hotel*) **huésped** *m., f.* 5 (*invited to a function*) **invitado/a** *m., f.* 9
guide **guía** *m., f.* 13
gymnasium **gimnasio** *m.* 4

## H

hair **pelo** *m.* 7
hairdresser **peluquero/a** *m., f.*
half **medio/a** *adj.* 3
  half-brother **medio hermano** 3
  half-sister **media hermana** 3
  half-past… (*time*) **…y media** 1

hallway **pasillo** *m.* 12
ham **jamón** *m.* 8
hamburger **hamburguesa** *f.* 8
hand **mano** *f.* 1
Hands up! **¡Manos arriba!**
handsome **guapo/a** *adj.* 3
happen **ocurrir** *v.*
happiness **alegría** *v.* 9
Happy birthday! **¡Feliz cumpleaños!** 9
happy **alegre** *adj.* 5; **contento/a**
*adj.* 5; **feliz** *adj. m., f.* 5
be happy **alegrarse** *v.* **(de)** 13
hard **difícil** *adj. m., f.* 3
hard-working **trabajador(a)**
*adj.* 3
hardly **apenas** *adv.* 10
haste **prisa** *f.* 3
hat **sombrero** *m.* 6
hate **odiar** *v.* 9
have **tener** *v.* 3
Have a good trip! **¡Buen viaje!** 1
have time **tener tiempo** 4
have to (*do something*) **tener
que (+ *inf.*) 3; **deber (+ *inf.*)**
have a tooth removed **sacar(se)
un diente** 10
he **él** 1
head **cabeza** *f.* 10
headache **dolor** *m.* **de cabeza** 10
health **salud** *f.* 10
healthy **saludable** *adj. m., f.* 10;
**sano/a** *adj.* 10
lead a healthy lifestyle **llevar** *v.*
**una vida sana** 15
hear **oír** *v.* 4
heard **oído/a** *p.p.* 14
hearing: sense of hearing **oído**
*m.* 10
heart **corazón** *m.* 10
heat **calor** *m.* 5
Hello. **Hola.** 1; (*on the telephone*) **Aló.** 11; **¿Bueno?** 11;
**Diga.** 11
help **ayudar** *v.* 12; **servir (e:i)**
*v.* 5
help each other **ayudarse** *v.* 11
her **su(s)** *poss. adj.* 3; (of) hers
**suyo(s)/a(s)** *poss.* 11
her **la** *f., sing., d.o. pron.* 5
to/for her **le** *f., sing., i.o. pron.* 6
here **aquí** *adv.* 1
Here it is. **Aquí está.** 5
Here we are at/in... **Aquí
estamos en...** 2
Hi. **Hola.** 1
highway **autopista** *f.* 11;
**carretera** *f.* 11
hike **excursión** *f.* 4
go on a hike **hacer una excursión** 5; **ir de excursión** 4
hiker **excursionista** *m., f.*
hiking **de excursión** 4
him: to/for him **le** *m., sing., i.o.
pron.* 6
hire **contratar** *v.*

his **su(s)** *poss. adj.* 3; (of) his
**suyo(s)/a(s)** *poss. pron.* 11
his **lo** *m., sing., d.o. pron.* 5
history **historia** *f.* 2
hobby **pasatiempo** *m.* 4
hockey **hockey** *m.* 4
holiday **día** *m.* **de fiesta** 9
home **casa** *f.* 2
home page **página** *f.*
**principal** 11
homework **tarea** *f.* 2
hood **capó** *m.* 11; **cofre** *m.* 11
hope **esperar** *v.* **(+ *inf.*)** 2;
**esperar** *v.* 13
I hope (that) **ojalá (que)** 13
horror (genre) **de horror** *m.*
hors d'oeuvres **entremeses** *m.,
pl.* 8
horse **caballo** *m.* 5
hospital **hospital** *m.* 10
hot: be (*feel*) (very) hot **tener
(mucho) calor** 3
It's (very) hot. **Hace (mucho)
calor.** 5
hotel **hotel** *m.* 5
hour **hora** *f.* 1
house **casa** *f.* 2
household chores **quehaceres** *m.
pl.* **domésticos** 12
housekeeper **ama** *m., f.* **de casa** 12
housing **vivienda** *f.* 12
How... ! **¡Qué...!** 3
how **¿cómo?** *adv.* 1
How are you? **¿Qué tal?** 1
How are you? **¿Cómo estás?**
*fam.* 1
How are you? **¿Cómo está
usted?** *form.* 1
How can I help you? **¿En qué
puedo servirles?** 5
How did it go for you...?
**¿Cómo le/les fue...?** 15
How is it going? **¿Qué tal?** 1
How is/are...? **¿Qué tal...?** 2
How is the weather? **¿Qué
tiempo hace?** 15
How much/many?
**¿Cuánto(s)/a(s)?** 1
How much does... cost?
**¿Cuánto cuesta...?** 6
How old are you? **¿Cuántos
años tienes?** *fam.* 3
however **sin embargo**
hug (each other) **abrazar(se)**
*v.* 11
humanities **humanidades** *f., pl.* 2
hundred **cien, ciento** 2
hunger **hambre** *f.* 3
hungry: be (very) hungry **tener** *v.*
**(mucha) hambre** 3
hunt **cazar** *v.* 13
hurricane **huracán** *m.*
hurry **apurarse** *v.* 15; **darse prisa**
*v.* 15
be in a (big) hurry **tener** *v.*
**(mucha) prisa** 3

hurt **doler (o:ue)** *v.* 10
It hurts me a lot... **Me duele
mucho...** 10
husband **esposo** *m.* 3

## I

I **yo** 1
I am... **Yo soy...** 1
I hope (that) **Ojalá (que)**
*interj.* 13
I wish (that) **Ojalá (que)**
*interj.* 13
ice cream **helado** *m.* 9
ice cream shop **heladería** *f.* 14
iced **helado/a** *adj.* 8
iced tea **té** *m.* **helado** 8
idea **idea** *f.* 4
if **si** *conj.* 4
illness **enfermedad** *f.* 10
important **importante** *adj.* 3
be important to **importar** *v.* 7
It's important that... **Es
importante que...** 12
impossible **imposible** *adj.* 13
it's impossible **es imposible** 13
improbable **improbable** *adj.* 13
it's improbable **es
improbable** 13
improve **mejorar** *v.* 13
in **en** *prep.* 2; **por** *prep.* 11
in the afternoon **de la tarde** 1;
**por la tarde** 7
in a bad mood **de mal humor** 5
in the direction of **para** *prep.* 1;
in the early evening **de la tarde** 1
in the evening **de la noche** 1;
**por la tarde** 7
in a good mood **de buen
humor** 5
in the morning **de la
mañana** 1; **por la
mañana** 7
in love (with)
**enamorado/a (de)** 5
in search of **por** *prep.* 11
in front of **delante de** *prep.* 2
increase **aumento** *m.*
incredible **increíble** *adj.* 5
inequality **desigualdad** *f.*
infection **infección** *f.* 10
inform **informar** *v.*
injection **inyección** *f.* 10
give an injection *v.* **poner una
inyección** 10
injure (oneself) **lastimarse** 10
injure (one's foot) **lastimarse** *v.*
**(el pie)** 10
inner ear **oído** *m.* 10
inside **dentro** *adv.*
insist (on) **insistir** *v.* **(en)** 12
installments: pay in installments
**pagar** *v.* **a plazos** 14
intelligent **inteligente** *adj.* 3
intend to **pensar** *v.* **(+ *inf.*)** 4

interest **interesar** v. 7
interesting **interesante** adj. 3
  be interesting to **interesar** v. 7
international **internacional** adj. m., f.
Internet **Internet** 11
interview **entrevista** f.; interview **entrevistar** v.
interviewer **entrevistador(a)** m., f.
introduction **presentación** f.
  I would like to introduce (name) to you... **Le presento a...** form. 1; **Te presento a...** fam. 1
invest **invertir (e:ie)** v.
invite **invitar** v. 9
iron (clothes) **planchar** v. **la ropa** 12
it **lo/la** sing., d.o., pron. 5
Italian **italiano/a** adj. 3
its **su(s)** poss. adj. 3, **suyo(s)/a(s)** poss. pron. 11
It's me. **Soy yo.** 1

### J

jacket **chaqueta** f. 6
January **enero** m. 5
Japanese **japonés, japonesa** adj. 3
jeans **bluejeans** m., pl. 6
jewelry store **joyería** f. 14
job **empleo** m.; **puesto** m.; **trabajo** m.
  job application **solicitud** f. **de trabajo**
jog **correr** v.
journalism **periodismo** m. 2
journalist **periodista** m., f. 3; **reportero/a** m., f.
joy **alegría** f. 9
  give joy **dar** v. **alegría** 9
joyful **alegre** adj. 5
juice **jugo** m. 8
July **julio** m. 5
June **junio** m. 5
jungle **selva, jungla** f. 13
just **apenas** adv.
  have just done something **acabar de (+ inf.)** 6

### K

key **llave** f. 5
keyboard **teclado** m. 11
kilometer **kilómetro** m. 11
kind: That's very kind of you. **Muy amable.** 5
kiss **beso** m. 9
  kiss each other **besarse** v. 11
kitchen **cocina** f. 12
knee **rodilla** f. 10
knife **cuchillo** m. 12
know **saber** v. 6; **conocer** v. 6
know how **saber** v. 6

### L

laboratory **laboratorio** m. 2
lack **faltar** v. 7
lake **lago** m. 13
lamp **lámpara** f. 12
land **tierra** f. 13
landlord **dueño/a** m., f. 8
landscape **paisaje** m. 5
language **lengua** f. 2
laptop (computer) **computadora** f. **portátil** 11
large **grande** adj. 3
large (clothing size) **talla grande** 6
last **durar** v.; **pasado/a** adj. 6; **último/a** adj.
  last name **apellido** m. 3
  last night **anoche** adv. 6
  last week **semana** f. **pasada** 6
  last year **año** m. **pasado** 6
late **tarde** adv. 7
later (on) **más tarde** 7
  See you later. **Hasta la vista.** 1; **Hasta luego.** 1
laugh **reírse (e:i)** v. 9
laughed **reído** p.p. 14
laundromat **lavandería** f. 14
law **ley** f. 13
lawyer **abogado/a** m., f.
lazy **perezoso/a** adj.
learn **aprender** v. (a + inf.) 3
least, at **por lo menos** adv. 10
leave **salir** v. 4; **irse** v. 7
  leave a tip **dejar una propina** 9
  leave behind **dejar** v.
  leave for (a place) **salir para**
  leave from **salir de**
left **izquierdo/a** adj. 2
  be left over **quedar** v. 7
  to the left of **a la izquierda de** 2
leg **pierna** f. 10
lemon **limón** m. 8
lend **prestar** v. 6
less **menos** adv. 10
  less... than **menos... que** 8
  less than **menos de (+ number)**
lesson **lección** f. 1
let **dejar** v. 12
let's see **a ver** 2
letter **carta** f. 4, 14
lettuce **lechuga** f. 8
liberty **libertad** f.
library **biblioteca** f. 2
license (driver's) **licencia** f. **de conducir** 11
lie **mentira** f. 4
life **vida** f. 9
  of my life **de mi vida** 15
lifestyle: lead a healthy lifestyle **llevar una vida sana** 15
lift **levantar** v. 15
  lift weights **levantar pesas** 15
light **luz** f. 12
like **como** prep. 8; **gustar** v. 2

I don't like them at all. **No me gustan nada.** 2
I like... **Me gusta(n)...** 2
like this **así** adv. 10
like very much **encantar** v.; **fascinar** v. 7
Do you like...? **¿Te gusta(n)...?** 2
likeable **simpático/a** adj. 3
likewise **igualmente** adv. 1
line **línea** f. 4; **cola** (queue) f. 14
listen (to) **escuchar** v. 2
  Listen! (command) **¡Oye!** fam., sing. 1; **¡Oiga/Oigan!** form., sing./pl. 1
  listen to music **escuchar música** 2
  listen (to) the radio **escuchar la radio** 2
literature **literatura** f. 2
little (quantity) **poco/a** adj. 5; **poco** adv. 10
live **vivir** v. 3
living room **sala** f. 12
loan **préstamo** m. 14; **prestar** v. 6, 14
lobster **langosta** f. 8
located **situado/a** adj.
  be located **quedar** v. 14
long **largo/a** adj. 6
look (at) **mirar** v. 2
look for **buscar** v. 2
lose **perder (e:ie)** v. 4
  lose weight **adelgazar** v. 15
lost **perdido/a** adj. 14
  be lost **estar perdido/a** 14
lot, a **muchas veces** adv. 10
lot of, a **mucho/a** adj. 2, 3
love (another person) **querer (e:ie)** v. 4; (inanimate objects) **encantar** v. 7 ; **amor** m. 9
  in love **enamorado/a** adj. 5
  I loved it! **¡Me encantó!** 15
luck **suerte** f. 3
lucky: be (very) lucky **tener (mucha) suerte** 3
luggage **equipaje** m. 5
lunch **almuerzo** m. 8
  have lunch **almorzar (o:ue)** v. 4

### M

ma'am **señora (Sra.); doña** f. 1
mad **enojado/a** adj. 5
magazine **revista** f. 4
magnificent **magnífico/a** adj. 5
mail **correo** m. 14; **enviar** v., **mandar** v. 14; **echar (una carta) al buzón** 14
  mail **correo** m. 14; **enviar** v., **mandar** v. 14
  mail carrier **cartero** m. 14
mailbox **buzón** m. 14
main **principal** adj. m., f. 8
maintain **mantener** v. 15
major **especialización** f. 2

make **hacer** v. 4
  make the bed **hacer la cama** 12
makeup **maquillaje** m. 7
  put on makeup **maquillarse** v. 7
man **hombre** m. 1
manager **gerente** m., f.
many **mucho/a** adj. 3
  many times **muchas veces** 10
map **mapa** m. 2
March **marzo** m. 5
margarine **margarina** f. 8
marinated fish **ceviche** m. 8
  lemon-marinated shrimp **ceviche** m. **de camarón** 8
marital status **estado** m. **civil** 9
market **mercado** m. 6
  open-air market **mercado al aire libre** 6
marriage **matrimonio** m. 9
married **casado/a** adj. 9
  get married (to) **casarse** v. **(con)** 9
marvelous **maravilloso/a** adj. 5
marvelously **maravillosamente** adv.
massage **masaje** m. 15
masterpiece **obra maestra** f.
match (sports) **partido** m. 4
match (with) **hacer** v. **juego (con)** 6
mathematics **matemáticas** f., pl. 2
matter **importar** v. 7
maturity **madurez** f. 9
maximum **máximo/a** adj. 11
May **mayo** m. 5
maybe **tal vez** 5; **quizás** 5
mayonnaise **mayonesa** f. 8
me **me** sing., d.o. pron. 5
  to/for me **me** sing., i.o. pron. 6
meal **comida** f. 8
means of communication **medios** m., pl. **de comunicación**
meat **carne** f. 8
mechanic **mecánico/a** m., f. 11
  mechanic's repair shop **taller mecánico** 11
media **medios** m., pl. **de comunicación**
medical **médico/a** adj. 10
medication **medicamento** m. 10
medicine **medicina** f. 10
medium **mediano/a** adj.
meet (each other) **encontrar(se)** v. 11; **conocerse(se)** v. 8
meeting **reunión** f.
menu **menú** m. 8
message (telephone) **recado** m. 11, **mensaje** m.
Mexican **mexicano/a** adj. 3
Mexico **México** m. 1
microwave **microonda** f. 12
  microwave oven **horno** m.**de microondas** 12
middle age **madurez** f. 9
midnight **medianoche** f. 1

mile **milla** f. 11
milk **leche** f. 8
million **millón** m. 2
  million of **millón de** 2
mine **mío(s)/a(s)** poss. 11
mineral **mineral** m. 15
  mineral water **agua** f. **mineral** 8
minute **minuto** m. 1
mirror **espejo** m. 7
Miss **señorita (Srta.)** f. 1
miss **perder (e:ie)** v. 4
mistaken **equivocado/a** adj.
modem **módem** m.
modern **moderno/a** adj.
mom **mamá** f. 3
Monday **lunes** m., sing. 2
money **dinero** m. 6
monitor **monitor** m. 11
month **mes** m. 5
monument **monumento** m. 4
moon **luna** f. 13
more **más** 2
  more… than **más… que** 8
  more than **más de** (+ number) 8
morning **mañana** f. 1
mother **madre** f. 3
mother-in-law **suegra** f. 3
motor **motor** m.
motorcycle **motocicleta** f. 5
mountain **montaña** f. 4
mouse **ratón** m. 11
mouth **boca** f. 10
move (from one house to another) **mudarse** v. 12
movie **película** f. 4
  movie star **estrella** f. **de cine**
  movie theater **cine** m. 4
MP3 player **reproductor** m. **de MP3** 11
Mr. **señor (Sr.); don** m. 1
Mrs. **señora (Sra.); doña** f. 1
much **mucho/a** adj. 2, 3
  very much **muchísimo/a** adj. 2
municipal **municipal** adj. m., f.
murder **crimen** m.
muscle **músculo** m. 15
museum **museo** m. 4
mushroom **champiñón** m. 8
music **música** f. 2
musical **musical** adj., m., f.
musician **músico/a** m., f.
must **deber** v. (+ inf.)
  It must be… **Debe ser…** 6
my **mi(s)** poss. adj. 3; **mío(s)/a(s)** poss. pron. 11

name **nombre** m. 1
  be named **llamarse** v. 7
  in the name of **a nombre de** 5
  last name **apellido** m.
  My name is… **Me llamo…** 1

napkin **servilleta** f. 12
national **nacional** adj. m., f.
nationality **nacionalidad** f. 1
natural **natural** adj. m., f. 13
natural disaster **desastre** m. **natural**
  natural resource **recurso** m. **natural** 13
nature **naturaleza** f. 13
nauseated **mareado/a** adj. 10
near **cerca de** prep. 2
neaten **arreglar** v. 12
necessary **necesario/a** adj. 12
  It is necessary that… **Hay que…** 12, 14
neck **cuello** m. 10
need **faltar** v. 7; **necesitar** v. (+ inf.) 2
negative **negativo/a** adj.
neighbor **vecino/a** m., f. 12
neighborhood **barrio** m. 12
neither **tampoco** adv. 7
neither… nor **ni… ni** conj. 7
nephew **sobrino** m. 3
nervous **nervioso/a** adj. 5
network **red** f. 11
never **nunca** adj. 7; **jamás** 7
new **nuevo/a** adj. 6
newlywed **recién casado/a** m., f. 9
news **noticias** f., pl.; **actualidades** f., pl.
newscast **noticiero** m.
newspaper **periódico** 4; **diario** m.
next **próximo/a** adj.
  next to **al lado de** prep. 2
nice **simpático/a** adj. 3; **amable** adj. m., f. 5
niece **sobrina** f. 3
night **noche** f. 1
  night stand **mesita** f. **de noche** 12
nine **nueve** 1
nine hundred **novecientos/as** 2
nineteen **diecinueve** 1
ninety **noventa** 2
ninth **noveno/a** 5
no **no** 1; **ningún, ninguno/a(s)** adj. 7
  no one **nadie** pron. 7
  No problem. **No hay problema.** 7
  no way **de ninguna manera**
nobody **nadie** 7
none **ningún, ninguno/a(s)** adj. 7
noon **mediodía** m. 1
nor **ni** conj. 7
north **norte** m. 14
  to the north **al norte** 14
nose **nariz** f. 10
not **no** 1
  not any **ningún, ninguno/a(s)** adj. 7
  not anyone **nadie** pron. 7

not anything **nada** *pron.* 7
not bad at all **nada mal** 5
not either **tampoco** *adv.* 7
not ever **nunca** *adv.* 7; **jamás**
   *adv.* 7
not very well **no muy bien** 1
not working **descompuesto/a**
   *adj.* 11
notebook **cuaderno** *m.* 1
nothing **nada** 1; 7
noun **sustantivo** *m.*
November **noviembre** *m.* 5
now **ahora** *adv.* 2
nowadays **hoy día** *adv.*
nuclear **nuclear** *adj. m., f.* 13
   nuclear energy **energía**
     **nuclear** 13
number **número** *m.* 1
nurse **enfermero/a** *m., f.* 10
nutrition **nutrición** *f.* 15
nutritionist **nutricionista** *m.,*
   *f.* 15

## O

o'clock: It's... o'clock **Son**
   **las...** 1
   It's one o'clock. **Es la una.** 1
obey **obedecer** *v.*
obligation **deber** *m.*
obtain **conseguir (e:i)** *v.* 4;
   **obtener** *v.*
obvious **obvio/a** *adj.* 13
   it's obvious **es obvio** 13
occupation **ocupación** *f.*
occur **ocurrir** *v.*
October **octubre** *m.* 5
of **de** *prep.* 1
   Of course. **Claro que sí.;**
     **Por supuesto.**
offer **oferta** *f.* 12; **ofrecer (c:zc)**
   *v.* 6
office **oficina** *f.* 12
   doctor's office **consultorio** *m.* 10
often **a menudo** *adv.* 10
Oh! **¡Ay!**
oil **aceite** *m.* 8
OK **regular** *adj.* 1
   It's okay. **Está bien.**
old **viejo/a** *adj.* 3
old age **vejez** *f.* 9
older **mayor** *adj. m., f.* 3
   older brother, sister **hermano/a**
     **mayor** *m., f.* 3
oldest **el/la mayor** 8
on **en** *prep.* 2: **sobre** *prep.* 2
   on behalf of **por** *prep.* 11
   on the dot **en punto** 1
   on time **a tiempo** 10
   on top of **encima de** 2
once **una vez** 6
one **un, uno/a** *m., f., sing. pron.* 1
   one hundred **cien(to)** 2
   one million **un millón** *m.* 2
   one more time **una vez más** 9

one thousand **mil** 2
one time **una vez** 6
onion **cebolla** *f.* 8
only **sólo** *adv.* 3; **único/a** *adj.* 3
   only child **hijo/a único/a**
     *m., f.* 3
open **abierto/a** *adj.* 5, 14;
   **abrir** *v.* 3
open-air **al aire libre** 6
opera **ópera** *f.*
operation **operación** *f.* 10
opposite **enfrente de** *prep.* 14
or **o** *conj.* 7
orange **anaranjado/a** *adj.* 6;
   **naranja** *f.* 8
orchestra **orquesta** *f.*
order **mandar** 12; *(food)* **pedir**
   **(e:i)** *v.* 8
   in order to **para** *prep.* 11
orderly **ordenado/a** *adj.* 5
ordinal *(numbers)* **ordinal** *adj.*
other **otro/a** *adj.* 6
ought to **deber** *v.* **(+ inf.)** *adj.* 3
our **nuestro(s)/a(s)** *poss. adj.* 3;
   *poss. pron.* 11
out of order **descompuesto/a**
   *adj.* 11
outskirts **afueras** *f., pl.* 12
oven **horno** *m.* 12
over **sobre** *prep.* 2
own **propio/a** *adj.*
owner **dueño/a** *m., f.* 8

## P

p.m. **tarde** *f.* 1
pack (one's suitcases) **hacer** *v.* **las**
   **maletas** 5
package **paquete** *m.* 14
page **página** *f.* 11
pain **dolor** *m.* 10
   have a pain **tener** *v.* **dolor** 10
paint **pintar** *v.*
painter **pintor(a)** *m., f.*
painting **pintura** *f.* 12
pair **par** *m.* 6
   pair of shoes **par** *m.* **de**
     **zapatos** 6
pants **pantalones** *m., pl.* 6
pantyhose **medias** *f., pl.* 6
paper **papel** *m.* 2; *(report)*
   **informe** *m.*
Pardon me. *(May I?)* **Con**
   **permiso.** 1; *(Excuse me.)*
   Pardon me. **Perdón.** 1
parents **padres** *m., pl.* 3; **papás**
   *m., pl.* 3
park **estacionar** *v.* 11; **parque**
   *m.* 4
parking lot **estacionamiento**
   *m.* 14
partner *(one of a married couple)*
   **pareja** *f.* 9
party **fiesta** *f.* 9
passed **pasado/a** *p.p.*

passenger **pasajero/a** *m., f.* 1
passport **pasaporte** *m.* 5
past **pasado/a** *adj.* 6
pastime **pasatiempo** *m.* 4
pastry shop **pastelería** *f.* 14
patient **paciente** *m., f.* 10
patio **patio** *m.* 12
pay **pagar** *v.* 6
   pay in cash **pagar** *v.* **al contado;**
     **pagar en efectivo** 14
   pay in installments **pagar** *v.* **a**
     **plazos** 14
   pay the bill **pagar la cuenta** 9
pea **arveja** *m.* 8
peace **paz** *f.*
peach **melocotón** *m.* 8
pear **pera** *f.* 8
pen **pluma** *f.* 2
pencil **lápiz** *m.* 1
penicillin **penicilina** *f.* 10
people **gente** *f.* 3
pepper *(black)* **pimienta** *f.* 8
per **por** *prep.* 11
perfect **perfecto/a** *adj.* 5
perhaps **quizás; tal vez**
permission **permiso** *m.*
person **persona** *f.* 3
pharmacy **farmacia** *f.* 10
phenomenal **fenomenal** *adj.* 5
photograph **foto(grafía)** *f.* 1
physical *(exam)* **examen** *m.*
   **médico** 10
physician **doctor(a), médico/a**
   *m., f.* 3
physics **física** *f. sing.* 2
pick up **recoger** *v.* 13
picture **cuadro** *m.* 12;
   **pintura** *f.* 12
pie **pastel** *m.* 9
pill (tablet) **pastilla** *f.* 10
pillow **almohada** *f.* 12
pineapple **piña** *f.* 8
pink **rosado/a** *adj.* 6
place **lugar** *m.* 4; **poner** *v.* 4
plaid **de cuadros** 6
plans **planes** *m., pl.* 4
   have plans **tener planes** 4
plant **planta** *f.* 13
plastic **plástico** *m.* 13
   (made) of plastic **de**
     **plástico** 13
plate **plato** *m.* 12
   platter of fried food **fuente** *f.*
     **de fritada**
play **drama** *m.;* **comedia** *f.;*
   **jugar (u:ue)** *v.* 4; *(a musical*
   *instrument)* **tocar** *v.; (a role)*
   **hacer el papel de;** *(cards)*
   **jugar a (las cartas)** 5; *(sports)*
   **practicar deportes** 4
player **jugador(a)** *m., f.* 4
playwright **dramaturgo/a**
   *m., f.*
plead **rogar (o:ue)** *v.* 12
pleasant **agradable** *adj. m., f.*
please **por favor** 1

Pleased to meet you. **Mucho gusto.** 1; **Encantado/a.** *adj.* 1

pleasing: be pleasing to **gustar** *v.* 7

pleasure **gusto** *m.* 1; **placer** *m.* 15
  It's a pleasure to… **Gusto de** (+ *inf.*)
  It's been a pleasure. **Ha sido un placer.** 15
  The pleasure is mine. **El gusto es mío.** 1

poem **poema** *m.*
poet **poeta** *m., f.*
poetry **poesía** *f.*
police (force) **policía** *f.* 11
political **político/a** *adj.*
politician **político/a** *m., f.*
politics **política** *f.*
polka-dotted **de lunares** 6
poll **encuesta** *f.*
pollute **contaminar** *v.* 13
polluted **contaminado/a** *m., f.* 13
  be polluted **estar contaminado/a** 13
pollution **contaminación** *f.* 13
pool **piscina** *f.* 4
poor **pobre** *adj., m., f.* 6
population **población** *f.* 13
pork **cerdo** *m.* 8
  pork chop **chuleta** *f.* **de cerdo** 8
portable **portátil** *adj.* 11
  portable computer **computadora** *f.* **portátil** 11
position **puesto** *m.*
possessive **posesivo/a** *adj.* 3
possible **posible** *adj.* 13
  it's (not) possible **(no) es posible** 13
post office **correo** *m.* 14
postcard **postal** *f.* 4
poster **cartel** *m.* 12
potato **papa** *f.* 8; **patata** *f.* 8
pottery **cerámica** *f.*
practice **entrenarse** *v.* 15; **practicar** *v.* 2
prefer **preferir (e:ie)** *v.* 4
pregnant **embarazada** *adj. f.* 10
prepare **preparar** *v.* 2
preposition **preposición** *f.*
prescribe (*medicine*) **recetar** *v.* 10
prescription **receta** *f.* 10
present **regalo** *m.*; **presentar** *v.*
press **prensa** *f.*
pressure **presión** *f.*
  be under a lot of pressure **sufrir muchas presiones** 15
pretty **bonito/a** *adj.* 3; **bastante** *adv.* 13
price **precio** *m.* 6
  (fixed, set) price **precio** *m.* **fijo** 6
print **estampado/a** *adj.*; **imprimir** *v.* 11
printer **impresora** *f.* 11
private (*room*) **individual** *adj.*

prize **premio** *m.*
probable **probable** *adj.* 13
  it's (not) probable **(no) es probable** 13
problem **problema** *m.* 1
profession **profesión** *f.* 3
professor **profesor(a)** *m., f.*
program **programa** *m.* 1
programmer **programador(a)** *m., f.* 3
prohibit **prohibir** *v.* 10
promotion (*career*) **ascenso** *m.*
pronoun **pronombre** *m.*
protect **proteger** *v.* 13
protein **proteína** *f.* 15
provided (that) **con tal (de) que** *conj.* 13
psychologist **psicólogo/a** *m., f.*
psychology **psicología** *f.* 2
publish **publicar** *v.*
Puerto Rican **puertorriqueño/a** *adj.* 3
Puerto Rico **Puerto Rico** *m.* 1
pull a tooth **sacar una muela**
purchases **compras** *f., pl.* 5
pure **puro/a** *adj.* 13
purple **morado/a** *adj.* 6
purse **bolsa** *f.* 6
put **poner** *v.* 4; **puesto/a** *p.p.* 14
  put (a letter) in the mailbox **echar (una carta) al buzón** 14
put on (*a performance*) **presentar** *v.*
put on (*clothing*) **ponerse** *v.* 7
put on makeup **maquillarse** *v.* 7

## Q

quality **calidad** *f.* 6
quarter (*academic*) **trimestre** *m.* 2
  quarter after (*time*) **y cuarto** 1; **y quince** 1
  quarter to (*time*) **menos cuarto** 1; **menos quince** 1
question **pregunta** *f.* 2
quickly **rápido** *adv.* 10
quiet **tranquilo/a** *adj.* 15
quit **dejar** *v.*
quiz **prueba** *f.* 2

## R

racism **racismo** *m.*
radio (*medium*) **radio** *f.* 2
  radio (set) **radio** *m.* 11
rain **llover (o:ue)** *v.* 5; **lluvia** *f.* 13
  It's raining. **Llueve.** 5; **Está lloviendo.** 5
raincoat **impermeable** *m.* 6

rainforest **bosque** *m.* **tropical** 13
raise (*salary*) **aumento de sueldo**
rather **bastante** *adv.* 10
read **leer** *v.* 3; **leído/a** *p.p.* 14
  read e-mail **leer correo electrónico** 4
  read a magazine **leer una revista** 4
  read a newspaper **leer un periódico** 4
ready **listo/a** *adj.* 5
  (Are you) ready? **¿(Están) listos?** 15
reap the benefits (of) *v.* **disfrutar** *v.* **(de)** 15
receive **recibir** *v.* 3
recommend **recomendar (e:ie)** *v.* 8; 12
record **grabar** *v.* 11
recreation **diversión** *f.* 4
recycle **reciclar** *v.* 13
recycling **reciclaje** *m.* 13
red **rojo/a** *adj.* 6
red-haired **pelirrojo/a** *adj.* 3
reduce **reducir** *v.* 13
  reduce stress/tension **aliviar el estrés/la tensión** 15
refrigerator **refrigerador** *m.* 12
region **región** *f.* 13
regret **sentir (e:ie)** *v.* 13
related to sitting **sedentario/a** *adj.* 15
relatives **parientes** *m., pl.* 3
relax **relajarse** *v.* 9
remain **quedarse** *v.* 7
remember **acordarse (o:ue)** *v.* **(de)** 7; **recordar (o:ue)** *v.* 4
remote control **control remoto** *m.* 11

rent **alquilar** *v.* 12; (payment) **alquiler** *m.* 12
repeat **repetir (e:i)** *v.* 4
report **informe** *m.*; **reportaje** *m.*
reporter **reportero/a** *m., f.*
representative **representante** *m., f.*
request **pedir (e:i)** *v.* 4
reservation **reservación** *f.* 5
resign (from) **renunciar (a)** *v.*
resolve **resolver (o:ue)** *v.* 13
resolved **resuelto/a** *p.p.* 14
resource **recurso** *m.* 13
responsibility **deber** *m.*; **responsabilidad** *f.*
rest **descansar** *v.* 2
restaurant **restaurante** *m.* 4
résumé **currículum** *m.*
retire (from work) **jubilarse** *v.* 9
return **regresar** *v.* 2; **volver (o:ue)** *v.* 4
returned **vuelto/a** *p.p.* 14
rice **arroz** *m.* 8
rich **rico/a** *adj.* 6

ride a bicycle **pasear** *v.* **en bicicleta** 4
ride a horse **montar** *v.* **a caballo** 5
ridiculous **ridículo/a** *adj.* 13
  it's ridiculous **es ridículo** 13
right **derecha** *f.* 2
  be right **tener razón** 3
  right? (*question tag*) **¿no?** 1; **¿verdad?** 1
  right away **enseguida** *adv.* 9
  right here **aquí mismo** 11
  right now **ahora mismo** 5
  right there **allí mismo** 14
  to the right of **a la derecha de** 2
rights **derechos** *m.*
ring (*a doorbell*) **sonar (o:ue)** *v.* 11
river **río** *m.* 13
road **camino** *m.*
roast **asado/a** *adj.* 8
roast chicken **pollo** *m.* **asado** 8
rollerblade **patinar en línea** *v.*
romantic **romántico/a** *adj.*
room **habitación** *f.* 5; **cuarto** *m.* 2; 7
  living room **sala** *f.* 12
roommate **compañero/a** *m., f.* **de cuarto** 2
roundtrip **de ida y vuelta** 5
  roundtrip ticket **pasaje** *m.* **de ida y vuelta** 5
routine **rutina** *f.* 7
rug **alfombra** *f.* 12
run **correr** *v.* 3
  run errands **hacer diligencias** 14
  run into (*have an accident*) **chocar (con)** *v.*; (*meet accidentally*) **encontrar(se) (o:ue)** *v.* 11; (*run into something*) **darse (con)** 10
  run into (*each other*) **encontrar(se) (o:ue)** *v.* 11
rush **apurarse, darse prisa** *v.* 15
Russian **ruso/a** *adj.* 3

## S

sad **triste** *adj.* 5; 13
  it's sad **es triste** 13
safe **seguro/a** *adj.* 5
said **dicho/a** *p.p.* 14
salad **ensalada** *f.* 8
salary **salario** *m.*; **sueldo** *m.*
sale **rebaja** *f.* 6
salesperson **vendedor(a)** *m., f.* 6
salmon **salmón** *m.* 8
salt **sal** *f.* 8
same **mismo/a** *adj.* 3
sandal **sandalia** *f.* 6
sandwich **sándwich** *m.* 8
Saturday **sábado** *m.* 2

sausage **salchicha** *f.* 8
save (*on a computer*) **guardar** *v.* 11; save (money) **ahorrar** *v.* 14
savings **ahorros** *m.* 14
  savings account **cuenta** *f.* **de ahorros** 14
say **decir** *v.* 4; **declarar** *v.*
say (that) **decir (que)** *v.* 4, 9
  say the answer **decir la respuesta** 4
scarcely **apenas** *adv.* 10
scared: be (very) scared (of) **tener (mucho) miedo (de)** 3
schedule **horario** *m.* 2
school **escuela** *f.* 1
science *f.* **ciencia** 2
  science fiction **ciencia ficción** *f.*
scientist **científico/a** *m., f.*
screen **pantalla** *f.* 11
scuba dive **bucear** *v.* 4
sculpt **esculpir** *v.*
sculptor **escultor(a)** *m., f.*
sculpture **escultura** *f.*
sea **mar** *m.* 5
season **estación** *f.* 5
seat **silla** *f.* 2
second **segundo/a** 5
secretary **secretario/a** *m., f.*
sedentary **sedentario/a** *adj.* 15
see **ver** *v.* 4
  see (you, him, her) again **volver a ver(te, lo, la)**
  see movies **ver películas** 4
  See you. **Nos vemos.** 1
  See you later. **Hasta la vista.** 1; **Hasta luego.** 1
  See you soon. **Hasta pronto.** 1
  See you tomorrow. **Hasta mañana.** 1
seem **parecer** *v.* 6
seen **visto/a** *p.p.* 14
sell **vender** *v.* 6
semester **semestre** *m.* 2
send **enviar; mandar** *v.* 14
separate (from) **separarse** *v.* **(de)** 9
separated **separado/a** *adj.* 9
September **septiembre** *m.* 5
sequence **secuencia** *f.*
serious **grave** *adj.* 10
serve **servir (e:i)** *v.* 8
set (*fixed*) **fijo** *adj.* 6
  set the table **poner la mesa** 12
seven **siete** 1
seven hundred **setecientos/as** 2
seventeen **diecisiete** 1
seventh **séptimo/a** 5
seventy **setenta** 2
several **varios/as** *adj. pl.* 8
sexism **sexismo** *m.*
shame **lástima** *f.* 13
  it's a shame **es una lástima** 13
shampoo **champú** *m.* 7
shape **forma** *f.* 15

be in good shape **estar en buena forma** 15
stay in shape **mantenerse en forma** 15
share **compartir** *v.* 3
sharp (*time*) **en punto** 1
shave **afeitarse** *v.* 7
shaving cream **crema** *f.* **de afeitar** 7
she **ella** 1
shellfish **mariscos** *m., pl.* 8
ship **barco** *m.*
shirt **camisa** *f.* 6
shoe **zapato** *m.* 6
  shoe size **número** *m.* 6
  shoe store **zapatería** *f.* 14
  tennis shoes **zapatos** *m., pl.* **de tenis** 6
shop **tienda** *f.* 6
shopping, to go **ir de compras** 5
  shopping mall **centro comercial** *m.* 6
short (*in height*) **bajo/a** *adj.* 3; (*in length*) **corto/a** *adj.* 6
short story **cuento** *m.*
shorts **pantalones cortos** *m., pl.* 6
should (*do something*) **deber** *v.* **(+ inf.)** 3
show **espectáculo** *m.*; **mostrar (o:ue)** *v.* 4
  game show **concurso** *m.*
shower **ducha** *f.* 7; **ducharse** *v.* 7
shrimp **camarón** *m.* 8
siblings **hermanos/as** *pl.* 3
sick **enfermo/a** *adj.* 10
  be sick **estar enfermo/a** 10
  get sick **enfermarse** *v.* 10
sign **firmar** *v.* 14; **letrero** *m.* 14
silk **seda** *f.* 6

(made of) **de seda** 6
silly **tonto/a** *adj.* 3
since **desde** *prep.*
sing **cantar** *v.* 2
singer **cantante** *m., f.*
single **soltero/a** *adj.* 9
  single room **habitación** *f.* **individual** 5
sink **lavabo** *m.* 7
sir **señor (Sr.), don** *m.* 1
sister **hermana** *f.* 3
sister-in-law **cuñada** *f.* 3
sit down **sentarse (e:ie)** *v.* 7
six **seis** 1
six hundred **seiscientos/as** 2
sixteen **dieciséis** 1
sixth **sexto/a** 5
sixty **sesenta** 2
size **talla** *f.* 6
  shoe size *m.* **número** 6
(in-line) skate **patinar (en línea)** 4
skateboard **andar en patineta** *v.* 4
ski **esquiar** *v.* 4
skiing **esquí** *m.* 4

water-skiing **esquí** *m.* **acuático** 4
skirt **falda** *f.* 6
sky **cielo** *m.* 13
sleep **dormir (o:ue)** *v.* 4; **sueño** *m.* 3
   go to sleep **dormirse (o:ue)** *v.* 7
sleepy: be (very) sleepy **tener (mucho) sueño** 3
slender **delgado/a** *adj.* 3
slim down **adelgazar** *v.* 15
slippers **pantuflas** *f.* 7
slow **lento/a** *adj.* 11
slowly **despacio** *adv.* 10
small **pequeño/a** *adj.* 3
smart **listo/a** *adj.* 5
smile **sonreír (e:i)** *v.* 9
smiled **sonreído** *p.p.* 14
smoggy: It's (very) smoggy. **Hay (mucha) contaminación.** 4
smoke **fumar** *v.* 8; 15
   (not) to smoke **(no) fumar** 15
smoking section **sección** *f.* **de fumar** 8
   (non) smoking section *f.* **sección de (no) fumar** 8
snack **merendar** *v.* 8; 15; afternoon snack **merienda** *f.* 15
   have a snack **merendar** *v.*
sneakers **los zapatos de tenis** 6
sneeze **estornudar** *v.* 10
snow **nevar (e:ie)** *v.* 5; **nieve** *f.*
snowing: It's snowing. **Nieva.** 5; **Está nevando.** 5
so (*in such a way*) **así** *adv.* 10; **tan** *adv.* 5
   so much **tanto** *adv.*
   so-so **regular** 1, **así así**
   so that **para que** *conj.* 13
soap **jabón** *m.* 7
   soap opera **telenovela** *f.*
soccer **fútbol** *m.* 4
sociology **sociología** *f.* 2
sock(s) **calcetín (calcetines)** *m.* 6
sofa **sofá** *m.* 12
soft drink **refresco** *m.* 8
software **programa** *m.* **de computación** 11
soil **tierra** *f.* 13
solar **solar** *adj., m., f.* 13
   solar energy **energía solar** 13
soldier **soldado** *m., f.*
solution **solución** *f.* 13
solve **resolver (o:ue)** *v.* 13
some **algún, alguno/a(s)** *adj.* 7; **unos/as** *pron./ m., f., pl; indef. art.* 1
somebody **alguien** *pron.* 7
someone **alguien** *pron.* 7
something **algo** *pron.* 7
sometimes **a veces** *adv.* 10
son **hijo** *m.* 3
song **canción** *f.*
son-in-law **yerno** *m.* 3
soon **pronto** *adv.* 10

See you soon. **Hasta pronto.** 1
sorry: be sorry **sentir (e:ie)** *v.* 13
   I'm sorry. **Lo siento.** 4
   I'm so sorry. **Mil perdones.** 4; **Lo siento muchísimo.** 4
soup **caldo** *m.* 8; **sopa** *f.* 8
south **sur** *m.* 14
   to the south **al sur** 14
Spain **España** *f.* 1
Spanish (*language*) **español** *m.* 2; **español(a)** *adj.* 3
spare (free) time **ratos libres** 4
speak **hablar** *v.* 2
spectacular **espectacular** *adj. m., f.* 15
speech **discurso** *m.*
speed **velocidad** *f.* 11
   speed limit **velocidad** *f.* **máxima** 11
spelling **ortografía** *f.*, **ortográfico/a** *adj.*
spend (*money*) **gastar** *v.* 6
spoon (*table or large*) **cuchara** *f.* 12
sport **deporte** *m.* 4
   sports-related **deportivo/a** *adj.* 4
spouse **esposo/a** *m., f.* 3
sprain (one's ankle) **torcerse (o:ue)** *v.* **(el tobillo)** 10
sprained **torcido/a** *adj.* 10
   be sprained **estar torcido/a** 10
spring **primavera** *f.* 5
(city or town) square **plaza** *f.* 4
stadium **estadio** *m.* 2
stage **etapa** *f.* 9
stairs **escalera** *f.* 12
stairway **escalera** *f.* 12
stamp **estampilla** *f.* 14; **sello** *m.* 14
stand in line **hacer** *v.* **cola** 14
star **estrella** *f.* 13
start (*a vehicle*) **arrancar** *v.* 11; (*establish*) **establecer** *v.*
station **estación** *f.* 5
statue **estatua** *f.*
status: marital status **estado** *m.* **civil** 9
stay **quedarse** *v.* 7
   stay in shape **mantenerse en forma** 15
steak **bistec** *m.* 8
steering wheel **volante** *m.* 11
step **etapa** *f.*
stepbrother **hermanastro** *m.* 3
stepdaughter **hijastra** *f.* 3
stepfather **padrastro** *m.* 3
stepmother **madrastra** *f.* 3
stepsister **hermanastra** *f.* 3
stepson **hijastro** *m.* 3
stereo **estéreo** *m.* 11
still **todavía** *adv.* 5
stockbroker **corredor(a)** *m., f.* **de bolsa**
stockings **medias** *f., pl.* 6
stomach **estómago** *m.* 10

stone **piedra** *f.* 13
stop **parar** *v.* 11
   stop (*doing something*) **dejar de (+ inf.)** 13
store **tienda** *f.* 6
storm **tormenta** *f.*
story **cuento** *m.*; **historia** *f.*
stove **cocina, estufa** *f.* 12
straight **derecho** *adj.* 14
   straight (ahead) **derecho** 14
straighten up **arreglar** *v.* 12
strange **extraño/a** *adj.* 13
   it's strange **es extraño** 13
strawberry **frutilla** *f.* 8, **fresa**
street **calle** *f.* 11
stress **estrés** *m.* 15
stretching **estiramiento** *m.* 15
   do stretching exercises **hacer ejercicios;** *m. pl.* **de estiramiento** 15
strike (*labor*) **huelga** *f.*
stripe **raya** *f.* 6
   striped **de rayas** 6
stroll **pasear** *v.* 4
strong **fuerte** *adj. m. f.* 15
struggle (for/against) **luchar** *v.* **(por/contra)**
student **estudiante** *m., f.* 1; 2; **estudiantil** *adj.* 2
study **estudiar** *v.* 2
stuffed-up (*sinuses*) **congestionado/a** *adj.* 10
stupendous **estupendo/a** *adj.* 5
style **estilo** *m.*
suburbs **afueras** *f., pl.* 12
subway **metro** *m.* 5
   subway station **estación** *f.* **del metro** 5
success **éxito** *m.*
successful: be successful **tener éxito**
such as **tales como**
suddenly **de repente** *adv.* 6
suffer **sufrir** *v.* 10
   suffer an illness **sufrir una enfermedad** 10
sugar **azúcar** *m.* 8
suggest **sugerir (e:ie)** *v.* 12
suit **traje** *m.* 6
suitcase **maleta** *f.* 1
summer **verano** *m.* 5
sun **sol** *m.* 5; 13
sunbathe **tomar** *v.* **el sol** 4
Sunday **domingo** *m.* 2
(sun)glasses **gafas** *f., pl.* **(oscuras/de sol)** 6; **lentes** *m. pl.* **(de sol)** 6
sunny: It's (very) sunny. **Hace (mucho) sol.** 5
supermarket **supermercado** *m.* 14
suppose **suponer** *v.* 4
sure **seguro/a** *adj.* 5
   be sure **estar seguro/a** 5
surf (*the Internet*) **navegar** *v.* **(en Internet)** 11

surprise **sorprender** *v.* 9;
  **sorpresa** *f.* 9
survey **encuesta** *f.*
sweat **sudar** *v.* 15
sweater **suéter** *m.* 6
sweep the floor **barrer el**
  **suelo** 12
sweets **dulces** *m., pl.* 9
swim **nadar** *v.* 4
swimming **natación** *f.* 4
  swimming pool **piscina** *f.* 4
symptom **síntoma** *m.* 10

## T

table **mesa** *f.* 2
tablespoon **cuchara** *f.* 12
tablet (*pill*) **pastilla** *f.* 10
take **tomar** *v.* 2; **llevar** *v.* 6;
  take care of **cuidar** *v.* 13
  take someone's temperature
    **tomar** *v.* **la temperatura** 10
  take (*wear*) a shoe size
    **calzar** *v.* 6
  take a bath **bañarse** *v.* 7
  take a shower **ducharse** *v.* 7
  take off **quitarse** *v.* 7
  take out the trash *v.* **sacar la**
    **basura** 12
  take photos **tomar** *v.* **fotos** 5;
    **sacar** *v.* **fotos** 5
talented **talentoso/a** *adj.*
talk **hablar** *v.* 2
  talk show **programa** *m.* **de**
    **entrevistas**
tall **alto/a** *adj.* 3
tank **tanque** *m.* 11
tape recorder **grabadora** *f.* 1
taste **probar (o:ue)** *v.* 8; **saber** *v.* 8
  taste like **saber a** 8
tasty **rico/a** *adj.* 8; **sabroso/a**
  *adj.* 8
tax **impuesto** *m.*
taxi **taxi** *m.* 5
tea **té** *m.* 8
teach **enseñar** *v.* 2
teacher **profesor(a)** *m., f.* 1, 2;
  **maestro/a** *m., f.*
team **equipo** *m.* 4
technician **técnico/a** *m., f.*
telecommuting **teletrabajo** *m.*
telephone **teléfono** 11
  cellular telephone **teléfono** *m.*
    **celular** 11
television **televisión** *f.* 2; 11
  television set **televisor** *m.* 11
tell **contar** *v.* 4; **decir** *v.* 4
tell (that) **decir** *v.* **(que)** 4, 9
  tell lies **decir mentiras** 4
  tell the truth **decir la verdad** 4
temperature **temperatura** *f.* 10
ten **diez** 1
tennis **tenis** *m.* 4
  tennis shoes **zapatos** *m., pl.* **de**
    **tenis** 6

tension **tensión** *f.* 15
tent **tienda** *f.* **de campaña**
tenth **décimo/a** 5
terrible **terrible** *adj. m., f.* 13
  it's terrible **es terrible** 13
terrific **chévere** *adj.*
test **prueba** *f.* 2; **examen** *m.* 2
text message **mensaje** *m.* **de**
  **texto** 11
Thank you. **Gracias.** *f., pl.* 1
  Thank you (very much).
    **(Muchas) gracias.** 1
  Thank you very, very much.
    **Muchísimas gracias.** 9
  Thanks (a lot). **(Muchas)**
    **gracias.** 1
  Thanks again. (lit. Thanks one
    more time.) **Gracias una vez**
    **más.** 9
  Thanks for everything. **Gracias**
    **por todo.** 9; 15
that **que, quien(es), lo que**
  *pron.* 12
  that (one) **ése, ésa, eso**
    *pron.* 6; **ese, esa,** *adj.* 6
  that (*over there*) **aquél,**
    **aquélla, aquello** *pron.* 6;
    **aquel, aquella** *adj.* 6
  that which **lo que** *conj.* 12
  that's me **soy yo** 1
  That's not the way it is. **No es**
    **así.**
  that's why **por eso** 11
the **el** *m.,* **la** *f. sing.,* **los** *m.,*
  **las** *f., pl.* 1
theater **teatro** *m.*
their **su(s)** *poss. adj.* 3;
  **suyo(s)/a(s)** *poss. pron.* 11
them **los/las** *pl., d.o. pron.* 5
  to/for them **les** *pl., i.o. pron.* 6
then (*afterward*) **después** *adv.* 7;
  (*as a result*) **entonces** *adv.* 7;
  (*next*) **luego** *adv.* 7; **pues**
  *adv.* 15
there **allí** *adv.* 5
  There is/are... **Hay...** 1;
  There is/are not... **No hay...** 1
therefore **por eso** 11
these **éstos, éstas** *pron.* 6;
  **estos, estas** *adj.* 6
they **ellos** *m.,* **ellas** *f. pron.*
thin **delgado/a** *adj.* 3
thing **cosa** *f.* 1
think **pensar (e:ie)** *v.* 4; (believe)
  **creer** *v.*
  think about **pensar en** *v.* 4
third **tercero/a** 5
thirst **sed** *f.* 3
thirsty: be (very) thirsty **tener**
  **(mucha) sed** 3
thirteen **trece** 1
thirty **treinta** 1; 2; thirty (*minutes*
  *past the hour*) **y treinta; y**
  **media** 1
this **este, esta** *adj.;* **éste, ésta,**
  **esto** *pron.* 6

This is... (*introduction*)
  **Éste/a es...** 1
This is he/she. (*on telephone*)
  **Con él/ella habla.** 11
those **ésos, ésas** *pron.* 6; **esos,**
  **esas** *adj.* 6
those (over there) **aquéllos,**
  **aquéllas** *pron.* 6; **aquellos,**
  **aquellas** *adj.* 6
thousand **mil** *m.* 6
three **tres** 1
three hundred **trescientos/as** 2
throat **garganta** *f.* 10
through **por** *prep.* 11
throughout: throughout the world
  **en todo el mundo** 13
Thursday **jueves** *m., sing.* 2
thus (*in such a way*) **así** *adj.*
ticket **boleto** *m.;* **pasaje** *m.* 5
tie **corbata** *f.* 6
time **vez** *f.* 6; **tiempo** *m.* 4
  have a good/bad time **pasarlo**
    **bien/mal** 9
  We had a great time. **Lo**
    **pasamos de película.**
  What time is it? **¿Qué hora**
    **es?** 1
  (At) What time...? **¿A qué**
    **hora...?** 1
times **veces** *f., pl.* 6
  many times **muchas veces** 10
  two times **dos veces** 6
tip **propina** *f.* 9
tire **llanta** *f.* 11
tired **cansado/a** *adj.* 5
  be tired **estar cansado/a** 5
to **a** *prep.* 1
toast (*drink*) **brindar** *v.* 9
  toast **pan** *m.* **tostado**
toasted **tostado/a** *adj.* 8
  toasted bread **pan tostado** *m.* 8
toaster **tostadora** *f.* 12
today **hoy** *adv.* 2
  Today is... **Hoy es...** 2
toe **dedo** *m.* **del pie** 10
together **juntos/as** *adj.* 9
toilet **inodoro** *m.* 7
tomato **tomate** *m.* 8
tomorrow **mañana** *f.* 1
  See you tomorrow. **Hasta**
    **mañana.** 1
tonight **esta noche** *adv.* 4
too **también** *adv.* 2; 7
  too much **demasiado** *adv.* 6;
    **en exceso** 15
tooth **diente** *m.* 7
toothpaste **pasta** *f.* **de dientes** 7
tornado **tornado** *m.*
tortilla **tortilla** *f.* 8
touch **tocar** *v.* 13
tour an area **recorrer** *v;* **excur-**
  **sión** *f.* 4
tourism **turismo** *m.* 5
tourist **turista** *m., f.* 1;
  **turístico/a** *adj.*
toward **hacia** *prep.* 14;

**para** *prep.* 11
towel **toalla** *f.* 7
town **pueblo** *m.* 4
trade **oficio** *m.*
traffic **circulación** *f.* 11; **tráfico** *m.* 11
   traffic signal **semáforo** *m.*
tragedy **tragedia** *f.*
trail **sendero** *m.* 13
   trailhead **sendero** *m.* 13
train **entrenarse** *v.* 15; **tren** *m.* 5
   train station **estación** *f.* **(de) tren** *m.* 5
trainer **entrenador(a)** *m., f.* 15
translate **traducir** *v.* 6
trash **basura** *f.* 12
travel **viajar** *v.* 2
   travel agent **agente** *m., f.* **de viajes** 5
traveler **viajero/a** *m., f.* 5
   (traveler's) check **cheque (de viajero)** 14
treadmill **cinta caminadora** *f.* 15
tree **árbol** *m.* 13
trillion **billón** *m.*
trimester **trimestre** *m.* 2
trip **viaje** *m.* 5
   take a trip **hacer un viaje** 5
tropical forest **bosque** *m.* **tropical** 13
true **verdad** *adj.* 13
   it's (not) true **(no) es verdad** 13
trunk **baúl** *m.* 11
truth **verdad** *f.*
try **intentar** *v.*; **probar (o:ue)** *v.* 8
   try (*to do something*) **tratar de (+ inf.)** 15
   try on **probarse (o:ue)** *v.* 7
t-shirt **camiseta** *f.* 6
Tuesday **martes** *m., sing.* 2
tuna **atún** *m.* 8
turkey **pavo** *m.* 8
turn **doblar** *v.* 14
   turn off (*electricity/appliance*) **apagar** *v.* 11
   turn on (*electricity/appliance*) **poner** *v.* 11; **prender** *v.* 11
twelve **doce** 1
twenty **veinte** 1
twenty-eight **veintiocho** 1
twenty-five **veinticinco** 1
twenty-four **veinticuatro** 1
twenty-nine **veintinueve** 1
twenty-one **veintiún, veintiuno/a** 1
twenty-seven **veintisiete** 1
twenty-six **veintiséis** 1
twenty-three **veintitrés** 1
twenty-two **veintidós** 1
twice **dos veces** 6
twin **gemelo/a** *m., f.* 3
twisted **torcido/a** *adj.* 10
   be twisted **estar torcido/a** 10
two **dos** 1
   two hundred **doscientos/as** 2
   two times **dos veces** 6

## U

ugly **feo/a** *adj.* 3
uncle **tío** *m.* 3
under **bajo** *adv.* 7; **debajo de** *prep.* 2
understand **comprender** *v.* 3; **entender (e:ie)** *v.* 4
underwear **ropa interior** 6
unemployment **desempleo** *m.*
United States **Estados Unidos (EE.UU.)** *m. pl.* 1
university **universidad** *f.* 2
unless **a menos que** *adv.* 13
unmarried **soltero/a** *adj.*
unpleasant **antipático/a** *adj.* 3
until **hasta** *prep.* 6; **hasta que** *conj.* 13
up **arriba** *adv.* 15
urgent **urgente** *adj.* 12
   It's urgent that... **Es urgente que...** 12
us **nos** *pl., d.o. pron.* 5
   to/for us **nos** *pl., i.o. pron.* 6
use **usar** *v.* 6
used for **para** *prep.* 11
useful **útil** *adj. m., f.*

## V

vacation **vacaciones** *f., pl.* 5
   be on vacation **estar de vacaciones** 5
   go on vacation **ir de vacaciones** 5
vacuum **pasar** *v.* **la aspiradora** 12
   vacuum cleaner **aspiradora** *f.* 12
valley **valle** *m.* 13
various **varios/as** *adj. m., f. pl.* 8
VCR **videocasetera** *f.* 11
vegetables **verduras** *pl., f.* 8
verb **verbo** *m.*
very **muy** *adv.* 1
   very much **muchísimo** *adv.* 2
   (Very) well, thank you. **(Muy) bien, gracias.** 1
video **video** *m.* 1
   video camera **cámara** *f.* **de video** 11
   video(cassette) **video(casete)** *m.* 11
   videoconference **videoconferencia** *f.*
   video game **videojuego** *m.* 4
vinegar **vinagre** *m.* 8
violence **violencia** *f.*
visit **visitar** *v.* 4
   visit monuments **visitar monumentos** 4
vitamin **vitamina** *f.* 15
volcano **volcán** *m.* 13
volleyball **vóleibol** *m.* 4
vote **votar** *v.*

## W

wait (for) **esperar** *v.* **(+ *inf.*)** 2
waiter/waitress **camarero/a** *m., f.* 8
wake up **despertarse (e:ie)** *v.* 7
walk **caminar** *v.* 2
   take a walk **pasear** *v.* 4;
   walk around **pasear por** 4
walkman *walkman* *m.*
wall **pared** *f.* 12
wallet **cartera** *f.* 6
want **querer (e:ie)** *v.* 4
war **guerra** *f.*
warm (oneself) up **calentarse (e:ie)** *v.* 15
wash **lavar** *v.* 12
   wash one's face/hands **lavarse la cara/las manos** 7
   wash (the floor, the dishes) **lavar (el suelo, los platos)** 12
   wash oneself **lavarse** *v.* 7
washing machine **lavadora** *f.* 12
wastebasket **papelera** *f.* 2
watch **mirar** *v.* 2; **reloj** *m.* 2
   watch television **mirar (la) televisión** 2
water **agua** *f.* 8
   water pollution **contaminación del agua** 13
   water-skiing **esquí** *m.* **acuático** 4
way **manera** *f.*
we **nosotros(as)** *m., f.* 1
weak **débil** *adj. m., f.* 15
wear **llevar** *v.* 6; **usar** *v.* 6
weather **tiempo** *m.*
   The weather is bad. **Hace mal tiempo.** 5
   The weather is good. **Hace buen tiempo.** 5
weaving **tejido** *m.*
Web **red** *f.* 11
website **sitio** *m.* **web** 11
wedding **boda** *f.* 9
Wednesday **miércoles** *m., sing.* 2
week **semana** *f.* 2
weekend **fin** *m.* **de semana** 4
weight **peso** *m.* 15
   lift weights **levantar** *v.* **pesas** *f., pl.* 15
welcome **bienvenido(s)/a(s)** *adj.* 12
well **pues** *adv.* 2; **bueno** *adv.* 2;
   (Very) well, thanks. **(Muy) bien, gracias.** 1
well-being **bienestar** *m.* 15
well organized **ordenado/a** *adj.*
west **oeste** *m.* 14
   to the west **al oeste** 14
western (*genre*) **de vaqueros**
what **lo que** *pron.* 12
what? **¿qué?** 1
   At what time...? **¿A qué hora...?** 1

What a pleasure to... ! **¡Qué gusto (+ inf.)...**
What day is it? **¿Qué día es hoy?** 2
What do you guys think? **¿Qué les parece?** 9
What happened? **¿Qué pasó?** 11
What is today's date? **¿Cuál es la fecha de hoy?** 5
What nice clothes! **¡Qué ropa más bonita!** 6
What size do you take? **¿Qué talla lleva (usa)?** 6
What time is it? **¿Qué hora es?** 1
What's going on? **¿Qué pasa?** 1
What's happening? **¿Qué pasa?** 1
What's. . . like? **¿Cómo es...?** 3
What's new? **¿Qué hay de nuevo?** 1
What's the weather like? **¿Qué tiempo hace?** 5
What's wrong? **¿Qué pasó?** 11
What's your name? **¿Cómo se llama usted?** *form.* 1
What's your name? **¿Cómo te llamas (tú)?** *fam.* 1
when **cuando** *conj.* 7; 13
When? **¿Cuándo?** 2
where **donde**
where (to)? *(destination)* **¿adónde?** 2; *(location)* **¿dónde?** 1
Where are you from? **¿De dónde eres (tú)?** *(fam.)* 1; **¿De dónde es (usted)?** *(form.)* 1
Where is...? **¿Dónde está...?** 2
(to) where? **¿adónde?** 2
which **que** *pron.*, **lo que** *pron.* 12
which? **¿cuál?** 2; **¿qué?** 2
In which...? **¿En qué...?** 2
which one(s)? **¿cuál(es)?** 2
while **mientras** *adv.* 10
white **blanco/a** *adj.* 6
white wine **vino blanco** 8
who **que** *pron.* 12; **quien(es)** *pron.* 12
who? **¿quién(es)?** 1
Who is...? **¿Quién es...?** 1
Who is calling? *(on telephone)* **¿De parte de quién?** 11
Who is speaking? *(on telephone)* **¿Quién habla?** 11
whole **todo/a** *adj.*
whom **quien(es)** *pron.* 12
whose? **¿de quién(es)?** 1
why? **¿por qué?** 2

widower/widow **viudo/a** *adj.* 9
wife **esposa** *f.* 3
win **ganar** *v.* 4
wind **viento** *m.* 5
window **ventana** *f.* 2
windshield **parabrisas** *m.*, *sing.* 11
windy: It's (very) windy. **Hace (mucho) viento.** 5
wine **vino** *m.* 8
red wine **vino tinto** 8
white wine **vino blanco** 8
wineglass **copa** *f.* 12
winter **invierno** *m.* 5
wish **desear** *v.* 2; **esperar** *v.* 13
I wish (that) **ojalá (que)** 13
with **con** *prep.* 2
with me **conmigo** 4; 9
with you **contigo** *fam.* 9
within (ten years) **dentro de (diez años)** *prep.*
without **sin** *prep.* 2; 13; 15; **sin que** *conj.* 13
woman **mujer** *f.* 1
wool **lana** *f.* 6
(made of) wool **de lana** 6
word **palabra** *f.* 1
work **trabajar** *v.* 2; **funcionar** *v.* 11; **trabajo** *m.* 16
work *(of art, literature, music, etc.)* **obra** *f.*
work out **hacer gimnasia** 15
world **mundo** *m.* 13
worldwide **mundial** *adj. m., f.*
worried (about) **preocupado/a (por)** *adj.* 5
worry (about) **preocuparse** *v.* **(por)** 7
Don't worry. **No se preocupe.** *form.* 7; **Tranquilo.; No te preocupes.;** *fam.* 7
worse **peor** *adj. m., f.* 8
worst **el/la peor, lo peor** 8
Would you like to...? **¿Te gustaría...?** *fam.* 4
write **escribir** *v.* 3
write a letter/post card/e-mail message **escribir una carta/postal/mensaje electrónico** 4
writer **escritor(a)** *m., f*
written **escrito/a** *p.p.* 14
wrong **equivocado/a** *adj.* 5
be wrong **no tener razón** 3

---

**X**

X-ray **radiografía** *f.* 10

---

**Y**

yard **jardín** *m.* 12; **patio** *m.* 12
year **año** *m.* 5
be... years old **tener... años** 3
yellow **amarillo/a** *adj.* 6
yes **sí** *interj.* 1
yesterday **ayer** *adv.* 6
yet **todavía** *adv.* 5
yogurt **yogur** *m.* 8
You **tú** *fam.* **usted (Ud.)** *form. sing.* **vosotros/as** *m., f. fam.* **ustedes (Uds.)** *form.* 1; (to, for) you *fam. sing.* **te** *pl.* **os** 6; *form. sing.* **le** *pl.* **les** 6
you **te** *fam., sing.,* **lo/la** *form., sing.,* **os** *fam., pl.,* **los/las** *form., pl, d.o. pron.* 5
You don't say! **¡No me digas!** *fam.;* **¡No me diga!** *form.* 11
You are. . . **Tú eres...** 1
You're welcome. **De nada.** 1; **No hay de qué.** 1
young **joven** *adj.* 3
young person **joven** *m., f.* 1
young woman **señorita (Srta.)** *f.*
younger **menor** *adj. m., f.* 3
younger: younger brother, sister *m., f.* **hermano/a menor** 3
youngest **el/la menor** *m., f.* 8
your **su(s)** *poss. adj. form.* 3
your **tu(s)** *poss. adj. fam. sing.* 3
your **vuestro/a(s)** *poss. adj. form. pl.* 3
your(s) *form.* **suyo(s)/a(s)** *poss. pron. form.* 11
your(s) **tuyo(s)/a(s)** *poss. fam. sing.* 11
your(s) **vuestro(s)/a(s)** *poss. fam.* 11
youth *f.* **juventud** 9

---

**Z**

zero **cero** *m.* 1

## Text Credits

474–475 © Carmen Laforet. Fragment of the novel *Nada*, reprinted by permission of Random House Publishing Group.

505–506 © Gabriel García Márquez, *Un día de éstos*, reprinted by permission of Carmen Balcells.

## Fine Art Credits

67 (ml) Diego Velázquez. *Las meninas*. 1656. Derechos reservados © Museo Nacional del Prado, Madrid. Photograph © José Blanco/VHL

105 Oswaldo Guayasamín. *Madre y niño en azul*. 1986. Cortesía Fundación Guayasamín. Quito, Ecuador.

136 Frida Kahlo. *Autorretrato con mono*. 1938. Oil on masonite, overall 16 x 12" (40.64 x 30.48 cms). Albright-Knox Art Gallery, Buffalo, New York. Bequest of A. Conger Goodyear, 1966.

## Illustration Credits

**Hermann Mejía:** 5, 14, 15, 17, 18, 22, 23, 29, 50, 52, 63 (b), 73, 83 (b), 86, 94, 95, 97, 119, 123, 130, 143, 150 (l), 153, 156, 161, 165, 167 (b), 177, 197, 199, 212, 213, 218, 222, 232, 235, 255, 265, 269, 278, 288, 297, 311, 328, 329, 333, 358, 361, 364, 365, 367, 392, 401, 403, 407, 432, 439, 441, 473, 499, 503.

**Pere Virgili:** 2–3, 36–37, 58, 70–71, 83 (t), 108–109, 110, 140–141, 142, 157, 160, 167 (t), 174–175, 198, 210–211, 242–243, 244, 276–277, 308–309, 342–343, 344, 376–377, 378, 416–417, 418, 450–451, 452, 482–483, 484.

**Yayo:** 9, 43, 77, 115, 149, 181, 217, 251, 283, 315, 349, 383, 423, 457, 489.

## Photography Credits

**Martín Bernetti:** 1, 3, 4, 16 (c, m), 19, 38, 53, 64, 65, 71, 72 (tl, tm, r, bml, bmr, br), 82, 89 (r), 90, 98, 99 (b), 101, 104, 105 (t, ml, b), 109 (b), 131, 134, 189, 193 (tl, tr, ml, mr), 194, 195, 202, 203, 221, 223, 226, 227, 238 (tl, tr), 239 (tl, br), 247, 279, 298 (t), 321, 325, 355, 360, 379, 406, 466, 485, 506, 507.

**Carlos Gaudier:** 168, 169, 170 (tl, tr, ml, mr), 171 (tl, bl).

**Corbis:** 11 (tr) © Hans Georg Roth. 19 (r) © 1999 Charles Gupton. 32 (tr) © Robert Holmes. 44 (t) © Pablo Corral V. 54 © Charles Gupton. 66 (m) © Elke Stolzenberg, (b) © Reuters. 67 (br) © Owen Franken, (tl) © Patrick Almasy, (tr) © Jean-Pierre Lescourret. 69 © Ronnie Kaufman. 78 (tr) © Rafael Pérez/Reuters, (b) © Martial Trezzini/epa. 79 (t) © Reuters. 97 © George Shelley. 100 © Tom & Dee Ann McCarthy. 107 © Jon Feingersh. 109 (t) © George Shelley. 116 (b) © Reuters. 117 (t) © Reuters. 133 © Images.com. 135 © AFP Photo/Juan Barreto. 136 (tl) © George D. Lepp, (mr) Peter Guttman, (b) Reuters. 137 (tr) © Bettman, (br) Greg Vaughn. 150 (r) © Jeremy Horner. 151 (b) © Mark A. Johnson. 155 © Ronnie Kaufman. 171 (br) © Steve Chenn. 205 (t) © Manuel Zambrana. 238 (bm) © Charles & Josette Lenars, (lm) © Richard Smith. 239 (bl) © Jeremy Horner. 253 (tr) © Carlos Cazalis, (br) © Carlos Cazalis. 257 © José Luis Pelaez, Inc. 272 (t) © Bob Winsett, (ml, mr, b) © Dave G. Houser. 273 (tl) © Reuters Newmedia, Inc./Jorge Silva, (tr) © Michael & Patricia Fogden, (bl) © Jon Butchofsky-Houser, (br) © Paul W. Liebhardt. 284 ® © PictureNet. 304 (ml) © Dave G. Houser, (tr, mtr) © Mcduff Everton, (tl) © Pablo Corral V., (mbr) © AFP/Macarena Minguell, (bl, br) © Bettman. 305 (tl) © Wolfgang Kaehler, (bl) © Roger Ressmeyer, (br) © Charles O'rear. 329 © Lawrence Kesterson. 336 (m) © Jan Butchofsky-Houser, (ml) © Bill Gentile, (mr) © Dave G. Houser, (b) © Bob Winsett. 337 (r,b) © Martin Rogers. 338 (tl) © Jeremy Horner, (tr, m) © Bill Gentile, (b) © Stephen Frink. 339 (tl) © Brian A. Vikander, (r) © Reuters NewMedia Inc./Claudia Daut, (bl) © Gary Braasch. 341 © PictureNet. 370 (m, mr) Galen Rowell. 371 (t) Pablo Corral V. 372 (tl) © Bettmann, (tr) © Reuters/Andres Stapff, (m) © Diego Lezama Orezzoli, (b) © Tim Graham. 373 (tl) © Stephanie Maze, (r) © SI/Simon Bruty, (ml) © Reuters/Andres Stapff, (bl) © Wolfgang Kaehler. 375 © Rolf Bruderer. 384 (l) © Dusko Despotovic. 410 (tl) © Kevin Schafer, (tr, b) Danny Lehman. 411 (tl) © Danny Lehman, (ml) Ralf A. Clavenger, (b) Jose & Fuste Raga. 412 (tl) © José F. Poblete, (tr) © Peter Guttman, (ml) © Leif Skoogfors, (mr) © Lake County Museum. 413 (tl) © Guy Motil. 415 © Michael de Young. 417 (tr) Stephanie Maze. 428 © Karl & Anne Purcell. 444 (tr) Carl & Anne Purcell. 445 (tl) Gianni Dagli Orti, (tr) Stringer/Mexico/Reuters, (br) © Jeremy Horner. 446 (tl) © Stuart Westmorland, (tr, ml) © Macduff Everton, (mr) © Tony Arruza. 447 (tl) © Macduff Everton. 475 © Bureau L.A. Collection. 476 (t) John Madere, (mt) Kevin Schafer, (mb) Buddy Mays, (b) Peter Guttmann. 477 (tl) Reuters/New Media Inc./Kimberly White, (bl, br) Pablo Corral V. 478 (tr) © Reinhard Eisele, (m) © Richard Bickel. 479 (tl) © Jeremy Horner, (r) © Reuters NewMedia Inc./Marc Serota, (bl) © Lawrence Manning. 495 © Sygma. 501 © Michael Keller. 510 (tl) © Anders Ryman, (m) © Reuters NewMedia Inc./Sergio Moraes, (b) © Pablo Corral V. 511 (tl) © Hubert Stadler, (r) AFP Photo/Gonzalo Espinoza, (bl) © Wolfgang Kaehler. 512 (t) © Peter Guttman, (ml) © Paul Almasy, (b) © Carlos Carrión. 513 (r) © Joel Creed; Ecoscene.

## About the Authors

**José A. Blanco** founded Vista Higher Learning in 1998. A native of Barranquilla, Colombia, Mr. Blanco holds degrees in Literature and Hispanic Studies from Brown University and the University of California, Santa Cruz. He has worked as a writer, editor, and translator for Houghton Mifflin and D.C. Heath and Company and has taught Spanish at the secondary and university levels. Mr. Blanco is also the co-author of several other Vista Higher Learning programs: **Panorama, Aventuras,** and **¡Viva!** at the introductory level, **Ventanas, Facetas, Enfoques, Imagina,** and **Sueña** at the intermediate level, and **Revista** at the advanced conversation level.

**Philip Redwine Donley** received his M.A. in Hispanic Literature from the University of Texas at Austin in 1986 and his Ph.D. in Foreign Language Education from the University of Texas at Austin in 1997. Dr. Donley taught Spanish at Austin Community College, Southwestern University, and the University of Texas at Austin. He published articles and conducted workshops about language anxiety management, and the development of critical thinking skills, and was involved in research about teaching languages to the visually impaired. Dr. Donley was also the co-author of **Aventuras** and **Panorama**, two other introductory college Spanish textbook programs published by Vista Higher Learning.

## About the Illustrators

**Yayo**, an internationally acclaimed illustrator, was born in Colombia. He has illustrated children's books, newspapers, and magazines, and has been exhibited around the world. He currently lives in Montreal, Canada.

**Pere Virgili** lives and works in Barcelona, Spain. His illustrations have appeared in textbooks, newspapers, and magazines throughout Spain and Europe.

Born in Caracas, Venezuela, **Hermann Mejía** studied illustration at the *Instituto de Diseño de Caracas*. Hermann currently lives and works in the United States.